THE LAW OF NET ZERO AND NATURE POSITIVE

THE LAW OF NET ZERO AND NATURE POSITIVE

edited by

NIGEL PLEMING KC
RICHARD WILMOT-SMITH KC
STEPHEN TROMANS KC
KARIM GHALY KC
CAMILLA TER HAAR
STEPHANIE DAVID

LONDON PUBLISHING PARTNERSHIP

The images on the facing page are reproductions of paintings by Stephen Tromans KC, entitled 'Climate Apathy' and 'Gannets'. More of Stephen's work can be found at https://www.stlaw.co.uk/.

British Library Cataloguing in Publication Data
A catalogue record for this book is available from the British Library

ISBN: 978-1-916749-21-4 (hbk)

Typeset in Adobe Caslon Pro by T&T Productions Ltd, London
www.tandtproductions.com

Printed and bound by CPI Group (UK) Ltd, Croydon, CR0 4YY

FSC
www.fsc.org
MIX
Paper | Supporting responsible forestry
FSC® C013604

FOREWORD

In May 2019, in the introduction to the Climate Change Committee ('CCC') report 'Net Zero: The UK's Contribution to Stopping Global Warming', Rt Hon Lord Debden said:[1]

> Our recommendation [for a new emissions target for the UK: net-zero greenhouse gases by 2050] emerges clearly from the extensive evidence presented here for the first time. We have reviewed the latest scientific evidence on climate change, including last year's IPCC Special Report on Global Warming of 1.5°C, and considered the appropriate role of the UK in the global challenge to limit future temperature increases. We have built a new understanding of the potential to achieve deep emissions reduction in the UK and made a fresh appraisal of the costs and benefits to the UK economy of doing so.

Five years on and the CCC is warning that even the interim 2030 target[2] is at risk.[3] There is clearly much to be done if net zero is to be achieved by 2050. Understanding the legal framework, national and international, is vitally important, and this book makes a major contribution to stating and analysing the relevant law. The authors have gone further and considered not only net zero itself but also the biodiversity crisis, and the need for a nature positive future – one in which nature loss is not only reversed but also recovered by 2030.[4] This interdependence is widely supported and identified in the 2023 report of the CCC on reducing emissions:[5]

> Climate change has caused major changes to ecosystems beyond that expected through natural climate variability. Climate solutions have the potential to put biodiversity at risk (e.g. large-scale bioenergy) or help restore nature (e.g. nature-based solutions). Biodiversity protection and enhancement can also deliver adaptation and mitigation co-benefits, such as forest and soil restoration. Conversely, destroying nature (e.g. deforesting the Amazon) can release huge amounts of stored carbon.

---

1 Climate Change Committee, 'Net Zero: The UK's Contribution to Stopping Global Warming' (2019) 8 <https://www.theccc.org.uk/publication/net-zero-the-uks-contribution-to-stopping-global-warming/> accessed 4 November 2024.

2 This is the UK's 'Nationally Determined Contribution' in accordance with the Paris Agreement, which is to reduce emissions in 2030 by 68% compared with 1990.

3 Climate Change Committee, 'Progress in Reducing Emissions: 2024 Report to Parliament' (2024) 8, laid before Parliament on 18 July 2024 <https://www.theccc.org.uk/publication/progress-in-reducing-emissions-2024-report-to-parliament/#publication-downloads> accessed 4 November 2024.

4 As set out in the G7 Nature Compact by G7 leaders on 13 June 2021. See DEFRA, 'Government Sets Out Commitments to Biodiversity and Sustainability in G7 Nature Compact' (2021) <https://www.gov.uk/government/news/government-sets-out-commitments-to-biodiversity-and-sustainability-in-g7-nature-compact> accessed 26 November 2024. See also, as an example, the domestic target for species abundance set out in Section 3 of the Environment Act 2021.

5 Climate Change Committee, 'Progress in Reducing Emissions: 2023 Report to Parliament' (2023) 60, laid before Parliament on 28 June 2023 <https://www.theccc.org.uk/publication/2023-progress-report-to-parliament/> accessed 4 November 2024.

Given this interdependence and the fact that nature is sometimes forgotten, the book aims to bring together the legal obligations in respect of both net zero and nature positive goals so that practitioners, policymakers and all others interested in this area have both objectives in mind as they seek to address the challenges of our generation: climate change and the biodiversity crisis. A brief run through the contents list shows the extremely broad range of topics that are addressed. These include the obvious areas of planning, property and construction law but also detailed consideration of commercial and financial services and fiscal measures.

I am delighted to see so many members of 39 Essex Chambers involved as authors and editors – and Stephen Tromans KC as illustrator as well. The book will assist anyone who is interested in the law of net zero and nature positive in navigating these complex and interrelated areas of law. I thoroughly recommend it.

The Rt Hon Lord Dyson, former Justice of the Supreme Court
and Master of the Rolls, 26 November 2024

ABOUT THE EDITORS AND CONTRIBUTORS

39 Essex Chambers

All of this volume's contributors, editors and general editors are members of 39 Essex Chambers.[1]

39 Essex Chambers is a leading set of barristers' chambers with locations in London, Manchester, Singapore and Kuala Lumpur. It has particular expertise in environmental and climate issues but offers expertise across a wide range of legal sectors and practice areas.

39 Essex Chambers represents a diverse range of clients across all industry sectors, including public and private companies, government bodies, utility providers, non-governmental organisations (NGOs), local authorities, trade unions, educational and health bodies as well as individual litigants, and it prides itself on delivering comprehensive and cost-effective legal services.

Nigel Pleming KC (Call 1971 Silk 1992)

Nigel Pleming KC has a distinguished legal career spanning over 50 years. He practises mainly in England and Wales, but also in Hong Kong, Belize and the Caribbean. He has been recommended as a leading silk in the Legal 500 since 2000 in the specialties of administrative and public law, civil liberties and human rights, environment, immigration and value added tax.

He has a special interest in environmental law, and he has acted with others for a coalition of residents, local authorities and Greenpeace in the well-known challenge to the government's decision to authorise the building of a third runway and sixth terminal at Heathrow.

He has recently been working with the British Institute of International and Comparative Law ('BIICL') on their Corporate Climate Change Litigation Toolbox.

Nigel has been nominated by *The Lawyer* magazine for the Barrister of the Year award.

Richard Wilmot-Smith KC (Call 1978 Silk 1994)

Richard Wilmot-Smith KC specialises in all aspects of construction and engineering litigation and arbitration. His expertise also extends to issues involving European law,

1 Except for one barrister contributor who is a former member of 39 Essex Chambers.

environmental law (including coal and nuclear power and waste incidents), libel, health and safety, railways and oil and gas.

He has more than 40 years of experience in the field, with 30 years at the highest level. Richard sits as an arbitrator and adjudicator in high-value cases worldwide.

Stephen Tromans KC (Call 1999 Silk 2009)

Stephen Tromans KC is an outstanding name in the environmental and planning spheres, who brings these skills to the energy sector. He is also known for his pre-eminent expertise in legal matters pertaining specifically to nuclear energy. Stephen has deep experience and knowledge of most aspects of environmental law, gained over almost 40 years in the field, and he has been involved in some of the leading cases in areas such as waste, water rights, environmental assessment, nuisance and nuclear law.

He has been teaching and writing in the field of environmental law since 1985 and is the author of leading texts on planning and environmental law, contaminated land, environmental assessment, and nuclear law.

Karim Ghaly KC (Call 2001 Silk 2017)

Karim Ghaly KC specialises in the litigation and arbitration of commercial disputes in the fields of construction and engineering, energy and natural resources, infrastructure, insurance, maritime projects and PPP/PFI. Over the past 20 years he has acted as counsel, arbitrator or adjudicator in complex and high-value disputes arising out of projects in Africa, Asia, the Caribbean, Europe, the Middle East, North America, South America and the UK.

Karim is recommended as a leading silk for commercial dispute resolution, construction, energy and natural resources, international arbitration, PPP/PFI and professional negligence by Chambers and Partners, Chambers Global, The Legal 500, The Legal 500 Middle East and *Who's Who Legal*.

Camilla ter Haar (Call 2005)

Camilla ter Haar specialises in domestic and international litigation and arbitration. Camilla's practice spans construction and infrastructure disputes as well as commercial and financial services work. Camilla acts as both sole counsel and as part of a larger counsel team.

Alongside her practice, Camilla is the co-host of the podcast 'Construction and the Climate', co-author of the book *Remedies in Construction Law*, and co-founder of the Klosters Forum, a Swiss-based environmental discussion forum.

Stephanie David (Call 2016)

Stephanie David has a multidisciplinary practice spanning public law and human rights; energy, the environment and planning matters; financial services and regulatory work. She is ranked as a leading junior and 'up and coming' in administrative law and public law, human rights and civil liberties, and planning law by The Legal 500 and

Chambers and Partners. She has particular expertise in climate change and nature-related litigation having been instructed in cases relating to financial services, national policy, infrastructure projects and agriculture.

She is an editor of the *Environmental Law Bulletin* (published by Sweet and Maxwell), a regular contributor to the *Journal of Environmental Law* and hosts the podcast 'Climate Law Matters'.

Contributor list

Alexander Burrell, LLB (Bristol), Barrister.

Rebecca Cattermole, BA (Bristol), Barrister.

Grace Cheng, LLB (LSE), BCL (Oxon), Barrister and Arbitrator, Visiting Professor and Lecturer.

Stephanie David, BA (Cantab), LLM (LSE), Barrister.

Rebecca Drake, MA (Cantab), LLM, Barrister.

Hannah Fry, LLB (QMUL), LLM (QMUL), Barrister.

Ella Grodzinski, BA (Oxon), LLM, Barrister.

Camilla ter Haar, MA (Edin.), MA (Johns Hopkins, SAIS), Barrister.

Ned Helme, BA (Oxon), Barrister.

Patrick Hennessy, BA (Oxon), Barrister.

David Hopkins, BA (York), MPhil (Oxon), Barrister

Joe-han Ho, LLB (Dunelm), LLM (Harvard), BCL (Oxon), Barrister.

Victoria Hutton, MA (Oxon), LLM, Barrister.

Philippa Jackson, MA (Oxon), Barrister.

Vivek Kapoor, LLM (Northwestern, US), LLB (Panjab, IN), BA (Economics and Mathematics) (Panjab, IN), Barrister, Advocate, Arbitrator.

Ruth Keating, LLB (Dubl.), Barrister (England & Wales and King's Inn Ireland).

Daniel Kozelko, MA (Cantab), BCL (Oxon), Barrister.

Philippe Kuhn, LLB (LSE), BCL (Oxon), Barrister.

Eleanor Leydon, BA (Cantab), LLM (UCL), Barrister.

Anna Lintner, BA (Cantab), LLM (UCL), Barrister.

Juan Lopez, LLB, Barrister.

Hannah McCarthy, BA (Cantab), Barrister.

Niraj Modha, MA (Cantab), FCIArb. Barrister.

Christopher Moss, LLB (UCL), Barrister.

Ashley Pratt, LLB (Hons) Law with Politics, Barrister.

Celia Reynolds, LLB (Dubl.), LLM (Harv.), Barrister.

David Sawtell, MA (Cantab), MPhil (Cantab), MSc (KCL), PhD (Cantab), FCIArb, Barrister and Bye-Fellow of Peterhouse, Cambridge.

James Shaerf, LLB (Hons), BA (Cantuar, NZ), LLM (Cantab), Barrister.

Melissa Shipley, BA (Cantab), Barrister.

Marion Smith KC, FCIArb; Honorary Professor of Law, School of International Arbitration, Centre for Commercial Law Studies, Queen Mary University of London; Vice-Chair of the International Committee of the Bar Council; Bencher of Gray's Inn; Board member of the Council of the Inns of Court.

Christopher Staker, BA, LLB (Hons) (Adel), DPhil (Oxon), PGDip International Commercial Arbitration (QMUL), Barrister.

Kelly Stricklin-Coutinho, LLB (LSE), LLM (Cantab), Barrister (England & Wales), Called to the Bar of Ireland, Mediator, Chair of the Civil Mediation Council.

Rachel Sullivan, BA (Oxon), MSt (Oxon), Barrister.

Gethin Thomas, BA (Oxon), Barrister.

Jake Thorold, BA (Cantab), MSt (Oxon), Barrister.

Acknowledgements

Finally, the general editors and editors also acknowledge the hard work and assistance of Marcelo Lozada Gomez, Justin Lim, Andrew Tan, Sarah Goy and Samuel Moss in perfecting and finalising the manuscript ready for publication.

CONTENTS

III PROPERTY

IV ENVIRONMENTAL PROTEST

V PUBLIC INTERNATIONAL LAW

VI COMMERCIAL AND FINANCIAL SERVICES

VIII CONSTRUCTION

TABLE OF CASES

United Kingdom

European Union

European Court of Human Rights

International Court of Justice

Other international tribunals

Other domestic jurisdictions

TABLE OF LEGISLATION

Primary legislation – domestic

Secondary legislation – United Kingdom

EU legislation

International legislation

Australia

Colombia

Ireland

Netherlands

New Zealand

United States

International instruments

PART I
INTRODUCTION

CHAPTER 1

NET ZERO AND NATURE POSITIVE

Stephanie David

To members of the judiciary: you are all climate judges now. The tidal wave of climate litigation is growing. There have been over 1,800 cases so far, including against fossil fuel companies. They will keep growing.

To barristers and solicitors: you are all climate lawyers now. Climate change has implications for daily legal practice. Lawyers have a responsibility to adopt a climate-conscious, not climate-blind, approach in daily legal practice.

To law students: you are the people who will be hit hardest by the impacts to come. On the other hand, you are also the generation that will live much of your lives with the empowering international human right to a clean, healthy and sustainable environment. A safe climate is aligned to this right. Healthy nature is aligned to this right. A pollution-free world is aligned to this right. Your responsibility is to do whatever you can through the law to help the UK and other countries transition to a safe climate and nature positive reality.

Friends, we cannot safeguard the future of humanity without the right laws and strong enforcement.[1]

Introduction

1.01 This book aims to provide a comprehensive overview of the law relating to net zero and nature positive in England and Wales, covering areas such as planning and environmental law, commercial and financial services, construction and property law. We believe, at the time of writing, that it is the first text of its kind to set out the domestic legal framework for the transition to a net zero and nature positive future. The book is intended for legal professionals, judges, arbitrators, policymakers, activists, representatives of industries affected by this transition and those recognising the essential role of national laws in achieving that transition and realising the ambitions in international agreements.

1 Inger Andersen, 'Law, Climate Change and Welfare of the People' (30 November 2021) <https://www.unep.org/news-and-stories/speech/law-climate-change-and-welfare-people> accessed 12 April 2024, delivered by the Executive Director of the United Nations Environment Programme ('UNEP'), for the United Kingdom Bar Council's 19th Annual Law Reform Lecture. The figure of 1,800 is now out of date and the number of cases depends upon how 'climate litigation' is defined. In 'Global trends in climate litigation: 2024 snapshot' (June 2024), Joana Setzer and Catherine Higham of the Grantham Institute estimate that at least 230 new climate cases were filed in 2023 alone.

1.02 Whilst the book focuses on England and Wales,[2] it necessarily sets out the wider domestic and international context, given that both climate change and the biodiversity crisis are global phenomena. It is essential that sight is not lost of the global implications of decisions taken in the territorial and jurisdictional limits of England and Wales.

1.03 The book uses net zero and nature positive as leitmotifs for climate change and the biodiversity crisis, respectively.

1.04 This chapter sets the scene for the book by describing the climate change and biodiversity crises. Although this may be a scene with which most readers will be familiar, we hope that it serves as a reminder as to why the areas of law covered in this book are so fundamentally important to ensure a just transition to net zero, successful adaptation to climate risks, and a nature positive future.

1.05 The biodiversity crisis and climate change are among the most significant challenges of our generation. Indeed, the World Economic Forum, in its 2024 Global Risks report, has set out what are perceived as the most severe global risks over a 10-year period. The top four are: (1) extreme weather events; (2) critical change to Earth systems; (3) biodiversity loss and ecosystem collapse; and (4) natural resource shortages.[3]

1.06 There is no doubt that there is a significant interdependency as between climate change and the biodiversity crises. Nature has already been greatly damaged by, and continues to be threatened by, the impacts of climate change; whilst also providing a means of reducing carbon dioxide ('CO_2') emissions, through natural sequestration and carbon sinks, such as oceans, forests and soils. Nature also plays an essential role in adaptation: nature-based solutions include 'restoration and protection of coral reefs, seagrass meadows, coastal wetlands, mangroves, and beaches to reduce coastal flooding and erosion; green and blue spaces to reduce urban flooding and heat-related risks; protecting and restoring floodplains, peatlands and riparian vegetation to reduce river flooding'.[4]

---

2 Some environmental legislation applies to the whole of the United Kingdom, for example, the Climate Change Act 2008 s 1 and explanatory notes, [3] (addressed further in Chapter 2, paras 2.83–2.89, and in Chapter 4, para 4.02).
3 World Economic Forum, 'The Global Risks Report 2024 (19th Edition)' (2024) 8 <https://www3.weforum.org/docs/WEF_The_Global_Risks_Report_2024.pdf> accessed 12 April 2024. See also, World Economic Forum, 'The Global Risks Report 2023 (18th Edition)' (2023) 6 <https://www3.weforum.org/docs/WEF_Global_Risks_Report_2023.pdf> accessed 12 April 2024, which sets out the top six risks over a 10-year period as follows: (1) failure to mitigate climate change; (2) failure of climate change adaptation; (3) natural disasters and extreme weather events; (4) biodiversity loss and ecosystem collapse; (5) large-scale involuntary migration; and (6) natural resources crises.
4 UNEP, 'Making Peace with Nature: A Scientific Blueprint to Tackle the Climate, Biodiversity and Pollution Emergencies' (2021) 32 <https://wedocs.unep.org/xmlui/bitstream/handle/20.500.11822/34948/MPN.pdf> accessed 12 April 2024 ('MPN Report').

1.07 The Intergovernmental Panel on Climate Change ('IPCC') in their Synthesis Report,[5] published in 2023 ('Synthesis Report 2023'), recognises 'the interdependence of climate, ecosystems and biodiversity, and human societies; the value of diverse forms of knowledge; and the close linkages between climate change adaptation, mitigation, ecosystem health, human well-being and sustainable development, and reflects the increasing diversity of actors involved in climate action'.[6]

1.08 The UK's expert statutory body, the Climate Change Committee ('CCC'), also recognises this interdependence, such as in their most recent reports to Parliament on, respectively, reducing emissions and adaptation.[7] The CCC explains as follows:[8]

> Climate change has caused major changes to ecosystems beyond that expected through natural climate variability. Climate solutions have the potential to put biodiversity at risk (e.g. large-scale bioenergy) or help restore nature (e.g. nature-based solutions). Biodiversity protection and enhancement can also deliver adaptation and mitigation co-benefits, such as forest and soil restoration. Conversely, destroying nature (e.g. deforesting the Amazon) can release huge amounts of stored carbon.

1.09 In this section, a high-level account of climate change is provided before setting out the development and adoption of net zero as the 'new organising principle of climate politics';[9] in similar form, the biodiversity crisis is summarised before considering the origins and reach of nature positive as nature's answer to net zero.[10] In the remainder of the text we proceed on the understanding, almost universally accepted, that the science is correct and unimpeachable and we expect the courts, at least in England and Wales, to proceed on the same basis.

---

5 IPCC, 'Climate Change 2023: Synthesis Report' (2023) ('Synthesis Report 2023') <https://www.ipcc.ch/report/ar6/syr/downloads/report/IPCC_AR6_SYR_FullVolume.pdf> accessed 12 April 2024. This report was prepared for the IPCC's 58th session between 13 and 19 March 2023. It combines the main findings of the Sixth Assessment Report (AR6), and the three Special Reports, entitled 1) 'Global Warming of 1.5°C (2018): an IPCC Special Report on the impacts of global warming of 1.5°C above pre-industrial levels and related global greenhouse gas emission pathways, in the context of strengthening the global response to the threat of climate change, sustainable development, and efforts to eradicate poverty (SR1.5)'; 2) 'Climate Change and Land (2019): an IPCC Special Report on climate change, desertification, land degradation, sustainable land management, food security, and greenhouse gas fluxes in terrestrial ecosystems (SRCCL)'; and 3) 'The Ocean and Cryosphere in a Changing Climate (2019) (SROCC)'. The Special Reports cover scientific literature accepted for publication respectively by 15 May 2018, 7 April 2019 and 15 May 2019.

6 ibid 3.

7 See Chapter 4, paras 4.04–4.09. These reports are produced pursuant to CCA 2008 ss 36 and 59.

8 Climate Change Committee, 'Progress in Reducing Emissions: 2023 Report to Parliament' (2023) 60 <https://www.theccc.org.uk/wp-content/uploads/2023/06/Progress-in-reducing-UK-emissions-2023-Report-to-Parliament.pdf> accessed 4 April 2024 ('CCC Progress Report 2023'), laid before Parliament on 28 June 2023.

9 Jessica F Green and Raúl Salas Reyes, 'The History of Net Zero: Can We Move from Concepts to Practice?' (2023) 23(7) Climate Policy 901 <https://www.tandfonline.com/doi/abs/10.1080/14693062.2023.2218334> accessed 12 April 2024.

10 Reuters, 'Explainer: What Is "Nature Positive"? Biodiversity's Answer to Net Zero' <https://www.reuters.com/business/cop/what-is-nature-positive-biodiversitys-answer-net-zero-2022-11-16/> accessed 5 February 2024.

Climate change

1.10 Certain atmospheric gases occur naturally in the atmosphere and trap the sun's heat energy to make the Earth habitable for all living things.[11] This is the greenhouse effect keeping the Earth's average temperature at 15°C (59°F). These gases include water vapour, CO_2, methane and nitrous oxide; and are greenhouse gases ('GHGs').[12]

1.11 This effect becomes problematic when the concentration of GHGs increases to such an extent that the gases amplify the greenhouse effect and distort the climate system.[13] There is a general scientific consensus about these effects.[14] In *R (Spurrier) v Secretary of State for Transport*,[15] it was accepted by all parties before the Divisional Court that:

> (i) the concentration of GHGs in the earth's atmosphere is directly linked to average global temperatures, (ii) the concentration of GHGs has been rising steadily—and, with it, mean global temperatures—since the start of the Industrial Revolution and (iii) the most abundant GHG, accounting for at least two thirds of all GHGs, is CO_2 which is largely the product of burning fossil fuels. The increase in global temperature has resulted in (amongst other things) sea level change; a decline in glaciers, the Antarctic ice sheet and Arctic sea ice; alterations to various ecosystems; and in some areas a threat to food and water supplies. It is potentially catastrophic.

1.12 The IPCC explained in their Fifth Assessment Report (2014) ('AR5') that the 'warning of the climate system is unequivocal', referring to unprecedented, observed changes since the 1950s, including the warming of the atmosphere and ocean, the diminishing of snow and ice, sea level rises, and the increase in concentration of GHGs.[16]

1.13 More recently, in their Synthesis Report 2023, the IPCC set out the state of knowledge of climate change and its widespread impacts and risk. The report explains the anthropocentric nature of climate change:[17]

> Human activities, principally through emissions of greenhouse gases, have unequivocally caused global warming, with global surface temperature reaching 1.1°C above 1850–1900 in 2011–2020. Global greenhouse gas emissions have continued to increase, with unequal historical and ongoing contributions arising from unsustainable energy use, land use and land-use change, lifestyles and patterns of consumption and production across regions, between and within countries, and among individuals (high confidence).

---

11 Elizabeth Fisher, Bettina Lange and Eloise Scotford, *Environmental Law: Text, Cases and Materials* (2nd edn, Oxford University Press 2019) 600; *R (Spurrier) v Secretary of State for Transport* [2020] PTSR 240 [558].
12 Fisher, Lange and Scotford (n 11).
13 ibid.
14 IPCC, 'Synthesis Report 2023' (n 5) 89.
15 *R (Spurrier) v Secretary of State for Transport* (n 11) [559]; and decision upheld by the Supreme Court in *R (Friends of the Earth Ltd and others) v Heathrow Airport Ltd* [2021] PTSR 190.
16 IPCC, 'Climate Change 2014: Synthesis Report Summary for Policymakers' (2014) 2 <https://www.ipcc.ch/site/assets/uploads/2018/02/AR5_SYR_FINAL_SPM.pdf> accessed 12 April 2024. See also Figures SPM1.1, SPM1.2, SPM1.3 and SPM1.4.
17 IPCC, 'Synthesis Report 2023' (n 5) 4, para A.1.

1.14 Additionally, it highlights the unequal impact of climate change: the emissions vary substantially across regions with '10% of households with the highest per capita emissions contribut[ing] 34–45% of global consumption-based household GHG emissions, while the bottom 50% contribute 13–15%'.[18]

1.15 The observed changes and impacts are as follows:

- There have been more weather and climate extremes, including heatwaves, heavy precipitation, droughts, and tropical cyclones; and the evidence showing that they are attributable to human activity has only strengthened since AR5.[19]

- Between 3.3 to 3.6 billion people live in areas highly vulnerable to climate change. The extreme weather events have led to acute food insecurity and reduced water security with the largest impacts felt in Africa, Asia, Central and South America, Least Developed Countries, Small Islands and the Arctic, as well as amongst indigenous populations. In the regions with the greatest vulnerability, human mortality from floods, droughts and storms was 15 times higher between 2010 and 2020 when compared to regions with the lowest vulnerability.[20] There has also been an increase in climate-related food-borne and water-borne diseases, as well as a negative impact on mental health. The extreme climate and weather events have also led to displacement.[21] Ocean warming and acidification have negatively impacted on food production.[22]

- Substantial damage, including increasingly irreversible loss, to terrestrial, freshwater, cryospheric, coastal and open ocean ecosystems has been caused by climate change, with hundreds of local losses of species as a result of heat extremes. The near irreversible impact is most obvious in the hydrological changes from glacial retreat and changes in mountain and Arctic ecosystems as a result of permafrost thaw.[23]

- Climate change has also had a widespread negative impact on 'climate-exposed sectors, such as agriculture, forestry, fishery, energy, and tourism', as well as on homes and infrastructure.[24]

1.16 The IPCC advises that climate-related risks have increased since they were assessed in AR5 (2014); and that global warming will increase between 2021 and 2040 because of increased cumulative CO_2 emissions in all the scenarios and pathways.[25] There will also be a compounding effect whereby 'climatic and non-climatic effects will interact' and the risks will become more difficult to manage.[26]

---

18 ibid 5, para A.1.5.
19 ibid, para A.2.1.
20 ibid, para A.2.2.
21 ibid 6, para A.2.5.
22 ibid, para A.2.4.
23 ibid 5, para A.2.3.
24 ibid 6, para A.2.6.
25 ibid 12, paras B.1, B.1.1, B.2.
26 ibid 15, para B.2.3.

1.17 Mitigation of climate change is 'human intervention to reduce emissions or enhance the sinks of [GHGs]',[27] where a 'sink' is defined to include 'any process, activity or mechanism which removes a [GHG], an aerosol, or a precursor of a [GHG] from the atmosphere'.[28]

1.18 The IPCC explains that 'global modelled pathways that limit warming to 1.5°C (>50%) with no or limited overshoot and those that limit warming to 2°C (>67%), involve rapid and deep and, in most cases, immediate greenhouse gas emissions reductions in all sectors this decade'.[29] Thus, urgent action is required to mitigate climate change:[30]

> Climate change is a threat to human well-being and planetary health (very high confidence). There is a rapidly closing window of opportunity to secure a liveable and sustainable future for all (very high confidence). Climate resilient development integrates adaptation and mitigation to advance sustainable development for all, and is enabled by increased international cooperation including improved access to adequate financial resources, particularly for vulnerable regions, sectors and groups, and inclusive governance and coordinated policies (high confidence). The choices and actions implemented in this decade will have impacts now and for thousands of years (high confidence).

1.19 If such 'deep, rapid and sustained mitigation' takes place, along with measures for adaptation, that would, in the IPCC's view, reduce projected loss and damage for humans and ecosystems, as well as delivering other benefits for health and air quality.[31] Yet, gaps remain between global and national ambitions, and between national commitments and implemented policies.[32]

1.20 Mitigation requires action across the economy. The IPCC identifies multiple opportunities for mitigation through renewable energy, green infrastructure, demand-side management, improved forest and grassland management, reduced food waste and loss, removal of GHGs and low emission technologies.[33]

1.21 In the UK, GHGs were 450 $MtCO_2e$[34] in 2022, which includes the UK's share of international aviation and shipping.[35] In a recent report to Parliament on the UK's progress in reducing emissions, the CCC advised that its confidence in the government's plans to meet the UK's emissions targets (as set out in the carbon budgets, see further Chapter 2, paragraphs 2.89–2.106) has decreased, noting that there has been 'little substantial progress, timelines are slipping … urgent action is needed to fill policy gaps

---

27 ibid 126.
28 ibid 128.
29 ibid 26, para B.6.
30 ibid 24, para C.1.
31 ibid 25, para C.2.
32 See more below at para 1.21; see also the discussion of relevant cases in Chapter 2, paras 2.123–2.138.
33 IPCC, 'Synthesis Report 2023' (n 5) 10–11, paras A.4.2 and A.4.5. See also SPM.7.
34 See also Climate Change Act 2008 s 93(1)–(2), where GHGs are measured by reference to carbon dioxide equivalent, and 'tonne of carbon dioxide equivalent' is defined as 'one metric tonne of carbon dioxide or an amount of any other greenhouse gas with an equivalent global warming potential (calculated consistently with international carbon reporting practice)'.
35 CCC Progress Report 2023 (n 8) 75.

and develop alternative plans to mitigate the risk'.[36] The CCC, in their annual reports, assess progress on a UK-wide basis and then sector-by-sector,[37] as well as cross-cutting measures and carbon capture and storage ('CCS').

1.22 Adaptation is concerned with addressing the impacts of climate change. It is generally approached by a consideration of climate risks, which arise from the impacts of climate change and human responses to it.[38] The IPCC defines it as follows:[39]

> In human systems, the process of adjustment to actual or expected climate and its effects, in order to moderate harm or exploit beneficial opportunities. In natural systems, the process of adjustment to actual climate and its effects; human intervention may facilitate adjustment to expected climate and its effects.

1.23 Internationally, effective adaptation measures include, for example, agroforestry, sustainable land management approaches, disaster risk management, and early warning systems.[40] The IPCC specifically recognises the role of ecosystem-based adaptation approaches such as restoration of wetlands and forestry in reducing flood risks and urban heat.[41]

1.24 At the domestic level, the government is required to assess the risks of the current and predicted impacts of climate change in the UK.[42] The most recent assessment was in January 2022: the UK Climate Change Risk Assessment 2022 ('CCRA3') was laid before Parliament, pursuant to section 56 of the CCA 2008, on 17 January 2022. It was the third assessment undertaken in accordance with the reporting cycle set out in section 56. The report relies upon the work undertaken by the CCC, and identifies 61 UK-wide climate risks cutting across different sectors of the economy.[43] Priority risk areas include high risks to 'viability and diversity of terrestrial and freshwater habitats and species from multiple hazards', 'risks to natural carbon stores and sequestration', risk to food supplies and vital services due to collapses in supply chains, and risks to human health and well-being.[44]

Net zero

1.25 'Net zero' has been described as 'the new organising principle of climate politics',[45] as set out above, and a 'frame of reference through which global action against climate

36 ibid.
37 ibid 4–5 and 314. These are surface transport, buildings, industry, electricity supply, fuel supply, agriculture and land use, aviation, shipping, waste, fluorinated gases ('F-gases', which are particularly potent and used in refrigeration, air conditioning, heat pumps and medical inhalers). The CCC is considered in more detail in Chapter 4.
38 IPCC, 'Synthesis Report 2023' (n 5) 128.
39 ibid 120.
40 ibid 8, para A.3.2.
41 ibid.
42 CCA 2008 s 56(1).
43 DEFRA, 'UK Climate Change Risk Assessment 2022' (2022) 7 <https://assets.publishing.service.gov.uk/media/61e54d8f8fa8f505985ef3c7/climate-change-risk-assessment-2022.pdf> accessed 12 April 2024.
44 ibid 19.
45 Green and Salas Reyes (n 9) 901.

change can be (and is increasingly) structured and understood'.[46] Where 'a net zero world' is 'a world in balance', GHG emissions are cancelled out by the sequestration or removal of an equal amount of GHGs.[47]

1.26 The concept originated in climate science but is now the focus of climate ambition.[48] It represents a shift from just a 'stabilised level of atmospheric concentrations' or a 'percentage emissions reduction target'.[49]

1.27 Out of 198 countries, 151 have at least proposed to adopt a net zero target, around 27 have enshrined it in law and 52 have embodied it in a policy document.[50] Yet, net zero targets are not limited to states – estimates suggest that half of the world's largest publicly-listed companies have adopted a net zero target, meaning that 66% of annual revenue of those companies, representing $27 trillion, is covered by the target.[51] The growing number of such pledges evidences the 'unifying and galvanizing power of the net zero narrative', but governance and accountability mechanisms are mostly inadequate leading to accusations of greenwashing.[52]

1.28 The net zero target was enshrined in Article 4(1) of the Paris Agreement (see Chapter 2, paragraphs 2.39–2.40), which sets out the objective of achieving 'a balance between anthropogenic emissions by sources and removals by sinks of GHGs in the second half of this century'.[53] It is linked to the peak temperature goal set out in that agreement, namely, well below an increase of 2°C and making efforts to limit it to 1.5°C.

1.29 Commentators argue that it therefore remains an 'intrinsically scientific concept', given its link to a temperature goal:[54]

> If the objective is to keep the rise in global average temperatures within certain limits, physics implies that there is a finite budget of carbon dioxide that is allowed into the atmosphere, alongside other greenhouse gases. Beyond this budget, any further release must be balanced by removal into sinks.

---

46 Sam Fankhauser and others, 'The Meaning of Net Zero and How to Get It Right' (2022) 12(1) Nature Climate Change 15 <https://www.nature.com/articles/s41558-021-01245-w> accessed 12 April 2024.
47 Green and Salas Reyes (n 9) 901, citing Holly Jean Buck, *Ending Fossil Fuels: Why Net Zero Is Not Enough* (Verso Books 2021) 33.
48 Fankhauser and others (n 46) 15.
49 Fankhauser and others (n 46), where the authors explain that stabilising the level of atmospheric concentrations was the formulation of climate ambition in the 1992 UNFCC, and in the 1997 Kyoto Protocol, the focus was on a percentage emissions reduction target.
50 See 'Net Zero Tracker' <https://zerotracker.net/> accessed 18 November 2023.
51 Net Zero Tracker, 'New Analysis: Half of World's Largest Companies Are Committed to Net Zero' (6 November 2023) <https://zerotracker.net/analysis/new-analysis-half-of-worlds-largest-companies-are-committed-to-net-zero> accessed 18 November 2023.
52 See Fankhauser and others (n 46) 17. The authors argue that these issues do not negate the scientific logic of global net zero but they do show the need for 'clear guardrails to ensure the robustness of net zero as a framework for climate action'. They identify seven attributes for a successful net zero framework.
53 See Article 4(1).
54 Fankhauser and others (n 46) 15.

1.30 Thus, 'meeting the 1.5°C goal with 50% probability translates into a remaining carbon budget of 400–800 $GtCO_2$', which, in turn, requires 'CO_2 emissions to peak before 2030 and fall to net zero by around 2050'.[55]

1.31 In their 2023 Synthesis Report, the IPCC explained that:[56]

> Limiting human-caused global warming requires net zero CO_2 emissions. Cumulative carbon emissions until the time of reaching net zero CO_2 emissions and the level of greenhouse gas emission reductions this decade largely determine whether warming can be limited to 1.5°C or 2°C (high confidence). Projected CO_2 emissions from existing fossil fuel infrastructure without additional abatement would exceed the remaining carbon budget for 1.5°C (50%) (high confidence).

1.32 The IPCC defines net zero in relation to CO_2 emissions and GHG emissions: net zero is a condition in which anthropogenic CO_2 or metric-weighted anthropogenic emissions are balanced by anthropogenic CO_2 removals or metric-weighted anthropogenic emissions, over a specified period.[57]

1.33 The UK's net zero target, set out in section 1 CCA 2008, has a specific legal meaning in domestic law.[58] This section was amended by the CCA 2008 (2050 Target Amendment) Order 2019,[59] following the UK's ratification of the Paris Agreement on 17 November 2016.

1.34 Section 1 requires 'the Secretary of State to ensure that the net UK carbon account for 2050 is at least 100% lower than the 1990 baseline'.[60] Where the 'net UK account' essentially means 'the amount of net UK emissions of targeted greenhouse gases' for a particular period 'reduced by the amount of carbon units credited' and 'increased by the amount of carbon units debited', in accordance with regulations made under section 27 CCA 2008.[61]

1.35 The '1990 baseline' means 'the aggregate amount of – (a) net UK emissions of carbon dioxide for that year, and (b) net UK emissions of each of the other targeted greenhouse gases for the year that is the base year for that gas'.[62]

---

55 ibid, citing IPCC, 'Global Warming of 1.5°C.' (2018) <https://www.ipcc.ch/site/assets/uploads/sites/2/2019/06/SR15_ Full_Report_High_Res.pdf> accessed 22 March 2024.
56 IPCC, 'Synthesis Report 2023' (n 5) 19, para B.5.
57 ibid 126.
58 *R (Greenpeace Ltd) v Secretary of State for Energy Security and Net Zero* [2023] EWHC 2608 (Admin) [12]. See also Chapter 2, paras 2.89–2.93.
59 The Climate Change Act 2008 (2050 Target Amendment) Order 2019, SI 2019/1056.
60 CCA 2008 s 1(1).
61 These are The Carbon Accounting Regulations 2009, SI 2009/1257. Regulation 3 defines a 'carbon unit', for purposes of Part 1 of the CCA 2008, as '(a) assigned amount units; (b) European Union allowances; (c) certified emission reductions; (d) emission reduction units; and (e) removal units'.
62 CCA 2008 s 1(2).

Biodiversity crisis

1.36 The UN Secretary-General, António Guterres, describes humanity's war on nature as 'senseless and suicidal'.[63] Indeed, the imperative for biodiversity conservation derives from the dependency not just of humankind, but of every life form on Earth, on healthy ecosystems.[64] Nature is also vital for a good quality of life, conceptualised as human well-being and living in harmony with Mother Earth.[65] Yet, biodiversity is declining faster than at any other time in human history.[66]

1.37 Humans rely on the planet's resources, as well as its life-supporting processes and capacity to absorb waste.[67] The United Nations Environment Programme ('UNEP') sets out that over the past 50 years, the global economy has tripled largely due to the extraction of natural resources that, in turn, have been used in energy for production and consumption.[68] The world's population has also increased to 7.8 billion people; yet whilst prosperity has doubled, 1.3 billion people remain poor and 700 million hungry.[69]

1.38 Nature, and biological diversity, also have their own intrinsic value. This is recognised in the preamble to the Convention on Biological Diversity ('CBD'), which entered into force on 29 December 1993 (and is addressed more below at Chapter 2, paragraphs 2.54ff). The CBD defines 'biological diversity' at Article 2 as:[70]

> [T]he variability among living organisms from all sources including, inter alia, terrestrial, marine and other aquatic ecosystems and the ecological complexes of which they are part; this includes diversity within species, between species and of ecosystems.

1.39 As the Intergovernmental Science-Policy Platform on Biodiversity and Ecosystem Services ('IPBES'), in their global independent assessment of biodiversity and ecosystems, published in 2019, explain:[71]

- Nature plays a critical role in human existence by providing food, energy, and materials. Through its ecological processes, nature 'sustains the quality of the air, fresh water and soils on which humanity depends, distributes fresh water, regulates the climate, provides pollination and pest control and reduces the impact of natural hazards'. For example, '75% of global food crop types … rely on animal pollination'. In 2016, the value of agricultural crop production globally was $2.6 trillion, which was a three-fold increase since 1970; similarly, raw timber harvest

---

63 UNEP, 'MPN Report' (n 4) 4.
64 ibid 14. See also Chidi Oguamanam, 'Biodiversity, Biosafety and Bioprospecting' in Erika Techera and others (eds), *Routledge Handbook of International Environmental Law* (2nd edn, Routledge 2023) 101.
65 IPBES, 'Summary for Policymakers of the Global Assessment Report on Biodiversity and Ecosystem Services of the Intergovernmental Science-Policy Platform on Biodiversity and Ecosystem Services' (2019) 10 <https://zenodo.org/records/3553579> accessed 12 April 2024.
66 ibid.
67 UNEP, 'MPN Report' (n 4) 14.
68 ibid.
69 ibid.
70 UN Convention on Biological Diversity 2011 4. It defines an 'ecosystem' as 'a dynamic complex of plant, animal and micro-organism communities and their non-living environment interacting as a functional unit' (Article 2).
71 IPBES, 'Summary for Policymakers' (n 65) 3–4, para A1.

increased by 45% since 1970 and reached 4 billion cubic metres in 2017. Land degradation caused productivity to reduce by 23% of the global terrestrial area; and as a result of pollinator loss, between $235 billion and $577 billion in annual crop output is at risk.

- Humans have had a significant negative impact on nature and more species are threatened with extinction:[72]

  - 25% of assessed animal and plant groups are threatened. The IPBES suggests this translates to around 1 million species facing extinction, unless action is taken to reduce the drivers of the biodiversity crisis.[73]

  - The average abundance of native species in most terrestrial biomes has decreased by at least 20% since 1900 and the decrease is accelerating.[74]

  - 66% of the ocean is 'experiencing increasing cumulative impacts' including (i) direct exploitation through over-fishing, (ii) land- and sea-based pollution (through, for example, river networks and plastic pollution[75]), and (iii) land and sea use change, such as coastal development and infrastructure.[76]

  - 75% of land surface has been significantly altered[77] – one third of land is used for agriculture (animal husbandry and crops) and there has been a doubling of urban areas since 1992, at the expense of forests, wetlands and grasslands.[78]

  - 85% of wetlands have been lost.[79]

  - Between 2010 and 2015, 32 million hectares of primary or recovering forest were lost.[80]

  - Since the 1870s, approximately half of live coral cover on coral reefs has been lost with recent accelerating loss due to climate change exacerbating other causes.

- The impacts of climate change, including the average rise in temperature, the frequency and intensity of extreme weather events, and the global average rise in sea level, have contributed to the biodiversity crisis and compounded other drivers of change (such as overexploitation of resources, invasive alien species, and pollution).[81]

72 ibid 4, paras A4–A5.
73 ibid, para A5.
74 ibid, para A4.
75 ibid 5, para B3: Plastic pollution has 'increased tenfold since 1980, affecting at least 267 species, including 86 per cent of marine turtles, 44 per cent of seabirds and 43 per cent of marine mammals'.
76 ibid 4–5, paras A4, B1.
77 ibid 4, para A4.
78 ibid 5, para B1.
79 ibid 4, para A4.
80 ibid.
81 ibid 5, para B2.

- Terrestrial ecosystems are the 'sole sinks for anthropogenic carbon emissions, with a gross sequestration of 5.6 gigatons of carbon per year (the equivalent of some 60 per cent of global anthropogenic emissions)'.[82]

- Local varieties and breeds of domesticated animals and plants are disappearing, and the loss of this biological diversity threatens resilience of agrosystems to climate change, pathogens and pests.[83]

1.40 In relation to species loss and habitats, the UNEP sets out as follows:[84]

> Species are currently going extinct tens to hundreds of times faster than the natural background rate. One million of the world's estimated 8 million species of plants and animals are threatened with extinction. The population sizes of wild vertebrates have dropped by an average of 68 per cent in the last 50 years, and the abundance of many wild insect species has fallen by more than half. The number of local varieties of domesticated plants and animal breeds and their wild relatives has been reduced sharply. For example, over 9 per cent of animal breeds have become extinct and at least another 17 per cent are threatened with extinction. Ecosystems are degrading at an unprecedented rate, driven by land-use change, exploitation, climate change, pollution and invasive alien species. Climate change exacerbates other threats to biodiversity, and many plant and animal species have already experienced changes in their range, abundance and seasonal activity. Degradation of ecosystems is impacting their functions and harming their ability to support human well-being. Loss of biodiversity is anticipated to accelerate in coming decades, unless actions to halt and reverse human transformation and degradation of ecosystems and to limit climate change are urgently implemented.

1.41 The Red List is a 'critical indicator of the health of the world's biodiversity', produced by the International Union for Conservation of Nature ('IUCN'); it identifies that more than 44,000 species are threatened with extinction (which is based on 28% of all assessed species).[85]

---

82 ibid 3, para A1. See also, IPCC, 'Synthesis Report 2023' (n 5) 21, B.6.4: 'Mitigation options often have synergies with other aspects of sustainable development, but some options can also have trade-offs. There are potential synergies between sustainable development and, for instance, energy efficiency and renewable energy. Similarly, depending on the context, biological CDR methods like reforestation, improved forest management, soil carbon sequestration, peatland restoration and coastal blue carbon management can enhance biodiversity and ecosystem functions, employment and local livelihoods. However, afforestation or production of biomass crops can have adverse socio-economic and environmental impacts, including on biodiversity, food and water security, local livelihoods and the rights of Indigenous Peoples, especially if implemented at large scales and where land tenure is insecure. Modelled pathways that assume using resources more efficiently or that shift global development towards sustainability include fewer challenges, such as less dependence on CDR and pressure on land and biodiversity. (high confidence) {3.4.1}.'

83 IPBES 'Summary for Policymakers' (n 65) 4, para A6.

84 UNEP, 'MPN Report' (n 4) 23.

85 IUCN, 'Red List – Background and History' <https://www.iucnredlist.org/about/background-history> accessed 12 April 2024; and IUCN, 'IUCN Home Page' <https://www.iucnredlist.org/> accessed 12 April 2024.

1.42 WWF, in their 'Living Planet Report 2022',[86] considered data gathered from nearly 32,000 populations of 5,230 species across the globe and, applying the Global Living Planet Index, have shown that there has been 'an average 69% decline in monitored populations between 1970 and 2018'.[87] In Latin America and the Caribbean, there has been a 94% decline.[88] From the Red List analysis, WWF has been able to identify the six key threats to terrestrial vertebrates: 'agriculture, hunting, logging, pollution, invasive species and climate change'.[89]

1.43 In 2019, HM Treasury commissioned the Dasgupta Review, which was an independent, global review of the economics of biodiversity led by Professor Sir Partha Dasgupta.[90] The Final Report of the Review, published in 2021, showed that, between 1992 and 2014, while capital produced per person doubled and human capital per person increased by 13% globally, the stock of natural capital per person declined by nearly 40%.[91] At this rate, 'we would require 1.6 Earths to maintain the world's current living standards'.[92] The review describes the imbalance between humanity's demands and nature's supply as the 'Impact Inequality', and explains the heart of problem:[93]

> Nature's worth to society – the true value of the various goods and services it provides – is not reflected in market prices because much of it is open to all at no monetary charge.

1.44 This is not just a market failure but an 'institutional failure' – governments have paid people to exploit nature rather than protect it:[94]

> A conservative estimate of the total cost globally of subsidies that damage Nature is around US$4 to 6 trillion per year. And we lack the institutional arrangements needed to protect global public goods, such as the ocean or the world's rainforests.

1.45 The review reflects on the current dominant understanding that 'humanity is "external" to Nature', and instead seeks to develop the understanding that 'our economies … are "embedded" within Nature'. Consequently, a fundamental transformation of our economies, 'akin to, or even greater than, those of the Marshall Plan', is needed in order to address biodiversity loss. This includes 'accounting fully for the impact of our interactions with Nature and rebalancing our demand with Nature's capacity to supply'.[95]

---

86 WWF, 'Living Planet Report 2022 – Building a Nature-Positive Society' (2022) 10 <https://wwflpr.awsassets.panda.org/downloads/lpr_2022_full_report.pdf> accessed 12 April 2024.
87 ibid 32.
88 ibid 34.
89 ibid 40–41.
90 HM Treasury, 'Final Report – The Economics of Biodiversity: The Dasgupta Review' (2021) <https://www.gov.uk/government/publications/final-report-the-economics-of-biodiversity-the-dasgupta-review> accessed 26 November 2023.
91 HM Treasury, 'The Economics of Biodiversity: The Dasgupta Review – Headline Messages' (2021) 1 <https://assets.publishing.service.gov.uk/media/60182857d3bf7f70c2afe5bb/Dasgupta_Review_-_Headline_Messages.pdf> accessed 12 April 2024.
92 ibid.
93 ibid 2.
94 ibid.
95 ibid 2–3.

Nature positive

1.46 The concept of 'nature positive' is gaining traction as the counterpart to net zero as the organising principle of nature politics. Indeed, WWF considers that 'a global goal reversing biodiversity loss to secure a nature-positive world by 2030' should be 'our guiding star, in the same way that the goal of limiting global warming to 2°C, and preferably 1.5°C, guides our efforts on climate'.[96] It has led to a range of initiatives, across both conservation groups and industry, to lead to transformative change through, for example, Science-based Targets for Nature and the Taskforce for Nature-Related Financial Disclosures.[97]

1.47 Nature positive is concerned, in broad terms, not only with the halt, but also the reversal of biodiversity loss.[98] It represents a paradigm shift in discourse from terms such as 'no net loss' ('NNL') and 'net positive impact' ('NPI'), which originated in public pollution and wetland trading policies in the 1970s in the US.[99] Such commitments were principally focused on the mitigation hierarchy (avoid, minimise, restore, offset) in companies' direct operational impacts.[100] The shift is attributed, in part at least, to the recognition of the economic and financial risks of biodiversity loss (as set out in the Dasgupta Review).[101]

1.48 Like with net zero, definitions of nature positive differ, which has led to calls for a consistent and agreed definition, to ensure that progress can be monitored, accountability can be ensured, and the risk of greenwashing reduced.[102]

1.49 G7 leaders, on 13 June 2021, agreed to halt and reverse biodiversity loss by 2030 as part of the G7 Nature Compact,[103] building on the G7 Metz Charter on Biodiversity and the Leaders' Pledge for Nature.[104] The compact recognises the interdependency between climate change and biodiversity loss, and acknowledges that:[105]

> Global system-wide change is required: our world must not only become net zero, but also nature positive, for the benefit of both people and the planet, with a focus on promoting sustainable and inclusive development. Nature, and the biodiversity that underpins it, ultimately sustains our economies, livelihoods and well-being – our decisions must take into account the true value of the goods and services we derive from it. The lives and livelihoods of today's youth and future generations rely on this.

---

96 WWF, 'Living Planet Report 2022 – Building a Nature-Positive Society' (n 86) 100.
97 Sophus zu Ermgassen and others, 'Are Corporate Biodiversity Commitments Consistent with Delivering "Nature-Positive" Outcomes? A Review of "Nature Positive" Definitions, Company Progress and Challenges' (2022) 379 Part 2 Journal of Cleaner Production 2 <https://www.sciencedirect.com/science/article/pii/S0959652622043700> accessed 13 April 2024.
98 Harvey Locke and others, 'A Nature-Positive World: The Global Goal for Nature' <https://f.hubspotusercontent20.net/hubfs/4783129/Nature%20Positive%20The%20Global%20Goal%20for%20Nature%20paper.pdf> accessed 12 April 2024.
99 zu Ermgassen and others (n 97) 2.
100 ibid.
101 ibid.
102 ibid.
103 DEFRA, 'Government Sets out Commitments to Biodiversity and Sustainability in G7 Nature Compact' (2021) <https://www.gov.uk/government/news/government-sets-out-commitments-to-biodiversity-and-sustainability-in-g7-nature-compact> accessed 26 November 2023.
104 Cabinet Office, 'Policy Paper – G7 2030 Nature Compact' (2021) <https://www.gov.uk/government/publications/g7-2030-nature-compact/g7-2030-nature-compact> accessed 26 November 2023.
105 ibid [3].

1.50 The pillars of the Compact include, as a first pillar, a transition to the sustainable and legal use of natural resources that acknowledges the 'harmful effect of some subsidies on the environment' and commits to a review of domestic policies, as well as taking appropriate action to develop nature positive replacements.[106] The second pillar builds upon the Dasgupta Review, and is concerned with investing in nature and driving a nature positive economy.[107] The third pillar focuses on protecting, conserving, and restoring nature, through global targets, and the fourth pillar is about ensuring accountability.[108]

1.51 Whilst the UN CBD's Kunming-Montreal Global Biodiversity Framework[109] does not refer to nature positive, it sets out four goals and 23 targets. Goals A and B provide as follows:

GOAL A Protect and Restore

- The integrity, connectivity and resilience of all ecosystems are maintained, enhanced, or restored, substantially increasing the area of natural ecosystems by 2050;
- Human induced extinction of known threatened species is halted, and, by 2050, extinction rate and risk of all species are reduced tenfold and the abundance of native wild species is increased to healthy and resilient levels;
- The genetic diversity within populations of wild and domesticated species, is maintained, safeguarding their adaptive potential.

GOAL B Prosper with Nature

- Biodiversity is sustainably used and managed and nature's contributions to people, including ecosystem functions and services, are valued, maintained and enhanced, with those currently in decline being restored, supporting the achievement of sustainable development for the benefit of present and future generations by 2050.

1.52 Targets 1–8 specifically address reducing the threats to biodiversity, and targets 9–13 address meeting people's needs through sustainable use of species and ecosystems and benefit-sharing.

1.53 As part of the Nature Positive Initiative, launched on 6 September 2023, 27 of the world's largest nature conservation organisations, institutes, businesses and finance coalitions have launched a campaign to standardise the definition of nature positive and to set a global goal for nature, which would work in parallel to the Global Biodiversity Framework.[110] The goal would have three measurable objectives: (i) zero net loss of nature from 2020; (ii) net positive by 2030; and (iii) full recovery by 2050.[111]

106 ibid Pillar 1, [3].
107 ibid Pillar 2.
108 ibid Pillars 3 and 4.
109 UNEP, 'Kunming-Montreal Global Biodiversity Framework' (19 December 2022) <http://www.unep.org/resources/kunming-montreal-global-biodiversity-framework> accessed 8 April 2024.
110 Locke and others (n 98). See their website at: 'Nature Positive Initiative' <https://www.naturepositive.org/> accessed 26 November 2023.
111 ibid.

1.54 Domestically, the Environment Act 2021 ('EA 2021'[112]) is relied upon by government as the 'key mechanism in driving forward our ambition on biodiversity and delivering our commitments under the CBD'.[113] The EA 2021 provides a legal mechanism for various long-term environmental targets to be set in four priority areas: air quality, water, biodiversity, and resource efficiency and waste reduction.[114] By section 5 of the EA 2021, it is the duty of the Secretary of State to ensure the targets are met. The EA 2021 also provides for other legal mechanisms (and amends existing legislation) to improve the protection of nature and biodiversity, including biodiversity net gain, conservation covenants and environmental principles in policy-making, dealt with elsewhere in this book.[115]

1.55 The government explained that a core part of its response to the Dasgupta Review was setting out a 'new world-leading target on species abundance for 2030'.[116] Section 3 addresses that target, with the stated aim of halting the decline of nature.[117] In the House of Lords, Lord Goldsmith observed as follows:[118]

> We hope that this measure will be the net zero equivalent for nature, spurring action of the scale required to address the biodiversity crisis. As noble Lords know, nature has been in decline for decades, and tackling that long-term decline will be challenging. But through this new target we are committing ourselves to that objective. A domestic 2030 species target will not only benefit species; the actions necessary to achieve it will also help drive wider environmental improvements – for example, to the habitats in which they live, and on which they depend.

1.56 Section 3(2) makes it clear that the specified date, which is the date by which the target must be achieved,[119] for the species abundance target must be 31 December 2030. The section does not, however, set the target itself but provides the statutory power for the government to make regulations; and 'the Secretary of State must be satisfied that meeting the target, or the amended target, would halt a decline in the abundance of species'.[120] The extant regulations made thereunder are the Environmental Targets (Biodiversity) (England) Regulations 2023.[121] These regulations set the species abundance target in regulation 11 and other long-term biodiversity targets relating to species' extinction risk and habitat restoration and creation. This is considered in more detail in Chapter 8, paragraphs 8.49–8.59.

112 See Chapter 8 for further detail on the EA 2021.
113 HM Treasury, *The Economics of Biodiversity: The Dasgupta Review – Government Response* (CP 504, 2021) 4 [1.3] <https://assets.publishing.service.gov.uk/media/60f02799e90e0764d2837899/Dasgupta_Response__web_July.pdf> accessed 12 April 2024.
114 EA 2021 ss 1(3) and 5.
115 See Chapter 8, in particular.
116 HM Treasury, *The Economics of Biodiversity: The Dasgupta Review – Government Response* (n 113) 4 para 1.3.
117 ibid 6 [2.1].
118 HL Deb 23 June 2021, vol 813, col 313.
119 EA 2021 s 1(4)(b).
120 ibid s 3(4).
121 The Environmental Targets (Biodiversity) (England) Regulations 2023, SI 2023/91.

CHAPTER 2

OVERARCHING LEGAL FRAMEWORK

Ella Grodzinski and Stephanie David

International legal framework

> Mr President, the environmental challenge which confronts the whole world demands an equivalent response from the whole world. Every country will be affected and no one can opt out.
>
> We should work through this great organisation [the United Nations] and its agencies to secure world-wide agreements on ways to cope with the effects of climate change, the thinning of the Ozone Layer, and the loss of precious species.
>
> We need a realistic programme of action and an equally realistic timetable.
>
> Each country has to contribute, and those countries who are industrialised must contribute more to help those who are not.[1]

(i) *Introduction*

2.01 The focus of this section is the international conventions on climate change and biodiversity – these two conventions were opened for signature at the Conference on the Environment and Development in 1992 in Rio de Janeiro, otherwise known as the 'Earth Summit', where agreement was also reached to negotiate the United Nations Convention to Combat Desertification (which is beyond the scope of this book).[2] Together, these three conventions are known as the 'Rio Conventions'.[3]

2.02 The United Nations Framework Convention on Climate Change ('UNFCCC')[4] entered into force on 21 March 1994, and sets the international legal framework for climate change. It provides an overarching structure, relying on protocols and other

1 Margaret Thatcher, 'Speech to United Nations General Assembly (Global Environment)' (11 August 1989) <https://www.margaretthatcher.org/document/107817> accessed 5 May 2024. She called for a framework convention on climate change, described as a 'good conduct guide for all nations' based on the Vienna Convention in 1985 and the Montreal Protocol in 1987; and specific protocols addressing different aspects of climate change. She also called for a convention to conserve biodiversity.

2 United Nations Convention to Combat Desertification (adopted 17 June 1994, entered into force 26 December 1996).

3 'The Rio Conventions | UNFCCC' <https://unfccc.int/process-and-meetings/the-rio-conventions> accessed 7 May 2024.

4 United Nations Framework Convention on Climate Change (adopted 9 May 1992, entered into force 21 March 1994) 1771 UNTS 107.

treaties created under its umbrella to be applied in practice.[5] The Paris Agreement[6] and the Kyoto Protocol[7] were created under its auspices.

2.03 For biodiversity, the international framework is set by the Convention on Biological Diversity ('CBD'), which entered into force on 29 December 1993.[8] It has three main objectives: (1) the conservation of biological diversity; (2) the sustainable use of the components of biological diversity; and (3) the fair and equitable sharing of the benefits arising out of the utilisation of genetic resources.[9]

2.04 There is also a direct intersection between these two Conventions – the Conference of the Parties ('COP', addressed more below) to the CBD[10] has a work programme on climate change and biodiversity, recognising both that biodiversity is affected by climate change and that, conversely, resilience to climate change is affected by biodiversity through the ecosystem services that biodiversity provides.[11] For example, voluntary guidelines have been adopted by the CBD Secretariat on the implementation of ecosystem-based approaches to adaptation and disaster risk reduction.[12] The Nairobi Work Programme,[13] under UNFCCC auspices, includes biodiversity and ecosystems as one of its priority areas.

2.05 The links between climate change and biodiversity were highlighted most recently at COP 28 in Dubai. Prior to COP 28, the three Presidents of the COPs on Climate Change (under the UNFCCC), biodiversity (under the CBD) and desertification (under the UN Convention to Combat Desertification, 'UNCCD') released a joint declaration emphasising the inextricable links between climate change, biodiversity loss and desertification; and called for a coordinated and holistic approach to tackling these global crises.[14]

---

5 Daniel Bodansky, Jutta Brunnée and Lavanya Rajamani, *International Climate Change Law* (Oxford University Press 2017) chs 4 and 5.
6 Paris Agreement (adopted 12 December 2015, entered into force 4 November 2016) 3156 UNTS 54113.
7 Kyoto Protocol to the United Nations Framework Convention on Climate Change (adopted 11 December 1997, entered into force 16 February 2005) 2303 UNTS 162.
8 'History of the Convention' (CBD, 6 May 2024) <https://www.cbd.int/history> accessed 6 May 2024.
9 United Nations Convention on Biological Diversity (adopted 5 June 1992, entered into force 29 December 1993) 2011 Article 1.
10 See section (v) below.
11 'Climate Change and Biodiversity' (CBD, 17 April 2024) <https://www.cbd.int/climate> accessed 1 May 2024. The 2003 Millennium Ecosystem Assessment defined ecosystem services as 'the benefits people obtain from ecosystems. These include provisioning services such as food and water; regulating services such as flood and disease control; cultural services such as spiritual, recreational, and cultural benefits; and supporting services, such as nutrient cycling, that maintain the conditions for life on Earth.' Millennium Ecosystem Assessment, 'Ecosystems and Human Well-Being: A Framework for Assessment' (2003) 49 <http://pdf.wri.org/ecosystems_human_wellbeing.pdf> accessed 5 July 2024.
12 Secretariat of the CBD, 'Voluntary Guidelines for the Design and Effective Implementation of Ecosystem-Based Approaches to Climate Change Adaptation and Disaster Risk Reduction and Supplementary Information' (2019) CBD Technical Series No. 93 <https://www.cbd.int/doc/publications/cbd-ts-93-en.pdf> accessed 5 January 2024.
13 The Nairobi Work Programme is the UNFCCC knowledge-to-action hub on adaptation and resilience, established at COP11 in Nairobi, in December 2005.
14 UNCCD, 'Presidents of Three COPs Call for a United Approach to Climate Change, Desertification and Biodiversity Loss' <https://www.unccd.int/news-stories/press-releases/presidents-three-cops-call-united-approach-climate-change> accessed 6 May 2024.

2.06 The freestanding right to a healthy environment has also now been recognised internationally. The Human Rights Council acknowledged the right in October 2021,[15] followed by the United Nations General Assembly ('UNGA') in July 2022.[16] Although there is no universal definition of this right, it is generally understood to involve both substantive requirements (including clean air, a safe and stable climate, access to safe water and adequate sanitation, and healthy biodiversity and ecosystems) and procedural requirements (including access to information, access to justice and the right to participate in decision-making).[17] The right has been recognised in some countries and incorporated into domestic law, either directly or as part of the right to life.[18] It has not been accepted in the United Kingdom.

2.07 Climate change and biodiversity are also directly and indirectly addressed in other legal frameworks that sit in parallel to, or integrate with, the UN system. For example, the World Trade Organization has recognised the negative impact of climate change on trade by disrupting distribution and supply chains.[19] The European Union ('EU') has its own internal regime, as well as having signed and ratified the UNFCCC and Kyoto Protocol and having submitted a collective Nationally Determined Contribution ('NDC') under the Paris Agreement. The jurisprudence of the European Court of Human Rights ('ECtHR') has also developed in such a way that the European Convention on Human Rights ('ECHR') is being interpreted through the lens of climate change.[20]

(ii) *United Nations Framework Convention on Climate Change*

2.08 The adoption of the UNFCCC was precipitated by the first Intergovernmental Panel on Climate Change ('IPCC') report in 1990.[21] The IPCC is the UN body responsible for assessing the science related to climate change.[22] Having been created in 1988 by the World Meteorological Organization[23] and the United Nations Environment

15 UNGA Resolution A/HRC/RES/48/13 (18 October 2021).
16 UNGA Resolution A/RES/76/300 (28 July 2022).
17 OHCHR, UNEP, and UNDP, 'What Is the Right to a Healthy Environment? Information Note' (2023) <https://wedocs.unep.org/bitstream/handle/20.500.11822/41599/WRHE.pdf?sequence=1&isAllowed=y> accessed 5 June 2024.
18 See, for example, in India under Articles 14 and 21 of the Constitution – Supreme Court judgment *Ranjitsinh & Ors v Union of India & Ors* 2024 INSC 280 [11–35].
19 For further details about the WTO's work on trade and climate change, see here: 'Trade and Climate Change' (WTO) <https://www.wto.org/english/tratop_e/envir_e/climate_intro_e.htm> accessed 6 May 2024.
20 European Court of Human Rights, 'Factsheet – Climate Change' <https://www.echr.coe.int/documents/d/echr/fs_climate_change_eng> accessed 8 April 2024; Further discussion on this can be found in s (iv) of 'Proceedings before national courts' within Chapter 28 ('Public International Law').
21 IPCC, 'Climate Change: The IPCC 1990 and 1992 Assessments' <https://www.ipcc.ch/report/climate-change-the-ipcc-1990-and-1992-assessments/> accessed 6 May 2024.
22 'The Intergovernmental Panel on Climate Change' (IPCC) <https://www.ipcc.ch/> accessed 6 May 2024.
23 The World Meteorological Organization (WMO) is a specialised UN agency, self-described as 'the United Nations system's authoritative voice on the state and behaviour of the Earth's atmosphere, its interaction with the land and oceans, the weather and climate it produces and the resulting distribution of water resources'. Established in 1950, the WMO 'regulates and facilitates free and unrestricted exchange of data and information, products, and services', and 'provides the framework for such international cooperation to advance meteorological, climatological, hydrological, and related environmental services, to improve well-being of all'. 'Overview' (World Meteorological Organization, 4 January 2023) <https://wmo.int/about-wmo/overview> accessed 6 May 2024.

Programme ('UNEP'),[24] the IPCC published its first report in November 1990.[25] The report was split into three sections, divided by working groups of scientists. The policy-makers' executive summary of the Working Group I report stated that the authors were 'certain' that 'emissions resulting from human activities are substantially increasing the atmospheric concentrations of greenhouse gases ... resulting in an additional warming of the Earth's surface'.[26] This led to calls by the IPCC and the second World Climate Conference for a global treaty addressing climate change.[27] In December 1990, the UNGA established the Intergovernmental Negotiating Committee ('INC') to conduct the relevant negotiations for a framework convention on climate change. The negotiations took just 15 months. At the Earth Summit in 1992, the UN adopted the UNFCCC.[28] The UNFCCC now has near-universal membership, with 198 State Parties.[29]

2.09 The 'ultimate objective' of the UNFCCC, and the agreements and protocols made thereunder, is provided in Article 2: to stabilise greenhouse gas ('GHG') concentrations in the atmosphere at a level that would prevent dangerous anthropogenic interference with the global climate system. Stabilisation of GHG concentrations, and of consequent average global temperature increases, should be achieved at such a level and within such a timeframe as to allow ecosystems and human societies to adapt to climate change and develop sustainably.[30]

2.10 The key terms within this objective are defined in Article 1 as follows:

> 1. 'Adverse effects of climate change' means changes in the physical environment or biota resulting from climate change which have significant deleterious effects on the composition, resilience or productivity of natural and managed ecosystems or on the operation of socio-economic systems or on human health and welfare.
>
> 2. 'Climate change' means a change of climate which is attributed directly or indirectly to human activity that alters the composition of the global atmosphere and which is in addition to natural climate variability observed over comparable time periods.
>
> ...

24 The United Nations Environment Programme (UNEP) was established in 1972. It is the body responsible for coordinating sustainable development within the UN system. It states its mission as 'to inspire, inform, and enable nations and peoples to improve their quality of life without compromising that of future generations', and aims to find solution to the 'root causes of the triple planetary crisis of climate change, nature and biodiversity loss and pollution': 'About the United Nations Environment Programme' (UNEP) <http://www.unep.org/who-we-are/about-us> accessed 6 May 2024.
25 'Climate Change: The IPCC 1990 and 1992 Assessments' (n 21).
26 JT Houghton, GJ Jenkins and JJ Ephraums, *Climate Change: The IPCC Scientific Assessment* (Cambridge University Press 1990) xi.
27 The Second World Climate Conference was held in Geneva in October and November 1990, sponsored by the World Meteorological Organization and the United Nations Environment Programme, along with other international organisations. See 'UNFCCC – 25 Years of Effort and Achievement' (UNFCCC) <https://unfccc.int/timeline/> accessed 6 May 2024.
28 UNFCCC (adopted 9 May 1992, entered into force 21 March 1994).
29 'Parties & Observers' (UNFCCC) <https://unfccc.int/parties-observers> accessed 6 May 2024.
30 UNFCCC Article 2.

4. 'Emissions' means the release of greenhouse gases and/or their precursors into the atmosphere over a specified area and period of time.

5. 'Greenhouse gases' means those gaseous constituents of the atmosphere, both natural and anthropogenic, that absorb and re-emit infrared radiation.

2.11 The UNFCCC and its related instruments work through a combination of what have come to be known as 'top-down', 'hybrid' and 'bottom-up' approaches.[31] The Kyoto Protocol encapsulated a 'top-down' approach, which means that it provided for strong coordination and targets set on an international level. By contrast, the Paris Agreement takes a 'bottom-up' or 'hybrid' approach, seeking to protect the autonomy of individual states in defining their national contributions.[32]

(a) Structure and contents of the UNFCCC

2.12 Articles 1–3 of the UNFCCC are the introductory provisions. Article 1 contains the definitions. Article 2 sets out the 'ultimate objective'. Article 3 provides principles, such as the establishment of the principle of 'common but differentiated responsibilities and respective capabilities', which means that 'developed country Parties[33] should take the lead in combating climate change and the adverse effects thereof'.[34]

2.13 The substantive commitments are largely contained in Articles 4–6. These can be divided up as follows into:[35]

- The general commitments are set out in Articles 4(1), 5 and 6. These include commitments to research and systematic observation of climate change under Article 5, and commitments to education, training and awareness under Article 6.

- The mitigation commitments are set out in Article 4(1)(b)–(d) and 4(3). Mitigation means reducing emissions or enhancing sinks of GHGs, in order to minimise climate change.[36] By Article 4(1), Parties committed to, *inter alia*, formulating, publishing and updating national and regional measures to address emissions, and to conserve sinks and reservoirs of GHGs. By Article 4(3), the more developed country Parties committed to providing financial and technological assistance to help less developed country Parties meet their mitigation commitments under Article 4(1).

- The adaptation commitments are set out in Article 4(1)(b), (e), 4(8)–4(9). Adaptation refers to increasing resilience and reducing vulnerability to effects of climate change[37] – for example, by preparing plans for coastal zone management

31 Lavanya Rajamani, 'Ambition and Differentiation in the 2015 Paris Agreement: Interpretative Possibilities and Underlying Politics' (2016) 65 The International and Comparative Law Quarterly 493.
32 ibid.
33 Capitalised as per the text of the UNFCCC.
34 UNFCCC Article 3(1) and 3(3).
35 Bodansky, Brunnée and Rajamani (n 5) chs 4 and 5.
36 See Chapter 1, para 1.17. 'Introduction to Mitigation' (UNFCCC) <https://unfccc.int/topics/introduction-to-mitigation> accessed 6 May 2024.
37 See Chapter 1, paras 1.22–1.24. Paris Agreement Article 7.

or the protection and rehabilitation of areas affected by drought, as referenced in Article 4(1)(e).

- Financial support is addressed in Article 4(3)–(4). Developed nation Parties agreed to provide financial resources to developing nations in order to help them meet the costs of their mitigation commitments and, for Parties which are particularly vulnerable to the adverse effects of climate change, the costs of adaptation.

- Technology transfer is dealt with in Article 4(5). Developed nation Parties committed to promoting, facilitating and financing the transfer of 'environmentally sound technologies' to developing nations, in order to enable them to meet their UNFCCC commitments.

- Transparency features in Article 4(1)(a) and 12. All Parties committed to communicating information about their emissions, steps taken to implement the UNFCCC, and other information relevant for meeting the UNFCCC's objectives. Such transparency aims to enable scrutiny and political accountability.

2.14 The substantive commitments vary depending upon the principle of 'common but differentiated responsibilities and respective capabilities'.[38] The Parties to the UNFCCC are categorised based upon their state of economic development. Annex I lists the industrialised countries which were members of the Organisation for Economic Co-operation and Development ('OECD') in 1992, and additionally countries which were deemed 'economies in transition' ('the EIT Parties'). Annex II is a sub-set of Annex I; and excludes the EIT Parties.[39] These two annexes together provide which nations are to be considered 'developed country Parties' which will be required to 'take the lead'.[40] Countries which are in neither annex ('non-annex Parties') are generally developing countries.[41] Commitments under the UNFCCC are allocated accordingly. For example, Article 4(2) commits the Annex I Parties to actions such as adopting national policies and corresponding measures on the mitigation of climate change by limiting GHG emissions and protecting and enhancing GHG sinks and reservoirs, as well as periodically communicating (in accordance with Article 12) information on such policies and measures adopted. Article 4(3) meanwhile commits the Annex II Parties to providing financial and technological support to developing countries.

2.15 Articles 7–14 make provision to enable the implementation of the UNFCCC, including establishing the Secretariat,[42] the Conference of the Parties,[43] and mechanisms for reporting and review of progress.[44]

---

38 UNFCCC Article 3(1).
39 'Parties & Observers' (n 29).
40 UNFCCC Article 3(1).
41 See 'What Are Parties & Non-Party Stakeholders?' (UNFCCC) <https://unfccc.int/process-and-meetings/what-are-parties-non-party-stakeholders> accessed 6 May 2024.
42 UNFCCC Article 8.
43 ibid Article 7, discussed further below.
44 ibid Article 12, discussed further below.

2.16 Articles 15–26 concern procedural matters such as amendments and ratifications of the Convention, and its entry into force. Notably, Article 17 allows any ordinary session of the COP to adopt protocols to the UNFCCC. Article 25 provides that any Party may withdraw from the UNFCCC at any time, by giving written notification to the Depositary.[45]

(b) Institutions and mechanisms created

2.17 There are a number of institutions and mechanisms created by and under the UNFCCC. The most significant are listed below.

2.18 *The Conference of the Parties ('COP')*: The COP is the 'supreme' decision-making body under the UNFCCC.[46] All State Parties to the UNFCCC are represented at the COP, which meets yearly (unless the Parties decide otherwise). The core aim of the COP is to implement the UNFCCC, and to review the effectiveness of the measures taken by the Parties towards achieving the ultimate objective of the UNFCCC. The decisions taken at COPs are not legally binding but do have significant political and practical weight. COPs can review existing commitments, initiate negotiations, establish new bodies (for example, the Green Climate Fund ('GCF'))[47] and define new procedures.

2.19 Some COPs produce particularly significant outcomes. COP 13, which took place in Bali in 2007, produced the Bali Road Map, which charted a route for new negotiations on climate change.[48] The Road Map included the Bali Action Plan, which looked at five key areas: shared vision, mitigation, adaptation, technology and financing. COP 15, which took place in Copenhagen in 2009, resulted in the 'Copenhagen Accord'.[49] The Copenhagen Accord was significant in setting out an aspirational goal of limiting global temperature increases to 2°C above pre-industrial levels, and in providing for all major economies to give explicit mitigation pledges, including China for the first time.[50] Developed countries also committed to a joint goal of providing $100 billion in funding to support developing countries in their mitigation, adaptation and technological development. However, the Accord was a political commitment rather than being

---

45 Article 19 provides that the UN Secretary-General shall be the Depositary of the UNFCCC.
46 UNFCC Article 7(2).
47 Established under the auspices of the UNFCCC by the Cancun Agreements at COP 16 in 2010. See 'Report of the Conference of the Parties on Its Sixteenth Session, Held in Cancun from 29 November to 10 December 2010' (2011) FCCC/CP/2010/7/Add.1 <https://unfccc.int/sites/default/files/resource/docs/2010/cop16/eng/07a01.pdf> accessed 5 June 2024. The GCF finances climate initiatives in developing countries, with programming and implementation led by the country in question (a 'country-driven approach'). Its work focuses on investment in four areas of transition: built environment; energy and industry; human security, livelihoods and wellbeing; and land-use, forests and ecosystems. See 'Homepage' (Green Climate Fund) <https://www.greenclimate.fund/> accessed 6 May 2024.
48 Decision 1/CP.13 of COP 13; Bali Action Plan, in 'Report of the Conference of the Parties on Its Thirteenth Session, Held in Bali from 3 to 15 December 2007' (2008) FCCC/CP/2007/6/Add.1 <https://unfccc.int/resource/docs/2007/cop13/eng/06a01.pdf> accessed 5 June 2024; see also UNFCCC, 'Decision 1/CP.8 Amendment to the Kyoto Protocol Pursuant to Its Article 3, Paragraph 9 (the Doha Amendment)' FCCC/KP/CMP/2012/13/Add.1 <https://unfccc.int/resource/docs/2012/cmp8/eng/13a01.pdf#page=2> accessed 5 June 2024.
49 'Report of the Conference of the Parties on Its Fifteenth Session, Held in Copenhagen from 7 to 19 December 2009' (2010) FCCC/CP/2009/11/Add.1 <https://unfccc.int/resource/docs/2009/cop15/eng/11a01.pdf> accessed 5 June 2024.
50 See ibid 5.

legally binding, and was widely criticised as weak and disappointing.[51] The following year, COP 16 in Cancun produced the 'Cancun Agreement' which established the above-mentioned GCF[52] and the Technology Mechanism,[53] as well as recognising the scale of GHG emission reductions needed to keep warming to below 2°C and calling on developed countries to reduce their GHGs, in line with the pledges made at Copenhagen the previous year.

2.20 COP 26 in Glasgow not only reaffirmed the Paris Agreement but went further and the countries expressed 'alarm and utmost concern that human activities have caused around 1.1°C of warming to date, that impacts are already being felt in every region, and that carbon budgets consistent with achieving the Paris Agreement temperature goal are now small and being rapidly depleted'.[54] The UN summary also states:

> In perhaps the most contested decision in Glasgow, countries ultimately agreed to a provision calling for a phase-down of coal power and a phase-out of 'inefficient' fossil fuel subsidies – two key issues that had never been explicitly mentioned in decisions of UN climate talks before, despite coal, oil and gas being the main drivers of global warming. Many countries, and NGOs, expressed dissatisfaction that the language on coal was significantly weakened (from phase-out to phase-down) and consequently, was not as ambitious as it needs to be.[55]

2.21 COP 28 in Dubai in 2023 produced the first agreement to 'transition away from fossil fuels' (although stopped short of committing to 'phasing out'), as part of the first 'global stocktake'.[56] COP 28 also resulted in significant boosts to climate finance: for example, pledges worth $3.5 billion were committed to the GCF.[57] Countries also agreed to establish the Loss and Damage Fund, which received pledges in the sum of $700 million.[58] The purpose of the Loss and Damage Fund is to assist and compensate those developing nations which, despite having contributed the least to the causes of the climate crisis, are disproportionately impacted by the adverse consequences of climate

---

51 Shamus Cooke, 'Why Copenhagen Failed' (Global Research, 19 December 2009) <https://www.globalresearch.ca/why-copenhagen-failed/16612> accessed 6 May 2024; International Institute for Sustainable Development, 'A Brief Analysis of the Copenhagen Climate Change Conference' (2009) <https://www.iisd.org/system/files/publications/enb_copenhagen_commentary.pdf> accessed 5 June 2024.

52 'Report of the Conference of the Parties on Its Sixteenth Session, Held in Cancun from 29 November to 10 December 2010' (n 47) para 102.

53 ibid 117.

54 'COP26: Together for Our Planet' (United Nations) <https://www.un.org/en/climatechange/cop26> accessed 6 May 2024.

55 ibid.

56 'COP28 Agreement Signals "Beginning of the End" of the Fossil Fuel Era' (UNFCCC, 13 December 2023) <https://unfccc.int/news/cop28-agreement-signals-beginning-of-the-end-of-the-fossil-fuel-era> accessed 6 May 2024. See also 'Summary of Global Climate Action at COP 28' (UNFCCC, 12 November 2023) <https://unfccc.int/documents/636485> accessed 6 May 2024; and UNFCCC, 'First Global Stocktake. Proposal by the President. Draft Decision –/CMA.5' (2023) FCCC/PA/CMA/2023/L.17 <https://unfccc.int/sites/default/files/resource/cma2023_L17_adv.pdf> accessed 5 June 2024.

57 Green Climate Fund, 'GCF at COP28: A Wrap up of Outcomes at COP28' (Green Climate Fund, 20 December 2023) <https://www.greenclimate.fund/news/gcf-cop28-wrap-outcomes-cop28> accessed 6 May 2024.

58 Agreement was reached to create a 'Loss and Damage Fund' at COP 27 in Egypt in 2022, with a Transitional Committee formed to make recommendations as to how such a fund could be implemented. The 'loss and damage fund' was duly operationalised the following year at COP 28 in Dubai in 2023. See 'COP28 Presidency Unites the World on Loss and Damage' (COP28, 30 November 2023) 28 <https://www.cop28.com/en/news/2023/11/COP28-Presidency-unites-the-world-on-Loss-and-Damage> accessed 6 May 2024.

change[59] (although critics point out that current pledges fall far short of the estimated losses actually facing such nations).[60]

2.22 The COP also serves as the meeting of the Parties to the Kyoto Protocol ('CMP'), and the meeting of the Parties to the Paris Agreement ('CMA')[61] – in other words, the COP is the governing body of the UNFCCC, the Paris Agreement and the Kyoto Protocol.

2.23 *The Secretariat*: The UNFCCC Secretariat is the UN body which provides organisational support and technical expertise (in addition to that provided by the SBSTA, see below) to facilitate the work done to implement the UNFCCC, Kyoto Protocol and Paris Agreement. Among other things, the Secretariat maintains the NDC registry established under the Paris Agreement, and organises and supports the annual COPs.

2.24 *The Subsidiary Body for Scientific and Technological Advice ('SBSTA')*: The SBSTA assists the COP, CMP and CMA by providing scientific and technological information and advice. Its functions include proving assessments of current scientific knowledge on climate change, and undertaking scientific assessments of the effectiveness of measures taken towards the implementation of the UNFCCC.[62]

2.25 *The Subsidiary Body for Implementation ('SBI')*: The SBI works towards the implementation of the UNFCCC and its treaties through monitoring, analysis of trends and policies, and enhancing the ambition of Parties on the key issues of transparency, mitigation, adaptation, finance, technology and capacity-building. The SBI and SBSTA collaborate on issues which come within the expertise of both, such as discussions under the Warsaw International Mechanism for Loss and Damage.[63]

(c) Notable themes

2.26 This is an instrument of compromise. Consequently, the language can border on tortuous, and is heavily softened in places. This is particularly evidenced in Article 4, containing most of the substantive commitments, the language of which is strong ('shall', as opposed to 'may' or 'shall endeavour to') but vague ('shall promote', 'shall cooperate'). The Convention was predominantly a political achievement and a foundation for future action, rather than itself having legal teeth to enforce commitments.

---

59 'Loss and Damage Fund for Developing Countries' (UNDP, 26 January 2024) <https://www.undp.org/belarus/stories/loss-and-damage-fund-developing-countries> accessed 6 May 2024.
60 Nina Lakhani, '$700m Pledged to Loss and Damage Fund at Cop28 Covers Less than 0.2% Needed' *The Guardian* (6 December 2023) <https://www.theguardian.com/environment/2023/dec/06/700m-pledged-to-loss-and-damage-fund-cop28-covers-less-than-02-percent-needed> accessed 6 May 2024.
61 As articulated repeatedly in both agreements (Paris Agreement Articles 4, 6 and 7; Kyoto Protocol Articles 2, 3), 'the Conference of the Parties serv[es] as the meeting of the Parties to this Agreement'. Article 1 of both provides that '"Conference of the Parties" means the Conference of the Parties to the Convention'.
62 UNFCCC Article 9.
63 See para 2.49 and n 106 below.

2.27 The Convention formalised the principle of 'common but differentiated responsibilities and respective capabilities'.[64] This provides that developed countries should take the lead in combatting climate change; and is a theme which runs throughout the UNFCCC architecture.

(iii) *Kyoto Protocol*

2.28 The Kyoto Protocol was adopted on 11 December 1997 and entered into force on 16 February 2005, following a lengthy ratification process.[65]

2.29 The Kyoto Protocol had a narrow focus on mitigation: strengthening and operationalising the mitigation commitments in Article 4 of the UNFCCC, by committing industrialised countries to limiting their GHG emissions in line with binding, individually agreed targets. Seven GHGs are regulated: carbon dioxide ('CO_2'), methane ('CH_4'), nitrous oxide ('N_2O'), hydrofluorocarbons ('HFCs'), perfluorocarbons ('PFCs'), sulphur hexafluoride ('SF_6'), nitrogen trifluoride ('NF_3').[66] This excludes those GHGs which were regulated by the Montreal Protocol.[67]

2.30 The commitments in the Protocol were highly differentiated, following the principle of common but differentiated responsibility and respective capabilities. The Protocol followed the annex-based structure of the UNFCCC. Annex A sets out the GHGs and source categories. In Annex B to the Kyoto Protocol, 37 industrialised countries from Annex I to the UNFCCC were assigned emissions targets, setting a percentage amount by which each country's GHG emissions must be reduced as compared to 1990 levels.[68]

2.31 The initial commitment period of the Protocol was from 2008–2012. Over that initial period the emissions targets, if met, would have produced an average of 5% GHG emissions reduction compared to 1990 levels.[69] The Doha amendment, adopted on 8 December 2012, extended the Protocol's effect for a second commitment period, from 2013–2020.[70] The second period stipulated an average 18% reduction of GHG emissions as compared to 1990 levels, although with fewer Annex I countries committing

64 Article 3(1). The concept of 'common but differentiated responsibilities and respective capabilities' formally emerged at the 1992 United Nations Conference on Environment and Development, in Rio de Janeiro, which produced the UNFCCC. It represented a compromise between the positions of developed and developing nations, and has since been incorporated into the Kyoto Protocol, and retroactively into the Vienna Convention and the Montreal Protocol. See Charlotte Epstein, 'Common but Differentiated Responsibilities (CBDR)' (*Encyclopedia Britannica*) <https://www.britannica.com/topic/common-but-differentiated-responsibilities> accessed 6 May 2024.

65 Kyoto Protocol to the United Nations Framework Convention on Climate Change (adopted 11 December 1997, entered into force 16 February 2005) 2303 UNTS 162.

66 Kyoto Protocol, Annex A; NF_3 was added by the Doha amendment to the Kyoto Protocol, UNFCCC, 'Decision 1/CP.8 Amendment to the Kyoto Protocol Pursuant to Its Article 3, Paragraph 9 (the Doha Amendment)' (n 48).

67 Montreal Protocol on Substances that Deplete the Ozone Layer (adopted 16 September 1987, entered into force 01 January 1989).

68 The EU is listed as one 'country', but the EU member states redistributed the relevant target of 8% reduction between themselves, utilising a scheme under the Protocol known as a 'bubble', whereby countries with different individual targets may join together to meet their combined target.

69 UNFCCC, 'What Is the Kyoto Protocol?' <https://unfccc.int/kyoto_protocol> accessed 6 May 2024.

70 UNFCCC, 'Decision 1/CP.8 Amendment to the Kyoto Protocol Pursuant to Its Article 3, Paragraph 9 (the Doha Amendment)' (n 48).

to binding targets. That second commitment period has now ended (as of 31 December 2020), with no extension for a third period.

2.32 Despite being a 'top-down' agreement, the Kyoto Protocol provided for various mechanisms to allow countries flexibility in how they met their assigned reduction targets. For example, Article 17 introduced 'emissions trading',[71] which allowed Annex I states to sell and purchase emissions units with each other (i.e. for Annex I countries which had 'spare' emissions budget to sell that capacity to countries which were over-budget). This operated on the rationale that GHG emissions have the same effect irrespective of where they occur. Similarly, Article 12 introduced a 'clean development mechanism' ('CDM'), allowing Annex I Parties to support emission reduction projects in developing countries and then apply those reductions to their own targets, provided that the reductions generated by the project were 'additional' to any which would have occurred in the absence of that project.

2.33 The reduction commitments were supported by reporting, review, and compliance mechanisms.[72]

2.34 Although the Kyoto Agreement was not extended past 2020, it nevertheless provided a key stepping stone by creating and testing the efficacy of certain fundamental building blocks within the system of international climate change regulation.[73] For example, the Kyoto Protocol established an international 'carbon market', predominantly through the CDM noted above. At least in principle, this was an important step, aiming to allow countries to adapt to more ambitious climate targets in the most economically efficient way – developed countries pay for emission reduction projects in developing countries and thus balance out their own emissions at home.[74] However, in practice, it appears that the CDM actually led to an overall increase in global emissions, because an estimated 85% of the CDM projects in developing countries which developed countries used to offset their own emissions would have happened anyway, rather than being additional reductions instituted through the CDM.[75] Similarly, the emissions trading mechanism (noted above) was rendered ineffective by weak national targets and too many credits being available within the system.[76] These were important lessons for future development of the carbon markets under Article 6 of the Paris Agreement.

(iv) *Paris Agreement*

2.35 The Paris Agreement on Climate Change was agreed and adopted on 12 December 2015.[77]

---

71 See Chapter 14.
72 Articles 5, 7, 8 and 18.
73 Bodansky, Brunnée and Rajamani (n 5) 206–7.
74 Gilles Dufrasne, 'Carbon Markets 101 – the Ultimate Guide to Global Offsetting Mechanisms' (Carbon Market Watch, 31 July 2020) <https://carbonmarketwatch.org/publications/carbon-markets-101-the-ultimate-guide-to-global-offsetting-mechanisms/> accessed 6 May 2024.
75 Martin Cames and others, 'How Additional Is the Clean Development Mechanism? Analysis of the Application of Current Tools and Proposed Alternatives' (Öko Institut 2016) CLIMA.B.3/SERI2013/0026r <https://climate.ec.europa.eu/system/files/2017-04/clean_dev_mechanism_en.pdf> accessed 5 June 2024.
76 Dufrasne (n 74).
77 Paris Agreement (adopted 12 December 2015, entered into force 4 November 2016).

2.36 The groundwork for such an agreement, created under the auspices of the UNFCCC, had been laid by the Kyoto Protocol and Copenhagen Accords, but their impact was insufficient to the scale of the task. In particular, the non-ratification of the Kyoto Protocol by the US, and the weakness of the political commitments under the Copenhagen Accord, produced an evident need for a stronger agreement to meet the challenge of climate change.[78]

2.37 At COP 17 in 2011, Parties implemented the Ad Hoc Working Group on the Durban Platform for Enhanced Action, which mandated negotiations for a new global climate change treaty by 2015.[79] The Durban Platform provided guidance, albeit limited, on the form, content and coverage of the intended agreement. The character of the agreement as bottom-up rather than top-down (partly as a reaction against the heavy top-down differentiation of obligation under the Kyoto Protocol) was confirmed at COP 19 in Warsaw in 2013 when Parties were invited to prepare and submit 'intended nationally determined contributions'.[80] COP 20 in Lima in 2014 provided non-prescriptive guidance on the types of information to be included when submitting such intended nationally determined contributions, and requested the UNFCCC Secretariat to produce a 'synthesis report on the aggregate effect of the intended nationally determined contributions',[81] as well as producing the 'elements of a draft negotiating text' for the 2015 agreement.[82]

2.38 COP 21 in Paris was the culmination of these efforts, bolstered by historical political will and record attendance of national leaders.[83] Two weeks of hard negotiations produced the Paris Agreement, hailed as a landmark legal and political achievement.[84] The agreement managed to combine delicately a high level of ambition with differentiation between developed and developing nations, underpinned by binding mitigation obligations and systematic oversight.[85]

2.39 The purpose of the Paris Agreement is contained in Articles 2 and 4(1): Article 2 contains an obligation to reduce GHG emissions with the objective of holding any increase in global temperature to well below 2°C above pre-industrial levels; and pursuing efforts to limit the temperature increase to 1.5°C above pre-industrial levels.[86] This is the long-term temperature goal.

---

78 Chitzi C Ogbumgbada, 'The Paris Agreement: An Imperfect but Progressive Document' (2016) 8 International Energy Law Review 320.
79 Rajamani (n 31).
80 ibid; UNFCCC, 'Decision 1/CP.19. Further Advancing the Durban Platform' FCCC/CP/2013/10/Add.1 para 2(b) <https://unfccc.int/resource/docs/2013/cop19/eng/10a01.pdf#page=3> accessed 5 June 2024.
81 UNFCCC, 'Decision 1/CP.20. Lima Call for Climate Action' FCCC/CP/2014/10/Add.1 paras 14, 16 <https://unfccc.int/resource/docs/2014/cop20/eng/10a01.pdf#page=2%22> accessed 5 June 2024; Rajamani (n 31).
82 UNFCCC, 'Decision 1/CP.20. Lima Call for Climate Action' (n 81) Annex: 'Elements for a draft negotiating text'.
83 'Leaders and High-Level Segment' (UNFCCC, 29 October 2015) <https://unfccc.int/news/cop-21cmp-11-information-hub-leaders-and-high-level-segment> accessed 6 May 2024.
84 'UN Chief Hails New Climate Change Agreement as "triumph"' (United Nations Sustainable Development, 12 December 2015) <https://www.un.org/sustainabledevelopment/blog/2015/12/un-chief-hails-new-climate-change-agreement-as-monumental-triumph/> accessed 6 May 2024.
85 Rajamani (n 31).
86 Paris Agreement Article 2(1)(a).

2.40 To achieve the long-term temperature goal, pursuant to Article 4(1), parties must aim to reach global peaking of GHG emissions as soon as possible and to undertake reductions thereafter in accordance with the best available science. Article 4(1) sets out the objective of achieving 'a balance between anthropogenic emissions by sources and removals by sinks of [GHGs] in the second half of this century' – that objective forms the basis of the 'net zero target' (see paragraphs 1.25–1.35 in Chapter 1 ('Net Zero')).

2.41 As articulated in Article 3, Parties must 'undertake and communicate ambitious efforts ... with the view to achieving the purpose of this Agreement as set out in Article 2'. These 'ambitious efforts' of the Parties must be 'a progression over time'. This is known as the 'ratchet mechanism'.

2.42 The overarching goals of the Paris Agreement are expressed in temperature terms. This means that unlike the Kyoto commitments, which had been expressed in terms of particular GHG emissions, meeting the commitments in the Paris Agreement can be done by engagement with any, or each of, the sources of global warming, rather than by specifically regulating certain gases. To this end, Parties are also committed under Article 5 to conserving and enhancing sinks and reservoirs of GHGs.

2.43 The principle of 'common but differentiated responsibilities and respective capabilities' is maintained in the Paris Agreement. For example, Article 4(4) provides that 'Developed country Parties should continue taking the lead by undertaking economy-wide absolute emission reduction targets'; while developing country Parties 'are encouraged to move over time towards economy-wide emission reduction or limitation targets in the light of different national circumstances'.

2.44 At the heart of the functioning of the Paris Agreement is the 'pledge and review' mechanism.[87] Such pledges are made in the form of 'nationally determined contributions' ('NDCs'), as introduced by Article 4(2). NDCs set out national pathways to achieve global net zero.[88] Each State Party to the Agreement is required to 'prepare, communicate and maintain successive [NDCs] that it intends to achieve', and then pursue domestic measures to achieve the NDC.

2.45 Article 4(3) provides that each NDC is a progression from the last, such that ambition would be successively ratcheted upwards, in line with the principle of 'ambitious efforts' in Article 3.[89] NDCs are communicated every five years,[90] although a Party may, at any time, adjust its NDC in order to enhance its level of ambition.[91]

---

87 Robert O Keohane and Michael Oppenheimer, 'Paris: Beyond the Climate Dead End through Pledge and Review?' (2016) 4 Politics and Governance 142.
88 Sam Fankhauser and others, 'The Meaning of Net Zero and How to Get It Right' (2022) 12(1) Nature Climate Change 16 <https://www.nature.com/articles/s41558-021-01245-w> accessed 12 April 2024.
89 This has become known as the 'ratchet mechanism', with the aim that ambition can only progress rather than backslide.
90 Paris Agreement Article 4(9).
91 Paris Agreement Article 4(11).

2.46 The content and structure of the NDCs are discretionary, but essentially they include mitigation targets for GHG emission reductions,[92] including (it is hoped) sector-specific targets, and plans for meeting those targets.[93] Each State is free to choose how they wish to reduce their emissions.[94] In practice, the NDCs submitted by States are often a combination of qualitative and quantitative arrangements, and vary greatly in their specificity, breadth and length, and even in relation to the baseline years against which to compare their GHG emissions.[95]

2.47 The NDCs provide the basis of a 'bottom-up' approach, with States having significant discretion to define the stringency and content of their contribution. There is no 'official yardstick against which the adequacy, ambition or fairness of the [NDCs] is measured',[96] rather the Paris Agreement relies upon the accountability process, and a 'top-down' promotion of ambition.

2.48 There are no penalties built into the Paris Agreement for non-compliance. The power of the agreement and the NDCs depends upon political accountability and pressure, both from other States and domestically. For this to be effective, transparency is essential.[97] To this end:

- A registry of NDCs submitted by Parties is maintained by the Secretariat.[98] Analysis of the NDCs submitted thus allows states to be held to account, and pledges to be monitored and analysed[99] – for example, as of 2022, pledges from African

---

92 As required by Article 4(2).
93 Guidance to assist with the preparation and revision of NDCs is provided by the UNDP, 'Quality Assurance Checklist. For Revising Nationally Determined Contributions' (2020) <https://climatepromise.undp.org/sites/default/files/research_report_document/undp-ndcsp-qa-checklist-ndc-revision-ENG.pdf> accessed 5 June 2024, drawing on the WRI-UNDP Guidance (Taryn Fransen and others, 'Enhancing NDCs: A Guide to Strengthening National Climate Plans' (WRI & UNDP 2019) <https://www.wri.org/research/enhancing-ndcs-guide-strengthening-national-climate-plans> accessed 5 June 2024). The Quality Assurance Checklist outlines the three dimensions that the UNDP considers essential, these being: 1) country ownership and inclusiveness; 2) robustness and ambition; 3) feasibility.
94 As required by Paris Agreement Article 4(2).
95 Climate Watch provides a tracker of 200 indicators across all NDCs, available at 'Explore Nationally Determined Contributions (NDCs)' (Climate Watch) <https://www.climatewatchdata.org/ndcs-explore?category=sectoral_mitigation_measures&indicator=m_economy-wide> accessed 6 May 2024.
96 Fankhauser and others (n 88) 16.
97 As explained by Pete Betts, former lead negotiator for the UK and EU, at a Press Briefing at COP 26 in Glasgow, 'There are no penalties in the climate regime, there's only naming and shaming ... Having a functioning transparency regime is absolutely key to the whole system working.' (Reported by Carbon Brief, 'COP26: Key Outcomes Agreed at the UN Climate Talks in Glasgow' (*Carbon Brief*, 15 November 2021) <https://www.carbonbrief.org/cop26-key-outcomes-agreed-at-the-un-climate-talks-in-glasgow/> accessed 6 May 2024).
98 Available at 'Nationally Determined Contributions Registry' (UNFCCC) <https://unfccc.int/NDCREG> accessed 6 May 2024.
99 For example, see detailed analysis in UNDP, 'Nationally Determined Contributions (NDC) Global Outlook Report 2021: The State of Climate Ambition' (2021) <https://www.undp.org/publications/nationally-determined-contributions-ndc-global-outlook-report-2021-state-climate-ambition#:~:text=November%201%2C%202021&text=This%20report%20explores%20trends%20emerging,on%20their%20NDC%20revision%20processes> accessed 5 June 2024.

countries were more robust than the global average[100] (meaning that on average African NDCs had a greater level of clarity and transparency[101]).

- Article 13(1) established an 'enhanced transparency framework for action and support', with the purpose of providing clarity and understanding of actions taken towards the Paris Agreement's goals, including progress towards NDCs, adaptation measures, and support provision. Article 13 details the information which Parties must provide under this 'enhanced transparency framework', including an inventory of anthropogenic emissions of GHGs.[102]

- Article 14 provides that there shall be 'global stocktakes' every 5 years. Such stocktakes allow the international community to monitor the collective progress towards the achieving of the Paris Agreement's goals under Article 2. The first such stocktake took place at COP 28 in Dubai in 2023; it revealed that current commitments and reductions are falling significantly short of those needed to limit warming to 1.5°C by 2030.[103]

- Article 15 established the Paris Agreement Implementation and Compliance committee ('PAICC'), the role of which is to facilitate implementation of, and promote compliance with, the provisions of the Paris Agreement.[104]

2.49 Beyond mitigation, the Paris Agreement also addresses, *inter alia*:

- Adaptation: Article 7(1) establishes a 'global goal' of adaptation, and further recognises that mitigation and adaptation are inherently linked, such that stronger mitigation of climate change will lessen the need for adaptation.

- Loss and damage: Pursuant to Article 8(1), Parties recognised the 'importance of averting, minimizing and addressing loss and damage associated with the adverse effects of climate change, including extreme weather events and slow onset events, and the role of sustainable development in reducing the risk of loss and damage'. Indeed, loss and damage is described as the third pillar (along with mitigation and adaptation) of climate change regulations in the Paris Agreement.[105] Article 8(2)

---

100 Daisy Mukarakate, 'In the Race against Climate Change, There's Still Hope for Africa – Here Are 5 Reasons Why' (UNDP Climate Promise, 18 August 2022) <https://climatepromise.undp.org/news-and-stories/race-against-climate-change-theres-still-hope-africa-here-are-5-reasons-why> accessed 6 May 2024.
101 UNDP (n 93).
102 Paris Agreement Article 13. See also 'Navigating the Paris Rulebook: Enhanced Transparency Framework' (WRI, 18 May 2023) <https://www.wri.org/paris-rulebook> accessed 6 May 2024.
103 UNFCCC, '2023 Synthesis Report on GST Elements' (2023) <https://unfccc.int/sites/default/files/resource/SYR_Views%20on%20%20Elements%20for%20CoO.pdf> accessed 5 June 2024.
104 Paris Agreement Article 15, with further detail in decision 1/CP.21 paragraphs 102 and 103. The modalities and procedures of the PAICC were by the CMA in decision 20/CMA.1 at Katowice. See 'Paris Agreement Implementation and Compliance Committee (PAICC) | UNFCCC' <https://unfccc.int/PAICC> accessed 6 May 2024.
105 See Paris Agreement, Article 8. Justice Nyema Nwabueze and Erika Techera, 'International Environmental Law and Climate Change' in Erika Techera and others (eds), *Routledge Handbook of International Environmental Law* (2nd edn, Routledge 2021) 220.

expressly incorporated the Warsaw International Mechanism[106] into the Paris Agreement.

- Finance, technology and support for capacity-building: Article 9(1) commits developed countries to providing financial resources to assist developing countries with both their mitigation and adaptation efforts (termed 'climate finance'). (See Chapter 29 ('The Role of Finance in Achieving Net Zero Nature Positive').)

2.50 The individual provisions within the Paris Agreement vary in how strongly they bind State Parties.[107] The overall instrument contains a combination of:

- normative, descriptive provisions which build a narrative and shared understanding but do not generate specific obligations (e.g. Article 7(4) which recognises the link between mitigation and the need for adaptation);

- provisions which impose specific obligations but couched in language which is advisory or includes an element of discretion (e.g. Article 7(10) which obliges each Party to submit and update an adaptation communication, but only 'as appropriate', and with certain things which 'may' be included therein); and

- obligations which are specific, clear and precise but these being the minority (e.g. Article 4(2), each Party 'shall' prepare, communicate and maintain its NDCs).

2.51 This combination largely reflects the highly contentious negotiations process which produced the final Agreement.[108]

2.52 On 17 November 2016, the United Kingdom ratified the Paris Agreement. The UK accordingly amended section 1 of the Climate Change Act 2008 (addressed below) and, on 12 December 2020, communicated its NDC to the UNFCCC, announcing that it would reduce national GHG emissions by 2030 by at least 68% compared to 1990 levels, replacing an earlier, EU-based figure of 53% for the same year.[109]

---

106 Established at COP 19 in Warsaw, Poland. The Warsaw international mechanism aims 'to address loss and damage associated with impacts of climate change, including extreme events and slow onset events, in developing countries that are particularly vulnerable to the adverse effects of climate change'. It does this by a) enhancing knowledge and understanding of risk management approaches, b) strengthening dialogue and coordination, and c) enhancing financial, technological and capacity–building action and support. See 'Report of the Conference of the Parties on Its Nineteenth Session, Held in Warsaw from 11 to 23 November 2013' (UNFCCC 2014) FCCC/CP/2013/10/Add.3 <https://unfccc.int/sites/default/files/resource/docs/2013/cop19/eng/10a03.pdf> accessed 26 April 2024; 'Frequently Asked Questions – Warsaw International Mechanism for Loss and Damage' (UNFCCC) <https://unfccc.int/topics/resilience/resources/questions-and-answers-ld-mechanism> accessed 6 May 2024.
107 Lavanya Rajamani, 'The 2015 Paris Agreement: Interplay Between Hard, Soft and Non-Obligations' (2016) 28 Journal of Environmental Law 337, 342–56.
108 ibid 343–52.
109 Secretary of State for Business, Energy and Industrial Strategy, 'United Kingdom of Great Britain and Northern Ireland's Nationally Determined Contribution' (2022) CP 744 <https://assets.publishing.service.gov.uk/media/633d937d8fa8f52a5803e63f/uk-nationally-determined-contribution.pdf> accessed 5 June 2024.

2.53 The successes and failures of the Paris Agreement can be (and are, in academic literature[110]) analysed according to various different metrics. By the simplest metric of keeping the world on track to limit global temperature increases to 1.5°C above pre-industrial levels (as per Article 2(1)), the Paris Agreement has not – yet – succeeded.[111] However, its institutional power has driven international momentum, collective action, and global normative shifts on the importance of climate change, keeping climate change prominent in international politics as well as providing a platform and prerogative for domestic action.[112]

(v) *Convention on Biological Diversity*

2.54 In 1987, the World Commission on Environment and Development published *Our Common Future*,[113] also known as the Brundtland Report. This report defined 'sustainable development' as 'development that meets the needs of the present without compromising the ability of future generations to meet their own needs', a definition which has since become paradigmatic.[114] The growing international commitment to sustainable development led the UNEP to convene ad hoc working groups to prepare an international legal instrument between 1988–1991.[115] The CBD was opened for signatures at the Earth Summit in June 1992, received 168 signatures by June 1993 and entered into force on 29 December 1993.[116]

2.55 The CBD defines biological diversity as 'the variability among living organisms from all sources including, *inter alia*, terrestrial, marine and other aquatic ecosystems and the ecological complexes of which they are part; this includes diversity within species, between species and of ecosystems'.[117] The preamble to the CBD recognises the 'intrinsic value of biological diversity' as well as its importance for 'maintaining life sustaining systems of the biosphere'.[118]

2.56 The three core objectives of the CBD are set out in Article 1 and are: (1) the conservation of biological diversity; (2) the sustainable use of the components of biological diversity; and (3) the fair and equitable sharing of the benefits arising out of the utilisation of genetic resources.

---

110 For a meta-analysis of the academic literature analysing the Paris Agreement, see Kilian Raiser and others, 'Is the Paris Agreement Effective? A Systematic Map of the Evidence' (2020) 15 Environmental Research Letters 83006.
111 As revealed by the first Global Stocktake at COP 28 in 2023, informed by UNFCCC, '2023 Synthesis Report on GST Elements' (n 103).
112 Raiser and others (n 110).
113 World Commission on Environment and Development, 'Our Common Future' (1987) UN Doc A42/427 <https://documents.un.org/doc/undoc/gen/n87/184/67/pdf/n8718467.pdf?token=N1elHLsyyfhOF4vkF-W&fe=true> accessed 26 April 2024.
114 See Chapter 3, paras 3.50–3.64. Hannah Ritchie, *Not the End of the World: How We Can Be the First Generation to Build a Sustainable Planet* (Chatto & Windus 2024).
115 Elizabeth Fisher, Bettina Lange and Eloise Scotford, *Environmental Law: Text, Cases and Materials* (2nd edn, Oxford University Press 2019) 380.
116 'History of the Convention' (n 8).
117 CBD Article 2.
118 ibid Preamble.

2.57 The key features of the CBD are as follows:

- Article 3 confirms States' sovereign right to exploit their own resources, in accordance with the UN Charter, principles of international law, their own environmental policies and ensuring that no damage is caused by activities within their jurisdiction or control beyond the limits of their own national jurisdiction. Related to that, Article 15 specifically addresses access to genetic resources.

- Conservation is addressed in Articles 6, 8 and 9. By Article 6, the Contracting Parties are required to develop national strategies, plans or programmes for the conservation and sustainable use of biological diversity or adapt existing strategies, plans or programmes for this purpose, as well as integrating, as far as possible, the conservation and sustainable use of biological diversity into relevant sectoral and cross-sectoral plans, programmes and policies. Article 8 contains further detail regarding in-situ conservation, which includes establishing systems of protected areas or areas where special measures may be needed to conserve biological diversity; promoting the protection of ecosystems, natural habitats, and maintenance of populations; restoring degraded ecosystems and the recovery of threatened species; managing the risks associated with the release of living modified organisms; respecting and preserving the knowledge of indigenous communities. Article 9 addresses ex-situ conservation, including facilities for conservation of, and research on, plants, animals, micro-organisms, in their country of origin; adopting measures for the reintroduction of threatened species; and managing and regulating the collection of biological resources.

- Integral to the conservation measures are the provisions relating to identification and monitoring in Article 7 and Annex I, such as identifying ecosystem and habitats that contain high diversity, large numbers of endemic or threatened species or wilderness; species that are threatened, of social, scientific or cultural importance; and described genomes and genes of social, scientific, or economic importance. The monitoring and evaluation requirements involve identifying those components of biological diversity that require urgent conservation measures or have the greatest potential for sustainable use; and identifying activities that have or are likely to have significant adverse effects on conservation and sustainable use of resources.

- Article 10 focuses on sustainable use of 'components of biological diversity'; ensuring that this consideration is integrating into national decision-making about the use of biological resources (including by the private sector); and protecting the customary use of such resources in traditional practices.

- Related to Articles 7 and 10, Article 14 specifically deals with environmental impact assessment,[119] in particular that appropriate arrangements are in place to ensure that the likely significant adverse impacts on biological diversity from programmes and policies are taken into account and ensuring that adverse impacts are avoided or minimised.

---

119 See Chapter 7.

- Conservation measures and the sustainable use of resources should be incentivised, as set out in Article 11.

- There are specific provisions relating to the handling and distribution of biotechnology, such as Article 19.

- Like with the UNFCCC, there are provisions for information-sharing in relation to the conservation and sustainable use of resources,[120] as well as promoting technical and scientific cooperation,[121] with particular regard for the 'special needs of developing countries'. There is also a mechanism for ensuring (i) contracting Parties provide the financial support necessary to achieve the Convention's objectives and (ii) developed country Parties can provide specific financial support to developing country Parties in relation to measures to implement the CBD.[122]

2.58 The organisational structure of the CBD is very similar to that of the UNFCCC. The governing body of the CBD is the Conference of the Parties ('COP'), which meets at regular intervals to review the implementation of the CDB.[123] There is also a Secretariat, which is principally responsible for arranging the COP meetings, performing specific functions under the protocols, reporting on those functions to the COP and coordinating with other relevant international bodies.[124] Finally, there is a subsidiary body for scientific, technical and technological advice, which is multidisciplinary, and provides scientific and technical assessments in relation to the status of biological diversity, conservation measures and other technology.

2.59 Article 28 of the CBD provides for the adoption of protocols to the Convention. The CBD has two supplementary protocols. The Nagoya Protocol was adopted in 2019,[125] and aims for the fair and equitable utilisation of genetic resources, providing a legal framework for the third of the CBD's core goals. The Cartagena Protocol was adopted in 2000,[126] and governs the movement between countries of living modified organisms resulting from biotechnology.[127]

2.60 The Kunming-Montreal Global Biodiversity Framework[128] ('GBF') was adopted in December 2022 at COP 15 to the CBD. The 'vision' of the GBF 'is a world of living in harmony with nature', meaning that 'biodiversity is valued, conserved, restored and wisely used, maintaining ecosystem services, sustaining a healthy planet and delivering

---

120 CBD Article 17.
121 ibid Article 18.
122 ibid Articles 20 and 21.
123 ibid Article 23.
124 ibid Article 24.
125 Nagoya Protocol on Access to Genetic Resources and the Fair and Equitable Sharing of Benefits Arising from their Utilization to the Convention on Biological Diversity (adopted 29 October 2019, entered into force 12 October 2014).
126 Cartagena Protocol on Biosafety to the Convention on Biological Diversity (adopted 29 January 2000, entered into force 11 September 2003).
127 'About the Protocol' (CBD, 18 May 2021) <https://bch.cbd.int/protocol/background> accessed 6 May 2024.
128 CBD, 'Decision Adopted by the Conference of the Parties to the Convention on Biological Diversity, Kunming-Montreal Global Biodiversity Framework' (2022) CBD/COP/DEC/15/4 <https://www.cbd.int/doc/decisions/cop-15/cop-15-dec-04-en.pdf> accessed 5 June 2024.

benefits essential for all people'.[129] This is articulated as a vision for 2050, with a 'mission' for 2030 of taking 'urgent action to halt and reverse biodiversity loss to put nature on a path to recovery for the benefit of people and planet by conserving and sustainably using biodiversity and by ensuring the fair and equitable sharing of benefits from the use of genetic resources, while providing the necessary means of implementation'.[130]

(vi) *Aarhus Convention*

2.61 The United Nations Economic Commission for Europe ('UNECE') Convention on Access to Information, Public Participation in Decision-Making and Access to Justice in Environmental Matters, more commonly known as the Aarhus Convention, has shaped the international conversation on the democratic nature and public law dimension of environmental policy.[131] The Aarhus Convention is concerned with public accountability, transparency, democratic participation and the relationship between public authorities and the public themselves.[132]

2.62 The Aarhus Convention arose out of the 1992 Rio Earth Summit, most specifically out of Principle 10 of the Rio Declaration, which declared that 'Environmental issues are best handled with the participation of all concerned citizens'.[133] The text of the convention was negotiated by the UNECE; the convention was signed in 1998, entered into force in 2001, and was ratified by the UK in 2005. As an international treaty it is not directly binding within the UK, but a number of its Articles have been incorporated into domestic law.[134]

2.63 The Aarhus Convention has three pillars:

- Pillar 1. Access to Environmental Information. Articles 4 and 5 require public authorities to collect and disseminate certain environmental information to the public, by publication or upon request, offering a (potentially) powerful tool for public scrutiny and governmental accountability.[135]

- Pillar 2. Public Participation in Decision Making. Articles 6–8 enshrine a right for the public to participate in (certain aspects of)[136] environmental decision-making, with public authorities being obliged to take 'due account of the outcome of the public participation'.[137]

---

129 ibid 10.
130 UNEP, 'Kunming-Montreal Global Biodiversity Framework' (19 December 2022) s F (10–11) <http://www.unep.org/resources/kunming-montreal-global-biodiversity-framework> accessed 8 April 2024.
131 Fisher, Lange and Scotford (n 115) 102.
132 'Introduction' (UNECE) <https://unece.org/environment-policy/public-participation/aarhus-convention/introduction> accessed 6 May 2024.
133 Rio Declaration on Environment and Development 1992 Principle 10.
134 For example, the Environmental Information Regulations 2004 ('the EIR') are retained EU law which transpose the Environmental Information Directive 2003/4/EC, which itself gives effect to Aarhus Convention Pillar 1. There are also specific costs provisions relating to claims falling within the Aarhus Convention. These provisions were in Part 45 of the Civil Procedure Rules but have now been moved to Part 46.
135 Fisher, Lange and Scotford (n 115) 104.
136 Not all environmental decision-making is included, only those decisions set out in Annex 1 to the Aarhus Convention.
137 ibid 6(8).

- Pillar 3. Access to Justice. Article 9 gives members of the public the right to challenge decisions which they allege are in breach of Pillars 1 or 2 or national environmental law. Article 9 also introduces certain safeguards to protect access to justice. Significantly, this includes a requirement for the judicial procedures to bring such challenges to be 'fair, equitable, timely and not prohibitively expensive'.[138] The impact of this Article has been transformational, both in the UK and EU-wide.[139] In the UK in particular, Article 9 triggered significant change in relation to costs in judicial review claims – Section IX of Part 46 of the Civil Procedure Rules now limits recoverable costs in a claim which is within the scope of Article 9 of the Aarhus Convention.[140]

(vii) *European Union*

2.64 The EU continues to have relevance to the legal framework for climate change and biodiversity in England and Wales, notwithstanding the UK's departure from the EU. This section aims to provide a high-level overview of that continued relevance, noting that the interaction between EU law and domestic law is complex and subject-matter specific, particularly following the passing of the Retained EU Law (Revocation and Reform) Act 2023. Insofar as EU law remains relevant for particular sectors, it is addressed later in this book.[141]

(a) Key policy and legal developments at the EU level

2.65 Policy and legal developments in the EU since the UK's departure from the EU are generally beyond the scope of this section.[142] In summary, the key developments are as follows:

- **European Green Deal**. Approved in 2020, the European Green Deal is a package of measures with the ultimate goal of making the EU climate neutral by 2050.[143] The policy initiatives are holistic and cross-sectoral, covering the climate, environment, energy, transport, industry, agriculture and finance.[144] The goals of the European Green Deal are written into law by the European Climate Law.[145]

---

138 ibid 9(4).
139 Fisher, Lange and Scotford (n 115) 195.
140 Previously Section VII of Part 45. This section was re-enacted as Section IX of Part 46 by The Civil Procedure (Amendment No. 2) Rules 2023 with effect from 1 October 2023.
141 See Chapters 9, 14 and 19.
142 For further discussion of recent climate developments in Europe, see: Catherine Higham and others, 'Climate Change Law in Europe. What Do New EU Climate Laws Mean for the Courts?' (Grantham Research Institute on Climate Change and the Environment 2023) <https://www.lse.ac.uk/granthaminstitute/wp-content/uploads/2023/03/Climate-change-law-in-Europe-what-do-new-EU-climate-laws-mean-for-the-courts.pdf> accessed 5 June 2024; European Council, 'Climate Change: What the EU Is Doing' <https://www.consilium.europa.eu/en/policies/climate-change/> accessed 8 May 2024.
143 European Commission, 'Communication from the Commission. The European Green Deal' COM (2019) 640 final <https://eur-lex.europa.eu/legal-content/EN/TXT/HTML/?uri=CELEX:52019DC0640> accessed 5 June 2024.
144 European Council, 'European Green Deal' <https://www.consilium.europa.eu/en/policies/green-deal/> accessed 6 May 2024.
145 Regulation (EU) 2021/1119 establishing the framework for achieving climate neutrality and amending Regulations (EC) No 401/2009 and (EU) 2018/1999 ('European Climate Law').

- **Corporate Sustainability Due Diligence Directive ('CSDDD'/'CS3D').** The CSDDD, approved by the European Parliament on 24 April 2024,[146] establishes due diligence standards for EU businesses, creating legal liability for human rights and environmental standards violations within their supply chains, in addition to liability for the direct actions of the business.[147]

- **Nature Restoration Law.** The Nature Restoration Law sets targets for EU countries to restore at least 20% of the EU's land and sea areas by 2030, as part of which countries must restore at least 30% of habitats in poor condition by 2030, followed by 60% by 2040, and 90% by 2050.[148] The Nature Restoration was adopted by the Council on 17 June 2024.[149]

(b) Summary of the UK's departure from the EU and trade and cooperation agreement

2.66 On 23 June 2016, the UK voted to leave the European Union in a referendum.[150] Following which, on 29 March 2017, the Prime Minister, Theresa May, notified the President of the European Council, Donald Tusk, of the UK's intention to withdraw from the EU, pursuant to Article 50(2) of the Treaty on the European Union ('TEU') and in accordance with the European Union (Notification of Withdrawal) Act 2017.[151] Multiple extensions were then sought from the EU in relation to the UK's withdrawal, pursuant to Article 50(3) of the TEU.

2.67 The European Union (Withdrawal) Bill received royal assent on 26 June 2018 and became an Act of Parliament ('EU(W)A 2018'),[152] which provided *inter alia* for the repeal of the European Communities Act 1972 on exit day, defined as 29 March 2019 at 11pm, but this was then amended due to difficulties in negotiating the departure.[153] On

---

146 'Due Diligence: MEPs Adopt Rules for Firms on Human Rights and Environment' (*News European Parliament*, 24 April 2024) <https://www.europarl.europa.eu/news/en/press-room/20240419IPR20585/due-diligence-meps-adopt-rules-for-firms-on-human-rights-and-environment> accessed 6 May 2024.

147 Jon McGowan, 'After Delays, EU Approves Corporate Sustainability Due Diligence Law' (*Forbes*) <https://www.forbes.com/sites/jonmcgowan/2024/03/15/after-delays-eu-approves-corporate-sustainability-due-diligence-law/> accessed 6 May 2024.

148 'Nature Restoration: Parliament Adopts Law to Restore 20% of EU's Land and Sea' (*News European Parliament*, 27 February 2024) <https://www.europarl.europa.eu/news/en/press-room/20240223IPR18078/nature-restoration-parliament-adopts-law-to-restore-20-of-eu-s-land-and-sea> accessed 6 May 2024.

149 Regulation (EU) 2024/1991 of the European Parliament and of the Council of 24 June 2024 on nature restoration and amending Regulation (EU) 2022/869.

150 European Council, 'Timeline – The EU-UK Withdrawal Agreement' <https://www.consilium.europa.eu/en/policies/eu-relations-with-the-united-kingdom/the-eu-uk-withdrawal-agreement/timeline-eu-uk-withdrawal-agreement/> accessed 6 May 2024; Nigel Walker, 'Brexit Timeline: Events Leading to the UK's Exit from the European Union' (House of Commons Library 2021) Briefing paper N 7960 <https://researchbriefings.files.parliament.uk/documents/CBP-7960/CBP-7960.pdf> accessed 5 June 2024.

151 The Supreme Court had confirmed in *R (Miller) v Secretary of State for Exiting the European Union* [2017] UKSC 5 that primary legislation was required to trigger Article 50 and the Government could not rely on the prerogative powers to give notice.

152 Walker (n 150) 30. Section 16 of the EU (Withdrawal) Act 2018 had required the Secretary of State to publish a draft Bill consisting of (i) a set of environmental principles; (ii) a duty to publish a statement dealing with the interpretation of those principles; (iii) a duty to have regard to the statement. This led to the enactment of s 17 of the Environment Act 2021 and the Environmental Principles Policy Statement published thereunder, see paras 3.05–3.08 in Chapter 3.

153 European Union (Withdrawal) Act 2018 ss 1, 20.

30 October 2019, the EU(W)A 2018 (Exit Day) (Amendment) (No. 3) Regulations 2019[154] were passed, which changed 'exit day' to 31 January 2020.

2.68 On 9 September 2019, a further Act was passed, the European Union (Withdrawal) (No.2) Act 2019 setting out provision for the negotiations in relation to the withdrawal. On the same day, the (then) Prime Minister, Boris Johnson, decided to prorogue Parliament but the Supreme Court determined that his decision was unlawful, because it frustrated or prevented Parliament's ability to carry out its constitutional functions without reasonable justification.[155]

2.69 On 23 January 2020, European Union (Withdrawal Agreement) Bill received royal assent ('EU(WA)A 2020'), which provided for implementation of the withdrawal agreement, negotiated between the UK and EU, in domestic law and made various amendments to the EU (Withdrawal) Act 2018. The EU Council ratified the Withdrawal Agreement on 29 January 2020, which provided for the transition period until 31 December 2020.[156]

2.70 On 24 December 2020, the EU–UK Trade and Cooperation Agreement ('TCA') is sealed; and on 30 December 2020, the European Union (Future Relationship) Act 2020 ('EU(FR)A 2020') is passed, which provides for the implementation of the TCA in domestic law and make provision for the future relationship between the EU and UK.[157] Section 29 of that Act provides for the general implementation of the TCA.[158]

2.71 Article 390(1) defines 'environmental levels of protection' by reference to preventing danger to human life or health from environmental impacts, across a range of areas, including nature and biodiversity conservation. Article 390(3) defines 'climate level of protection' as 'the level of protection with respect to emissions and removals of greenhouse gases and the phase-out of ozone depleting substances'. Further, in relation to GHGs, Article 390(3)(a)–(b) provides as follows:

(a) for the Union, the 40% economy-wide 2030 target, including the Union's system of carbon pricing;

(b) for the United Kingdom, the United Kingdom's economy-wide share of this 2030 target, including the United Kingdom's system of carbon pricing.

---

154 The European Union (Withdrawal) Act 2018 (Exit Day) (Amendment) (No. 3) Regulations 2019, SI 2019/1423.
155 *R (Miller) v Prime Minister* [2019] UKSC 41.
156 European Council, 'Brexit: Council Adopts Decision to Conclude the Withdrawal Agreement' <https://www.consilium.europa.eu/en/press/press-releases/2020/01/30/brexit-council-adopts-decision-to-conclude-the-withdrawal-agreement/> accessed 7 May 2024. During this period, other Acts of Parliament were passed to addressed specific issues, including free movement (see Immigration and Social Security Co-ordination (EU Withdrawal) Act 2020, which received royal assent on 11 November 2020) and the internal market (see the United Kingdom Internal Market Act 2020, which received royal assent on 17 December 2020). See Walker (n 150).
157 Walker (n 150) 82–4.
158 There is also a requirement, set out in s 30 of the EU (FR) Act 2020, for a court or tribunal to have regard to Article 4 of the TCA (public international law) when interpreting the TCA or any supplementing agreement. By s 31, there is a power to make regulations to implement the TCA.

2.72 Chapter 7 of Title XI of Part 2 of the TCA, concerned with fair competition and sustainable development,[159] deals specifically with the environment and climate. Article 391 provides for non-regression in relation to environmental and climate levels of protection 'in a manner affecting trade or investment' between the EU and UK; reaffirms the right of each of the EU and UK to set its own policies and priorities in this area, including the allocation of resources for environmental enforcement so long as the approach adopted is consistent with the TCA; and requires the parties to 'strive' to increase their climate and environmental levels of protection.

2.73 Article 394 contains further provision in relation to enforcement, as referred to in Article 391. It requires both the UK and EU to ensure that environmental and climate law are properly enforced, to include adequate and effective remedies and administrative and judicial proceedings in relation to alleged violations of these laws that are not prohibitively costly and are undertaken in a 'fair, equitable and transparent way'.[160] This provision sits alongside Article 395 which ensures there is cooperation on monitoring and enforcement of environmental and climate change law as between the UK and EU.

2.74 Article 392 deals with carbon pricing and required the UK and EU to have an effective system of carbon pricing in place by 1 January 2021, stipulating that the system must: (i) cover GHG emissions from electricity generation, heat generation, industry and aviation[161] and (ii) uphold the level of protection set out in Article 391. The provision also requires the EU and UK to (i) maintain the system of carbon pricing insofar as it constitutes an effective tool in fighting climate change and (ii) cooperate with each other on carbon pricing, which includes giving consideration to linking together their systems.

2.75 Article 393 deals with environmental and climate principles; and environmental impact assessments. It starts by affirming that the UK and EU share 'a common biosphere' in relation to cross-border pollution and that they both respect internationally recognised environmental principles, including the integration principle, prevention principle, precautionary approach, rectification at source and the polluter pays principle. By Articles 393(2)–(3), the UK and EU reaffirmed their commitments to have procedures in place for evaluating the likely impact of a proposed activity on the environment, which includes, where the impact is significant, environmental impact assessment or strategic environmental assessment.[162]

2.76 Finally, Article 396 sets out the dispute resolution mechanism in relation to any disagreement in relation to the application of this chapter. It requires dialogue, consultation, exchange of information and cooperation, in the first instance; should that fail the parties are required to follow the procedure set out in Articles 408–410.

---

159 Referred to as 'Level playing field for open and fair competition and sustainable development'.
160 Article 394(1)(b).
161 But Article 392(4) contained a derogation in relation to aviation.
162 See Chapter 7.

(c) Overview of status of EU law in the UK

2.77 The status of EU law in the UK is now governed by the EU(W)A 2018, as amended by the EU(WA)A 2020 and the Retained EU Law (Revocation and Reform) Act 2023 ('REUL(RR)A 2023'). These provisions are complex and depend upon the source of EU law. In short, the position is as follows:[163]

- The European Communities Act 1972 ('ECA 1972') had provided for the transposition of EU law into domestic law; and included a general implementation provision, as set out in section 2, in relation to rights, powers, liabilities, obligations and restrictions created or arising under the treaties. Any question as to the meaning or effect of the treaties or any EU instrument was to be treated as a question of law.[164]

- By section 1 of the EU(W)A 2018, the ECA 1972 was repealed on exit day, 31 January 2020. Notwithstanding its repeal on exit day, section 2 of the EU(W)A 2018 (as amended) provided for the continued effect of the ECA 1972 as set out in section 2 during the implementation (otherwise known as transition) period. Where the 'IP completion day' is the end of the implementation period and was defined in section 39 of the EU (WA)A 2020 as 31 December 2020 at 11pm; and these statutory provisions were repealed on IP completion day.

- By sections 1B and 2 of the EU(W)A 2018, EU-derived domestic legislation,[165] as it had effect in domestic law immediately before IP completion day, continued to have effect in domestic law on and after IP completion day, subject to certain interpretative principles (unless the contrary intention appeared in such law enacted after exit day and before IP completion day) and any relevant regulations.[166] Section 2 was also subject to sections 5, 5A and schedule 1.

- By section 3 of the EU(W)A 2018, direct EU legislation, so far as operative immediately before IP completion day, formed part of domestic law on or after IP completion day.[167] This provision was also subject to sections 5, 5A and schedule 1.

---

163 ss 7A and 7B of the EU(W)A 2018 provide for the general implementation of the remainder of the withdrawal agreement, EEA EFTA, and Swiss agreements; s 7C addresses the interpretation of separate agreements; s 8 contains a power for a Minister to make regulations in relation to any deficiencies arising from withdrawal.
164 As per s 3 of the ECA 1972.
165 This is defined in s 1B(7) of the EU(W)A 2018.
166 See s 1B(4). In relation to EU-derived domestic legislation enacted on or after exit day and before IP completion day, it has unless the contrary intention appears.
167 'Direct EU legislation' is defined in s 3(2) of the EU(W)A 2018 as *inter alia* any EU regulation, EU decision or EU tertiary legislation, as it has effect in EU law immediately before IP completion day and so far as (i) it is applicable to and in the UK by virtue of Part 4 of the withdrawal agreement; (ii) it neither has effect nor is to have effect by virtue of s 7A or 7B; (iii) it is not an exempt EU instrument (as set out in s 20(1) and schedule 6); and (iv) its effect is not reproduced in an enactment to which s 2(1) applies. Section 3(3) of the EU(W)A 2018 addresses the meaning of any direct EU legislation being operative immediately before IP completion day.

- Any EU law retained by operation of EU(W)A 2018 is subject to the sunsetting provisions in the REUL(RR)A; see section 1 (dealing with EU-derived subordinate legislation and retained direct EU legislation) and schedule 1.[168]

- Section 4 of the EU(W)A 2018 had provided for the saving of various rights, powers, liabilities, obligations, restrictions, remedies and procedures, which had been recognised and available in domestic law by virtue of section 2 of the ECA 1972 and enforced accordingly (subject to certain exceptions). Section 4 was, however, repealed by section 2 of the REUL(RR)A 2023, which is also a sunsetting provision. Thus, anything which immediately before the end of 2023 had been retained EU law by virtue of section 4 is no longer recognised in domestic law (subject to any reproduction of a provision that has been subject to the sunsetting provision by regulations made under section 12, RREUL(RR)A 2023).

- Section 5 provides *inter alia* that the principle of the supremacy of EU law and the general principles of EU law are not part of domestic law from the end of 2023. It also requires that any assimilated direct legislation is interpreted compatibly with domestic enactments, except where regulations have been made pursuant to section 7 of REUL(RR)A 2023 stating that section 5(A2) does not apply which means that the domestic enactment must instead be read and given effect in a way that is compatible with assimilated direct legislation. If any assimilated direct legislation is incompatible with any domestic enactment or any domestic enactment is incompatible with assimilated direct legislation (as provided for by section 7 of REUL(RR)A 2023), the court is required to make an incompatibility order, as set out in section 6D of EU(W)A 2018.

- By section 6 of the EU(W)A 2018, any EU law, which by virtue of sections 2 or 3 (or sections 6(3) or (6)[169]), continues to be, or forms part of domestic law is defined as 'assimilated law'.[170]

- Section 6[171] also deals with the interpretation of assimilated law. A court or tribunal is not bound by any principles laid down, or decision made, on or after

---

168 But a Minister of the Crown has various powers to restate retained EU law (s 11 albeit this power did not extend beyond the end of 2023), restate assimilated law or reproduce sunsetted retained EU rights, powers and liabilities (s 12), as well as general powers to restate, reproduce, revoke, replace, update and remove or reduce burdens, as set out in ss 13–16 of the REUL(RR)A 2023.

169 These provisions deal with any relevant assimilated case law and limits of EU competence insofar as they are not inconsistent with modifications to the relevant law on or after IP completion day. 'Assimilated case law' is defined, by s 6(7), as 'assimilated domestic case law' and 'assimilated EU case law.' Where, in turn, 'assimilated domestic case law' is defined as 'any principles laid down by, and any decisions of, a court or tribunal in the United Kingdom, as they have effect immediately before IP completion day and so far as they— (a) relate to anything to which section 2 or 3 applies, and (b) are not excluded by section 5 or Schedule 1, (as those principles and decisions are modified by or under this Act or by other domestic law from time to time)'; and 'assimilated EU case law' is defined as 'any principles laid down by, and any decisions of, the European Court, as they have effect in EU law immediately before IP completion day and so far as they—(a) relate to anything to which section 2 or 3 applies, and (b) are not excluded by section 5 or Schedule 1, (as those principles and decisions are modified by or under this Act or by other domestic law from time to time)'.

170 See also s 5 of the REUL(RR)A 2023 for further details as to the nomenclature.

171 Further related amendments were set out in REUL(RRA)A 2023 (see sections 6A, 6B and 6C of the EU(W)A 2018) but, at the time of writing, they are yet to come into force.

IP completion day by the European Court; and cannot refer any matter to the European Court on or after IP completion day. The court or tribunal may, subject to certain provisions, have regard to anything done on or after IP completion day by the European Court or another EU entity insofar as it is relevant to the particular matter. Any validity, meaning or effect of any assimilated law, insofar as relevant, should be decided in accordance with assimilated case law and any limits of EU competence. The Supreme Court is not bound by any assimilated EU case law; and in deciding whether to depart from any such case law, it must apply the same test as it would apply in determining whether to depart from its own case law.[172] Finally, there is a power for a Minister to make regulations in relation to the interpretation of this law.

- Section 7 of the EU(W)A 2018 deals with the status of assimilated law.

(viii) *European Convention on Human Rights*

2.78 The ECHR does not directly address climate change. There is no explicit right to a clean environment or stable climate enshrined therein. Yet, as recognised by the UN Human Rights Council by its resolution of 8 October 2021, 'a clean, healthy and sustainable environment' is a prerequisite for the enjoyment of all other human rights.[173] Inevitably, climate litigation is now testing the boundaries of the applicability of the ECHR to issues of climate change. The UK is required to take any case law from the ECtHR into account when determining any question concerned with a Convention right.[174]

2.79 There is already a strong line of jurisprudence on the protections afforded by the ECHR with regards to environmental hazards and natural disasters, although not specifically in relation to climate change: notably, in relation to, for example, a methane explosion;[175] a mudslide;[176] chemical hazards;[177] and flash floods.[178]

---

172 See s 6(5).

173 UNGA Resolution A/HRC/RES/48/13 (18 October 2021).

174 Human Rights Act 1998 s 2.

175 *Öneryıldız v Turkey*, App no 48939/99 (ECHR, 30 November 2004) concerned a methane explosion at a rubbish tip which engulfed nearby houses, killing 9 of the applicant's relatives. The court found a violation of both the substantive and procedural limbs of Article 2 (the right to life) given the Turkish government's failure to take appropriate steps to prevent the deaths and inadequate legal protections safeguarding the right to life, as well as a violation of Article 1 of Protocol 1 to the convention (protection of property) and of Article 13 (right to an effective remedy).

176 *Budayeva and others v Russia*, App no 15339/02 (ECHR, 20 March 2008) arose out of a mudslide which destroyed the town in which the applicants lived, including killing the first applicant's husband. The court found a violation of the substantive limb of Article 2 given the Russian authorities' failure to implement land-planning and emergency relief policies in a hazardous area, and of the procedural limb given the lack of judicial inquiry into the disaster.

177 *Guerra v Italy*, App no 14967/89 (ECHR, 19 February 1998) concerned a chemical factory which had seen major accidents seriously impacting the health of locals. The applicants alleged a violation of Article 8, the right to private and family life, on the basis that the authorities had failed to implement practical measures to reduce pollution and the risk of major hazard events, and failure to provide adequate information about the risks. The court agreed that there had been such a violation of Article 8.

178 *Kolyadenko and others v Russia*, App no 17423/05 (ECHR, 28 February 2012), concerned heavy flash flooding in Vladivostok which occurred when the Russian authorities released water without prior warning, having failed to maintain the river channel of the Pionerskaya river and water reservoir. The court found a substantive and procedural violation of Article 2, a violation of Article of Protocol 1, and a violation of Article 13.

2.80 Articles 2, 3, 8, 10 and Article 1 of Protocol No. 1 have all been successfully invoked in relation to environmental harms.[179] In relation to Article 2 for example, in *Öneryıldız v Turkey*, the ECtHR found a violation of both the substantive and procedural limbs of Article 2, following a failure by the Turkish government to take appropriate steps to avoid risk to life, or even to warn the inhabitants of a slum about the risks of living close to a rubbish tip (where a methane explosion had occurred). The court similarly found a violation of both limbs of Article 2 in the case of *Budayeva*, in which a mudslide had resulted in numerous deaths, the relevant authorities having failed to implement land-planning and emergency relief policies.[180]

2.81 Three cases concerning climate change have recently been decided by the Grand Chamber of the ECtHR: *Verein KlimaSeniorinnen Schweiz and Others v Switzerland*,[181] *Carême v France*[182] and *Duarte Agostinho and Others v Portugal and 32 Others*.[183] These were the first cases which required the ECtHR to address the relationship between the ECHR and climate change. Judgments were handed down on 9 April 2024 and are considered at paragraphs 28.109–28.121 in Chapter 28. In short, the Grand Chamber in *Verein KlimaSeniorinnen Schweiz* found that Switzerland had violated Articles 8 (right to respect for private and family life) and 6 (right to a fair trial). In relation to Article 8, Switzerland had failed to comply with its positive obligations and exceeded its margin of appreciation.[184] There were significant gaps in its domestic regulatory framework, which included a failure to quantify its national GHG emissions and to meet its past GHG emission reduction targets.[185] The Grand Chamber also considered the question of victim status. The court determined that the applicant in *Carême* did not have victim status; and the claim in *Duarte Agostinho and Others* was inadmissible.[186]

2.82 It is notable that Council of Europe States other than the UK are already grappling with these issues at a domestic level, and this is likely to be noted by the ECtHR at Strasbourg. The German Bundesverfassungsgericht (BVerfG) and the Dutch Hoge Raad have, in the cases of *Klimabeschluss*[187] and *Urgenda*[188] respectively, held that their individual nation states could not escape responsibility for climate change by pointing to the emissions of other states,[189] rejecting the argument that multifactorial global causation renders individual state emissions irrelevant.[190] The ECtHR was referred to these judgments of the BVerfG and the Hoge Raad in the case of *KlimaSeniorinnen*, in relation to causality. While such rulings by national courts do not bind the ECtHR, the

179 European Court of Human Rights, 'Factsheet – Environment and the European Convention on Human Rights' <https://www.echr.coe.int/documents/d/echr/fs_environment_eng> accessed 8 April 2024.
180 *Budayeva and others v Russia*, App no 15339/02 (ECHR, 20 March 2008) (n 176).
181 *Verein KlimaSeniorinnen Schweiz and Others v Switzerland*, App no 53600/20 (ECHR, 09 April 2024) (ECtHR) (2024) 79 EHRR 1.
182 *Carême v France*, App no 7189/21 (ECHR, 09 April 2024) (2024) 79 EHRR SE1.
183 *Duarte Agostinho and Others v Portugal and 32 Others*, App no 39371/20 (ECHR, 09 April 2024) (2024) 78 EHRR SE9.
184 See Chapter 28, paragraphs 28.109–28.121.
185 *Verein KlimaSeniorinnen Schweiz and Others v Switzerland* (n 181) [573].
186 See Chapter 28, paragraphs 28.109–28.121.
187 *BvR* 2656/18/1, *BvR* 78/20/1, *BvR* 96/20/1, *BvR* 288/20 [2021] First Senate (Bundesverfassungsgericht [BVerfG]).
188 *Stichting Urgenda v De Staat der Nederlanden* [2019] Hoge Raad der Nederlanden ECLI:NL:HR:2019:2007.
189 *BvR* 2656/18/1, *BvR* 78/20/1, *BvR* 96/20/1, *BvR* 288/20 (n 187) [203].
190 *Stichting Urgenda v De Staat der Nederlanden* (n 188) [5.7.7].

'living instrument' doctrine means that the ECHR must be interpreted in the light of present-day circumstances, which includes the developments and commonly accepted standards in Council of Europe member States (see Chapter 28).[191]

Domestic legal framework

(i) *Climate Change Act 2008*

2.83 The central pillar of the UK's domestic climate change policy is the Climate Change Act 2008 ('CCA 2008').[192] The CCA 2008 sets the framework for the UK's long-term climate mitigation targets, adaptation processes, and the associated governance mechanisms enabling a transition to a low carbon UK economy.[193]

2.84 The policy background to the passing of the CCA 2008 was noted by the Supreme Court in *R (Friends of the Earth Ltd and others) v Heathrow Airport Ltd*:[194]

> [T]he UK has for a long time appreciated the desirability of tackling climate change, and wished to take a more rigorous domestic line. In the 2003 White Paper, 'Our Energy Future – Creating a Low Carbon Economy', the Government committed to reduce CO_2 emissions by 60% on 1990 levels by 2050; and to achieve 'real progress' by 2020 (which equated to reductions of 26–32%). The 60% figure emanated from the EU Council of Ministers' 'Community Strategy on Climate Change' in 1996, which determined to limit emissions to 550 parts per million (ppm) on the basis that to do so would restrict the rise in global temperatures to 2°C above pre-industrial levels which, it was then considered, would avoid the serious consequences of global warming. However, by 2005, there was scientific evidence that restricting emissions to 550ppm would be unlikely to be effective in keeping the rise to 2°C; and only stabilising CO_2 emissions at something below 450ppm would be likely to achieve that result.

2.85 In 2005, Friends of the Earth drafted a Climate Change Bill which was brought before Parliament as a private member's bill on 7 April 2005. Before the Bill could progress, Parliament was dissolved for the 2005 general election.[195] Following the election, the Labour government announced the (re-)introduction of a Climate Change Bill in the Queen's speech of 16 November 2006.[196] The government consulted on the draft Bill in March 2007, and the Bill became law on 26 November 2008.[197]

2.86 Section 1 sets 'the target for 2050', providing that the Secretary of State has a duty to 'ensure that the net UK carbon account for the year 2050 is at least 100% lower than the 1990 baseline'. This is the 'net zero by 2050' target which lies at the

---

191 *Tyrer v United Kingdom*, App no 5856/72 (ECHR, 25 April 1978).
192 See also the Climate Change (Scotland) Act 2009; Environment (Wales) Act 2016 pt 2; Climate Change Act (Northern Ireland) 2022.
193 Fisher, Lange and Scotford (n 115) 625.
194 *R (Friends of the Earth Ltd and others) v Heathrow Airport Ltd* [2020] UKSC 52 [39]. This case is considered in more detail in the Chapters 6 and 18.
195 Matthew Tempest, 'Blair Calls Election for May 5' *The Guardian* (5 April 2005) <https://www.theguardian.com/politics/2005/apr/05/election2005.uk5> accessed 7 May 2024.
196 HL Deb 15 November 1996, vol 687.
197 Climate Change Act 2008.

heart of the CCA; and was part of the UK's response to the Paris Agreement.[198] See paragraphs 1.25–135 in Chapter 1, and see below from paragraph 2.90.

2.87 The core goal of 'net zero by 2050' is to be achieved through the means of binding emissions targets. These impose duties of result – the Secretary of State is bound to ensure that the targets are met – rather than merely being obligations to take certain steps or consider certain matters.[199] The CCA 2008 was the first domestic legislation anywhere in the world to introduce such legally-binding national minimum target.[200]

2.88 Various government departments have been assigned the lead role in focusing on climate change and energy supply by the Prime Minister as a matter of administration.[201] The Department of Energy and Climate Change ('DECC') was created for this purpose in October 2008. Its functions were subsequently taken over by the Department for Business, Energy and Industrial Strategy ('BEIS') in July 2016, and then the Department of Energy Security and Net Zero ('DESNZ'), established by Prime Minister Rishi Sunak in February 2023.

2.89 Part 1 of the CCA 2008 concerns the carbon target and budgeting. Part 2 establishes the Climate Change Committee ('CCC').[202] Part 3 deals with trading schemes,[203] whilst Part 4 addresses reporting obligations on the impact of, and adaptation to, climate change.

(a) Net zero target and carbon budgeting

2.90 Section 1 provides the core goal of the CCA 2008. As originally enacted in 2008, section 1 required the 'Secretary of State to ensure that the net UK carbon account for 2050' would be at least 80%[204] lower than the '1990 baseline' for CO_2 and other GHGs (targeted GHGs).[205]On 27 June 2019, section 1 was amended to mandate the Secretary

---

198 *R (Friends of the Earth Ltd) v Secretary of State for Business, Energy and Industrial Strategy* [2022] EWHC 1841 (Admin). For a discussion of the Paris Agreement's status in domestic law, see para 28.98 in Chapter 28, and also see para 2.124 below.

199 See Colin T Reid, 'A New Sort of Duty? The Significance of "outcome" Duties in the Climate Change and Child Poverty Acts' (2012) 4 Public law 749, 751–2, 757; an amendment to alter the duty on the Secretary of State to ensure that the 2050 target was met from an absolute duty to a duty merely to propose policies to meet the target was narrowly defeated in the House of Lords, by 132 votes to 130, see HL Deb 31 March 2008, vol 700, col 755.

200 Department for Energy Security and Net Zero, 'Net Zero Government Initiative: UK Roadmap to Net Zero Government Emissions' (2023) <https://assets.publishing.service.gov.uk/media/6569cb331104cf000dfa7352/net-zero-government-emissions-roadmap.pdf> accessed 5 June 2024.

201 *R (Global Feedback Ltd) v Secretary of State for the Environment, Food and Rural Affairs and the Secretary of State for Energy Security and Net Zero* [2023] EWCA Civ 1549; the mechanism by which these changes occur is set out in the Ministers of the Crown Act 1975.

202 The CCC is addressed in more detail in Chapter 4.

203 Trading schemes are schemes which encourage the limitation of activities which result in emissions being limited or GHGs removed from the atmosphere, s 44(1) CCA 2008. See Chapter 14.

204 As noted in *R (Spurrier) v Secretary of State for Transport and others* [2019] EWHC 1070 (Admin) [566] (being the first instance decision in the case of *R (Friends of the Earth Ltd and others) v Heathrow Airport Ltd* [2020] UKSC 52): 'The figure of 80% was substituted for 60% during the passage of the Bill, as evolving scientific knowledge suggested that the lower figure would not be sufficient to keep the rise in temperature to 2°C in 2050.'

205 The 'targeted greenhouse gases' are defined in s 24(1) of the CCA 2008 as (a) carbon dioxide, (b) methane, (c) nitrous oxide, (d) hydrofluorocarbons, (e) perfluorocarbons, and (f) sulphur hexafluoride. The Secretary of State is also empowered, by order, to designate other GHGs as a 'targeted greenhouse gas'.

of State to ensure that the 2050 carbon account is at least 100% lower than the 1990 baseline. This is known as 'the net zero target', or 'net zero by 2050'.[206]

2.91 The Secretary of State has the power to amend the section1(1) target or base year.[207] The Secretary of State is permitted to exercise this power only in certain circumstances, as specified in section 2(2). These circumstances are where: (a) it appears to her that there have been significant developments in either scientific knowledge about climate change or European or international law or policy that make it appropriate to do so;[208] or (b) where the power is exercised in connection with an order designating further targeted GHGs,[209] or in connection with regulations concerning emissions from international aviation or shipping.[210] In addition, before exercising this power, the Secretary of State is required by section 3 to: (a) obtain, and take into account, the advice of the CCC; and (b) take into account any representations made by the other national authorities.[211] The advice must also be published by the CCC, and sent to the other national authorities.[212] If the order made by the Secretary of State differs from the advice given by the CCC, she must publish a statement explaining the reasons for that decision.[213]

2.92 GHG emissions are expressed for the purposes of the CCA 2008 in tonnes of 'carbon dioxide equivalent'.[214] That term refers to either a tonne of CO_2 or an amount of another GHG with 'an equivalent global warming potential' ('GWP').[215]

2.93 The 'net UK carbon account' is the formal definition of UK emissions used under the CCA 2008. It is calculated by aggregating targeted GHG emissions over a given period, converting them into an equivalent of CO_2 emitted, and deducting and/or adding the 'carbon units'[216] credited and/or debited to the UK's account during that same period.[217] It concerns all targeted GHGs, which are carbon dioxide, methane, nitrous oxide, hydrofluorocarbons, perfluorocarbons, and sulphur hexafluoride.[218]

2.94 The '1990 baseline' is defined in section 1(2) as being the aggregate amount of (a) net UK emissions of CO_2 for that year, and (b) net UK emissions of each of the other

---

206 See The Climate Change Act 2008 (2050 Target Amendment) Order 2019, SI 2019/1056.
207 CCA 2008 s 2.
208 CCA 2008 s 2(2)(a)(i)–(ii).
209 CCA 2008 s 24; s 2(2)(b)(i).
210 CCA 2008 s 30; s 2(2)(b)(ii).
211 CCA 2008 s 3(1); a 'national authority' is defined by s 95(1) of the CCA 2008 as any of the following the Secretary of State, Scottish Ministers, Welsh Ministers, and the relevant Northern Ireland department.
212 CCA 2008 s 3(2)–(3).
213 CCA 2008 s 3(6).
214 CCA 2008 s 93(1).
215 CCA 2008 s 93(2).
216 See further para 2.97.
217 See s 27(1). Pursuant to s 29(1)(c), 'net UK emissions' for a period is defined as 'in relation to a greenhouse gas, means the amount of UK emissions of that gas for the period reduced by the amount for the period of UK removals of that gas'. The amount must be determined in accordance with 'international carbon reporting practice' (s 94). Section 27(2) provides that 'The net amount of carbon units credited to the net UK carbon account for a budgetary period must not exceed the limit set under s 11 (limit on use of carbon units) for the period'.
218 CCA 2008 s 24.

targeted GHG for the year that is the base year for that gas.[219] Each targeted GHG has its own base year, set out in section 25.[220]

2.95 The CCA 2008 operates a system of setting and revising legally-binding 'carbon budgets' to ensure the net zero target is met. These carbon budgets act as stepping stones towards meeting the target.[221] Section 4 requires the Secretary of State to set such carbon budgets for succeeding 5-year periods, at least 12 years in advance.[222] The Secretary of State is bound by section 4(1)(b) to ensure that the UK carbon account does not exceed those budgets.[223]

2.96 The budgets are set after consultation with the CCC and any representations made by other national authorities.[224] The government must take account of the CCC's advice in relation to setting the carbon budgets, and if it chooses to diverge from the CCC's advice, it must provide a statement of the reasons as it why it has done so.[225] The government has accepted the CCC's advice on the level of all six carbon budgets legislated to date.[226] When advising on, and considering the carbon budgets, the CCC and the government must take into account:[227] (i) scientific knowledge about climate change; (ii) technology relevant to climate change; (iii) economic circumstances;[228] (iv) fiscal circumstances;[229] (v) social circumstances;[230] (vi) energy policy;[231] (vii) different circumstances between England, Wales, Northern Ireland and Scotland; (viii) circumstances at the European and international levels and (ix) reportable emission estimates from international aviation and shipping.

2.97 The First Carbon Budget (2008–2012) and Second Carbon Budget (2013–2017) were both met.[232] The Third Carbon Budget (2018–2022) is due to be assessed by

---

219 ibid s 1(2).
220 The base years for the targeted GHGs, other than CO_2, are set by s 25(1) as follows: (a) methane – 1990; (b) nitrous oxide – 1990; (c) hydrofluorocarbons – 1995; (d) perfluorocarbons – 1995; and (e) sulphur hexafluoride – 1995.
221 Climate Change Committee, 'CCC Insights Briefing 4. Advising on the Level of the UK's Carbon Budgets' <https://www.theccc.org.uk/wp-content/uploads/2020/10/CCC-Insights-Briefing-4-Advising-on-the-level-of-the-UKs-carbon-budgets.pdf> accessed 5 June 2024.
222 CCA 2008 s 4(1)–(2).
223 For periods after 2018–2022; ibid s 4.
224 ibid ss 9 and 34.
225 ibid s 9.
226 Climate Change Committee, 'CCC Insights Briefing 4. Advising on the Level of the UK's Carbon Budgets' (n 221); Department for Energy Security and Net Zero, 'Carbon Budget Delivery Plan' (2023) HC 1269 <https://assets.publishing.service.gov.uk/media/6424b2d760a35e000c0cb135/carbon-budget-delivery-plan.pdf> accessed 4 April 2024.
227 CCA 2008 s 10.
228 The provision specifically refers to the likely impact of the decision on the economy and the competitiveness of different sectors.
229 The provision specifically refers to the likely impact of any decision on taxation, public spending and public borrowing.
230 The provision specifically refers to the impact of any decision on fuel poverty.
231 The provision refers to the likely impact of any decision on energy supplies and the carbon and energy intensity of the economy.
232 Respectively, they required 26% and 32% reductions of GHG emissions below 1990 levels. See 'Advice on Reducing the UK's Emissions' (Climate Change Committee) <https://www.theccc.org.uk/about/our-expertise/advice-on-reducing-the-uks-emissions/> accessed 7 May 2024.

the CCC in their 2024 Progress Report.[233] The Sixth Carbon Budget (set for period 2033–2037) was adopted on 24 June 2021, when the Carbon Budget Order 2021 came into force. It is the first carbon budget to be set in line with the net zero target, and the first to include emissions from international aviation and shipping attributable to the UK. Consequently, the target of CB6 is substantially more challenging than those previously set.[234]

2.98 The carbon budgets are not purely calculated on the basis of actual reductions of emissions – the 'carbon units' used for calculation, as defined in section 26, can be a reduction in an amount of GHG emissions, or the removal of an amount of GHG from the atmosphere, or an amount of GHG emissions allowed under a scheme or arrangement limiting such emissions. The system of 'carbon accounting' allows carbon units to be credited or debited to the 'net UK carbon account'.[235] This system allows for flexibility in the means used to meet the carbon budgets.

2.99 Having been set, the carbon budgets must then be achieved. The principal mechanism is in sections 13 and 14 of the CCA 2008. By section 13(1), the Secretary of State must 'prepare such proposals and policies' as they consider 'will enable the carbon budgets' to be met. This is a continuing obligation; and the wording 'proposals and policies' is 'deliberately broad'.[236] The duty requires the Secretary of State to 'prepare' measures, which means that it is recognised that 'proposals will evolve over time and will be introduced and developed at different stages'.[237] They must be prepared with a 'view to meeting' the target set out in section 1 of the CCA 2008, which is currently the net zero target, as well as any targets set under section 5(1)(c); and in preparing the policies and proposals, the government can take into account those prepared by other national authorities.[238] Finally, by section 13(3), the 'proposals and policies, taken as whole' must contribute to sustainable development.

2.100 By section 14, the Secretary of State must then lay before Parliament a report setting out such proposals and policies for meeting the carbon budgets for the current and future budgetary periods up to and including that period.[239] The report must set out the 'current proposals and policies under section 13' and the time-scales over which they are expected to take effect; as well as explaining how the proposals and policies affect different sectors of the economy and the implications of the proposals and policies for the crediting of carbon units to the UK carbon account.[240] Where the proposals and policies are those of the Scottish ministers, Welsh ministers or a Northern Ireland department, they must be prepared in consultation with that authority.[241]

---

233 ibid.
234 *R (Friends of the Earth Ltd) v Secretary of State for Business, Energy and Industrial Strategy* (n 198) [12].
235 CCA 2008 s 27.
236 *R (Friends of the Earth Ltd) v Secretary of State for Business, Energy and Industrial Strategy* (n 198) [144]–[146].
237 ibid [165].
238 CCA 2008 s 13(2)–(4).
239 ibid s 14(1).
240 ibid s 14(2)–(4).
241 ibid s 14(5).

2.104 As stated above, the sixth carbon budget was set on 24 June 2021, and was the first to be set under the new net zero target. Pursuant to section 14 of the CCA 2008, the 'Net Zero Strategy: Build Back Greener' ('NZS') was published on 19 October 2021.[246]

2.105 The NZS sets out an 'indicative delivery pathway', which is an indicative trajectory of emissions reductions to meet targets up to and including the sixth carbon budget.[247] The pathway is 'indicative' rather than fixed because the government's approach to meeting carbon budgets may need to adapt in response to change in technology or markets, which may result in a different 'optimal distribution of policy effort'.[248]

2.106 The NZS sets out policies and proposals for seven different sectors, namely power; fuel supply and hydrogen; industry; heat and buildings; transport; natural resources, waste and fluorinated gases; and GHG removals. In respect of each sector, the NZS summarises the progress made to date, and how much the sector needs to change in order to contribute to the net zero target.[249] The NZS also sets out 'cross-cutting' policies and proposals which affect more than one sector, or the economy as a whole, such as government-funded programmes for research and innovation, or investment in green finance.[250]

2.107 As set out in further detail below at paragraphs 2.123 and 2.125, following the High Court declaration that the NZS was unlawful in *R (Friends of the Earth Ltd) v Secretary of State for Business, Energy and Industrial Strategy* (the 'Net Zero Case'),[251] the government published a further report, on 30 March 2023, updating the NZS, called the Carbon Budget Delivery Plan ('CBDP') (along with the Net Zero Growth Plan and other supporting documents).

2.108 As explained in the CCC's Progress Report 2023:

> [T]he Carbon Budget Delivery Plan (CBDP) [laid] out a set of decarbonisation policies and proposals. Most, but not all, of these have an associated quantification of how they contribute to the emissions reductions required to meet future targets. The CBDP provides a welcome and significant increase in detail and transparency. It was published in response to a High Court ruling that the Government's 2021 Net Zero Strategy (NZS) did not comply sufficiently with the Climate Change Act due to lacking this detail.[252]

While welcoming the increased transparency embodied by the CBDP, the CCC's 2023 Progress Report also raised concerns that 'policy development continues to be too slow'

246 Department for Energy Security and Net Zero, 'Net Zero Strategy: Build Back Greener' (2021) <https://www.gov.uk/government/publications/net-zero-strategy> accessed 28 September 2023.
247 NZS, Chapter 2, [17].
248 *R (Friends of the Earth Ltd) v Secretary of State for Business, Energy and Industrial Strategy* (n 198) [70].
249 NZS Chapter 3.
250 ibid Chapter 4.
251 *R (Friends of the Earth Ltd) v Secretary of State for Business, Energy and Industrial Strategy* (n 198).
252 Climate Change Committee, 'Progress in Reducing Emissions: 2023 Report to Parliament' (2023) 75 <https://www.theccc.org.uk/wp-content/uploads/2023/06/Progress-in-reducing-UK-emissions-2023-Report-to-Parliament.pdf> accessed 4 April 2024.

and that 'confidence in the UK meeting its medium-term targets has decreased in the past year'. They continued:

> To achieve the NDC goal of at least a 68% fall in territorial emissions from 1990 levels, the rate of emissions reduction outside the power sector must almost quadruple. Continued delays in policy development and implementation mean that the NDC's achievement is increasingly challenging. Some of the key planks of the UK Net Zero Strategy have substantial lead-times (e.g. hydrogen storage, greenhouse gas removals and carbon capture and storage (CCS) more generally). Progress in other areas is also too slow, including tree planting and the roll-out of low-carbon heating. There continues to be an overly narrow approach to solutions, which crucially does not embrace the need to reduce demand for high-carbon activities.[253]

2.109 Section 15 contains the express requirement that, in exercising functions under Part 1 of the CCA 2008, in particular meeting (as it currently is) the net zero target or any carbon budget, the Secretary of State 'must have regard to the need for UK domestic action on climate change'. Sections 16–20 contain provisions for determining whether the objectives set in the CCA have been met. By section 16, the government must make an annual statement to Parliament setting out progress made on GHG emissions, within 15 months of the end of the year to which the statement relates. The statement must include, with respect to each year and each targeted GHG, (a) the amount of UK emissions, removals and net emissions of that gas, (b) methods used to measure or calculate those amounts, and (c) whether any of those amounts represents an increase or decrease compared to the equivalent amount for the previous year.[254] It must also state the amount of emissions, removals and net emissions for all GHGs in aggregate, and any emissions from international aviation or shipping that the UK is required to report on in accordance with international carbon reporting practice (unless they are included in the total emissions under the power in section 30). Further, under section 18, the government must make a final statement within 17 months of the end of each budget.[255] If the carbon budget for the relevant period has not been met, the statement must explain why this is.[256]

2.110 There are strict requirements for altering a carbon budget, set out in section 21. A carbon budget for a given period can be altered after the date by which a budget for the period was required to be set only if it appears to the Secretary of State that, since the budget was originally set (or previously altered), there have been significant changes affecting the basis on which the previous decision was made. A budget can be altered after the relevant period has begun only if it appears to the Secretary of State that there have been such changes since the period began. A budget cannot be altered after the period has ended. The CCC must be consulted before any such alteration.[257] So far, no carbon budgets have been amended. The government considered a revision to the Fourth Carbon Budget (2023–2027), given concerns that the UK's trajectory might be

253 ibid 13.
254 CCA 2008 s 16(2).
255 Rules on the content of this statement are given in s 18.
256 ibid s 18(8).
257 ibid s 22.

significantly more ambitious than the EU-wide one, placing the UK at a competitive disadvantage. However, the government accepted the advice of the CCC that there were no changes in the evidence base that supported a change to the level of the Fourth Carbon Budget, and the budget remained unchanged.[258]

(b) Climate Change Committee

2.111 Part 2 of the CCA 2008 created a new independent, non-departmental advisory body, the CCC.[259] As set out in the explanatory notes to the CCA 2008, the purpose of this body is:

> to advise the Government and devolved administrations on how to reduce emissions over time and across the economy and, on request, on any other matter relating to climate change, including adaptation to climate change. This expert body will advise on the optimum trajectory to 2050, the level of carbon budgets, and on how much effort should be made by the part of the economy covered by trading schemes and by the rest of the economy, as well as reporting on progress.[260]

For further details as to the role and functions of the CCC, see paragraphs 4.04–4.09 in Chapter 4.

(c) Trading schemes (see also Chapter 14)

2.112 Part 3 and Schedules 2 and 3 of the CCA 2008 give the government and devolved administrations powers to introduce new domestic emissions trading schemes. As set out in the Explanatory Notes to the CCA 2008, such trading schemes:

> may limit activities that lead, directly or indirectly, to emissions of greenhouse gases (for example, by capping emissions from a particular set of activities and allow trading of emissions within the cap), or they may encourage activities that directly or indirectly lead to a reduction in greenhouse gas emissions or the removal of greenhouse gases from the atmosphere.[261]

2.113 The idea underpinning the emissions trading schemes is to reduce emissions in an economically efficient way, which 'increases the policy options which the Government could use to meet the medium and long-term targets in the Act'.[262]

2.114 The UK Emissions Trading Scheme was accordingly introduced through section 44 of the CCA 2008, by the Greenhouse Gas Emissions Trading Scheme Order 2020[263] and its subsequent amendments.

---

258 Climate Change Committee, 'CCC Insights Briefing 4. Advising on the Level of the UK's Carbon Budgets' (n 221); Department for Energy Security and Net Zero, 'Carbon Budget Delivery Plan' (n 226).
259 For further discussion, see Chapter 4.
260 Explanatory Notes to the Climate Change Act 2008 para 3.
261 ibid 13.
262 ibid 3.
263 The Greenhouse Gas Emissions Trading Scheme (Amendment) Order 2020 (GHG ETS Order 2020).

(d) Impact of and adaptation to climate change

2.115 While the world is aiming to limit global temperature increases to 1.5°C above pre-industrial temperatures, the evidence shows that we must nevertheless be prepared for rises of up to 4°C.[264] Even the lowest warming scenarios will have significant and costly impacts on the UK unless appropriate, timely action is taken to adapt to climate change.[265] Accordingly, the CCA 2008 addresses adaptation to climate change as well as mitigation thereof.

2.116 Adaptation to climate change is a devolved matter,[266] and each devolved government is responsible for their own respective adaptation programmes. Scotland has a devolved statutory framework on adaptation, set out through the Climate Change (Scotland) Act 2009.

2.117 The UK government is given duties under Part 4 of the CCA 2008 to allow monitoring of adaptation and preparedness for climate change impacts. The mechanisms set out within Part 4 are as follows:

2.118 UK-wide Climate Change Risk Assessment ('CCRA'): By section 56, the Secretary of State must submit to Parliament reports assessing the risks to the UK created by the current and predicted impact of climate change. Such a report must take into account the advice of the CCC.[267] The first such report was to be laid within three years, with subsequent reports every five years.[268]

2.119 The third UK Climate Change Risk Assessment 2022 ('CCRA3') was published on 17 January 2022.[269] The Technical Report to the CCRA3 identifies sixty-one UK-wide climate risks and opportunities cutting across multiple sectors of the economy, and assesses the urgency of further action in respect of each risk and opportunity.[270] The report sets out the costs of climate change to the UK, showing that such costs are high and increasing,[271] as well as highlighting certain 'very high' damage risk areas including risks to infrastructure networks (water, energy, transport, ICT) from climate hazards

---

264 Climate Change Committee, 'Independent Assessment of UK Climate Risk: Advice to Government For the UK's Third Climate Change Risk Assessment (CCRA3)' (2021) <https://www.theccc.org.uk/wp-content/uploads/2021/07/Independent-Assessment-of-UK-Climate-Risk-Advice-to-Govt-for-CCRA3-CCC.pdf> accessed 1 April 2024.

265 See the Independent Assessments of UK Climate Risk published by the CCC, the latest being ibid; for example, as flagged in the executive summary of CCRA3, unless the UK takes further action, a 2°C increase by 2100 would produce an increase in annual damages from flooding for non-residential properties across the UK by 27% by 2050 and 40% by 2080. Under a 4°C scenario, these increases would be 44% and 75% respectively.

266 DEFRA, 'Policy Paper: Understanding Climate Adaptation and the Third National Adaptation Programme (NAP3)' (2024) <https://www.gov.uk/government/publications/third-national-adaptation-programme-nap3/understanding-climate-adaptation-and-the-third-national-adaptation-programme-nap3> accessed 7 May 2024.

267 CCA 2008 ss 56(5), 57.

268 The first CCRA was published in 2012, the second CCRA in 2017, and the third in 2022.

269 Taking into account the CCC's Independent Assessment of UK Climate Risk, delivered in summer 2021.

270 Climate Change Committee, 'Independent Assessment of UK Climate Risk: Advice to Government For the UK's Third Climate Change Risk Assessment (CCRA3)' (n 264) 8–15. Of the 61 risks considered, 34 are ranked as 'more action needed', meaning that new stronger or different government action is required in the next five years over and above those already planned.

271 ibid 8. For example, for eight of the 61 climate risks, under a 2°C warming scenario, UK-wide economic damages by 2050 are estimated to exceed £1billion per annum. A decade ago, only 3 of the 61 risks were predicted to produce damages that large.

which cause cascading failures across sectors, risks to health and wellbeing from high temperatures particularly amongst the vulnerable, risks from flooding and risks associated with climate change overseas. It then goes on to make the case for acting sooner rather than later, illustrating the relative economic efficiency and impact of earlier rather than later investment in adaptation measures.

2.120 The 'Adaptation Reporting Power': The UK and Welsh governments have a discretionary power under section 62 to require relevant bodies ('reporting authorities', as defined in section 70[272]) to report on their adaptation to and preparedness for climate change. The third round of such reports was completed at the end of 2021 with voluntary contributions from over 90 organisations.

2.121 The National Adaptation Programme ('NAP'): Following on from a CCRA, the Secretary of State must lay a programme before Parliament setting out the UK government's objectives, proposals and policies in response to the risks identified in the most recent CCRA.[273] Scotland, Wales and Northern Ireland develop their own respective NAPs. The first NAP was published in 2013, the second in 2018, and the third in July 2023 ('NAP3'), in response to CCRA3. NAP3 sets out an action plan for the subsequent 5 years, with action areas being divided into: infrastructure; natural environment; health, communities and the built environment; business and industry; and international impacts. NAP3 also sets out the government's strategy for the fourth round of climate adaptation reporting.

(e) Other provisions

2.122 Part 5 of the CCA 2008 is a smorgasbord of other policy measures, such as a power given to the Secretary of State under section 77, along with schedule 6, to make regulations regarding charges for single use carrier bags.[274]

2.123 Part 6 contains the general supplementary provisions, such as defining terms as noted in the earlier sections of this chapter.

(ii) *Case law on the CCA 2008*

2.124 There has been a significant number of cases citing the CCA 2008, but very few have relied upon the provisions in the CCA 2008 as a core part of the grounds of challenge and even fewer have been successful. A key case is the judicial review challenge to the NZS, in which Holgate J considered the operation of section 13 of the CCA 2008 when a report, pursuant to section 14, was required: Net Zero Case.[275] The result of this case, as explained further below, is that the NZS was declared unlawful

---

272 'Reporting authority' is defined in s 70 as (1) '(a) a person or body with functions of a public nature, (b) a person who is or is deemed to be a statutory undertaker for the purposes of any provision of— (i) Part 11 of the Town and Country Planning Act 1990 (c. 8) (see section 262 of that Act), or (ii) Part 10 of the Town and Country Planning (Scotland) Act 1997 (c. 8) (see section 214 of that Act), or (c) a person who is a statutory undertaker within the meaning of the Planning Act (Northern Ireland) 2011 201. (see section 250 of that Act)'.
273 CCA 2008 s 58.
274 See the Single Use Carrier Bags Charges (England) Order 2015, SI 2015/776.
275 *R (Friends of the Earth Ltd) v Secretary of State for Business, Energy and Industrial Strategy* (n 198).

and the government was ordered to lay a report, compliant with section 14 of the CCA 2008, before Parliament by 31 March 2023.

2.125 Other significant cases citing the CCA include:

- *R (Elliott-Smith) v Secretary of State for Business, Energy and Industrial Strategy*.[276] The claimant challenged the legality of the UK Emissions Trading Scheme. The court held that the defendants had taken adequate account of the Paris Agreement, and that the Scheme had been designed in order to achieve the purpose of 'limiting or encouraging the limitation of activities' causing or contributing to GHG emissions pursuant to section 44 CCA.[277]

- *R (Transport Action Network Ltd) v Secretary of State for Transport*.[278] The court held that the Paris Agreement was not an obviously material consideration which should have been taken into account when setting a road investment strategy under the Infrastructure Act 2015 Pt 1 section 3(1), and the secretary of state had taken sufficient account of the net zero target.[279]

- *R (Cox) v Oil and Gas Authority*.[280] The claimant challenged the Oil and Gas Authority's ('OGA') revised oil and gas strategy. The revised strategy made provision for 'maximising the economic recovery of UK petroleum' (as required by section 9A of the Petroleum Act 1998), and also required relevant persons to assist the secretary of state in meeting the section 1 CCA net zero target. The claimants argued *inter alia* that the definition of 'economically recoverable' (which included 'resources which could be recovered at an expected (pre-tax) market value greater than the expected (pre-tax) resource cost of their extraction') was irrational in light of the Secretary of State's duty under section 1 of the 2008 Act. The court disagreed, holding that the balancing of various objectives was not a matter for the court.

- *R (Greenpeace) v Secretary of State for Energy Security and Net Zero*.[281] The Secretary of State's policy for licensing offshore oil and gas exploration was contained within his non-statutory offshore energy plan. The Environmental Assessment of Plans and Programmes Regulations 2004 required the secretary of state to carry out a strategic environmental assessment (SEA) of the plan. The secretary of state did not assess the emissions produced by the end use of oil and gas as part of the SEA. The court held that this was not irrational, despite the net zero target.

---

276 *R (Elliott-Smith v Secretary of State for Business, Energy and Industrial Strategy* [2021] EWHC 1633 (Admin).
277 See Chapter 14.
278 *R (Transport Action Network) v Secretary of State for Transport* [2021] EWHC 2095 (Admin).
279 For a general discussion of transport-related issues, see Chapter 18.
280 *R (Cox) v Oil and Gas Authority* [2022] EWHC 75 (Admin).
281 *R (Greenpeace Ltd) v Secretary of State for Energy Security and Net Zero* [2023] EWHC 2608 (Admin). See also paras 17.32–17.36 in Chapter 17.

- *R (Dawes) v Secretary of State for Transport.*[282] The claimants argued, *inter alia*, that the Secretary of State had failed to properly consider the UK's sixth carbon budget when granting development consent for Manston Airport in Kent, and had relied on untested policies for decarbonising the aviation sector. The court dismissed this ground, holding that the secretary of state had been entitled to rely on those policies and to conclude that the climate change impact could be regarded as neutral in the light of them.[283]

2.126 In July 2022, the High Court declared that the NZS was unlawful in the Net Zero Case,[284] and the government was ordered to lay a report, compliant with section 14 of the CCA 2008, before Parliament by 31 March 2023, as mentioned above. The NZS was found to be unlawful because the delivery pathway did not converge with the modelled output of the proposals and policies; the modelled effect of quantified proposals and policies achieved only 95% of the emissions reductions necessary to meet the sixth carbon budget.[285] In this landmark case, Holgate J carefully considered sections 13 and 14 of the CCA 2008. The court confirmed *inter alia* that:

- The obligation in section 13 is a continuing one.[286]

- Whilst it is a matter of judgement for the Secretary of State to decide on (a) the proposals and policies that should be prepared and (b) whether they will enable the carbon budgets to be met, the word 'enable' should be given its ordinary meaning of 'to make possible or effective'.[287] Thus, the Secretary of State will need to decide whether the policies will be 'effective' or 'efficacious' for achieving the reductions set by the carbon budget.[288]

- Section 13(1) requires the Secretary of State to assess the time-scales over which his policies are expected to take effect, which is an obviously material considera-tion and necessarily implied by the legislation.[289]

- The obligations in section 13 and section 14 cannot properly and rationally be sat-isfied without quantitative projections and analysis of the effects of the proposals and policies in reducing GHG emissions.[290]

- The Secretary of State must take into account the risk to the delivery of *individual* proposals and policies and to the achievement of the carbon budgets and the 2050 net zero target.[291] Achieving the carbon budget and net zero target must

---

282 *R (Dawes) v Secretary of State for Transport* [2023] EWHC 2352 (Admin).
283 See paras 18.27–18.28 in Chapter 18.
284 *R (Friends of the Earth Ltd) v Secretary of State for Business, Energy and Industrial Strategy* (n 198).
285 ibid 118.
286 ibid 164.
287 ibid 167, 170.
288 ibid 170.
289 ibid 173.
290 ibid 176, 222.
291 ibid 204.

depend upon the relative contributions made by individual policies to achieving those targets.[292]

- If the *quantified* effects fall significantly below meeting the whole of the emissions reductions required, then the Secretary of State would need to be satisfied that the meeting of that shortfall by *qualitative* analysis is demonstrated to him with sufficient cogency. As that shortfall increases, so that task would be likely to become increasingly challenging for the Secretary of State and his officials.[293]

- The measures proposed by the Secretary of State in accordance with section 13 will be scrutinised by the CCC, Parliament, the scientific community, public interest groups and the wider public.[294] Hence the report prepared pursuant to section 14 is necessary to meet the statutory objective of transparency in respect of how the targets set out in legislation are to be met so that the measures can be subject to scrutiny.[295]

- A briefing to the Secretary of State when approving a package of policies for the purposes of a section 14 report, and the report itself, must address: '(a) the assessment made by officials of the quantitative contributions that individual policies are expected to make to meeting carbon budgets (and the 2050 target) and (b) the justification for relying upon unquantified policies to make up any predicted shortfall in meeting a statutory target. These requirements enable the scrutiny, firstly by the Secretary of State of the policy package, and secondly by Parliament, the CCC and others of the s 14 report, to be effective and more rigorous'.[296] The report prepared pursuant to section 14 must 'set out' the proposals and policies for meeting the carbon budgets, which requires the Secretary of State to tell Parliament how the policies are intended to meet the statutory targets (which requires a quantitative explanation).[297]

2.127 The CBDP has also been subject to a legal challenge and was declared unlawful by Sheldon J.[298] There were three main issues in the case:

- The first concerned the Secretary of State's assessment pursuant to section 13(1) of the CCA 2008, in particular whether, as a matter of fact, the Secretary of State had proceeded on the assumption that all quantified proposals and policies would be delivered in full, based on the ministerial submissions; and whether the Secretary of State had sufficient information about the delivery risks associated with individual policies to enable a lawful decision pursuant to section 13(1) in respect of those policies and proposals enabling the carbon budgets to be met.

292 ibid.
293 ibid 185.
294 ibid 186.
295 ibid 241, 247.
296 ibid 187.
297 ibid 235–6, 251.
298 *Friends of the Earth and others v Secretary of State for Energy Security and Net Zero* [2024] EWHC 995 (Admin).

- The second issue concerned the legal test under section 13(3), which requires that the Secretary of State must be satisfied that her policies and proposals, taken as a whole, must be such as to contribute to sustainable development.

- The third issue related to the obligation in section 14 and the information required in the CBDP, which contained a sectoral summary of risks but not information about the degree of risk for each proposal and policy.

2.128 On the first issue, it was common ground that an obviously material consideration (from the Net Zero Case) was the delivery risk to individual policies and proposals. The issue turned on the advice and material provided to the Secretary of State, in particular a ministerial submission from March 2023. In Sheldon J's determination, the reasonable interpretation of the relevant text was that the Secretary of State was being told that 'each of the individual proposals and policies that form the package of measures would be delivered in full'.[299] Thus, the 'Secretary of State's decision was taken on the basis of a mistaken understanding of the true factual position', which renders the decision irrational.[300]

2.129 Sheldon J went on to consider whether it would have been highly likely that the Secretary of State would have reached the same decision, pursuant to section 31(2A) of the Senior Courts Act 1981. Thus, the judge was required to consider the counterfactual, namely 'the information available to the Secretary of State would have enabled him to reach the conclusion that the 97% emissions savings would be met by the quantified proposals and policies even if not all of the individual proposals and policies would be achieved in full'.[301] He concluded that it was not possible for the court to reach that decision because the Secretary of State did not have sufficient information to undertake the necessary evaluation – the Secretary of State could not ascertain which policies would not be delivered at all or in full.[302]

2.130 Sheldon J also noted that, even if he had been wrong about the assumption made by the Secretary of State, based on the advice provided to him, the Secretary of State's decision under section 13 of the CCA 2008 was still flawed because 'he was not provided with sufficient information as to the obviously material consideration of risk to the individual proposals and policies'.[303] The Secretary of State was therefore unable to assess for himself whether a policy or proposal would under or over-deliver; and if so, by how much so he could undertake the whole evaluation and assess for himself the cumulative risk from the package of policies and proposals.[304]

2.131 On the second issue, Sheldon J interpreted section 13(3) of the CCA 2008, which requires that, '[t]he proposals and policies, taken as a whole, must be such as to contribute to sustainable development'. In the CBPD, it had been said that the overall

---

299 ibid 119.
300 ibid 126–7.
301 ibid 129.
302 ibid 129–30.
303 ibid 132.
304 ibid 132–5.

contribution of the policies and proposals to sustainable development 'is likely to be positive'.[305] The judge determined that the use of the word 'must' connotes a degree of certainty and that therefore the Secretary of State's assessment of 'likely' does not come near the high threshold mandated by section 13(3).[306]

2.132 On the third issue, dealing with section 14 of the CCA 2008 and the contents of the CBDP, Sheldon J determined that the material provided in the CBDP complied with section 14.[307] It set out how the Secretary of State proposes to meet the carbon budgets, including a description of the proposals and policies, the contribution made by unquantified policies and how the shortfall would be met. There was no obligation to provide risk data or delivery risks for individual policies; and, in any event, the section 14 report provided summaries of risk at the sectoral level.

2.133 Following the CBDP having been laid before Parliament in March 2023, Prime Minister Rishi Sunak announced on 20 September 2023 that key climate policies would be abandoned or delayed.[308] It is reported that the decision to abandon or delay these net zero policies and proposals had been taken by Claire Coutinho MP, Secretary of State for Energy Security and Net Zero and Mark Harper MP, Secretary of State for Transport.[309] Chris Packham, a naturalist, campaigner and TV broadcaster, has brought a judicial review challenge to that decision, alleging that the decisions breached key decision-making mechanisms set out in the CCA 2008, given that no alternative measures were proposed.[310] The public should have been able to rely on the CBDP in relation to the policies and proposals coming forward; and if there was a change in position that should have involved notifying and consulting the public and the CCC.[311] Permission to proceed has been granted by Eyre J and the case is listed for November 2024.

2.134 In December 2023, the Court of Appeal handed down judgment in *R (Global Feedback) v Secretary of State for Environment, Food and Rural Affairs* ('SSEFRA') *and Secretary of State for Energy Security and Net Zero* ('SSESNZ'),[312] in which it considered the scope of section 13 of the CCA 2008; in particular, whether the duty was engaged in the development and adoption of the food strategy. The food strategy had been described in the NZS as follows:[313]

---

305 ibid 144.
306 ibid 151–2.
307 ibid 161–2.
308 PM Rishi Sunak, 'PM Speech on Net Zero: 20 September 2023' (20 September 2023) <https://www.gov.uk/government/speeches/pm-speech-on-net-zero-20-september-2023> accessed 25 April 2024.
309 Chris Packham, 'Is the Prime Minister a Climate Leader or a Climate Loser?' (*CrowdJustice*) <https://www.crowdjustice.com/case/is-the-pm-a-climate-leader-or-a-climate-loser/> accessed 7 May 2024; 'Chris Packham Legal Challenge to Prime Minister over Axing of Timetable on Vehicles and Boilers' (Leigh Day, 10 April 2023) <https://www.leighday.co.uk/news/news/2023-news/chris-packham-legal-challenge-to-prime-minister-over-axing-of-timetable-on-vehicles-and-boilers/> accessed 7 May 2024.
310 Packham (n 309).
311 ibid.
312 *R (Global Feedback Ltd) v Secretary of State for the Environment, Food and Rural Affairs and the Secretary of State for Energy Security and Net Zero* [2023] EWCA Civ 1549 (n 201).
313 ibid 39.

> The Government's upcoming Food Strategy will support the delivery of net zero, nature recovery, and biodiversity commitments and will help to create a food system that incentivises farmers to produce high quality, high welfare food in the most sustainable way.

2.135 The CCC had repeatedly advised that the government should consider policies aimed at shifting diets away from meat and dairy to achieve the necessary GHG emission reductions.

2.136 The claimant alleged: (i) that the SSEFRA, alternatively SSESNZ, had breached section 13(1) of the CCA 2008, given the office of Secretary of State is one and indivisible and therefore applied to SSEFRA as well as SSESNZ; and (ii) contingent on the first ground, the SSEFRA had failed to take into account, give significant weight to, and cogent reasons for departing from, the CCC's advice.

2.137 The Court of Appeal rejected both grounds. The court determined that properly interpreting the relevant provisions meant that the Secretary of State tasked with laying the report before Parliament pursuant to section 14(1) of the CCA 2008 must be the same Secretary of State who would prepare and evaluate policies and proposals, pursuant to section 13(1) of the CCA 2008.[314] It is that Secretary of State who is 'ultimately accountable for operating the legislative machinery designed to bring about a reduction in greenhouse gas emissions and to secure the meeting of carbon budgets through the Net Zero Strategy'.[315] Further, they determined that the carbon budgets apply to the economy as a whole at a national level and are not broken down into individual sectors, relying upon the language of section 13(3), in particular, proposals and policies 'taken as a whole'.[316] In their judgment, the food strategy was not a policy or proposal for the purpose of section 13(1) of the CCA 2008.[317]

2.138 Given the claim was rejected on the first ground, the second ground did not fall for consideration but the court determined that, in the context of discharging section 13(1) of the CCA 2008, the Secretary of State was not under a legal duty to take into account, give significant weight to, or cogent reasons for departing from, the CCC advice.[318]

2.139 Most recently, Mr Justice Chamberlain dismissed a judicial review challenge of NAP3.[319] The challenge was brought by the campaign group Friends of the Earth, along with a disability rights activist particularly vulnerable to the effects of extreme heat and a campaigner who was forced by coastal erosion to leave his home. The judge held that there had been no error of law in construing section 58(1) CCA, the goals set out in the NAP3 being properly describable as 'objectives' as required by that section (albeit not

---

314 ibid 71.
315 ibid 81.
316 ibid 80, 82.
317 ibid 95.
318 ibid 112.
319 *Friends of the Earth & Ors, R (On the Application Of) v Secretary of State for Environment, Food and Rural Affairs* [2024] EWHC 2707 (Admin).

very specific ones); and that the level of consideration given to the risk to delivery of individual policies and proposals in NAP3 had been rational.[320]

(iii) *Other domestic legislation*

2.140 The Environment Act 2021 is the UK's framework for environmental protection. It was intended to protect those aspects of the environment which had previously been safeguarded by EU law and which were at risk of being left unprotected following Brexit.[321]

2.141 In presenting the Environment Bill (which became the Environment Act) for its second reading before the House of Commons, the Secretary of State for Environment, Food and Rural Affairs (George Eustice) provided the following context for the bill:[322]

> In recent decades, our natural world has faced multiple pressures. As a consequence, we face two great global challenges: climate change and biodiversity loss. A million species face extinction, and climate change is piling the pressure on nature, doubling the number of species under threat in the past 15 years. If global temperatures rise by even 1.5°, we will lose even more of our precious life on Earth. As an island nation, we are acutely aware of the devastating effects of plastic pollution on marine life. We need to act now to turn things around. This Government were elected on the strongest-ever manifesto for the environment, and this Bill is critical to implementing that commitment.

2.142 The Act is divided into seven parts, which are:

- Parts 1 and 2: Improving the Natural Environment. Part 1 provides a framework for delivering environmental improvements in England. Under section 1, the Secretary of State is empowered to make regulations to set long-term targets relating to the natural environment,[323] and is obliged to do so in the four priority areas of air quality, water, biodiversity and resource efficiency and waste reduction.[324] Under section 8, the Secretary of State must prepare an environmental improvement plan, setting out the government's steps to improve the natural environment. The Secretary of State is also obliged to prepare a policy statement on environmental principles, to be considered by government ministers in creating policy (ss 17–19). Sections 22–42 create and describe the functions of the Office for Environmental Protection, as a watchdog to hold government and public authorities to account. Part 2 empowers the OEP to act in Northern Ireland (on the approval of the Northern Ireland Assembly).

- Part 3: Waste and Resource Efficiency. Part 3 provides the framework necessary to fulfil the Resources and Waste strategy, through extended producer responsibility

---

320 ibid, at [93]–[96] and [115]–[121].
321 'The UK Environment Act – What's Happening Now?' (*ClientEarth*, 4 January 2022) <https://www.clientearth.org/latest/news/why-the-uk-environment-bill-matters/> accessed 7 May 2024.
322 HC Deb 26 February 2020, vol 672.
323 EA 2021 s 1(1).
324 EA 2021 s 1(2)–(3).

(ss 50–51), resource efficiency (ss 52–56) and waste management, enforcement and regulation (ss 57–71).

- Part 4: Air Quality and Environmental Recall. Part 4 provides for air quality management (ss 72–73) and recall of motor vehicles which do not meet the relevant environmental standards (ss 74–77).

- Part 5: Water. Part 5 provides duties and powers on water undertakers and on the Secretary of State to safeguard water resources and properly manage wastewater (ss 78–97).

- Part 6: Nature and biodiversity. Part 6 sets out the new planning requirement for a biodiversity net gain plan ('BNG') to be submitted and approved before the commencement of development (ss 98–101), as well as making provisions on the duty of public authorities to have regard to enhancing biodiversity (s 102) and providing for local nature recovery strategies ('LNRS') (ss 104–108). See also Chapters 10 and 11.

- Part 7: Conservation covenants. Part 7 introduces conservation covenants, being private, voluntary agreements for the conservation of the natural environment and heritage assets (ss 117–139). See also Chapter 23.

2.143 The Environment Act 2021 is discussed in greater detail in Chapter 8.

2.144 It is also worth noting the environmental protections which exist within legislation not primarily concerned with environmental protection. For example, part 6 of the Levelling-Up and Regeneration Act 2023 is concerned with environmental outcomes reports, and part 7 with nutrient pollution standards.

CHAPTER 3

ENVIRONMENTAL PRINCIPLES

Stephanie David

Introduction

3.01 Environmental principles[1] are a staple feature of international, European Union ('EU') and domestic environmental law;[2] and an integral part of policymaking.[3] Yet, there is no definitive and universal catalogue of environmental principles nor is there any agreed definition of what an environmental principle is.[4] Environmental principles have been described as 'an amorphous group of policy ideas concerning how environmental protection ... ought to be pursued'.[5] What is therefore difficult is 'translating those principles into detailed policies and binding law'.[6]

3.02 In this chapter, the key environmental principles are considered. The focus is on the development of these principles; their meanings (insofar as it is possible to define them); and the role that they play, or could play, in addressing climate change and the biodiversity crisis. These principles also inform later chapters.

3.03 The most commonly cited catalogue of environmental principles is the Rio Declaration on Environment and Development ('the Rio Declaration'), which was adopted

1 For a discussion of the role of legal principles, see Ronald Dworkin, *Taking Rights Seriously* (Harvard University Press 1978).
2 Richard Macrory and Justine Thornton QC, 'Environmental Principles: Will They Have a Legal Role after Brexit?' [2017] JPL 907.
3 Environment Act 2021 ss 18, 19. Stephen Tromans, 'High Talk and Low Cunning: Putting Environmental Principles into Legal Practice' [1995] JPL 779. Tromans attributes the richness of principles in this area to four features of environmental law and policy: (i) its 'strong international aspect' which necessitates trying to 'achieve adherence to common goals' across differing cultures and priorities; (ii) its need to 'wrestle with some very large scientific uncertainties and unexpected reactions and interactions'; (iii) the need to consider the long-term view (beyond election cycles); and (v) its popularity in the media and politics, which means the principles provide a 'common currency' for action.
4 Eloise Scotford, *Environmental Principles and the Evolution of Environmental Law* (Hart Publishing 2017) 5–6.
5 Elizabeth Fisher, Bettina Lange and Eloise Scotford, *Environmental Law: Text, Cases and Materials* (2nd edn, Oxford University Press 2019) 214–5. They have been described as 'policies' in two respects: (i) 'they reflect courses of action adopted to secure, or that tend to secure, a state of affairs considered to be desirable'; and (ii) 'in the Dworkinian sense of "collective goal[s] of the community as a whole"', citing Neil MacCormick, *Legal Reasoning and Legal Theory* (Clarendon 1994) 261.
6 Tromans (n 3). See also Nicolas de Sadeleer, *Environmental Principles: From Political Slogans to Legal Rules* (2nd edn, Oxford University Press 2020).

in 1992, at the United Nations Conference on Environment and Development in Rio de Janeiro.[7] The Rio Declaration sets out 27 principles.

3.04 This chapter focuses[8] on the five principles set out in the Environmental Principles Policy Statement ('the EPPS') made under the Environment Act 2021 ('EA 2021') and the principles of sustainable development and intergenerational justice. The principle of sustainable development is directly relevant to the EPPS, given that section 17(4) of the EA 2021 required the Secretary of State to be satisfied that it would contribute to *inter alia* sustainable development.[9] Intergenerational equity is also considered in this chapter, because (i) of the nature of the climate change and biodiversity crises and the need to consider the legal obligations owed by the present to future generations and (ii) intergenerational justice is tied to the definition of sustainable development within the Well-being of Future Generations (Wales) Act 2015 and a similar Bill proposed in England.

Environmental Principles Policy Statement

3.05 After the UK's departure from the European Union, five environmental principles were formally enshrined in the EA 2021 in section 17(5) and the policy statement produced in accordance with sections 17(1) and 18 of the Act, the EPPS. The principles are: (i) the integration principle; (ii) the prevention principle; (iii) the precautionary principle; (iv) rectification at source principle; and (v) the polluter pays principle.[10]

3.06 This followed the obligation under section 16(1) of the European Union (Withdrawal) Act 2018, before it was amended by the 2020 Act,[11] which required the Secretary of State to publish a draft Bill consisting of *inter alia* a set of environmental principles. A commitment to environmental and climate principles was also set out in Article 393 of the EU–UK Trade and Cooperation Agreement.[12]

---

7 Fisher, Lange and Scotford (n 5) 214–5. The principles set out in the Rio Declaration followed on from other earlier 'UN-sponsored soft law agreements', such as the United Nations Environment Programme, Declaration of the United Nations Conference on the Human Environment (Stockholm, 16 June 1972) (UN Doc A/CONF.48/14); World Commission on Environment and Development, 'Our Common Future' (1987) UN Doc A42/427 Annex I <https://documents.un.org/doc/undoc/gen/n87/184/67/pdf/n8718467.pdf?token=N1elHLsyyfhOF4vkFW&fe=true> accessed 26 April 2024.

8 For further reading on international environmental principles, readers are referred to Philippe Sands and others, *Principles of International Environmental Law* (4th edn, Cambridge University Press 2018).

9 s 17(4)(a) also required that the EPPS would contribute to the improvement of environmental protection.

10 Environment Act 2021 s 17(5).

11 European Union (Withdrawal Agreement) Act 2020.

12 See paras 2.70–2.76 in Chapter 2. Trade and Cooperation Agreement between the European Union and the European Atomic Energy Community, of the one part, and the United Kingdom of Great Britain and Northern Ireland, of the other part [2021] OJ L 149/10. In Article 393, the 'precautionary approach' is specifically defined by reference to Article 356(2) of the TCA as 'where there are reasonable grounds for concern that there are potential threats of serious or irreversible damage to the environment or human health, the lack of full scientific certainty shall not be used as a reason for preventing a Party from adopting appropriate measures to prevent such damage'.

3.07 By section 19(1) of the EA 2021, ministers are required to have 'due regard'[13] to the policy statement when making policy ('section 19(1) duty'). It is not therefore a duty which requires the achievement of a specific outcome. In *R (Rights Community Action Ltd) v Secretary of State for Levelling Up, Housing and Communities,*[14] the High Court considered for the first time the nature and scope of the section 19(1) duty. The claimant drew on the case law on the public sector equality duty ('PSED') set out in section 149 of the Equality Act 2010. It was agreed between the parties that the broad principles applicable to the discharge of the PSED were applicable to the section 19(1) duty, namely that the duty has to be applied 'in substance, with rigour and with an open mind'.[15] Lieven J, otherwise, accepted the Defendant's submissions, and observed as follows:[16]

> The two duties are very different, both in terms of the statutory provisions (save for the broad words 'have due regard') and the aims to be achieved. Whereas the impact on those with protected characteristics may generally be relatively straightforward to set out, the environmental issues as set out in the EPPS will often be very multifaceted and complex. This case is a good example of that complexity. Although setting higher CO_2 standards for new homes may appear to be more environmentally positive, it might have consequences that lead to an environmentally less good ultimate outcome. Environmental impacts are rarely linear and binary, but rather frequently involve complex and multifaceted impacts which need to be assessed in a holistic manner. The nature of the two statutory schemes, and therefore the due regard duties are very different.

3.08 Her judgment has been appealed and the Office for Environmental Protection and Green Alliance have applied to intervene in the appeal. The section 19(1) duty does not apply to specific individual decisions made pursuant to a policy. Sections 17(2) and (3) temper the role of the principles: they specifically require Ministers of the Crown to apply the principles 'proportionately'; and, when interpreting and applying them, to 'take into account other considerations relevant to their policy'.[17] There is no obligation to take the EPPS into account in the context of policy relating to the armed forces, defence or national security, taxation or the allocation of resources within government or Wales.[18]

(i) *Integration principle*

3.09 This principle is generally recognised as requiring that environmental protection and the other environmental principles are integrated into policymaking and, in some

---

13 In Christopher Badger and Richard Macrory, *Environment Act 2021: Text, Guide and Analysis* (Hart Publishing 2022) 57–9, the authors argue that the phrase should be interpreted by reference to the case law on s 149 of the Equality Act 2010 as set out in *R (Bracking) v Secretary of State for Work and Pensions* [2013] EWCA Civ 1345. See also *R (Sofia Sheakh) v Lambeth LBC* [2022] EWCA Civ 457 [10]–[18]. The parallels between section 149 of the Equality Act 2010 and this duty are limited as Lieven J set out in *R (Rights Community Action Ltd) v Secretary of State for Levelling Up, Housing and Communities* [2024] EWHC 1693 (Admin) (subject to appeal). See para 3.07.
14 *R (Rights Community Action Ltd) v Secretary of State for Levelling Up, Housing and Communities* [2024] EWHC 1693 (Admin).
15 ibid [35].
16 ibid [42].
17 Environment Act 2021 s 19(2).
18 ibid s 19(3).

the policy statement itself – by section 17(4), the Secretary of State had to be satisfied that the EPPS would contribute to (i) the improvement of the environmental protection; and (ii) sustainable development.

3.15 The EPPS defines the integration principle as 'the principle that environmental protection should be integrated into the making of policies'.[27] Thus, the statement advises that 'policymakers should look for opportunities to embed environmental protection and/or enhancement across fields of policy'.[28] Notably, the EA 2021 defines 'policy' to exclude administrative decisions taken in relation to particular individuals or in particular cases (providing specific examples of an application for planning permission and decisions on funding, a licence, or about regulatory enforcement).[29]

3.16 In the context of nature positive and net zero goals, it is specifically envisaged by the EPPS that the principles will play an 'important role' in delivering on the Environmental Improvement Plans[30] and on the UK's commitment to achieve net zero. The EPPS notes that policies can affect the environment through CO_2 and other emissions,[31] as well as through physical changes like biodiversity and habitat loss; and that the environmental effects must be considered regardless of where the potential effects occur – specifically, in the context of climate change, it is noted that:

> If it is feasible and appropriate to consider the overseas effects of a policy, this must be done proportionately and within reason.

3.17 The integration principle therefore bakes in considerations of net zero and nature positive into policy design, but these factors are still weighed into the mix as part of policymaking, as is apparent from the EA 2021 itself and the language of the EPPS.

(ii) *Precautionary principle*

3.18 The precautionary principle, often referred to as a precautionary approach, escapes a universal definition. Much depends upon the context in which it is used and the legal framework, even then it can remain a nebulous concept. Defining and applying the principle have caused significant debate; and the lack of clarity has led to arguments that the principle leads to overly burdensome regulation.[32] It was used as a standard of review in judicial review proceedings in the challenge to the third runway at Heathrow Airport[33] but was given short shrift by the Supreme Court.[34] It is generally accepted that it applies to assist decision-making in the context of scientific uncertainty.

27 'Environmental protection' is defined within the Environment Act 2021 s 45.
28 DEFRA, 'Environmental Principles Policy Statement' (2023) <https://www.gov.uk/government/publications/environmental-principles-policy-statement/environmental-principles-policy-statement> accessed 26 April 2024.
29 ibid 47.
30 See paras 8.08, 8.32 and 8.60–8.85 in Chapter 8.
31 DEFRA, 'Environmental Principles Policy Statement' (n 28).
32 See Department for Business, Energy and Industrial Strategy, 'UK Innovation Strategy: Leading the Future by Creating It' (2021) 34 < https://www.gov.uk/government/publications/uk-innovation-strategy-leading-the-future-by-creating-it> accessed 29 April 2024.
33 *R (Plan B Earth) v Secretary of State for Transport* [2020] EWCA Civ 214 [258].
34 *R (Friends of the Earth Ltd and others) v Heathrow Airport Ltd* [2020] UKSC 52, [2021] 2 All ER 967 [164]–[166].

3.19 The principle is thought to have originated in German law in the concept known as *Vorsorge* (literally 'beforehand or prior care or worry') in the context of air pollution laws in the 1970s.[35]

3.20 In the international context, the precautionary principle started to appear in agreements in the 1980s. It has been suggested that, whilst not specifically referred to in name, the approach was set out in the World Charter for Nature, adopted by the UNGA in 1982.[36] 'Precautionary measures' then appeared in the recitals to the Vienna Convention for the Protection of the Ozone Layer 1985. Following which the principle was formally adopted at the international North Sea conference in London in 1987 at which participants agreed on further measures to protect the North Sea and its marine ecosystem, particularly from polluting substance emissions.[37] It was referred to therein as the 'principle of precautionary action'; and was encapsulated as follows:[38]

> [W]hen there is reason to assume that certain damage or harmful effects on the living resources of the sea are likely to be caused by such substances, even where there is no scientific evidence to prove a causal link between emissions and effects.

3.21 In the Rio Declaration, the precautionary principle was adopted as principle 15:

> In order to protect the environment, the precautionary approach shall be widely applied by States according to their capabilities. Where there are threats of serious or irreversible damage, lack of full scientific certainty shall not be used as a reason for postponing cost-effective measures to prevent degradation.

3.22 The principle is reflected at Article 3(3) of the UNFCCC, as follows:

> The Parties should take precautionary measures to anticipate, prevent or minimize the causes of climate change and mitigate its adverse effects. Where there are threats of serious or irreversible damage, lack of full scientific certainty should not be used as a reason for postponing such measures, taking into account that policies and measures to deal with climate change should be cost-effective so as to ensure global benefits at the lowest possible cost.

3.23 In this Article, the UNFCCC recognises that different socio-economic contexts should be taken into account, along with ensuring that policies and measures are

---

35 Tromans (n 3) 780; Didier Bourguignon, 'The Precautionary Principle: Definitions, Application and Governance' (European Parliamentary Research Service 2016) PE 573.876 <https://www.europarl.europa.eu/RegData/etudes/IDAN/2015/573876/EPRS_IDA(2015)573876_EN.pdf>.

36 Adopted at the 48th plenary meeting on 28 October 1982; see para 11 which specifically sets out that the 'best available technologies that minimise significant risks to nature or other adverse effects shall be used'.

37 'Precautionary measures' had been referred to at the previous international conference in Bremen in 1984; see Declaration of the International Conference on the Protection of the North Sea paras D3, H7.

38 Declaration from the Second International Conference on the Protection of the North Sea, London, 24–25 November 1987 para 1.

'comprehensive, cover all relevant sources, sinks and reserves of [GHGs] and adaptation, and comprise all economic sectors'.[39]

3.24 In the Convention on Biological Diversity ('CBD'), there is a general recognition of the urgent need to understand biological diversity better, including by developing the necessary scientific, technical, and institutional capacities.[40] The recitals also state that:

> *Noting* also that where there is a threat of significant reduction or loss of biological diversity, lack of full scientific certainty should not be used as a reason for postponing measures to avoid or minimize such a threat.

3.25 In the EU, the precautionary principle is a general principle of law[41] and a fundamental principle of environmental law,[42] introduced by the Maastricht Treaty in 1992. It is now referred to in Article 191(2) of the TFEU in the context of ensuring a 'high level of protection' for the environment, along with the prevention principle, the rectification at source principle, and the polluter pays principle.[43] The principle requires:[44]

> [C]ompetent authorities to take appropriate measures to prevent specific potential risks to public health, safety and the environment, by giving precedence to those interests over economic interests … where there is uncertainty as to the existence or extent of risk to human health, the institutions may take precautionary measures without having to wait until the reality and seriousness of those risks become fully apparent …

3.26 In 2000, the European Commission provided specific guidance on the principle, through a communication which emphasised that the principle 'forms part of a structured approach to the analysis of risk, as well as being relevant to risk management'.[45] It acknowledges the need to balance 'the freedom and rights of individuals, industry and organisations with the need to reduce the risk of adverse effects to the environment'.[46] In short, the Commission's position is that analysis of risk comprises three elements: (i) risk assessment, (ii) risk management, and (iii) risk communication.[47] The precautionary principle is relevant to risk management; and recourse should be had to the principle where potentially dangerous effects have been identified and 'scientific evaluation does

---

39 Most of these terms are defined within the UNFCCC itself, which is considered in more detail in paragrahs 2.08–2.27 in Chapter 2. A 'reservoir' is 'a component or components of the climate system where a greenhouse gas or a precursor of a greenhouse gas is stored' (Article 1). A 'sink' means 'any process, activity or mechanism which removes a greenhouse gas from the atmosphere' (ibid). A 'source' means 'any process or activity which releases a greenhouse gas, an aerosol or a precursor of a greenhouse gas into the atmosphere' (ibid).

40 Convention on Biological Diversity 1992, preamble.

41 Applying in other contexts too such as public health and safety.

42 Retained EU Law (Revocation and Reform) Act 2023 s 4 amended s 5 of the European Union (Withdrawal) Act 2018 to provide that, 'No general principle of EU law is part of domestic law after the end of 2023'.

43 See below at para 3.39 (prevention principle), para 3.84 (rectification at source principle) and para 3.65 (polluter pays principle).

44 Case T-74/00 *Artegodan GmbH and others v Commission* [2002] ECR II-4945 [184]–[185].

45 'Commission Adopts Communication on Precautionary Principle' (*European Commission*) <https://ec.europa.eu/commission/presscorner/detail/en/IP_00_96> accessed 27 April 2024.

46 Commission of the European Communities, 'Communication from the Commission on the Precautionary Principle' (2000) COM/2000/0001 Summary, 1 <https://op.europa.eu/en/publication-detail/-/publication/21676661-a79f-4153-b984-aeb28f07c80a/language-en> accessed 22 April 2024.

47 ibid Summary, 4.

not allow the risk to be determined with sufficient certainty'.[48] The Commission noted that there are two distinct aspects to the precautionary principle:[49]

> (i) the political decision to act or not to act as such, which is linked to the factors triggering recourse to the precautionary principle; (ii) in the affirmative, how to act, i.e. the measures resulting from application of the precautionary principle.

3.27 A key difficulty may arise from a possible tension between the seriousness of the adverse effects on the environment and the level of uncertainty that may trigger application of the principle.

3.28 In England and Wales, the principle was referred to in the government's 1990 White Paper, 'This Common Inheritance' but, as was pointed out in *R v Secretary of State for Trade and Industry, ex p Duddridge and others*,[50] that was the extent of the government's consideration of it. The White Paper stated:[51]

> Where there are significant risks of damage to the environment, the government will be prepared to limit the use of potentially dangerous materials or the spread of potentially dangerous pollutants, even where scientific knowledge is not conclusive, if the balance of likely costs and benefits justifies it.

3.29 Now, the precautionary principle is referred to at section 17(5) of the EA 2021 and the EPPS. The latter describes how the principle 'assists the decision-making process in the face of a lack of scientific certainty'.[52] It adopts the definition from the Rio Declaration.

3.30 The EPPS advises that application of the precautionary principle only applies where there is 'sufficient evidence that the risk of serious or irreversible damage is plausible and real'.[53] At the Report Stage of the Bill in the House of Commons on 26 January 2021, the DEFRA Minister Pow explained that, '[O]ur approach to the precautionary principle includes a proportionate and risk-focused application respecting the balance with social, economic and other considerations.'[54]

3.31 In certain environmental decision-making and planning, such as environmental impact assessments[55] and the protection of habitats,[56] the law has developed to provide

---

48 ibid.
49 ibid Main Text, 5.
50 *R v Secretary of State for Trade and Industry, Ex p Duddridge and others* [1996] 2 CMLR 361; House of Commons Environment Committee, 'The Environment White Paper: This Common Inheritance' (1990) Cm 1200 para 1.15 <https://archive.org/details/b32226937> accessed 25 April 2024.
51 Cited in Tromans (n 3).
52 DEFRA, 'Environmental Principles Policy Statement' (n 28).
53 ibid.
54 HC Deb 26 January 2021, vol 688, col 260–261.
55 For a further discussion of EIA, see Chapter 7. On EIA, at the domestic level, see *R (Champion) v North Norfolk DC* [2015] UKSC 52, [2015] 1 WLR 3710.
56 On habitats, at the EU level see Case 127/02 *Landelijke Vereniging tot Behoud van de Waddenzee v Staatssecretaris van Landbouw* [2004] ECR I-07405; Case C-521/12 *Briels v Minister van Infrastractuur en Milieu* (2014) ECLI:EU:C:2014:330; [2005] 2 CMLR 31; at the domestic level, see *R (Shimbles) v City of Bradford MDC* [2018] EWHC 195 (Admin) [15]–[19].

greater clarity, namely that a precautionary approach should be adopted when there is objective scientific uncertainty.

3.32 In the context of nature positive goals, the principle plays a fundamental role in the regulatory regimes for the protection of habitats and the environment. For example, pursuant to the Conservation of Habitats and Species Regulations 2017, where there is a risk of significant adverse effects to a protected site, there should be an appropriate assessment;[57] such a risk exists 'if it cannot be excluded on the basis of objective information that the plan or project will have significant effects on the site concerned'; and 'in case of doubt as to the absence of significant effects such an assessment must be carried out'.[58] The principle is also fundamental to environmental impact assessments, as was confirmed by the Supreme Court in *R (Champion) v North Norfolk District Council*.[59] These topics are addressed in later chapters of the book: Chapter 7 looks at the EIA and Chapter 9 deals with HRA.

3.33 The role of the precautionary principle is less clear cut in meeting net zero targets, because there is a scientific consensus as to the cause and effects of climate change.

3.34 In the mitigation context, it is most commonly deployed in relation to non-CO_2 emissions, because there is continuing uncertainty in the scientific community about the effects of these emissions. In the third runway at Heathrow litigation,[60] for example, the Court of Appeal upheld Friends of the Earth's challenge stating that 'the precautionary principle and common sense suggested that scientific uncertainty was not a reason for not taking something into account at all, even if it could not be precisely quantified at this stage'.[61] The Court of Appeal did not hold in terms that the Secretary of State had acted irrationally in this regard but, given it was remitting the Airports National Policy Statement ('ANPS') back to the Secretary of State for reconsideration, noted that 'the question of non-CO_2 emissions and the effect of post-2050 emissions would need to be taken into account as part of that exercise' (as summarised by the Supreme Court).[62]

3.35 The Supreme Court disagreed with the approach and determined that '[t]he precautionary principle adds nothing to the argument in this context'.[63] The court's view on irrationality is not the same as common sense, which is the only basis on which Friends of the Earth sought to impugn the designation.[64] Thus, the Supreme Court concluded as follows:[65]

---

57 The Conservation of Habitats and Species Regulations 2017 regulation 63.

58 Case 127/02 *Waddenzee* (n 56) [44]; *Wealden DC v Secretary of State for Communities and Local Government* [2017] EWHC 351 (Admin) [44(ii)]; *R (Hart District Council) v SSCLG* [2008] EWHC 1204 (Admin) [78]; *R (Mynydd y Gwynt) v Secretary of State for Business Energy and Industrial Strategy* [2016] EWHC 2581 (Admin) [20].

59 *R (Champion) v North Norfolk DC* (n 55).

60 *R (Spurrier) v Secretary of State for Transport and others* [2019] EWHC 1070 (Admin); *R (Plan B Earth) v Secretary of State for Transport* (n 33); *R (Friends of the Earth Ltd and others) v Heathrow Airport Ltd* (n 34).

61 *R (Plan B Earth) v Secretary of State for Transport* (n 33).

62 *R (Friends of the Earth Ltd and others) v Heathrow Airport Ltd* (n 34) [164].

63 ibid.

64 ibid [165].

65 ibid [166].

> In summary, we agree with the Divisional Court that it is not reasonably arguable that the Secretary of State acted irrationally in not addressing the effect of the non-CO_2 emissions in the ANPS for six reasons. First, his decision reflected the uncertainty over the climate change effects of non-CO_2 emissions and the absence of an agreed metric which could inform policy. Secondly, it was consistent with the advice which he had received from the CCC. Thirdly, it was taken in the context of the Government's inchoate response to the Paris Agreement. Fourthly, the decision was taken in the context in which his department was developing as part of that response its Aviation Strategy, which would seek to address non-CO_2 emissions. Fifthly, the designation of the ANPS was only the first stage in a process by which permission could be given for the NWR Scheme to proceed and the Secretary of State had powers at the DCO stage to address those emissions. Sixthly, it is clear from both the AoS and the ANPS itself that the applicant for a DCO would have to address the environmental rules and policies which were current when its application would be determined.

3.36 The Supreme Court decision was applied, again in the context of non-CO_2 emissions from aviation, in R (*Bristol Airport Action Network Co-Ordinating Committee v Secretary of State for Levelling up, Housing and Communities*.[66] It was alleged that the panel of planning inspectors, appointed to consider the expansion of Bristol airport, had failed to have regard to the precautionary principle.[67] Lane J considered the Heathrow decision and noted that:[68]

> The precautionary principle is capable of being invoked where the nature of the decision-making leaves space for it.

3.37 Like in the Heathrow case, Lane J determined that the decision had been taken to leave non-CO_2 emissions, in respect of which there was scientific uncertainty, 'for further consideration, within the overall development consent process'.[69] Thus:[70]

> to have recourse to the precautionary principle in such a situation would subvert the decision-making process, by requiring consideration here and now of the very issue which the decision-making process has rationally concluded should be dealt with later.

3.38 The principle may have an important role to play in climate change adaptation, particularly in considering what measures could, or even should, be taken in the context of increased vulnerability arising from climate change.

---

66 *R (Bristol Airport Action Network Co-Ordinating Committee) v Secretary of State for Levelling Up, Housing and Communities (expansion of Bristol Airport)* [2023] EWHC 171 (Admin).
67 ibid [224].
68 ibid [228].
69 ibid [228].
70 ibid [229].

(iii) *Prevention principle*

3.39 The prevention principle, or the principle that 'preventive action should be taken',[71] is concerned with ensuring that the environmental damage does not happen in the first place; and relatedly, taking measures to prevent the further spread of existing damage or harm.[72] It means that the harm should be avoided or at least contained. Indeed, it might be that precautionary measures need to be taken in order to achieve that objective.

3.40 The prevention principle is said to have originated in the prohibition on causing harm to the territory of another state in the *Trail Smelter* case of 1941.[73] It was then further developed in principle 21 of the Stockholm Declaration, described as 'the most important principle,'[74] which says that:

> States have, in accordance with the Charter of the United Nations and the principles of international law, the sovereign right to exploit their own resources pursuant to their own environmental policies, and the responsibility to ensure that activities within their jurisdiction *do not cause damage to the environment of other States or of areas beyond the limits of national jurisdiction*. [emphasis added]

3.41 It has been argued that principle 21 represented a 'radical shift' from 'the early curative and reactive perspective towards a preventative and anticipatory approach to environmental harm and risk'.[75]

3.42 The prevention principle is not expressly referred to in the UNFCCC, but the ultimate objective of the UNFCCC is the 'stabilization of [GHG] concentrations in the atmosphere at a level that would *prevent* dangerous anthropogenic interference with the climate system' [emphasis added].[76] Furthermore, the UNFCCC sets out that in order to achieve that objective, the parties shall take 'precautionary measures to anticipate, *prevent*, or minimize the causes of climate change and mitigate its adverse effects' [emphasis added].[77]

3.43 The preamble to the CBD recognises the importance of anticipating, *preventing* and attacking the 'causes of significant reduction of loss of biological diversity at source'. In the context of in-situ conservation, the prevention principle concerns the need to ensure 'alien species' that 'threaten ecosystems, habitats or species' are not introduced.[78] It is also relevant to the 'imminent or grave danger or damage ... to biological diversity';

---

71 TFEU, Article 191(2).
72 Case C-534/13 *Ministero dell'Ambiente v Fipa Group* (2015) ECLI:EU:C:2015:140, [56].
73 *Trail Smelter (United States v Canada)* RIAA III 1905 cited in Leslie-Anne Duvic-Paoli, *The Prevention Principle in International Environmental Law* (Cambridge University Press 2018) 1.
74 Emanuela Orlando, 'Principles, Standards and Voluntary Commitments in International Environmental Law' in Erika Techera and others (eds), *Routledge Handbook of International Environmental Law* (2nd edn, Routledge 2020) 17–8.
75 ibid citing Duvic-Paoli (n 73) 21 and Chapter 2.
76 UNFCCC, Article 2.
77 ibid, Articles 3(3) and 4s.
78 Convention on Biological Diversity 1992 Article 8(h).

and provides that state parties should take action to 'prevent or minimize such danger or damage'.[79]

3.44 The principle is a general principle of EU environmental law; and is set out in Article 191(2) of the TFEU. In *Paolo Lirussi and Francesca Bizzaro*,[80] the court considered the preventive action principle, alongside the precautionary principle and observed that:

> By virtue of those principles, it is for the Community and the Member States to prevent, reduce and, in so far as is possible, eliminate from the outset, the sources of pollution or nuisance by adopting measures of a nature such as to eliminate recognised risks.

3.45 In domestic law, it is included in section 17(5) of the EA 2021. The policy statement explains that the principle means that policy 'should aim to prevent environmental harm;' and advises policymakers that it should be preferred over the rectification at source and polluter pays principles.[81] In the context of the prevention principle, the statement advises:

> [P]olicymakers should particularly consider those habitats and species that are endangered or vulnerable, and national environmental priorities such as those outlined in the Environmental Improvement Plan, environmental targets, and net zero.

3.46 Policymakers are advised to apply the principle as follows:[82]

- Understand the potential harm of a proposed policy to the environment (taking into account the different aspects of the environment that could be harmed);
- Consider the extent to which the harm can be prevented, which includes taking into account whether the damage is short or long term and how widespread the damage might be (including the cumulative effects of low levels of damage);
- Investigate how the harm could be prevented; and the cost and benefits of preventing and not preventing the damage.

3.47 The prevention principle presents obvious difficulties in the context of net zero and nature positive, given how much damage has already been caused, but it is generally relied upon in the context of preventing further harm. Indeed, as set out in relation to the integration principle, the EPPS will require ministers to identify the potential environmental effects of policies, which includes GHG emissions and climate change-related effects, as well as the impacts on habitats and biodiversity.

3.48 In the context of litigation, the principle was referred to in the UNGA's resolution requesting an advisory opinion from the International Court of Justice on 'the

---

79 ibid Article 14(1)(d).
80 Joined Cases C-175/98 *Paolo Lirussi and C-177/98 Francesca Bizzaro* (C-177/98) [1999] ECR 1999 I-06881 [51].
81 DEFRA, 'Environmental Principles Policy Statement' (n 28).
82 ibid.

obligations of States in respect of climate change' albeit formulated as the principle of prevention of *significant* harm to the environment and in the context of transboundary harm as between those states that have caused significant harm by virtue of anthropogenic GHG emissions and those states, such as small island developing states, that are particularly vulnerable to the effects of climate change.[83]

3.49 In *Urgenda Foundation v State of Netherlands*,[84] the Dutch Supreme Court referred to the no-harm principle, with the result that countries 'can be called upon to make their contribution to reducing [GHG] emissions'.[85] The principle was also deployed in *PSB v Brazil*,[86] which concerned the intersection between climate change and biodiversity; and involved a claim against Brazil for failing to implement the national deforestation policy. In reliance on the prevention principle, the court identified the 'duties of the State arising from its constitutional duty to protect the environment'.[87] Against that, Duvic-Paoli and Gervasi observe that in other cases, such as *Whaling in the Antarctic*,[88] the principle was initially relied upon before being abandoned in favour of more specific treaty obligations. It remains to be seen what role, if any, the principle will play in climate change and nature-related litigation in England and Wales.

(iv) *Sustainable development*

3.50 Sustainable development is a recurring theme in international and domestic legislation and policy. Yet, there is no comprehensive definition and arguably it is not a principle as such, rather it is a concept or an 'umbrella concept'[89] involving the balancing of different interests: environmental, economic and social, as well as taking into account the needs of the present and future generations.

3.51 Whilst not expressly referred to as sustainable development, various principles in the Stockholm Declaration of 1972 sought to reconcile environmental protection and economic development in the context of present and future generations, for example:

- Principle 1, in many ways the predecessor of the right to a clean and healthy environment, provides for the need to ensure an 'environment of a quality that permits a life of dignity and well-being'. Principle 8 is similarly concerned with economic and social development, as well as ensuring a favourable living and working environment.

83 Request for an advisory opinion of the International Court of Justice on the obligations of States in respect of climate change. UNGA Res A/RES/77/276.
84 *Stichting Urgenda v De Staat der Nederlanden* [2019] Hoge Raad der Nederlanden ECLI:NL:HR:2019:2007 [5.7.5] cited in Leslie-Anne Duvic-Paoli and Mario Gervasi, 'Harm to the Global Commons on Trial: The Role of the Prevention Principle in International Climate Adjudication' (2023) 32 RECIEL 226.
85 ibid 227.
86 *PSB et al v Brazil* ADPF 760 (on deforestation and human rights), Supreme Federal Court of Brazil, Vote of Minister Cármen Lúcia (4 June 2022) cited in cited in Leslie-Anne Duvic-Paoli and Mario Gervasi, 'Harm to the Global Commons on Trial: The Role of the Prevention Principle in International Climate Adjudication' (2023) 32 RECIEL 227.
87 ibid.
88 *Whaling in the Antarctic (Australia v Japan: New Zealand intervening), Judgment*, ICJ Reports 2014, p 226 [38] cited in Leslie-Anne Duvic-Paoli and Mario Gervasi, 'Harm to the Global Commons on Trial: The Role of the Prevention Principle in International Climate Adjudication' (2023) 32 RECIEL 228.
89 Fisher, Lange and Scotford (n 5) 222.

- Principle 2 emphasises the need to safeguard Earth's natural resources.

- Principle 3 requires that 'the capacity of the earth to produce vital renewable resources must be maintained and, whenever practicable, restored or improved'. Related to that, principle 5 requires that non-renewable resources must be employed 'to guard against the danger of their future exhaustion and to ensure that benefits from such employment are shared by all mankind'.

- Principle 12 is concerned with preserving and improving the environment, whilst also taking into account the particular needs of developing countries and making technical and financial assistance available to them.

- Principles 14 and 15 are both focused on the need for planning to reconcile any conflict between the needs of development and the need to protect and improve the environment.

3.52 Sustainable development gained international prominence in the Brundtland Report of 1987,[90] which described it as follows:[91]

> Sustainable development is development that meets the needs of the present without compromising the ability of future generations to meet their own needs. It contains within it two key concepts:
>
> - the concept of 'needs', in particular the essential needs of the world's poor, to which overriding priority should be given; and
> - the idea of limitations imposed by the state of technology and social organization on the environment's ability to meet present and future needs.
>
> Thus the goals of economic and social development must be defined in terms of sustainability in all countries - developed or developing, market-oriented or centrally planned. Interpretations will vary, but must share certain general features and must flow from a consensus on the basic concept of sustainable development and on a broad strategic framework for achieving it.
>
> ...
>
> In essence, sustainable development is a process of change in which the exploitation of resources, the direction of investments, the orientation of technological development; and institutional change are all in harmony and enhance both current and future potential to meet human needs and aspirations.

3.53 Sustainable development also featured in the Rio Declaration at principles 1 and 4. Whilst not defining the concept, these principles emphasise an anthropogenic

---

90 World Commission on Environment and Development (n 7) ch 2.
91 ibid, paras 1, 2 and 15.

approach with humans at the centre of sustainable development; noting that environmental protection must be an integral part of development.

3.54 The concept of sustainable development formed the backbone of the 17 Sustainable Development Goals, adopted by the United Nations in 2015.[92]

3.55 At the domestic level, the principle was given much consideration by the government in the early 1990s. In January 1994, 'Sustainable Development, the UK Strategy'[93] was published, alongside a suite of other documents.[94] But part of the difficulty with the principle continued to be its 'immense breadth … applicable as it is to all aspects of human activity'.[95] This can be seen in a debate in the Commons on 7 February 1994, as described by Tromans KC:[96]

> After the Secretary of State for the Environment had offered his own pithy definition ('working for economic growth without cheating on our children') the debate ranged across the evils of limited liability of companies, peat mining, the poetry of Gerard Manley Hopkins, biodiversity in the British Indian Ocean territories of Chagos Archipela[g]o, Tristan da Cunha and St Helena, world population growth, the 'dash for gas', wind energy, VAT on fuel, the widening of the M25; recycling of packaging waste, the GATT trade negotiations, hedgerows, the 'desecration' of Twyford Down, the importance of the ancient forest of Cal[ed]on, the largest fire in the world (apparently started by Volkswagen in a Brazilian forest), nuclear energy, public transport, the hazard-potential of the petrochemical industry, and the role of seagulls as carriers of salmonella in infringing the bathing water directive. The best laugh of the evening was, incidentally, produced by Conservative M.P. Mr Robert Jones (Hertfordshire, West) who, referring to the annual reports of the Department of the Environment, said that these were '… extremely well set out and coherent, and contribute greatly to debate on a factual rather than a suppository basis'.

3.56 The principle of sustainable development has a statutory basis in the Climate Change Act 2008 ('CCA 2008') in the context of both mitigation and adaptation. By section 13(3) of the CCA 2008, the policies and proposals, taken as a whole and prepared in accordance with section 13(1), must contribute to sustainable development.[97] Similarly, by section 58(2), the objectives, policies and proposals set out as the programme

---

92 United Nations, 'THE 17 GOALS | Sustainable Development' <https://sdgs.un.org/goals> accessed 28 April 2024. Goal 13 requires urgent action on climate change. Goals 14 and 15 focus on the conservation of marine and land ecosystems. Goal 6 focuses on the sustainable management of water and sanitation. Goal 7 requires access to affordable and clean energy. Goal 11 concerns the sustainability of human communities. Goal 12 addresses sustainable consumption and production patterns; and relatedly, Goal 16 is concerned with peaceful and inclusive communities for sustainable development.

93 Department for Environment, Food and Rural Affairs, 'Sustainable Development: The UK Strategy' (1994) Cm 2426.

94 Department of the Environment, 'Climate Change: The UK Programme. United Kingdom's Report under the Framework Convention on Climate Change.' (1994) Cm 2427; Department for Environment, Food and Rural Affairs, 'Biodiversity, The U.K. Action Plan' (1994) Cm 2428 <https://data.jncc.gov.uk/data/cb0ef1c9-2325-4d17-9f87-a5c84fe400bd/UKBAP-BiodiversityActionPlan-1994.pdf> accessed 27 April 2024; Department for Environment, Food and Rural Affairs, 'Sustainable Forestry, the U.K. Programme' (1994) Cm 2429.

95 Tromans (n 3).

96 ibid.

97 The meaning of this provision was considered in *Friends of the Earth and others v Secretary of State for Energy Security and Net Zero* [2024] EWHC 995 (Admin). See para 2.127 in Chapter 2.

for adaptation to climate change must also contribute to sustainable development. But no definition is provided within that Act.

3.57 Sustainable development also features in the Planning Act 2008 ('PA 2008'). Section 5(1) of the PA 2008 empowers the Secretary of State to designate a national policy statement ('NPS') in relation to certain specified development; and section 6 allows the Secretary of State to review a NPS in certain circumstances.[98] By section 10, the Secretary of State must exercise his functions in sections 5 and 6 'with the objective of contributing to the achievement of sustainable development'. Furthermore, when considering that objective, the Secretary of State must have regard *inter alia* to 'the desirability of – (a) mitigating, and adapting, to climate change'.[99] Again, PA 2008 does not define sustainable development.

3.58 In the EA 2021, sustainable development is not included as a principle as such, but the Secretary of State has to be satisfied that the EPPS itself contributes *inter alia* to sustainable development.[100] The EPPS defines sustainable development as follows:[101]

> [D]evelopment that meets the needs of the present generation without compromising the ability of future generations to meet their own needs. It involves trying to achieve environmental benefit alongside economic growth and social progress and should be considered in a global context.

3.59 In Wales, sustainable development is a core element of the Well-being of Future Generations (Wales) Act 2015 and is defined as:[102]

> [T]he process of improving the economic, social, environmental and cultural well-being of Wales by taking action, in accordance with the sustainable development principle (see section 5), aimed at achieving the well-being goals.

3.60 The Act requires public bodies to 'carry out sustainable development', which is described as the 'well-being duty'.[103] Three of the seven well-being goals, set out in section 4, directly relate to climate change and nature.[104] A similar Bill was introduced in the Westminster Parliament as a Private Members' Bill in 2020 but its progress has been stalled.

---

98 See paras 6.26 and 6.49 in Chapter 6.
99 Planning Act 2008 s 10(3a).
100 Environment Act 2021 s 17(4).
101 By reference to the sustainable development goals.
102 See Well-being of Future Generations (Wales) Act 2015 ss 2, 4, 5.
103 ibid s 3.
104 See the goal of a prosperous Wales (through *inter alia*: 'An innovative, productive and low carbon society which recognises the limits of the global environment and therefore uses resources efficiently and proportionately (including acting on climate change)'; a resilient Wales (described as 'A nation which maintains and enhances a biodiverse natural environment with healthy functioning ecosystems that support social, economic and ecological resilience and the capacity to adapt to change (for example climate change)'); and a globally responsible Wales (defined as 'A nation which, when doing anything to improve the economic, social, environmental and cultural well-being of Wales, takes account of whether doing such a thing may make a positive contribution to global well-being').

3.61 Sustainable development is a key thread in the National Policy Planning Framework ('NPPF'). The NPPF sets out that the purpose of the planning system is to contribute to sustainable development; indeed, 'the heart' of the NPPF is 'a presumption in favour of sustainable development'.[105] It is defined, also by reference to the sustainable development goals, as 'meeting the needs of the present without compromising the ability of future generations'.[106] The NPPF sets out three overarching objectives to achieve sustainable development: economic, social and environmental.[107]

3.62 The NPPF definition was referred to by the Supreme Court, in the context of the PA 2008, in the third runway at Heathrow case:[108]

> Sustainable development is a recognised term in the planning context and its meaning is not controversial in these proceedings. As explained in paras 7 and 8 of the National Planning Policy Framework (July 2018), at a very high level the objective of sustainable development involves 'meeting the needs of the present without compromising the ability of future generations to meet their own needs'; it has three overarching elements, namely an environmental objective, an economic objective and a social objective. For a major infrastructure project like the development of airport capacity in the South East, which promotes economic development but at the cost of increased greenhouse gases emissions, these elements have to be taken into account and balanced against each other.

3.63 Yet, the definition within the NPPF and the observations of the Supreme Court call into question the extent to which the concept really can constitute a legal principle capable of being applied in practice. Indeed, commentators have described it as a 'paradox'; an attempt at 'marrying two incompatible ideas, environmental protection and development, the resulting formulation has no consequences;' and a concept that 'requires a political exercise to assess environmental, economic and social effects in any particular case'.[109]

3.64 Thus, it is questionable the extent to which sustainable development will assist law and policymaking achieve net zero and nature positive. The concept could prove more powerful if it were shifted to focus on ecological priorities through 'ecological sustainability'.[110] Bosselmann argues that the concept would be capable of constituting a legal principle if it were to have that focus:[111]

---

105 Department for Levelling Up, Housing and Communities, 'National Planning Policy Framework' (2023) paras 10–11 <https://assets.publishing.service.gov.uk/media/65a11af7e8f5ec000f1f8c46/NPPF_December_2023.pdf> accessed 2 April 2024; importantly, the presumption does not change the statutory status of the development plan in decision-making.
106 ibid para 7.
107 ibid para 8.
108 *R (Friends of the Earth Ltd and others) v Heathrow Airport Ltd* (n 34) [115].
109 Fisher, Lange and Scotford (n 5) 220–2 citing A Dan Tarlock, 'Ideas without Institutions: The Paradox of Sustainable Development' (2001) 9 Indiana Journal of Global Legal Studies 35 and Maria Lee, *EU Environmental Law, Governance and Decision-Making* (2nd edn, Hart Publishing 2014) 80.
110 Fisher, Lange and Scotford (n 5) 221–2 citing Klaus Bosselmann, *The Principle of Sustainability: Transforming Law and Governance* (Ashgate 2008) 52–3.
111 Bosselmann (n 110) 52–3.

> The principle of sustainability itself is best defined as the duty to protect and restore the integrity of the Earth's ecological systems. … It should become clear that the principle has a normative quality. It is reflective of a fundamental morality (respect for ecological integrity), requires action ('protect and restore') and is, therefore, capable of causing legal effect. The standards of a legal principle are all met.

(v) *Polluter pays principle*

3.65 The polluter pays principle ('PPP') requires, as the term would suggest, that those who pollute or cause environmental damage pay for the remediation. Whilst it 'trips nicely off the tongue', it 'can be dauntingly difficult to unpack and apply'.[112]

3.66 The basic, underlying premise of the PPP is that a 'polluter' (or equally, a contributing polluter) should be legally accountable to compensate for the environmental 'harm' or 'cost' either caused, or which will be caused, on account of one or more identifiable and quantifiable pollutants. The harm or cost need not be monetisable, in this exercise. Within the sphere of the PPP, the potential class of polluters has purposely been cast widely, to include primary and secondary polluters, as well as, in principle, a body of persons, a section of the community, or even, the public at large. The PPP has been described as 'a cardinal general principle' underlying the 1995 amendments to the Environment Protection Act 1990.[113]

3.67 Internationally, the principle was first adopted by the Organisation for Economic Co-operation and Development ('OECD') Council on 26 May 1972, following a recommendation by the Environment Committee on 'Guiding Principles concerning International Economic Aspects of Environmental Policies'.[114] It was recognised that environmental resources are limited; and their use in production and consumption leads to their deterioration. Measures are necessary to reduce pollution and ensure a better allocation of resources, but those measures come at a cost. Thus, the principle was recommended as follows:[115]

> The principle to be used for allocating costs of pollution prevention and control measures to encourage rational use of scarce environmental resources and to avoid distortions in international trade and investment is the so-called 'Polluter-Pays Principle'. This principle means that the polluter should bear the expenses of carrying out the above-mentioned measures decided by public authorities to ensure that the environment is in an acceptable state. In other words, the cost of these measures should be reflected in the cost of goods and services which cause pollution in production and/or consumption. Such measures should not be accompanied by subsidies that would create significant distortions in international trade and investment.

---

112 Tromans (n 3).
113 *R (National Grid Gas plc (formerly Transco plc)) v Environment Agency* [2007] UKHL 30 Lord Neuberger at [28].
114 OECD, 'Recommendation of the Council on Guiding Principles Concerning International Economic Aspects of Environmental Policies' OECD/LEGAL/0102 <https://legalinstruments.oecd.org/public/doc/4/4.en.pdf>.
115 ibid.

3.68 The recommendation was accepted by the OECD and the principle was adopted by the OECD, noting that it is 'a fundamental principle for allocating costs of pollution prevention and control measures introduced by the public authorities in Member countries'.[116] In relation to subsidies, tax advantages or other assistance for pollution control, the OECD was clear that it should be 'strictly controlled' and should comply with each of the following conditions:[117]

a) It should be selective and restricted to those parts of the economy, such as industries areas or plants, where severe difficulties would otherwise occur;

b) It should be limited to well-defined transitional periods, laid down in advance and adapted to the specific socio-economic problems associated with the implementation of a country's environmental programme;

c) It should not create significant distortions in international trade and investment.

3.69 The principle was included at principle 16 of the Rio Declaration:

> National authorities should endeavour to promote the internalization of environmental costs and the use of economic instruments, taking into account the approach that the polluter should, in principle, bear the cost of pollution, with due regard to the public interest and without distorting international trade and investment.

3.70 It is often recognised as an economic principle based on the concept of internalisation of external costs.[118]

3.71 The principle is not expressly referred to in the UNFCCC. Instead, there are repeated references to 'common but differentiated responsibilities' as between the State Parties with developed countries taking the lead.[119] Thus, for example, there is express provision for the developed State Parties to provide 'financial resources' to developing countries.[120] Likewise, Article 9 of the Paris Agreement requires developed countries to provide financial resources to assist developing countries with both mitigation and adaptation.[121]

3.72 The principle also informs the international legal and policy approach to loss and damage. At COP 19 held in Warsaw in 2013, the parties adopted the 'Warsaw International Mechanism for Loss and Damage associated with climate change impacts'.[122] In

---

116 OECD, 'Recommendation of the Council on the Implementation of the Polluter-Pays Principle. OECD/LEGAL/0132'.
117 See Chapter 34.
118 Kahl and Weller attribute the principle to the economics of Arthur Cecil Pigou in Wolfgang Kahl and Marc-Philippe Weller, *Climate Change Litigation: A Handbook* (Beck 2021) 47.
119 UNFCCC, Article 3(1).
120 ibid, Article 4(3).
121 Article 10 emphasises the importance of the transfer of technology; and Article 11 sets out a provision for building the capacity of developing countries.
122 'Report of the Conference of the Parties on Its Nineteenth Session, Held in Warsaw from 11 to 23 November 2013' (UNFCCC 2014) FCCC/CP/2013/10/Add.3 <https://unfccc.int/sites/default/files/resource/docs/2013/cop19/eng/10a03.pdf> accessed 26 April 2024.

the Paris Agreement, Article 8 recognises the importance of 'averting, minimizing and addressing loss and damage' and restates the importance of the Warsaw Mechanism.

3.73 At the domestic level, the UK described the principle in the 1990 White Paper, '*This Common Inheritance*', as follows:[123]

> [T]he objective is to make those who cause environmental damage face the costs of control in full, without subsidy.

3.74 The government saw the principle 'as applicable both to traditional forms of command-and-control regulation' and 'the use of economic instruments':[124]

> If we impose higher standards centrally, this puts extra costs on producers and on their customers in turn; if we use price signals, for example by imposing charges or taxes on certain activities, extra costs again fall on the manufacturers, and then on their customers. The 'polluter pays' principle is an important means of influencing potential polluters.

3.75 In some contexts, the principle is fairly easy to apply – for example, levy charges in the relation to environmental discharge consents or for infringements of environmental standards, by exceeding a permitted discharge standard or disposing of waste without an appropriate licence.[125] The principle also informs particular statutory provisions in relation to controlled waste.[126]

3.76 Indeed, the principle featured in the decision of the High Court in *Re Mineral Resources Ltd*[127] concerning an insolvent waste disposal operator. Neuberger J (as he then was) decided that that the environment should trump creditors noting that:

> [I]t appears to me that there is considerable public interest in the maintenance of a healthy environment and in the principle pithily expressed as the polluter must pay. It is the view which prevails both in popular perception and in the legislative system in this country and indeed in most of the developed world.

3.77 The Court of Appeal did not agree, holding that 'there is nothing in the Directive to suggest that the polluter pays principle is to be applied to cases where the polluter cannot pay so as to require that the unsecured creditors of the polluter should pay'.[128]

---

123 Tromans (n 3).
124 ibid.
125 ibid.
126 Environmental Protection Act 1990; ss 45(1)(b) and 45(4) EPA, interpreted and applied in order to give the fullest possible effect to the environmental objectives of Part II EPA s 4. The decision of the Court of Session (Outer House) in *Re Doonin Plant Ltd v Scottish EPA* [2019] Env LR 10 provides a (Scots law) example of how the PPP has been given effect; in this instance, within the context of the Directive 2008/98/EC of the European Parliament and of the Council of 19 November 2008 on waste and repealing certain Directives ('WFD') and, on the facts, an ongoing liability of a waste management company to fund the removal – through the Scottish Environmental Protection Agency, acting in pursuance of the PPP – of unlawfully deposited, controlled waste, pursuant to a remediation notice, issued under s.59 EPA. At [16], [63]–[64], Lord Doherty observed that the PPP is repeatedly referred to in the preamble to the WFD and is one of the main objectives of the WFD.
127 *Re Mineral Resources Ltd* [1999] 1 All ER 746.
128 *Official Receiver (as liquidator of Celtic Extraction Ltd and Bluestone Chemi-cals Ltd v Environment Agency* [1999] EWCA Crim.

3.78 The polluter pays principle is enshrined as one of the environmental principles in section 17(5) of the EA 2021. The EPPS states that, 'where possible, the costs of pollution [which is treated as synonymous with environmental damage] should be borne by those causing it, rather than the person who suffers the effects of the resulting environmental damage, or the wider community'. Pollution, in this context, takes account of a wide range of negative environmental effects, including short-term and secondary effects.

3.79 The statement recognises that the principle can be used at different stages of policymaking and has different functions, including to prevent or deter environmental damage and to restore or redistribute the costs of environmental damage. Considerations should include:

- who the polluter is (including the drivers for the pollution and the allocation of responsibility);
- how much the polluter should pay, emphasising the importance of proportionality in that assessment; and
- how the polluter should pay, whether, for example, it is through direct payment such as fees or charges, or indirect payment such as regulatory or contractual obligations.

3.80 The statement notably provides as follows in relation to fiscal measures, which ties to the statutory exclusion for the section 19(1) duty in relation to policy on taxation, spending or the allocation of resources within government:[129]

> [T]he duty to have due regard to the policy statement does not create an obligation on ministers to create a tax in response to the polluter pays principle. If it is decided it would be is [sic] appropriate for the consumer to pay, the costs of environmental damage (such as pollution control and remediation) would be reflected in the cost of goods and services. Each policy area should consider how the costs of environmental damage could be recovered as well as how polluters could be disincentivised from causing further environmental damage.

3.81 The principle is relevant to the past and present generation of emissions in the context climate change litigation. Setzer and Higham have categorised such cases as follows:[130] (i) compensation for past and present loss and damage arising from climate change;[131] (ii) contributions to the costs of adapting to future climate impacts; and (iii) compensation to 'offset' emissions where those activities have caused damage to carbon climate sinks.

---

129 See EA 2021 s 19(3)(b).
130 Joana Setzer and Catherine Higham, 'Global Trends in Climate Change Litigation: 2023 Snapshot' (Grantham Research Institute on Climate Change and the Environment 2021) 24.
131 For example, 'Municipalities of Puerto Rico v. Exxon Mobil Corp.' (*Climate Change Litigation*) <https://climatecasechart.com/case/municipalities-of-puerto-rico-v-exxon-mobil-corp/> accessed 26 April 2024; 'Asmania et al. vs Holcim' (*Climate Change Litigation*) <https://climatecasechart.com/non-us-case/four-islanders-of-pari-v-holcim/> accessed 26 April 2024.

3.82 At the domestic level, the application of the principle to the present and future generation of GHG emissions is likely to be most relevant in the context of policymaking and design. But it is notable, as set out above, that the statutory duty to have regard to the EPPS, and therefore the polluter pays principle amongst the others, is excluded in relation to fiscal measures, which is one of the more obvious applications of the principle (see Chapter 34).

3.83 The role of the principle in relation to nature positive is less clear. It would be concerned with requiring those that damage nature to pay in some form. An obvious example is the fines (or other imprisonment) if certain wildlife offences are committed.[132] To date, policy interventions in this area mostly relate to incentivising investment in natural capital and biodiversity – for example, the Environmental Improvement Plan 2023 relies on 'green finance' and sets a target to raise at least £500 million a year by 2027 in private finance to support nature recovery in England and up to £1 billion in 2030.[133]

(vi) *Rectification at source principle*

3.84 This principle is concerned with ensuring that any environmental damage should be rectified at its origin to avoid further effects elsewhere.

3.85 In the international context, the principle is not found in the Stockholm Declaration, the Rio Declaration or the UNFCCC but it is in the recitals to the CBD, as follows:

> *Noting* that it is vital to anticipate, prevent and attack the causes of significant reduction of loss of biological diversity at source.

3.86 The principle is also contained in Article 191(2) of the TFEU but not defined. In *Commission v Belgium*[134] (the Wallonia waste case), the court considered that a prohibition imposed by a Member State on the storage, tipping and dumping of waste originating from another Member State as justifiable on the grounds of environmental protection. The court determined, invoking the rectification at source principle, that the prohibition was not discriminatory, because 'each region, municipality or other local authority [is] to take appropriate steps to ensure that its own waste is collected, treated and disposed of in order to limit as far as possible the transport of waste'.[135]

3.87 The EPPS says the following in relation to the principle:[136]

> [E]nvironmental damage should, as a priority, be addressed at its origin to avoid the need to remedy its effects later. Rectification at source should result in approaches that are more cost-effective, efficient, and equitable in the long-term.

132 See, for example, offences under the Wildlife and Countryside Act 1981; Deer Act 1991; Wild Mammals (Protection) Act 1996.
133 DEFRA, 'Environmental Improvement Plan 2023: First Revision of the 25 Year Environment Plan' (2023) 35, 60 <https://assets.publishing.service.gov.uk/media/64a6d9c1c531eb000c64fffa/environmental-improvement-plan-2023.pdf> accessed 4 April 2024.
134 Case C-2/90 *Commission v Belgium* [1992] ECR I-04431.
135 See ibid Summary, [2].
136 DEFRA, 'Environmental Principles Policy Statement' (n 28).

3.88 The EPPS sets out how the principle should be applied; the focus of policy design, if possible, should be on addressing or managing any environmental damage at source. If that is not possible, the focus should be on containing or limiting environmental damage as far as possible. Application of this principle, according to the EPPS, involves (i) understanding the actual or potential environmental damage; (ii) understanding where the damage comes from and (iii) considering the feasibility (including costs and benefits) of rectifying the issue at source versus other options.

3.89 The EPPS explains that, if environmental damage has already occurred or is occurring, then the rectification at source (along with the polluter pays principle) should be considered 'to reduce, mitigate or disincentivise damage'.

3.90 The application of this principle to achieving net zero targets, through mitigation, is less clear cut because of the very nature of climate change compared to other environmental harm, as set out in *Verein Klimaseniorinnen Schweiz and others v Switzerland*:[137]

> First, there is no single or specific source of harm. GHG emissions arise from a multitude of sources. The harm derives from aggregate levels of such emissions. Secondly, CO_2 – the primary GHG – is not toxic per se at ordinary concentrations. The emissions produce harmful consequences as a result of a complex chain of effects. These emissions have no regard for national borders.

3.91 The principle is relevant to certain GHG mitigation targets: for example, it is argued that carbon capture and storage technology is incompatible with the rectification at source principle, because it involves burying harmful emissions rather than avoiding their production.[138]

(vii) *Intergenerational equity*

3.92 This principle (also known as intergenerational justice) has application across a range of issues relating to justice and fairness, but in the environmental context, it is best captured in the Rio Declaration, at principle 2:

> The right to development must be fulfilled so as to equitably meet developmental and environmental needs of present and future generations.

3.93 The concept is generally thought to be rooted in the philosophy of John Rawls[139] and his theory that justice should be approached behind a veil of ignorance whereby

137 *Verein KlimaSeniorinnen Schweiz and others v Switzerland* (2024) 79 EHRR 1 [416].
138 Angelica Rutherford, 'The Application of the Environment Act 2021 Principles to Carbon Capture and Storage' (2022) 11 Laws 15.
139 John Rawls, *A Theory of Justice* (Harvard University Press 1971).

there is ignorance as to temporal or spatial existence. It can, however, also be traced back to Jefferson.[140]

3.94 Brown Weiss explains that the principle requires that each generation has the right to use the Earth's resources for its own benefit but is also constrained by the need to ensure future generations have options and receive the planet in no worse a condition.[141]

3.95 The concept is referred to in principles 1 and 2 of the Stockholm Declaration of 1972:

> Man has the fundamental right to freedom, equality and adequate conditions of life, in an environment of a quality that permits a life of dignity and well-being, and he bears a solemn responsibility to protect and improve the environment for present and future generations …
>
> The natural resources of the earth, including the air, water, land, flora and fauna and especially representative samples of natural resources, must be safeguarded for the benefit of present and future generations through careful planning or management, as appropriate.

3.96 It is a core element in the Brundtland Report[142] and was tied closely to the principle of sustainable development:[143]

> Humanity has the ability to make development sustainable to ensure that it meets the needs of the present without compromising the ability of future generations to meet their own needs.

3.97 The report conceptualised the principle in economic, moral and legal terms, for example:[144]

> Many present efforts to guard and maintain human progress, to meet human needs, and to realize human ambitions are simply unsustainable - in both the rich and poor nations. They draw too heavily, too quickly, on already overdrawn environmental resource accounts

---

140 See Thomas Jefferson, 'To James Madison from Thomas Jefferson, 6 September 1789' <https://founders.archives.gov/documents/Madison/01-12-02-0248> accessed 26 April 2024. In his letter, Jefferson opined on this very issue: 'The question, whether one generation of men has a right to bind another, seems never to have been started either on this or our side of the water. Yet it is a question of such consequences as not only to merit decision, but place also among the fundamental principles of every government. The course of reflection in which we are immersed here, on the elementary principles of society, has presented this question to my mind; and that no such obligation can be transmitted, I think very capable of proof. I set out on this ground, which I suppose to be self evident, that the earth belongs in usufruct to the living; that the dead have neither powers nor rights over it. … Then I say, the earth belongs to each of these generations during its course, fully and in its own right. The second generation receives it clear of the debts and incumbrances of the first, the third of the second, and so on. For if the first could charge it with a debt, then the earth would belong to the dead and not to the living generation. Then, no generation can contract debts greater than may be paid during the course of its own existence.'

141 Edith Brown Weiss, 'In Fairness To Future Generations and Sustainable Development' (1992) 8 American University International Law Review 19, 20–3 cited in Fisher, Lange and Scotford (n 5) 222–3.

142 World Commission on Environment and Development (n 7).

143 ibid 27.

144 ibid 16, 26, 43, 55.

to be affordable far into the future without bankrupting those accounts. They may show profit on the balance sheets of our generation, but our children will inherit the losses. We borrow environmental capital from future generations with no intention or prospect of repaying. They may damn us for our spendthrift ways, but they can never collect on our debt to them. We act as we do because we can get away with it: future generations do not vote; they have no political or financial power; they cannot challenge our decisions.

But the results of the present profligacy are rapidly closing the options for future generations. Most of today's decision makers will be dead before the planet feels; the heavier effects of acid precipitation, global warming, ozone depletion, or widespread desertification and species loss. Most of the young voters of today will still be alive. In the Commission's hearings it was the young, those who have the most to lose, who were the harshest critics of the planet's present management. ...

... Governments now need to fill major gaps in existing national and international law related to the environment, to find ways to recognize and protect the rights of present and future generations to an environment adequate for their health and well-being, to prepare under UN auspices a universal Declaration on environmental protection and sustainable development and a subsequent Convention, and to strengthen procedures for avoiding or resolving disputes on environment and resource management issues.

Development tends to simplify ecosystems and to reduce their diversity of species. And species, once extinct, are not renewable. The loss of plant and animal species can greatly limit the options of future generations; so sustainable development requires the conservation of plant and animal species.

... [T]he case for the conservation of nature should not rest only with development goals. It is part of our moral obligation to other living beings and future generations.

3.98 Intergenerational justice also features in the UNFCCC: the first principle in Article 3 requires that, 'The Parties should protect the climate system for the benefit of present and future generations of humankind, on the basis of equity and in accordance with their common but differentiated capabilities.' It is recognised in the preamble to the Paris Agreement but not within the Articles themselves.

3.99 The principle is recognised in the introduction to the CBD which states that 'the Earth's biological resources are vital to humanity's economic and social development ... there is growing recognition that biological diversity is a global asset of tremendous value to present and future generations.'[145] It also defines sustainable use, in Article 2, as follows:

[T]he use of components of biological diversity in a way and at a rate that does not lead to the long-term decline of biological diversity, thereby maintaining its potential to meet the needs and aspirations of present and future generations.

145 See also the preamble to the World Charter for Nature.

3.100 The United Nations, in the resolution adopted to recognise 'the right to a clean, healthy, and sustainable environment,' referred to intergenerational justice:[146]

> Recognizing that sustainable development, in its three dimensions (social, economic and environmental), and the protection of the environment, including ecosystems, contribute to and promote human well-being and the full enjoyment of all human rights, for present and future generations, ...
>
> Recognizing further that environmental degradation, climate change, biodiversity loss, desertification and unsustainable development constitute some of the most pressing and serious threats to the ability of present and future generations to effectively enjoy all human rights.

3.101 At the national level, intergenerational justice is recognised in some constitutions, such as those in South Africa and Norway.[147]

3.102 In Wales, the Well-being of Future Generations (Wales) Act 2015 ties the principle of intergenerational justice to sustainable development in providing a statutory definition of 'the sustainable development principle'.[148]

3.103 As set out above at 3.60, a similar Bill, also called the Wellbeing of Future Generations Bill, has been introduced at Westminster. The Bill concerns sustainable development, which is defined to include environmental wellbeing,[149] and proposes the establishment of a wellbeing duty on public bodies, which, in turn, requires public bodies to set wellbeing objectives to achieve the wellbeing goals. The Bill defines a public body acting 'in accordance with the future generations principle' as a body 'acting in a manner which seeks to ensure that the needs of the present are met without compromising the ability of future generations to meet their own needs'.[150] By clause 11, when proposing amendments to public expenditure, taxation or policy, public bodies are required to publish a future generations impact assessment, which considers the likely impact of the proposal on its wellbeing objectives. The Bill also creates a Joint Committee on Future Generations.

3.104 In terms of achieving nature positive goals, the principle has been adopted in litigation aimed at protecting rainforests, such as a case in the Philippines in 1993, *Minors Oposa v Secretary of the Department of Environment and Natural Resources.*[151] The plaintiffs were all minors and citizens in the Republic of the Philippines; and the action sought cancellation of the existing logging permits, given the scale and extent of the

146 UNGA Resolution A/RES/76/300 (26 July 2022).
147 See Article 24 of the Constitution of South Africa and the Constitution of the Kingdom of Norway where it is recognised in the context of preserving natural resources.
148 Well-being of Future Generations (Wales) Act 2015 s 5(1).
149 ibid; 'wellbeing' is not defined as such but the Bill envisages that there will be a public consultation to set 'wellbeing goals' (s 5).
150 ibid s 3.
151 *Minors Oposa v Secretary of the Department of Environment and Natural Resources* [1993] Supreme Court of the Philippines G.R. No. 101083 cited in Tromans (n 3).

loss of rainforest.[152] In the Supreme Court on appeal, it was held that the plaintiffs had standing for present and future generations, based on the principle of international responsibility.[153] They were successful – the Philippine Constitution contains a right 'to balanced and healthful ecology'. The government had recognised the intergenerational issue in its environmental policy:

> In pursuing this policy, it shall be the responsibility of the Government ... that the nation may ... recognise, discharge and fulfil the responsibilities of each generation as trustee and guardian of the environment for succeeding generations.[154]

3.105 As to net zero ambitions, the UNGA's resolution requesting an advisory opinion from the International Court of Justice on 'the obligations of States in respect of climate change' also alludes to intergenerational equity by specifically asking the ICJ to consider the legal consequences of those obligations on states but also 'peoples and individuals of the present and future generations affected by the adverse effects of climate change'.[155]

3.106 International equity forms a key element of the decision of the ECtHR in *Verein Klimaseniorinnen Schweiz and others v Switzerland*,[156] which is concerned with the scope of states' obligations in relation to climate change under the European Convention on Human Rights. The Grand Chamber observed as follows:[157]

> 410. The Court is also aware that the damaging effects of climate change raise an issue of intergenerational burden-sharing ... and impact most heavily on various vulnerable groups in society, who need special care and protection from the authorities.
>
> ...
>
> 419. Climate change is a polycentric issue. Decarbonisation of the economies and ways of life can only be achieved through a comprehensive and profound transformation in various sectors. Such 'green transitions' necessarily require a very complex and wide-ranging set of coordinated actions, policies and investments involving both the public and the private sectors. Individuals themselves will be called upon to assume a share of responsibilities and burdens as well. Therefore, policies to combat climate change inevitably involve issues of social accommodation and intergenerational burden-sharing, both in regard to different generations of those currently living and in regard to future generations.
>
> 420. In this connection, the Court notes that, in the specific context of climate change, intergenerational burden-sharing assumes particular importance both in regard to the

---

152 The court was referred to loss at a rate of loss of 25 hectares per hour, leading to a reduction of cover from 53% of the country's land mass in 1968 to only 4% by 1987 (as cited in Tromans (n 3)).
153 Tromans (n 3).
154 ibid.
155 Request for an advisory opinion of the International Court of Justice on the obligations of States in respect of climate change. UNGA Res A/RES/77/276.
156 *Verein KlimaSeniorinnen Schweiz and others v Switzerland* (n 137).
157 ibid [410], [419]–[420].

> different generations of those currently living and in regard to future generations. While the legal obligations arising for States under the Convention extend to those individuals currently alive who, at a given time, fall within the jurisdiction of a given Contracting Party, it is clear that future generations are likely to bear an increasingly severe burden of the consequences of present failures and omissions to combat climate change ... and that, at the same time, they have no possibility of participating in the relevant current decision-making processes. By their commitment to the UNFCCC, the States Parties have undertaken the obligation to protect the climate system for the benefit of present and future generations of humankind (...; Article 3 of the UNFCCC). This obligation must be viewed in the light of the already existing harmful impacts of climate change, as well as the urgency of the situation and the risk of irreversible harm posed by climate change. In the present context, having regard to the prospect of aggravating consequences arising for future generations, the intergenerational perspective underscores the risk inherent in the relevant political decision-making processes, namely that short-term interests and concerns may come to prevail over, and at the expense of, pressing needs for sustainable policy-making, rendering that risk particularly serious and adding justification for the possibility of judicial review.

It remains to be seen how this judgment,[158] handed down on 9 April 2024, will impact upon domestic case law.

158 This case is addressed in more detail in Chapter 28.

CHAPTER 4

DOMESTIC REGULATORS, ADVISORS AND OTHER PUBLIC AUTHORITIES

Stephanie David

Introduction

4.01 Achieving net zero and nature positive requires action and intervention across the whole economy involving both the public and private sector. The Climate Change Act 2008 ('CCA 2008'), the Environment Act 2021 ('EA 2021') and the Planning Act 2008 ('PA 2008') principally place legal obligations on the government as set out elsewhere in this book[1] to lead the transition. But statutory obligations also fall on local government, devolved administrations and other public bodies.

4.02 The division of competence between Westminster and the devolved administrations in relation to the subject matter covered in this book is complicated. Climate change itself is addressed at the UK level by the CCA 2008,[2] but climate change mitigation and adaptation are devolved[3] and the Welsh, Scottish and Northern Irish administrations have their own regimes and targets.[4] Environmental protection is a devolved matter.[5] Thus, the Scottish, Welsh and Northern Irish administrations have competence. Some

1 See Chapters 2, 6 and 8.
2 There are also specific obligations under the CCA 2008 in certain devolved administrations, for example, s 60 of the CCA 2008 sets out a duty on the relevant Northern Ireland department to lay programmes before the Northern Ireland Assembly. For further information on the devolved administrations and climate change setting out the department's objectives in relation to adaptation to climate change, including proposals, policies and timescales: see Dominic Carver and Alex Adcock, 'General Debate on the Role and the Response of the Devolved Administrations to COP26' (2021) <https://researchbriefings.files.parliament.uk/documents/CDP-2021-0144/CDP-2021-0144.pdf> accessed 8 May 2024.
3 ibid.
4 See Climate Change (Scotland) Act 2009, which sets a net zero emissions target by 2045 (see A1); Part 2 of the Environment (Wales) Act 2016 deals with climate change and, in March 2021, the Senedd Cymru approved a net zero target for 2050 for Wales: 'Climate Change Targets and Carbon Budgets' (gov.wales, 23 March 2021) <https://www.gov.wales/climate-change-targets-and-carbon-budgets> accessed 9 May 2024; and in Northern Ireland, the Climate Change Act (Northern Ireland) 2022 sets emissions targets for 2030, 2040 and 2050.
5 Scotland Act 1998 s 30 and Schedule 5; Government of Wales Act 2006 (as amended by the Wales Act 2017) s 108A(2)(c) and Schedule 7A, and the Northern Ireland Act 1998 ss 4, 6, Schedule 3.

relevant areas are, however, reserved matters, such as certain energy, financial, transport, and consumer protection policy, as well as particular pollution control regimes.[6]

4.03 The aim of the chapter is to provide a summary of the various statutory and non-statutory bodies, focusing on England and Wales, that play a key role in the shift to a net zero and nature positive future.

Climate Change Committee

4.04 The Climate Change Committee ('CCC') is an independent statutory public body 'tasked to advise the UK and devolved Governments and Parliament on tackling climate change, including matters relating to the UK's statutory carbon reduction target for 2050'.[7]

4.05 The CCC was established by section 32(1) of the CCA 2008 as a body corporate. Its powers and duties are governed by Part 2 of the CCA 2008 along with Schedule 1, which deals mostly with administrative matters but also sets out out the expertise required on the CCC.[8] The expertise spans business competitiveness, climate change policy at the national and international level, climate science (and other branches of environmental science), different circumstances as between England, Wales, Scotland and Northern Ireland and the capacity of national authorities to take action in relation to climate change, economic analysis and forecasting, emissions trading, energy production and supply, financial investment, and technology development and diffusion.

4.06 The CCC's functions are as follows:[9]

- By section 33(1) of the CCA 2008, the CCC was required to advise the Secretary of State, by 1 December 2008, on the target set out in section 1(1) of the CCA 2008, in particular whether that target should be amended and, if so, to what it should be amended. In turn, that advice must be taken into account by the Secretary of State and, if departed from, reasons must be given.[10]

---

6 For example, under the Scotland Act 1998, Schedule 5 sets out the reserved matters and the various exceptions. Head A deals with financial and economic matters, Head C deals with trade and industry (and includes at para C7 consumer protection and at para C8 product standards, safety and liability), Head D addresses energy (including electricity, oil and gas, coal, nuclear energy and energy conservation; paragraph D1 specifically refers to various pollution control regimes under the Environmental Protection Act 1990), Head E deals with transport (including road, rail, marine, and air). Pursuant to Schedule 7A of the Government of Wales Act 2006, the reserved matters and exceptions thereto are set out. Head A deals with financial and economic matters, Head C is trade and industry (with consumer protection at s C6), Head D addresses energy (with certain exceptions), Head E deals with transport. The legislative framework for Northern Ireland is more complex. The starting point is the Northern Ireland Act 1998; some reserved matters are set out in Schedule 3 and include civil aviation, natural resources in the foreshore, seabed, subsoil and various pipe-lines.
7 *R (Friends of the Earth Ltd and others) v Heathrow Airport Ltd* [2020] UKSC 52, [2021] 2 All ER 967 [41].
8 CCA 2008, Schedule 1, para 1(3).
9 The CCC is also required to advise the Secretary of State on the definition of 'targeted greenhouse gas' under s 24 of the CCA 2008; and base years for non-CO_2 gases, as set out in s 25.
10 CCA 2008 s 3(1), (6).

- By section 34(1), the CCC must advise the Secretary of State: (i) on the level of each carbon budget,[11] (ii) the extent to which each carbon budget should be met by reducing the amount of net UK emissions of targeted GHGs or by the use of carbon units, (iii) the respective contributions to a carbon budget by sectors of the economy, respectively, covered by trading schemes and those that are not, and (iv) sectors of the economy where there are particular opportunities for contributions to be made. In considering its advice, the CCC must take various matters set out in section 10 into account including scientific knowledge about climate change, technology relevant to climate change, economic circumstances, and fiscal circumstances. In turn, the Secretary of State must take the advice into account and give reasons for departing from any such advice (as well as the matters set out in CCA 2008, section 10).[12]

- Relatedly, the CCC has a role to advise on regulations produced in relation to carbon units, carbon accounting and the net UK carbon account, set out sections 26 and 27 of the CCA 2008.[13]

- By section 35(1), the CCC must advise the Secretary of State on the consequences of treating emissions of targeted GHG from international aviation and international shipping, as emissions from sources in the UK for the purpose of Part 1 of the CCA 2008.[14]

- By section 36(1), the CCC is required to publish an annual report on the UK's progress in meeting carbon budgets and the net zero target (as it now is), including further progress that is required and whether the budgets and target are likely to be met. This report must be laid before Parliament and each of the devolved legislatures. The Secretary of State must respond to the points raised in the report produced pursuant to section 36(1) and lay that report before Parliament.[15] In preparing the response, the Secretary of State must consult the other national authorities.[16]

- By section 38(1), the CCC is required to provide other advice, analysis, information or assistance, following a request from a national authority in connection with (i) the authority's functions under the CCA 2008, (ii) progress made towards meeting the objectives under the CCA 2008, (iii) adaptation to climate change or (iv) other matters relating to climate change.

---

11 The CCC must also advice on the targets set in s 5 in relation to the level of carbon budgets (CCA 2008 s 5(1) and 7); and the alteration of any carbon budgets (CCA 2008 s 22).

12 CCA 2008 s 9(1), (4).

13 ibid s 28(5).

14 See Chapter 2, paras 2.89ff. There is a related obligation on the Secretary of State to take that advice into account in the context of regulations dealing with these emissions (ss 30 and 31).

15 CCA 2008 s 37(1).

16 This is defined in CCA 2008 s 95(1) as any of the following: (a) the Secretary of State (b) the Scottish Ministers; (c) the Welsh Ministers; (d) the relevant Northern Ireland department. See discussion of this provision in *R (Global Feedback Ltd) v Secretary of State for the Environment, Food and Rural Affairs and the Secretary of State for Energy Security and Net Zero* [2023] EWCA Civ 1549, [2024] 1 WLR 2923 [74–5].

- By section 39(1), the CCC has general ancillary powers in relation to doing anything that appears to be 'necessary or appropriate for the purpose of, or in connection with, the carrying out of its functions'. In *R (Friends of the Earth) v Secretary of State for Business, Energy and Industrial Strategy*,[17] Holgate J noted that sections 38 and 39 together 'enable the CCC to engage in ongoing dialogue with the Secretary of State and to respond publicly to documents he publishes'.[18] The Court of Appeal agreed in *R (Global Feedback) v Secretary of State for the Environment, Food and Rural Affairs*,[19] noting that the CCC has 'the power to give such advice as it thinks fit in this context' but there was no corresponding duty on the Secretary of State to take that advice into account, let alone 'give it significant weight' or 'cogent reasons for departing from it'.[20]

- By section 48(1), in the context of regulating emissions trading schemes, a national authority is required to obtain and take into account the advice of the CCC, in particular in relation to any limit on the total amount of activities to which the trading scheme applies for a trading period or periods.

- By section 57(1), the CCC is under a duty to advise the Secretary of State in relation to reports prepared under section 56 dealing with the assessment of risks for the UK of the current and predicted impact of climate change.

- By section 59(1), the CCC must, in its report produced under section 36, also assess the Secretary of State's progress in relation to implementing the objectives, policies and proposals set out in the section 58 report to Parliament dealing with adaptation to climate change.

4.07 Reasons must be given for the CCC's advice, produced pursuant to sections 33, 34, 35 of CCA 2008, copies must be sent to the Secretary of State and other national authorities, and the advice must be published.[21]

4.08 The CCC works alongside other public bodies and regulators such as the Office for Environmental Protection, where there is a crossover in their work, as set out below. The national authorities, which include the Secretary of State, are empowered to give the CCC guidance or directions in relation to matters to take into account in the exercise of certain functions in the Act.[22]

4.09 The CCC's role in achieving net zero is obvious, given its statutory role and remit. In terms of nature positive, there is no explicit reference to nature or biodiversity within the CCA 2008 itself. The expertise on the CCC should include not only 'climate science'

---

17 *R (Friends of the Earth Ltd) v Secretary of State for Business, Energy and Industrial Strategy* [2022] EWHC 1841 (Admin), [2023] 1 WLR 225.
18 ibid 55.
19 *R (Global Feedback) v Secretary of State for the Environment, Food and Rural Affairs* (n 16).
20 ibid 112.
21 CCA 2008 ss 33(2), (4)–(5); 34(3), (5)–(6); 35(3), (5)–(6).
22 ibid s 41–2.

but 'other branches of environmental science'.[23] The CCC recognises that human-induced climate change and biodiversity are 'inextricably linked',[24] as set out in the Introduction. In its report on progress in relation to adaptation, the CCC specifically considers the government's policies and proposals to ensure a climate resilient nature.[25] The relevant outcomes ensure that three types of habitat (terrestrial, freshwater, and marine and coastal) are in good ecological health, which are based on the principles set out in the Lawton Review.[26]

Office for Environmental Protection ('OEP')

4.10 The OEP was created as an independent body 'to provide expert, objective and impartial advice on environmental issues'[27] and 'to monitor the implementation of, and enforce compliance with, environmental law, holding public authorities to account'.[28] It is required by statute to have a memorandum of understanding with the CCC to avoid any overlap in the exercise of their respective functions.[29]

4.11 The OEP was established by section 22(1) of the EA 2021 as a body corporate. It operates in England and Northern Ireland[30] and was intended to replace the EU Commission. The OEP's principal objective, in exercising its functions, is to contribute to (a) environmental protection and (b) the improvement of the natural environment.[31] 'Environmental protection' is defined as:[32]

(a) protection of the natural environment from the effects of human activity;

(b) protection of people from the effects of human activity on the natural environment;

(c) maintenance, restoration or enhancement of the natural environment;

(d) monitoring, assessing, considering, advising or reporting on anything in paragraphs (a) to (c).

---

23 ibid Schedule 1, para 1(3)(c).
24 Climate Change Committee, 'Progress in Reducing Emissions: 2023 Report to Parliament' (2023) 60 <https://www.theccc.org.uk/wp-content/uploads/2023/06/Progress-in-reducing-UK-emissions-2023-Report-to-Parliament.pdf> accessed 4 April 2024.
25 See, for example, Climate Change Committee, 'Progress in Adapting to Climate Change: 2023 Report to Parliament' (2023) ch 2 <https://www.theccc.org.uk/wp-content/uploads/2023/03/WEB-Progress-in-adapting-to-climate-change-2023-Report-to-Parliament.pdf> accessed 16 May 2024.
26 See further Chapter 8.
27 Rt Hon George Eustice MP in HC Deb 26 February 2020, vol 672, col 343.
28 Lord Goldsmith of Richmond Park in HL Deb 28 June 2021, vol 813, col 611.
29 EA 2021 s 26, the memorandum of understanding is dated 15 June 2022 and sets out how the CCC and OEP 'maximise their respective contributions to addressing climate change and minimise scope for duplicating and conflicting activity' (see para 1.2).
30 EA 2021 s 49.
31 ibid s 23(1).
32 ibid s 45(1).

4.12 The 'natural environment' means:[33]

(a) plants, wild animals and other living organisms,

(b) their habitats,

(c) land (except buildings or other structures), air and water,

and the natural systems, cycles and processes through which they interact.

4.13 The OEP must act objectively and impartially; and have regard to the need to act proportionately and transparently.[34] It must also prepare a strategy, pursuant to section 23(3) of the EA 2021, setting out how it intends to exercise its functions.

4.14 Essentially, the OEP's functions can be divided into two: (i) the scrutiny and advice functions and (ii) its enforcement functions.

4.15 The scrutiny and advice functions require the OEP to monitor progress in improving the natural environment in accordance with the government's extant environmental improvement plan ('EIP') and the statutory targets (including interim targets) set under the EA 2021.[35] This involves the OEP publishing an annual progress report,[36] monitoring and reporting on the implementation of environmental law (except where the matter falls within the CCC's remit).[37] The OEP must advise Ministers of the Crown in relation to changes to environmental law or other matters affecting the natural environment.[38]

4.16 At the time of writing, the OEP had, on 18 January 2024, published its annual report for 2022/2023. The report addresses the various goals set out in the EIP and is considered further in Chapter 8. The apex goal in the EIP is 'thriving plants and wildlife', which is directly concerned with improving biodiversity. The OEP, in their report, conclude that there remains a 'backdrop of continuing decline across trends in biodiversity' and the 'lack of strategy, guidance and action plans for "30 by 30" commitments is impeding progress'.[39] The OEP considers that the government is largely off track in meeting its ambitions, targets and commitments but identifies various opportunities.

4.17 Goal 7 of the EIP specifically concerns climate change mitigation and adaptation. The OEP notes that the first two carbon budgets have been met and the third is likely to be met based on provisional figures.[40] It observes that overall GHG emissions from

---

33 ibid s 44.
34 ibid s 23(2).
35 ibid ss 1–3, 11, 14.
36 ibid s 28.
37 ibid s 29.
38 ibid s 30.
39 Office for Environmental Protection, 'Progress in Improving the Natural Environment in England 2022/2023' (2024) 28, 40 <https://assets.publishing.service.gov.uk/media/65a7c8f8ed27ca001327b106/E02987560-progress-in-improving-natural-environment.pdf> accessed 27 April 2024. For further discussion see Chapter 8.
40 ibid 106.

consumption in England are decreasing. But the OEP raises concerns about the Carbon Budget Delivery Plan's overreliance on 'technological innovation' and 'the lack of long-term funding for action'.[41] The OEP notes the CCC's decreased confidence in carbon budgets 5 and 6 being met, that 'apart from the power sector, emissions reduction rates must quadruple within eight years to meet targets' and considers that the UK is 'largely not on track'.[42] In terms of adaptation, the OEP observes as follows:[43]

> Climate adaptation is characterised by a lack of clear domestic objectives against which to assess progress. The UK is committed to strengthening resilience and reducing vulnerability to climate change through the Paris Agreement. Overall, Climate Change Committee progress assessments spanning the lifetime of the second National Adaptation Programme (2018–2023) indicate a persistent lack of progress in reducing vulnerability and exposure to climate risks across all sectors and a need to increase the pace and scale of delivery.

4.18 The OEP's enforcement functions are concerned with failures by public authorities to comply with environmental law.[44] Such failures mean (i) 'unlawfully failing to take proper account of environmental law when exercising its functions'; and (ii) 'unlawfully exercising, or failing to exercise, any function it has under environmental law'.[45] A 'public authority' means 'a person carrying out any function of a public nature' subject to certain exceptions.[46] Thus, the statutory wording is similar to section 6(3)(b) of the Human Rights Act 1998.[47] Whilst it would ultimately be for the courts to determine what a public function is, the explanatory notes to the EA 2021 envisage that bodies that undertake both public and private functions, such as statutory undertakers, will fall within the scope of the OEP's remit.[48]

4.19 The OEP sets out its enforcement policy in the strategy it produces, pursuant to section 23 of the EA 2021. Its enforcement functions operate following complaints made where a person believes that a public authority has failed to comply with environmental law[49] or the OEP's own initiative. The OEP has the power to undertake an investigation where it appears that a public authority has failed to comply with environmental law and such a failure would be serious.[50] It has the power to issue information notices, requiring a public authority to provide further specified information relating to an alleged breach of environmental law;[51] and decision notices, if the OEP is satisfied, on the balance of probabilities, that the authority has failed to comply with environmental law and the

---

41 ibid.
42 ibid 107.
43 ibid 107.
44 EA 2021 s 31(1).
45 ibid s 31(2).
46 ibid s 31(3), the exceptions are 'a devolved function, a parliamentary function or a function of any of the following persons— (a) the OEP; (b) a court or tribunal; (c) either House of Parliament; (d) a devolved legislature; (e) the Scottish Ministers, the Welsh Ministers, a Northern Ireland department or a Minister within the meaning of the Northern Ireland Act 1998'.
47 Explanatory Notes to the Environment Act 2021 n 268.
48 ibid.
49 EA 2021 s 32(1).
50 ibid s 33.
51 ibid s 35.

failure is serious.[52] The OEP also has the power to apply to the court for environmental review, if certain conditions are fulfilled;[53] and to apply to court, or intervene in cases, on an urgent basis, if the urgency condition is met: the application is 'necessary to prevent, or mitigate, serious damage to the natural environment or to human health'.[54]

Environment Agency ('EA')

4.20 The EA is the principal environmental regulator in England. It is a non-departmental public body of DEFRA that administers various environmental statutory schemes.[55] It was established as a body corporate by the Environment Act 1995 ('EA 1995');[56] and became operational on 1 April 1996. It took over responsibilities from the National Rivers Authority, HM Inspectorate of Pollution and the waste regulation authorities.[57]

4.21 The EA's principal aim is set out in section 4(1) of the EA 1995 and is to discharge its functions 'so to protect or enhance the environment, taken as a whole, as to make the contribution towards attaining the objective of achieving sustainable development'. It achieves that objective through its role[58] as an environmental regulator, environmental operator, a monitor and advisor on the statement of the environment, a technical advisor on the development of environmental policy, a promoter of scientific research, and a category one responder in relation to incidents and emergencies.[59]

4.22 The EA has various functions in relation to pollution control,[60] the regulation of major carbon intensive industry, renewables sector, water, agriculture, contaminated land and waste.[61]

4.23 In terms of net zero and nature positive, the EA recognises its role in addressing climate change and nature loss in its corporate report, entitled 'Environment Agency: EA 2025 creating a better place'. The plan sets out three long-term goals for the EA:[62]

- A nation resilient to climate change, which includes more resilient places and infrastructure and a country ready for flooding, coastal change and drought;

---

52 ibid s 36.
53 ibid s 38.
54 ibid s 39(2).
55 Richard Burnett-Hall and Brian Jones, *Burnett-Hall on Environmental Law* (3rd edn, Sweet & Maxwell 2012) para 5–016; DEFRA, 'Framework Document: Environment Agency' (2017) para 2.1 <https://assets.publishing.service.gov.uk/media/5a81f5c540f0b6230269a15e/Environment_Agency_Framework_Document.pdf> accessed 16 May 2024 (this is the guidance produced, pursuant to s 4(2) of the EA 1995).
56 Environment Act 1995 ('EA 1995') s 1.
57 Burnett-Hall and Jones (n 55) paras 5–015; see EA 1995 s 2.
58 DEFRA (n 55) para 3.1.
59 ibid, and in relation to its role as a category 1 responder see the Civil Contingencies Act 2004.
60 EA 1995 s 5(1) and exercises functions under the environmental permitting regime. See further Chapter 13.
61 Burnett-Hall and Jones (n 55) paras 5-018–5-019; see, for example, EA 1995 s 6 on water and related legislation such as the Water Industry Act 1991 s 141D.
62 Environment Agency, 'EA 2025 Creating a Better Place' <https://assets.publishing.service.gov.uk/media/5f06be3dd3bf7f2beca9b854/EA2025-creating-a-better-place.pdf> accessed 16 May 2024.

- Healthy air, land and water, which includes better air quality, better water quality for both people and wildlife, and the protection and enhancement of nature; and,

- Green growth and a sustainable future through its role in influencing local planning authorities, as well as targeting waste crime and developing a circular economy.

4.24 Examples of its specific roles in this context include its role as the regulator for the UK Emissions Trading Scheme in England.[63] It also provides guidance on strategic flood risk assessments for local planning authorities and for developers on flood risk assessments and the use of climate change allowances to address vulnerability and provide resilience, particularly in the context of flooding and coastal change.[64]

Natural Resources Wales ('NRW')

4.25 The NRW has a wide range of responsibilities, including advisory and regulatory, relating to nature, natural resources and the environment in Wales.[65]

4.26 The Natural Resources Body for Wales (Establishment) Order 2012 created the NRW, whose general purpose is to ensure the environment and natural resources of Wales are sustainably used, enhanced and maintained.[66] The word 'sustainably' is defined 'with a view to benefitting, and in a manner designed to benefit the people, environment and economy of Wales in the present and the future'.[67] The 'environment' includes 'without limitation, living organisms and ecosystems'.[68] Further, the NRW must prepare and publish reports containing an assessment of the state of natural resources in Wales, which must include *inter alia* its assessment of biodiversity.[69]

4.27 In terms of biodiversity, the NRW has a nature conservation duty, whereby it must exercise its functions to further nature conservation and the conservation and enhancement of natural beauty and amenity.[70] The NRW must be consulted by the Welsh Ministers as part of their preparation and review of 'a list of the living organisms and types of habitat which in their opinion are of principal importance for the purpose of maintaining and enhancing biodiversity in relation to Wales'.[71]

---

63 The Greenhouse Gas Emissions Trading Scheme Order 2020/1265, reg 9(1)(b). See further Chapter 14.
64 Environment Agency, 'Guidance: Flood Risk Assessments: Climate Change Allowances' (2022) <https://www.gov.uk/guidance/flood-risk-assessments-climate-change-allowances> accessed 23 April 2024.
65 'Our Roles and Responsibilities' (*Natural Resources Wales*, 15 March 2024) <https://naturalresources.wales/about-us/what-we-do/our-roles-and-responsibilities/our-roles-and-responsibilities/?lang=en> accessed 16 May 2024.
66 The Natural Resources Body for Wales (Establishment) Order 2012 (as amended by the Environment (Wales) Act 2016) Article 4.
67 ibid 4(2).
68 ibid 4(2b).
69 Environment (Wales) Act 2016 s 8.
70 The Natural Resources Body for Wales (Establishment) Order 2012 (as amended by The Natural Resources Body for Wales (Functions) Order 2013) Article 5A.
71 Environment (Wales) Act 2016 s 7. There is also a duty on public authorities, set out in s 6 of the Act, which requires them to seek to maintain and enhance biodiversity in the exercise of their functions in Wales.

4.28 The NRW must also exercise its functions to promote the provision and improvement of opportunities for access to the countryside and the study and enjoyment of the natural environment.[72] It is also required to cooperate and coordinate its activities with the EA.[73]

4.29 In terms of net zero, the NRW is designated as the regulator in relation to installations in Wales and the Welsh territorial sea in the emissions trading scheme.[74]

Nature conservation bodies

4.30 The nature conservation bodies include Natural England, the NRW (addressed above at paragraphs 4.25–4.29) and the Joint Nature Conservation Committee.

(i) *Natural England*

4.31 Natural England was established by section 1 of the Natural Environment and Rural Communities Act 2006 ('NERCA 2006'). Its functions are exercisable in England and, where the context requires, the territorial sea adjacent to England.[75] Both English Nature and the Countryside Alliance were dissolved by NERCA and their respective functions transferred to Natural England.[76]

4.32 Natural England's general purpose is 'to ensure that the natural environment is conserved, enhanced and managed for the benefit of present and future generations, thereby contributing to sustainable development'.[77] The purpose includes:[78]

(a) promoting nature conservation and protecting biodiversity,

(b) conserving and enhancing the landscape,

(c) securing the provision and improvement of facilities for the study, understanding and enjoyment of the natural environment,

(d) promoting access to the countryside and open spaces and encouraging open-air recreation, and

(e) contributing in other ways to social and economic well-being through management of the natural environment.

---

72 The Natural Resources Body for Wales (Establishment) Order 2012 (as amended by The Natural Resources Body for Wales (Functions) Order 2013), Article 5C.
73 ibid Article 8A.
74 The Greenhouse Gas Emissions Trading Scheme (Amendment) Order 2020/1557, regs 9–10.
75 NERCA 2006 s 1(3).
76 ibid s 1(4).
77 ibid s 2(1).
78 ibid s 2(2).

4.33 Natural England's role is principally advisory in respect of matters relating to its general purpose.[79] For example, it is required to advise the Secretary of State on living organisms or habitat types for inclusion on the list of organisms and habitats that are of principal importance for the purpose of conserving and enhancing biodiversity.[80] It also has a role in environmental impact assessments and habitats regulation assessments (see Chapter 7 on EIAs and Chapter 9 on HRA).

4.34 Natural England has a statutory duty to review all matters relating to its general purpose and has the power to undertake relevant research.[81] In terms of its monitoring functions, Natural England must have regard to the common standards established under section 34(2)(c) of NERCA 2006.[82] To further its general purpose, Natural England also has powers to carry out proposals,[83] provide financial assistance,[84] enter into management agreements with persons with an interest in land in relation to the management or use of that land,[85] carry out experimental schemes,[86] and provide information.[87] Natural England also has the power to institute criminal proceedings in the magistrates' court.[88]

4.35 Natural England's enforcement functions include environmental damage,[89] in particular, severe damage to a protected species, natural habitat, site of special scientific interest, land, water or biodiversity; site of special scientific interest ('SSSI');[90] heather and grass burning;[91] and breaches of species licences.

(ii) *Joint Nature Conservation Committee ('JNCC')*

4.36 The JNCC is the statutory advisor to the government and devolved administrations on UK and international nature conservation.[92] It is an executive non-departmental public body. It was originally established under the Environmental Protection Act 1990 and was reconstituted under NERCA 2006, section 31. The JNCC, along with the UK conservation bodies,[93] have the purposes of nature conservation and fostering the understanding of nature conservation.[94] In discharging their functions under part 2 of

---

79 ibid s 4(1).
80 ibid s 41.
81 ibid s 3.
82 ibid s 3(4).
83 ibid s 5.
84 ibid s 6.
85 ibid s 7.
86 ibid s 8.
87 ibid s 9.
88 ibid s 12.
89 Environmental Damage (Prevention and Remediation) (England) Regulations 2015, SI 2015/810.
90 Wildlife and Countryside Act 1981 s 28.
91 The Heather and Grass etc. Burning (England) Regulations 2007, SI 2007/20003.
92 'Joint Nature Conservation Committee' (gov.uk, 31 May 2019) <https://www.gov.uk/government/organisations/joint-nature-conservation-committee> accessed 16 May 2024.
93 The UK conservation bodies are defined by NERCA 2006 s 32(1) as Natural England (England); Natural Resources Wales (Wales); Scottish Natural Heritage (Scotland); and Council for Nature Conservation and the Countryside (Northern Ireland).
94 ibid s 33(1).

NERCA 2006, the bodies must have regard to (i) actual or possible ecological changes and (ii) the desirability of contributing to sustainable development.[95]

4.37 The JNCC must provide advice to the Secretary of State, National Assembly for Wales, Scottish Ministers and relevant Northern Ireland Department on *inter alia* the development and implementation of policies for, or affecting, nature conservations throughout the UK or outside the UK.[96] It also has certain functions in relation to wildlife in Great Britain.[97]

Marine Management Organisation ('MMO')

4.38 The MMO is tasked with protecting and enhancing the marine environment, as well as supporting and regulating economic growth in sustainable marine activities.[98]

4.39 The MMO was established by section 1 of the Marine and Coastal Access Act 2009 ('MCCA 2009'). Its general duty is to ensure that its functions are exercised so that the carrying on of activities by persons in its area are managed, controlled or regulated with the objective of contributing to the achievement of sustainable development.[99] The objective should take into account the scientific evidence available, or reasonably obtainable, by the MMO, as well as other evidence relating to the social, economic and environmental aspects of sustainable development.[100]

4.40 The MMO's area is 'those parts of the UK marine area, or of the United Kingdom, where MMO functions are exercisable'.[101]

4.41 The MMO is also an executive non-departmental public body. It is required to follow guidance issued by the government in relation to how it exercises its functions;[102] and it also may be delegated marine functions of the Secretary of State, pursuant to section 14 of the MCAA 2009.

4.42 The MMO is responsible for regulating activities in seas around England, such as in relation to fisheries, conservation and renewable energy installations.[103] Its functions include licensing of fishing boats, trans-shipment licences for vessels and licensing for the purpose of a range of other functions such as conserving wild birds, repopulating areas, conserving flora and fauna.[104]

---

95 ibid s 33.
96 ibid s 34(2).
97 ibid s 36.
98 Marine Management Organisation, 'About Us' (GOV.UK) <https://www.gov.uk/government/organisations/marine-management-organisation/about> accessed 16 May 2024.
99 MCAA 2009 s 2(1)(a).
100 ibid s 2(3).
101 ibid s 2(12).
102 ibid s 2(4).
103 See Marine Management Organisation and Department for Environment, Food and Rural Affairs, 'Corporate Report: MMO Framework Document' (2022) para 4.2, Annex 1 <https://www.gov.uk/government/publications/mmo-framework-document/mmo-framework-document> accessed 16 May 2024.
104 MCAA 2009; Wildlife and Countryside Act 1981 s 16 (as amended by the MCAA 2009).

4.43 In terms of net zero, the MMO recognises the significant role that climate change is having on the coastal and marine environment, including sea level rise, sea water temperature, ocean acidification and storm surge and winds.[105] The MMO has a strategic plan for healthy, productive seas and coasts with seven goals – for example, the first of which concerns the restoration of functioning marine ecosystems; the second concerns marine planning to address priorities in using the seas; and the sixth concerns sustainable and transparent management of fishing opportunities.[106]

4.44 The MMO has a role in the transition to renewable energy: for example, it has a statutory function in relation to various consents under the Electricity Act 1989 for certain generating stations.[107]

4.45 In the context of nature positive, the MMO has statutory obligations and powers in relation to marine conservations zones;[108] and will receive guidance and advice from the appropriate statutory conservation body.[109] There is also a general statutory obligation on the MMO (and ministers) in relation to marine conservation.[110] By section 1, the MMO is required, so far is consistent with its function under the Sea Fisheries (Wildlife Conservation) Act 1992,[111] to have regard to the conservation of marine flora and fauna and achieve a reasonable balance as between that consideration and other considerations.

Office of Gas and Electricity Markets ('Ofgem')

4.46 Ofgem is the independent energy regulator and therefore plays a pivotal role in the energy transition to net zero. It is a non-ministerial government department, which is governed by the Gas and Electricity Markets Authority ('GEMA').[112] GEMA was established as a body corporate pursuant to section 1 of the Utilities Act 2000 ('UA 2000'). Functions of the Director Generals of Gas and Electricity Supply were transferred to GEMA by that Act.[113]

4.47 The principal objective on the Secretary of State and GEMA in carrying out their functions under the Gas Act 1986 is to protect the interests of existing and future consumers in relation to gas conveyed through pipes.[114] The provision was amended by section 202(2) of the Energy Act 2023 so that the interests of existing and future

105 Marine Management Organisation, 'Climate Change Adaptation Report' (2022) 4, 9–10 <https://assets.publishing.service.gov.uk/media/64b67f020ea2cb001315e4b1/MMO_Climate_Change_Adaptation_Report_v1.0.pdf> accessed 16 May 2024.
106 Marine Management Organisation, 'MMO2030: Healthy, Productive Seas and Coasts MMO Strategic Plan' <https://assets.publishing.service.gov.uk/media/64c261e07aea5b000d07505e/MMO_Strategy__April_2023_.pptx.pdf> accessed 16 May 2024.
107 MCAA 2009 s 12; Electricity Act 1989 s 36.
108 See Chapter 9 for further consideration of MCZs.
109 MCAA 2009 ss 127 and 147(1).
110 Sea Fisheries (Wildlife Conservation) Act 1992 s 1.
111 This is defined in s 1(2) as 'any enactments for the time being in force relating to sea-fishing, including any enactment relating to fishing in the sea for shellfish, salmon or migratory trout'.
112 'Our Role and Responsibilities' (Ofgem) <https://www.ofgem.gov.uk/our-role-and-responsibilities> accessed 16 May 2024.
113 UA 2000 ss 1 and 3.
114 Gas Act 1986 s 4AA(1).

consumers, taken as a whole, are defined to include their interests in the Secretary of State's compliance with the duties in sections 1 and 4(1)(b) of the CCA 2008 (Net Zero Target for 2050 and the five-year carbon budgets).[115]

4.48 The same principal objective applies in the context of electricity conveyed by distribution systems or transmission systems.[116] That statutory provision was also amended by the Energy Act 2023 so that the interests of existing and future consumers, taken as a whole, are defined to include their interests in the Secretary of State securing compliance with the Net Zero Target and carbon budgets.[117]

4.49 Ofgem's functions are broad and include: (i) administering and regulating licenses and licensed activities relating to the supply of gas and electricity;[118] (ii) administering various renewable energy and social schemes on behalf of the government; and (iii) setting price controls for the electricity and gas network companies.

4.50 Even prior to the Energy Act 2023, Ofgem was exercising its functions in the context of achieving net zero and the transition to green energy. For example, the schemes administered by Ofgem include renewable obligations, feed-in tariffs scheme, boiler upgrade scheme, and a green gas support scheme.[119] Indeed, licensed suppliers have certain obligations under these schemes, depending on their licence, which funds and/or supports the schemes: for example, the green gas levy funds the green gas support scheme.[120] In terms of price controls, RIIO-2 is an investment programme to transform the energy networks io deliver low-carbon energy in Great Britain.[121]

Water Services Regulation Authority ('Ofwat')

4.51 Ofwat is the economic regulator of the water sector. It works alongside the EA, which is principally concerned with regulating water quality and ecological protection.

4.52 Ofwat is a body corporate, established by s1A of the Water Industry Act 1991 ('WIA 1991'). In undertaking its functions, Ofwat has to consider how best to further various objectives, including the consumer objective, the resilience objective and various functions relating to how water undertakers and sewerage undertakers carry out their functions.[122] The consumer objective is defined by reference to protecting the interests

---

115 The interests also include security of supply of gas to them and their interests in GEMA carrying out its regulatory functions and objectives.
116 Electricity Act 1989 s 3A.
117 ibid s 3A(1A)(a).
118 'Licences and Licence Conditions' (Ofgem) <https://www.ofgem.gov.uk/licences-and-licence-conditions> accessed 16 May 2024.
119 Considered further in Chapter 34. 'Environmental and Social Schemes' (Ofgem) <https://www.ofgem.gov.uk/environmental-and-social-schemes> accessed 16 May 2024.
120 'Supplier Obligations: Environmental and Social Schemes' (Ofgem, 5 January 2023) <https://www.ofgem.gov.uk/publications/supplier-obligations-environmental-and-social-schemes> accessed 16 May 2024.
121 'Network Price Controls 2021–2028 (RIIO-2)' (Ofgem, 2 May 2024) <https://www.ofgem.gov.uk/energy-policy-and-regulation/policy-and-regulatory-programmes/network-price-controls-2021-2028-riio-2> accessed 16 May 2024.
122 WIA 1991 s 2.

of consumers (and related to that promoting effective competition).[123] The resilience objective is as follows:[124]

> (a) to secure the long-term resilience of water undertakers' supply systems and sewerage undertakers' sewerage systems as regards environmental pressures, population growth and changes in consumer behaviour, and
>
> (b) to secure that undertakers take steps for the purpose of enabling them to meet, in the long term, the need for the supply of water and the provision of sewerage services to consumers, including by promoting—
>
> (i) appropriate long-term planning and investment by relevant undertakers, and
> (ii) the taking by them of a range of measures to manage water resources in sustainable ways, and to increase efficiency in the use of water and reduce demand for water so as to reduce pressure on water resources.

4.53 By section 3 of the WIA 1991, Ofwat, like the Secretary of State and relevant undertakers, is required, in the context of exercising certain functions, to:

> further the conservation and enhancement of natural beauty and the conservation of flora, fauna and geological or physiographical features of special interest and, in the case of the exercise of such a power by a company holding an appointment as a relevant undertaker, as to further water conservation.[125]

4.54 The government has set Ofwat's strategic priorities in England, pursuant to section 2A of the WIA 1991.[126] The strategic priorities include: (i) protecting and enhancing the environment and (ii) delivering a resilient water sector.

4.55 In terms of the protection and enhancement of the environment, the government refers to the Environmental Improvement Plan and the strategy to achieve clean and plentiful water, as well as the specific obligations in the Environment Act 2021 on water and sewerage companies in relation to storm overflows. The government sets out that it expects Ofwat to, for example:[127]

- Challenge water companies to demonstrate how they will improve environmental performance to meet Environment Agency requirements in the Environmental Performance Assessment;

- Challenge water companies to demonstrate how they will achieve zero serious pollution incidents by 2030;

---

123 ibid s 2(2B).
124 ibid s 2(2DA).
125 ibid s 3(2)(ii).
126 DEFRA, 'February 2022: The Government's Strategic Priorities for Ofwat' (2022) <https://www.gov.uk/government/publications/strategic-policy-statement-to-ofwat-incorporating-social-and-environmental-guidance/february-2022-the-governments-strategic-priorities-for-ofwat> accessed 16 May 2024.
127 ibid.

- Challenge water companies to demonstrate how they will significantly reduce the frequency and volume of sewage discharges from storm overflows, so they operate infrequently, and only in cases of unusually heavy rainfall; …

- Challenge companies to deliver against both relevant environmental legislation, and applicable targets set under the Environment Act 2021, and how they will meet the ambition set out in the WISER;[128] …

- Support an increase in the use of nature-based solutions where appropriate and in the interests of the environment and customers. Ofwat should work with the sector, the Environment Agency, Natural England and others to rapidly identify and overcome any barriers to the uptake of these approaches by water companies;

- Challenge water companies to prioritise improvements to protected sites and recognise the importance of priority habitats such as chalk streams, including the need to address nutrient pollution;

- Challenge water companies to contribute to meeting the objectives in the River Basin Management Plans.

4.56 Regarding water sector resilience, the policy sets out that Ofwat 'should challenge the water industry to plan, invest in, and operate its water and wastewater services to secure the needs of current and future customers, in a way which delivers value to customers, the environment and wider society over the long-term'.[129]

4.57 Ofwat's strategy[130] sets out its ambition for the water sector and recognises the need to respond and adapt to climate change, as well as the other environmental challenges. It has also produced various guidance for water companies to assist in the transition to net zero[131] as well as establishing an innovation fund[132] and calling on industry to identify proposals to deliver for the environment.[133] Ofwat also produces a climate change adaptation report every five years in which it identifies the current and future risks posed by climate change.[134] This report then feeds into the UK's climate change risk assessment produced under the CCA 2008.[135]

128 'WISER' stands for water industry strategic environmental requirements.
129 DEFRA (n 126).
130 Ofwat, 'Time to Act, Together: Ofwat's Strategy' (2024) <https://www.ofwat.gov.uk/wp-content/uploads/2019/10/Time-to-act-together-2024.pdf> accessed 16 May 2024.
131 Ofwat, 'Net Zero Principles Position Paper' (2022) <https://www.ofwat.gov.uk/wp-content/uploads/2022/01/Net_Zero_Principles_Position_Paper_Jan_2022.pdf>.
132 'Water Innovation Competitions' (Ofwat) <https://www.ofwat.gov.uk/regulated-companies/innovation-in-the-water-sector/water-innovation-competitions/> accessed 16 May 2024.
133 'Green Recovery' (Ofwat) <https://www.ofwat.gov.uk/regulated-companies/price-review/2024-price-review/green-recovery/> accessed 16 May 2024.
134 Ofwat, 'Ofwat's 3rd Climate Change Adaptation Report' (2022) <https://www.ofwat.gov.uk/wp-content/uploads/2022/01/Ofwats-3rd-Climate-Change-Adaptation-Report.pdf> accessed 16 May 2024.
135 ibid 5.

Financial Conduct Authority ('FCA')

4.58 The FCA is the regulator of financial services in the UK. It is a body corporate that was previously named the Financial Services Authority.[136] It works alongside and in parallel with the Prudential Regulation Authority, which is part of the Bank of England.[137]

4.59 The FCA's strategic objective is 'ensuring that the relevant markets[138] function well';[139] and its secondary objective is concerned with facilitating international competitiveness of the UK economy, in particular financial services, and its growth.[140] The FCA also has three operational objectives, which are (i) the consumer protection objective;[141] (ii) the integrity objective;[142] and (iii) the competition objective.[143]

4.60 Its general functions under FSMA 2000 include (i) making rules; (ii) making technical standards; (iii) giving guidance and (iv) determining the general policy and principles in relation to particular functions under the Act.[144]

4.61 The FCA is under a statutory obligation to discharge its general functions in a way that is compatible with its strategic objective, advances one or more of its operational objectives and its secondary objective, so far as is reasonably possible.[145] It must also have regard to *inter alia* the regulatory principles set out in section 3B of FSMA 2000.

4.62 Those principles were amended by section 27 of the Financial Services and Markets Act 2023, to include the following as a regulatory principle:[146]

> [T]he need to contribute towards achieving compliance by the Secretary of State with section 1 of the Climate Change Act 2008 (UK net zero emissions target) and section 5 of the Environment Act 2021 (environmental targets) where each regulator considers the exercise of its functions to be relevant to the making of such a contribution.

4.63 The debates from Hansard set out the Government's intention behind this amendment, including both its ambition and limitations:

> Clause 25 replaces the sustainable growth principle with a new regulatory principle to require the FCA and PRA to have regard to the need to contribute towards achieving

136 Financial Services and Markets Act 2000 ('FSMA 2000') s 1A.
137 ibid s 2A(1).
138 'relevant markets' are defined in FSMA 2000 s 1F, in summary, as (a) the financial markets; (b) the markets for regulated financial services and (c) the markets for services that are provided by persons other than authorised persons in carrying on regulated activities but are provided without contravening the general prohibition.
139 FSMA 2000 s 1B(2).
140 ibid s 1B and 1EB.
141 ibid s 1C defined as 'securing an appropriate degree of protection for consumers'.
142 ibid s 1D defined as 'protecting and enhancing the integrity of the UK financial system'.
143 ibid s 1E defined as 'promoting effective competition in the interests of consumers in the markets for— (a) regulated financial services, or (b) services provided by a recognised investment exchange in carrying on regulated activities in respect of which it is by virtue of section 285(2) exempt from the general prohibition'.
144 ibid s 1B(6).
145 ibid s 1B.
146 ibid, s 3B(1)(c). This provision also applies to the PRA.

> compliance with section 1 of the Climate Change Act 2008. This new regulatory principle will cement the Government's long-term commitment to transform the economy in line with our net zero strategy and vision to make the UK a net zero financial centre by ensuring that the FCA and the PRA must have regard to these considerations when discharging their functions.[147]
>
> ... [W]e should not underestimate the significance of Clause 25, which will embed in statute consideration of the UK's climate target across the full breadth of the regulators' rule-making and therefore support the Government's action and ambition to transform the UK economy in line with their net zero strategy and vision.[148]
>
> ... It is important to recognise that addressing climate change and nature issues is not the regulators' primary function, which is, broadly, to advance their objectives, including to protect the integrity of the financial markets and the safety and soundness of firms within the financial system and to deliver appropriate protection for consumers. Most of the levers for reaching our net- zero and environmental targets sit outside the regulators' remit and control.[149]

4.64 The debates further make clear that the nature of the statutory duty means that it is ultimately a matter for the FCA itself, the independent regulator, to determine how best to meet the requirements placed on it in primary legislation.[150] It therefore remains to be seen how the FCA will approach this regulatory principle.

4.65 By section 1JA of the FSMA 2000, the Treasury has the power to set out in writing various recommendations to the FCA in relation to aspects of the government's economic policy to which the FCA should have regard when considering *inter alia* its strategic objective, operational objectives and the regulatory principles. In the remit letter in December 2022, the Chancellor set out that the government's economic policy includes increasing long-term energy security and delivering net zero.[151] In his specific recommendations as to what aspects of the economic policy the FCA should have regard to, the Chancellor referred to sustainable economic growth and sustainable finance, but not specifically climate change or biodiversity. This contrasts with the previous remit letter, dated 23 March 2021, which specifically required the FCA to have regard to climate change and stated as follows:[152]

> The government wishes to deliver a financial system which supports and enables a net-zero economy by mobilising private finance towards sustainable and resilient growth and

---

147 Promoting Minister, the Rt Hon Andrew Griffith MP at the Public Bill Committee in HC Deb 27 October 2022, vol 721, col 158.
148 Promoting Minister, Baroness Penn, during the Second Siting on the Bill in the House of Lords, in HL Deb 30 January 2023, vol 827, col 169GC.
149 Baroness Penn in the House of Lords, in HL Deb 27 June 2023, vol 831, col 605–606.
150 ibid.
151 HM Treasury, 'Recommendations for the Financial Conduct Authority' (2022) <https://assets.publishing.service.gov.uk/media/639227cee90e0769b493a15e/FCA_Remit_Letter_December_2022_with_cover.pdf> accessed 16 May 2024.
152 Rishi Sunak (Chancellor), 'Letter to the Chief Executive of the Financial Conduct Authority Nikhil Rathi' <https://assets.publishing.service.gov.uk/government/uploads/system/uploads/attachment_data/file/972445/CX_Letter_-_FCA_Remit_230321.pdf> accessed 16 May 2024.

is resilient to the physical and transition risks that climate change presents. The FCA should have regard to the government's commitment to achieve a net-zero economy by 2050 under the Climate Change Act 2008 (order 2019) when considering how to achieve its objectives and discharge its functions.

4.66 The FCA has an environmental, social and governance strategy,[153] which specifically addresses climate change. The regulator has set the following initial priorities (FS19/6): (i) disclosure and transparency; (ii) integrating consideration of climate change in firms' business, risk and investment decisions; and (iii) promoting consumer access to genuinely green products and services.[154] Further, in its strategy for 2022–2025,[155] the FCA sets out its actions in this area, which include: (i) building trust in the market for sustainable investment products and addressing greenwashing through disclosures and product labelling; and, (ii) improving ESG data, ratings and assurance.

153 'A Strategy for Positive Change: Our ESG Priorities' (FCA, 21 November 2022) <https://www.fca.org.uk/publications/corporate-documents/strategy-positive-change-our-esg-priorities> accessed 16 May 2024.
154 ibid.
155 FCA, 'Our Strategy 2022 to 2025' <https://www.fca.org.uk/publication/corporate/our-strategy-2022-25.pdf> accessed 16 May 2024.

PART II

PLANNING AND ENVIRONMENTAL

CHAPTER 5

LAND USE PLANNING

Christopher Moss

The role of the planning system

5.01 In 'Mission Zero – Independent Review of Net Zero', the chair of the independent review, Chris Skidmore MP, stated that the planning system 'should be an essential tool in delivering the changes needed for net zero'.[1] As well as being key in climate change mitigation, land use planning also has an essential role in ensuring development is adapted to climate change and helping to achieve nature positive development.[2]

5.02 This chapter provides a broad overview of how the planning system works to help achieve net zero and nature positive by looking, in outline, at the following topics:

- The role of the planning system;
- National planning policies;
- Local plan policies;
- Net zero and nature positive as material considerations;
- Balancing material considerations; and
- Planning conditions and obligations.

5.03 The rest of the section addresses more discrete topics in planning and environmental law.

5.04 The role of planning in this sphere is twofold. First, both preserving and enhancing land are important in tackling climate change and enhancing biodiversity: for example, the protection of woodlands and wetlands that provide carbon sinks and habitats for a

1 Department for Energy Security and Net Zero, 'Mission Zero: Independent Review of Net Zero' (2022) para 818 <https://assets.publishing.service.gov.uk/media/63c0299ee90e0771c128965b/mission-zero-independent-review.pdf> accessed 3 April 2024.

2 Department for Levelling Up, Housing and Communities, 'Planning Policy Guidance – Climate Change' (2014) para 001 <https://www.gov.uk/guidance/climate-change> accessed 3 April 2024.

diverse array of species;[3] and second, in enabling and encouraging development aimed at the transition to net zero and nature positive. Examples include local plans requiring residential developments to be zero-carbon,[4] and national policy, setting out the policy framework for energy projects,[5] under the Planning Act 2008 ('PA 2008').[6] The planning system operates alongside other pollution control regimes to help mitigate pollution (including, for example, greenhouse gas ('GHG') emissions, the release of nutrients into water courses and particulate pollution) caused by development.[7]

5.05 There are concerns, however, that the current system is stymying progress 'with inconsistent and misaligned decisions undermining local efforts to deliver [n]et [z]ero [a]ctions'.[8] Indeed, the Climate Change Committee ('CCC') has recommended that 'planning policy needs radical reform to support [n]et [z]ero'.[9]

5.06 In summary, the planning system works as follows:[10]

- At the heart of the planning system is the Town and Country Planning Act 1990 ('TCPA 1990'), which provides the framework for making local development plans, determining planning applications and challenging decisions.[11]

- Central government, specifically the Secretary of State for Housing, Communities and Local Government[12] sets national policy and guidance to be followed, such as the National Planning Policy Framework ('NPPF'), supplemented by Planning Practice Guidance ('PPG') and, in respect of some infrastructure projects, National Policy Statements ('NPSs').[13]

---

3 The Royal Society, 'Climate Change and Land: Opportunities and Challenges for the UK' (2019) 2 <https://royalsociety.org/-/media/policy/projects/climate-change/IPCC-special-report-briefing-climate-change-and-land.pdf> accessed 4 April 2023.
4 Reading Borough Council, 'Reading Borough Local Plan' (2019) Policy H5, 82 <https://images.reading.gov.uk/2019/12/Local_Plan_Adopted_November_2019.pdf> accessed 4 April 2024.
5 Department for Energy Security and Net Zero, 'Overarching National Policy Statement for Energy (EN-1)' (2023) <https://assets.publishing.service.gov.uk/media/65bbfbdc709fe1000f637052/overarching-nps-for-energy-en1.pdf> accessed 4 April 2024.
6 Discussed in more detail in Chapter 6.
7 For example, those set up through the Control of Pollution Act 1974, Environmental Protection Act 1990, Pollution Prevention and Control Act 1999; environmental permitting is discussed further in Chapter 13.
8 Climate Change Committee, 'Progress in Reducing Emissions: 2023 Report to Parliament' (2023) 366 <https://www.theccc.org.uk/wp-content/uploads/2023/06/Progress-in-reducing-UK-emissions-2023-Report-to-Parliament.pdf> accessed 4 April 2024.
9 ibid 15.
10 See Department for Levelling Up, Housing and Communities, 'Plain English Guide to the Planning System' (2015) <https://assets.publishing.service.gov.uk/media/601034938fa8f5655299d23e/Plain_ English_guide_to_the_planning_system.pdf> accessed 4 April 2024. For a more detailed guide to the planning system see Richard Harwood, *Planning Permission* (1st edn, Bloomsbury Publishing 2016).
11 Other planning-specific acts such as the Planning and Compulsory Purchase Act 2004, which introduced local development plans, and the PA 2008, which deals with nationally significant infrastructure projects. NSIPs are addressed in detail in Chapter 6.
12 The name of the department has been subjected to change on a number of occasions. Previously, it was 'Communities and Local Government' from 2005 to 2016, 'Housing Communities and Local Government' from 2016 to September 2021, 'Levelling Up, Housing and Communities' from September 2021 and has been under the current name from July 2024 to the time of writing.
13 NPSs are made in accordance with the planning act. They are addressed in detail in Chapter 6 (particularly paras 6.12–6.27), which addresses the making and review of NPSs.

- Local planning authorities must prepare and maintain a local development plan,[14] which sets out the broad policy framework for development within their area.[15] Neighbourhood plans may also be developed by communities at a smaller level set by the local planning authority.[16]

- The control of land use in England is plan-led, meaning that planning applications must be determined in accordance with the development plan for an area, unless material considerations indicate otherwise.[17] In most cases, the NPPF and PPG are material considerations that must be taken into account where relevant. Whether other factors constitute material considerations depends on the relevant planning policy and facts of a particular case. The weight to be given to a material consideration is a matter for the decision-maker.[18]

- Those proposing development, which is not permitted development,[19] should make an application for planning permission. Generally, an application should be made to the local planning authority. Applications for major infrastructure projects in the fields of energy, transport, water, waste water, and waste[20] are made to the Secretary of State as Development Consent Orders.[21]

- A planning application can be 'called-in' by the Secretary of State,[22] and this can be done regardless of whether a party has requested it. Applications are usually called-in where planning issues of more than local importance are involved.[23]

- If a local planning authority refuses to give planning permission, grants it subject to conditions, or fails to deal with the application within statutory time limits, the applicant has a right to appeal to the Secretary of State via the Planning Inspectorate.[24] Planning appeals can be 'recovered' from the Planning Inspectorate

---

14 Planning and Compulsory Purchase Act 2004 s 15(1).

15 Department for Levelling Up, Housing and Communities, 'National Planning Policy Framework' (2023) para 35–37 <https://assets.publishing.service.gov.uk/media/65a11af7e8f5ec000f1f8c46/NPPF_December_2023.pdf> accessed 2 April 2024. Before coming into effect, local plans are examined by an independent inspector whose role is to consider whether the plan has been prepared in line with the relevant legal requirements and whether it is 'sound', namely whether it is: positively prepared, justified, effective, and consistent with national policy.

16 TCPA 1990 s 61E, s 61G. These are also subject to an independent examination and take effect following a community referendum. Once made, neighbourhood plans form part of the local planning authority's development plan.

17 Planning and Compulsory Purchase Act 2004 s 38(6), TCPA 1990 s 70(2). If a development plan is out of date, then the 'tilted balance' policy in paragraph 11(d) of the NPPF applies. This provides that the application should be approved, unless it is in a protected area or the harms caused by the application significantly outweigh its benefits.

18 *Cala Homes (South) Ltd v (1) SSCLG (2) Winchester CC* [2011] 1 P&CR 22, Lindblom J at [31].

19 There are certain types of development, where it has been determined nationally or locally, that there is no need to apply for planning permission.

20 Thresholds for what constitutes a national significant infrastructure project and that must thus follow the development consent order process, are set out in the PA 2008 ss 14–30A.

21 PA 2008 s 104. Development Consent Orders and the process by which they are made are addressed in paras 6.28–6.39 in Chapter 6.

22 TCPA 1990 s 76A.

23 If the Secretary of State decides to call-in a planning application, a planning inspector is appointed to carry out an inquiry into the proposal. The inspector will then report with their recommendation to the Secretary of State, who will make a decision on the proposal.

24 TCPA 1990 s 78.

for determination by the Secretary of State, to determine if a case raises particular issues that justify a ministerial decision. In this case, the inspector will then report with their recommendation to the Secretary of State, who will make a decision on the proposal, in much the same way as a planning permission that has been 'called-in'.

- Planning decisions may be subject to legal challenge by way of statutory review on the basis that the decision was not within the appropriate power, or a procedural requirement has not been complied with.[25] A planning statutory review must be brought within 6 weeks of the decision under challenge.[26]

5.07 The status quo in the planning system has been criticised for being riddled with 'bottlenecks',[27] and preventing necessary development through 'restrictive planning rules';[28] with the CCC recommending a review and update of the NPPF 'to ensure that net zero outcomes are consistently prioritised through the planning system, making clear that these should work in conjunction with, rather than being over-ridden by, other outcomes such as development viability'.[29]

5.08 One of the key drivers of decarbonisation is a fast transition from reliance on fossil fuels to clean and renewable energy.[30] This will require adaption of existing, and development of new, significant infrastructure, which the government acknowledges will require 'faster, fairer and more effective planning regimes'.[31]

5.09 Despite the government's commitment to achieving net zero by 2050,[32] the recognised importance of the planning system in achieving this objective, the criticism of the current system, and the acknowledgment by government of the need for change;[33] the necessary change, such as an explicit commitment to net zero in planning policy, has not been forthcoming. Recent legislation and policy in the form of the Levelling Up and Regeneration Act 2023, and changes to the NPPF are simply tinkering around the edges.[34] A failure to address substantially issues with the system will materially impact the UK's ability to achieve net zero.

5.10 Other promised changes have simply not come to fruition. For example, the government committed to publishing a land use framework in 2023 that would reflect

---

25 TCPA 1990 ss 287–288.
26 TCPA 1990 s 287(2B), s 288(4B).
27 Department for Energy Security and Net Zero, 'Mission Zero: Independent Review of Net Zero' (n 1) 11, para 24.
28 Climate Change Committee, 'Progress in Reducing Emissions: 2023 Report to Parliament' (n 8) 15.
29 ibid 33.
30 Department for Energy Security and Net Zero, 'Powering Up Britain' (2023) 6 <https://assets.publishing.service.gov.uk/media/642468ff2fa8480013ec0f39/powering-up-britain-joint-overview.pdf> accessed 4 April 2024.
31 ibid 23; Department for Energy Security and Net Zero, *Carbon Budget Delivery Plan* (HC 2023, 1269) 173 and 186 <https://assets.publishing.service.gov.uk/media/6424b2d760a35e000c0cb135/carbon-budget-delivery-plan.pdf> accessed 4 April 2024.
32 Climate Change Act 2008 s 1.
33 Department for Energy Security and Net Zero, 'Powering Up Britain' (n 30) 23.
34 This is despite reform of the NPPF 'to make sure it contributes to climate change mitigation and adaption as fully as possible' being an aim of the Government's Net Zero Strategy – Department for Energy Security and Net Zero, 'Net Zero Strategy: Build Back Greener' (2021) 267 <https://www.gov.uk/government/publications/net-zero-strategy> accessed 28 September 2023.

'objectives for English agriculture … [and] inform incentives we build into our agri-environment schemes and … be a valuable resource for responsible authorities as they prepare their Local Nature Recovery Strategies'.[35] At the time of writing, the land use framework is due to be published at an unspecified time in 2024,[36] and will only take the form of guidance, rather than being prescriptive in any way.[37]

5.11 An array of environmental focused legislation also impacts planning decisions, particularly in respect of nature positive considerations, for example, Section 40 of the Natural Environment and Rural Communities Act 2006 ('NERCA 2006'),[38] and the biodiversity net gain requirement set out in section 98 and schedule 14 of the Environment Act 2021 ('EA 2021').[39]

National planning policies

5.12 Planning policy is 'a statement by a person or body of how they would or are likely to reach a decision or how they would like others to act' used to inform and guide decisions on planning applications.[40]

5.13 The NPPF sets the national direction for planning policy in England; and is a material consideration in planning decisions. Since its creation in 2012, the NPPF has recognised the importance of the planning system in adapting to, and mitigating the effects of, climate change and improving biodiversity. The NPPF states that, at a high level, 'the purpose of the planning system is to contribute to the achievement of sustainable development'.[41] Sustainable development is defined in paragraph 8 of the NPPF:[42]

> Achieving sustainable development means that the planning system has three overarching objectives, which are interdependent and need to be pursued in mutually supportive ways (so that opportunities can be taken to secure net gains across each of the different objectives):
>
> a) an economic objective – …;
> b) a social objective – …;
> c) an environmental objective – to protect and enhance our natural, built and historic environment; including making effective use of land, improving biodiversity, using natural resources prudently, minimising waste and pollution, and mitigating and adapting to climate change, including moving to a low carbon economy.

35 Department for Environment, Food and Rural Affairs, *Government Food Strategy* (CP 698, 2022) para 1.2.3 <https://assets.publishing.service.gov.uk/media/62a6eb418fa8f5039a1bd7b5/government-food-strategy.pdf> accessed 4 April 2024.
36 HC Deb 21 March 2024, vol 747, cols 1148–1149.
37 HL Deb 12 March 2024, vol 836, col 1901.
38 Section 40 of NERCA 2006 is addressed in Chapter 8 at paras 8.20 and 8.96–8.101.
39 These topics are considered further in Chapter 10, in Chapter 8 (on section 40 of NERAC 2006: see paras 8.20 and 8.96–8.101) and in Chapter 24 (see paras 24.06, 24.23 and 24.38 on biodiversity net gain in an agricultural context).
40 Richard Harwood and Victoria Hutton, *Planning Policy* (1st edn, Bloomsbury Publishing 2018) 1, para 1.1.
41 Department for Levelling Up, Housing and Communities, 'National Planning Policy Framework' (n 15) para 7.
42 The principle of sustainable development is discussed in detail in Chapter 3 (see paras 3.04 and 3.50–3.64).

5.14 This aim is reflected in the presumption of sustainable development set out in paragraph 11 of the NPPF.[43] In *R (Friends of the Earth Ltd and others) v Heathrow Airport Ltd*, Lord Hodge and Lord Sales held that when considering the principle of sustainable development, 'these elements have to be taken into account and balanced against each other'.[44] The weight that is to be given to each element is a matter for the decision-maker, depending on the context of the matter they are dealing with.

5.15 The NPPF also contains specific sections on 'Meeting the Challenge of Climate Change, Flooding and Coastal Change'[45] and 'Conserving and Enhancing the Natural Environment'.[46] Section 14 materially provides:

> 157. The planning system should support the transition to a low carbon future in a changing climate, taking full account of flood risk and coastal change. It should help to: shape places in ways that contribute to radical reductions in greenhouse gas emissions, minimise vulnerability and improve resilience; encourage the reuse of existing resources, including the conversion of existing buildings; and support renewable and low carbon energy and associated infrastructure.
>
> 158. Plans should take a proactive approach to mitigating and adapting to climate change, taking into account the long-term implications for flood risk, coastal change, water supply, biodiversity and landscapes, and the risk of overheating from rising temperatures. Policies should support appropriate measures to ensure the future resilience of communities and infrastructure to climate change impacts, such as providing space for physical protection measures, or making provision for the possible future relocation of vulnerable development and infrastructure.
>
> 159. New development should be planned for in ways that:
> a) avoid increased vulnerability to the range of impacts arising from climate change. When new development is brought forward in areas which are vulnerable, care should be taken to ensure that risks can be managed through suitable adaptation measures, including through the planning of green infrastructure; and
> b) can help to reduce greenhouse gas emissions, such as through its location, orientation and design. Any local requirements for the sustainability of buildings should reflect the Government's policy for national technical standards.

5.16 Section 15 provides that planning policies and decisions should 'contribute to and enhance the natural and local environment'.[47] Plans should:

> a) Identify, map and safeguard components of local wildlife-rich habitats and wider ecological networks, including the hierarchy of international, national and locally designated sites of importance for biodiversity; wildlife corridors and stepping stones

---

43 Department for Levelling Up, Housing and Communities, 'National Planning Policy Framework' (n 15) para 11.
44 *R (Friends of the Earth Ltd and others) v Heathrow Airport Ltd* [2020] UKSC 52 [115].
45 Department for Levelling Up, Housing and Communities, 'National Planning Policy Framework' (n 15) s 14.
46 ibid s 15.
47 ibid para 180.

that connect them; and areas identified by national and local partnerships for habitat management, enhancement, restoration or creation; and

b) promote the conservation, restoration and enhancement of priority habitats, ecological networks and the protection and recovery of priority species; and identify and pursue opportunities for securing measurable net gains for biodiversity.[48]

5.17 When determining planning applications, local planning authorities should:

- Refuse planning permission if significant harm to biodiversity cannot be avoided, adequately mitigated, or as a last resort, compensated for;

- Normally refuse planning permission for development 'on land within or outside a Site of Special Scientific Interest, and which is likely to have an adverse effect on it (either individually or in combination with other developments)' unless the benefits clearly outweigh 'both its likely impact on the features of the site that make it of special scientific interest, and any broader impacts on the national network of Sites of Special Scientific Interest';

- Refuse development that will result in the loss or deterioration of irreplaceable habitats unless there are 'wholly exceptional reasons and a suitable compensation strategy';

- Support development whose primary objective is to conserve or enhance biodiversity; and

- Integrate opportunities to improve biodiversity in and around developments as part of their design.[49]

5.18 The presumption in favour of sustainable development will also not apply 'where the plan or project is likely to have a significant effect on a habitats site (either alone or in combination with other plans or projects), unless an appropriate assessment has concluded that the plan or project will not adversely affect the integrity of the habitats site'.[50]

5.19 In addition to the NPPF, the Secretary of State may publish national policy statements in relation to one or more specified descriptions of development.[51] A national policy statement must give reasons for the policy,[52] and these 'reasons must (in particular) include an explanation of how the policy set out in the statement takes account of government policy relating to the mitigation of, and adaptation to, climate change.'[53] The Secretary of State may review and update national policy statements from time to

---

48 ibid para 185.
49 ibid, para 186.
50 ibid, para 188.
51 PA 2008 s 5(1); see Chapter 6 for further detail on NPSs, particularly paras 6.12–6.27 and 6.46–6.56.
52 PA 2008 s 5(7).
53 PA 2008 s 5(8).

time.[54] For example, the Energy NPSs were revised in January 2024, with the intention that revisions would help with 'speeding up planning and networks'.[55]

5.20 When publishing or reviewing national policy statements, the Secretary of State must do so with 'the objective of contributing to the achievement of sustainable development'[56] and in particular, 'have regard to the desirability of mitigating, and adapting to, climate change'.[57]

5.21 Despite the number of national policies referring to the desirability of mitigating and adapting to climate change, national policy does not go into detail as to how the planning system should achieve these aims. Some broad guidance is given in respect of adaptation and mitigation in PPGs;[58] but in terms of setting tangible policies for achieving net zero, and mitigating and adapting to climate change, this is essentially left to local planning authorities to address in their development plans, or to the Secretary of State in terms of NPSs.

5.22 Improving biodiversity is also recognised as a key part of sustainable development.[59] In addition, the government has published a number of action plans and strategies addressing biodiversity. The core policy document is the 25 Year Environment Plan 2018, which sets out the government's aims for improving the environment within a generation.[60] In January 2023, the government published an Environmental Implementation Plan,[61] providing a five-year update on the 25 Year Plan.[62]

Local plan policies

5.23 Section 15(1) of the Planning and Compulsory Purchase Act 2004 ('PCPA 2004') requires all local planning authorities to prepare and maintain a scheme to be known as their local development scheme. Section 19(1A) of the same Act establishes that local plans must 'include policies designed to secure that the development and use of land in the local planning authority's area contribute to the mitigation of, and adaptation to, climate change'. Further, section 19(1B) provides that '[e]ach local planning authority must identify the strategic priorities for the development and use of land in the authority's area'.

---

54 PA 2008 s 6.
55 Department for Energy Security and Net Zero, 'Powering Up Britain' (n 30) 8.
56 PA 2008 s 10(2).
57 PA 2008 s 10(3)(a).
58 Department for Levelling Up, Housing and Communities, 'Planning Policy Guidance – Climate Change' (n 2).
59 Department for Levelling Up, Housing and Communities, 'National Planning Policy Framework' (n 15) para 8(c).
60 Department for Environment, Food and Rural Affairs, 'A Green Future: Our 25 Year Plan to Improve the Environment' (2018) <https://assets.publishing.service.gov.uk/media/5ab3a67840f0b65bb584297e/25-year-environment-plan.pdf> accessed 4 April 2024.
61 DEFRA, 'Environmental Improvement Plan 2023: First Revision of the 25 Year Environment Plan' (2023) <https://assets.publishing.service.gov.uk/media/64a6d9c1c531eb000c64fffa/environmental-improvement-plan-2023.pdf> accessed 4 April 2024.
62 Addressed in further detail in Chapter 8 at paras 8.61–8.64 and in Chapter 11 at para 11.03.

5.24 These requirements work together. This can be seen from paragraph 20 of the NPPF, which identifies the issues that should be addressed through strategic policies:

> Strategic policies should set out an overall strategy for the pattern, scale and design quality of places, and make sufficient provision for: a) housing (including affordable housing), employment, retail, leisure and other commercial development; b) infrastructure for transport, telecommunications, security, waste management, water supply, wastewater, flood risk and coastal change management, and the provision of minerals and energy (including heat); c) community facilities (such as health, education and cultural infrastructure); and d) conservation and enhancement of the natural, built and historic environment, including landscapes and green infrastructure, *and planning measures to address climate change mitigation and adaptation.*[63] (emphasis added)

5.25 Further, in making a local plan, paragraphs 157–164 of the NPPF, addressed above, set out the need for 'radical reductions' in GHG emissions and for plans to take a 'proactive approach' to mitigating and adapting to climate change, 'in line' with the objectives and provisions of the Climate Change Act 2008 ('CCA 2008').[64] Local development plans ought therefore to play a strong role in ensuring the planning system works towards net zero. Indeed, the London Plan 2021 expressly requires that major developments should be net zero-carbon,[65] schemes which will be referred to the Mayor of London must include a whole life cycle carbon emission assessment,[66] boroughs must establish and administer a carbon offset fund, and any shortfall against the net zero-carbon target on site must be met via another scheme or cash payment to the local authority's carbon offset fund.[67]

5.26 As per the 'soundness test' in the NPPF, local plans can only stipulate specific net zero and/or nature positive aligned policies in their Local Plans, if they are demonstrated through evidence to be viable, deliverable, and in line with national law and policy.[68]

5.27 Research conducted by Climate Emergency UK and Anthesis to score all UK councils on their climate action[69] identified that whilst more than 300 local authorities across the UK have declared climate emergency since 2018,[70] authorities scored poorly

---

63 Mitigation being measures to prevent or reduce the emission of GHGs, adaption being the process of adjusting to the current and future effects of climate change.
64 Department for Levelling Up, Housing and Communities, 'National Planning Policy Framework' (n 15) para 158, fn 56: 'In line with the objectives and provisions of the Climate Change Act 2008.'
65 Mayor of London, 'The London Plan 2021' (2021) 357 <https://www.london.gov.uk/sites/default/files/the_london_plan_2021.pdf> accessed 4 April 2024.
66 ibid 395–396, 399.
67 ibid 395.
68 Department for Levelling Up, Housing and Communities, 'National Planning Policy Framework' (n 15) para 35.
69 Climate Emergency UK, 'Council Climate Action Scorecards Methodology: 2023 Action Scorecards' (2023) <https://councilclimatescorecards.uk/methodology/> accessed 4 April 2024.
70 Climate Emergency UK, 'Scorecards Successes: What Factors Enable Climate Action within UK Local Authorities?' (2024) 6 <https://climateemergency.uk/wp-content/uploads/2024/03/Scorecards_ Successes_report_CEUK_DIGITAL.pdf> accessed 4 April 2024.

on using their planning powers to enable and encourage low emission development.[71] Climate Emergency UK's report highlighted that a key influence is the lack of national guidance and support, and emphasised the need for central government support for local authorities on how councils can 'deliver and enable action towards net zero'.[72]

5.28 The soundness of a local plan's net zero policy relating to the energy efficiency of new buildings in a new garden village was considered in *R (Rights Community Action Ltd) v Secretary of State for Levelling Up, Housing and Communities*.[73] This concerned two inspectors appointed by the Secretary of State to review the area action plan of Salt Cross garden village. Lieven J held that they had been wrong in law to find that Policy 2 of the action plan, which required development at Salt Cross to demonstrate net zero operational carbon, conflicted with national policy on energy efficiency and was thus unsound. The inspectors had concluded that the building energy efficiency standards demanded by the action plan were significantly higher than that required in the Building Regulations and that consequently, this was contrary to national policy as set out in a 2015 written ministerial statement on energy performance requirements. Lieven J held that it was plainly wrong, based on both the wording and subsequent context of the 2015 statement, to find that it prevented the local planning authority ('LPA') from setting a higher standard than in the Building Regulations.[74] The case highlights the complexity of government policy in the area of energy efficiency building regulations and the minefield faced by LPAs seeking to act progressively and exceed them. The 2015 statement was also superseded in December 2023 with the government's current position being that it 'does not expect plan-makers to set local energy efficiency standards for buildings that go beyond current or planned buildings regulations' and that planning policies which go beyond current or planning buildings regulation 'should be rejected at examination if they do not have a well-reasoned and robustly costed rationale' that ensures development remains viable, the impact on housing supply and affordability is considered, and the additional requirement is expressed as a percentage uplift of a dwelling's Target Emissions Rate.[75]

Net zero and nature positive as material considerations

5.29 Net zero and nature positive may also be relevant considerations when determining an application for planning permission. A decision-maker dealing with an application for planning permission must have regard to material considerations when determining an application.[76] Section 38(6) of the PCPA Act 2004 additionally provides that: 'If

---

71 Climate Emergency UK, 'Action Scorecards 2023: Planning & Land Use' (2023) <https://council climatescore cards.uk/sections/s3_p_lu/> accessed 4 April 2024 – The mean level of success in planning and land use across Single Tier, District, County and Northern Irish local authorities was 11.75%.

72 Climate Emergency UK, 'Scorecards Successes: What Factors Enable Climate Action within UK Local Authorities?' (n 70) 3.

73 *R (Rights Community Action Ltd) v Secretary of State for Levelling Up, Housing and Communities* [2024] EWHC 359 (Admin).

74 *ibid* [75]–[78].

75 Department for Levelling Up, Housing and Communities, 'Planning – Local Energy Efficiency Standards Update, Statement UIN HLWS120' (2023) <https://questions-statements.parliament.uk/written-statements/detail/2023-12-13/hlws120> accessed 19 April 2024.

76 TCPA 1990 s 70(2)(c).

regard is to be had to the development plan for the purpose of any determination to be made under the planning Acts the determination must be made in accordance with the plan unless material considerations indicate otherwise.'

5.30 What then is a material consideration? Lindblom J held that 'it encompasses any consideration bearing on the use or development of land. Whether a particular consideration is material in a particular case will depend on the circumstances.'[77] In *R (ClientEarth) v Secretary of State for Business, Energy and Industrial Strategy*, Holgate J explained at [99]:[78]

> A legally relevant consideration is only something that is not irrelevant or immaterial, and therefore something which the decision-maker is empowered or entitled to take into account. But a decision-maker does not fail to take a relevant consideration into account unless he was under an obligation to do so. Accordingly, for this type of allegation it is necessary for a claimant to show that the decision-maker was expressly or impliedly required by the legislation (or by a policy which had to be applied) to take the particular consideration into account, or whether on the facts of the case, the matter was so 'obviously material', that it was irrational not to have taken it into account.

5.31 Accordingly, unless a factor is specified in law or policy to be a material consideration (for example, the NPPF), what may be a material consideration is largely a matter for the planning decision-maker subject to a rationality assessment.

5.32 A failure to take into account a material consideration is a failure to consider relevant factors, which is sufficient to render the ensuing decision unlawful, unless the court is satisfied that the decision-maker would have reached the same decision even if it had taken it into account[79] or it is highly likely that the outcome would not have been substantially different.[80]

5.33 A requirement to consider climate change mitigation and adaptation, and the need to achieve net zero, have not yet been set out as generally applicable material considerations in legislation or policy. However, they have both been recognised as important factors in planning decision making generally,[81] and a decision-maker is unlikely to be successfully challenged for taking these matters into account. Whether climate change mitigation and/or adaptation constitute a consideration that must be taken into account, at present, depends on the facts and circumstances of the case (in particular, the relevant planning and legal context). Indeed, this point was made by

---

77 *Cala Homes (South) Ltd v (1) SSCLG (2) Winchester CC* (n 18) [32].
78 *R (ClientEarth) v Secretary of State for Business, Energy and Industrial Strategy* [2020] EWHC (Admin) 1303, Holgate J at [99]; See also the Supreme Court decision in *R (Friends of the Earth) v Secretary of State for Transport* [2021] PTSR 190 [116]–[121].
79 *Simplex G E (Holdings) Ltd and another v Secretary of State for the Environment and another* [1988] 3 PLR 25.
80 Senior Courts Act 1981 s 31(2A).
81 Discussed at 1.24 above in respect of local development plans.

Lieven J in *Frack Free Balcombe Residents Association v Secretary of State for Levelling Up, Housing and Communities* where she held:[82]

> There is no requirement, whether in statute or caselaw, that every planning decision has to expressly refer to or quantify the GHG emissions that will result. Climate change is likely to be a material consideration in every planning decision given the policy context as well as the much wider issues, but that does not mean that every decision has to have reference to specific figures or assessment. Each case will depend on its own factual and policy context.

5.34 In respect of where the impact on climate change was a material consideration that needed to be taken into account on the facts of the case, see *R (McLennan) v Medway Council*.[83] Here, the claimant homeowner had objected to his neighbour's planning application, on the basis that such an extension would overshadow his solar panels and adversely affect his ability to generate electricity from them. The local authority held, in part, that the effect of daylight on the claimant's solar panels was a purely private interest that should not be considered as part of the planning process.

5.35 The claimant applied for judicial review of the local authority's decision, on the basis that the impact on his solar panels was a material consideration which the local authority had failed to take into account. This challenge was successful. Lane J quashed the grant of permission, on the basis that consideration of the impact on the claimant's solar panels was a material consideration:[84]

> [B]oth the local plan and, more recently and much more particularly, the NPPF recognise the positive contribution that can be made to climate change by even small-scale renewable energy schemes ...[85]
>
> What emerges from section 19(1A) [PCPA 2004] and the NPPF is that mitigation of climate change is a legitimate planning consideration. The fact that both section 19 and the NPPF speak in broad terms (as they plainly must) cannot mean their message vanishes at the very point where consideration has to be given to a specific proposal. Such an approach would render the provisions a dead letter. Nor does the fact that they relate to new rather than existing development defeat the rationality challenge. If the issue of climate change is regarded as having a material planning bearing on particular proposed development, it is illogical to regard that issue as suddenly becoming immaterial, once the development had taken place.[86]

82 *Frack Free Balcombe Residents Association v Secretary of State for Levelling Up, Housing and Communities* [2023] EWHC 2548 (Admin) [65]. This case is discussed in more detail in Chapter 17 at paras 17.62–17.63 and 17.67.
83 *R (McLennan) v Medway Council* [2019] EWHC 1738 (Admin). Other recent examples of where a development's impact on climate change have been considered material considerations include *Bramley Solar Power Residents Group v SSLUHC* [2023] EWHC 2842 (Admin) and *Project Genesis Ltd v Secretary of State for Levelling Up, Housing and Communities* [2024] EWHC 368 (Admin). In these cases, the relevance of climate change was not disputed as part of the legal challenge.
84 *R (McLennan) v Medway Council* (n 83) [37].
85 ibid [34].
86 ibid [36].

> ... given what is now said at national level about climate change in relation to new development, the first defendant is not entitled to reject as immaterial, in planning terms, the effect that another development proposal may have upon a renewable energy system, such as the claimant's solar panels. That, however, is the stance of the first defendant. It is a stance which, I find, no reasonable authority could take. It is, in short, irrational.

5.36 It is clear from Lane J's decision that mitigation of climate change is a consideration that a decision-maker is entitled to consider; however, that it amounted to a material consideration that needed to be considered turned on the specific facts of the case; in particular, the specific recognition in the defendant's local plan of the importance of renewable energy schemes in combatting climate change.

5.37 An area of development impacting climate change that has gained traction relatively recently is the concept of embodied carbon. Embodied carbon represents the carbon dioxide (CO_2) emissions associated with materials and construction processes throughout the whole lifecycle of a building or infrastructure – so, from the manufacture and transport of materials, to the construction process, maintenance, and demolition of the building itself.[87] The House of Commons Environmental Audit Committee stated that the introduction of a mandatory requirement to undertake a whole life carbon assessment for buildings would be 'the single most significant policy the Government could introduce'.[88]

5.38 As mentioned above, the London Plan 2021 requires schemes which will be referred to the Mayor of London to include a whole life cycle carbon emission assessment.[89] This includes developments of more than 150 residential units, over 30 metres in height (outside the City of London), and on Green Belt or Metropolitan Open Land.[90] The City of Westminster has also proposed a retrofit first policy as part of its local plan review.[91]

5.39 A recent example of the relevance of embodied carbon was the Secretary of State for Levelling Up, Housing and Communities' calling-in, and refusal of, Marks and Spencer's application to demolish and redevelop its Oxford Street shop.[92] There was no explicit blanket local or national policy requiring it to be considered as a material consideration.

---

87 Environmental Audit Committee, *Building to Net Zero: Costing Carbon in Construction, First Report of Session 2022–23*, 7 (HC 2022–23, 103) <https://committees.parliament.uk/publications/22427/documents/165446/default/> accessed 28 November 2023.
88 ibid 5.
89 Mayor of London, 'The London Plan 2021' (n 65) 395–396, 399.
90 The Town and Country Planning (Mayor of London) Order 2008, SI 2008/580, Schedule – Potential Strategic Importance, part 1.
91 City of Westminster, 'City Plan – Regulation 18 Statement, Notice of Partial Review of Westminster's City Plan Development Plan Document' (2022).
92 Department for Levelling Up, Housing and Communities, 'Called-in Decision: 456–472 Oxford Street, London W1 (Ref: 3301508 – 20 July 2023)' <https://assets.publishing.service.gov.uk/media/64b90f082059dc00125d265b/23-07-20_DL_+_IR_456-472_OXFORD_STREET_LONDON_W1_-_3301508.pdf> accessed 4 April 2024.

5.40 Marks and Spencer's application was to demolish its existing Oxford Street buildings and replace them with a two basement and nine storey mixed-use retail development. The plan was supported by Westminster City Council and recommended for approval by an Inspector.[93] The Secretary of State disagreed with the Inspector's recommendation and refused permission. The three key issues were the impact on heritage, the extent to which the proposals were consistent with the UK's transition to a zero-carbon economy, and whether the benefits of the proposed development outweighed any heritage or climate change harm.

5.41 The second issue is of particular importance. The Secretary of State interpreted paragraph 152 of the NPPF as encompassing 'a strong presumption in favour of repurposing and reusing buildings … [and] that a strong reason would be needed to justify demolition and rebuilding'.[94] He held that Marks and Spencer had not presented 'an appropriately thorough exploration of alternatives to demolition' and that the proposals would 'in part fail to support the transition to a low carbon future, and would overall fail to encourage the reuse of existing resources, including the conversion of existing buildings' and that this carried 'moderate weight against the scheme'.[95] This failure, and the heritage impacts, were not outweighed by the benefits of the proposal, including Marks and Spencer's agreement to make carbon offset payments.[96]

5.42 Marks and Spencer successfully challenged the Secretary of State's refusal by way of statutory review.[97] Lieven J held that the Secretary of State had 'plain[ly] misinterpreted the NPPF',[98] and that although there is 'some encouragement [in 152] for the reuse of buildings',[99] there is 'nothing that comes close to a presumption'.[100] She concluded that, 'The [Secretary of State] has not applied the policy, he has rewritten it.'[101]

5.43 This error flowed into the rest of the Secretary of State's decision, in particular regarding embodied carbon. The Secretary of State had also been incorrect to find that the requirement in the London Plan for carbon offsetting applied to embodied carbon, not just operational carbon. Lieven J held that it was 'clear beyond any rational doubt … that the offsetting requirements … are in relation to operational carbon … This is because the reference to the Building Regulations necessarily includes a calculation based on the energy efficiency of the building in its operational phase, not the construction carbon impacts.'[102] Accordingly, the Secretary of State's refusal was quashed.

---

93 ibid para 3.
94 ibid para 24.
95 ibid para 45.
96 ibid paras 54–56.
97 *Marks and Spencer plc v Secretary of State for Levelling Up, Housing and Communities* [2024] EWHC 452 (Admin).
98 ibid [54].
99 ibid [55].
100 ibid.
101 ibid [56].
102 ibid [115].

5.44 Lieven J's decision in *Marks and Spencer* makes abundantly clear that there is no presumption in the NPPF in favour of a retrofit first policy and that where the NPPF creates a presumption, this will be 'made clear on the face of the NPPF'.[103] There is nothing from the *Marks and Spencer* decision that would stop a local authority supporting a retrofit first approach or requiring assessments of embodied carbon in their local plan; it is simply that the NPPF and London Plan do neither (in their current form at least).

5.45 Consideration of whether a development is nature positive is much closer to becoming a generally applicable material consideration, given the biodiversity net gain requirement set out in the Environment Act 2021.[104]

Balancing material considerations

5.46 If, in relation to a particular development, climate change, net zero, or nature positive amount to a material consideration, how is a decision-maker to balance these considerations with any competing material considerations and even each other? Unless statute or national policy set out a presumption in favour of net zero or nature positive development, balancing such a conflict is a matter of planning judgment, challengeable only on the basis of irrationality (save for where there is an express legal obligation). As Lord Hoffmann stated in *Tesco Stores Ltd v Secretary of State for the Environment*:[105]

> Provided that the planning authority has regard to all material considerations, it is at liberty (provided that it does not lapse into Wednesbury irrationality) to give them whatever weight the planning authority thinks fit or no weight at all. The fact that the law regards something as a material consideration therefore involves no view about the part, if any, which it should play in the decision-making process.

5.47 The *Bristol Airport Action Network* decision[106] is a clear example of the High Court considering this balancing exercise. Broadly, it was held that it was not irrational for the Council to have decided that the impact of aviation carbon emissions that would be caused by the expansion of Bristol airport was a matter for national, not local, decision-making.

5.48 The focus in this statutory review was whether, and to what extent, aviation emissions should play a role in deciding whether planning permission should be granted for the proposed extension of Bristol Airport. In particular, whether the defendant had properly interpreted two local plan policies regarding North Somerset Council's commitment to reduce carbon emissions and mitigate and adapt to climate change,[107] and that any proposal to develop Bristol Airport must demonstrate the satisfactory

---

103 ibid [57].
104 BNG is considered in detail in Chapter 10.
105 *Tesco Stores Ltd v Secretary of State for the Environment* [1995] 1 WLR 759 [206].
106 *R (Bristol Airport Action Network) v Secretary of State for Levelling Up, Housing and Communities (expansion of Bristol Airport)* [2023] EWHC 171 (Admin).
107 ibid [9], with reference to Local Plan Policy CS1.

resolution of environmental issues[108] and (as then applicable) paragraph 188 of the NPPF.[109]

5.49 The relevant version of paragraph 188 of the NPPF read as follows:

> The focus of planning policies and decisions should be on whether proposed development is an acceptable use of land, rather than the control of processes or emissions (where these are subject to separate pollution control regimes). Planning decisions should assume that these regimes will operate effectively. Equally, where a planning decision has been made on a particular development, the planning issues should not be revisited through the permitting regimes operated by pollution control authorities.

5.50 Lane J held that whilst the two relevant local plan policies were both wide enough to include the consideration of aircraft emissions, neither expressly stated how these should be addressed. He noted, 'the obvious fact that aviation emissions, which can occur at any point in an aircraft's journey to and from Bristol Airport, are of a different character from, for example, carbon emissions that can be addressed by reducing energy demand through good design of buildings in the area of N[orth] S[omerset] C[ouncil ('NSC')]'.[110] Accordingly, he held that it falls upon the individual decision-maker to exercise their judgement, in order to determine how such emissions should be dealt with under these policies.

5.51 In respect of paragraph 188 of the NPPF, it was argued that the panel had erred by assuming that (i) the Secretary of State would meet his obligations under the CCA 2008 and meet the carbon budgets; and that (ii) the assumption was irrebuttable. It was argued that paragraph 188, properly interpreted, 'does not require a planning decision-maker to assume that the Secretary of State will have acted within the time span of the carbon budgets to take the action required in order to discharge his responsibilities under the legislative scheme for climate'. It is therefore a question of law as to whether the CCA 2008 is included in the definition of 'pollution control regimes'. The appellants argued that the principle from *Gateshead MBC v Secretary of State for the Environment*[111] did not apply. The principle provides that where parallel pollution control regimes exist, it is not for the planning system to duplicate them; rather, it can be assumed that, absent contrary evidence, they will operate effectively. The claimant argued that the CCA 2008 obligation was not the sort of parallel pollution control regime to which the *Gateshead* principle would apply – rather, it should have been considered on a local level, in a similar manner to how air quality must be.

5.52 Lane J rejected this argument, holding that aircraft emissions are controlled at the national level, whereas, air quality issues have a 'significant and discrete local element'.[112]

108 ibid [63], with reference to Local Plan Policy CS23.
109 It is paragraph 194 of the December 2023 version of the NPPF.
110 *R (Bristol Airport Action Network) v Secretary of State for Levelling Up, Housing and Communities (expansion of Bristol Airport)* (n 106) [82].
111 *Gateshead MBC v Secretary of State for the Environment* [1996] 71 P & CR 350.
112 *R (Bristol Airport Action Network) v Secretary of State for Levelling Up, Housing and Communities (expansion of Bristol Airport)* (n 106) [139].

Ultimately, the decision provided that aircraft emissions should be addressed by the parallel pollution control mechanisms for GHG emissions under the CCA 2008.[113] Conceivably, the outcome would have been different had either of the two local plan policies considered expressly provided for how aircraft emissions should be addressed by the decision-maker.

5.53 For another similar example, see *R (Boswell) v Secretary of State for Transport.* It was held at first instance,[114] and in the Court of Appeal,[115] that it had not been irrational for the Secretary of State to assess the estimated carbon emissions from three road schemes individually against the national carbon budget, rather than in combination. This was largely on the basis that the assessment of whether impacts should be assessed cumulatively or individually is not a question of law, but a 'matter of degree and judgment'[116] dependent on the facts of a case, properly within the remit of the decision-maker, and thus impugnable only on the basis of irrationality. At first instance in *Boswell,* Thornton J's remark that the Court 'must be astute to avoid being drawn into the area of the merits of climate decision making' demonstrates the degree of judicial caution that is applied to consideration of this area.[117]

5.54 In practice, absent a specific policy or legislative provision setting out a particular approach to how to address an issue such as aircraft emissions, it will be a matter for the planning decision-maker.[118] To challenge the balancing exercise, it will therefore be necessary to demonstrate that the decision-maker acted irrationally, which is a high bar.

Planning conditions and obligations

5.55 Section 70(1)(a) of the TCPA 1990 enables the local planning authority, in granting planning permission, to impose 'such conditions as they think fit' to make otherwise unacceptable developments acceptable. This is subject to taking into account material considerations, such as the NPPF and PPG, on the use of planning conditions.[119] The NPPF makes clear that conditions should be kept to a minimum and only used where they satisfy six tests, namely that they are: (1) necessary; (2) relevant to planning; (3) relevant to the development to be permitted; (4) enforceable; (5) precise; and (6) reasonable in all other respects.[120]

5.56 Provided the six tests can be satisfied, a planning condition could be imposed to make acceptable a development that would otherwise have been unacceptable on

---

113 ibid [258].
114 *R (Boswell) v Secretary of State for Transport* [2023] EWHC 1710 (Admin).
115 *R (Boswell) v Secretary of State for Transport* [2024] EWCA Civ 145; This case is considered in more detail in the context of environmental impact assessment in Chapter 7 at paras 7.65–7.67.
116 *Bowen-West v Secretary of State for Communities and Local Government Northamptonshire CC & others* [2012] EWCA Civ 321, Laws LJ at [30].
117 *R (Boswell) v Secretary of State for Transport* [2023] EWHC 1710 (Admin) [6].
118 The important role of planning policy, in particular the role of National Policy Statements is considered in detail in Chapter 6 (on PA 2008).
119 Department for Levelling Up, Housing and Communities, 'Guidance: Use of Planning Conditions' (2014) <https://www.gov.uk/guidance/use-of-planning-conditions> accessed 4 April 2024.
120 Department for Levelling Up, Housing and Communities, 'National Planning Policy Framework' (n 15) paras 55–56; For more detail see Harwood, *Planning Permission* (n 10) ch 11–12.

climate change, net zero, or nature positive grounds. Examples include requiring landscaping works to demonstrate how they will protect and enhance the biodiversity of the development site before being approved, or that parking plans must include a certain number of electric vehicle charging stations to be approved.

5.57 Some local planning authorities have adopted model planning conditions, which ensure climate change considerations are taken into account in the planning process. For example, in June 2020, Swale Borough Council introduced a model condition for all new homes in the borough to achieve carbon reductions, pending the adoption of a new local development plan. At the point of introduction, new dwellings are required to reduce carbon emissions to 'be at least 50% lower than building regulations 2013 Part L1'.[121] This will increase to 75% for new buildings by 2025 and a 200% reduction by 2030.[122] In imposing model conditions, a local planning authority should ensure they are not applied in a rigid way, and that they have regard to whether the six tests will be met.[123]

5.58 Where it is not possible to address unacceptable impacts through a planning condition, planning obligations may be used in the form of section 106 agreements.[124] As set out in section 106:

> (1) Any person interested in land in the area of a local planning authority may, by agreement or otherwise, enter into an obligation (referred to in this section and sections 106A to 106C as 'a planning obligation'), enforceable to the extent mentioned in subsection (3)–
>
> (a) restricting the development or use of the land in any specified way;
> (b) requiring specified operations or activities to be carried out in, on, under or over the land;
> (c) requiring the land to be used in any specified way; or
> (d) requiring a sum or sums to be paid to the authority (or, in a case where section 2E applies, to the Greater London Authority) on a specified date or dates or periodically.

5.59 A planning obligation cannot be the reason for the grant of planning permission, unless it is necessary to make the development acceptable in planning terms, directly related to the development, and fairly and reasonably related in scale and kind to the development.[125] One example of using a section 106 agreement could be requiring a developer to offset the development's carbon emissions, by paying into a fund set up by the local planning authority for spending on carbon reduction projects.

---

121 Swale Borough Council, 'Guidance for Complying with the Climate Change Planning Condition to Reduce Operational Carbon of New Dwellings in Swale by 50%' (2020) 23 <https://services.swale.gov.uk/assets/Planning-General/Planning%20General/21%20SBC%2050%20pc%20carbon%20reduction%20guidance%20%20v1.0%20ISSUE.pdf> accessed 4 April 2024.
122 ibid.
123 Department for Levelling Up, Housing and Communities, 'Guidance: Use of Planning Conditions' (n 119) para 021.
124 Department for Levelling Up, Housing and Communities, 'National Planning Policy Framework' (n 15) para 55; TCPA 1990 s 160.
125 The Community Infrastructure Levy Regulations 2010 reg 122.

Conclusion

5.60 It is clear that land use planning has a key role to play in achieving net zero and promoting nature positive development, from enabling clean energy infrastructure, to driving gains in biodiversity. Yet, it currently fails to 'clearly bind together the provisions of the climate and planning acts so as to provide a mutually supportive regime of both target setting and delivery'.[126] There are certainly green shoots in the willingness of public authorities to use the planning system to encourage climate conscious development,[127] but it seems correct to say that the existing legislative and policy framework operates more as a stumbling block than as a 'key public policy solution in implementing the wide range of complex actions necessary to mitigate and adapt to climate change'.[128] It is therefore additionally apparent that if there is appetite in central government, there is scope for an improved or radically reformed[129] planning system better equipped to achieve net zero and promote nature positive development. It would not quite be correct to describe land use planning as an area of law and policy 'in flux', but it is certainly an area with significant potential for change.

126 Centre for Sustainable Energy and The Town and Country Planning Association, 'Spatial Planning for Climate Resilience and Net Zero (CSE & TCPA)' (2023) 93 <https://www.theccc.org.uk/publication/spatial-planning-for-climate-resilience-and-net-zero-cse-tcpa/> accessed 4 April 2024.
127 For example, the London Plan 2021 discussed at 1.25 and 1.38 above, and the approach of Swale Borough Council discussed at 1.57 above.
128 Centre for Sustainable Energy and The Town and Country Planning Association, 'Spatial Planning for Climate Resilience and Net Zero (CSE & TCPA)' (n 127) 93.
129 Climate Change Committee, 'Progress in Reducing Emissions: 2023 Report to Parliament' (n 8) 15.

CHAPTER 6

NATIONALLY SIGNIFICANT INFRASTRUCTURE

Daniel Kozelko and Stephanie David

Introduction

6.01 As net zero and nature positive are nationally significant objectives for the UK, achieving these objectives requires a similarly national approach to significant development. The consenting process for 'nationally significant infrastructure project(s)' ('NSIP(s)'), set out in the Planning Act 2008 ('PA 2008'), establishes this process. It provides for key infrastructure to be permitted at the national level, guided by nationally established policy (the 'National Policy Statement(s)' or 'NPS(s)'), and consented by the Secretary of State with appropriate guidance from expert inspectors.

6.02 The NSIP scheme responded to a range of defects which were identified in the 2000s with how large infrastructure projects were being consented. Among other schemes, the Heathrow Terminal 5 application (which took over 7 years from application to a decision) and the Dibden Bay port decision (taking over 3 years from the start of the inquiry to a decision) demonstrated the delay, complexity, and lack of clarity which bedevilled the existing processes.[1] With these issues in mind the government proposed a new scheme which aimed to:[2]

> (a) Produce national policy statements for key sectors to ensure that there is a clear policy framework for decisions on nationally significant infrastructure. …
>
> (b) Help promoters of infrastructure projects to improve the way that they prepare applications by making better advice available to them, requiring them to consult the public and local communities effectively and requiring earlier engagement with key parties such as statutory environmental and heritage bodies and the Highways Agency. …
>
> (c) Clarify the decision making process and achieve a clear separation of policy and decision making by creating an independent infrastructure planning commission to take the decisions on nationally significant infrastructure cases. …
>
> (d) Streamline the procedures for infrastructure projects of national significance by rationalising the different development consent regimes and improving the inquiry process for all of them. …

---

1 Ministry of Housing, Communities and Local Government, 'Planning for a Sustainable Future' (2007) Cm 7120, ch 2.
2 ibid para 2.13.

(e) Improve public participation across the entire process by providing better opportunities for public engagement at each stage of the development consent process. ...

(f) Explore devolving decisions on smaller infrastructure projects, where appropriate to local authorities.

6.03 The NSIP scheme in the PA 2008 was the outcome of that work. At the time the government suggested that the scheme would provide for average times from application to decision of around one year, while saving around £1 billion over 10 years.[3] This was intended to be done while 'maintaining the quality of decision making and clarifying and improving the opportunities for public consultation and engagement'.[4] As of 2023 the NSIP scheme has led to 120 major projects with a 95% approval rating for development consent.[5]

6.04 The NSIP scheme sits alongside other approaches to planning and consenting significant infrastructure in the UK. The most significant such infrastructure may be the subject of specific bills (for example, HS2[6] and Crossrail[7]). Other approaches include the Road Investment Strategy (made under the Infrastructure Act 2015) which provides for a holistic and long-term vision for motorways and major roads in the UK.[8] What is notable about these schemes is how they elevate significant infrastructure outside of the general planning regime and attempt to provide a holistic, effective, and expeditious way of consenting development.

6.05 However, whether the NSIP scheme now achieves the aims originally set out for it in the 2000s seems doubtful. While the NSIP scheme initially was successful in speeding up applications (with, on average, applications running for 2.5 years from the pre-application stage to decision on consent), this has ballooned to over 4 years for some schemes (with at least half of all schemes experiencing delays, and the average delay being 9 months).[9] The expense of progressing schemes has also gone up significantly,[10] while legal challenges to development consent orders ('DCOs') are more common.[11] This is all while, since 2020, the number of projects going through the NSIP system has gone up 40% compared to 2016–2019.[12] Finally, research indicates that the scheme has significant problems in properly achieving community engagement.[13]

---

3 ibid para 2.15.
4 ibid para 2.16.
5 Department for Levelling Up, Housing and Communities, 'Getting Great Britain Building Again: Speeding up Infrastructure Delivery' (2023) para 2 <https://www.gov.uk/government/publications/getting-great-britain-building-again-speeding-up-infrastructure-delivery/getting-great-britain-building-again-speeding-up-infrastructure-delivery> accessed 27 November 2023.
6 For phase 1: High Speed Rail (London – West Midlands) Act 2017.
7 Crossrail Act 2008.
8 Infrastructure Act 2015 s 3.
9 Department of Levelling Up, Housing and Communities, 'Getting Great Britain Building Again: Speeding Up Infrastructure Delivery' (n 5) introduction para 5, part 1 para 3.
10 ibid introduction para 4: 'On large infrastructure projects, the National Infrastructure Commission estimates that teams can cost around £1.5 million to run per month.'
11 ibid part 1 para 5.
12 ibid part 1 para 2.
13 See, for example, Lucy Natarajan and others, 'Navigating the Participatory Processes of Renewable Energy Infrastructure Regulation: A "Local Participant Perspective" on the NSIPs Regime in England and Wales' (2018) 114 Energy Policy 201–210.

6.06 The government has now indicated an intention to modify the NSIP system. Some changes have already been introduced in the Levelling-up and Regeneration Act 2023.[14] Those upcoming changes are addressed in more detail at the end of this chapter.

Relevance of NSIPs to achieving net zero and nature positive

6.07 There is no doubt that achieving net zero and nature positive requires nationally significant infrastructure.[15] Climate change was a key factor at the introduction of the NSIP scheme; the 'Planning for a Sustainable Future' White Paper recognised:[16]

> 2.1 … we must further reduce our greenhouse gas emissions and develop not only places, but also a way of life, that are more environmentally sustainable.
>
> 2.2 Improving our nation's infrastructure is critical to meeting these objectives. Planning for and enabling greater use of renewable and low carbon sources of electricity can help us both meet our emissions targets and provide energy security in the context of rising demand and increased dependence on energy imports.

6.08 The legislative process for passing the Planning Bill which became the PA 2008 also reflects its connection from the outset with climate change. The Bill was introduced to Parliament alongside the bills which became the Climate Change Act 2008 and the Energy Act 2008. The Secretary of State for Communities and Local Government, on introducing the Planning Bill for its Second Reading, said: 'Together with the Climate Change Bill and Energy Bill, [the Planning Bill] will accelerate our transition to a low-carbon economy'.[17]

6.09 Today, references to infrastructure as a key part of achieving net zero is ubiquitous in government policy; this includes the very National Policy Statements which underpin the NSIP scheme. This is unsurprising; as Sir John Armitt recognised in the foreword to the Second National Infrastructure Assessment: 'To deliver net zero by 2050, the UK must be a long way down the road of decarbonising electricity, transport, industry and heating by the Sixth Carbon Budget in 2035. In infrastructure terms, 12 years is not a long time'.[18] However, the scheme for NSIPs (and planning generally) is the subject of some concern. In its June 2023 progress report, the Climate Change Committee explained:[19]

---

14 Levelling-up and Regeneration Act 2023 s 127. Most notably, the ability to shorten the time provided for the examination of an application.

15 Department for Energy Security and Net Zero, 'Overarching National Policy Statement for Energy (EN-1)' (November 2023) para 2.3.4.

16 Ministry of Housing, Communities and Local Government, 'Planning for a Sustainable Future' (n 1) paras 2.1 and 2.2.

17 HC Deb 10 December 2008, vol 469, col 25.

18 National Infrastructure Commission, 'The Second National Infrastructure Assessment' (2023) 4 <https://nic.org.uk/app/uploads/Final-NIA-2-Full-Document.pdf> accessed 5 April 2024.

19 Climate Change Committee, 'Progress in Reducing Emissions: 2023 Report to Parliament' (2023) 15 <https://www.theccc.org.uk/wp-content/uploads/2023/06/Progress-in-reducing-UK-emissions-2023-Report-to-Parliament.pdf> accessed 4 April 2024. In its 2024 assessment of reducing emissions scores, the Committee gave a score of 'no progress' against reviewing and updating NPPF to achieve these ends: 'Progress in Reducing Emissions 2023 Recommendation Scores' <https://www.theccc.org.uk/wp-content/uploads/2024/07/Progress-in-reducing-emissions-2023-recommendation-scores.xlsx> accessed 21 October 2024.

> **Planning policy requires radical reform to support Net Zero.** In a range of areas, there is now a danger that the rapid deployment of infrastructure required by the Net Zero transition is stymied or delayed by restrictive planning rules. The planning system must have an overarching requirement that all planning decisions must be taken giving full regard to the imperative of Net Zero. (emphasis in original).

6.10 The PA 2008 itself sets out commitments to responding to climate change. Most notably sections 5(8) and 10 which are considered further below. These were the subject of comment in *R (Friends of the Earth Ltd and another) v Heathrow Airport Ltd*,[20] where the Supreme Court considered the extent of the obligations to consider international climate change obligations as part of setting National Policy Statements. While, on the facts, that case concluded that the government had complied with its obligations when making the Airports National Policy Statement, it is clear that there is a weighty obligation on the government to properly exercise its mind to these commitments. That is something that can be seen in detail in the most recently published National Policy Statements concerning energy.

6.11 It is also correct to note that some NSIP schemes have a negative impact on achieving net zero and nature positive. This includes highways infrastructure and airports. This reflects the fact that the PA 2008 is the central planning mechanism for all nationally significant infrastructure; it is not tied solely to the issue of climate change.

Designated National Policy Statements

6.12 There are, at the time of writing, 13 designated National Policy Statements covering energy, transport, water, waste water and waste.[21]

6.13 For energy, the relevant NPSs are:[22]

- Overarching NPS for energy (EN-1);
- NPS for natural gas electricity generating infrastructure (EN-2);
- NPS for renewable energy infrastructure (EN-3);
- NPS for natural gas supply infrastructure and gas and oil pipelines (EN-4);
- NPS for electricity networks infrastructure (EN-5);
- NPS for nuclear power generation (EN-6).

---

20 *R (Friends of the Earth Ltd and another) v Heathrow Airport Ltd* [2020] UKSC 52, [2021] PTSR 190.
21 The Planning Inspectorate, 'Nationally Significant Infrastructure Projects: National Policy Statements' <https://www.gov.uk/government/publications/nationally-significant-infrastructure-projects-national-policy-statements/nationally-significant-infrastructure-projects-national-policy-statements#which-sectors-do-national-policy-statements-cover> accessed 5 April 2024.
22 See further Chapter 15, Chapter 16 and Chapter 17.

6.14 EN-1 to EN-5 were produced by the Department for Energy Security and Net Zero ('DESNZ') and came into force on 17 January 2024.[23] The government's guidance has set out that, in relation to any application accepted for examination before 17 January 2024, the 2011 NPSs shall apply.[24]

6.15 EN-6 was designated on 19 July 2011 and has effect for certain nuclear projects capable of being deployed by the end of 2025.[25] A new NPS for nuclear is being prepared by DESNZ.[26]

6.16 There are three transport NPSs: NPS for ports, national networks NPS ('NNNPS'), and airports NPS.[27] On 14 July 2021, the government announced a review of the NNNPS, pursuant to section 6 of the PA 2008.[28] This was triggered by a significant change in circumstances, namely, the net zero target, the sixth carbon budget and the Transport Decarbonisation Plan, which, had they been anticipated at the time the policy statement was adopted, the NNNPS would have been materially different.[29] On 14 March 2023, the government laid a draft NNNPS before Parliament;[30] and the NNNPS was designated on 24 May 2024.[31]

6.17 Finally, there are NPSs for hazardous waste,[32] waste water,[33] water resources infrastructure,[34] and geological disposal infrastructure.[35]

6.18 Not all nationally significant infrastructure relevant to achieving net zero are addressed by the NPSs. One example which is currently expressly excluded from the scheme is battery energy storage systems. While such battery storage can appear as part of another scheme as associated development, they cannot be consented in this way on their own (unless made the subject of a s 35 PA 2008 direction). Currently, the only

---

23 The Planning Inspectorate, 'Nationally Significant Infrastructure Projects: National Policy Statements' (n 21).
24 ibid.
25 ibid.
26 ibid.
27 ibid.
28 Department for Transport, 'Review of National Policy Statement for National Networks' (2021) <https://www.gov.uk/government/speeches/review-of-national-policy-statement-for-national-networks> accessed 5 April 2024. See also *R (Transport Action Network Ltd) v Secretary of State for Transport* [2022] EWHC 503 (Admin).
29 Department for Transport 'Review of National Policy Statement for National Networks' (n 28). The law here is addressed in more detail at para 6.24 below.
30 Department for Transport, 'Draft National Policy Statement for National Networks' (2023) <https://assets.publishing.service.gov.uk/government/uploads/system/uploads/attachment_data/file/1141537/draft-nps-for-national-networks-web.pdf> accessed 5 April 2024. See also Department for Transport, 'Draft Revised National Networks National Policy Statement' (2023) <https://www.gov.uk/government/speeches/draft-revised-national-networks-national-policy-statement> accessed 5 April 2024.
31 Department for Transport, 'National Networks National Policy Statement' (2024) <https://www.gov.uk/government/publications/national-networks-national-policy-statement> accessed 14 October 2024.
32 DEFRA, 'Hazardous Waste National Policy Statement' (2013) <https://www.gov.uk/government/publications/hazardous-waste-national-policy-statement> accessed 5 April 2024.
33 DEFRA, 'National Policy Statement for Waste Water' (2012) <https://www.gov.uk/government/publications/national-policy-statement-for-waste-water> accessed 5 April 2024.
34 DEFRA, 'National Policy Statement for Water Resources Infrastructure' (2023) <https://www.gov.uk/government/publications/national-policy-statement-for-water-resources-infrastructure> accessed 5 April 2024.
35 Department for Energy Security and Net Zero and Department for Business, Energy and Industrial Strategy, 'National Policy Statement for Geological Disposal Infrastructure' (2019) <https://www.gov.uk/government/publications/national-policy-statement-for-geological-disposal-infrastructure> accessed 5 April 2024.

energy storage method which can be consented by the PA 2008 scheme (without being ancillary to something else) is pumped-storage hydroelectricity.[36]

Statutory framework

6.19 The PA 2008 establishes the procedure for obtaining consent for 'nationally significant infrastructure projects', which includes those relating to energy, transport, water, waste water and waste.[37]

(i) *Preparation and designation of National Policy Statement*

6.20 Part 2 of the PA 2008 addresses National Policy Statements. Within that Part, section 5(1) of the PA 2008 explains that the Secretary of State may designate an NPS if the statement 'sets out national policy in relation to one or more specified descriptions of development'.[38]

6.21 The Secretary of State produces a draft NPS, which is subject to (i) an appraisal of sustainability;[39] (ii) public consultation and publicity;[40] and (iii) parliamentary approval.[41]

6.22 In addition, there is a need to carry out a Strategic Environmental Assessment ('SEA') under the SEA Directive[42] and the Environmental Assessment of Plans and Programmes Regulations 2004[43] ('the SEA Regulations').

6.23 The content of the NPS is governed by sections 5(5) to (8) of the PA 2008, which, in summary, provide that an NPS contains: (i) the amount, type or size of development of a specified description or for a specified area; (ii) the criteria to be applied in relation to considering a particular area and/or the design of the development; (iii) the relative weight to be attributed to the criteria; (iv) suitable, potentially suitable or unsuitable locations are identified.[44] Additionally, the NPS must provide reasons for the policy it sets out;[45] those reasons must, importantly for present purposes, 'include an explanation of how the policy set out in the statement takes account of Government policy relating to the mitigation of, and adaptation to, climate change'.[46]

---

36 See further Chapter 15.
37 PA 2008 s 14(6). See also the list of NSIPs in s 14(1) and the related provisions at ss 15–30A.
38 ibid s 5(1)(b).
39 ibid s 5(3).
40 ibid s 7.
41 ibid ss 5(4) and 9. The PA 2008 thus provides for an opportunity for a committee of either House of Parliament to scrutinise a proposed NPS and to make recommendations, and for either House to make resolutions (see s 9(4)). See also PA 2008 s 9(5), which requires the Secretary of State to lay before Parliament a statement setting out his response to any resolution or recommendations.
42 Directive 2001/42/EC.
43 The Environmental Assessment of Plans and Programmes Regulations 2004, SI 2004/1633.
44 PA 2008 s 5(5).
45 ibid s 5(7).
46 ibid s 5(8).

6.24 The Secretary of State is required to review each NPS 'whenever the Secretary of State thinks it appropriate to do so'.[47] This procedure addresses 'a contention that a policy, or the basis for a policy, has been overtaken by events, or has become out of date'.[48] The review can relate to all, or part of, the NPS.[49] In deciding whether to review an NPS, in whole or in part, the Secretary of State is required to have regard to whether, since the time it was published or reviewed, there has 'been a significant change in any circumstances on the basis of which any of the policy set out in the statement was decided' that was not anticipated at that time and, if it had been, the policy 'would have been materially different'.[50] Following the review, the Secretary of State must either (i) amend the NPS; (ii) withdraw the NPS's designation; or (iii) leave the NPS as it is.[51] Should the Secretary of State decide to amend the NPS, generally,[52] an appraisal of sustainability is required in relation to the amendment,[53] and the consultation, publicity and parliamentary requirements need to be complied with.[54]

6.25 The Secretary of State may suspend the operation of all or any part of an NPS until a review of the statement or the relevant part has been completed.[55]

6.26 Section 10 of PA 2008 applies to the Secretary of State's functions as set out in sections 5 and 6;[56] it requires that in exercising those functions the Secretary of State must 'do so with the objective of contributing to the achievement of sustainable development',[57] and must (in particular) have regard to 'the desirability of— (a) mitigating, and adapting to, climate change'.[58]

6.27 A judicial review challenge to an NPS 'or anything done, or omitted to be done, by the Secretary of State in the course of preparing such a statement' can be brought in accordance with section 13 of PA 2008 (addressed more in paragraphs 6.46–6.56 below). Such a challenge must be brought within 6 weeks of designation or, if later, publication.[59]

---

47 ibid s 6(1).
48 *R (ClientEarth) v Secretary of State for Business, Energy and Industrial Strategy* [2020] EWHC 1303 (Admin), [2020] PTSR 1709 [39] and [108].
49 PA 2008 s 6(2).
50 ibid s 6(3)–(4). See also *R (Spurrier) v Secretary of State for Transport* [2019] EWHC 1070 (Admin), [2020] PTSR 240 [107]–[108], which states that the material difference condition is 'critical'; it also continued as follows: 'This formulation clearly lays down the statutory principle that significant changes in circumstance affecting the basis for a policy in an NPS are to be taken into account if, after assessment, the relevant Secretary of State considers that the policy would have been materially different and only through the statutory process of review.'
51 PA 2008 s 6(5).
52 Unless PA 2008 s 6(8) applies, which is that the Secretary of State thinks that the proposed amendment does not 'materially affect the policy as set out in the national policy statement'.
53 PA 2008 s 6(5).
54 ibid s 6(7).
55 ibid s 11(4).
56 ibid s 10(1).
57 ibid s 10(2).
58 ibid s 10(3)(a).
59 PA 2008 s 13.

(ii) *Development Consent Orders*

6.28 Section 31 of the PA 2008 provides that consent under the Act ('development consent') is required to the extent that such development 'is or forms part of a nationally significant infrastructure project'.[60]

6.29 The pre-application procedure is governed by chapter 2 of part 5 of the PA 2008; and sets out various consultation duties.[61] Regulation 12 of the Infrastructure Planning (Environmental Impact Assessment) Regulations 2017[62] provides for publication of and consultation on preliminary environmental information.

6.30 Applications for development consent must be made in accordance with section 37 of the PA 2008.[63] The Secretary of State may appoint a panel or single person to examine the application.[64] The examining authority will then prepare a report for the Secretary of State on the application setting out the findings and conclusions in relation to the application and providing a recommendation as to the decision to be made.[65]

6.31 If the application is accepted by the Secretary of State,[66] the statutory regime sets out various notification requirements, which include notifying, insofar as relevant to the particular application: the Greater London Authority;[67] the Marine Management Organisation;[68] and certain local authorities.[69] There are also notification requirements in relation to those whose land may be subject to compulsory acquisition.[70]

6.32 Whilst the examining authority makes a recommendation, the Secretary of State is required to decide the application for a development consent order.[71] Where an NPS has effect in relation to a development, section 104 applies and requires that, in deciding an application, the Secretary of State must have regard to: (i) the relevant NPS; (ii) the appropriate marine policy document (if any);[72] (iii) any local impact report;[73] (iv) 'any matters prescribed in relation to the development of the description to which the application relates'; and (v) 'any other matters which the Secretary of State thinks are both important and relevant to the Secretary of State's decision.'[74]

---

60 ibid s 31.
61 ibid ss 42–44 and 47–49.
62 Infrastructure Planning (Environmental Impact Assessment) Regulations 2017, SI 2017/572.
63 PA 2008 s 37.
64 ibid chs 2 and 3.
65 ibid s 74(2).
66 ibid s 55.
67 ibid s 56(2)(c), if the land to which the application relates, or any part of it is in Greater London.
68 ibid ss 56(2)(aa) and 56(2A), if the development involves carrying out an activity or activities in an area specified in s 56(2A), which includes waters in or adjacent to England up to the limits of the territorial sea; an exclusive economic zone; a Renewable Energy Zone; and an area designated under Continental Shelf Act 1964 s 1(7) (subject to certain exceptions).
69 PA 2008 s 56(2)(b). See also ibid s 56(A), which includes the local authority in which the land for the development is situated.
70 PA 2008 s 59.
71 ibid s 103(1).
72 See Marine and Coastal Access Act 2009 s 59.
73 See PA 2008 s 60(3).
74 ibid s 104(2).

6.33 The application must be determined in accordance with the relevant NPS, unless one or more of the exceptions in sections 104(4)–(8) applies.[75] The exceptions apply where deciding the application in accordance with the NPS would: (i) lead to the UK being in breach of its international obligations or lead to the Secretary of State being in breach of any domestic legal duty;[76] and (ii) be unlawful by virtue of any enactment.[77] There is also an exception where the Secretary of State is satisfied that 'the adverse impact of the proposed development would outweigh its benefits'.[78]

6.34 If there is no relevant NPS, then section 105 applies, which requires that the Secretary of State has regard to: (i) any local impact report; (ii) 'any matters prescribed in relation to the development of the description to which the application relates'; and (iii) 'any other matters which the Secretary of State thinks are both important and relevant to the Secretary of State's decision'.[79]

6.35 Sections 99 and 101, and schedule 15 of the EA 2021 will make various amendments to the PA 2008, by introducing 'biodiversity gain' into the NSIP statutory scheme.[80] The amendments are not, at the time of writing, in force. They are addressed in more detail in paragraphs 10.50–10.57 of Chapter 10 but, in short, the provision about biodiversity gain, will be built into decisions on DCOs taken by the Secretary of State, pursuant to sections 104 and 105 of the PA 2008.[81]

6.36 An Environmental Impact Assessment ('EIA') must be carried out in relation to an application for development consent.[82] Reg 5(1) defines an EIA as a process consisting of (a) the preparation of an environmental statement, (b) compliance with publicity, notification and consultation requirements in the EIA Regulations 2017 on the application and the ES, and (c) compliance with reg 21 or, in certain circumstances, reg 25.[83] The EIA must 'identify, describe and assess in an appropriate manner' the 'direct and indirect significant effects' on *inter alia:* (i) the population and human health; (ii) biodiversity, with particular attention to protected species and habitats; (iii) land, soil, water, air and climate; and, (iv) importantly, the interaction between the other factors.[84] The significant effects must also include those arising 'from the vulnerability of the proposed development to major accidents or disasters that are relevant to that development'.[85]

---

75 ibid s 104(3).
76 ibid ss 104(4)–(5).
77 ibid s 104(6).
78 ibid s 104(7).
79 PA 2008 s 105(2).
80 EA 2021 ss 99 and 101, and sch 15.
81 ibid sch 15, paras 2–4.
82 Infrastructure Planning (Environmental Impact Assessment) Regulations 2017, SI 2017/572 reg 4(2).
83 ibid reg 5(1).
84 ibid reg 5(2).
85 ibid reg 5(4).

6.37 When the Secretary of State has made a decision on an application for development consent, they must either make a DCO or refuse development consent.[86] Reasons must be provided for the decision.[87]

6.38 By regulation 7 of the Infrastructure Planning (Decisions) Regulations 2010,[88] when deciding an application for development consent, the Secretary of State must have regard to the Convention on Biological Diversity[89] and, in relation to development in Scotland, the Secretary of State must have regard to any strategy designated under section 2(1) of the Nature Conservation (Scotland) Act 2004.[90]

6.39 Section 118 of the PA 2008 governs legal challenges to DCOs. These are judicial review proceedings and there are strict time limits for any such challenge.[91]

(iii) *Wales*

6.40 In contrast to England, Wales currently operates a tripartite system. The largest infrastructure schemes use the NSIP scheme set out in the PA 2008 in the manner set out above. However, intermediate size schemes are instead dealt with by the Welsh Government through the Developments of National Significance ('DNS') scheme.[92] This DNS scheme reflects the devolution of some powers concerning infrastructure from the UK Government to the Welsh Government. One such criterion by which a development will be consented via the DNS route (rather than at a local level, or through the NSIP scheme) is that it is a generating station with a power rating between 50MW and 350MW. Schemes below 50MW are dealt with in the normal way at local level. At the time of writing, the Infrastructure (Wales) Bill is passing through the Senedd. This piece of legislation is intended to clarify and simplify the existing scheme for such intermediate size developments.[93]

Case law

6.41 From the perspective of net zero and nature positive, challenges to NPSs or DCOs can be a help or hindrance, depending on the particular infrastructure and the grounds of challenge. In any event, successful judicial review challenges brought under the PA 2008 in relation to either NPSs or DCOs are extremely limited.[94] For example:

86 PA 2008 s 114(1).
87 ibid s 116(1).
88 Infrastructure Planning (Decisions) Regulations, SI 2010/305 reg 7.
89 See paras 2.54–2.60 of Chapter 2.
90 Nature Conservation (Scotland) Act 2004 s 2(1).
91 PA 2008 s 118.
92 Town and Country Planning Act 1990 s 62D.
93 'Infrastructure (Wales) Bill' (12 June 2023) <https://business.senedd.wales/mgIssueHistoryHome.aspx?IId=41502> accessed 5 April 2024.
94 Another example was the quashing, by consent, of the first DCO in relation to Manston Airport, but, the DCO was then granted for a second time and the judicial review challenge was dismissed by Dove J in *R (Dawes) v Secretary of State for Transport* [2023] EWHC 2352 (Admin) (and the appeal was dismissed, [2024] EWCA Civ 560).

- In terms of aviation, whilst the challenge to the ANPS was successful in the Court of Appeal on climate change grounds, it was then overturned by the Supreme Court (addressed below in paragraphs 6.47–6.54).

- In the context of roads, the first DCO granted in relation to the construction of a new 13-kilometre dual carriageway for the A303, including a tunnel through the Stonehenge, Avebury and Associated Sites World Heritage Site, was quashed by the High Court on heritage grounds.[95]

- Finally, in relation to renewable energy, the DCO for an offshore wind farm that would share onshore installations with another wind farm was quashed where the decision-maker had decided to defer consideration of the cumulative impacts of the wind farms in accordance with the EIA Directive 2011[96] and the Infrastructure Planning (Environmental Impact Assessment) Regulations 2009[97] until the examination of the second one.[98] The court determined that, given the Secretary of State had agreed that the cumulative impacts were substantial, he could not lawfully defer the evaluation of those impacts until the second application.

6.42 As above, sections 13 and 118 of PA 2008 apply to challenges to an NPS or DCO. The time limits for bringing such a challenge are strict: *R (Blue Green London Plan) v Secretary of State for Environment, Food and Rural Affairs*[99] and *R (Williams) v Secretary of State for Energy and Climate Change.*[100]

6.43 Furthermore, a legal challenge can only be brought in relation to an NPS after it is designated or published: *R (Hillingdon LBC) v Secretary of State for Transport,*[101] where the decision to include in the draft Airports NPS a proposal for a third runway at Heathrow was challenged.

6.44 The general principles that apply to the interpretation of planning policy also apply to the interpretation of an NPS: *R (Scarisbrick) v Secretary of State for Communities and Local Government.*[102]

6.45 Reasons given in a DCO must be intelligible, adequate and enable the reader to understand why the matter was decided as it was: *Bucks DC v Porter (No 2),*[103] and applied to DCOs in *R (Mars Jones) v Secretary of State for Business, Energy and Industrial*

---

95 *R (Save Stonehenge World Heritage Site Ltd) v Secretary of State for Transport* [2021] EWHC 2161 (Admin), [2022] PTSR 74. The challenge to the second DCO, following the redetermination, raised climate change grounds but the claim was unsuccessful: See *R (Save Stonehenge World Heritage Site Ltd and another) v Secretary of State for Transport* [2024] EWHC 339 (Admin) (and the appeal was dismissed, [2024] EWCA Civ 1227).
96 Directive 2011/92/EU.
97 Infrastructure Planning (Environmental Impact Assessment) Regulations 2009, SI 2009/2263.
98 *R (Pearce) v Secretary of State for Business, Energy and Industrial Strategy* [2021] EWHC 326 (Admin), [2022] Env LR 4.
99 *R (Blue Green London Plan) v Secretary of State for Environment, Food and Rural Affairs* [2015] EWHC 495 (Admin) (waste water scheme).
100 *R (Williams) v Secretary of State for Energy and Climate Change* [2015] EWHC 1202 (Admin) (wind farm).
101 *R (Hillingdon LBC) v Secretary of State for Transport* [2017] EWHC 121 (Admin), [2017] 1 WLR 2166.
102 *R (Scarisbrick) v Secretary of State for Communities and Local Government* [2017] EWCA Civ 787.
103 *Bucks DC v Porter (No 2)* [2004] UKHL 33, [2004] 1 WLR 1953.

Strategy.[104] The same standard of reasons applies to a challenge to a DCO, so long as the specific requirements of the statutory code are kept in mind.[105]

(i) *National Policy Statements*

6.46 The courts have repeatedly observed that the scheme within the PA 2008 accords with well-established constitutional principles:[106]

> Under our constitution policy-making at the national level is the responsibility of democratically-elected governments and ministers accountable to Parliament. As Lord Hoffmann said in *R (Alconbury Developments Ltd) v Secretary of State for the Environment, Transport and the Regions* [2003] 2 AC 295, paras 69 and 74: 'It does not involve deciding between the rights or interests of particular persons. It is the exercise of a power delegated by the people as a whole to decide what the public interest requires.' …
>
> Planning and the development of land are matters which concern the community as a whole, not only the locality where the particular case arises. They involve wider social and economic interests, considerations which are properly to be subject to a central supervision. By means of a central authority some degree of coherence and consistency in the development of land can be secured. …
>
> Once it is recognised that there should be a national planning policy under a central supervision, it is consistent with democratic principle that the responsibility for that work should lie on the shoulders of a minister answerable to Parliament.

6.47 In proceedings that ultimately went to the Supreme Court, judicial review challenges were brought by Friends of the Earth, Plan B, five local authorities and the Mayor of London in relation to the Secretary of State's decision to designate the Airports NPS, favouring the third runway at Heathrow.[107] The claims raised issues relating to both climate change and biodiversity, including approach under the Habitats Directive 92/43 and the adequacy of the Strategic Environmental Assessment.

6.48 Reversing the decision of the Divisional Court, the Court of Appeal determined that the Paris Agreement was part of 'Government policy' for the purpose of s 5(8) of the PA 2008, which requires that the reasons provided in the NPS must explain how the policy 'takes account of Government policy relating to the mitigation of, and adaptation to, climate change.'[108] Thus, the executive needed to take those policy commitments into account.[109]

---

104 *R (Mars Jones) v Secretary of State for Business, Energy and Industrial Strategy* [2017] EWHC 1111 (Admin).
105 *R (ClientEarth) v Secretary of State for Business, Energy and Industrial Strategy* [2020] (n 48).
106 ibid [44]–[45], citing *R (Spurrier) v Secretary of State for Transport* (n 50) and *R (Alconbury Developments Ltd) v Secretary of State for the Environment, Transport and the Regions* [2003] 2 AC 295, [2001] UKHL 23 [69], [74], and [140]–[141].
107 *R (Spurrier) v Secretary of State for Transport* (n 50); *R (Plan B Earth) v Secretary of State for Transport* [2020] EWCA Civ 214, [2020] PTSR 1446; and *R (Friends of the Earth Ltd and others) v Heathrow Airport Ltd* (n 20).
108 *R (Plan B Earth) v Secretary of State for Transport* (n 107) [228]–[231].
109 ibid.

6.49 Furthermore, in exercising functions under sections 5 and 6 of the PA 2008, the Secretary of State had to 'do so with the objective of contributing to the achievement of sustainable development', with regard to be had to the desirability of *inter alia* mitigating, and adapting to, climate change.[110] The Court of Appeal found that the Secretary of State did not consider whether he could take the Paris Agreement into account as a matter of discretion because he had been 'advised that he was not permitted as a matter of law to do so'.[111] The court found that the Paris Agreement was an 'obviously material' consideration.[112] In the context of the SEA Directive, the court also accepted that the reference to the 'international level' in Annex 1 must include the Paris Agreement.[113]

6.50 Except as set out in relation to the Paris Agreement, the Court of Appeal dismissed the challenges to the ANPS based on the Habitats Directive and the SEA Directive.[114] On habitats, the claimants argued *inter alia* that the Secretary of State had unlawfully rejected the Gatwick proposal as an alternative solution contrary to Article 6(3) and 6(4) of the Habitats Directive. On SEA, the Court considered whether the Secretary of State adopted a lawful approach to the environment report: in particular, whether the Secretary of State had provided an outline of the relationship between the ANPS and other relevant plans and programmes and whether there had been a failure to identity the environmental characteristics of areas likely to be significantly affected by the ANPS.[115]

6.51 The Supreme Court upheld Heathrow Airport Limited's appeal and found that the Paris Agreement did not constitute 'Government policy' for the purpose of section 5(8) PA 2008.[116] The court determined that 'the epitome of "Government policy" is a formal written statement of established policy',[117] determining that the test for a legitimate expectation would be 'the absolute minimum' to be satisfied to constitute 'policy' within the meaning of the provision.[118] Thus, 'a statement qualifies as policy only if it is clear, unambiguous and devoid of relevant qualification'.[119] Hence, the Paris Agreement does not constitute 'Government policy' for section 5(8).[120]

6.52 On section 10(3) of the PA 2008, the Supreme Court considered that the question the Secretary of State asked himself was whether he should take the Paris Agreement into account beyond the extent it was reflected in obligations under the CCA 2008.[121] He concluded in the exercise of his discretion that it was not appropriate to do so, and

110 PA 2008 s 10(2)–(3).
111 *R (Plan B Earth) v Secretary of State for Transport* (n 107) [236].
112 ibid [237].
113 ibid [243]–[247].
114 ibid [283].
115 ibid [12].
116 Some commentators have considered this case 'a missed opportunity to develop a more creative approach to the polycentric and dynamic issue of climate change in the context of nationally significant infrastructure projects', as described in Joanne Hawkins, 'A Lesson in Un-Creativity: *R (Friends of the Earth Ltd and Others) v Heathrow Airport Ltd* [2020] UKSC 52' (2021) 23(4) Environmental Law Review <https://doi.org/10.1177/14614529211052929> accessed 26 April 2024.
117 *R (Friends of the Earth Ltd and others) v Heathrow Airport Ltd* (n 20) [106].
118 ibid.
119 ibid.
120 ibid [110]–[112].
121 ibid [129].

this was deemed a rational conclusion.[122] The same reasoning applied in relation to the SEA ground of challenge – the Secretary of State did not consider that the Paris Agreement was legally irrelevant but rather followed the advice of the Climate Change Committee to the effect that that the UK's obligations under the Agreement were sufficiently taken into account in the CCA 2008.[123]

6.53 Thus, the Divisional Court was right that the PA 2008 and CCA 2008 should be read together, which means that, prior to designation, an NPS must *inter alia* promote the objective of the CCA 2008.[124]

6.54 Should there in future be any inconsistency between the ANPS and the UK's obligations under the Paris Agreement, section 6 of the PA 2008 provides for the ANPS to be amended (as per Lords Hodge DPSC and Sales JSC, giving the leading judgment of the court and endorsing the observation of the Divisional Court).[125]

6.55 The same point was made in *R (ClientEarth) v Secretary of State for Business, Energy and Industrial Strategy*.[126] The claimant challenged the decision to grant a DCO for the construction and operation of two gas-fired generating units.[127] Holgate J analysed section 6 of the PA 2008 and noted that the PA 2008 'proceeds on the legal principle that significant changes in circumstances affecting the basis for, or content of, a policy may only be taken into account through the statutory process of review under section 6'.[128] Thus, he rejected the argument that 'key policies in EN-1 and EN-2 are out of date by virtue of the net zero target enshrined in the CCA 2008'.[129] He stated as follows:[130]

> It is not the function of the court to say whether that view is right or wrong. But it is the function of the court to say that this line of argument undoubtedly falls outside the scope of the process created by Parliament by which an application for a DCO is examined and determined. Instead, it is a matter which could only be addressed through a decision to carry out a review under section 6 of the PA 2008 (see above). There has been no such decision and no claim for judicial review relating to any allegation of failure to institute such a review.

6.56 A statutory review of an NPS, pursuant to section 6 PA 2008, sits alongside section 11 of the PA 2008, which allows the Secretary of State to suspend an NPS during the course of a review. In *R (Transport Action Network Ltd) v Secretary of State for Transport*,[131] whilst welcoming the decision to review the NNNPS, pursuant to section 6, the claimant challenged the Secretary of State's decision, pursuant to section 11,

122 ibid [129] and [132].
123 ibid [149]. There was also an argument regarding non-CO_2 emissions that is considered in more detail in Chapter 3, paras 3.34–3.38, in the context of the precautionary principle.
124 As Holgate J (as he then was) set out in *R (ClientEarth) v Secretary of State for Business, Energy and Industrial Strategy* (n 48) [39]–[40].
125 *R (Friends of the Earth Ltd and others) v Heathrow Airport Ltd* (n 20) [132].
126 *R (ClientEarth) v Secretary of State for Business, Energy and Industrial Strategy* (n 48).
127 ibid [1].
128 ibid [37]–[38], [108].
129 ibid [243].
130 ibid.
131 *R (Transport Action Network Ltd) v Secretary of State for Transport* (n 28).

not to suspend the operation of the NNNPS, in whole or in part. The court found the claim was unarguable.

(ii) *Development Consent Orders*

6.57 Legal challenges have been brought to DCOs across the range of NSIPs, including roads,[132] fossil fuel development,[133] airports,[134] nuclear power stations,[135] electricity interconnector project,[136] wind farms,[137] and waste water projects.[138]

6.58 Many of these challenges turn on climate change grounds. In *R (ClientEarth) v Secretary of State for Business, Energy and Industrial Strategy*,[139] for example, the claim directly concerned the transition to net zero.[140] The claimant challenged the DCO for two gas-fired units at the Drax power station in North Yorkshire on the issue of need and the assessment of greenhouse gas ('GHG') emissions. The claim turned on the interpretation and application of two NPSs: EN-1 and EN-2.

6.59 The examining authority, appointed to consider the application, had recommended that consent for the development should be withheld. The panel concluded that Drax had not established that the development met an identified need for gas generation capacity, it would not accord with the energy NPSs, and would undermine the government's commitment to cut GHG as set out in the CCA 2008. Thus, the examining authority applied the balancing exercise in section 104(7) PA 2008 and concluded that the adverse impact of the development outweighed the benefits, so consent should be withheld.[141]

6.60 The Secretary of State disagreed with the recommendation. She determined that the general need for fossil fuel generation was set out in EN-1; thus, that factor should

---

132 *R (Boswell) v Secretary of State for Transport* [2023] EWHC 1710 (Admin), [2024] Env LR 12, upheld by the Court of Appeal in [2024] EWCA Civ 145, [2024] RTR 14; *R (Save Stonehenge World Heritage Site Ltd) v Secretary of State for Transport* [2022] (n 95) and the challenge to the DCO following the redetermination process in *R (Save Stonehenge World Heritage Site Ltd) v Secretary of State for Transport* [2024] (n 95).
133 *R (ClientEarth) v Secretary of State for Business, Energy and Industrial Strategy* [2020] (n 48), where the NSIP consisted of the construction and operation of two gas-fired generating units.
134 See challenges relating to the third runway at Heathrow (see above at paras 6.47–6.54); and *R (Dawes) v Secretary of State for Transport* (n 94).
135 *R (Together against Sizewell C) v Secretary of State for Energy Security and Net Zero* [2023] EWHC 1526 (Admin), [2023] Env LR 29, which was a challenge to the The Sizewell C (Nuclear Generating Station) Order 2022, SI 2022/853; the decision of the High Court was upheld in the Court of Appeal, [2023] EWCA Civ 1517, [2024] Env LR 22.
136 *R (Aquind Ltd) v Secretary of State for Business, Energy and Industrial Strategy* [2023] EWHC 98 (Admin).
137 *R (Pearce) v Secretary of State for Business, Energy and Industrial Strategy* (n 98); *R (Suffolk Energy Action Solutions SPV) v Secretary of State for Energy Security and Net Zero* [2023] EWHC 1796 (Admin); *R (Substation Action Save East Suffolk Ltd) v Secretary of State for Energy Security and Net Zero* [2022] EWHC 3177 (Admin), [2023] PTSR 975 and upheld by the Court of Appeal in [2024] EWCA Civ 12, [2024] PTSR 561.
138 *R (Thames Blue Green Economy Ltd) v Secretary of State for Communities and Local Government* [2015] EWCA Civ 876, [2016] JPL 157 which was a challenge to the Thames Tideway Tunnel infrastructure project.
139 *R (ClientEarth) v Secretary of State for Business, Energy and Industrial Strategy* (n 48).
140 Another recent example is the judicial review challenge to the decision to grant development consent for a new gas-fired electricity generating station with post combustion carbon capture: *R (Boswell) v Secretary of State for Energy Security and Net Zero* [2024] EWHC 2128 (Admin).
141 *R (ClientEarth) v Secretary of State for Business, Energy and Industrial Strategy* (n 48) [18].

be given substantial weight.[142] She took into account the significant adverse impact that the development would have as a result of the GHGs that would be emitted, but determined that that did not provide a reason to rebut the presumption in favour of granting consent.[143]

6.61 The grounds of challenge[144] turned on the alleged misinterpretation of the assessment of need for the development and the assessment of GHG emissions set out in the NPS EN-1. There was also an alleged breach of the EIA Regulations in relation to measures for monitoring GHG emissions.

6.62 The court determined that EN-1, properly interpreted, did not require a quantitative individual assessment of the proposed project, contrary to the claimant's submission.[145] On the NPS's approach to the GHG emissions assessment, Holgate J determined that it was 'not legally objectionable' for the national policy to state that 'a particular factor is insufficient by itself to justify refusal of a planning consent because it is addressed by other regimes', citing section 5(5)(c) PA 2008, which sets out that the NPS can prescribe how much weight should be given to a particular factor.[146]

6.63 Holgate J rejected the ground alleging a breach of the EIA.[147] He found that there was no requirement on the Secretary of State to give reasons for a decision not to impose a particular monitoring measure in relation to GHG emissions.[148] He accepted that in substance the requirements and objectives in regulation 21 had been met.[149] Furthermore, Drax was required to obtain a GHG permit from the Environment Agency under the Greenhouse Gas Emissions Trading Scheme Regulations 2012 to address the emissions from the development.[150] That regime, which focused on the transition to net zero, required monitoring and reporting of GHG emissions.[151]

142 ibid [20].
143 ibid [21].
144 ibid [23]. See also [198]: A 'monitoring measure' is defined by regulation 3(1) as: 'a provision requiring the monitoring of any significant adverse effects on the environment of proposed development, including any measures contained in a requirement imposed by an order granting development consent'.
145 ibid [128]–[130], [135], and [142].
146 ibid [170]. He observed further, at [178], as follows: 'EN-1 and EN-2 do not state that GHG emissions may not be taken into account in the DCO process. They do not prescribe how much weight should be given to such emissions as a disbenefit, except to say that this factor does not in itself justify a refusal of consent, given the other mechanisms for achieving decarbonisation. The NPSs proceed on the basis that there is no justification in land use planning terms for treating GHG emissions as a disbenefit which in itself is dispositive of an application for a DCO.'
147 ibid [221].
148 ibid [207].
149 ibid [218].
150 ibid [208].
151 ibid [213]–[218].

Upcoming changes to the NSIP scheme

6.64 The NSIP scheme has been the subject of criticism in recent years. In a recent ministerial foreword to the 'Nationally Significant Infrastructure: action plan for reforms to the planning process' it was said:[152]

> The Nationally Significant Infrastructure Project (NSIP) consenting process has served the UK well for more than a decade. However, the demands on the system are changing, and its speed has slowed. The number and complexity of cases coming into the system is increasing. Policy changes are more frequent in response to a changing world.

6.65 Some changes have already been made. New NPSs for energy infrastructure were designated in November 2023 recognising the 'critical national priority' for such infrastructure.[153] Amendments were also made to the PA 2008 to allow the Secretary of State to direct a shortened timescale for 'fast-track' consenting[154] (with the intent that such use would be piloted on several projects),[155] and to better control non-material amendments of schemes.[156]

6.66 However, more changes are on the way. The 'Nationally Significant Infrastructure: action plan for reforms to the planning process' report recognised as its third area for reform that:[157]

> Nationally significant infrastructure will play a critical role in delivering the government's environmental commitments and supporting our journey to net zero. In bringing forward the infrastructure the country needs, we want to secure the best possible outcomes for the environment so we can live up to our ambition to be the first generation to leave the environment in a better state than we found it.
>
> Consideration of environmental impacts needs to be at the heart of early stages of project design, and decision-making, but the current system is too often delivering process rather than helping deliver better environmental outcomes. Our reforms will ensure the NSIP system is better placed to meet our strategic environmental goals and actively address the environmental impacts of development.

---

152 Department for Levelling Up, Housing and Communities, 'Policy Paper – Nationally Significant Infrastructure: Action Plan for Reforms to the Planning Process' (2023) foreword para 2 <https://www.gov.uk/government/publications/nationally-significant-infrastructure-projects-nsip-reforms-action-plan/nationally-significant-infrastructure-action-plan-for-reforms-to-the-planning-process#annex-a-nsip-reform-actions> accessed 27 November 2023.
153 Department for Energy Security and Net Zero, 'Overarching National Policy Statement for Energy (EN-1)' (n 15) section 4.2.
154 Levelling-up and Regeneration Act 2023 s 127.
155 Department for Levelling Up, Housing and Communities, 'Policy Paper – Nationally Significant Infrastructure: Action Plan for Reforms to the Planning Process' (n 152) para 1.11.
156 Levelling-up and Regeneration Act 2023 s 128.
157 Department for Levelling Up, Housing and Communities, 'Policy Paper – Nationally Significant Infrastructure: Action Plan for Reforms to the Planning Process' (n 152) reform area 3.

6.67 In a November 2023 policy paper on NSIPs various next steps were identified for reform. Some of these have now already been achieved (e.g. publishing the new energy NPSs). Particularly important next steps included:[158]

- By spring 2024 putting in place a new fast track route to reduce the consenting process from 17 months to 12 months (this route was subsequently introduced)[159];
- By summer 2024 completed a review on how to 'discourage repeated and potentially inappropriate legal challenges';
- By summer 2024 the introduction of a pre-application service through the Planning Inspectorate leading to the fast track route;
- By end of 2024 received recommendations from a new study on simplifying and standardising the process of updating future NPSs.

6.68 The government has also recently consulted on changes to the NSIP consenting procedure.[160] It again affirmed the approach set out in its November 2023 policy paper, and included the development of improved pre-application services and advice from the Planning Inspectorate so as to encourage efficient and effective systems and applications.[161] Aside from this, Lord Banner KC has also been appointed to conduct an independent review to look into the speeding up of the delivery of major infrastructure projects.[162] The new Labour government elected in July 2024 has also indicated that it will make significant changes to the NSIP process and issue fresh NPSs in the near future.[163] Thus, it seems likely that the scheme will change significantly in the next few years.

158 Department for Levelling Up, Housing and Communities, 'Getting Great Britain Building Again: Speeding up Infrastructure Delivery' (n 5).
159 Levelling-up and Regeneration Act 2023, s 127.
160 Department for Levelling Up, Housing and Communities, 'Operational Reforms to the Nationally Significant Infrastructure Project (NSIP) Consenting Process' (2023) <https://www.gov.uk/government/consultations/operational-reforms-to-the-nationally-significant-infrastructure-project-consenting-process> accessed 17 September 2024.
161 ibid.
162 Department for Levelling Up, Housing and Communities, '(Lord) Banner KC to Lead Review on National Infrastructure' (7 March 2024) <https://www.gov.uk/government/news/lord-banner-kc-to-lead-review-on-national-infrastructure> accessed 19 March 2024.
163 Labour Manifesto 2024 General Election, <https://labour.org.uk/change/kickstart-economic-growth/> accessed 17 September 2024.

CHAPTER 7

ENVIRONMENTAL IMPACT ASSESSMENTS

Ruth Keating

Introduction

7.01 Environmental Impact Assessments ('EIAs') are a cornerstone of environmental protection in England and Wales but also globally. Broadly stated, the purpose of an EIA is to assess the potential environmental impacts of proposed development, and to ensure that these impacts are properly considered before planning permission is granted.

7.02 EIAs are a crucial tool for ensuring that the environmental impacts of proposed developments are properly considered. Climate change and net zero considerations are become increasingly relevant in the EIA process. There is a developing recognition of the importance of the role EIAs serve in combating and adapting to climate change, halting the loss of biodiversity and the degradation of ecosystems. This is an issue which has been flagged by the European Commission.[1] Since climate change and biodiversity loss, like so many other environmental issues, are closely related, effective EIAs can contribute to the consideration of climate change and biodiversity at an early stage. Domestically, a central plank of the Environment Act 2021 ('EA 2021') includes the setting of targets – intended to improve biodiversity, air and water quality, and reduce waste.[2] Further, all planning permissions in England will be subject to a mandatory condition that requires the delivery of a 10% net gain in biodiversity from the pre-development baseline position.[3] There are differences between an EIA biodiversity assessment and a biodiversity net gain assessment – not least that in respect of the latter there is a focus on quantitative assessment and it considers on site habitats only. Nonetheless, the existence of both demonstrates the way in which there is increasing recognition of the importance of biodiversity loss.

7.03 The UK has set ambitious targets for reducing greenhouse gas ('GHG') emissions to net zero by 2050. This will require a significant transformation of the economy, including changes to the way we generate and consume energy, transport goods and people, and build and use our homes and businesses. EIAs have the potential to play an important role in ensuring that these changes are implemented in a sustainable and environmentally responsible manner, depending upon how the courts interpret the legal

1 European Commission, Directorate-General for Environment, 'Guidance on Integrating Climate Change and Biodiversity into Environmental Impact Assessment' (EU 2013) <https://op.europa.eu/en/publication-detail/-/publication/3ed0e578-7f24-4073-81c9-f279c6d4b3cf/language-en>.
2 EA 2021 ss 1–6.
3 EA 2021 s 98, Schedule 14.

obligations in the context of net zero and nature positive. However, the nature of EIAs is that they do not dictate binary outcomes – it is not a process which dictates a specific result. The purpose is: (a) to improve decision-making by ensuring there is better information and the process is more transparent; and (b) to allow the public to understand the environmental effects of proposed projects and hence participate more effectively in the process. Decisions such as that of the Court of Appeal in *R (Boswell) v Secretary of State for Transport*[4] (concerning cumulative impact assessments) and *R (Finch on behalf of the Weald Action Group) v Surrey County Council and others*[5] (assessment of scope 3 emissions) are therefore critical in guiding the direction of what information should be included in EIAs and how that process should be carried out.

EIA law and policy

7.04 In recent years, there has been a number of developments that are relevant to EIA law and policy, including:

(i) *Domestic policy*

7.05 The National Planning Policy Framework ('NPPF') (2023) sets out the government's policy on planning for climate change. There are several references to climate change therein. This includes at the outset of Chapter 14 entitled 'Meeting the challenge of climate change, flooding and coastal change' that:

> The planning system should support the transition to a low carbon future in a changing climate, taking full account of flood risk and coastal change. It should help to: shape places in ways that contribute to radical reductions in greenhouse gas emissions, minimise vulnerability and improve resilience; encourage the reuse of existing resources, including the conversion of existing buildings; and support renewable and low carbon energy and associated infrastructure.

7.06 The NPPF goes on to make clear under the heading 'Planning for climate change' that '[p]lans should take a proactive approach to mitigating and adapting to climate change … biodiversity'.[6]

7.07 The NPPF also refers to biodiversity:

- Planning policies and decisions should contribute to and enhance the natural and local environment by: a) protecting and enhancing valued landscapes, sites of biodiversity.[7]

- Planning policies and decisions should contribute to and enhance the natural and local environment by: … (d) minimising impacts on and providing net gains for

4 *R (Boswell) v Secretary of State for Transport* [2024] EWCA Civ 145.
5 *R (Finch on behalf of the Weald Action Group) v Surrey County Council and others* [2024] UKSC 20.
6 Department for Levelling Up, Housing and Communities, 'National Planning Policy Framework' (2023) para 158 <https://assets.publishing.service.gov.uk/media/65a11af7e8f5ec000f1f8c46/NPPF_December_2023.pdf> accessed 2 April 2024.
7 ibid para 80.

biodiversity, including by establishing coherent ecological networks that are more resilient to current and future pressures.[8]

- It is expressly said that to protect and enhance biodiversity and geodiversity, plans should: (a) 'identify, map and safeguard components of local wildlife-rich habitats and wider ecological networks'; and (b) 'promote the conservation, restoration and enhancement of priority habitats'.[9]

- When determining planning applications, local planning authorities should apply the following principles: (a) if significant harm to biodiversity resulting from a development cannot be avoided (through locating on an alternative site with less harmful impacts), adequately mitigated, or, as a last resort, compensated for, then planning permission should be refused; … (d) development whose primary objective is to conserve or enhance biodiversity should be supported.[10]

7.08 The publication of the Environmental Principles Policy Statement ('EPPS')[11] sets out the government's principles for environmental policy. Therein the EPPS outlines that: 'The environmental effects of a policy should be considered regardless of where the potential effect occurs within the UK, whether that be in England, or other nations in the UK. Among other issues, this includes the extent to which it will contribute to climate change, and our net zero commitment.' The legal duty to have due regard to EPPS applies to Ministers when making policy.

(ii) *International law and policy*

7.09 The role of EIA in international law and policy is also important and has developed over time. The formal process of EIA resulted from increasing environmental awareness during the 1950s and 1960s.[12]

7.10 Notably, the United States was at the forefront of developing EIA; and EIA was first legally mandated there through the National Environmental Policy Act ('NEPA') in 1969. Since then, national legislation requiring EIA has increased worldwide.

7.11 Due to the concern about the potential transboundary environmental effects of projects, several international agreements specifically require EIAs for projects and/or plans and so there are international legal instruments and guidance as well as domestic regimes. The most significant of these international legal instruments are referred to in this section.

---

8 ibid para 80.
9 ibid para 185.
10 ibid para 186.
11 Updated 31 January 2023.
12 See for example 'Principles of Environmental Impact Assessment' published in 1987 by the United Nations Environment Programme under the heading 'Historic Background', 4. Available at <https://wedocs.unep.org/bitstream/handle/20.500.11822/13595/rsrs122.pdf?sequence=1&isAllowed=y> accessed 9 April 2024.

7.12 The Action Plan adopted in June 1972 by the United Nations Conference on the Human Environment recognised environmental management as 'functions designed to facilitate comprehensive planning that takes into account the side effects of man's activities and thereby to protect and enhance the human environment'.[13]

7.13 On 28 October 1982, the United Nations developed a code of conduct for the protection and preservation of global natural habitats and resources, the 'World Charter for Nature'.[14] Importantly under 'II Functions' at paragraph 11(c) the World Charter for Nature provides:

> Activities which may disturb nature shall be preceded by assessment of their consequences, and environmental impact studies of development projects shall be conducted sufficiently in advance, and if they are to be undertaken, such activities shall be planned and carried out so as to minimize potential adverse effects.

7.14 'Goals and Principles of Environmental Impact Assessment' were then adopted by the United Nations Environment Programme in 1987.[15] They provide guidance on the conduct of EIAs. Those goals and principles have been widely adopted by governments and international organisations since 1987; and include the following:

- To establish that before decisions are taken which are likely to 'significantly affect' the environment, the environmental effects of those activities should be taken fully into account.
- To promote the implementation of appropriate procedures through which the first goal could be realised.
- To encourage the development of reciprocal procedures for information exchange, notification and consultation between States when proposed activities are 'likely to have significant transboundary effects'.[16]
- Thirteen 'principles' were also outlined.[17]

7.15 The United Nations Conference on Environment and Development, also known as the 'Earth Summit', was held in Rio de Janeiro, Brazil, from 3 to 14 June 1992. Two outcomes of that Earth Summit are mentioned in this chapter: (i) the Rio Declaration

---

13 See page 28. The 1972 United Nations Conference on the Human Environment in Stockholm was the first world conference to make the environment a major issue. The participants adopted a series of principles for sound management of the environment including the Stockholm Declaration and Action Plan for the Human Environment and several resolutions. The Action Plan contained three main categories: a) Global Environmental Assessment Programme (watch plan); b) Environmental management activities; (c) International measures to support assessment and management activities carried out at the national and international levels. In addition, these categories were broken down into 109 recommendations.
14 For further information see Chapter 3 (paras 3.11 and 3.20).
15 'Goals and Principles of Environmental Impact Assessment: Decision 14/25 of the Governing Council of UNEP of 17 June 1987.
16 ibid 5.
17 ibid 5–7.

on Environment and Development (1992) (the 'Rio Declaration') and (ii) the Convention on Biological Diversity.

7.16 The Rio Declaration provided for 27 universal principles.[18] Principle 17 provides:

> Environmental impact assessment, as a national instrument, shall be undertaken for proposed activities that are likely to have a significant adverse impact on the environment and are subject to a decision of a competent national authority.

7.17 A further outcome of the Earth Summit was the Convention on Biological Diversity, Article 14 of which provides:

> 1. Each Contracting Party, as far as possible and as appropriate, shall:
>
> (a) Introduce appropriate procedures requiring environmental impact assessment of its proposed projects that are likely to have significant adverse effects on biological diversity with a view to avoiding or minimizing such effects and, where appropriate, allow for public participation in such procedures.

7.18 EIAs also feature in international conventions and include the below.[19]

7.19 The UNECE Espoo Convention on Environmental Impact Assessment in a Transboundary Context (the 'Espoo Convention') aims to ensure international cooperation in assessing and managing the transboundary environmental impacts of planned activities and projects. The Espoo Convention was adopted in 1991 at a meeting at Espoo, Finland, and entered into force on 10 September 1997. It has 45 parties, including the EU and the UK.

7.20 The Espoo Convention is the only international instrument under the umbrella of the United Nations offering a legal framework to ensure international cooperation in assessing and managing the environmental impacts of planned activities and projects, in particular in a transboundary context. The Espoo Convention sets out the obligations of parties to assess the environmental impact of certain activities at an early stage of planning. It also lays down the general obligation of states to notify and consult each other on all major projects under consideration that are likely to have a significant adverse environmental impact across boundaries. Notably under Article 1(vii) 'impact' is broadly defined as 'any effect caused by a proposed activity on the environment including...climate'.

7.21 The Espoo Convention is augmented by the Protocol on Strategic Environmental Assessment to the Convention on Environmental Impact Assessment in a Transboundary

18 For further information see Chapter 3.

19 There are other further conventions which could be referred to but are not as relevant for the purposes of this chapter. For example, the Convention on the Law of the Sea (which came into force in 1994) contains provisions on the protection of the marine environment, including a requirement for EIAs for certain activities that may have a significant adverse impact on the marine environment. The Convention on Biological Diversity 2005 also provides for impact assessment.

Context (the 'Kyiv SEA Protocol'), which ensures that individual parties integrate environmental assessment into their plans and programmes at the earliest stages, and so help to encourage sustainable development. The EU and the UK signed the Kyiv SEA Protocol on 21 May 2003 and the EU approved it on 21 November 2008. The Kyiv SEA Protocol entered into force on 11 July 2010. Like the Espoo Convention, Article 2 of the Kyiv SEA Protocol provides for a definition of 'effect'. The Kyiv SEA Protocol requires its parties to evaluate the environmental consequences of their official draft plans and programmes and to assess the likely effects of their plans and programmes on: 'the environment, including … climate … and the interaction among these factors' (Article 2, paragraph 7.) Therefore, the likely significant effects to be described in the EIA report should include secondary and cumulative effects such as climate change.[20]

The legal framework for EIAs

7.22 Much of the UK's domestic environmental law is derived from EU law. EIA is no exception to this.

7.23 Article 2(1) Directive 2011/92/EU (the '2011 EIA Directive') provides for an assessment of projects likely to have 'significant effects on the environment' before development consent is granted:

> Member States shall adopt all measures necessary to ensure that, before consent is given, projects likely to have significant effects on the environment by virtue, inter alia, of their nature, size or location are made subject to a requirement for development consent and an assessment with regard to their effects.

7.24 Recital 14 to the 2011 EIA Directive encapsulates the nature of the required assessment as follows:

> The effects of a project on the environment should be assessed in order to take account of concerns to protect human health, to contribute by means of a better environment to the quality of life, to ensure maintenance of the diversity of species and to maintain the reproductive capacity of the ecosystem as a basic resource for life.

7.25 The recital expressly adopts a nature positive approach.

7.26 In respect of net zero, it is notable that when the 2011 EIA Directive was amended and updated in 2014 (Directive 2014/52/EU (the '2014 EIA Directive')) recitals were added which for the first time expressly mentioned climate change and GHG emissions. Those recitals state that:

> 7. Over the last decade, environmental issues, such as … climate change … have become more important in policy making. They should therefore also constitute important elements in assessment and decision making processes.

20 See footnote to item 6 of Annex IV of the Kyiv SEA Protocol.

…

13. Climate change will continue to cause damage to the environment and compromise economic development. In this regard, it is appropriate to assess the impact of projects on climate (for example greenhouse gas emissions) and their vulnerability to climate change.

7.27 Climate change is therefore expressly referred to as constituting an important element in the assessment and decision-making process. Recital 13 also makes clear that climate change will continue to cause damage to the environment and compromise economic development and so it is appropriate to assess the impact of projects on climate in the context of both mitigation and adaptation to climate change (hence, consideration of vulnerability).

7.28 The first EIA Directive (85/337/EEC) (the '1985 EIA Directive') came into force in 1985. It, and various amendments to it, were subsequently codified into the currently in force 2011 EIA Directive, which has itself been amended by the 2014 EIA Directive.

7.29 The approach to transposition involves multiple legislative instruments covering different types of project and different regimes for development consenting (for example forestry activities, port and harbour works, water abstraction and reservoirs). Since the majority of projects within the scope of the Directive require planning permission or development consent, the principal transposing regulations in England are the Town and Country Planning (Environmental Impact Assessment) Regulations 2017,[21] the Infrastructure Planning (Environmental Impact Assessment) Regulations 2017 ('EIA Regulations'),[22] and in Wales the Town and Country Planning (Environmental Impact Assessment) (Wales) Regulations 2017[23] (collectively, 'the Regulations').

7.30 The EIA regime only applies to certain projects. Consistent with the terms of the EIA Directive, for each of the Regulations, the categories of projects which are required to undergo EIA are: (a) those set out in Schedule 1 to the Regulations; and (b) those which meet the thresholds in Schedule 2 and are 'likely to have significant effects on the environment by virtue of factors such as [their] nature, size or location'.[24] The term 'project' has been broadly defined in the jurisprudence.[25]

7.31 As set out above, the purpose of EIA is to assess the significant effects of certain projects upon the environment. Crucially, the environmental information gained by assessment – comprising both the developer's environmental statement ('ES') and the

21 SI 2017/571.
22 SI 2017/572.
23 SI 2017/567.
24 reg 2.
25 Case C-72/95 *Aannemersbedrijf PK Kraaijeveld BV v Gedeputeerde Staten van Zuid-Holland* [1996] ECR I-5403 [31] and [39].

outputs of consultation with specialist statutory bodies and the public – informs but does not dictate the ultimate decision.[26]

7.32 The process is designed to inform project design and decision-making, including measures which may be necessary to avoid, mitigate or compensate for certain effects.

(i) *The EIA process*

7.33 The EIA process involves a number of steps, including:

- **Screening.** The first step is to determine whether an EIA is required. This is done by screening the proposed development against the threshold criteria in the EIA Regulations. If a developer is unsure whether their development requires an EIA, they can ask the planning authority for a screening decision.
- **Scoping.** If an EIA is required, the next step is to scope the EIA. This involves identifying the key environmental issues that need to be assessed, and setting the scope of the assessment. If a developer is unsure what should be included in an ES, the developer can ask the planning authority for a scoping opinion from the Local Planning Authority ('LPA') or a scoping direction (from the Secretary of State).
- **ES.** The EIA culminates in the preparation of an ES. The ES is a detailed report that assesses the potential environmental impacts of the proposed development.
- **Consultation.** The ES is then consulted upon with a range of statutory and non-statutory consultees. This provides an opportunity for stakeholders to comment on the proposed development and its potential environmental impacts.
- **Decision-making.** The decision-making authority, such as the LPA, needs to take account of the ES and any representations made about the development by the relevant consultation bodies, the public and any interested third parties before it can decide whether to grant planning consent.

(ii) *Key aspects of EIA Regulations*

7.34 The following are some of the key aspects of the EIA Regulations:[27]

- If an EIA is required for development and not carried out, then planning permission or subsequent consent must not be granted (as per reg 3).

---

26 As put by Thornton J in *R (Friends of the Earth Ltd) v Secretary of State for International Trade/Export Credits Guarantee Department (UK Export Finance)* [2022] EWHC 568 (Admin) [274]: 'EIA is not a procedure for preventing actions with significant environmental impacts from being implemented, although in certain circumstances this could be the appropriate outcome of the process. Rather the intention is that actions are authorised in the full knowledge of their environmental consequences.'
27 References in this list are to the Town and Country Planning (Environmental Impact Assessment) Regulations 2017 (n 21).

- The EIA process must identify, describe and assess in an appropriate manner, in the light of each individual case, the direct and indirect significant effects of the proposed development (reg 4(2)). This explicitly includes 'climate' (as per reg 4(2)(c)).

- The EIA process must include the preparation of an ES which is part of the environmental information that must be examined and taken into account (regs 2(1), 4(1) and 26(1)).[28]

- The ES must include at least a description of the likely significant effects of the proposed development on the environment (reg 18(3)(b)). As per regulation 4(2)(c) referred to above, this explicitly includes 'climate'.

- It must also include at least any additional information specified in Schedule 4 relevant to the specific characteristics of the particular development or type of development and to the environmental features likely to be significantly affected (reg 18(3)(f)).

- Schedule 4 concerns 'Information for inclusion in Environmental Statements' and specifies that a description of the likely significant effects of the development on the environment must be provided. This expressly includes at [5(f)]: 'the impact of the project on climate (for example the nature and magnitude of greenhouse gas emissions) and the vulnerability of the project to climate change'.

- The description should cover the direct effects and any indirect, secondary, cumulative, transboundary, short-term, medium-term and long-term, permanent and temporary, positive and negative effects of the development. It should 'take into account the environmental protection objectives … which are relevant to the project, including in particular those established under [the Directive]' (Schedule 4, [5]).

- It must also include the information reasonably required for reaching a reasoned conclusion on the significant effects of the development on the environment, taking into account current knowledge and methods of assessment (reg 18(4)(b)).

The legal framework for SEA

7.35 Again, broadly stated, the purpose of Strategic Environmental Assessment ('SEA') is to inform decision-making in relation to the adoption of plans and programmes (defined below). It is an iterative process which is undertaken as the plans and programmes evolve. It is therefore designed to shape the plans and programmes as they are developed and to ensure that environmental effects are properly taken into account

---

28 It is important to recall, as per the case law, that an ES is not expected to include more information than is reasonably required to assess the likely significant environmental effects of the development proposed in the light of current knowledge: as per Lindblom LJ in *Preston New Road Action Group v Secretary of State for Communities and Local Government* [2018] Env LR 18 [67].

while the proposals are at a formative stage, as well as requiring the plan-making body to explain what reasonable alternatives have been considered at the various stages.

7.36 Therefore, the purposes of EIA and SEA are broadly similar – however, they are focused on different stages of the process, with SEA operating 'upstream' and EIA 'downstream'. Moreover, while the SEA regime applies to public plans and programmes, the EIA regime applies to both public and private projects. The Court of Justice of the European Union ('CJEU') has confirmed that the application of the EIA Directive 'does not dispense with the obligation to carry out such an assessment under [the SEA] Directive'.[29]

7.37 The SEA Directive[30] is transposed in England by the Environmental Assessment of Plans and Programmes Regulations 2004[31] and in Wales by the Environmental Assessment of Plans and Programmes (Wales) Regulations 2004.[32] The purpose of the SEA Directive is set out at Article 1, which states:

> The objective of this Directive is to provide for a high level of protection of the environment and to contribute to the integration of environmental considerations into the preparation and adoption of plans and programmes with a view to promoting sustainable development, by ensuring that, in accordance with this Directive, an environmental assessment is carried out of certain plans and programmes which are likely to have significant effects on the environment.

7.38 The SEA regime applies to certain plans and programmes. Plans and programmes are defined in regulation 2 of the SEA Regulations as meaning plans and programmes (as well as modifications to them) which: (a) are subject to preparation or adoption by an authority at national, regional or local level; or (b) are prepared by an authority for adoption through a legislative procedure by Parliament or government; and, in either case (c) are required by legislative, regulatory or administrative provisions. The terms plans and programmes are not to be interpreted narrowly.[33]

7.39 Regulation 5 sets out the types of plans and programmes which must be subject to SEA (where the first formal preparatory act was taken on or after 21 July 2004). By regulation 5(2), these include plans or programmes which are prepared for agriculture, forestry, fisheries, energy, industry, transport, waste management, water management, telecommunications, tourism, town and country planning or land use and which set the framework for future development consent of projects listed in Annex I or Annex II of the EIA Directive.[34] By regulation 5(3), it also includes plans or programmes which require assessment pursuant to Article 6 or 7 of the Habitats Directive (as transposed). Regulation 5(6) and (7) carve out limited exceptions.

---

29 Case C-295/10 *Valčiukienė & Others v Pakruojo rajono savivaldybė and Others* (2011) ECLI:EU:C:2011:608; [2011] ECR I-08819 [60]–[63].
30 2001/42/EC.
31 SI 2004/1633.
32 SI 2004/1656.
33 *Walton v Scottish Ministers* [2012] UKSC 44.
34 2011/92/EU.

7.40 Schedule 1 to the SEA Regulations sets out the criteria for determining the likely significance of effects on the environment. Schedule 2 sets out information for environmental reports. The information to be contained within environmental reports is broadly cast. For example, it includes '[T]he relevant aspects of the current state of the environment and the likely evolution thereof without implementation of the plan or programme'.[35] This also includes, as per [6], Schedule 2:

> [T]he likely significant effects on the environment, including short, medium and long-term effects, permanent and temporary effects, positive and negative effects, and secondary cumulative and synergistic effects on issues such as (a) biodiversity, (b) population, (c) human health, (d) fauna, (e) flora, (f) soil, (g) water, (h) air, (i) climatic factors, (j) material assets (k) cultural heritage, including architectural and archaeological heritage, (l) landscape and (m) the inter-relationship between the issues referred to in (a)–(l).

7.41 Under the SEA regime, the environmental report must identify, describe and evaluate not only the likely significant effects on the environment of implementing the plan or programme, but also those of 'reasonable alternatives taking into account the objectives and the geographical scope of the plan or programme' (as per reg 12).

7.42 As with the EIA regime, the SEA regime includes consultation and publicity requirements, restrictions on adoption/submission unless the process has been followed, and post-adoption requirements.

The Levelling Up and Regeneration Act 2023

7.43 This chapter on EIAs is written against the backdrop of the Levelling Up and Regeneration Act 2023 ('LURA 2023'). From the commencement date (26 December 2023), the Secretary of State will have new powers under Part 6 of LURA 2023 to establish a system of Environmental Outcomes Reports ('EOR') to replace EIA and SEA. Section 153(1) of LURA 2023 provides that EOR regulations may make provision requiring an EOR to be prepared in relation to a proposed relevant consent[36] or plan.[37]

7.44 Paragraphs 56 and 57 of the Explanatory Notes to the Act provide some background on how an outcomes-based approach is intended to operate:[38]

> The Bill introduces an outcomes-based approach that will allow the government to set clear and tangible environmental outcomes which a plan or project is assessed against. This will allow decision-makers and local communities to clearly see where a plan or

35 Schedule 2, [2].
36 As per section 154(8): '"Consent" means any consent, approval, permission, authorisation, confirmation or decision (however described, given or made) that is required, or otherwise provided for, by or under any enactment in relation to a project.'
37 As per section 154(6): '"Relevant plan" means a plan or programme which— (a) relates, or may relate, to a project or to environmental protection in the United Kingdom or a relevant offshore area, and (b) is specified or described in EOR regulations for the purposes of this subsection.'
38 Explanatory Notes to LURA 2023 56–57.

project is meeting these outcomes and what steps are being taken to avoid and mitigate any harm to the environment. These outcomes will be set following consultation and parliamentary scrutiny but will, for the first time, allow the government to reflect its environmental priorities directly in the decision-making process.

By moving to an outcomes-based approach, and taking powers to address procedural issues with the current system, the Bill provides the opportunity to go further for the environment and to turn passive assessment into a more active tool to support environmental regeneration.

7.45 At the time of writing, the government had consulted on some of the 'principles' behind the EOR regime[39] – however, no response to that consultation has been published. The consultation said the goal was to 'simplify and streamline the assessment process'.

7.46 In terms of the key provisions of LURA 2023:

- Section 152 provides for a power to 'specify environmental outcomes': as per subsection 1 'regulations made by an appropriate authority under this Part ("EOR regulations") may specify outcomes relating to environmental protection in the United Kingdom or a relevant offshore area that are to be "specified environmental outcomes" for the purposes of this Part.'

- Therefore, the specified environmental outcomes will be set out in regulations (as per section 152), as will rules about when an EOR is required (as per section 153(1)).

- Section 153(4) defines an EOR as a written report which assesses the impact on the delivery of specified environmental outcomes and steps which will be taken to avoid, mitigate or compensate for any 'effects' on those outcomes that cannot delivered.

7.47 Despite the lack of full detail available, the LURA 2023 gives an indication as to how EORs will broadly will operate. EORs will work in the following way:

- Part 6 establishes an outcomes-based approach to assessment where anticipated environmental effects are measured against specified environmental outcomes.

39 Department for Levelling Up, Housing and Communities, 'Environmental Outcomes Reports: a new approach to environmental assessment' (published 17 March 2023). A consultation ran from 17 March 2023 to 9 June 2023. The Consultation Description was given as: 'Part 6 of the Levelling Up and Regeneration Bill will secure powers to implement a new system of environmental assessment known as Environmental Outcomes Reports. This will allow the government to replace the EU-derived Strategic Environmental Assessment and Environmental Impact Assessment processes with a streamlined system that places greater focus on delivering our environmental ambitions.'

- As well as assessing against outcomes, an EOR must set out and assess the impact of any proposed mitigation or compensation as well as considering reasonable alternatives to the consent or plan, or any element of them.

- Where an EOR is required following screening (see below), this must be taken into account when considering whether to grant consent or bring a plan into effect.

- As indicated in the consultation, the intention is for outcomes to be set in secondary legislation with a supporting suite of indicators set out in guidance. There will be a number of indicators for each outcome.

- In terms of 'screening', section 154 creates a power to define 'relevant consent' and 'relevant plan'. Section 154 creates two categories – Category 1 and Category 2. Category 1 consents will require an assessment in all circumstances and Category 2 consents will require an assessment if the criteria set out in the regulations are met. The intention is for section 154 to provide powers to clearly set what plans and projects require environmental assessment and avoid borderline cases because of unclear criteria which are then at high risk of legal challenge. As now, all projects in, or partly within, sensitive areas such as protected sites, will require screening, and the greater the potential impact on the environment, the greater the probability that the plan or project will require an environmental assessment. The consultation (at paragraph 6.4) provided that 'Screening' decisions for the smaller number of Category 2 consents will remain the judgement and discretion of the consenting authority, but regulations will narrow the scope for discussion by being more prescriptive on how borderline cases should be considered.

- In terms of 'scoping', discussed below, the new proposal for EORs would be that a set list of pre-defined outcomes would all be 'scoped in' to every assessment, whether or not there is likely to be a significant impact.

7.48 There is therefore potential for the provisions of LURA 2023 to lead to a wholesale replacement of EIA and SEA.

7.49 At this stage, there is little detail on how EORs will differ from the EIA process. However, section 156 of LURA 2023 does contain a non-regression guarantee. Section 156(1) provides:

> [a]n appropriate authority may make EOR regulations only if satisfied that making the regulations will not result in environmental law providing an overall level of environmental protection that is less than that provided by environmental law at the time this Act is passed.

7.50 One would therefore expect that the objective of this non-regression principle is to try and guarantee that much of the existing protections offered by the EIA regime, which have been built up over decades, will still be retained even in a different EOR system. Further, section 156(2) of LURA provides that: 'EOR regulations may not contain provision that is inconsistent with the implementation of the international obligations of the United Kingdom relating to the assessment of the environmental impact of relevant plans and relevant consents'.

7.51 Therefore, much of the guidance that already exists in respect of EIAs both at a domestic and international level will continue, at the very least, to be relevant to assessing the protection offered by the new EOR regime.

7.52 However, it will have to be seen in practice how EORs are implemented. The purpose of the EIA regime is set out in the recital of the respective EU Directive. These purposes provide important context for the interpretation and application of the relevant legal provisions. One criticism of LURA is that the lack of clearly stated legislative purposes could mean that any eventual EOR regime lacks legal coherence. Further, the EIA regime has been part of UK law for decades, is very detailed and is now well understood by decision-makers and developers – having been subject to decades of interpretation and explanation by the courts. This in itself could have serious consequences in terms of environmental protection.

Case law on climate change considerations in EIAs

7.53 Climate change is a complex and multifaceted issue, and it can be difficult to assess the potential impacts of development on climate change, or the potential impacts of climate change on development. However, there are a number of factors that could be relevant depending on the particular project, plan or programme in issue; these include: (i) GHG emissions; (ii) climate change resilience; and (iii) adaptation measures.

7.54 The 'mandatory' nature of assessment where a project is likely to have significant effects on the environment is confirmed by the CJEU in *Commission v Spain*.[40] Across the case law, the EIA Directive has been given a broad and purposive approach.[41] Indeed this broad and purposive approach to EIA is reflected in the judgment of the Supreme Court in *R (Champion) v North Norfolk*[42] which stated at [51]: 'Application of the precautionary principle, which underlies the EIA Directive, implies that cases of material doubt should generally be resolved in favour of EIA.'

7.55 In terms of 'significant effects', it is well-established that issues as to whether an effect is significant and the adequacy of any assessment of significant effects are matters of judgment for the decision-maker. Such judgments are only open to challenge in

---

40 *Commission v Spain* (Case C-227/01) [2005] Env LR 20, see [47]: 'In particular, Articles 1(1) and 2(1) and the first, fifth, sixth, eighth and 11th recitals in the preamble make clear that the Directive's fundamental objective is that, before consent is granted, projects likely to have significant effects on the environment by virtue, inter alia, of their nature, size or location should be made subject to a mandatory assessment with regard to their effects (see to that effect Case C-287/98 *Linster* [2000] ECR I-6917, para 52).'

41 See for example *Aannemersbedrijf PK Kraaijeveld BV v Gedeputeerde Staten van Zuid-Holland* (n 25); Case C-2/07 *Abraham v Wallonia* [2008] ECR I-01197; [2008] Env LR 66 and Case C-411/17 *Inter-Environnement Wallonie ASBL v Council of Ministers* (2019) ECLI:EU:C:2019:622; [2020] Env LR 9.

42 *R (Champion) v North Norfolk* [2015] 1 WLR 3710.

the courts applying the conventional *Wednesbury* standard[43] and as such whether the decision falls outside the range of reasonable decisions open to the decision-maker or whether there is a demonstrable flaw in the reasoning which led to it.[44]

7.56 There is a growing body of case law on climate change, net zero and EIAs. The courts have adopted a mixed-approach to climate change and EIA cases – sometimes arguments run by claimants that there has been a failure to consider properly climate change and GHG emissions are successful, while often a significant degree of discretion is given to the decision-maker. Cases illustrating the relevance of climate change and net zero considerations in the context of EIAs are outlined below.

7.57 In *HJ Banks and Co Ltd v SSHCLG*[45] the court held that the Secretary of State for Housing Communities and Local Government had erred in refusing planning permission for a surface mine for the extraction of coal after giving very considerable weight to the adverse effects of the emission of GHGs. He had erred in his approach to the NPPF,[46] and had given inadequate reasoning on the critical issue of how a proposal for coal required to meet the country's energy needs could be refused on the basis of the adverse impact of GHGs, unless the gap was filled by renewables or low carbon sources. However, it is clear from that decision that all parties, including the Secretary of State,[47] agreed that the GHG impact of combustion had to be assessed and taken into account.

7.58 Another decision which is relevant to the intersection of EIAs and climate change/net zero *is R (Squire) v Shropshire Council*[48] ('*Squire*'). *Squire* was a challenge to the grant of permission for a poultry-rearing facility in the countryside. At [65] to [69] of the Court of Appeal's judgment, Lindblom LJ held that the ES prepared in connection with the project was unlawful. The statement did not specify the third party land on which manure from the chickens was going to be spread. Although it dealt with odour likely to emanate from the poultry buildings themselves, the ES did not set out any parallel assessment or indeed any meaningful assessment of the effects of odour and dust from the storage and spreading of chicken manure, either on the land of the farmer who was the proposed developer or on that of any other farmer. It did not seek to anticipate the content of any future manure management plan, including the fields to which it would relate. It could not be inferred from the ES that its authors had concluded that the proposed storage and spreading of manure was not a potential source of pollution, including odour and dust, which ought to be addressed in determining the application for planning permission. Finally, the future manure management plan was not a substitute for the assessment lacking in the ES. Not only was the manure management plan yet to come into existence, even when it did, it was only going to relate to the storage and spreading of manure on the land of the farmer seeking to build

43 *Associated Provincial Picture Houses Ltd v Wednesbury Corporation* (1948) 1 KB 223.
44 *Blewett v Derbyshire County Council* [2004] Env LR 29; *R (Friends of the Earth Ltd) v Secretary of State for Transport* [2021] PTSR 190 at [142]–[145] and *R (Law Society) v The Lord Chancellor* [2018] EWHC (Admin) 2094 [98].
45 *HJ Banks and Co Ltd v SSHCLG* [2019] Env LR 20.
46 ibid [149].
47 ibid [119].
48 *R (Squire) v Shropshire Council* [2019] Env LR 36.

the facility, not to the substantial qualities that were going to have to be disposed of elsewhere. Lindblom LJ therefore held at [69] that:

> In my view, therefore, the environmental statement was deficient in its lack of a proper assessment of the environmental impacts of the storage and spreading of manure as an indirect effect of the proposed development. In this respect it was not compliant with the requirements of the EIA Directive and the EIA regulations.

7.59 One of the most significant cases at the intersection of EIAs and climate change/ net zero considerations is the Supreme Court decision in *R (Finch on behalf of the Weald Action Group) v Surrey County Council and others (Respondents)*[49] ('*Finch*'). The judgment gives important guidance on EIAs.

7.60 The relevant background to the *Finch* decision is as follows. In December 2018, Horse Hill Developments Ltd (the second Respondent), sought planning permission from Surrey County Council ('the Council') (the first Respondent), to retain and expand an existing onshore oil well site (comprising two wells) and to drill for four new wells, enabling the production of hydrocarbons from six wells over a period of 25 years. The EIA for the project considered the environmental impacts of 'the direct releases of greenhouse gases from with the well site boundary resulting from the site's construction, production, decommissioning and subsequent restoration over the lifetime of the proposed development.' However the EIA did not assess the environmental impacts of the downstream GHG emissions that would inevitably result when the oil extracted from the development site was later refined and then used, for example, as fuel. The Council granted planning permission for the development on 27 September 2019. The Appellant applied for judicial review of the Council's decision, acting on behalf of the Weald Action Group. Her claim was unsuccessful before the High Court and the Court of Appeal. The Supreme Court allowed her appeal. This was the first case in which the Office for Environmental Protection ('OEP') intervened, making use of its powers to intervene for the first time since it was established in 2021.[50] This intervention also reflected the significance of the judgment.

7.61 By a three-to-two majority, the Supreme Court allowed the Appellant's appeal and held that the Council's decision was unlawful because the emissions that will occur when the oil produced is burnt as fuel are within the scope of the EIA required by law. Lord Leggatt gave the majority judgment (with whom Lord Kitchin and Lady Rose agreed) and Lord Sales dissented (with whom Lord Richards agreed).

7.62 The following aspects of the majority judgment are of note:

- It was an agreed fact between all the parties that if the project went ahead, it would not be merely likely but 'inevitable' that the oil produced from the well site

---

49 *R (Finch on behalf of the Weald Action Group) v Surrey County Council and others (Respondents)* [2024] UKSC 20.
50 For further information see Chapter 4 (paras 4.10–4.19).

would be refined and, as an end product, eventually undergo combustion. That combustion would produce GHG emissions (at [45]).

- It was also agreed that the amount of these emissions could be estimated using an established methodology. It was also observed by the Supreme Court that the Council had in fact provided such an estimate as part of its evidence – it was therefore clearly possible (at [81]).

- The question for the Supreme Court was whether the combustion emissions constitute 'direct or indirect ... effects of the project' within the meaning of the EIA Directive and 2017 Regulations. If they were, they must be assessed as part of the EIA. The Supreme Court was unanimous in rejecting the view of the Court of Appeal that this question required an evaluative judgment about whether there is a sufficient causal connection between the extraction of the oil and its eventual combustion. It would be unreasonable to interpret the EIA Directive in such a way that such inconsistent answers would be equally valid (see [59]–[60] and [321]–[325]).

- The majority of the Supreme Court considered this question to be one of causation to which, on the agreed facts, only one answer could reasonably be given. It was known with certainty that, if the project went ahead, all the oil extracted from the ground would inevitably be burnt thereby releasing GHG emissions which could readily be estimated (at [79]–[81]).

- The EIA Directive does not impose any geographical limit on the scope of the environmental effects of a project that must be assessed. It is in the very nature of 'indirect' effects that they may occur away from their source (at [101]–[103]).

- The Supreme Court addressed Holgate J's concern (as he then was) that where a component is manufactured which forms a small part of a much larger object (such as a motor vehicle or aircraft), the view might reasonably be taken that the contribution of the component is not material enough to justify attributing the impact on the environment of the end product to the activity of manufacturing the component part. However, the majority held that there is no element of conjecture about what will ultimately happen to the oil; refining the oil does not change it into a different type of object (unlike the incorporation of a part in a motor vehicle or aircraft); and a reasonable estimate could readily be made (at [122]–[123]).

- Throughout the majority judgment it was emphasised that the purpose of the EIA is to ensure that, whatever the decision taken, it is taken with full knowledge and public awareness of the likely significant environmental consequences (see [140]–[154]).

- Consequently, the Council's failure to assess the effect on climate of the combustion of the oil that would be produced from the proposed well site meant that its decision to grant planning permission for the project was unlawful (at [174]).

7.63 Lord Sales in his dissenting judgment (with whom Lord Richards agreed) emphasised the following:

- The EIA Directive contemplates that decisions on the grant of planning consent will often be taken by local or regional authorities (at [252]). However, downstream emissions are addressed by central governments at the level of national policy (at [253]).

- It would therefore be constitutionally inappropriate for a local planning authority to assume practical decision-making authority based on its own views regarding downstream emissions and it would also be contrary to the EU principle of proportionality (at [256] and [260]).

- Lord Sales explained that this view was supported by the general scheme of the EIA Directive (at [261]) and the wording of the EIA Directive [273].

- Lord Sales' judgment therefore agreed with the approach of the High Court in which the question is to be determined by a proper interpretation of the EIA Directive as a matter of law (at [327]).

7.64 It is noted the UK Supreme Court reached a similar conclusion to that of the Norwegian courts in *The Greenpeace Nordic Association and Others v The State and Energy Ministry*.[51] That case was decided after the *Finch* appeal was heard in the Supreme Court but before judgment in *Finch* was handed down. It is referred to in the Supreme Court's majority judgment (at [169] to [173]). In *The Greenpeace Nordic Association and Others v The State and Energy Ministry* all three projects involved the extraction of petroleum in quantities which made an EIA mandatory before consent could be granted. The EIAs carried out did not assess the combustion emissions from the oil and gas to be produced. On 18 January 2024 the Oslo District Court ruled that there was a legal requirement to assess the combustion emissions under both the EIA Directive and the Norwegian regulations which implement the EIA Directive. As such an assessment had not been made, the consents granted for the development and operation of the three oil fields were declared to be invalid. At [172] the Supreme Court noted the Norwegian court's reasoning that: 'The express requirement to assess 'indirect' effects shows that 'it cannot be decisive that the combustion emissions do not occur on site in connection with production, and that instead they occur later via one or more intermediate steps as combustion emissions elsewhere': p 52.' Lord Leggatt expressly said that he found the reasoning of the Norwegian court persuasive and agreed with it (at [173]).

7.65 In *R (Boswell) v Secretary of State for Transport*[52] ('*Boswell*'), the High Court refused an application for judicial review in a case relating to three new nationally significant infrastructure ('NSIP') road schemes in Norfolk. The Secretary of State for Transport assessed the GHG emissions expected to be generated by each scheme

---

51 *The Greenpeace Nordic Association and Others v The State and Energy Ministry* Case No 23-099330TVI (Oslo District Court, 18 January 2024).
52 *R (Boswell) v Secretary of State for Transport* [2023] EWHC 1710 (Admin).

and acknowledged that each scheme would lead to an increase in GHG emissions. However, the Secretary of State ultimately concluded that when compared with the UK's national carbon budgets, the increase from each scheme was not significant. The Claimant challenged the Secretary of State's decision on the basis that he was under a legal duty to assess the cumulation of environmental effects with other existing or approved projects and that he acted unlawfully in failing to meaningfully assess the combined GHG emissions from the three schemes.

7.66 The court dismissed the application, saying that the Secretary of State's assessment was lawful. The Court held that the question of what impacts should be addressed cumulatively; how the cumulative impacts might occur; whether the effects are likely to be significant and, if so, how they should be assessed are all matters of evaluative judgment for the Secretary of State. The Court also added that: 'Acceptability of impact is not a matter for the Courts, who must be astute to avoid being drawn into the arena of the merits of climate decision making.'[53] The judgment also emphasised that some government policies may result in GHG emissions, but they are nonetheless promoted in order to achieve other policy goals. For that reason, any net emissions increase from a particular policy or project is managed within the government's overall strategy for meeting carbon budgets and the net zero target for 2050, as part of an economy-wide transition. As a consequence, 'EIA for any proposed project must therefore give proportionate consideration to whether and how that project will contribute to or jeopardise the achievement of these targets'.[54]

7.67 The Claimant appealed to the Court of Appeal and that appeal was dismissed in *R (Boswell) v Secretary of State for Transport*.[55] The Claimant's single ground of appeal was that the judge at first instance was wrong to hold that the requirement to consider the significance of the cumulative GHG emissions from the scheme was discharged in the Secretary of State's decision letters. The Court held that the Secretary of State clearly addressed his mind to the question of cumulative effects, and he took into account the submissions which the Claimant had made at the examination stage of the EIA process, but he nevertheless decided that there was no meaningful basis, in this particular context, upon which a wider cumulative assessment of carbon emissions could be undertaken.[56]

7.68 *R (Bristol Airport Action Network Co-ordinating Committee) v Secretary of State for Levelling Up, Housing and Communities*:[57] the Court held that a panel of planning inspectors had not erred in their consideration of whether and to what extent aviation emissions were relevant when allowing a developer's appeal against the refusal of planning permission for the expansion of Bristol Airport. The Court concluded that there was scientific uncertainty about how to assess the effects of non-CO_2 emissions and

---

53 See para 6(vii).
54 See [71]; *R (Transport Action Network) v Secretary of State for Transport* [2021] EWHC (Admin) 2091 [46] and [54] and *R (Packham) v Secretary of State for Transport* [2021] Env LR 10 [87] also cited.
55 *R (Boswell) v Secretary of State for Transport* [2024] EWCA Civ 145.
56 ibid [54].
57 *R (Bristol Airport Action Network Co-ordinating Committee) v Secretary of State for Levelling Up, Housing and Communities* [2023] Env LR 28.

the panel had been entitled to consider that there was no defect in the approach to the EIA.[58] Leaving non-CO_2 aircraft emissions to be dealt with when the science enabled them to be brought into account was a decision that was open to those preparing the ES, and one that the local authority and the panel were entitled to accept. For the panel to have attempted directly to address the non-CO_2 effects of aircraft emissions would have been highly anomalous. Therefore, even if they might have acted lawfully if they had embarked on such an exercise, it was not irrational for them to conclude that they would not do so.[59]

7.69 The following points can be observed from the above cases:

- Issues as to whether an effect is significant and the adequacy of any assessment of significant effects are matters of judgment for the decision-maker. The courts have reiterated on several occasions that this is a matter of planning judgment.
- Depending on the nature of the development, it will be much more difficult for the decision-maker to argue that climate change or GHG emissions did not need to be assessed and taken into account at all.
- Again, depending on the circumstances of the individual case, regard should also be had to overall strategy for meeting carbon budgets and the net zero target for 2050, as part of an economy-wide transition.

7.70 Such challenges are only likely to increase in prevalence. For instance, there is currently a challenge underway in the courts to the Secretary of State's grant of permission for a new underground coal mine and associated development at Whitehaven in Cumbria (which has been adjourned pending the outcome in *Finch*). The Secretary of State granted permission for the UK's first deep coal mine in 30 years following a month-long planning inquiry that took place in September 2021. The Claimants contend that in permitting the proposed mine, the Secretary of State failed to account for the significant climate impacts of the mine.[60] The impact for Whitehaven is of particular

---

58 For further information see Chapter 3 (paras 3.36–3.38).

59 *R (Bristol Airport Action Network Co-ordinating Committee) v Secretary of State for Levelling Up, Housing and Communities* (n 58) [202], [216], [220] and [231].

60 Details of the challenge are available on the Friends of the Earth website: <https://friendsoftheearth.uk/climate/climate-groups-contest-high-court-refusal-hear-legal-challenge-against-cumbria-coal-mine> accessed 9 April 2024. The decision is challenged on four grounds:

1. That the Secretary of State erred when concluding that the climate impacts of the mine were 'neutral or at worst slightly beneficial' because there would be 'potential for a significant degree of substitution' (i.e. for some of the coal from the mine to displace coal which otherwise would have come from other mines) when the evidence before the Inquiry had been that if even 1.1% of the coal was not subject to substitution, the emissions from the use of the coal would lead to a net increase in GHG emissions;
2. The Secretary of State erred in failing to address or even mention undisputed evidence before the inquiry that permitting the new coal mine would have a negative effect on the UK's climate diplomacy and would send a signal that the UK is not serious about its climate ambition, resulting in reduced ambition from other countries and increased global GHG emissions;
3. The Secretary of State applied the wrong legal test in considering whether downstream emissions (i.e. the emissions from the use of the coal) should have been considered; and
4. The Inspector applied disparate standards to the evidence of the applicant coal mining company and the objectors, consistently resolving matters of uncertainty or evidential gaps in the applicant's favour despite it being for the applicant to produce evidence to a standard to satisfy the Inspector that relevant policies were met. The Secretary of State adopted the findings of the Inspector, failing to correct this erroneous approach.

note given that West Cumbria Mining Limited (who are involved in the Whitehaven coal mine) were permitted to intervene in the Supreme Court in *Finch*.

7.71 This case law suggests that the courts are likely to play a key role in ensuring that EIAs are used effectively to achieve net zero. Developers and decision-makers will need to be aware of the latest case law and guidance in order to ensure that EIAs are carried out in a way that is consistent with net zero and biodiversity, as reflected by the references to biodiversity discussed above.

Conclusion

7.72 EIAs are an important tool for ensuring that the environmental impacts of development are properly considered. Climate change and biodiversity are major considerations in EIAs, and it is essential that the potential impacts of development on climate change, and the potential impacts of climate change on development, are properly assessed.

7.73 It is worth emphasising that the fact that GHG emissions are assessed does not mean the proposal is unacceptable: the environmental effects of GHG emissions simply have to be weighed against other material considerations. The EIA process is concerned with how a decision is made and not what the decision should be. It has been succinctly stated that:

> EIA is not a procedure for preventing actions with significant environmental impacts from being implemented, although in certain circumstances this could be the appropriate outcome of the process. Rather the intention is that actions are authorised in the full knowledge of their environmental consequences.[61]

7.74 EIAs can play a crucial role in ensuring that the UK's transition to net zero is implemented in a sustainable and environmentally responsible manner. By identifying the GHG emissions of proposed developments, assessing the vulnerability of developments to climate change, and promoting the use of renewable energy technologies and sustainable construction materials and techniques, EIAs can help to reduce the environmental impact of development and achieve net zero.

---

61 Thornton J in *R (Friends of the Earth Ltd) v Secretary of State for International Trade/Export Credits Guarantee Department (UK Export Finance)* (n 26) [274].

CHAPTER 8

OVERVIEW OF THE LAW AND POLICY OF NATURE POSITIVE

Eleanor Leydon and Stephanie David

Introduction

8.01 As set out in the introduction to this book, there is a significant interdependency between the climate crisis and biodiversity crisis (see Chapter 1, paragraphs 1.05–1.09). The climate crisis poses a grave threat to nature: as recognised in the 25 Year Environment Plan ('the 25YEP'), climate change is 'perhaps the most serious long-term risk to the environment given higher land and sea temperatures, rising sea levels, extreme weather patterns and ocean acidification, which harms marine species.'[1] However, nature can also (to the extent it is preserved from external threats) play a crucial role in climate mitigation and adaptation.

8.02 Many experts consider that climate change is currently the second biggest direct driver of biodiversity loss; as climate impacts worsen, this role will expand.[2] However, other drivers of biodiversity loss remain fundamental. These include, first and foremost, land use and sea use change (i.e. the degradation, destruction, and conversion of habitats); overexploitation (particularly in the case of mammals and fish); pollution; and invasive alien species. There is 'overwhelming consensus' that these drivers interact synergistically, such that the combined effects of multiple drivers are greater than the sum of their parts.[3]

8.03 Biodiversity loss and climate change are 'fundamentally connected, not only in terms of the driving processes, feedback and mechanistic links, but, critically, also in terms of potential solutions'.[4] In particular, nature recovery has 'gained significant traction in recent years as a solution to jointly address the biodiversity crisis and climate change emergency, with research suggesting that the restoration of the planet's most degraded areas in combination with the protection of biodiversity hotspots could significantly boost carbon sequestration capacity while preventing about 70% of predicted

1 Department for Environment, Food and Rural Affairs, 'A Green Future: Our 25 Year Plan to Improve the Environment' (2018) 9 <https://assets.publishing.service.gov.uk/media/5ab3a67840f0b65bb584297e/25-year-environment-plan.pdf> accessed 4 April 2024.
2 Forest Isbell and others, 'Expert Perspectives on Global Biodiversity Loss and Its Drivers and Impacts on People' (2023) 21 Frontiers in Ecology and the Environment 94, 94–103.
3 ibid 94–103.
4 Nathalie Pettorelli and James M Bullock, 'Restore or Rewild? Implementing Complementary Approaches to Bend the Curve on Biodiversity Loss' (2023) 4(2) Ecological Solutions and Evidence 12244 <https://besjournals.onlinelibrary.wiley.com/doi/full/10.1002/2688-8319.12244> accessed 7 May 2024.

species extinctions'.[5] The UK in particular is acknowledged by the government to be 'one of the most nature depleted countries in the world'.[6]

8.04 Crucially, nature 'recovery' implies a policy turn from mere nature 'conservation' towards nature restoration[7] and enhancement, as argued for domestically in the 2010 Lawton Review (see below at paragraph 8.25). This ambition is reflected in the new global goal for nature, Nature Positive, which is defined as a goal to 'Halt and Reverse Nature Loss by 2030 on a 2020 baseline, and achieve full recovery by 2050' (see paragraphs 1.46–1.56 in Chapter 1).[8]

8.05 This policy turn also underpins the 25YEP published in 2018, and substantial sections of the Environment Act 2021 ('EA 2021'). Illustratively, section 102 of the EA 2021 amends section 40 of the Natural Environment and Rural Communities Act 2006, which required all public authorities carrying out functions in England[9] to have regard to 'conserving' biodiversity when delivering their functions. The amended section refocuses the duty towards an active requirement to seek the further conservation 'and enhancement' of nature, with the aim of aligning public authorities' action on biodiversity with the government's increased ambition (see further paragraphs 8.96–8.101 below).[10]

8.06 Halting and reversing biodiversity loss encompasses consideration of diversity within species, between species and of ecosystems.[11] However, there are other relevant measures of nature positive performance, such as species abundance, which have been integrated into national law and policy (see paragraphs 8.50ff below). Other concepts found in the international legal framework, such as the degradation of ecosystems, still require domestic definition.

8.07 Historically, the legal framework governing nature conservation has comprised two main pillars: habitat conservation and species protection.[12] In particular, for over a century, protected areas have been the main instrument used to regulate biodiversity conservation (see further Chapter 9).[13] As set out below, both pillars will continue to play a key role in both international and national legal frameworks leading up to 2030.[14] However, there is an increasing focus on not only the quantity but also the quality of

---

5 ibid.

6 DEFRA, 'Nature Recovery Green Paper: Protected Sites and Species' (2022) 4 <https://consult.defra.gov.uk/nature-recovery-green-paper/nature-recovery-green-paper/supporting_documents/Nature%20Recovery%20Green%20Paper%20Consultation%20%20Protected%20Sites%20and%20Species.pdf>.

7 Restoration is generally defined as the science-based assisted recovery of an ecosystem that has been degraded, damaged, or destroyed. Restoration generally focuses on the recovery of an ecosystem's known or presumed former state. This might be contrasted with the more novel approach of rewilding, which has a lower fidelity to precedent and focuses on present and future ecosystem functioning and resilience: Nathalie Pettorelli and James M Bullock (n 4).

8 'Nature Positive Initiative' <https://www.naturepositive.org/> accessed 26 November 2023.

9 Together with HMRC carrying out functions in Wales. For the equivalent duty which applies to all other public authorities in Wales, see ss 6–7 Environment (Wales) Act 2016 (discussed at para 8.148).

10 Explanatory Notes to the EA 2021 para 49.

11 Article 2 of the UN Convention on Biological Diversity.

12 Burnett-Hall and Jones, *Burnett-Hall on Environmental Law* (3rd edn, Sweet & Maxwell 2012) paras 9–005.

13 David W Macdonald, *Biodiversity Conservation: A Very Short Introduction* (Oxford University Press 2023) 143.

14 See, for example, s 40A(6) NERCA 2006, as amended by s 102 of the EA 2021, and the Explanatory Notes to the EA 2021 at para 932.

protected areas, as well as the need to take action for nature outside of protected areas, including by increasing ecological connectivity and regulating human activity (e.g. pollution and resource extraction) outside of these areas. Further, the historic bifurcated approach to protecting particular species and particular protected areas is giving way to a more holistic, ecosystem-based approach to nature conservation, restoration and recovery.[15] The new approach has also heralded calls to reform and consolidate the wealth of more discrete, species-specific legislation which has developed historically.[16]

8.08 This chapter will first address the international and national development of nature conservation and 'nature positive' law and policy, before turning to the current legal frameworks set out, internationally, in the Kunming-Montreal Global Biodiversity Framework ('GBF'), and in England in the EA 2021, in particular Part 1 (Environmental Governance) and Part 6 (Nature and Biodiversity). Part 1 provides for a new governance framework comprising, *inter alia*, statutory environmental targets, environmental improvement plans, and a new environmental watchdog (the Office for Environmental Protection ('OEP')). Part 6 provides a range of new legal mechanisms for the protection of nature and biodiversity, including biodiversity net gain in the planning system; the enhanced biodiversity duty on public authorities and biodiversity reporting; Local Nature Recovery Strategies, species conservation strategies and protected site strategies; and the forest risk commodity regime. For a discussion of the current position in Wales, see paragraphs para 8.144–8.157 below. For an account of the ways in which domestic planning policy incorporates 'nature positive'/biodiversity goals, see Chapter 5.

Development of the law of nature positive

(i) *Domestic duties and designations*

8.09 As set out above, the focus of this chapter is on the national and international legal framework which applies post-2020 and creates scientifically-informed obligations and targets which are specifically geared towards nature recovery.

8.10 The ways in which domestic law has previously 'made space for nature'[17] are manifold, according to their development over (roughly) the last 70 years. There are some key 'nature' statutes (briefly explored below), and a much wider range of individual nature-conscious provisions scattered among statutes which substantively focus on other areas or industries (for example, the Plant Health Act 1967 and Forestry Act 1967, which also intend to protect agriculture and the forestry industry). A comprehensive

---

15 This includes a focus on nature recovery outside of protected areas. See, for example, DEFRA, 'Nature Recovery Green Paper: Protected Sites and Species' (n 6), which set out an 'overall aim' of 'moving to an approach which focuses more on outcomes and recovery' (p7). At p13, the Green Paper states that '[w]hile there will always be a role for more defensive, site-specific protections, the Government believes that in order to see a genuine national recovery in species abundance, the old approach will not be sufficient. In considering a more holistic approach to nature recovery and making space for nature, we can also look to better support those species which have wide ranges and are not necessarily dependant on specific habitats under protection at present'.

16 Burnett-Hall and Jones (n 12) paras 9-012–9-013, 9-123, 9-140; Law Commission, 'Wildlife Law, Volume 1: Report' (2015) LC No. 362; DEFRA, 'Nature Recovery Green Paper: Protected Sites and Species' (2022) (n 6) 26–28.

17 JH Lawton and others, 'Making Space for Nature: A Review of England's Wildlife Sites and Ecological Network. Report to DEFRA' (2010); see further paras 8.25ff.

account of the ways in which nature is protected, recognised or indeed adversely affected across our statute book is therefore beyond the scope of this book.

8.11 The development of different protected site designations over time is explored in detail in Chapter 9. Key legislation includes the National Parks and Access to the Countryside Act 1949 ('NPACA 1949'), which first provided for a number of landscape and protected area designations, including National Parks, National and Local Nature Reserves, Areas of Outstanding Natural Beauty ('AONBs')[18]; the Wildlife and Countryside Act 1981 ('WCA 1981'), which significantly modernised sites of special scientific interest ('SSSIs'); the Marine and Coastal Access Act 2009 ('MCAA 2009') which creates new marine designations; and the Habitats Regulations which comprehensively protect European Sites (both onshore and offshore).[19]

8.12 The role of the planning system in protecting nature is explored in Chapter 5. Chapter 7 considers Environmental Impact Assessment and Strategic Impact Assessment regulations. The 'nature' provisions in key agricultural legislation – both pre and post Brexit – are explored in Chapter 12. The role of the nature conservation bodies is discussed in Chapters 4 and 9. The Environmental Permitting (England and Wales) Regulations 2016 (the principal regulations made under the Pollution Prevention and Control Act 1999) are discussed in Chapter 13.

(ii) *Species-specific protection*

8.13 The WCA 1981 achieved much for nature conservation beyond advancing the legal framework for protecting SSSIs (as explored in Chapter 9). It is the principal modern act providing for species-specific protection, having repealed and re-enacted previous legislation on the protection and conservation of birds, wild creatures and wild plants, in the process implementing the UK's obligations under the original Birds Directive.[20]

8.14 Part 1 WCA 1981 provides for the protection of birds, animals and wild plants. Sections 1–8 implement the key wild bird protection measures now required under the Birds Directive.[21] These include creating offences of intentionally interfering with wild birds, by killing, injuring or taking a wild bird; taking, damaging or destroying nests; or taking or destroying an egg (section 1(1); Schedule ZA1). It is also an offence to possess or control any live or dead wild bird, their egg, or anything derived from a wild bird or their egg, unless the person can show that the bird or egg was lawfully[22] killed, taken or sold (section 1(2)–(3)). It is also an offence to intentionally or recklessly disturb any wild bird building a nest, or their young (section 1(5)). Sections 2 and 4 provide

18 As amended by the Countryside Act 1968, which gave further environmental duties to public bodies, and first introduced the concept of areas of Special Scientific Interest by reason of their flora, fauna or geological or physiographical features (s 15).
19 The Conservation of Habitats and Species Regulations 2017, SI 2017/1012 and the Conservation of Offshore Marine Habitats and Species Regulations 2017, SI 2017/1013.
20 79/409/EEC.
21 2009/147/EC.
22 As defined in s 1(3A).

for exceptions to these offences. Section 3 empowers the Secretary of State to make provision relating to Areas of Special Protection. Sections 5–6 create further offences of using certain methods of killing or taking wild birds, and selling certain birds. Section 7 requires that possession or control of any bird included in Schedule 4 must be registered and ringed or marked in accordance with regulations, or the possessor shall be guilty of an offence. Section 8 creates offences in relation to the treatment and release of captive birds.

8.15 Sections 9–12 provide for the protection of the wild animals listed in Schedule 5, creating similar offences. Section 13 similarly creates protections for the wild plants listed in Schedule 8. Section 14 prohibits the introduction of the non-native species listed in Part I, IA or IB of Schedule 9, and sections 14ZA–14P provide for further controls on species.

8.16 Section 16 provides for the licensing of many of the actions defined as offences in Part 1. The appropriate authority (as defined in section 16) may grant licences for the purposes specified in section 16(1), but only where satisfied that there is no other satisfactory solution (section 16(1A)).

8.17 There is a wealth of other species-specific legislation which dates back to 1831: much of the earlier law was developed to govern activities such as hunting and fishing, and developed over the years to include species conservation, animal welfare and biodiversity concerns. In 2012, the Law Commission consulted on proposals to reform domestic wildlife law: in November 2015, it published its final report and accompanying draft bill.[23] The report noted that wildlife legislation has developed in a 'piecemeal' fashion, resulting in legislation which is 'unnecessarily complex and inconsistent', and contains 'overlapping and sometimes conflicting provisions'.[24] While a certain level of complexity is inevitable, in many cases there is little obvious rationale for the existing complexity.[25] The Law Commission proposed replacing the patchwork of existing legislation with a single statute, as set out in the draft bill. While some recommendations relating to the control of invasive non-native species were given effect in the Infrastructure Act 2015, the other recommendations have not been implemented, given the impact of Brexit in the intervening period.[26] Some species-specific protections relating to marine mammals have now been repealed or amended via the Fisheries Act 2020.

(iii) *Further early domestic nature law*

8.18 The Environmental Protection Act 1990 contains a wide range of provisions including pollution control by local authorities (Part I), controls on waste (Part II) and contaminated land (Part IIA), statutory nuisances (Part III) and controls on GMOs (Part VI). The Environment Act 1995, *inter alia*, provides for National Parks (Part III), and provides for hedgerow protection and conservation grants: see further Chapter 12.

---

23 Law Commission, 'Wildlife Law, Volume 1: Report' (n 16).
24 ibid paras 1.7–1.8.
25 ibid para 1.9.
26 ibid.

8.19 Although the Countryside and Rights of Way Act 2000 ('CROWA 2000') provides for public rights of access to land, these rights can be restricted for conservation purposes (section 26). Part IV advances the law on AONBs, including making it the general duty of relevant authorities to seek to further the purpose of conserving and enhancing the site's natural beauty (section 85), providing for the establishment of conservation boards (section 86), and providing for the publishing of management plans (section 89).

8.20 Part 3 of the Natural Environment and Rural Communities Act 2006 ('NERCA 2006') makes further provision for the protection of wildlife, including through the section 40 duty to conserve (and now enhance) biodiversity, and the new section 40A provision for biodiversity reports (see paragraphs 8.96–8.101 below). Section 41 further obliges the Secretary of State for England to publish a list of the living organisms and types of habitat which in the Secretary of State's opinion are of principal importance for the purpose of conserving (or enhancing) biodiversity, having consulted Natural England. The Secretary of State must then take such steps as appear reasonably practicable to further the conservation of the listed organisms and habitats, or promote the taking of such steps by others. The Secretary of State must keep the list under review, and revise it as appropriate.

8.21 Sections 43–46 NERCA 2006 create an offence of possessing prescribed pesticides, provide for enforcement powers, and empower the Secretary of State to issue a relevant code of practice.

8.22 The MCAA 2009 introduces wide-ranging new arrangements for the sustainable management of activities, and protection of resources, in the UK's marine area. This includes establishing the Marine Management Organisation (Part 1), introducing a new system of marine planning (Part 3), and new, streamlined marine licensing provisions (Part 4), as well as enabling the designation of Marine Conservation Zones (see further Chapter 9).

8.23 The Environmental Damage (Prevention and Remediation) (England) Regulations 2015[27] and Environmental Damage (Prevention and Remediation) (Wales) Regulations 2009[28] ('the Environmental Damage Regulations') implement a standalone regime which was originally introduced to implement the Environmental Liability Directive 2004.[29] This aims to prevent and remediate environmental damage (which is widely defined) based on the polluter pays principle. The Environmental Damage Regulations remain in force as assimilated law following Brexit.

8.24 The Fisheries Act 2020 makes substantial further provision in relation to fisheries, fishing, aquaculture and marine conservation. It is seen by government as one of the three 'foundation stones' of the post-Brexit legislative framework intended to halt nature's decline by 2030, alongside the EA 2021 and AA 2020.[30]

---

27 SI 2015/810.
28 SI 2009/995.
29 2004/35/EC.
30 DEFRA, 'Environmental Improvement Plan 2023: First Revision of the 25 Year Environment Plan' (n 30) 6 <https://assets.publishing.service.gov.uk/media/64a6d9c1c531eb000c64fffa/environmental-improvement-plan-2023.pdf> accessed 4 April 2024.

A step-change in the law and policy of nature positive: 2010–2020

8.25 In September 2010, the Lawton Review of England's wildlife and ecological network, 'Making Space for Nature', was published.[31] It noted that the world had failed to meet its commitment to achieve a significant reduction in the rate of global biodiversity loss by 2010, and that Europe has not met its 2010 target to halt biodiversity loss.[32] It also set out that, despite the important contribution made by designated sites, England's wildlife habitats had become increasingly fragmented and isolated, leading to declines in the provision of some ecosystem services, and losses to species populations.[33]

8.26 The Lawton Review concluded that England's legally protected wildlife areas, and other wildlife areas, did not represent a coherent and resilient ecological network capable of responding to the challenges of climate change and other pressures: the review therefore recommended the establishment of such a network. Effectively establishing a coherent and resilient ecological network would require a shift in emphasis, away from piecemeal conservation actions and towards a more integrated, landscape-scale approach:

> [W]e need a step-change in our approach to wildlife conservation, from trying to hang on to what we have, to one of large-scale habitat restoration and recreation, under-pinned by the re-establishment of ecological processes and ecosystem services, for the benefits of both people and wildlife.[34]

8.27 The essence of the required action to enhance the resilience and coherence of England's ecological network was summarised in four words: *more*, *bigger*, *better* and *joined*.[35] The review recommended five key approaches which encompassed these, and took account of the land around the ecological network:

(i) Improving the quality of current sites by better habitat management.

(ii) Increasing the size of current wildlife sites.

(iii) Enhancing connections between, or join up, sites, either through physical corridors, or through 'stepping stones'.

(iv) Creating new sites; and

(v) Reducing the pressures on wildlife by improving the wider environment, including through buffering wildlife sites.[36]

---

31 Lawton Review (n 17).
32 ibid 5.
33 ibid 5.
34 ibid 2.
35 ibid 8.
36 ibid 8.

8.28 In October 2010, there was a global agreement to the Convention on Biological Diversity's ('CBD's') Strategic Plan for Biodiversity 2011–2020, which included an ambition to 'take effective and urgent action to halt the loss of biodiversity in order to ensure that by 2020 ecosystems are resilient and continue to provide essential services…'.[37] Signatories agreed to 20 associated 'Aichi Biodiversity Targets'.

8.29 In June 2011, the UK National Ecosystem Assessment ('NEA') was published: the NEA aimed to provide a comprehensive account of ecosystem services (see Chapter 2, paragraph 2.04), and demonstrated that nature was consistently undervalued in decision-making and was in decline, with 30% of ecosystem services declining and many others in a reduced or degraded state.[38]

8.30 Also in June 2011, the government responded to the Lawton Review in the Natural Environment White Paper.[39] It committed to 'establish a clear institutional framework to achieve the recovery of nature'.[40] This was to involve establishing Local Nature Partnerships and creating new Nature Improvement Areas to enhance and reconnect nature on a significant scale: ultimately, the trial of these measures evolved into a commitment in the 25YEP to develop a Nature Recovery Network, and shortly after to statutory provision for Local Nature Recovery Strategies (see further Chapter 11).

8.31 In August 2011, the government published its Biodiversity Strategy running up to 2020.[41] It noted that '[o]ver 40% of priority habitats and 30% of priority species were declining in the most recent analysis', with eight priority species lost entirely from the UK between 2002–2008.[42] The ambition was to halt biodiversity loss in England by 2020, before moving to a position of net gain: in more detail, the overarching objective was, by 2020, to 'halt overall biodiversity loss, support healthy well-functioning ecosystems and establish coherent ecological networks, with more and better places for nature for the benefit of wildlife and people', with a long-term ambition of moving progressively towards biodiversity net gain.[43] Implementing the more integrated, landscape-scale approach to conservation recommended by Professor Lawton would help achieve this objective.[44]

8.32 The post-2020 international legal framework is set out in the Kunming-Montreal GBF. The modern domestic legal and policy framework for England is set out in the EA 2021 and two associated statutory Environmental Improvement Plans ('EIPs'), the 25YEP and 2023 EIP. For a discussion of the position in Wales, see paragraphs 8.144–8.157 below.

37 Convention on Biological Diversity, COP Decision X/2, Strategic Plan for Biodiversity 2011–2020 (2010).
38 UK NEA, 'UK National Ecosystem Assessment: Understanding Nature's Value to Society' (2011) <http://uknea.unep-wcmc.org/Resources/tabid/82/Default.aspx>.
39 DEFRA, 'The Natural Choice: Securing the Value of Nature' (2011) Cm 8082 <https://assets.publishing.service.gov.uk/media/5a7cb8fce5274a38e57565a4/8082.pdf> accessed 26 March 2024.
40 ibid 3.
41 DEFRA, 'Biodiversity 2020: A Strategy for England's Wildlife and Ecosystem Services' (2011).
42 ibid 4, 9.
43 ibid 2, 4, 6.
44 ibid 7.

International legal framework: the CBD and the GBF

8.33 The international global biodiversity framework for the period 2022–2030 is set out in the GBF, which was adopted by the Conference of the Parties to the CBD on 19 December 2022.[45] Article 3 of the GBF sets out its purpose: the GBF 'aims to catalyze, enable and galvanize urgent and transformative action by Governments, and subnational and local authorities...to halt and reverse biodiversity loss'.

8.34 By Article 7(d), each party is to contribute to attaining the goals and targets 'in accordance with national circumstances, priorities and capabilities'. By Article 7(g), the GBF 'acknowledges the human right to a clean, healthy and sustainable environment'. By Article 7(n), implementation 'should be guided by the principle of intergenerational equity which aims to meet the needs of the present without compromising the ability of future generations to meet their own needs and to ensure meaningful participation of younger generations in decision-making processes at all levels'.[46]

8.35 Article 12 sets out four long-term goals for 2050 (see paragraph 1.51 in Chapter 1), namely:

- Goal A: the integrity, connectivity and resilience of all ecosystems are maintained, enhanced, or restored, substantially increasing the area of natural ecosystems by 2050; human-induced extinction of known threatened species is halted, and, by 2050, the extinction rate and risk of all species are reduced tenfold and the abundance of native wild species is increased to healthy and resilient levels; the genetic diversity within populations of wild and domesticated species is maintained, safeguarding their adaptive potential.

- Goal B: biodiversity is sustainably used and managed and nature's contributions to people, including ecosystem functions and services, are valued, maintained and enhanced, with those currently in decline being restored, supporting the achievement of sustainable development for the benefit of present and future generations by 2050.

- Goal C: the monetary and non-monetary benefits from the utilisation of genetic resources and digital sequence information on genetic resources, and of traditional knowledge associated with genetic resources, as applicable, are shared fairly and equitably, including, as appropriate with indigenous peoples and local communities, and substantially increased by 2050, while ensuring traditional knowledge associated with genetic resources is appropriately protected, thereby contributing to the conservation and sustainable use of biodiversity, in accordance with internationally agreed access and benefit-sharing instruments.

- Goal D: adequate means of implementation, including financial resources, capacity-building, technical and scientific cooperation, and access to and transfer

45 See Chapter 2, para 2.60.
46 See Chapter 3, paras 3.92–3.106.

of technology to fully implement the [GBF] are secured and equitably accessible to all Parties, especially developing country Parties, in particular the least developed countries and small island developing States, as well as countries with economies in transition, progressively closing the biodiversity finance gap of $700 billion per year, and aligning financial flows with the [GBF] and the 2050 Vision for biodiversity.

8.36 By Articles 10–11, parties should move towards the long-term 2050 goals by means of a mission up to 2030 to urgently halt and reverse biodiversity loss, to put nature on a path to recovery. Article 13 sets 23 'action-oriented global targets for urgent action over the decade to 2030', each of which 'need to be initiated immediately and completed by 2030'.

8.37 Targets 1–8 relate to reducing threats to biodiversity: in particular, Target 1 requires Parties to ensure that all areas are under participatory, integrated and biodiversity inclusive spatial planning and/or effective management processes addressing land use and sea use change, to bring the loss of areas of high biodiversity importance, including ecosystems of high ecological integrity, close to zero by 2030, while respecting the rights of indigenous peoples and local communities.

8.38 Per Target 2, by 2030 at least 30% of areas of degraded ecosystems should be under effective restoration. The GBF Guidance prepared by the Secretariat states that degraded land includes ecosystems which have suffered a loss of ecosystem functions and services, and transformed ecosystems (such as agricultural areas). An assessment of degraded areas within a country is a necessary first step for monitoring the total percentage of degraded ecosystems which are under restoration. At the time of going to print, no such assessment is publicly available, nor is there a domestic definition for 'degraded' ecosystems.

8.39 Target 3 sets an action of ensuring that, by 2030, 'at least 30 per cent of terrestrial and inland water areas, and of marine and coastal areas, especially areas of particular importance for biodiversity and ecosystem functions and services, are effectively conserved and managed through ecologically representative, well-connected and equitably governed systems of protected areas and other effective area-based conservation measures'. This appears to be the target referred to in government policy as 'the 30 by 30 target': the OEP have critiqued this transposition of the international commitment, stating that Targets 2 and 3 are interrelated but are not duplicative.[47]

8.40 By Target 6, rates of introduction and establishment of invasive alien species should be reduced by at least 50% by 2030. In line with this target, in February 2023 the government published the Great Britain Invasive Non-Native Species Strategy: 2022 to 2030.[48]

---

47 Office for Environmental Protection, 'Progress in Improving the Natural Environment in England 2022/2023' (2024) 29 <https://www.gov.uk/government/publications/progress-in-improving-the-natural-environment-in-england-2022-to-2023> accessed 27 April 2024.

48 'The Great Britain Invasive Non-Native Species Strategy' (GOV.UK, 27 February 2023) <https://www.gov.uk/government/publications/the-great-britain-invasive-non-native-species-strategy> accessed 7 May 2024.

8.41 Targets 9–13 address meeting people's needs through sustainable use of species and ecosystems and benefit-sharing. Targets 14–23 relate to tools and solutions for implementation and mainstreaming.

8.42 Parties to the CBD were obliged to publish updated National Biodiversity Strategy and Action Plans ('NBSAPs') aligning with the GBF ahead of COP16 in October 2024.[49] Parties are now also expected to submit 'National Targets'. The UK published a number of national targets in August 2024. However, at the time of going to print in late October 2024, COP16 is ongoing; the UK is the only G7 nation which has not yet published an updated NBSAP aligning with the GBF.

Environment Act 2021: Overview and Part 1

8.43 The EA 2021 comprises two halves: the first (Part 1) provides a post-Brexit framework for environmental governance, while the remaining parts provide for specific environmental improvements, including measures on waste and resource efficiency, air quality and environmental recall, water, nature and biodiversity (Part 6), and conservation covenants (Part 7).[50] This chapter will focus on Parts 1 and 6, insofar as germane to the goals of nature positive policy.[51] Part 7 is discussed in detail in Chapter 23.

8.44 Although a number of the other provisions of the EA 2021 apply to Wales,[52] almost all of Parts 1, 6 and 7 apply to England only.[53] The few individual provisions which also apply to Wales are expressly highlighted below. Otherwise, for a discussion of the current position in Wales, see paragraphs 8.144–8.157 below.

(i) *Part 1: Environmental governance*

8.45 Chapter 1 of Part 1 creates a new statutory cycle of monitoring, planning and reporting, the aim of which is to ensure continuing improvement to the environment.[54]

8.46 In keeping with the emergent, more holistic approach to nature recovery outlined at paragraph 8.07 above, the 'natural environment' is now defined for the purposes of Part 1 of the EA 2021 as – '(a) plants, wild animals and other living organisms, (b) their habitats, (c) land (except buildings or other structures), air and water, and the natural systems, cycles and processes through which they interact' (section 44).

8.47 'Environmental protection' is defined for the purposes of Part 1 as – '(a) protection of the natural environment from the effects of human activity; (b) protection of people from the effects of human activity on the natural environment; (c) maintenance,

---

49 WCL, 'COP15 One Year on– Where We Are Now' (2023) <https://www.wcl.org.uk/assets/uploads/img/files/2023_COP15_one_year_on_Report.pdf>.
50 Explanatory Notes to the EA 2021 para 1.
51 Further, the provisions of Part 6 dealing with Biodiversity Net Gain and Local Nature Recovery Strategies are discussed in detail in Chapters 10 and 11.
52 Explanatory Notes to the EA 2021 para 63.
53 See Annex A of the Explanatory Notes to the EA 2021 for full details of the territorial extent and application of the statutory provisions.
54 Explanatory Notes to the EA 2021 para 19.

restoration or enhancement of the natural environment; (d) monitoring, assessing, considering, advising or reporting on anything in paragraphs (a) to (c)' (section 45).

8.48 'Environmental law', a term used for the primary purpose of delineating the OEP's statutory functions,[55] is defined for the purposes of Part 1 as 'any legislative provision to the extent that it (a) is mainly concerned with environmental protection, and (b) is not concerned with an excluded matter' (disclosure of or access to information, armed forces or national security, and taxation, spending or the allocation of resources within government) (section 46 EA 2021). For a discussion of the effect of this provision, see paragraphs 8.86–8.90 below.

(ii) *Environmental targets: EA 2021, sections 1–3*

8.49 Section 1 allows the Secretary of State to set long-term targets in relation to the environment by way of regulations, and requires the Secretary of State to set at least one long-term target in respect of four priority areas: air quality, water, biodiversity, and resource efficiency and waste reduction (s 1). Long-term targets must be of at least 15 years' duration (s 1(6)), and must specify a standard to be achieved, which must be 'capable of being objectively measured', as well as a target date (s 1(4)). Separately and additionally to the section 1 long-term targets, the Secretary of State must also set a PM2.5 air quality target (s 2), and a short-term species abundance target to be met by 31 December 2030 (s 3). The Secretary of State must be satisfied that meeting the target would halt a decline in the abundance of species (s 3(4)): this measure is intended to be the 'net zero equivalent for nature'.[56] It is the duty of the Secretary of State to ensure that each of the above targets are met (s 5), and the Secretary of State may not set or amend a target without being satisfied that it can be met (s 4(2)).

8.50 The government has discharged these obligations by way of a number of statutory instruments which came into force in January 2023. The principal instrument for the purposes of this chapter is the Environmental Targets (Biodiversity) (England) Regulations 2023[57] ('the Biodiversity Targets Regulations'), which deals with the 2030 species abundance target and long-term biodiversity targets together.[58] In short, the targets are to halt the decline in species abundance by 2030; reverse the decline in species abundance by 2042; reduce the risk of species extinction by 2042; and restore or create in excess of 500,000 hectares of wildlife-rich habitat outside of current protected sites by 2042.[59]

55 Explanatory Notes at para 368; Sections 23(6)–(7), 29–36, 38–39, 41 EA 2021. Section 20 EA 2021 also creates duties on a Minister of the Crown when introducing a bill which would become 'environmental law': see para 8.92 below.
56 Zac Goldsmith, HoL; see Chapter 1, para 1.55.
57 SI 2023/91.
58 See further SI 2023/90 and SIs 2023/92–96, setting targets in respect of Woodland, Residual Waste, Water, Marine Protected Areas and Fine Particulate Matter, each of which are accompanied by an Explanatory Memorandum.
59 Explanatory Notes to the Biodiversity Targets Regulations para 2.1.

8.51 The Explanatory Notes observe that in England, species abundance has fallen by 52% since 1970: in setting binding targets to halt the decline in species abundance by 2030, and reverse this decline by 2042, the targets will establish a 'clear recovery trend'.[60]

8.52 The 2030 species abundance target has been described by a former Secretary of State for DEFRA as 'our compass'.[61] The target is that the overall relative species abundance index ('the Index') on 31 December 2030 indicates that the decline in the abundance of species has been halted (reg 11). Regulation 12 sets out how the Index for a given year is to be derived, and stipulates that the same methodology must be used each year. The 2030 target will be measured by calculating the differences in the Index for the years 2029 and 2030 (reg 12(1)). However, the long-term target to reverse the decline of species abundance provides that the Index by 31 December 2042 must be (a) higher than the Index for 31 December 2022, as well as (b) at least 10% higher than the Index for 31 December 2030 (reg 14). The 2022 baseline represents a strengthening of the target from the originally proposed baseline of 2030, which was criticised by the OEP as being 'highly uncertain and inappropriate', and apparently contrary to the requirements of section 1 of the EA 2021 that long-term targets must be objectively measurable and achievable.[62] Both of the species abundance targets are crucial not only to the delivery of obligations under the EA 2021 and associated EIPs, but also for adaptation to climate change.[63]

8.53 The other long-term biodiversity targets in relation to land are:

- To reduce the risk of species' extinction by 2042, compared to a 2022 baseline (reg 4); and
- To restore or create in excess of 500,000 hectares of wildlife-rich habitat outside of current protected sites by 2042 (reg 7), as compared to 30 January 2023 when the regulations came into force.

8.54 The extinction risk value is to be measured in accordance with regulation 5, against the 2022 Red List Index for England.[64] Regulation 8 provides for how the Secretary of State is to measure the area of wildlife-rich habitat which is restored or created, and for what qualifies as 'restoration' and 'creation'. Pursuant to regulation 10, 'wildlife-rich habitat' is either (a) a habitat type of principal importance for the conservation of biodiversity listed by the Secretary of State under section 41 NERCA 2006 (as amended by the EA 2021), or (b) another habitat type listed in Schedule 1 of the Regulations,[65]

---

60 ibid paras 7.1–7.2.
61 DEFRA, 'Nature Recovery Green Paper: Protected Sites and Species' (n 6).
62 Letter from Dame Glenys Stacey (Chair, Office for Environmental Protection) to the Rt Hon George Eustice MP (Secretary of State for Environment, Food and Rural Affairs) and Rebecca Pow MP (Minister for Nature Recovery and the Domestic Environment) (27 June 2022) 5, 7.
63 DEFRA, 'The Third National Adaptation Programme (NAP3) and the Fourth Strategy for Climate Adaptation Reporting' (HC 2023, 1649) 54–55 <https://assets.publishing.service.gov.uk/government/uploads/system/uploads/attachment_data/file/1172931/The_Third_National_Adaptation_Programme.pdf>; Office for Environmental Protection, 'Progress in Improving the Natural Environment in England 2022/2023' (n 47).
64 This may be found at http://publications.naturalengland.org.uk/publication/6315201438941184.
65 These include certain kinds of grassland, lines of trees, native hedgerows and woodland, scrub, and floodplain wetland mosaic, as well as reef, subtidal mud, sand and sediment, and subtidal grassland beds.

which is of sufficient quality that it is, or will be, capable of supporting flora and fauna which are typically found in the habitat in question.

8.55 Briefly, the long-term woodland and tree canopy cover target set under the Environmental Targets (Woodland and Trees Outside Woodland) (England) Regulations 2023[66] is that by 31 December 2050 at least 16.5% of all land in England should be covered by woodland and trees outside woodland (reg 3), as compared to a 2022 baseline of 14.5% coverage.[67] The 2050 target is to be calculated by the Forestry Commission (reg 4). The trees planted to meet this target will contribute to the objectives of the EA 2021 by providing thousands of hectares of priority habitat to support species recovery and improving the quality of our air and water courses, as well as contributing to the government's statutory net zero target (see paragraphs 1.33–1.35 in Chapter 1 and paragraphs 2.90–2.94 in Chapter 2). Purpose-grown energy forestry plantations are excluded from contributing to the target.[68]

8.56 The marine biodiversity target set under the Environmental Targets (Marine Protected Areas) Regulations 2023[69] is that by 31 December 2042, at least 70% of the designated features within all relevant MPAs will be in a favourable condition, with the remainder in recovering condition (reg 3): see further paragraphs 9.180–9.181.

8.57 The Secretary of State may revoke or lower an existing target only if satisfied either that (a) meeting the existing target would have no significant benefit compared with not meeting it or with meeting a lower target, or (b) because of changes in circumstances since the existing target was set or last amended, the environmental, social, economic or other costs of meeting it would be disproportionate to the benefits (s 4(3) of the EA 2021). The Secretary of State must first lay before Parliament, and publish, a statement explaining why they are so satisfied (s 4(4)). 'Lowering' a target includes (a) replacing the specified standard with a lower standard, or (b) replacing the specified date with a later date (s 4(5)). The PM2.5 air quality target may be amended but not revoked (s 4(6)).

8.58 Section 6 of the EA 2021 provides for the reporting procedure to be followed shortly after the respective target dates, by a further date specified in the relevant statutory instrument. If the Secretary of State reports that a target has not been met, they must publish a subsequent report within 12 months, explaining why the target has not been met, and setting out the steps taken, or intended to be taken, to ensure the specified standard is achieved as soon as reasonably practicable.

8.59 Section 7 of the EA 2021 provides that the Secretary of State must review the statutory targets, and any other similar and appropriate targets set, to consider whether the 'significant improvement test' is met – i.e. whether meeting the targets would significantly improve the natural environment in England. The test does not assess progress made towards achieving the targets. A review is completed when the Secretary of State

66 SI 2023/90.
67 Explanatory Memorandum to the Environmental Targets (Woodland and Trees Outside Woodland) (England) Regulations 2023 para 7.1.
68 ibid paras 7.2–7.4.
69 SI 2023/94.

lays before Parliament and publishes a report stating (a) whether the test is met and (b) if not, the steps the Secretary of State intends to take to ensure that it is met. The first review had to be completed by 31 January 2023, and subsequently before the end of the following 5-year period. The first report was presented to Parliament on 31 January 2023, and concluded that the test had been met.[70]

(iii) *Environmental improvement plans*

8.60 Pursuant to section 8 of the EA 2021, the Secretary of State must prepare an environmental improvement plan ('EIP') to significantly improve the natural environment in England, spanning a period of not less than 15 years. An EIP must set out the steps which the government intends to take to improve the natural environment in the relevant period (and may also set out intended steps to improve people's enjoyment of the natural environment). The 25YEP published in 2018 is to be treated as the first statutory EIP (s 8(7)–(8)): for the 2023 EIP, see paragraphs 8.71–8.77 below.

(iv) *The 25 Year Environment Plan*

8.61 The 25YEP set 10 goals in relation to the environment, which are, to a great extent, complementary. The goals include clean air, clean and plentiful water, climate mitigation and adaptation, and the 'Thriving Plants and Wildlife' goal – namely to achieve a 'growing and resilient network of land, water and sea that is richer in plants and wildlife'.[71] The 25YEP also set out an intention to join up policies to maximise environmental benefits and value for money, and identified six key areas for action, including sustainable land use, nature recovery, and marine biodiversity, as well as reducing pollution and waste.[72]

8.62 *Inter alia*, the 25YEP set out a new commitment to develop a Nature Recovery Network ('NRN') providing 500,000 hectares of additional wildlife habitat, to 'complement and connect our best wildlife sites' and 'provide opportunities to re-introduce lost species'.[73] The 25YEP committed to explore what the NRN could look like, and to investigate implementing up to 25 new catchment or landscape-scale nature recovery areas. Specific measures to be explored included peatland restoration, natural flood management, woodland planting and wildflower recovery areas, learning from the NIAs and other initiatives such as the Knepp Estate.[74] Developing the NRN would also provide opportunities for species recovery and reintroduction. The 25YEP also committed government to publish a new strategy for nature building on Biodiversity 2020.[75] At the time of writing, no new standalone biodiversity strategy has been published, and the Environmental Improvement Plan 2023 ('2023 EIP') is silent on this.

70 DEFRA, 'Report on the First Review of Environmental Targets (the Significant Improvement Test)' (2023) <https://assets.publishing.service.gov.uk/media/63d8dc338fa8f518877e76bc/Review_of_environmental_targets_Outcome_of_the_Significant_Improvement_Test.pdf>.
71 DEFRA, 'A Green Future: Our 25 Year Plan to Improve the Environment' (n 1) 10, 26.
72 ibid 10.
73 ibid 56–58.
74 ibid 59–60.
75 ibid 58.

8.63 The 25YEP also included a commitment to develop a set of metrics to monitor environmental change material to the 10 goals, ensuring transparency and accountability. In 2019, DEFRA published an 'Outcome Indicator Framework' for the 25YEP[76] under which it has since been publishing data in relation to a set of 66 indicators describing relevant environmental change.[77] The framework will be reviewed and updated to reflect the development of new indicators: the aim is to provide a transparent and comprehensive set of indicators to show whether and how the environment is changing, and to help assess the effectiveness of policies and other interventions.[78] DEFRA currently publishes data in relation to 7 indicators for wildlife: (1) the quantity, quality and connectivity of habitats (building on the Lawton Review); (2) the extent and condition of protected sites; (3) the area of woodland in England; (4) the relative abundance and/or distribution of widespread species; (5) the conservation status of native species; (6) the relative abundance and distribution of priority species in England; and (7) species supporting ecosystem functions.[79] The publication of data under the Outcome Indicator Framework is now underpinned by the Secretary of State's statutory duty under section 16 of the EA 2021 to obtain and publish data appropriate for monitoring environmental improvement in accordance with an EIP, and progress towards any statutory targets.

8.64 While one of the 10 goals set out in the 25YEP is mitigating and adapting to climate change, detail on climate in the 25YEP is light: it is sketched out that government will pursue this goal through '[c]ontinuing to cut greenhouse gas emissions including from land use, land use change, the agriculture and waste sectors and the use of fluorinated gases'.[80] Specific areas for action were to include restoring peatlands, new landscape-scale nature recovery, and the forthcoming environmental land management system (see further Chapter 12), as well as international leadership.[81]

(v) *Annual reporting on EIPs*

8.65 Pursuant to section 9 of the EA 2021, the Secretary of State must report annually on the implementation of the current EIP, (a) describing what has been done that year by way of implementation, and (b) considering (with regard to any data obtained under section 16) whether the natural environment, or aspects of it, have improved during the year. This includes considering the progress made towards achieving targets set under sections 1–3, and any interim targets set under sections 11 and 14. DEFRA has so far published six annual progress reports.[82]

---

76 DEFRA, 'Measuring Environmental Change: Outcome Indicator Framework for the 25 Year Environment Plan' (2019) <https://assets.publishing.service.gov.uk/media/5f840cd5d3bf7f6ba4f45077/25-yep-indicators-2019.pdf> accessed 14 October 2024.
77 See <https://oifdata.defra.gov.uk/> accessed 14 October 2024.
78 DEFRA, 'Measuring Environmental Change: Outcome Indicator Framework for the 25 Year Environment Plan' (n 76) 5.
79 <https://oifdata.defra.gov.uk/themes/wildlife/> accessed 5 Mar 2024.
80 DEFRA, 'A Green Future: Our 25 Year Plan to Improve the Environment' (n 1).
81 ibid.
82 See <https://www.gov.uk/government/publications/25-year-environment-plan-progress-reports> accessed 14 October 2024 and <https://www.gov.uk/government/publications/environmental-improvement-plan-annual-progress-report-2023-to-2024> accessed 14 October 2024.

8.66 The section 9 reporting functions, together with the OEP's section 28 functions of monitoring and reporting on EIPs and targets (see paragraphs 8.78–8.85 below), are the provisions under which public authorities will actually consider the government's concrete progress towards improving the environment and meeting its statutory targets (as opposed to the 'significant improvement test' review under section 7, which only considers whether meeting the targets *would* significantly improve the environment).

(vi) *Review, revision and renewal of EIPs*

8.67 Sections 10–15 of the EA 2021 set out duties on the Secretary of State to review, revise and renew EIPs. The deadline for the first review of the first EIP was 31 January 2023, with subsequent reviews due to be completed within five years of the previous review or a fresh EIP (s 10(3)–(5)). In reviewing an EIP, the Secretary of State must consider –

(a) what has been done to implement the plan since it was published or last reviewed,

(b) whether, having regard to data obtained under section 16 and OEP reports made under section 28, the natural environment (or aspects of it) have improved during that period (which must include considering the progress made towards meeting any long-term or interim targets set under the Act), and

(c) whether the Government should take further or different steps to improve the environment in the remainder of the relevant period (including different steps towards meeting the statutory targets) (s12(1)).

8.68 On the first review of the first EIP, the Secretary of State must also revise the plan so as to set at least one interim target in respect of each target set under sections 1–3: they must be satisfied that meeting the target would make an 'appropriate contribution' to meeting the relevant target set under sections 1–3. On any other review, the Secretary of State must set at least one interim target in respect of any new targets set under sections 1–3 (s 11(1)–(4), (8)), and may revise or replace existing interim targets (s 11(5)). The deadline for achieving an interim target must be no later than five years after the date the EIP review is completed (or, for any subsequent interim targets, no later than 5 years after the specified deadline for the previous interim target).

8.69 If as a result of a review the Secretary of State revises the EIP, they must lay the revised EIP before Parliament along with a statement explaining the reasons for the revisions. If a review does not result in a revised EIP, the Secretary of State must lay a statement before Parliament explaining why not (s 10(6)–(7)).

8.70 Before the end of a period to which an EIP relates, the Secretary of State must prepare a new EIP in accordance with sections 13–15, to be published no later than the end of the previous period. Section 15 provides for similar matters to be considered in preparing a new EIP; section 14 provides for interim targets in renewed EIPs.

(vii) *The 2023 EIP*

8.71 On 31 January 2023, the government published the Environmental Implement Plan 2023, the first revised EIP ('the 2023 EIP'). This builds on the 10 goals set out in the 25YEP, and for the first time describes the biodiversity target, Thriving Plants and Wildlife, as an 'apex goal' which all the other goals will help to achieve.[83] The 2023 EIP is presented as an 'integrated and outcome focused delivery plan', and a 'detailed delivery plan' with policy actions allocated to various stakeholders:[84] however, this has been critiqued by the OEP (see paragraphs 8.80–8.85 below).

8.72 The 2023 EIP sets a number of new interim targets. In respect of the 'apex goal', these are:[85]

- To restore or create 140,000 hectares of wildlife-rich habitats outside protected sites by 2028, compared to 2022 levels;
- For all SSSIs to have an up-to-date condition assessment by 31 January 2028;
- For 50% of SSSIs to have actions on track to achieve favourable condition by 31 January 2028;
- In respect of the long-term target in relation to tree canopy and woodland cover, to increase this cover by 0.26% (equivalent to 34,000 hectares) by 31 January 2028; and
- In respect of the long-term target in relation to MPAs, for 48% of designated features to be in favourable condition by 31 January 2028.

8.73 Key policies to deliver the apex biodiversity target (and presumably the interim targets) include biodiversity net gain; nature friendly farming; creating, restoring and extending areas for wildlife including through National Nature Reserves and Landscape Recovery; mapping wetlands; improving the condition of Marine Protected Areas; and creating Highly Protected Marine Areas.[86] The government also announced a new Species Survival Fund, specifically targeted towards the 2030 species abundance target:[87] the fund covers projects both within and outside protected sites. Applications were open for a limited period between July–October 2023, and the 20 successful projects were announced on 15 March 2024.[88]

8.74 The 2023 EIP also sets a number of new interim targets in respect of air quality, water, and waste. No new interim targets are set in respect of climate mitigation and

83 DEFRA, 'Environmental Improvement Plan 2023: First Revision of the 25 Year Environment Plan' (n 30).
84 ibid (n 30) 9–10, 16–17.
85 ibid 31, 34.
86 ibid 29–70.
87 ibid 55.
88 Zelda Baveystock, 'Over £25 Million to Preserve Wildlife-Rich Habitats in England' (*DEFRA Environment blog*, 15 March 2024) <https://defraenvironment.blog.gov.uk/2024/03/15/over-25-million-to-preserve-wildlife-rich-habitats-in-england/#:~:text=The%20Species%20Survival%20Fund%20is,250%2C000%20to%20%C2%A33%20million> accessed 14 October 2024.

adaptation: rather, the 2023 EIP refers to pre-existing national and international targets and commitments under the Climate Change Act 2008 and Paris Agreement.[89] The 2023 EIP clarifies that while the government's Net Zero Strategy sets out policies and proposals for decarbonising all sectors of the UK economy to meet the statutory net zero target,[90] the EIP 'sets out land use considerations for net zero alongside nature, biodiversity and climate adaptation goals'.[91]

8.75 The 2023 EIP notes that 'our habitats are crucial carbon sinks, and deliver increased co-benefits compared to other carbon solutions…we must deploy nature at scale domestically and around the world in order to keep 1.5°C alive. Nature and land-based sectors therefore must go beyond net zero and become carbon negative by 2050 in order to support the rest of the economy'.[92] It also notes that in 2020, net emissions from agriculture, forestry and land use, waste and fluorinated gases in England were responsible for 54.5 metric tons of carbon dioxide equivalent (MtCO2e).[93] Under the Climate Change Committee's Balanced Pathway to Net Zero by 2050, agricultural and land use emissions should fall to 40 MtCO2e by 2035, with residual emissions of just 16 MtCO2e by 2050: delivering this transition requires a transformation in the use of land.[94]

8.76 The majority of proposed climate actions set out in the 2023 EIP are those mandated under the government's existing international and national climate commitments: beyond these, two key land-use and climate commitments were the introduction of nature friendly farming through Environmental Land Management schemes ('ELMs'), and the publication of a Land Use Framework in 2023.[95] For a detailed discussion of ELMs, see Chapter 12.

8.77 On 3 July 2024, the new government announced a rapid review of the EIP to be completed by the end of the year, to deliver on its legally binding nature targets. The announcement promised that the forthcoming EIP would include delivery plans for each target.[96] As at 31 October 2024, the forthcoming EIP is outstanding. The 2023 EIP's keystone commitment of the Land Use Framework also is yet to be published. As set out at paragraph 12.128 in Chapter 12, government's climate and nature advisors have placed great reliance on the role of the Land Use Framework in providing a coherent, overarching structure for managing the competing demands on land in a manner consistent with government's net zero and nature commitments: however, early

---

89 DEFRA, 'Environmental Improvement Plan 2023: First Revision of the 25 Year Environment Plan' (n 30) 189.
90 Climate Change Act 2008 s 1. The updated policies and proposals are now set out in the Carbon Budget Delivery Plan (March 2023), published a month after the 2023 EIP.
91 DEFRA, 'Environmental Improvement Plan 2023: First Revision of the 25 Year Environment Plan' (n 30) 191.
92 ibid 188. This accords with the CCC's analysis, which envisages that on the Balanced Pathway to net zero by 2050, the land use sector will move from generating annual emissions of 12.8 MtCO2e in 2018, to annual savings of 12 MtCO2e in 2035, and 30 MtCO2e by 2050, moving the sector to a net sink of 19 MtCO2e by 2050: Climate Change Committee, 'The Sixth Carbon Budget: The UK's Path to Net Zero' (2020) 170 <https://www.theccc.org.uk/wp-content/uploads/2020/12/The-Sixth-Carbon-Budget-The-UKs-path-to-Net-Zero.pdf> accessed 26 April 2024.
93 DEFRA, 'Environmental Improvement Plan 2023: First Revision of the 25 Year Environment Plan' (n 30) 193.
94 Climate Change Committee, 'The Sixth Carbon Budget: The UK's Path to Net Zero' (n 92) 163.
95 DEFRA, 'Environmental Improvement Plan 2023: First Revision of the 25 Year Environment Plan' (n 30) 12, 187–201.
96 <https://www.gov.uk/government/news/government-launches-rapid-review-to-meet-environment-act-targets> accessed 14 October 2024.

indications before the 2024 General Election were that the forthcoming framework would be 'light-touch' and 'essentially guidance'.[97]

(viii) *OEP scrutiny of EIPs and progress towards targets*

8.78 In addition to the Parliamentary scrutiny provided for under Part 1 of the EA 2021, the OEP has relevant scrutiny and advice functions. Pursuant to section 28, the OEP must monitor and annually report on progress in improving the natural environment in accordance with the current EIP, and towards meeting any targets set under Part 1 of the EA 2021. Its reports may include consideration of how progress could be improved, and consideration of the adequacy of the data published under section 16. The Secretary of State must publish a response to each report, addressing any recommendations as to how to improve progress.

8.79 Pursuant to sections 29–30 EA 2021, the OEP must also report on the implementation of environmental law (save to the extent a matter falls within the Climate Change Committee's remit),[98] and must advise on any proposed change to environmental law. The OEP may investigate, and bring proceedings in relation to, serious breaches of environmental law by public authorities, including of the statutory duty to ensure long-term targets are met.[99]

8.80 On 18 January 2024, the OEP published its most recent annual progress report, which found that 'government is largely off track to meet EIP23 ambitions, Environment Act targets and other commitments'.[100] Of the 10 goal areas set out in the EIPs, in seven areas the government's overall prospects of meeting its ambitions, targets and commitments was 'largely off track', including the 'apex goal' of Thriving Plants and Wildlife, and the goal of mitigating and adapting to climate change.[101] There is no area in which the Government is largely on track to meet its goals.[102]

8.81 The 2023 EIP purported to be a 'detailed delivery plan with policy actions allocated to different government departments, local government' and third-party stakeholders. The OEP challenge this representation, stating baldly 'in our view, the EIP23 is not a detailed delivery plan. Our assessment is that overall progress and prospects are impeded by the lack of an effective and transparent delivery plan'.[103] The OEP advises that the degree of disclosure and transparency is not consistent with that needed for public scrutiny or government accountability, noting that:

> The EIP23 does not demonstrate transparently how policies and strategies will be effectively implemented and how actions, individually and together, will significantly

---

97 'Land Use Framework Set to Be "Essentially Guidance", Government Confirms' (14 March 2024) <https://www.endsreport.com/article/1865192?utm_source=website&utm_medium=social> accessed 24 March 2024.
98 See Chapter 4, para 4.10.
99 See Chapter 4, paras 4.10–4.19.
100 OEP, 'Progress in Improving the Natural Environment in England 2022/2023' (n 47).
101 ibid 11.
102 The only two areas which are partially on track are clean air and reduced risk of harm from environmental hazards. The goal of enhancing beauty, heritage and engagement could not yet be assessed.
103 OEP, 'Progress in Improving the Natural Environment in England 2022/2023' (n 47) 11–12.

> improve the natural environment and meet Environment Act targets. There is limited and unstructured information on the role of delivery partners and stakeholders, making it difficult to identify governance and operational arrangements and the barriers to, and enablers of, effective delivery.
>
> We consider that, for progress to be improved and for the EIP23 to be effective, it now needs the support of detailed delivery plans: plans that spell out who will do what, how much, and by when. These plans must show that when these many and diverse actions are taken, specified outcomes will be achieved. To succeed, the EIP23 must be implemented with delivery plans that can be shown to stack up.[104]

8.82 In particular, the OEP could not assess the prospects of achieving the long-term target to reverse the decline of species abundance, nor the long-term species extinction risk target, due to the lack of an adequately detailed delivery plan.[105]

8.83 One of the OEP's 'key recommendations' in the report is that the government should now develop and publish a detailed delivery plan for the 2023 EIP and each of its goal areas, within the next year: plans 'need to identify specific policies and activities and make explicit their contribution, individually and together, towards achieving the specified (p14) outcomes. It should be clear how much progress is expected to be made, and by when. The government's plans must be shown to stack up.'[106]

8.84 In effect, the OEP are requesting a quantified, policy-by-policy analysis comparable to that produced in respect of the government's climate obligations in the Net Zero Strategy and Carbon Budget Delivery Plan. While those plans were produced to comply with specific statutory obligations under the Climate Change Act 2008, which have not been replicated in respect of nature in the EA 2021, the OEP argue that a similar analysis is necessary by virtue of the requirements of transparency and accountability, in the interests of effective delivery, and to be able to effectively discharge its statutory duty set out in s28(1) EA 2021.

8.85 As set out above at paragraph 8.77, on 3 July 2024 the new government announced that a rapid review of the EIP would be completed by the end of the year: the announcement promised that the forthcoming EIP would include delivery plans for each target.

(ix) *Extent of OEP's remit*

8.86 The OEP's functions are delineated so as to (1) avoid overlap with the Climate Change Committee[107] and (2) restrict the exercise of their monitoring functions to (a) reporting on EIPs and targets, and (b) monitoring, reporting on, advising on, and enforcing failures to comply with 'environmental law'.[108] 'Environmental law' is

---

104 ibid (n 47) 12.
105 ibid 36.
106 ibid 13.
107 EA 2021 ss 23(5), 26, 29(3)–(4), 35(7).
108 ibid ss 23(6)–(7), 29–36, 38–39, 41.

defined in section 46(1) as 'any legislative provision[109] to the extent that it (a) is mainly concerned with environmental protection, and (b) is not concerned with an excluded matter'. Pursuant to section 46(2), excluded matters are (a) disclosure of or access to information; (b) the armed forces or national security; and (c) taxation, spending or the allocation of resources within government.

8.87 While this provision has yet to be subject to judicial construction, it would appear to exclude provisions which in reality have a significant impact on the environment, but which are not concerned with environmental protection *per se*.[110]

8.88 The Explanatory Notes acknowledge that the definition 'does mean that within broadly environmental policy areas, whilst many provisions may meet these criteria, there may be certain provisions that will not be mainly concerned with environmental protection, and therefore not constitute environmental law'.[111] The example given is of the Forestry Act 1967: section 1(3A) creates a duty on forestry authorities to 'endeavour to achieve a reasonable balance' between afforestation and timber supply, and its conservation functions. According to the Explanatory Notes, 'as this places a duty on a public authority concerning the conservation of the natural environment, this provision would fall within scope'.[112] However, section 1(2) of the Forestry Act 1967, which creates a general duty on authorities of 'promoting the interests of forestry, the development of afforestation and the production and supply of timber and other forest products' would not fall within scope as it is mainly concerned with promoting the interests of the forestry sector – notwithstanding that this duty is likely to, in reality, have a significant effect on the environment.

8.89 The same will be true for many areas of planning legislation, outside of the provisions dealing with environmental impact assessments and strategic impact assessments.[113] This approach presumably also excludes from scope the provisions of Part 1A of the Petroleum Act 1998, which create a 'principal objective' of maximising UK petroleum recovery, notwithstanding the likely significant impact of these provisions on the climate.[114]

8.90 The Explanatory Notes to the EA 2021 conclude that:

> 402 It will be for the OEP to assess whether or not it considers a legislative provision to fall under the definition on a case by case basis when determining whether or not

109 A reference to UK legislation, meaning the OEP does not have a statutory function to assess compliance with purely international environmental law (Explanatory Notes to the EA 2021 at para 397). However, it does have a statutory function to give advice to Ministers on any proposed change to 'environmental law', or any other matter relating to the natural environment which is requested by a Minister: s 30 EA 2021.

110 Explanatory Notes to the EA 2021 paras 395–402.

111 Explanatory Notes to the EA 2021 para 399.

112 ibid para 400. It might be said that there is an argument to be had about whether a provision creating a duty to balance two sets of considerations, one economic and one environmental, is 'mainly concerned with environmental protection'.

113 ibid para 401.

114 The objective includes maximising recovery through, in particular, the development, construction, deployment and use of industry equipment (Petroleum Act 1998, s9A(1)(a)), and requires the Oil and Gas Authority ('OGA') to produce a strategy for enabling the objective to be met: the OGA must then act in accordance with the strategy when exercising functions (Petroleum Act 1998 s9A(2), s9B).

it has legal powers to act in that area. In most cases, it is expected that the answer to this question will be clear, and agreed by all parties. However, there may be cases of uncertainty or disagreement, and in these instances it may ultimately be for the courts to decide whether a specific provision falls within the definition or not.

(x) *Environmental principles policy statement*

8.91 Sections 17–19 of the EA 2021 deal with the environmental principles policy statement ('EPPS'): this is addressed in detail in Chapter 3, paragraphs 3.05–3.08.

(xi) *Statements and reports on new domestic and international environmental law*

8.92 Pursuant to section 20 (which also applies to Wales), where a Bill introduced into either House of Parliament contains a provision that, if enacted, would be environmental law (as defined in section 46), the Minister in charge of the Bill must make a statement to that House, which must either:

- Confirm that in the Minister's view, the Bill will not have the effect of reducing the level of environmental protection provided for by any existing environmental law; or

- Confirm that the Minister is unable to make such a statement, but that government nevertheless wishes the House to proceed with the Bill.[115]

8.93 In making a statement, the Minister may in particular take into account the possibility that a Bill, by making provision that is different from existing environmental law, might provide for the same or a greater level of environmental protection.

8.94 Pursuant to section 21 (which applies to England only), the Secretary of State must report on significant developments in international environmental protection legislation (defined as legislation of countries and territories outside the United Kingdom, and international organisations, that is mainly concerned with environmental protection). Reports must be laid before Parliament, and published, as soon as reasonably practicable after the end of each reporting period, i.e. the two-year period beginning with the section coming into force (1 April 2022), and each subsequent two-year period.

Environment Act 2021: Parts 6 and 7 – nature, biodiversity, and conservation covenants

8.95 Part 6 makes provision in relation to:

- Biodiversity net gain in the planning system (discussed in detail in Chapter 10);

- An enhanced biodiversity duty on public authorities, and new biodiversity reports, under amendments to NERCA 2006;

115 The Explanatory Notes to the EA 2021 at para 216 suggest that such a statement might be made where an existing UK environmental protection is no longer justified by new scientific evidence.

- Local Nature Recovery Strategies (discussed in detail in Chapter 11);
- Species conservation strategies and protected site strategies;
- Powers to amend the Habitats Regulations (see further Chapter 9);
- Tree felling and planting; and
- The use of forest risk commodities in commercial activity.[116]

(i) *Enhanced biodiversity duty and biodiversity reports*

8.96 As set out above in paragraph 8.05, section 102 of the EA 2021 amends public authorities' duties under s 40 NERCA 2006. Authorities exercising functions in England must, from time to time, consider what action they can properly take, consistently with the proper exercise of their functions, to further the 'general biodiversity objective' of not only conserving, but also enhancing, biodiversity (s 40(A1), (1), (7)).[117] After such consideration, the authority must (unless it concludes there is no new action it can properly take):

(a) determine policies and specific objectives which it considers appropriate for taking action to further the general biodiversity objective;[118] and

(b) take such action as it considers appropriate, in the light of those policies and objectives, to further that objective (including revising any existing policies and objectives) (s 40(1A)).

8.97 In complying with these obligations, an authority must in particular have regard to any relevant Local Nature Recovery Strategy, and any relevant species conservation strategy or protected site strategy (s 40(2A)): see further paragraphs 8.102–8.114 and Chapter 11.[119] The Secretary of State is obliged to issue guidance to local planning authorities as to how to take into account these considerations, by no later than 1 January 2025 (s 40(2B)–(2D)). The action which may be taken to further the general biodiversity objective includes, in particular, action for the purpose of conserving, restoring

---

116 Section 116 EA 2021, dealing with the use of forest risk commodities in commercial activity, is the only provision of Part 6 which also applies to Wales.
117 Per Explanatory Notes to the EA 2021 para 924, the periodic consideration duty (across the full range of an authority's functions) represents a 'proactive, strategic assessment of a public authority's functions, rather than considering each function in isolation as required by the original section 40 duty'.
118 A determination must be made as soon as practicable after completion of the consideration: s 40(1E). It is possible for an authority to decide that there is no action it can reasonably take that is consistent with the proper exercise of its functions (for example, if a particular action is not possible within existing budget constraints, not good value for money or conflicts with other priorities). If there is action it can take, however, then under the statute it must decide how that action can be put into effect, and must then take that action: para 925 of the Explanatory Notes to the EA 2021.
119 Conversely, the strengthened duty is also characterised as a mechanism to support the delivery of LNRSs: Department for Environment, Food and Rural Affairs, 'Local Nature Recovery Strategy Statutory Guidance: What a Local Nature Recovery Strategy Should Contain' (2023) para 7.

or otherwise enhancing (a) a population of a particular species or (b) a particular type of habitat (s 40(3)).

8.98 Without prejudice to the generality of the section 40(1) obligation, public authorities were required to complete a first consideration by 1 January 2024: subsequent considerations must be completed no later than five years after an authority's previous consideration (s 40(1C)–(1D), (1F)).

8.99 Section 103 of the EA 2021 creates a new section 40A in NERCA 2006 requiring local authorities and local planning authorities in England, and any other authorities designated by the Secretary of State, to publish biodiversity reports. Biodiversity reports must contain:

(a) a summary of the action taken by the authority over the relevant period to comply with its section 40(1)–(1A) duties;

(b) a summary of the authority's plans for complying with those duties over the subsequent five years;

(c) any quantitative data specified in regulations;[120] and

(d) any other information the authority thinks appropriate to include (s 40A(3)).

8.100 Local planning authorities' reports must also contain further information in relation to biodiversity net gain (s 40A(4)).

8.101 Biodiversity reports must specify the period covered, and must be published within 12 weeks of the end of that period. An authority's first biodiversity report must cover a period of no longer than three years, beginning with the day the authority first became subject to the duty (1 January 2023 for local authorities, or the date of designation for designated authorities). Subsequent reports must cover a period of no longer than five years, beginning the day after the previous period (s 40(A)(5)–(7)).

(ii) *Species conservation strategies and protected site strategies*

8.102 Pursuant to section 109(1)–(2) EA 2021, Natural England ('NE') may prepare and publish a 'species conservation strategy' for improving the conservation status of any species of fauna or flora. These provisions enable NE to prepare a strategy for any species where it is beneficial, without being constrained by any specific list of endangered or threatened species.[121]

8.103 A species conservation strategy may either relate to all of England, or any part of England (s 109(3)). In particular, a species conservation strategy may:

---

120 As at 29 April 2024, no regulations have yet been made under the new s 40A NERCA 2006.
121 Explanatory Notes to the EA 2021 para 988.

- identify areas or features in the strategy area which are important to the conservation of the species;
- identify priorities in relation to the creation or enhancement of habitat for the purpose of improving the species' conservation status; and
- set out how NE proposes to exercise its relevant functions, across the whole or part of the strategy area, to improve the species' conservation status (s 109(4)(a)–(c) EA 2021).

8.104 A species conservation strategy may also, in particular, include NE's opinion on:

- the giving by any other public authority of consents or approvals which might affect the species' conservation status in the strategy area; and
- measures that it would be appropriate to take to avoid, mitigate or compensate for any adverse impact on the species' conservation status in the strategy area that may arise from a plan, project or other activity (s 109(4)(d)–(e) EA 2021).

8.105 Local Planning Authorities ('LPAs'), and any authorities prescribed by the Secretary of State in regulations,[122] must cooperate with NE in preparing and implementing a species conservation strategy (s 109(6), (10) EA 2021). The Secretary of State may give guidance to these authorities on how to discharge this duty (s 109(7)–(8) EA 2021). The Explanatory Notes indicate that this power allows bespoke guidance to be prepared for each strategy, according to the varying cooperation required in relation to different species and areas.[123]

8.106 LPAs and prescribed authorities must also have regard to any species conservation strategy in the exercise of its functions, so far as relevant (s 109(9) EA 2021). This includes the development of local plans.[124]

8.107 Finally, NE may amend a species conservation strategy from time to time (s 109(5) EA 2021): this will allow strategies to be updated as evidence emerges showing how effective they are in improving the species' conservation status.[125]

8.108 As at April 2024, it is not apparent that any species conservation strategies have yet been published by NE. However, some strategies are in development, including a strategy for water vole in the East Anglian region.[126]

---

122 At the time of writing, no such regulations have been made. However, the legislative intention is that while cooperation will largely be required only from local planning authorities, specific strategies might require cooperation from other public authorities such as a marine management organisation or the Environment Agency (Explanatory Notes to the EA 2021 para 997).
123 Explanatory Notes to the EA 2021 para 995.
124 ibid para 997.
125 ibid para 993.
126 See <https://www.suffolkwildlifetrust.org/species-conservation-strategy-water-vole> accessed 29 April 2024.

8.109 Pursuant to section 110(1)–(3) EA 2021, NE may similarly prepare and publish 'protected site strategies' for improving the conservation and management of a protected site,[127] and managing the impact of plans, projects or other activities (wherever undertaken) on the site.

8.110 Protected site strategies may in particular:

(a) include an assessment of the impact that any plan, project or other activity may have on the site's conservation or management (whether individually or cumulatively with other activities);

(b) include NE's opinion on measures that it would be appropriate to take to avoid, mitigate or compensate for any adverse impact[128] on the site's conservation or management that may arise from a plan, project or other activity;

(c) identify any plan, project or other activity that NE considers is necessary for the purposes of the site's conservation or management; and

(d) cover any other relevant matters (s 110(4) EA 2021).

8.111 NE must consult a number of bodies in preparing a protected site strategy (s 110(5) EA 2021), namely:

- any LPA exercising functions in the relevant area for either the protected site itself, or the plan, project or activity which may adversely impact on the site;
- any public authority which is proposing to undertake a relevant plan, project or other activity, whose consent or approval is required for such an activity, or who 'may otherwise be affected by the strategy';
- the Environment Agency;
- the Secretary of State;
- any affected Inland Fisheries and Conservation Authority, and the Marine Management Organisation, where relevant; and
- any other person that NE considers should be consulted, including the public.

8.112 The above bodies (excluding the Secretary of State and the miscellaneous other persons considered relevant) must, on being consulted, cooperate with NE in preparing a protected site strategy (s 110(7)). The Secretary of State may give guidance as to how to discharge this duty of cooperation (s 110(8)–(9)). As with species conservation strategies, public bodies must have regard to protected site strategies in discharging certain

127 A European Site, Site of Special Scientific Interest or Marine Conservation Zone (s 110(3) EA 2021).
128 Defined in s 110(6) EA 2021 so as to align with existing legislation.

relevant statutory duties (s 110(10)). Also similarly, protected site strategies may be amended from time to time: the duty to consult applies so far as proposed amendments are relevant to the body's functions (s 110(11)–(12)).

8.113 At the time of writing, it is not apparent that NE have published any protected site strategies.

8.114 Measures included in both species conservation strategies and protected site strategies should be integrated into relevant Local Nature Recovery Strategies:[129] see further Chapter 11.

(iii) *Part 7: Conservation covenants*

8.115 Part 7 provides for new conservation covenants: these are discussed in detail in Chapter 23.

Forest risk commodities

(i) *Introduction*

8.116 The EA 2021 introduced a new legal regime, concerned with tackling 'illegal deforestation in UK supply chains', through the regulation of products associated with deforestation.[130] In this section, we set out the context for this new regime, the policy development at the international and EU level, before considering the statutory framework under the EA 2021 and issues that may arise in practice.

8.117 Deforestation, defined as 'the conversion of forest to other land use independently whether human-induced or not',[131] is a major barrier to achieving both net zero and nature positive goals. Forests play a crucial role in sequestering and storing carbon,[132] providing critical habitats and natural ecosystems. A total of 1.6 billion people, including indigenous people and local communities, rely upon them directly for their livelihoods.[133] When the forests are converted, their stored carbon is released into the atmosphere. Indeed, the Secretary of State for the Environment, Food and Rural

129 Explanatory Notes to the EA 2021 paras 987, 1003.
130 See DEFRA, 'Implementing Due Diligence on Forest Risk Commodities' (2021) <https://consult.defra.gov.uk/international-biodiversity-and-climate/implementing-due-diligence-forest-risk-commodities/> accessed 13 April 2024. Readers may also be interested in the parallel regulation of timber and timber products. This regime was originally derived from EU law in the Regulation (EU) No. 995/2010 of the European Parliament and of the Council of 20 October 2010; and implemented domestically by the Timber and Timber Products (Placing on the Market) Regulations 2013/233 and Forest Law Enforcement, Governance and Trade Regulations 2012/178. Since the UK's departure from the EU, those regulations have been amended by The Timber and Timber Products and FLEGT (EU Exit) Regulations 2018/1025; and The Timber and Timber Products and FLEGT (Amendment) (EU Exit) Regulations 2020/1315.
131 Food and Agriculture Organization of the United Nations, 'Global Forest Resources Assessment 2020: Terms and Definitions' 6 <https://www.fao.org/3/I8661EN/i8661en.pdf> accessed 13 April 2024.
132 Holly Gibbs, 'Monitoring and Estimating Tropical Forest Carbon Stocks: Making REDD a Reality' <https://iopscience.iop.org/article/10.1088/1748-9326/2/4/045023/pdf> accessed 13 April 2024.
133 World Wide Fund for Nature UK, 'Due Diligence on Forest-Risk Commodities' (2022) 1 <https://www.wwf.org.uk/sites/default/files/2022-03/WWF-UK-Due-Diligence-Secondary-Legislation-External-Policy%20Briefing-V2.pdf> accessed 13 April 2024.

Affairs ('SSEFRA'), the Rt Hon Steve Barclay MP, reported on 12 December 2023 as follows:[134]

> Deforestation is now the second leading cause of climate change globally, after burning fossil fuels, and is responsible for around 11% of all greenhouse gas emissions. Forests host around 80% of the world's wildlife on land and are home to many species found nowhere else. In the last 60 years, more than half of tropical forests worldwide have been destroyed, reducing biodiversity and endangering beloved and crucial species like orangutans and other great apes, tigers, leopards and jaguars.

8.118 The Food and Agriculture Organisation of the United Nations ('FAO') estimated, in its 2020 Global Forest Resources Assessment, that the world has a total forest area of 4.06 billion hectares; and since 1990, the world has lost 178 million hectares, which is around the size of Libya.[135]

8.119 Agriculture is a major driver of deforestation.[136] Seven commodities have been identified as replacing forests: palm oil, soy, cattle, plantation wood fibre/timber, cocoa, coffee and rubber.[137] Estimates suggest that, between 2016 and 2018, an average of 21.3 million hectares (the size of the UK) is required on an annual basis to meet the UK's demand for these commodities.[138]

(ii) *Policy development*

8.120 Deforestation has been on the international agenda for some time: under the UNFCCC, at COP 13 in 2007, the Bali Action Plan called for policy approaches relating to reducing emissions from deforestation in developing countries. It adopted the acronym, 'REDD', referring to 'Reducing Emissions from Deforestation and forest Degradation in developing countries'.[139] The need to consider 'the role of conservation, sustainable management of forests and enhancement of forest carbon stocks in

134 Rt Hon Steve Barclay MP, Secretary of State for Environment, Food and Rural Affairs, 'Introduction of Forest Risk Commodities Regulations: Statement UIN HCWS117' HC Deb 12 December 2023, vol 742, col 38WS <https://questions-statements.parliament.uk/written-statements/detail/2023-12-12/hcws117> accessed 13 April 2024.

135 Food and Agriculture Organization of the United Nations, 'Global Forest Resources Assessment 2020 Key Findings' (2020) 1–2 <https://www.fao.org/3/ca8753en/ca8753en.pdf> accessed 13 April 2024.

136 Some sources suggest that agriculture and forestry commodities drive around a quarter of deforestation and related ecosystems. See World Wide Fund for Nature UK (n 133) 1.

137 The precise seven commodities vary between source: compare World Resources Institute, 'Estimating the Role of Seven Commodities in Agriculture-Linked Deforestation: Oil Palm, Soy, Cattle, Wood Fiber, Cocoa, Coffee, and Rubber' (2020) with World Wide Fund for Nature UK, 'Riskier Business: The UK's Overseas Land Footprint – Summary Report' (2020) <https://www.wwf.org.uk/sites/default/files/2020-07/RiskierBusinessSummaryReport_July2020_revised.pdf> accessed 13 April 2024.

138 World Wide Fund for Nature UK (n 133) 1.

139 United Nations Framework Convention on Climate Change ('UNFCCC'), 'Report of the Conference of the Parties on Its Thirteenth Session, Held in Bali from 3 to 15 December 2007' (2007) FCCC/CP/2007/6/Add.1 <https://unfccc.int/resource/docs/2007/cop13/eng/06a01.pdf> accessed 13 April 2024; Decision 1/CP.13, Bali Action Plan para 1(b)(iii) and Decision 2/CP.13, Reducing emissions from deforestation in developing countries: approaches to stimulate action; cited in Benoit Mayer, *The International Law on Climate Change* (Cambridge University Press 2018) 209.

developing countries' was signified in the '+', such that the acronym became REDD+.[140] Eventually, at COP 19 in 2013, a comprehensive agreement was adopted to provide financial support to developing countries to protect their forests: the Warsaw Framework for REDD+.[141]

8.121 In 2014, the New York Declaration on Forests was a political declaration that contained two main goals: halve the rate of loss of natural forests globally by 2020 and end forest loss by 2030.[142] At COP 26 in Glasgow in 2021, forestry and land use were key themes; 141 countries signed the Glasgow Leader's Declaration on Forest and Land Use, where there was a commitment *inter alia* to:[143]

> Facilitate trade and development policies, internationally and domestically, that promote sustainable development, and sustainable commodity production and consumption, that work to countries' mutual benefit, and that do not drive deforestation and land degradation.

8.122 At the EU level, the Commission committed in 2019 to assess demand-side regulatory and non-regulatory measures, in order to develop a shared understanding of deforestation-free supply chains and reduce the risk of deforestation and forest degradation associated with commodity imports.[144] The commitment was confirmed in, and formed an integral part of, the European Green Deal, the 2030 EU Biodiversity Strategy and the Farm to Fork Strategy.[145] Policies prior to that had focused on illegal logging and associated trade.[146] In 2021, the EU proposed a regulation on commodities associated with deforestation and forest degradation. The regulation was intended to complement other initiatives on sustainable corporate governance, but its focus was to be on specific products and commodities, rather than business operations.[147] The regulation was also to sit alongside the initiatives focused on sustainable finance (such as the Corporate Sustainability Reporting Directive),[148] which could target the deforestation

140 United Nations Framework Convention on Climate Change, Decision 1/CP.13, Bali Action Plan, cited in Mayer (n 139) 209.
141 Mayer (n 139) 210.
142 Climate Initiatives Platform, 'The New York Declaration on Forests' <https://climateinitiativesplatform.org/index.php/The_New_York_Declaration_on_Forests> accessed 13 April 2024; see also UNFCCC, 'New York Declaration on Forests – Halving the Loss of Natural Forest by 2020, Striving to End It by 2030' <https://unfccc.int/news/new-york-declaration-on-forests> accessed 13 April 2024.
143 UN Climate Change Conference UK 2021, 'Glasgow Leaders' Declaration on Forests and Land Use' (12 November 2021) <https://webarchive.nationalarchives.gov.uk/ukgwa/20230418175226/https://ukcop26.org/glasgow-leaders-declaration-on-forests-and-land-use/> accessed 13 April 2024; see also Cabinet Office, 'World Leaders Summit on "Action on Forests and Land Use"' (2022) <https://www.gov.uk/government/publications/cop26-world-leaders-summit-on-action-on-forests-and-land-use-2-november-2021/world-leaders-summit-on-action-on-forests-and-land-use> accessed 13 April 2024.
144 Proposal for a regulation of the European Parliament and of the Council on the making available on the Union market as well as export from the Union of certain commodities and products associated with deforestation and forest degradation and repealing Regulation (EU) No 995/2010 COM/2021/706 Explanatory Memorandum, 1.
145 ibid.
146 ibid 2.
147 ibid 3.
148 Directive (EU) 2022/2464 of the European Parliament and of the Council of 14 December 2022 amending Regulation (EU) No 537/2014, Directive 2004/109/EC, Directive 2006/43/EC and Directive 2013/34/EU, as regards corporate sustainability reporting PE/35/2022/REV/1.

impacts of financial services.[149] Finally, it was intended that the regulation would complement the Renewable Energy Directive, particularly given the use of wood pellets or derivatives of soil and palm oil in biofuel.[150]

8.123 The EU regulation on deforestation-free products[151] was formally adopted by the European Council on 16 May 2023[152] and came into force on 29 June 2023 ('EU Deforestation Regulation').[153] It applies to listed products that 'contain, have been fed with or have been made using' the following commodities: cattle, cocoa, coffee, oil palm, rubber, soya and wood.[154] By Article 3, there is a prohibition on placing relevant commodities and products on the market or exporting them, unless three conditions have been fulfilled: (i) they are deforestation-free; (ii) they have been produced in accordance with the relevant laws of the country of production; and (iii) they have been addressed in a due diligence statement. There are then detailed provisions in relation to the due diligence obligations on operators, which are more broadly defined to include both natural and legal persons.[155] There is also a system of assessing and categorising countries, based on the risk that relevant commodities do not comply with Article 3(a) and are not therefore deforestation-free.[156]

(iii) *Statutory framework*

8.124 The EA 2021 introduced a framework for regulating forest risk commodities in commercial activity, as set out in section 116 and Schedule 17. It is concerned with 'agricultural commodities whose production is associated with widescale conversion of forests'.[157] The Schedule is divided into three parts, addressing (i) use of forest risk commodities (Part 1), (ii) enforcement mechanisms (Part 2), and (iii) general provisions (Part 3). Much of the detail is to be included in statutory instruments made under the EA 2021.[158]

149 Proposal for a regulation of The European Parliament and of the Council on the making available on the Union market as well as export from the Union of certain commodities and products associated with deforestation and forest degradation and repealing Regulation (EU) No 995/2010 COM/2021/706 3.
150 ibid.
151 Regulation (EU) 2023/1115 of the European Parliament and of the Council of 31 May 2023 on the making available on the Union market and the export from the Union of certain commodities and products associated with deforestation and forest degradation and repealing Regulation (EU) No 995/2010 PE/82/2022/REV/1.
152 Council of the EU, 'Council Adopts New Rules to Cut Deforestation Worldwide' (2023) <https://www.consilium.europa.eu/en/press/press-releases/2023/05/16/council-adopts-new-rules-to-cut-deforestation-worldwide/> accessed 13 April 2024.
153 European Commission, 'Regulation on Deforestation-Free Products' <https://environment.ec.europa.eu/topics/forests/deforestation/regulation-deforestation-free-products_en> accessed 13 April 2024.
154 Regulation (EU) 2023/1115 of the European Parliament and of the Council of 31 May 2023 on the making available on the Union market and the export from the Union of certain commodities and products associated with deforestation and forest degradation and repealing Regulation (EU) No 995/2010 PE/82/2022/REV/1 Articles 1 and 2.
155 ibid Articles 2(15) and 4–13.
156 ibid Article 29.
157 Explanatory Notes to the Environment Act 2021 para 972.
158 By Environment Act 2021 Schedule 17, para 6, the Secretary of State can also issue guidance to the enforcement authority about the Part 1 requirements to which the authority must have regard in exercising its Part 2 functions. There are various consultation requirements in the Schedule in relation to any regulations made thereunder.

(a) Definition of 'forest risk commodity'

8.125 A 'forest risk commodity' is not expressly defined in the Act itself, which states only that it means 'a commodity specified in regulations made by the Secretary of State'.[159] The definition is, however, circumscribed by the Act as follows:

- Commodities may only be specified if they meet the following conditions: (i) they have been produced from a plant, animal or other living organism and (ii) if the 'Secretary of State considers that forest is being or may be converted to agricultural use for the purposes of producing the commodity',[160] where 'agricultural use' includes 'use for horticulture and aquaculture.'[161]

- 'Forest' is defined as 'an area of land of more than 0.5 hectares with a tree canopy cover of at least 10% (excluding trees planted for the purpose of producing timber or other commodities)';[162] where 'land' includes land that is permanently or temporarily submerged in water.

- Timber or timber products, within the meaning of Regulation (EU) No. 995/2010 of the European Parliament and of the Council of 20 October 2010, which lays down obligations on operators who place timber and timber products on the market, may not be specified.[163] The rationale for this exclusion is to avoid overlap with an existing regime.[164]

(b) Prohibitions

8.126 Paragraph 2 of Schedule 17 of the EA 2021 contains the prohibition on use of illegally produced commodities and provides as follows:

> (1) A regulated person in relation to a forest risk commodity must not use that commodity in their UK commercial activities unless relevant local laws were complied with in relation to that commodity.
>
> (2) A regulated person in relation to a forest risk commodity must not use a product derived from that commodity in their UK commercial activities unless relevant local laws were complied with in relation to that commodity.

8.127 A 'product derived from a forest risk commodity' is a reference to 'a product derived from a forest risk commodity in whole or in part (and includes any product of an animal fed on a forest risk commodity or a product derived from a forest risk commodity)'.[165]

8.128 A 'regulated person' in relation to a particular forest risk commodity is partly defined by paragraph 7 of Schedule 17, with the full definition left over to the regulations,

159 ibid para 1(1).
160 ibid paras 1(2)–(3).
161 ibid para 18(1).
162 ibid paras 1(4)–(5).
163 ibid para 1(6).
164 Explanatory Notes to the Environment Act 2021 para 1686.
165 Environment Act 2021 Schedule 17, para 18(2).

as follows: 'a person (other than an individual) who carries on commercial activities in the United Kingdom' and either (i) meets such conditions as to turnover as specified in the regulations; or (ii) is 'an undertaking which is a subsidiary of another undertaking which meets those conditions'.[166]

8.129 In this context, 'local law' is defined in paragraph 2(3) of the Schedule as 'any law having effect in the country or territory where the source organism was grown, raised or cultivated'; and a 'relevant local law' is defined in paragraph 2(4) as follows:

(a) which relates to the ownership of the land on which the source organism[[167]] was grown, raised or cultivated,

(b) which relates to the use of that land, or

(c) which otherwise relates to that land and is specified in regulations made by the Secretary of State.

8.130 'UK commercial activity', unsurprisingly, means 'commercial activity carried on in the United Kingdom'.[168] A 'commercial activity' includes (i) producing, manufacturing and processing; (ii) distributing, selling or supplying; and (iii) purchasing for a purpose within (i) or (ii) but not as a consumer.[169]

8.131 There are two exemptions to the prohibitions set out in paragraphs 2(1) and (2), in relation to the commodities themselves and a product derived from the commodities.[170] These are: (i) where the commodity is a waste;[171] and (ii) where the use of the commodity is for the purpose of making renewable transport fuel, which qualifies for a renewable transport fuel certificate in the Renewable Transport Fuel Obligations Order 2007.[172]

(c) Due diligence system

8.132 By paragraph 3(1) of Schedule 17, there is an obligation on a regulated person to establish and implement a system of due diligence in relation to a forest risk commodity, where they use that commodity or a product derived from that commodity in their UK commercial activities. Such a system should provide for the identification of the

---

166 The paragraph further states that the regulations may provide for 'a group of undertakings to be treated as a regulated person, in such circumstances, for such purposes and to such extent as may be provided (and may modify the application of the Schedule accordingly).' Where a 'group' is defined by reference to Companies Act 2006 ('CA 2006') s 474, namely 'a parent undertaking and its subsidiary undertakings'; and an 'undertaking' is given the meaning in CA 2006 s 1161: '(a) a body corporate or partnership, or (b) an unincorporated association carrying on a trade or business, with or without a view to profit.' Further, whether an undertaking is a subsidiary of another undertaking is to be determined in accordance with CA 2006 s 1162.
167 This is defined as 'the plant, animal or other living organism from which the forest risk commodity was produced', see Environment Act 2021 Schedule 17, para 2(6).
168 ibid para 18(1).
169 ibid.
170 ibid paras 2(7)–(8).
171 As defined in The Renewable Transport Fuel Obligations Order 2007 Article 2(1).
172 See Chapter 18, paras 18.161–18.171.

commodity (which includes obtaining information about it), assessing the risk that relevant local laws have not been complied with, and mitigating that risk.[173]

(d) Reporting requirement

8.133 Where a regulated person uses a particular commodity or a product derived from a commodity in their UK commercial activities, they must provide a report on the actions they have taken to establish a due diligence system in relation to that particular commodity.[174] The report must be provided to the relevant authority, which is the Secretary of State, unless the regulations specify another person.[175] The reporting period will commence from the day on which paragraph 4 of Schedule 17 comes fully into force and end the following 31 March, followed by each successive period of 12 months.[176] Regulations made under paragraph 4 can stipulate the content and form of the reports, as well as the manner by which they are provided, and the extent to which they must be made public.

(e) Exemption

8.134 There is an exemption to the prohibition, due diligence system and reporting requirements, if two conditions are satisfied:

- Condition 1: The relevant person gives a notice to the relevant enforcement authority, which contains (i) a declaration that they are satisfied on reasonable grounds that the amount of the commodity used in their UK commercial activities does not exceed the prescribed threshold; and (ii) prescribed information.
- Condition 2: The amount of the commodity used in the UK commercial activities does not in fact exceed the prescribed threshold.

8.135 If condition 1 is satisfied but not condition 2, then the person may still be exempt as set out in paragraphs 5(4)–(6) of Schedule 17.

8.136 The 'prescribed thresholds' will be set by reference to weight or volume by the regulations made under the EA 2021, and the 'relevant enforcement authority' will be defined.

(f) Enforcement

8.137 Part 2 of Schedule 17 says very little about the enforcement function in relation to the regime; save that it provides that the regulations made thereunder can, for example, impose requirements relating to record-keeping, providing records or other information to the enforcement authority and preparing reports for the Secretary of State. It also provides other enforcement powers relevant to investigation, including power of entry, inspection, examination, search and seizure, and how these powers are

173 Environment Act 2021 Schedule 17, para 3(1); and further, by para 3(3), the Secretary of State is empowered to make regulations to address these points further, in particular: (i) what information should be obtained; (ii) the criteria that should be used in assessing the risk; and (iii) how the risk may be mitigated.
174 ibid para 4(1).
175 ibid para 4(5).
176 ibid para 4(6).

exercisable (such as under a warrant);[177] and provides for civil sanctions,[178] appeals, and criminal offences.[179]

(g) Review

8.138 The Secretary of State is required to review the effectiveness of the requirements set out in Part 1 and any regulations made under Part 2, as set out in paragraph 17 of Schedule 17. The review must consider the following:[180]

(a) the amount of forest being converted to agricultural use for the purposes of producing commodities;

(b) the impact of the relevant provisions on the amount of forest being converted to agricultural use for the purposes of producing forest risk commodities;

(c) the impact of the relevant provisions on the use of forest risk commodities, or products derived from forest risk commodities, in UK commercial activities where relevant local laws were not complied with in relation to those commodities;

(d) any changes to relevant local laws in relation to forest risk commodities.

8.139 Following a review, the Secretary of State must lay a report before Parliament and publish a report, setting out the conclusions of the review and any steps the Secretary of State intends to take to improve the effectiveness of the relevant provisions.[181]

(h) Secondary legislation

8.140 On 12 December 2023, the government introduced draft regulations under the Act but, by 12 March 2024, the regulations had not been laid before Parliament.[182] It is understood that the initial draft covers four commodities: cattle products (excluding dairy), cocoa, palm oil and soy, which, according to the SSEFRA, are estimated to account for '64% of the UK's tropical deforestation footprint, with as much as 93% of this deforestation likely to be in violation of local laws'.[183] The global annual turnover threshold is set at £50m; and businesses that are using 500 tonnes or less of each commodity per year can apply for an exemption.[184] In terms of enforcement action and penalties, it is reported that an unlimited monetary penalty has been provided for in relation to the most serious breaches, along with a reasonable range.[185]

---

177 ibid para 12.
178 This is defined by para 13(4) of Schedule 17 as 'a sanction of a kind for which provision may be made under Part 3 of the Regulatory Enforcement and Sanctions Act 2008 (fixed monetary penalties, discretionary requirements, stop notices and enforcement undertakings)'.
179 ibid Schedule 17, paras 13–14.
180 ibid para 17(2).
181 ibid para 17(3).
182 HL Deb 12 March 2024, vol 836.
183 Barclay, Secretary of State for Environment, Food and Rural Affairs (n 134).
184 ibid.
185 ibid.

(iv) *Issues in practice*

8.141 At this stage, it is difficult to say what issues will arise in practice, given so much of the detail has been left to the draft regulations that have not, at the time of writing, been laid before Parliament.

8.142 There are some limitations in the EA 2021 itself, when compared to the EU Deforestation Regulation.[186] For instance, the EU regulation applies to both natural and legal persons who place products on the markets in the course of commercial activity, whereas the EA 2021 limits the scope to those who carry out UK commercial activities and have a certain annual turnover. Importantly, the EU regulation covers any deforestation, but in contrast, the domestic regime applies to commodities that have been produced contrary to local laws, and therefore only focusses on illegal deforestation.

8.143 Some analysis has raised concerns about the focus on only four commodities in the draft regulations, particularly given the urgent need to stop and reverse deforestation and land degradation.[187] There has also been a call for shifting the focus from a company's turnover to the volume of the commodities that they handle, which is suggested to be a more direct indication of the potential risks of illegal deforestation and conversion.[188] There is also a call for clear public accountability, through mandatory public reporting and a robust enforcement body.[189]

Wales

8.144 A detailed examination of the Welsh devolution settlement is beyond the scope of this book. In brief, the Senedd Cymru (Welsh Parliament, formerly known as the National Assembly for Wales) was first established under the Government of Wales Act 1998, which also provided for functions to be devolved in certain expressly conferred areas, including the environment, agriculture, forestry, fisheries and food.[190] The Senedd's powers were extended by the Government of Wales Act 2006, and then again by the Wales Act 2017, which moved Wales to a reserved powers model.

8.145 Key pre-Brexit environmental statutes in Wales include the Planning Act 2015, Well-being of Future Generations (Wales) Act 2015 ('WBFGA 2015') and the Environment (Wales) Act 2016 ('EWA 2016'), which draw inspiration from international goals and principles, including the UN Sustainable Development Goals and the 12 principles of an ecosystem approach set out under the CBD.[191]

---

186 Naomi Hart and Grace Ferrier, 'Seeing the Wood for the Trees: Developments in Deforestation Legislation and Litigation' (2024) Essex Court Chambers <https://essexcourt.com/publication/seeing-the-wood-for-the-trees-developments-in-deforestation-legislation-and-litigation-week-5-series-3/> accessed 13 April 2024.
187 World Wide Fund for Nature UK (n 133).
188 ibid.
189 ibid.
190 Government of Wales Act 1998 (as originally enacted), s 22, Schedule 2 paras 1, 6.
191 <https://www.cbd.int/ecosystem/principles.shtml>.

8.146 The WBFGA 2015 enshrines the principle of sustainable development and requires public bodies in Wales to carry out sustainable development and otherwise act in accordance with the principle.[192] Carrying out sustainable development includes setting well-being objectives which will contribute to the achievement of seven well-being goals and (b) take steps to meet those objectives.[193] The key goal for the purposes of this book is the goal of a resilient Wales, defined as 'a nation which maintains and enhances a biodiverse natural environment with healthy functioning ecosystems that support social, economic and ecological resilience and the capacity to adapt to change (for example climate change).'[194] The Welsh Ministers must publish indicators that must be applied to measure progress towards achieving the well-being goals.[195] Part 3 of the WBFGA 2015 provides for the appointment of a Future Generations Commissioner, whose general duty includes acting as a guardian of the ability of future generations to meet their needs, encouraging public bodies to take account of the long-term impact of their decisions, and monitoring public bodies' progress towards meeting their well-being objectives.[196]

8.147 The EWA 2016 provides a framework for sustainable management of Wales' environment and natural resources, and creates a statutory target for reductions of greenhouse gas emissions. The objective of sustainable management of natural resources ('SMNR') is to 'maintain and enhance the resilience of ecosystems and the benefits they provide', and in so doing meet the needs of both present and future generations, and contribute to the achievement of the well-being goals.[197] The principles of SMNR include taking account of the benefits and intrinsic value of natural resources and ecosystems, taking action to prevent significant damage to ecosystems, and taking account of the resilience of ecosystems, including the diversity between and within ecosystems, their scale, condition (including structure and functioning), and adaptability.[198]

8.148 Section 6 EWA 2016 provides Wales with its own enhanced 'biodiversity and resilience of ecosystems duty', several years earlier than the enhanced duty set out in the EA 2021 (see paragraphs 8.05 and 8.96 above). Public authorities must seek to maintain and enhance biodiversity in the exercise of functions in relation to Wales, and in so doing promote the resilience of ecosystems (section 6(1)). Public authorities must take account of the resilience of ecosystems, including the same considerations set out above. Pursuant to sections 7 and 9 EWA 2016, Welsh Ministers must publish a list of organisms and habitats of principal importance for the purpose of maintaining and enhancing biodiversity in Wales, and publish a national natural resources policy. Pursuant to sections 8 and 11, NRW must publish reports assessing the state of natural resources in Wales, and area statements for the areas it considers appropriate to facilitate the implementation of the national natural resources policy.

---

192 WBFGA 2015 ss 1–3, 5.
193 ibid s 3(2).
194 ibid s 4.
195 ibid s 10.
196 ibid ss 17–18.
197 EWA 2016 s 3(2).
198 ibid s 4.

8.149 Part 2 EWA 2016 imposes duties on the Welsh Ministers to meet targets for reducing emissions of greenhouse gases from Wales, including an equivalent net zero 2050 target.[199] Interim targets for 2020, 2030 and 2040 are to be set by way of regulations, as are carbon budgets for every five-year period up to 2050.[200]

8.150 Wales has also published a Nature Recovery Action Plan, setting out how it will address international commitments made under the CBD (see paragraphs 8.28 and 8.33–8.42 above). The first iteration of the plan, published in 2015, set out how Wales proposed to deliver its EU and international commitments to halt biodiversity decline by 2020 and reverse it thereafter.[201] In October 2020, the Welsh Government published a 'refreshed' action plan for 2020–2021,[202] to 'provide focus and prioritisation within a fast changing policy context and the emerging ecological crisis', while noting that the 2015 strategy would 'remain in place until it is realigned to address the post 2020 framework for the UN Convention on Biological Diversity'.[203] As at 6 March 2024, no post-2020 plan has been published.

8.151 In March 2019, following the UK government publishing draft clauses for what would become the Environment Act 2021, the Welsh Government published its own consultation on post-Brexit environmental principles and governance.[204] The consultation noted that Welsh law, in particular the WBFGA 2015 and EWA 2016, already comprised a framework of certain environmental principles and related concepts, including sustainable development, sustainable management of natural resources based on an ecosystem approach, and the principles of prevention, precaution, non-regression and resilience. The consultation proposed legislating to further incorporate the polluter pays principle and the rectification at source principle. The consultation also sought views on the national post-Brexit arrangements for environmental governance.

8.152 On 1 March 2021, an Interim Environmental Protection Assessor for Wales ('IEPAW') was appointed to consider issues relating to the functioning of environmental law in Wales and make recommendations to the Welsh Ministers. The IEPAW does not have an equivalent remit or powers to those which existed under the EU framework, nor does she have statutory investigation and enforcement powers to address complaints about compliance with environmental law by public authorities, equivalent to the OEP.[205]

---

199 ibid ss 28–29.
200 ibid ss 30–31.
201 Welsh Government, 'The Nature Recovery Plan for Wales Setting the Course for 2020 and Beyond' (2015) 2, 6, 43–50 <https://www.gov.wales/sites/default/files/publications/2019-05/nature-recovery-action-plan-2015.pdf> accessed 14 October 2024.
202 Welsh Government, 'The Nature Recovery Action Plan for Wales 2020–21' (2020) <https://www.gov.wales/sites/default/files/publications/2020-10/nature-recovery-action-plan-wales-2020-2021.pdf> accessed 14 October 2024.
203 See <https://www.gov.wales/nature-recovery-action-plan accessed> 14 October 2024.
204 See <https://www.gov.wales/environmental-principles-and-governance-wales-post-european-union-exit> accessed 14 October 2024.
205 Welsh Government, 'Consultation on the White Paper: Securing a Sustainable Future Environmental Principles, Governance and Biodiversity Targets for a Greener Wales' (2024) WG48598 10 <https://www.gov.wales/sites/default/files/consultations/2024-01/environmental-principles-governance-and-biodiversity-targets-white-paper.pdf> accessed 14 October 2024.

8.153 On 30 January 2024, the Welsh Government issued a White Paper setting out proposals to introduce a Bill which will:

- Embed environmental principles into Welsh law;
- Strengthen environmental governance in Wales by establishing a new governance body to oversee compliance with environmental law by Welsh public authorities; and
- Introduce a biodiversity targets framework.[206]

8.154 In respect of the third limb, the current proposals include a headline or 'apex' nature positive target enshrined in primary legislation; a suite of supporting biodiversity targets set out in secondary legislation; monitoring, reporting and scrutiny requirements in relation to all targets; a Nature Recovery Strategy, Nature Recovery Action Plan addressing the action needed to meet the targets, and Local Nature Recovery Plans produced by Welsh public authorities.[207]

8.155 It is proposed that the headline target reflect the existing WBFGWA 2015 commitment to '[r]everse the decline in biodiversity with an improvement in the status of species and ecosystems by 2030 and their clear recovery by 2050'. The supporting targets will likely be based around species, habitat, and ecosystem health and resilience, but no further benchmarks have yet been particularised. Interim targets may also be set.[208]

8.156 Consultation on the White Paper runs until 30 April 2024, and it remains to be seen what the final form of the proposed legislation (the equivalent of the EA 2021) will be, or when it will be enacted.

8.157 The Welsh Government has also enacted the Agriculture (Wales) Act 2023, which mirrors the Agriculture Act 2020 in facilitating a move towards environmental land management: see further Chapter 12.

Conclusion

8.158 The EA 2021 is a highly significant piece of environmental legislation, which sets out an ambitious post-Brexit governance framework intended to drive a cycle of continuous improvement to the environment. The governance framework includes a wealth of specific statutory nature targets, and an enhanced biodiversity objective reflecting government's increased ambition in relation to nature recovery. The EA 2021 also places other pre-existing policy (including spatial planning for nature recovery) on a statutory footing, creating an array of new legal tools for nature protection. The structure of long-term and interim targets which government has committed to under the

---

206 ibid.
207 ibid 44–65.
208 ibid 51–54, 34–35, 39–50.

EA 2021 corresponds with the 2050 and 2030 goals agreed to internationally by Parties to the GBF, reflecting that halting and reversing nature's decline is a global concern.

8.159 It must, however, be noted that similar international commitments have been made before. Internationally, Parties to the CBD committed to significantly reduce biodiversity loss by 2010, with Europe committing to halt biodiversity loss by this date: the world and Europe failed to meet these commitments.[209] In 2010, Parties to the CBD agreed to take 'effective and urgent action to halt the loss of biodiversity' to ensure that by 2020 ecosystems were resilient: consequently, the government published the 2011–2020 Biodiversity Strategy setting out its ambition to halt overall biodiversity loss in England by 2020, and thereafter move towards biodiversity net gain. The result is self-evident: the new ambition to halt biodiversity decline by 2030 (and reverse it thereafter) divulges a further decade of delay and decline.

8.160 The post-2020 strategy for nature which was committed to in the 25YEP has not emerged as a standalone strategy to explain or respond to government's failure to meet its 2020 commitment, or what it will do differently in future. However, it is sincerely to be hoped that domestically, the three 'foundation stones' of the post-Brexit legislative framework intended to halt nature's decline by 2030 (the EA 2021, AA 2020 and Fisheries Act 2020) will make a tangible difference to this concerning historic trend. Early and effective implementation of the legislation will be critical to its success in doing so.

8.161 The EA 2021 is at an early stage of its implementation, but with much to do to remain (or indeed become) on track to meet the interim and long-term targets. The OEP's most recent analysis suggests that government is largely off track to meet many of these targets, and the current lack of monitoring data means it is currently not possible to assess progress in some areas. The position is further complicated by the inconsistency in the baselines provided for in relation to the different statutory targets. While more data will emerge as the provisions of the Act are implemented, it is currently unclear how different policy actions are expected, individually and collectively, to contribute to meeting the statutory targets. There are recent indications that the new government are minded to adopt the OEP's recommendation to publish a more detailed, quantified delivery plan. The extent to which that intention is made out in the forthcoming EIP, promised by the end of 2024, will have become apparent by the time this book is published.

---

209 Lawton and others (n 17) 5.

CHAPTER 9

PROTECTED AREAS

Victoria Hutton and Eleanor Leydon

Introduction

9.01 Protected areas have historically been the main legal instrument used to regulate biodiversity conservation (see further Chapter 8, in particular paragraph 8.07). However, this has not been their only historic purpose. In the UK, some of the earliest protected area designations were created for broader purposes, such as conserving 'natural beauty' and open-air recreation. Over time, these early statutes have been amended to reflect developments in conservation policy and practice, taking into consideration biodiversity, and the need not only to conserve but also to enhance nature. The UK has also incorporated robust international and EU-derived mechanisms for protecting certain valuable habitat types and species, which continue to be known as 'European Sites'.

9.02 One result of this incremental development is that there is significant overlap between designations: both legally (for example, the EU-derived Habitats Regulations overlap with other domestic measures for species protection) and geographically (in that particular areas are often protected by more than one designation).[1] This has led to calls for wholesale reform of protected area designations,[2] as well as species protection measures:[3] however, neither has progressed. Further, as set out in Chapter 8, the government has adopted recommendations to move towards an approach of nature recovery (as opposed to mere conservation), which includes implementing initiatives outside of protected areas.[4]

9.03 Nevertheless, it is envisaged that protected area designations will continue to play a key role in achieving the government's international and national nature commitments leading up to 2030 and beyond.

---

1 Richard Burnett-Hall and Brian Jones, *Burnett-Hall on Environmental Law* (3rd edn, Sweet & Maxwell 2012) ch 9.

2 Department for Environment, Food and Rural Affairs, 'Nature Recovery Green Paper: Protected Sites and Species' (2022) <https://consult.defra.gov.uk/nature-recovery-green-paper/nature-recovery-green-paper/supporting_documents/Nature%20Recovery%20Green%20Paper%20Consultation%20%20Protected%20Sites%20and%20Species.pdf> accessed 15 May 2024.

3 Law Commission, *Wildlife Law, Volume 1: Report* (HC 585–I, Law Com No 362, 2015) <https://s3-eu-west-2.amazonaws.com/cloud-platform-e218f50a4812967ba1215eaecede923f/uploads/sites/30/2015/11/lc362_wildlife_vol-1.pdf> accessed 13 May 2024.

4 JH Lawton and others, 'Making Space for Nature: A Review of England's Wildlife Sites and Ecological Network. Report to DEFRA' (2010) <https://webarchive.nationalarchives.gov.uk/ukgwa/20130402151656/http://archive.defra.gov.uk/environment/biodiversity/documents/201009space-for-nature.pdf> accessed 13 May 2024; DEFRA, 'Environmental Improvement Plan 2023: First Revision of the 25 Year Environment Plan' (2023) 39 <https://assets.publishing.service.gov.uk/media/64a6d9c1c531eb000c64fffa/environmental-improvement-plan-2023.pdf> accessed 4 April 2024.

9.04 Internationally, the government has committed to two distinct 2030 targets under the Kunming-Montreal Global Biodiversity Framework:

- That by 2030, at least 30% of areas of degraded ecosystems should be under effective restoration; and
- That by 2030, at least 30% of terrestrial and inland water areas, and of marine and coastal areas, especially areas of particular importance for biodiversity and ecosystem functions and services, are effectively conserved and managed through ecologically representative, well-connected and equitably governed systems of protected areas and other effective area-based conservation measures.

9.05 To achieve the second target, the government plans to strengthen existing policy and statutory safeguards and powers; designate new protected areas, as well as create wildlife-rich habitat outside these areas; and invest in habitat restoration both within and outside protected areas.[5] In particular, the government plans to increase nature recovery efforts in National Parks and Areas of Outstanding Natural Beauty ('AONBs').[6]

9.06 Nationally, the government has legislated for a suite of ambitious environmental targets under the Environment Act 2021 ('EA 2021'), including to halt the decline in species abundance by 2030;[7] reverse the decline in species abundance by 2042; reduce the risk of species extinction by 2042; and restore or create in excess of 500,000 hectares of wildlife-rich habitat outside of current protected sites by 2042[8] (see further paragraphs 8.49–8.59 in Chapter 8). Further, the marine biodiversity target set under the EA 2021 is that by 31 December 2042, at least 70% of the designated features within all relevant MPAs will be in a favourable condition, with the remainder in recovering condition.[9]

9.07 The 2023 Environmental Improvement Plan ('EIP') also sets the following relevant statutory interim targets[10] and further commitments:

- To restore 75% of protected sites to favourable condition by 2042;
- For all Sites of Special Scientific Interest ('SSSIs') to have an up-to-date condition assessment by 31 January 2028;
- For 50% of SSSIs to 'have actions on track to achieve favourable condition by 31 January 2028'; and
- For 48% of designated features in MPAs to be in favourable condition, with the remainder in recovering condition, by 31 January 2028.

---

5 DEFRA, 'Environmental Improvement Plan 2023: First Revision of the 25 Year Environment Plan' (n 4) 40.
6 ibid 41.
7 EA 2021 s 3.
8 The Environmental Targets (Biodiversity) (England) Regulations 2023, SI 2023/91.
9 Environmental Targets (Marine Protected Areas) Regulations 2023, SI 2023/94 reg 3.
10 EA 2021 ss 11 and 14.

9.08 While it is recognised that protected areas have been, and will remain fundamental to, legal nature recovery efforts, it is also recognised that (a) measures are also needed outside of protected areas; and (b) the effectiveness of protections within designated areas could be improved.[11] As set out above, wholesale reform to our existing patchwork of designations has been mooted (including to address the disconnect between the historical purposes underpinning designations, and the government's post-2020 nature positive ambitions) but has not progressed.[12] In the meantime, there continues to be an increased focus on the need to improve the poor condition of some of our protected areas, as well as increasing their quantity.

Development of the law on protected areas

(i) *The NPACA 1949: National Parks, NNRs and LNRs, and AONBs*

9.09 The National Parks and Access to the Countryside Act 1949 ('NPACA 1949') provides for the establishment of national parks, nature reserves and AONBs. Each one is discussed below.

(a) National Parks

9.10 Part II of the NPACA 1949 provides for the designation, by Order, of areas of land as National Parks, where it is especially desirable to take measures in relation to them by reason of their 'natural beauty' or the opportunities they afford for open-air recreation.[13] Following amendments made under the Natural Environment and Rural Communities Act 2006 ('NERCA 2006'), Natural England ('NE') or the Natural Resources Body for Wales ('NRBW')[14] may take wildlife into account in their consideration of 'natural beauty'. Additionally, when considering the opportunities an area affords for open-air recreation, they may also take into account the extent to which it is possible to promote opportunities for the understanding and enjoyment of its special qualities by the public.[15] The procedure for making and varying designations is set out in section 7 of the NPACA 1949.

9.11 There are currently nine National Parks in England: Dartmoor, Exmoor, Lake District, New Forest, North Yorkshire Moors, Northumberland, Peak District, South Downs and the Yorkshire Dales. There are three national parks in Wales: Bannau Brycheiniog (Brecon Beacons), Eryri (Snowdonia) and Pembrokeshire Coast. While the Norfolk Broads is commonly referred to as a National Park, it is designated and governed by separate legislation, and is therefore discussed separately below.

---

11 JH Lawton and others, 'Making Space for Nature: A Review of England's Wildlife Sites and Ecological Network. Report to DEFRA' (n 4); DEFRA, 'Environmental Improvement Plan 2023: First Revision of the 25 Year Environment Plan' (n 4) 39.

12 DEFRA, 'Environmental Improvement Plan 2023: First Revision of the 25 Year Environment Plan' (n 4) 9. However, at page 33, the 2023 EIP states somewhat enigmatically that the reforms explored in the Nature Recovery Green Paper have fed into the 2023 EIP.

13 NPACA 1949, SI 1949/97 s 5.

14 These bodies are discussed further in Chapter 4.

15 NPACA 1949 s 5(2A).

9.12 Section 5(1) of the NPACA 1949 provides that the purposes of National Parks are to: (a) conserve and enhance the natural beauty,[16] wildlife and cultural heritage of those areas and (b) promote opportunities for the understanding and enjoyment of the special qualities of those areas by the public. The Environment Act 1995 ('EA 1995') inserted section 11A into the NPACA 1949, subsection 1 of which provides that in applying the section 5(1) purposes, a National Park authority must 'seek to foster the economic and social well-being of local communities within the National Park'.

9.13 Between 1971 and 1974, the National Parks Policy Review Committee reviewed national parks of England and Wales. The Committee was chaired by Lord Sandford. The report included a recommendation that where the two purposes of National Parks proved irreconcilable, then priority should be given to the conservation of natural beauty.[17] This has become known as the 'Sandford Principle'.

9.14 The EA 1995 first introduced the Sandford Principle into the NPACA 1949 by the insertion of section 11A(2). The principle is now found in sections 11A(1A), (1B) and (2). In short, relevant authorities (ministers, public bodies, statutory undertakers or any person holding public office) must, in exercising or performing any functions in relation to or so as to affect land in a National Park, have regard to the purposes set out in section 5(1) of the NPACA 1949. If it appears that there is a conflict between those purposes then they must attach greater weight to the purpose of conserving and enhancing the natural beauty, wildlife and cultural heritage of the National Park.

9.15 In *Stubbs v Lake District National Park Authority,* Dove J confirmed that section 11A(2), as was then enacted, was included within the NPACA 1949 'as a means of resolving situations where it is no longer possible to treat both of the purposes equally, and not possible through management or stewardship to satisfactorily accommodate both purposes'.[18] As such, the word 'conflict' in section 11A(2) 'is not to be understood as referring to any conflict or friction' between the two purposes in section 11A(2). Therefore:[19]

> [W]here the National Park Authority judges that the conflict can no longer be satisfactorily mediated through management or stewardship then, in circumstances where it is judged that both purposes cannot be accommodated and the National Park Authority concludes that it must make a choice, section 11A(2) makes clear that it is the first of the purposes which is to be afforded greater weight.

9.16 The EA 1995 empowered the Secretary of State to establish, by Order, new National Park Authorities.[20]

---

16 NPACA 1949 s 114(2) states that 'References in this Act to the preservation, or the conservation, of the natural beauty of an area shall be construed as including references to the preservation or, as the case may be, the conservation, of its flora, fauna and geological and physiographical features'.
17 'Report of the National Parks Policies Review Committee (Sandford Report)' (1974).
18 *R (Stubbs) v Lake District National Park Authority* [2020] EWHC 2293 (Admin) [39].
19 ibid [39].
20 EA 1995 ss 63–64.

9.17 Section 65 of the EA 1995 sets out the general purposes and powers of National Park Authorities in line with the purposes specified in section 5(1) of the NPACA 1949, with further provisions applying to English National Park Authorities in sections 65A–C of the EA 1995.

9.18 The EA 1995 also provides for National Park Authorities to be planning authorities for their area.[21] They therefore formulate and adopt the local development plan and make decisions on planning applications under the Town and Country Planning Act 1990 ('TCPA 1990'). Along with a number of other miscellaneous statutory functions, the EA 1995 expressly provides that National Park Authorities have planning authority functions under the Wildlife and Countryside Act 1981 ('WCA 1981'). This includes being able to enter into management agreements for the establishment of nature reserves[22] and also to establish local nature reserves.[23]

9.19 National Park Authorities are required to prepare and publish National Park Management Plans which set out their policy for managing their National Park and carrying out their functions in relation to it, in accordance with section 66 of the EA 1995. Such plans must be reviewed every five years.[24]

9.20 The Levelling Up and Regeneration Act 2023 ('LURA 2023')[25] inserted section 66A into the EA 1995. This empowers the Secretary of State to make regulations: (a) requiring a National Park Management Plan for a park in England to contribute to meeting any of the targets set in Chapter 1 of Part 1 of the EA 2021; (b) setting out how much a Management Plan must contribute to the meeting of such targets; and (c) setting out how such a Management Plan must further the purposes set out in section 5(1) of the NPACA 1949. Regulations may also require a relevant authority, other than a devolved Welsh authority to contribute to the preparation, implementation or review of a National Park Management Plan. Relevant authorities are: ministers of the Crown, public bodies, statutory undertakers and any person holding public office.

(b) Local and national nature reserves

9.21 The NPACA 1949[26] and the WCA 1981[27] provide for the establishment of local and national nature reserves.

9.22 Local nature reserves are established by councils of counties and county boroughs.[28] National nature reserves are established by NE and NRBW and are declared to be such by those bodies under section 35 of the WCA 1981.

---

21 ibid s 67 inserted into TCPA 1990 s 4A.
22 EA 1995 s 69.
23 ibid sch 9, para 3.
24 ibid s 66(4).
25 LURA 2023 s 245(4).
26 NPACA 1949 Part III.
27 WCA 1981 Part II.
28 NPACA 1949 ss 16 and 21. Other bodies such as parish and town Councils may establish local nature reserves if the relevant powers have been delegated to them.

9.23 The establishment of both local and national nature reserves is governed by sections 15–21 of the NPACA 1949.

9.24 Nature reserves (whether national or local) are defined as either (a) land managed solely for a conservation purpose, or (b) land managed not only for a conservation purpose but also for a recreational purpose, if the management of the land for the recreational purpose does not compromise its management for the conservation purpose.[29] The NPACA 1949 provides that land is 'managed for a conservation purpose' if it is managed for the purpose of (a) providing, under suitable conditions and control, special opportunities for the study of, and research into, matters relating to the fauna and flora of Great Britain and the physical conditions in which they live, and for the study of geological and physiographical features of special interest in the area, and/or (b) preserving flora, fauna or geological or physiographical features of special interest in the area.[30]

9.25 For a local nature reserve to be established, the relevant local authority must determine that it would be expedient in the local interest for that area of land to be managed as a nature reserve.[31] Local Authorities must exercise their powers under Part III of the NPACA 1949 in consultation with either NE or NRBW as appropriate. The NPACA 1949 makes separate further provision for Welsh local authorities (meaning the council of a county or county borough or a National Park authority for a National Park in Wales) to establish nature reserves where they consider that it would be expedient in the national interest or in the interests of the locality, for an area to be managed as a nature reserve. They may enter into agreements with owners, lessees and occupiers of that land for its management.[32] This power is only exercisable in relation to land in the authority's area which is not held by, or managed in accordance with, an agreement entered into with NRBW.

9.26 NE and NRBW may compulsorily acquire land where they are satisfied that it is expedient in the national interest that it should be managed as a nature reserve.[33]

9.27 Similarly, county councils and county borough councils may compulsorily acquire land where they are satisfied that it is expedient in the local interest that it should be managed as a nature reserve.[34]

9.28 Land may not, however, be compulsorily acquired for the purpose of managing land as a nature reserve, unless the relevant acquiring body is satisfied that they are unable to secure the management of the area by way of a nature reserve agreement or an agreement made under section 16 of the NPACA 1949.[35] A nature reserve agreement is defined in section 15A NPACA 1949 as an agreement entered into by NE with a person who has a legal interest in that land for its management under section 7 of the

---

29 NPACA 1949 s 15(1).
30 NPACA 1949 s 15(2).
31 NPACA 1949 s 21.
32 NPACA 1949 s 16.
33 NPACA 1949 s 17(1).
34 NPACA 1949 s 21, read with s 17(1).
35 NPACA 1949 ss 17 and 21.

NERCA 2006, or a similar agreement entered into by NRBW under section 16 of the Environment (Wales) Act 2016 ('E(W)A 2016').

9.29 Further, where NE, NRBW, a county council or a county borough council has entered into a nature reserve agreement or an agreement under section 16 of the NPACA 1949, and a breach of the agreement occurs which prevents or impairs the satisfactory management of the land as a nature reserve, they may acquire the interest compulsorily.[36] The NPACA 1949 provides for arbitration where there is a dispute as to whether there has been a breach of a management agreement such that it gives rise to a power of compulsory acquisition.[37]

9.30 NE, NRBW, county councils and county borough councils are empowered to make byelaws for the protection of each nature reserve, which is under a management agreement entered into with them, or in respects of land which is held by them and managed as a nature reserve.[38]

9.31 NE or NRBW may declare a nature reserve as a 'national nature reserve' where the nature reserve is of national importance and is: (a) being managed as a nature reserve under an agreement entered into with either NE or NRBW; (b) held by NE or NRBW and managed by them as a nature reserve; or (c) is held by a body approved by NE or NRBW and is being managed by that body as a nature reserve.[39] Any proposed declaration relating to subtidal land is subject to a ministerial power of call-in under section 35A of the WCA 1981.

9.32 In 2023, there were 221 National Nature Reserves in England. Of these, 135 are managed by NE on its own or jointly with others, and the remainder are managed by Approved Bodies such as the National Trust and the Royal Society of the Protection of Birds;[40] 93% of all National Nature Reserves in England are also designated as SSSIs.[41]

(c) Areas of outstanding natural beauty

9.33 Areas of outstanding natural beauty ('AONBs') were first established under section 87 of the NPACA 1949. This was repealed by the Countryside and Rights of Way Act 2000 ('CROWA 2000'), which now governs designations. section 82 of the CROWA 2000 provides that where NE or NRBW are of the view that an area in England or Wales, as applicable, which is not in a National Park is 'of such outstanding natural beauty' that the protective provisions of the CROWA 2000 should apply, they may designate the area as an AONB in accordance with the procedure set out in section 83 and subject to confirmation by either the Secretary of State in England or the National Assembly in Wales. There are currently 34 AONBs in England[42] and five in Wales.

---

36 NPACA 1949 ss 18 and 21.
37 NPACA 1949 s 18(3).
38 NPACA 1949 ss 20 and 21.
39 WCA 1981 s 35.
40 Natural England, 'Natural England Standard: National Nature Reserves Management Standards' (2023) <https://publications.naturalengland.org.uk/publication/5642141770448896> accessed 13 May 2024.
41 ibid.
42 Natural England, 'Guidance: Areas of Outstanding Natural Beauty (AONBs): Designation and Management' (2017) <https://www.gov.uk/guidance/areas-of-outstanding-natural-beauty-aonbs-designation-and-manageme nt> accessed 13 May 2024.

9.34 Although the relevant legislation refers to AONBs, the government has, since 2022, 're-branded' AONBs as 'National Landscapes'.[43] As the legislation continues to refer to AONBs, this chapter will use the term set out in the legislation.

9.35 The CROWA 2000 requires that NE/NRBW is consulted on development proposals within AONBs.[44] It also requires that NE is consulted on development plans which include any area within an AONB.[45]

9.36 AONBs are administered by Conservation Boards which are established by order of the Secretary of State in England, and by order of the Assembly for Wales in Wales.[46] The Secretary of State or Assembly for Wales may order that functions of local authorities where the AONB is situated be transferred to a Conservation Board. However, this does not include a power to transfer functions under Parts III, VII or XIII of the TCPA 1990 or Parts 2 or 6 of the Planning and Compulsory Purchase Act 2004 ('PCPA 2004'). Therefore, unlike National Park Authorities, AONB Conservation Boards are not planning authorities. Those powers remain in the hands of the local authorities whose administrative areas include areas within any AONB.

9.37 The CROWA 2000 places a duty upon relevant authorities:[47] where they are exercising or performing any functions in relation to or so as to affect land in an AONB, they must seek to further the purpose of conserving and enhancing the natural beauty of that AONB.[48]

9.38 Conservation Boards are under a duty to seek to further (a) the purpose of conserving and enhancing the natural beauty of the AONB, and (b) the purpose of increasing the understanding and enjoyment by the public of the special qualities of the AONB.[49] If the Conservation Board considers that there is a conflict between those purposes, then they are required to attach greater weight to purpose (a). Whilst fulfilling their duties, Conservation Boards are required to seek to foster the economic and social well-being of local communities within the AONB, and are required to cooperate with local authorities and public bodies whose functions include the promotion of economic or social development within the AONB.[50]

9.39 The phrase 'conservation of the natural beauty of an area' includes 'a reference to the conservation of its flora, fauna, geological and physiographical features'.[51]

---

43 DEFRA, 'Policy Paper: Landscapes Review (National Parks and AONBs): Government Response' (2022) <https://www.gov.uk/government/publications/landscapes-review-national-parks-and-aonbs-government-response/landscapes-review-national-parks-and-aonbs-government-response> accessed 13 May 2024.
44 CROWA 2000, SI 2000/37 s 84(1)(a) applying NPACA 1949 s 6(4)(e).
45 ibid s 84(1)(b) applying NPACA 1949 s 9.
46 ibid s 86(1). The procedure for this is set out in CROWA 2000 s 88.
47 Ministers of the Crown, public bodies, statutory undertakers and any person holding public office.
48 CROWA 2000 s 85(A1) and (1).
49 ibid s 87(A1) in England and s 87(1) in Wales.
50 ibid s 87(2).
51 ibid s 92(2).

9.40 Conservation Boards are required to publish management plans for their area and for the carrying out of their functions in relation to it, in accordance with section 89 and section 90 of the CROWA 2000. AONB Management Plans must be reviewed every five years.[52][53] The LURA 2023 inserted section 90(2A) into the CROWA 2000,[54] which enables the Secretary of State to make regulations: (a) requiring an AONB Management Plan in England to contribute to the meeting of any target set under Chapter 1 of Part 1 of the EA 2021; (b) setting out how such a plan must contribute to the meeting of such targets; and (c) setting out how an AONB Management Plan must further the purpose of conserving and enhancing the natural beauty of that area.

9.41 The LURA 2023[55] also inserted section 85(1A) into the CROWA 2000 which enables the Secretary of State to make regulations about how relevant authorities are to comply with their duties to seek to further the purpose of conserving and enhancing the natural beauty of AONBs in England.

(ii) *The Norfolk Broads*

9.42 The Norfolk Broads spans an area of 303 square kilometres with over 200km of navigable waterways located in both Norfolk and Suffolk.[56] It is commonly referred to as a National Park; however, it is governed by its own legislative regime which is tailored to its unique features. This requires that its functions cover not only the conservation and enhancement of natural beauty and promoting public enjoyment, but also the protection of interests of navigation along its waterways.

9.43 The Norfolk and Suffolk Broads Act 1988 ('NSBA 1988') established the Broads Authority to manage the Norfolk Broads for the purposes of (a) conserving and enhancing the natural beauty, wildlife and cultural heritage of the Broads; (b) promoting opportunities for the understanding and enjoyment of the special qualities of the Broads by the public; and (c) protecting the interests of navigation.[57] The Act provides that in discharging its functions the Authority shall have regard to (a) the national importance of the Broads as an area of natural beauty and one which affords opportunities for open-air recreation; (b) the desirability of protecting the natural resources of the Broads from damage; and (c) the needs of agriculture, forestry and the economic and social interests of those who live or work in the Broads.

9.44 The Authority is required to maintain 'the Broads Plan', which sets out its policy with respect to the exercise of its functions and to review that plan at least once every five years.[58] Similarly, the Authority is required to maintain a map which depicts areas

52 ibid s 89(7).
53 NB the LURA 2023 s 245(9) has added a power for the Secretary of State to require a relevant authority, other than a devolved Welsh authority to contribute to the preparation, implementation or review of an AONB Management Plan; see CROWA 2000 s 90A.
54 CROWA 2000 s 245(8).
55 LURA 2023 s 245(6)(c).
56 'About the Broads: Facts and Figures' <https://www.broads-authority.gov.uk/about-the-broads/facts-and-figures> accessed 13 May 2024.
57 NSBA 1988, SI 1988/4 s 2.
58 ibid s 3.

within the Broads whose natural beauty is particularly important to conserve. It is under a duty to review that map every five years.[59]

9.45 Section 5 of the NSBA 1988 bestows powers upon Ministers to, by Order, specify certain areas of grazing marsh, fen marsh, reed bed or broadleaved woodland and certain operations likely to affect the character or appearance of one or more of those areas. If made, an order would prohibit any person from carrying out a specified operation within the specified area(s), unless written notice is given to the Authority and the Authority has given consent, not given or refused consent within three months, or has refused consent and 12 months has passed from the date of notice.

9.46 The Authority has powers to make byelaws in relation to land where the Authority is the owner or occupier, where the general public have a right of access or which is commonly used by the general public.[60] Byelaws may be made for the purpose of preventing damage to land or anything in, on, or under it, or anything interfering unduly with the enjoyment of the land by other persons. In preparing byelaws, the Authority must consult NE and the byelaws must be confirmed by the Secretary of State, with or without modifications.

9.47 Where relevant authorities[61] exercise functions relating to or affecting land in the Broads, they must seek to further the purposes of (a) conserving and enhancing the natural beauty, wildlife and cultural heritage of the Broads; (b) promoting opportunities for the understanding and enjoyment of the special qualities of the Broads by the public; and (c) protecting the interests of navigation.[62]

9.48 The Authority is the sole planning authority for its area.[63] It therefore prepares the development plan for the area and determines planning applications.

9.49 The Authority has some powers which apply to other local authorities. These include the power to establish nature reserves under section 21 of the NPACA 1949.[64]

The Wildlife and Countryside Act 1981: Sites of Special Scientific Interest and Ramsar Sites

(i) *Sites of Special Scientific Interest ('SSSIs')*

9.50 The concept of SSSIs first appeared in legislation in the NPACA 1949.[65] This imposed a duty upon the Nature Conservancy to notify the local planning authority where it was of the opinion that any area of land not managed as a nature reserve is of special interest by reason of its flora, fauna or geological or physiographical features.[66]

---

59 ibid s 4.
60 ibid s 6.
61 Ministers, public bodies, statutory undertakers and any person holding public office.
62 NSBA 1988 s 17A(1).
63 TCPA 1990 s 5 and sch 1.
64 NPACA 1949 s 111A.
65 NECR414 Edition 1 Sites of Special Scientific Interest (SSSIs) in England (2).
66 NPACA 1949 s 23.

The law relating to SSSIs has undergone significant development and they are now governed by the WCA 1981.

9.51 The WCA 1981 provides, at section 28, for sites to be notified as SSSIs. The process for designation is instigated by NE or NRBW[67] where it is 'of the opinion that any area of land is of special interest by reason of any of its flora, fauna, or geological or physiographical features.'[68] Land which may be notified includes land lying above the mean low water mark and land covered by estuarial waters.[69] The Joint Nature Conservation Committee ('JNCC') has published guidelines for the selection of Biological SSSIs and guidelines for the selection of geological and physiographical SSSIs.[70]

9.52 Where NE/NRBW reaches such an opinion, they are required to notify (a) the local planning authority in whose area the land is situated; (b) every owner and occupier of that land; and (c) the Secretary of State.[71] They are also required to publish a notification of its opinion in a local newspaper, giving at least three months for representations or objections to be made.[72]

9.53 The notification must specify the flora, fauna or geological or physiographical features by reason of which the land is of special interest, and any operations appearing to NE/NRBW to be likely to damage the flora and fauna or those features. It shall also contain a statement of NE's/NRBW's views about the management of the land.[73]

9.54 Once NE/NRBW has given a notification under section 28(1), they may within 9 months of giving the notification to the Secretary of State, either withdraw or confirm the notification (with or without modifications).[74] If it is not confirmed within 9 months, then the notification expires after the end of that period.[75]

9.55 Once confirmed under section 28(5)(b), NE/NRBW may vary notifications. However, variations may not include the areas of land covered by the notification. The procedure for varying notifications is set out in section 28A.[76]

9.56 The WCA 1981 also enables land to be added to a pre-existing SSSI where NE/NRBW are 'of the opinion that if land adjacent to a site of special scientific interest ('the extra land') were combined with the site of special scientific interest ('the SSSI'),

67 WCA 1981 s 27AA; applies s 28 of the WCA 1981 to Wales and reference to NE is to be read as Natural Resources Wales.
68 ibid s 28(1).
69 WCA 1981 s 28(1A).
70 Joint Nature Conservation Committee, 'SSSI Guidelines' (2022) Part 2: Species Chapters <https://jncc.gov.uk/our-work/guidelines-for-selection-of-sssis/#part-2-species-chapters> accessed 13 May 2024.
71 WCA 1981 s 28(1). If any part of the land is in Wales and all or part of it is included in the area of a corporate joint committee to which Part 6 of the Planning and Compulsory Purchase Act 2004 applies by virtue of regulations under Part 5 of the Local Government and Elections (Wales) Act 2021, then NRBW must also give notice to that corporate joint committee (see s 27AA of the WCA 1981).
72 ibid s 28(3).
73 ibid s 28(4).
74 ibid s 28(5).
75 ibid s 28(6).
76 Note also that NE/NRBW may vary a notification under s 28 of the WCA 1981 for the purpose of securing compliance with the Directives, pursuant to reg 23 of the Conservation of Habitats and Species Regulations 2017.

the combined area of land would be of special interest by reason of any of its flora, fauna, or geological or physiographical features'.[77] The procedure for this is set out in the remainder of that section. Similarly, existing SSSIs may be enlarged through the procedure set out in section 28C.

9.57 Particular provisions apply to proposals to give notifications concerning 'subtidal land,' meaning land lying below mean low water mark, whereby the ministerial power has power to call-in notifications relating to these areas.[78]

9.58 Land may be de-notified as an SSSI. This is either because NE/NRBW has reached the opinion that all or part of an SSSI 'is not of special interest by reason of the matters mentioned in section 28(1)' (i.e. 'by reason of any of its flora, fauna, or geological or physiographical features'), or that it should no longer be the subject of a notification because it has been designated as (or as part of) a marine conservation zone under section 116 of the Marine and Coastal Access Act 2009.[79] The procedure is set out under section 28D.

9.59 The owners and occupiers of SSSIs are subject to the duties set out in section 28E of the WCA 1981. They must not carry out, or cause, or permit to be carried out, any operation specified in the notification unless one of them has given NE/NRBW notice of a proposal to carry out the operation specifying its nature and the land on which it is proposed to carry it out and either (a) NE/NRBW gives its written consent (which may be subject to conditions or given for a limited period); (b) the operation is carried out in accordance with the terms of an agreement under section 16 of the NPACA 1949,[80] section 7 of the NERCA 2006[81] or section 16 of the E(W)A 2016;[82] or (c) the operation is carried out in accordance with a management scheme under section 28J or a management notice under section 28K of the WCA 1981, which are addressed further below.[83] A breach of section 28E(1) is a criminal offence under section 28P(1) of the WCA 1981. Regulation 24 of the Conservation of Habitats and Species Regulations 2017 applies the habitats regime (addressed at paragraphs 9.78ff below) to proposals under section 28E(1)(a) of the WCA 1981.

9.60 Where an owner or occupier has been refused consent, has been granted consent subject to conditions or for a limited period, or is aggrieved by the modification or withdrawal of consent, then they may appeal that decision to the Secretary of State.[84] An appeal may take the form of a hearing (either wholly or partially in private) or by local inquiry. The Secretary of State must hear the appeal by either hearing or inquiry, if

---

77 WCA 1981 s 28B(1).
78 ibid s 28CB.
79 ibid s 28D(1).
80 A management agreement entered into by owners, lessees and occupiers of any land and a Welsh local authority for land to be managed as a nature reserve.
81 A management agreement entered into by NE with a person who has an interest in land about the management or use of that land.
82 A management agreement entered into by the NRBW with a person who has an interest in land about the management or use of that land.
83 WCA 1981 ss 28E(1) and (3).
84 ibid s 28F(1).

either party to the appeal asks to be heard in connection with that appeal.[85] On hearing the appeal, the Secretary of State may: (a) affirm the decision of NE/NRBW; (b) direct NE/NRBW to give consent; (c) quash or modify the terms of any consent or (d) quash a withdrawal or modification of consent or direct NE/Natural Resources Wales as to the terms on which they are to give consent.[86]

9.61 Certain authorities, termed 'section 28G authorities', are under a duty 'to take reasonable steps, consistent with the proper exercise of the authority's functions, to further the conservation and enhancement of the flora, fauna or geological or physiographical features by reason of which the site is of special scientific interest'. The duty applies where those authorities exercise functions which are 'likely to affect the flora, fauna or geological or physiographical features by reason of which a [SSSI] is of special interest'.[87] Section 28G authorities are: (a) ministers of the Crown or government departments; (b) the National Assembly for Wales; (c) local authorities; (d) persons holding an office (i) under the Crown, (ii) created or continued in existence by a public general Act of Parliament, or (iii) under the remuneration in respect of which is paid out of money provided by Parliament; (e) statutory undertakers; and (f) any other public bodies of any description.[88]

9.62 Section 28G authorities are required to give notice to NE/NRBW before carrying out operations likely to damage any of the flora, fauna or geological or physiographical features by reason of which an SSSI is of special interest.[89] NE/NRBW may assent (with or without conditions) or refuse to assent to the proposed operation.[90] If NE/NRBW do not respond within 28 days, they are taken to not have assented.

9.63 If NE/NRBW does not assent to the operations or the section 28G authority proposes to carry out operations otherwise than in accordance with the terms of any assent, then it shall not carry out the operations unless: (a) it has notified NE/NRBW of the date on which it proposes to start the operations and how (if at all) it has taken account of any written advice it has received from NRBW/NE;[91] and (b) it must carry out the operations in such a way as to give rise to as little damage as is reasonably practicable in all the circumstances to the flora, fauna or geological or physiographical features by reason of which the site is of special interest and restore the site to its former condition, so far as is reasonably practicable if any such damage does occur.[92]

85 ibid s 28F(4).
86 WCA 1981 s 28F(5). Regulations governing the appeals process are set out in the Sites of Special Scientific Interest (Appeals) Regulations 2009/197 and the Wildlife and Countryside (Sites of Special Scientific Interest, Appeals) (Wales) Regulations 2002/1172.
87 WCA 1981 ss 28G(1)–(2).
88 ibid s 28G(3).
89 ibid s 28H(1). A failure to give such notice without reasonable excuse for carrying out the operation without complying is a criminal offence under WCA 1981 s 28P(2)(a).
90 ibid s 28H(3).
91 A failure to give such notice under s 28H(5)(a) without reasonable excuse for carrying out the operation without complying is a criminal offence under WCA 1981 s 28J(2)(b).
92 WCA 1981 ss 28H(4)–(6). A failure to carry out operations in accordance with these requirements without reasonable excuse is a criminal offence under WCA 1981 s 28P(3).

9.64 Where the permission of a section 28G authority is required before operations may be carried out then they must give notice to NE/NRBW before permitting any operations which are likely to damage any of the flora, fauna, or geological or physiographical features by reason of which an SSSI is special.[93] NE/NRBW then has a 28 day period in which to advise as to whether permission for the operations should be granted or whether conditions should be attached.[94] In the event that NE/NRBW advise against permitting the operations or advise that certain conditions should be attached, but the section 28G authority does not follow that advice, the authority is required to give notice of the permission and its terms to NE/NRBW with an explanation of how (if at all) the advice has been taken into account, and shall not grant the permission until 21 days after that notice has been given to NE/NRBW.[95]

9.65 NE/NRBW are empowered to formulate management schemes for all or part of an SSSI.[96] Management schemes are schemes for conserving the flora, fauna, or geological or physiographical features by reason of which the land (or part of it to which the scheme relates) is of special interest, or restoring them, or both.[97] Owners and occupiers are consulted upon proposed management schemes and have a three-month period within which to make representations/object.[98] NE/NRBW may thereafter, within nine months of serving the notice, either withdraw the notice or confirm the management scheme (with or without modifications), so long as those modifications do not make compliance with the management scheme more onerous.[99]

9.66 Where NE/NRBW consider that an owner or occupier is not giving effect to a provision of a management scheme and as a result any flora, fauna or geological or physiographical features by reason of which the land is of special interest are being inadequately conserved or restored, they may serve a management notice requiring action, including the carrying out of works.[100] However, a management notice may not be served, unless NE/NRBW is satisfied that they are unable to conclude, on reasonable terms, an agreement with the owner or occupier as to the management of the land, in accordance with the management scheme.[101] If works or any other things required by the management notice have not been carried out in the time specified in it, NE/NRBW may enter the land to carry out the works or other things, and may recover reasonable expenses of doing so from the owner or occupier.[102] Owners and occupiers may appeal against management notices in accordance with section 28L of the WCA 1981.

---

93 ibid s 28I(2). A failure to give such notice without reasonable excuse for permitting the carrying out of the operation without complying is a criminal offence under WCA 1981 s 28P(5A)(a).
94 ibid s 28I(4). A failure to comply with this requirement without reasonable excuse for permitting the carrying out of the operation without complying is a criminal offence under WCA 1981 s 28P(5A)(b).
95 ibid s 28I(6). Additionally, a failure to comply with this requirement without reasonable excuse for permitting the carrying out of the operation without complying is a criminal offence under WCA 1981 s 28P(5A)(b).
96 ibid s 28J.
97 ibid s 28J(2).
98 ibid ss 28J(3)–(7).
99 ibid s 28J(8).
100 ibid ss 28K(1) and (3).
101 ibid s 28K(2).
102 ibid s 28K(7).

9.67 NE/NRBW has power to compulsorily purchase land within an SSSI where (a) they are satisfied that they are unable to conclude, on reasonable terms, an agreement with the owner or occupier for the management of the land, or (b) they have entered into a management agreement but it has been breached in such a way that the land is not being managed satisfactorily.[103] Any dispute about whether there has been a breach of a management agreement giving rise to a power of compulsory purchase, is subject to arbitration.[104] Where NE/NRBW has compulsorily purchased land under section 28N of the WCA 1981, they may either manage it themselves or dispose of it on terms designed to secure that the land is managed satisfactorily.[105]

9.68 NE/NRBW may make byelaws for the protection of an SSSI.[106]

9.69 It is a criminal offence for a person (other than a section 28G authority acting in the exercise of its functions) to, without reasonable excuse, (a) intentionally or recklessly destroy or damage any of the flora, fauna, or geological or physiographical features by reason of which land is of special interest, or intentionally or recklessly disturb any of those fauna, and (b) know that what was destroyed, damaged or disturbed was within an SSSI.[107] This is an either-way offence and is subject to a fine.

9.70 Separately, the WCA 1981 provides for a similar lesser offence, where it is not necessary to prove that the relevant person knew that any destroyed, damaged or disturbed flora/fauna/geological or physiological features were within an SSSI. This is a summary offence subject to a fine not exceeding level 4 on the standard scale.[108] These offences and those which apply to section 28G authorities, which are addressed above, may also lead to restoration orders under section 31 of the WCA 1981.

(ii) *Ramsar Sites*

9.71 Ramsar Sites are wetlands of international importance designated under the Convention on Wetlands of International Importance especially as Waterfowl Habitat ('Ramsar Convention'). The Ramsar Convention was adopted in February 1971 and came into force in December 1975.

9.72 Signatories to the Convention are required, under Article 2, to 'designate suitable wetlands within its territory for inclusion in a List of Wetlands of International Importance'. Wetlands are to be selected for the list 'on account of their international significance in terms of ecology, botany, zoology, limnology or hydrology'. The Convention defines wetlands as 'areas of marsh, fen, peatland or water, whether natural or artificial, permanent or temporary, with water that is static or flowing, fresh, brackish

103 ibid ss 29N(1)–(2).
104 ibid s 28N(3).
105 ibid s 28N(4).
106 ibid s 28R.
107 ibid s 28P(6).
108 ibid s 28P(6A).

or salt, including areas of marine water the depth of which at low tide does not exceed six metres'.[109]

9.73 The UK is one of 172 Contracting Parties,[110] and it designated its first Ramsar sites in 1976. There are currently 175 Ramsar sites across the UK.[111]

9.74 The Ramsar Convention requires contracting parties to 'formulate and implement their planning so as to promote the conservation of the wetlands included in the List, and as far as possible the wise use of wetlands in their territory'.[112]

9.75 Section 37A of the WCA 1981 requires the Secretary of State to notify NE and the NRBW of sites which have been designated as Ramsar Sites. NE and the NRBW are then under a duty to notify certain persons of the designation, including: the local planning authority where the Ramsar site is situated, every owner and occupier of that wetland, relevant statutory undertakers and internal drainage boards whose works operations or activities may affect the wetland[113] and the Environment Agency.[114]

9.76 Although Ramsar Sites do not have their own bespoke legislative protection regime, it is government policy that Ramsar Sites should have the same protection as sites protected under the Habitats Regulations.[115]

9.77 The physical areas of Ramsar Sites often overlap with other designations, such as European Marine Sites and SSSIs, and therefore enjoy statutory protection through the regimes which protect those areas.

European Sites

(i) *European Sites: SACs and SPAs*

9.78 European Site designations offer a robust level of protection for the relevant protected habitats and species, deriving from EU law, in particular the Habitats Directive[116] and Birds Directive.[117] The Directives were in turn designed to meet and complement

109 Ramsar Convention, 'The Importance of Wetlands', Article 1 <https://www.ramsar.org/about/our-mission/importance-wetlands> accessed 15 May 2024.
110 ibid.
111 ibid.
112 ibid Article 3(1).
113 ibid s 37A(2).
114 ibid s 37A(2A).
115 Department for Levelling Up, Housing and Communities, 'National Planning Policy Framework' (2023) <https://assets.publishing.service.gov.uk/media/65a11af7e8f5ec000f1f8c46/NPPF_December_2023.pdf> accessed 2 April 2024 para 187; Department for Environment, Food and Rural Affairs, 'Policy Paper: Changes to the Habitats Regulations 2017' (2021) <https://www.gov.uk/government/publications/changes-to-the-habitats-regulations-2017/changes-to-the-habitats-regulations-2017> accessed 15 May 2024. See the application of this policy in *CG Fry and Son Ltd v Secretary of State for Levelling Up, Housing and Communities* [2024] EWCA Civ 730.
116 Habitats Directive 92/43/EEC.
117 Birds Directive 2009/147/EC. The 2009 Birds Directive (referred to in the Habitats Regulations as the 'new Wild Birds Directive') consolidates and updates Council Directive 79/409/EEC on the conservation of wild birds ('the old Wild Birds Directive').

international obligations under the Ramsar Convention, Bern Convention[118] and Bonn Convention.[119]

9.79 Prior to Brexit, the UK domestically implemented obligations derived from the two Directives through the Conservation of Habitats and Species Regulations 2017 ('the Habitats Regulations 2017') and Conservation of Offshore Marine Habitats and Species Regulations 2017 ('the Offshore Habitats Regulations 2017'). The Habitats Regulations 2017 extend and apply to England and Wales and their adjacent territorial waters (to 12 nautical miles); the Offshore Habitats Regulations 2017 apply beyond 12 nautical miles offshore, within the UK offshore marine area. Both sets of Regulations were retained in domestic law following Brexit,[120] and are now assimilated law,[121] subject to a number of post-Brexit amendments.[122] The relationship of the retained regulations with the EU Directives is a complex one, as explored below. This chapter will focus on the onshore Habitats Regulations 2017.

9.80 The Habitats Regulations 2017 have been described as 'the most effective nature protection laws in the UK'.[123] They protect the most important and vulnerable sites and species in the UK, including sites of international importance for nature. European Site designations offer a higher level of legal protection than other domestic protections, such as SSSIs, including stringent restrictions on development (see paragraphs 9.129ff below) and broader protection against disturbance than that offered by the WCA 1981.[124] The Habitats Regulations 2017 have also been found to boost biodiversity outside protected sites and of non-listed species.[125]

9.81 Two previous reviews of the implementation of the Habitats Regulations 2010 concluded that they remain fit for purpose.[126] DEFRA's 2012 review concluded that:[127]

> [I]n the large majority of cases the implementation of the Directives is working well, allowing both development of key infrastructure and ensuring that a high level of environmental protection is maintained. For instance, [NE] receives around 26,500 land use consultations annually; of these, they 'object' to less than 0.5% of these on Habitats Regulations grounds. Most of these objections are successfully dealt with at the planning stage.

---

118 The Convention on the Conservation of European Wildlife and Natural Habitats 1979.
119 The Convention on the Conservation of Migratory Species of Wild Animals 1979.
120 European Union (Withdrawal) Act 2018 s 2.
121 Retained EU Law (Revocation and Reform) Act 2023 s 5.
122 The Conservation of Habitats and Species (Amendment) (EU Exit) Regulations 2019, SI 2019/579.
123 Wildlife and Countryside Link, 'The Habitats Regulations: What's at Risk and How Can We Build on and Strengthen the Regulations to Be More Effective for Nature and People?' (2023) <https://www.wcl.org.uk/docs/Link%20briefing%20on%20Habs%20Regs%20risks%20and%20opportunities%20Jan%202023.pdf> accessed 15 May 2024.
124 ibid.
125 ibid 2; 'UK Protected Sites Deliver Far-Reaching Benefits for Birds, Say Landmark New Studies' [2022] *InsideEcology* <https://insideecology.com/2022/12/06/uk-protected-sites-deliver-far-reaching-benefits-for-birds-say-landmark-new-studies/> accessed 15 May 2024.
126 Explanatory Memorandum to The Conservation of Habitats and Species Regulations 2017, para 3.3.
127 DEFRA, 'Report of the Habitats and Wild Birds Directives Implementation Review' (2012) 13 <https://assets.publishing.service.gov.uk/media/5a79926f40f0b642860d920f/pb13724-habitats-review-report.pdf> accessed 15 May 2024.

9.82 Nevertheless, there was plainly appetite for reform under previous governments, as is evident by the amendment, disapplication and modification powers provided under sections 112–113 of the EA 2021, Part 13 of the Energy Act 2023, and the LURA 2023. See further the proposed reforms set out in the Nature Recovery Green Paper,[128] as informed by the recommendations of the HRA Review Working Group.[129] On 23 May 2024, DEFRA published a survey for its post-implementation review of both the Offshore and Onshore Habitats Regulations.[130]

9.83 A recent Office for Environmental Protection ('OEP') review of the implementation of the Environmental Impact Assessment ('EIA'),[131] Strategic Environmental Assessment ('SEA') and Habitats Regulations Assessment ('HRA') regimes in England concluded that the three main barriers to the effectiveness of the regimes (access to information, post-decision monitoring and access to expertise) arise 'less from the legislation itself, and more from shortcomings in the wider planning system that affect the way the legislation is implemented'.[132] Further, the OEP advises that 'unless these issues are addressed, reform to environmental assessment legislation is unlikely to deliver the government's ambitions and may create new problems, for example to legal certainty.'[133]

(ii) *The Habitats Regulations: key concepts*

9.84 'European Sites' are defined in the Habitats Regulations 2017 as encompassing both Special Protection Areas ('SPAs') and Special Areas of Conservation ('SAC'), as well as: (a) any Sites of Community Importance ('SCIs') which had been placed on the European Commission's list before exit day, and (b) any site which had been proposed to the Commission as an SCI before exit day, until either the site is domestically designated as an SAC or the appropriate authority gives notice of its intention not to designate the site.[134] 'European marine sites' are defined as 'a European site so far as consisting of marine areas',[135] while 'European offshore marine sites' are effectively any European sites which are located in an offshore marine area.[136]

9.85 The 'appropriate authority' in England is the Secretary of State, and in Wales is the Welsh Ministers, subject to modifications given in certain discrete regulations.[137] A 'competent authority' includes any Minister of the Crown, government department,

128 DEFRA, 'Nature Recovery Green Paper: Protected Sites and Species' (n 2).
129 DEFRA, 'Habitats Regulations Assessment Review Working Group Summary of Findings' <https://consult.defra.gov.uk/nature-recovery-green-paper/nature-recovery-green-paper/supporting_documents/Background%20Doc%201%20%20HRA%20Review%20Working%20Group%20%20Summary%20of%20Findings.pdf> accessed 15 May 2024.
130 <https://consult.defra.gov.uk/habitats-regulations-legislation-and-engagement/ba4e11eb/> accessed 19 June 2024.
131 See further Chapter 7.
132 OEP, 'A Review of the Implementation of Environmental Assessment Regimes in England' (2023) 10 <https://www.theoep.org.uk/environmental-assessment-regimes-england> accessed 15 May 2024.
133 ibid.
134 The Habitats Regulations 2017 reg 8(1).
135 ibid reg 8(3).
136 ibid reg 3(1); Offshore Habitats Regulations reg 18.
137 The Habitats Regulations 2017 reg 3(1).

statutory undertaker, public body of any description[138] or person holding a public office;[139] the Welsh Ministers; and any person exercising any function of the aforementioned persons.[140] The regulations further define the set of relevant authorities in relation to a marine area or European marine site.[141]

9.86 Generally, the relevant 'nature conservation bodies' are NE and the NRBW.[142] The JNCC also has obligations as a relevant nature conservation body in respect of (a) certain discrete and limited surveillance and monitoring functions, and (b) assessment of the effects of plans and projects on European offshore marine sites.[143]

9.87 Post-Brexit amendments have created the concept of the 'national site network', with specified management objectives: see further paragraphs 9.115–9.118 below.

(iii) *The Habitats Regulations: continuity or divergence?*

9.88 Many of the terms used in the Habitats Regulations 2017 are defined in regulation 3(1) as exactly the same as in Article 1 of the Habitats Directive (including 'conservation', 'conservation status', 'natural habitats' and 'priority natural habitats', and 'sites') and Article 1 of the Birds Directive (specifically, 'wild bird'). However, any reference to an Annex to the Habitats Directive is a reference to that Annex as it had effect immediately before exit day, or as subsequently amended under regulation 144.[144]

9.89 The new regulation 3A makes necessary further provision for construing the Habitats and Birds Directives in light of Brexit, including that references to Member States include reference to the UK, and references to sites 'of Community interest' include reference to UK sites 'of national interest'. It also provides that any reference in the Habitats Regulations 2017 to 'the requirements of the Directives' is to be construed as if the objectives of the Directives included the objectives referred to in regulation 16A(2) (the management objectives of the national site network). The Secretary of State and/or Welsh Ministers may also issue guidance as to the interpretation of the requirements of the Directives, having consulted with the appropriate nature conservation body, and 'such other bodies or persons as it considers appropriate'.

9.90 Regulation 9 sets out two further distinct duties relating to compliance with the Directives. The first is the regulation 9(1) duty:

> The appropriate authority, the nature conservation bodies and, in relation to the marine area, a competent authority must exercise their functions which are relevant to nature

138 Including the Broads Authority and National Park authorities, Local Authorities, joint planning boards, and joint committees appointed under s 102(1)(b) LGA 1972 (reg 7(3)).
139 As also defined in reg 7(3)).
140 The Habitats Regulations 2017 reg 7(1).
141 ibid reg 6.
142 ibid reg 5(1). See also Chapter 4.
143 ibid regs 5(2)–(3), 50, 52, and part 6.
144 ibid reg 3(4).

conservation, including marine conservation,[145] so as to secure compliance with the requirements of the Directives.

9.91 The second is the regulation 9(3) duty:

> Without prejudice to the preceding provisions, a competent authority, in exercising any of its functions, must have regard to the requirements of the Directives so far as they may be affected by the exercise of those functions.

9.92 Competent authorities and/or nature conservation bodies must, in complying with either duty, have regard to any guidance issued by the appropriate authority.[146]

9.93 The leading case considering the two duties is *Harris v The Environment Agency*,[147] which concerned the Environment Agency's discharge of its duty under regulation 9(3) to have regard to the requirements of the Directives, and in particular Article 6(2) of the Habitats Directive (the duty to take appropriate steps to avoid, in SACs, the deterioration of the designated features as well as significant disturbance of species).

9.94 The court rejected the Claimant's argument that this amounted to an obligation to secure compliance with Article 6(2).[148] The court observed that statutory obligations to 'have regard' to something arise in many different contexts (usually advice, guidance or a code of practice), and do not mean that these sources must be 'followed' or 'slavishly obeyed'.[149] It is (in contexts whether the 'have regard' source is advice or guidance) different to a duty to act in accordance with the source.[150] In this particular context, the court observed that it was 'striking' that the statutory language differed between regulations 9(1) and 9(3), and that there was some force in the submission that regulation 9(1) must impose a less onerous obligation.[151] The 'natural and conventional approach' to the 'have regard' duty would mean that:[152]

> [T]he Environment Agency is obliged to take account of the requirements of the Habitats Directive but may depart from its requirements if there is good reason to do so. In other words, it must take account of the Habitats Directive but is entitled not itself to discharge all of the requirements of the Directive where that can be justified.

9.95 However, the court went on to find that the scope of a competent authority's discretion under Regulation 9(3) is in certain circumstances narrower than is the case with other 'have regard' duties, in light of the specific legal context and depending on the interrelationship of public bodies in a particular habitats decision:[153]

---

145 This applies, in particular, to functions under the Habitats Regulations, but also to functions under various other statutory provisions relating to nature conservation, as specified in reg 9(2).
146 The Habitats Regulations 2017 reg 9(4A).
147 *Harris v The Environment Agency* [2022] EWHC 2264 (Admin).
148 ibid [74]–[79].
149 ibid [80].
150 ibid [81].
151 ibid [81].
152 ibid [82].
153 ibid [83]–[87].

83 It is, however, relevant (when considering whether a departure can be justified) that the object of the 'have regard' duty is 'requirements', rather than advice or guidance. Advice or guidance is not, ordinarily, mandatory. 'Requirements' more usually are mandatory. The 'requirements' are set out, in mandatory terms, in a Directive which the Regulations themselves transposed. In this context, there is not the same broad scope for taking something into account, but then deciding for good reason to depart from it, as there is in the case of non-binding guidance.

84 There is an important part of the regulatory context which helps explain the different language as between regulations 9(1) and 9(3). Regulation 9(3) is concerned with a 'competent authority'. That has a broad meaning (including every public body). In some contexts different competent authorities may have overlapping roles that are relevant to the discharge of the requirements of the Habitats Directive. In such cases, it would not be meaningful or appropriate to impose on one single competent authority (or on every competent authority) an obligation to secure compliance with the Habitats Directive. Instead, what is required is that all competent authorities have regard to the Habitats Directive, so as to ensure that, in the result, compliance with the Directive is achieved.

85 Conversely, regulation 9(1) is concerned with the Secretary of State and the nature conservation bodies, who each have overarching responsibility for compliance with the Habitats Directive. That seems to me to explain the difference in language. This implies that the duty to 'have regard' here does not implicitly permit the Environment Agency to act in a way which is inconsistent with the Habitats Directive (in other words to have regard to the requirements of the Directive but then deliberately decide to act in a way that is inconsistent with those requirements). Rather, it recognises that the Environment Agency is one part of a complex regulatory structure and, depending on the issue, it may have a greater or lesser role to play.

86 In the present context the Environment Agency is, effectively, the sole (and certainly the principal) public body which is responsible for determining whether abstraction licences should be granted, varied, or revoked. If it does not secure the requirements of article 6(2) in respect of those decisions then no other public body is capable of filling the gap.

87 For these reasons, in this context, the duty on the Environment Agency to have regard to the requirements of the Habitats Directive means that the Environment Agency must take those requirements into account, and, in so far as it is (in a particular context) the relevant public body with responsibility for fulfilling those requirements, then it must discharge those requirements. In other words, the scope for departure that is ordinarily inherent in the words 'have regard to' is considerably narrowed.

9.96 This aspect of the reasoning in *Harris* was applied in *R (River Action) v Environment Agency*, which concerned pollution of the rivers Wye and Lugg (both SSSIs) from high concentrations of phosphorus, some of which was caused by runoff from agricultural land.[154] It was agreed that the Wye SAC's conservation status was deteriorating as

154 See further Chapter 12.

a result of the impact of phosphate pollution from diffuse sources on water quality.[155] However, the evidence suggested that phosphate pollution had to be addressed through the coordinated activity of a number of different regulatory organisations. This was being done, including through a Nutrient Management Plan instigated by the nature conversation bodies, and overseen by a Board comprising of a number of public bodies and NGOs.[156] The fact that the pollution was contributed to by numerous potential sources meant that action was required under multiple regulatory regimes, and the work being done demonstrated that the regulation 9(3) duty was being discharged.[157] River Action are appealing on this point.[158]

9.97 Perhaps the more discussed aspect of *Harris* was the court's further finding that Article 6(2) remained available in domestic law and was enforceable by domestic courts following Brexit. This turned on the application of section 4(2)(b) of the European Union (Withdrawal) Act 2018 ('EUWA 2018'): were the obligations arising under Article 6(2) of a kind recognised by the CJEU or any UK court or tribunal in a case decided before 31 December 2020?[159] Johnson J reasoned that Article 6(3) had been held to have direct effect in the relevant CJEU case of *Waddenzee*,[160] which was applied in a domestic Upper Tribunal decision; Article 6(2) was 'of a kind' with this provision due to their close relationship; and accordingly, Article 6(2) continued to be available in domestic law by virtue of section 4 of the EUWA 2018.[161] It must be noted, however, that section 4 has now been repealed by section 2(1) of the Retained EU Law (Revocation and Reform) Act 2023 ('REULA 2023'), with effect from 1 January 2024. Section 2(2) of the REULA 2023 expressly provides that:

> [A]ccordingly, anything which, immediately before the end of 2023, is retained EU law by virtue of that section is not recognised or available in domestic law at or after that time (and, accordingly, is not to be enforced, allowed or followed).

9.98 Section 112 of the EA 2021 empowers the Secretary of State to make regulations amending the Habitats Regulations 2017, as they apply to England, for prescribed purposes which relate specifically to the regulation 9(1) and 9(3) duties. In particular, regulations may require authorities with duties under regulation 9(1) to exercise their relevant functions (i) to comply with further specified requirements, or (ii) to further objectives specified in the future regulations, instead of exercising their functions to secure compliance with the requirements of the Directives. Similarly, regulations may require authorities with duties under regulation 9(3) to have regard to newly specified matters, 'instead of the requirements of the Directives'.[162] Any such regulations may

---

155 *R (River Action) v Environment Agency* [2024] EWHC 1279 (Admin) [83].
156 ibid [85]–[88], [90].
157 ibid [139]–[141].
158 'Campaign Group to Appeal Legal Challenge against the Environment Agency & Prepares for Further Legal Action to Protect the Wye' (*River Action UK*, 18 June 2024) <https://riveractionuk.com/campaign-group-to-appeal-legal-challenge-against-the-environment-agency-prepares-for-further-legal-action-to-protect-the-wye/> accessed 21 June 2024.
159 *Harris v The Environment Agency* (n 147) [89].
160 Case 127/02 *Landelijke Vereniging tot Behoud van de Waddenzee v Staatssecretaris van Landbouw* [2004] ECR I-07405; [2005] 2 CMLR 31.
161 *Harris v The Environment Agency* (n 147) [89]–[94].
162 Environment Act 2021 ss 112(1)–(2).

also amend other provisions of the Habitats Regulations which refer to requirements, objectives or provisions of the Directives, where this is 'in connection with provision made for the purposes in subsection (2)'.[163]

9.99 In making regulations under section 112, the Secretary of State must have regard to the particular importance of furthering the conservation and enhancement of biodiversity, and may make regulations only if satisfied that they do not reduce the level of environmental protection provided by the Habitats Regulations 2017.[164] Before making regulations, the Secretary of State must lay before Parliament and publish a statement explaining why s/he is so satisfied, and must consult such persons as s/he considers appropriate.[165]

9.100 At the time of writing, no such regulations have been made. Similar powers to amend Part 6 of the Habitats Regulations 2017 are set out in section 113 of the EA 2021.

9.101 Section 293 of the Energy Act 2023 similarly empowers the appropriate authority (as defined in that section) to make regulations relating to the assessment of the environmental effects of offshore wind activities on protected sites, and contains provisions relating to compensation measures, which may *inter alia* include disapplying or modifying regulations 9 and 10 and Part 6 of the Habitats Regulations 2017. This provision was commenced on 26 December 2023: at the time of writing, no such regulations have been made.

9.102 The duties in regulation 10 relate to wild bird habitat. Regulation 10(3) specifies an objective of the preservation, maintenance and re-establishment of a sufficient diversity and area of habitat for wild birds in the UK, including by means of the upkeep, management and creation of such habitat, as appropriate, having regard to the requirements of Article 2 of the new Wild Birds Directive.[166] Regulation 10(1) provides that without prejudice to regulation 9(1), the same authorities listed therein must 'take such steps in the exercise of their functions[167] as they consider appropriate to secure the objective in paragraph (3), so far as lies within their powers'. Similarly, pursuant to regulation 10(2), the Environment Agency, the Forestry Commissioners, local authorities, the Broads Authority and National Park authorities must take such steps in the exercise of their functions as they consider appropriate to contribute to the achievement of the objective in paragraph 3. In considering which measures may be appropriate for the purpose of securing or contributing to the objective in paragraph 3, appropriate account must be taken of economic and recreational requirements.[168] The appropriate authority must take any steps it considers necessary to facilitate or coordinate arrangements to secure

163 ibid s 112(5).
164 ibid ss 112(6)–(7).
165 Environment Act 2021 ss 112(8)–(9).
166 2009/147/EC. Regulation 3 refers to the 2009 Birds Directive (which consolidates and updates Council Directive 79/409/EEC) as the 'new Wild Birds Directive', and Council Directive 79/409/EEC on the conservation of wild birds as 'the old Wild Birds Directive'.
167 Similarly to the situation under reg 9, relevant functions are specified in reg 10(4)–(5).
168 The Habitats Regulations 2017 reg 10(7).

the taking of steps under paragraphs (1) and (2) by the bodies mentioned in those paragraphs.[169] The appropriate authority must give guidance to the bodies specified in Regulation 10(2), to which they must have regard.[170]

9.103 So far as lies within its powers, a competent authority in exercising any function in or in relation to the UK must use all reasonable endeavours to avoid any pollution or deterioration of habitats of wild birds.[171]

9.104 NE and the NRBW must, from time to time, review and report on the extent to which the Regulation 10(3) objective has been met: their review may also take account of measures taken under other enactments.[172]

9.105 Regulation 9A(1) of the Habitats Regulations 2017 (as amended) imposes a duty on the Secretary of State and Welsh Ministers to publish reports on the 'implementation of the measures taken for the purpose of giving effect to the provisions of the Directives, and the achievement of the objectives set out in Article 2 of the Habitats Directive and Articles 2 and 3 of the new Wild Birds Directive', within six years from exit day and at least every six years thereafter. Reports must include certain specified information.[173] In England, the Secretary of State must also publish a composite report drawn from the six-yearly reports of all the devolved administrations within two years of their publication, which must include an evaluation of the progress achieved and in particular of the contribution of the national site network to the achievement of the first management objective.[174]

(iv) *Revised designation process*

9.106 Regulations 12–19 set out a revised process for the designation of SACs and SPAs, in which the appropriate authority is the sole decision-maker. However, the selection and designation of SACs is based on the criteria set out in Annex III of the Habitats Directive so far as it applies to the UK.[175]

9.107 In relation to SACs: the appropriate authority must establish priorities for designating as SACs such sites as it has determined to be Sites of National Importance ('SNIs').[176] These priorities must be established in light of (a) the importance of the sites for achieving the first management objective; (b) the importance of such sites for the coherence of the national site network; and (c) the threats of degradation or destruction to which the sites are exposed.[177]

---

169 ibid reg 10(9).
170 ibid regs 10(9)–(10).
171 ibid reg 10(8).
172 ibid reg 11.
173 ibid reg 9A(2).
174 ibid regs 9A(3)–(4).
175 DEFRA, 'Policy Paper: Changes to the Habitats Regulations 2017' (n 115).
176 The Habitats Regulations 2017 reg 13(1).
177 ibid reg 13(2).

9.108 Having regard to those priorities, the appropriate authority must then designate as SACs such sites as it considers to be SNIs.[178] SNIs are sites which contribute significantly to the first management objective or to the maintenance of biological diversity within the Atlantic biogeographic region.[179]

9.109 For wide-ranging animal species, SNIs must correspond to places within that species' natural range, which present the physical or biological factors essential to their life and reproduction.[180] For wide-ranging aquatic species, sites are only to be considered SNIs where there is a 'clearly identifiable area which is distinct in providing the physical and biological factors essential to their life and reproduction'.[181]

9.110 In determining which sites are SNIs, the appropriate authority must (a) apply the Annex III criteria[182] (having regard to the advice of the nature conservation bodies or the JNCC); (b) make its determination only on the basis of relevant scientific information; and (c) have regard to the importance of the population of a species or area of a habitat found in the UK for the purpose of meeting the above two objectives.[183]

9.111 In relation to SPAs, the prescribed designation objective is that the sites across UK territory which are most suitable in number and size for (a) the conservation of the species listed in Annex 1 to the new Wild Birds Directive which naturally occur in that territory; and (b) the conservation of regularly occurring migratory species of birds not listed in Annex 1 which naturally occur in that territory, are classified as SPAs.[184] The appropriate authority must classify as SPAs such sites as it considers necessary to ensure this objective is met.[185] Its decisions on designation must be made only on the basis of relevant scientific information, and the criteria set out in Articles 4(1) and (2) respectively of the new Wild Birds Directive.[186]

9.112 Where the appropriate authority proposes to classify a site as an SPA, it must give NE or the NRBW notice of that proposal and an accompanying statement of reasons.[187] NE or the NRBW must then in turn give notice of that proposal, with the statement of reasons, to (a) any persons who in its opinion ought to be notified (including site owners and occupiers, and competent authorities exercising functions on the site or an adjacent area); and (b) anyone else the appropriate authority directs.[188] This notice must specify the date by which representations may be made: the time for representations must be no less than 12 weeks.[189] NE or the NRBW must then provide

---

178 ibid reg 12(1).
179 ibid regs 12(2)–(3).
180 ibid reg 12(4).
181 ibid reg 12(5).
182 But these criteria are to be construed in accordance with reg 12(7).
183 The Habitats Regulations 2017 regs 12(6) and (8).
184 ibid reg 15(2).
185 ibid reg 15(1).
186 ibid reg 15(3); as construed in accordance with reg 15(4)).
187 ibid reg 16(1).
188 ibid reg 16(2).
189 ibid reg 16(3).

to their appropriate authority a report on the representations.[190] DEFRA's guidance describes this as a 'public consultation' on new SAC proposals.[191]

9.113 The appropriate authority may issue guidance to the appropriate nature conservation body for the purposes of its functions under Regulation 16, to which the nature conservation body must have regard.[192]

9.114 Newly designated European Sites will be entered onto the register of European sites, which must be compiled and maintained by the appropriate authority.[193] NE or the NRBW must then be notified, and they must in turn notify all relevant land owners or occupiers, local planning authorities and/or the Marine Management Organisation ('MMO')[194] as relevant, and any other persons directed.[195]

(v) *The national site network*

9.115 Post-Brexit amendment regulations have created the concept of the 'national site network'.[196] This is defined as the network of sites in the UK's territory consisting of sites which (a) formed part of the Natura 2000 network immediately before exit day; or (b) at any time on or after exit day are European sites, European marine sites and European offshore marine sites for the purposes of any of the retained transposing regulations.[197] Any pre-Brexit domestic guidance referring to 'Natura 2000' is to be construed as referring to the national site network.[198] Maintaining a coherent network of protected sites with overarching conservation objectives is still required in order to (a) fulfil the commitment made by the government to maintain environmental protections; and (b) continue to meet the UK's international legal obligations, such as the Bern Convention, the Oslo and Paris Conventions, the Bonn Convention and the Ramsar Convention.[199]

9.116 The Secretary of State and/or the Welsh Ministers must, in cooperation with any other authority having a corresponding responsibility, manage and where necessary adapt the national site network, so far as it consists of European sites, with a view to contributing to the achievement of the management objectives of the national site network.[200] The management objectives remain grounded in the Habitats and Birds Directives, and are:

---

190 ibid regs 16(4)–(5).
191 DEFRA, 'Policy Paper: Changes to the Habitats Regulations 2017' (n 115).
192 The Habitats Regulations 2017 reg 16(6).
193 ibid reg 17.
194 See further Chapter 4.
195 The Habitats Regulations 2017 regs 18–19.
196 Conservation of Habitats and Species (Amendment) (EU Exit) Regulations 2019/579 Pt 3 reg 4(2)(a).
197 The Habitats Regulations 2017 reg 3(1).
198 ibid reg 3(10).
199 DEFRA, 'Policy Paper: Changes to the Habitats Regulations 2017' (n 115). Ramsar Sites do not, however, form part of the national site network under Regulation 3, nor do they enjoy equivalent legislative protection overall: nevertheless, it is Government policy that they should be given the same protection as European Sites (NPPF, para 187). See the application of this policy in *CG Fry and Son Ltd v Secretary of State for Levelling Up, Housing and Communities* (n 115).
200 The Habitats Regulations 2017 reg 16A(1).

- In relation to the habitat types listed in Annex 1 to the Habitats Directive, and the species listed in Annex II whose natural range includes any UK territory, to maintain these at, or where appropriate restore these to, a favourable conservation status ('FCS') in their natural range, so far as it lies within UK territory and so far as is proportionate;

- To contribute, in their area of distribution, to ensuring the survival and reproduction of (i) the species of birds listed in Annex I to the new Wild Birds Directive which naturally occur in UK territory, and (ii) other regularly occurring migratory species of birds which naturally occur in UK territory; and

- To contribute to securing compliance with the requirements of Article 2 of the new Wild Birds Directive for the purposes of the duty in Regulation 9(1) in relation to the above species of birds within their area of distribution.[201]

9.117 In compliance with the duty to manage and where necessary adapt the national site network, the Secretary of State or Welsh Ministers must have regard to certain relevant considerations.[202]

9.118 Adapting the network may include designating new European Sites or amending existing European Sites: for example, where the protected features have changed over time (including re-introduced species or a new or increasing population of birds); where the site boundary needs to be moved in response to storm events or natural processes; or to include an area which compensates for the loss of other areas within the network as a result of a plan or project proceeding for imperative reasons of overriding public interest ('IROPI').[203] According to 2021 guidance from DEFRA, it may also include declassifying existing European Sites in exceptional circumstances.[204]

Protections for European Sites

9.119 This section will primarily focus on Habitats Regulations Assessment ('HRA'), perhaps the principal protection for European Sites. The Habitats Regulations 2017 do, however, set out a wide range of other protective measures for European Sites, including:

- Management Agreements: NE and NRBW may make management agreements in relation to a European Site with persons interested in that land, or adjacent land, for the purposes of management, conservation, restoration or protection of the site.[205] Management agreements may provide for a number of specified matters.[206] Various pre-2017 agreements made in relation to land which has become land

201 ibid reg 16A(2).
202 ibid regs 16A(3A)–(5).
203 DEFRA, 'Policy Paper: Changes to the Habitats Regulations 2017' (n 115).
204 ibid.
205 The Habitats Regulations 2017 reg 20.
206 ibid reg 20(3).

within or adjacent to a European Site are now to have effect as if the agreement were a management agreement under Regulation 20;[207]

- Restrictions on farm capital grants:[208] the appropriate authority must determine applications for relevant farm capital grants, so far as possible, so as to further the conservation of the protected features, and must consider any objection from NE or the NRBW before making any grants;[209]

- Special Nature Conservation Orders ('SNCOs'):[210] the appropriate authority may, after consultation with NE or the NRBW, make an SNCO in respect of any land within a European Site, specifying operations (on or off the European Site) which are likely to destroy or damage protected features.[211] The appropriate authority may then serve a stop notice, or may publish and affix public notices, prohibiting the carrying out of the specified operations (unless certain conditions are fulfilled, including NE/NRBW consent).[212] There is a defence of reasonable excuse, which includes emergency operations and operations authorised by planning permission.[213] Any application for consent which is likely to significantly affect a European Site must be subject to appropriate assessment.[214] NE or the NRBW must pay compensation to any person served a stop notice who can show they have an interest in relevant land which has consequently diminished in value.[215] A person convicted of an offence under Regulation 28 may be ordered to carry out operations to restore the land: failure to comply with a restoration order is a further offence;[216]

- Byelaws: NE and NRBW may make byelaws for the protection of a European Site.[217] Compensation will be payable to anyone whose right in affected land is prevented or hindered as a result;[218] and

- Compulsory Acquisition: where NE or the NRBW have been unable to conclude a reasonable management agreement, or such an agreement has been breached, they may compulsorily acquire an interest in land in a European Site.[219]

9.120 Parts 3 and 4 of the Habitats Regulations 2017 introduce additional protections for European protected species of animals and plants, defined as those animals/plants

---

207 ibid reg 21.
208 Grants under a scheme made under section 29 of the Agriculture Act 1970 (works or facilities of a capital nature for agricultural improvement and farm diversification).
209 The Habitats Regulations 2017 reg 26.
210 There is government guidance on SNCOs, which was first published in 2015 and was significantly updated in February 2021: <https://www.gov.uk/guidance/special-nature-conservation-orders-consent-and-stop-notices>.
211 The Habitats Regulations 2017 reg 27.
212 ibid reg 28.
213 ibid regs 28(8)–(9).
214 ibid reg 29.
215 ibid reg 30.
216 ibid reg 31.
217 ibid regs 32–33.
218 ibid reg 34.
219 ibid reg 36.

listed in Annexes IV(a) and (b) to the Habitats Directive whose natural range includes any area in Great Britain.[220] Regulation 43 creates offences in relation to protected animal species, including deliberately capturing, injuring, killing or disturbing any wild animal of that species; taking or destroying their eggs; damaging or destroying their breeding site or resting place; or possessing, transporting, or selling or exchanging such animals. Regulation 44 sets out statutory defences, including where the animal has been disabled by a separate incident; tending to and/or releasing a disabled animal; sampling; investigating a relevant offence; or showing that it was lawfully taken from the wild. In relation to the majority of these defences, it must additionally be shown that (a) there was no satisfactory alternative; and (b) the action was not detrimental to the maintenance of the population of the species concerned at a favourable conservation status in their natural range.[221]

9.121 There are additional prohibitions in relation to the capturing or killing of wild animals listed in Annex V(a) to the Habitats Directive, whose range includes any area in Great Britain.[222]

9.122 Statutory offences in relation to protected species of plants include deliberately picking, collecting, uprooting or destroying wild plants of those species; and possession, transport and sale or exchange.[223] Defences similarly include sampling, investigations, and lawfully taking from the wild.[224]

9.123 Part 4 makes provision requiring surveillance of the conservation status of habitat types and species of national interest, and the taking of protective measures in light of the information acquired from surveillance.[225] It also requires the establishment of a system to monitor the incidental capture or killing of animals in the species listed in Annex IV(a) to the Habitats Directive, and that similar protective measures are taken consequently.[226] The nature conservation bodies who have a role in surveillance and monitoring are not only NE and the NRBW, but also the JNCC.[227] Regulation 54 creates a distinct offence of the deliberate introduction of non-native animals and plants from ships, where their introduction would give rise to a risk of prejudice to native habitats or plants.

9.124 Part 5 provides for the licensing of certain activities by the relevant licensing bodies: NE, the NRBW and the MMO.[228] Licences may be granted for specified purposes, including science and education, conservation, protection, preventing disease or damage to livestock, crops and timber, and preserving public health or public safety or other imperative reasons of overriding public interest.[229] Separately to those purposes,

220 ibid regs 42, 46 and sch 2 and 5.
221 ibid reg 44(10).
222 ibid reg 45 and sch 4.
223 ibid reg 47.
224 ibid reg 48.
225 ibid regs 50–51.
226 ibid reg 52–53.
227 ibid reg 5(2).
228 ibid reg 58.
229 ibid reg 55(2).

the licensing body may also license the taking, possession or control of the specimens listed in Annex II(b) or IV to the Habitats Directive, where satisfied that this would be consistent with the restrictions in Article 16(1)(e) of the Habitats Directive.[230] However, no licence may be granted under Regulation 55 unless the licensing body is satisfied both that there is no satisfactory alternative, and that the action authorised will not be detrimental to the maintenance of the population of the species concerned at a favourable conservation status in their natural range.[231]

9.125 The appropriate authority must from time to time consult NE or the NRBW as to the exercise of their functions under Regulation 5.[232] The licensing bodies must publish two-yearly reports on licences granted.[233]

9.126 Licensing bodies may also license the introduction of new species from ships, where satisfied this will not prejudice natural habitats or plants.[234]

9.127 It is an offence to knowingly or recklessly make a material and false statement to obtain a licence, and it is an offence to breach a licence condition, unless the breach occurred despite all reasonable precautions or was otherwise beyond the licensee's control.[235]

9.128 Part 7 provides for enforcement.

(i) *Habitats Regulations Assessment ('HRA')*

9.129 Part 6 of the Habitats Regulations 2017 provides for the appropriate assessment of plans and projects, implementing Articles 6(3)–(4) of the Habitats Directive. As with the SSSI consenting process, the purpose of HRA is to prevent the condition of protected sites from deteriorating as a result of the impact of new activities.[236] However, the HRA regime offers a more robust level of protection to European Sites.[237]

9.130 Regulation 63(1) provides that:

> (1) A competent authority, before deciding to undertake,[238] or give any consent, permission or other authorisation for, a plan or project which—
>
> (a) is likely to have a significant effect on a European site or a European offshore marine site (either alone or in combination with other plans or projects), and
> (b) is not directly connected with or necessary to the management of that site,

230 ibid regs 55(4)–(8).
231 ibid reg 55(9).
232 ibid reg 55(11).
233 ibid regs 55(15)–(16).
234 ibid reg 56.
235 ibid regs 59–60.
236 DEFRA, 'Nature Recovery Green Paper: Protected Sites and Species' (n 2) 18.
237 Wildlife and Countryside Link, 'The Habitats Regulations: What's at Risk and How Can We Build on and Strengthen the Regulations to Be More Effective for Nature and People?' (n 123) 1.
238 This includes deciding to vary any plan or project undertaken or to be undertaken: The Habitats Regulations 2017 reg 63(9).

> must make an appropriate assessment of the implications of the plan or project for that site in view of that site's conservation objectives.

9.131 An applicant for any such consent must provide 'such information as the competent authority may reasonably require for the purposes of the assessment or to enable it to determine whether an appropriate assessment is required'.[239] The competent authority must consult NE, the NRBW, or (in relation to offshore marine sites) the JNCC[240] for the purposes of the assessment, and must also take the opinion of the general public if they consider it appropriate to do so.[241]

9.132 In the light of the conclusions of the assessment, and subject to Regulation 64, the competent authority may agree to the plan or project only after having ascertained that it will not adversely affect the integrity[242] of the European site or the European offshore marine site.[243] In considering whether a plan or project will adversely affect the integrity of the site, the competent authority must have regard to the manner in which it is proposed to be carried out or to any conditions or restrictions subject to which it proposes that the consent, permission or other authorisation should be given.[244]

9.133 Regulation 64 provides an exception to the restriction on the consenting of plans or projects, where an adverse effect on European Site integrity cannot be ruled out. Regulation 64(1) states that:

> If the competent authority is satisfied that, there being no alternative solutions, the plan or project must be carried out for imperative reasons of overriding public interest (which, subject to paragraph (2), may be of a social or economic nature), it may agree to the plan or project notwithstanding a negative assessment of the implications for the European site or the European offshore marine site (as the case may be).

9.134 Where a plan or project is agreed to in accordance with Regulation 64, notwithstanding a negative assessment, the appropriate authority must secure that any necessary compensatory measures are taken to ensure that the overall coherence of Natura 2000 is protected.[245]

---

239 ibid reg 63(2).
240 ibid reg 5(3).
241 ibid regs 63(3)–(4).
242 'Integrity' is not defined in the legislation, but is considered at s 4.6.4 of European Commission, 'Managing and Protecting Natura 2000 Sites' (2019). Consideration should be limited to the designated features and the site's conservation objectives: identifying the conservation objectives can itself be a source of confusion in practice.
243 The Habitats Regulations 2017 reg 63(5).
244 ibid reg 63(6).
245 ibid reg 68.

9.135 Regulation 63(1) does not apply in relation to plans or projects to which certain other specific regulations apply.[246] However, the assessment provisions[247] do apply to a wide range of specified decision-making contexts set out in Part 6, including:

- Applications for planning permission under Part 3 of the TCPA 1990, and various other applications for planning permission;[248]
- Applications for development consent for nationally significant infrastructure projects ('NSIPs')[249] under the Planning Act 2008;[250]
- Special development orders, local development orders and neighbourhood development orders (save that Regulation 64 does not apply);[251]
- Environmental permits;[252]
- Land use plans and neighbourhood plans;[253]
- National policy statements;[254] and
- Marine policy statements and marine plans.[255]

9.136 Modifications to the relevant authorities apply in certain cases: see Regulation 69.

9.137 Where a decision has been taken to authorise a plan or project before a site becomes a European Site, the appropriate authority must review its decision or consent as soon as reasonably practicable, and must for that purpose undertake an appropriate assessment.[256] The rest of Part 6 sets out how the review provisions apply in the various specific contexts where appropriate assessment needs to be undertaken.

---

246 The Environmental Impact Assessment (Agriculture) (England) (No. 2) Regulations 2006; the Environmental Impact Assessment (Agriculture) (Wales) Regulations 2017; the Merchant Shipping (Ship-to-Ship Transfers) Regulations 2020; and the Offshore Petroleum Activities (Conservation of Habitats) Regulations 2001 (in so far as this regulation is not disapplied by reg 4 (plans or projects relating to offshore marine area or offshore marine installations) in relation to plans or projects to which those Regulations apply); The Habitats Regulations 2017 reg 63(7). See also reg 63(8).
247 The Habitats Regulations 2017 regs 63 and 64.
248 ibid reg 70; This includes Developments of National Significance ('DNS'), the Welsh equivalent of NSIPs, which also fall under the TCPA 1990. On a purposive interpretation, reading Regulation 70 in accordance with Regulation 63, this also includes reserved matters applications and the discharge of conditions: *CG Fry and Son Ltd v Secretary of State for Levelling Up, Housing and Communities* (n 115).
249 See further Chapter 6.
250 The Habitats Regulations 2017 reg 84.
251 ibid regs 79–81.
252 ibid reg 101.
253 ibid regs 105–109.
254 ibid reg 110.
255 ibid regs 112–113.
256 ibid regs 65–66.

9.138 Regulation 62(1) further specifies that the assessment provisions and review provisions apply:[257]

(a) subject to and in accordance with the provisions of Chapters 2 to 7, in relation to the matters specified in those provisions; and

(b) subject to Regulation 63(7)(c), in relation to all other plans and projects not relating to matters specified in Chapters 2 to 9.

9.139 In sum, the HRA process comprises of four stages:[258]

- Stage 1: screening. The competent authority must first identify the likely impacts of a project on a European Site (either alone or in combination with other plans and projects) and consider whether the impacts are likely to be significant. If so, the authority must undertake an appropriate assessment.
- Stage 2: appropriate assessment. At this stage the competent authority substantively considers the impacts on the integrity of the European Site, either alone or in combination with other plans and projects. Where there are adverse impacts, the competent authority undertakes an assessment of mitigation options. If the available mitigation options cannot avoid adverse effects, then consent can only be given if stages 3 and 4 (Regulation 64(1)) are followed.
- Stage 3: assessment of alternative solutions. The competent authority will consider whether there are alternative ways of achieving the objectives of the project which would avoid, or have a lesser effect on, European Site integrity.
- Stage 4: imperative reasons of overriding public interest ('IROPI'). Where no alternative solution exists and where adverse impacts remain, development cannot be consented unless there are considered to be IROPIs which render the development necessary. If so, the authority must still consider the potential compensatory measures needed to maintain the overall coherence of the site or integrity of the European site network.

(ii) *Screening*

9.140 Neither Article 6(3) of the Habitats Directive nor Regulation 63(1) of the Habitats Regulations 2017 explicitly require a screening assessment, and the 'screening'

---

257 For a discussion of the interrelationship of reg 62 and reg 63 with particular provisions in Part 6, and in particular reg 70, see *CG Fry and Son Ltd v Secretary of State for Levelling Up, Housing and Communities* (n 115) [47]–[64]. At the time of writing, these conclusions are under appeal.

258 As set out in European Commission, 'Assessment of Plans and Projects Significantly Affecting Natura 2000 Sites: Methodological Guidance on the Provisions of Article 6(3) and (4) of the Habitats Directive 92/43/EEC: Novembre 2001' (2002) <https://op.europa.eu/en/publication-detail/-/publication/2b6c4b16-e867-42da-b604-f67ee6fe60c3> accessed 15 May 2024. See, however, Lord Carnwath's dicta on the lack of a formal 'screening' stage equivalent to the EIA regime: para 9.140 below.

stage is not to be equated with a formal 'screening opinion' under the EIA regime.[259] Nevertheless, the likelihood or possibility that a plan or project will have a significant effect on a European Site is the trigger for the obligation to carry out an appropriate assessment.[260] It may therefore be necessary in practice to carry out a screening assessment, particularly if it is not obvious whether a plan or project is likely to have a significant effect on a European Site.[261]

9.141 In light of the precautionary principle in particular, such a risk exists if it cannot be excluded on the basis of objective information that the plan or project will have significant effects on the site concerned. In cases of doubt as to the absence of significant effects, an appropriate assessment must be carried out.[262]

9.142 Where a plan or project has an effect on a European Site which is not likely to undermine the site's conservation objectives, this will not be a 'significant' effect: conversely, where a plan or project is likely to undermine the conservation objectives, it must necessarily be considered likely to have a significant effect on that site. The significance of effects must be established in light, *inter alia*, of the characteristics and specific environmental conditions of the site concerned by that plan or project.[263]

9.143 Mitigation measures (i.e. those which would mitigate any potential significant effects) may not be taken into account at the screening stage.[264]

9.144 Consideration of whether an appropriate assessment is required necessitates a strict precautionary approach, including assessment of any 'in-combination' effects.[265] However, where a series of development projects are contemplated, the strict precautionary approach would be complied with if the first project would not, by itself, have a detrimental impact on a protected site, and if there would be future opportunity to consider measures arising from a later project, so as to identify any 'in-combination' effects of the two together.[266]

---

259 Per Lord Carnwath JSC in *R (Champion) v North Norfolk DC* [2015] UKSC 52, [2015] 1 WLR 3710 [34]–[41]. See further Chapter 7.

260 See Case C-127/02 *Waddenzee* (n 160) [42]–[43]; Case C-258/11 *Sweetman v An Bord Pleanala* (2013) ECLI:EU:C:2013:220, Opinion of AG Sharpston, [49]; *R (Mynydd y Gwynt) v Secretary of State for Business, Energy and Industrial Strategy* [2018] EWCA Civ 231 [8](1).

261 *No Adastral New Town Ltd v Suffolk Coastal DC* [2015] EWCA Civ 88, [2015] Env LR 28 [68]; *R (Champion) v North Norfolk DC* (n 259) [40]–[41].

262 Case C-127/02 *Waddenzee* (n 160) [44]; *R (Buckinghamshire Council) v Secretary of State for Transport and Secretary of State for Levelling Up, Housing and Communities* [2013] EWHC 481 (Admin) [203]; *R (Mynydd y Gwynt) v Secretary of State for Business, Energy and Industrial Strategy* (n 260) [8](2); *Wealden DC v Secretary of State for Communities and Local Government* [2017] EWHC 351 (Admin) [44](ii).

263 Case C-127/02 *Waddenzee* (n 160) [47]–[58].

264 Case C-323/17 *People Over Wind and Sweetman v Coillte Teoranta* (2018) ECLI:EU:C:2018:244 [36]; *Canterbury City Council v Secretary of State for Housing, Communities and Local Government* [2019] EWHC 1211 (Admin); *R (Preston) v Cumbria County Council* [2019] EWHC 1362 (Admin).

265 *Smyth v Secretary of State for Communities & Local Government* [2015] EWCA Civ 174 [56]–[62].

266 *R (Forest of Dean (Friends of the Earth)) v Forest of Dean District Council* [2015] EWCA Civ 683.

(iii) *Appropriate assessment*

9.145 No particular methodology for carrying out an appropriate assessment is prescribed in either the Habitats Directive or the Habitats Regulations 2017, and 'appropriate' is not a technical term.[267] The following principles are, however, well-established, and have recently been re-stated in *R (Wyatt) v Fareham Borough Council*.[268]

- Appropriate assessments must be based on the best scientific knowledge in the field, which is both up-to-date and not based on the bare assertion of an expert;[269]
- The requirement in Regulation 63(5) embodies the precautionary principle.[270] Accordingly, a high standard of investigation is required.[271] The burden on the competent authority is to prove that there would be no adverse effects, not to a standard of absolute certainty (which would be impossible of scientific attainment, as well as disproportionate), but to be at least satisfied that there is no reasonable doubt as to the absence of adverse effects on the integrity of the site concerned;[272]
- Competent authorities must give considerable weight to the expert advice of the relevant nature conservation body (and the courts will also give appropriate deference to their views). A competent authority may lawfully disagree with and depart from such expert advice, but it must have cogent reasons for doing so;[273]
- The judgment as to whether a proposal will adversely affect the integrity of the protected site is for the competent authority. This is an evaluative judgment which the court is neither entitled nor equipped to make for itself. In a resulting legal challenge, the role of the court is not to undertake its own assessment, but to review the competent authority's assessment according to ordinary public law principles, albeit according appropriate cognisance to the nature of the subject-matter and

267 *R (Champion) v North Norfolk DC* (n 259) at [41].
268 *R (Wyatt) v Fareham Borough Council & Natural England* [2022] EWCA Civ 983: see in particular the judgment of Lindblom LJ at [9]. See also the summary of principles set out by Jay J in the High Court judgment *R (Wyatt) v Fareham BC* [2021] EWHC 1434 (Admin) [29]–[39], which was endorsed by Lindblom LJ in the Court of Appeal at [46].
269 *R (Wyatt) v Fareham BC* [2021] (n 268) [30]; *R (Wyatt) v Fareham BC & Natural England* (n 268) [9](9). See further Case C-461/17 *Holohan v An Bord Pleanála* (2018) ECLI:EU:C:2018:883; [2019] PTSR 1054, [33]; *Smyth v Secretary of State for Communities & Local Government* (n 265) [83].
270 *R (Wyatt) v Fareham BC & Natural England* [2022] (n 268) [9](6).
271 *R (Wyatt) v Fareham BC* [2021] (n 268) [32]; *R (Wyatt) v Fareham BC & Natural England* [2022] (n 268) [9](6), [125]. See further Case C-127/02 *Waddenzee* (n 160) [44], [58]–[59], [61]; Case C-293/17 *Cooperatie Mobilisation for the Environment UA, Vereniging Leefmilieu v College van Gedeputeerde Staten van Limburg* (2018) ECLI:EU:C:2018:882.
272 *R (Wyatt) v Fareham BC* [2021] (n 268) [32]; *R (Wyatt) v Fareham BC & Natural England* [2022] [9](7)–(8). See further Case C-127/02 *Waddenzee* (n 160) [99], [104], [107] and [108]; Case C-258/11 *Sweetman* (n 260) [39]. Similarly, the burden is at first on the developer to provide the information requested by the competent authority, and where the developer fails to provide information, the competent authority is entitled to conclude they do not have the necessary information to grant the application: *R (Mynydd y Gwynt) v Secretary of State for Business, Energy and Industrial Strategy* (n 260).
273 *R (Wyatt) v Fareham BC & Natural England* [2022] (n 268) [9](4), [141]; *R (Morge) v Hampshire County Council* [2011] UKSC 2 [45]. Where good reasons from departing from the conservation body's views exist, however, an authority may err in law by following its views: see *Wealden DC v Secretary of State for Communities and Local Government* (n 262).

the 'demanding' requirement inherent in Regulation 63(5). There is no heightened standard of 'anxious scrutiny' in this context;[274] and

- In a claim for judicial review, the court will not look behind or re-evaluate the conclusions reached in expert evidence, unless there is clear evidence revealing a failure of expertise, such as a conspicuous factual or scientific error. The court will bear in mind the scientific, technical and predictive nature of the assessment, and accordingly apply a substantial margin of appreciation.[275]

9.146 The appropriate assessment cannot have lacunae and must contain complete, precise and definitive findings and conclusions.[276] The European Court of Justice has held that the requirement to dispel all reasonable scientific doubt as to the absence of adverse effects, and the requirement for complete, precise and definitive findings as to adverse effects on site objectives, means that an appropriate assessment must (a) catalogue the entirety of habitat types and species for which a site is protected; and (b) also examine the implications of the proposed project for habitat types and species to be found outside the boundaries of that site, provided that those implications are liable to affect the conservation objectives of the site.[277]

9.147 The appropriate assessment must be undertaken before the plan is given effect: beyond this, no particular timing for the assessment is stipulated in the Directive or the regulations. It is clearly preferable, but not essential, for the assessment to be undertaken at an early stage.[278]

9.148 It is not permissible to argue that an appropriate assessment is not required on the basis that the environmental harms will be regulated under another regime, which should be presumed to be effective.[279] However, a competent authority is not required to assess any implications of a plan or project which would be more appropriately assessed under the Habitats Regulations by another competent authority.[280] In accordance with regulation 67(3), DEFRA's guidance on protecting European Sites includes guidance on coordination by competent authorities.[281]

---

274 *R (Wyatt) v Fareham BC* [2021] (n 268) [29], [36], [38]; *R (Wyatt) v Fareham BC & Natural England* [2022] (n 268) [9](1)–(3), [125]. Per Males LJ at [125], a rational approach by the competent authority 'must include application of the precautionary principle, which is implicit in the Regulations, and must involve a high standard of investigation', but precisely what that means in practice in any given case is left to the competent authority's judgment, subject to *Wednesbury* review.
275 *R (Wyatt) v Fareham BC & Natural England* [2022] (n 268) [9](5); *R (BACI Bedfordshire Ltd) v Environment Agency* [2019] EWCA Civ 1962 [87].
276 *C–323/17 People Over Wind and Sweetman v Coillte Teoranta* (n 264) [44]; *Wealden DC v Secretary of State for Communities and Local Government* (n 262) [44](vi).
277 Case C-461/17 *Holohan v An Bord Pleanála* (n 269), [33]–[45].
278 *No Adastral New Town Ltd v Suffolk Coastal DC* (n 261) [68].
279 *R (Preston) v Cumbria County Council* [2019] EWHC 1362 (Admin) [58]–[60], [71]–[74].
280 The Habitats Regulations 2017 reg 67. See further *Cornwall Waste Forum St Dennis Branch v Secretary of State for Communities and Local Government & Anor* [2012] EWCA Civ 379.
281 DEFRA, 'Guidance: Habitats Regulations Assessments: Protecting a European Site' (2021) <https://www.gov.uk/guidance/habitats-regulations-assessments-protecting-a-european-site> accessed 16 May 2024.

9.149 Unlike at the screening stage, at the appropriate assessment stage, mitigation measures must be taken into account. However, compensatory measures cannot be considered.[282]

9.150 Nor may socio-economic considerations form part of any weighing or balancing of considerations in the appropriate assessment under regulation 63: they may only be taken into account in considering whether the limited scope for derogation under regulation 64 is made out. Unless regulation 64 applies, the planning authority has no discretion to exercise once it has concluded, by means of an appropriate assessment, that the effect of the proposed development will be adverse – even if the adverse effect is only modest.[283]

9.151 In *CG Fry and Son,* the Court of Appeal held that where the appropriate assessment provisions were engaged, regulations 63 and 70 have the effect of requiring such an assessment to be undertaken when the discharge of conditions was being considered in a multi-stage process. The obligation imposed by regulation 63 was a broad one, making necessary the carrying out of an appropriate assessment before deciding to give 'any consent, permission or other authorisation' for a project. The Court relied on a straightforward reading of the language used, having regard to the legislative purpose of the assessment provisions and the underlying precautionary principle.[284]

(iv) *Conditions for derogation: Regulations 64 and 68*

9.152 If, following an appropriate assessment, a decision-maker cannot be certain that a plan or project will not have an adverse effect on the integrity of a European site or European offshore marine site, the consent, permission or other authorisation must be refused unless the three strict derogation tests set out in regulations 64 and 68 of the Habitats Regulations are met:

- There are no feasible alternative solutions which are less damaging;
- There are IROPI; and
- Compensatory measures must be secured to ensure that the overall coherence of Natura 2000 is protected.

9.153 The assessment of each of these tests requires a weighing up against the damage caused to the site by the plan or project: these assessments, therefore, cannot lawfully be made before the appropriate assessment has been carried out.[285]

---

282 Case C-521/12 *Briels v Minister van Infrastructuur en Milieu* (2014) ECLI:EU:C:2014:330; [2014] PTSR 1120.
283 *R (Wyatt) v Fareham BC & Natural England* [2022] EWCA Civ 983 (n 268) [121], per Males LJ. Case C-293/17 *Cooperatie Mobilisation for the Environment UA, Vereniging Leefmilieu v College van Gedeputeerde Staten van Limburg* (2018) ECLI:EU:C:2018:882, Opinion of AG Kokott, [159].
284 *CG Fry and Son Ltd v Secretary of State for Levelling Up Housing and Communities* (n 115) [74]–[77], [85].
285 Case C-182/10 *Solvay v Region Wallonne* (2012) ECLI:EU:2012:82; [2012] Env LR 545, [73]–[74]; *R (Wilkinson) v South Hams District Council & Anor* [2016] EWHC 1860 (Admin) [35].

9.154 The requirement to establish an absence of alternatives is analogous to a stage of proportionality analysis, requiring recourse to the least onerous measure.[286] It also requires all of the alternatives to have been ruled out; it is not enough to examine a few.[287]

9.155 Competent authorities should work with the proposer to consider alternative solutions, including whether the proposal could happen at a different location, use different routes, or change its scale, size, design, method or timing.[288] Alternatives need to meet the proposal's original objectives; be financially, legally and technically feasible; and be less damaging to the European Site.[289] If there are, or appear to be, one or more alternative solutions, a derogation cannot be granted and the proposal must be rejected.[290] If there are no alternative solutions, the competent authority must move on to consider whether there are any IROPI such as to justify the granting of consent.[291]

9.156 The IROPI test is a high bar, to be strictly defined.[292] It requires that the reasons are:[293]

- Imperative (it is essential that the project proceeds for public interest reasons);
- In the public interest (rather than merely benefitting private interests); and
- Overriding (the public interest outweighs the harm, or risk of harm, to the integrity of the European site that is predicted by the appropriate assessment).

9.157 Unless the site concerned hosts a priority natural habitat type or a priority species, IROPI can be of a social or economic nature.[294] In such cases, the opinion of the national government should be sought).[295] Where the site concerned hosts a priority natural habitat type or a priority species, the IROPI must be either (a) reasons relating to human health, public safety or beneficial consequences of primary importance to the environment; or (b) any other reasons which the competent authority considers to be IROPI, having due regard to the opinion of the appropriate authority.[296]

9.158 Where a competent authority (other than one who is also an appropriate authority) desires the appropriate authority's opinion as to whether reasons are IROPI, it

---

286 C-239/04 *Commission v Portugal* [2006] ECR I-10183, Opinion of AG Kokott, [42].
287 ibid [43].
288 DEFRA, 'Guidance: Habitats Regulations Assessments: Protecting a European Site' (n 281).
289 ibid.
290 ibid.
291 ibid.
292 Case C-182/10 *Solvay v Region Wallonne* (n 285) [75]. However, while the requirements are intentionally rigorous, they are not insuperable: Case C-258/11 *Sweetman* (n 260) [66].
293 DEFRA, 'Guidance: Habitats Regulations Assessments: Protecting a European Site' (n 281). See further relying on Case C-411/17 *Inter-Environnement Wallonie ASBL v Council of Ministers Conseil des Ministres* (2019) ECLI:EU:C:2019:622; [2020] Env LR 9 [155], on Case C-43/10 *Nomarchiaki Aftodioikisi ASBL and Others v Ipourgos Perivallontos, Chorotaxias kai Dimosion ergon and Others* (2012) ECLI:EU:C:2012:560.
294 The Habitats Regulations 2017 reg 64(1).
295 DEFRA, 'Guidance: Habitats Regulations Assessments: Protecting a European Site' (n 281). See further Case C-135/11 *IFAW Internationaler Tierschutz-Fonds v European Commission* (2012) ECLI:EU:C:2012:376.
296 The Habitats Regulations 2017 reg 64(2).

may submit a written request for that opinion.[297] In giving its opinion, the appropriate authority must have regard to the national interest, and must first consult the JNCC and the other national administrations.[298] Where a competent authority proposes to agree a plan or project under regulation 64, it must first notify the appropriate authority and wait 21 days from the notification, during which the appropriate authority may give directions prohibiting the approval, either definitely or indefinitely.[299]

9.159 The balancing exercise is fact-sensitive.[300] Generally, national strategic plans, policy statements and major projects are more likely to have a high level of public interest and be able to show they are imperative and overriding. Plans or projects that only provide short-term or very localised benefits are less likely to be able to show IROPI.[301] However, scale is not determinative: a relatively modest project may be capable of engaging IROPI, including where the adverse impact on the protected species is negligible or otherwise very small.[302] At this stage, therefore, it is permissible to consider the extent of adverse impact on a protected feature, and to weigh this in the balance against the magnitude of any IROPI.

9.160 Interests which the ECJ has found to be in principle capable of being IROPI include ensuring the supply of electricity,[303] the supply of drinking water and irrigation,[304] the construction of a platform to facilitate the movement of disabled persons,[305] and the importance of mining activities to the local economy.[306]

9.161 Finally, the duty set out in regulation 68 is to secure that 'any necessary compensatory measures are taken to ensure that the overall coherence of Natura 2000 is protected.' Plainly, compensatory measures are not limited to the individual site in question, but may concern other European Sites.[307]

9.162 Compensatory measures will need to fully offset the damage which will or could be caused to the site.[308] The proposer will be expected to pay for compensatory measures, and should work with the competent authority to identify, define and secure these.[309] Albeit that any proposal approved under regulations 64 and 68 will have negative effects on an individual European Site, the compensatory measures themselves must not have a negative effect on the national network of European Sites as a whole.[310]

---

297 ibid reg 64(3).
298 ibid reg 64(4), (4A).
299 ibid regs 64(5)–(6).
300 *R (Wilkinson) v South Hams District Council & Anor* (n 285) [35].
301 ibid.
302 ibid [35].
303 Case C-411/17 *Inter-Environnement Wallonie ASBL* (n 293) [159].
304 Case C-43/10 *Nomarchiaki Aftodioikisi ASBL* (n 293) [122].
305 Case C-504/14 *European Commission v Greece* (2016) ECLI:EU:C:2016:847 [77].
306 Case C-227/01 *Commission v Spain* [2004] ECR I-08253; [2005] Env LR 20 [109].
307 Case C-521/12 *Briels v Minister van Infrastructuur en Milieu* (2014) ECLI:EU:C:2014:330; [2014] PTSR 1120, Opinion of AG Sharpston, [46], adopted by the Court in Case C-387/15 *Orleans v Vlaams Gewest* (2016) ECLI:EU:C:2016:583 [38].
308 DEFRA, 'Guidance: Habitats Regulations Assessments: Protecting a European Site' (n 281).
309 ibid.
310 ibid.

9.163 Compensatory measures can include creating or restoring the same or very similar habitat on areas of little or no conservation value (a) within the same site - if it exists, or (b) at a suitable location outside the site. If the area providing compensatory measures is not within the European Site, it should become designated as part of the European Site. Until that happens, it is protected by government planning policy.[311]

(v) *Nutrient neutrality*[312]

9.164 Following the 2018 ECJ decision in the Dutch Nitrogen case, NE published guidance on nutrient neutrality, recommending that LPAs only approve 'nitrogen neutral' housing developments in certain areas. By July 2022, NE had advised a total of 74 LPAs on the nutrient impacts of new plans and projects on protected sites which are in unfavourable condition due to excess nutrients, and on achieving 'nutrient neutrality' to mitigate the impact of nutrient pollution, so that development can go ahead.[313] In *R (Wyatt) v Fareham BC*,[314] the Court of Appeal held that the guidance note issued in relation to the Solent Region did not misstate the legal position under Regulation 63 (nor could there be a proper challenge to the lawfulness of the advice, which was merely an advisory document).

9.165 Nutrient neutrality continues to be a hot topic, and following the passage of the LURA 2023, further amendments have been made to the Habitats Regulations 2017, requiring competent authorities to make certain assumptions about nutrient pollution standards when making various decisions under Part 6.[315]

(vi) *Implications of the Retained EU Law (Revocation and Reform) Act 2023*

9.166 Practitioners seeking to rely on any provision of the Habitats Directive which is not directly transposed in the Habitats Regulations 2017 (and/or any pre-2024 domestic case law finding such provisions to be directly enforceable), or on any relevant retained EU case law, must be aware of the provisions of the Retained EU Law (Revocation and Reform) Act 2023 ('REULA 2023').

9.167 As set out above, section 2 of the REULA 2023 repeals section 4 of the EUWA 2018 from the end of 2023, meaning that anything which was retained EU law 'by virtue of that section' (including rights etc. arising under Directives) are no longer recognised or available in domestic law, and are not to be enforced, allowed or followed.

9.168 Section 4 of the REULA 2023 abolishes the previously retained 'general principles' of EU law. It was said in *Harris* at [59] that the precautionary principle was a retained general principle of EU law pursuant to section 6(7) of the EWUA 2018,

---

311 ibid.
312 See paras 19.121–19.127 in Chapter 19.
313 George Eustice, 'Statement on Improving Water Quality and Tackling Nutrient Pollution, Statement UIN HCWS258' (2022) <https://questions-statements.parliament.uk/written-statements/detail/2022-07-20/hcws258> accessed 17 May 2024.
314 *R (Wyatt) v Fareham BC & Natural England* [2022] (n 268).
315 The Habitats Regulations 2017 regs 85A–85D, 110A–110C.

although this is doubtful.[316] In any case, first, the precautionary principle is deeply embedded in domestic case law which remains relevant (notwithstanding the changes that will be made to the interpretative rules governing retained EU case law if section 6 of the REULA 2023 comes into force). Second, sections 11–16 of the REULA 2023 include powers to reproduce the effects of anything which was previously retained by virtue of section 4 of the EUWA 2018 (including relevant Directive provisions), and to restate by way of regulations any secondary assimilated law, including producing effects equivalent to the retained general principles.[317]

Marine Protected Areas

(i) *Marine Conservation Zones*

9.169 Marine Conservation Zones ('MCZs') are designated under Part 5 of the Marine and Coastal Access Act 2009 ('MCAA 2009'). MCZs are one type of designation which form part of the marine protected areas ('MPA') network.

9.170 In September 2010, DEFRA issued 'Guidance on the proposed approach to the selection and designation of Marine Conservation Zones under Part 5 of the Marine and Coastal Access Act' ('the 2010 Guidance') (now revoked). The 2010 Guidance set out the following aim:

> Our aim is to develop an ecologically coherent and well-managed network of Marine Protected Areas (MPAs) that is well understood and supported by sea-users and other stakeholders. Achieving this aim will make a major contribution to recovering and protecting the richness of our marine wildlife and environment and will be a contribution to achieving Good Environmental Status in our seas as required by the EC Marine Strategy Framework Directive.

9.171 The MPA network should be understood against the background of the Convention for the Protection of the Marine Environment of the North-East Atlantic ('OSPAR Convention'), which the UK ratified in 1998.[318] Article 2 of Annex V of the OSPAR Convention states:

> In fulfilling their obligation under the Convention to take, individually and jointly, the necessary measures to protect the maritime area against the adverse effects of human activities so as to safeguard human health and to conserve marine ecosystems and,

316 The court did not engage with the proviso in EU(W)A 2018 para 2, sch 1 that no general principle of EU law is retained if it was not recognised as a general principle of EU law by the European Court in a case decided before IP completion day. It is debatable whether this includes the pre-Lisbon Treaty case of Case T-74/00 *Artegodan GmbH & Others v Commission* [2002] ECR II-04945. In any case, there is academic debate as to whether *Artegodan* sufficiently establishes the precautionary principle as a general principle. Paul Craig, *EU Law: Text, Cases and Materials* (6th edn, Oxford University Press 2015) 575 accepts that it did, but Professors Joanne Scott and Eloise Scotford have doubted this: Joanne Scott, 'Legal Aspects of the Precautionary Principle: A British Academy Brexit Briefing' (2018) <https://www.thebritishacademy.ac.uk/documents/309/Legal-Aspects-of-the-Precautionary-Principle.pdf> accessed 17 May 2024; Eloise Scotford, *Environmental Principles and the Evolution of Environmental Law* (Hart Publishing 2017) 61–62.

317 Retained EU Law (Revocation and Reform) Act 2023 s 12.

318 It ratified Annex V and Appendix 3 in June 2000.

when practicable, restore marine areas which have been adversely affected, as well as their obligation under the Convention on Biological Diversity of 5 June 1992 to develop strategies, plans or programmes for the conservation and sustainable use of biological diversity, Contracting Parties shall:

a. take the necessary measures to protect and conserve the ecosystems and the biological diversity of the maritime area, and to restore, where practicable, marine areas which have been adversely affected; and
b. cooperate in adopting programmes and measures for those purposes for the control of the human activities identified by the application of the criteria in Appendix 3.

9.172 The MPA network is comprised of SACs, SPAs, Ramsar Sites, SSSIs, MCZs and the recently created Highly Protected Marine Areas ('HPMAs'). The 2010 Guidance set out seven principles for the MPA which were 'based closely on those developed for OSPAR'.[319] The seven principles are:[320]

- Representativity – the MPA network should represent the range of marine habitats and species through protecting all major habitat types and associated biological communities present in our marine area.

- Replication – all major habitats should be replicated and distributed throughout the network. The amount of replication will depend on the extent and distribution of features within our seas.

- Viability – the MPA network should incorporate self-sustaining, geographically dispersed component sites of sufficient size to ensure species' and habitats' persistence through natural cycles of variation.

- Adequacy – the MPA network should be of adequate size to deliver its ecological objectives and ensure the ecological viability and integrity of populations, species and communities (the proportion of each feature included within the MPA network should be sufficient to enable its long-term protection and/or recovery).

- Connectivity – the MPA network should seek to maximise and enhance the linkages among individual MPAs using the best current science. For certain species this will mean that sites should be distributed in a manner to ensure protection at different stages in their life cycles.

319 Department for Environment, Food and Rural Affairs, 'Guidance on the Duties on Public Authorities in Relation to Marine Conservation Zones (Note 2): Guidance on the Duties Which Will Be Placed on Public Authorities in Relation to Marine Conservation Zones under Part 5 of the Marine and Coastal Access Act 2009' (2010) section 3 <https://infrastructure.planninginspectorate.gov.uk/wp-content/ipc/uploads/projects/EN010080/EN010080-001544-Orsted%20Hornsea%20Project%20Three%20(UK)%20Ltd%20-%20Appendix%2051%20-%20Defra%20MCZ%20Guidance%202010.pdf> accessed 17 May 2024.
320 ibid.

- Protection – the MPA network is likely to include a range of protection levels. Ranging from highly protected sites or parts of sites where no extractive, depositional or other damaging activities are allowed, to areas with only minimal restrictions on activities that are needed to protect the features.

- Best available evidence – Network design should be based on the best information currently available. Lack of full scientific certainty should not be a reason for postponing proportionate decisions on site selection.

9.173 There are currently 91 MCZs in waters around England. They were designated in three tranches. The first 27 zones were designated on 21 November 2013. 23 sites were designated on 17 January 2016. The remaining 41 sites and 12 additional features were designated on 31 May 2019.[321]

9.174 Part 5 of the MCAA 2009 provides for the designation of MCZs. The legislation provides for the Secretary of State, Welsh Ministers or Scottish Ministers ('the appropriate authority') to, by order, designate certain areas as MCZs.[322] To be designated an MCZ an area must be: (a) an area of the sea within the seaward limits of the territorial sea adjacent to the United Kingdom; (b) an area of the sea within the limits of the exclusive economic zone; or (c) an area of the sea bed or subsoil within the limits of the UK sector of the continental shelf.[323]

9.175 The appropriate authority may designate an area as an MCZ where it thinks that it is 'desirable to do so for the purpose of conserving (a) marine flora or fauna; (b) marine habitats or types of marine habitat; (c) features of geological or geomorphological interest'.[324]

9.176 The legislation envisages MCZs as 'feature-based' protections, i.e. the designation of the site depends upon the presence of a particular feature (habitat, species or feature of geological/geomorphological interest). However, this legislation has also been used to create the HPMAs (discussed further below). HPMAs take a whole site protection approach as opposed to a 'feature-based' one.

9.177 The MCAA 2009 provides that appropriate authorities are under a duty to designate MCZs in order to achieve the objective that MCZs and any other relevant conservation sites (European marine site, SSSIs and Ramsar Sites) in the UK area form a network which: (a) contributes to the conservation or improvement of the marine environment in the UK marine area; (b) protects features which represent the range of features present in the UK marine area; and (c) reflects the fact that the conservation of a feature may require the designation of more than one site.[325]

---

321 DEFRA, 'Collection: Marine Conservation Zone Designations in England' (31 May 2019) <https://www.gov.uk/government/collections/marine-conservation-zone-designations-in-england> accessed 17 May 2024.
322 MCAA 2009 s 116.
323 ibid s 116(2).
324 ibid s 117(1).
325 ibid ss 123(2) and (3).

9.178 The appropriate authority was required (by 31 May 2010) to prepare a statement setting out principles relating to the achievement of the above objective, which the appropriate authority intends to follow when complying with its duty to designate MCZs.[326] The appropriate authority is required to keep this statement under review and, if it considers it appropriate, lay a copy of any revised statement before the relevant legislature.

9.179 The appropriate authority is required, every six years, to lay a report before the legislature which sets out the extent to which it considers the objective in section 123(2) has been achieved and any further steps which, in the opinion of the authority, are required to be taken in order to contribute to the achievement of that objective.[327] The report must also contain the information set out in section 124(2) of the MCAA 2009. The appropriate authority may direct the appropriate statutory nature conservation body for its area to carry out monitoring MCZ in order to comply with this duty.[328]

9.180 An order designating an MCZ must state: (a) the protected feature or features; and (b) the conservation objectives for the MCZ.[329]

9.181 Explanatory notes issued by DEFRA explain that the conservation objective for each MCZ is for each of the features being protected to be in favourable condition. With 'favourable condition' being defined as: '(i) its extent is stable or increasing; (ii) its structures and functions, its quality, and the composition of its characteristic biological communities are such as to ensure that it remains in a condition which is healthy and not deteriorating'.[330]

9.182 Before making an order designating an MCZ, the appropriate authority must comply with the consultation requirements in section 119 of the MCAA 2009 and may hold a hearing as part of the decision-making process.[331] On making the Order, the appropriate authority must publicise it in accordance with section 120 of the MCAA 2009.

9.183 MCZs may be amended or revoked by further order.[332]

9.184 Public authorities whose functions are capable of affecting the protected features of an MCZ, or any ecological or geomorphological process on which the conservation of any protected feature of an MCZ is wholly or partly dependent are under the general duties set out in section 125 of the MCAA 2009. Those authorities must (a) exercise their functions in the manner which the authority considers best furthers the conservation objectives stated for the MCZ; and (b) where it is not possible to exercise

---

326 ibid s 126(6).
327 ibid s 124(1).
328 ibid s 124(3).
329 ibid s 117(2).
330 DEFRA, 'Marine Conservation Zones Designation Explanatory Note' (2013) [6]–[7] <https://assets.publishing.service.gov.uk/media/5a7c9bc4ed915d12ab4bbedf/pb14078-mcz-explanatory-note.pdf> accessed 17 May 2024.
331 MCAA 2009 s 121.
332 ibid s 122.

its functions in such a manner, it must exercise them in a manner which the authority considers least hinders the achievement of those objectives.[333]

9.185 If a public authority considers that the exercise of any of its functions would or might significantly hinder the achievement of the conservation objectives for an MCZ, it must inform the appropriate statutory conservation body.[334] Further, where a public authority intends to carry out an act which is capable of affecting (other than insignificantly) (a) the protected features of an MCZ; or (b) any ecological or geomorphological process on which the conservation of any protected feature of an MCZ is wholly or in part dependent, and the authority believes that there is a significant risk of the act hindering the achievement of the conservation objectives for the MCZ, then it must notify the appropriate statutory nature conservation body).[335] There is then a 28-day period where the statutory nature conservation body can give advice before the public authority undertakes the proposed action.[336]

9.186 Section 126 sets out a similar procedure relating to where a public authority has the function of determining an application for authorisation of an act, and the act is capable of (other than insignificantly) affecting the protected features of an MCZ or any ecological or geomorphological process on which the conservation of any protected feature of an MCZ is (wholly or in part) dependent. Again, this allows for a 28-day period within which the statutory nature conservation body may give advice.

9.187 The public authority must not grant authorisation for an act which is capable of (other than insignificantly) affecting the protected features of an MCZ or any ecological or geomorphological process on which the conservation of any protected feature of an MCZ is (wholly or in part) dependent, unless one of two conditions are met.[337] The first condition is that 'the person seeking the authorisation satisfies the authority that there is no significant risk of the act hindering the achievement of the conservation objectives stated for the MCZ'.[338] The second condition is that although the person seeking the authorisation is not able to satisfy the authority that there is no significant risk of the act hindering the achievement of the conservation objectives stated for the MCZ, that person satisfied the authority that (a) there is no other means of proceeding with the act which would create a substantially lower risk of hindering the achievement objectives; (b) the benefit to the public of proceeding with the act clearly outweighs the risk of damage to the environment; and (c) the person seeking the authorisation will undertake or make arrangements for the undertaking of measures of environmental benefit equivalent to the damage which the act will or is likely to have on the MCZ.[339]

---

333 ibid s 125(2).
334 ibid s 125(3).
335 ibid ss 123(4) and (5). This requirement applies save for in circumstances where the relevant statutory nature conservation bodies have issued standing advice on activities where public authorities do not need to notify them every time they carry out certain activities: MCAA 2009 s 125(6).
336 Save for where the statutory nature conservation body notifies the public authority that it need not wait for 28 days or the situation is urgent: MCAA 2009 s 123(7).
337 ibid s 126(5).
338 ibid s 126(6).
339 ibid s 126(7).

9.188 The appropriate statutory conservation body is empowered to give advice and guidance as to certain matters relating to MCZs including, broadly, the matters which may damage protected features, how conservation objectives may be furthered or hindered and how effects might be mitigated. This advice can apply to MCZs generally or to specific MCZs, and to all public authorities or specific public authorities. Advice must be given to a public authority who requests it.[340]

9.189 The appropriate statutory conservation body may request a written explanation from a public authority where it considers that the public authority has failed to comply with the duties imposed by section 125(2) or 126(5), or to act in accordance with advice or guidance given under section 127.[341]

9.190 The MMO[342] is empowered to make byelaws for the purpose of furthering conservation objectives for an MCZ or to apply to England as a whole.[343] Byelaws may prohibit or restrict entry into or any movement or other activity within an MCZ by persons, animals, vessels or vehicles.[344] Byelaws may restrict the speed at which a vessel may move in an MCZ or in specified areas outside the MCZ, and prohibit or restrict the anchoring of any vessel within the MCZ.[345] Byelaws may also prohibit the killing, taking, destruction, molestation or disturbance of any animals or plants of any description in the MCZ, and prohibit or restrict doing anything which would interfere with the seabed or damage or disturb any object in the MCZ.[346] The MMO may, through the byelaws, issue conditional or unconditional permits authorising anything which would otherwise be unlawful under the byelaws.[347]

9.191 The procedure for making byelaws under section 129 is set out in section 130 of the MCAA 2009, which includes confirmation by the Secretary of State. However, where the MMO considers that there is an urgent need to protect an MCZ or the English offshore reason then a byelaw made for that purpose does not require confirmation by the Secretary of State.[348] Such byelaws are termed 'emergency byelaws' and remain in force for 12 months, unless revoked by the MMO or the Secretary of State. They must be publicised and kept under review.[349]

9.192 The MMO also has powers to make interim byelaws where it considers that there are or may be reasons for the Secretary of State to consider whether to designate an area as an MCZ and there is an urgent need to protect any feature.[350] The procedure is set out in the remainder of section 132 of the MCAA 2009.

---

340 ibid ss 127(1)–(3).
341 ibid s 128.
342 See further paras 4.38–4.45 in Chapter 4.
343 MCAA 2009 ss 129(1)–(2).
344 ibid s 129(3)(a) and (b).
345 ibid s 129(3)(c) and (d).
346 ibid s 129(3)(e) and (f).
347 ibid s 123(5) and (6).
348 ibid s 131(1) and (1A).
349 ibid s 131.
350 ibid s 132(1).

9.193 In Wales, the Welsh Ministers have the power to make conservation orders to protect MCZs, to help further their conservation objectives. Section 134 of the MCAA 2009 applies certain of the byelaw-making provisions in section 130 of the MCAA 2009 to conservation orders in Wales, which are intended to work in a similar way to byelaws in England. Welsh Ministers are empowered to make interim conservation orders under section 136 of the MCAA 2009.

9.194 A breach of any byelaw or conservation order is a criminal offence.[351] It may also attract a fixed monetary penalty where the appropriate authority has provided for this by Order under section 142 of the MCAA 2009.

9.195 The MCAA 2009 also creates offences where a person: (a) intentionally or recklessly kills or injures any animal in an MCZ which is a protected feature of the MCZ; (b) intentionally picks or collects, or intentionally or recklessly cuts, uproots or destroys, any plant in an MCZ which is a protected feature of that MCZ; (c) intentionally or recklessly takes anything from an MCZ which is or forms part of a protected feature of that MCZ; or (d) intentionally or recklessly destroys or damages any habitat or feature which is a protected feature of an MCZ. For the offence to be made out, the person must not (a) have lawful excuse for doing the act; (b) know or ought to have known that the feature to which the act relates is in or forms part of an MCZ; and (c) the act has significantly hindered, or may significantly hinder the achievement of the conservation objectives stated for the MCZ.[352]

9.196 Section 141 of the MCAA 2009 sets out exceptions to criminal offences under sections 139 and 140: examples include where the act was expressly authorised under section 126[353] or was necessary in the interests of national security or the prevention or detection of crime, or was necessary for securing public health.[354]

(ii) *Highly Protected Marine Areas*

9.197 In 2019 the government commissioned Richard Benyon to conduct a review of the potential role for Highly Protected Marine Areas ('HPMAs'). HPMAs are similar to MCZs but with stricter protection. The review was reported in June 2020. It concluded that HPMAs would play an important role in helping the marine ecosystem to recover and recommended that the government pilots around five HPMAs to test the proposition.

9.198 On 8 June 2021, George Eustice, the then Secretary of State for Environment, Food and Rural Affairs announced in a written statement to Parliament that the government would begin introducing HPMAs.[355]

---

351 ibid s 139.
352 ibid s 140.
353 ibid s 141(1)(b).
354 ibid s 141(1)(d).
355 HC Deb 8 June 2021, vol 696.

9.199 Following public consultation, on 5 July 2023, DEFRA designated three HPMAs: Allonby Bay,[356] North East of Farnes Deep[357] and Dolphin Head.[358] These form the 'pilot phase' of HPMAs, which are intended to inform the future of HPMA policy.[359]

9.200 Each of the three HPMAs identify the 'protected feature' as being 'the marine ecosystem of the area'. This is defined as meaning 'all marine flora and fauna, all marine habitats and all geological or geomorphological interests, including all abiotic elements and all supporting ecosystem functions and processes, in or on the sea bed, water column and the surface of the sea'.

9.201 The conservation objective of each HPMA is to 'achieve full recovery of the protected feature, including its structure and functions, its qualities and the composition of its characteristic biological communities present … to a natural state' and to 'prevent further degradation and damage to the protected feature, subject to natural change'.

9.202 DEFRA envisages that a wide range of activities will be prohibited within each HPMA, including commercial and recreational fishing, dredging, construction and anchoring.[360]

---

356 The Allonby Bay Highly Protected Marine Area (Marine Conservation Zone) Designation Order 2023, SI 2023/2.
357 The North East of Farnes Deep Highly Protected Marine Area (Marine Conservation Zone) Designation Order 2023, SI 2023/3.
358 The Dolphin Head Highly Protected Marine Area (Marine Conservation Zone) Designation Order 2023, SI 2023/1.
359 DEFRA, 'Highly Protected Marine Areas (HPMAs)' (2023) <https://www.gov.uk/government/publications/highly-protected-marine-areas/highly-protected-marine-areas-hpmas> accessed 17 May 2024.
360 ibid.

CHAPTER 10

BIODIVERSITY NET GAIN

Ned Helme

Introduction

10.01 This chapter addresses the regime for biodiversity gain in planning (as it stands at 28 October 2024) introduced by the Environment Act 2021 ('EA 2021'). The regime, which applies only in England,[1] is designed to ensure that all development (with limited exceptions) is required to deliver measurable gains in biodiversity of at least 10%. The first part of the regime, which applies to development governed by the Town and Country Planning Act 1990 ('TCPA 1990'), came into force on 12 February 2024 (with transitional provisions[2] and with a temporary exemption for non-major developments until 2 April 2024[3]). The second part, which will apply to development governed by the Planning Act 2008 ('PA 2008'), is due to come into force in late November 2025.[4]

10.02 The legislation uses the term 'biodiversity gain', but this is referred to in government guidance on the TCPA 1990 part of the regime as 'biodiversity net gain' to distinguish it from other or more general biodiversity gains,[5] and this and its acronym 'BNG' are both widely used. We use 'BNG' in this chapter to refer to biodiversity gain under both parts of the regime.

10.03 It is important to emphasise that the BNG regime does not displace other statutory powers and duties of relevance to biodiversity (such as the duty to conserve and enhance biodiversity under section 40 of the Natural Environment and Rural Communities Act 2006, as amended by the EA 2021[6]) or other policy and guidance on biodiversity. BNG is a distinct requirement, though there is inevitably an interplay with other regimes.

10.04 It is also important to emphasise the newness of the regime. Changes are likely to be required as experience shows its strengths and weaknesses. Moreover, the regime

---

1 For the TCPA 1990 part of the regime, see s 90A and Schedule 7A paras 1(1) and 13(1) of that Act. For the PA 2008 part of the regime, see Schedule 2A para 1(1) of that Act (to be inserted by Schedule 15 para 5 of the EA 2021 on a date to be appointed).
2 See para 10.39 below.
3 See para 10.41 below.
4 DEFRA, 'Understanding Biodiversity Net Gain' (GOV.UK, 22 February 2024) <https://www.gov.uk/guidance/understanding-biodiversity-net-gain> accessed 28 October 2024.
5 Ministry of Housing, Communities and Local Government and Department for Levelling Up, Housing and Communities, Planning Practice Guidance on 'Biodiversity Net Gain' (GOV.UK, 1 May 2024) para 001 Reference ID: 74-001–20240214 <https://www.gov.uk/guidance/biodiversity-net-gain> accessed 28 October 2024.
6 Addressed in Chapter 8.

is likely to be developed beyond its current terrestrial limitation to embrace marine net gain[7] ('MNG') and may in due course also be broadened to address wider environmental net gain ('ENG') (i.e. to address not only biodiversity but also other improvements in natural capital and ecosystem services).[8]

Background to statutory BNG

10.05 Aspirations to achieve gains in biodiversity through the English planning system are not new. Paragraph 109 of the original version of the National Planning Policy Framework ('NPPF'), published on 27 March 2012, emphasised the role of the planning system in 'providing net gains in biodiversity where possible' and this echoed earlier policy statements.[9] What is new under the BNG regime is a mandatory requirement for quantified gains coupled with a standardised assessment approach through a metric.

10.06 The origins of BNG are to be found in biodiversity offsetting (i.e. compensation for damage to biodiversity so as to ensure an overall neutral impact). The government explored biodiversity offsetting in the early 2010s and ran a consultation on the subject in 2013.[10] DEFRA and Natural England also ran six biodiversity offsetting pilot areas from 2012 to 2014, and developed a metric to ensure that offsetting was carried out in a measurable way. The government responded to the 2013 consultation on 18 February 2016[11] but did not take forward its proposals, instead developing (as a logical extension of the offsetting concept) proposals for BNG.

10.07 The next step towards BNG came in the government's 25 Year Environment Plan,[12] published on 11 January 2018. Chapter 1 included a policy for 'embedding an ENG principle for development, including housing and infrastructure' and, as part of this, promised a consultation on mandatory BNG.[13] The promised consultation ran from December 2018 to February 2019[14] and the government responded in July 2019.[15] At that stage the government only proposed to introduce mandatory BNG for TCPA 1990 development, and when the government introduced its Environment Bill in the 2019–21 session, it did not include BNG for PA 2008 development. However, that changed following advice from the Natural Capital Committee.[16] The EA 2021 was

---

7 See paras 10.58 and 10.59 below.
8 See paras 10.60 to 10.62 below.
9 See, for example, Office of the Deputy Prime Minister, 'Planning Policy Statement 9: Biodiversity and Geological Conservation' (2005).
10 DEFRA, 'Biodiversity Offsetting' (GOV.UK, 9 April 2013) <https://www.gov.uk/government/collections/biodiversity-offsetting> accessed 28 October 2024.
11 DEFRA, 'Biodiversity offsetting in England' (GOV.UK, 18 February 2016) <https://www.gov.uk/government/consultations/biodiversity-offsetting-in-england> accessed 28 October 2024.
12 HM Government, 'A Green Future: Our 25 Year Plan to Improve the Environment' (GOV.UK, 17 February 2023) <https://www.gov.uk/government/publications/25-year-environment-plan> accessed 28 October 2024.
13 HM Government, 'A Green Future: Our 25 Year Plan to Improve the Environment' (n 12).
14 DEFRA, 'Net Gain – Defra – Citizen Space' <https://consult.defra.gov.uk/land-use/net-gain/> accessed 28 October 2024.
15 DEFRA, 'Net Gain. Summary of Responses and Government Response' (2019) <https://www.gov.uk/government/consultations/biodiversity-net-gain-updating-planning-requirements> accessed 28 October 2024.
16 'Natural Capital Committee (NCC)' (GOV.UK, 10 September 2019) <https://www.gov.uk/government/publications/natural-capital-committee-advice-to-government-on-net-environmental-gain> accessed 28 October 2024.

enacted on 9 November 2021. Further BNG consultations have followed on matters such as implementation[17] and the biodiversity metric.[18] As noted in paragraph 10.01 above, BNG launched for TCPA 1990 development on 12 February 2024 and is due to launch for PA 2008 development in November 2025.

Legislative framework

10.08 The legislative framework for BNG is complex and only partially in force. The key primary legislation for BNG for TCPA 1990 development is found in that Act at section 90A and Schedule 7A, which were inserted by the EA 2021[19] and subsequently amended,[20] and which came into force (subject to transitional provisions) on 12 February 2024.[21] So far as development under the PA 2008 is concerned, sections 103–105 of that Act will be amended and a new Schedule 2A added by the EA 2021,[22] but these changes are not expected to come into force before late November 2025.[23] The EA 2021, section 100[24] also makes provision in relation to biodiversity gain sites and section 101[25] makes provision in relation to biodiversity credits.

10.09 As for secondary legislation, the following regulations address BNG:

- The Environment Act 2021 (Commencement No. 7) Regulations 2023;[26]
- The Environment Act 2021 (Commencement No. 8 and Transitional Provisions) Regulations 2024;[27]
- The Biodiversity Gain Site Register Regulations 2024;[28]
- The Biodiversity Gain Site Register (Financial Penalties and Fees) Regulations 2024;[29]

---

17 The consultation is available at <https://consult.defra.gov.uk/defra-net-gain-consultation-team/consultation-on-biodiversity-net-gain-regulations/> accessed 28 October 2024, and the government response is available at <https://www.gov.uk/government/consultations/consultation-on-biodiversity-net-gain-regulations-and-implementation/outcome/government-response-and-summary-of-responses> accessed 28 October 2024.
18 DEFRA, 'Technical Consultation on the Biodiversity Metric' <https://consult.defra.gov.uk/defra-net-gain-consultation-team/technicalconsultation_biodiversitymetric/> accessed 28 October 2024.
19 s 98 and Schedule 14. Schedule 14 para 3 also made various additional amendments to the TCPA 1990.
20 By the Levelling-up and Regeneration Act 2023 and the Biodiversity Gain (Town and Country Planning) (Consequential Amendments) Regulations 2024.
21 See paras 10.37 to 10.39 below.
22 s 99 and Schedule 15. Schedule 15 paras 6–9 will also make various additional amendments to the PA 2008.
23 See para 10.01 above.
24 Which came into force on 3 November 2023 for the purposes of making regulations (reg 2(c) of the Environment Act 2021 (Commencement No. 7) Regulations 2023) and on 12 February 2024 for all remaining purposes (Regulation 2(1)(b) of the Environment Act 2021 (Commencement No. 8 and Transitional Provisions) Regulations 2024).
25 Which came into force on 12 February 2024 (reg 2(1)(c) of the Environment Act 2021 (Commencement No. 8 and Transitional Provisions) Regulations 2024).
26 SI 2023/1170.
27 SI 2024/44.
28 SI 2024/45.
29 SI 2024/46.

- The Biodiversity Gain Requirements (Exemptions) Regulations 2024;[30]
- The Biodiversity Gain Requirements (Irreplaceable Habitat) Regulations 2024;[31]
- The Biodiversity Gain (Town and Country Planning) (Consequential Amendments) Regulations 2024;[32]
- The Biodiversity Gain (Town and Country Planning) (Modifications and Amendments) (England) Regulations 2024.[33]

10.10 The legislative framework will develop further in due course so as to bring BNG for PA 2008 development into effect (and likely for other reasons as well, for example to correct issues that arise in practice, to extend BNG to new areas, or to broaden BNG to embrace other aspects of ENG).

Policy and guidance

10.11 The government maintains a BNG 'collection'[34] comprising a range of guidance documents issued by DEFRA (some jointly with Natural England), together with Planning Practice Guidance on BNG issued by the Department for Levelling Up, Housing and Communities (now the Ministry of Housing, Communities and Local Government). Although not part of the BNG collection, the Planning Practice Guidance section on the Natural Environment[35] also contains guidance on BNG and wider ENG.

10.12 The British Standards Institution has produced a British Standard (BS 8683:2021)[36] specifying a process to design, implement, maintain and monitor BNG outcomes from development projects.

10.13 The Chartered Institute of Ecology and Environmental Management maintains a number of resources on BNG.[37] The Planning Advisory Service also maintains a suite of resources on BNG for local authorities.[38]

---

30 SI 2024/47.
31 SI 2024/48.
32 SI 2024/49.
33 SI 2024/50.
34 DEFRA, 'Biodiversity Net Gain Collection' (GOV.UK, 15 March 2024) <https://www.gov.uk/government/collections/biodiversity-net-gain> accessed 28 October 2024.
35 Ministry of Housing, Communities and Local Government and Department for Levelling Up, Housing and Communities, 'Natural Environment Guidance' (GOV.UK, 14 February 2024) <https://www.gov.uk/guidance/natural-environment> accessed 28 October 2024.
36 British Standards Institution, 'BS 8683:2021 Process for designing and implementing Biodiversity Net Gain. Specification'.
37 CIEEM's website is available at <https://cieem.net> accessed 28 October 2024.
38 Planning Advisory Service, 'Biodiversity Net Gain for Local Authorities' (8 February 2024) <https://www.local.gov.uk/pas/events/pas-past-events/biodiversity-net-gain-local-authorities> accessed 28 October 2024.

Biodiversity gain as a condition of planning permission

(i) *Introduction and Overview*

10.14 The BNG regime for TCPA 1990 development came into force on 12 February 2024. The scope of the regime, its transitional provisions, and the various exceptions and exemptions that apply are addressed in paragraphs 10.37–10.42 below.

10.15 The regime is highly complex (and so a complete treatment is not possible in this chapter), but in essence it imposes a condition on all planning permissions granted for the development of land in England (with certain exceptions) preventing commencement until a biodiversity gain plan has been submitted to and approved by the planning authority. The biodiversity gain plan must assess the biodiversity value before and after development and an increase in value of at least 10% (the biodiversity gain objective) must be secured for at least 30 years through (in descending order of priority) onsite gains, registered offsite gains, or biodiversity credits.

(ii) *The biodiversity gain objective*

10.16 The heart of the regime is the 'biodiversity gain objective', which is set out in paragraph 2 of Schedule 7A to the TCPA 1990. The objective is met if the biodiversity value attributable to the development exceeds the pre-development biodiversity value of the onsite habitat by at least 10%.[39] The biodiversity value attributable to the development is the total of: (a) the post-development biodiversity value of the onsite habitat; (b) the biodiversity value, in relation to the development, of any registered offsite biodiversity gain allocated to the development; and (c) the biodiversity value of any biodiversity credits purchased for the development. Schedule 7A does not provide an order of priority for these, but Article 37A of the Town and Country Planning (Development Management Procedure) (England) Order 2015[40] ('the DMPO') provides a 'biodiversity gain hierarchy' which does so. As the Planning Practice Guidance on BNG explains,[41] the biodiversity gain hierarchy is distinct from the mitigation hierarchy set out in paragraph 186(a) of the NPPF.

(iii) *The statutory biodiversity metric*

10.17 By paragraphs 3 and 4 of Schedule 7A, the biodiversity value of any habitat or habitat enhancement must be calculated in accordance with the statutory biodiversity metric, which is available online together with a detailed user guide[42] (and also a

39 By para 2(4) the Secretary of State may by regulations change the relevant percentage.
40 SI 2015/595.
41 Ministry of Housing, Communities and Local Government, Planning Practice Guidance on 'Biodiversity Net Gain' (n 5) para 008.
42 DEFRA, 'Statutory Biodiversity Metric Tools and Guides' (GOV.UK, 6 August 2024) <https://www.gov.uk/government/publications/statutory-biodiversity-metric-tools-and-guides> accessed 28 October 2024.

separate, simplified, metric and user guide for small sites). As the Planning Practice Guidance explains:[43]

> The statutory biodiversity metric is used to calculate the pre-development and post-development biodiversity value of the development's onsite habitat, as well as the value for offsite biodiversity gains and biodiversity credits. It uses habitat information to generate 'biodiversity units', a proxy measure for biodiversity value. The statutory biodiversity metric data value inputs include habitat type, size, distinctiveness, condition, and its location in the local area.

10.18 A final version of the metric calculation is submitted post-permission with the biodiversity gain plan (see paragraph 10.32 below). However, DEFRA Guidance emphasises that:[44]

> The metric tool is not intended to be a one-off step in your design and planning process. It's advisable to use it repeatedly as you refine your plans. You should aim to get the best possible gains on site, before considering making off-site gains, or (as a last resort) buying statutory credits. The metric tool will tell you where you could create more gains. Then you can make changes to your designs, and use the metric tool again to check your decision.

10.19 Consistent with the biodiversity gain hierarchy, the metric includes a spatial risk multiplier to disincentivise reliance on biodiversity credits and offsite biodiversity gains (with a greater disincentive for offsite gains outside the neighbouring area than those within it).

(iv) *Calculating the pre- and post-development biodiversity value of the site*

10.20 As noted above, under the biodiversity gain hierarchy the initial focus is onsite. Only if the biodiversity gain objective cannot be achieved in full by onsite measures should registered offsite gains or (failing that) biodiversity credits be considered. In assessing the onsite position, it is necessary to compare the position pre- and post-development using the statutory metric.

10.21 By paragraph 5 of Schedule 7A, the pre-development biodiversity value is generally calculated as at the date of the application for planning permission or, where there is no application, the date on which permission is granted. However, different rules apply in certain circumstances.[45]

10.22 By paragraph 8(1) of Schedule 7A, the post-development biodiversity value of the onsite habitat is the projected value of the onsite habitat as at the time the

---

43 Ministry of Housing, Communities and Local Government, Planning Practice Guidance on 'Biodiversity Net Gain' (n 5) para 005.
44 DEFRA, 'Calculate biodiversity value with the statutory biodiversity metric' (GOV.UK, 27 February 2024) <https://www.gov.uk/guidance/biodiversity-metric-calculate-the-biodiversity-net-gain-of-a-project-or-development> accessed 28 October 2024.
45 See Schedule 7A, paras 6, 6A, 6B and 7. See also the Ministry of Housing, Communities and Local Government, Planning Practice Guidance on 'Biodiversity Net Gain' (n 5) paras 012, 036 and 057.

development is completed. By paragraph 8(2) that value is to be calculated by taking the pre-development biodiversity value and adding the amount of any projected increase in the biodiversity value of the onsite habitat, or subtracting any projected decrease. This is, however, subject to paragraph 9, which provides that where works are proposed that increase the biodiversity value of the onsite habitat and the planning authority considers that the increase is 'significant', the increase can only be taken into account if the planning authority is satisfied that the habitat enhancement resulting from the works will be maintained for at least 30 years[46] after the development is completed by virtue of: (a) a condition; (b) a planning obligation; or (c) a conservation covenant.[47] DEFRA has provided guidance on what constitutes a 'significant' increase for these purposes.[48]

(v) *Registered offsite biodiversity gains*

10.23 If the biodiversity gain objective cannot be met in full through onsite measures, registered offsite biodiversity gains fall to be considered. These are defined by paragraph 10(1) of Schedule 7A as any habitat enhancement of an offsite habitat, where: (a) the enhancement is required to be carried out under a conservation covenant or planning obligation; and (b) the enhancement is recorded in the biodiversity gain site register established pursuant to the EA 2021, section 100. Provision is made for the approach to measuring the biodiversity value of registered offsite biodiversity gains in paragraphs 10(1A)–(3) of Schedule 7A. As with significant onsite gains,[49] a minimum 30-year period is stipulated for biodiversity gain sites by section 100(2)(b).[50]

10.24 The register for offsite biodiversity gains is available online.[51] Detailed provision is made for its operation in the Biodiversity Gain Site Register Regulations 2024 and the Biodiversity Gain Site Register (Financial Penalties and Fees) Regulations 2024.

10.25 Registered offsite biodiversity gains provide considerable opportunities for landowners to raise revenue through the sale of biodiversity units to developers. Units may be sold independently, as part of a group, or through habitat bank operators.[52] It is possible to stack biodiversity units with units/credits from other nature markets (such as nutrient credits).[53] Moreover, where a development makes significant onsite gains in excess of the mandatory 10% level, the excess can be sold as registered offsite biodiversity gains for another development.[54]

---

46 By para 9(4) of Schedule 7A, the Secretary of State may by regulations increase (but not decrease) the 30-year period.

47 See Chapter 23 for the Conservation Covenant regime.

48 DEFRA, 'Make On-Site Biodiversity Gains as a Developer' (GOV.UK, 27 February 2024) <https://www.gov.uk/guidance/make-on-site-biodiversity-gains-as-a-developer> accessed 28 October 2024.

49 See para 10.22 above.

50 And as with onsite gains, by s 100(7) the Secretary of State may by regulations increase (but not decrease) the 30-year period.

51 DEFRA, 'Search the Biodiversity Gain Sites Register' (GOV.UK, 18 March 2024) <https://www.gov.uk/guidance/search-the-biodiversity-gain-sites-register> accessed 28 October 2024.

52 DEFRA, 'Sell Biodiversity Units as a Land Manager' (GOV.UK, 15 March 2024) <https://www.gov.uk/guidance/sell-biodiversity-units-as-a-land-manager> accessed 28 October 2024.

53 DEFRA and Natural England, 'Combining Environmental Payments: Biodiversity Net Gain (BNG) and Nutrient Mitigation' (GOV.UK, 12 February 2024) <https://www.gov.uk/guidance/combining-environmental-payments-biodiversity-net-gain-bng-and-nutrient-mitigation> accessed 28 October 2024.

54 DEFRA, 'Make On-Site Biodiversity Gains as a Developer' (n 48).

(vi) *Biodiversity credits*

10.26 The third means of satisfying the biodiversity gain objective is through purchasing biodiversity credits from the Secretary of State through the arrangements established under the EA 2021, section 101. By section 101(4), in determining the cost of a biodiversity credit, the Secretary of State is required to have regard to the need to determine an amount which does not discourage the registration of land in the biodiversity gain sites register. Biodiversity credits are also at the bottom of the biodiversity gain hierarchy. The purchase of biodiversity credits is therefore, as DEFRA Guidance makes clear,[55] a last resort option for developers who are unable to fully satisfy the biodiversity gain objective through onsite or offsite units. Developers buying statutory credits use the credit sales service, which requires a form (available online)[56] to be submitted to Natural England. Prices are reviewed every six months and at least 10 weeks' notice is given of changes.[57]

(vii) *The submission and determination of planning applications and the statutory BNG condition*

10.27 Although BNG under the TCPA 1990 operates by deemed imposition of a pre-commencement condition under paragraph 13 of Schedule 7A, BNG is not simply a post-permission matter. The biodiversity gain hierarchy would be undermined if BNG were not considered throughout the development process, including being factored into site selection and design, and this is expressly encouraged by the Planning Practice Guidance.[58]

10.28 Article 7 of the DMPO imposes detailed minimum requirements relating to BNG for planning applications made to planning authorities[59] and such authorities may also impose additional requirements in local lists.[60] There will therefore be considerable information on BNG which will be available for comment by consultees and consideration by the planning authority. The planning authority also has an important role in considering and determining issues relating to BNG in determining applications, as the Planning Practice Guidance emphasises.[61]

10.29 The general condition under paragraph 13 of Schedule 7A to the TCPA 1990 is, however, not imposed by the planning authority, but is deemed by the statute. It is imposed on every planning permission granted for the development of land in England (save those out of scope, and subject to certain transitional provisions and exceptions,

---

55 DEFRA and Natural England, 'Buy Statutory Biodiversity Credits' (GOV.UK, 21 May 2024) <https://www.gov.uk/guidance/buy-statutory-biodiversity-credits> accessed 28 October 2024.
56 ibid.
57 DEFRA, 'Statutory Biodiversity Credit Prices' (GOV.UK, 12 February 2024) <https://www.gov.uk/guidance/statutory-biodiversity-credit-prices> accessed 28 October 2024.
58 Ministry of Housing, Communities and Local Government, Planning Practice Guidance on 'Biodiversity Net Gain' (n 5) para 002.
59 Article 4 of the Town and Country Planning (Section 62A Applications) (Procedure and Consequential Amendments) Order 2013, SI 2013/2140 does the same for applications made directly to the Secretary of State.
60 Ministry of Housing, Communities and Local Government, Planning Practice Guidance on 'Biodiversity Net Gain' (n 5) paras 013, 015.
61 ibid paras 018–030.

addressed in paragraphs 10.37–10.42 below) and requires that development may not begin unless: (a) a biodiversity gain plan has been submitted to the planning authority; and (b) the planning authority has approved the plan. Article 35 of the DMPO provides requirements for information about BNG to be set out in decision notices,[62] and the Planning Practice Guidance provides suggested paragraphs.[63]

(viii) *The biodiversity gain plan*

10.30 The biodiversity gain plan sets out how the biodiversity gain objective of at least a 10% gain will be met for the development granted planning permission. By Article 37B of the DMPO, it must be submitted in writing and no earlier than the day after the day on which notification is given of the decision to grant planning permission (though a draft will often be submitted before planning permission is granted).

10.31 The planning authority for determining the biodiversity gain plan is normally, but not invariably, the local planning authority which granted the relevant planning permission, or which would have granted the planning permission had it not been granted by the Secretary of State or a person appointed by them.[64] A fee (currently £145) is payable under Regulation 16 of the Town and Country Planning (Fees for Applications, Deemed Applications, Requests and Site Visits) (England) Regulations 2012[65] (though this is refundable if the application is not determined within 12 weeks).

10.32 The required content of a biodiversity gain plan is specified in paragraph 14 of Schedule 7A of the TCPA 1990 and Article 37C of the DMPO. A standard template is available online.[66]

10.33 The determination of the biodiversity gain plan is governed[67] by paragraphs 15 and 16 of Schedule 7A to the TCPA 1990 and Article 37D of the DMPO. Under paragraph 15 of Schedule 7A, the planning authority must approve the plan if, and only if, it is satisfied:

- that the pre-development biodiversity value of the onsite habitat is as specified in the plan;
- that the post-development biodiversity value of the onsite habitat is at least the value specified in the plan;

62 Article 24 of the Town and Country Planning (Section 62A Applications) (Procedure and Consequential Amendments) Order 2013 does the same for applications made directly to the Secretary of State.
63 Ministry of Housing, Communities and Local Government, Planning Practice Guidance on 'Biodiversity Net Gain' (n 5) para 026.
64 See Schedule 7A to the TCPA 1990, paras 12A–12J and Ministry of Housing, Communities and Local Government, Planning Practice Guidance on 'Biodiversity Net Gain' (n 5) para 032.
65 SI 2012/2920.
66 DEFRA, 'Biodiversity Gain Plan' (GOV.UK, 9 October 2024) <https://www.gov.uk/government/publications/biodiversity-gain-plan> accessed 28 October 2024.
67 Special provisions apply in relation to irreplaceable habitats (see para 10.43 below) and phased developments (see para 10.44 below).

- that, in a case where any registered offsite biodiversity gain is specified in the plan as allocated to the development: (i) the registered offsite biodiversity gain is so allocated (and, if the allocation is conditional, that any conditions attaching to the allocation have been met or will be met by the time the development begins); and (ii) the registered offsite biodiversity gain has the biodiversity value specified in the plan in relation to the development;
- that any biodiversity credits specified in the plan as purchased for the development have been so purchased; and
- that the biodiversity gain objective is met.

10.34 By Article 37D(2) of the DMPO, in determining whether to approve the plan, the planning authority must take into account:

- how the biodiversity gain hierarchy is to be applied; and
- where any part of that hierarchy is not to be applied, the reason for that, or the absence of a reason.

10.35 By Article 37D(1) of the DMPO the time limit for giving written notice of determination of an application to approve a biodiversity gain plan is within 8 weeks beginning with the day after the day on which the plan is received, or such longer period as is agreed in writing.

10.36 There is a right of appeal under section 78 of the TCPA 1990 against a decision by a local planning authority to refuse to approve a biodiversity gain plan, or against a failure to take a decision in time.[68] There is no right of appeal where it is the Secretary of State who refuses (as planning authority) to approve a biodiversity gain plan, but such a refusal can be challenged in the High Court under the TCPA 1990, section 288.[69] A decision on a section 78 appeal is also challengeable in the High Court under the TCPA 1990, section 288.[70]

(ix) *Scope of BNG, transitional provisions, exceptions and exemptions*

10.37 By Regulation 2 of the Environment Act 2021 (Commencement No. 8 and Transitional Provisions) Regulations 2024, BNG was commenced on 12 February 2024 in respect of planning permission granted on an application made under Part 3 of the TCPA 1990, other than planning permission relating to development to which section 73A of the TCPA 1990 (planning permission for development already carried out) applies.

10.38 BNG has not yet been commenced for planning permissions granted through other routes than an application under Part 3 of the TCPA 1990, including local

68 See TCPA 1990 s 78 and Article 37E of the DMPO.
69 See TCPA 1990 s 284(3)(k).
70 See ibid s 284(3)(b).

development orders, simplified planning zones, neighbourhood development orders, enforcement appeals and deemed planning permissions. As the Planning Practice Guidance explains,[71] the grant of permission in principle is not within the scope of BNG (as it is not the grant of a planning permission), but the subsequent technical details consent (as a grant of planning permission) is. As the Planning Practice Guidance also explains,[72] the approval of reserved matters for outline planning permissions is not subject to the BNG condition (since such approval is not a grant of planning permission), but the grant of outline permission itself (as a grant of planning permission) is.

10.39 Regulations 3 and 4 of the Environment Act 2021 (Commencement No. 8 and Transitional Provisions) Regulations 2024 provide transitional provisions:

- By Regulation 3, the BNG condition does not apply in relation to a planning permission for which the application was made before 12 February 2024; and
- By Regulation 4, the BNG condition does not apply in relation to a section 73 planning permission where: (a) the original planning permission to which the section 73 planning permission relates was granted before 12 February 2024; or (b) the application for the original planning permission to which the section 73 application relates was made before 12 February 2024.

10.40 Paragraph 17(a) of Schedule 7A to the TCPA 1990 provides that the general biodiversity gain condition does not apply in relation to development for which planning permission is granted: (a) by a development order;[73] or (b) under section 293A (urgent Crown development).

10.41 Paragraph 17(b) enables the Secretary of State to provide further exceptions, and these are provided in the Biodiversity Gain Requirements (Exemptions) Regulations 2024. These provide exemptions in connection with:

- Small sites (a temporary exemption until 2 April 2024);[74]
- Developments below a de minimis threshold;
- Householder applications;
- The High Speed Railway Transport Network;
- Certain applications concerning Biodiversity Gain Sites; and
- Certain self-build and custom build applications.

---

71 Ministry of Housing, Communities and Local Government, Planning Practice Guidance on 'Biodiversity Net Gain' (n 5) para 003.
72 ibid.
73 So BNG does not apply in respect of permitted development rights, for example.
74 Though, by reg 3(2) of the Biodiversity Gain Requirements (Exemptions) Regulations 2024, the exemption continues to apply to s 73 planning permissions where the original planning permission was subject to the temporary exemption.

10.42 Guidance on the exceptions and exemptions is provided in the Planning Practice Guidance[75] and in DEFRA Guidance.[76]

(x) *Modifications for irreplaceable habitat*

10.43 Paragraph 18 of Schedule 7A permits the Secretary of State to make modifications and exclusions in relation to irreplaceable habitats, and this power has been exercised in making the Biodiversity Gain Requirements (Irreplaceable Habitat) Regulations 2024[77] and (so far as phased development is concerned) the Biodiversity Gain (Town and Country Planning) (Modifications and Amendments) (England) Regulations 2024. The irreplaceable habitats defined and listed in the regulations are: blanket bog; lowland fens; limestone pavements; coastal sand dunes; ancient woodland; ancient trees and veteran trees; spartina saltmarsh swards; and mediterranean saltmarsh scrub. The modifications are complex, but in essence,[78] for irreplaceable habitats the usual approach of requiring the biodiversity gain objective to be met is disapplied and instead the planning authority must be satisfied that any adverse effect is minimised and that appropriate arrangements (which cannot involve the purchase of biodiversity credits) have been made for the purpose of compensating for any impact.[79] It should also be noted that the statutory provisions do not displace the policy tests under paragraph 186(c) of the NPPF, by which development resulting in loss or deterioration of irreplaceable habitats should be refused, unless there are 'wholly exceptional reasons *and* a suitable compensation strategy exists' (emphasis added).

(xi) *Modifications for phased development*

10.44 Paragraph 19 of Schedule 7A permits the Secretary of State to make modifications in relation to phased developments, and this power has been exercised in making the Biodiversity Gain (Town and Country Planning) (Modifications and Amendments) (England) Regulations 2024. These adjust the standard approach by requiring: (i) an Overall Biodiversity Gain Plan to be submitted to and approved by the planning authority before the development can be begun; and (ii) a Phase Biodiversity Gain Plan for each phase of development to be submitted to and approved by the planning authority before the development of that phase can be begun. The Overall Biodiversity Gain Plan sets a framework for how the 10% gain for the whole development will be met, while each Phase Biodiversity Gain Plan sets out the phase's contribution to BNG and tracks progress towards the overall biodiversity gain objective for the development.

---

75 Ministry of Housing, Communities and Local Government, Planning Practice Guidance on 'Biodiversity Net Gain' (n 5) para 003.

76 DEFRA, 'Biodiversity Net Gain: Exempt Developments' (GOV.UK, 21 August 2024) <https://www.gov.uk/guidance/biodiversity-net-gain-exempt-developments> accessed 28 October 2024.

77 Article 37D(3) of the DMPO also disapplies Article 37D(2) in connection with irreplaceable habitat.

78 For detailed guidance on the BNG approach for irreplaceable habitats, see Ministry of Housing, Communities and Local Government, Planning Practice Guidance on 'Biodiversity Net Gain' (n 5) para 042 and DEFRA, 'Irreplaceable habitats' (GOV.UK, 4 September 2024) <https://www.gov.uk/guidance/irreplaceable-habitats> accessed 28 October 2024.

79 Ministry of Housing, Communities and Local Government, Planning Practice Guidance on 'Biodiversity Net Gain' (n 5) para 042 and DEFRA, 'Irreplaceable Habitats' (n 78).

Detailed guidance on BNG for phased developments is provided in the Planning Practice Guidance.[80]

(xii) *Section 73 applications*

10.45 As set out at paragraph 10.39 above, applications under the TCPA 1990, section 73 are only in scope for BNG if the original permission to which they relate was in scope.

10.46 For those section 73 applications in scope:

- Since the information required by Article 7(1A) of the DMPO will have been provided for the original application, by Article 7(1B) it is not required for a section 73 application.
- By section 73(2B) an application under section 73 cannot be used to vary or remove the general BNG condition.
- By section 73(2C) and (2D), where a planning permission granted under section 73 does not affect the post-development value of the onsite habitat, or the effect on the biodiversity of any irreplaceable habitat (including any arrangements made to compensate for any such effect), as specified in the biodiversity gain plan for the original permission, the earlier biodiversity gain plan is regarded as approved for the purposes of the new section 73 permission, and a new biodiversity gain plan is not required.

(xiii) *Minerals*

10.47 BNG requirements apply without modification for mineral permissions.[81] Such applications are often phased, however, and for these the modifications for phased development (addressed in paragraph 10.44 above) will apply. Review of Old Mineral Permissions ('ROMPs') are not within scope for BNG since they do not require planning permission.[82]

(xiv) *Monitoring and enforcement*

10.48 Monitoring and enforcement are generally matters for the local planning authority (so far as conditions and planning obligations are concerned) or the responsible body[83] (so far as conservation covenants are concerned[84]). Monitoring fees can be charged by local planning authorities through planning obligations, and an authority can use

---

80 Ministry of Housing, Communities and Local Government, Planning Practice Guidance on 'Biodiversity Net Gain' (n 5) paras 053–063.
81 ibid para 009.
82 ibid.
83 DEFRA, 'Enter a Legal Agreement for Biodiversity Net Gain' (GOV.UK, 4 October 2024) <https://www.gov.uk/guidance/legal-agreements-to-secure-your-biodiversity-net-gain> accessed 28 October 2024.
84 See Chapter 23 for the Conservation Covenant regime.

its ordinary enforcement powers to enforce against commencement in breach of the pre-commencement condition under TCPA 1990, paragraph 13 of Schedule 7A, and other breaches of conditions and planning obligations.[85] Responsible bodies can enforce conservation covenants.

(xv) *Plan-making and BNG*

10.49 The Planning Practice Guidance includes specific guidance on how plan-makers should deal with BNG.[86] It emphasises the policy at paragraph 185 of the NPPF that plans should pursue opportunities for securing measurable net gains for biodiversity. It also notes that plan-makers may seek a higher percentage than the statutory objective of 10% BNG, but emphasises that they should not do so unless justified, and that to justify such policies they will need to be evidenced including as to local need for a higher percentage, local opportunities for a higher percentage and any impacts on viability for development; and it indicates that consideration will also need to be given to how the policy will be implemented.

BNG in Nationally Significant Infrastructure Projects[87]

10.50 As noted at paragraph 10.01 above, mandatory BNG for Nationally Significant Infrastructure Projects ('NSIPs') is due to come into force in late November 2025.[88] At this stage, the primary legislation to be inserted into the PA 2008 by the EA 2021 is not in force and no draft secondary legislation is available. The full details of BNG for NSIPs are therefore not yet clear, and so we provide only a brief overview in this section.

10.51 The primary legislation is contained in section 99 of and Schedule 15 to the EA 2021, which will, from a date to be appointed, embed BNG for NSIPs through changes to sections 37, 103–105, 120 and 232 of the PA 2008 and the insertion of a new Schedule 2A to that Act.

10.52 The amendments to section 104 will, for decisions where a national policy statement has effect, prevent the granting of applications for development consent unless the biodiversity gain objective set out in an applicable biodiversity gain statement is met (with certain exceptions). The amendments to section 105 will do likewise in cases where no national policy statement has effect (again with certain exceptions).

10.53 The new Schedule 2A will make detailed provision in relation to BNG. By paragraph 1, the new Schedule will apply to all development consent order applications, to the extent that the development is carried out in England, that fall to be determined

---

85 Ministry of Housing, Communities and Local Government, Planning Practice Guidance on 'Biodiversity Net Gain' (n 5) para 007 emphasises that 'appropriately worded planning conditions and planning obligations would ... help achieve effective monitoring and enforcement of biodiversity net gain, particularly in relation to the maintenance and monitoring of significant onsite habitat enhancements and registered offsite biodiversity gains'.
86 Ministry of Housing, Communities and Local Government, Planning Practice Guidance on 'Biodiversity Net Gain' (n 5) para 006.
87 See Chapter 6 for commentary on NSIPs.
88 DEFRA, 'Understanding Biodiversity Net Gain' (n 4).

under section 104 or 105, unless the development is of a description excluded by regulations made by the Secretary of State. In its 2023 response to the 2022 consultation on BNG regulations and implementation, the government indicated that it intended to apply BNG for NSIPs without any broad exemptions other than the provision made (as with the TCPA 1990 regime) for development on irreplaceable habitats.[89]

10.54 Paragraph 2 to the new Schedule 2A defines 'biodiversity gain statement' and makes certain mandatory provision for such statements. Paragraph 3(1) then defines the 'biodiversity gain objective' as being 'an objective that the biodiversity value attributable to development to which a biodiversity gain statement relates exceeds the pre-development biodiversity value of the onsite habitat by a percentage specified in the statement'. By paragraph 3(2) the percentage must be at least 10%, but paragraph 3(3) empowers the Secretary of State by regulations to amend that up or down. No minimum period for securing BNG is set by Schedule 2A, but in its 2023 response to the 2022 consultation on BNG regulations and implementation, the government indicated that the minimum duration for which biodiversity gains must be secured will initially be set at 30 years, that this would be kept under review, and that it would be increased in line with any increases to the minimum for TCPA 1990 development.[90] The government response also indicated that it did not intend to facilitate lighter touch approaches to offsite biodiversity gains for NSIPs, and that it intended to stipulate that NSIP offsite gains will need, as with TCPA 1990 development, to be recorded in a biodiversity gain site register.[91]

10.55 Paragraphs 4 to 8 of Schedule 2A make detailed provision in relation to matters that may or must be specified in biodiversity gain statements. Paragraph 4 gives flexibility on the use of different metrics for calculating BNG, but in its March 2023 response on the Consultation on the Biodiversity Metric, the government indicated that the statutory metric for TCPA 1990 development would apply for BNG for NSIPs.[92]

10.56 Paragraph 9 of Schedule 2A then addresses the process where, at the time the new Schedule comes into force, an existing national policy statement sets out policy in respect of a description of development to which the Schedule applies. Paragraph 10 addresses the process where, at the time the new Schedule comes into force or any subsequent time, no national policy statement sets out policy in respect of a description of development to which the Schedule applies.

10.57 As can be seen from the above, at this stage, it appears that BNG for NSIPs is likely to operate in a broadly similar way to the regime for TCPA 1990 development, but much will depend on the precise terms of future legislation, guidance and biodiversity gain statements.

---

89 DEFRA, 'Government Response and Summary of Responses' para 4.3 (GOV.UK, 21 February 2023) <https://www.gov.uk/government/consultations/consultation-on-biodiversity-net-gain-regulations-and-implementation/outcome/government-response-and-summary-of-responses> accessed 28 October 2024.
90 ibid.
91 ibid.
92 DEFRA, 'Technical Consultation on the Biodiversity Metric' (n 18) page 25.

Marine Net Gain

10.58 The legislation governing BNG is currently limited to development on land and intertidal locations. However, once the new Schedule 2A to the PA 2008 is in force, the Secretary of State will have power (under paragraph 11 of that Schedule) by regulations to apply the Schedule, with or without modifications, to PA 2008 development in the English marine region.

10.59 Between 7 June and 13 September 2022, the government conducted a 'Consultation on the Principles of Marine Net Gain.'[93] This proposed that MNG (a concept adapting BNG to the marine environment) will apply to the majority of marine developments in English waters. It therefore proposed introducing MNG not only for PA 2008 development but also for other consenting/licensing regimes under the Marine and Coastal Access Act 2009 and the Petroleum Act 1998. The government published its response to the consultation on 9 December 2023,[94] confirming that it continued to intend to bring forward a mandatory MNG regime, that it would commission evidence needed to take its proposals forward, and that after it had developed its policy, it would consult again prior to implementation.

Environmental Net Gain

10.60 As noted in paragraph 10.07 above, the government's 25 Year Environment Plan, published on 11 January 2018, included a policy for embedding an ENG principle for development. That policy was reiterated in the 2022 consultation on MNG[95] and the 2023 government response to that consultation. The latter included the following definition of ENG:[96]

> Improving all aspects of environmental quality through a scheme or project. Achieving environmental net gain means achieving biodiversity net gain first, and going further to achieve net increases in the capacity of affected natural capital to deliver ecosystem services.

10.61 The government response to the MNG consultation confirmed that MNG will 'incorporate a wider environmental net gain approach but only where these extra benefits are underpinned by biodiversity enhancement'.

10.62 There are undoubtedly complexities in legislating for ENG, but it is a more holistic principle than BNG and therefore a worthy aspiration for future legislation.

---

93 DEFRA, 'Consultation on the Principles of Marine Net Gain' <https://consult.defra.gov.uk/defra-net-gain-consultation-team/consultation-on-the-principles-of-marine-net-gain/> accessed 28 October 2024.
94 DEFRA, 'Consultation Outcome Government Response' (GOV.UK, 9 December 2023) <https://www.gov.uk/government/consultations/consultation-on-the-principles-of-marine-net-gain/outcome/government-response> accessed 28 October 2024.
95 DEFRA, 'Consultation on the Principles of Marine Net Gain' (n 93).
96 DEFRA, 'Consultation Outcome Government Response' (n 94).

Case law on BNG

10.63 Given its novelty and complexity, BNG is likely to lead to a certain amount of litigation as the regime beds in. At this stage, however, there is only limited case law. The first case of note is *NRS Saredon Aggregates Ltd v Secretary of State for Levelling Up, Housing and Communities.*[97] In that case, in a decision dated 5 May 2023, an Inspector had dismissed an appeal for minerals development in which BNG of nearly 40% was secured. In so doing, he had afforded 'only moderate weight' to the BNG on the basis that 'some of the biodiversity net gain that would be achieved is required to meet national policy and future legislative requirements in order to mitigate the environmental impact of the development'. Eyre J found that to be an error of law, since the statutory regime for BNG had not, at the time of the Inspector's decision, commenced and would not operate retrospectively. The *Saredon* decision has since been followed by Holgate J in two judgments handed down on the same day (7 August 2024): *Vistry Homes Ltd v Secretary of State for Levelling Up, Housing and Communities*[98] and *R (Weston Homes plc) v Secretary of State for Levelling Up, Housing and Communities.*[99] In paragraphs 148 to 163 of the *Vistry* decision, Holgate J set out guidance to assist decision-makers when assessing the weight to attribute to BNG in planning decisions.

Issues in practice

10.64 BNG is a new regime, and it is therefore too early to give a firm view on issues arising in practice. Indeed, the effectiveness of the new regime will only be ascertainable in the long term. The TCPA 1990 part of the regime requires gains to be secured for at least 30 years and it is likely that the PA 2008 part will do likewise. But what will happen beyond that timescale is uncertain, and there is a clear risk of long-term environmental losses if harms are caused in perpetuity, but gains are secured for only 30 years. Even in the shorter term, it is not certain at this stage how effective the regime will be: a host of issues, from the appropriateness of the scope of BNG and its exemptions and exceptions to the detail of the metric and the operation of the biodiversity units market, will only become clear with experience.

10.65 The level of burden of the operation of the regime also remains to be seen. It inevitably imposes costs which will be easier for some developments to carry than others. It also requires considerable ecological expertise from both developers and decision-makers to operate effectively.

10.66 The BNG regime is undoubtedly a bold new approach, but it has yet to win its spurs. It is to be hoped that it will prove successful, that it will be sufficiently nimble in adapting to challenges that arise, and that it will broaden out in due course to embrace the wider ENG principle in both terrestrial and marine environments.

---

97 *NRS Saredon Aggregates Ltd v Secretary of State for Levelling Up, Housing and Communities* [2023] EWHC 2795 (Admin), [2024] Env LR 18.
98 *Vistry Homes Ltd v Secretary of State for Levelling Up, Housing and Communities* [2024] EWHC 2088 (Admin).
99 *R (Weston Homes plc) v Secretary of State for Levelling Up, Housing and Communities* [2024] EWHC 2089 (Admin).

CHAPTER 11

LOCAL NATURE RECOVERY STRATEGIES

Eleanor Leydon

Policy background to LNRSs

(i) *The Lawton Review*

11.01 As discussed in Chapter 8, the 2010 Lawton Review recommended that 'the essence of what needs to be done to enhance the resilience and coherence of England's ecological network can be summarised in four words: more, bigger, better and joined'.[1] The review recommended several key approaches which encompass these principles, broadly: improving the quality and quantity of current sites; enhancing connections between them; and reducing pressures on wildlife by improving the wider environment, including through buffering wildlife sites.

11.02 In its subsequent 2011 White Paper, the government committed to 'establish a clear institutional framework to achieve the recovery of nature'.[2] This was originally to involve establishing Local Nature Partnerships ('LNPs') and creating new Nature Improvement Areas ('NIAs') to enhance and reconnect nature on a significant scale. Twelve NIAs were selected for a trial period of government funding from 2012–2015,[3] representing an 'initial contribution' to the 'step-change' envisaged in the Lawton Review.[4] The 2015 final report set out that the trials had achieved 'substantial contributions to Biodiversity 2020 outcomes',[5] including maintaining or improving 13,664 hectares of existing priority habitat, and restoring or creating 4,625 hectares of new priority habitat, as well as restoring, creating or managing 225km of linear and boundary habitats, such as rivers and hedgerows.[6] These activities delivered multiple benefits, including improved habitat connectivity; development of recreational corridors; creation of open spaces; and the enhancement of ecosystem services.[7]

---

1 JH Lawton and others, 'Making Space for Nature: A Review of England's Wildlife Sites and Ecological Network. Report to DEFRA' (2010) 8.
2 Department for Environment Food and Rural Affairs, 'The Natural Choice: Securing the Value of Nature' (2011) Cm 8082 3 <https://assets.publishing.service.gov.uk/media/5a7cb8fce5274a38e57565a4/8082.pdf> accessed 26 March 2024.
3 'Nature Improvement Areas: About the Programme' (GOV.UK) <https://www.gov.uk/government/publications/nature-improvement-areas-improved-ecological-networks/nature-improvement-areas-about-the-programme> accessed 26 March 2024.
4 DEFRA and Natural England, 'Monitoring and Evaluation of Nature Improvement Areas: Final Report (2012–2015)' (2015) 127.
5 ibid.
6 ibid.
7 ibid 6, 16.

(ii) *The 25 Year Environment Plan ('25YEP')*

11.03 The 25YEP, published in 2018, set out a new government commitment to develop a Nature Recovery Network ('NRN') providing 500,000 hectares of additional wildlife habitat, to 'complement and connect our best wildlife sites' and provide opportunities to re-introduce lost species.[8] The 25YEP committed to explore what the NRN could look like, and to investigate implementing up to 25 new catchment or landscape-scale nature recovery areas.[9] Specific measures to be explored included peatland restoration, natural flood management, woodland planting and wildflower recovery areas, learning from the NIAs and other initiatives such as the Knepp Estate.[10]

Environment Act 2021: Local Nature Recovery Strategies

11.04 The EA 2021 provides for Local Nature Recovery Strategies ('LNRSs') covering the whole of England, placing spatial planning for nature on a statutory footing, and aiming to support local action on biodiversity by consistently mapping important existing habitats and opportunities to create or restore habitat.[11]

11.05 LNRSs are cross-cutting, in that they have been designed to work with other measures implemented via the EA 2021, such as Environmental Improvement Plans ('EIPs'), biodiversity targets and biodiversity net gain, to 'help join-up and delivery in a coherent and effective way'.[12] LNRSs will support both the delivery of the NRN and the effective implementation of biodiversity net gain in the planning system.[13] Public authorities must also have regard to them in complying with the general biodiversity objective.[14]

11.06 The main purpose of LNRSs is to identify locations to create or improve habitat most likely to provide the greatest benefit for nature and the wider environment.[15] As opposed to nature recovery actions, 'nature-based solutions' are those which support and draw on nature to provide wider environmental or societal benefits: having both

---

8 DEFRA, 'A Green Future: Our 25 Year Plan to Improve the Environment' (2018) 56–8 <https://assets.publishing.service.gov.uk/media/5ab3a67840f0b65bb584297e/25-year-environment-plan.pdf> accessed 4 April 2024.
9 ibid 59.
10 ibid 60.
11 EA 2021 Explanatory Notes, para 50.
12 Explanatory Memorandum to The Environment (Local Nature Recovery Strategies) (Procedure) Regulations 2023 No. 341 para 7.1. See however the OEP's previous criticism of the lack of clarity as to how the different measures will work together, and how much each measure is expected to contribute to the government's various targets and commitments: OEP, 'Progress in Improving the Natural Environment in England 2022/2023' (2024). DEFRA's Statutory Biodiversity Metric User Guide (published in February 2024 and updated in July 2024) explains how an LNRS should be used to assess the 'strategic significance' of a habitat to calculate its biodiversity value for the purposes of biodiversity net gain: DEFRA, 'Statutory Biodiversity Metric Tools and Guides' (GOV.UK, 6 August 2024) <https://www.gov.uk/government/publications/statutory-biodiversity-metric-tools-and-guides> accessed 14 October 2024.
13 Explanatory Memorandum to The Environment (Local Nature Recovery Strategies) (Procedure) Regulations 2023 No. 341. The strategies will identify where action to achieve the net gain will have the most impact: DEFRA, 'Local Nature Recovery Strategy Statutory Guidance: What a Local Nature Recovery Strategy Should Contain' (2023), para 7. See further Chapter 10 on Biodiversity Net Gain.
14 Natural Environment and Rural Communities Act 2006 s 40(2A). See further paras 8.05 and 8.96–8.98 in Chapter 8.
15 DEFRA, 'Local Nature Recovery Strategy Statutory Guidance' (n 13).

kinds of actions will, it is hoped, help to join up and improve how land is managed for different environmental reasons.[16]

11.07 Importantly, LNRSs do not oblige the owners and managers of the land identified (or indeed any other body) to make any changes to land. Instead, government is encouraging action through mandating the creation of cohesive spatial strategies and habitat maps which will, for example, identify opportunities for funding and investment.[17] LNRSs are thus likely to be most effective through the value assigned to mapped sites in the government's statutory biodiversity metric, used for the purposes of calculating biodiversity net gain.[18]

(i) *Preparing and reviewing an LNRS*

11.08 Section 104 of the EA 2021 provides that there are to be LNRSs for areas in England. The Act does not specify how many there must be. However, together they must cover the whole of England.

11.09 It is for the Secretary of State to determine the areas within England to which individual LNRSs will relate.[19] This is intended to allow flexibility, to ensure each area balances the need to align with existing administrative boundaries with the need for an area to be ecologically meaningful (based on the common geographic, geological, topographical or other physical features that help define an area's ecology, and of sufficient scale to include a range of habitats and land uses). It will also allow boundary alignment between neighbouring LNRS areas to avoid gaps or overlap. It was anticipated that LNRSs would be approximately county-scale, with variance to accommodate local circumstances.[20]

11.10 Pursuant to section 105(2) of the EA 2021, the Secretary of State may appoint a responsible authority for an LNRS, which may be a relevant local authority, the Mayor of London or mayor of another combined authority, a National Park authority or the Broads Authority, or Natural England.[21] The Secretary of State has appointed 48 responsible authorities covering the determined 48 strategy areas; the majority are county councils.[22]

---

16 ibid 5.
17 ibid 4.
18 See note 12 above, and see further Chapter 10 on Biodiversity Net Gain.
19 Subject to the requirement that the area of a local authority, other than a county council, may not be split between LNRSs. See EA 2021 s 104(3)–(4). The rationale for this is set out in EA 2021 Explanatory Notes, paras 948–949.
20 EA 2021 Explanatory Notes, para 946.
21 A county council or mayoral authority would be suitable for appointment where the LNRS area corresponds with county or mayoral boundaries. Where this is not the case, another local authority, mayoral authority or national park would be preferable to 'foster strong links between the LNRS and the land-use planning system and to benefit from existing local democratic mechanisms'. Natural England provides a final alternative. See ibid, para 954.
22 'Local Nature Recovery Strategies: Areas and Responsible Authorities' (GOV.UK, 11 March 2024) <https://www.gov.uk/government/publications/local-nature-recovery-strategies-areas-and-responsible-authorities> accessed 26 March 2024.

11.11 Responsible authorities must prepare and publish the LNRS for the strategy area, and must review and re-publish the LNRS 'from time to time'.[23] Updates may be periodic and/or may be triggered by the Secretary of State publishing an updated national habitat map under section 107(3). Information collected and published under the NERCA reporting duty[24] is expected to provide an important resource when reviewing and re-publishing an LNRS.[25]

11.12 Section 105 of the EA 2021 empowers the Secretary of State to make regulations providing for the procedure to be followed in the preparation of an LNRS (see further paragraphs 11.35–11.63 below).[26]

(ii) *Content of an LNRS: The statutory requirements*

11.13 An LNRS must include (a) a statement of biodiversity priorities for the strategy area and (b) one or more local habitat map/s,[27] which together cover the whole strategy area.[28] If a local habitat map does not relate to the whole strategy area, it must relate to the area of one or more local authorities within the strategy area.[29]

11.14 The statement of biodiversity priorities must include:[30]

(a) a description of the strategy area and its biodiversity,

(b) a description of the opportunities for recovering or enhancing biodiversity, in terms of habitats and species, in the strategy area,

(c) the priorities for recovering or enhancing biodiversity (taking into account the contribution this can also make to other environmental benefits), and

(d) proposals for potential measures relating to those priorities.[31]

11.15 A local habitat map is a map identifying any area within the strategy area which is:

---

23 EA 2021 s 105(1), (3).
24 Natural Environment and Rural Communities Act 2006 s 40A. See further paras 8.05 and 8.96–8.98 in Chapter 8.
25 EA 2021 Explanatory Notes, para 955.
26 EA 2021 s 105.
27 While LNRSs should consider both habitats and species, the focus is on habitats as these will indicate an area's general characteristics, including which species it may support. See DEFRA, 'Local Nature Recovery Strategy Statutory Guidance' (n 13), para 37.
28 EA 2021 s 106(1).
29 ibid s 106(4).
30 ibid s 106(2).
31 For example, rotational coppicing of native woodland to provide dormouse habitat or ditch-blocking to re-wet degraded peat to mitigate climate change. See DEFRA, 'Local Nature Recovery Strategy Statutory Guidance' (n 13), para 50.

(a) a national conservation site,[32]

(b) a Local Nature Reserve, and

(c) another area which in the responsible authority's opinion —

(i) is, or could become, of particular importance for biodiversity, or
(ii) where the recovery or enhancement of biodiversity could make a particular contribution to other environmental benefits.[33]

11.16 Subsection 106(3)(c)(i) aims to build on and seek to accommodate existing best practice, which is sometimes referred to as 'biodiversity opportunity mapping'.[34] The government is aware of more than a dozen examples of biodiversity opportunity maps previously produced by or for local authorities.[35] National Parks and Areas of Outstanding Natural Beauty ('AONBs') are expected to be particularly suitable places for areas identified under this provision, reflecting the increasing contribution of protected landscapes to nature recovery goals.[36] Subsection 106(3)(c)(ii) intentionally targets multiple benefits in the hope of increasing cost-efficiency, in turn making proposals more likely to be acted on.[37]

11.17 While local habitat mapping is fundamental to the operation of an LNRS, the proposals as to potential measures relating to local biodiversity priorities should include measures which can be used widely across the strategy area, even in sites which are not mapped for any particular reason, such as sowing native nectar-rich wildflowers or planting native hedgerows. This will enable and support an inclusive, broad approach, while retaining targeted nature goals.[38]

11.18 In March 2023, the Secretary of State issued statutory guidance as to the matters to be included in an LNRS, to which responsible authorities must have regard in preparing an LNRS.[39]

(iii) *Content of an LNRS: The statutory guidance*

11.19 Responsible authorities ('RAs') should prepare their strategy so that the statement of biodiversity priorities and local habitat map work 'closely' together. To do so, they should follow the following steps:

32 Defined as an SSSI; a National Nature Reserve declared pursuant to the Wildlife and Countryside Act 1981 s 35; a Ramsar site; a Marine Conservation Zone; or a European Site (EA 2021 s 108(3)).
33 For example, planting a new area of woodland for biodiversity would also sequester carbon, and could reduce the likelihood of downstream flooding. See EA 2021 Explanatory Notes, para 966.
34 EA 2021 s 106(3)(c)(i).
35 EA 2021 Explanatory Notes, para 965.
36 DEFRA, 'Local Nature Recovery Strategy Statutory Guidance' (n 13), para 84.
37 EA 2021 Explanatory Notes, para 966. This is in line with the Lawton Review: see JH Lawton and others (n 1).
38 DEFRA, 'Local Nature Recovery Strategy Statutory Guidance' (n 13), para 76.
39 ibid; EA 2021 s 106(5)–(6).

- Map areas of particular importance for biodiversity;
- Map areas where nature recovery action has taken place (when the strategy is reviewed);
- Describe the strategy area, its biodiversity and opportunities for recovery in the written statement;
- Agree priorities and identify potential measures for achieving them in the written statement;
- Map areas that could become of particular importance using the information in step 4.[40]

11.20 Steps 1 and 2 form part of the local habitat map, and feed in to Steps 3 and 4, which form the statement of biodiversity priorities. In turn, the information written in Step 4 is used in Step 5 to complete the map.[41]

11.21 RAs should take a 'consistent approach' to identifying other areas of particular importance for biodiversity, and should include all existing local wildlife sites; areas of irreplaceable habitat;[42] and any other areas identified by the Secretary of State as being of particular importance.[43] RAs are advised *not* to map any areas other than these as being of particular importance to biodiversity: that is not to say that other areas may not be important, but is intended to establish *a* 'nationally consistent baseline of areas' whose importance is already recognised, to help LNRSs align with planning policy and avoid duplicating with the identification of local wildlife sites. If an RA believes another area requires protection, it should coordinate with the relevant planning authority to discuss designation as a local wildlife site.[44]

11.22 RAs may need to consult with or request data from other parties, such as NE, other local authorities or other park authorities, to identify areas of particular importance (indeed, they are required to involve other bodies in preparing an LNRS – see the regulations at paragraphs 11.35–11.37). However, this step is 'not expected to require wide engagement' with partner organisations and should be 'comparatively quick to complete'.[45]

---

40 DEFRA, 'Local Nature Recovery Strategy Statutory Guidance' (n 13), para 20.
41 ibid.
42 ibid, paras 22, 24. The Statutory Guidance refers to upcoming government regulations which would establish a legal definition of irreplaceable habitat: this is now defined via Schedule 1 of The Biodiversity Gain Requirements (Irreplaceable Habitat) Regulations 2024.
43 DEFRA, 'Local Nature Recovery Strategy Statutory Guidance' (n 13), para 22.
44 ibid, paras 22–27.
45 ibid, para 29.

11.23 In setting their statement of biodiversity priorities, RAs should consider:

- the range of habitats in the strategy area and their general distribution (especially priority habitats, but RAs should also include habitats of local importance, including ones that support scarce or declining species);
- how this distribution and extent of habitats has changed in recent decades, including habitats which may have been lost entirely from the area;
- the species or groups of species for which the strategy area is, or could feasibly be, of national importance;
- anticipated future pressures likely to influence species or the extent, distribution or quality of different habitat types (including recognising the impact of climate change scenarios and anticipated new developments, including house building and infrastructure); and
- wider environmental issues affecting part or all of the strategy area which changes in land use or management could help to address (for example improvements to the water environment, flood risk management, or climate mitigation and adaptation).[46]

11.24 In setting their biodiversity priorities, RAs should also refer to relevant nationally held data provided by government, and a wide range of other available data and expertise from local partner organisations.[47]

11.25 When describing the strategy area, RAs should draw on other spatial plans such as local plans or RBMPs. RAs are also invited to recognise sub-areas which have similar topography, geology and soil type, and to take a joined-up approach with neighbouring RAs.[48] Particular guidance is given to coastal RAs on how to align with local authorities' boundaries and marine spatial planning.[49]

11.26 Statements of biodiversity priorities should reflect local circumstances and local issues, but also (where appropriate) the contribution that the strategy area can make to national environmental objectives and targets, including under the EA 2021 and the Climate Change Act 2008.[50]

11.27 RAs should 'seek support for their priorities' across the public, private and voluntary sectors, including though transparent, direct engagement.[51] RAs should also set out the potentially complex relationships between priorities and potential measures as

---

46 ibid, para 36.
47 ibid, paras 38–39. This should include working out arrangements for privately sharing sensitive or commercially valuable information.
48 ibid, paras 40–41.
49 ibid, paras 42, 59.
50 ibid, paras 52–58.
51 ibid, para 59–63.

clearly as possible, so they can be understood by local decision-makers, land managers and non-experts. RAs should avoid including any potential measures which are not likely to be implemented in the foreseeable future, since LNRSs should be 'practical, realistic and deliverable' documents.[52]

11.28 Finally, RAs should map areas which could *become* of particular importance (either to biodiversity or other environmental benefits); this should build on the distribution of existing habitats and areas identified in Step 1, so that areas can be joined-up or expanded, establishing more resilient networks of high-quality habitat. RAs should think across different scales, from narrow features such as hedgerows to landscape-scale changes.[53]

11.29 The proposed measures set out in the statement of biodiversity priorities may be applicable across the whole of the strategy area or may relate to particular areas identified on the local habitat map. Attention is drawn in particular to local wildlife sites, which do not require management plans, and to areas within the Green Belt and/or near homes which could become of particular importance. RAs may propose more than one measure in the same area, but should clarify whether one is particularly suitable for that area, whether there are equally effective options, or whether multiple measures could be carried out together.[54]

11.30 Some potential measures may entail a change in land use or management which requires a separate consent to be undertaken (such as planning permission). RAs do not need those consents to be in place in order to include an area on their maps as being of potential importance, but they should seek to involve the relevant consenting bodies, to avoid proposing measures in locations which are unlikely to be granted consent. RAs should also listen to land managers' views for land they are considering mapping as being of potential importance, such that if a land manager is very unlikely to choose to carry out a potential measure, alternative measures can be identified before consultation.[55]

(iv) *Information to be provided by the Secretary of State*

11.31 To assist responsible authorities in preparing an LNRS, the Secretary of State must prepare and publish a national habitat map for England.[56] The map must in particular identify (a) national conservation sites, and (b) other areas which the Secretary of State considers of particular importance for biodiversity. The Secretary of State may (but is not obliged to) review and re-publish the map from time to time.[57]

11.32 The Secretary of State must also inform responsible authorities of any area within their strategy area which:

---

52 ibid, paras 64–65, 67.
53 ibid, paras 73–75.
54 ibid, paras 80–82.
55 ibi, paras 87–89.
56 EA 2021 s 107(1).
57 ibid s 107(2)–(3).

- could be of greater importance for biodiversity, or is an area where the recovery or enhancement of biodiversity could make a contribution to other environmental benefits; and

- could contribute to the establishment of a network of areas for the recovery and enhancement of biodiversity in England as a whole.[58]

11.33 Whilst the intention is that the large majority of 'biodiversity opportunities' are identified locally by the responsible authority through a collaborative approach, these provisions also allow the Secretary of State to propose national priorities for an area. This could include future landscape-scale biodiversity projects.[59]

11.34 Finally, there is a general duty on the Secretary of State to provide a responsible authority with any other information they hold which might assist in preparing an LNRS.[60] This might include other mapped information, like climate change assessments, soils, geology or topography which are relevant to an area's biodiversity potential.[61]

Procedure for preparing an LNRS: The LNRS Regulations

11.35 The Environment (Local Nature Recovery Strategies) (Procedure) Regulations 2023 ('the LNRS Regulations'), made pursuant to section 105(5) EA 2021, set out the procedure to be followed in preparing and reviewing an LNRS. The aims are (1) to create consistency and maintain standards between LNRSs, and (2) to encourage a 'broad, collaborative approach to producing LNRSs, involving a wide range of stakeholders from public, private and voluntary sectors'.[62] The LNRS Regulations have been developed to work alongside the Statutory Guidance.[63]

11.36 In line with the above policy aims, the LNRS Regulations set out a role for 'supporting authorities' in the preparation of an LNRS.[64] Supporting authorities are those operating within an LNRS, which fall within the categories eligible for appointment as responsible authorities under section 105(2) (see paragraph 11.10 above), but which are not the responsible authority appointed for that area.[65]

11.37 An RA must take reasonable steps to involve all supporting authorities ('SAs') in the preparation of the LNRS.[66] In particular, the RA must ensure SAs are provided with relevant information; ensure that SAs are aware of how to contact the RA; and have regard to any opinions expressed by SAs.[67] An RA must also take reasonable steps

---

58 ibid s 107(4)–(5).
59 EA 2021 Explanatory Notes, para 977.
60 EA 2021 s 107(6).
61 EA 2021 Explanatory Notes, para 980.
62 ibid 957; Explanatory Memorandum to The Environment (Local Nature Recovery Strategies) (Procedure) Regulations 2023 No. 341, para 7.3.
63 ibid, para 7.4.
64 The Environment (Local Nature Recovery Strategies) (Procedure) Regulations 2023 reg 4.
65 ibid reg 3.
66 ibid reg 4(1).
67 ibid reg 4(2).

to involve 'such persons and organisations' as they consider appropriate in preparing an LNRS.[68] RAs should involve stakeholders across the public, private and voluntary sectors and help them work together.[69] An RA must consider and keep under review which persons and organisations it intends to involve, how, and with which aspects of the statement of biodiversity priorities and local habitat map.[70]

11.38 Per the Statutory Guidance, RAs should apply the following principles when working with partners:

- Transparency: be able to show how partner contributions have been considered, how decisions have been made, and what the basis for them is;
- Inclusivity: enable everyone with an interest to be involved where possible;
- Clear communication: avoid using technical terms that may not be understood by partners and end users.

11.39 This aims to ensure that LNRSs are technically sound, benefit from local knowledge, and have the support from partners to help achieve successful delivery.[71]

11.40 An RA must publish its relevant contact details online, together with details of the progress of an LNRS and any nascent reviews or re-publications.[72]

11.41 In preparing an LNRS, an RA must take reasonable steps to ascertain the location and area of every local nature reserve, and every other site recognised by the relevant local planning authority ('LPA') as justifying protection for its value to biodiversity, which is wholly or partly within the strategy area.[73] An LPA which receives a request for information regarding such sites must provide it within 28 days, unless there is a legitimate reason why the information should not become publicly available.[74]

(i) *Pre-consultation steps*

11.42 In preparing its consultation draft and final draft LNRS, an RA should bear in mind the above three principles, and create practical documents which can be understood by a range of landowners, managers, decision-makers and other interested parties.[75] The statement of biodiversity priorities should be concise, clearly structured and written in plain English, while the local habitat map should be similarly clear and accessible.[76]

---

68 ibid reg 3(3).
69 DEFRA, 'Local Nature Recovery Strategy Statutory Guidance' (n 13) 6.
70 The Environment (Local Nature Recovery Strategies) (Procedure) Regulations 2023 reg 4(4)–(5).
71 DEFRA, 'Local Nature Recovery Strategy Statutory Guidance' (n 13) 12–4.
72 The Environment (Local Nature Recovery Strategies) (Procedure) Regulations 2023 reg 5.
73 ibid reg 6(1).
74 ibid reg 6(2)–(3).
75 DEFRA, 'Local Nature Recovery Strategy Statutory Guidance' (n 13) 94.
76 ibid 94–5.

11.43 An RA must provide all SAs with the consultation draft of its LNRS for their comments; it must then also provide a copy to all neighbouring RAs within a reasonable time.[77] SAs have an opportunity to raise a reasoned written objection within 28 days, about either the LNRS itself or the RA's preparation of the LNRS, including the extent to which it has involved the SA.[78]

11.44 Where an SA raises an objection, the RA may write to the Secretary of State requesting permission to consult on the LNRS: it must enclose a copy of the LNRS, the objection, and all relevant correspondence. It must also set out any steps taken to address the SA's objection, and explain why the RA considers it reasonable for the consultation to proceed.[79] The RA must then immediately provide a copy of the request to their SAs, and confirm this has been done.[80] Within 14 days of receiving a copy of the request, an SA may submit relevant information to the Secretary of State.[81]

11.45 The Secretary of State must decide whether to permit the RA to consult within 14 days of the SAs receiving their copies of the request. Permission may be subject to conditions. The Secretary of State must in particular have regard to the reasonableness of the objection, any steps taken to address the objection, the RA's explanation as to the reasonableness of proceeding to consultation, and the RA's conduct. The Secretary of State must inform all SAs of their decision.[82]

11.46 An RA must comply with regulations 5–8 before consulting. It must also wait 28 days from the date SAs were provided with the consultation draft, or all the SAs give written confirmation that they are content for consultation to proceed.[83] Additional requirements apply where the RA has received an objection.[84]

11.47 Consultation is mandatory, and responses must be published within a reasonable time upon conclusion.[85]

(ii) *Pre-publication obligations to supporting authorities*

11.48 Once consultation has concluded, an RA must provide a copy of the LNRS to all SAs and inform them in writing of the intended publication date. It must subsequently provide a copy to all neighbouring RAs within a reasonable time.[86]

11.49 Where an SA considers that (a) part of the final LNRS cannot be justified based on the consultation results, or (b) that the final LNRS is 'materially deficient', it may give a publication advisory notice to the RA in writing within 28 days of receiving the

---

77 The Environment (Local Nature Recovery Strategies) (Procedure) Regulations 2023 regs 7–8.
78 ibid reg 9.
79 ibid reg 10(1)–(3).
80 ibid reg 10(4).
81 ibid reg 10(5).
82 ibid reg 10(5)–(9).
83 ibid reg 11(1)–(2).
84 ibid reg 11(3)–(4).
85 ibid reg 12.
86 ibid regs 13–4.

final LNRS, explaining its reasoning. The SA must also give a copy of the notice to the Secretary of State within a reasonable time.[87]

11.50 On receipt of a publication advisory notice, an RA must investigate the matters raised, and reply to the SA in writing within 28 days, setting out the results of its investigation and any further steps it has taken or intends to take. An RA must provide a copy of its reply to the Secretary of State within a reasonable time.[88]

11.51 Where an RA has received a publication advisory notice from an SA, and the SA has not subsequently informed the RA that it is content for the RA to publish the LNRS, the RA may write to the Secretary of State requesting permission to publish the LNRS. An RA must first have investigated the matters raised and replied to the notice. A request to publish an LNRS must enclose a final copy, and such other information considered relevant.[89]

11.52 As soon as reasonably practical after making a request to publish, the RA must provide a copy of the request to all its SAs, along with a copy of the publication advisory notice made by the objecting SA. The RA must confirm in writing to the Secretary of State the date and method by which they have done this.[90] An SA which receives a copy of the request may within 14 days submit relevant information to the Secretary of State.[91]

11.53 Upon receiving a request for permission to publish an LNRS, the Secretary of State must wait 28 days from the date SAs were informed before making a decision. The Secretary of State must ultimately grant permission to publish the LNRS once this time has elapsed, but permission may be conditional or unconditional. The Secretary of State must inform all SAs of their decision.[92]

(iii) *Further pre-publication obligations*

11.54 The above requirements apply where an SA has raised an objection to a final LNRS. In any event, an RA must give reasonable notice in writing to the Secretary of State of its intention to publish a final LNRS, including the intended publication date, the website details, and the final LNRS itself. This must be provided in an 'editable electronic format', with the relevant parts[93] either separated or capable of being separated to be combined with other LNRSs.[94]

11.55 It is mandatory to have concluded the statutory consultation process, and notified the Secretary of State of intention to publish, prior to publishing an LNRS. An RA

87 ibid reg 15(1)–(6).
88 ibid reg 15(7)–(10).
89 ibid reg 16(1)–(4).
90 ibid reg 16(5).
91 ibid reg 16(6).
92 ibid reg 16(7)–(9).
93 Defined in detail at ibid reg 17(5).
94 ibid reg 17.

must also wait 28 days from the date on which the final LNRS was provided to all SAs, or until all SAs confirm in writing that they are content with publication. Additional requirements apply where an RA has received a publication advisory notice from an SA.[95]

(iv) *Publishing an LNRS*

11.56 An RA must publish its final LNRS online, to a known website address, and must also make hard copies available for inspection at its office. An RA may not change a published LNRS, other than in accordance with the regulations, without the written agreement of the Secretary of State.[96]

11.57 The Statutory Guidance was published in March 2023, and the LNRS Regulations were laid before Parliament the same month, coming into force on 13 April 2023. RAs began to consult on their draft strategies in early 2024. As at 14 October 2024, some consultations are ongoing, and no RA has yet published their LNRS.[97]

(v) *Reviewing an LNRS*

11.58 As set out above, RAs are under an obligation to periodically review and re-publish an LNRS 'from time to time'.[98] Under regulation 20 of the LNRS Regulations, the Secretary of State must from time to time give written notice to an RA of the need to review its LNRS.[99] The notice must specify a date before which the review must begin, which must be between four and eight months following the date of the notice. It must also give 'indicative dates' for completion of the review and re-publication.[100]

11.59 The first such notices must be given to each RA between three and ten years of the LNRS Regulations coming into force on 13 April 2023. Subsequent notices must also be given at intervals of between three and ten years.[101]

11.60 A review must include a review of the two mandatory elements of an LNRS, and must assess progress in achieving the biodiversity priorities; any actions taken to enable areas to become of particular importance for biodiversity; and any actions taken to recover or enhance biodiversity for the purpose of achieving environmental benefits.[102] RAs are strongly encouraged to record the specific locations of any such actions in their re-published local habitat map, but only where the action has or is expected to bring about significant or lasting positive change rather than minor, short-term or uncertain benefits (having consulted with Natural England if necessary).[103] Consideration

---

95 ibid reg 18.
96 ibid reg 19.
97 DEFRA's Statutory Biodiversity Metric User Guide (n 12) specifies how the 'strategic significance' of habitat should be assessed using alternative documents where an LNRS has not yet been published.
98 EA 2021 s 105(3).
99 The Environment (Local Nature Recovery Strategies) (Procedure) Regulations 2023 reg 20.
100 ibid reg 20(1)–(2).
101 ibid reg 20(3)–(4).
102 ibid reg 20(6).
103 DEFRA, 'Local Nature Recovery Strategy Statutory Guidance' (n 13), paras 30–31.

of which measures have or have not been carried out will inform an open process of amending the list of potential measures before re-publishing.[104]

11.61 RAs should use both information provided by local partners and published information – such as section 40A NERCA 2006 reports and the biodiversity gain site register – to undertake their reviews.[105]

11.62 Where changes to a local authority's area or the boundary of the strategy area may affect a published LNRS, the RA must consider the effect of those changes as part of its review.[106] In any review, the RA must have regard to the indicative dates for publication.[107]

11.63 An RA must have completed its review under regulation 20 before providing SAs with the consultation draft of the LNRS, and beginning the new process of consultation and pre-publication steps.[108]

(vi) *Delivering an LNRS*

11.64 Responsible authorities should contribute to the delivery of their strategy as well as leading its preparation. However, they are not solely responsible for delivery: it is also envisaged that public, private and voluntary sector partners will play a role.[109]

Conclusion

11.65 LNRSs sit alongside a variety of nature recovery measures implemented in the EA 2021: they are expected to contribute to the government's nature recovery goals, including its statutory biodiversity targets, through agreeing local priorities for nature recovery and proposing actions in areas which can make a particular contribution to achieving those priorities.[110] The EA 2021 does not require that any specific action must be carried out under an LNRS, but intends that the proposals will guide the efforts of public bodies and their partners, with responsible authorities then being required to review progress periodically.[111] LNRSs are thus likely to be most effective through the value assigned to mapped sites in the government's statutory biodiversity metric, used for the purposes of calculating biodiversity net gain. It also remains to be seen whether the detailed consultation and pre-publication requirements set out in the LNRS Regulations, intended to drive dialogue between public authorities, are proving a barrier to effective implementation, or whether these requirements will produce long-term benefits.

104 ibid para 72; EA 2021 s 106(2)(d).
105 DEFRA, 'Local Nature Recovery Strategy Statutory Guidance' (n 13), para 32.
106 The Environment (Local Nature Recovery Strategies) (Procedure) Regulations 2023 reg 20(7)–(8).
107 ibid reg 20(9).
108 ibid reg 7(2).
109 DEFRA, 'Local Nature Recovery Strategy Statutory Guidance' (n 13), para 10.
110 'Local Nature Recovery Strategies' (GOV.UK) <https://www.gov.uk/government/publications/local-nature-recovery-strategies/local-nature-recovery-strategies> accessed 26 March 2024.
111 ibid.

11.66 The OEP's 2024 report on the government's progress in improving the natural environment under the EIPs, and progress towards the statutory biodiversity targets, states that a decision-making framework to manage competing demands on land is 'critical' to mitigating climate change and meeting the statutory Net Zero and nature targets.[112] This should be provided by LNRSs, together with the Land Use Framework, but at present these spatial plans remain a 'major gap'.[113] The OEP recommends that the design, development and delivery of these plans is accelerated, if they are to be effective.[114] At the time of going to print, no LNRS has yet been published.

112 Office for Environmental Protection (n 12) 6, 41.
113 ibid 41.
114 ibid.

CHAPTER 12

AGRICULTURE AND LAND USE

Eleanor Leydon and Daniel Kozelko

The role of agriculture in achieving the UK's net zero and biodiversity targets

12.01 Agriculture is both a significant driver of climate change and biodiversity loss – making agricultural changes vital to meeting our statutory and international net zero and biodiversity targets – and an activity which is vulnerable to ecosystem collapse and the effects of climate change. Rising temperatures will increase crop pests and livestock diseases, while extreme weather events and catastrophic harvest failures will increase food supply chain volatility and lead to higher prices, higher vulnerability to famine, food riots and conflict.[1] This is not just a future problem: it is estimated that climate change has already lowered global farming productivity by 21%.[2]

(i) *The global picture*

12.02 Globally, the food system[3] (in particular, beef and other livestock farming) is the single biggest contributor to biodiversity loss, deforestation, drought, freshwater pollution and the collapse of aquatic wildlife.[4] Globally, the food system is also, after the energy industry, the second-biggest contributor to climate change.[5] This occurs through:[6]

- the damage done when wild areas are converted to farmland, or when farmland is prevented from reverting to forest;
- the release of carbon from farmland soil – particularly peat soils;
- the use of fossil fuels across the food system; and
- the release of methane and nitrous oxide from agriculture (by far the largest factor in the UK).

1 National Food Strategy Independent Review, 'Part Two: The Plan' (2021) 10 and 34 <https://www.nationalfoodstrategy.org/wp-content/uploads/2021/07/National-Food-Strategy-The-Plan.pdf> accessed 24 April 2024.
2 National Food Strategy Independent Review, 'The Evidence' (2021) 11 <https://www.nationalfoodstrategy.org/the-report/> accessed 26 April 2024.
3 This is defined as 'agriculture, food production, distribution and retail combined', of which agriculture accounts for 46% of emissions: NFS Independent Review: The Plan (n 1) 73–74.
4 ibid 10 and 73; NFS Independent Review: The Evidence (n 2) 9–10.
5 NFS Independent Review: The Plan (n 1) 10 and 73.
6 ibid 10 and 73.

12.03 Agriculture – particularly livestock agriculture – is a significant source of land use, which carries a significant opportunity cost in terms of using land as a carbon sink, and/or for nature recovery.[7] Of the 50% of Earth's habitable land used for agriculture, a tremendous 77% is used either to graze animals directly or to produce crops to feed to animals.[8] The global mass of farm animals is now 22 times heavier than that of all wild animals combined.[9]

12.04 Agriculture is responsible for 50% of global methane emissions, mainly through ruminant livestock (chiefly cows and sheep) and rice production.[10] The methane produced by ruminants is estimated to have caused a third of global warming since the industrial revolution.[11] Rapidly reducing methane emissions from both agriculture and the fossil fuel industry could reduce temperature rises this century by 0.25 degrees.[12] Meanwhile, the process of producing ammonia (which is used for fertiliser) accounts for 1% of global carbon emissions, while the conversion of fertiliser spread on land into nitrous oxide adds a further 2%.[13]

12.05 Intensive agriculture also damages soil health, which is integral to ecosystem services including food production and flooding mitigation.[14]

(ii) *The domestic picture*

12.06 Domestically, agricultural production is responsible for 11% of greenhouse gas emissions,[15] with overall food system production accounting for 20% of domestic emissions (rising to 30% if consumption emissions are also considered).[16] Agriculture in the UK currently emits 54.6 million tonnes of carbon ($MtCO_2e$) per year, while land use – mainly carbon emissions from soil converted for agriculture – emits a further

---

7 ibid 92. Mapping of domestic priority areas for both biodiversity and carbon storage shows that the two can be effectively protected together: NFS Independent Review: The Evidence (n 2) 37. For further discussion of agriculture's carbon opportunity costs, see Timothy D Searchinger and others, 'Assessing the Efficiency of Changes in Land Use for Mitigating Climate Change' (2018) 564 Nature 249 <https://www.nature.com/articles/s41586-018-0757-z> accessed 26 April 2024, which estimates that while the official carbon footprint of an average UK diet is 5.4 tonnes per capita per year, the total carbon opportunity costs amount to 9 tonnes. For further discussion of the nature opportunity costs, see J Poore and T Nemecek, 'Reducing Food's Environmental Impacts through Producers and Consumers' (2018) 360 Science 987, which demonstrates that a plant-based diet would release 76% of the land currently used for farming.

8 NFS Independent Review: The Plan (n 1) 8 and 17; NFS Independent Review: The Evidence (n 2) 8.

9 NFS Independent Review: The Evidence (n 2) 7.

10 NFS Independent Review: The Plan (n 1) 74.

11 ibid.

12 ibid.

13 ibid.

14 House of Commons Environment, Food and Rural Affairs, *Soil Health* (HC 2023–24, 245) 3 <https://committees.parliament.uk/publications/42415/documents/210844/default/> accessed 24 April 2024.

15 As at 2021: DEFRA, 'Agriculture in the UK Dashboard: Agri-Environment – Emissions from Agriculture' <https://defra-farming-stats.github.io/auk-dashboard/#emissions-from-agriculture> accessed 26 March 2024; Climate Change Committee, 'Progress in Reducing Emissions: 2023 Report to Parliament' (2023) 241 <https://www.theccc.org.uk/wp-content/uploads/2023/06/Progress-in-reducing-UK-emissions-2023-Report-to-Parliament.pdf> accessed 4 April 2024. Note that the CCC only consider production and not consumption emissions: the NFS Review considers both.

16 NFS Independent Review: The Plan (n 1) 73.

12.8 $MtCO_2e$ (totalling 67 $MtCO_2e$ per year).[17] This figure has remained virtually unchanged since 2008.[18] Methane and nitrous oxide released from ruminant animals account for two third of the UK's farming emissions:[19] while agriculture is responsible for just 2% of UK carbon dioxide emissions, it accounts for 49% of UK methane emissions, 71% of nitrous oxide emissions, and 87% of ammonia emissions.[20]

12.07 Of all UK land, 70% is estimated to be agricultural, far exceeding our built-up land, peat, and broadland woods.[21] Of this, 85% is used either to graze livestock or produce crops to feed animals (providing 32% of our calories), with just 15% of UK agricultural land being used to grow the grains, fruit and vegetables we directly consume (providing 68% of our calories).[22] This is a 'wildly inefficient use of land'.[23] UK consumption of beef and lamb takes up not only 40% of our own land mass, but also an area three times the size of Wales overseas.[24] In contrast, ground-mounted solar panels currently take up just 0.1% of UK land (230km^2).[25]

12.08 Agriculture is the single largest source of water pollution in England (responsible for 25% of phosphorus pollution, 50% of nitrate pollution and 75% of sediment pollution).[26] The impacts of diffuse water pollution include eutrophication, increased flood risk, the silting of fish spawning grounds, and pollution of bathing waters.[27]

12.09 Government data shows that in the UK, all farmland birds have decreased by 56% since 1970.[28] The ecological health of agricultural land must also include consideration of soil health: see further paragraphs 12.102–12.104 below.

(iii) *The role of agriculture and land use in decarbonising and nature recovery*

12.10 As reported by the National Food Strategy Independent Review in July 2021, 'every credible model for reaching net zero' requires both that the food system cuts its own emissions, and that it relinquishes agricultural land to be used in ways that

---

17 Climate Change Committee, 'The Sixth Carbon Budget: The UK's Path to Net Zero' (2020) 163 <https://www.theccc.org.uk/wp-content/uploads/2020/12/The-Sixth-Carbon-Budget-The-UKs-path-to-Net-Zero.pdf> accessed 26 April 2024. It is a UNFCCC convention to separate agricultural emissions from land use emissions – for more information on the relationship between agriculture, LULUCF and AFOLU, see Peter Iversen, Donna Lee, and Marcelo Rocha, 'Understanding Land Use in the UNFCCC' (2014) <https://ghginstitute.org/wp-content/uploads/2015/04/Understanding_Land_Use_in_the_UNFCCC.pdf> accessed 26 April 2024.
18 NFS Independent Review: The Plan (n 1) 87; Department of Business, Energy and Industrial Strategy, '2019 UK Greenhouse Gas Emissions, Final Figures' (2021) <https://assets.publishing.service.gov.uk/media/60198cd5d3bf7f70bc2e1ee7/2019_Final_greenhouse_gas_emissions_statistical_release.pdf> accessed 26 April 2024.
19 NFS Independent Review: The Plan (n 1) 76.
20 DEFRA, 'Agriculture in the UK Dashboard: Agri-Environment – Emissions from Agriculture' (n 15).
21 NFS Independent Review: The Plan (n 1) 89–91; NFS Independent Review: The Evidence (n 2) 38; see also DEFRA, 'Agriculture in the UK Dashboard: Structure – Land Use' <https://defra-farming-stats.github.io/auk-dashboard/#land-use> accessed 26 March 2024, which calculates a very similar 69%.
22 NFS Independent Review: The Plan (n 1) 91; NFS Independent Review: The Evidence (n 2) 38.
23 NFS Independent Review: The Plan (n 1) 109.
24 ibid.
25 Carbon Brief, 'Factcheck: Is Solar Power a 'Threat' to UK Farmland?' (25 August 2022) <https://www.carbonbrief.org/factcheck-is-solar-power-a-threat-to-uk-farmland/> accessed 26 March 2024.
26 *R (River Action) v Environment Agency* [2024] EWHC 1279 (Admin) [8].
27 ibid 9.
28 DEFRA, 'Agriculture in the UK Dashboard: Agri-Environment – Biodiversity' <https://defra-farming-stats.github.io/auk-dashboard/#biodiversity> accessed 27 March 2024.

sequester carbon.[29] Some industries, such as air travel or steel production, will remain heavily dependent on fossil fuels for years: using land to sequester carbon is the only large-scale method available for mopping up these emissions.[30]

12.11 In January 2020, the Climate Change Committee ('CCC') produced its first in-depth advice on UK agricultural policies,[31] which argued that a major shift in UK land use was needed to deliver net zero emissions.[32] The CCC's analysis showed that UK land-use emissions could be reduced by 64% to around 21 $MtCO_2e$ by 2050, without producing less food in the UK or increasing imports from elsewhere.[33] The objectives for new policy were increasing tree planting, encouraging low-carbon farming, restoring 50% of upland peat and 25% of lowland peat, expanding bioenergy crops, and reducing food waste and beef, lamb and dairy consumption by at least 20% per person.[34]

12.12 The CCC's report on setting and meeting the sixth carbon budget, published in December 2020,[35] set out a range of pathways to meeting net zero by 2050, including a main 'Balanced Pathway', a more pessimistic 'Headwinds' scenario, and more optimistic Widespread Engagement, Widespread Innovation and 'Tailwinds' scenarios.[36]

12.13 The CCC report that meeting the sixth carbon budget 'requires action across four key areas', which include reducing demand for carbon-intensive activities (meat and dairy, waste, flights and other travel), and a transformation in land use, including a substantial increase in tree planting, bioenergy production, peatland restoration, and wide adoption of low-carbon farming practices.[37] The choices made in the sectors of agriculture, land use, aviation and greenhouse gas removals have the greatest impact on the UK's residual greenhouse gas emissions in 2050 and the scale and type of negative emissions that are required to offset them.[38]

12.14 Under the Balanced Pathway, combined agriculture and land emissions fall from 67 $MtCO_2e$ in 2018 to 40 $MtCO_2e$ by 2035, reaching residual emissions of 16 $MtCO_2e$

29 NFS Independent Review: The Plan (n 1) 87.
30 ibid.
31 CCC, 'Land Use: Policies for a Net Zero UK' (2020) <https://www.theccc.org.uk/wp-content/uploads/2020/01/Land-use-Policies-for-a-Net-Zero-UK.pdf> accessed 26 April 2024.
32 CCC, 'Major Shift in UK Land Use Needed to Deliver Net Zero Emissions' (23 January 2020) <https://www.theccc.org.uk/2020/01/23/major-shift-in-uk-land-use-needed-to-deliver-net-zero-emissions/> accessed 26 March 2024.
33 ibid.
34 These measures would cost around £1.4 billion per year, but generate wider benefits worth £4 billion per year.
35 CCC, 'The Sixth Carbon Budget: The UK's Path to Net Zero' (n 17).
36 ibid. The 'Balanced Pathway' makes moderate assumptions on behavioural change and innovation and assumes action is taken in the 2020s to develop options including hydrogen and/or electrification expansion for later roll-out: CCC, 'The Sixth Carbon Budget: The UK's Path to Net Zero' (n 17) 24. The 'Headwinds' scenario assumes less progress in societal/behavioural change and/or innovations, and is more reliant on large hydrogen and CCS infrastructure: Climate Change Committee, 'The Sixth Carbon Budget: The UK's Path to Net Zero' (n 17) 45–46. The Tailwinds scenario aims to achieve net zero as quickly as possible (finding that even in a 'highly optimistic' scenario, net zero is only achieved in 2042): Climate Change Committee, 'The Sixth Carbon Budget: The UK's Path to Net Zero' (n 17) 87.
37 CCC, 'The Sixth Carbon Budget: The UK's Path to Net Zero' (n 17) 25.
38 ibid 95.

by 2050.[39] As emissions from agriculture and aviation will not reach net zero, these will need to be offset by removals from the forestry carbon sink and greenhouse gas removals deployed at scale starting in the 2020s.[40] In the Balanced Pathway model, 9% of agricultural land will need to be used for actions to reduce emissions and sequester carbon by 2035, with 21% needed by 2050.[41] This analysis balances climate mitigation considerations with the requirements of maintaining food production and climate adaptation: it requires investment of £1.5 billion per year by 2035, but will bring co-benefits for health and recreation, air quality, flood alleviation and biodiversity.[42]

12.15 The CCC's most recent annual report to Parliament[43] notes that to meet the UK's NDC (nationally determined contribution) goal of at least a 68% reduction in territorial emissions by 2030, the rate of emissions reductions outside the power sector must almost quadruple, with faster progress needed in tree planting among other sectors, and a focus needed on reducing demand for high-carbon activities.[44] One key message of the report is that '[t]he slow progress to date on delivery towards Net Zero means that it is no longer tenable for the government to develop strategies that do not contain committed policies. Policies with immediate delivery are needed, in parallel with development of new strategic visions.'[45]

12.16 A further key message is the need to develop demand-side and land-use policies: given risks of shortfalls in delivery elsewhere, further policy strengthening in these areas may be required.[46] The areas in which action is 'significantly off track' include agriculture and land use (as well as surface transport, electricity supply, and buildings).[47] New woodland and peatland restoration in particular are significantly off track.[48] Interestingly, despite the ongoing roll-out of Environmental Land Management schemes ('ELMs') discussed below, the CCC report that funding and financial incentives in agriculture are significantly off-track.[49] In the land-use sector, the CCC refer to the extant Land Use Framework, and note that '[l]and use and agriculture in England remains one of the few sectors where the government has not set out a coherent, strategic approach to coordinated policy to meet the multiple needs for land'.[50]

---

39 The two biggest sources of emissions savings by 2035 are forestry and diet change, food waste and other land release: diet change is the most significant land release measure. The Balanced Pathway involves a 20% shift away from meat and dairy products by 2030, with a further 15% reduction of meat products by 2050: the Widespread Engagement, Widespread Innovation and Tailwinds scenarios imply just a 50% reduction in meat and dairy by 2050. See CCC, 'The Sixth Carbon Budget: The UK's Path to Net Zero' (n 17) 163–165 and 169.
40 ibid 65.
41 ibid 163.
42 ibid.
43 CCC, 'Progress in Reducing Emissions: 2023 Report to Parliament' (n 15).
44 ibid 13 and 25.
45 ibid 27.
46 ibid 14. Recommendations for specific DEFRA actions are set out at 409.
47 ibid 20.
48 ibid 21.
49 ibid 23.
50 ibid 27.

12.17 The CCC observed that the government's Carbon Budget Delivery Plan ('CBDP'), published in March 2023,[51] sets out plans to reduce agricultural and land-use emissions by 29% by 2035, compared to 2021 levels – 32% fewer emissions savings than those envisaged in the 2021 Net Zero Strategy ('NZS').[52] Around a third of relevant abatement in the CBDP is assigned to speculative technological and innovative measures: the CCC advise that 'failing to address demand-side measures properly raises risks that emissions reductions will be insufficient, and that land is not released for sequestration. This will result in a missed opportunity for climate policy across the agriculture and land-use sectors, with benefits for human health'.[53] Further, national targets for tree planting and peatland restoration are currently not being met and require a 'dramatic increase'.[54] In relation to ELMs, the CCC report that a lack of clarity on policy funding details is hampering uptake, which requires stability and confidence in policies, but that there has been some improvement since 2022.[55] Finally, the CCC advise that 'a comprehensive UK land use strategy is still urgently needed'.[56]

Environmental provisions within domestic agricultural law

12.18 This chapter will focus on the key legal framework governing agricultural law post-Brexit – the Agriculture Act 2020 and Agriculture (Wales) Act 2023 – and the corresponding development of schemes for incentivising farmers to take environmental actions on their land. It will also consider other retained and post-Brexit environmental controls on diffuse agricultural pollution, and the role of agricultural land classification in planning policy.

12.19 Environmental provisions in earlier domestic agricultural statutes include:

- Section 20 of the Hill Farming Act 1946 and related regulations placing restrictions on heather, grass and peat burning;[57]
- Part IV of the Agriculture Act 1970, providing for controls on the sale of fertilisers and feeding stuffs;
- Section 17 of the Agriculture Act 1986, which creates a duty on the Secretary of State to balance rural economic and social interests with the conservation and enhancement of the natural beauty and amenity of the countryside (including its flora and fauna and geological and physiographical features);

51 Department for Energy Security and Net Zero, 'Carbon Budget Delivery Plan' HC 2023, 1269 <https://assets.publishing.service.gov.uk/media/6424b2d760a35e000c0cb135/carbon-budget-delivery-plan.pdf> accessed 4 April 2024.
52 CCC, 'Progress in Reducing Emissions: 2023 Report to Parliament' (n 15) 242.
53 ibid.
54 ibid 242–243.
55 ibid.
56 ibid 244.
57 The Heather and Grass etc. Burning (England) Regulations 2007, SI 2007/2003; The Heather and Grass etc. Burning (Wales) Regulations 2008, SI 2008/1081; The Heather and Grass etc. Burning (England) Regulations 2021, SI 2021/158. The 2021 regulations prohibit burning specified vegetation on areas of peat over 40 cm deep in SSSIs which are also European sites.

- Section 18 of the Agriculture Act 1986, which empowers the Secretary of State to designate environmentally sensitive areas where this appears particularly desirable for conservation purposes, and to enter into management agreements with interested persons;

- Parts I, II, IIA, III and VI of the Environmental Protection Act 1990, dealing with integrated pollution control, waste on land, contaminated land, statutory nuisance and clean air, and genetically modified organisms;

- Sections 5–6, Chapter 1A of the Environment Act 1995, setting out general duties on the conservation bodies in respect of pollution control and water;

- Sections 97–98 of the Environment Act 1995, empowering the Secretary of State to make provision for the protection of important hedgerows and for conservation grants, and the associated regulations;[58]

- The Countryside and Rights of Way Act 2000 and Natural Environment and Rural Communities Act 2006;

- Various Environmental Impact Assessment Regulations[59] (see further Chapter 7); and

- The Conservation of Habitats and Species Regulations 2017 (see further paragraphs 9.78ff in Chapter 9).

Agricultural law and policy pre- and post-Brexit

12.20 Up until 31 January 2020, when the UK left the EU, domestic agricultural policy operated within the EU's Common Agricultural Policy ('CAP'), which comprised two pillars of support for farmers. Pillar 1, the main pillar of CAP funding, consisted of three compulsory direct payments: payments under the basic payment scheme ('BPS'), the 'greening payment' and the Young Farmer's Payment. Payments made under the BPS were based on the area of land farmed.

12.21 Pillar 2 provided for a Rural Development Programme, with support measures including payments to farmers who voluntarily adopted agri-environmental commitments. Domestically, rural development payments were made under land-based agreements such as Environmental Stewardship ('ES') and Countryside Stewardship ('CS'),

---

58 For hedgerows, see the The Hedgerows Regulations 1997, SI 1997/1160. For conservation grants, see the Environmental Stewardship (England) Regulations 2005, SI 2005/621, and Countryside Stewardship (England) Regulations 2020, SI 2020/41 regs 3(1) and 6(1).

59 Mainly The Environmental Impact Assessment (Agriculture) (England) (No.2) Regulations 2006, SI 2006/2522 and The Environmental Impact Assessment (Agriculture) (Wales) Regulations 2017, SI 2017/565, but see also The Environmental Impact Assessment (Land Drainage Improvement Works) Regulations 1999, SI 1999/1783, The Environmental Impact Assessment (Forestry) (England and Wales) Regulations 1999, SI 1999/2228, and The Water Resources (Environmental Impact Assessment) (England and Wales) Regulations 2003, SI 2003/164.

administered by the Rural Payments Agency ('RPA') in England and Rural Payments Wales ('RPW') in Wales.

12.22 Further, any farmer claiming payments under either pillar had to comply with certain environmental conditions, known as the 'cross-compliance' conditions.

12.23 In addition to the cross-compliance conditions, from 2014, under the 'greening' rules farmers had to adhere to three practices (crop diversification, maintenance of permanent grassland, and ecological focus areas) or environmentally equivalent practices.

12.24 It has long been recognised that the CAP, and in particular the BPS, caused significant environmental damage: as set out in the 25 Year Environment Plan ('25YEP'), in paying farmers according to the amount of land they own, the BPS 'concentrates money in the hands of those who already have significant private wealth, without improving environmental outcomes'.[60] Efforts to improve this by way of the 'greening' rules were found to be largely ineffective. In the UK, of the £3.2 billion spent under the CAP, £2.59 billion was spent under the BPS, with just £0.64 billion spent on environmental stewardship programmes under Pillar 2.[61]

12.25 It was therefore recognised that Brexit presented an opportunity to fundamentally transform the focus of agricultural policy, towards a system of 'public money for public goods', and in particular environmental enhancement.[62]

12.26 In England, the new policy focus on public money for public goods is underpinned by the Agriculture Act 2020 ('AA 2020'),[63] which empowers the Secretary of State to give financial assistance in connection with a range of environmental purposes (as well as improving productivity). These powers are being exercised to introduce new ELMs across the 'agricultural transition period' from 2021–2027,[64] while at the same time steadily reducing and phasing out direct payments.[65] England is currently halfway through its agricultural transition period.

12.27 In Wales, the primary statute is the Agriculture (Wales) Act 2023, which establishes a similar framework of Sustainable Land Management ('SLM'), to be delivered

---

60 DEFRA, 'A Green Future: Our 25 Year Plan to Improve the Environment' (2018) 36 <https://assets.publishing.service.gov.uk/media/5ab3a67840f0b65bb584297e/25-year-environment-plan.pdf> accessed 4 April 2024.
61 ibid.
62 See, in England, DEFRA, *Health and Harmony: The Future for Food, Farming and the Environment in a Green Brexit* (Cm 9577, 2018) <https://assets.publishing.service.gov.uk/media/5a952ad9e5274a5b849d3ad1/future-farming-environment-consult-document.pdf> accessed 26 April 2024; the 25YEP. As for Wales, see the National Assembly for Wales' Climate Change, Environment and Rural Affairs Committee, 'The Future of Land Management in Wales' (2017) <https://senedd.wales/laid%20documents/cr-ld10995/cr-ld10995-e.pdf> accessed 26 April 2024 Recommendations 16, 18, 20 and 23. The Rock Review has recommended that food security is also defined as a public good: DEFRA, 'Independent Report – The Rock Review: Summary and Recommendations' (2023) <https://www.gov.uk/government/publications/the-rock-review-working-together-for-a-thriving-agricultural-tenanted-sector/the-rock-review-summary-and-recommendations> accessed 26 March 2024.
63 Explanatory Notes to AA 2020 para 1.
64 AA 2020 s 8(1).
65 DEFRA, 'The Path to Sustainable Farming: An Agricultural Transition Plan 2021 to 2024' (2020) <https://assets.publishing.service.gov.uk/media/60085334e90e073ec94cc80b/agricultural-transition-plan.pdf> accessed 26 April 2024.

through the Sustainable Farming Scheme ('SFS'): see further paragraphs 12.61–12.64 below.

12.28 ELM is intended to make a 'significant contribution' to meeting most, if not all,[66] of the environmental goals set out in the 25YEP and 2023 Environmental Improvement Plan ('EIP'), as well as the '30by30' target[67] and statutory targets set under the EA 2021, in particular the biodiversity targets (see further Chapter 8, in particular paragraphs 8.49–8.59). Indeed, the government expects farmers and land managers to contribute to at least 50% of the target of bringing protected sites into favourable condition by 2042, and 80–100% of the 2042 target for restoring or creating 500,000 hectares of 'wildlife-rich habitat' outside of protected areas. The 2023 EIP envisages that:[68]

- by 2028, 70% of agricultural land and 70% of farm holdings will be 'covered by our new farming schemes'; and
- by 2030, 65–80% of farmers will adopt nature friendly farming on at least 10–15% of their land.

12.29 A further key statutory target is the Agricultural Water Target focused on reducing agricultural diffuse pollution: see further paragraphs 12.84ff below. There are also a number of woodland grants available under current CS agreements, and the government is running a tree health pilot scheme from 2021–2024 to inform the design of future ELMs schemes, indicating that agriculture will also contribute to the statutory woodland and tree cover targets.[69]

Agriculture Act 2020 and ELMs

12.30 This section will focus on the AA 2020 insofar as germane to climate change and biodiversity, in particular Part 1, which underpins the new system of financial assistance based on the principle of public money for public goods. Other aspects of the AA 2020 – for example, the provisions relating to reports on free trade agreements – are beyond the scope of this book.

---

66 In addition to farming's general relevance to nature recovery and climate mitigation and adaptation, ammonia emissions from agriculture (87% of UK ammonia emissions, over half of which derive from dairy and intensive beef farms) contribute to poor air quality and biodiversity loss, and nutrient pollution from agriculture contributes to poor water quality. Control of pesticides through Integrated Pest Management will also contribute to what is now Goal 4. For a detailed discussion of the contribution of agricultural measures to each goal, see DEFRA, 'Environmental Improvement Plan 2023: First Revision of the 25 Year Environment Plan' (2023) <https://assets.publishing.service.gov.uk/media/64a6d9c1c531eb000c64fffa/environmental-improvement-plan-2023.pdf> accessed 4 April 2024.

67 DEFRA, 'The Path to Sustainable Farming: An Agricultural Transition Plan 2021 to 2024' (n 65) 16.

68 DEFRA, 'Environmental Improvement Plan 2023: First Revision of the 25 Year Environment Plan' (2023), 19 and 32 (n 66).

69 Namely that by 31 December 2050, at least 16.5% of all land in England should be covered by woodland and trees outside woodland, compared to a 2022 baseline of 14.5% coverage: see the Environmental Targets (Woodland and Trees Outside Woodland) (England) Regulations 2023, SI 2023/90.

(i) *New financial assistance powers*

12.31 Section 1(1), (3) of the AA 2020 empowers the Secretary of State to give financial assistance in England for or in connection with any one or more of the following purposes –

(a) managing land or water in a way that protects or improves the environment;[70]

(b) supporting public access to and enjoyment of the countryside, farmland or woodland and better understanding of the environment;[71]

(c) managing land or water in a way that maintains, restores or enhances cultural or natural heritage;[72]

(d) managing land, water or livestock in a way that mitigates or adapts to climate change;[73]

(e) managing land or water in a way that prevents, reduces or protects from environmental hazards;[74]

(f) protecting or improving the health or welfare of livestock;

(g) conserving[75] native livestock, native equines or genetic resources relating to any such animal;

(h) protecting or improving the health of plants;[76]

(i) conserving plants grown or used in carrying on an agricultural, horticultural or forestry activity, their wild relatives or genetic resources relating to any such plant;

(j) protecting or improving the quality of soil.

12.32 In addition to the purposes set out above, the Secretary of State may also give financial assistance in England for or in connection with the purpose of starting, or improving the productivity of, an agricultural, horticultural or forestry activity, and/or

---

70 This is a broad provision. The Explanatory Notes refer to environmental outcomes listed in the 25YEP such as cleaner air, clean and plentiful water and thriving plants and wildlife. For example, the subsection could be used to improve air quality by creating financial incentives for the targeted planting of trees to help capture ammonia emissions and protect nearby sensitive habitats from damaging nitrogen deposition: Explanatory Notes to AA 2020 para 17.
71 Including a better understanding of agroecology: AA 2020 s 1(5).
72 Including uplands and other landscapes: AA 2020 s 1(5).
73 Peatland restoration would fall within this provision: Explanatory Notes to AA 2020 para 20.
74 For example, improving soil water infiltration and porosity to mitigate against flooding: Explanatory Notes to AA 2020 para 21.
75 'Conserving' includes restoring or enhancing a species' population or a habitat: AA 2020 s 1(5).
76 Including wild plants, agricultural and horticultural crops, trees and bushes: Explanatory Notes to AA 2020 para 24. This could include support for measures across the forestry and horticultural sectors.

supporting ancillary activities by or for a producer.[77] Improving productivity includes (a) improving the quality of products deriving from the activity, and (b) improving the efficiency of the activity; ancillary activities mean selling, marketing, preparing, packaging, processing or distributing products deriving from an agricultural, horticultural or forestry activity.[78] While the government envisages that there will be some actions which will improve both productivity and environmental benefits,[79] there is plainly some potential tension between the purposes set out in subsections (1) and (2).

12.33 Financial assistance may be given to beneficiaries including, but not limited to, farmers, foresters and those responsible for the management of land.[80]

12.34 In framing any financial assistance scheme, the Secretary of State must have regard to the need to encourage the production of food by producers in England and its production by them in an environmentally sustainable way.[81]

12.35 Section 2 of the AA 2020 provides that financial assistance may be given by way of grant, loan or guarantee or in any other form, and may be given subject to such conditions as the Secretary of State considers appropriate, which may include provision under which the financial assistance is to be repaid or otherwise made good. Financial assistance may be given to the maker or operator of any third party scheme,[82] in connection with expenditure involved in operating the scheme. The Secretary of State may delegate functions relating to the giving of financial assistance, and may make regulations requiring the publishing of specified information about financial assistance which has been given.[83]

12.36 Under section 3 of the AA 2020, the Secretary of State may make regulations providing for monitoring of whether eligibility criteria for receipt of financial assistance are met (and the consequences if not); enforcing compliance with conditions, monitoring the extent to which the relevant purpose has been achieved; and the investigation of suspected offences (including fraud).[84]

12.37 The Agriculture (Financial Assistance) Regulations 2021 came into force on 26 March 2021, making provision for the award of financial assistance under four financial assistance schemes: the environmental land management pilot scheme, the countryside stewardship scheme, the farming investment fund scheme, and the tree health pilot scheme (see further paragraphs 12.68ff below). The regulations make provision for the submission of additional information and the correction of obvious defects; for

---

77 AA 2020 s 1(2).
78 AA 2020 s 1(5).
79 Explanatory Notes to AA 2020 para 27. For example, precision equipment for slurry application will increase efficiency at the same time as reducing ammonia emissions.
80 Explanatory Notes to AA 2020 para 16.
81 AA 2020 s 1 (4), (6).
82 Any scheme for giving financial support which is not made by the Secretary of State: AA 2020 s 2(5). For example, this would enable the Secretary of State to fund local partnerships or other organisations or bodies (such as National Parks) to deliver a project that supports public access to and enjoyment of the countryside, farmland or woodland: Explanatory Notes to AA 2020 para 37.
83 AA 2020 s2(6)–(8).
84 Explanatory Notes to AA 2020 para 48.

checking, monitoring and record keeping; for the transfer of agreements; the publication of relevant data; powers of entry and inspection; and investigating breaches of the regulations and suspected offences. The regulations do not themselves set out eligibility criteria, which are instead set out in the relevant scheme guidance.

(ii) *Multi-annual financial assistance plans, reports and monitoring*

12.38 The Secretary of State must from time to time prepare a 'multi-annual financial assistance plan', giving information about the expected use of their section 1 powers during the plan period, including setting out the government's strategic priorities during the period and describing the schemes which are, or will be, in operation during the period.[85] The first plan period is 1 January 2021 – 1 January 2028 (covering the agricultural transition period), and the plan was published on 30 November 2020,[86] supported by the Agricultural Transition Plan.[87] The government's strategic priorities during the agricultural transition period are:[88]

- encourage increased sustainable productivity in the agricultural sector;
- significantly contribute to meeting the goals set out in the 25YEP;
- contribute to meeting the UK's net zero carbon emissions goal by 2050;
- protecting and improving the health and welfare of livestock.

12.39 Subsequent plan periods must be at least five years, with the plan being published at least 12 months before the beginning of the plan period. A subsequent plan must be in place before the previous plan period expires.[89] Plans must be laid before Parliament and published. Where, during a plan period, the government's strategic priorities change or any information describing the relevant financial assistance schemes becomes inaccurate or incomplete, the Secretary of State must amend and republish the plan.[90]

12.40 The Secretary of State must have regard to the strategic priorities set out in the plan when determining (a) what financial assistance to give, and (b) the overall budget for, or for any period of operation of, a financial assistance scheme.[91]

12.41 From 2021–2022 onwards, the Secretary of State must prepare an annual report about the financial assistance given during each financial year, which must include the

---

85 AA 2020 s4(1)–(2).
86 DEFRA, 'Multi Annual Financial Assistance Plan for the Plan Period 2021 to 2027' (2020) <https://www.gov.uk/government/publications/agriculture-multi-financial-assistance-plan-2021-to-2027/multi-annual-financial-assistance-plan-for-the-plan-period-2021-to-2027> accessed 26 April 2024.
87 DEFRA, 'The Path to Sustainable Farming: An Agricultural Transition Plan 2021 to 2024' (n 65) 64.
88 DEFRA, 'Multi Annual Financial Assistance Plan for the Plan Period 2021 to 2027' (n 86).
89 AA 2020 ss 4(3)–(5).
90 AA 2020 ss 4(6)–(8).
91 AA 2020 s 4(9).

total amount of financial assistance given, as well as certain information about each financial assistance scheme in operation during the year.[92]

12.42 The Secretary of State may also prepare interim reports within a financial year, and other reports about the amount of financial assistance that has been given.[93] Any report prepared under section 5 of the AA 2020 must be laid before Parliament and published.[94]

12.43 Pursuant to section 7 of the AA 2020, the Secretary of State must monitor the impact of each financial assistance scheme, and make one or more reports on the impact and effectiveness of the scheme, having regard to the findings. They must do the same in respect of any financial assistance given otherwise than under a financial assistance scheme.[95] The Secretary of State has a broad discretion as to the manner of monitoring, appropriate period of monitoring, and the number and frequency of reports; however, every report must be laid before Parliament and published.[96]

(iii) *Direct payments after Brexit*

12.44 On leaving the EU on 31 January 2020, direct EU legislation was incorporated into UK law under section 3 of the European Union (Withdrawal) Act 2018, and is now assimilated law.[97] However, the Direct Payments Regulation (Regulation (EU) No 1307/2013 of the European Parliament and of the Council of 17 December 2013) was expressly disapplied in the UK for the year 2020.[98] Accordingly, the Direct Payments to Farmers (Legislative Continuity) Act 2020 was passed on 30 January 2020, to provide a legal basis to continue paying direct payments to farmers across the UK in 2020.[99] The AA 2020 provides powers for the Secretary of State to modify the retained direct and subordinate EU legislation governing direct payments[100] in relation to England,[101] and provides the legal basis for direct payments to continue beyond 2020 during the agricultural transition period, with the direct payments ceiling being determined by the Secretary of State.[102]

12.45 The modification power can only be exercised to serve certain purposes, such as simplifying the administration of the basic payment scheme, or removing or reducing 'burdens':[103] there is an express power for the Secretary of State to terminate greening payments in relation to England before the end of the agricultural transition period, so

92 AA 2020 s 5(1)–(5).
93 'Other reports' may cover a period of several years: AA 2020 s 5(6); Explanatory Notes to AA 2020 para 72.
94 AA 2020 s 5(7)–(8).
95 AA 2020 s 6(1)–(2).
96 AA 2020 s 6(3)–(5).
97 Retained EU Law (Revocation and Reform) Act 2023 s 5.
98 The EU–UK Withdrawal Agreement Article 137.
99 Explanatory Notes to the Direct Payments to Farmers (Legislative Continuity) Act 2020 paras 1–20.
100 Note that the 'basic payment scheme', and payments under the basic payment scheme, are defined as including greening payments and young farmers payments: AA 2020 ss 7(2) and 7(5).
101 AA 2020 ss 7(2)–(3) and 9.
102 AA 2020 s 10.
103 AA 2020 ss 9(1) and 9(3).

long as this does not reduce the amount of a direct payment a person would have been entitled to overall.[104]

12.46 The Secretary of State may also provide for phasing out direct payments under the basic payment scheme across the agricultural transition period, by reducing them in amount.[105] In line with the approach set out in the Agricultural Transition Plan, direct payments under the basic payment scheme were progressively reduced between 2021 and 2024, with funding instead invested into piloting and delivering the new ELMs.[106]

12.47 Under section 12(1) of the AA 2020, the Secretary of State may provide for the making of 'delinked payments' in place of direct payments under the basic payment scheme, during a 'delinking period' within the latter portion of the agricultural transition period. The 'Delinked Payments Regulations'[107] came into force on 1 January 2024, defining the 'delinking period' as 1 January 2024 – 31 December 2027.[108] Unlike direct payments, delinked payments are not based on the amount of land owned, and there is no requirement for the recipient to continue to own land or keep farming it.

12.48 Upon the coming into force of the Delinked Payments Regulations, the basic payment scheme in England ceased to exist.[109] Instead of direct payments, the Secretary of State must make annual delinked payments to eligible persons,[110] to be calculated in accordance with reg 5 and Schedule 1. Essentially, a 'reference amount' will be calculated for a person for each year within the delinking period, which will be the average amount paid to that person in direct payments in the 'reference period' of 1 January 2020–31 December 2022. The Secretary of State may adjust the reference amount to reflect any alterations to payments made to or in respect of a person under the basic payment scheme, and must adjust it to offset any lump sum payment, or in accordance with paragraph 4, Schedule 1.[111] As with direct payments, the intention is to progressively reduce delinked payments until the end of the agricultural transition period.

12.49 Eligible persons are those who were eligible for and claimed direct payments in 2023, have a reference amount calculated in respect of them, and (where applicable) have complied with any request for further information or evidence.[112] Reference amounts may be transferred between persons (reg 8, Schedule 2). The Delinked Payments

104 AA 2020 s 9(2).
105 AA 2020 ss 11(1) and 11(3).
106 DEFRA, 'The Path to Sustainable Farming: An Agricultural Transition Plan 2021 to 2024' (n 65) 64.
107 The Agriculture (Delinked Payments and Consequential Provisions) (England) Regulations 2023.
108 ibid regs 2 and 4.
109 ibid regs 15–17. Schedules 3 and 4 deal with revocations, savings (in particular for the purposes of finally determining outstanding rights and liabilities arising in respect of applications for direct payments made prior to 31 December 2023) and consequential amendments.
110 ibid regs 3 and 6.
111 Further guidance for farmers on delinked payments is available at DEFRA and Rural Payments Agency, 'Delinked Payments: Replacing the Basic Payment Scheme' (2022) <https://www.gov.uk/guidance/delinked-payments-replacing-the-basic-payment-scheme> accessed 6 February 2024.
112 The Agriculture (Delinked Payments and Consequential Provisions) (England) Regulations 2023 reg 6.

Regulations also provide for the making and recovery of delinked payments,[113] and for an appeals process.[114]

12.50 The coming into force of the Delinked Payments Regulations also removes the powers under section 11(1) of the AA 2020 and any associated regulations to phase out direct payments under the basic payments scheme (as the basic payments scheme has ceased to exist).[115]

(iv) *The end of cross-compliance*

12.51 The Agricultural Transition Plan also set out that 'when we delink Direct Payments, we will stop using cross-compliance as the basis for regulation and enforcement or scheme compliance and will move to a new approach that we will co-design with the sector' between 2021 and 2024.[116] Consulting during the early transition would allow a new regulatory approach to be implemented from 2024, which would set out 'a clear distinction, and coherent relationship, between the basic requirements farmers are obliged to meet by law, and scheme standards where they are paid to go beyond this minimum'.[117]

12.52 The 'Removal of Cross-Compliance Regulations'[118] also came into force on 1 January 2024, meaning that the previously retained cross-compliance requirements will not apply to delinked payments.

12.53 The Removal of Cross-Compliance Regulations thus revoke a number of previously assimilated EU Regulations and related domestic regulations,[119] and make further amendments to assimilated EU Regulations which are not revoked.[120] They also provide for savings for the revoked provisions so far as is necessary for the purposes of determining any outstanding rights and liabilities arising in respect of the cross-compliance framework.[121] The terms and conditions of Countryside Stewardship and Environmental Stewardship agreements (see below at paragraphs 12.74–12.79) have also been updated to reflect the end of cross-compliance.[122]

12.54 No impact assessment was produced in relation to either the Removal of Cross-Compliance Regulations or the Delinked Payments Regulations, and the promised new regulatory approach to compliance has not yet been clearly articulated. In bringing forward the Delinked Payments Regulations, Lord Benyon stated that:[123]

---

113 ibid regs 9–10.
114 ibid regs 11–14.
115 AA 2020 s 12(7).
116 DEFRA, 'The Path to Sustainable Farming: An Agricultural Transition Plan 2021 to 2024' (n 65) 10 and 14.
117 ibid 15.
118 The Agriculture (Removal of Cross-Compliance and Miscellaneous Revocations and Amendments, etc.) (England) Regulations 2023.
119 ibid pt 1 sch 1.
120 ibid regs 3–7.
121 ibid pt 2 sch 1.
122 Rural Payments Agency, 'Guidance: Cross Compliance' (2023) <https://www.gov.uk/guidance/cross-compliance> accessed 6 February 2024.
123 HL Deb 13 December 2023, vol 834, col 1923.

> [W]hen cross-compliance ends, farm standards will be maintained through existing and ongoing domestic regulations that protect the environment, the public, animal and plant health and animal welfare … the rules within cross-compliance that are not in underlying domestic legislation will have cover through existing and forthcoming guidance, regulation or incentives. We will deliver a fair, clear and effective system to regulate agriculture.

12.55 'Incentives' is understood to refer to the Sustainable Farming Incentive ('SFI') strand of ELMs (see below at paragraphs 12.69–12.73). Concerns have however been expressed about the increased uncertainty for farmers and risk of regulatory gaps in environmental protections that are presently ensured via cross-compliance (in particular, in relation to hedgerows, soil cover and watercourse buffer strips that will not be covered by the Farming Rules for Water).[124] Following a consultation, in March 2024 DEFRA confirmed its intention to replicate the hedgerows protections previously set out in the cross-compliance rules in forthcoming regulations.[125] The Management of Hedgerows (England) Regulations 2024 came into force in May 2024.

12.56 Neither direct payments nor delinked payments are to be made in relation to England after the end of the agricultural transition period (currently 31 December 2027). However, the Secretary of State may, before the end of the agricultural transition period, extend that period by way of regulations.[126]

(v) *The Lump Sum Exit Scheme*

12.57 Finally, section 13 of the AA 2020 empowers the Secretary of State to provide for the payment of lump sums to applicants who are entitled to either a direct payment or delinked payment in a year up to 2026. A lump sum is received in lieu of the relevant payment(s), and is intended to provide farmers wishing to retire or leave the industry with the capital to do so.[127]

12.58 The 'Lump Sump Payment Regulations'[128] came into force on 26 March 2022: they made it mandatory for the Secretary of State to make a lump sum payment to any eligible applicant,[129] but applications were only accepted until 30 September 2022, or later if the Secretary of State was satisfied there were good reasons for the lateness.[130] Applicants then had to transfer all the agricultural land at their disposal, and certain

---

124 ibid cols 1923–1933. DEFRA consulted on new protective legislative requirements for hedgerows across June-September 2023, with a view to meeting the hedgerow targets set out in the 2023 EIP: DEFRA, 'Press Release – Government Seeks Views to Improve Hedgerow Protections' (2023) <https://www.gov.uk/government/news/government-seeks-views-to-improve-hedgerow-protections> accessed 26 April 2024.
125 DEFRA, 'The Future of Hedgerow Protections in England: Consultation Response' (4 March 2024) <https://defrafarming.blog.gov.uk/2024/03/04/the-future-of-hedgerow-protections-in-england-consultation-response/> accessed 26 April 2024.
126 AA 2020 s 8.
127 DEFRA, 'An Update on the Lump Sum Exit Scheme and Delinked Payments' (8 February 2022) <https://defrafarming.blog.gov.uk/2022/02/08/an-update-on-the-lump-sum-exit-scheme-and-delinked-payments/> accessed 26 April 2024.
128 The Agriculture (Lump Sum Payment) (England) Regulations 2022, SI 2022/390.
129 ibid reg 3.
130 ibid reg 4.

rights in common, by the scheme end date of 31 May 2024.[131,132] Applicants could not transfer their land or rights in common to a 'connected person'.[133] Applicants were also required to surrender all registered payment entitlements by the scheme end date.[134,135]

12.59 The Secretary of State may require an applicant to provide additional information, or to correct any material errors ('defects') within a specified period.[136] A lump sum payable under the regulations must be paid no later than six months after the applicant is notified by the Secretary of State that the requirements have been met, or an extended period if the Secretary of State is satisfied that there are good reasons to extend it.[137] The Secretary of State must not pay a lump sum payment if the applicant is ineligible; the application is incomplete or defective; or the applicant has provided false or misleading information. The applicant must be notified of the decision within a reasonable time and informed of their right to appeal.[138]

12.60 The National Farmers' Union state that a farmer may withdraw their application at any time before being paid the lump sum through discussion with the Rural Payments Agency.[139] However, no procedure for withdrawal is set out in the regulations.

The Agriculture (Wales) Act 2023 ('AWA 2023')

12.61 The AWA 2023 loosely mirrors the AA 2020: section 1 sets out a new set of sustainable land management objectives, which are (1) producing food and other goods sustainably; (2) mitigating and adapting to climate change; (3) maintaining and enhancing the resilience of ecosystems and their benefits; and (4) conserving and enhancing the countryside and cultural resources and promoting public access to and engagement with the same, and sustaining and facilitating the Welsh language. Each of these objectives should contribute to meeting the needs of the present without compromising the ability of future generations to meet their own needs, and to achieving the well-being goals in section 4 of the Well-being of Future Generations (Wales) Act 2015.

12.62 The Welsh Ministers must exercise relevant functions in the way which best contributes to achieving the sustainable land management objectives, so far as consistent with the proper exercise of the function.[140] Sections 4–7 of the AWA 2023 make provision for monitoring and reporting on progress towards achieving the sustainable land management objectives.

---

131 This period may be extended by the Secretary of State on the provision of certain further evidence by the applicant: ibid reg 6(5).
132 ibid regs 2 and 6.
133 ibid regs 6(1) and 7.
134 This may also be extended by the Secretary of State in the same circumstances as above: ibid reg 8(4).
135 ibid reg 8.
136 ibid regs 9–10.
137 ibid reg 13.
138 ibid regs 11 and 14.
139 'Lump Sum Exit Scheme Application Window Reminders' (30 January 2023) <https://www.nfuonline.com/updates-and-information/find-out-more-about-the-lump-sum-exit-scheme/> accessed 27 April 2024.
140 AWA 2023 ss 2–3.

12.63 Sections 8–10 of the AWA 2023 empower the Welsh Ministers to provide financial support for agriculture and ancillary activities in Wales in connection with similar environmental purposes to those set out in the AA 2020, and sections 16–20 provide equivalent powers to modify the relevant retained EU legislation.

12.64 However, in Wales, the phase-out of the BPS will take place across a transition period of 1 April 2025 – 31 March 2029. A consultation on the Welsh government's SFS proposals ran until 7 March 2024, and the proposals will not be implemented until 2025. From 1 January 2024, an interim agri-environmental support scheme called Habitat Wales is available.[141]

Environmental land management schemes

(i) *Agricultural Transition Plan*

12.65 The Agricultural Transition Plan envisaged that the three components of ELMs would make a 'significant contribution' to the goals set out in the 25YEP, working with other proposals set out in the Environment Act 2021.[142] At that time, the three components proposed were the Sustainable Farming Incentive ('SFI'), Local Nature Recovery, and Landscape Recovery.[143] The SFI would be available and accessible to all farmers, helping all farmers take actions to manage their land sustainably and contribute to environmental outcomes. Landscape Recovery would involve longer-term land use change projects, supporting the delivery of landscape and ecosystem recovery at a larger scale. The ambition was for ELMs to attract wide participation, increasing from 30% participation in pre-existing agri-environment schemes to over 70% participation by the end of the transition, with even higher participation in the SFI scheme.[144]

12.66 The Agricultural Transition Plan planned to introduce the first ELM pilots and tests across 2021–2024, roll out aspects of each component from 2022, and have all three components fully available from 2024.[145]

12.67 It was originally intended that the existing Countryside Stewardship agreements would operate until 2023, but ultimately fade out as a legacy scheme.[146] However, by January 2023, it had been decided to continue and evolve Countryside Stewardship, in recognition of the successful adoption of CS agreements under the new domestic arrangements.[147]

---

141 Lesley Griffiths MS, 'Written Cabinet Statement: Habitat Wales Scheme 2024/25' (25 September 2023) <https://www.gov.wales/written-statement-habitat-wales-scheme-202425> accessed 27 April 2024.
142 DEFRA, 'The Path to Sustainable Farming: An Agricultural Transition Plan 2021 to 2024' (n 65) 16.
143 ibid 32.
144 ibid 31; DEFRA, 'Environmental Improvement Plan 2023: First Revision of the 25 Year Environment Plan' (n 66) 19.
145 DEFRA, 'The Path to Sustainable Farming: An Agricultural Transition Plan 2021 to 2024' (n 65) 8.
146 ibid 27.
147 DEFRA, 'Environmental Land Management Update: How Government Will Pay for Land-Based Environment and Climate Goods and Services' (2023) 11 <https://assets.publishing.service.gov.uk/media/63ed0244e90e077bb472a7d2/Environmental-Land-Management-Update-January-2023-Accessible-Final.pdf> accessed 27 April 2024.

12.68 As set out above at paragraph 12.37, the Financial Assistance Regulations 2021 came into force on 26 March 2021, making provision for the award of financial assistance under four financial assistance schemes: the environmental land management pilot scheme, the countryside stewardship scheme, the farming investment fund scheme, and the tree health pilot scheme. The regulations have been amended over time to reflect the evolution of ELMs.

(ii) *Sustainable Farming Incentive*

12.69 In June 2021, DEFRA published details of the first options under the SFI, before it opened for applications in Spring 2022. The first options focused on soil health (through an arable and horticultural soils standard and improved grassland soils standard), a moorland and rough grazing standard, and an annual health and welfare review.[148] In December 2021, DEFRA further clarified that SFI would operate at a land parcel (field) level, and that agreements would last three years, with flexibility to amend the terms every 12 months. Payments would be made in quarterly instalments – an increase compared to Countryside Stewardship and the BPS (which pay yearly in arrears) – to help farmers manage cashflow.[149] In March 2022, the Financial Assistance Regulations 2021 were amended to apply to the three strands of ELMs.[150] The SFI scheme was launched in earnest in June 2022, and was updated for 2023,[151] with the addition of new standards related to hedgerows, integrated pest management ('IPM'), nutrient management, and grassland, again contributing to the government's priority climate and nature targets.

12.70 The SFI 2023 offer addressed the same environmental issues (and in addition, buffer strips), but no longer contained standards or levels: it was designed for farmers to have maximum flexibility, including in relation to the combination of actions they wish to take up, and the area of land on which to take each action.[152] Further SFI actions were introduced on 31 May 2024, including actions for agroforestry and precision farming.[153] There are now also a range of actions intended to improve water quality, including in-field flower-rich strips, companion cropping and grassy field corners.[154]

12.71 SFI agreements have been designed to be accessible to tenant farmers, including through three-year agreements which align with the average length of Farm Business

148 DEFRA, 'Agricultural Transition Plan: June 2021 Progress Update' (2021) <https://www.gov.uk/government/publications/agricultural-transition-plan-june-2021-progress-update/agricultural-transition-plan-june-2021-progress-update> accessed 6 February 2024.
149 DEFRA, 'Sustainable Farming Incentive: How the Scheme Will Work in 2022' (2021) <https://www.gov.uk/government/publications/sustainable-farming-incentive-how-the-scheme-will-work-in-2022/sustainable-farming-incentive-how-the-scheme-will-work-in-2022> accessed 6 February 2024.
150 The Agriculture (Financial Assistance) (Amendment) Regulations 2022, SI 2022/389.
151 DEFRA, 'Environmental Land Management Update: How Government Will Pay for Land-Based Environment and Climate Goods and Services' (n 147).
152 DEFRA, 'SFI Handbook for the SFI 2023 Offer' (2023) 8 <https://www.gov.uk/government/publications/sfi-handbook-for-the-sfi-2023-offer> accessed 27 April 2024.
153 Department for Environment, Food and Rural Affairs, 'SFI Scheme Information: Expanded Offer for 2024' (GOV.UK, 31 May 2024) <https://www.gov.uk/government/publications/sustainable-farming-incentive-scheme-expanded-offer-for-2024/sfi-scheme-information-expanded-offer-for-2024> accessed 21 June 2024.
154 DEFRA, 'Environmental Improvement Plan 2023: First Revision of the 25 Year Environment Plan' (n 66) 112.

Tenancies, and do not require tenants to obtain landlord consent.[155] SFI agreements can be combined with participation in other schemes (such as CS agreements), so long as the actions are compatible and farmers are not being paid twice for the same outcome. Detailed guidance on the SFI scheme is now set out in the SFI Handbook.[156]

12.72 On 25 March 2024, DEFRA announced plans to limit the amount of land which SFI applicants can take wholly of direct food production, for food security purposes.[157] The measures mean that applicants will only be able to put 25% of their land into six specified actions.[158] While these restrictions only operate on the six actions specified, landowner lobby groups have responded that food production and nature are not binary choices, and questioned whether these measures will delay DEFRA's target of getting 70% of farmland into ELM schemes by 2028.[159]

12.73 DEFRA's press release noted that to date, the SFI scheme had received over 15,000 applications and issued over 14,000 agreement offers.[160] There are, in total, 104,000 agricultural holdings in England.[161]

(iii) *Countryside Stewardship, Environmental Stewardship and Higher Level Stewardship Agreements*

12.74 Environmental Stewardship ('ES') and Countryside Stewardship ('CS') agreements existed prior to Brexit as earlier agri-environmental support schemes. Regulations in respect of both ES and CS are made, in whole or in part, pursuant to section 98 of the Environment Act 1995, which empowers the Secretary of State to provide for the making of grants conducive to (a) the conservation or enhancement of the natural beauty or amenity of the countryside (including its flora and fauna and geological and physiographical features) or of any features of archaeological interest; or (b) the promotion of the public's enjoyment of the countryside.

12.75 The Environmental Stewardship (England) Regulations 2005 continue in force following Brexit. One form of ES agreement was an agreement under the Higher Level

---

155 DEFRA, 'Agricultural Transition Plan Update January 2024' (2024) <https://www.gov.uk/government/publications/agricultural-transition-plan-2021-to-2024/agricultural-transition-plan-update-january-2024> accessed 5 February 2024. For a detailed discussion of agricultural tenancies, see Chapter 24.

156 DEFRA, 'SFI Handbook for the SFI 2023 Offer' (2023) <https://www.gov.uk/government/publications/sfi-handbook-for-the-sfi-2023-offer> accessed 27 April 2024.DEFRA, 'SFI Handbook for the SFI 2023 Offer' (2023) (n 152).

157 DEFRA, 'Press Release – Government Ensures Food Production Remains Primary Purpose of Farming' (2024) <https://www.gov.uk/government/news/government-ensures-food-production-remains-primary-purpose-of-farming> accessed 27 March 2024.

158 ibid: Flower-rich grass margins; pollen and nectar flower mix; winter bird food on arable and horticultural land; grassy field corners and blocks; improved grassland field corners or blocks out of management; and winter bird food on improved grassland.

159 ENDS Report, 'Government Places Land Use Cap on Sustainable Farming Interventions' (26 March 2024) <https://www.endsreport.com/article/1866612?utm_source=website&utm_medium=social> accessed 27 April 2024. The 2028 target is set out in the 2023 EIP: DEFRA, 'Environmental Improvement Plan 2023: First Revision of the 25 Year Environment Plan' (n 66) 19.

160 DEFRA, 'Press Release – Government Ensures Food Production Remains Primary Purpose of Farming' (n 157).

161 DEFRA, 'Agriculture in the UK Dashboard: Structure – Farm Size and Ownership' <https://defra-farming-stats.github.io/auk-dashboard/#farm-size-and-ownership> accessed 27 March 2024.

Stewardship ('HLS') scheme, which aimed to deliver significant environmental benefit in high priority areas. The scheme has been closed to new applicants since 2014, but from 1 January 2023, HLS agreement holders became eligible to extend their HLS agreement for up to five years.[162] The final HLS agreements will expire in 2028, with government encouraging transition into the new ELM schemes.

12.76 CS agreements granted from 1 January 2021 are governed by the Countryside Stewardship (England) Regulations 2020. It has now been confirmed that an enhanced version of CS will continue, and will form the second component of ELMs, in place of Local Nature Recovery. The three main elements of CS are:[163]

- Mid Tier: multi-year agreements for environmental improvements in the wider countryside, that include multi-year options and capital items.
- Higher Tier: multi-year agreements for environmentally significant sites, commons and woodlands where more complex management requires support from Natural England or the Forestry Commission, that include multi-year options and capital items.
- Capital-only grants: a range of grants specific to outcomes for hedgerows and boundaries, developing implementation plans, feasibility studies, woodland management plans, woodland creation (establishment), and tree health – normally two year agreements.

12.77 From 1 January 2024, the terms and conditions of ES and CS agreements have been updated to reflect the end of cross-compliance.[164] Those in ES agreements are encouraged to apply for SFI, CS or Landscape Recovery.[165]

12.78 The current CS scheme requires tenant farmers to obtain their landlord's consent before applying: however, the government is considering what more can be done to make the scheme accessible for tenants.

12.79 The Welsh equivalent of CS under the CAP was Glastir: Glastir ended on 31 December 2023, and is replaced by an interim Habitat Wales scheme issuing 12-month contracts prior to the introduction of the SFS in 2025.

---

162 Rural Payments Agency, 'Guidance – Higher Level Stewardship 2024: Agreement Extensions' (2022) <https://www.gov.uk/guidance/higher-level-stewardship-2023-agreement-extensions> accessed 27 April 2024.
163 Forestry Commission, 'Woodland Grants and Incentives Overview Table' (2024) <https://www.gov.uk/government/publications/woodland-grants-and-incentives-overview-table/woodland-grants-and-incentives-overview-table#countryside-stewardship-grants> accessed 27 April 2024.
164 Rural Payments Agency, 'Guidance – Countryside Stewardship: Terms and Conditions, and Rules for Agreement Holders, from 1 January 2024' (2023) <https://www.gov.uk/guidance/countryside-stewardship-terms-and-conditions-and-rules-for-agreement-holders-from-1-january-2024> accessed 27 April 2024.
165 DEFRA, 'Agricultural Transition Plan Update January 2024' (n 155).

(iv) *Landscape Recovery projects*

12.80 The Landscape Recovery component of ELMs is designed to fund a smaller number of longer-term, larger-scale, bespoke projects to enhance the natural environment and deliver significant benefits at scale.[166] Landscape Recovery projects begin with a Project Development Phase ('PDP') of up to two years, before proceeding to full implementation,[167] which can take place across decades.

12.81 In 2022, funding was awarded to 22 projects covering over 40,000 hectares. The pilot projects aimed to restore over 400 miles of rivers and protect and provide habitat for at least 263 species.[168] The second round of applications in 2023 focused on net zero, protected sites and habitat creation: the projects cover over 200,000 hectares across England. A third round will open in 2024.

Other environmental support schemes

(i) *Farming in Protected Landscapes*

12.82 DEFRA are also operating a Farming in Protected Landscapes ('FiPL') programme for farmers and land managers in National Parks and National Landscapes (previously AONBs) as part of the Agricultural Transition Plan. The programme offers funding for one-off projects to support nature recovery and mitigate climate impacts. Applications opened in July 2021: the 3,000 projects funded to date have created and improved more than 70,000 hectares of habitat for biodiversity; planted more than 100 miles of hedgerow and more than 100,000 trees; and conserved or enhanced 300 historic features, buildings and structures. FiPL has now been extended until March 2025.

(ii) *Slurry Infrastructure Grant scheme*

12.83 In England, DEFRA and the RPA are also running a Slurry Infrastructure Grant scheme for livestock farmers (both landowners and tenants). Grants can be used to improve or expand slurry storage capacity, to improve the use of organic nutrients, reduce water pollution and air pollution and reduce greenhouse gases.[169] Previous schemes included the Farming Ammonia Reduction Grant Scheme, which offered grants to pay for slurry store covers.

---

166 ibid.

167 DEFRA, 'Landscape Recovery: Sharing the Successful Second Round Projects' (29 November 2023) <https://defrafarming.blog.gov.uk/2023/11/29/round-two-projects/> accessed 27 April 2024.

168 One example is the Upper Axe Landscape Recovery Project, which works with 32 farmers and landowners to improve the condition of the River Axe (an SAC and an SSSI) across 2,777 hectares: DEFRA, 'Restoring the River Axe: A Landscape Recovery Spotlight' (29 January 2024) <https://defrafarming.blog.gov.uk/2024/01/29/restoring-the-river-axe-a-landscape-recovery-spotlight/> accessed 27 April 2024. This project has a minimum length of 20 years.

169 DEFRA and Rural Payments Agency, 'Guidance – About the Slurry Infrastructure Grant, Who Can Apply and What It Can Pay For' (2024) <https://www.gov.uk/government/publications/slurry-infrastructure-grant/about-the-slurry-infrastructure-grant-who-can-apply-and-what-it-can-pay-for> accessed 27 April 2024. Addressing ammonia emissions from slurry is a commitment of the 2023 EIP and will contribute to the long-term and interim air quality targets.

Controls on agricultural diffuse pollution

12.84 As set out above, the agricultural sector is expected to contribute to most if not all of the ten goals set out in the 25YEP and 2023 EIP, and to several of the environmental targets set under the EA 2021. A key target is the Agricultural Water Target set out in Part 2 of the Environmental Targets (Water) (England) Regulations 2023.

12.85 This target stipulates that by 31 December 2038, the load of each of (a) total nitrogen, (b) total phosphorus, and (c) sediment ('the agriculture target substances') entering the water environment through agricultural diffuse pollution is at least 40% lower than the 2018 baseline.[170] This reflects the recognition in the 25YEP that farming is the most significant source of water pollution in the UK, accounting for 25% phosphate, 50% nitrate and 75% of sediment loadings in the water environment.[171]

12.86 In the 2023 EIP, the government further set relevant interim targets of 10% reductions in the agriculture target substances by 31 January 2028, and 15% reductions by the same date in catchments containing protected sites in unfavourable condition due to nutrient pollution.[172]

12.87 The interim and long-term targets will be supported through the roll-out of ELMs.[173] There are, however, other legal instruments which are also intended to drive reductions in agricultural diffuse pollution.[174]

(i) *Nitrate Vulnerable Zones ('NVZs')*

12.88 Pollution caused by nitrates from livestock and fertilisers has long been controlled within designated NVZs, which were originally introduced to implement the Nitrates

170 The Environmental Targets (Water) (England) Regulations 2023 regs 5 and 8(1). Interestingly, the load to be measured in 2038 must include the load from human activity on land which was agricultural in 2018, but for land management reasons with environmental, conservation or sustainability objectives, is no longer agricultural land in 2038: The Environmental Targets (Water) (England) Regulations 2023 reg 6(2).
171 DEFRA, 'A Green Future: Our 25 Year Plan to Improve the Environment' (n 60) 38.
172 DEFRA, 'Environmental Improvement Plan 2023: First Revision of the 25 Year Environment Plan' (n 66) 99 and 103. Acceleration is expected after 2028, as interventions such as technology, farm infrastructure and land use change will take time to deliver, particularly in the current context of high input prices. A list of protected sites in unfavourable condition due to nutrient pollution is maintained by Natural England.
173 ibid 103.
174 Government anticipate that a 'combination of regulation and public and private schemes' will deliver at least 80% of the required progress towards the long-term target, with the remainder being met through other improvements made by the sector, such as developments in soil and nutrient management: DEFRA, 'Environmental Improvement Plan 2023: First Revision of the 25 Year Environment Plan' (n 66) 111.

Directive 1991.[175] NVZ designations have been effective at reducing excess application of fertiliser, and as a result have lowered N2O emissions.[176]

12.89 Following the transition period, the principal English regulations (the Nitrate Pollution Prevention Regulations 2015) became part of the body of retained EU law (now assimilated law). The principal Welsh regulations have now been replaced by the Water Resources (Control of Agricultural Pollution) (Wales) Regulations 2021.

12.90 In England, as at 2020 NVZ designation covered around 55% of England, mainly in the east of the country:[177] the CCC recommended extending NVZ coverage to 'all of the UK' by 2023.[178] The Welsh regulations now introduce an NVZ over Wales, such that the requirements will apply to all holdings in Wales (although implementation is delayed under the terms of the regulations). They also revoke and replace the Water Resources (Control of Pollution) (Silage and Slurry) (Wales) Regulations 2010: in England, the Water Resources (Control of Pollution) (Silage, Slurry and Agricultural Fuel Oil) (England) Regulations 2010 continue to be in force.

12.91 Under the English Nitrates Regulations, an area is designated as an NVZ if, as an area which drains into and pollutes polluted waters, it is marked on the relevant map.[179] The Secretary of State must monitor the nitrate concentration in freshwaters every four years (including by 1 January 2021 and 1 January 2025).[180] The Secretary of State must then identify water which is or potentially could be affected by pollution and the land which drains into those waters and contributes to the pollution; take into account any changes and previously unforeseen factors; and if necessary revise the designations.[181] The Environment Agency must, every four years (including by 10 August 2024), make recommendations as to which areas should be designated, to which the Secretary of State must have regard.[182] Proposals to revise the designations must be published, and written notice sent to relevant owners or occupiers.[183]

---

175 Council Directive 91/676/EEC of 12 December 1991 concerning the protection of waters against pollution caused by nitrates from agricultural sources.
176 Climate Change Committee, 'Land Use: Policies for a Net Zero UK' (n 31) 79. See also 'Agriculture in the UK Dashboard: Agri-Environment – Fertiliser Usage' <https://defra-farming-stats.github.io/auk-dashboard/#fertiliser-usage> accessed 27 March 2024, which shows the declines in nitrogen fertiliser usage and phosphate fertiliser usage between 1984 and 2021. However, soil health statistics show that there continues to be a minor phosphorus surplus of 2.8 kg/ha of managed agricultural land, and a major nitrogen surplus of 79.1kg/ha of managed agricultural land: DEFRA, 'Soil Nutrient Balances UK, 2022 – Statistics Notice' (2024) <https://www.gov.uk/government/statistics/uk-and-england-soil-nutrient-balances-2022/soil-nutrient-balances-uk-2022-statistics-notice> accessed 27 March 2024.
177 Climate Change Committee, 'Land Use: Policies for a Net Zero UK' (n 31) 79.
178 ibid 15, 87 and 102.
179 The Nitrate Pollution Prevention Regulations 2015, SI 2015/668 reg 3. The 'relevant map' is published on the Environment Agency's website: 'Check for Drinking Water Safeguard Zones and NVZs' <https://environment.data.gov.uk/farmers/> accessed 27 April 2024.
180 Except that, in the case of any sampling station at which the concentration in all previous samples have been below 25mg/l and no new factor likely to increase the nitrate content has appeared, monitoring needs only take place every eight years: The Nitrate Pollution Prevention Regulations 2015, SI 2015/668 reg 4(3).
181 ibid reg 4.
182 The Nitrate Pollution Prevention Regulations 2015, SI 2015/668 regs 5(1)–(2).
183 ibid regs 5(3)–(4).

12.92 Newly designated holdings are allowed a two-year grace period before certain aspects of the regulations will be engaged.[184] The regulations also apply for an appeal process to the First-Tier Tribunal against the proposals or designation.[185]

(ii) *Restrictions within NVZs*

12.93 The occupier of a holding in an NVZ is responsible for complying with most of the regulatory requirements,[186] although neither the English nor the Welsh regulations define who the occupier is: it will usually be either the landowner or the tenant farmer.

12.94 There are detailed regulatory restrictions on agricultural activities within NVZs. The key requirements include restrictions on the spreading and storage of organic manure, nitrogen fertiliser and slurry; maintaining a 'risk map' of the holding; and record keeping. There are certain exemptions for organic holdings,[187] and occupiers of a holding where 80% or more of the area is sown with grass may apply for a derogation.[188]

12.95 The Secretary of State must establish a monitoring programme to assess the effectiveness of the restrictions, and must review their effectiveness at least every four years. A review must include public consultation.[189] The Secretary of State must also review and report on the regulations and their implementation every four years.[190]

(iii) *The Reduction and Prevention of Agricultural Diffuse Pollution (England) Regulations 2018 (the 'Farming Rules for Water')*

12.96 The Farming Rules for Water apply to all agricultural land managers in England, separately and additionally to the restrictions in place within NVZs. The rules arose as part of a broader initiative to meet the requirements of the Water Framework Directive, specifically the requirement to achieve good status:[191] they were also designed to create simplified rules for all land managers to reduce water pollution from agriculture.

12.97 The Farming Rules for Water similarly set out certain restrictions on the application of organic manure and manufactured fertiliser, and the storage of organic manure.[192] They also set out rules for managing livestock and soil.[193] Failure to comply with the regulatory requirements is an offence, unless the person can show they took

---

184 ibid reg 5A sch 4.
185 ibid reg 6.
186 ibid regs 7–35.
187 ibid reg 21.
188 ibid regs 36–38.
189 ibid reg 39.
190 ibid regs 40–40A.
191 *R (River Action) v Environment Agency* [2024] EWHC 1279 (Admin) (n 26) paras 8, 13–5. See further paras 19.128ff.
192 The Reduction and Prevention of Agricultural Diffuse Pollution (England) Regulations 2018, SI 2018/151 regs 3–9.
193 ibid reg 10.

all reasonable steps and exercised all due diligence to avoid committing the offence.[194] Enforcement of offences is a matter for the Environment Agency.[195]

12.98 Pursuant to regulation 15, the Secretary of State may issue guidance to the Environment Agency with respect to the exercise of its functions, to which the Environment Agency must have regard. The most recent statutory guidance[196] was issued in June 2022, following a pre-action letter from WildFish which argued that the guidance encouraged farmers to unlawfully apply slurries and manures in excess of the needs of their soil or crops, contrary to the requirements of the regulations.[197] In May 2024, a further judicial review brought by River Action against the Environment Agency in respect of their approach to enforcement of the rules was dismissed.[198] Dove J also determined a separate issue which had arisen in respect of the correct interpretation of Regulation 4(1)(a)(i), pursuant to which land managers must ensure that each application of organic manure or fertiliser is planned so that it does not exceed the needs of the soil and crop on that land. The parties in fact agreed in interpreting as meaning need at the time of application; the Secretary of State for DEFRA and National Farmers Union argued for need over an annual crop cycle or crop rotation, to allow farmers to plan their applications over such a cycle.[199] Dove J found in favour of the parties' interpretation, drawing both on the precise wording of Regulation 4(1)(a)(i) and on the purpose of the regulations.[200]

Peatland and soil health

12.99 Peatland, which forms over thousands of years, is a natural carbon sink: when degraded, however, it becomes a carbon source, emitting an average 4 tonnes per hectare of CO_2e per year.[201] Over the past few centuries, 56% of the UK's peatland has been drained and converted to agricultural use.[202] Peatland restoration and management is therefore an important component of the UK's approach to net zero. The CBDP includes a policy of restoring 280,000 hectares of peatland by 2050, with the main delivery vehicle from 2025 onwards being ELMs; further, a Peatland Restoration Roadmap will be developed to set out a detailed trajectory for restoration to 2050.[203] The government also intends to end the sale of peat by 2026, with limited exemptions.[204]

---

194 ibid regs 11–12.
195 ibid regs 13–14.
196 DEFRA, 'Applying the Farming Rules for Water' (2022) <https://www.gov.uk/government/publications/applying-the-farming-rules-for-water/applying-the-farming-rules-for-water> accessed 27 April 2024.
197 Wildfish, 'WildFish Forces Change to How Farming Rules for Water Will Be Enforced to Protect English Rivers' (20 June 2022) <https://wildfish.org/latest-news/2022-06-20-farming-rules-for-water/> accessed 27 April 2024.
198 *R (River Action) v Environment Agency* [2024] EWHC 1279 (Admin) (n 26).
199 ibid 34–5.
200 ibid 91–113.
201 NFS Independent Review: The Plan (n 1) 73.
202 ibid.
203 Department for Energy Security and Net Zero, *Carbon Budget Delivery Plan* (n 51) 101–102. Pre-2025, action has been taken through the Nature for Climate Peatland Grant Fund. See further the 2021 Peat Action Plan at DEFRA, 'Policy Paper – England Peat Action Plan' (2021) <https://www.gov.uk/government/publications/england-peat-action-plan> accessed 27 April 2024.
204 Department for Energy Security and Net Zero, *Carbon Budget Delivery Plan* (n 51) 102. For further policies and proposals on peat, see CBDP 140–143.

12.100 The CCC's most recent annual report advises that peatland restoration is 'significantly off track'; restoration remains a factor of five less than recommended rates (and national targets are below those set out in the CCC's Balanced Pathway); and a comprehensive delivery mechanism is needed.[205]

12.101 In January 2024, DEFRA introduced premium payments through ELMs for high impact environmental actions including on lowland peat.[206] The Welsh government also propose to incentivise peat restoration through the SFS.[207]

12.102 Soil health has also been an early focus of ELMs. There is a recognised need to improve data and monitoring on soil health, to inform future policy, targets and actions.[208] The 25YEP also promised a Soil Health Action Plan for England: however, this was ultimately incorporated into the 2023 EIP.[209]

12.103 The 2023 EIP sets out a new target to bring at least 40% of England's agricultural soil into sustainable management by 2028, and increase this to 60% by 2030, to be achieved primarily through ELMs.[210] DEFRA monitors soil health as part of Natural Capital and Ecosystem Assessment, but the 2023 EIP further commits to establish a soil health indicator under the 25YEP Outcome Indicator Framework (x-ref to Nature Positive paras);[211] publish a baseline map of soil health for England by 2028; and support farmers and land managers to establish their own soil health baseline, as well as diverting more soil away from landfill.

12.104 A November 2023 report by the House of Commons Environment, Food and Rural Affairs Committee[212] calls for soil health to be put on the same footing as water and air quality within government policy, and calls for statutory targets on soil health, alongside the existing water and air quality targets, by 2028.[213] The EU has a discrete soil strategy for 2030,[214] and the European Commission has adopted a proposal for an EU Directive on Soil Monitoring and Resilience.[215]

---

205 Committee on Climate Change, '2023 Progress Report to Parliament' (2023) 20–21, 36 and 242 <https://www.theccc.org.uk/publication/2023-progress-report-to-parliament/>.
206 DEFRA, 'Environmental Land Management in 2024: Details of Actions and Payments' (4 January 2024) <https://defrafarming.blog.gov.uk/2024/01/04/environmental-land-management-in-2024-details-of-actions-and-payments/> accessed 27 April 2024.
207 Welsh Government, 'Sustainable Farming Scheme – Outline Proposals from 2025: Frequently Asked Questions' (2022) <https://www.gov.wales/sustainable-farming-scheme-outline-proposals-2025-frequently-asked-questions-html> accessed 27 April 2024.
208 DEFRA, 'A Green Future: Our 25 Year Plan to Improve the Environment' (n 60) 12, 32, 43 and 130; House of Commons Environment, Food and Rural Affairs, Soil Health (n 14).
209 House of Commons Environment, Food and Rural Affairs, Soil Health (n 14).
210 DEFRA, 'Environmental Improvement Plan 2023: First Revision of the 25 Year Environment Plan' (n 66) 165, 167 and 180.
211 At the time of writing, this indicator is in development: DEFRA, 'E7: Healthy Soils' <https://oifdata.defra.gov.uk/themes/natural-resources/E7/> accessed 23 March 2024.
212 House of Commons Environment, Food and Rural Affairs, Soil Health (n 14).
213 ibid.
214 Directorate-General for Environment, 'EU Soil Strategy for 2030' (2021) <https://environment.ec.europa.eu/publications/eu-soil-strategy-2030_en> accessed 27 April 2024.
215 Directorate-General for Environment, 'Proposal for a Directive on Soil Monitoring and Resilience' (2023).

Agricultural land classification

12.105 So far, the focus has been on the direct relationship between agriculture and achieving net zero. However, another important indirect relationship between these two concepts is how agricultural land use bears on the planning process, and particularly the loss of valuable agricultural land for development concerned with achieving net zero. In recent years this has been an important political topic in the context of constructing large solar farms,[216] but the issue arises whenever large developments are proposed on valuable agricultural land.

12.106 This issue has been exacerbated by the war in Ukraine and the internal focus on food security in the UK.[217] Numerous MPs have called for specific protections for high-value agricultural land to safeguard the country's agricultural capacity in light of shifting supply chains across Europe and the rest of the world.[218] With the change of government in July 2024, it will be important to see if the pressure to protect agricultural land continues to grow, or whether the high point has now passed in light of the requirements of meeting net zero.

(i) *Classifying agricultural land*

12.107 In planning policy, the primary way in which valuable agricultural land is protected is through the agricultural land classification ('ALC') system.

12.108 For many decades agricultural land in the UK has been subject to grading using the ALC scale. This scale is based, primarily, on the capacity of agricultural land to grow a wide range of crops and a large volume of crops.[219] The scale runs through grades 1, 2, 3a, 3b, 4 and 5. Natural England currently state that the 'highest grade' goes to land that:[220]

- gives a high yield or output
- has the widest range and versatility of use
- produces the most consistent yield
- requires less input

216 See, for example, the consideration of this issue in relation to the Sunnica Energy Farm NSIP, 'Sunnica Energy Farm Examining Authority's Report' (28 June 2023) paras 4.12.82–4.12.151 and Secretary of State Decision Letter, 'Application for Development Consent for Sunnica Energy Farm' (12 July 2024) paras 4.208–4.226.
217 See, for example, AA 2020 s 19, which imposes an obligation on the Government to report on food security in the United Kingdom. See also DEFRA, 'Government Food Strategy' (CP 698, 2022) <https://www.gov.uk/government/publications/government-food-strategy/government-food-strategy#food-security-and-sustainable-production> accessed 15 November 2023.
218 HC Deb 8 June 2022, vol 715, cols 386WH–404WH.
219 The current grading is assessed using: Ministry of Agriculture, Fisheries and Food, 'Agricultural Land Classification of England and Wales – Revised Guidelines and Criteria for Grading the Quality of Agricultural Land' (1988) and associated policies including Natural England, 'Agricultural Land Classification: Protecting the Best and Most Versatile Agricultural Land' (2012) TIN049.
220 Natural England, 'Guidance to Assessing Development Proposals on Agricultural Land' (5 February 2021) <https://www.gov.uk/government/publications/agricultural-land-assess-proposals-for-development/guide-to-assessing-development-proposals-on-agricultural-land> accessed 15 November 2023.

12.109 Land at the upper end of the ALC scale, grades 1, 2 and 3a, is described as 'best and most versatile land' (commonly abbreviated to 'BMV'). The more an area of agricultural land meets descriptors such as those above, the higher up the scale the land will be placed. Planning policy has specific protections for BMV land, the loss of which weighs against proposed developments.

12.110 The approach to grading agricultural land is complex and the subject of some debate. This issue is beyond the scope of this book, requiring expert input from agricultural consultants. However, in short, assessment requires experts to dig the land to examine the quality of the soil, deposits in the soil and access of crops to water. Some high-level information about ALC classification across the UK is published by DEFRA in the Magic Map facility.[221] In a recent ministerial statement it has been noted that the rigour of some soil surveys has been doubted, and that the government proposes to introduce an independent certification scheme to ensure such surveys are of a high standard.[222]

(ii) *Policy*

12.111 The protection of BMV land is recognised throughout planning policy. At the local level it has protection in the National Planning Policy Framework, ('NPPF') where paragraph 180 provides:

> Planning policies and decisions should contribute to and enhance the natural and local environment by: (a) protecting and enhancing… soils (in a manner commensurate with their statutory status or identified quality in the development plan) (b) recognising… the wider benefits from natural capital and ecosystem services – including the economic and other benefits of the best and most versatile agricultural land…[223]

12.112 Attached to paragraph 181, concerning plans, footnote 62 further provides (albeit at the time of writing the July 2024 draft NPPF proposes to remove the second sentence of this footnote):[224]

> Where significant development of agricultural land is demonstrated to be necessary, areas of poorer quality land should be preferred to those of higher quality. The availability of agricultural land used for food production should be considered, alongside the other policies in this Framework, when deciding what sites are most appropriate for development.[225]

---

221 DEFRA, 'Magic Map Application' <https://magic.defra.gov.uk/magicmap.aspx> accessed 15 November 2023.

222 Ministerial Statement, Claire Coutinho, Department for Energy Security and Net Zero, 'Solar and protecting our Food Security and Best and Most Versatile (BMV) Land', 15 May 2024, UIN HCWS466.

223 Department for Levelling Up, Housing and Communities, 'National Planning Policy Framework' (2023) 52 <https://assets.publishing.service.gov.uk/media/65a11af7e8f5ec000f1f8c46/NPPF_December_2023.pdf> accessed 2 April 2024.

224 Ministry of Housing, Communities and Local Government, 'Draft National Planning Policy Framework' (July 2024) 55 <https://assets.publishing.service.gov.uk/media/66acffddce1fd0da7b593274/NPPF_with_footnotes.pdf> accessed 21 October 2024.

225 Department for Levelling Up, Housing and Communities, 'National Planning Policy Framework' (2023) 52 (n 223). See also Department for Levelling Up, Housing and Communities, 'Planning Practice Guidance: Renewable and Low Carbon Energy' (2023) para 013 Reference ID: 5-013-20150327, which goes into further detail in respect of solar farms.

12.113 Similarly, the Planning Practice Guidance ('PPG') sets out that 'Planning policies and decisions should take account of the economic and other benefits of the best and most versatile agricultural land'.[226]

12.114 As to achieving this protection, the Development Management Procedure Order provides that Natural England must be consulted on all applications which are not for agricultural purposes and not included in a development plan that result in the loss of more than 20 hectares of BMV land.[227] It is typical for Natural England to provide comment on the loss of ALC that a development will entail and (depending on the circumstances) they may undertake a review of the underlying assessment of ALC for the land.

12.115 Protection for BMV is also set out in the national policy statements for energy, such as in NPS EN-1:[228]

> 5.11.12 Applicants should seek to minimise impacts on the best and most versatile agricultural land … and preferably use land in areas of poorer quality …
>
> 5.11.34 The Secretary of State should ensure that applicants do not site their scheme on the best and most versatile agricultural land without justification. Where schemes are to be sited on best and most versatile agricultural land the Secretary of State should take into account the economic and other benefits of that land. Where development of agricultural land is demonstrated to be necessary, areas of poorer quality land should be preferred to those of higher quality.

12.116 Protections for BMV did not appear in the old 'National Policy Statement for Renewable Energy Infrastructure (EN-3)'.[229] However, the November 2023 version addresses site selection and the loss of BMV land in the context of solar farms.[230]

12.117 This protection of valuable agricultural land can also be seen in broader policy. It suffices to address three recent examples here. The first is the government's 25 Year Environmental Improvement Plan.[231] The housing and planning section of that policy provides:[232]

---

226 Department for Levelling Up, Housing and Communities, 'Planning Practice Guidance: Natural Environment' (2019) para 001 Reference ID: 8-001-20190721.
227 The Town and Country Planning (Development Management Procedure) (England) Order 2015, SI 2015/595, Schedule 4, para (y).
228 Department for Energy Security and Net Zero, 'Overarching National Policy Statement for Energy (EN-1) (November 2023)' (2023) <https://assets.publishing.service.gov.uk/media/65bbfbdc709fe1000f637052/overarching-nps-for-energy-en1.pdf> accessed 4 April 2024.
229 Department of Energy and Climate Change, 'National Policy Statement for Renewable Energy Infrastructure (EN-3) (July 2011)' (2011) <https://assets.publishing.service.gov.uk/government/uploads/system/uploads/attachment_data/file/37048/1940-nps-renewable-energy-en3.pdf> accessed 4 April 2024.
230 Department for Energy Security and Net Zero, 'National Policy Statement for Renewable Energy Infrastructure (EN-3) (November 2023)' (2023) para 2.10.29 and 2.10.30 <https://assets.publishing.service.gov.uk/media/65a7889996a5ec000d731aba/nps-renewable-energy-infrastructure-en3.pdf> accessed 4 April 2024.
231 DEFRA, 'A Green Future: Our 25 Year Plan to Improve the Environment' (n 60).
232 ibid 35.

> **New development will happen in the right places**, delivering maximum economic benefit while taking into account the need to avoid environmental damage. We will protect ancient woodlands and grasslands, high flood risk areas and our best agricultural land. (emphasis in original).

12.118 Similar sentiment is expressed in the Government Food Strategy which sets out in 'Food security and sustainable production' that:[233]

> 1.2.2 … We have some of the best performing farms in the world, with 57% of agricultural output coming from just 33% of the farmed land area. It follows from this that it is possible to target land-use change at the least productive land, to increase the environmental benefit from farming and to increase yields with minimal impact on food production.

12.119 The Government Food Strategy foreshadowed the introduction of a land use framework in 2023 which may have also addressed BMV land.[234] That strategy, among a host of other things, was to look at the relationship between low-carbon infrastructure and other land uses.[235] However, at the time of writing, the framework is still outstanding (reported to have been due in summer 2024), and appears to have been weakened in scope. Lord Douglas-Miller, in answer to a Parliamentary question on the framework in March 2024, explained '[t]he framework is not intended to be prescriptive or force people into certain categories. It is essentially guidance.'[236] Given that lack of prescription,[237] it seems likely the framework will have little scope to make any significant change to planning policy on approach to BMV land.

12.120 Most recently, on 15 May 2024 a ministerial statement was issued by the Secretary of State for Energy Security and Net Zero addressing the use of BMV land for large solar farms. The statement, which applies to prospective schemes and existing schemes currently within the planning process and contains considerations that are 'likely to be important and relevant', emphasises the importance of giving due weight to the value of BMV land:[238]

> This means that due weight needs to be given to the proposed use of Best and Most Versatile land when considering whether planning consent should be granted for solar developments. For all applicants the highest quality agricultural land is least appropriate for solar development and as the land grade increases, there is a greater onus on developers to show that the use of higher quality land is necessary. Applicants for Nationally

---

233 DEFRA, 'Government Food Strategy' (n 217) 14.
234 ibid 11.
235 HM Government, 'Government Response to the Land Use Committee Report "Making the Most out of England's Land"' (2023) <https://committees.parliament.uk/publications/34710/documents/191039/default/> accessed 15 May 2024.
236 HL Deb 12 March 2024, vol 836, col 1899.
237 A change which has been criticised by some, such as the Wildlife and Countryside link, who would prefer to see the framework have significant impact in the planning process: 'Land Use Framework Set to Be "Essentially Guidance", Government Confirms' (14 March 2024) <https://www.endsreport.com/article/1865192?utm_source=website&utm_medium=social> accessed 24 March 2024.
238 Ministerial Statement UIN HCWS466 (n 222).

> Significant Infrastructure Projects should avoid the use of Best and Most Versatile agricultural land where possible.

12.121 Finally, it is worth recognising that protections for BMV do not appear expressly in statute, although attempts have been made to include them. At the third reading of the Energy Bill (now the Energy Act 2023) in the House of Commons, Alicia Kearns MP proposed a new clause which would have required the Secretary of State to exclude development of solar energy projects from sites over 500 acres where over 20% of the land is BMV.[239] Ms Kearns stressed that this was as part of 'moving to a rooftop-first strategy'. The amendment was not moved and protection of BMV currently remains a matter of policy.[240] It may be that the recent ministerial statement on BMV land was delivered in response to these concerns raised within Parliament.

(iii) *Policy – Wales*

12.122 While the approach to assessment of ALC grades in Wales is the same as in England, policy protections are somewhat stronger. Planning Policy Wales provides for the following approach to assessing such land:[241]

> 3.59 When considering the search sequence and in development plan policies and development management decisions considerable weight should be given to protecting such land from development, because of its special importance. Land in grades 1, 2 and 3a should only be developed if there is an overriding need for the development, and either previously developed land or land in lower agricultural grades is unavailable, or available lower grade land has an environmental value recognised by a landscape, wildlife, historic or archaeological designation which outweighs the agricultural considerations. If land in grades 1, 2 or 3a does need to be developed, and there is a choice between sites of different grades, development should be directed to land of the lowest grade.

12.123 The contrast between this policy and that provided for in NPPF is considerable, setting a much higher test asking whether there is an overriding need for development. This will practically achieve significantly different planning outcomes on either side of the border.

(iv) *Implications for net zero*

12.124 At the time of writing the government has indicated some change to the approach to agricultural land with the modification of footnote 62 (now 63) in the draft NPPF.[242] However, it still remains the case that there is clear policy to protect BMV land which is not yet proposed to be altered. This is in conflict with achieving net zero as, ultimately, that aim requires developments which take large areas of land away from

---

239 HC Deb 5 September 2023, vol 737, cols 261–262.
240 HC Deb 5 September 2023, vol 737, col 295.
241 Welsh Government, 'Planning Policy Wales' (2024) 37 <https://www.gov.wales/sites/default/files/publications/2024-07/planning-policy-wales-edition-12.pdf> accessed 2 November 2024.
242 Ministry of Housing, Communities and Local Government, 'Draft National Planning Policy Framework' (n 224).

agricultural use. This is obvious in the case of energy infrastructure, but extends beyond this, such as to significant transport infrastructure.

12.125 ALC is a notable limit on the freedom of developers to site large developments. It is also a notable limit on farmers and their ability to engage in farm diversification. However, that limit need not be absolute. In at least some cases, novel agricultural methods have developed to permit (at least in the solar context) the combining of agriculture and electricity generation.[243] Similarly, some development is temporary and is not usually considered a permanent loss of the land.[244] Thus, there is some flexibility for developers to minimise or avoid losses and achieve compliance with these ALC-focused policies.

12.126 While the significance of ALC is currently most obvious in the realm of solar energy developments, it can be seen that the policy protecting this land goes far beyond this. It is important to be aware of the requirements of policy to protect BMV land and its implications for the siting of large infrastructure.

Conclusion

12.127 Agriculture and land use changes are key to meeting the government's statutory net zero and biodiversity targets, and its international '30by30' commitment. Meeting these targets will require a 'transformation' in UK land use, while supporting farmers.[245] Analysis by the CCC and National Food Strategy Independent Review has demonstrated that it is possible to meet these targets while maintaining food security and accounting for other land uses – but the radical nature of the agricultural transition required cannot be underestimated. The gradual phase-out of BPS payments and converse increase in ELMs payments across the agricultural transition period aims to secure a just transition for farmers, away from BPS subsidies towards a system of public money for public goods. However, as advised by the CCC, farmers need certainty and security (not to mention sufficiency of payments) for uptake to continue at pace, if government targets (statutory and non-statutory) are to be met.

12.128 At the time of writing, the already delayed Land Use Framework was expected to be published in summer 2024: at the time of going to print in Autumn 2024, the publication date remains unclear following the snap election. Great reliance has been placed on the role of a land use framework in providing a coherent, overarching structure for managing the competing demands on land in a manner consistent with government's net zero and nature commitments, including by government advisors.[246] However, early indications (prior to the 2024 General Election) were that the forthcoming framework

---

243 In the solar context this is called 'agrivoltaics'. See, for example, the appeal decision in *Land south of Leeming Substation* (The Planning Inspectorate) [19]–[22] APP/G2713/W/23/3315877.

244 In the solar context this is addressed at paras 2.10.65–2.10.67 of NPS EN-3: Department of Energy Security and Net Zero, 'National Policy Statement for Renewable Energy Infrastructure (EN-3) (November 2023)' (n 230).

245 Climate Change Committee, 'The Sixth Carbon Budget: The UK's Path to Net Zero' (n 17) 25.

246 NFS Independent Review: The Plan (n 1) 156; Committee on Climate Change, '2023 Progress Report to Parliament' (n 205) 27, 36 and 243; Office for Environmental Protection, 'Progress in Improving the Natural Environment in England 2022/2023' (2024) 6, 12, 41, 67, 101, 115 and 177 <https://assets.publishing.service.gov.uk/media/65a7c8f8ed27ca001327b106/E02987560-progress-in-improving-natural-environment.pdf> accessed 27 April 2024.

would be 'light-touch' and 'essentially guidance'.[247] It is therefore likely that government advisors will continue to scrutinise this sector for ongoing policy gaps, and that managing demands on land will form a recurring part of CCC and OEP advice on progress towards the targets over the coming years.

247 'Land Use Framework Set to Be "Essentially Guidance", Government Confirms' (n 236).

CHAPTER 13

ENVIRONMENTAL PERMITTING

Jake Thorold

Introduction

13.01 The environmental permitting regime is, according to the Department for Environment, Food and Rural Affairs ('DEFRA'), concerned with 'facilities [which] could harm the environment or human health unless they are regulated'.[1] The avoidance of such harm is achieved by requiring the operators of such facilities to obtain an environmental permit. As one of the primary ways in which the government can regulate and control environmentally harmful activities 'on the ground', the environmental permitting regime is an essential component of the regulatory framework for achieving net zero and nature positive objectives.

13.02 The environmental permitting regime is contained within the Environmental Permitting (England and Wales) Regulations 2016 ('the EPR 2016'). As their name makes clear, the EPR 2016 apply to England and Wales only.[2] The EPR 2016 constitute the latest iteration of a regime first introduced in 2007[3] pursuant to the Secretary of State's powers under the Pollution Prevention and Control Act 1999. As explained in the Explanatory Memorandum to the original 2007 regulations, the purpose of the regime was to 'introduce a single streamlined environmental permitting and compliance regime'.[4] This was in response to the previous system of distinct regimes for different sectors, which the Explanatory Memorandum described as being 'perceived as unnecessarily complex for industry, regulators and the public and so in need of simplification'.[5]

13.03 The nature of the EPR 2016 as a consolidatory piece of legislation is apparent in the way it is structured. The core permitting regime is set out in Parts 1–7, which are then supplemented by the Schedules with extensive substantive and technical details and permitting requirements for the various specific regulated polluting activities

1 Department for Environment, Food and Rural Affairs, 'Environmental Permitting: Core Guidance for the Environmental Permitting (England and Wales) Regulations 2016 (SI 2016 No 1154)' (2020) 8 <https://assets.publishing.service.gov.uk/media/5fb3a39dd3bf7f37d7e7270e/environmental-permitting-core-guidance.pdf> accessed 21 November 2023. As a broad point, this core guidance is very helpful in understanding the EPR 2016 and should, in the view of the authors, form a central component in any consideration of the EPR 2016.
2 Albeit they also apply to the sea adjacent to England and Wales out as far as the seaward boundary of the territorial sea: The Environmental Permitting (England and Wales) Regulations 2016, SI 2016/1154 reg 1(3)–(4).
3 The Environmental Permitting (England and Wales) Regulations 2007, SI 2007/3538.
4 Department for Environment, Food and Rural Affairs, 'Explanatory Memorandum to the Environmental Permitting (England and Wales) Regulations 2007' para 2.1.
5 ibid 4.1.

covered by the EPR 2016. The wide range of activities within the scope of the EPR 2016 include (but are not limited to):

- Energy activities[6] (including combustion activities and gasification, liquefaction and refining activities);
- Production and processing of metals;[7]
- Mineral industries;[8]
- The chemical industry (including pharmaceutical production and explosives production);[9]
- Waste management (including landfill disposal, the production of fuel from waste and the treatment of wastewater);[10]
- Timber activities;[11]
- Various food industries;[12]
- Intensive farming (pig and poultry);[13]
- Carbon capture and storage.[14]

13.04 The content of much of the Schedules of the EPR 2016 was designed to implement the permitting requirements of European Union Directives, often simply by requiring the relevant regulator to ensure that the relevant provisions of the respective Directive were complied with. At the end of the 'transition period', following the UK's departure from the European Union, the Environmental Permitting (England and Wales) (Amendment) (EU Exit) Regulations 2019 came into force, including the insertion of a new Schedule 1A to the EPR 2016 to modify the effect of more than 300 cross-references to over 20 EU Directives implemented by the EPR 2016. These provisions ensure that the EPR 2016 Schedules continue to operate, however the legislation must be read carefully, in particular, where the relevant part is impacted by the provisions of Schedule 1A of the EPR 2016.

13.05 Practitioners should also be conscious that the EPR 2016 regime is one which continues to evolve to encompass additional activities. At the time of writing the

---

6 EPR 2016 (n 2) Schedule 1, Part 2(1).
7 ibid Schedule 1, Part 2(2).
8 ibid Schedule 1, Part 2(3).
9 ibid Schedule 1, Part 2(4).
10 ibid Schedule 1, Part 2(5).
11 ibid Schedule 1, Part 2(6.6).
12 ibid Schedule 1, Part 2(6.8).
13 ibid Schedule 1, Part 2(6.9).
14 ibid Schedule 1, Part 2(6.10).

following activities were among those under consideration by the government for inclusion within the EPR 2016 regime:

- Water abstraction and impoundment: Section 61 of the Water Act 2014 provides the Secretary of State and the Welsh Ministers with powers to make regulations to bring water abstraction and water impounding licences within the EPR 2016 regime. The Environment Agency consulted on this in September 2021; however no consultation response had yet been published at the time of writing.

- Dairy and beef farming: The government's April 2023 Plan for Water indicated that it would consult on extending the EPR 2016 to include dairy and intensive beef farms. This was reiterated in the government's Environmental Improvement Plan 2023.

- Sludge and septic tank sludge: In 2020, the Environment Agency announced plans to bring the storage, treatment and use of sludge and septic tank sludge into the EPR 2016 regime in 2023. This aspiration was reaffirmed in the Environment Agency's August 2023 'Strategy for Safe and Sustainable Sludge Use' policy paper albeit with no timescale, and it appears that no further progress had occurred as at the time of writing.[15]

- Decarbonisation ready combustion plants: In March 2023, the government published a consultation on proposed amendments to the carbon capture readiness requirements for new combustion plants at or above 300 megawatts under the nationally significant infrastructure project ('NSIP') regime, including moving decarbonisation ready regulatory requirements from the planning consent process to the EPR 2016 regime. The government in October 2024 published its consultation response confirming that the decarbonisation ready requirements will be moved into the EPR 2016 regime for all applications submitted after 28 February 2026.[16]

- In 2022, the government consulted on proposed changes to the registration system for waste carriers, brokers and dealers, principally by bringing it within the environmental permitting regime. In October 2023, the government indicated that it intends to proceed with its proposals. It had been anticipated that legislation would be introduced during the course of 2024, however at the time of writing (October 2024) this appears unlikely.

---

15 In August 2024, the High Court rejected a judicial review challenge against the EA's decision to remove a target date for implementing its 'Strategy for Safe and Sustainable Sludge Use' without identifying a replacement target date, see *R (Fighting Dirty Ltd) v Environment Agency & Ors* [2024] EWHC 2029 (Admin).

16 <https://www.gov.uk/government/consultations/decarbonisation-readiness-updates-to-the-2009-carbon-capture-readiness-requirements> accessed 23 October 2024.

(i) *The EPR 2016: basic regime*

13.06 The EPR 2016 revolve around the requirement in regulation 12 that a person must not operate a regulated facility or cause or knowingly permit a water discharge activity or groundwater activity except under and to the extent authorised by an environmental permit.[17] The twelve (at the time of writing) regulated facilities are set out in general terms in the interpretative provisions of the EPR 2016,[18] which are then typically afforded further definition in the relevant part of the EPR 2016 Schedules.[19] In line with the goals of the EPR 2016, if a facility can be characterised as more than one regulated activity there is ordinarily no requirement to obtain multiple environmental permits – an operator will usually only need a single permit for its operations at a single site (albeit will need to comply with the requirements that apply to both types of activity).[20]

13.07 The operator of the relevant regulated facility is the person who has, or will have, control of the regulated facility.[21] If more than one operator operates a regulated facility, then each of those operators will require an environmental permit.

13.08 Certain regulated facilities that pose a low risk to the environment and human health are exempted from the requirement to obtain an environmental permit.[22] There are various requirements which must be met before an exemption applies, including that operators must register the exempt activity with the relevant regulator, and renew that registration periodically.[23] The Courts have held that as soon as a facility begins to operate outside of the requirements of the relevant exemption, it ceases to be an 'exempt facility' for the purposes of the EPR 2016.[24]

13.09 In order to obtain a new environmental permit, or to vary an existing one, an operator must make an application to the relevant regulator.[25] The 'regulator' under the EPR 2016 is either the local authority or the Environment Agency in England, and Natural Resources Wales in Wales.[26] The EPR 2016 detail which regulator should be applied to in order to obtain an environmental permit, with local authorities acting as regulators only for smaller scale facilities and activities.[27]

13.10 Operators can choose to apply for either a 'standard rules permit' or a 'bespoke permit'. Standard rules permits are ordinarily for facilities which present a low risk to the environment, whereas bespoke permits are intended for higher-risk facilities.

---

17 EPR 2016 (n 2) reg 12.
18 ibid reg 8(1).
19 For example, 'a water discharge activity' is a 'regulated facility' under reg 8(1). reg 2(1) defines 'water discharge activity' by reference to the definition contained in para 3 of Schedule 21 of the EPR 2016.
20 EPR 2016 (n 2) reg 8(4), 17.
21 ibid 7. See also Department for Environment, Food and Rural Affairs (n 1) para 5.1–5.3.
22 EPR 2016 (n 2) Schedule 3.
23 ibid Schedule 2.
24 *Mustafa and Breslin v The Environmental Agency* [2020] EWCA Crim 597.
25 EPR 2016 (n 2) Schedule 5.
26 ibid reg 32 and Schedule 1(1).
27 EPR 2016 (n 2) Schedule 1. For a useful overview of the division of regulatory responsibilities between local authorities and the Environment Agency (and by extension Natural Resources Wales), see *R v Recycled Materials Supplies Ltd* [2017] EWCA Crim 58.

Standard rules permits are simple to obtain and require the operator to comply with a set of standard rules for the relevant sector. Where an operator considers that the conditions contained within the relevant standard rules are not appropriate, however, they should apply for a bespoke permit. Where an operator is unsure, DEFRA's Core Guidance indicates that pre-application discussions between operators and regulators are likely to be helpful.[28]

13.11 Once an application has been made, the relevant regulator is under a duty to determine it within specified timeframes (which differ depending on the specifics of the permit applied for).[29] For bespoke permit applications, as part of its determination the regulator is required to consult anyone who they consider is affected by, is likely to be affected by, or has an interest in, the application.[30] Any representations received must be considered.[31] In a range of instances, various additional mandatory considerations are detailed in the EPR 2016 Schedules for particular types of activities and permits, for example industrial activities over certain thresholds will need to comply with best available techniques.[32]

13.12 If the regulator considers that the applicant will not operate the regulated facility in accordance with the environmental permit then the application must be refused.[33] DEFRA's Core Guidance suggests that this will be the case in circumstances where the applicant has an inadequate management system, demonstrates inadequate technical competence, has a record of poor behaviour or non-compliance with previous regulatory requirements, or has inadequate financial competence.[34] Where these are not of concern, however, the regulator may grant an application subject to 'such conditions as it sees fit'.[35]

13.13 Of particular interest in the present context is the Environment Agency's requirement for environmental permit holders to integrate climate change adaption planning into their management systems.[36] Considering that regulators are required by the EPR 2016 to periodically review environmental permits, this is a potentially significant development.[37]

---

28 Department for Environment, Food and Rural Affairs (n 1) para 5.4–5.6.

29 EPR 2016 (n 2) Schedule 5 Part 1 para 12. For timeframes, see Schedule 5 Part 1 para 15. If the regulator does not reach a decision within these timeframes, then the application is deemed to be refused.

30 ibid Schedule 5 Part 1 para 6 and definition of 'public consultees' in Schedule 5 Part 1 para 1. The only exceptions to this relate to information relating to national security and confidential information, which itself is subject to various exceptions. See ibid. Schedule 5 Part 1 para 6(2)-(3). The Environment Agency has published a public participation statement on when and how it will consult on environmental permit applications. See 'Environmental Permits: When and How We Consult' (GOV.UK) <https://www.gov.uk/government/publications/environmental-permits-when-and-how-we-consult/environmental-permits-when-and-how-we-consult> accessed 25 March 2024.

31 EPR 2016 (n 2) Schedule 5 Part 1 para 11.

32 See, for example, ibid Schedule 7 paras 3, 5 relating to 'Part A installations'.

33 ibid Schedule 5 Part 1 para 13.

34 DEFRA (n 1) para 9.3.

35 EPR 2016 (n 2) Schedule 5 Part 1 para 12.

36 See section entitled 'A changing climate' in 'Develop a Management System: Environmental Permits' (GOV.UK, 3 April 2023) <https://www.gov.uk/guidance/develop-a-management-system-environmental-permits> accessed 25 March 2024.

37 EPR 2016 (n 2) reg 34. The DEFRA *Environmental Permitting: Core Guidance* explains that reviews are intended 'to check whether permit conditions continue to reflect appropriate standards and remain adequate in light of experience and new knowledge' (para 11.41).

13.14 There is a right of appeal to the Secretary of State or Welsh Ministers against a regulator's refusal to grant, vary or transfer a permit or any conditions imposed in a bespoke permit.[38] Typically this will be heard by the Planning Inspectorate,[39] although in exceptional circumstances an appeal can be recovered by the Secretary of State or Welsh Ministers. Conversely, a decision to grant (or vary) an environmental permit can be challenged by way of judicial review.[40]

(ii) *The EPR 2016: enforcement and other powers of the regulator*

13.15 It is an offence to operate a regulated facility without an environmental permit in contravention of regulation 12(1), to knowingly[41] cause or permit the same, or to fail to comply with or contravene an environmental permit condition.[42] A person found guilty of one of these offences is liable to a fine or imprisonment for up to 12 months (or both) on summary conviction, or a fine or imprisonment for a term not exceeding 5 years (or both) on indictment.[43] Upon conviction the court may also order that the person take steps to remedy the matter where it appears to the court to be in the person's power to do so.[44]

13.16 Notably, in England, the Environment Agency may accept an enforcement undertaking from a person in circumstances where it appears that an offence has been committed.[45] Such an undertaking must specify:[46]

- action to secure that the offence does not continue or recur;
- action to secure that the position is, so far as possible, restored to what it would have been if the offence had not been committed;

---

38 EPR 2016 (n 2) reg 31. See Schedule 6 for the procedure for making an appeal, which is well explained in DEFRA (n 1) ch 13. It may also be that an operator has a right of appeal in relation to other regulatory decisions too, such as Compliance Assessment Reports. See *R (Suez Recycling and Recovery UK Ltd) v Environment Agency* [2023] EWHC 3012 (Admin).
39 Environment Act 1995 s 114.
40 See, for example, *R (BACI Bedfordshire Ltd) v Environment Agency* [2019] EWCA Civ 1962. The Court of Appeal concluded that a scientific error in application materials for an environmental permit did not invalidate the Environment Agency's decision to grant the permit.
41 The Court of Appeal have concluded that 'knowingly permit' in this context requires proving that a defendant: (1) knowingly permitted a regulated activity to take place; and (2) that as a matter of fact the operation was not in accordance with an environmental permit. See *Walker & Sons (Hauliers) Ltd v Environment Agency* [2014] EWCA Crim 100. It is also clear that to 'knowingly permit' does not require a positive act, although the defendant must know about the unauthorised regulated activity. See *Stone and another v Environment Agency* [2018] EWHC (Admin) 994. See also the House of Lords' decisions on the meaning of 'causing' and 'knowingly permitting' in the context of water pollution offences: *Alphacell Ltd v Woodward* [1972] AC 284; *Environment Agency v Empress Car Co (Abertillery) Ltd* [1998] 1 All ER 481.
42 EPR 2016 (n 2) reg 38. This is subject to various defences in reg 40, including where the acts alleged to constitute the contravention were done in an emergency in order to avoid danger to human health, in a case where the person took all reasonably practicable steps to minimise pollution and informed the regulator of the acts as soon as reasonably practicable. For an example of this defence see *Express Ltd v Environment Agency* [2003] EWHC 448 (Admin).
43 EPR 2016 (n 2) reg 39.
44 ibid reg 44.
45 ibid reg 39(6) and Schedule 26.
46 ibid Schedule 26, para 2(1).

- action (including the payment of a sum of money) to benefit any person affected by the offence;
- where restoration of the harm arising from the offence is not possible, action that will secure equivalent benefit or improvement to the environment.

13.17 Where the Environment Agency opts to accept an enforcement undertaking, the person providing it cannot be convicted for the offence to which the undertaking relates (unless, of course, they are not complying with the undertaking).[47]

13.18 The environmental undertaking provisions are indicative of the range of tools provided to regulators under the EPR 2016 above and beyond the relatively blunt tool of criminal prosecution. Perhaps most obviously, regulators also have a wide discretion to vary, suspend and ultimately revoke environmental permits.[48]

13.19 Regulators also have powers to issue enforcement notices which, unlike their counterparts in the planning sphere, can be served as a preventative measure by a regulator where it has reasonable grounds to suspect that a breach of the conditions of an environmental permit is likely to occur.[49] An enforcement notice must clearly specify what steps the operator needs to take, which can extend to requiring operators to remedy the environmental effects caused by any contravention.[50] A regulator can also apply to the High Court for an injunction to enforce compliance with an enforcement or other specified notice.[51]

13.20 As for a refusal to grant an environmental permit, an operator can appeal against an enforcement, suspension or revocation notice, with this ordinarily being dealt with by the Planning Inspectorate.[52]

13.21 As of December 2023, the Environment Agency has a new power under the EPR 2016 to impose 'variable monetary penalties'.[53] There is no cap on the level of financial penalty which can be imposed, albeit a recipient has a right of appeal to the First-tier Tribunal. The introduction of VMPs is an important step in permitting the Environment Agency to take punitive action against offenders without needing to take the more serious step of criminal proceedings.

13.22 In addition to powers in relation to operators, regulators are also provided under the EPR 2016 with a wide discretion to take 'steps' to remove the risk of serious pollution where it considers that risk to exist as a result of the operation of either a regulated

---

47 ibid Schedule 26, para 3.
48 ibid regs 20, 22, 37.
49 ibid reg 36.
50 ibid reg 36(3.b).
51 ibid reg 42.
52 ibid reg 31 and Schedule 6.
53 ibid Schedule 26A.

facility or an exempted facility.[54] The regulator is able to recover its costs of doing so from the operator provided it can show that there was in fact a risk of serious pollution.[55]

(iii) *The EPR 2016 and a net zero and nature positive future*

13.23 In summary, the EPR 2016 provide regulators with a range of powers and considerable flexibility to regulate polluting activities and take action against unauthorised activities which harm the environment. As increasingly more facilities and activities come under the remit of the EPR 2016, their role in ensuring that unauthorised fossil fuel combustion does not undermine the UK's climate change and net zero goals will only become more important.

13.24 In the author's view, the potential extension of the environmental permitting regime to encompass dairy and beef farming could be particularly impactful in helping the UK to meet its net zero and nature positive aspirations. As the government's Environmental Improvement Plan 2023 observes, the extension of environmental permitting conditions to pig and poultry farming is estimated to have decreased emissions from those industries by around 30%.[56] Given that dairy and intensive beef farms together contributed over half of the UK's ammonia emissions from agriculture in 2020, if similar reductions could be achieved this would be impactful. It remains to be seen whether the government will extend the environmental permitting regime in this way, however.

13.25 The success of environmental permitting in reducing emissions in pig and poultry farming is demonstrative of the impacts that the permitting regime can have when appropriate conditions accompany the grant of a permit. As ever, however, the extent to which the EPR 2016 can effectively contribute to the UK's net zero and nature positive will depend on the extent to which regulators are given the financial resources to ensure that the environmental permitting regime is able to operate effectively.

---

54 EPR 2016 (n 2) reg 57(1).
55 ibid reg 57(4)–(5).
56 Department for the Environment, Food and Rural Affairs, 'Environmental Improvement Plan 2023: First revision of the 23 Year Environment Plan', 88 <https://assets.publishing.service.gov.uk/media/64a6d9c1c531eb000c64fffa/environmental-improvement-plan-2023.pdf> accessed 19 April 2024.

CHAPTER 14

GREENHOUSE GAS EMISSIONS TRADING

Jake Thorold

Introduction

14.01 Emissions trading, often referred to as carbon trading, is a mechanism through which private parties buy and sell rights to emit pollutants (most commonly CO_2). Typically, they operate by way of 'cap and trade' schemes, by which the government sets an overall cap on the maximum amount of a particular pollutant which can be emitted in a given year, with a specified number of credits on offer up to that cap (usually done on the basis that one credit is equal to one tonne of CO_2 (or other greenhouse gas ('GHG')).[1] Participants in a scheme can only emit up to the level permitted by the credits they hold. If they wish to emit more, then they are required to find a willing seller of credits, thereby creating a marketplace.

14.02 Put simply, the aspiration of emissions trading schemes is to make it cost money to emit GHG. If the costs of doing so are too high, the hope is that companies will look to innovate to be more environmentally friendly.

14.03 The idea of emissions trading is not new, with their first use coming in the United States during the 1970s following prior research by various economists.[2] On the international stage, the idea came to prominence with the formation of the International Emissions Trading Mechanism established under article 17 of the Kyoto Protocol.[3] At the domestic level, however, between 2002–2006 the United Kingdom ran one of the world's first emissions trading schemes for a five year trial period, designed to familiarise UK businesses with the mechanism and help to develop a planned European Union-wide scheme. That scheme, the EU Emissions Trading System ('EU ETS'), is now the largest emissions trading scheme in the world, covering a wide array of industries,

1 This is commonly referred to as a 'carbon credit'.
2 Hugh S Gorman and Barry D Solomon, 'The Origins and Practice of Emissions Trading' (2002) 14 Journal of Policy History 293.
3 Kyoto Protocol to the United Nations Framework Convention on Climate Change (adopted 11 December 1997, entered into force 16 February 2005) 2303 UNTS 162 Article 17. See paras 2.28–2.34 in Chapter 2.

sectors and activities[4] that require large amounts of energy and therefore account for significant levels of CO_2, N_2O and perfluorocarbons ('PFCs') emissions.[5]

14.04 When the UK decided to leave the EU there was considerable uncertainty regarding the UK's involvement with the EU ETS going forward, with organisations such as the Climate Change Committee ('CCC') indicating a preference for remaining part of the EU scheme.[6] As negotiations progressed, however, it became clear that the UK would leave the EU ETS, albeit it was only in December 2020 – just days before the end of the Brexit transition period – that the UK announced that it would introduce a new UK-wide emissions trading system.[7] In its White Paper, the government declared that the UK Emissions Trading Scheme ('UK ETS') would be 'the world's first net zero emissions trading scheme'.[8] Although the scheme initially launched in 2021 was not tied to the government's net zero targets, following a detailed consultation process in July 2023 the UK Emissions Trading Scheme Authority ('UKETSA') – the joint UK, Scottish, Welsh and Northern Irish government body which runs the scheme – announced revised caps from 2024 which require affected industries to 'bring their emissions down at the rate needed to reach net zero goals' (described as 'the net zero cap').[9] The UKETSA also announced plans to expand the UK ETS to additional industries, including domestic maritime transport and waste.

14.05 The importance of the UK ETS to the UK meeting its net zero targets under the Climate Change Act 2008 ('CCA 2008') has been widely recognised. In *Mission Zero: Independent Review of Net Zero*, for example, it was stated that carbon pricing as in the UK ETS was 'the most cost-efficient way to support transition to net zero on an economy-wide scale' and 'central to achieving [n]et [z]ero by 2050'.[10]

4 A full list of the sectors and activities covered by the EU ETS can be found in European Commission, 'Scope of the EU Emissions Trading System' <https://climate.ec.europa.eu/eu-action/eu-emissions-trading-system-eu-ets/scope-eu-emissions-trading-system_en> accessed 17 April 2024.

5 In March 2023, the EU created a second ETS scheme (known as 'EU ETS 2') covering CO_2 emissions from fuel combustion in buildings, road transport and additional sectors (mainly small industry not covered by the existing EU ETS). More information can be found in European Commission, 'ETS2: Buildings, Road Transport and Additional Sectors' <https://climate.ec.europa.eu/eu-action/eu-emissions-trading-system-eu-ets/ets2-buildings-road-transport-and-additional-sectors_en> accessed 17 April 2024.

6 See, for example, Committee on Climate Change, 'Meeting Carbon Budgets – Implications of Brexit for UK Climate Policy' (2016) <https://www.theccc.org.uk/wp-content/uploads/2016/10/Meeting-Carbon-Budgets-Implications-of-Brexit-for-UK-climate-policy-Committee-on-Climate-Change-October-2016.pdf> accessed 17 April 2024.

7 Secretary of State for Business, Energy and Industrial Strategy, 'Energy White Paper: Powering Our Net Zero Future' (2020) CP 337 <https://assets.publishing.service.gov.uk/media/5fdc61e2d3bf7f3a3bdc8cbf/201216_BEIS_EWP_Command_Paper_Accessible.pdf> accessed 17 April 2024.

8 ibid 118.

9 UK Government and others, 'Developing the UK Emissions Trading Scheme: Main Response' (2023) <https://assets.publishing.service.gov.uk/government/uploads/system/uploads/attachment_data/file/1166812/uk-emissions-trading-scheme-consultation-government-response.pdf> accessed 17 April 2024.

10 Rt Hon Chris Skidmore MP, 'Mission Zero: Independent Review of Net Zero' (2023) paras 1063–4 <https://assets.publishing.service.gov.uk/government/uploads/system/uploads/attachment_data/file/1128689/mission-zero-independent-review.pdf> accessed 17 April 2024.

The UK ETS

(i) *The UK ETS: basic regime*

14.06 The UK ETS is primarily contained in the Greenhouse Gas Emissions Trading Scheme Order 2020 (as amended) ('the GHG ETS Order'), made under section 44 of the Climate Change Act 2008. This is a highly technical regime and as such provided here is only a summary of the overarching legal architecture of the UK ETS.

14.07 The purpose of the UK ETS is described in the GHG ETS Order as 'to limit, or encourage the limitation of, the emission of greenhouse gases in the trading period[11] from the carrying out of – (a) regulated activities by operators of installations; and (b) aviation activities by aircraft operators'.[12]

14.08 The GHGs and sectors covered by the UK ETS are set out in Schedule 2 of the GHG ETS Order, which defines what is meant by 'installation' (para 2) and 'regulated activity' (para 3). While 'installation'[13] is defined by reference to an equally vague (and undefined in the GHG ETS Order) concept of a 'stationary technical unit',[14] in effect what matters most is whether a 'regulated activity' takes place. Table C in para 3 of Schedule 2 details in column 1 which activities are in scope of the UK ETS, while column 2 details which greenhouse gas(es) an activity must produce in order to constitute a 'regulated activity'.[15] Schedule 1 of the GHG ETS Order describes what constitutes an 'aviation activity',[16] as well as various exceptions.

14.09 Operators of 'regulated activities' under the GHG ETS Order must apply for a GHG emissions permit,[17] and surrender 'allowances' as required by that permit in each UK ETS year.[18] Each 'allowance' permits its holder to emit 1 tonne of CO_2 or equivalent.[19]

14.10 The number of allowances available each year must not exceed the sum reached via the calculation detailed in article 20 of the GHG ETS Order, albeit that is subject to an overall cap for the trading period contained in article 19. The calculation of available allowances relies heavily on the base figures for each scheme year set out in article 22

11 The 'trading period' is 1 January 2021 to 31 December 2030. See The GHG ETS Order Article 4. This is split into two 'allocation periods' of 2021–2025 and 2026–2030.
12 ibid Article 16(2).
13 It should be noted that there are various specific exceptions to what will constitute an 'installation' for the purposes of the GHG ETS Order, for example installations which solely use biomass as a fuel. See ibid Article 2(2).
14 Installations are defined in paragraph 2 of Schedule 2 of the GHG ETS Order, as '*a stationary technical unit or units where one or more regulated activities are carried out*'.
15 It should be noted that there are certain opt-outs from the UK ETS for particular activities which would constitute a 'regulated activity'. For example, hospitals and so-called 'ultra-small emitters' producing less than 25,000 tonnes of carbon dioxide are able to opt out of the UK ETS should they wish to. See the GHG ETS Order Schedule 7.
16 Aviation activity is defined by para 1 of Schedule 1 of the GHG ETS Order. The excluded flights are listed at para 2 of Schedule 1 of the GHG ETS Order, but include e.g. military flights, search and rescue flights, firefighting flights.
17 The GHG ETS Order Article 26.
18 ibid Article 27. ETS years simply mirror the calendar year from 1 January to 31 December (see Article 4).
19 ibid Article 18.

of the GHG ETS Order, which decrease over time. At present, these are calculated at 5% less than the UK's expected notional share of the EU ETS cap for the period of 2021–2030, however in 2024 the ETS allowances were stated by government to be set at a level consistent with the 'net zero cap'.[20] At the time of writing, the figures in article 22 of the GHG ETS Order had not changed, however a limitation on the number of allowances available in 2024 to that consistent with the net zero cap was achieved by regulations limiting the number of allowances which could be auctioned in 2024 (and thereafter) to that level.[21]

14.11 Most allowances under the UK ETS are auctioned, although the GHG ETS Order also contains provision for the award of free allowances in particular circumstances.[22] The UK ETS participants eligible for free allowances for the period 2021–2025 are set out in an allocation table published by the government.[23] As set out in the government's guidance on the UK ETS, the purpose of free allocations is to 'reduce the risk of carbon leakage for UK businesses', i.e. to prevent businesses seeking ways to export emissions overseas as a means to avoid domestic climate taxation.[24] Decisions on applications for free allowances are made by the relevant UK ETS authority (see paragraph 14.15 below).

14.12 The rules relating to the auctioning of allowances are contained the Greenhouse Gas Emissions Trading Scheme Auctioning Regulations 2021. Although a detailed account of these regulations is beyond the scope of this chapter, it should be noted that the regulations contain various mechanisms to regulate the price of allowances in the UK ETS, such as setting minimum reserve prices. The system of auctions for allowances is overseen by the Financial Conduct Authority.[25]

---

20 In January 2024, the 2024 UK ETS auction was announced, with the number of allowances auctioned being just under 69 million. The government has stated that this 'reflect[s] that the new net zero consistent cap for the scheme announced in July 2023 is being implemented'. See Department for Business, Energy and Industrial Strategy and Department for Energy Security and Net Zero, 'Policy Paper: UK Emissions Trading Scheme Markets' (GOV.UK) <https://www.gov.uk/government/publications/uk-emissions-trading-scheme-markets/uk-emissions-trading-scheme-markets> accessed 17 April 2024.

21 The Greenhouse Gas Emissions Trading Scheme Auctioning (Amendment) Regulations 2023, SI 994/2023 which made the necessary amendments to the Greenhouse Gas Emissions Trading Scheme Auctioning Regulations 2021, SI 484/2021. This is helpfully explained in the explanatory memorandum to the 2023 amendment regulations. See 'Explanatory Memorandum to The Greenhouse Gas Emissions Trading Scheme Auctioning (Amendment) Regulations 2023. 2023 No. 994' <https://www.legislation.gov.uk/uksi/2023/994/pdfs/uksiem_20230994_en_001.pdf> accessed 17 April 2024.

22 The GHG ETS Order Article 4A.

23 See 'UK ETS Allocation Table for Operators of Installations' (GOV.UK, 20 February 2024) <https://www.gov.uk/government/publications/uk-ets-allocation-table-for-operators-of-installations> accessed 17 April 2024. It should be noted that the government has by regulations postponed the application window for applying for free allocation of allowances in the 2026 to 2030 allocation period by one year to 1 April to 30 June 2025 (see the Greenhouse Gas Emissions Trading Scheme (Amendment) Order 2024, SI 2024/192. In September 2024 the government published a consultation proposing moving the start of the second free allocation period from 2026 to 2027, and extending the current allocation period to include 2026 <https://www.gov.uk/government/consultations/uk-emissions-trading-scheme-free-allocation-review> accessed 18 October 2024.

24 Department for Business, Energy and Industrial Strategy and Department for Energy Security and Net Zero, 'Guidance: Participating in the UK ETS' (GOV.UK) <https://www.gov.uk/government/publications/participating-in-the-uk-ets/participating-in-the-uk-ets> accessed 17 April 2024. See also paras 34.20–34.21 in Chapter 34, which addresses carbon leakage.

25 See The Recognised Auction Platforms (Amendment and Miscellaneous Provisions) Regulations 2021, SI 2021/494.

14.13 The GHG ETS Order expressly allows for the trading of allowances, save for where that is prohibited by other legislation.[26]

14.14 To help facilitate this, the GHG ETS Order has also established a UK Emissions Trading Registry, an online platform monitoring the holding of allowances, the surrender of them and enabling the easy transfer of allowances between different accounts.[27]

(ii) *The UK ETS: enforcement and other powers of the regulator and appeals*

14.15 The regulators for the UK ETS are as follows:[28]

- Environment Agency in England;
- Natural Resources Wales in Wales;
- Scottish Environmental Protection Agency in Scotland;
- Chief Inspector in the Department of Environment in Northern Ireland;
- Department for Energy Security and Net Zero for offshore installations.

14.16 The enforcement powers of regulators for non-compliance with the UK ETS scheme are contained in Part 7 of the GHG ETS Order. Regulators have powers to issue:

- An enforcement notice,[29] if an operator contravenes a requirement of the Order, the Monitoring and Reporting Regulation 2018,[30] the Verification Regulation 2018,[31] the Free Allocation Regulation,[32] a GHG permit or an emissions monitoring plan.[33] There are various requirements for such an enforcement notice, including that it must set out details of the contravention or likely contravention, the steps that must be taken to remedy the contravention or to ensure that a contravention does not occur, and the period within which steps must be taken.[34]
- Impose a civil penalty.[35]

---

26 The GHG ETS Order Article 23.
27 The GHG ETS Order Schedule 5A.
28 ibid Articles 9–14.
29 ibid Article 44.
30 See ibid Article 24, which holds that the Monitoring and Reporting Regulation 2018 has effect for the purpose of the UK ETS with various modifications contained in the GHG ETS Order.
31 See ibid Article 25, which holds that the Verification Regulation 2018 has effect for the purpose of the UK ETS with various modifications contained in the GHG ETS Order.
32 This refers to Commission Delegated Regulation (EU) 2019/331 of 19 December 2018 which, as per Article 4 of the GHG ETS Order, 'forms part of domestic law'. This was originally made for the EU ETS, but is adapted for the UK ETS. See the Greenhouse Gas Emissions Trading Scheme (Amendment) Order 2020.
33 Emissions monitoring plans must be applied for by aircraft operators (and may be applied for by others) in order to set out how the operator's aviation emissions will be monitored for the purposes of the GHG ETS Order. See the GHG ETS Order Articles 28–32.
34 ibid Article 44(3).
35 ibid Article 47.

14.17 Articles 50–68 of the GHG ETS Order set out the various circumstances in which a civil penalty notice can be imposed, including carrying out a regulated activity without a GHG permit,[36] failing to surrender allowances,[37] failing to comply with an emissions monitoring plan[38] and failing to comply with an enforcement notice.[39]

14.18 For most of the matters set out in articles 50–68 of the GHG ETS Order, the regulator has a discretion as to whether to impose a civil penalty.[40] In certain circumstances, however, the GHG ETS Order requires that a civil penalty must be imposed where the regulator considers a person is liable:

- By failing to surrender allowances;[41]

- Where a hospital or small emitter exceeds the installation's emissions target (except where that target was incorrectly calculated);[42]

- Where an ultra-small emitter's reportable emissions exceed the maximum amount permitted for the year.[43]

14.19 The mandatory nature of these civil penalties and their compatibility with Article 1 Protocol 1 ('A1P1') of the European Convention on Human Rights ('ECHR') providing for the right to property has recently been considered by the Upper Tribunal in *ABX Air Inv v Environment Agency*.[44] The Environment Agency had imposed a civil penalty of £382,000 on an aircraft operator for failure to surrender sufficient allowances. The Tribunal considered that on a literal interpretation the mandatory civil penalty provision contravened A1P1 because it prohibited any consideration of the nature of the offending. It therefore went on to consider whether an ECHR-compliant interpretation was possible under section 3 of the Human Rights Act 1998, concluding that the mandatory provision had to be read to include the wording 'save where to impose a civil penalty on the person would be contrary to section 6(1) of the Human Rights Act 1998'.[45] On the facts, the Upper Tribunal did not accept that the aircraft operator had established that the penalty was a disproportionate interference with their A1P1 right.

14.20 The level of civil penalty for various of the instances in articles 50–68[46] is set by reference to the price per tonne of CO_2 or equivalent for a particular year, referred to

36 ibid Article 50.
37 ibid Article 52.
38 ibid Article 62.
39 ibid Article 65.
40 ibid Article 47(1).
41 ibid Article 52.
42 ibid Article 54.
43 ibid Article 59.
44 *ABX Air Inv v Environment Agency* [2023] UKFTT 847 (GRC).
45 ibid, para 45.
46 See the GHG ETS Order Articles 50, 54, 56, 57, 59, 60.

as the 'carbon price'.[47] The UK ETS authority is required to determine and publish the carbon price for each UK ETS year.[48]

14.21 Part 8 of the GHG ETS Order provides a right of appeal for a wide range of decisions made under the GHG ETS Order, including against the imposition of a civil penalty.[49] It should be noted that the 'appeal body' differs depending on the part of the UK and the particular decision in question.[50] With various exceptions (including, notably, enforcement notices), the making of an appeal suspends the effect of a decision or notice pending the final determination or withdrawal of the appeal.[51] In determining an appeal, the relevant appeal body may affirm the decision, quash the decision or vary any of its terms, and giving directions as to the exercise of the regulator's functions under the GHG ETS Order.[52]

14.22 The nature of the appeal jurisdiction under the GHG ETS Order has been considered by the Upper Tribunal in the context of an excess emissions civil penalty.[53] The Tribunal concluded that the first question for the appeal body is whether the operator did in fact fail to comply with the relevant obligation. Where the relevant obligation has been breached, then an appeal must be dismissed unless the imposition of the penalty would breach section 6 of the Human Rights Act 1998, a determination which the appeal body must itself make. In respect of challenges to a regulator's discretion to impose a penalty, the appeal jurisdiction extended only to judicial review grounds of challenge.[54]

(iii) *The UK ETS and climate change*

14.23 As described above, the UK ETS has been recognised by the government and independent bodies, such as the CCC, as a central plank in the UK's climate change and net zero policy. The government's announcement in December 2023 extending the UK ETS from 2030 to 2050 reflects this.[55]

14.24 The UK ETS has not been without controversy, however. Following its introduction, its lawfulness was challenged in the High Court[56] on grounds: (1) that in approving

---

47 ibid Article 46.
48 ibid Article 46(7). For the most recent publication, see Department for Energy Security and Net Zero, 'Guidance: UK ETS: Carbon Prices for Use in Civil Penalties, 2023' (GOV.UK) <https://www.gov.uk/government/publications/determinations-of-the-uk-ets-carbon-price/uk-ets-carbon-prices-for-use-in-civil-penalties-2024> accessed 18 October 2024.
49 The GHG ETS Order 2020 Article 70.
50 ibid Article 71.
51 ibid Article 72.
52 ibid Article 73. In the case of a deemed refusal under the GHG ETS Order, the appeal body may also substitute its own decision for that of the regulator.
53 *ABX Air Inv v Environment Agency* (n 45) paras 48–54.
54 As formulated in *R (Begum) v Special Immigration Appeals Commission* [2021] UKSC 7 [68].
55 <https://www.gov.uk/government/publications/uk-emissions-trading-scheme-long-term-pathway/the-long-term-pathway-for-the-uk-emissions-trading-scheme> accessed 18 October 2024. See also the UK ETS authority's response to Mission Zero: Independent Review of Net Zero, entitled 'The long-term pathway for the UK Emissions Trading Scheme' <https://www.gov.uk/government/publications/uk-emissions-trading-scheme-long-term-pathway/the-long-term-pathway-for-the-uk-emissions-trading-scheme> accessed 18 October 2024.
56 *R (Elliott-Smith) v Secretary of State for Business, Energy and Industrial Strategy* [2021] EWHC 1633 (Admin).

the levels of the allowances cap and the proposed auction reserve prices the Secretary of State for Business, Energy and Industrial Strategy had failed to have regard to a mandatory material consideration in the form of requirements in the Paris Agreement to take urgent action to limit GHGs; and (2) that the UK ETS did not fulfil or serve the statutory purpose of section 44 of the Climate Change Act 2008 of 'limiting or causing the limitation of activities' causing or contributing to greenhouse gas emissions.[57]

14.25 The High Court refused to grant permission for the challenge, concluding in summary that: (1) on the facts the Secretary of State's approach to the Paris Agreement was tenable,[58] and those taking the decision adequately took it into account in deciding to introduce the UK ETS; (2) a trading scheme introduced under section 44 of the Climate Change Act 2008 did not necessarily have to achieve a reduction in activities contributing to GHG emissions; it was sufficient that the design of the scheme limited or encouraged the limitation of those activities. The UK ETS had been developed and designed in order to fulfil the statutory purposes in section 44 of the 2008 Act, and achieved that aim.

14.26 The government's decision to align the UK ETS with its net zero strategy is significant, as demonstrated by the October 2023 announcement that the number of allowances available to buy in 2024 would be 12.4% fewer than in 2023. By 2027, the number will be 45% lower than in 2023.[59] There is considerable scope for the UK ETS to go further, however, including to expand into sectors not currently included.[60] In May 2024, for example, the government launched consultations on the intergration of greenhouse gas removals[61] and energy from waste and waste incineration[62] into the UK ETS. At the time of writing it is unclear what the status of these proposed changes is following the change of government in July 2024. As pointed out in the Independent Review of Net Zero in January 2023, by 2030 the current sectors covered by the UK ETS will only cover 18% of UK territorial emissions, with important sectors such as agriculture and international aviation and shipping not included.[63]

14.27 There also remains the prospect of the UK ETS being linked with the EU ETS, a development which the UK and the EU are required to 'give serious consideration' to

---

57 ibid paras 32–33. Section 44 of the CCA 2008 is set out at para 35 of the judgment.

58 See also *R (Friends of the Earth Ltd) v Secretary of State for International Trade/Export Credits Guarantee Department (UK Export Finance)* [2023] EWCA Civ 14 in which the Court of Appeal confirmed that the standard of review in relation to the government's interpretation of the Paris Agreement (it being an unincorporated international treaty) was whether the government had adopted a 'tenable view'.

59 Department for Energy Security and Net Zero and others, 'News Story: Emissions Scheme to Reduce Sale of Carbon Allowances on Path to Net Zero' (GOV.UK) <https://www.gov.uk/government/news/emissions-scheme-to-reduce-sale-of-carbon-allowances-on-path-to-net-zero> accessed 17 April 2024.

60 In Rt Hon Chris Skidmore MP (n 10) para 1073, it is suggested that these sectors could include domestic transport and heat and buildings. The UK ETS in its response to the Independent Review of Net Zero committed that it 'will explore expanding the UK ETS to more sectors of the economy' <https://www.gov.uk/government/publications/uk-emissions-trading-scheme-long-term-pathway/the-long-term-pathway-for-the-uk-emissions-trading-scheme> accessed 18 October 2024.

61 See <https://www.gov.uk/government/consultations/integrating-greenhouse-gas-removals-in-the-uk-emissions-trading-scheme access> accessed 18 October 2024.

62 See <https://www.gov.uk/government/consultations/uk-emissions-trading-scheme-scope-expansion-waste> accessed 18 October 2024.

63 Rt Hon Chris Skidmore MP (n 10) paras 1071–4.

under the terms of the EU-UK Trade and Co-operation Agreement.[64] In June 2023, the government indicated that no decision on linking had yet been made albeit the government was open to cooperating on carbon pricing and to considering a linkage between the two ETS systems.[65]

64 Trade and Cooperation Agreement between the European Union and the European Atomic Energy Community, of the one part, and the United Kingdom of Great Britain and Northern Ireland, of the other part [2021] OJ L 149/10 Article 392(6).

65 'Government Response to the European Affairs Committee Report. Report from the European Affairs Committee on the UK–EU Future Relationship' (2023) <https://committees.parliament.uk/publications/40685/documents/198331/default/> accessed 17 April 2024.

CHAPTER 15

FACILITATING THE ENERGY TRANSITION

Daniel Kozelko

Introduction

15.01 The importance of the switch to renewable energy generation as part of meeting the UK's net zero commitments cannot be overstated. In 2022 greenhouse gas ('GHG') emissions from energy generation in the UK accounted for 10.6% of total UK emissions.[1] In the 'Net Zero Strategy: Build Back Greener', the government committed to decarbonising the power system by 2035.[2] That was the case even while demand for electricity was predicted to go up by 50% over the same period.[3] This chapter focuses on the infrastructure required for the transition to a decarbonised power system by 2035. The following chapter then focuses on forms of energy generation.

15.02 While demand for electricity is predicted to go up significantly, this arises against a backdrop of a general decline in the demand for energy since the UK peak in 2005.[4] Indeed, the government is currently committed to a 15% decrease in final energy demand by 2030 compared to 2021 levels.[5] Thus, the predicted increase in demand for electricity indicates a key point: electrification, using renewable energy generating little by way of GHG emissions, is a central mechanism by which other sectors (such as transport[6]) can decarbonise en route to net zero.

(i) *Grid makeup of the UK*

15.03 In 2022 the UK generated 294.1TWh of electricity. Of that energy, 33% was generated from fossil fuels, while 53% was generated from renewable sources (of which

1 48MtCO_2e of a total 450MtCO_2e; reported as 11%. Climate Change Committee, 'Progress in Reducing Emissions: 2023 Report to Parliament' (2023) 75 and 199 <https://www.theccc.org.uk/wp-content/uploads/2023/06/Progress-in-reducing-UK-emissions-2023-Report-to-Parliament.pdf> accessed 4 April 2024.
2 Department for Energy Security and Net Zero, 'Net Zero Strategy: Build Back Greener' (2021) 19 <https://www.gov.uk/government/publications/net-zero-strategy> accessed 28 September 2023.
3 From 300TWh in 2020 to 460TWh in 2035. Climate Change Committee, 'The Sixth Carbon Budget: The UK's Path to Net Zero' (December 2020) 134.
4 Climate Change Committee, 'Progress in Reducing Emissions: 2023 Report to Parliament' (n 1) 91.
5 HM Treasury, 'Autumn Statement 2022' (2022) CP 751 para 5.6 <https://assets.publishing.service.gov.uk/media/63761099d3bf7f720cfc0040/CCS1022065440-001_SECURE_HMT_Autumn_Statement_November_2022_Web_accessible__1_.pdf>.
6 National Grid ESO, 'Future Energy Scenarios 2023' (July 2023) 85 <https://www.nationalgrideso.com/document/283101/download> accessed 28 September 2024.

39% was wind or solar). To meet the requirements of net zero, 'Future Energy Scenarios'[7] predicts that:[8]

- By 2025: between 66% and 76% of generation needs to be from renewable sources (of which between 53% and 65% needs to be wind or solar). The scenarios call for 18% or less generation from fossil fuels.

- By 2035: between 87% and 91% of generation needs to be from renewable sources (of which between 81% and 86% needs to be wind or solar). The scenarios call for 2% or less generation from fossil fuels.

- By 2050: between 87% and 89% of generation needs to be from renewable sources (of which between 78% and 84% needs to be wind or solar). The scenarios call for no generation from fossil fuels. The drop in renewable generation compared to 2035 is because of the growth required in nuclear over the period, which 'Future Energy Scenarios' does not include within renewables.

(ii) *Planning policy and NSIPs*

15.04 While developments of all shapes and sizes will be important to achieving net zero, nationally significant infrastructure projects will be key. This is because achieving such a fundamental shift in sources of energy in the UK by 2035 requires building and replacing vast amounts of generating capacity. For energy generation in England, any generating station onshore with a capacity of 50MW or over is classified as a nationally significant infrastructure project ('NSIP'), while offshore anything with a capacity over 100MW is an NSIP.[9]

15.05 National Policy Statement ('NPS') EN-1, designated in November 2023, makes clear the need for new nationally significant electricity infrastructure. It reaffirms the principle that any infrastructure covered by the NPS shall be considered on the basis that 'the government has demonstrated that there is a need for those types of infrastructure which is urgent'[10] and that 'substantial weight should be given to this need'.[11]

7 National Grid ESO, 'FES 2023 Data Workbook' ES.05-08 <https://www.nationalgrideso.com/future-energy/future-energy-scenarios-fes>.
8 'Future Energy Scenarios 2023' provides four different scenarios: Consumer Transformation, System Transformation, Leading the Way, and Falling Short. Excluding Falling Short, the three other scenarios describe different routes to achieving (or surpassing) net zero by 2050. The ranges for figures in the rest of this paragraph reflect the different figures for these three scenarios.
9 Planning Act 2008 s 15. However, this does not apply to onshore wind which was excluded from the definition of NSIP in March 2016: The Infrastructure Planning (Onshore Wind Generating Stations) Order 2016 reg 3. An amendment to reinclude onshore wind was added to the Levelling-up and Regeneration Bill in the House of Lords but was removed by the House of Commons shortly before the Bill became law (Lords amendment 244, HC Deb 17 October 2023, vol 738, cols 285–287; not insisted upon in the House of Lords, HL Deb 23 October 2023, vol 833, col 480).
10 Department for Energy Security and Net Zero, 'Overarching National Policy Statement for Energy (EN-1) (November 2023)'(2023) para 3.2.6. <https://assets.publishing.service.gov.uk/media/65bbfbdc709fe1000f637052/overarching-nps-for-energy-en1.pdf> accessed 4 April 2024.
11 ibid para 3.2.7.

15.06 However, a notable departure from the March 2023 draft of NPS EN-1 is that a 'critical national priority ('CNP') for the provision of nationally significant new offshore wind infrastructure'[12] has become a 'critical national priority for low carbon infrastructure'. This widens up the scope of the CNP designation significantly:[13]

> 4.2.1 Government has committed to fully decarbonising the power system by 2035, subject to security of supply, to underpin its 2050 net zero ambitions. More than half of final energy demand in 2050 could be met by electricity, as transport and heating in particular shift from fossil fuel to electrical technology.
>
> 4.2.2 Ensuring the UK is more energy independent, resilient and secure requires the smooth transition to abundant, low-carbon energy. The UK's strategy to increase supply of low carbon energy is dependent on deployment of renewables and nuclear power generation, alongside hydrogen and CCUS. Our energy security and net zero ambitions will only be delivered if we can enable the development of new low carbon sources of energy at speed and scale.
>
> 4.2.3 With smart and strategic planning, the UK can maintain high environmental standards and minimise impacts while increasing the levels of deployment at the scale and pace needed to meet our energy security and net zero ambitions.
>
> 4.2.4 Government has therefore concluded that there is a critical national priority (CNP) for the provision of nationally significant low carbon infrastructure.

15.07 It is correct to say that the designation as a critical national priority does not create an additional or cumulative need case or weighting to that which is outlined in the remainder of the policy for each type of energy infrastructure.[14] However, it is telling that the government considered it necessary to widen the designation significantly in the policy, which came as a result of consultation on the draft NPSs.[15]

(iii) *Types of generation*

15.08 The remainder of this chapter addresses storage and network infrastructure as important further energy infrastructure which will support the expansion of renewable energy generation and the UK achieving net zero. The next chapter considers various types of generation which are relevant to the UK meeting its net zero goals. Some of these are not, necessarily, renewable energy, but are an important part of moving away from generation using fossil fuels (and supporting generation from renewable sources): for example, nuclear power.

---

12 Department for Energy Security and Net Zero, 'Overarching Policy Statement For Energy (EN-1) (March 2023 draft)' (2023) para 3.3.59 <https://assets.publishing.service.gov.uk/media/64252f3b60a35e00120cb158/NPS_EN-1.pdf> accessed 4 April 2024.

13 Department for Energy Security and Net Zero, 'Overarching National Policy Statement for Energy (EN-1) (November 2023)' (n 10).

14 ibid para 4.2.7.

15 Department for Energy Security and Net Zero, 'Consultation Response Planning for New Energy Infrastructure' (2023) 14 <https://assets.publishing.service.gov.uk/media/655ddb1f544aea0019fb323b/national-policy-statement-consultation-government-response.pdf> accessed 4 April 2024.

Energy Storage

(i) *Introduction*

15.09 Energy storage describes any installation which stores electrical energy. Such installations are, usually, either freestanding installations connected to the electricity grid,[16] or installations built in tandem with energy generating sources. In the UK there are currently two main forms of energy storage infrastructure:

- Pumped-storage hydroelectricity: electrical energy is used to pump water uphill to a storage reservoir. Stored energy is then released by allowing the water to run downhill under gravity and through electricity generating turbines.
- Battery storage: electrical energy is stored as chemical energy. Typically, this is done using lithium-ion cells. They are often called battery energy storage systems ('BESS').

15.10 Energy storage is an area of significant growth in the UK. With 29GWh of installed energy storage volume in 2022, National Grid Electricity System Operator's ('ESO') assessment in 'Future Energy Scenarios' for 2023 indicates that successfully achieving net zero will require between 116GWh and 197GWh of installed storage volume.[17]

(ii) *Contribution to net zero*

15.11 Storage of electrical energy is recognised by the government as 'essential' to net zero.[18] This is because energy storage allows for the mitigation of the drawbacks of certain forms of renewable generation, and the additional facilities such storage provides to the electricity grid:[19]

- Across a day, energy storage can charge at times of low demand or high generation, and discharge at times of high demand or low generation. The need for such storage is particularly acute in the context of solar generation (due to the day/night cycle of this source).
- Across longer periods, energy storage can charge at times of low demand or high generation, and discharge at times of high demand or low generation. The need

16 This general term is used to refer to the national electricity transmission and distribution networks in Great Britain. This is often referred to as the National Grid, which risks being confused with National Grid plc or National Grid ESO. This generalist term is adopted as is one sometimes used by National Grid ESO in its resources: National Grid ESO, 'Glossary' (March 2024). National Grid ESO became the National Energy System Operator in October 2024.
17 National Grid ESO, 'Future Energy Scenarios 2023' (July 2023) (n 6).
18 Department for Business, Energy and Industrial Strategy and Ofgem, 'Transitioning to a Net Zero Energy System: Smart Systems and Flexibility Plan 2021' (2021) 38 <https://assets.publishing.service.gov.uk/media/60f575cd8fa8f50c7f08aecd/smart-systems-and-flexibility-plan-2021.pdf> accessed 4 April 2024.
19 ibid 38–39.

for such storage is particularly acute in the context of wind generation (due to the weather-dependent nature of this source).

- Storage can assist in managing local constraints on the electricity grid. The need for such storage is particularly acute in areas where, historically, generation was not located (and, thus, infrastructure to distribute the generated energy is not in place). Using storage avoids other methods of remedying constraints on the network: paying (usually low carbon) generators to reduce their power output.[20]

- Storage can provide important ancillary functions for the electricity grid. This includes frequency response,[21] whereby the storage charges or discharges with the intention of aiding the grid to stay at its 50Hz frequency, or inertia,[22] whereby the storage provides a mitigation to sudden loss of power events.

15.12 As of 2022 the UK had 5.25GW of storage capacity, equating to 29.46GWh of storage volume.[23] This storage capacity was almost evenly split between pumped-storage hydroelectricity and battery storage.[24] However, in 2023 a further 1.6GW of battery storage was under construction, with a further 10.4GW consented and 18.6GW in the planning and development stages. In contrast, only 0.8GW of pumped-storage hydroelectricity was consented, and a further 3.9GW was in scoping.[25]

15.13 Aside from these established forms of storage, compressed air energy storage and liquid air energy storage are both envisaged for installation by 2030.[26] In addition, other emerging technologies are being explored, including gravitational storage and redox flow batteries.[27] These storage solutions do not attempt to replace each other, but are complementary with each having valuable characteristics. Considering pumped-storage hydroelectricity and battery storage: the former is notable for being able to store a high volume of energy while having a (comparatively) low power capacity; the latter is notable for its high power capacity and immediacy of discharge. These are both valuable characteristics for developers and the electricity grid.

---

20 National Grid ESO, 'Energy Storage for Constraint Management' (2022) 7–8 <https://www.nationalgrideso.com/document/247646/download> accessed 26 April 2024.
21 National Grid ESO, 'Mandatory Frequency Response (MFR) | ESO' <https://www.nationalgrideso.com/industry-information/balancing-services/frequency-response-services/mandatory-frequency-response#Technical-Requirements> accessed 26 April 2024.
22 National Grid ESO, 'Our New Approach to Inertia and Other Stability Services' (2020) <https://www.nationalgrideso.com/news/our-new-approach-inertia-and-other-stability-services> accessed 14 November 2023.
23 National Grid ESO, 'FES 2023 Data Workbook' (n 7) FL.11. The National Grid ESO, 'Future Energy Scenarios 2023' (July 2023) (n 6) at page 13 records only 3GW capacity, which appears to only refer to battery storage, albeit it still refers to approximately 29GWh volume (which would include pumped-storage hydroelectricity). As the 'Data Workbook' figures are repeated elsewhere in 'Future Energy Scenarios' those figures are preferred. The nomenclature of capacity in watts and volume in watt hours is used in 'Future Energy Scenarios'.
24 National Grid ESO, 'Future Energy Scenarios 2023' (July 2023) (n 6). However, around 90% of the storage volume was in pumped-storage hydroelectricity (due to its design nature): National Grid ESO, 'FES 2023 Data Workbook', FL.11 (n 7).
25 National Grid ESO, 'Future Energy Scenarios 2023' (July 2023) (n 6).
26 ibid.
27 Department for Business, Energy and Industrial Strategy, 'Facilitating the Deployment of Large-Scale and Long-duration Electricity Storage' (2022) 8 <https://assets.publishing.service.gov.uk/media/62ea22d48fa8f5033041f6c1/large-scale-long-duration-electricity-storage-govt-response.pdf> accessed 26 April 2024.

15.14 Given the low ratio between capacity and volume, battery storage is notable for its (relatively) short storage times. Recently the government has recognised the need for greater long duration storage. In its response to a call for evidence on large-scale, long duration electricity storage ('LLES') it concluded: 'we will ensure the deployment of sufficient LLES to balance the overall system by developing appropriate policy to enable investment by 2024.'[28]

(iii) *Policy*

15.15 Various high-level policies reflect the need for energy storage as part of achieving net zero. To take two examples the 'Net Zero Strategy: Build Back Greener' identifies energy storage as a way of de-risking the introduction of low carbon energy.[29] The policy recognises:[30]

> A low-cost, net zero consistent electricity system is most likely to be composed predominantly of wind and solar generation, whether in 2035 or 2050. To ensure the system is reliable, intermittent renewables need to be complemented by known technologies such as nuclear and power CCUS, and flexible technologies such as interconnectors, electricity storage, and demand-side response. These flexible technologies can help to minimise the amount of generation and network capacity needed to meet our demand needs, for example, by matching new sources of demand to renewable generation both nationally and locally.

15.16 Similarly the 'British Energy Security Strategy' emphasises the need for flexibility within the network. One way of achieving this is storage, with the Strategy explaining that the government would be: '[e]ncouraging all forms of flexibility with sufficient large-scale, long-duration electricity storage to balance the overall system by developing appropriate policy to enable development.'[31]

15.17 From the perspective of planning policy, the change in the technological position over the past 12 years is made apparent by footnote 13 of the 2011 NPS EN-1 which notes: 'At present we have no ability to store electricity. Currently the only viable utility scale energy storage is hydro pumped storage.'[32] In contrast, paragraph 3.3.25 of the November 2023 NPS EN-1 provides: 'Storage has a key role to play in achieving net zero and providing flexibility to the energy system, so that high volumes of low carbon power, heat and transport can be integrated.'[33]

---

28 ibid 6.
29 Department for Energy Security and Net Zero, 'Net Zero Strategy: Build Back Greener' (n 2) 105.
30 ibid.
31 Department for Business, Energy and Industrial Strategy, Department for Energy Security and Net Zero and Prime Minister's Office, 'British Energy Security Strategy' (2022) 25 <https://www.gov.uk/government/publications/british-energy-security-strategy/british-energy-security-strategy> accessed 26 April 2024.
32 Department for Energy and Climate Change, 'Overarching National Policy Statement for Energy (EN-1) (July 2011)' (2011) <https://assets.publishing.service.gov.uk/media/65a794dd96a5ec000d731abe/1938-overarching-nps-for-energy-en1-withdrawn.pdf> accessed 26 April 2024.
33 Department for Energy Security and Net Zero, 'Overarching National Policy Statement for Energy (EN-1) (November 2023)' (n 10).

15.18 NPS EN-3 focuses on pumped-storage hydroelectricity, while noting that the opportunities for such developments are currently limited.[34] It explains the significant environmental and landscape impacts posed by such schemes, which involve sizeable reservoirs. The policy notes the significance that this form of storage has:[35]

> 2.9.25 Few technologies that are commercial or have been demonstrated at scale are able to provide storage services at the scale of PHS.
>
> 2.9.26 As the electricity grid sees increasing levels of generation from variable renewable generators such as offshore wind, onshore wind and solar power, there will be an increasing need for storage infrastructure to balance electricity supply and demand. PHS could therefore be a key piece of infrastructure for enabling increased use of renewable energy.

15.19 The 2023 NPSs limit themselves to pumped-storage hydroelectricity because other forms of storage are expressly excluded from NSIP designation.[36] Indeed in 2020 an amendment to the Planning Act 2008 introduced the concept of 'exempt electricity storage facility' which excludes all such facilities except pumped-storage hydroelectricity.[37] However, electricity storage facilities may still be 'associated development' which may be consented alongside an NSIP development.[38]

(iv) *Specific issues*

15.20 As recent years have seen significant growth in battery storage, many contemporary issues concerning energy storage concern those installations. As such, this section focuses on battery storage.

15.21 Safety is a common objection to battery storage.[39] Such batteries are susceptible to 'thermal runaway', the process by which a single battery cell overheats and propagates to its neighbours. Such thermal runaway events have been experienced across the globe. As such events can generate their own oxygen, they are notoriously hard to extinguish. Importantly, due to the chemical makeup of battery storage, the gasses released by thermal runaway can be toxic (most notably hydrogen fluoride) or highly flammable (for example, hydrogen and methane). Currently the Health and Safety Executive does not consider battery storage to require hazardous substances consent or to be subject

---

34 Department for Energy Security and Net Zero, 'National Policy Statement for Renewable Energy Infrastructure (EN-3) (November 2023)' (2023) para 2.9.13. <https://assets.publishing.service.gov.uk/media/65a7889996a5ec000d731aba/nps-renewable-energy-infrastructure-en3.pdf> accessed 26 April 2024.
35 ibid.
36 Planning Act 2008 s 14(1) and s 15.
37 Planning Act 2008 s 15(6). Introduced by The Infrastructure Planning (Electricity Storage Facilities) Order 2020, SI 2020/1218.
38 Planning Act 2008 s 115(1)(b).
39 Much is written on this topic. See, for example, section 4.7 of the 'Sunnica Energy Farm: Examining Authority's Report of Findings and Conclusions and Recommendation to the Secretary of State for Energy Security and Net Zero' (28 June 2023) <https://infrastructure.planninginspectorate.gov.uk/wp-content/ipc/uploads/projects/EN010106/EN010106-005902-Sunnica-ExA-Recommendation-Report-28-June-2023-FINAL-with%20Errata%20sheet.pdf> accessed 22 November 2023. For an example of objections based on safety grounds see: Fordham and Allison, 'Safety of Grid Scale Lithium-Ion Battery Energy Storage Systems' (5 June 2021) <https://www.researchgate.net/publication/352158070_Safety_of_Grid_Scale_Lithium-ion_Battery_Energy_Storage_Systems> accessed 22 November 2022.

to major accident hazards regulations, however this has been the subject of dispute in a recent NSIP application.[40] In 2022 an attempt was made by Dame Maria Miller MP to expressly introduce hazardous substance consenting and consultation requirements for battery storage.[41] The government's 'Planning Practice Guidance' indicates that appropriate engagement with the emergency services is an important part of addressing safety risks in an application, and also encourages consideration of the National Fire Chiefs Council on this issue.[42]

15.22 Whether or not safety objections to battery storage are well-founded, this issue is a common topic in local planning and development consent order applications. This is particularly so as, sometimes, due to the guidance to build battery storage on brownfield land, installations are proposed nearby to residential or high population areas. An important response in land use planning terms is that, typically, planning policies or decisions will not concentrate on control of processes or emissions. This is a point made in the National Planning Policy Framework ('NPPF')[43] at paragraph 194:

> The focus of planning policies and decisions should be on whether proposed development is an acceptable use of land, rather than the control of processes or emissions (where these are subject to separate pollution control regimes). Planning decisions should assume that these regimes will operate effectively. Equally, where a planning decision has been made on a particular development, the planning issues should not be revisited through the permitting regimes operated by pollution control authorities.

15.23 Aside from safety, siting of battery storage has also been challenged from the perspective of harm to the landscape and heritage. Battery storage typically appears as a large number of containers clustered together. Mitigating this impact, particularly for large developments using greenfield land, is key to securing consent. This is particularly so when the argument may be made that positioning battery storage on greenfield land will industrialise the landscape.[44]

15.24 From a technical perspective, siting of battery storage may also give rise to noise concerns and light pollution concerns. These will be highly case dependent but, again, are a consideration which developers must take into account when progressing battery storage (particularly in close proximity to residential development).

---

40 See also E Fordham and P Swords, 'Application of the COMAH and Hazardous Substances Consents Regulations to Battery Energy Storage Systems (BESS): Does Classification as 'Articles' Exempt a Technology?' (2022) accessed 22 November 2023.

41 Lithium-ion Battery Storage (Fire Safety and Environmental Permits) Bill. See also HC Deb 7 September 2022, vol 719, cols 275–277.

42 Department for Levelling Up, Housing and Communities, 'Planning Practice Guidance – Renewable and Low Carbon Energy' (2023) para 34 (Ref ID: 5-034-20230814) and para 35 (Ref ID: 5-035-20230814) <https://www.gov.uk/guidance/renewable-and-low-carbon-energy> accessed 22 November 2023.

43 Department for Levelling Up, Housing and Communities, 'National Planning Policy Framework' (2023) <https://assets.publishing.service.gov.uk/media/65a11af7e8f5ec000f1f8c46/NPPF_December_2023.pdf> accessed 2 April 2024.

44 See, in the context of battery storage accompanying solar farms, for example East Cambridgeshire DC, Cambridgeshire CC Suffolk CC, West Suffolk C, 'Joint Impact Report Sunnica Energy Farm' (October 2022) para 10.13 <https://infrastructure.planninginspectorate.gov.uk/wp-content/ipc/uploads/projects/EN010106/EN010106-003658-Suffolk%20County%20Council%20-%20Local%20Impact%20Reports%20(LIR)%20from%20local%20authorities.pdf> accessed 22 November 2023.

15.25 Finally, a valuable step that those developing energy generating stations can take is siting battery storage with that generation. This is common in the realm of solar, and means that battery storage can be taken out of local planning and made subject of the NSIP procedure. However, when doing this, care should be taken to ensure the battery storage is properly 'associated development.'[45] Guidance on associated development indicates that there must be a 'direct relationship between the associated development and the principal development'; it should be 'subordinate'; should not be 'only necessary as source of additional revenue for the applicant'; and, should be 'proportionate to the nature and scale of the principal development'.[46] Given the ancillary functions that energy storage can provide, and the opportunities for trading capacity and arbitrage, consideration should be given to ensuring that the definition is met.

15.26 Interestingly, the government in July 2021 indicated it plans to take further steps to recognise battery storage as a 'distinct subset of generation in primary legislation'.[47] It is unclear whether this proposal entails designating such installations as being NSIPs, or some other step. Currently, the government does not appear to have taken steps to move towards that goal.

Network infrastructure

(i) *Introduction*

15.27 The central focus of planning concerning network infrastructure in the UK is the electricity grid, along with any development which connects into the grid. Indeed, any form of energy generating development is likely to include at least some form of network infrastructure. However, the issue goes much further than this, and includes expanding the network into new areas and reinforcing the existing network.

15.28 The change to renewable energy is increasingly placing generation in locations where it historically was not situated. The transmission network of the electricity grid, constructed around a (relatively) small number of power plants located across the UK in the 20th Century, must now evolve to serve both generation which is located far from those historic power plants (including, in respect of wind generation, at sea[48]), and generation which is far more decentralised.[49] For these reasons it is unsurprising

45 Planning Act 2008 s 115(2).
46 Department for Communities and Local Government, 'Planning Act 2008: Guidance on Associated Development Applications for Major Infrastructure Projects' (2013) <https://assets.publishing.service.gov.uk/media/5a7b5f04ed915d3ed9063f36/Planning_Act_2008_-_Guidance_on_associated_development_applications_for_major_infrastructure_projects.pdf> accessed 22 November 2023.
47 Department for Business, Energy and Industrial Strategy and Ofgem, 'Transitioning to a Net Zero Energy System: Smart Systems and Flexibility Plan 2021' (n 18).
48 Securing transmission networks for offshore wind has been consistently identified as a specific an important subcategory of this area. See the funding commitments in HM Government, 'Net Zero Strategy: Build Back Greener' (n 2) 94 and special assessment principles for offshore-onshore transmission in Department for Energy Security and Net Zero, 'National Policy Statement for Electricity Networks Infrastructure (EN-5) (November 2023)' (2023) para 2.12. <https://assets.publishing.service.gov.uk/media/65a78a5496a5ec000d731abb/nps-electricity-networks-infrastructure-en5.pdf> accessed 26 April 2024.
49 National Grid ESO, 'Beyond 2030' (2024) 21 <https://www.nationalgrideso.com/document/315516/download> accessed 26 April 2024.

that NPS EN-1 identifies electricity grid infrastructure as part of the critical national priority for nationally significant low carbon infrastructure.[50]

15.29 In March 2024 National Grid ESO explained in its 'Beyond 2030' report that 'Great Britain is about to embark upon the biggest change to the electricity network since the high voltage transmission grid was established in the 1950s'.[51] This is comprised in a proposed £60 billion in investment in the onshore and offshore electricity grid by 2030.[52] In part, this builds upon and implements the Holistic Network Design published by National Grid ESO in 2022,[53] and the progress towards the Centralised Strategic Network Plan. National Grid ESO itself became the National Energy System Operator in October 2024.

(ii) *Contribution to net zero*

15.30 The key contribution improving and expanding the electricity grid can make to net zero is facilitating the installation of new renewable generation. The 'British Energy Security Strategy' specifically recognises that the speed we can achieve a domestic supply of clean and affordable energy is coupled with the speed at which we can provide the connecting and supporting infrastructure. Similarly, NPS EN-5 begins:[54]

> The security and reliability of the UK's current and future energy supply is highly dependent on having an electricity network which will enable the new electricity generation, storage, and interconnection infrastructure that our country needs to meet the rapid increase in electricity demand required to transition to net zero, while maintaining energy security.

15.31 The contribution of the electricity grid in respect of offshore wind is particularly important. NPS EN-5 recognises that, '[t]he electricity network infrastructure to support the government's offshore wind ambition is as important as the offshore wind generation infrastructure'.[55] This reflects the importance of connecting offshore generation recognised in the Holistic Network Design, which plans for the connection of 23GW of offshore generation to the electricity grid.[56]

(iii) *Policy*

15.32 At a macro level, policy surrounding strategic network development is in flux because of the progress towards the Centralised Strategic Network Plan. This plan concerns developing the electricity grid for the future and looks to 'proactively identify,

---

50 Department for Energy Security and Net Zero, 'Overarching National Policy Statement for Energy (EN-1) (November 2023)' (n 10) para 4.2.5.
51 National Grid ESO, 'Beyond 2030' (n 49) 26.
52 ibid 34.
53 National Grid ESO, 'Pathway to 2030: Holistic Network Design' (2022) <https://www.nationalgrideso.com/document/262681/download> accessed 22 November 2023.
54 Department for Energy Security and Net Zero, 'National Policy Statement for Electricity Networks Infrastructure (EN-5)' (November 2023) (n 48) para 1.1.1.
55 ibid para 1.1.3.
56 National Grid ESO, 'Pathway to 2030: Holistic Network Design' (n 53) 6. This is itself being built upon and progressed by the Detailed Network Design: National Grid ESO, 'Beyond 2030' (March 2024) (n 49) 36.

design and progress investments in the network and will ensure that the transmission network is planned holistically'.[57] This also sits alongside the government's plan to set up a new independent system operator for the grid to conduct whole-system planning.[58] Considering the massive imbalance in the location of generation and demand currently (and in the future),[59] this plan will be key to achieving an effective transmission network. In that regard NPS EN-5 emphasises the importance of strategic network planning.[60]

15.33 As to planning policy, the new NPS EN-5 makes specific provision for electricity networks infrastructure. The policy particularly focuses on the landscape and visual impacts of such infrastructure. This builds on historic rules, called the Holford Rules[61] and Horlock Rules[62] which provide principles on approaching the siting and design of transmission infrastructure. While the former were guidelines for siting originally established in 1959, the latter arose out of obligations under Schedule 9 of the Electricity Act 1989.[63]

15.34 Interestingly, specific legislative protection also exists for amenity value. Schedule 9 of the Electricity Act 1989 provides:

> (1) In formulating any relevant proposals, a licence holder or a person authorised by exemption to generate, distribute, supply or participate in the transmission of electricity –
>
> (a) shall have regard to the desirability of preserving natural beauty, of conserving flora, fauna and geological or physiographical features of special interest and of protecting sites, buildings and objects of architectural, historic or archaeological interest; and
> (b) shall do what he reasonably can to mitigate any effect which the proposals would have on the natural beauty of the countryside or on any such flora, fauna, features, sites, buildings or objects.

15.35 In assessing a development, the Secretary of State is specifically directed to consider whether the development 'so far as is reasonably possible' complies with the Holford and Horlock rules.[64] In addition, they are required to be 'satisfied that all feasible

---

57 National Grid ESO, 'Future Energy Scenarios 2023' (July 2023) (n 6) 171.
58 More detail about the Centralised Strategic Network Plan and the move towards a future system operator is set out in Ofgem's recent decision, 'Decision on the framework for the Future System Operator's Centralised Strategic Network Plan', 13 December 2023 <https://www.ofgem.gov.uk/sites/default/files/2023-12/Decision%20on%20the%20framework%20for%20the%20Future%20System%20Operators%20Centralised%20Strategic%20Network%20Plan.pdf> accessed 26 April 2024, and National Grid ESO, 'Beyond 2023' (March 2024) (n 49).
59 For example, applying the 'Leading the Way' assessment in 'Future Energy Scenarios', it is predicted there was a net supply surplus in Scotland of 33.8TWh in 2022 compared to net demand in the South of England of 68.4TWh. In 2035 it is predicted the net supply in Scotland will be 192.6TWh with net demand in the South of England being 180TWh. See National Grid ESO, 'Future Energy Scenarios 2023 (July 2023)' (n 6) 172.
60 Department for Energy Security and Net Zero, 'National Policy Statement for Electricity Networks Infrastructure (EN-5) (November 2023)' (n 48) para 2.8.
61 ibid para 2.9.16.
62 ibid para 2.9.17.
63 ibid para 2.9.16–2.6.19.
64 ibid para 2.11.2.

options for mitigation – including rationalisation, reconfiguration, or undergrounding of existing networks infrastructure, have been considered and evaluated appropriately.'[65]

(iv) *Specific issues*

15.36 As has already been noted, a significant portion of NPS EN-5 is devoted to assessing and managing the landscape and visual impacts of transmission infrastructure.[66] This is unsurprising given that this can be experienced at great distances and (along with large transport infrastructure) must be spread out across large areas of the country. Notwithstanding this issue, the starting presumption with network infrastructure is that it will be overhead lines.[67] This reflects the difficulty, from the perspective of time and cost, of undergrounding or using subsea cabling. It is of note that, notwithstanding significant negative feedback from communities following consultation, the government maintained the presumption given the 'large number of factors which inform the starting presumption'.[68]

15.37 This starting point is reversed in the context of nationally designated landscapes.[69] NPS EN-5 also recognises that cases may arise where, lacking a designation, the 'high potential for widespread and significant adverse landscape and/or visual impacts along certain sections of its route' may call for undergrounding or subsea cables.[70] Thus, developers might expect to spend much time on the judicious selection of locations for transmission infrastructure and decisions on undergrounding.

15.38 It is important to recognise, however, that site selection for network infrastructure is unusual in that may developers will have little control over point of connection to the electricity grid as a whole. This is because connection into the grid will be determined by 'system capacity and resilience requirements as determined by the Electricity Systems Operator'.[71] In planning terms this may mean that any scope to minimise landscape and visual impact is closed off by the limited options provided for location of connection. It will be important for developers to carefully assess how to connect to such initiating and terminating points of the grid, and to take steps aside from siting to minimise harm.

15.39 Developers might also note the government's position that, wherever reasonably possible, new generating stations and their related infrastructure should be brought together as part of a single application.[72] This may be particularly valuable for developers where the planning merits of that new generating station may outweigh any negative factors about the network infrastructure.

---

65 ibid para 2.11.3.
66 Other considerations include noise, vibration, electric and magnetic fields, and sulphur hexafluoride.
67 Department for Energy Security and Net Zero, 'National Policy Statement for Electricity Networks Infrastructure (EN-5) (November 2023)' (n 48) para 2.9.20.
68 Department for Energy Security and Net Zero, 'Consultation Response Planning for New Energy Infrastructure' (n 15) 32.
69 ibid 32.
70 Department for Energy Security and Net Zero, 'National Policy Statement for Electricity Networks Infrastructure (EN-5) (November 2023)' (n 48) para 2.9.23.
71 ibid para 2.2.2.
72 ibid para 2.7.2.

Carbon capture, usage and storage

(i) *Introduction*

15.40 Carbon capture, usage[73] and storage ('CCUS') describes the process of capturing carbon dioxide produced by large point sources so that it does not enter the atmosphere, or the direct removal of carbon dioxide from the atmosphere.[74] The captured carbon might then be used for industrial purposes or permanently stored. Properly understood, CCUS is a mechanism for directly or indirectly mitigating emissions, rather than an inherently low-emission approach to energy generation or industrial production. It also describes two separate activities: (1) the capturing of carbon dioxide; and, (2) the usage or storage of carbon dioxide.

15.41 The significant role to be played by CCUS in the UK meeting its emissions targets was recognised early in the 21st Century. In 2003 the energy white paper explained the capacity of the UK for CCUS by noting: '[t]he North Sea oil and gas well capacity in the UK Continental Shelf is sufficient to absorb all UK CO_2 emissions at current levels for 15 years, potentially hundreds of years if saline aquifers are included.'[75] Yet installation of CCUS capacity has been significantly hampered by technological issues, lack of policy clarity and, more recently, commercial concerns. In 2019 the Business, Energy and Industrial Strategy Committee described CCUS as having had a:[76]

> turbulent history in the UK, and the lack of sustained policy support for the technology, despite a decade of repeated – and increasingly urgent – calls from official bodies and parliamentary inquiries to bring forwards its deployment.

15.42 CCUS is now recognised as a necessary rather than optional part of the UK meeting its net zero commitments.[77] It has also begun to see successful deployments in the UK,[78] although overall capacity remains low. In March 2023 the government promised 'up to £20 billion funding for early development … to help meet the government's climate commitments',[79] and the Energy Act 2023 made extensive provision for the regulation of CCUS. The technology also takes a significantly increased role in the new

---

73 The term 'utilisation' is sometimes substituted for 'usage'. As 'usage' is typically used in the UK that is the term adopted here.

74 Various definitions are available. See, for example, Houses of Parliament Parliamentary Office of Science & Technology, 'Carbon Capture and Usage', POSTbrief No.30, October 2018 <https://post.parliament.uk/research-briefings/post-pb-0030/> accessed 8 November 2023.

75 Department for Trade and Industry, 'Our Energy Future – Creating a Low Carbon Economy' (2003) White Paper Cm 5761 90 <https://assets.publishing.service.gov.uk/media/5a7c1f5940f0b645ba3c6d4f/5761.pdf> accessed 8 November 2023.

76 Business, Energy and Industrial Strategy Committee, 'Carbon Capture Usage and Storage: Third Time Lucky?: Government Response to the Committee's Twentieth Report' (HC 2019, 2644) para 2.

77 Committee on Climate Change, 'Net Zero, The UK's Contribution to Stopping Global Warming' (2019) 23 <https://www.theccc.org.uk/wp-content/uploads/2019/05/Net-Zero-The-UKs-contribution-to-stopping-global-warming.pdf> accessed 8 November 2023.

78 Jamie Durrani, 'UK's first 'industrial scale' carbon capture plant opens in Cheshire' (28 June 2022) <https://www.chemistryworld.com/news/uks-first-industrial-scale-carbon-capture-plant-opens-in-cheshire/4015867.article> accessed 8 November 2023.

79 HM Treasury, 'Spring Budget 2023' (HC 2023, 1183) para 3.88 and 4.99 <https://assets.publishing.service.gov.uk/media/6419c87d8fa8f547c267efca/Web_accessible_Budget_2023.pdf> accessed 8 November 2023.

NPS EN-1, although CCUS infrastructure does not currently appear as a project which can be an NSIP in itself under the Planning Act 2008.[80]

15.43 Currently, capture technology is included as part of a larger overall development, or as a retrofitting step on an existing development. Thus, capture itself has limited contact with the planning system, save for the requirements of certain installations with a generating capacity over 300MW to be 'Carbon Capture Ready'.[81] This is likely to change, however, as installations which have the aim of capturing carbon dioxide from the atmosphere become increasingly prevalent.

15.44 As to storage, a significant focus in the UK has been the use of existing infrastructure installed in the North Sea for the storage of captured carbon dioxide. This is a matter broadly in the control of marine planning.[82] For land-use planning, transport of carbon to these offshore sites is key. While existing oil and gas pipelines can be used as conduits for transporting carbon dioxide, it is likely that a significant role for land-use planning will exist for development to facilitate transportation in the future. As such transport will require significant infrastructure, government policy has focused on producing 'clusters' to ensure that industry and generation can easily access this infrastructure.[83]

(ii) *Contribution to net zero*

15.45 As a necessary rather than optional part of meeting net zero commitments, the Committee on Climate Change in 2018 considered that the UK should aim to have initial carbon capture and storage ('CCS') clusters established in 2026 enabling the sequestering of 10 million tonnes of CO_2 by 2030, and at least 20 million tonnes by 2035. This would be equivalent, respectively, to 2.7 and 5.5% of the UK's emissions in 2018.[84] The House of Commons BEIS Committee in 2019 affirmed this:[85]

> We recommend the Government sets a specific target to store 10 million tonnes of carbon by 2030, and 20 million by 2035, to keep the UK on track to meet its 2050 climate change targets, as recommended by the CCC.

15.46 A clear statement of these aims was expressed in the Net Zero Strategy. At the time of that publication, point 8 of the Prime Minister's 'Ten Point Plan for a Green Industrial Revolution' was investing in CCUS including 'two industrial clusters by mid

---

80 Planning Act 2008 s 14. However, it may be designated an NSIP on a case-by-case basis: Planning Act 2008 s 35.
81 The Carbon Capture Readiness (Electricity Generating Stations) Regulations 2013, SI 2013/2696.
82 Department for Energy Security and Net Zero, 'Overarching National Policy Statement for Energy (EN-1) (November 2023)' (n 10) para 4.9.10.
83 HM Government, 'CCUS Net Zero Investment Roadmap' (2023) <https://assets.publishing.service.gov.uk/government/uploads/system/uploads/attachment_data/file/1167167/ccus-investment-roadmap.pdf> accessed 8 November 2023.
84 Committee on Climate Change, 'Reducing UK Emissions 2018 Progress Report to Parliament' (2018) 41 <https://www.theccc.org.uk/wp-content/uploads/2018/06/CCC-2018-Progress-Report-to-Parliament.pdf> accessed 8 November 2023.
85 Business, Energy and Industrial Strategy Committee, 'Carbon Capture Usage and Storage: Third Time Lucky?: Government Response to the Committee's Twentieth Report' (n 76).

2020s, and an aim for four sites by 2030, aiming to capture up to 10Mt CO_2 emissions per year'.[86] The point also included a CCUS infrastructure fund of £1 billion.[87] A key part of the policy provides specific reference to the Phase 1 Cluster Sequencing process identifying the Hynet and East Coast Clusters to be progressed to completion in the mid-2020s.[88] This process has been realised with the North Sea Transition Authority having already issued a number of licences for these clusters and beyond.[89]

15.47 The Net Zero Strategy also included important policy recognising the significance of CCUS in the production of low carbon hydrogen. This is because hydrogen production can create GHGs which may need to be stored to remain low carbon. The Net Zero Strategy identified commitments to have up to 1GW of CCUS-enabled hydrogen by the mid-2020s, and an ambition to achieve 5GW by 2030 (a figure subsequently doubled in the 'British Energy Security Strategy').[90] While noting the issue of cost and commercial risk, the Net Zero Strategy identified funding for hydrogen production specifically through a levy.[91] The government has progressed this specific aim by consulting upon and producing drafts for the hydrogen production business model.[92]

(iii) *Policy*

15.48 While policy has recognised some role for CCUS in the UK since the 2000s, the 2010s were a period of significant turbulence. £1 billion competitions to advance CCUS were run but cancelled in 2011 and 2016, the latter being at a late stage due to concerns about future costs concerns for consumers.[93] This was of considerable harm to developers that were early adopters and suffered losses, and indicated the lack of security of the commitment of the government to the technology at the time. More recently the House of Commons BEIS Committee have expressed the view that CCUS should be brought forwards at least cost rather than focusing specifically on meeting sufficient costs reductions to implement the policy (such costs fears having been part of the failure of earlier competitions).[94]

86 Department for Energy Security and Net Zero, 'The Ten Point Plan for a Green Industrial Revolution' (2020) 22 <https://assets.publishing.service.gov.uk/media/5fb5513de90e0720978b1a6f/10 _POINT_PLAN_BOOKLET.pdf> accessed 28 September 2023.
87 Department for Energy Security and Net Zero, 'Net Zero Strategy: Build Back Greener' (n 2) 33.
88 ibid 126. This clustering process essentially aims to identify and approve locations which can be a focal point for CCUS infrastructure (a 'cluster'). Phase 1 is the first phase of this identification and approval approach.
89 North Sea Transition Authority, 'Net Zero Boost as Carbon Storage Licences Accepted' <https://www.nstauthority.co.uk/news-publications/net-zero-boost-as-carbon-storage-licences-accepted/> accessed 26 April 2024.
90 Department for Business, Energy and Industrial Strategy, Department for Energy Security and Net Zero and Prime Minister's Office, 'British Energy Security Strategy' (n 31) 22.
91 ibid 128.
92 Department for Energy Security and Net Zero, 'Hydrogen Production Business Model' (GOV.UK, 9 August 2023) <https://www.gov.uk/government/publications/hydrogen-production-business-model> accessed 26 April 2024.
93 Business, Energy and Industrial Strategy Committee, 'Carbon Capture Usage and Storage: Third Time Lucky?: Government Response to the Committee's Twentieth Report' (n 76).
94 House of Commons Business, Energy and Industrial Strategy Committee, 'Carbon capture usage and storage: third time lucky?' (HC 2019, 1094) para 14. While somewhat opaque language, this refers to the focus not being on achieving specific cost reduction targets, but rather pursuing a general policy of low cost which does not stifle development.

15.49 Today CCUS is recognised at a high level in government policy for meeting net zero targets. Reflecting the fast-moving status of technology behind CCUS, the July 2011 NPS EN-1 made limited reference to CCUS framed around the nascent state of the technology[95] and the requirement for generating infrastructure to be carbon capture ready.[96] The version of NPS EN-1 designated in November 2023 puts the status of CCUS on a much stronger footing, recognising there is an 'urgent need for new carbon capture … infrastructure to support the transition to a net zero economy'.[97] The policy specifically identifies 'CCS infrastructure, CCS technologies, pipelines and storage infrastructure are to be considered CNP infrastructure'.[98] It recognises the role of CCUS in reducing emissions associated with generating electricity from natural gas, as well as from hydrogen gas production.[99] CCUS is also recognised as having a role in decarbonising energy intensive sectors such as 'chemicals, oil refining, and cement.'[100] Indeed, specifically in respect of hydrogen, the policy notes that sufficient sources of low carbon hydrogen will not be possible without CCUS.[101] Overall, the policy notes the aim to 'capture and store 20–30MtCO_2 per year by 2023'.[102]

15.50 The effect of NPS EN-1 is that decision-makers on an application for a development consent order under the Planning Act 2008 should recognise that there is an urgent need for CCUS infrastructure, and that substantial weight should be given to this need when considering such proposals. The policy also recognises that future demand may be significant, and permits proposals for pipelines with a greater capacity than demand at the time of consenting would suggest.[103]

(iv) *The Energy Act 2023*

15.51 The Energy Act 2023 produces the skeleton of a regulatory framework for the widescale introduction of CCUS in the UK.[104] The framework established is one of economic regulation, envisaging that carbon dioxide transport and storage networks are likely to be operated as regional monopolies serving a wide range of network users. Those networks will be licensed and prices approved by the regulator.[105] This approach reflects the significant upfront investment and coordination required in establishing transport networks for a given area, explained by the initial approach of establishing 'clusters' around infrastructure. The explanatory note to the Act envisages Ofgem as the most appropriate entity to take on the role of regulator.[106]

---

95 Department of Energy and Climate Change, 'Overarching National Policy Statement for Energy (EN-1) (July 2011)' para 4.7.6 (n 32).
96 ibid paras 4.7.10–4.7.17.
97 Department for Energy Security and Net Zero, 'Overarching National Policy Statement for Energy (EN-1) (November 2023)' (n 10) para 3.1.5.
98 ibid para 3.5.8.
99 ibid para 3.5.2.
100 ibid para 3.5.3.
101 ibid para 3.5.9.
102 ibid para 3.5.4.
103 ibid para 4.9.21.
104 Energy Act 2023 Parts 1 and 2.
105 Explanatory Notes to the Energy Act 2023 para 8.
106 ibid para 9.

15.52 The principal objectives applying to the Secretary of State and the economic regulator, which must be achieved in whatever way is 'best calculated to further' those objectives, are expressed as:[107]

(a) protect the interests of current and future transport and storage network users;

(b) protect the interests of any consumers whose interests the Secretary of State or the economic regulator (as the case may be) considers may be impacted by the exercise of their respective functions under this Part;

(c) promote the efficient and economic development of transport and storage networks, having regard to the need for licence holders to be able to finance their licensable activities.

15.53 The principal objectives, given the difficulties experienced in the 2010s in securing appropriate commercial funding and security of business, are unsurprising. However, it is of note that the Act chooses to express these requirements so firmly. Section 1 requires regard to be had to certain other considerations, most notably sustainable development,[108] the carbon targets and budgets under the Climate Change Act 2008,[109] and the net zero emissions targets set by devolved legislatures.[110] This all puts on a firm footing the role of net zero at the heart of the introduction of CCUS in the UK.

15.54 In Part 2, the Act introduces a range of supporting powers, including spending powers to provide financial assistance to support the establishment of CCUS, and delegated powers for establishing the detailed framework for business models to make provision of these services a reality.[111] This also includes a strategy and policy statement for CCUS.[112]

15.55 The Act addresses CCUS alongside hydrogen production, transportation and storage. This is unsurprising for two reasons. First, there are many parallels to be drawn between the transporting of hydrogen to places where it is to be used, and transporting carbon dioxide to places where it is to be stored. However, the second and more substantial reason is the key role that CCUS has to play in the production of low carbon hydrogen. As has already been noted, it is unlikely the UK can meet the requirements of hydrogen demand in the future without extensive CCUS introduction.

15.56 Not all provision for CCUS is made within the 2023 Act. The earlier Energy Act 2008 provides for the licensing and control of storage of carbon dioxide, including the mechanisms (including criminal offences) for enforcement.[113] In addition, regulations

---

107 Energy Act 2023 s 1(1).
108 ibid s 1(4)(b).
109 ibid s 1(5).
110 ibid s 1(6)(b).
111 Explanatory Notes to the Energy Act 2023 para 16.
112 Energy Act 2023 s 99.
113 Energy Act 2008 Part 1 Chapter 3.

to leave open the possibility of retrofitting development to include CCUS has been in place since the early 2010s.[114]

(v) *The future of CCUS*

15.57 At the time of writing, CCUS appears to be on the cusp of significant growth. The situation has moved from government aspirations expressed in the 2000s, through turbulence in the 2010s, to proper frameworks and planning policy in the 2020s. While a slow and troubled progression, it seems that the UK is now prepared for substantial developments of CCUS. It is likely that any subsequent edition of this work will have considerably more to say about the successful implementation of CCUS in the UK.

114 The Carbon Capture Readiness (Electricity Generating Stations) Regulations 2013 (n 81).

CHAPTER 16

TYPES OF RENEWABLE ENERGY GENERATION

Daniel Kozelko, Stephanie David and Ella Grodzinski

Introduction

16.01 This chapter considers various types of generation which are relevant to the UK meeting its net zero goals. Some of these are not, necessarily, forms of renewable energy,[1] but are an important part of moving away from fossil fuel generation (and supporting renewable generation), such as nuclear. The chapter covers solar, hydrogen, nuclear, energy from waste, biomass and offshore wind.[2] The importance of the switch to generation from renewable sources as part of meeting the UK's net zero commitments cannot be overstated.

16.02 At a national level, government policy is significantly in favour of the consenting and construction of renewable and low carbon generation. This is recognised as key in the Net Zero Strategy[3] and the British Energy Security Strategy ('BESS').[4] It is also recognised in the Overarching National Policy Statement for Energy (EN-1) as a 'critical national priority' for low carbon infrastructure.[5] Low carbon infrastructure includes electricity generating infrastructure (being all onshore and offshore generation that does not include fossil fuel combustion, as well as natural gas fired generation which is carbon capture ready), electricity grid infrastructure and associated infrastructure such as substations.[6] The National Policy Statement for Renewable Energy Infrastructure (EN-3) complements the ambition for full decarbonising of the power system by 2035

1 Renewable energy is described by the UN as 'energy derived from natural sources that are replenished at a higher rate than they are consumed': United Nations, 'What Is Renewable Energy?' <https://www.un.org/en/climatechange/what-is-renewable-energy> accessed 23 April 2024.
2 Onshore wind is addressed in this chapter briefly. However, given government policy until recently practically constrained such installations, and onshore wind is left to planning consenting through local planning rather than at a national level, the matter is not addressed in detail. Installed capacity for onshore wind in England and Wales has seen minimal increase since 2016: Felicia Rankl, House of Commons Library, 'Planning for Onshore Wind' (2024) SN 4370 8 <https://researchbriefings.files.parliament.uk/documents/SN04370/SN04370.pdf> accessed 28 September 2023.
3 HM Government, 'Net Zero Strategy: Build Back Greener' (2021) ch 3(i) <https://www.gov.uk/government/publications/net-zero-strategy> accessed 28 September 2023.
4 Department for Business, Energy and Industrial Strategy, Department for Energy Security and Net Zero and Prime Minister's Office, 'British Energy Security Strategy' (2022) 16–21 <https://www.gov.uk/government/publications/british-energy-security-strategy/british-energy-security-strategy> accessed 28 September 2023.
5 Department for Energy Security and Net Zero, 'Overarching National Policy Statement for Energy (EN-1) (November 2023)' (2023) paras 4.2.1–4.2.9 <https://assets.publishing.service.gov.uk/media/65bbfbdc709fe1000f637052/overarching-nps-for-energy-en1.pdf> accessed 4 April 2024.
6 ibid para 4.2.5.

by providing specific policy in favour of renewable infrastructure.[7] Similarly, such recognition is present in the NPPF for renewable and low carbon development:[8]

> [L]ocal planning authorities should:
>
> a) not require applicants to demonstrate the overall need for renewable or low carbon energy, and recognise that even small-scale projects provide a valuable contribution to significant [sic] cutting greenhouse gas emissions;
> b) approve the application if its impacts are (or can be made) acceptable.

16.03 EN-1 also recognises, and sets out the policy dealing with the GHG emissions from the construction, operation, and decommissioning of energy infrastructure.[9] Thus, there is a requirement *inter alia* for a whole life GHG assessment, which addresses the construction, operational and decommissioning impacts of the development, as well as the proposed land use changes.[10] In terms of the decision-making, EN-1 provides that:[11]

> 5.3.9 The Secretary of State should be content that the applicant has taken all reasonable steps to reduce the GHG emissions of the construction and decommissioning stage of the development.
>
> 5.3.10 The Secretary of State should give appropriate weight to projects that embed nature-based or technological processes to mitigate or offset the emissions of construction and decommissioning within the proposed development. However, in light of the vital role energy infrastructure plays in the process of economy wide decarbonisation, the Secretary of State must accept that there are likely to be some residual emissions from construction and decommissioning of energy infrastructure.
>
> 5.3.11 Operational GHG emissions are a significant adverse impact from some types of energy infrastructure which cannot be totally avoided (even with full deployment of CCS technology). Given the characteristics of these and other technologies, as noted in Part 3 of this NPS, and the range of non-planning policies that can be used to decarbonise electricity generation, such as the UK ETS (see Section 2.4), government has determined that operational GHG emissions are not reasons to prohibit the consenting of energy projects or to impose more restrictions on them in the planning policy framework than are set out in the energy NPSs (e.g. the CCR requirements). Any carbon assessment will include an assessment of operational GHG emissions, but the policies set out in Part 2, including the UK ETS, can be applied to these emissions.

---

7 Department for Energy Security and Net Zero, 'National Policy Statement for Renewable Energy Infrastructure (EN-3) (November 2023)' (2023) <https://assets.publishing.service.gov.uk/media/65a7889996a5ec000d731aba/nps-renewable-energy-infrastructure-en3.pdf> accessed 2 April 2024.
8 Department for Levelling Up, Housing and Communities, 'National Planning Policy Framework' (2023) para 163 <https://assets.publishing.service.gov.uk/media/65a11af7e8f5ec000f1f8c46/NPPF_December_2023.pdf> accessed 2 April 2024.
9 Department for Energy Security and Net Zero, 'Overarching National Policy Statement for Energy (EN-1) (November 2023)' (n 5) para 5.3.
10 ibid para 5.3.4.
11 ibid para 5.3.9–5.3.12.

> 5.3.12 Operational emissions will be addressed in a managed, economy-wide manner, to ensure consistency with carbon budgets, net zero and our international climate commitments. The Secretary of State does not, therefore need to assess individual applications for planning consent against operational carbon emissions and their contribution to carbon budgets, net zero and our international climate commitments.

16.04 EN-1 also sets out the policy requirements relating to climate change adaptation; and ensuring new energy infrastructure is sufficiently resilient.[12] The specific issue of coastal change is also addressed.[13]

16.05 As this chapter considers a range of generating sources, it is important to discuss their distinct characteristics. One such characteristic is their contribution to the grid and the availability of power. Typically, generating sources are rated by their peak generating output; that is, what the generating source will maximally generate. However, such a peak will only be reached when conditions are optimal. To account for this variation, it is useful to calculate the actual generation of a plant over a period. This can be calculated by looking at the 'plant load factor' which describes:[14]

> [T]he ratio between the actual energy generated by the plant to the maximum possible energy that can be generated with the plant working at its rated power and for a duration of an entire year.

16.06 In 2022 the load factor for solar in the UK was estimated at 10.6%. This means, over the course of 2022 in the UK, solar produced 10.6% of its rated generating capacity. For comparison, onshore wind was estimated at 27.4% and offshore wind at 40.8%.[15] Nuclear power in the UK was estimated at 58.5% in 2021, although this figure was as high as 80.1% in 2016.[16] Overall plant load factor for all power stations in the UK for 2022 was 43%.[17]

Solar

(i) *Introduction*

16.07 In 2022 there was 14GW of solar generation installed in the UK.[18] It is one of the most established forms of renewable energy generation, along with being the cheapest form of electricity generation.[19] Aside from wind generation, solar is expected

---

12 ibid para 4.10.
13 ibid para 5.6.
14 Statista, 'Plant load factor of all power stations in the United Kingdom (UK) 2010–2022' (20 November 2023) <https://www.statista.com/statistics/548885/plant-load-factor-power-stations-uk/> accessed 28 November 2023.
15 Lucia Fernández, 'UK: Renewable Energy Load Factor 2022' (*Statista*, 2023) <https://www.statista.com/statistics/383314/average-renewable-energy-load-factor-in-the-united-kingdom-uk/> accessed 23 April 2024.
16 Jaganmohan, 'UK: Plant Load Factor of Nuclear Stations 2022' (*Statista*, 2024) <https://www.statista.com/statistics/548830/plant-load-factor-nuclear-stations-uk/> accessed 23 April 2024.
17 Statista, 'Plant load factor of all power stations in the United Kingdom (UK) 2010–2022' (n 14).
18 Department for Business, Energy and Industrial Strategy, Department for Energy Security and Net Zero and Prime Minister's Office, 'British Energy Security Strategy' (n 4).
19 Department for Energy Security and Net Zero, 'National Policy Statement for Renewable Energy Infrastructure (EN-3) (November 2023)' (n 7) para 2.10.13.

to have the highest installed capacity for a renewable generation source in the UK by 2050.[20]

16.08 When considering solar in the UK, the focus is on photovoltaic generation.[21] While there are other forms of solar generation, most notably concentrated solar power,[22] this has not seen substantial deployment in the UK.[23] There is also a mixed focus on both rooftop and ground mounted solar in the UK, and the government has resisted suggestions that the former alone would be sufficient to satisfy the UK's needs.[24]

16.09 Solar is a variable energy generating source, reliant on weather and climate to reach its maximum output.[25] A worked example[26] assists in understanding this variance:

- There is a significant change in output over the course of the year due to the seasons. A 1MWp[27] solar farm might generate 124MWh in July while producing 23.6MWh in December.

- There is also a significant change in output over the course of the year due to daylight hours. A 1MWp solar farm might generate for 16 hours a day in July while only generating for 8 hours a day in December.

- Over the course of a day generation will differ significantly. A 1MWp solar farm in July might generate on a given day: 6kWh between 04:00 and 05:00; 320kWh between 08:00 and 09:00; 469kWh between 12:00 and 13:00; 220kWh between 16:00 and 17:00; and 0kWh between 20:00 and 21:00.

- These figures will be impacted day to day depending on the weather. Solar generation may entirely cease when there is sufficient cloud cover.

16.10 As was noted above, in 2022 the load factor for solar in the UK was estimated at 10.6%. This is significantly lower than other forms of renewable energy generation,

---

20 National Grid ESO, 'FES 2023 Data Workbook' (2023) table ES.05–08 <https://www.nationalgrideso.com/future-energy/future-energy-scenarios-fes> accessed 28 September 2023. National Grid ESO became the National Energy System Operator in October 2024.

21 Current planning policy specifically identifies the technology as solar photovoltaic generation: Department for Energy Security and Net Zero, 'National Policy Statement for Renewable Energy Infrastructure (EN-3) (November 2023)' (n 7) 88.

22 REN21, 'Market Developments | Concentrating Solar Thermal Power' (2023) <https://www.ren21.net/gsr-2023/> accessed 23 April 2024.

23 Globally there is approximately 6.3GW of installed concentrated solar power generation. Almost two thirds of this is in the US and Spain: see n 22.

24 Felicia Rankl, House of Commons Library, 'Planning and Solar Farms' (2023) Number CDP 2023/0168 29–37 <https://researchbriefings.files.parliament.uk/documents/CDP-2023-0168/CDP-2023-0168.pdf> accessed 28 September 2023.

25 Department for Energy Security and Net Zero, 'Overarching National Policy Statement for Energy (EN-1) (November 2023)' (n 5) para 3.3.22.

26 This worked example considers a 1MWp solar farm installed at the longitude and latitude of Charing Cross Station in London. It applies the standard assumptions used by Global Solar Atlas. The figures are sourced from Global Solar Atlas: <https://globalsolaratlas.info/map> accessed 28 November 2023.

27 Installed capacity of energy generating infrastructure, usually solar and wind, will often be measured as 'megawatt peak' (MWp). This is because such infrastructure will produce a variable amount of power over a year, and MWp measures the maximum such output.

and reflects the variable output of solar across both the day and the year. Given its load factor and variance across the day and across the year, it is important that solar is part of a diverse energy mix.[28] In this respect wind and solar can work in synergy as there is some correlation between days with high wind and lower average irradiation.[29] Base load generation also remains key to ensuring a reliable supply of energy in the UK, as does the increased use of grid scale storage. However, solar is now being sited with battery energy storage as a way of managing variance across the day and storing energy until the time at which it is needed.[30] In addition, battery energy storage can provide ancillary functions for the electricity grid which solar cannot typically provide on its own (for example, artificial inertia and frequency management of the grid).[31]

(ii) *Contribution to net zero*

16.11 Government policy is clear that solar will play a key part in achieving net zero.[32] The energy White Paper, 'Powering our Net Zero Future' expressly recognised that, '[a] low-cost, net zero consistent system is likely to be comprised predominantly of wind and solar'.[33] That policy position has been carried through into various other policies and ultimately now appears in the text of NPS EN-1.[34] In the 'British Energy Security Strategy', the government set out that it expects a fivefold increase in the deployment of solar generation by 2035.[35] Indeed, this direction of travel was further affirmed by the new Labour government in July 2024, with three solar farm development consent orders being granted within days of the election.[36]

16.12 In policy terms, the contribution that solar energy can now make to net zero is striking. In the 2011 versions of NPS EN-1 and EN-3, solar energy was barely mentioned, reflective of its status (at the time) as a developing form of generation which had significant costs. However, over the past decade the cost of solar has reduced by 85%[37] to

28 Department for Energy Security and Net Zero, 'Overarching National Policy Statement for Energy (EN-1) (November 2023)' (n 5) para 3.3.22.
29 Philip E Bett and Hazel E Thornton, 'The Climatological Relationships between Wind and Solar Energy Supply in Britain' (2016) 87 *Renewable Energy* 96, 104–105.
30 Department for Energy Security and Net Zero, 'Overarching National Policy Statement for Energy (EN-1) (November 2023)' (n 5) para 3.3.27. See also, for example, the Sunnica Energy Farm Order 2024, SI 2024/802, the Longfield Solar Farm Order 2023, SI 2023/734, the Little Crow Solar Park Order 2022, SI 2022/436 and the Cleve Hill Solar Park Order 2020, SI 2020/547 all of which incorporate battery energy storage systems.
31 To which see Chapter 15.
32 Department for Energy Security and Net Zero, 'National Policy Statement for Renewable Energy Infrastructure (EN-3) (November 2023)' (n 7) para 2.10.9.
33 Secretary of State for Business, Energy and Industrial Strategy, 'Energy White Paper: Powering Our Net Zero Future' (2020) CP 337 43 <https://assets.publishing.service.gov.uk/media/5fdc61e2d3bf7f3a3bdc8cbf/201216_BEIS_EWP_Command_Paper_Accessible.pdf> accessed 17 April 2024.
34 Department for Energy Security and Net Zero, 'Overarching National Policy Statement for Energy (EN-1) (November 2023)' (n 5) para 3.3.20.
35 Department for Business, Energy and Industrial Strategy, Department for Energy Security and Net Zero and Prime Minister's Office, 'British Energy Security Strategy' (n 4) page 19.
36 On 12 July 2024 the Secretary of State for Energy and Net Zero made the Mallard Pass Solar Farm Order 2024, SI 2024/796, the Sunnica Solar Farm Order 2024, SI 2024/802, and the Gate Burton Energy Park Order 2024, SI 2024/807.
37 Department for Business, Energy and Industrial Strategy, Department for Energy Security and Net Zero and Prime Minister's Office, 'British Energy Security Strategy' (n 4) page 19.

become the cheapest form of energy generation.[38] Indeed, the November 2023 version of NPS EN-3 recognises that solar is now sufficiently cost effective that 'large-scale solar is now viable in some cases to deploy subsidy-free'.[39] This generation form is also notable for ease of building and consistent developments in efficiency.[40]

16.13 Solar's particular contribution to net zero is also reflected by its low carbon intensity. Carbon intensity reflects the amount of CO_2 equivalent in GHGs that, spread across the life of the generator, it effectively emits to produce electricity. Assuming an assessment considers the entire lifecycle of an energy source (which includes the processes of raw mineral extraction, manufacturing, installation, decommissioning etc) the US National Renewable Energy Laboratory has estimated a carbon intensity for photovoltaic solar of around 43gCO^2eq/kWh. For comparison, natural gas is estimated at 486gCO^2eq/kWh while oil is 840gCO^2eq/kWh and coal is 1001gCO^2eq/kWh. It is, however, worth noting that both wind and nuclear are estimated below solar at 13gCO^2eq/kWh.[41]

16.14 Globally, solar is playing a key role in the energy transition. In 2023, the global cumulative installed capacity for photovoltaic solar generation reached 1,185GW.[42] This is a striking development and reflects the global move towards solar as a mechanism for decarbonising generation.

(iii) *Policy*

16.15 Following the designation of the new National Policy Statements for energy in November 2023, NPS EN-3 now sets out a detailed policy basis for consenting solar energy farms in the UK. Much of that policy is addressed under the specific issues section below. Solar power falls within the general designation of low carbon infrastructure as a critical national priority in NPS EN-1,[43] and attracts the designation of need and substantial weight in favour of meeting that need.[44]

16.16 A key feature of solar farms is that, generally, they are recognised as having a limited project lifespan. This means permissions for such schemes are described as 'temporary'.[45] The NPS recognises an upper limit in the region of 40 years, although consent without a time frame or different periods can be sought.[46] A key consideration

---

38 Department for Energy Security and Net Zero, 'National Policy Statement for Renewable Energy Infrastructure (EN-3) (November 2023)' (n 7) para 2.10.13.
39 ibid para 2.10.14.
40 ibid.
41 NREL, 'Life Cycle Greenhouse Gas Emissions from Electricity Generation: Update' (2021) 3 <https://www.nrel.gov/docs/fy21osti/80580.pdf> accessed 28 September 2023.
42 Gaëtan Masson and others, 'Snapshot of Global PV Markets 2022 Task 1 Strategic PV Analysis and Outreach PVPS' (2022) 10 <https://www.researchgate.net/publication/360562245_Snapshot_of_Global_PV_Markets_2022_Task_1_Strategic_PV_Analysis_and_Outreach_PVPS> accessed 28 September 2023.
43 Department for Energy Security and Net Zero, 'Overarching National Policy Statement for Energy (EN-1) (November 2023)' (n 5) paras 3.2.6–3.2.8.
44 ibid s 4.2.
45 Department for Energy Security and Net Zero, 'National Policy Statement for Renewable Energy Infrastructure (EN-3) (November 2023)' (n 7) para 2.10.66.
46 ibid para 2.10.149.

that arises out of the temporary nature of solar farms is that the harms of such schemes may be similarly temporary. The Secretary of State is directed as follows:[47]

> The Secretary of State should consider the period of time that the applicant is seeking to operate the generating station as well as the extent to which the site will return to its original state when assessing impacts such as landscape and visual effects and potential effects on the settings of heritage assets and nationally designated landscapes.

16.17 This means harms which are typically assessed in the planning process, be it to amenity, value of landscape, or value of heritage assets, might be assessed on the assumption that there is a substantial return to the baseline at the end of the temporary permission. This is a point the policy makes, for example, in respect of heritage.[48] Developers may point to this as minimising the weight to be attached to a given harm, and this argument has found favour in decisions of the Secretary of State.[49] It is worth noting, however, that NPS EN-1 designates lifetime extensions and repowering of infrastructure as a critical national priority,[50] and the NPPF recognises that 'significant weight' should be given to the utilisation of an established site which is proposed to be repowered.[51] As such, a temporary permission could, functionally, become permanent.

16.18 Another feature of applications for solar farms is the direction in NPS EN-3 that developers may aim to 'overplant' to respond to the issue of solar panel degradation (i.e. to initially station more photovoltaic cells than are needed to reach the stated capacity of the site).[52] This will also respond, to some extent, to the variable production of electricity across the year. The scheme must be assessed to its full extent as part of an application, including any overplanting.[53] This is important to bear in mind as it resists the suggestion that a solar farm is too big on the basis of its grid connection. Indeed, the policy also indicates 'AC installed export capacity should not be seen as an appropriate tool to constrain the impacts of a solar farm'.[54] Put another way, the installed generating capacity of the site should not be limited by capacity of the of the transmission infrastructure to send that power to the grid.

16.19 One final point to note is that solar farms will often be built with associated infrastructure.[55] One such case is energy storage, which may store energy when solar power is plentiful and discharge when solar power is not (to which, see Chapter 15).

---

47 ibid para 2.10.151.
48 ibid para 2.10.160.
49 The argument that the scheme would be temporary found favour with the Secretary of State in the Sunnica Energy Farm decision and led him to reduce the weight given to certain harms: 'Application for Development Consent for Sunnica Energy Farm' (12 July 2024) para 4.114–4.115 and para 4.160 <https://infrastructure.planninginspectorate.gov.uk/wp-content/ipc/uploads/projects/EN010106/EN010106-006023-Sunnica%20SoS%20Decision%20Letter%20signed%2012%20July%202024.pdf> accessed 18 September 2024.
50 Department for Energy Security and Net Zero, 'Overarching National Policy Statement for Energy (EN-1) (November 2023)' (n 5) para 4.2.5.
51 Department for Levelling Up, Housing and Communities, 'National Planning Policy Framework' (n 8) para 163(c).
52 Department for Energy Security and Net Zero, 'National Policy Statement for Renewable Energy Infrastructure (EN-3) (November 2023)' (n 7) para 2.10.55.
53 ibid para 2.10.55.
54 ibid para 2.10.56.
55 ibid para 2.10.16.

(iv) *Specific issues*

16.20 A corollary of the significant growth in solar generation in the UK has been the growth in planning and environmental issues surrounding consenting of developments. Resistance to solar generation proposals can be considerable, and a wide range of issues can arise. This section addresses agricultural land classification,[56] siting, national designations and green belt, heritage, and landscape.[57]

16.21 It is worth noting that the key characteristic of solar, from which many of the concerns below arise, is the land use needs of this kind of development. This is a point recognised in NPS EN-3:[58]

> Along with associated infrastructure, a solar farm requires between 2 to 4 acres for each MW of output. A typical 50 MW solar farm will consist of around 100,000 to 150,000 panels and cover between 125 to 200 acres. However, this will vary significantly depending on the site, with some being larger and some being smaller. This is also expected to change over time as new technology continues to evolve to become more efficient. Nevertheless, the scale of development will inevitably have impacts, particularly if sited in rural areas.

16.22 All of the specific issues addressed below, in some way, relate back to the fact that solar farms require a large amount of land.

(a) Agricultural land classification

16.23 The principles behind agricultural land classification are addressed in the agriculture section of this book (see Chapter 12). Because of the significant land take involved in solar, the classification of land can be a matter of significant dispute when considering an application.

16.24 NPS EN-3 now provides welcome clarity in approaching the issue of siting solar farms on Best and Most Versatile ('BMV') land. It explicitly recognises that ground mounted solar is not prohibited on such land, albeit impacts are expected to be considered. Paragraph 2.10.29 provides:

> Where land type should not be a predominating factor in determining the suitability of the site location applicants should, where possible, utilise suitable previously developed land, brownfield land, contaminated land and industrial land. Where the proposed use of any agricultural land has been shown to be necessary, poorer quality land should be preferred to higher quality land avoiding the use of 'Best and Most Versatile' agricultural land where possible.

---

56 See the section on 'Agricultural land classification' in Chapter 12.
57 For an analysis of specific issues see also Thea Osmund-Smith and Odette Chalaby, Energy development: focus on solar and wind: law, policy reforms, key appeal decisions and consents (2023) 13 JPL OP23–OP41.
58 Department for Energy Security and Net Zero, 'National Policy Statement for Renewable Energy Infrastructure (EN-3) (November 2023)' (n 7) para 2.10.17.

16.25 In deciding an application, the Secretary of State is directed to 'take into account the economic and other benefits of the best and most versatile agricultural land.'[59] This builds on the general direction to value and assess development on BMV land in NPS EN-1.[60] In its consultation on the draft NPSs, the government received responses pushing for increased protection of agricultural land but ultimately resolved that the provisions as included in the drafts 'strike the right balance between protecting our most versatile and high-quality agricultural land and enabling the sustained increases in the development of large-scale solar capacity needed to meet our net zero targets.'[61]

16.26 The policy in the NPPF and PPG is set out in the agriculture section (Chapter 12). It is clear that policy such as this has been causing difficulty, at least at the local level. In *Minchens Lane, Bramley, Hampshire,* the inspector found that a solar farm would 'not be harmful in respect of BMVAL'[62] and would accord with local policy. They found:

> While the use of higher quality agricultural land is discouraged, the proposals for a temporary period of forty years … The agricultural land would not be permanently or irreversibly lost, particularly as pasture grazing would occur between the solar panels. This would allow the land to recover from intensive use, and the soil condition and structure to improve. The use of the soil for grassland under the solar panels should serve to improve soil health and biodiversity.[63]

16.27 On the other hand, in *Land North of Lullington, Swadlincote, Derbyshire, DE12 8EW*, the inspector relied on a March 2015 Written Ministerial Statement in applying a test requiring 'the most compelling evidence' to develop solar on BMV land.[64] The inspector went on to conclude that the developer had not brought sufficient evidence to 'demonstrate that there are no suitable poorer quality areas of land in the study area that could be used' and concluded that 'loss of just under 50% of BMV is a significant negative aspect'.[65]

16.28 These cases are diametrically opposed and reflect the lack of clarity on ALC and solar development. For NSIPs, the policy set out in NPS EN-3 is by comparison useful for its clarity. It remains to be seen how this shifts the balance in cases raising significant concerns about loss of ALC.

16.29 Finally, there is some suggestion that solar might be used alongside certain farming practices such as allowing animals to graze among and below the photovoltaic cells

---

59 ibid para 2.10.145.
60 Department for Energy Security and Net Zero, 'Overarching National Policy Statement for Energy (EN-1) (November 2023)' (n 5) para 5.11.34.
61 Department for Energy Security and Net Zero, 'Consultation Response Planning for New Energy Infrastructure' (2023) 42 <https://assets.publishing.service.gov.uk/media/655ddb1f544aea0019fb323b/national-policy-statement-consultation-government-response.pdf> accessed 2 April 2024.
62 *Minchens Lane, Bramley, Hampshire* APP/H1705/W/22/3304561 para 60.
63 ibid para 59.
64 *Land North of Lullington, Swadlincote, Derbyshire, DE12 8EW* APP/F1040/W/22/3313316 para 8.
65 ibid para 22.

(often called agrivoltaics).[66] This might maximise the efficiency of land use,[67] although its utility remains to be fully explored. Indeed, in *Land at Cruxton Farm, Cruxton Lane, Cruxton* the Secretary of State on a recovered appeal took into account a continued pastoral agricultural use for a solar farm proposed on land which was a little less than half BMV. The decision provides:[68]

> the Secretary of State agrees that the solar farm would be superimposed on continued (albeit restricted to pastoral) agricultural use and although this would limit agricultural opportunities and thus reduce agricultural productivity, this would, over the lifetime of the development, improve the quality of the land. The Secretary of State, overall, considers that this temporary reduction in agricultural productivity carries little weight against the scheme.

(b) Siting, national designations, and green belt

16.30 A difficult issue, particularly in the context of solar farms, is siting. NPS EN-3 indicates that: 'It is for applicants to decide what applications to bring forward. In general, the government does not seek to direct applicants to particular sites for renewable energy infrastructure.'[69] The NPS also recognises that proximity to network capacity is important to the selection of a site[70] (indeed, following consultation, the government moved the text on network connection forwards in the document to reflect this importance).[71]

16.31 A key provision is now included in respect of sites with nationally recognised designations. It is especially so as a result of all low carbon infrastructure being designated a critical national priority by NPS EN-1. Paragraph 2.3.6 of NPS EN-3 states:[72]

> When considering applications for CNP Infrastructure in sites with nationally recognised designations (such as SSSIs, National Nature Reserves, National Parks, the Broads, Areas of Outstanding Natural Beauty, Registered Parks and Gardens, and World Heritage Sites), the Secretary of State will take as the starting point that the relevant tests in Sections 5.4 and 5.10 of EN-1 have been met, and any significant adverse effects on the qualities for which the area has been designated are clearly outweighed by the urgent need for this type of infrastructure.

---

66 'Agrivoltaics' <https://www.nrel.gov/solar/market-research-analysis/agrivoltaics.html> accessed 23 April 2024. US National Renewable Energy Laboratory, <https://www.nrel.gov/solar/market-research-analysis/agrivoltaics.html> accessed 29 November 2023.

67 Department for Energy Security and Net Zero, 'National Policy Statement for Renewable Energy Infrastructure (EN-3) (November 2023)' (n 7) para 2.10.32.

68 *Land at Cruxton Farm, Cruxton Lane Cruxton DT2 0EB* APP/D1265/W/23/3317593 (3 April 2024) para 31.

69 Department for Energy Security and Net Zero, 'National Policy Statement for Renewable Energy Infrastructure (EN-3) (November 2023)' (n 7) para 2.3.5.

70 ibid para 2.10.21–2.10.26.

71 Department for Energy Security and Net Zero, 'Consultation Response Planning for New Energy Infrastructure' (n 61) page 42.

72 Department for Energy Security and Net Zero, 'National Policy Statement for Renewable Energy Infrastructure (EN-3) (November 2023)' (n 7) para 2.3.6.

16.32 This departs from the March 2023 draft, in which paragraph 3.3.6 said:[73]

> In sites with nationally recognised designations (such as SSSIs, National Nature Reserves, National Parks, the Broads, Areas of Outstanding Natural Beauty and Registered Parks and Gardens), consent for renewable energy projects should only be granted where the relevant tests in Sections 5.4 and 5.10 of EN-1 are met and any significant adverse effects on the qualities for which the area has been designated are clearly outweighed by the environmental, social and economic benefits.

16.33 This change marks a significant departure in approach to nationally recognised designations in NPS EN-3, putting substantially more weight in favour of development in such areas. It is also not a change foreshadowed in the consultation response published by the government with the designation of the policies in November 2023.[74] With this provision now in the policy, it is likely that there will be a substantial shift in approach to biodiversity and geological conservation (section 5.4 of EN-1) and landscape and visual impact (section 5.10 of EN-1) when siting renewable infrastructure covered by EN-3. This change is striking, albeit denoting the significance the government places on such development in meeting net zero commitments. It will be interesting to see how central this paragraph becomes in decisions on renewable energy DCOs in the future.

16.34 Separate to the issue of national designations is proposals within the Green Belt. This designation is primarily protected and maintained by the NPPF.[75] The starting point for development in the green belt is that: 'Inappropriate development is, by definition, harmful to the Green Belt and should not be approved except in very special circumstances.'[76] Currently, solar does not fall within the categories of construction which are not inappropriate development, and thus to be policy compliant with NPPF would need to show 'very special circumstances'.

16.35 NPS EN-1 specifically addresses energy infrastructure and very special circumstances. Para 5.11.37 provides:[77]

> Very special circumstances are not defined in national planning policy as it is for the individual decision maker to assess each case on its own merits and give relevant circumstances their due weight. However, when considering any planning application affecting Green Belt land, the Secretary of State should ensure that substantial weight is given to any harm to the Green Belt when considering any application for such development, while taking account, in relation to renewable and linear infrastructure, of the extent

---

73 Department for Energy Security and Net Zero, 'National Policy Statement for Renewable Energy Infrastructure (EN-3) (March 2023)' (2023) para 3.3.6. <https://assets.publishing.service.gov.uk/media/64252f5f2fa848000cec0f52/NPS_EN-3.pdf> accessed 4 April 2024.
74 Department for Energy Security and Net Zero, 'Consultation Response Planning for New Energy Infrastructure' (n 61). It is possible that this is an error arising out of the significant widening of 'critical national priority' infrastructure: see pages 14 and 15.
75 Department for Levelling Up, Housing and Communities, 'National Planning Policy Framework' (n 8) para 152–156.
76 ibid para 147.
77 Department for Energy Security and Net Zero, 'Overarching National Policy Statement for Energy (EN-1) (November 2023)' (n 5) para 5.11.37.

> to which its physical characteristics are such that it has limited or no impact on the fundamental purposes of Green Belt designation. Very special circumstances may include the wider environmental benefits associated with increased production of energy from renewables and other low carbon resources.

16.36 While outside the remit of NSIPs, this approach of considering wider environmental benefits has seen effective use at the local planning level. In *Land east and west of A130 and north and south of Canon Barns Road, East Hanningfield, Chelmsford, Essex CM3 8BD*,[78] the inspector considered a solar farm proposed to be built in the Green Belt. He concluded that the 'the benefits of renewable energy raise substantial benefits in favour of the proposal' and concluded that those benefits were in line with local and national policy.[79] He also noted the limitations on siting solar farms, and that 'a rational approach was taken to site selection' given an appropriate nearby place to connect into the grid.[80] This led to the conclusion that very special circumstances were made out and the scheme was permitted.[81]

(c) Heritage

16.37 While the most serious heritage harm is direct harm to an asset, the much more common heritage concern for solar is harm caused by a change in the asset's setting.[82] This will often be because the immediate area surrounding the asset will include the solar site. The protections afforded to assets with official designation is high, as are the protections afforded to assets which are not designated but are of equivalent significance to such designated assets.[83] For assets which do not fall within this category (for example, assets identified in a local plan or the subject of local listing) policy provides for protection 'on the basis of clear evidence that such heritage assets have a significance that merits consideration in the process, even though those assets are of lesser significance than designated heritage assets'.[84]

16.38 The policy makes clear that 'considerable importance and weight' should be given to the 'desirability of preserving heritage assets'.[85] The weight to be given to harm to assets is on a sliding scale in the normal way.[86] However, specifically in respect of renewables, NPS EN-3 goes on to provide:[87]

> In considering the impact on the historic environment as set out in Section 5.9 of EN-1 and whether the Secretary of State is satisfied that the substantial public benefits would outweigh any loss or harm to the significance of a designated heritage asset, the Secretary

78 *Land east and west of A130 and north and south of Canon Barns Road, East Hanningfield, Chelmsford, Essex CM3 8BD* APP/W1525/W/22/3300222.
79 ibid para 91.
80 ibid para 92.
81 ibid para 93.
82 Department for Energy Security and Net Zero, 'Overarching National Policy Statement for Energy (EN-1) (November 2023)' (n 5) para 5.9.3.
83 ibid paras 5.9.4–5.9.6.
84 ibid para 5.9.7.
85 ibid para 5.9.28.
86 ibid paras 5.9.29–5.9.31.
87 Department for Energy Security and Net Zero, 'National Policy Statement for Renewable Energy Infrastructure (EN-3) (November 2023)' (n 7) para 2.3.8.

> of State should take into account the positive role that large-scale renewable projects play in the mitigation of climate change, the delivery of energy security and the urgency of meeting the net zero target.

16.39 On the other hand, NPS EN-3 does go on to recognise that characteristics of solar farms make them particularly likely to cause harm to assets.[88] NPS EN-3, at paragraph 2.10.118, provides:[89]

> As the significance of a heritage asset derives not only from its physical presence but also from its setting, careful consideration should be given to the impact of large-scale solar farms which depending on their scale, design and prominence, may cause substantial harm to the significance of an asset.

16.40 How this policy interacts with the principle that solar farms are temporary and therefore reversible has played out in a number of cases. In the Longfield Solar Farm DCO,[90] the Examining Authority expressly recognised (in respect of heritage,[91] and landscape and visual impact)[92] that adverse effects of the scheme would be mostly reversible. In that case, the Examining Authority accepted that there would be harm to the setting of a number of assets and afforded that great weight.[93] They also noted that, while temporary, the amount of time that the harm would be experienced was 'a considerable period of time'.[94] However, that the scheme was overall temporary and the harm to heritage was (mostly) reversible, along with the benefits of the scheme, led to heritage matters only having a moderate amount of weight in the overall planning balance.[95] This approach was accepted by the Secretary of State in approving the scheme.[96] A similar approach was recently taken by the Secretary of State in the Sunnica Energy Farm DCO.[97]

---

88 The Government resisted consultation responses suggesting that the protection of heritage assets should be strengthened further still in respect of solar: Department for Energy Security and Net Zero, 'Consultation Response Planning for New Energy Infrastructure' (2023) (n 61) 44.

89 Department for Energy Security and Net Zero, 'National Policy Statement for Renewable Energy Infrastructure (EN-3) (November 2023)' (n 7) para 2.10.118.

90 Secretary of State for Energy Security and Net Zero, 'Application for Development Consent for the Longfield Solar Farm' (26 June 2023) <https://infrastructure.planninginspectorate.gov.uk/wp-content/ipc/uploads/projects/EN010118/EN010118-001300-Decision%20Letter%20-%20Longfield%20Solar%20Farm%20-%20June%202023.pdf> accessed 29 November 2023.

91 Planning Inspectorate, 'Longfield Solar Farm (EN010118): Examining Authority's Report of Findings and Conclusions and Recommendation to the Secretary of State for Energy Security and Net Zero' para 5.6.83 <https://infrastructure.planninginspectorate.gov.uk/wp-content/ipc/uploads/projects/EN010118/EN010118-001296-Longfield%20Solar%20Farm%20Recommendation%20Report%20Final%20and%20Appendix%20FINAL.pdf>.

92 ibid para 5.5.81.

93 ibid para 5.6.83.

94 ibid para 5.6.55.

95 ibid para 5.6.83.

96 Secretary of State for Energy Security and Net Zero, 'Application for Development Consent for the Longfield Solar Farm' (26 June 2023) (n 90) para 4.53.

97 Secretary of State for Energy and Net Zero, 'Application for Development Consent for Sunnica Energy Farm' (12 July 2024) (n 49) para 4.114–4.115.

(d) Landscape

16.41 The visual intrusion of solar farms can be significant. NPS EN-3 recognises that proposals should 'demonstrate good design, particularly in respect of landscape and visual amenity'.[98] However, due to its characteristics, it is recognised that generation is 'likely to be in low lying areas of good exposure and as such may have a wider zone of visual influence than other types of onshore energy infrastructure'.[99]

16.42 NPS EN-1 recognises that '[v]irtually all nationally significant energy infrastructure projects will have adverse effects on the landscape' (albeit noting there may be benefits from mitigation).[100] Schemes are encouraged to be designed carefully, taking into account this harm,[101] and especially focusing on the protections for nationally designated landscapes.[102] NPS EN-1 generally describes the weight to be attributed to varying qualities of landscape and designations on a sliding scale. Developers are directed to try and avoid, and then mitigate, harms.[103]

16.43 Key in understanding the sliding scale of protection for landscape in the national policy statements is the protection offered to landscape which does not have the benefit of a national designation. NPS EN-1 recognises that local landscape designations may be 'highly valued locally' and that they should be 'paid particular attention'. However, crucially, the policy indicates that 'locally valued landscapes should not be used in themselves to refuse consent, as this may unduly restrict acceptable development'.

16.44 This issue was an important one in the examination of the Sunnica Energy Farm DCO where a specific importance for horseracing was attributed to an area of land called the Limekilns overlooked by part of the proposed scheme. Objectors argued that such landscape must be given significant weight akin to a nationally recognised designation, while the developer relied on this part of the policy to argue that such landscape carried relatively little value in policy terms.[104] The Examining Authority concluded that there would be 'extensive adverse impact on the landscape setting of and views from the Limekilns, which comprises a valued landscape, and that this weighs substantially' against the scheme.[105] In contrast, while the Secretary of State noted this impact on the Limekilns, on this and the overall landscape issue the Secretary of State disagreed with the Examining Authority and concluded that the landscape and visual impacts did not

98 Department for Energy Security and Net Zero, 'National Policy Statement for Renewable Energy Infrastructure (EN-3) (November 2023)' (n 7) para 2.5.2.
99 ibid para 2.10.94.
100 Department for Energy Security and Net Zero, 'Overarching National Policy Statement for Energy (EN-1) (November 2023)' (n 5) para 5.10.5.
101 ibid para 5.10.6.
102 ibid para 5.10.7.
103 Department for Energy Security and Net Zero, 'National Policy Statement for Renewable Energy Infrastructure (EN-3) (November 2023)' (n 7) para 5.10.32–5.10.34.
104 Secretary of State for Energy and Net Zero, 'Application for Development Consent for Sunnica Energy Farm' (12 July 2024) (n 49).
105 Planning Inspectorate, 'Sunnica Energy Farm Examining Authority's Report of Findings and Conclusions and Recommendation to the Secretary of State for Energy Security and Net Zero' (28 June 2023) para 4.10.122 <https://infrastructure.planninginspectorate.gov.uk/wp-content/ipc/uploads/projects/EN010106/EN010106-005902-Sunnica-ExA-Recommendation-Report-28-June-2023-FINAL-with%20Errata%20sheet.pdf> accessed 18 September 2024.

outweigh the benefit of the scheme (albeit they still weighed against the scheme in the overall planning balance).[106]

16.45 Landscape and visual impact may also be relevant as a harm to the amenity and enjoyment of public rights of way. NPS EN-3 encourages applicants to design around and minimise such impact on high sensitivity receptors.[107]

16.46 Finally, NPS EN-1 establishes what is often understood as a principle of precedent for approaches to NSIPs and visual effects. Paragraph 5.10.25 of NPS EN-1 provides:[108]

> In considering visual effects it may be helpful for applicants to draw attention, in the supporting evidence to their applications, to any examples of existing permitted infrastructure they are aware of with a similar magnitude of impact on equally sensitive receptors. This may assist the Secretary of State in judging the weight they should give to the assessed visual impacts of the proposed development.

16.47 This is important as it means, at least in respect of landscape and visual effects, there might slowly be a pushing of the envelope as increasingly impactful schemes build upon each other as more DCOs are consented for solar farms.

(e) Other issues

16.48 Many other issues arise in the context of solar generation. Some are technical, including the co-location of battery storage, glint and glare assessments, and transport. Some are environmental, including protected species and BNG. Some are more policy-driven, including concerns that solar farms cut off communities, harm local amenity land, and industrialise the landscape. All parties involved in applications concerning solar farms must be cautious to consider the full gamut of issues that can arise.

Hydrogen

(i) *Introduction*

16.49 This section focuses on the production of hydrogen as a fuel that can be used to assist the UK in meeting its net zero targets. While the UK has historically made use of hydrogen, for example in town gas which heated homes and lit streets in the 20th century, or in industrial processes, methods of producing hydrogen were carbon intensive.[109] With the advent of methods of producing hydrogen in a low carbon way this is now changing. Hydrogen might be produced using carbon-intensive methods

106 Secretary of State for Energy and Net Zero, 'Application for Development Consent for Sunnica Energy Farm' (12 July 2024) (n 49) para 4.161–4.162.

107 Department for Energy Security and Net Zero, 'National Policy Statement for Renewable Energy Infrastructure (EN-3) (November 2023)' (n 7) para 2.10.42–2.10.43.

108 Department for Energy Security and Net Zero, 'Overarching National Policy Statement for Energy (EN-1) (November 2023)' (n 5) para 5.10.25.

109 Secretary of State for Business, Energy, and Industrial Strategy, 'UK Hydrogen Strategy' (2021) 8 <https://assets.publishing.service.gov.uk/media/64c7e8bad8b1a70011b05e38/UK-Hydrogen-Strategy_web.pdf> accessed 28 September 2023.

but with carbon captured through CCUS infrastructure (so-called 'blue hydrogen'), or hydrogen might be produced using electrolysis with the electricity used coming from low carbon sources (so-called 'green hydrogen') or, sometimes, 'pink hydrogen' where the electricity is sourced from nuclear power.[110]

16.50 In 2022 the UK produced 27TWh of hydrogen, primarily for use in the petrochemical and fertiliser industry.[111] Of that figure, 96% was 'grey hydrogen', being hydrogen produced using methods which produce significant amounts of GHGs (primarily arising from the use of natural gas as the primary production material).[112] While such methods will continue to be used, an important feature of hydrogen production moving forwards will be increased use of CCUS to manage the GHG emissions of such production methods (turning 'grey hydrogen' into 'blue hydrogen').

16.51 There are many features which make hydrogen well suited to supporting net zero:

- Hydrogen can be used in a multitude of generator types, including: fuel cells, boilers, turbines, or engines.[113] It can 'replace many current natural gas uses, become a key component of synthetic fuels for aviation and replace existing carbon intensive hydrogen used in petrochemicals [and] agriculture'.[114]

- As a gas it can be stored at very large scales and transported similarly to natural gas or liquid fuels today.[115]

- Hydrogen can be used to decarbonise sectors which are not suited to electrification. This might include generation of high temperature heat or long-distance and heavy-duty transport.[116]

16.52 Progressing with hydrogen production and use is, however, difficult. There is 'the "chicken and egg" problem of growing supply and demand in tandem'.[117] The infrastructure is also likely to be initially expensive, and to require clustering (encouraging development in specific locations to maximise contact between infrastructure and users) to better achieve effective introduction. In this regard it shares much with CCUS;[118] indeed, because blue hydrogen relies heavily on CCUS is likely to be developed alongside

---

110 Department for Business, Energy and Industrial Strategy, Department for Energy Security and Net Zero and Prime Minister's Office, 'British Energy Security Strategy' (n 4).
111 National Engineering Policy Centre, 'The Role of Hydrogen in a Net Zero Energy System' (2022) 9 <https://nepc.raeng.org.uk/media/tkphxfwy/the-role-of-hydrogen-in-the-net-zero-energy-system.pdf> accessed 28 September 2023.
112 ibid 9.
113 Secretary of State for Business, Energy, and Industrial Strategy, 'UK Hydrogen Strategy' (n 109) 9.
114 National Grid ESO, 'Future Energy Scenarios 2023 (July 2023)' (2023) 147 <https://www.nationalgrideso.com/document/283101/download>. National Grid ESO became the National Energy System Operator in October 2024.
115 Secretary of State for Business, Energy, and Industrial Strategy, 'UK Hydrogen Strategy' (n 109) 9.
116 ibid 9.
117 ibid 10.
118 See the section on 'Carbon capture, usage and storage' in Chapter 15.

clusters being progressed by the government.[119] Operators planning to produce hydrogen in England will need an environmental permit from the Environment Agency,[120] and guidance is being produced on the use of emergent techniques for such production (e.g. the recent guidance on green hydrogen and the electrolysis of water).[121]

(ii) *Contribution to net zero*

16.53 Government policy makes clear that '[l]ow carbon hydrogen will be essential for meeting net zero'.[122] Most pathways modelled for Carbon Budget 6 indicated 'hydrogen demand doubles between 2030 and 2035, and continues to increase rapidly over the 2030s and 2040s. By 2050, between 250–460TWh of hydrogen could be needed across the economy.'[123] Similarly, one of the three scenarios proposed by Future Energy Scenarios 2023, 'System Transformation', envisages that an essential aspect of achieving net zero would be moving to annual demand for hydrogen of 446TWh (with 119TWh devoted to residential hydrogen demand for heat).[124]

16.54 The government has already made significant commitments to the immediate increase in production and use of hydrogen in the UK. As part of the UK's 'Ten Point Plan for a Green Industrial Revolution', point 2 committed the UK to aim for 5GW of low carbon hydrogen production capacity by 2030. This commitment was supported by a £240 million Net Zero Hydrogen Fund. The commitment was re-emphasised in the UK Hydrogen Strategy which fleshed out the detail of how progressing production in the UK would commence and continue.[125] Subsequent to that the government doubled its ambition in the British Energy Security Strategy:[126]

> We will offer *long-term signals* alongside *immediate support by:*
>
> - Doubling our ambition to *up to 10GW of low carbon hydrogen production capacity by 2030,* subject to affordability and value for money, with at *least half of this coming from electrolytic hydrogen.* By efficiently using our surplus renewable power to make hydrogen, we will reduce electricity system costs.
> - *Aiming to run annual allocation rounds for electrolytic hydrogen,* moving to price competitive allocation by 2025 as soon as legislation and market conditions allow, so that up to *1GW of electrolytic hydrogen is in construction or operational by 2025.*

---

119 Such a clustering approach has been adopted since the UK's initial commitments to grow hydrogen production. See Department for Energy Security and Net Zero, 'The Ten Point Plan for a Green Industrial Revolution' (2020) 10 <https://assets.publishing.service.gov.uk/media/5fb5513de90e0720978b1a6f/10 _POINT_PLAN_BOOKLET.pdf> accessed 28 September 2023.
120 Environment Agency, 'Environment Agency Publishes Guidance on Production of Green Hydrogen' (2024) <https://www.gov.uk/government/news/environment-agency-publishes-guidance-on-production-of-green-hydrogen> accessed 16 April 2024.
121 Environment Agency, 'Hydrogen Production by Electrolysis of Water: Emerging Techniques' (2024) <https://www.gov.uk/guidance/hydrogen-production-by-electrolysis-of-water-emerging-techniques> accessed 16 April 2024.
122 Secretary of State for Business, Energy, and Industrial Strategy, 'UK Hydrogen Strategy' (n 109) 9.
123 ibid 38.
124 National Grid ESO, 'Future Energy Scenarios 2023 (July 2023)' (n 114) 13.
125 Secretary of State for Business, Energy, and Industrial Strategy, 'UK Hydrogen Strategy' (n 109) 38.
126 Department for Business, Energy and Industrial Strategy, Department for Energy Security and Net Zero and Prime Minister's Office, 'British Energy Security Strategy' (n 4).

- *Designing, by 2025, new business models for hydrogen transport and storage infrastructure*, which will be essential to grow the hydrogen economy.
- Levelling the playing field by setting up a *hydrogen certification scheme by 2025*, to demonstrate high-grade British hydrogen for export and ensure any imported hydrogen meets the same high standards that UK companies expect. (emphasis in original)

16.55 However, while government policy has been clear and forward thinking in some areas, other issues remain unresolved. In its June 2023 Report to Parliament, the Climate Change Committee ('CCC') identified its 2016 recommendation that the government take a strategic decision on the roles of hydrogen and electrification in heat for buildings 'by 2025 at the latest'.[127] The CCC noted the commitment of the government to take that decision by 2026, yet expressed concerns that the dates involved are now approaching, stating 'in our assessment there has not been enough progress on the decisions needed to enable progress on buildings decarbonisation.'[128]

16.56 It is worth noting that hydrogen is often an alternative to electrification. Future Energy Scenarios 2023 explains that, between its three scenarios for success in achieving net zero, hydrogen demand could vary from 120 to 446TWh.[129] This is a point also recognised in the November 2023 version of NPS EN-1, which sets out:[130]

> The precise level of electricity demand during the transition to net zero is uncertain and could be affected by alternative means of decarbonising these sectors, such as the use of low carbon hydrogen, and the pace of that decarbonisation. However, it is prudent to plan on a conservative basis to ensure that there is sufficient supply of electricity to meet demand across a wide range of future scenarios, including where the use of hydrogen is limited.

(iii) *Policy*

16.57 The direction of travel for hydrogen production is now set out in various high-level policies. This includes, for the first time, planning policy. While the July 2011 versions of NPS EN-1 and EN-3 made no reference at all to hydrogen production and use, the November 2023 version states: 'There is an urgent need for all types of low carbon hydrogen infrastructure to allow hydrogen to play its role in the transition to net zero.'[131]

---

127 Committee on Climate Change, 'Next Steps for UK Heat Policy' (2016) 40 <https://www.theccc.org.uk/publication/next-steps-for-uk-heat-policy/> accessed 4 April 2024.
128 Climate Change Committee, 'Progress in Reducing Emissions: 2023 Report to Parliament' (2023) 160 <https://www.theccc.org.uk/wp-content/uploads/2023/06/Progress-in-reducing-UK-emissions-2023-Report-to-Parliament.pdf> accessed 4 April 2024.
129 National Grid ESO, 'Future Energy Scenarios 2023 (July 2023)' (n 114) 13.
130 Department for Energy Security and Net Zero, 'Overarching National Policy Statement for Energy (EN-1) (November 2023)' (n 5) para 3.3.10.
131 ibid para 3.4.12.

16.58 The NPS goes on to identify low carbon hydrogen infrastructure, hydrogen distribution, pipelines and storage to be critical national priority infrastructure.[132]

16.59 NPS EN-1 repeats much of the high-level policy within its text, quoting from the UK Hydrogen Strategy and the British Energy Security Strategy. It also gives a summary of hydrogen, and describes how it might be used as a replacement for natural gas and other fuels.[133] However, consideration of detailed planning policy is limited to recognising that hydrogen pipelines and underground storage may need DCO consent when they fall within the Planning Act 2008 ('PA 2008'),[134] and explaining that future need for infrastructure should be taken into account when applying for permissions (with applicants proposing 'pipelines with a greater capacity than demand might suggest at the time of consenting').[135]

16.60 That there is this lack of detail on hydrogen in the NPSs themselves reflects the nascent state of hydrogen production, transport, storage and use. While the national priority is clear, achieving it practically project-to-project is not. NPS EN-4 (concerning natural gas supply infrastructure), which has clear relevance to hydrogen transport and storage, emphasises this point:[136]

> The guidance that follows in this NPS has been drafted in respect of, and has effect only in relation to, natural gas infrastructure. It does not have effect for hydrogen infrastructure, but may be part of other matters which the Secretary of State thinks are important and relevant to their decision on applications for hydrogen infrastructure, in which case they would need to take it into account.

16.61 There is also an absence of reference to hydrogen in planning policy focused at the local level.[137] This might be thought unsurprising given the need for governmental support to introduce it at the national level. However, it is obvious that detailed planning policy must be brought forward in the future if the UK is to achieve 10GW by 2030.

(iv) *The Energy Act 2023 ('EA 2023')*

16.62 Overall, the purposes of the EA 2023 are described by the explanatory note as 'liberating investment in clean technologies' and 'reforming the UK's energy system so it is fit for the future'.[138]

---

132 ibid para 3.4.22.
133 ibid para 3.4.13–3.4.19.
134 ibid para 3.4.20.
135 ibid para 3.4.21.
136 Department for Energy Security and Net Zero, 'National Policy Statement for Natural Gas Supply Infrastructure and Gas and Oil Pipelines (EN-4) (November 2023)' (2023) para 1.6.6. <https://assets.publishing.service.gov.uk/media/65a789a8867cd8000d5ae9be/nps-natural-gas-supply-infrastructure-pipelines-en4.pdf> accessed 4 April 2024.
137 For example, in: Department for Levelling Up, Housing and Communities, 'National Planning Policy Framework' (n 8) para 163 or see the absence of the relevant Planning Practice Guidance from the Department for Levelling Up, Housing and Communities: https://www.gov.uk/government/collections/planning-practice-guidance> accessed 4 April 2024.
138 Explanatory Notes to the Energy Act 2023 para 2.

16.63 The EA 2023 introduces various mechanisms for achieving the production and use of hydrogen on a major scale. Part 2 of the Act provides regulatory mechanisms for production, transport and storage. A focus of the Act is on introducing the business models, including through the hydrogen levy, which will support widespread industry adoption. It also focuses on infrastructure such as pipelines to achieve the practical steps of getting hydrogen from source to point of use.[139]

16.64 The EA 2023 more generally reflects how the government proposes to trial the use of hydrogen in various settings. The Act provides for a 'hydrogen village trial' whereby the gas distribution network operator will operate a grid conversion trial. This will involve disconnecting a local grid area from the natural gas supply and substituting it for hydrogen.[140] The Act also provides various powers in the Secretary of State to amend other Acts (including the Gas Act 1986) to achieve the government's objectives in relation to hydrogen.

(v) *The future of hydrogen*

16.65 The British Energy Security Strategy recognises that, '[w]e have virtually no low-carbon hydrogen in our system today'.[141] It is clear that the future will involve significant and expansive introduction of low carbon hydrogen production and use. It will be key for clear policy to continue to be set out, and appropriate funding implemented, to achieve the strikingly high predicted demands for hydrogen by 2050.

Offshore Wind

(i) *Introduction*

(a) General

16.66 Offshore wind is predicted to be the single largest generating source contributing to the UK's drive towards net zero. While in 2022 there was 13.4GW installed, it is predicted that between 96.8GW and 115GW will be required by 2050 to achieve net zero.[142] Indeed, National Grid ESO (now, since October 2024, the National Energy System Operator) consider that over half of all domestic energy production will be being sourced from offshore wind in 2050 (489TWh of an overall domestic production total of 886TWh) if net zero is to be achieved.[143] Thus, the contribution that offshore wind will make cannot be overstated.

16.67 Offshore wind has a number of advantages over other generating sources which has highlighted it as critical in the move towards net zero. Being placed offshore, landscape, heritage, and safety concerns do not arise in the same way as onshore wind, solar or nuclear. Offshore wind also has a higher load factor than solar (comparatively 40.8%

---

139 Energy Act 2023 Part 3.
140 Explanatory Notes to the Energy Act 2023 paras 2 and 5.
141 Department for Business, Energy and Industrial Strategy, Department for Energy Security and Net Zero and Prime Minister's Office, 'British Energy Security Strategy' (n 4) 22.
142 National Grid ESO, 'Future Energy Scenarios 2023 (July 2023)' (n 114) 130.
143 ibid 125–7. Figures taken from the 'Consumer Transformation' model.

versus 10.6%), and indeed onshore wind (27.4%), meaning it achieves a much higher energy output against its installed power capacity.[144] However this form of generation is still variable, and times of extremely low generation are recorded.[145] It is thus important for wind to be part of a broad generation mix including storage.

16.68 Being an island, the UK is well-placed to provide space for such generation. This avoids a lot of local resistance which has made consenting onshore more difficult. The expense of offshore wind has also significantly reduced, falling 67% between 2010 and 2022.[146] The technology is also one with significant ongoing development; aside from seabed installed wind turbine generators (or 'WTGs') the government has also expressed an intent to install 5GW of innovative floating wind by 2030.[147] These are all factors which weigh in favour of the government's intention to remain a world leader in this form of generation.[148]

16.69 However, offshore wind is not without its difficulties. One critical aspect is properly connecting offshore wind to the electricity grid. Substantial work in this field has been done, and the National Grid ESO 'Holistic Network Design' planned in 2022 for 23GW of connection.[149] Consenting of offshore wind also remains slow, and the government has expressed an intention to reduce the period required to achieve this from 4 years to one (with a move to fast-track consenting for schemes of particular quality).[150]

16.70 Government policy is strongly behind offshore wind; most notably NPS EN-1 and NPS EN-3. These policies are addressed below. In the 'British Energy Security Strategy' the government expressed the view that: '[w]e will be the Saudi Arabia of wind power, with the ambition that by 2030 over half our renewable generation capacity will be wind'.[151]

---

144 Lucía Fernández, 'Average Load Factor of Renewable Energies in the United Kingdom (UK) from 2015 to 2022, by Source' (*Statista*, 2023) <https://www.statista.com/statistics/383314/average-renewable-energy-load-factor-in-the-united-kingdom-uk/> accessed 23 April 2024. The principles of load factors are explained in paras 16.05–16.06 above. Figures for UK in 2022.

145 See the discussion in Olusola Bamisile and others, 'Enabling the UK to Become the Saudi Arabia of Wind? The Cost of Green Hydrogen from Offshore Wind' (Imperial College London 2023) 12 <https://spiral.imperial.ac.uk/bitstream/10044/1/106502/7/Briefing%20Paper_The%20cost%20of%20green%20hydrogen%20from%20offshore%20wind.pdf> accessed 24 May 2024. There it is recorded, for example, that the entire UK output for wind on 3 March 2021 was 0.6GW.

146 Rt Hon Chris Skidmore MP, 'Mission Zero: Independent Review of Net Zero' (2023) 20 <https://assets.publishing.service.gov.uk/government/uploads/system/uploads/attachment_data/file/1128689/mission-zero-independent-review.pdf> accessed 17 April 2024.

147 Department for Business, Energy and Industrial Strategy, Department for Energy Security and Net Zero and Prime Minister's Office, 'British Energy Security Strategy' (n 4).

148 ibid 17.

149 National Grid ESO, 'Pathway to 2030: Holistic Network Design' (2022) 6 <https://www.nationalgrideso.com/document/262681/download> accessed 24 May 2024. National Grid ESO became the National Energy System Operator in October 2024.

150 Department for Business, Energy and Industrial Strategy, Department for Energy Security and Net Zero and Prime Minister's Office, 'British Energy Security Strategy' (n 4) 17.

151 ibid 16.

(b) Onshore wind

16.71 This chapter focuses on offshore wind given that, until recently, this was the focus of government policy and the likely source of the vast increase in installed capacity required. However, onshore wind may also have a significant role to play in the future, particularly given changes in policy in 2024. In 2022 there was 13.6GW of installed onshore wind capacity,[152] and National Grid ESO predict a need for between 32.5GW and 44.4GW by 2050 to reach net zero.[153] In the 'British Energy Security Strategy', published in 2022 the following was set out:[154]

> In Scotland, which has its own planning system, we will work with the Scottish Government to ensure communities and landscape issues are considered for future projects.
>
> In Wales, we will support the work underway by the Welsh Government, Ofgem, and networks to improve grid connections.
>
> In the more densely populated England, the Government recognizes the range of views on onshore wind. Our plans will prioritise local communities in control. We will not introduce wholesale changes to current planning regulations for onshore wind but will consult this year on developing local partnership for a limited number of supportive communities who wish to host new onshore wind infrastructure in return for benefits, including lower energy bills. The consultation will consider how clear support can be demonstrated by local communities, local authorities and MPs.

16.72 However, in July 2024 the new Labour government significantly changed planning policy applying to onshore wind. As is discussed below, it excised those bits of NPPF which indicated against onshore wind and treated this form of generation differently to other energy development proposals.[155] While currently onshore wind (unlike offshore) remains excluded from the NSIP process in the PA 2008, and thus is left to local planning, the government has indicated that it will consult on changing this position.[156] Thus, it seems likely there will be a substantial change in number and type of onshore wind developments coming forward.

---

152 National Grid ESO, 'Future Energy Scenarios 2023 (July 2023)' (n 114).

153 ibid.

154 Department for Business, Energy and Industrial Strategy, Department for Energy Security and Net Zero and Prime Minister's Office, 'British Energy Security Strategy' (n 4) 18.

155 Ministry of Housing, Communities and Local Government, HM Treasury, Department for Energy Security and Net Zero, Department for Levelling Up, Housing and Communities, 'Policy paper: Policy statement on onshore wind' (8 July 2024) <https://www.gov.uk/government/publications/policy-statement-on-onshore-wind/policy-statement-on-onshore-wind> accessed 18 September 2024.

156 Planning Act 2008 s 15. However, this does not apply to onshore wind which was excluded from the definition of NSIP in March 2016: The Infrastructure Planning (Onshore Wind Generating Stations) Order 2016, SI 2016/306 reg 3. An amendment to reinclude onshore wind was added to the Levelling-up and Regeneration Bill in the House of Lords but was removed by the House of Commons shortly before the Bill became law (Lords amendment 244, HC Deb 17 October 2023, vol 738, cols 285–7; not insisted upon in the House of Lords, HL Deb 23 October 2023, vol 833, col 480).

(ii) *Contribution to net zero*

16.73 The importance of offshore cannot be overstated. In the government's original 'Ten Point Plan for a Green Industrial Revolution' point 1 was 'Advancing Offshore Wind'. That policy went on to say:[157]

> Offshore wind is a critical source of renewable energy for our growing economy, with the UK already leading the world. By 2030 we plan to quadruple our offshore wind capacity so as to generate more power than all our homes use today, backing new innovations to make the most of this proven technology and investing to bring new jobs and growth to our ports and coastal regions.

16.74 That policy then went on to set the aim of reaching an installed capacity of 40GW of offshore wind, with 1GW of floating offshore wind, by 2030. This was repeated in the 'Energy White Paper: Powering our Net Zero Future'[158] and the 'Net Zero Strategy: Build Back Greener'. The Net Zero Strategy identified this target as one of two power targets that the government would update annually (the other being a general commitment to achieve generation of all electricity from low carbon sources by 2035, security of supply permitting).[159]

16.75 In April 2022 the British Energy Security Strategy then increased the target for 2030 by moving to a target of 50GW by 2030 (with 5GW of floating wind).[160] This has been maintained in the 'Powering Up Britain – The Net Zero Growth Plan'.[161] As to achieving that target, in 2022 2.7GW was deployed in the UK. This is slightly off track from the target and an annual deployment rate of 4.5GW is required to 2030. However, this is still ahead of other areas of generation (including solar and onshore wind) which are comparatively lagging.[162]

16.76 The early recognition given to the contribution of offshore wind in draft NPS EN-1 and EN-3 is telling. As is addressed at the start of this chapter, the November 2023 version of NPS EN-1 identifies all low carbon infrastructure as a 'critical national priority'.[163] However, the March 2023 drafts of both policies broadly reserved this designation for offshore wind, with draft NPS EN-3 stating:[164]

> there is a critical national priority (CNP) fir the provision of nationally significant new offshore wind development and supporting onshore and offshore network infrastructure and related network reinforcements ('CNP Infrastructure').

---

157 HM Government, 'The Ten Point Plan for a Green Industrial Revolution' (n 119) 8.
158 HM Government, 'Energy White Paper: Powering Our Net Zero Future' (n 33).
159 HM Government, 'Net Zero Strategy: Build Back Greener' (n 3) 254.
160 Department for Business, Energy and Industrial Strategy, Department for Energy Security and Net Zero and Prime Minister's Office, 'British Energy Security Strategy' (n 4) 16.
161 Department for Energy Security and Net Zero, 'Powering Up Britain' (2023) 17 <https://assets.publishing.service.gov.uk/media/642468ff2fa8480013ec0f39/powering-up-britain-joint-overview.pdf> accessed 4 April 2024.
162 Climate Change Committee, 'Progress in Reducing Emissions: 2023 Report to Parliament' (n 128) 204.
163 Department for Energy Security and Net Zero, 'National Policy Statement for Renewable Energy Infrastructure (EN-3) (November 2023)' (n 7) para 4.2.
164 Department for Energy Security and Net Zero, 'National Policy Statement for Renewable Energy Infrastructure (EN-3) (March 2023)' (n 73) para 3.8.12.

16.77 That the policies have moved towards designating all low carbon infrastructure as of a 'critical national priority' does not indicate that the importance of offshore wind has diminished. Rather, it reflects the general recognition of the importance of all such infrastructure.

16.78 It is also worth noting that the contribution to net zero that offshore wind can make is heavily dependent on improvements to the electricity grid and the connecting of offshore sites. As Sir Chris Skidmore MP recognised in his review of net zero, '[r]olling out the [Holistic Network Design] is critical to deliver the Government's ambition of up to 50GW of offshore wind by 2030 and ensuring long-term certainty for businesses'.[165] As is explored in the network infrastructure section at paragraph 16.99 below, National Grid ESO has produced its Holistic Network Design which provides for the connection of 23GW of offshore capacity. The Holistic Network design recognises that its development, along with other projects further advanced in their building out, come together to provide a route to achieving the 50GW by 2030. However, it is only with those significant network works that this is achievable.[166]

(iii) *Policy*

16.79 Given the significant contribution that offshore wind can make to meeting net zero, it is unsurprising that policy heavily favours its development. Aside from the more general policy discussed above, nearly half of NPS EN-3 is devoted to offshore wind. The section begins with the importance of offshore wind and how this should inform development:[167]

> 2.8.1 As set out in the British Energy Security Strategy (BESS), the Government expects that offshore wind (including floating wind) will play a significant role in meeting demand and decarbonising the energy system. The ambition is to deploy up to 50GW of offshore wind capacity (including up to 5GW of floating wind) by 2030, with an expectation that there will be a need for substantially more installed offshore capacity beyond this to achieve net zero carbon emissions by 2050.
>
> 2.8.2 To meet its objectives government considers that *all offshore wind developments are likely to need to maximise their capacity within technological, environmental, and other constraints of the development.* (emphasis added)

16.80 In that regard it is of note EN-3 includes that the Secretary of State will not include a maximum capacity limit in a DCO,[168] and indeed some DCOs have had their maximum generation limits removed.[169] However, the policy goes on to note that

---

165 Rt Hon Chris Skidmore MP, 'Mission Zero: Independent Review of Net Zero' (n 146) 75.
166 National Grid ESO 'Pathway to 2030: Holistic Network Design' (n 149) 31.
167 Department for Energy Security and Net Zero, 'National Policy Statement for Renewable Energy Infrastructure (EN-3) (November 2023)' (n 7) s 2.8.
168 ibid para 2.8.25.
169 Tim Pick, 'Independent Report of the Offshore Wind Champion: Seizing Our Opportunities' (2023) 32 <https://assets.publishing.service.gov.uk/media/65a662c1867cd800135ae90b/offshore-wind-champion-independent-report.pdf> accessed 24 May 2024.

maximum generation limits may appear in sea bed leases from the Crown Estate as such limits are used by it to estimate environmental effect of schemes at the plan level. The EN-3 reinforces the point that the limits assessed for a DCO 'may differ from the limits on development assumed by the Crown Estate in the agreement for a lease'.[170]

16.81 As is common, the policy leaves matters of wind resource and economic modelling to the applicant,[171] and directs the Secretary of State away from technical and commercial considerations, including those aspects of location (e.g. concerning water depth or foundations issues) save as far as they raise matters which may have planning impacts.[172]

16.82 Without going through the detail of EN-3, significant portions of the offshore wind section then addresses (1) harm to ecology and habitats;[173] (2) impact on commercial activities (including fishing and shipping);[174] and (3) network connection to the electricity grid.[175] This is not unsurprising; while other forms of offshore generation are included in EN-3,[176] offshore wind is by far the most deployed and planned for. The planning harms of offshore schemes of the size now in development are not merely different in degree, but have differences in kind to the other generation included in EN-3. Indeed, the specifics of impact on commercial activities and achieving network connection are almost unique to this kind of development. Thus, while the policy sits alongside the remainder of EN-3 and the general policies in EN-1, there are important and specific provisions for offshore wind which do not appear elsewhere (some of which are explored further below, including those new provisions in the Energy Act 2023).

(iv) *Energy Act 2023, ecology and environmental impacts*

16.83 As part of achieving the reduction in consenting time for offshore wind identified in the British Energy Security Strategy from four years to one year, the government proposed to bring forward an Offshore Wind Environmental Improvement Package ('OWEIP').[177] Certain measures to achieve that package required legislation, which has now been passed in the Energy Act 2023.

16.84 The first measure is a power to modify the requirements of Habitats Regulations Assessment(s) ('HRA') to specifically account for the marine aspects of offshore wind

---

170 Department for Energy Security and Net Zero, 'National Policy Statement for Renewable Energy Infrastructure (EN-3) (November 2023)' (n 7) para 2.8.25.
171 ibid para 2.8.28–30.
172 ibid paras 2.8.33, 2.8.284.
173 ibid para 2.8.51–6, 2.8.95–164, 2.8.218–49, 2.8.265–83, 2.8.302–24.
174 ibid para 2.8.178–95, 2.8.250–1, 2.8.559–60, 2.8.326–40.
175 ibid para 2.8.34–43, 2.8.59–73, 2.8.285–90.
176 ibid para 2.11 (concerning tidal stream energy).
177 Department for Business, Energy and Industrial Strategy and Department for Energy Security and Net Zero, 'Energy Security Bill Factsheet: Offshore Wind Environmental Improvement Package' (GOV.UK, 9 January 2023) <https://www.gov.uk/government/publications/energy-security-bill-factsheets/energy-security-bill-factsheet-offshore-wind-environmental-improvement-package> accessed 24 May 2024. See also Department for Energy Security and Net Zero, 'National Policy Statement for Renewable Energy Infrastructure (EN-3) (November 2023)' (n 7) para 2.8.8.

developments.[178] This is with the intention of reducing time by frontloading aspects of such assessment. The apparent hope is to avoid situations where problems with the application only become apparent at a late stage thereby ultimately delaying the process of consenting.[179]

16.85 The second is a provision allowing for strategic compensatory measures allowing collaborative work between developers and the government to compensate for negative environmental effects of offshore wind farms which cannot be avoided, reduced or mitigated.[180] Again, part of the intention here is to frontload compensatory measures so less time is spent resolving issues project by project. The government also reports that the Department for Environment, Food and Rural Affairs is already working on a pilot project to explore identification of effective compensatory measures.[181]

16.86 The third is a power to create one or more marine recovery funds for the purpose of achieving strategic compensatory measures.[182] The intention is for these funds to be an option for developers to pay into so as to discharge compensation obligations. Notwithstanding an intention expressed that the fund should be able to receive payments from late 2023, this does not appear to have yet been set up.[183]

16.87 It is early days for the Energy Act 2023, and the powers to modify HRA and to set up the marine recovery fund are yet to be used. However, these are important changes which appear to signify a move towards the speeding up of development consent for offshore wind. They also sit alongside changes now present within EN-3.

16.88 EN-3 addresses the government's obligations to protect Marine Protected Areas ('MPAs') and notes that the extent of the offshore wind ambition may make mitigation difficult and compensation necessary.[184] Similarly, the possibility of harms to SACs, SPAs, Ramsar sites and MCZs are noted, and the need for derogation from those protections is explored (given that avoidance, reduction and mitigation may be insufficient).[185] The policy explores requirements to provide information on a 'without prejudice' basis to assess the issue of derogations as soon as is reasonably practicable, and the possibility of refusing applications for the lack of this information is specifically noted (along with consultation obligations at an early stage).[186] Importantly paragraphs 2.8.276–283 address the introduction of strategic compensation (in the Energy Act 2023), albeit the policy is relatively light on detail reflecting the nascent state of this approach to compensation.

---

178 Energy Act 2023 s 293.
179 Department for Business, Energy and Industrial Strategy and Department for Energy Security and Net Zero, 'Energy Security Bill Factsheet: Offshore Wind Environmental Improvement Package' (n 177).
180 Energy Act 2023 s 291.
181 Department for Business, Energy and Industrial Strategy and Department for Energy Security and Net Zero, 'Energy Security Bill Factsheet: Offshore Wind Environmental Improvement Package' (n 177).
182 Energy Act 2023 s 292.
183 Department for Business, Energy and Industrial Strategy and Department for Energy Security and Net Zero, 'Energy Security Bill Factsheet: Offshore Wind Environmental Improvement Package' (n 177).
184 Department for Energy Security and Net Zero, 'National Policy Statement for Renewable Energy Infrastructure (EN-3) (November 2023)' (n 7) para 2.8.51–6.
185 ibid para 2.8.265.
186 ibid para 2.8.267–71.

16.89 EN-3 also notes that part of the OWEIP includes the bringing forwards of Offshore Wind Environmental Standards ('OWES') 'to accelerate deployment whilst offering greater protection to marine environment'.[187] The Department for Environment, Food and Rural Affairs is tasked with consulting on such standards.[188] Once established, applicants will have to explain how they have complied with OWESs, or justify departures from them.[189] Compliance with the OWES is likely to be material to a decision to consent, and to inform HRA and MCZ assessments.[190]

(v) *Specific issues*

16.90 Offshore wind gives rise to a number of specific issues, some of which are strikingly different to those addressed elsewhere in this chapter concerning onshore development. It is also pertinent to note that, unlike onshore development, offshore development will not be captured by the PA 2008 NSIP procedure unless the generating station produces in excess of 100MW.[191]

(a) Landscape and visual impacts

16.91 Offshore wind farms are often visible from land. They can provide the setting for onshore areas with significant landscape designations, such as AONBs, National Parks, or Heritage Coasts (the latter of which are typically characterised by a largely undeveloped coastal character).[192] Thus, while an offshore wind farm may be far out to sea and therefore have minimal landscape and visual impact calling for limited assessment,[193] they can also be an integral part of these highly prized landscapes. Of a seascape, landscape and visual impact assessment ('SLVIA'), EN-3 sets out an assessment should include the following:[194]

- the limit of visual perception from the coast under poor, good and best lighting conditions;
- The effect of navigation and hazard prevention lighting on dark night skies;
- Individual landscape and visual characteristics of the coast and the special qualities of designated landscapes, such as World Heritage Sites and National Park, within limits the coast's capacity to absorb a development; and
- How people perceive and interact with the coast and natural seascape.

16.92 The seascape, landscape and visual impacts of offshore wind have been of considerable significance in DCO applications in the past, albeit often the focus has been on

187 ibid para 2.8.90.
188 ibid para 2.8.91.
189 ibid para 2.8.92.
190 ibid para 2.8.299.
191 PA 2008 s 15(3). The figure is 350 MW in Wales: s 15(3A).
192 Department for Energy Security and Net Zero, 'National Policy Statement for Renewable Energy Infrastructure (EN-3) (November 2023)' (n 7) para 2.8.205.
193 ibid para 2.8.350.
194 ibid para 2.8.209.

nationally designated or internationally recognised sites. The Secretary of State refused permission in the 970MW Proposed Navitus Bay Wind Park off the coast of Dorset and the Isle of Wight in September 2015.[195] Key in the analysis was the identification that changes in the coastline would 'affect important special qualities of the AONBs over a widespread area of coastline'[196] and that the scheme would 'bring about changes in the way the [Dorset coast as a] World Heritage Site would be experienced or enjoyed in its surroundings'.[197]

16.93 NPS EN-3 does carry over from the 2011 version important policy on assessing visual impact of such schemes (albeit modified to take into account the critical national priority for low carbon energy). Paragraph 2.8.351 states:[198]

> Where a proposed offshore wind farm is within sight of the coast, there may be adverse effects. The Secretary of State should not refuse to grant consent for a development solely on the ground of an adverse effect on the seascape or visual amenity unless:
>
> - it considers that an alternative layout within the identified site could be reasonably produced which would minimise any harm, taking into account the other constraints that the applicant has faced such as ecological effects, while maintaining safety or economic viability of the application; or
> - it takes account of the sensitivity of receptor(s) and impacts on the statutory purposes of designated landscapes as set out in Section 5.10 of EN-1; and decides that the harmful effects outweigh the benefits of the proposed scheme. See also Critical National Priority (Section 3 of this NPS).

(b) Marine considerations

16.94 Offshore wind development requires a marine licence from the Marine Management Organisation (in Scotland, Marine Scotland, and in Wales, Natural Resources Wales). These are licences under the scheme set out in the Marine and Coastal Access Act 2009. These licences are granted with the relevant marine plans and the Marine Policy Statement applicable,[199] and it is the role of these organisations to undertake authorisation and enforcement. Such licence terms can include coordinating offshore activities and marine nature conservation (the Marine and Coastal Access Act 2009 itself providing for Marine Conservation Zones).[200] It is worth noting, however, that in England a DCO may itself provide a deemed grant of a marine licence.[201]

---

195 Giles Scott, 'Secretary of State Decision Letter – Proposed Navitus Bay Wind Park. Ref EN 010024' para 7 <https://infrastructure.planninginspectorate.gov.uk/wp-content/ipc/uploads/projects/EN010024/EN010024-000055-Secretary%20of%20State%20Decision%20Letter%20and%20Statement%20of%20Reasons.pdf> accessed 24 May 2024.
196 ibid para 17.
197 ibid para 24.
198 Department for Energy Security and Net Zero, 'National Policy Statement for Renewable Energy Infrastructure (EN-3) (November 2023)' (n 7) para 2.8.351.
199 See HM Government and others, 'UK Marine Policy Statement' (2011) <https://assets.publishing.service.gov.uk/media/5a795700ed915d042206795b/pb3654-marine-policy-statement-110316.pdf> accessed 24 May 2024.
200 Department for Energy Security and Net Zero, 'National Policy Statement for Renewable Energy Infrastructure (EN-3) (November 2023)' (n 7) para 2.3.16–24.
201 Planning Act 2008 s 149A.

16.95 Seabed leasing is undertaken by the Crown Estate (and in Scotland, the Crown Estate Scotland). Applicants require leases as an important early step in achieving a development. Notably, each offshore leasing round is subject to a plan level HRA. These plan level assessments can be relevant to project level applications, minimising time spend.[202]

16.96 Marine spatial planning is likely to become significantly more important as the build out of offshore wind (in competition with other uses) continues. In the 'Independent report of the Offshore Wind Champion' Tim Pick recommended that steps be taken to encourage prioritisation in allocation, as 'balancing need is no longer sufficient when delivering the UK's policy ambitions on Net Zero'.[203] Spatial planning is also relevant between wind farms; NPS EN-3 notes that overtime cumulative effects between wind farms will become more pronounced (especially given the proposed focus on nodes for connecting offshore wind to the electricity grid). The policy directs a focus on assessing those cumulative impacts and on recognising the increased need for mitigation and compensation.[204]

16.97 Alongside this sits the government's Offshore Energy Strategic Environmental Assessment 4 ('OESEA4').[205] This SEA addresses UK offshore waters and territorial waters of England and Wales for a wide range of forms of generation, production and storage activities. It is intended to inform plans for offshore licensing and leasing decisions, following the proposed plans of the Department for Business, Energy and Industrial Strategy.[206] It considers the 40GW and 1GW floating wind aim set out in policy prior to the British Energy Security Strategy,[207] and it has a lifespan of approximately 4 years.[208] The detail of OESEA4 is considerable and there is insufficient space to consider its detail here. Applicants are required to explain how they have complied with OESEA4 in site selection and any successor to it.[209]

16.98 While much of the current installed offshore wind capacity is within the territorial waters of the UK, it is important to note that the UK may install wind farms

---

202 Department for Energy Security and Net Zero, 'National Policy Statement for Renewable Energy Infrastructure (EN-3) (November 2023)' (n 7) para 2.8.22.
203 Pick, 'Independent Report of the Offshore Wind Champion: Seizing Our Opportunities' (n 169) 20. Specific plans on managing and mitigating conflicts have been established in Scotland and Wales.
204 Department for Energy Security and Net Zero, 'National Policy Statement for Renewable Energy Infrastructure (EN-3) (November 2023)' (n 7) para 2.8.100–1.
205 Department for Business, Energy and Industrial Strategy, 'UK Offshore Energy Strategic Environmental Assessment 4 (OESEA4)' (GOV.UK, 17 March 2022) <https://www.gov.uk/government/consultations/uk-offshore-energy-strategic-environmental-assessment-4-oesea4> accessed 24 May 2024.
206 Department for Business, Energy and Industrial Strategy, 'UK Offshore Energy Strategic Environmental Assessment – Future Leasing/Licensing for Offshore Renewable Energy, Offshore Oil & Gas and Gas Storage and Associated Infrastructure - OESEA4 Environmental Report' (2022) viii <https://assets.publishing.service.gov.uk/media/623356e4e90e0709e1e4530d/OESEA4_Environmental_Report.pdf> accessed 24 May 2024.
207 ibid ix.
208 Department for Business, Energy and Industrial Strategy, 'UK Offshore Energy Strategic Environmental Assessment: Government Response to OESEA4 Public Consultation' (2022) 2 <https://assets.publishing.service.gov.uk/media/6319b419e90e077dc0c6d693/OESEA4_Public_Consultation_Government_Response.pdf> accessed 24 May 2024.
209 Department for Energy Security and Net Zero, 'National Policy Statement for Renewable Energy Infrastructure (EN-3) (November 2023)' (n 7) para 2.8.14.

in international waters.[210] This was provided for in the Energy Act 2004, whereby a 'Renewable Energy Zone' was established adjacent to UK territorial waters.[211]

(c) Transmission[212]

16.99 As has already been referenced above, transmission is a key issue which risks endangering the success of offshore wind. The National Grid ESO 'Holistic Network Design' has been brought forwards in part to address this,[213] and EN-3 recognises that many wind farm projects in the future will be limited to connection points proposed through strategic network designs such as this.[214] Ultimately, the aim appears to be to move from a situation where individual offshore wind farms are connected directly to land (described in EN-3 as a radial connection) to a coordinated approach where 'multiple, spatially close, offshore wind farms and other offshore infrastructure' will be connected before then being connected to land (what might be described as a node approach).[215]

16.100 Concerns remain about achieving connections for offshore wind farms, particularly in the medium term. So far, connections for new infrastructure has been achieved through an 'incremental approach' to improvement of the grid without a 'big overhaul'. However, the grid is becoming increasingly constrained, and it is common for offshore wind farms to be paid to stop generating when it is too windy (as the grid cannot absorb the amount of energy being produced). Ultimately, this is leading to grid connections being offered for new offshore wind farms with a connection date a decade into the future.[216]

16.101 This was a key issue that the government's Offshore Wind Champion explored in his independent report. Among other things he encouraged the government to press on following Ofgem's bulk approval of Accelerated Strategic Infrastructure Projects in December 2022.[217] Further, referring to the work of the Networks Commissioner, Nick Winser,[218] he also suggests moving from a 'first-come, first-served' basis for granting grid connections to one where how realistic it is that the project will be built out is taken into account. He notes that the queue for connection is currently over 140 projects representing over 300GW of generation, but many of those projects are not going to be built and sit on the grid connection offer as a 'speculative asset'.[219]

---

210 ibid 2.8.3.
211 Energy Act 2004 s 84. The zone itself was designated by The Renewable Energy Zone (Designation of Area) Order 2004, SI 2004/2668 using the limits provided for in the Merchant Shipping (Prevention of Pollution) (Limits) Regulations 1996, SI 1996/2128. NPS EN-3 describes this as 'from the seaward limit of the territorial sea up to a maximum of 200 nautical miles from the baseline' (NPS EN-3 para 2.8.3 and footnote 29).
212 More detail on transmission and network connections is set out in the network infrastructure section in Chapter 15.
213 Department for Energy Security and Net Zero (n 7) para 2.8.37.
214 ibid para 2.8.61.
215 ibid para 2.8.35.
216 Pick, 'Independent Report of the Offshore Wind Champion: Seizing Our Opportunities' (n 169) 42.
217 ibid 44.
218 ibid 46.
219 ibid 44.

16.102 Aside from achieving a connection, EN-3 is clear that transmission infrastructure can itself be a cause of negative impact on seabed habitats and protected sites.[220] While the coordination described above is hoped to minimise the cumulative effect of this type of development,[221] the policy is clear that a relatively high level of specificity is required of applicants in defining their route[222] (albeit a corridor approach is permitted)[223] and identifying avoidance measures.[224] Given the plan level HRA undertaken by the Crown Estate as part of seabed leasing, applicants are also expected to demonstrate compliance with mitigation measures identified in that plan (and other requirements set out in the OWES).[225]

16.103 An important decision for applicants will be the extent to which transmission infrastructure should be included in a DCO application. The policy recognises that offshore cabling, including cabling connecting to the onshore electricity grid, and offshore substations may constitute associated development for a DCO.[226] However, some infrastructure may or should properly be consented as independent development,[227] and policy directs applicants to consider whether to seek a direction under s 35 of the PA 2008 to have that infrastructure identified as an NSIP in its own right.[228] That kind of independent consenting is likely to arise from the node approach to network design, and the use of multi-purpose interconnectors which have a far bigger role than onshore transmission of electricity generated by offshore wind farms.[229]

(d) Decommissioning

16.104 Decommissioning of offshore wind has long been addressed in statute. Sections 105 to 114 of the Energy Act 2004 provided for a statutory decommissioning scheme for offshore wind and marine energy installations. That was further strengthened by amendments to these provisions by the Energy Act 2008 with the introduction of a power for the Secretary of State to issue notices to require the submission by a developer of a decommissioning programme,[230] and to require information to assess suitability and viability of such a programme.[231] Under the PA 2008 it is also common for a DCO to specifically include conditions and plans for decommissioning.

(e) Investment

16.105 In its Offshore Wind Net Zero Investment Roadmap, the government noted that £50 billion is required in construction capital expenditure to build the required

220 Department for Energy Security and Net Zero, 'National Policy Statement for Renewable Energy Infrastructure (EN-3) (November 2023)' (n 7) para 2.8.62.
221 ibid para 2.8.63.
222 ibid para 2.8.67.
223 ibid para 2.8.69.
224 ibid para 2.8.73.
225 ibid para 2.8.71.
226 ibid para 2.8.268.
227 ibid para 2.8.290.
228 ibid para 2.8.39.
229 ibid para 2.8.38–40; Department for Energy Security and Net Zero, 'Overarching National Policy Statement for Energy (EN-1) (November 2023)' (n 5) para 3.3.76–7.
230 Energy Act 2008 s 69 (amending Energy Act 2004 s 105 and introducing a s 105A into that Act).
231 ibid s 71 (amending Energy Act 2004 to introduce a new s 112A).

offshore windfarms in the UK by 2030.[232] The Roadmap itself sets out the steps the government is taking to make offshore wind a desirable investment.[233] The Roadmap provides a lifecycle of an offshore wind farm, setting out various investment opportunities, and identifying that the cost of 1GW scheme for 2022 would be: £100 million in early stages and development, with £2.5–£3 billion required for construction and installation, £75 million a year for operation and maintenance, and around £300 million for decommissioning.[234]

16.106 However, in recent years there has been something of a faltering in funding of these schemes. While in CfD auction round 2 and 3 95–96% of capacity awarded was offshore wind, and round 4 10.8GW was awarded, there were no awards in auction round 5.[235] This was as a result of the complete absence of bids made by industry.[236] It might be thought telling that in late 2023 the government announced it had increased maximum strike prices under CfD by 66% for offshore wind and 52% for floating offshore wind, with a specific separate funding pot made available.[237]

16.107 Aside from direct investment, the offshore wind industry has other benefits for the UK as a whole. In his review of net zero Sir Chris Skidmore MP considered the economic value of this kind of development:[238]

> 228. As a first mover, the UK has specific advantages and export opportunities in offshore wind. The UK is home to hundreds of supply chain companies in offshore wind and is already exporting offshore wind goods. The UK has particular expertise in the second-largest sub-sector market, operations and maintenance. The value of those exports could increase fivefold to £2.6 billion by 2030 as global markets are expected to increase rapidly to £30bn per year with potentially 380GW by 2030.
>
> 229. The UK is also a first mover on floating offshore and tidal stream technologies, and further investment in those technologies could create distinct advantages. The ambition of 5GW floating offshore by 2030, as expressed in the British Energy Security Strategy, could deliver a GVA of £43.6 billion and 29,000 jobs in the UK.

(f) Floating offshore wind

16.108 The government has set a target of 5GW of floating offshore wind by 2030. One of the key benefits of this technology if that deployment is considerably easier

---

232 HM Government, 'Offshore Wind Net Zero Investment Roadmap' (2023) 14 <https://assets.publishing.service.gov.uk/media/64a54c674dd8b3000f7fa4c9/offshore-wind-investment-roadmap.pdf> accessed 24 May 2024.
233 ibid 7–13.
234 ibid 18.
235 Helpfully summarised in: Nicole Watson and Paul Bolton, House of Commons Library, 'Contracts for Difference' (2023) Research Briefing N. 9871 7 <https://researchbriefings.files.parliament.uk/documents/CBP-9871/CBP-9871.pdf> accessed 24 May 2024.
236 ibid 12.
237 Department for Energy Security and Net Zero and others, 'Boost for Offshore Wind as Government Raises Maximum Prices in Renewable Energy Auction' (GOV.UK, 16 November 2023) <https://www.gov.uk/government/news/boost-for-offshore-wind-as-government-raises-maximum-prices-in-renewable-energy-auction> accessed 24 May 2024.
238 Rt Hon Chris Skidmore MP, 'Mission Zero: Independent Review of Net Zero' (n 146) 84.

in deep sea waters, which ae often locations with advantageous wind conditions. The turbines are floated on structures and tethered to the sea bed.[239]

16.109 This type of generation is being successfully pursued, and there are currently two installed pilot projects: Hywind Scotland (a 30MW scheme)[240] and Kincardine Wind Farm (a 47.5MW scheme),[241] both of which are found off the east coast of Scotland. In respect of leasing of seabed, 14 projects with a total capacity of 17.8GW have been proposed under the Scotwind Leasing process,[242] and 4.5GW was made available in July 2023 through the Offshore Wind Leasing Round 5.[243] Currently, one CfD has been agreed for a floating scheme through the fourth round of allocation in December 2021 (Hexicon's TwinHub project at 32MW).[244] Along with offshore wind in general, no awards were made in CfD allocation round 5.[245] Grant schemes have also been made available for floating offshore wind.[246]

16.110 The UK is the first mover in floating offshore wind, and has the largest deployment globally.[247] However, a key limiting factor for floating offshore wind is the practical reality of port infrastructure being able to manage these developments. It is thought that approximately £4 billion requires to be spent to develop the port infrastructure required to meet the needs of planned offshore wind projects.[248]

(vi) *Onshore wind*

16.111 As was addressed at the outset of this section, onshore wind is predicted to play an important part in the UK's progress to net zero. Until recently, in England, planning policy (and the exclusion from the PA 2008 processes) was a significant drag on the consenting of this form of generation. Indeed, it was said by some renewable energy groups that there is a 'de facto ban' on onshore wind in England.[249]

16.112 Certainly, evidence suggests that onshore wind has been hampered in England for a number of years. In October 2023 there were 758 operational onshore wind farms

---

239 Alan Walker and Nikki Sutherland, House of Commons Library, 'Floating Offshore Wind' (2023) Research Briefing <https://commonslibrary.parliament.uk/research-briefings/cdp-2023-0208/> accessed 24 May 2024.
240 'Hywind Scotland' (Equinor) <https://www.equinor.com/energy/hywind-scotland> accessed 24 May 2024.
241 'Projects: Kincardine Offshore Wind Farm' (Principle Power) <https://www.principlepower.com/projects/kincardine-offshore-wind-farm> accessed 24 May 2024.
242 13 floating, 1 mixed. 'ScotWind Offshore Wind Leasing Delivers Major Boost to Scotland's Net Zero Aspirations' (Crown Estate Scotland, 17 January 2022) <https://www.crownestatescotland.com/news/scotwind-offshore-wind-leasing-delivers-major-boost-to-scotlands-net-zero-aspirations> accessed 24 May 2024.
243 'Offshore Wind Leasing Round 5' (The Crown Estate, 7 December 2023) 5 <https://www.thecrownestate.co.uk/our-business/marine/round-5> accessed 24 May 2024.
244 'TwinHub - The First Floating Offshore Wind Project in the Celtic Sea' (TwinHub) <https://www.twinhub.co.uk> accessed 24 May 2024.
245 Department for Energy Security and Net Zero, 'Contracts for Difference (CfD) Allocation Round 5: Results' (GOV.UK) 5 <https://www.gov.uk/government/publications/contracts-for-difference-cfd-allocation-round-5-results> accessed 24 May 2024.
246 Department for Business, Energy and Industrial Strategy and The Rt Hon Greg Hands MP, '£60 Million Boost for Floating Offshore Wind' (GOV.UK, 25 January 2022) <https://www.gov.uk/government/news/60-million-boost-for-floating-offshore-wind> accessed 24 May 2024.
247 Pick, 'Independent Report of the Offshore Wind Champion: Seizing Our Opportunities' (n 169) 62.
248 ibid 58.
249 Rankl, 'Planning for Onshore Wind' (n 2).

in the UK: 43% of those were in Scotland, 37% in England, 11% in Northern Ireland and 9% in Wales.[250] However, of those 253 wind farms under construction or awaiting construction at that time: 48% were in Scotland, 37% in Northern Ireland, 9% in England and 6% in Wales.[251] The decline in England is notable.

16.113 Part of the reason for this was planning policy. The high point of planning policy in England indicating against onshore wind was around 2015. At that time NPPF was changed and a ministerial statement issued setting out a high test for the grant of permission:[252]

> When determining planning applications for wind energy development involving one or more wind turbines, local planning authorities should only grant planning permission if:
>
> - the development site is in an area identified as suitable for wind energy development in a local or neighbourhood plan; and
> - following consultation, it can be demonstrated that the planning impacts identified by affected local communities have been fully addressed and therefore the proposal has their backing.

16.114 In 2023 there was something of a rowing back from the height of this test. Again, NPPF was amended[253] and a new ministerial statement issued on this matter:[254]

> This includes amending the planning tests for proposed onshore wind developments to make clear that suitable locations can be identified in a number of ways (rather than solely through an area's development plan). Development plans can take a number of years to be produced and adopted and we want to be clear that other, more agile and targeted routes are appropriate. For example, through Local Development Orders, Neighbourhood Development Orders and Community Right to Build Orders. We hope that this will mean sites are identified more quickly, speeding up the process of allocating sites for onshore wind projects, and ultimately, and as a consequence more clean and renewable energy is generated sooner.
>
> We are also adjusting the policy so that local authorities can more flexibly address the planning impact of onshore wind projects as identified by local communities, on which we intend to publish further guidance. We have heard accounts that current policy has been applied in such a way that a very limited number of objections, and even at times objections of single individuals, have been taken as showing a lack of community backing. This is not the policy intent, and as a result of today's policy change it will now be important that local decision makers are able to take a more balanced approach,

---

250 ibid 9.
251 ibid 10.
252 Secretary of State for Communities and Local Government, 'House of Commons: Written Statement (HCWS42)' (June 2015) <https://www.parliament.uk/globalassets/documents/commons-vote-office/June-2015/18-June/1-DCLG-Planning.pdf> accessed 24 May 2024.
253 A summary of the changes before and after September 2023 can be found in: Rankl, 'Planning for Onshore Wind' (n 2) 21.
254 Michael Gove, UK Parliament, 'Statement UIN HCWS1005' (9 May 2023) <https://questions-statements.parliament.uk/written-statements/detail/2023-09-05/hcws1005> accessed 24 May 2024.

considering the views of communities as a whole. The Government is also open to novel ways to demonstrate community consent, building on best practice and using new digital engagement techniques.

16.115 It seems the 2015 change had a particularly dramatic effect on the onshore solar farm market in England. Whereas in the period 2007 to 2014 there were between 49 and 64 applications for permission for onshore wind developments in England, this fell to 23 in 2015 and did not rise above 10 from 2016 to 2022. Indeed, in 2017 there was only one application, and no applications in 2019.[255] It is currently unclear what impact the 2023 changes will have had to reverse this trend.

16.116 Following its success in the 2024 General Election, the new Labour government introduced changes to reverse the key policy indicating against onshore wind. In a policy statement made on 8 July 2024 those changes introducing new tests for onshore wind in 2015 were withdrawn from NPPF.[256] The policy statement provides:

> 1. Delivering our clean power mission will help boost Britain's energy independence, save money on energy bills, support high-skilled jobs and tackle the climate crisis. We are therefore committed to doubling onshore wind energy by 2030. This means immediately removing the de facto ban on onshore wind in England, in place since 2015. We are revising planning policy to place onshore wind on the same footing as other energy development in the National Planning Policy Framework (NPPF).
>
> …
>
> 3. [The 2015] policy tests no longer apply. The removal of these tests from planning policy means that onshore wind applications will be treated in the same way as other energy development proposals.
>
> 4. These changes take effect today (8 July 2024). The government will confirm this position to Parliament on 18 July, following the State Opening. These changes will also be reflected in the forthcoming NPPF update.
>
> 5. Through that update we will go further and set out proposals for wider changes to support renewable energy development. Alongside this we will consult on bringing large onshore proposals into the Nationally Significant Infrastructure Project regime, to support quick determination, followed by a revised National Policy Statement. Local communities will play an essential part in delivering this mission and we will empower

---

255 Rankl, 'Planning for Onshore Wind' (n 2).
256 Ministry of Housing, Communities and Local Government, HM Treasury, Department for Energy Security and Net Zero, Department for Levelling Up, Housing and Communities, 'Policy paper: Policy statement on onshore wind' (8 July 2024) <https://www.gov.uk/government/publications/policy-statement-on-onshore-wind/policy-statement-on-onshore-wind> accessed 18 September 2024. At the time of writing this change appears in the consultation version of NPPF published 30 July 2024, (Ministry of Housing, Communities and Local Government, 'National Planning Policy Statement: draft text for consultation') alongside suggested text placing greater weight in favour of local planning authorities supporting renewable and low carbon development <https://www.gov.uk/government/consultations/proposed-reforms-to-the-national-planning-policy-framework-and-other-changes-to-the-planning-system> accessed 18 September 2024.

> them to participate in decisions on local infrastructure. Communities should rightly benefit from hosting local renewable energy infrastructure and this is why we will shortly publish an update to the Community Benefits Protocol for Onshore Wind in England.

16.117 While at the time of writing it remains to be seen the effect that this change in policy will have, the government has an ambitious target to double onshore wind generating capacity by 2030. It seems likely it will lead to significant growth in applications for (and grants of consent for) onshore wind projects. In addition, while the government has indicated it will consult on the issue, it also seems likely that onshore wind will be reintroduced in to the NSIP regime.

Energy from Waste

(i) *Introduction*

16.118 Energy from Waste ('EfW') is distinct from the other forms of generation included in this chapter in that policy recognises that its primary purpose is the treatment of waste.[257] As such, this form of generation is as much controlled by policy concerning waste management as it is policy on renewable energy.[258]

16.119 EfW uses combustion or other processes applied to waste to derive energy. The feedstock used by EfW varies widely; whether a specific plant can be described as renewable (and obtain renewable financial incentives) will depend on the waste processed.[259] Unless equipped with CCUS technology,[260] such generating stations also produce significant carbon emissions.[261] Thus, it might be queried whether EfW should be included in this chapter at all.

16.120 There are various forms of EfW generation which include, but are not limited to, combustion and so-called 'Advanced Conversion Technologies'[262] such as pyrolysis.[263] As policy indicates that planning decision-makers should not be concerned about the type of technology applied,[264] these differing processes are not explored further in this chapter.

---

257 Department for Energy Security and Net Zero, 'Overarching National Policy Statement for Energy (EN-1) (November 2023)' (n 5) para 3.3.39; Department for Energy Security and Net Zero, 'National Policy Statement for Renewable Energy Infrastructure (EN-3) (November 2023)' (n 7) para 2.7.27.

258 ibid. See, for example, the test for end of waste set out in Article 6 of the Waste Framework Directive 2008/98/EC; The Waste and Environmental Permitting etc. (Legislative Functions and Amendment etc.) (EU Exit) Regulations, SI 2020/1540; The Waste (Wales) (Miscellaneous Amendments) (EU Exit) Regulations, SI 2019/414; The Waste (Wales) (Miscellaneous Amendments) (EU Exit) Regulations, SI 2020/1339.

259 Department for Energy Security and Net Zero, 'Overarching National Policy Statement for Energy (EN-1) (November 2023)' (n 5) para 3.3.42.

260 ibid para 3.3.41. That paragraph also notes that energy recovery from residual waste has a lower GHG impact than landfill.

261 ibid para 3.3.37.

262 ibid para 3.3.38.

263 The heating of organic materials to a high temperature in the absence of oxygen. See, Sarah E Boslaugh, 'Pyrolysis' <https://www.britannica.com/science/pyrolysis> accessed 23 May 2024.

264 Department for Energy Security and Net Zero, 'Overarching National Policy Statement for Energy (EN-1) (November 2023)' (n 5) para 3.3.36; Department for Energy Security and Net Zero, 'National Policy Statement for Renewable Energy Infrastructure (EN-3) (November 2023)' (n 7) para 2.7.80.

16.121 As EfW is focused on residual waste and waste management, it must comply with the government's waste hierarchy.[265] Importantly, such generating infrastructure: 'must not compete with greater waste prevention, re-use, or recycling, or result in over-capacity of EfW treatment at a national or local level'.[266] Thus, there is a balance to be struck between having sufficient EfW to use the available feedstock of waste, without overdeveloping capacity or otherwise departing from the policy which indicates that amounts of residual waste should be reduced wherever possible.

(ii) *Contribution to net zero*

16.122 Much government policy discussing renewable energy does not explore EfW in detail. For example, it does not appear in the 'British Energy Security Strategy'[267] and plays no substantive role in 'Powering Up Britain: The Net Zero Growth Plan'.[268] However, when one looks beyond generation to the whole of the net zero strategy (including how waste is addressed), the dual role of EfW is recognised. The Net Zero Strategy sets out that:[269]

> 16. By 2050, we will have met the 25 Year Environment Plan (25YEP) commitments to eliminate all avoidable waste, including plastic, and to double resource productivity. A circular economy will be part of everyday life: reusing, repairing, and remanufacturing goods will be standard practice. Goods will be designed to last for longer and be more efficient. At end of life, the vast majority of products will be sent for recycling, with food, garden, and dry materials collected separately and used as lower carbon inputs for new products. Producer responsibility schemes will be embedded across the economy. *Any non-recyclable residual waste will be treated to enable the processing of waste into valuable outputs, such as energy. Where possible, these processes would include carbon capture and storage.* (See the Power chapter for more on energy from waste.) Only where no such treatment is possible may landfill be permitted.' (emphasis added)

16.123 EfW's contribution to net zero is also recognised in the principal planning policies. A significant part of NPS EN-3 addresses EfW.[270] Significantly, the critical national priority for low carbon infrastructure includes 'other plants that convert residual waste to energy, including combustion, provided they meet existing definitions of low carbon'.[271] This poses the question of whether EfW does fall within those existing

265 Addressed below under policy.
266 Department for Energy Security and Net Zero, 'Overarching National Policy Statement for Energy (EN-1) (November 2023)' (n 5) para 3.3.40.
267 Department for Business, Energy and Industrial Strategy, Department for Energy Security and Net Zero and Prime Minister's Office, 'British Energy Security Strategy' (n 4).
268 Department for Energy Security and Net Zero, 'Powering Up Britain' (2023) (n 161). While it does appear this is either descriptive (page 44) or related to emissions trading (page 55).
269 UK Government, 'Net Zero Strategy: Build Back Greener' (n 3) 172.
270 Department for Energy Security and Net Zero, 'National Policy Statement for Renewable Energy Infrastructure (EN-3) (November 2023)' (n 7) para 2.7.1 onwards (albeit in that section considered with biomass).
271 Department for Energy Security and Net Zero, 'Overarching National Policy Statement for Energy (EN-1) (November 2023)' (n 5) para 4.2.5.

definitions of low carbon. Certainly, unabated EfW burning waste which has not been managed to minimise emissions could not be described as low carbon.[272]

16.124 In asking whether EfW is low carbon, regard must be had to the role of carbon capture, utilisation and storage in mitigating EfW GHG emissions. Unlike other forms of combustion generation, there is no requirement for EfW plants to be carbon capture ready within the scope of the Carbon Capture Readiness (Electricity Generating Stations) Regulations 2013.[273] On this issue the government set out in the Net Zero Strategy that:[274]

> Reducing emissions from the energy from waste sector – emissions from energy from waste plants represent a significant part of the residual emissions in the power sector. We are exploring options to reduce emissions from these plants within the power sector, including whether support for CCUS at Energy from Waste plants could be provided by the Industrial Carbon Capture Business Model. The Government's approach in respect of this is still under consideration and we intend to provide further details later this year.

16.125 While the government has now consulted on this issue, an outcome is still pending.[275] That is notwithstanding the CCC in December 2020 indicating that all EfW plants should be built with CCUS or made Carbon Capture Ready.[276] It is of course open to individual developers to elect to use CCUS (or other processes) to minimise emissions and aim for low carbon. However, the continued install of unabated EfW does appear contrary to achieving net zero.

(iii) *Policy*

(a) Planning policy

16.126 Assuming an EfW plant can be categorised as 'low carbon' due to its design (including use of CCUS), any NSIP development will benefit from the identification of such infrastructure as of a 'critical national priority'.[277] That is in addition to the general provision in NPS EN-1 that all developments within the scope of the policy should be considered as 'urgent', with 'substantial weight' to be given to that need.[278]

---

272 Zero Waste Europe, 'The Impact of Waste-to-Energy Incineration on Climate – Policy Briefing' (2019) 3 <https://zerowasteeurope.eu/wp-content/uploads/edd/2019/09/ZWE_Policy-briefing_The-impact-of-Waste-to-Energy-incineration-on-Climate.pdf> accessed 22 May 2024. The report describes that such unabated unmanaged EfW will outstrip the GHG emissions of fossil gas.
273 The Carbon Capture Readiness (Electricity Generating Stations) Regulations 2013, SI 2013/2696. See also Department for Energy Security and Net Zero, 'National Policy Statement for Renewable Energy Infrastructure (EN-3) (November 2023)' (n 7) para 2.7.16.
274 HM Government, 'Net Zero Strategy: Build Back Greener' (n 3) 105.
275 Department for Energy Security and Net Zero, 'National Policy Statement for Renewable Energy Infrastructure (EN-3) (November 2023)' (n 7) para 2.7.17 and footnote 17.
276 Climate Change Committee, 'The Sixth Carbon Budget: The UK's Path to Net Zero' (2020) 71 <https://www.theccc.org.uk/wp-content/uploads/2020/12/The-Sixth-Carbon-Budget-The-UKs-path-to-Net-Zero.pdf> accessed 26 April 2024.
277 Department for Energy Security and Net Zero, 'Overarching National Policy Statement for Energy (EN-1) (November 2023)' (n 5) s 4.2.
278 ibid paras 3.2.6–8.

16.127 NPS EN-3 then provides detail about approaching consenting of EfW infrastructure. Much of the general policy in NPS EN-3 is discussed elsewhere in this chapter and not repeated here.[279] However, the policy highlights some important factors for decision-makers considering EfW.

16.128 The Secretary of State is directed by NPS EN-3 not to consider the throughput volume of an EfW plant. However, a consideration of the consequences of the amount of throughput is then required. This poses an interesting question about the extent to which the Secretary of State should involve themselves in considering whether schemes using different technologies, or different approaches to feedstock, would result in avoiding or mitigating planning harm. Paragraph 2.7.82 provides:

> Throughput volumes are not, in themselves, a factor in Secretary of State decision-making as there are no specific minimum or maximum fuel throughput limits for different technologies or levels of electricity generation; this is a matter for the applicant. However, the increase in traffic volumes, any change in air quality, and any other adverse impacts as a result of the increase in throughput should be considered by the Secretary of State …

16.129 Indeed, it is not clear how this then sits alongside the direction to the Secretary of State that they must consider compliance with the relevant waste strategies and plans themselves. Paragraph 2.7.102–103 provides:

> 2.7.102 The Secretary of State should be satisfied, with reference to the relevant waste strategies and plans, that the proposed waste combustion generating station is in accordance with the waste hierarchy and of an appropriate type and scale so as not to prejudice the achievement of local or national waste management targets in England and local, regional or national waste management targets in Wales.
>
> 2.7.103 Where there are concerns in terms of a possible conflict, evidence should be provided to the Secretary of State by the applicant as to why this is not the case or why a derivation from the relevant waste strategy or plan is nonetheless appropriate and in accordance with the waste hierarchy.
>
> 2.7.104 The Secretary of State should also consider whether a requirement, including monitoring, is appropriate to ensure compliance with the waste hierarchy.

16.130 As policy around waste progresses, and the focus is increasingly on prevention as the primary approach to waste management (to which see below), it will be interesting to see the level of detail with which the Secretary of State will consider compliance with the waste hierarchy and the proper availability of feedstock.

16.131 Finally, most of the other forms of generation considered in this chapter use a natural phenomenon as a resource. In contrast, EfW (and biomass) have to have

---

279 E.g. many of the landscape and visual considerations are similar to those considered elsewhere in this chapter. See Department for Energy Security and Net Zero, 'National Policy Statement for Renewable Energy Infrastructure (EN-3) (November 2023)' (n 7) para 2.7.92–97.

resources transported to them. As such, transport infrastructure has a far larger role to play. EN-3 recognises that a plant processing 500,000 tonnes of waste per annum may necessitate 220 HGV movements per weekday.[280] The policy states that applicants should consider existing transport routes when siting new infrastructure, and should have regard to rail, water and multimodal transport options.[281] Where existing transport infrastructure is inadequate the tests for new infrastructure in EN-1 section 5.14 must be applied.[282]

(b) Waste policy

16.132 Aside from planning policy, the Waste Management Plan for England[283] (and the similar plan for Wales) is important. It is referred to as applicable in NPS EN-1[284] and NPS EN-3.[285] While the full detail of waste policy is beyond the scope of this book, it is relevant to highlight the below. The Plan recognises the value of EfW in that it can derive valuable output from residual waste which otherwise may be disposed of.

16.133 The waste hierarchy is itself is set out in the Waste (England and Wales) Regulations 2011.[286] Regulation 12 provides:

> (1) An establishment or undertaking which imports, produces, collects, transports, recovers or disposes of waste, or which as a dealer or broker has control of waste must, on the transfer of waste, take all such measures available to it as are reasonable in the circumstances to apply the following waste hierarchy as a priority order—
>
> (a) prevention;
> (b) preparing for re-use;
> (c) recycling;
> (d) other recovery (for example energy recovery);
> (e) disposal.
>
> (2) But an establishment or undertaking may depart from the priority order in paragraph (1) so as to achieve the best overall environmental outcome where this is justified by life-cycle thinking on the overall impacts of the generation and management of the waste.
>
> (3) When considering the overall impacts mentioned in paragraph (2), the following considerations must be taken into account—

280 ibid para 2.7.8.
281 ibid para 2.7.9–11.
282 ibid para 2.7.72.
283 Department for Environment, Food and Rural Affairs, 'Waste Management Plan for England' (2021) <https://assets.publishing.service.gov.uk/media/60103f71d3bf7f05bc42d294/waste-management-plan-for-england-2021.pdf> accessed 22 May 2024. Itself placing significant weight on HM Government, 'Our Waste, Our Resources: A Strategy for England' (2018) <https://assets.publishing.service.gov.uk/media/5c18f11740f0b60bbee0d827/resources-waste-strategy-dec-2018.pdf> accessed 23 May 2024.
284 Department for Energy Security and Net Zero, 'Overarching National Policy Statement for Energy (EN-1) (November 2023)' (n 5) para 3.3.38.
285 Department for Energy Security and Net Zero, 'National Policy Statement for Renewable Energy Infrastructure (EN-3) (November 2023)' (n 7) para 2.7.6.
286 The Waste (England and Wales) Regulations, SI 2011/988.

(a) the general environmental protection principles of precaution and sustainability;
(b) technical feasibility and economic viability;
(c) protection of resources;
(d) the overall environmental, human health, economic and social impacts.

16.134 The Waste Management Plan for England then recognises that '[i]n the past, most waste was dealt with by disposal, but over time that will shift increasingly to recycling, reuse and ultimately prevention'.[287] As such, the desire is for the availability of residual waste to decrease; prevention, reuse and recycling are to be the primary methods of dealing with waste.

16.135 Of 'other recovery' the Waste Management Plan for England sets out:[288]

> Residual waste generally refers to the waste collected from households or businesses in a black bag or wheelie bin. The government supports efficient energy recovery from residual waste – energy from waste is generally the best management option for waste that cannot be reused or recycled in terms of environmental impact and getting value from the waste as a resource. It plays an important role in diverting waste from landfill. In 2016, 6.2 million tonnes of residual waste were disposed of in energy from waste facilities. The Resources and Waste Strategy promotes the greater efficiency of energy from waste plants through utilisation of the heat generated in district heating networks or by industry, and by seeking an increase in the number of plants obtaining R1 recovery status.

16.136 Ultimately, the Plan recognises that EfW is 'generally the best management option for waste that cannot be reused or recycled in terms of environmental impact and getting value from waste as a resource'.[289] The Plan places some emphasis on using EfW plants as a source of both power and heat (often called 'CHP' or 'combined heat and power').[290]

(iv) *Specific issues*

16.137 Some important issues for EfW have already been addressed above. These include whether we should be avoiding the use of EfW in favour of other forms of waste management higher up the waste hierarchy; whether this form of generation can properly be described as renewable at all; and whether there should be a move to include CCUS with all newly developed EfW. This section addresses other specific issues discrete to EfW.

16.138 In March 2021 Wales introduced a moratorium on EfW with a rated capacity of 10MW or greater.[291] Smaller scale plants of 10MW or less will only be allowable 'if

287 Department for Environment, Food and Rural Affairs, 'Waste Management Plan for England' (n 285) 15.
288 ibid 17. R1 recovery status refers to an efficiency as an EfW plant which permits classification in the waste hierarchy a level up from disposal as the bottom rung.
289 ibid 45.
290 ibid.
291 Lesley Griffiths MS, 'Written Statement: Taking Action to Make the Circular Economy a Reality' (GOV.WALES, 24 March 2021) <https://www.gov.wales/written-statement-taking-action-make-circular-economy-reality> accessed 23 May 2024.

the applicant can demonstrate the need for such a facility for the non-recyclable wastes produced in the region'. Such plants are required to supply heat and have CCUS or be CCUS ready 'where feasible'. The ministerial statement goes on to say that such small-scale plants would:

> not be allowable if waste is to be imported from outside of the proposed region (unless in close proximity to a region), in order to avoid also locking in transport emissions and associated pollution.

16.139 Permitting and emissions are a key point of contention with EfW plants, and a significant scheme of permitting exists through the Environmental Permitting (England and Wales) Regulations 2016.[292] Alongside the requirements for waste incinerator plants in Schedule 13 to the Regulations (concerning compliance with limits on air and water emissions, plus monitoring conditions), size and design will be relevant to whether and what general controls in Part 2 of Schedule 1 apply, and whether Schedule 15 (large combustion plants with a rated thermal input of 50MW or more) or Schedule 25A (medium combustion plants with a rated thermal input between 1MW and 50MW) are relevant. These controls are substantial and focus on air and water emissions, and their related monitoring.

16.140 While challenges to permitting decisions do occur, significant leeway is given to the expertise of the Environment Agency and other expert regulators. In *R (BACI Bedfordshire Ltd) v Environment Agency* the court considered whether there was an error in permitting a decision where it appeared the Environment Agency had incorporated a scientific error that heavy metals were not soluble in water. Those heavy metals would result from incineration at the proposed EfW plant. Both the High Court and Court of Appeal decisions are pertinent as:

- The High Court (Lang J)[293] considered that there was an error in the supporting documentation submitted by the applicant,[294] but that the Environment Agency is an expert regulator and therefore it was implausible that such a mistake would have been carried through.[295] The case also recited earlier jurisprudence on the expert role of regulators, and the 'enhanced margin of appreciation' which will be offered in scientific, technical and predictive assessments.[296]

- The Court of Appeal approved Lang J's approach.[297] Notwithstanding the applicant's error, a proper reading of the permit led to the conclusion that the Environment Agency had not made that same error.[298] In concluding this, the judge below

292 The Environmental Permitting (England and Wales) Regulations 2016, SI 2016/1154. Implementing, among other things, the Industrial Emissions Directive 2010/75/EU. Much of the EU emission standards rules have remained following Brexit.
293 *R (BACI Bedfordshire Ltd) v Environment Agency* [2018] EWHC 2962 (Admin).
294 ibid [48]–[51].
295 ibid [52], [58].
296 ibid [43] (referring to *R (Mott) v Environment Agency* [2016] EWCA Civ 564 [58]).
297 *R (BACI Bedfordshire Ltd) v Environment Agency* [2019] EWCA Civ 1962.
298 ibid [81].

had not had to use the 'enhanced margin of appreciation'.[299] The Court of Appeal did note that the principle could not be used to 'excuse a patent mistake of fact or basic science'.[300]

16.141 As is common in planning decisions,[301] issues of environmental permitting and pollution control in themselves are left to the expert regulator and not matters for the Secretary of State. Indeed, in EN-3 the Secretary of State is also directed to consider such consenting leads to the generating station 'having acceptable impacts on health'.[302] EN-1 directs that 'the Secretary of State should focus on whether the development itself is an acceptable use of land or sea, and the impact of that use'.[303] The Secretary of State is also directed to work on the assumption that pollution controls and environmental regimes will be properly applied and enforced by the regulator.[304]

16.142 However, in matters squarely concerned with planning judgment, the decision-maker retains significant latitude. In *Project Genesis Ltd v Secretary of State for Levelling Up, Housing and Communities* ('*Project Genesis*'),[305] Fordham J considered challenges to a decision to refuse an EfW plant where significant weight was placed by the Secretary of State (in a recovered appeal) on landscape harm (including to a nearby AONB and an Area of Higher Landscape Value). As part of the recovered appeal process, an inspector's report had recommended a grant of permission. However, the Secretary of State disagreed, and Fordham J held these issues were clearly a matter of planning judgment.[306]

16.143 As was noted above, government policy favours EfW with CHP. This maximises the amount of energy that can be derived from the feedstock waste, and significantly improves overall efficiency.[307] Indeed, EfW with CHP has been and remains the only form of EfW which has been included in the Contracts for Difference scheme (being the mechanism by which low carbon energy is currently funded in the UK).[308] It remains to be seen how much of this CHP is being used; often the heat produced can only be transported a small distance and thus many plants are CHP ready but operate in power mode only.[309] In *Project Genesis* the appellant argued that insufficient weight had

---

299 ibid [96]–[100].
300 ibid [100].
301 See, for example: Department for Levelling Up, Housing and Communities, 'National Planning Policy Framework' (n 8) para 194.
302 Department for Energy Security and Net Zero, 'National Policy Statement for Renewable Energy Infrastructure (EN-3) (November 2023)' (n 7) para 2.7.91.
303 Department for Energy Security and Net Zero, 'Overarching National Policy Statement for Energy (EN-1) (November 2023)' (n 5) para 4.12.9. The sentence goes on '…rather than the control of processes, emissions or discharges themselves.'
304 ibid para 4.12.10.
305 *Project Genesis Ltd v Secretary of State for Levelling Up, Housing and Communities* [2024] EWHC 368 (Admin).
306 ibid [25].
307 Department for Environment, Food and Rural Affairs, 'Energy from Waste – A Guide to the Debate' (2014) para 81 <https://assets.publishing.service.gov.uk/media/5a7c77ade5274a559005a113/pb14130-energy-waste-201402.pdf> accessed 22 May 2024.
308 Department for Energy Security and Net Zero, 'Contracts for Difference' (16 November 2023) <https://www.gov.uk/government/collections/contracts-for-difference> accessed 28 April 2024.
309 Department for Environment, Food and Rural Affairs, 'Energy from Waste – A Guide to the Debate' (2014) (n 307) para 83.

been given to the CHP credentials of the scheme (saying it had instead been bundled in with another benefit, being that the project would operate as a catalyst for further development). Fordham J disagreed and noted that substantial weight had been given to the CHP aspect of the development, in line with policy and distinct from other considerations.[310] It remained that weight and balance overall was a matter of planning judgment.

16.144 Finally, an area to watch with EfW is the UK Emissions Trading Scheme, as it has been announced that EfW will come within the scheme in 2028.[311]

Nuclear energy

(i) *Introduction*

16.145 UK energy generation from nuclear energy is approximately 14.7%, having dropped slightly since 2021 (14.9%) and generally declined since 2016 due to outages and reduced capacity and having peaked around 1998.[312] There are 15 civil nuclear reactors,[313] consisting of 14 Advanced Gas-cooled Reactors ('AGRs')[314] and one Pressurised Water Reactor ('PWR').[315] Three of these have already stopped generating energy;[316] and the other AGRs are due to stop generating by 2028, which will have a significant impact.[317]

16.146 Nuclear energy is seen as a reliable[318] and very low carbon source of energy generation that produces more energy than (for example) a solar farm of equivalent size.[319]

310 *Project Genesis Ltd v Secretary of State for Levelling Up, Housing and Communities* (n 305) para 41.
311 Department for Energy Security and Net Zero, 'Policy Paper: The Long-Term Pathway for the UK Emissions Trading Scheme' (GOV.UK, 18 December 2023) para 5 <https://www.gov.uk/government/publications/uk-emissions-trading-scheme-long-term-pathway/the-long-term-pathway-for-the-uk-emissions-trading-scheme> accessed 23 May 2024.
312 Department for Energy Security and Net Zero, 'UK Energy in Brief 2023' (2023) 27–8 <https://assets.publishing.service.gov.uk/media/6581cb5aed3c34000d3bfbfc/UK_Energy_in_Brief_2023.pdf> accessed 13 June 2024.
313 'Operational Power Stations' (Office for Nuclear Regulation) <https://www.onr.org.uk/our-work/what-we-regulate/operational-power-stations/> accessed 13 June 2024.
314 Gas cooled reactors in the UK use carbon dioxide as the coolant, but other countries are developing technology that uses other gases, such as helium, as a coolant: 'Gas Cooled Reactors' (IAEA, 13 April 2016) <https://www.iaea.org/topics/gas-cooled-reactors> accessed 13 June 2024.
315 A PWR is a specific type of water-cooled reactor that produces steam for the turbine in separate steam generators: 'Water Cooled Reactors' (IAEA, 13 April 2016) <https://www.iaea.org/topics/water-cooled-reactors> accessed 13 June 2024.
316 Hunterston B, Hinkley Point B and Dungeness B: These reactors are in the defueling stage, which is the last stage before decommissioning. See 'Operational Power Stations' (n 313).
317 House of Commons Committee of Public Accounts, 'The Future of the Advanced Gas-Cooled Reactors (Third Report of Session 2022–23)' 4, 6 <https://committees.parliament.uk/publications/22301/documents/165594/default/> accessed 17 June 2024.
318 Rather than intermittent like wind or solar generation, which depends upon weather conditions.
319 Department for Business, Energy and Industrial Strategy, Department for Energy Security and Net Zero and Prime Minister's Office, 'British Energy Security Strategy' (n 4); Katy Laffan, 'International Day of Clean Energy: Why Nuclear Power?' (IAEA, 25 January 2024) <https://www.iaea.org/newscenter/news/international-day-of-clean-energy-why-nuclear-power> accessed 13 June 2024.

For instance, it is reported that Hinkley Point C, which covers a site approximately one quarter of a square mile, will power around 6 million homes.[320]

16.147 Nuclear energy is not a renewable energy source as such because the fuels needed for this type of energy generation are not renewable, such as uranium, which needs to be mined and is finite in supply (albeit needed in significantly lower quantities than fossil fuels).[321] Nuclear energy is, however, recognised as a 'green' technology as part of the energy transition in the EU Green Taxonomy Regulation,[322] provided that certain conditions are satisfied and in the context of particular nuclear-related activities.[323] The government has also proposed that nuclear will be included in the UK's Green Taxonomy (but at the time of writing, the consultation proposed for Autumn 2023 had still not taken place).[324]

(ii) *Energy generated with nuclear fission or fusion*

16.148 Heat energy is generated through nuclear fission, which involves the splitting of uranium atoms in the reactor of the nuclear power plant.[325] The uranium is split into ceramic pellets, which are stacked in metal fuel rods.[326] The heat energy is used to produce steam, which, in turn, powers the large turbines and generates electricity.[327]

16.149 Nuclear fusion presents another potential source of nuclear energy generation, which involves fusing together the atomic nucleus of certain elements (such as hydrogen) to form larger elements.[328] The process involves the release of a large amount of energy, but the reaction takes place at very high temperatures.[329] The government has set out its strategy and is consulting on its planning policy approach to nuclear fusion

---

320 Department for Business, Energy and Industrial Strategy and others, 'Nuclear Energy: What You Need to Know' (GOV.UK, 4 June 2022) <https://www.gov.uk/government/news/nuclear-energy-what-you-need-to-know> accessed 13 June 2024.
321 'What Is Nuclear Energy?' (National Grid) <https://www.nationalgrid.com/stories/energy-explained/what-nuclear-energy-and-why-it-considered-clean-energy> accessed 13 June 2024.
322 Regulation (EU) 2020/852 of the European Parliament and of the Council of 18 June 2020 on the establishment of a framework to facilitate sustainable investment, and amending Regulation (EU) 2019/2088; supplemented by Commission Delegated Regulation (EU) 2022/1214 of 9 March 2022 amending Delegated Regulation (EU) 2021/2139 as regards economic activities in certain energy sectors and Delegated Regulation (EU) 2021/2178 as regards specific public disclosures for those economic activities.
323 European Commission, 'EU Taxonomy: Accelerating Sustainable Investments' <https://finance.ec.europa.eu/document/download/e01e9e40-7698-4b08-a9ea-078fb7070f18_en?filename=sustainable-finance-taxonomy-complementary-climate-delegated-act-factsheet_en.pdf> accessed 17 June 2024.
324 HM Government, 'Mobilising Green Investment: 2023 Green Finance Strategy' (2023) 10, s 2.3.1 <https://assets.publishing.service.gov.uk/media/643583fb877741001368d815/mobilising-green-investment-2023-green-finance-strategy.pdf> accessed 17 June 2024.
325 Department for Business, Energy and Industrial Strategy and others, 'Nuclear Energy: What You Need to Know' (n 320).
326 ibid.
327 ibid.
328 Department for Energy Security and Net Zero, 'Consultation on a New National Policy Statement for Fusion Energy: The Proposed Approach to Siting Fusion Energy Facilities' (2024) 10 <https://assets.publishing.service.gov.uk/media/663b4f248603389a07a6d231/new-nps-for-fusion-energy-consultation-document-1.pdf> accessed 13 June 2024.
329 ibid.

as set out below, but this form of energy generation is at an experimental stage[330] and commercialisation is some time off.

(iii) *Contribution to net zero*

16.150 Globally, there are ambitions to increase nuclear capacity because of the view that it plays a fundamental role in the energy transition.[331] At COP 28 in Dubai, for example, more than 20 countries launched the declaration to triple nuclear energy capacity from 2020 to 2050, recognising its role in achieving net zero.[332]

16.151 Indeed, without new nuclear developments, particularly given the age of many nuclear reactors globally, it will be difficult to meet net zero. In Germany, there was a concern about the increased reliance on fossil fuels following the closure of their last three remaining nuclear power plants in April 2023 and additional coal power was deployed as a safety net but, it is reported, that the demand for coal was ultimately lower than expected.[333]

16.152 At the domestic level, the importance of nuclear energy generation in achieving net zero has been recognised.[334] The government has ambitions to grow nuclear energy in the UK, given it is a reliable source of low-carbon electricity.[335] In the BESS, published in April 2022, a goal was set to achieve the deployment of civil nuclear up to 24GW by 2050, which would constitute 25% of the projected energy demand.[336] With the closure of AGRs (as set out above in paragraph 16.145), there is likely to be a pressing need to bring new nuclear projects to fruition to meet net zero; or to consider extending the operation of existing nuclear power plants for quicker implementation.[337]

16.153 The focus of policy development, since the Ten Point Plan for a Green Industrial Revolution and Energy White Paper[338] in November and December 2020 respectively, has been on pursuing large-scale nuclear as well as investing in research into new nuclear

---

330 For example, the work of the Culham laboratory in the UK, and ITER in France, representing a collaboration of 35 nations. See, respectively, 'About CCFE' (*Culham Centre for Fusion Energy*) <https://ccfe.ukaea.uk/about-ccfe/> accessed 17 June 2024; 'What Is ITER?' (*ITER*) <http://www.iter.org/proj/inafewlines> accessed 17 June 2024.

331 IAEA, 'Nuclear Energy for a Net Zero World' (2021) <https://www.iaea.org/sites/default/files/21/10/nuclear-energy-for-a-net-zero-world.pdf> accessed 17 June 2024.

332 'At COP28, Countries Launch Declaration to Triple Nuclear Energy Capacity by 2050, Recognizing the Key Role of Nuclear Energy in Reaching Net Zero' (*Energy.gov*, 12 January 2023) <https://www.energy.gov/articles/cop28-countries-launch-declaration-triple-nuclear-energy-capacity-2050-recognizing-key> accessed 13 June 2024.

333 Benjamin Whermann, 'Q&A – Germany's Nuclear Exit: One Year After' (*Clean Energy Wire*, 16 April 2024) <https://www.cleanenergywire.org/factsheets/qa-germanys-nuclear-exit-one-year-after> accessed 17 June 2024.

334 Department for Energy Security and Net Zero and others, 'Biggest Expansion of Nuclear Power for 70 Years to Create Jobs, Reduce Bills and Strengthen Britain's Energy Security' (GOV.UK, 11 January 2024) <https://www.gov.uk/government/news/biggest-expansion-of-nuclear-power-for-70-years-to-create-jobs-reduce-bills-and-strengthen-britains-energy-security> accessed 17 June 2024.

335 HM Government, 'The Ten Point Plan for a Green Industrial Revolution' (n 119) 12; Department for Business, Energy and Industrial Strategy, Department for Energy Security and Net Zero and Prime Minister's Office, 'British Energy Security Strategy' (n 4).

336 Department for Business, Energy and Industrial Strategy, Department for Energy Security and Net Zero and Prime Minister's Office, 'British Energy Security Strategy' (n 4).

337 IAEA, 'Nuclear Energy for a Net Zero World' (n 331) 40.

338 HM Government, 'Energy White Paper: Powering Our Net Zero Future' (n 33).

technology,[339] including Small Modular Reactors ('SMRs') and Advanced Modular Reactors ('AMRs').[340] SMRs are smaller versions of the traditional water cooled nuclear reactors and produce around a fifth to a third of the traditional reactors such as Hinkley Point C.[341] SMRs can be defined as producing up to 300MW(electrical) per module.[342] AMRs entail a range of nuclear reactor technologies including SMRs and other technologies that involve using novel cooling systems or fuels; they tend to be smaller than conventional reactors and are designed so they can be constructed in factories and transported to site to reduce the construction risk and capital costs.[343]

16.154 The intention is also to utilise the heat from these reactors to produce hydrogen and synthetic fuels and complement investments in CCUS, hydrogen and offshore wind.[344]

16.155 There was a policy impetus to secure a final investment decision in a large-scale nuclear plant by the end of the last Parliament, subject to value for money and relevant approvals.[345] Hinkley Point C and Sizewell C are considered in more detail below.

16.156 The Carbon Budget Delivery Plan ('CBDP')[346] continued the same policy trajectory; and reliance was placed by the government on the following key policies:[347]

- As part of the commitment to new nuclear projects, the government established Great British Nuclear, which is described as 'an arms-length body with the responsibility to drive delivery of new nuclear projects' beyond Sizewell C, and was put a statutory footing by the Energy Act 2023 (addressed further at paragraphs 16.160 and 16.186 below).[348]

---

339 For example, through the launch of the £120 million Future Nuclear Enabling Fund, as set out in HM Government, 'Net Zero Strategy: Build Back Greener' (n 3) 19.
340 HM Government, 'The Ten Point Plan for a Green Industrial Revolution' (n 119) 12.
341 Department for Business, Energy and Industrial Strategy and others, 'Nuclear Energy: What You Need to Know' (n 322).
342 'Small Modular Reactors' (IAEA) <https://www.iaea.org/topics/small-modular-reactors> accessed 13 June 2024.
343 Department for Business, Energy and Industrial Strategy and Department for Energy Security and Net Zero, 'Advanced Nuclear Technologies' (2023) <https://www.gov.uk/government/publications/advanced-nuclear-technologies/advanced-nuclear-technologies> accessed 13 June 2024.
344 HM Government, 'The Ten Point Plan for a Green Industrial Revolution' (n 119) 12.
345 Department for Business, Energy and Industrial Strategy, Department for Energy Security and Net Zero and Prime Minister's Office, 'British Energy Security Strategy' (n 4); HM Government, 'Energy White Paper: Powering Our Net Zero Future' (n 33) 48; HM Government, 'Net Zero Strategy: Build Back Greener' (n 3) 19, 94, 103.
346 This plan was published in accordance with Holgate J's direction following the legal challenge to the Net Zero Strategy and has since been declared unlawful by Sheldon J. Sheldon J's decision in *Friends of the Earth and others v Secretary of State for Energy Security and Net Zero* [2024] EWHC 995 (Admin) is discussed at paragraphs 2.126–2.131.
347 Department for Energy Security and Net Zero, *Carbon Budget Delivery Plan* HC 2023, 1269 policies 29–33 pp 52–3 <https://assets.publishing.service.gov.uk/media/6424b2d760a35e000c0cb135/carbon-budget-delivery-plan.pdf> accessed 4 April 2024; Department for Energy Security and Net Zero, 'Powering Up Britain' (2023) <https://assets.publishing.service.gov.uk/media/642468ff2fa8480013ec0f39/powering-up-britain-joint-overview.pdf> accessed 4 April 2024.
348 Energy Act 2023 s 317.

- A decision to invest £700 million in Sizewell C, which means the government is a shareholder in the project and has been involved in raising capital for the project through the regulated asset base ('RAB') model (see further below).

- The RAB has been implemented, following the passing of the Nuclear Energy (Financing) Act 2022, which provides a new model of financial nuclear power plant projects; and involves risk-sharing between projects and consumers.

- The establishment of the Advanced Nuclear Fund, which is a commitment to spend £385 million to invest in nuclear technologies (including SMRs and AMRs).

- The Future Nuclear Enabling Fund is intended to help reduce project risks; and is targeted at those applicants that closest to a Final Investment Decision.[349]

16.157 A separate but relevant policy objective has been to legislate to support other low carbon alternative fuels to include nuclear derived fuels as part of the decarbonisation of transport (see further below in relation to the amendments made by the Energy Act 2023).[350]

16.158 Fusion energy was specifically addressed by the government in a strategy published in October 2023, which is concerned with the commercialisation of fusion energy.[351] One of the main policy objectives is for a prototype fusion power plant to be built in the UK to demonstrate its commercial viability.[352]

16.159 In January 2024, the government published the 'Civil Nuclear: Roadmap to 2050'.[353] This policy paper is intended to set out how the government intends nuclear deployment to occur, including a timeline for relevant decisions, to ensure the government's ambitions for both net zero and energy security can be achieved. It touches upon the question of dealing with nuclear waste from the proposed increased nuclear capacity, which includes building a geological disposal facility and updating policy on nuclear decommissioning and managing radioactive waste.[354]

---

349 At the time of writing the fund was closed to new applicants: Department for Energy Security and Net Zero and Department for Business, Energy and Industrial Strategy, 'Future Nuclear Enabling Fund (FNEF) (Closed to Applications)' (GOV.UK, 18 July 2023) <https://www.gov.uk/government/publications/future-nuclear-enabling-fund-fnef> accessed 13 June 2024.
350 Department for Business, Energy and Industrial Strategy and Department for Energy Security and Net Zero, 'Energy Security Bill Factsheet: Recycled Carbon Fuels and Nuclear Derived Fuels for Transport' (GOV.UK, 9 January 2023) <https://www.gov.uk/government/publications/energy-security-bill-factsheets/energy-security-bill-factsheet-recycled-carbon-fuels-and-nuclear-derived-fuels-for-transport> accessed 17 June 2024; Department for Transport, 'Low Carbon Transport Fuels: DfT Science Advisory Council Position Paper' (GOV.UK, 6 May 2023) <https://www.gov.uk/government/publications/low-carbon-transport-fuels-dft-science-advisory-council-position-paper/low-carbon-transport-fuels-dft-science-advisory-council-position-paper> accessed 17 June 2024.
351 Department for Energy Security and Net Zero, 'Towards Fusion Energy 2023: The next Stage of the UK's Fusion Energy Strategy' (2023) <https://assets.publishing.service.gov.uk/media/65301b78d06662000d1b7d0f/towards-fusion-energy-strategy-2023-update.pdf> accessed 13 June 2024.
352 ibid 14.
353 Department for Energy Security and Net Zero, 'Civil Nuclear: Roadmap to 2050' (2024) CP 1009 <https://assets.publishing.service.gov.uk/media/65c0e7cac43191000d1a457d/6.8610_DESNZ_Civil_Nuclear_Roadmap_report_Final_Web.pdf> accessed 13 June 2024.
354 ibid 9.

16.160 The policy position of the new Labour government towards nuclear energy is not entirely clear but seems generally supportive. The Secretary of State for Energy Security and Net Zero, Rt Hon Ed Miliband, has spoken positively about nuclear energy, for example in his keynote speech to the Energy UK conference 2024; and the statement announcing Great British Energy[355] emphasises the role of nuclear energy in clean energy production and the work of Great British Nuclear.[356] At the Labour Party Conference in September 2024 the Secretary of State reaffirmed the government's commitment to nuclear, telling the conference that he 'will use every lever we have to win jobs and build new industries for Britain. Great British Energy, the National Wealth Fund, the British Jobs Bonus. And let's spell out what this future means … jobs constructing the next generation of nuclear power stations.' Through Great British energy, the Labour government has said that it is committed to getting Hinkley Point C 'over the line'. The government has expressed itself committed to Sizewell C but it appears may not take an investment decision until 2025. The government did however in August 2024 announce a new subsidy scheme for development expenditure which will benefit the project. The £5.5 billion Sizewell DevX scheme will provide the government with greater flexibility to cover development expenditure costs up to and including Final Investment Decision, subject to appropriate Value for Money assessments and approvals at the relevant time.[357] It has been suggested that the government may be considering not pursuing plans for gigawatt scale nuclear new build at Wylfa on Anglesey.[358] But no firm announcement has been made in that regard and before the election Labour had expressed support for the project. In Parliament on 11 September 2024 the Parliamentary Under-Secretary for Wales stated that 'as a previously designated nuclear site that has hosted nuclear power, Wylfa is ideally placed either to be used for large-scale nuclear, or to be used for a series of small modular reactors. We will be setting out our plans for the site in due course'.[359] This leaves open the possibility that the site might be used only for small modular reactors. It can therefore be said that there is support for new nuclear build but that financial factors may intervene in the case of new gigawatt scale plant – a position not very different to that of the previous Conservative government.

(a) Hinkley Point C

16.161 The complex consenting process for Hinkley Point C, which is capable of generating 3,260MW of electricity, is underway. It will be the third nuclear power station on the north Somerset coast. The first station was Hinkley Point A, which was operational between 1965 and 2000 and is now being decommissioned, followed by Hinkley Point B, which began operations in 1976 and stopped generating electricity in 2022.

---

355 A publicly-owned energy company designed to drive clean energy development.

356 Department for Energy Security and Net Zero, 'Great British Energy founding statement' (2024) <https://www.gov.uk/government/publications/introducing-great-british-energy/great-british-energy-founding-statement#what-is-great-british-energy> accessed 6 October 2024.

357 <https://www.newcivilengineer.com/latest/sizewell-c-to-receive-up-to-a-further-5-5bn-of-taxpayer-cash-02-09-2024/>.

358 <https://www.newcivilengineer.com/latest/government-considering-scrapping-wylfa-plans-and-24gw-nuclear-capacity-target-09-09-2024/>.

359 <https://hansard.parliament.uk/commons/2024-09-11/debates/852EE7B9-E2BA-4B7C-9A90-7058506E9CDA/NuclearPowerPlantWylfa>.

16.162 Hinkley Point C is being built by EDF's company, NNB Generation Company (HPC) Limited ('NNB'). It received a nuclear site licence on 26 November 2012 from the Office of Nuclear Regulation ('ONR') for two pressurised water reactors.[360] The Environment Agency and ONR considered that the design of the reactor was acceptable in December 2012.[361]

16.163 Environmental permits were issued by the Environment Agency in March 2013, in relation to disposing of and discharging radioactive wastes, operating standby power supply systems using diesel generators and discharging cooling water and liquid effluents into the English Channel.[362]

16.164 A DCO was approved for the nuclear power station on 19 March 2013.[363] An Taisce (the National Trust for Ireland) brought judicial review proceedings[364] challenging the DCO on the grounds that the defendant had failed to carry out a transboundary consultation with Ireland as part of the environmental impact assessment for the project (considered further below at paragraph 16.189).

16.165 An ongoing issue regarding the power station has been in relation to one of the fish protection measures, which is an acoustic fish deterrent ('AFD'). This issue gave rise to two applications, first in February 2019 and then in December 2022, to vary the environmental permit relating to water discharge activities and an application, in October 2023, to vary the DCO.

16.166 In relation to the February 2019 application, the Environment Agency determined that, following an appropriate assessment, they could not conclude that removing the AFD would have no adverse effect on the protected habitats and species in the Severn Estuary. NNB then appealed what they considered to be the Environment Agency's deemed refusal to vary the permit, in respect of which refusal of the appeal was

---

360 'Hinkley Point C' (Office for Nuclear Regulation, 2024) <https://www.onr.org.uk/our-work/what-we-regulate/new-reactors/construction/hinkley-point-c/> accessed 13 June 2024; Environment Agency, 'Hinkley Point: Nuclear Regulation' (GOV.UK, 7 May 2024) <https://www.gov.uk/guidance/hinkley-point-nuclear-regulation> accessed 13 June 2024.
361 Environment Agency, 'Hinkley Point' (n 360).
362 ibid; see decisions on the environmental permit applications in Environment Agency, 'Hinkley Point C: Decisions on Environmental Permit Applications' (GOV.UK, 31 July 2023) <https://www.gov.uk/government/publications/hinkley-point-decisions-on-environmental-permit-applications-for-a-proposed-new-nuclear-power-station> accessed 13 June 2024.
363 The Hinkley Point C (Nuclear Generating Station) Order 2013 No. 648; The Rt Hon Edward Davey, 'Edward Davey Statement on Hinkley Point C Nuclear Power Station' (GOV.UK, 19 March 2013) <https://www.gov.uk/government/speeches/edward-davey-statement-on-hinkley-point-c-nuclear-power-station> accessed 13 June 2024; There was also separate consideration of the Hinkley Point Connection, see Giles Scott, 'Letter on the Application for the Proposed Hinkley Point C Electric Line Connection' <https://infrastructure.planninginspectorate.gov.uk/wp-content/ipc/uploads/projects/EN020001/EN020001-000001-160119%20FINAL%20DL.pdf> accessed 13 June 2024.
364 *R (An Taisce (The National Trust for Ireland)) v Secretary of State for Energy and Climate Change* [2014] EWCA Civ 1111.

recommended by a planning inspector.[365] The Secretary of State reviewed the inspector's report and accepted his advice, and therefore refused the appeal on 2 September 2022.[366]

16.167 On the second application for a variation, the Environment Agency decided to grant the variation requested by the operator following consultation and further consideration of the environmental impacts.[367] Thus, the conditions relating to the AFD were removed on the basis that there would be no adverse effect on the integrity of the relevant European designated site.[368] Other conditions were imposed on the permit.[369]

16.168 The DCO amendment application includes the removal of the requirement to install an AFD system onsite and certain offsite measures, including works to and/or removals of certain weirs.[370] At the time of writing, NNB had consulted on the proposed amendments; and the Environment Agency had raised concerns in relation to the calculated level of harm from removing the AFD and the lack of other environmental assessments (including flood risk assessment and in relation to the marine habitats and fish pass removal/easement proposals).[371]

(b) Sizewell C

16.169 EDF is also bringing forward the nuclear power station, Sizewell C, in Suffolk, through a nuclear build company, Sizewell C Company ('Sizewell C Co').[372] Sizewell A was operational between 1966 and 2006, and is being decommissioned.[373] Sizewell B is a PWR and will stop generating electricity in 2035.[374]

16.170 The ONR received the application from Sizewell C Co for a nuclear site licence to construct and operate a twin EPR power station in Suffolk, next to Sizewell B, on

---

365 Sarah Swash, 'Decision Letter on the Appeal by NNB Generating Company (HPC) Ltd Removal of Acoustic Fish Deterrent Conditions from Water Discharge Activity (WDA) Permit' <https://assets.publishing.service.gov.uk/media/6310cbc88fa8f5578c40543f/hpc-decision-letter-220902.pdf> accessed 13 June 2024; 'Environmental Permit Appeal: Removal of Acoustic Fish Deterrent Conditions from Water Discharge Activity (WDA) Permit' (GOV.UK) <https://www.gov.uk/government/publications/environmental-permit-appeal-removal-of-acoustic-fish-deterrent-conditions-from-water-discharge-activity-wda-permit> accessed 13 June 2024.
366 ibid.
367 'TA5 1UD, NNB Generation Company (HPC) Limited, EPR/HP3228XT/V005: Environmental Permit Proposed Decision Advertisement' (Environment Agency, 8 January 2023) <https://consult.environment-agency.gov.uk/psc/ta5-1ud-hinkley-point-c-v005-proposed-decision/> accessed 13 June 2024.
368 ibid.
369 ibid.
370 John Wheadon, 'Decision Letter on The Hinkley Point C (Nuclear Generating Station) Order 2013 – Regulation 10 S.I. 2013 No. 648 (as Amended) ('the Order') – Material Change Application' <https://infrastructure.planninginspectorate.gov.uk/wp-content/ipc/uploads/projects/EN010102/EN010102-000148-HPC%20MC%20-%20DESNZ%20Letter%20Redacted.pdf> accessed 13 June 2024.
371 Environment Agency, 'Environment Agency Response to Hinkley Point C Development Consent Order Material Change Consultation' (GOV.UK, 5 July 2024) <https://www.gov.uk/government/publications/hinkley-point-c-responses-to-hinkley-point-c-company-dco-consultations/environment-agency-response-to-hinkley-point-c-development-consent-order-material-change-consultation> accessed 13 June 2024; Environment Agency, 'Hinkley Point' (n 360).
372 Environment Agency, 'Sizewell: Nuclear Regulation' (GOV.UK, 28 March 2023) <https://www.gov.uk/guidance/sizewell-nuclear-regulation> accessed 13 June 2024.
373 ibid.
374 ibid.

30 June 2020.[375] The ONR has granted the licence; and it came into effect on 7 May 2024.[376]

16.171 The Environment Agency granted three environmental permits for NNB in relation to this power station, following an application in May 2020.[377] The permits relate to the disposal and discharge of radioactive waste, the operation of a standby power supply system using diesel generators, and the discharge of cooling water liquid effluent into the North Sea.[378]

16.172 The application for a DCO under the PA 2008 was subject to examination that concluded on 14 October 2022 and reported to the Secretary of State on 25 February 2022.[379] The DCO was granted for the project on 20 July 2022.[380] The DCO was challenged by a judicial review brought by a campaigning group opposing the development of the power station, *Together against Sizewell C*[381] (addressed below at paragraphs 16.190–16.192).

(iv) *Policy and law*

16.173 The consenting process for nuclear power plants is extremely complex.[382] The focus in this section is on the key aspects of the national policy statements ('NPS') dealing with nuclear energy from fission.[383] The government also intends to produce an NPS for nuclear fusion, which would become EN-8.[384]

16.174 The relevant NPSs for nuclear fission are: the overarching NPS for energy (EN-1) and the nuclear specific NPS, EN-6. EN-6 was designated under the PA 2008

---

375 ibid; 'Sizewell C' <https://www.sizewellc.com/> accessed 28 September 2023.
376 'Sizewell C' (n 375).
377 'Information Regarding Three New Environmental Permit Applications for the Proposed Sizewell C Power Station Site, Sizewell, Suffolk, IP16 4UR' (Environment Agency, 28 March 2024) <https://consult.environment-agency.gov.uk/psc/sizewell-c-environmental-permits-information-page/> accessed 13 June 2024.
378 ibid.
379 Environment Agency, 'Sizewell' (n 372).
380 The Sizewell C (Nuclear Generating Station) Order 2022, SI 2022/853; Planning Inspectorate, 'The Sizewell C Project Development Consent Decision Announced' (GOV.UK, 20 July 2022) <https://www.gov.uk/government/news/the-sizewell-c-project-development-consent-decision-announced> accessed 13 June 2024.
381 *R (Together against Sizewell C) v Secretary of State for Energy Security and Net Zero* [2023] EWCA Civ 1517.
382 There is both nuclear-specific and general legislation and regulations that apply for nuclear energy. The Nuclear Installations Act 1965 provides for nuclear site licences and is due to be amended by section 156 of the Energy Act 2023 to deal with certain fusion energy sites not requiring a licence but, at the time of writing, that provision is not yet in force. Part 1 of the Energy Act 2004 sets out further provision in relation to the civil nuclear industry, which includes the establishment of the Nuclear Decommissioning Authority (with responsibilities not only for decommissioning of nuclear installations but also the cleaning-up of designated nuclear sites). The Energy Act 2013 established the ONR (as set out in section 77) and deals, in part 3, with nuclear regulation. The ONR's purposes include nuclear safety, nuclear site health and safety, nuclear security, nuclear safeguards and transport purposes (see s 67); and second legislation such as the Ionising Radiations Regulations 2017 No. 1075 and the Nuclear Industries Security Regulations 2003 No. 403.
383 There is also a separate specific NPS dealing with any deep geological facility for disposing of higher activity radioactive waste: Department for Energy Security and Net Zero and Department for Business, Energy and Industrial Strategy, 'National Policy Statement for Geological Disposal Infrastructure' (2019) <https://www.gov.uk/government/publications/national-policy-statement-for-geological-disposal-infrastructure> accessed 5 April 2024.
384 Department for Energy Security and Net Zero, 'Consultation on a New National Policy Statement for Fusion Energy: The Proposed Approach to Siting Fusion Energy Facilities' (n 328).

and has effect in relation to nuclear energy projects that are capable of being deployed by the end of 2025.[385] The government has recently consulted on various issues, such as a new approach to siting of such power plants,[386] that will feed into a new NPS, EN-7, for nuclear power stations after 2025 and will include smaller reactors.[387]

16.175 The newly designated overarching NPS for energy (EN-1) will have effect in relation to any new applications for nuclear energy generation that will be capable of being deployed after 2025 (along with a nuclear specific NPS that is being developed).[388]

16.176 EN-1 sets out the CNP for nationally significant low carbon infrastructure and the substantial weight that should be given to this need when assessing applications for any energy infrastructure (that meets the definition of nationally significant infrastructure within the PA 2008).[389]

16.177 EN-1 specifically recognises the role of nuclear fission to achieve net zero, stating *inter alia* as follows:[390]

> Nuclear fission already provides the UK with continuous, reliable, safe low-carbon power. Nuclear plants produce no direct emissions during operation and have indirect life cycle GHG emissions comparable to offshore wind. Power stations with an estimated lifetime of 60 years provide large amounts of low carbon electrical power, using a relatively small amount of land. Nuclear, alongside other technologies could also offer broader system benefits, such as low carbon hydrogen production through electrolysis, or low carbon heat. In addition, nuclear generation provides security of supply benefits by utilising an alternative fuel source to other thermal plants, with a supply chain independent from gas supplies.

16.178 This overarching policy statement also flags the important role of the ONR for safety[391] and security[392] considerations in the UK's civil nuclear industry.

---

385 The Planning Inspectorate, 'Nationally Significant Infrastructure Projects: National Policy Statements' <https://www.gov.uk/government/publications/nationally-significant-infrastructure-projects-national-policy-statements/nationally-significant-infrastructure-projects-national-policy-statements#which-sectors-do-national-policy-statements-cover> accessed 5 April 2024.

386 Department for Energy Security and Net Zero, 'A National Policy Statement for New Nuclear Power Generation: Consultation on the New Approach to Siting beyond 2025' (2024) <https://assets.publishing.service.gov.uk/media/659fa3313308d2000d1fbe04/nps-new-nuclear-siting-consultation.pdf> accessed 3 October 2024; Department for Energy Security and Net Zero, 'Approach to Siting New Nuclear Power Stations beyond 2025' (GOV.UK, 11 January 2024) <https://www.gov.uk/government/consultations/approach-to-siting-new-nuclear-power-stations-beyond-2025> accessed 13 June 2024.

387 Department for Levelling Up, Housing and Communities, 'Policy Paper – Nationally Significant Infrastructure: Action Plan for Reforms to the Planning Process' (2023) <https://www.gov.uk/government/publications/nationally-significant-infrastructure-projects-nsip-reforms-action-plan/nationally-significant-infrastructure-action-plan-for-reforms-to-the-planning-process#annex-a-nsip-reform-actions> accessed 27 November 2023; 'Nuclear Power Stations: Question for Department for Energy Security and Net Zero UIN HL3852' (UK Parliament, 16 April 2024) <https://questions-statements.parliament.uk/written-questions/detail/2024-04-16/HL3852/> accessed 13 June 2024.

388 Department for Energy Security and Net Zero, 'Overarching National Policy Statement for Energy (EN-1) (November 2023)' (n 5) para 1.3.6.

389 ibid paras 3.2.6–8, 4.2.4–9. See above at para 16.76 and see Chapter 6.

390 ibid para 3.3.51.

391 ibid para 4.13.3.

392 ibid para 4.16.3.

16.179 The impact on nature is addressed in the sections of EN-1 dealing with environmental effects and considerations,[393] marine considerations,[394] environmental and biodiversity net gain,[395] and biodiversity conservation.[396] In considering the impact on nature of these projects, EN-1 recognises as follows:[397]

> The government's 25 Year Environment Plan and the Environment Act 2021 mark a step change in ambition for wildlife and the natural environment. The Secretary of State should have regard to the aims and goals of the government's Environmental Improvement Plan 2023, and in Wales the objectives of the Nature Recovery Plan, and any relevant measures and targets, including statutory targets set under the Environment Act or elsewhere.
>
> In addition, in exercising functions in relation to Wales, the Secretary of State should consider Section 6 of the Environment (Wales) Act 2016 and seek to maintain and enhance biodiversity, and in so doing promote the resilience of ecosystems, so far as consistent with the proper exercise of the Secretary of State's functions.

16.180 EN-1 then goes on to set out the principles that the Secretary of State should apply to making a decision on an application for a DCO, including that development should be in line with the mitigation hierarchy,[398] development proposals provide opportunities for building in biodiversity,[399] and appropriate weight is given to the designation of a particular site.[400] EN-1 then deals with the Secretary of State's decision-making in relation to different sites and legal frameworks concerned with protecting nature including marine environments and ancient woodland.[401]

16.181 EN-6 likewise recognises the urgent need for energy infrastructure in achieving climate change mitigation and a drive to net zero, as well as the importance of climate change adaptation.[402] It sets out the specific risks for nuclear power plants and how the Generic Design Assessment ('GDA')[403] factors these issues into nuclear power plant design, as well as how they are addressed by the parallel licensing and permitting regimes:[404]

> Nuclear power stations need access to cooling water. As the sites listed in this NPS indicate, this means that nuclear power stations in the UK are most likely to be developed on

---

393 ibid para 4.3. See Chapter 7.
394 ibid para 4.5.
395 ibid para 4.6.
396 ibid para 5.4.
397 ibid para 5.4.39–40.
398 ibid para 5.4.42.
399 ibid para 5.4.46.
400 ibid para 5.4.48.
401 ibid para 5.4.49–55.
402 Department of Energy and Climate Change, 'National Policy Statement for Nuclear Power Generation (EN-6) Vol I' (2011) s 1.3, 2.10 <https://assets.publishing.service.gov.uk/media/65a7b049ed27ca001327b0e5/2009-nps-for-nuclear-volumeI.pdf> accessed 13 June 2024.
403 As EN-6, footnote 32 explains 'The purpose of the GDA is to provide a robust, transparent and independent review of the "licensibility" of nuclear power station designs. This begins prior to the assessment of other site licensing and environmental permitting issues and before large capital commitments need to be made, thus reducing project risks and uncertainty associated with the regulatory processes.' See ibid 13.
404 ibid 2.10.2–4.

coastal or estuarine sites. Without appropriate mitigation measures the potential effects of climate change could mean these sites become at greater risk of flooding than if they were located inland (see Section 3.6 of this NPS). Applicants should therefore provide the IPC with information as to how the development incorporates adaptation measures to take account of the effects of climate change, including:

- coastal erosion and increased likelihood of storm surge and rising sea levels;
- effects of higher temperatures; and
- increased risk of drought, which could lead to a lack of available process water.

The GDA process looks at the capability of the power station's generic design features to take into account the effects of climate change. The subsequent site licensing and environmental permitting processes ensure that new nuclear power stations will be located, constructed, operated and decommissioned with the long-term impacts of climate change in mind.

16.182 The policy test for dealing with flood risk as part of the decision-making on a DCO application is set out in section 3.6 at paragraphs 3.6.9–3.6.16, which follows a sequential and exception test. There are also specific policy requirements for dealing with coastal change.[405]

16.183 In the context of water quality and resources, EN-6 recognises the specific negative impact on coastal processes, hydrodynamics and sediment transport, as well as the thermal impact of cooling water discharges on nationally and internationally designated habitats.[406] As part of the decision-making on a DCO application, consideration must be given to the cumulative effects of any proposed new nuclear power station with other major infrastructure, and there should be close liaison between the decision-maker and the Environment Agency on the issue of water quality, including abstraction and discharge, in the environmental permitting process.[407] Further, in relation to mitigation, EN-6 provides that:[408]

> In the design of any direct cooling system the locations of the intake and outfall should be sited to avoid or minimise adverse impacts on legitimate commercial and recreational uses of the receiving waters, including their ecology. There should also be specific measures to minimise impact to fish and aquatic biota by entrainment or by excessive heat or biocidal chemicals from discharges to receiving waters.

16.184 More generally, the impact on nature is addressed by reference to the policy tests in EN-1, but also noting the specific issue that can arise in the nuclear energy context, including water discharge, abstraction and quality issues, habitat and species loss and coastal squeeze, as well as air quality and disturbance events (such as from light and noise).[409]

---

405 ibid 3.8.
406 ibid 3.7.2.
407 ibid 3.7.4–5.
408 ibid 3.7.6.
409 ibid 3.9.

16.185 Finally, EN-6 addresses radioactive waste management, noting the different types of waste arising from nuclear energy development, including 'higher activity waste', which consists of spent fuel and intermediate level waste, and other waste streams (such as low level waste and non-radioactive waste).[410] The government has taken the view that higher activity waste should be dealt with by way of geological disposal (including waste from new nuclear power stations);[411] suitable sites can be identified for that geological disposal; and safe, secure and environmentally acceptable interim storage arrangements will be available until a geological disposal facility can accept the waste.[412]

16.186 The following recently enacted legislation is also relevant to facilitating the overall objective of increasing nuclear energy generation at the domestic level as part of the transition to net zero:

- The Nuclear Energy (Financing) Act 2022 ('NE(F)A 2022') provides for the implementation of a regulated asset base ('RAB') funding model for new nuclear energy generation projects and for revenue collection for that model.[413] The RAB model has been used to finance large-scale infrastructure assets such as water, gas and electricity networks in the UK; and aims to reduce the financing costs of a project and the overall cost (by attracting private investment).[414] The model operates on the basis that if a nuclear company has RAB licence conditions in place they are entitled to a regulated revenue stream, which is a levy on electricity suppliers that is, in turn, passed on to consumers.[415] The NE(F)A 2022 provides for the designation of a company that holds an electricity generation licence[416] in relation to a nuclear energy generation project as a 'nuclear company'.[417] By section 6(1), the Secretary of State has the power to modify a term or condition on the nuclear company's electricity generation licence for the purpose of facilitating investment in the design, construction, commissioning and operation of nuclear energy generation projects; and, when exercising that power, the Secretary of State must have regard *inter alia* to the net zero target and ensuring the carbon budgets are met.[418]

- As set out above, the Energy Act 2023 gave Great British Nuclear a statutory basis; and established that its objects are to 'facilitate the design, construction, commissioning and operation of nuclear energy generation projects for the purpose of furthering any policies published by His Majesty's government.'

---

410 ibid 2.11.2.
411 In respect of which, as set out at footnote 383 above, there is a specific NPS, which is beyond the scope of this book.
412 Department of Energy and Climate Change (n 402) para 2.11.3.
413 Nuclear Energy (Financing) Act 2022 Preamble.
414 Department for Business, Energy and Industrial Strategy, 'Revenue Stream for the Nuclear RAB Model: Consultation in Respect of Revenue Regulations Relating to the Implementation of the Nuclear RAB Model Revenue Stream' (2022) 5 <https://assets.publishing.service.gov.uk/media/62a8341c8fa8f5038fee9c0b/nuclear-rab-revenue-stream-regulations-consultation.pdf> accessed 13 June 2024.
415 ibid.
416 This is defined as a licence under s 6(1)(a) of the Electricity Act 1989.
417 NE(F)A 2022, ss 1 and 2. As part of the designation process, s 3 requires consultation *inter alia* with Ofgem, the ONR and for England (the Environment Agency), Wales (Natural Resources Wales) and in Scotland (Scottish Environment Protection Agency).
418 See Climate Change Act 2008, ss 1 and 4(1)(b), as per s 6(4)(a) of the NE(F)A 2022.

- The Energy Act 2023[419] has also amended the Nuclear Installations Act 1965 so that the requirement of certain nuclear installations to be licensed sites does not apply to defined fusion energy facilities.

- Further, the Energy Act 2004 has been amended by section 157 of the Energy Act 2023 to introduce section 131D, which provides for nuclear-derived fuel, designated as such by a renewable transport fuel order where 'a description of liquid or gaseous fuel which is produced wholly using, or by a process powered wholly by, nuclear fuel', to be treated as a renewable transport fuel.[420]

(v) *Specific issues*

16.187 This section touches upon some of the key issues relating to nuclear energy, insofar as relevant to the scope of this book: the achievement of net zero and nature positive. The focus therefore is on the environmental impact of nuclear energy projects, which brings to the fore the conflict between net zero and nature positive goals. Other issues such as the complexity of the regulatory process and the costs associated with these projects are also flagged because these are directly relevant to the speed and progress in achieving net zero.

(a) Environmental impact

16.188 Given the nature of nuclear energy generation, an important issue is the impact that any such development has on other aspects of the environment, in particular in relation to water supply and impact on the aquatic and marine environments, as set out above.[421]

16.189 The concern around the environmental impact of nuclear power plants has formed the principal basis for public interest judicial review challenges to nuclear project schemes. For example, the judicial challenge to the Hinkley Point C DCO brought by An Taisce alleged that the defendant had failed to undertake a lawful environmental impact assessment, in particular that there had been a failure to undertake transboundary consultation with Ireland in accordance with Article 7 of the EIA Directive.[422] The main point was the meaning of 'likely' in Article 7, which contains the triggers for a transboundary consultation, where *inter alia* 'a member state is aware that a project is likely to have significant effects on the environment in another member state'.[423] The High Court refused permission to proceed; whilst the Court of Appeal granted permission to proceed but then refused the claim. The Court of Appeal accepted that

---

419 Section 156.

420 See further paras 18.161–18.171 in Chapter 18. There are also specific provisions relating to including nuclear fuel in the definition of 'renewable liquid heating fuel', as per section 159 of the Energy Act 2023.

421 There have also been challenges based on landscape impacts, such as the impact of the relocation works for Sizewell B power station on an area of outstanding natural beauty in Suffolk in *Girling v East Suffolk Council* [2020] EWHC 2579 (Admin).

422 n 364; Directive 2011/92/EU of the European Parliament and of the Council of 13 December 2011 on the assessment of the effects of certain public and private projects on the environment; for further discussion of EIA, see Chapter 7 and reg 24 of the Infrastructure Planning (Environmental Impact Assessment) Regulations 2009 (which have since been revoked).

423 ibid Article 7(1).

'likely' meant a 'real risk', not one that 'cannot be excluded on the basis of objective information'.

16.190 The principal issue in *Together against Sizewell C* concerned the permanent potable water supply, and whether the Secretary of State lawfully decided that the nuclear power station and the provision of a water supply were separate projects for the purposes of the Conservation of Habitats Regulations[424] ('Habitats Regulations 2017').[425]

16.191 The claim was dismissed by Holgate J at first instance; and the appeal was dismissed by the Court of Appeal. The decision-maker's discretion in relation to defining a project is wide, but the decision-maker must be alert to: (i) the mischief of 'salami-slicing' whereby a project is split to avoid the necessary assessment; (ii) two or more separate projects may have some physical or functional connection, but the likelihood or certainty of them having cumulative effects on the environment does not mean they should be treated as a single project and (iii) certain factors that may be relevant to defining a project.[426]

16.192 The Court of Appeal also recognised the policy emphasis on nuclear energy as an important component of the drive to net zero, noting that EN-1[427] states that 'there is "an urgent need for new electricity generation plant, including new nuclear power" to enable the United Kingdom to meet its energy and climate change objectives' and Sizewell is one of the specific sites identified in EN-6 for a new nuclear power station.[428]

16.193 In *R (Tarian Hafren Severen Shield Cyf) v Marine Management Organisation and another,*[429] the claimant represented a group of scientists, organisations and individuals opposing the disposal of material dredged from the Severn Estuary as part of the Hinkley Point C project back into the Severn, because of the concern that the material

---

424 The Conservation of Habitats and Species Regulations 2017 reg 63 as amended.
425 For more detailed consideration of HRA, see Chapter 9. The key facts in *Together against Sizewell C* were as follows (see n 381 [24]–[28]): At the time the DCO application was made, the applicant could not identify a permanent supply of potable water for the power station but indicated that that would become clear following preparation of the water resources management plan by the relevant water undertaker. During the examination, water supply was considered at an issue specific hearing. The water undertaker explained that a review of the ongoing modelling work was required to understand if there was a sustainable source of water supply, but that could not be done before the end of the examination. Natural England therefore took the position that it could not advise on whether there would be adverse effects on designated sites as a result of the water infrastructure; further, without such a water supply, the ONR confirmed that the applicant could not fulfil its licence conditions. The examining authority therefore reported to the Secretary of State that the applicant had not undertaken 'a cumulative assessment of the environmental effects of the proposed water supply' and, given the lack of information, no meaningful assessment of potential environmental effects. This would therefore mean the power station could not operate and the examining authority recommended that the DCO could not be granted 'without greater clarity about a sustainable water supply solution and any consequential environmental effects'. The Secretary of State undertook further enquiries with the applicant and the water undertaker. In deciding to grant the DCO, the Secretary of State was satisfied that there was 'reasonable level of certainty' that the necessary water supply could be found, given the options put forward by the water undertaker and applicant. Further, the water supply was a separate project to the nuclear power station for the purposes of the Habitats Regulations assessment; and the potential environmental effects (including cumulative effects) will be assessed.
426 *Together against Sizewell C* (n 381) [71].
427 At [3.5.1].
428 *Together against Sizewell C* (n 381) [17].
429 *R (Tarian Hafren Severn Shield CYF) v MMO* [2022] EWHC 683 (Admin).

contains fine radioactive particles, which involve a risk of low levels of radiation.[430] The judicial review challenge was to the Marine Management Organisation's ('MMO') approval of a variation to a marine licence granted under the Marine and Coastal Access Act 2009 ('MCAA 2009').[431] The grounds included that (i) the decision to vary the licence was *ultra vires* the variation power in section 72 of the MCAA 2009 because it involved adding a new activity, namely the disposal of dredged material; (ii) the MMO failed to comply with the regulation 22 of the Waste (England and Wales) Regulations 2011, in particular the waste hierarchy; and (iii) the MMO failed to comply with the Water Framework Directive ('WFD'),[432] given effect by the Water Environment (Water Framework Directive) (England and Wales) Regulations 2017,[433] in particular whether the disposal would jeopardise attainment of 'good surface water status' under Article 4(1) of the WFD. The application for judicial review was refused.

(b) Siting

16.194 EN-6 identified a number of potential sites for nuclear power plants, based on a strategic siting assessment.[434] The criteria as part of that assessment involved consideration of the impact of such development on internationally and nationally designated sites of ecological importance as well as considering the resilience and adaptation risks (associated with flooding, storm surge, sea level rise and coastal changes). Thus, the environmental impacts and climate change considerations were factored into the process of identifying potentially suitable sites for that NPS.

16.195 The question will be how sites will be selected for nuclear energy generation beyond 2025. That question formed the basis of the government's recent consultation on siting as part of the design of EN-7 and its new proposed policy approach, which involves setting criteria for site selection, rather than identifying specific sites.[435] It is proposed that the criteria will apply to traditional large-scale power plants, SMRs and AMRs;[436] and that it will factor in coastal flood risk that will take into account climate change and flood risk modelling,[437] as well as the impact on nationally and internationally designated sites of ecological importance[438] and access to suitable sources of cooling, especially for traditional nuclear power plants.[439] Interestingly, in the consultation proposal, the view was taken that there was no need for a specific criterion for climate change itself, because climate change related considerations were embedded in other criteria.[440]

---

430 ibid 2.
431 It had been subjected to an environmental impact assessment under The Marine Works (Environmental Impact Assessment) Regulations 2007, SI 2007/1518.
432 Directive 2000/60/EC of the European Parliament and of the Council of 23 October 2000 establishing a framework for Community action in the field of water policy (as amended).
433 SI 2017/407 (as amended by the Floods and Water (Amendment etc) (EU Exit) Regulations 2019).
434 Department of Energy and Climate Change (n 402) para 2.3.1.
435 Department for Energy Security and Net Zero, 'A National Policy Statement for New Nuclear Power Generation: Consultation on the New Approach to Siting beyond 2025' (n 386).
436 ibid 4.1.5.
437 ibid 4.3.3–8.
438 ibid 4.3.24.
439 ibid 4.3.31.
440 ibid 4.3.14–17.

(c) Financing nuclear energy generation

16.196 Financing of nuclear energy projects has been, and continues to be, a 'major barrier' to the increased development of this form of energy generation, particularly because of the high upfront capital costs and long construction periods.[441] The Climate Change Committee has advised that it is 'relatively expensive on a levelized cost basis'.[442] There is no easy solution to this issue.[443] The Contract for Difference model was adopted to assist in financing Hinkley Point C but this model reportedly left significant capital costs.[444] It is early days of the adoption of the RAB model to assist with financing of these projects but commentators suggest that the model will lower the risk profile and open up the possibility of further potential investors.[445]

(d) Waste

16.197 The approach to managing nuclear waste both at operational sites and those going through the decommissioning process is one of the challenges of this form of energy generation. As part of the government's strategy for increasing nuclear energy generation, the need for a sufficient geological disposal facility has been identified, but the delays in securing such a deep underground facility, and identifying an appropriate location for it, are recognised; and the government envisages that such a facility may not be ready until the 2050s.[446]

Biomass

(i) *Introduction*

16.198 Bioenergy is reportedly the second largest source of renewable energy in the UK, generating 12.9% of the total UK electricity supply in 2021.[447] An important source of bioenergy is biomass, which is set to play an increasingly significant role in securing the UK's net zero goals.

16.199 In 2022, biomass generated 15.9TWh of electricity output, or 5% of the UK's domestic electricity generation.[448] Bioenergy from biomass is relied upon by the CCC

---

441 Department for Energy Security and Net Zero, 'Civil Nuclear: Roadmap to 2050' (n 353) s 6.

442 Climate Change Committee, 'Delivering a Reliable Decarbonized Power System' (2023) 35 <https://www.theccc.org.uk/wp-content/uploads/2023/03/Delivering-a-reliable-decarbonised-power-system.pdf> accessed 13 June 2024.

443 The issue has been further complicated by restrictions in relation to state aid, but the European Commission ultimately determined that the provision of state aid for the construction of Hinkley Point was compatible with the internal market and that was upheld by the European Court of Justice in the Case C-594/18 *Austria v Commission* (2020) ECLI:EU:C:2020:742.

444 'Financing Nuclear Energy – World Nuclear Association' (World Nuclear Association, 5 February 2024) <https://world-nuclear.org/information-library/economic-aspects/financing-nuclear-energy> accessed 13 June 2024.

445 ibid.

446 Department for Energy Security and Net Zero and Andrew Bowie, 'Updated Approach to Managing Nuclear Waste' (GOV.UK, 16 May 2024) <https://www.gov.uk/government/news/updated-approach-to-managing-nuclear-waste> accessed 17 June 2024.

447 UK Parliament POST, 'Biomass for UK Energy' (2023) POSTnote 690 2 <https://researchbriefings.files.parliament.uk/documents/POST-PN-0690/POST-PN-0690.pdf> accessed 21 June 2024.

448 National Grid ESO, 'FES 2023 Data Workbook' (n 20) ES.05–08.

in its Balanced Net Zero Pathway, as part of its report on the Sixth Carbon Budget.[449] The government also relies upon policies for use of bioenergy in the Carbon Budget Delivery Plan.[450]

16.200 Biomass is defined as material of recent biological origin, derived from plant or animal matter.[451] Ultimately deriving its energy from the sun, captured by plants through photosynthesis, biomass has the potential to be a reliable low-carbon source of energy, particularly where it is combined with Carbon Capture and Storage ('CCS'), known in combination as Bioenergy with Carbon Capture and Storage ('BECCS'). Large-scale BECCS projects will only be delivered by 2030.[452] Hence, based on projections by the National Grid, the use of BECCS is set to dramatically uptick from 2031 onwards, potentially generating 26.0 TWh of electricity by 2038.[453]

16.201 The sources of biomass include the biodegradable portion of crops, wastes and any other products of biological origin.[454] The sources are therefore highly versatile, and include biogenic waste products or residues (for example, those produced by agriculture or industry) which would otherwise be left to decompose or combusted in waste disposal. Their usage as a source of energy, replacing more expensive and volatile fossil fuels, is an efficient means of reducing carbon emissions. Biomass can also be purpose-grown, such biomass being mainly comprised of conventional food crops.[455] For the purposes of heat and power generation, biomass is usually classified as:[456]

- biomass deriving 'forest residues' as a co-product of forestry management;
- biomass deriving agricultural crops and residues, including 'energy crops'; and
- biomass from biodegradable waste, including sewage sludge, manure, waste wood, and food waste.

16.202 Biomass is used across the economy, including in heating, combined heat and power, low carbon transport fuels, industrial decarbonisation, low carbon hydrogen technologies and powering the wider bioeconomy.

16.203 Operational emissions from biomass combustion plant are controlled through environmental permitting. An overview of the relationship between the permitting and the planning systems is set out in the National Policy Statement for renewable energy infrastructure, NPS EN-3.[457]

---

449 Climate Change Committee, 'The Sixth Carbon Budget: The UK's Path to Net Zero' (n 276) 72.
450 Department for Energy Security and Net Zero, *Carbon Budget Delivery Plan* (n 347) 50, 67–69.
451 Department for Energy Security and Net Zero, 'Biomass Strategy' (2023) 6 <https://assets.publishing.service.gov.uk/media/64dc8d3960d123000d32c602/biomass-strategy-2023.pdf> accessed 21 June 2024; in NPS EN-1, it is defined as 'matter of recent biological origin derived from plant or animal matter'.
452 National Grid ESO, 'Future Energy Scenarios 2023 (July 2023)' (n 114) 51.
453 National Grid ESO, 'FES 2023 Data Workbook' (n 20) ES.05–08.
454 Department for Energy Security and Net Zero, 'Biomass Strategy' (2023) 6 (n 451) Executive Summary.
455 ibid ch 1.
456 Department for Energy Security and Net Zero, 'National Policy Statement for Renewable Energy Infrastructure (EN-3) (November 2023)' (n 7) para 3.7.5.
457 ibid para 4.12.

(ii) *Contribution to net zero*

16.204 Biomass has the potential to make a significant contribution towards achieving net zero, particularly where it is combined with BECCS. Biomass has already played a role in decarbonising the power, heat and transport sectors – as of 2022, bioenergy was estimated to provide 8.6% of the UK's energy supply.[458]

16.205 Bioenergy generated from biomass is relied upon as part of the package of policies and proposals set out by the Secretary of State in accordance with the duty under sections 13 and 14 of the Climate Change Act 2008 ('CCA 2008') in the Carbon Budget Delivery Plan, including:

- Boiler Upgrade Scheme ('BUS'), which involves a capital grant for low carbon technology such as biomass boilers where they replace fossil fuel heating systems;[459]
- Green Heat Network Fund ('GHNF'), which supports the development of low carbon heat network infrastructure;[460]
- The development of a business model for BECCS;[461]
- Incentivising a change in industrial fuel to low carbon fuels, including bioenergy where other low carbon alternatives are not available;[462]
- Increasing land planted with perennial energy crops and short rotation forestry;[463] and
- Research into the use of microalgae and macroalgae to fix CO_2 into biomass.[464]

16.206 The government recognises the risks associated with these policies, however, noting that:[465]

> Many proposals and policies, such as policy relating to domestic biomass planting and some aspects of waste decarbonisation, are at early stages of development. Key risks to delivery of the biomass pathway include establishment of the business model for sustainable biomass cultivation, linked with demand from end use sectors including bioenergy with carbon capture and storage, and confidence in uptake of new models for land use. R&D and policy work is ongoing to increase delivery confidence. For delivery of waste emissions savings, we committed in the Environmental Improvement Plan to launch a

---

458 Department for Energy Security and Net Zero, 'Digest of UK Energy Statistics (DUKES) 2023' (2023) <https://www.gov.uk/government/statistics/digest-of-uk-energy-statistics-dukes-2023> accessed 21 June 2024 Table 1.1.
459 Department for Energy Security and Net Zero, *Carbon Budget Delivery Plan* (n 347) Policy 4.
460 ibid Policy 23.
461 ibid Policy 24.
462 ibid Policy 73.
463 ibid Policy 177.
464 ibid Table 6: unquantified proposals and policies, Policies 92 and 93.
465 ibid Policy 36.

call for evidence to support detailed policy development to achieve the near elimination of biodegradable municipal waste to landfill from 2028.

16.207 In terms of biomass specific policy, the Biomass Policy Statement ('BPS') was published in November 2021, as part of the development of the Biomass Strategy. The BPS confirms that the feedstocks within its scope and that of the Biomass Strategy are as follows:[466]

> Conventional food and feed crops, perennial energy crops (Miscanthus and short rotation coppice (SRC)), short rotation forestry (SRF) and wastes, products (incl. forest derived products), agricultural residues, forest residues, and residues from processing, as well as marine-based and novel feedstocks.

16.208 The BPS sets out the principles for prioritising biomass use over different timescales (including short, medium and long-term) to deliver net zero; and confirms that the government remains committed to sustainable biomass.[467] The principles are as follows:[468]

- Compliance with sustainability criteria and waste hierarchy principles;
- Contribution to carbon budgets and net zero considering feedstock availability, lifecycle greenhouse gas emissions, and cost-benefits; and
- Biomass to be used with carbon capture utilisation or storage where feasible, otherwise used only in hard-to-decarbonise sectors with limited or no low carbon alternatives.

16.209 The BPS flagged the use of biomass in BECCS but noted that that would be subject to technological developments to allow for its deployment.[469]

16.210 In 2023, the government published its Biomass Strategy, which sets out how sustainable biomass could be used across the sector to support the achievement of net zero and other environmental targets.[470] As also set out in NPS EN-3,[471] the government's view is that the combustion of biomass for electricity generation is important for meeting energy needs and for promoting energy decarbonisation, especially in conjunction with the use of CCS.[472]

16.211 The Biomass Strategy claimed that with CCS, BECCS has the potential to produce negative emissions. The theory is that carbon is first captured from the atmosphere

---

466 Department for Business, Energy and Industrial Strategy, 'Biomass Policy Statement' (2021) 9 <https://assets.publishing.service.gov.uk/media/6183a2f4d3bf7f55fd843da1/biomass-policy-statement.pdf> accessed 21 June 2024.
467 ibid 10.
468 ibid Executive Summary, 5.
469 ibid 6; see s 2.7.
470 Department for Energy Security and Net Zero, 'Biomass Strategy' (n 451).
471 Department for Energy Security and Net Zero, 'National Policy Statement for Renewable Energy Infrastructure (EN-3) (November 2023)' (n 7) para 2.7.1.
472 Department for Energy Security and Net Zero, 'Biomass Strategy' (n 451) 175.

by the growth of the plant which will become the biomass, and then the CO_2 emitted by the conversion of biomass into electricity, heat, hydrogen and biofuels is itself captured in more long-term storage.[473] Hence BECCS can be termed an engineered Greenhouse Gas Removal ('GGR') technology.

16.212 The Biomass Strategy also stated that the usage of biomass *without* concurrent CCS can still play a role in reducing the carbon emissions in sectors and technologies which are otherwise considered 'hard to decarbonise', but such usage should be weighed against the availability of alternative energy sources.[474]

16.213 Whether biomass can be regarded as a carbon-neutral or even a carbon-negative source of energy generation has been the subject of a judicial review challenge by the Lifescape Project, a rewilding environmental charity (addressed further below at paragraph 16.221).

16.214 For biomass to be considered low-carbon, it must comply with strict criteria set out in sector-specific legislation, such as the Renewables Obligation Order, Renewable Heat Incentive, Green Gas Support Scheme, Renewable Transport Fuel Obligation, UK Emissions Trading scheme, and the Low Carbon Hydrogen Standard.[475] The regulations are overseen and enforced by their respective sector-specific regulatory bodies.

16.215 While specific requirements differ across the schemes, the sustainability requirements generally include:[476]

- Land criteria: Biomass feedstocks must be legally and sustainably harvested, account for the protection of biodiversity, high carbon stock lands and ecosystem services, protect land rights of local communities, and ensure labour rights; and

- GHG criteria: GHG emissions arising from the lifecycle of biomass use must meet minimum restrictions, which progressively tighten over time. The lifecycle of biomass use includes its production, cultivation, harvesting, transportation and processing.

(iii) *Policy*

16.216 There is a combination of national policy and planning policy that sets out the government's approach to biomass and the role it can play in achieving net zero. The national policy is addressed in the previous section.

---

473 ibid Executive Summary.
474 ibid Executive Summary.
475 ibid 28.
476 ibid 20.

16.217 The overarching NPS on energy, EN-1, recognises the role of biomass in combustion power stations; it sets out that certain commercial scale power stations must be CCR ready.[477] In relation to biomass, EN-1 notes as follows:

> 3.3.43 Bioenergy could provide either baseload or dispatchable low carbon generation. The need for negative emissions to offset residual emissions through BECCS, might provide a case for baseload deployment. In addition, the amount of bioenergy for generating electricity will be constrained by the availability of sustainable biomass and the extent to which it may be more cost effective in decarbonising other sectors (such as heat and transport) over the long-term.

16.218 As set out above, EN-3 is the NPS for renewable energy infrastructure and it deals with biomass where it meets the definition of nationally significant infrastructure projects within the Planning Act 2008.[478] The NPS is supportive of biomass use: it stipulates that biomass has a 'potentially significant role' in supporting the net zero transition, when combined with carbon capture and storage technology.[479] It also spotlights the need for carbon capture readiness and refers to the 'priority application' of BECCS:[480]

> The government recognises the need to prioritise biomass use to applications where it can deliver GHG emission reductions in hard-to-decarbonise sectors, without other viable alternatives, to comply with our net zero and wider environmental goals. One of these priority applications is the use of biomass to deliver negative emissions through Bioenergy with Carbon Capture & Storage (BECCS).

16.219 NPS EN-3 is closely interlinked with the Biomass Strategy, which sets out how biomass will be supported in the future and how the resource can be used for net zero and other environmental targets.[481] Collectively, the two instruments demonstrate the government's support for, and dependency on, biomass in attaining net zero.

(iv) *Issues*

(a) Biomass emissions

16.220 The strong support for biomass is seen by some as problematic because the assumption that biomass is carbon neutral is flawed. There are concerns that the true emission levels of biomass have been overlooked, resulting in criticisms that biomass use is a 'climate fallacy'[482] that fails to contribute meaningfully to net zero.

---

477 Department for Energy Security and Net Zero, 'Overarching National Policy Statement for Energy (EN-1) (November 2023)' (n 5) para 3.3.36.
478 See further Chapter 6.
479 Department for Energy Security and Net Zero, 'National Policy Statement for Renewable Energy Infrastructure (EN-3) (November 2023)' (n 7) paras 2.7.1, 16.
480 ibid paras 2.7.14, 20.
481 ibid para 2.7.4.
482 Leigh Day, 'Environmental Charity Seeks Judicial Review of Government's Plans to Promote the Use of Biomass Fuel in Its Strategy to Cut Greenhouse Gases' <https://www.leighday.co.uk/news/news/2023-news/environmental-charity-seeks-judicial-review-of-government-s-plans-to-promote-the-use-of-biomass-fuel-in-its-strategy-to-cut-greenhouse-gases/> accessed 21 June 2024.

16.221 As mentioned above at paragraph 16.213, the Lifescape Project issued an application for judicial review of the Biomass Strategy in November 2023, still pending at the time of writing.[483] The challenge was brought on three grounds:[484]

- Ground 1. The Secretary of State irrationally failed to undertake adequate inquiry into (and/or failed to take into account the relevant consideration of) the extent to which the government's continued support for the combustion of biomass, including forest biomass, will achieve genuine reductions in carbon emissions, or otherwise contribute to the net zero.

- Ground 2. The failure to conduct such an analysis is a breach of the requirements of section 13 of the CCA 2008.[485]

- Ground 3. The consultation was unfair because key aspects of the analysis relied upon in the strategy were not included in the consultation documents.

16.222 The claimant is concerned that a significant proportion of the biomass being burned for energy in the UK is forest biomass from managed forests in North America.[486] The Strategy suggests that this biomass is low carbon energy because the energy comes from the sun, it absorbs CO_2 as it grows, can regrow in a relatively short period of time and the carbon released upon combustion can be sequestered.[487] The claimant suggested that part of the reason why the government characterises biomass as 'low carbon' is because they rely upon the international protocol for counting GHG emissions, produced by the IPCC in 2006 (and updated in 2019), which states that emissions from harvesting wood for biomass should be counted in the country of origin, rather than where the energy is ultimately used.[488]

16.223 The claimant argued that BECCS only captures emissions released from burning biomass, and fails to account for indirect, lifecycle carbon emissions arising from the manufacture and combustion of biomass. Consequently, the true environmental harms arising from biomass have been underreported, and the government has overinflated the true effectiveness of biomass in delivering on carbon savings.[489]

16.224 Issues regarding the emissions of biomass have been corroborated by research from Chatham House, which found that, in 2019, US-sourced pellets burned for energy

---

483 *R (the Lifescape Project) v Secretary of State for Energy Security and Net Zero (challenge to Biomass Strategy)* [2023]; issued 10 November 2023.
484 Forest Litigation Collaboration, 'Legal Summary: The King on Application of the Lifescape Project v Secretary of State for Energy Security and Net Zero' (2023) <https://forestlitigation.org/wp-content/uploads/2023/11/Legal-summary-Lifescape-v-SSESNZ-Nov-20-2023.pdf> accessed 21 June 2024.
485 This point was made in reliance on *R (Global Feedback Limited) v Secretary of State for the Environment, Food and Rural Affairs and the Secretary of State for Energy Security and Net Zero* [2024] 1 WLR 2923 (see paras 2.133–2.137 in Chapter 2). Section 13 of the CCA 2008 is considered further at paras 2.98–2.99, 2.123 and 2.125–2.130.
486 Forest Litigation Collaboration, 'Legal Summary: The King on Application of the Lifescape Project v Secretary of State for Energy Security and Net Zero' (n 484).
487 ibid para 11.
488 ibid 11–12.
489 ibid.

in the UK accounted for 13 to 16 million tonnes of carbon.[490] Yet, due to the classification of biomass as zero-carbon, almost none of these emissions were included in the UK's GHG reports.[491]

16.225 Carbon emissions arise from biomass use in four ways:[492]

- Reduced carbon stock. Harvesting feedstock from forests reduces the carbon stock in trees and soil. As forests take an average of 50 to 120 years to regrow to their previous level of carbon storage, this creates a time lag and leads to foregone carbon sequestration. If forests are continuously harvested for biomass, the loss in carbon stock will never be fully recovered, thus hampering carbon reduction in the long-run.

- Land-use change. Converting forests to agricultural land for growing bioenergy crops exacerbates deforestation and global warming.

- Opportunity costs. Instead of using land for biomass harvesting, greater climate benefits could be gained from alternative actions, such as the restoration of forests.

- Additional emissions. The use of BECCS technology itself can generate additional carbon emissions. While the most notable concern is of carbon leakage from carbon storage sites, other emission sources include supply chain emissions and the increased use of fertiliser to grow biomass.

16.226 Against that, the government sets out that a key commitment in the Biomass Strategy itself is to develop and implement a cross-sectoral common sustainability framework, which will involve strengthening the sustainability criteria.[493]

16.227 Other legal challenges regarding biomass projects have also arisen. In 2024, Biofuelwatch UK launched a challenge against the Energy Secretary, Claire Countinho's, grant of a Development Consent Order ('DCO') to Drax Power Limited, for plans to install BECCS technology in up to two biomass units at its power plants. Biofuelwatch argued that the granted DCO is 'unlawful', as it fell short of the requirements of the Infrastructure Planning (Environmental Impact Assessment) Regulations 2017 on three grounds:[494]

---

490 Chatham House, 'Why Burning Biomass Is Not Zero-Carbon' <https://www.chathamhouse.org/2022/10/why-burning-biomass-not-zero-carbon> accessed 21 June 2024.
491 ibid.
492 Fern, 'Six Problems with BECCS' (2018) <https://www.fern.org/fileadmin/uploads/fern/Documents/2021/Six_problems_with_BECCS.pdf> accessed 21 June 2024.
493 Department for Energy Security and Net Zero, 'Biomass Strategy' (n 451) 6.
494 Leigh Day, 'Biofuelwatch Issues Legal Challenge to Decision to Allow Carbon Capture Installation at Drax Power Plant' <https://www.leighday.co.uk/news/news/2024-news/biofuelwatch-issues-legal-challenge-to-decision-to-allow-carbon-capture-installation-at-drax-power-plant/#:~:text=It%20would%20effectively%20allow%20the,further%20%C2%A3617m%20in%202022.> accessed 21 June 2024.

- First, the Secretary of State 'failed to assess the significant GHG impacts of the proposed project, by irrationally deciding that it would lead to a net reduction in GHG emissions by zero rating the combustion emissions';
- Second, there was 'a failure to account for the GHG emissions from the combustion of biomass at the units to be fitted with carbon capture technology'. In particular, it was 'wrongly decided that the combustion emissions were not an effect of the project that needed to be assessed in their own right';
- Third, there was 'a failure to consider the combined environmental impacts of the proposed project with the additional works to construct and operate transport and storage facilities for the captured carbon'.

16.228 Overall, the campaign group argued that the unabated burning of biomass would be 'economically unviable beyond 2027, meaning emissions from its continued use were additional and should have been assessed'.[495] Biofuelwatch's Co-Director, Robert Palgrave, stated that:[496]

> Far from slowing climate change, Drax BECCS will do the opposite, and it will continue to damage forests and biodiversity in the countries supplying Drax's woodfuel. At the heart of our challenge is a fundamental point - that carbon emissions from burning wood impact the climate with immediate effect, just like those from coal or gas. They must no longer be discounted when planning decisions are made.
>
> In granting development consent for Drax BECCS, Claire Coutinho ignored the self-evident fact that burning wood produces carbon emissions, hiding behind an obscure accounting convention that says such emissions can be zero-rated in national greenhouse gas inventories.

(b) Biomass subsidies

16.229 The government's continued reliance on biomass to meet its net zero goals, coupled with its heavy financial contributions, raises questions over the extent of resources currently channelled into biomass. The Biofuelwatch challenge also highlighted the issue of biomass subsidies, by noting that Drax had received £893 million in renewable energy subsidies in 2021, followed by a further £617 million in 2022.[497] The granted DCO would allow Drax to continue benefitting from such subsidies, until 2035.

16.230 More broadly, a 2024 report by the National Audit Office ('NAO'), found that since 2002, the government has provided £22 billion in financial subsidies to support

---

495 ibid.

496 Tess Colley, 'Government Threatened with Legal Action over Approval of Drax Carbon Capture Plans' [2024] *ENDS Report* <https://www.endsreport.com/article/1861100/government-threatened-legal-action-approval-drax-carbon-capture-plans> accessed 21 June 2024.

497 Leigh Day, 'Biofuelwatch Issues Legal Challenge to Decision to Allow Carbon Capture Installation at Drax Power Plant' (n 494).

biomass use.[498] However, the NAO observed a 'lack of evaluation' as to the credibility and effectiveness of sustainability criteria, made further complicated by the 'long, complex supply chains for biomass'. As a result, it recommended the need for more stringent mechanisms to ensure compliance with sustainability criteria, including the need to ensure 'assurance over the billions of pounds involved'.[499]

498 National Audit Office, *The Government's Support for Biomass* (HC 2024, 358) 20 <https://www.nao.org.uk/wp-content/uploads/2024/01/Repo rt-the-governments-support-for-biomass.pdf> accessed 21 June 2024.
499 ibid 10.

CHAPTER 17

TRANSITION FROM FOSSIL FUELS

Stephanie David, Gethin Thomas and Daniel Kozelko

Introduction

17.01 The continued expansion of fossil fuel productions is antithetical to net zero. As explained by the United Nations Environment Programme, in its 2021 Production Gap Report, fossil fuel production must be reduced if the 1.5°C Paris Agreement target is to be met:[1]

> As countries set net-zero emission targets, and increase their climate ambitions under the Paris Agreement, they have not explicitly recognized or planned for the rapid reduction in fossil fuel production that these targets will require. Rather, the world's governments plan to produce more than twice the amount of fossil fuels in 2030 than would be consistent with limiting warming to 1.5°C.

17.02 The International Energy Agency has also warned that no new oil and gas fields are consistent with the 1.5°C target.[2]

17.03 Similarly, as the Climate Change Committee ('CCC') observed, in its report 'Progress in reducing emissions 2023 Report to Parliament' (June 2023):

> **Expansion of fossil fuel production is not in line with Net Zero.** As well as pushing forward strongly with new low-carbon industries, Net Zero also makes it necessary to move away from high-carbon developments. The decision on the Cumbrian coal mine sent a very concerning signal on the Government's priorities. The UK will continue to need some oil and gas until it reaches Net Zero, but this does not in itself justify the development of new North Sea Fields. (emphasis in original)

17.04 The CCC's scenarios for meeting the sixth carbon budget and achieving net zero by 2050 require 'large and rapid reductions in consumption of oil and gas', as do those relied upon by the government.[3] The CCC pathways provide as follows:[4]

---

1 UNEP, 'Production Gap Report 2021' (2021) 4 <https://productiongap.org/wp-content/uploads/2021/11/PGR2021_web_rev.pdf> accessed 10 May 2024.
2 International Energy Agency, 'Net Zero by 2050: A Roadmap for the Global Energy Sector' (2021) 21 <https://iea.blob.core.windows.net/assets/deebef5d-0c34-4539-9d0c-10b13d840027/NetZeroby2050-ARoadmapfortheGlobalEnergySector_CORR.pdf> accessed 10 May 2024.
3 Climate Change Committee, 'Letter: Climate Compatibility of New Oil and Gas Fields' (2022) <https://www.theccc.org.uk/publication/letter-climate-compatibility-of-new-oil-and-gas-fields/> accessed 10 May 2024.
4 ibid.

> [O]il consumption falls by 46–62% by 2035 and 84–98% by 2050, while unabated consumption of fossil gas (i.e. use without CCS) falls by around 65% by 2035 and is virtually eliminated by 2050. Even with a significant role for CCS, total UK gas consumption must fall by 50% by 2035 and 75% by 2050.

17.05 Progress is being made. At COP 28 in Dubai in 2023, the parties to the UNFCCC agreed to 'transition away from fossil fuels' (although stopped short of committing to 'phasing out') as part of the first global stocktake in accordance with Article 14 of the Paris Agreement.[5]

17.06 In 2023, the amount of electricity generated in the UK from fossil fuels fell 22% year-on-year, to the lowest level since 1957. Fossil fuels constituted just 33% of UK electricity supplies, a reduction of some 7% on 2022. Over the period 1990 to 2021 emissions from electricity generation fell by 73%; much of that was driven by this move away from coal.[6]

17.07 However, the government continues to support both onshore and offshore oil and gas production in the UK. Under section 9A of the Petroleum Act 1998 ('PA 1998'), the 'principal objective' of the oil and gas licensing regime is 'maximising the economic recovery of UK petroleum' (known as the 'MER' duty). The North Sea Transition Authority ('NSTA') (formerly the Oil and Gas Authority ('OGA')) is obliged to produce a strategy to enable the MER duty to be met.

17.08 In *R (Cox) v Oil and Gas Authority*,[7] the High Court dismissed a challenge to the OGA's definition of 'economically recoverable' in its strategy which contended it was inconsistent with the statutory term 'maximising the economic recovery of UK petroleum' in section 9A of the PA 1998 and frustrated the statutory purpose. The OGA's strategy gave a definition of 'economically recoverable' which included 'resources which could be recovered at an expected (pre-tax) market value greater than the expected (pre-tax) resource cost of their extraction'. The court's primary conclusion was that the definition was a matter for the OGA, as the expert regulator (subject to the usual public law supervisory controls), but that, in any event, its definition was correct.

17.09 It remains to be seen whether the progress made will continue in order to meet the government's target of 95% low-carbon energy by 2030, and a decarbonised electricity system by 2035.[8]

---

5 Nidhi Singal, 'COP28 Success: Nations Agree to Transition Away from Fossil Fuels' (*Business Today*, 15 December 2023) <https://www.businesstoday.in/cop28/story/cop28-success-nations-agree-to-transition-away-from-fossil-fuels-409540-2023-12-15> accessed 10 May 2024. See also Summary of Global Climate Action at COP 28, 11 December 2023; and First Global Stocktake, Proposal by the President FCCC/PA/CMA/2023/L.17.

6 National Grid ESO, 'FES 2023 Data Workbook' NZ.01 <https://www.nationalgrideso.com/future-energy/future-energy-scenarios-fes> accessed 10 May 2024. National Grid ESO became the National Energy System Operator in October 2024.

7 *R (Cox) v Oil and Gas Authority* [2022] EWHC 75 (Admin).

8 Simon Evans and Verner Viisainen, 'Analysis: UK Electricity from Fossil Fuels Drops to Lowest Level since 1957' (Carbon Brief, 3 January 2024) <https://www.carbonbrief.org/analysis-uk-electricity-from-fossil-fuels-drops-to-lowest-level-since-1957/> accessed 10 May 2024.

17.10 This chapter will address: (a) UK offshore oil and gas production, (b) UK onshore oil and gas production, (c) the further development of fossil fuel energy infrastructure in the UK, and (d) the residual role of coal in the UK's energy supply mix. The focus is on the shift away from fossil fuels. It does not address the planning and wider consenting regimes for fossil fuels in any detail.[9]

UK offshore oil and gas production

17.11 The UK Continental Shelf ('UKCS') is a mature hydrocarbon basin. It contains oil and gas reserves which have been exploited since 1967. The NSTA estimates that there remains approximately 10 to 20 billion barrels of oil equivalent remaining in the UKCS. UK production has significantly decreased, having more than halved since 2000.[10] The majority of crude oil produced in the UKCS is exported, whereas a significant proportion of the natural gas produced is combusted domestically.

(i) *North Sea Transition Deal*

17.12 On 24 March 2021, the government agreed the North Sea Transition Deal ('NSTD'), a partnership with the offshore oil and gas sector. The NSTD introduced a voluntary target to reduce the production of upstream greenhouse gas ('GHG') emissions by 50% in 2030 (against a 2018 baseline), reaching net zero by 2050. In 2018, upstream oil and gas activities in the UK accounted for 4% of total UK GHG emissions.[11]

17.13 The NSTD recognises the need for the transition from fossil fuel production and reliance. It observes:[12]

> Moving away from unabated greenhouse gas emissions resulting from combustion of fossil fuels will be achieved through a combination of energy efficiency, electrification, alternative decarbonised energy and the use of carbon capture technologies. The pace of this transition must be managed to balance the need to decarbonise with the need to maintain energy security and affordability. The oil and gas sector is committed to net-zero but it is a sector that is hard to abate, in view of the location and nature of the assets involved and it is exposed to international competition. It is therefore necessary to ensure that the costs of abatement are manageable and mitigate the risk of a relocation of production (and therefore carbon leakage) abroad and reduced investment in a strategic UK industry.

---

9 For example, environmental permits and permissions are also needed from the Environment Agency in relation to onshore oil and gas, see further: https://www.gov.uk/guidance/onshore-oil-and-gas-sector-guidance.
10 OGA, 'UK Oil and Gas Reserves and Resources' (2019) <https://www.nstauthority.co.uk/media/6681/uk_oil-gas-rr_2020.pdf>.
11 Department for Business, Energy and Industrial Strategy, 'North Sea Transition Deal One Year On' (2022) 6 <https://assets.publishing.service.gov.uk/media/6238513ee90e077999320564/north-sea-transition-deal-one-year-on.pdf>.
12 Department for Business, Energy and Industrial Strategy, 'North Sea Transition Deal' (2021) 8 <https://assets.publishing.service.gov.uk/media/605b148ce90e0724c7d30c2b/north-sea-transition-deal_A_FINAL.pdf>.

> Oil and gas production will still be needed during the transition, but at lower levels than today. The delivery of this transformative plan, which is supported by elements of the North Sea Transition Deal, will enable the oil and gas sector to drive the energy transition by developing and deploying a range of technologies, transforming the UK supply chain, securing jobs, and protecting and building successful local communities.

17.14 The NSTD also emphasises the importance of significantly reducing gas flaring and venting (both onshore and offshore), as they are major sources of methane emissions.

17.15 On 21 March 2022, the government published, 'North Sea Transition Deal One Year On'. On supply decarbonisation, it noted as follows:[13]

> In 2018, upstream oil and gas activities in the UK accounted for four percent of UK greenhouse gas emissions at some 19 million tonnes. Progress has been good, with overall upstream greenhouse gas emissions falling by 11%, since 2018, as reported in the Emissions Monitoring Report. Flaring in the UK North Sea fell by 19% in 2021, building on a 22% decrease the previous year, with venting cut by 24%.

17.16 The government's policy in relation to flaring and venting abatement is also in line with its commitment to the World Bank's 'Zero Routine Flaring by 2030' initiative and the sector's target of a 50% reduction in emissions by 2030 and 100% by 2050.[14]

(ii) *Net Zero Strategy*

17.17 In October 2021, the government published its Net Zero Strategy ('NZS'). The NZS specifically recognises the importance of the transition from reliance on fossil fuels. It notes:[15]

> Removing dirty fossil fuels will require the transformation of every sector of the global economy. It means no longer burning fossil fuels for power or heating; it means new ways of making concrete, cement, steel; it means the end of the petrol and diesel engine.

17.18 The NZS primarily relies on alternative energy sources and technologies, in particular, electricity, hydrogen, carbon capture usage and storage, and biomass, to reduce reliance on fossil fuels considerably.

17.19 On UK fossil fuel production, the NZS states (amongst other things):[16]

> We have always been clear that as we reduce our dependence on fossil fuels, the North Sea basin has a key role to play. Our approach will ensure that it does contribute to the

---

13 Department for Business, Energy and Industrial Strategy, 'North Sea Transition Deal: One Year On' (n 11) 6.
14 See Department for Energy Security and Net Zero, 'Carbon Budget Delivery Plan' (2023) HC 1269, policy 62 at page 63 and para 18 at page 176 <https://assets.publishing.service.gov.uk/media/6424b2d760a35e000c0cb135/carbon-budget-delivery-plan.pdf> accessed 4 April 2024.
15 Department for Energy Security and Net Zero, 'Net Zero Strategy: Build Back Greener' (2021) 15 <https://www.gov.uk/government/publications/net-zero-strategy> accessed 28 September 2023.
16 ibid 112 [20], [23].

> transition, driving investment in transition technologies and providing the skills needed for net zero. However, we are clear that we do need to reduce our reliance on hydrocarbons as swiftly as possible. The best way to protect British businesses and consumers from volatile international fossil fuel markets is to get our economy off hydrocarbons.
>
> …
>
> Step-change abatement will be delivered by the electrification of existing and new offshore assets, through connections to onshore networks or offshore renewables. We will work with regulators to review supporting infrastructure in the Offshore Transmission Network Review and to address regulatory barriers. We will support removing further barriers through £1 million of additional funding from 2021 to 2022.

17.20 The NZS committed to the introduction of a formal climate compatibility checkpoint on future licensing rounds for oil and gas exploration. Its stated intention was to ensure that future licensing rounds are only awarded following a compatibility assessment against the government's broad climate change ambitions, including reaching net zero by 2050. The climate compatibility checkpoint that was ultimately produced is addressed further below at paragraphs 17.23–17.27.

(iii) *British Energy Security Strategy*

17.21 On 7 April 2022, shortly after the Russian invasion of Ukraine, the government published the British Energy Security Strategy ('BESS').[17] It committed to securing 95% of energy from low-carbon sources by 2030, with full decarbonisation by 2035.[18]

17.22 It also committed to reducing the UK's reliance on imported fossil fuels by fully utilising the reserves of oil and gas in the North Sea. That need to have continued access to fossil fuels reflects the fact that in 2022 annual natural gas demand was 986TWh,[19] with 90% of homes in the UK heated by fossil fuels accounting for a third of overall gas use.[20] Indeed, assuming the best case, National Grid ESO (now, since October 2024, the National Energy System Operator) predict that consumer demand for gas alone will only fall below 100TWh in 2040.[21] The BESS also confirmed the launch of a new North Sea oil and gas licensing round.

17 Department for Business, Energy and Industrial Strategy, Department for Energy Security and Net Zero and Prime Minister's Office, 'British Energy Security Strategy' (2022) <https://www.gov.uk/government/publications/british-energy-security-strategy/british-energy-security-strategy> accessed 10 May 2024.
18 ibid 6.
19 National Grid ESO, 'Future Energy Scenarios 2023 (July 2023)' (2023) 13 <https://www.nationalgrideso.com/document/283101/download> accessed 10 May 2024. National Grid ESO became the National Energy System Operator in October 2024.
20 Department for Business, Energy and Industrial Strategy, Department for Energy Security and Net Zero and Prime Minister's Office, 'British Energy Security Strategy' (n 17).
21 National Grid ESO, 'FES 2023 Data Workbook' (n 6) EC.04.

(iv) *Climate change compatibility checkpoint*

17.23 Between 20 December 2021 and 28 February 2022, the Secretary of State ran a consultation on the design of the climate change compatibility checkpoint. The aim of the checkpoint is 'to ensure that before a new oil and gas licensing round is offered, the compatibility of future licensing with the UK's climate objectives is evaluated.[22] It sits alongside other regulatory frameworks, including the OGA Strategy and the Offshore Petroleum Regulator for Environment and Decommissioning ('OPRED').

17.24 On 22 September 2022, the checkpoint design was published. It constituted three tests:[23]

- The first test 'compares the performance and projected performance of the UK oil and gas industry against the emissions targets set out by the North Sea Transition Deal (NSTD) which were agreed to by the sector in 2021'.
- The second test 'benchmarks the UK oil and gas sector against other global producers in terms of associated production emissions'.
- The third test 'evaluates whether the UK is expected to remain a net importer of oil and gas', defined as whether the UK is expected to continue to need to import oil and gas to meet UK energy demand.

17.25 The checkpoint was stated to be 'presented as an informative, data and narrative-based exercise designed to inform Ministers on whether to endorse the NSTA in launching a new round'.[24]

(v) *Thirty third offshore licensing round*

17.26 On 17 March 2022, the Secretary of State issued a consultation on its Offshore Energy Strategic Environmental Assessment ('OESEA4') Environmental Report ('the Environmental Report'), which was prepared as part of BEIS's Offshore Energy Strategic Environmental Assessment ('SEA') of its draft plan/programme for offshore energy. OESEA4 was carried out for the purposes of complying with the Environmental Assessment of Plans and Programmes Regulations 2004[25] ('the SEA Regulations 2004'). The draft plan/programme was:

> Exploration and production – further Seaward Rounds of oil and gas licensing of the UK territorial sea and UK Continental Shelf (UKCS), subject to the outcome of periodic Climate Compatibility Checkpoints.

22 Department for Business, Energy and Industrial Strategy, 'Climate Compatibility Checkpoint Design' (2022) <https://assets.publishing.service.gov.uk/media/64a5a4c37a4c23000cbba22e/climate-compatibility-checkpoint-design.pdf> accessed 10 May 2024.
23 ibid 8.
24 ibid 8.
25 SI 2004/1633.

17.27 On 22 September 2022, the Secretary of State issued a written ministerial statement headed 'Energy Update' ('the WMS'), formally endorsing a new licensing round.

17.28 In the WMS, the Secretary of State stated that (in summary):[26]

- The government had completed OESEA4 on a draft plan/programme to enable further offshore licensing/leasing for offshore marine renewables including wind, wave and tidal energy, oil and gas, gas storage including carbon dioxide storage, and offshore production and transport of hydrogen.

- The government had decided to adopt the draft plan/programme 'with the area offered restricted spatially through the exclusion of certain areas together with a number of mitigation measures to prevent, reduce and offset significant adverse impacts on the environment and other users of the sea'.

- No overriding environmental considerations would prevent the achievement of the draft plan/programme:

> Having reviewed the results of these tests in the context of a 33rd licensing round, it has been decided that a 33rd licensing round is compatible with the UK's climate objectives.

17.29 The Secretary of State explained that the NSTA would shortly be launching a new licensing round for oil and gas exploration, and the round could result in the award of 'more than 100 licences'. He also stated that the plan/programme based on OESEA4 would have a lifespan of approximately four years.[27]

17.30 On 7 October 2022, the NSTA launched the 33rd oil and gas licensing round, by issuing an invitation for interested persons to apply for seaward area production licences pursuant to section 3 of the PA 1998.[28] A notice of the announcement was published in the London Gazette.[29]

17.31 On 13 October 2022, the NSTA announced (via its website) that an additional 34 blocks would be offered within the 33rd licensing round.[30]

17.32 In *R (Greenpeace Ltd and Uplift) v Secretary of State for Energy Security and Net Zero*,[31] two environmental campaigning organisations judicially reviewed the decision to launch a new licensing round. The central issue was whether the Secretary of State

---

26 Jacob Rees-Mogg, 'Energy Update: Statement UIN HCWS295' <https://questions-statements.parliament.uk/written-statements/detail/2022-09-22/hcws295> accessed 10 May 2024.
27 ibid.
28 North Sea Transition Authority, 'Licencing' <https://www.nstauthority.co.uk/regulatory-information/licensing-and-consents/licensing/> accessed 10 May 2024.
29 OGA, 'Announcement of United Kingdom 33rd Offshore Oil and Gas Licensing Round' (2022) <https://www.nstauthority.co.uk/media/8417/33rd-offshore-oil-and-gas-round-gazzette-notice-final.pdf>.
30 North Sea Transition Authority, 'Licencing' (n 28).
31 *R (Greenpeace Ltd and Uplift) v Secretary of State for Energy Security and Net Zero* [2023] EWHC 2608 (Admin), [2024] PTSR 345.

acted unlawfully by not including in his assessment of the plan downstream emissions of greenhouse gases from the end use by consumers of oil and gas as a fuel.

17.33 In dismissing the claims, Holgate J concluded that the Secretary of State had not acted irrationally in deciding not to assess end-use emissions on the basis that there was an insufficient causal connection between the plan's policy and emissions from end uses. In particular, Holgate J explained that the Secretary of State's decision was sufficient, on the basis that the new licensing round did not 'set a framework for decisions on development consents for downstream development such as refinement, storage and distribution, or electricity generation or other land uses involving the consumption of oil and gas extracted pursuant to a UK licence'.[32] Moreover, Holgate J also dismissed the claimants' challenge to the failure to include any consideration of end-use emissions within the climate compatibility checkpoint.

17.34 Greenpeace and Uplift were refused permission to appeal by the Court of Appeal.

17.35 So far, some 51 new licences have been issued by the NSTA under the 33rd licensing round.[33]

17.36 In December 2023, Greenpeace and Uplift sought permission for separate judicial review challenges, in the Scottish Court of Session, to the government's decision to allow development of Rosebank, the UK's largest unexploited North Sea oilfield.[34] Following the decision in *R (Finch) v Surrey CC* (addressed in more detail in paragraphs 7.59–7.64 of Chapter 7), the government determined not to defend the grant of consent.[35] Permission was granted for the Greenpeace and Uplift judicial review in September 2024.[36]

(vi) *Powering Up Britain*

17.37 On 30 March 2023, the government published its 'Powering Up Britain' policy paper. Notably, it commits to the replacement of imported fossil fuels with 'cheaper, cleaner, domestic sources of energy'. In particular, it states:[37]

> We will be powered by renewables including wind and solar, hydrogen, power with carbon capture, usage and storage (CCUS) and new nuclear plants - while recognising

---

32 ibid [105].

33 North Sea Transition Authority, '24 Licences Offered in Second Tranche of 33rd Oil and Gas Licensing Round' (2024) <https://www.nstauthority.co.uk/news-publications/24-licences-offered-in-second-tranche-of-33rd-oil-and-gas-licensing-round/> accessed 10 May 2024.

34 Phil Richards, 'Uplift and Greenpeace Take Government to Court to Stop Rosebank Oil Field' (*Greenpeace UK*, 18 December 2023) <https://www.greenpeace.org.uk/news/uplift-greenpeace-rosebank-legal-case/> accessed 10 May 2024.

35 *R (Finch) v Surrey CC* [2023] EWHC 2608 (Admin) [2024] PTSR 988. BBC, 'UK government will not fight Rosebank oil field legal challenge' (29 August 2024) <https://www.bbc.co.uk/news/articles/c30393m4z50o> accessed 23 October 2024.

36 BBC, 'Legal challenge to Rosebank oil field given go-ahead' (25 September 2024) <https://www.bbc.co.uk/news/articles/cx2m8zn95x1o> accessed 23 October 2024.

37 Department for Energy Security and Net Zero, 'Powering Up Britain' (2023) 5 <https://assets.publishing.service.gov.uk/media/642468ff2fa8480013ec0f39/powering-up-britain-joint-overview.pdf> accessed 4 April 2024.

the vital role that UK oil and gas will play in the transition. This will make us much more energy independent, to protect us from volatile international energy markets, while underpinning our clean energy transition, so the UK becomes a net zero economy by 2050. It will also help us make sure the UK has among the cheapest wholesale electricity prices in Europe by 2035.

(vii) *Offshore Petroleum Licensing Bill 2023–24*

17.38 On 8 November 2023, the government introduced the Offshore Petroleum Licensing Bill 2023–24 into Parliament. The primary purpose of the Bill is to impose a new duty upon the NSTA to run annual application rounds for new offshore oil and gas licences.

17.39 The obligation to invite applications, on an annual basis, for new licences would be triggered only where two tests are met:[38]

- Carbon intensity test: that the average carbon intensity of domestic (UK) gas is lower than the average carbon intensity of imported liquefied natural gas (LNG).
- Net importer test: that the UK remains a net importer of both oil and gas.

17.40 The Impact Assessment, published alongside the Bill, notes:[39]

Oil and gas will continue to play an important role as the UK transitions to a low carbon economy. There are currently 284 active oil and gas fields in the North Sea and by 2030 around 180 of those will have ceased production due to natural decline. If maturing oil and gas fields are not replaced with new ones, it could potentially mean that the rate of production will likely decline much faster than can be replaced with lower carbon alternatives. For the UK's energy security it is therefore critical that the domestic oil and gas sector remains able to access significant levels of investment.

(viii) *OGA plan to reduce UKCS greenhouse gas emissions*

17.41 On 27 March 2024, the NSTA published a new plan to reduce UKCS GHG emissions. It acknowledges, upfront, the requirement for 'rapid and sustained reductions in oil and gas production emissions'.[40]

17.42 The plan emphasises the role of electrification and low-carbon power, and further relies upon investment and efficiency, focus on inventory as a whole, and action on flaring and venting.

38 Offshore Petroleum Licensing Bill 2023–2024 (as introduced), clause 1. Proposing to introduce a new ss 4ZA–4ZC into the PA 1998.
39 Department for Energy Security and Net Zero, 'Offshore Petroleum Licensing Bill Impact Assessment' (2023) para 4.1 <https://publications.parliament.uk/pa/bills/cbill/58-04/0009/20231107OffshorePetroleumLicensingBillImpactAssessment.pdf>.
40 North Sea Transition Authority, 'OGA Plan to Reduce UKCS Greenhouse Gas Emissions' (2024) <https://www.nstauthority.co.uk/media/laidjfqb/oga-plan-to-reduce-ukcs-greenhouse-gas-emissions.pdf>.

UK onshore oil and gas production

17.43 The focus of decarbonisation initiatives in the oil and gas sector is mostly on offshore oil and gas.[41] The Infrastructure Act 2015 ('IA 2015') did, however, introduce a new statutory duty on the government to seek advice from the CCC on the impact 'which combustion of, and fugitive emissions from, petroleum got through onshore activity in England is likely' to have on the government's ability to meet the net zero target and the carbon budgets.[42] Where 'petroleum' is defined as including:[43]

> (a) any mineral oil or relative hydrocarbon and natural gas existing in its natural condition in strata; but
>
> (b) does not include coal or bituminous shales or other stratified deposits from which oil can be extracted by destructive distillation.

17.44 The IA 2015 then defines 'petroleum got through onshore activity in England' as 'petroleum got from the strata in which it exists in its natural condition by activity carried out on land in England (excluding land covered by the sea or any tidal waters)'.[44]

17.45 In their most recent advice, prepared pursuant to section 49(1) of the IA 2015 and published on 21 March 2021, the CCC explained as follows:[45]

> Onshore petroleum is another source of fossil fuels, the consumption of which must fall sharply on the path to Net Zero. The Committee's Balanced Net Zero Pathway requires reductions in oil consumption of 47% by 2035 and 77% by 2050 and in unabated fossil gas combustion of 65% by 2035 and 99% by 2050 (see Annex). These are larger drops in demand than that identified as part of our Fifth Carbon Budget advice in 2015.

(i) *Nature of onshore oil and gas production*

17.46 Sources of onshore oil and gas production in the UK include conventional oil and gas, shale gas, shale oil and coalbed methane.[46] Conventional oil and gas accumulations are contained in permeable rocks; whereas in unconventional accumulations (such as shale gas and coal bed methane), the rock acts as a source, reservoir and cap rock.[47]

---

41 See, for example Department for Energy Security and Net Zero, 'Carbon Budget Delivery Plan' (HC 2023, 1269) 176 <https://assets.publishing.service.gov.uk/media/6424b2d760a35e000c0cb135/carbon-budget-delivery-plan.pdf> accessed 4 April 2024.
42 IA 2015 s 49(1).
43 IA 2015 s 49(7), which defines 'petroleum' by reference to s 1 of the PA 1998.
44 IA 2015 s 49(7).
45 CCC, 'Letter: Advice to the UK Government on Compatibility of Onshore Petroleum with UK Carbon Budgets' (2021) <https://www.theccc.org.uk/publication/letter-advice-to-the-uk-government-on-compatibility-of-onshore-petroleum-with-uk-carbon-budgets/> accessed 10 May 2024.
46 ibid footnote 1.
47 Department for Energy and Climate Change, 'Onshore Oil and Gas Exploration in the UK: Regulation and Best Practice' (2015) 6 <https://assets.publishing.service.gov.uk/media/5a758c14ed915d6faf2b3d48/Onshore_UK_oil_and_gas_exploration_England_Dec15.pdf>; British Geological Survey, 'Shale Gas' (British Geological Survey) <https://www.bgs.ac.uk/geology-projects/shale-gas/> accessed 10 May 2024.

17.47 Shale is a 'fine-grained, sedimentary rock formed as a result of the compaction of clay, silt, mud and organic matter over time and is usually considered equivalent to mudstone'.[48] Shale gas is found in deposits of shale; where it is trapped in microscopic or sub-microscopic pores.[49] Given that shale gas is stored within impermeable shale, it is an unconventional accumulation of hydrocarbons that requires extraction by a process of hydraulic fracturing ('fracking').[50] Coalbed methane arises as a result of a process called adsorption whereby gas becomes bound with coal.[51] When the pressure is reduced often as a by-product of mining, the gas (methane) is released from the coal.[52]

17.48 In very brief summary, fracking involves pumping a mixture of water, chemicals and sand down a borehole at a high pressure, which cracks open the rocks, sand grains enter the space to keep them open and the gas is released.[53] The process of extracting the coalbed methane involves drilling a well into a coal seam and water is pumped out, which lowers the pressure in the seam and the methane desorbs from the surfaces of the coal (a process known as 'dewatering').[54]

(ii) *Government policy*

17.49 Government policy in relation to onshore oil and gas extraction has been variable, particularly in the context of fracking.

17.50 The government has oscillated in its commitment to exploration around shale gas, principally because of safety concerns dating back to seismic activity in 2011 during shale gas exploration.[55]

17.51 On 2 November 2019, the government introduced the fracking moratorium based on a report by NSTA, which concluded that it was not possible to predict accurately the probability of earthquakes associated with fracking.[56] The report had considered seismic activities related to fracking at Preston New Road.[57] The PA 1998 had been amended by the IA 2015 introducing the requirement of a Hydraulic Fracturing Consent from the Secretary of State.[58] The government confirmed that it was adopting a 'presumption

48 British Geological Survey, 'Shale Gas' (n 47).
49 ibid.
50 ibid; British Geological Survey, 'Shale Gas Extraction' (British Geological Survey) <https://www.bgs.ac.uk/geology-projects/shale-gas/shale-gas-extraction/> accessed 10 May 2024.
51 Department for Energy and Climate Change, 'The Unconventional Hydrocarbon Resources of Britain's Onshore Basins – Shale Gas' (2013) 1 <https://www.nstauthority.co.uk/media/1693/shalegas_uk.pdf>.
52 ibid 1.
53 British Geological Survey, 'Shale Gas Extraction' (n 50).
54 Department for Energy and Climate Change, 'The Unconventional Hydrocarbon Resources of Britain's Onshore Basins – Shale Gas' (n 51) 1.
55 Andrea Leadsom, 'Energy Policy Update: Statement UIN HCWS68' <https://questions-statements.parliament.uk/written-statements/detail/2019-11-04/HCWS68> accessed 10 May 2024.
56 Department for Business, Energy and Industrial Strategy and others, 'Government Ends Support for Fracking' (GOV.UK, 2019) <https://www.gov.uk/government/news/government-ends-support-for-fracking> accessed 10 May 2024.
57 North Sea Transition Authority, 'Preston New Road – Well PNR2 – Data Studies' <https://www.nstauthority.co.uk/regulatory-information/exploration-and-production/onshore/onshore-reports-and-data/preston-new-road-well-pnr2-data-studies/> accessed 10 May 2024.
58 PA 1998 s 4A (as introduced by IA 2015 s 50).

against issuing any further Hydraulic Fracturing Consents', on a precautionary approach, but would still consider any applications for such a consent on its merits.[59]

17.52 In the BESS, published on 7 April 2022, the government noted that:[60]

> We will send clear signals on the role of gas in the transition: …
>
> - remaining open-minded about our onshore reserves. We have commissioned an impartial technical review on shale gas by the British Geological Survey to consider any further scientific updates on seismicity that the govt ought to consider. The pause continues to remain in place unless new evidence emerges. Any exploration or development of shale gas would need to meet rigorous safety and environmental protection both above ground and sub-surface.

17.53 In September 2022, the government under (then) Prime Minister Liz Truss lifted the moratorium setting out the policy position that 'all means' should be pursued for increasing UK gas production. Emphasis was put on the need for 'local support' in the context of considering applications for hydraulic fracturing consents.[61] What exactly 'local support' meant, however, was unclear, as became apparent during the debate on the Ban on Fracking for Shale Gas Bill on 19 October 2022.[62]

17.54 On 27 October 2022, it was confirmed that the moratorium was to be re-imposed, so that the government does 'not support shale extraction unless the science shows categorically that it can be done safely'.[63]

17.55 The CCC has advised that, even if the safety concerns are overcome, the moratorium should not be lifted unless a detailed independent review of the climate impact is undertaken, which should involve consideration of the government's net zero strategy, international plans on decarbonisation and fossil production, 'lifecycle emissions of UK unconventional fossil fuel production and alternative sources of supply', and progress of deployment of zero-carbon hydrogen and CCS.[64]

17.56 In terms of national planning policy, the NPPF deals with oil, gas, and coal[65] exploration and extraction at paragraph 221. It requires that minerals planning authorities should *inter alia* encourage: (i) carbon capture and storage, along with linked infrastructure; and (ii) 'the capture and use of methane from coal mines in active and abandoned coalfields'.

---

59 Leadsom, 'Energy Policy Update: Statement UIN HCWS68' (n 55).
60 Department for Business, Energy and Industrial Strategy, Department for Energy Security and Net Zero and Prime Minister's Office, 'British Energy Security Strategy' (n 17).
61 Rees-Mogg, 'Energy Update: Statement UIN HCWS295' (n 26).
62 HC Deb 19 October 2022, vol 720, col 748–804.
63 HC Deb 27 October 2022, vol 721, HCWS346.
64 Climate Change Committee, 'Letter: Advice to the UK Government on Compatibility of Onshore Petroleum with UK Carbon Budgets' (n 45).
65 Coal is addressed below from paragraph 17.76.

17.57 In Wales, the Welsh Ministers have the power to grant petroleum licences in relation to Welsh onshore areas.[66] The Welsh government confirmed, not long after they were granted that power, that it would not undertake any new petroleum licensing in Wales, nor support applications for fracking consents.[67]

(iii) *Case law relating to onshore oil and gas*

(a) Onshore crude oil extraction

17.58 There is a growing trend whereby GHG emissions themselves are directly informing part of a ground of challenge in relation to onshore oil and gas extraction, which has been accelerated by the Supreme Court's decision in *R (Finch) v Surrey CC* [2024] PTSR 988. This case has been addressed in some detail at paragraphs 7.59–7.64 in Chapter 7. In short, this case concerned the lawfulness of the Environmental Impact Assessment ('EIA') undertaken for the retention and expansion of an existing onshore oil well site and the drilling of four new wells in Surrey. The EIA had not assessed the environmental impacts of the downstream GHG emissions that would result when the extracted oil was later refined and used. It was agreed that if the project went ahead, the oil would be refined and the end product would undergo combustion. It was also agreed that it was possible to estimate the emissions produced by the combustion. The majority of the Supreme Court determined that this was a question of causation; and that on the agreed facts, if the project went ahead, all the extracted oil would be burnt and release GHG emissions (the amount of which could be estimated). The downstream emissions were indirect effects for the purpose of the EIA Directive and should have been factored into the EIA. There is no geographical limit on the scope of the environmental effects of a project.

17.59 The implications of the Supreme Court decision in *Finch* have already been felt. In the context of onshore oil and gas,[68] a judicial review challenge to the decision to grant permission for 15 years' of oil production in the Lincolnshire Wolds Area was conceded by the defendant and the developer, following *Finch*.[69]

17.60 In other cases, more traditional public law grounds of review are the focus but, for some claimants at least, seen through a net zero or nature positive lens depending upon their ultimate objectives. For instance, the lawfulness of planning permission for an exploratory oil and gas drilling site in Dunsfold was challenged, albeit unsuccessfully, in *Protect Dunsfold Ltd v Secretary of State for Levelling Up, Housing and Communities*.[70] The claimants challenged, by way of section 288 of the Town and Country Planning

---

66 PA 1998 s 8A (as amended by the Wales Act 2017 s 23).
67 Griffiths, 'Written Statement: Petroleum Extraction Policy Statement (10 December 2018) | GOV.WALES' (10 December 2018) <https://www.gov.wales/written-statement-petroleum-extraction-policy-statement> accessed 10 May 2024; see also the condition that needs to be imposed on any consent for a well in Wales: <https://law.gov.wales/environment/energy-and-climate-change/petroleum-licensing> accessed 10 May 2024.
68 See also para 17.79 below regarding Whitehaven coal mine.
69 Cornerstone Barristers, 'Lincolnshire oil drilling permission quashed after Supreme Court judgment in Finch' (2024) <https://cornerstonebarristers.com/lincolnshire-oil-drilling-permission-quashed-after-supreme-court-judgment-in-finch/#:~:text=Lincolnshire%20oil%20drilling%20permission%20quashed,judgment%20in%20Finch%20%7C%20Cornerstone%20Barristers> accessed 22 October 2024.
70 *Protect Dunsfold Ltd v Secretary of State for Levelling Up, Housing and Communities* [2023] EWHC 1854 (Admin), [2024] JPL 183.

Act 1990, the Secretary of State's decision to grant planning permission for the development. The site was south of the Surrey Hills Area of Outstanding Natural Beauty ('AONB').

17.61 The claim focused principally on the policy test in relation to AONBs in the NPPF at paragraph 176 (as it then was),[71] which required 'great weight' to be 'given to conserving and enhancing landscape and scenic beauty in' the AONB. The ground was dismissed; and Steyn J determined that the policy had been properly applied. She noted that the approach adopted by the inspector in deciding that the 'short-lived nature of the harm' was 'a key factor in concluding that only moderate weight should be given to the assessed harm is manifest in his conclusions'.[72] The second ground of challenge alleged that the decision was inconsistent with the Ellesmere Port decision, which concerned an appeal against the refusal of Cheshire West and Cheshire Council to refuse planning permission in relation to a development for natural gas extraction. The court determined that the Ellesmere Port decision was not sufficiently similar to require application of the consistency principle.

17.62 In *Frack Free Balcombe Residents Association v Secretary of State for Levelling Up, Housing and Communities*,[73] the grounds of challenge encompass both public law grounds through the net zero and nature positive lens, as well as those directly concerned with GHG emissions. Notwithstanding the claimant's name, this challenge concerned the grant of planning permission for the exploration and assessment of suitability of a site, located in an AONB, for commercial hydrocarbon production. The application was not directly concerned with fracking but the claimant had contended that future production may involve fracking.[74] The grounds included an unlawful failure to take into account the benefits, and not the disbenefits, of hydrocarbon production, a failure to consider alternative sites outside the AONB, a failure to comply the Town and Country Planning (Environmental Impact Assessment) Regulations 2017,[75] and a failure to consider the climate change impacts from the development.

17.63 Lieven J dismissed the claim and noted *inter alia* as follows:

- On benefit and disbenefits, the application was only concerned with exploration and therefore the focus should be the benefits and disbenefits of that particular phase; but, as part of the assessment of the benefits of exploration, the inspector was entitled to consider the matters relating to 'what would happen if viable

71 Department for Levelling Up, Housing and Communities, 'National Planning Policy Framework' (2023) para 182 <https://assets.publishing.service.gov.uk/media/65a11af7e8f5ec000f1f8c46/NPPF_December_2023.pdf> accessed 2 April 2024.
72 *Protect Dunsfold Ltd v Secretary of State for Levelling Up, Housing and Communities* (n 70) [56].
73 *Frack Free Balcombe Residents Association v Secretary of State for Levelling Up, Housing and Communities* [2023] EWHC 2548 (Admin), [2024] JPL 484.
74 ibid [26]–[27].
75 SI 2017/571.

hydrocarbons were found in the exploration phase'.[76] The disbenefits of production would be considered at that stage.[77]

- The question of alternatives had to be restricted to alternatives for the purpose of exploration, not production.[78] Further, she noted that:[79]

> It makes no sense of the policy, in the context of hydrocarbon exploration, to say that there should be no permission if there are alternatives for production elsewhere. It is completely obvious that there will be alternative hydrocarbon production sites both in the UK (onshore and offshore) and in other countries. Such an exercise would be pointless at the exploration stage but is likely to be highly relevant if there is ever a production application.

- On the EIA, she dismissed the argument that there had been 'salami-slicing'[80] and a failure to consider the project as a whole. In her judgment, the project was clearly defined as exploration and monitoring, not the subsequent commercial production.[81] In relation to the alleged failure to consider the GHG emissions from flaring at the site, she noted that, whilst the local planning authority did not expressly consider GHG emissions, the scale relative to the indicative threshold was small and, to be EIA development, there needed to be 'significant likely effects'.[82]

- Finally, Lieven J dismissed the argument that the inspector had failed to consider the climate change impacts of the development and considered that the inspector's reference in the decision letter was adequate.[83] She observed that:

> There is no requirement, whether in statute or caselaw, that every planning decision has to expressly refer to or quantify the GHG emissions that will result. Climate change is likely to be a material consideration in every planning decision given the policy context as well as the much wider issues, but that does not mean that every decision has to have reference to specific figures or assessment. Each case will depend on its own factual and policy context.

76 *Frack Free Balcombe Residents Association v Secretary of State for Levelling Up, Housing and Communities* (n 73) [18]–[19].
77 ibid [20].
78 ibid [38].
79 ibid [39].
80 *Ecologistas Accion-CODA v Ayuntameinto de Madrid* (Case C-142/07) EU:C:2008:445; [2009] PTSR 458.
81 *Frack Free Balcombe Residents Association v Secretary of State for Levelling Up, Housing and Communities* (n 73) [50].
82 ibid [55]–[56], [61].
83 ibid [65].

(b) Fracking litigation

17.64 Prior to the moratorium, there was unsurprisingly a significant number of judicial review challenges to individual decisions to grant planning permission for fracking and to regulatory challenges to the terms of various licences.[84]

17.65 Before considering challenges to individual decisions,[85] a successful challenge was brought, on consultation grounds, to national planning policy, namely the proposed revision of the NPPF to include paragraph 209(a), which concerned shale fracking in *R (Stephenson) v Secretary of State for Housing and Communities and Local Government.*[86] The paragraph stated as follows:[87]

> Minerals planning authorities should: (a) recognise the benefits of onshore oil and gas development, including unconventional hydrocarbons, for the security of energy supplies and supporting the transition to a low-carbon economy; and put in place policies to facilitate their exploration and extraction.

17.66 Dove J accepted that from examining the consultation documents the message to a reasonable reader was that the contents and substance of paragraph 209(a) were within the scope of the consultation.[88] Yet, the 'the defendant had a closed mind as to the content of the policy and was not undertaking the consultation at a formative stage'.[89] Thus, he concluded that the design and process of consultation was 'so flawed' that it was unlawful.[90] The claimant had put forward scientific evidence, as part of its consultation response, in relation to the climate impact of fracking having been underestimated. Given the consultation exercise was unlawful, this evidence was never taken into account.[91]

17.67 In *R (Frack Free Balcombe Residents Association) v West Sussex County Council,*[92] the claimant challenged a decision to grant planning permission in relation to the exploration and appraisal of an existing hydrocarbon lateral borehole. The focus of the

---

84 The focus in this section is on judicial review proceedings but there has been litigation relating to fracking across a number of different areas, including cases in which injunctions were granted to restrain allegedly unlawful protest activity at shale gas exploration sites in the UK, see, for example, *Ineos Upstream Ltd and others v Persons Unknown* [2017] EWHC 2945 (Ch), which was overturned on appeal in *Boyd and Corré v Ineos Upstream Ltd* [2019] EWCA Civ 515; for cases concerning possession proceedings in respect of land that was being occupied by those involved in an anti-fracking protests, see, for instance, *Jones and Jones v Persons Unknown and Brian Morgan* [2014] EWHC 4691 (Ch), *Wensley and others v Persons Unknown and others* [2014] EWHC 3086 (Ch) and *Manchester Ship Canal Developments and another v Persons Unknown and others* [2014] EWHC 645 (Ch); criminal convictions relating to conduct arising from such protest activities were also before the court, *Roberts, Blevins, and Loizou v R* [2018] EWCA Crim 2739 (an appeal against a sentence imposed following a conviction of public nuisance contrary to the common law).

85 There was also an unsuccessful challenge to a planning inspector's refusal to adjourn a planning inquiry to give an interested party more time to consider an expert traffic expert report: *R (Barlow) v Secretary of State for Housing, Communities and Local Government* [2019] EWHC 146 (QB), [2019] JPL 707.

86 *R (Stephenson) v Secretary of State for Housing and Communities and Local Government* [2019] EWHC 519 (Admin), [2019] JPL 929.

87 ibid [2].

88 ibid [57].

89 ibid [58].

90 ibid [62].

91 ibid [67]–[68].

92 *R (Frack Free Balcombe Residents Association) v West Sussex County Council* [2014] EWHC 4108 (Admin).

challenge was that the planning committee had been wrongly advised in relation to *inter alia* leaving matters such as pollution control, well integrity and air emissions to other public bodies; and Public Health England's views in relation to the air emissions monitoring. The claim was dismissed. Gilbart J determined that the local planning authority was entitled to assume that 'the matters of regulatory control could be left to the statutory regulatory authorities to consider'.[93] He noted that the very fact of the statutory regimes meant there are 'other mechanisms for dealing with the very proper concerns which the Claimant's members have about the effects on the environment'.[94]

17.68 In 2016, a decision of North Yorkshire County Council to grant planning permission to Third Energy UK Gas Limited in relation to fracking at site at Alma Farm in North Yorkshire was challenged in *R (Friends of the Earth and Frack Free Ryedale) v North Yorkshire County Council*.[95] Permission to proceed was refused at a rolled up hearing. The Claimant raised two grounds of challenge: the first concerned the failure to take into account the indirect, secondary, cumulative climate change impacts arising from the burning of gas in the production phase of the development at a gas-fired electricity generating station in Knapton as part of the EIA; and the second that the council misdirected itself in law by indicating that it could not require Third Energy to provide a financial bond in relation to remediation from fracking.[96] The first ground is an early variation on a theme in these challenges; and, as set out above, has recently been considered by the Supreme Court. Lang J dismissed the first ground, noting that in making the decision not to include these emissions from a separate site some distance away, which was governed by its own planning permission and environmental permits, the council had lawfully exercised its judgment in determining that assessment of these impacts was not required.[97] The second ground was also dismissed as, taking into account the planning practice guidance, the planning officer was justified in advising that this was not an exceptional case requiring a financial bond, and the council could assume that other regulatory regimes would operate effectively, including that financial protection could be achieved another way through a condition.[98]

17.69 The Court of Appeal considered an appeal of Dove J's decision rejecting a challenge to the decision to grant planning permission to assess the feasibility of extracting shale gas at two sites in Lancashire in *Preston New Road Action Group v Secretary of State for Communities and Local Government*.[99] The projects were concerned with exploration, not commercial extraction.[100] The grounds of appeal raised issues relating *inter alia* to the misinterpretation and misapplication of certain planning policies relating to minerals; the misinterpretation and misapplication of national policy relating to valued landscapes; the meaning of 'cumulative effects' (and related to that the meaning of direct and

93 ibid [100], [132]–[134].
94 ibid [102].
95 *R (Friends of the Earth and Frack Free Ryedale) v North Yorkshire County Council* [2016] EWHC 3303 (Admin), [2017] Env LR 22.
96 ibid [11].
97 ibid [36], [38].
98 ibid [62].
99 *Preston New Road Action Group v Secretary of State for Communities and Local Government* [2018] EWCA Civ 9, [2018] Env LR 18.
100 ibid [2]–[3].

indirect effects) in an EIA; and a failure to apply the precautionary principle in assessing the effects of the development on human health and, again raising an argument in relation to assuming the regulatory regime would operate effectively.

17.70 There are three points worth noting from the judgment:

- Specific consideration was given to the purpose of a minerals policy in local plans; and it was observed as follows:[101]

  > Policy CS5 is a policy specifically concerned, in part, with the working of minerals. It is a truism that minerals can only be worked where they are found, and, equally, that they can only be found where they lie (see the judgment of Ouseley J in *Europa Oil and Gas Ltd v Secretary of State for Communities and Local Government* [2013] EWHC 2643 (Admin), at [67], and the judgment of Stephen Richards LJ in the appeal in that case ([2014] EWCA Civ 825, at [37])). The working of minerals will likely alter the landscape during the extraction phase, but such effects will often be reversed or repaired in the course of the site's restoration. The same may also be said of works required in the exploration for minerals.

  Thus, considering the terms of policy CS5, a planning judgment was required in relation to the temporary effects on the landscape, which included the duration of any harm and the likely effectiveness of any site restoration.[102]

- The crucial point, in the court's view, was that the 'single, clearly defined project' for the purposes of an EIA[103] was the exploration for shale gas and monitoring.[104] The fact that commercial extraction could only follow successful exploration did not mean that 'two operations are necessarily and indivisibly parts of the same project'.[105] Given the nature of the project, there was no legal requirement to consider indirect or secondary effects associated with a 'hypothetical future project'.[106]

- The court rejected the argument based on the precautionary principle in relation to the Secretary of State's assessment of the health impacts, including that the relevant regulatory controls would operate effectively to address the impact.[107] This is an assumption that the decision-maker was entitled to make, based upon the NPPF (paragraph 122 as it then was) and more generally.[108]

---

101 ibid [18].
102 ibid [19].
103 See Chapter 7.
104 *Preston New Road Action Group v Secretary of State for Communities and Local Government* (n 99) [63].
105 ibid [65].
106 ibid [65], [68].
107 ibid [93]–[94].
108 The existence of other pollution control regimes are material planning considerations and decision-makers are entitled to assume the effective operation of those regimes: *R (Frack Free Balcombe Residents Association) v West Sussex County Council* (n 92); and more recent consideration in the context of GHG emissions in the case of *R (Bristol Airport Action Network Co-Ordinating Committee) v Secretary of State for Levelling Up, Housing and Communities* [2023] EWHC 171 (Admin) [2023] PTSR 853.

17.71 In the regulatory context, challenges have been brought in relation to licences and permits in respect of fracking operations:

- An unsuccessful attempt was made to quash a deed varying the terms of a petroleum exploration and development licence to extend the initial term of the licence, given the time it takes to apply for and obtain planning and environmental permits, on the ground that entering into such a deed was *ultra vires: R (Dean) v Secretary of State for Business, Energy and Industrial Strategy.*[109] The court determined that the licence was a property right (not just a contractual arrangement); and they could be varied by agreement.

- A challenge was also brought against the Environment Agency in relation to an unalleged unlawful variation of a licence, in relation to the daily injection rate of fracturing fluid, granted to a fracking company in *R (Friends of the Earth) v Environment Agency.*[110] The claimant argued that there was a failure to give any, or any adequate, consideration, to whether the best available technique ('BAT') for the treatment and re-use of the flowback fluid was electrocoagulation and that should have been considered as part of a revised waste management plan ('WMP'). The circumstances in which a WMP needs to be reviewed are set out exhaustively in Article 5(4) of the Mining Waste Directive (2006/21/EC); and, on the facts, there were no substantial changes requiring the Environment Agency to reconsider the WMP.[111]

- In *R (Thornton) v Oil and Gas Authority*[112] the OGA's (now the NSTA) decision to allow the acquisition of a company who held a licence to bore for natural gas was challenged. The focus of the judicial review was whether the licence commitments, in particular those relating to decommissioning of the shale gas wells could be met. A condition precedent of the sale was that the OGA would issue a letter of comfort, in relation to the change of control, to the effect that it would not revoke the licence or demand a further change of control.[113] The grounds of challenge turned on the model clauses,[114] the scope and extent of the OGA's assessment of financial capability, and whether the OGA had discharged its duty in relation to minimising public expenditure, set out in section 8 of the Energy Act 2016. There was no specific direct or indirect climate change ground, but the principal concern was who would bear the decommissioning cost.[115] The claim was dismissed.

---

109 *R (Dean) v Secretary of State for Business, Energy and Industrial Strategy* [2017] EWHC 1998 (Admin), [2017] 4 WLR 158.
110 *R (Friends of the Earth) v Environment Agency* [2019] EWHC 25 (Admin) [2019] PTSR 1020.
111 ibid [40].
112 *R (Thornton) v Oil and Gas Authority* [2020] EWHC 2615 (Admin).
113 ibid [8].
114 These clauses are made pursuant to s 4(1)(e) of the PA 1998.
115 Eddie Thornton, 'Don't Let the Oil and Gas Industry Offload Clean Up Costs on Taxpayers' (*CrowdJustice*, 2019) <https://www.crowdjustice.com/case/dont-let-the-taxpayer-pay-to-clean-up-fracking/> accessed 10 May 2024.

Development of oil and gas energy infrastructure

17.72 In 2022 the single greatest electricity generating source in the UK was gas, producing a total output of 90.2TWh (the total output from fossil fuels being 97TWh).[116] Of those routes to net zero modelled by National Grid ESO, all envisage gas as producing between 17.9 and 29.5TWh in 2030. Further, while all models envisage unabated gas being phased out by 2050, gas assisted by CCUS is likely to remain part of the energy makeup, with generation in the range of 8.2 to 17.2TWh in 2040, and up to 10.8TWh in 2050.[117] Thus, net zero will not lead to gas infrastructure becoming a thing of the past. In addition, this is to exclude consideration of consumer demand for gas, which in 2022 was 514.3TWh, and is not predicted to dip below 100TWh on any model before 2040.[118]

17.73 At the time of writing, the government had closed its second consultation on electricity market arrangements and was reviewing responses.[119] That consultation recognises that gas generation is an important part of demand management, as gas generation can be activated quickly to support the electricity grid in times of high demand.[120] It also recognises that, over time, there will be a move to low-carbon gas generation utilising CCUS, but that for the moment further gas capacity is required:[121]

> Based on our internal analysis we expect that a limited amount of new build gas capacity will be required in the immediate term to ensure a secure and reliable system, to replace existing generation capacity as it expires. It is the only mature technology capable of providing sustained flexible capacity whilst low carbon long-duration alternatives, such as Power CCUS, H2P and LDES scale up as we move into the 2030s.

17.74 Given approximately 15GW of the existing combined cycle gas turbine fleet is due to retire by 2035, this immediate need for further infrastructure is unsurprising.[122] Capacity market auctions have bought 0.5–2GW of new unabated gas generating capacity over the last 4 years.[123] Ultimately, there is a balance to be struck between achieving net zero in a timely manner (including decarbonisation of the power sector) and maintaining energy security. The construction of gas infrastructure is a key part of striking that balance. Further, this is before addressing the use of gas more generally in the UK, including heating demand and demand for hydrogen generation (addressed below under coal).

116 Coal comprised 4.9TWh, with the remainder of fossil fuels being other thermal at 1.9TWh. National Grid ESO, 'FES 2023 Data Workbook' (n 6) ES.05–08.
117 ibid.
118 ibid.
119 See Department for Energy and Climate Change, 'Review of Electricity Market Arrangements (REMA): Second Consultation' (GOV.UK, 12 March 2024) <https://www.gov.uk/government/consultations/review-of-electricity-market-arrangements-rema-second-consultation> accessed 10 May 2024.
120 ibid 68–70.
121 ibid 76.
122 ibid 76.
123 ibid 76.

17.75 As to oil, the electricity grid has moved away from oil-based generation.[124] Thus, while oil was the second largest fuel by inland energy consumption in 2022 (36% compared to gas at 39.3%),[125] this was not as a source of electricity. Instead, the vast majority of oil is used in transport (in 2022 46.8 million tonnes of oil equivalent were used in transport).[126] It is very unlikely any oil energy generating infrastructure will be built in the UK in the future, and indeed increasingly domestic heating and transport is also planned to move away from oil and oil-based products.

Coal

17.76 A significant transition from certain fossil fuels has already been achieved. In the 1950s around 90% of Great Britain's power came from burning coal.[127] Shortly before this book was published, the final coal fired power plant in Great Britain stopped operating, with Ratcliffe on Soar power plant in Nottinghamshire closing on 30 September 2024.[128] Prior to this, Ratcliffe on Soar produced 1% of Great Britain's power.[129] An important factor in progressing towards the phase out of coal has been a transition to other fuels. For example, Drax power station in North Yorkshire, which was a coal fired power plant at one time providing about 6% of the UK's electricity supply, now burns biomass.[130] The phase out of coal has had a significant impact on the overall decline in emissions.

17.77 Aside from recently having a very small role in the energy makeup of Great Britain which has since ceased, it is important to note that National Grid ESO give no role for generation from coal in their 'Future Energy Scenarios'. Thus, from October 2024, Great Britain has ceased to use coal in the direct production of electricity, and will no longer have an intention to develop future coal generation.[131]

17.78 This position is further reflected in the NPPF where, at paragraph 223, it provides that:[132]

> Planning permission should not be granted for the extraction of coal unless: a) the proposal is environmentally acceptable, or can be made so by planning conditions or obligations; or b) if it is not environmentally acceptable, then it provides national, local or community benefits which clearly outweigh its likely impacts (taking all relevant matters into account, including any residual environmental impacts).

---

124 The final power station was Littlebrook D closed in March 2015 <https://www.powerstations.uk/coal-countdown/> accessed 24 April 2024.
125 Department for Energy Security and Net Zero, 'UK Energy in Brief 2023' (2023) 9 <https://assets.publishing.service.gov.uk/media/6581cb5aed3c34000d3bfbfc/UK_Energy_in_Brief_2023.pdf> accessed 24 April 2024.
126 ibid 10.
127 National Grid ESO, 'Beyond 2030' (2024) 21 <https://www.nationalgrideso.com/document/315516/download> accessed 10 May 2024. National Grid ESO became the National Energy System Operator in October 2024.
128 Uniper, 'Ratcliffe-on-Soar | Uniper' <https://www.uniper.energy/united-kingdom/power-plants-in-the-united-kingdom/ratcliffe-soar> accessed 23 October 2024.
129 National Grid ESO, 'Beyond 2030' (2024) 22.
130 'Drax Power Station' (Drax Global) <https://www.drax.com/about-us/our-sites-and-businesses/drax-power-station/> accessed 10 May 2024.
131 National Grid ESO, 'FES 2023 Data Workbook' (n 6) NZ.01.
132 Department for Levelling Up, Housing and Communities, 'National Planning Policy Framework' (2023) (n 71).

17.79 However the role for coal in the UK may not entirely cease. On 7 December 2022 the Secretary of State for Levelling Up, Housing and Communities granted permission for a metallurgical coal mine in Whitehaven.[133] Such coal is of a grade used in the blast furnace process for primary steelmaking. The Secretary of State agreed with the inspector that there did exist a need for new coal, and that,[134] while the hurdle in NPPF (set out above) is a high one, it is not a pure prohibition.[135] The Secretary of State also considered GHGs, and, importantly, agreed with the Inspector and applied the Court of Appeal decision in *Finch* (discussed above) in concluding that downstream emissions of the scheme 'cannot reasonably be regarded as indirect significant effects of the proposed development'.[136] On climate change, he concluded 'that given no evidence was provided to suggest that any other metallurgical coal mines in the world aspire to be net zero, the proposed mine is likely to be much better placed to mitigate GHG emissions' than comparators around the world.[137]

17.80 A statutory challenge was brought to the decision by Friends of the Earth and Lakeland Action on Climate Change – Towards Transmission. In the intervening period between that claim being filed and judgment, the Supreme Court handed down *Finch* (discussed above) and the Secretary of State on 10 July 2024 offered to consent to judgment to quash the decision to grant consent on the basis that he had concluded that GHG emissions from burning the produced coal were not a significant likely effect of the proposed development.[138] The developer of Whitehaven mine continued to defend the Secretary of State's decision.

17.81 Judgment was handed down by Holgate J on 13 September 2024 quashing the decision of the Secretary of State.[139] In respect of a proper approach to an environmental statement and environmental impact assessment he held:[140]

> Taking into account the common ground that the burning of the Whitehaven coal is an inevitable consequence of its extraction from the mine, in my judgment it is plain, following the decision of the Supreme Court in Finch, that the GHG emissions from that combustion are significant likely indirect effects of the project the subject of the planning application. Accordingly, the 2011 Regulations required WCM's ES and the EIA process to assess those emissions and their implications. The Secretary of State was obliged to take into account that environmental information (including the GHG emissions from combustion of the Whitehaven coal) before deciding whether or not to grant planning permission on the application.

---

133 Department for Levelling Up, Housing and Communities, *Former Marchon Site, Pow Beck Valley and Area from the Former Marchon Site to the St Bees Coast, Whitehaven, Cumbria* (APP/H0900/V/21/3271069) 7 December 2022.
134 ibid [21].
135 ibid [23].
136 ibid [35].
137 ibid [37].
138 *R (Friends of the Earth Limited) v Secretary of State for Levelling Up, Housing and Communities and Others* [2024] EWHC 2349 (Admin) [52].
139 ibid.
140 ibid [101]–[102].

> Furthermore, in view of the scale and significance of those emissions, (according to the evidence accepted by the Inspector at IR 21.110 to IR 21.115 and by the Secretary of State at DL 5 and DL 32), in my judgment that assessment was an obviously material consideration which the Secretary of State was obliged to take into account in the determination of the planning application (see Friends of the Earth [2021] PTSR at [116] to [121]).

17.82 Having identified the error of law in not conducting this assessment of the downstream emissions, Holgate J went on to consider whether an argument based on substitution (that is, that the Whitehaven coal would be burnt in substitution for US coal, and therefore the downstream emissions were net neutral against the US coal which would not be burnt) could remedy this error. He concluded that this was not the case. The Secretary of State had found only partial substitution, and therefore he could not conclude there would be no net increase in GHGs. As a result, the case on these grounds succeeded.[141]

17.83 Holgate J also upheld a challenge to the permission on the basis that it undermined the UK's leadership role in promoting international action on climate change. While the inspector (and Secretary of State) had correctly engaged with whether this was the case, he ultimately rejected the argument that a consent sent the wrong message on the basis that the scheme was net zero.[142] The inspector had been correct to engage the issue, and Holgate J thought it wise that the developer had not pushed the argument that these concerns were 'virtue signalling'.[143] However, as the inspector had relied upon the mine being net zero, and that had now been rejected by Holgate J as a result of the assessment of emissions issue, the basis for rejecting this argument also fell.[144] He also accepted the submission that the offsetting regime proposed (which only concerned projects outside the UK) was in breach of clear UK policy.[145] As a result, Holgate J quashed the permission.[146]

17.84 This case follows on from the earlier decision in *HJ Banks & Company v Secretary of State for Housing Communities and Local Government* where the High Court quashed a decision letter of the Secretary of State refusing permission for a surface mine to extract coal, sandstone and fireclay in Northumberland.[147] In that case, while the Secretary of State accepted that there was an identified need for coal,[148] he had concluded that the then text of NPPF pointed against permission notwithstanding the public benefits that weighed in favour. The High Court disagreed and held that the Secretary of State had failed to weigh the benefits of the scheme according to policy,[149] and had failed to

---

141 ibid [187]–[188].
142 ibid [208].
143 ibid [202]–[203].
144 ibid [209]–[211].
145 ibid [212]–[221].
146 ibid [231]. He rejected the fifth ground of challenge concerning an unlawful disparity in the treatment of the parties' cases by the inspector and Secretary of State.
147 *HJ Banks & Company v Secretary of State for Housing Communities and Local Government* [2018] EWHC 3141 (Admin).
148 ibid [13].
149 ibid [38]–[48].

explain why the reasons for refusal could include the adverse effect of GHG emissions when it was accepted that the scheme would result in savings compared to import of coal.[150]

17.85 Additionally, coal currently has a role in the production of hydrogen alongside natural gas.[151] As is explored in Chapter 16 at paragraphs 16.49–16.65, a large part of developing hydrogen infrastructure in the UK will be taking steps to minimise the emissions production methods, moving across to blue, green and pink hydrogen.[152] Ammonia production globally also remains the largest individual CO_2-emitting industrial process, and uses hydrogen. Coal and natural gas act as the feedstock for that process.[153]

17.86 As to the legacy of coal and coal mining in the UK, the Coal Authority has recently published its 'Sustainability Plan 2023 to 2026'.[154] In it, the Authority sets out the steps it will take in aiming to meet net zero in its own emissions (which it aims to hit by 2030). Part of this aim includes achieving net zero in the indirect emissions of electricity, heat, goods and services that the Coal Authority itself uses.[155] The Coal Authority also manages over 1300 hectares of land as a result of existing mine legacy works.[156] The Sustainability Plan sets out steps for nature positive in respect of that legacy works land; that includes working towards a nature recovery plan for much of that land which is in need of significant regeneration as a result of the harm of mining works.[157]

150 ibid [93]–[121].
151 National Engineering Policy Centre, 'The Role of Hydrogen in a Net Zero Energy System' (2022) 3 <https://nepc.raeng.org.uk/media/tkphxfwy/the-role-of-hydrogen-in-the-net-zero-energy-system.pdf> accessed 10 May 2024.
152 ibid.
153 ibid.
154 The Coal Authority, 'Sustainability Plan: 2023 to 2026' (2023) <https://assets.publishing.service.gov.uk/media/645a59c8c6e8970012a0fba1/Coal_Authority_Sustainability_Report_2023_to_2026.pdf> accessed 10 May 2024.
155 ibid 8–9.
156 ibid 10.
157 ibid 12.

CHAPTER 18

TRANSPORT

Philippa Jackson and Gethin Thomas

Introduction

18.01 Decarbonising the transport sector is critical to achieving net zero, given that transport is the largest emitting sector of greenhouse gas ('GHG') emissions. The Department for Transport's ('DfT') latest statistics reveal that the transport sector produced 26% of the UK's total emissions in 2021 (427MtCO_2e).[1] Aviation has a particularly important role to play due to its high carbon footprint. However, regulating emissions from aviation and international shipping is complex due to the international scope and impact of emissions from air and maritime transport.

18.02 At a domestic level, the development of major new rail infrastructure to reduce emissions from private car use has the potential to create tension between net zero and nature positive objectives, while reducing reliance upon petrol and diesel vehicles continues to represent a political and technological challenge.

18.03 This chapter addresses the main transport modes (aviation, shipping, rail and road) and the legal and policy framework specific to each mode of transport; as well as examining the legal and policy framework for the development and promotion of both renewable fuels and green transport.

18.04 The Transport Decarbonisation Plan ('TDP'), published on 14 July 2021, provides the overarching policy framework for tackling emissions across the transport network and addresses all of the transport modes, discussed below.

Aviation

(i) *Introduction*

18.05 The government's priority remains tackling emissions from international aviation and shipping ('IAS') at an international level, through the International Civil Aviation Organisation ('ICAO'). However, the Sixth Carbon Budget formally included emissions from international aviation within the budget figure for the first time.

1 Department for Transport, 'Official Statistics: Transport and Environment Statistics: 2023' (2023) <https://www.gov.uk/government/statistics/transport-and-environment-statistics-2023/transport-and-environment-statistics-2023> accessed 5 May 2024.

18.06 Airport-related development also gives rise to other localised environmental impacts, in particular air quality impacts and noise, which require assessment as part of the planning process.

(ii) *Policy framework*

(a) Aviation Policy Framework ('APF') and Aviation 2050

18.07 The APF, published in 2013, remains part of national aviation policy. It makes clear that action at a global level is the 'preferred and most effective means by which to reduce emissions'.[2] It recognises that emissions trading schemes, in particular the then EU ETS (now UK ETS),[3] discussed further below, are a key component of its objective to reduce global emissions.

18.08 In 2017, the government published an initial call for evidence to inform publication of a new national aviation strategy, 'Aviation 2050'. This was followed by 'Beyond the horizon – the future of UK aviation: next steps towards an aviation strategy', published in June 2018.[4]

18.09 In December 2018, the government published the green paper 'Aviation 2050: the future of UK aviation: A consultation', building upon the call for evidence and next steps documents. This reiterates the objective stated in the APF of ensuring that the aviation sector makes a significant contribution towards reducing global emissions, while confirming that international action on emissions, through negotiation in ICAO for a long-term climate change goal, is the first priority.[5]

18.10 The Aviation 2050 White Paper was due to be published in mid-2019, but is presently still awaited and appears to have been overtaken by subsequent strategies and policy documents.

(b) The Airports National Policy Statement ('ANPS')

18.11 The ANPS, published on 5 June 2018, is a national policy statement ('NPS') made pursuant to section 5 of the Planning Act 2008 ('PA 2008').[6] It provides support for the North West Runway at Heathrow, as a means of providing additional runway capacity in the South East, as well as the policy framework for any Development Consent Order ('DCO') application relating to the new runway, new terminal capacity or the reconfiguration of terminal facilities at Heathrow Airport.[7]

---

2 Department for Transport, *Aviation Policy Framework* (Cm 8584, 2013) <https://assets.publishing.service.gov.uk/media/5a7aa94b40f0b66eab99bc3e/aviation-policy-framework.pdf> accessed 6 May 2024 para 2.8.
3 See Chapter 14 for further discussion on emissions trading schemes.
4 Department for Transport, 'Beyond the Horizon – the Future of UK Aviation: Next Steps towards an Aviation Strategy' (2018) <https://assets.publishing.service.gov.uk/media/5acb7dae40f0b64fed0afe45/next-steps-towards-an-aviation-strategy.pdf> accessed 7 May 2024.
5 HM Government, *Aviation 2050: The Future of UK Aviation* (Cm 9714, 2018) <https://assets.publishing.service.gov.uk/government/uploads/system/uploads/attachment_data/file/769695/aviation-2050-web.pdf> accessed 5 May 2024 para 3.83.
6 See Chapter 6 for further discussion on Nationally Significant Infrastructure Projects.
7 HM Government, *Aviation 2050: The Future of UK Aviation* (n 5) para 1.40.

18.12 The ANPS requires the decision-maker to have regard to carbon emissions on any DCO application. However, it also states that:[8]

> any increase in carbon emissions alone is not a reason to refuse development consent, unless the increase in carbon emissions resulting from the project is so significant that it would have a material impact on the ability of government to meet its carbon reduction targets, including carbon budgets.

18.13 The lawfulness of the ANPS was the subject of a long-running legal challenge by Plan B Earth and Friends of the Earth, amongst others, who challenged its adoption on a number of climate change-related grounds. These claims were originally rejected by the Divisional Court in 2019.[9] However, in February 2020, the Court of Appeal overturned part of the Divisional Court's ruling,[10] and held that the Secretary of State had acted unlawfully in failing to take the Paris Agreement into account when designating the ANPS in breach of section 5(7) of the PA 2008.[11] Consequently, the Court of Appeal ruled that the ANPS was of no legal effect.

18.14 On 16 December 2020, the Supreme Court unanimously overturned the Court of Appeal's decision and allowed Heathrow Airport's appeal. It held that the government's commitment to the Paris Agreement, as expressed in ministerial statements, did not constitute 'government policy' for the purposes of section 5(8). The epitome of 'government policy' is a 'formal written statement of established policy', while the 'absolute minimum standard' is a 'statement which is clear, unambiguous, and devoid of relevant qualification'.[12] The ministerial statements relied upon by the Court of Appeal failed to satisfy this test. Moreover, international treaties are binding only as a matter of international law and do not have an effect in domestic law. Treaty commitments are not therefore a statement of 'government policy'.

18.15 The Supreme Court also held that there was no established 'government policy' on climate change beyond that already reflected in the Climate Change Act 2008 ('CCA 2008'), which sets a national carbon target and obliges the government to establish carbon budgets to meet that target.[13]

18.16 Consequently, the ANPS remains valid and provides policy support in principle for a third runway at Heathrow. However, no DCO application has been submitted to date.

---

8 Department for Transport, 'Airports National Policy Statement: New Runway Capacity and Infrastructure at Airports in the South East of England' (2018) https://assets.publishing.service.gov.uk/media/5e2054fc40f0b65dbed71467/airports-nps-new-runway-capacity-and-infrastructure-at-airports-in-the-south-east-of-england-web-version.pdf> accessed 6 May 2024 para 5.82.

9 *R (Spurrier and others) v Secretary of State for Transport and others* [2019] EWHC 1070 (Admin).

10 *R (Spurrier) v Secretary of State for Transport* [2020] PTSR 240.

11 See paras 6.46–6.54 in Chapter 6.

12 *R (Friends of the Earth Ltd and others) v Heathrow Airport Ltd* [2020] UKSC 52, [106].

13 See paras 2.83–2.88 in Chapter 2.

(c) Making best use of existing runways

18.17 In June 2018, the government also published 'Beyond the Horizon, the Future of UK Aviation: Making Best Use of Existing Runways' ('MBU'), which provides support for airports other than Heathrow making best use of their existing runways, subject to environmental issues being addressed.[14]

18.18 Where a proposal to intensify use of an existing runway does not meet the thresholds under section 23 of the PA 2008 for a Nationally Significant Infrastructure Project ('NSIP'), the application must be determined by the local planning authority; and 'for the majority of environmental concerns, the government expects these to be taken into account as part of existing local planning application processes'.[15]

18.19 However, MBU states that carbon emissions are to be addressed at a national level, through the (yet to be published) Aviation Strategy (Aviation 2050).[16] In formulating MBU, the DfT nonetheless modelled the impact of allowing all airports to make best use of existing airport capacity, against the 80% target then in force. On balance, and having regard to possible abatement measures, the policy advises that it is likely that the planning assumption (the 'headroom' assumed by the CCC of 37.5Mt of CO_2 in 2050 for aviation emissions for the purposes of the fifth carbon budget, which runs until 2032) will still be met with MBU in place.[17] This modelling has since been updated by the DfT when formulating the Jet Zero Strategy: see paragraphs 18.24–18.28 below.

18.20 In *R (Bristol Airport Action Network Co-Ordinating Committee) v Secretary of State for Levelling Up, Housing and Communities*,[18] Lane J rejected the claimant's argument that the MBU policy requires decision-makers to take into account aviation emissions as environmental impacts. Paragraphs 1.12–1.13 of MBU make clear that aviation emissions are to be considered at a national level.

(d) Flightpath to the future

18.21 In May 2022, the government published a new statement on aviation called 'Flightpath to the Future: a Strategic Framework for the Aviation Sector', which it describes as a 'strategic framework for the future of aviation, focusing on the next 10 years'. This sets out a ten-point plan for delivery, including '4. Put the sector on course to achieve jet zero by 2050' and '5. Capture the potential of new technology and its uses'.[19]

18.22 Under 4, the policy cross-refers to the forthcoming Jet Zero Strategy ('JZS'). Under 5, additional funding is promised to the Civil Aviation Authority ('CAA') to 'scale up support to innovators' and set up a 'Future of Flight Industry Group to work

---

14 Department for Transport, 'Beyond the Horizon, The Future of UK Aviation: Making Best Use of Existing Runways' (2018) para 1.5 <https://assets.publishing.service.gov.uk/media/5b16b68d40f0b634b469fa35/making-best-use-of-existing-runways.pdf> accessed 5 May 2024.

15 ibid para 1.9.

16 ibid paras 1.11–1.12.

17 ibid para 1.21.

18 *R (Bristol Airport Action Network Co-Ordinating Committee) v Secretary of State for Levelling Up, Housing and Communities* [2023] EWHC 171 (Admin).

19 Department for Transport, 'Flightpath to the Future: A Strategic Framework for the Aviation Sector' (2022) <https://assets.publishing.service.gov.uk/media/628f7d26e90e07039f799ebc/flightpath-to-the-future.pdf> accessed 5 May 2024.

with industry and the CAA to develop, publish and implement a plan for Future of Flight', as well as support in delivering the CAA's Airspace Modernisation Strategy (refreshed in 2023) 'to achieve quicker, quieter, and cleaner flights'. Airspace modernisation is identified as being critical to achieving decarbonisation.

18.23 Flightpath to the Future does not refer to Aviation 2050, which appears to have been overtaken by this new 'strategic framework' for aviation.

(e) Jet Zero Strategy

18.24 The JZS is the latest statement of government policy on aviation emissions, published in July 2022.[20] It confirms the government's support for aviation growth, while relying upon technological advances to deliver reductions in emissions and to meet the net zero target under the CCA. In formulating the JZS the government has also updated the carbon modelling underpinning MBU to reflect updated airport capacity assumptions and the net zero amendment. The strategy includes a five-year review as well as annual monitoring to ensure that the CO_2 emissions reduction trajectory for aviation is being reached.

18.25 The JZS also addresses non-CO_2 climate impacts, while recognising that there are large uncertainties in this regard.[21]

18.26 An application for judicial review of the JZS has been made by climate change charity, Possible, as well as Group for Action on Leeds Bradford Airport ('GALBA') on grounds including alleged unlawfulness in disregarding the advice of the Climate Change Committee ('CCC') concerning demand management measures, and the adequacy of the consultation process. However, the claim is currently stayed.

18.27 In *R (Dawes) v Secretary of State for Transport and others*,[22] the claimant challenged the grant of development consent for the development and reopening of Manston Airport in Kent on the grounds (amongst others) that the defendant had erred in law by relying upon measures in the JZS to ensure carbon budgets were met, which were aspirational and untested.

18.28 Dove J dismissed the claim. He held that the defendant was entitled to rely on his own policies in concluding that the question of GHG emissions and climate change could properly be regarded as neutral in the overall planning balance:[23]

> The defendant relied upon the new policies, and in particular DTP and JZS, as measures that would accelerate decarbonisation in the aviation sector and ensure carbon budgets were met without directly limiting aviation demand. The defendant thus relied directly upon those new policies to reach his conclusion that this was an issue to which neutral weight should be afforded. In my view, as a matter of law, that was a permissible approach.

---

20 Department for Transport, 'Jet Zero Strategy: Delivering Net Zero Aviation by 2050' (2022) <https://assets.publishing.service.gov.uk/media/62e931d48fa8f5033896888a/jet-zero-strategy.pdf> accessed 5 May 2024.
21 ibid para 3.64.
22 *R (Dawes) v Secretary of State for Transport and others* [2023] EWHC 2352 (Admin).
23 ibid [104].

> The defendant was entitled to rely upon his own policies, which had not been the subject of any successful legal challenge, to deliver the outcome for which they were designed, namely achieving the carbon budgets which had been and were to be legislated without impacting upon aviation demand.

(f) National Planning Policy Framework ('NPPF')

18.29 The NPPF does not contain policies specific to aviation. It does, however, expect the planning system to 'help to shape places in ways that contribute to radical reductions in greenhouse gas emissions'.[24] This would include surface access (road) emissions associated with airport expansion schemes.

18.30 Paragraph 194 also states that:

> The focus of planning [...] decisions should be on whether proposed development is an acceptable use of land, rather than the control of processes or emissions (where these are subject to separate pollution control regimes).

18.31 The pollution control regime includes the regime relating to the control of carbon emissions from IAS under the CCA, including the UK ETS: see *R (Bristol Airport Action Network Co-Ordinating Committee) v Secretary of State for Levelling Up, Housing and Communities.*[25]

(iii) *Statutory framework*

(a) The international context

18.32 The United Nations Framework Convention on Climate Change ('UNFCCC') entered into force in 1994 and established the first international environmental treaty, signed by 154 states, to combat climate change (see paragraphs 2.08–2.27 in Chapter 2). The Kyoto Protocol, signed in 1997, was the first implementation of measures under the UNFCCC. However, emissions from international aviation were excluded from the reduction targets made under the protocol and states were instead asked to work through ICAO to agree on an approach specific to aviation (see paragraphs 2.28–2.34 in Chapter 2).

18.33 The Kyoto Protocol was superseded by the Paris Agreement, which came into force in 2016 (see paragraphs 2.35–2.53). The Paris Agreement commits signatories to 'limiting global warming to well below 2°C and pursuing efforts to limit it to 1.5°C'. Unlike the Kyoto Protocol, it does not establish national targets for signatories. Instead, each signatory is tasked with assessing their own national circumstances and proposing a legally binding nationally determined contribution ('NDC'). The Paris Agreement makes no specific reference to international aviation emissions.

---

24 Department for Levelling Up, Housing and Communities, 'National Planning Policy Framework' (2023) <https://assets.publishing.service.gov.uk/media/65a11af7e8f5ec000f1f8c46/NPPF_December_2023.pdf> accessed 2 April 2024 para 157.

25 *R (Bristol Airport Action Network Co-Ordinating Committee) v Secretary of State for Levelling Up, Housing and Communities* (n 18) [139]–[145].

18.34 As the Supreme Court made clear in the *Heathrow* judgment, international treaties, including the Paris Agreement, are not legally binding in UK law unless incorporated into domestic legislation.[26] However, the UK's obligations under the Paris Agreement are given effect in domestic law, in that the carbon target under section 1 of the CCA 2008 and the carbon budgets under section 4 of that Act meet (and, indeed, go beyond) the UK's obligations under the Paris Agreement to adhere to the NDCs notified on its behalf under that Agreement.[27]

(b) Climate Change Act 2008

18.35 Section 30(1) of the CCA 2008 provides that:

> Emissions of greenhouse gases from international aviation or international shipping do not count as emissions from sources in the United Kingdom except as provided by regulations made by the Secretary of State.

18.36 Under section 10, however, the Secretary of State is required, when setting carbon budgets, to take into account the estimated amount of reportable emissions from IAS for the budgetary period or periods in question.

18.37 Section 32 of the CCA 2008 establishes the CCC[28] to advise the government on matters relating to climate change, including the consequences of treating emissions from IAS as emissions from sources in the UK for the purposes of Part 1: see section 35. However, the CCC's role is advisory only and the Secretary of State is not obliged to follow its advice.

18.38 Emissions from IAS were not formally included within the first to fifth carbon budgets. The Sixth Carbon Budget (2033–2037) included, for the first time, emissions from IAS within the budget figure set by Article 2 of the Carbon Budget Order 2021.

(c) UK ETS

18.39 Aviation was included in the EU ETS from 2012 until 1 January 2021, when the UK ETS replaced the UK's participation in the EU ETS. By virtue of Schedule 1 of the Greenhouse Gas Emissions Trading Scheme Order 2020, flights to and from the EEA are included in the UK ETS.[29]

(d) CORSIA

18.40 In 2016, the ICAO established and adopted an international trading scheme for limiting and offsetting emissions from international aviation.

18.41 The 'Carbon Offsetting and Reduction Scheme for International Aviation' ('CORSIA') is a market-based mechanism, which requires airlines to compensate for any increase in emissions above the base year of 2019, by purchasing approved carbon

---

26 *R (Friends of the Earth Ltd and others) v Heathrow Airport Ltd* [2020] UKSC 52 [108].
27 ibid [122].
28 See Chapter 4 for further discussion of other public bodies.
29 See Chapter 14 for more detailed discussion of emissions trading schemes.

off-sets from a list of approved emission units. It involves comparing the total CO_2 emissions for a year (from 2021 onwards) against a baseline level of CO_2 emissions. From 2021 onwards, CO_2 emissions from international aviation covered by CORSIA exceeding this baseline level represent the sector's offsetting requirements for that year.

18.42 CORSIA has three phases: a pilot scheme from 2021 to 2023, a first phase from 2024 to 2026 and a mandatory second phase for all states (with some exemptions, principally for small and less developed states) from 2027 until 2035. However, although CORSIA has now moved into its first phase, China, Russia, India, Brazil and Vietnam have not agreed to participate. This means that flights to these destinations from participating states are also currently excluded from the offsetting requirements under CORSIA.

18.43 The baseline for the pilot phase has been set at the total CO_2 emissions covered by CORSIA in 2019. At its 41st assembly in October 2022, ICAO set the baseline for 2024 onwards at the more ambitious level of 85% of 2019 emissions.[30]

18.44 On 27 May 2021, the Air Navigation (Carbon Offsetting and Reduction Scheme for International Aviation) Order 2021 came into force. This notifies ICAO of the UK's participation in CORSIA. The intention is for CORSIA to apply to emissions not covered by the UK ETS (see below).

18.45 For a helpful summary of the relevant provisions of the CCA 2008 and the legislation made under it in this context see: [41] – [55] of *R (Bristol Airport Action Network Co-Ordinating Committee) v Secretary of State for Levelling Up, Housing and Communities* per Lane J.[31]

(e) Planning Act 2008

18.46 'Airport-related development' falls within the definition of an NSIP for the purposes of section 14(1)(i) PA 2008 if it meets the thresholds set out in section 23 PA 2008.[32] Section 23 of the PA 2008 requires a judgment to be made by the Secretary of State as to 'what increase in capacity could realistically be achieved, not what might technically or arithmetically be possible': see *Ross and Sanders v Secretary of State for Transport.*[33]

18.47 Where airport-related development does not meet the definition of an NSIP under sections 14 and 23, the provisions of the Town and Country Planning Act 1990 ('TCPA 1990') apply.

30 CORSIA, 'Resolution A41-22: Consolidated Statement of Continuing ICAO Policies and Practices Related to Environmental Protection — Carbon Offsetting and Reduction Scheme for International Aviation (CORSIA)' <https://www.icao.int/environmental-protection/CORSIA/Documents/Resolution_A41-22_CORSIA.pdf> accessed 5 May 2024.

31 *R (Bristol Airport Action Network Co-Ordinating Committee) v Secretary of State for Levelling Up, Housing and Communities* (n 18).

32 Climate Change Act 2008 ss 14 and 23.

33 *R (Ross and Sanders) v Secretary of State for Transport* [2020] EWHC 226 (Admin) [101].

(iv) *Issues arising in practice*

(a) The correct decision-maker

18.48 In relation to any airport-related development, a preliminary issue arises as to whether the application falls to be determined at a national level through the DCO process, or by the local planning authority under the TCPA 1990: see *Ross and Sanders v Secretary of State for Transport*.[34]

18.49 Even where an airport scheme does not quality as an NSIP, it may still be called in and so taken out of the hands of the local planning authority, through the exercise of the 'call in' power under section 77 of the TCPA 1990. Applications which do qualify as an NSIP will not fall within the scope of the TCPA 1990 at all and so section 77 will not apply.

(b) Challenging scientific or technical judgments in judicial review

18.50 Challenges to airport expansion schemes on the basis of deficiencies in the assessment of aviation emissions and/or the adequacy of mitigation or adaptation measures invariably involve evidence of a technical or scientific nature.

18.51 The courts will accord a substantial margin of appreciation to judgments based upon scientific, technical or predictive assessments by those with appropriate expertise: see *R (Mott) v Environment Agency*.[35]

(c) Cumulative impacts and EIA

18.52 No criteria or thresholds have been set by which to measure the 'significance' of GHG emissions under the Town and Country Planning (Environmental Impact Assessment) Regulations 2017 ('EIA Regulations'). It is therefore permissible to use carbon budgets or national targets as a benchmark and to reach a judgment, which may inevitably be of a generalised nature, about the likelihood of a proposal harming the achievement of that target: *R (Goesa Ltd) v Eastleigh Borough Council & Southampton Airport*[36] per Holgate J. See, also, *R (Boswell) v Secretary of State for Transport*, considered in the 'Renewable Transport Fuels' section below.[37]

18.53 Holgate J also held in *Goesa* that there was no error of law in treating MBU as a cumulative assessment of other airport expansion proposals, while noting that this pre-dated the net zero amendment so that national targets would become more restrictive.

(d) Time limits and remedies in aviation-related judicial review challenges

18.54 Where the challenge is to the grant of consent for aviation-related development, the appropriate remedy is likely to be a quashing order.

34 ibid.

35 *R (Mott) v Environment Agency* [2016] EWCA Civ 564; *R (Plan B Earth) v Secretary of State for Transport* [2020] EWCA Civ 214 [176]–[177]; *R (Ross and Sanders) v Secretary of State for Transport* (n 33) [69]–[77]; *R (Goesa Ltd) v Eastleigh Borough Council & Southampton Airport* [2022] EWHC 1221 (Admin) [102] and [125]–[127].

36 *R (Goesa Ltd) v Eastleigh Borough Council & Southampton Airport* (n 35).

37 *R (Boswell) v Secretary of State for Transport* [2024] EWCA Civ 145.

18.55 However, in recent years, there have been several high-profile legal challenges to national policies and strategies aimed in part at tackling aviation emissions, on the grounds that these are inadequate to achieve net zero. In such cases,[38] a declaration is the most likely remedy. This achieves a more targeted result than a quashing order, leaving positive elements of the impugned strategy intact.

18.56 The courts have also been astute in this context not to allow out of time challenges to adopted policy, under the guise of a challenge to a subsequent decision: see, for example, *Ross and Sanders v Secretary of State for Transport*.[39] Any legal challenge to the adoption of government policy must be brought within the time frame under CPR Part 54, following its adoption.

Shipping

(i) *Introduction*

18.57 For the purposes of the CCA 2008, emissions from international shipping are treated in the same way as emissions from international aviation. However, although shipping generated 3% of UK GHG emissions (in 2018)[40] (compared to 7% from international aviation), emissions from shipping have not attracted the same degree of attention from the courts.

18.58 Although IAS are treated in the same way for the purposes of section 30 of the CCA 2008 and their inclusion in carbon budgets, the overall policy and statutory framework are different. In particular, and as explained below, the UK ETS does not currently extend to shipping.

(ii) *Policy framework*

(a) The international context

18.59 Similar to the ICAO, international efforts to tackle GHG emissions from shipping have been channelled through the International Maritime Organisation ('IMO'), of which the UK is a member state.

18.60 The IMO was established under the Convention on the International Maritime Organisation at the 1948 Geneva conference as an agency of the United Nations, and was originally known as the Inter-Governmental Maritime Consultative Organization ('IMCO'). It came into existence ten years later in 1958 and was renamed in 1982.

18.61 The IMO's original remit was to promote maritime safety. However, by the late 1960s, concerns about maritime pollution and the environmental impacts of shipping had begun to emerge. This led to the adoption of the International Convention for

38 A successful example of such a challenge is *R (Friends of the Earth Ltd) v Secretary of State for Business, Energy and Industrial Strategy* [2022] EWHC 1841 (Admin).
39 *R (Ross and Sanders) v Secretary of State for Transport* (n 33) [117].
40 Climate Change Committee, 'The Sixth Carbon Budget: Shipping' (2020) 5 <https://www.theccc.org.uk/wp-content/uploads/2020/12/Sector-summary-Shipping.pdf> accessed 5 May 2024.

the Prevention of Pollution from Ships in 1973, as modified by the Protocol of 1978 ('MARPOL 73/78').

18.62 However, it was not until 2011 that the IMO took explicit regulatory action to address GHG emissions, by adopting the first set of international mandatory measures to improve ships' energy efficiency on 15 July 2011.

18.63 In April 2018, the IMO published a Greenhouse Gas Strategy for the sector, committing to a target of reducing emissions by at least 50% by 2050.

18.64 At the Marine Environment Protection Committee ('MEPC 80') in July 2023, IMO Member States adopted the revised 2023 IMO Strategy on Reduction of GHG Emissions from Ships, which includes enhanced targets to tackle harmful emissions. The revised strategy includes an enhanced common ambition to reach net-zero GHG emissions from international shipping by or around 2050, a commitment to ensure an uptake of alternative zero and near-zero GHG fuels by 2030, as well as indicative check-points for international shipping to reach net-zero GHG emissions for 2030 (by at least 20%, striving for 30%) and 2040 (by at least 70%, striving for 80%).

18.65 At the eighty-first session of the Maritime Environment Protection Committee ('MEPC 81'), held on 18–22 March 2024, the IMO agreed on a draft outline illustration of a possible net zero framework. This identifies regulations under MARPOL, which could be adopted or amended to allow for a new global fuel standard and pricing mechanism for maritime GHG emissions.[41] By requiring shipping companies to pay a fee for every ton of carbon they emit by burning fuel, this illustrative framework could pave the way to creating the world's first global carbon price.

(b) Maritime 2050 and the Clean Maritime Plan

18.66 Maritime 2050 is the UK government's overarching strategy for the British maritime sector to 2050, published in January 2019.

18.67 In July 2019, the government published the Clean Maritime Plan ('CMP'). The CMP is described as the UK's national action plan on shipping emissions and 'the environment route map of Maritime 2050, outlining the UK's pathway to zero emissions shipping'.[42]

18.68 As with the JZS, the CMP focuses heavily on technological advancements to deliver emissions reductions by 2050. However, a Transport Committee report in March 2023[43] described the CMP as a good 'starting point' but emphasised that a 'more

41 International Marine Organization, 'IMO Agrees Possible Outline for Maritime 'Net-Zero Framework'' <https://www.imo.org/en/MediaCentre/PressBriefings/pages/IMO-agrees-possible-outline-for-net-zero-framework.aspx?campaign_id=54&emc=edit_clim_20240328&instance_id=118767&nl=climate-forward&regi_id=131821933&segment_id=162028&te=1&user_id=5a9e6d82c16604e5ec2ea7ee110f0d7e> accessed 5 May 2024.

42 Department for Transport, 'Clean Maritime Plan' (2019), Foreword <https://assets.publishing.service.gov.uk/media/5d24a96fe5274a2f9d175693/clean-maritime-plan.pdf> accessed 5 May 2024.

43 House of Commons Transport Committee, *Maritime 2050: Government Response to the Committee's Fifth Report* (HC 2023, 1420) para 60 <https://committees.parliament.uk/publications/40458/documents/197439/default/> accessed 5 May 2024.

focused plan is now necessary to give the industry certainty about the part it will play, the fuels and vessel types that will be supported, and the regulatory environment that will be in place to achieve net zero by 2050'.

18.69 In response, the government has committed to publishing a revised CMP by the end of 2023.[44] This is still awaited at the time of writing. The government will also establish a new Maritime Council to prioritise and deliver the recommendations in the Transport Committee report.

18.70 In its progress report to Parliament, dated June 2023, the CCC was critical of the government's failure to implement policies to deliver adequate emissions reductions in respect of shipping and noted that there is currently a policy vacuum pending an update to the CMP:

> Policy development has been insufficient in the shipping sector as, without an update to the Clean Maritime Plan, there are currently no credible policies in place to meet the required emissions reduction by the Sixth Carbon Budget period.[45]

(c) National Policy Statement for Ports 2012

18.71 The NPS for Ports provides the framework for determining applications for new port developments falling within the definition of an NSIP. It is also a relevant consideration for the Marine Management Organisation,[46] which decides other port development proposals, and for local planning authorities where they have a role to play.[47] The NPS covers England and Wales only.

18.72 Under the heading 'Climate Change Mitigation', the NPS advises at paragraphs 4.12.2–4.12.3 that:

> The decision-maker does not need to consider the impact of a new port development on greenhouse gas emissions from ships transiting to and from the port as these are considered at an international level.

18.73 This does not align with the approach in the Airports NPS, which does require emissions to be taken into account: see paragraph 18.12 above.

18.74 In March 2023, the government announced a review of the Ports NPS. The current NPS remains in force pending the outcome of the review.[48]

---

44 ibid.

45 Climate Change Committee, 'Progress in Reducing Emissions: 2023 Report to Parliament' (2023) page 292 <https://www.theccc.org.uk/wp-content/uploads/2023/06/Progress-in-reducing-UK-emissions-2023-Report-to-Parliament.pdf> accessed 4 April 2024.

46 See Chapter 4 on other public bodies generally, and paras 4.38–4.45 on the MMO in particular.

47 Department for Transport, 'National Policy Statement for Ports' (2012) para 1.2.1 <https://assets.publishing.service.gov.uk/media/5a78c20ae5274a277e68f3b1/national-policy-statement-ports.pdf> accessed 5 May 2024.

48 Baroness Vere of Norbiton, 'Review of the National Policy Statement for Ports: Statement UIN HLWS617' <https://questions-statements.parliament.uk/written-statements/detail/2023-03-14/hlws617> accessed 5 May 2024.

(iii) *Statutory framework*

(a) MARPOL

18.75 The International Convention for the Prevention of Pollution from Ships ('MARPOL') was developed by the IMO for the prevention of pollution of the marine environment by ships. The current version of MARPOL was signed in 1983. As of January 2018, 156 states were parties to the convention.

18.76 Annex 6 of MARPOL came into force on 19 May 2005 and addresses the prevention of air pollution in ships. The current version of Annex VI comprises 5 chapters and 26 regulations. Chapter 3 contains the regulations controlling and limiting emissions from ships, except CO_2 emissions. These are covered by Chapter 4.

18.77 On 1 November 2022, amendments to Annex VI were adopted to cover mandatory technical and operational energy efficiency measures aimed at reducing GHG emissions from international shipping in 2030 by at least 40%, compared to 2008 levels.

18.78 The IMO's illustrative draft outline for a net zero framework agreed at MEPC 81 (see paragraph 18.65 above) in March 2024 includes a proposed new Chapter 5 of MARPOL Annex VI, containing regulation on the IMO net zero framework to include a goal-based marine fuel standard and an economic mechanism to incentivise the transition to net zero.[49]

(b) Climate Change Act 2008

18.79 See paragraphs 18.35–18.38 above for the relevant provisions of the CCA 2008, so far as they apply to international aviation and shipping.

(c) EU/UK ETS

18.80 With effect from 1 January 2024, the EU ETS has been extended to cover CO_2 emissions from all large ships (of 5,000 gross tonnage and above) entering EU ports.

18.81 Maritime transport is not currently included in the UK ETS, pursuant to the Greenhouse Gas Emissions Trading Scheme Order 2020.

18.82 However, on 3 July 2023, the UK ETS authority announced that from 2026, the UK ETS would be expanded to include domestic maritime transport only, for ships of 5,000 gross tonnage and above, subject to further consultation on the details of implementation.[50]

---

49 House of Commons Transport Committee, *Maritime 2050: Government Response to the Committee's Fifth Report* (n 43).

50 Department for Energy Security and Net Zero, 'Press Release: Tighter Limit on Industrial, Power and Aviation Emissions, as UK Leads the Way to Net Zero' (2023) <https://www.gov.uk/government/news/tighter-limit-on-industrial-power-and-aviation-emissions-as-uk-leads-the-way-to-net-zero> accessed 5 May 2024.

(d) Planning Act 2008

18.83 The construction or alteration of harbour facilities falls within the definition of an NSIP for the purposes of section 14(1)(j) PA 2008 if it meets the thresholds set out in section 24 of the PA 2008.

18.84 Where the thresholds in section 14 and section 24 are not met for harbour facilities, the provisions of the TCPA 1990 will apply.

(iv) *Issues arising in practice*

18.85 In the aviation context, legal issues have arisen in the context of airport expansion schemes and the adoption of new government policy aimed at addressing aviation emissions. With the promotion of freeports and the planned review of the NPS, attention may also begin to shift to the environmental impacts of shipping.[51]

18.86 Port and harbour development may also give rise to legal issues relating to marine and coastal protection, as well as engaging the Habitats Regulations, particularly where development is proposed in or close to marine protected areas.[52]

Rail

(i) *Introduction*

18.87 Rail has the potential to play an important role in decarbonising and meeting the UK's net zero targets. However, progress towards electrification – which will be the main way of decarbonising the rail network – has been slow to date.[53]

18.88 Although rail may have a positive role to play in the drive towards net zero, rail-related development often has significant local environmental impacts. In recent years legal issues arising in relation to the environmental impacts of rail development have largely focused on HS2, which has been the subject of a series of legal challenges.

18.89 As with aviation and shipping, there have been significant policy developments in recent years, with the aim of providing a comprehensive policy framework to achieve net zero by 2050.

(ii) *Policy framework*

(a) The sustainable rail strategy

18.90 In May 2021, the government published a rail white paper, entitled the 'Williams-Shapps Plan for Rail'. This calls for a 30-year strategy to 'provide clear, long-term

51 Wildlife and Countryside Link, 'Freeports Inquiry: Evidence for the International Trade Committee by Wildlife and Countryside Link' <https://committees.parliament.uk/writtenevidence/5465/pdf/> accessed 5 May 2024.
52 See Chapter 9 for a more detailed discussion on 'Protected Areas' and see also Chapter 19 on 'Water'.
53 Catherine Moore, 'Slow Progress in Decarbonising UK Railways Revealed' [2022] *New Civil Engineer* <https://www.newcivilengineer.com/latest/slow-progress-in-decarbonising-uk-railways-revealed-28-03-2022/> accessed 5 May 2024.

plans for transforming the railways', incorporating a 'comprehensive environment plan for the rail network' to 'establish rail as the backbone of a cleaner future transport system'.[54]

18.91 This was followed in July 2021 by the 'Rail Environment Policy Statement' ('REPS'), which focuses on electrification as the main way to reduce carbon emissions from the railway, while also identifying 'a role for battery and hydrogen trains on some lines, where they make economic and operational sense'.[55]

18.92 A draft sustainable rail strategy ('SRS') was published for consultation from March to July 2022.

(b) The National Networks National Policy Statement

18.93 The National Policy Statement for National Networks ('NPSNN') was designated in December 2014. However, in a written ministerial statement dated 21 July 2021 the Minister for Transport (Rt Hon Grant Shapps MP) announced a review of the NPSNN, noting that it was written before the government's legal commitment to net zero, the Ten Point Plan for a Green Industrial Revolution, the new Sixth Carbon Budget and the TDP.

18.94 On 14 March 2023 the DfT laid a draft revised National Networks National Policy Statement ('NNNPS') before Parliament. The revised NNNPS was designated on 24 March 2024.[56]

18.95 The revised NNNPS states that 'In the short to medium term, the government's policy, as part of its broader transport policy, is to improve the connectivity, capacity and reliability of the railway network'.[57] However, 'larger interventions including new rail links and upgrades will be required in a number of cases to meet [the identified] needs'.[58]

18.96 In relation to decarbonisation of the railway network, the revised NNNPS notes that:

> improvements to the rail network will be needed to support decarbonisation. These may include decarbonisation of the existing network through improvements in power supply and rolling stock, such as the adoption of electric, battery, and hydrogen technologies. Further, the government's walking and cycling plan, Gear Change, includes a commitment

---

54 Department for Transport, *Policy Paper: Great British Railways: Williams-Shapps Plan for Rail* (CP 423, 2021) 89 <https://assets.publishing.service.gov.uk/media/60a514bce90e07356c43a038/gbr-williams-shapps-plan-for-rail-print.pdf> accessed 5 May 2024.

55 Department for Transport, 'Policy Paper: Environmental Sustainability on the Railway: Stating Our Priorities' (2021) 12–13 <https://assets.publishing.service.gov.uk/media/60eee7498fa8f50c7f08ae4b/rail-environment-policy-statement.pdf> accessed 5 May 2024.

56 Department for Transport, 'National Networks National Policy Statement March 2024' <National Networks - National Policy Statement (publishing.service.gov.uk)> accessed 15 October 2024.

57 ibid, para 3.75.

58 ibid, para 3.77.

to implement greenways to improve traffic free links between communities disrupted by the construction of new railways.[59]

18.97 The Government's support for the growth of rail freight is also emphasised due to the 'environmental and economic benefits of the sector'.[60]

18.98 The revised NNNPS is considered further at paragraphs 18.128–18.145 below.

(c) Other relevant policies

18.99 In March 2020, the DfT published a policy paper titled 'Decarbonising Transport: Setting the Challenge', which invited consultation on the then inchoate decarbonisation of transport plan. In the policy paper, the Secretary of State acknowledged that:[61]

> the UK must go much further in reducing domestic transport emissions than currently projected if we are to meet the emission levels set out in the 2032 Clean Growth Strategy scenario …

18.100 The TDP sets out the government's plan to decarbonise the entire transport system, including rail, in order to meet net zero by 2050.

18.101 The expansion of the rail network and electrification are also identified under point 5 of the government's 'Ten Point Plan for a Green Industrial Revolution', published in November 2020.

(iii) *Statutory framework*

(a) The HS2 Acts

18.102 Unlike other rail developments, which will fall to be determined either under the TCPA 1990 or the PA 2008, the construction and operation of HS2 is governed by project-specific legislation. Phase 1 of HS2 is governed by the High-Speed Rail (London–West Midlands) Act 2017.

18.103 The High-Speed Rail (West Midlands–Crewe) Act 2021 ('the 2021 Act') received Royal Assent in February 2021 and was intended to govern the construction and operation of phase 2(a) from Birmingham to Crewe. However, on 2 October 2023, the government announced the cancellation of the northern leg of HS2 beyond Birmingham, including phase 2(a). At the current time, the 2021 Act remains on the statute book.

18.104 The 2017 Act deems that planning permission is granted for the HS2 project. However, Schedule 17 provides that HS2 Limited must make requests to local authorities for approval of various matters relating to the construction of HS2, as a condition

---

59 ibid, para 3.77.
60 ibid, para 3.78.
61 Department for Transport, 'Decarbonising Transport: Setting the Challenge' <https://assets.publishing.service.gov.uk/media/5fa03423d3bf7f03a7a99151/decarbonising-transport-setting-the-challenge.pdf> accessed 5 May 2024 para 4.5.

of the grant of consent. Appeals against refusal or non-determination of requests are made to the two Secretaries of State.

18.105 There have been a series of challenges to the HS2 project on environmental and related grounds: see *R (HS2 Action Alliance Ltd) v Secretary of State for Transport and others*;[62] *R (Christopher Packham) v Secretary of State for Transport*;[63] and *London Borough of Hillingdon v Secretaries of State*,[64] where Sir Keith Lindblom observed that, 'Few projects of major infrastructure have come before the courts more often than HS2.'[65]

(b) Climate Change Act 2008

18.106 Emissions from domestic rail transport count as emissions from sources in the UK for the purposes of setting carbon budgets under section 4 of the CCA 2008.

(c) Planning Act 2008

18.107 The construction of a railway will fall within the definition of an NSIP, if it meets the thresholds set out in section 25 of the PA 2008.

18.108 The construction of a rail freight interchange will fall within the definition of an NSIP, where it meets the thresholds set out in section 26.

18.109 Where the thresholds in sections 25 and 26 are not met, the provisions of the TCPA 1990 will apply.

(iv) *Issues arising in practice*

(a) Local environmental impacts

18.110 Many of the challenges in recent years in this area have concerned HS2: see paragraphs 18.98–18.101 above. However, strategic rail freight interchanges have also proved contentious and have resulted in long-running legal disputes on environmental grounds.[66] While new rail development has the potential to have positive impacts in terms of carbon emissions, it often has significant local environmental impacts, including loss of habitats or woodland.[67]

(b) Decision-making process

18.111 In practice, significant railway projects are likely to fall within the definition of an NSIP, and so engage the DCO process. This is addressed in more detail in Chapter 6.

---

62 *R (HS2 Action Alliance Ltd) v Secretary of State for Transport and others* [2014] UKSC 3.
63 *R (Christopher Packham) v Secretary of State for Transport* [2020] EWCA Civ 1004.
64 *London Borough of Hillingdon v Secretaries of State* [2021] EWCA Civ 1501.
65 See, also, *R (Buckinghamshire Council) v Secretary of State for Transport Secretary of State for Levelling Up, Housing and Communities* [2022] EWHC 1923 (Admin).
66 See, for example, *St Albans City and District Council v Secretary of State for Communities & Local Government* [2015] EWHC 655 (Admin).
67 See *Packham v The Secretary of State for Transport and another* [2020] EWHC 829 (Admin) where the claimant's application for an injunction was unsuccessful, although the Court accepted that the works 'would bring about irreversible damage on a substantial scale'.

(c) Interaction with other statutory regimes

18.112 The construction of lines for long-distance railway traffic falls within Schedule 1 of the EIA Regulations and so is automatically EIA development requiring EIA assessment. The construction of all other railways falls within Schedule 2, where the area of works exceeds 1 hectare.

18.113 New railway lines or terminal buildings may also impact upon protected species or habitats and so require habitats regulation assessment.[68]

Road projects

(i) *Introduction*

18.114 In the UK, transport is the largest emitting sector of GHG emissions, producing 24% of the total emissions in 2020. The overwhelming majority of those emissions came from road vehicles.[69]

18.115 Reducing emissions from road vehicles is therefore critical to achieving net zero. This has been explicitly recognised by the government, in the Net Zero Strategy. It expects a reduction in emissions from transport[70] by 2035 by 47–59% from 1990.[71] The CCC has also advised that, in order to meet the Sixth Carbon Budget, surface transport emissions must be reduced by 70% by the mid-2030s.[72] The government has recognised that the UK must go much further in reducing domestic transport emissions than currently projected, in order to meet the emission levels set out in the 2032 Clean Growth Strategy scenario.[73]

18.116 Road infrastructure projects vary in scope and scale, but often result in (and, indeed, are designed to produce) increased road capacity. Their carbon emission impact is twofold: (a) the building and maintenance of roads; and (b) the use of roads. In addition, road infrastructure projects generally raise issues relating to air quality, habitats and noise.

18.117 As set out further below, it is important to note a stark difference of approach to road projects as between England and Wales:

- In England, investment in road infrastructure projects is enshrined in the Road Investment Strategy 2 ('RIS2'), and is a major part of the government's growth

---

68 See Chapter 9 for a more detailed discussion of the Habitats Regulations.
69 Department for Transport, 'Official Statistics: Transport and Environment Statistics 2022' (2022) <https://www.gov.uk/government/statistics/transport-and-environment-statistics-2022/transport-and-environment-statistics-2022> accessed 5 May 2024.
70 'Transport' includes emissions from domestic transport and international aviation and shipping.
71 Department for Energy Security and Net Zero, 'Net Zero Strategy: Build Back Greener' (2021) 79 <https://www.gov.uk/government/publications/net-zero-strategy> accessed 28 September 2023.
72 Climate Change Committee, 'The Sixth Carbon Budget: Surface Transport' (2020) <https://www.theccc.org.uk/wp-content/uploads/2020/12/Sector-summary-Surface-transport.pdf> accessed 5 May 2024.
73 Department for Transport, 'Decarbonising Transport: Setting the Challenge' (n 59) para 4.5.

plan. Some £27.4 billion is secured for road infrastructure projects in the five-year period between 2020 to 2025;[74] and

- In Wales, by contrast, all road projects were frozen pursuant to an independent 'roads review' in June 2021. Following the review, the Welsh government committed to only developing road schemes which meet a stringent policy future road building test, involving reduction of carbon emissions, and not increasing road capacity. As a result, all major road building projects have ceased.[75]

18.118 This section primarily addresses the legal and policy framework in England.

(ii) *Statutory framework*

(a) Planning Act 2008[76]

18.119 'Highway-related development' in England is within the scope of the PA 2008, where it meets the specific thresholds prescribed under sections 14 and 22. In particular, the thresholds include:

- in relation to the construction or alteration of a motorway, the area of development[77] is greater than 15 hectares (section 22(4)(a));
- in relation to the construction or alteration of a highway, other than a motorway, where the speed limit is expected to be 50 miles per hour or greater, the area of development is greater than 12.5 hectares (section 22(4)(b));
- in relation to the construction or alteration of any other highway, the area of development is greater than 7.5 hectares (section 22(4)(c)); and
- the improvement of a highway, where the improvement is likely to have a 'significant effect on the environment' (section 22(5)).

18.120 Accordingly, if a highway-related development meets the thresholds, it will be governed by the PA 2008's provisions, and (in particular) the Infrastructure Planning (Environmental Impact Assessment) Regulations 2017. Where highway-related development does not meet the definition of a NSIP, the provisions of the TCPA 1990 will apply.

74 Department for Transport, 'Road Investment Strategy 2: 2020–2025' (2020) <https://assets.publishing.service.gov.uk/media/5ffb39808fa8f56405c5f5bf/road-investment-strategy-2-2020-2025.pdf> accessed 5 May 2024.

75 Welsh Government, 'Welsh Government Response to the Roads Review' (2023) <https://www.gov.wales/sites/default/files/pdf-versions/2023/2/2/1676385038/welsh-government-response-roads-review.pdf> accessed 5 May 2024.

76 See Chapter 6 and para 3.57 in Chapter 3.

77 Under s 22(9), 'Area of development' is specifically defined as being: (a) in relation to construction of a highway, means the land on which the highway is to be constructed and any adjoining land expected to be used in connection with its construction; (b) in relation to alteration of a highway, means the land on which the part of the highway to be altered is situated and any adjoining land expected to be used in connection with its alteration.

(b) Infrastructure Act 2015

18.121 Section 1 of the Infrastructure Act 2015 ('IA 2015') makes provision for the appointment of one or more companies as a highway authority (a 'strategic highways company'). The functions of a strategic highways company include, for example, following directions issued by the Secretary of State for the management and development of particular highways.

18.122 The strategic highways company in respect of the strategic roads network ('SRN'), made up of motorways and major A-roads, is National Highways (formally registered as Highways England Company Ltd). The Secretary of State for Transport is the sole shareholder of National Highways.

18.123 Section 3(1) of the IA 2015 empowers the Secretary of State to set a Road Investment Strategy ('RIS') for a strategic highways company. Where a strategic highways company does not currently have a RIS, then section 3(7) requires him or her to set one. Section 8 of, and Schedule 2 to, the IA 2015 prescribe the procedure for setting a RIS.

18.124 A RIS must specify the objectives to be achieved by the strategic highways company, which may include activities to be performed, results to be achieved and standards to be met (sections 3(a) and (4)). A RIS must also specify the financial resources to be provided by the Secretary of State for the purpose of achieving those objectives (section 3(b)). As noted above, the current RIS, 'RIS2', covers the period 2020–2025, and is discussed further below.

18.125 Under section 3(5)(a) when making a RIS, the Secretary must consider, among other things, the effect of the RIS on the environment.

18.126 The Secretary of State and the strategic highways company must comply with the RIS, pursuant to section 3(6). The Office of Rail and Road ('ORR') monitors their compliance, under sections 10 and 11. The ORR may issue the strategic highways company with a fine for non-compliance with the RIS.

(iii) *Policy framework*

(a) The Transport Decarbonisation Plan

18.127 The TDP commits to reducing car use, and increasing greener transport, and acknowledges that zero emissions vehicles are not a panacea. Whilst the TDP does not directly address road infrastructure construction, alteration or improvement projects, it states:[78]

> We cannot simply believe that zero emission cars and lorries will meet all our climate goals or solve all our problems. They will not, particularly in reaching the medium-term

---

78 Department for Transport, 'Decarbonising Transport: A Better, Greener Britain' (2021) <https://assets.publishing.service.gov.uk/media/610d63ffe90e0706d92fa282/decarbonising-transport-a-better-greener-britain.pdf> accessed 6 May 2024 para 29.

Sixth Carbon Budget targets. By its mid year of 2035, the industry body the SMMT estimates that 46% of cars on the roads could be zero emission under a central scenario; percentages for goods vehicles will be lower still. Another risk, until the electricity grid is fully decarbonised, is that carbon savings from electric vehicles are to a partial extent offset if people drive them more. Nor, of course, will zero emission vehicles reduce other harms, such as congestion or road danger, at all.

(b) The National Networks National Policy Statement

18.128 As explained at paragraph 18.92, above, the NNNPS was first designated in 2014 (when the CCA 2008 pre-net zero target was to cut GHGs by at least 80% by 2050).

18.129 It prescribed a broad general need for NSIPs on the road (and rail) networks. The NNNPS's 'summary of need' explained that networks which were needed included those, amongst other things, 'which support and improve journey quality, reliability and safety', and 'which support the delivery of environmental goals and the move to a low carbon economy'. It set[79] a presumption in favour of granting development consent for national networks NSIPs that fall within the need for infrastructure established in the NNNPS.

18.130 With regard to climate change, the NNNPS provided (amongst other things) at paragraph 5.18, that:

> any increase in carbon emissions is not a reason to refuse development consent, unless the increase in carbon emissions resulting from the proposed scheme are so significant that it would have a material impact on the ability of Government to meet its carbon reduction targets.

18.131 When the TDP was published on 14 July 2021, the Secretary of State announced the decision to review the NNNPS in the following terms:[80]

> The current National Policy Statement (NPS) on National Networks, the government's statement of strategic planning policy for major road and rail schemes, was written in 2014 – before the government's legal commitment to net zero, the Ten Point Plan for a Green Industrial Revolution, the new Sixth Carbon Budget and most directly the new, more ambitious policies outlined in this document. While the NPS continues to remain in force, it is right that we review it in the light of these developments, and update forecasts on which it is based to reflect more recent, post-pandemic conditions, once they are known.

79 Department for Transport, 'Policy Paper: National Networks National Policy Statement' (n 57) para 4.2.
80 For a detailed account of the background to the Secretary of State's decision to review the NNNPS, see: *R (Transport Action Network Ltd) v Secretary of State for Transport* (n 58) [14]–[25].

18.132 The revised NNNPS maintains that there is 'at a strategic level ... a compelling need development of the national networks – both as individual networks and as a fully integrated system'.[81]

18.133 The revised NNNPS observes that 'continued absolute traffic growth' is likely in all the DfT's modelled future potential scenarios, and as such, the revised NNNPS endorses the need for road infrastructure projects in the following terms, at paragraph 3.31:

> enhancements on the national road network will be necessary in order to ensure the national road network operates effectively in the face of growing demand. Infrastructure interventions can include measures such as addressing pinch points and improving flow aimed at addressing localised issues to help address reliability, predictability, and capacity issues at specific locations, which can in turn improve overall performance of the wider network of local roads and the SRN in that location. Equally interventions could include measures to reallocate road space to systems for journeys addressing traffic growth via a vision-led approach to that plans for modal shift.

18.134 The revised NNNPS further states at paragraphs 3.46 and 3.47:

> 3.46 The government's wider policy is to bring forward improvements and enhancements to the existing SRN where necessary to address the needs set out earlier. Enhancements to the existing national road network will include but are not limited to:
>
> - New and improved junctions and slip roads
> - Improvements to trunk roads, in particular, dualling of single carriageway strategic trunk roads and additional lanes on existing dual carriageways
> - Measures to enhance capacity of the motorway network
>
> 3.47 In some cases, to meet the need set out in this NPS, it will no/t be sufficient to simply expand capacity on the existing network. In those circumstances new road alignments and corresponding links, including alignments which cross a river or estuary, may be needed to support increased capacity and connectivity.

18.135 On climate change, the revised NNNPS provides at paragraph 3.40, that:

> Any scheme needs to comply with the environmental legislative requirements and address the policy context appropriately. Infrastructure improvements may help to facilitate a reduction in emissions (such as carbon, air pollution, noise or discharges to water resources), improvements to the natural and built environment (such as landscapes, biodiversity, or cultural heritage improvements) or increased accessibility for non-motorised users and reduced severance. For example, reducing the time vehicles spend in congestion may reduce carbon and air quality emissions at that particular location.

---

81 Department for Transport, National Networks National Policy Statement (24 May 2024) para 3.31 <https://assets.publishing.service.gov.uk/media/65e9c5ac62ff48001a87b373/national-networks-national-policy-statement-web.pdf> accessed 14 October 2024.

18.136 There are several specific obligations introduced by the NNNPS that concern GHG emissions. However, the final, as designated version of the revised NNNPS markedly rowed back from some of the measures contained in the draft, which was published and laid before parliament on 14 March 2023.

18.137 First, the revised NNNPS obliges applicants to use a whole life carbon assessment to measure GHG emissions at every stage of the proposed development,

18.138 Notably, the draft version of the NNNPS included the following at paragraph 5.29:

> to ensure that emissions are minimised as far as possible as we transition to net zero. This includes the construction, maintenance, operation and use of the asset across its entire lifecycle. This is critical at early stages of project planning, for example, the conception stage, because the ability to reduce whole life carbon emissions is increasingly more limited as the project passes through detailed design and enters construction.

18.139 The final, as designated version, omits the reference to ensuring emissions are minimised as far as possible in the transition to net zero, and includes the following at paragraph 5.30:

> national network infrastructure plays an important role in supporting decarbonisation. While all steps should be taken to avoid, and where unavoidable, reduce and mitigate climate change impacts, there will likely be residual emissions from national networks infrastructure, particularly during the economy wide transition to net zero, and potentially beyond.

18.140 Secondly, a 'carbon management plan' must be produced as part of the applicant's DCO submission. A carbon management plan would include, for example, an explanation of the steps taken to drive down climate change impacts, alongside how operational emissions have been reduced as much possible by the application of best available technology.

18.141 Finally, in making a decision, the Secretary of State must be satisfied that the applicant has as far as possible assessed the GHG emissions at all stages of the development. The draft NNNPS states at paragraph 5.38 to 5.42:

> 5.38 The Secretary of State must be satisfied that the applicant has as far as possible assessed the carbon emissions at all stages of the development. The Secretary of State for Energy Security and Net Zero regularly assesses whether the UK has sufficient policies and proposals overall to meet the UK carbon budgets, with a view to meeting the net zero target, in line with the duties under section 13 of the Climate Change Act 2008. It would not be feasible or sensible for such an assessment to be done at the time of taking individual development decisions, and there is no legal requirement to do so.
>
> 5.39 S.1(1) of the Climate Change Act 2008 reflects and puts into effect the net zero target set in light of the temperature goal of the Paris Agreement. The target was

increased from 80% emission reductions by 2050 to 100% emission reductions by 2050 in June 2019. Carbon budgets 1 to 5 were set to meet the 80% emission reduction target, but carbon budget 6 (2033–2037) has been set to meet the 2050 net zero target, so it is more stretching. The UK's current Nationally Determined Contribution (set in line with Article 4 of the Paris Agreement) commits to reducing economy-wide greenhouse gas emissions by at least 68% by 2030, compared to 1990 levels, so it is more stretching than carbon budget 5. The UK's Nationally Determined Contribution is on the pathway to the 2050 net zero target. Where it provides useful context, applicants may wish to compare their scheme emissions against carbon budgets, net zero and the UK Nationally Determined Contribution. Where an applicant assesses the carbon impacts of its scheme against carbon budget 6, and later carbon budgets, it is to be taken also to have assessed the carbon impacts of the scheme against the net zero target in the Climate Change Act 2008, as they are in line with this target.

5.40 The Secretary of State should be content that the applicant has taken all reasonable steps to reduce the total carbon emissions at all stages of development. The Secretary of State should also give positive weight to projects that embed nature-based or technological processes to mitigate or offset the emissions of construction and within the proposed development. However, given the important role national network infrastructure plays in supporting the process of economy wide decarbonisation, the Secretary of State accepts that there are likely to be some residual emissions from construction of national network infrastructure.

5.41 Operational carbon emissions from some types of national network infrastructure cannot be totally avoided. Given the range of non-planning policies aimed at decarbonising the transport system, government has determined that a net increase in operational carbon emissions is not, of itself, reason to prohibit the consenting of national network projects or to impose more restrictions on them in the planning policy framework.

5.42 Any carbon assessment will include an assessment of operational carbon emissions, but the policies set out in chapter 2 of this NPS, apply to these emissions. Operational emissions will be addressed in a managed, economywide manner, to ensure consistency with carbon budgets, net zero and our international climate commitments. Therefore, approval of schemes with residual carbon emissions is allowable and can be consistent with meeting net zero. However, where the increase in carbon emissions resulting from the proposed scheme are so significant that it would have a material impact on the ability of government to achieve its statutory carbon budgets, the Secretary of State should refuse consent.

18.142 Notably, the final designated version abandoned the requirement for a 'Greenhouse Gas Reduction Strategy', which was proposed to be secured under a Development Consent Order for a project. A Greenhouse Gas Reduction Strategy would have required steps to be taken to minimise, capture and offset emissions in design and construction.[82]

---

82 House of Commons Transport Committee, *Draft Revised National Policy Statement for National Networks* (HC 2023, 903) para 5.33 <https://committees.parliament.uk/publications/41770/documents/206912/default/> accessed 5 May 2024.

18.143 In its Progress Report on Net Zero published in June 2023, the CCC considered that the draft NNNPS needed to be clearer on the network's role in reducing traffic growth, rather than simply meeting projected demand. The CCC recommended that the government conduct:[83]

> a systematic review of current and future road-building projects to assess their consistency with the Government's environmental goals. This should ensure that decisions do not lock in unsustainable levels of traffic growth and develop conditions…that permit schemes to be taken forward only if they meaningfully support cost-effective delivery of Net Zero and climate adaptation.

18.144 On 20 October 2023, the House of Commons Transport Committee published its report on the draft revised NNNPS. Notably, the Committee observed that whilst the draft NNNPS permits 'residual' GHG emissions, there is no definition of 'residual', and it is unclear what distinction lies between 'residual' and unacceptable increases in emissions from a NSIP.

18.145 Moreover, the Committee recommended that the draft NNNPS be amended to explicitly state the government's understanding of the legal precedent for permitting major infrastructure schemes which result in an increase in emissions, where that increase is judged as not likely to harm the achievement of a national target. The designated version did not adopt the Committee's recommendation.

(c) Strategic road network and the delivery of sustainable development

18.146 The DfT has also published a policy document titled 'Strategic Road Network and the Delivery of Sustainable Development' ('the SRN circular'). It is a circular which provides direction to National Highways in respect of certain of its functions. In particular, it requires that National Highways acts in a manner which 'conforms to the principles of sustainable development'. The SRN circular notes that National Highways' licence agreement defines sustainable development as 'encouraging economic growth while protecting the environment and improving safety and quality of life for current and future generations'.[84]

18.147 In addition, the SRN circular provides that National Highways have an important role to play in the drive towards net zero emission transport, through (amongst other things) its commitment to net zero road user emissions by 2050.

18.148 It further provides that new development should be facilitating a reduction in the need to travel by private car and focused on locations that are or can be made sustainable. The SRN circular is otherwise relatively limited in its guidance on net zero. In respect of capacity enhances on the SRN, it provides broadly that:[85]

---

83 Climate Change Committee, 'Progress in Reducing Emissions: 2023 Report to Parliament' (n 45) 40.
84 Department for Transport, 'Policy Paper: Strategic Road Network and the Delivery of Sustainable Development' (2022) para 11 <https://www.gov.uk/government/publications/strategic-road-network-and-the-delivery-of-sustainable-development/strategic-road-network-and-the-delivery-of-sustainable-development> accessed 5 May 2024.
85 ibid para 23.

> Capacity enhancements such as modifications to existing junctions or road widening to facilitate development should be determined on a case-by-case basis. The general principle should be accepted where proposals would include measures to improve community connectivity and public transport accessibility, and this will be weighed against any negative safety, traffic flow, environmental and deliverability considerations, impacts on the permeability and attractiveness of local walking, wheeling and cycling routes, and alternative options to manage down the traffic impact of planned development or improve the local road network as a first preference.

(d) RIS2

18.149 In brief, RIS2: (a) specifies performance standards that National Highways are required to meet; (b) lists specific planned enhancement schemes to be built; and (c) sets out the funding made available during the financial years 2020/21 to 2024/25 (the second road period).

18.150 RIS2 makes several references to the net zero target, but it primarily relies upon the (then forthcoming) TDP, to address road transport's contribution to meeting net zero.

18.151 The revised draft NNNPS endorsed RIS2 in the following terms:[86]

> The Road Investment Strategy outlines the government's 5-year strategy for investment in, improvement of, and management of the strategic road network. User needs and performance of the network are critical considerations in the preparation of the Road Investment Strategy. The Road Investment Strategy identifies the balance between large-scale infrastructure interventions covered by this NPS, and smaller-scale enhancements and maintenance. The Road Investment Strategy also identifies individual schemes that meet the corridor of localised benefits and which collectively deliver strategic benefits from a programmatic approach.

(iv) *Issues arising in practice*

18.152 There have been several judicial review challenge to DCOs authorising road NSIPs. A common issue which has arisen in different permeations, is the approach to be taken by the decision-maker in assessing the impact of a development on carbon budgets, and in turn, the net zero target.

18.153 The approach generally taken in respect of NSIPs is to assess their carbon impact against the national carbon budget. In *R (Boswell) v Secretary of State for Transport*,[87] the claimant contended that the Secretary of State was required to assess three road schemes cumulatively, against local carbon budgets, by the EIA Regulations. Each scheme had been compared against the national carbon budgets, with the purpose of compliance with net zero. Thornton J concluded that the Secretary of State's approach had not been

---

86 House of Commons Transport Committee, *Draft Revised National Policy Statement for National Networks* (n 79) para 3.32.
87 *R (Boswell) v Secretary of State for Transport* [2023] EWHC 1710 (Admin).

in breach of the EIA Regulations, and was a rational exercise of judgment. Specifically, Thornton J applied *R (Goesa Ltd) v Eastleigh BC*[88] (see paragraphs 18.52–18.53 above) in which Holgate J held that the use of national carbon budgets as a benchmark for the assessment of carbon emissions was lawful.

18.154 Thornton J generally discouraged judicial review claims seeking to challenge the acceptability of the carbon impact of an individual scheme at [84]:

> On analysis therefore, Dr Boswells approach to cumulative assessment becomes, in essence, a case about the acceptability of the impact, as may be evident in his conclusion that the combined emissions from the schemes (and related development) will amount to 0.47% of the UKs 6th national carbon budget and his concern about the extent of the emissions used up on relatively small schemes in a small area of Norfolk. However, the legislation does not deal with the acceptability of an effect identified by environmental information. That is a matter of judgement for the decision-maker, not a hard-edged point of law (GOESA at §122 – 123). The Courts must be astute to avoid being drawn into the arena of the forbidden merits. Decisions to upgrade strategic roads and their effect upon climate change is a subject attracting many widely differing views, whether for or against.

18.155 The Court of Appeal[89] upheld Thornton J's analysis in the claimant's appeal. The claimant was granted permission only to appeal the issue as to whether the Secretary of State lawfully discharged the obligation to examine and assess the cumulative GHG emissions likely to result from each of the proposed developments.

18.156 The crux of the Court of Appeal's analysis was as follows:[90]

> In substance, [the Secretary of State] considered that the likely future emissions from the Scheme, calculated in the wider local context of the relevant ARN, fell below the threshold of significance, and that there was no meaningful way in which a wider assessment of cumulative emissions could be carried out in the light of current scientific knowledge and the lack of any geographical boundary for such emissions.
>
> ... the Secretary of State clearly addressed his mind to the question of cumulative effects, and he took into account the submissions which Dr Boswell had made at the examination stage of the EIA process, but he nevertheless decided that there was no meaningful basis, in this particular context, upon which a wider cumulative assessment of carbon emissions could be undertaken. By virtue of regulation 5(2), the EIA must identify, describe and assess in an appropriate manner, in light of each individual case, the direct and indirect significant effects of the proposed development on, among other things air and climate (my emphasis). The Secretary of State concluded, for reasons which he adequately articulated and integrated into his decision, that there was no appropriate manner in which cumulative GHG emissions from each Scheme could usefully be modelled and taken into

---

88 *R (Goesa Ltd) v Eastleigh BC* (n 35).
89 *R (Boswell) v Secretary of State for Transport* (n 37).
90 ibid [52] and [54].

> account, separately from the elements of cumulation which were already inherent in the use of an ARN baseline which included the other Schemes, and in the use of national net carbon budgets as the comparator. In my judgment, a process of reasoning along these lines would have been more than adequate to discharge the duties imposed on the Secretary of State by regulation 21.

18.157 A similar challenge to a DCO authorising a road NSIP in Bedfordshire (the A428 scheme) was brought by Transport Action Network Ltd, but refused permission by Sir Ross Cranston following an oral renewal hearing.

18.158 In *R (Save Stonehenge World Heritage Site Ltd) v Secretary of State for Transport* ('Stonehenge 2'),[91] the court refused the claimants' application for permission to apply for judicial review of the Secretary of State for Transport's decision to re-grant a DCO for the construction of a new dual carriageway and tunnel at the Stonehenge world heritage site, after the original DCO had been quashed in earlier judicial review proceedings.

18.159 The claimants pursued two grounds of general relevance to road infrastructure projects. The claimants argued that: (a) the Secretary of State failed to consider not applying the NPSNN under section 104(4), (5) or (7) of the PA 2008 and/or acted irrationally in not departing from the NPSNN in relation to climate change, given that that policy is being reviewed because it does not take into account current obligations under the CCA 2008 (Ground 6); and (b) the approach to environmental impact assessment was unlawful in relation to the cumulative effect of GHG emissions from the DCO scheme and other committed road schemes (Ground 7).

18.160 However, on 6 November 2023, Ground 7 was stayed behind the Court of Appeal's decision in *Boswell* (addressed above).

18.161 Holgate J concluded that Ground 6 was unarguable at [255]:

> In substance ground 6 is concerned with whether the proposed scheme would impact upon the Government's ability to comply with obligations under the CCA 2008, which give effect to the UK's obligations under the Paris Agreement. The carbon budgets have been set so as to lead towards the achievement of the 2050 net zero target. Paragraph 5.35 of the draft NPSNN continues to accept that it is sufficient to make an assessment of the schemes carbon emissions against the carbon budgets. That is what has been done in the technical analysis placed before the SST and in the decision letter. The SST accepted that assessment and decided that those emissions are negligible and will not impair the UKs ability to meet the carbon budgets.

---

91 *R (Save Stonehenge World Heritage Site Ltd and another) v Secretary of State for Transport* [2024] EWHC 339 (Admin).

Renewable transport fuels

(i) *Introduction*

18.162 Renewable transport fuels have a crucial role to play in achieving net zero by 2050. However, the government's fuel policy has been cautious to date, perhaps due to the novel nature of many of these technologies.[92] There are also political challenges with making the changes required to move to renewable transport fuels and low emission vehicles, particularly in relation to car use, as reflected in the Prime Minister's announcement on 20 September 2023 of the decision to push back the deadline for the sale of petrol and diesel cars from 2030 to 2035.[93]

18.163 The development of sustainable aviation fuel ('SAF') is identified as one of six key measures in the JZS. In November 2023, the Civil Aviation Authority granted a permit to Virgin Atlantic for the first 100% SAF flight from London Heathrow to New York, which was successfully completed on 28 November 2023.[94] However, SAF development and production is currently limited due to high capital costs, as well as its reliance on new technology.[95]

(ii) *Policy framework*

18.164 At the current time, the government does not have a comprehensive low carbon fuel strategy, although a 'call for ideas' consultation ran from February to April 2022.[96]

(a) Transport Decarbonisation Plan

18.165 The TDP recognises the need to maximise the benefits of renewable, low carbon fuels. However, it does not set out the government's strategy for achieving this objective. Instead, it sets out a commitment to develop a strategy for low carbon fuels to 2050. This was due to be published in 2022 but is still awaited.[97]

---

92 See House of Commons Transport Committee, *Fuelling the Future: Motive Power and Connectivity* (HC 2023, 159) <https://committees.parliament.uk/publications/34205/documents/188123/default/> accessed 6 May 2024, which states that 'direction, guidance and regulation from the Department for Transport in respect of sustainable fuels is urgently required' and concludes that the government's 'technology agnostic approach has led to a lack of investment in alternative decarbonisation technologies by the private sector'.

93 See, for example, Alistair Smout, 'Britain Delays Ban on New Petrol and Diesel Cars to 2035, Prime Minister Says' (2023) *Reuters* <https://www.reuters.com/world/uk/britain-delays-ban-new-petrol-diesel-cars-2035-pm-sunak-2023-09-20/> accessed 6 May 2024.

94 UK Civil Aviation Authority, 'Virgin Atlantic Granted Permit to Fly for Historic Transatlantic 100% Sustainable Aviation Fuel Flight' <https://www.caa.co.uk/newsroom/news/virgin-atlantic-granted-permit-to-fly-for-historic-transatlantic-100-sustainable-aviation-fuel-flight/> accessed 6 May 2024.

95 Department for Transport, 'Jet Zero Consultation: Summary of Responses and Government Response' (2022) para 3.16 <https://assets.publishing.service.gov.uk/government/uploads/system/uploads/attachment_data/file/1096928/jet-zero-consultation-summary-of-responses-and-government-response.pdf> accessed 28 April 2024.

96 Department for Transport, 'Low Carbon Fuels Strategy: Call for Ideas' (2022) <https://assets.publishing.service.gov.uk/media/620ce902d3bf7f4f04b2b51e/low-carbon-fuels-strategy-call-for-ideas.pdf> accessed 6 May 2024.

97 See, further, the 'Promoting Green Transport' section below.

(b) Jet Zero Strategy

18.166 The creation of a SAF industry to develop and produce SAF plays a crucial role in the JZS.

18.167 The JZS commits to £180m of new funding between 2022–2025 to support the commercialisation of SAF plants and fuel testing in the UK. It also commits to the implementation of an SAF mandate, to come into force in 2025. This will set an obligation on fuel suppliers to reduce the GHG emissions of aviation fuel by the equivalent of at least 10% SAF use by 2030.

18.168 On 30 March 2023, the government launched its second consultation on the UK SAF mandate.

(iii) *Statutory framework*

(a) Renewable Transport Fuels Obligation ('RTFO')

18.169 The RTFO, established by the Renewable Transport Fuels Obligation 2007, is currently the main measure to incentivise the supply of low carbon fuels. It sets an annual obligation on suppliers to supply renewable fuels. Fuel suppliers who supply 450,000 litres or more of relevant transport fuels are required to register under the RTFO and to demonstrate that a percentage of the fuel they supply comes from renewable and sustainable transport sources. The fuels covered by the RTFO, as amended include petrol, diesel, gas oil and renewable fuels for road vehicles and non-road transport, as well as renewable fuels used for aviation and maritime (if the fuel used is a renewable fuel of non-biological origin ('RFNBO').

18.170 The Renewable Transport Fuels Obligation (Amendment) Order 2021 came into force on 1 January 2022. This increased the RTFO from 9.6% in 2021 to 14.6% in 2032, as well as expanding the scope of eligibility of RFNBOs to include maritime RFNBOs.

(iv) *Issues arising in practice*

18.171 Reliance by the government on future technological advances as a basis for formulating a policy approach to meeting the legally binding net zero requirement under section 1 of the CCA 2008 is fertile ground for judicial review: see, for example, *Friends of the Earth v Secretary of State for Business Energy and Industrial Strategy*,[98] where the claimants successfully challenged the government's net zero strategy. Holgate J held that the Secretary of State did not have legally sufficient information to enable him to adopt the net zero strategy. Moreover, he was still obliged to explain and provide 'legally adequate estimates of the quantifiable effects' of proposed policies even where, for example, the effect of future technologies was uncertain.

98 *R (Friends of the Earth Ltd) v Secretary of State for Business, Energy and Industrial Strategy* (n 38).

18.172 The stayed judicial review of the JZS also challenges the government's reliance upon future technological advances to meet the net zero target. However, see also *R (Dawes) v Secretary of State for Transport*,[99] discussed at paragraph 18.27 above, where Dove J rejected the argument that the defendant was not entitled to rely on its own policies on the basis that decarbonisation measures contained in these policies were untested and aspirational.

Promoting green transport

(i) *Introduction*

18.173 'Green transport' is a broad concept, encompassing sustainable transport that has a minimal or reduced impact on the environment, compared to conventional fossil fuel transport. These include both forms of active travel, walking and cycling, as well as low or zero emission vehicles, such as electric cars and buses. Increasing green transport, so as to ultimately make it the default and primary form of transport in the UK, is, and needs to be, a key pillar of the efforts to meet the net zero target.

(ii) *Policy framework*

(a) Gear Change

18.174 In July 2020, the DfT published 'Gear Change', a policy statement seeking to promote an increase in active travel: walking and cycling. It recognised that mode shift to active transport was one of the most cost-effective ways of reducing transport emissions. Amongst its policy proposals, Gear Change committed to creating cycle, bus and walking corridors, closing some main roads to traffic except for buses. It also commits to ensuring that new housing business developments are built around making sustainable travel, and a series of national urban road audits to help inform future allocation of road space.

18.175 In July 2021, the DfT published a one-year review, summarising what had been achieved, setting out evidence from several case studies, and explaining the benefits of investment. The review noted that the government made some £320 million available to a newly established Active Travel Fund. Furthermore, Active Travel England, a new commissioning body and inspectorate will hold the budget, as well as act as a statutory consultee on larger planning applications so as to ensure walking and cycling is properly provided for.

(b) Transport Decarbonisation Plan

18.176 The TDP establishes the very broad overarching aims of increasing cycling and walking, making buses and coaches zero emission, increasing the electrification of the railways, so as to deliver a net zero rail network by 2050 (and remove all diesel-only trains from the network by 2040) and improve rail connectivity with walking and cycling.

99 *R (Dawes) v Secretary of State for Transport and others* (n 22).

(c) Zero emission vehicle mandate

18.177 The government has recognised that promoting green forms of transport is a key aspect of decarbonising the UK's roads. The government's flagship commitment on green transport, also set out in the TDP, is the removal of all emissions from road transport. The key proposed steps in achieving this commitment were prescribed as follows:

- In 2030, the sale of new petrol and diesel cars and vans would end;
- In 2035, all new cars and vans would be obliged to be 100% zero emission at the tailpipe. In addition, but subject to consultation, all new L-category vehicles would need to be fully zero emission at the tailpipe; and
- In 2040, the sale of all non-zero emission HGVs would end.

18.178 The phase out dates for non-zero emission cars have been pushed back by the current administration. A total of 80% of new cars and 70% of new vans sold in Great Britain will now be zero emission by 2030, increasing to 100% by 2035.[100]

18.179 As set out below, the zero emission vehicle mandate has recently been placed on a statutory footing, through the Vehicle Emissions Trading Schemes Order 2023 SI No 1394.

(d) UK electric vehicle infrastructure strategy: Taking charge

18.180 An important corollary of promoting green transport is ensuring that the vital infrastructure to facilitate their use is in place. The DfT has estimated that approximately 300,000 public charge points will be needed at a minimum, to support the commitment to phase out sales of new diesel and petrol cars and vans.

18.181 On 25 March 2022, the DfT published 'Taking Charge: The electric vehicle infrastructure strategy', a policy paper. Its two key pillars are: (a) a commitment to accelerate the rollout of high powered chargers on the strategic network; and (b) subject to consultation, imposing an obligation on local authorities to develop and implement local charging strategies to plan for the transition to zero emissions.

(e) UK government's plan for drivers

18.182 The government's Plan for Drivers was published on 2 October 2023. It is a broad policy paper, that seeks (in general terms) to improve driving on UK roads. It makes specific provision in respect of the transition to zero emission driving. In particular, it proposes consultations on easing the ability of charge point operators to install chargepoint infrastructure on the public highway using permits, instead of street works licences, and the expansion of permitted development rights in respect of private charge point installation.

100 See the 'Renewable Transport Fuels' section above.

(iii) *Legal framework*

(a) Public Charge Point Regulations 2023 SI No 1168

18.183 The Public Charge Point Regulations 2023 came into force on 24 November 2023, and set out certain requirements for public electric vehicle charge points.

18.184 The key requirements of the Public Charge Point Regulations 2023 are:

- New public charge points of 8kW and above and existing charge points of 50kW and above must offer contactless to consumers;[101]

- Charge point operators must enable consumers to pay through at least one roaming provider at their charge points.[102] Roaming is the ability to pay to charge an EV across multiple charge point networks using a single app or RFID card. The roaming provider must be operated by a person or organisation that is external to the charge point operator;

- Rapid charge points must be 99% reliable, measured as an average across each charge point operator's rapid network.[103] A charge point operator will not be penalised if their reliability is below 99% for a given month, as long as they make this up over the rest of the 12-month period, so that their reliability remains at 99% or above for the whole year. If the reliability rate drops below the point where it is possible to maintain 99% reliability for the year, enforcement action may be taken;

- A free to use 24/7 staffed telephone helpline must be available and advertised at all charge points;[104]

- All data must be accurate and charge point operators must use the Open Charge Point Interface ('OCPI') to hold and open their data (reg 10). Reference and availability data must be made publicly available and in a machine-readable format. Government bodies, Distribution Network Operators, Transmission Owners and Electricity System Operators must have access to all data; and

- The maximum price of a charging session[105] must be displayed clearly in pence per kilowatt hour.[106]

18.185 The Office for Product Safety and Standards ('OPSS') (part of the Department for Business and Trade) acts on behalf of the Secretary of State to enforce the Public

---

101 The Public Charge Point Regulations 2023 SI 2023/1168 reg 5.
102 ibid reg 6.
103 ibid regs 7 and 8.
104 ibid reg 9.
105 ibid reg 11.
106 Department for Transport, 'Guidance: Public Charge Point Regulations 2023 Guidance' (2023) <https://www.gov.uk/government/publications/the-public-charge-point-regulations-2023-guidance/public-charge-point-regulations-2023-guidance> accessed 6 May 2024.

Charge Point Regulations 2023. The separate OPSS enforcement policy provides guidance as to the approach that will be taken to non-compliance.

18.186 In particular, the OPSS can serve a compliance notice requiring action to be taken to remedy the breach. Any failure to comply with the requirements of a compliance notice by the date specified in the notice may result in a civil penalty notice being issued. The maximum civil penalty amount in respect of the obligations imposed by the Public Charge Point Regulations 2023 is £10,000, save for the penalty maximum in respect of obstructing enforcement work, which is £250,000.[107]

(b) Vehicle Emissions Trading Schemes Order 2023 SI No 1394

18.187 The Vehicle Emissions Trading Schemes Order 2023 establishes four new emissions trading schemes across Great Britain, which are intended to help the UK to meet the net zero target. The Vehicle Emissions Trading Schemes Order 2023 was made pursuant to section 44 of the CCA 2008.

18.188 The Non-Zero-Emission Car Registration Trading Scheme ('CRTS') and the Non-Zero-Emission Car CO_2 Trading Scheme ('CCTS') apply to cars, and the Non-Zero-Emission Van Registration Trading Scheme ('VRTS') and the Non-Zero-Emission Van CO_2 Trading Scheme ('VCTS') apply to vans.

18.189 In brief, the CRTS and VRTS provide for annual targets for non-zero emission vehicles ('non-ZEV') registrations, decreasing yearly. The effect of the schemes is that manufacturers must register increasing numbers of ZEVs as a proportion of their overall registrations each year. The CCTS and VCTS set a baseline per-vehicle emissions target, derived from a manufacturer's performance and compliance in 2021. Manufacturers must keep per-vehicle average emissions the same or lower than in 2021, while selling fewer non-ZEVs as set out in the ZEV mandate schemes. It will continue to limit emissions until all new sales are zero emission.

(iv) *Issues arising in practice*

18.190 On 26 October 2023, the High Court granted permission for Transport Action Network's judicial review to challenge the DfT's decision to cut funding for walking and cycling by 75% in March 2023. In particular, Transport Action Network have argued that the DfT has acted incompatibly with section 21 of the IA 2015, which requires the DfT to produce a Cycling and Walking Investment Strategy for England. Judgment is awaited.

---

107 ibid reg 12(1).

CHAPTER 19

WATER

Philippa Jackson and Celia Reynolds

Introduction

19.01 Access to water is vital to society and a wide range of people depend upon it, from households to farmers and industry. Yet, climate change has had, and is continuing to have, a significant impact on water resources and water bodies (including coasts). Thus, there will also need to be investment in water-related infrastructure, as part of adaptation to climate change. This chapter covers a range of topics including water management and scarcity, water infrastructure, flood protection, sea level rise and coastal management, and water as a constraint on development.

Water management and water scarcity

(i) *Introduction*

19.02 Water resources face increasing pressures from population growth, growing consumer expectations, ageing infrastructure and climate change. The climate emergency will have a significant and permanent impact on the water cycle, with serious implications for the water and sewerage sectors in the UK. The Water Services Regulation Authority ('Ofwat') has summarised those impacts as broadly being the following:[1]

- Precipitation – Changing rainfall patterns may make it harder to meet demand and could increase the risk of droughts affecting the supply of water.
- Abstraction – Higher temperatures and less rainfall in the summer means there will be more stress on already scarce water resources when they are needed the most.
- Treatment – More frequent heavy downpours and changes to the ecology of rivers may reduce the quality of the water we take from the environment, requiring more treatment.
- Distribution – Key assets may be at greater risk of being flooded and changes in soil moisture levels may lead to changing patterns of pipe bursts and leaks.

1 The Water Services Regulation Authority (Ofwat), 'Climate Change: Main Impacts of Climate Change' <https://www.ofwat.gov.uk/regulated-companies/resilience-in-the-round/climate-change/> accessed 23 April 2024.

- Consumption – As the climate warms, demand for water is likely to increase from both household and non-household consumers. In some areas, there may also be increased competition for raw water resources from other sectors, especially during the summer months.

- Drainage – Changing rainfall patterns challenge the current approach to drainage. Climate change will increase the risk of surface water flooding and sewer flooding, which is one of the most serious types of service failure. Climate change may also increase the damage caused by overflows of untreated wastewater into the environment.

- Wastewater treatment and discharge – Reduced river flows could mean that more carbon-intensive sewage treatment is required to ensure rivers are protected.

19.03 The findings from the most recent 'Third UK Climate Change Risk Assessment ('CCRA3') Evidence Report 2021' are summarised in the CCRA3 briefing for the water sector:[2]

- Water infrastructure, such as reservoirs, dams, pipelines, water treatment plants and sewage treatment plants, are all at risk from the impacts of climate change, especially increases in the frequency and intensity of surface water and coastal flooding.

- Water infrastructure assets represent a key element of the UK infrastructure system and could affect, or be affected by, failures of other assets due to extreme weather, such as energy systems, transport and information and communications technology (ICT).

- There are also risks to buried infrastructure, such as water pipelines, with damage potentially becoming more frequent in future due to flooding and subsidence.

- More frequent flooding could also impact on water treatment facilities, leading to potential reductions in water quality, in turn impacting upon health.

- Future projections of more frequent and intense dry periods lead to concerns around the availability of public water supplies in future, especially in England and parts of Wales. Private water supplies are also at risk.

- Aquifers near the coast could be at greater risk from saltwater intrusion due to sea level rise, though the risk is thought to be low in places where aquifers are important water sources.

2 UK Climate Risk, 'Water Briefing: Findings from the Third UK Climate Change Risk Assessment (CCRA3) Evidence Report 2021' (2021) <https://www.ukclimaterisk.org/wp-content/uploads/2021/06/CCRA3-Briefing-Water.pdf> accessed 23 April 2024.

19.04 In response to growing challenges, the UK government and devolved administrations have developed law and policy to manage water resources and the impacts of scarcity. This section will focus on the management and regulation of water in response to climate change. The following sections will focus on the regulation of water scarcity, flood protection, sea level rise and coastal management, and water as a constraint on development.

(ii) *Policy framework*

19.05 National policy provides that national strategy and local plan-making should take a proactive approach to mitigating and adapting to climate change and its impacts on water supply.[3] In 2020, the Environment Agency ('EA') developed a national framework for water resources, setting out a strategic direction for regional water resources groups (discussed further below) and the range of approaches available to meet the likely pressures confronting water resources.[4] The framework specifically focuses on the development of regional resource plans to deal with disparities in water availability across England and in water companies bordering Wales. It also establishes the government's aims to accelerate delivery of new water supply sources, including from reservoirs, desalination and transfer schemes.

19.06 The government, principally through DEFRA, is responsible for setting the overall legal and policy framework for water in England.[5] Water policy is otherwise devolved across the UK.[6] The most recent pronouncement on the approach for England was published on 5 April 2023.[7] Ofwat acts as the economic regulator. The EA implements the permitting and licensing regimes and has responsibility for assessing water resource planning for each water company. Natural England ('NE') advises the government on the protection and improvement of England's natural environment and the impacts on water dependent habitat sites. The Drinking Water Inspectorate ('DWI') investigates disruption to supply, the quality of water supplied and the role of local authorities in regulating private water supplies.[8]

3 Department for Levelling Up, Housing and Communities, 'National Planning Policy Framework' (2023) para 158 <https://assets.publishing.service.gov.uk/media/65a11af7e8f5ec000f1f8c46/NPPF_December_2023.pdf> accessed 2 April 2024.
4 Environment Agency, 'Meeting Our Future Water Needs: A National Framework for Water Resources' (2020) <https://assets.publishing.service.gov.uk/media/5e6e478ed3bf7f26963789f3/National_Framework_for_water_resources_main_report.pdf> accessed 23 April 2024.
5 Department for Environment, Food and Rural Affairs, 'Our Integrated Plan for Delivering Clean and Plentiful Water' (2023) 15 <https://www.gov.uk/government/publications/plan-for-water-our-integrated-plan-for-delivering-clean-and-plentiful-water> accessed 23 April 2024.
6 ibid 16. See also Scotland Act 1998, Government of Wales Act 2006, Northern Ireland Act 1998.
7 Department for Environment, Food and Rural Affairs, 'Our Integrated Plan for Delivering Clean and Plentiful Water' (n 5).
8 ibid 16. Local authority functions in relation to water quality and sufficiency are set out under WIA 1991 ss 77–86. For example, WIA s 80 empowers local authorities to take steps where water privately supplied for human consumption is unwholesome or where it is at risk of being unwholesome or insufficient. Private water supplies are registered with local authorities.

19.07 Cyfoeth Naturiol Cymru ('Natural Resources Wales' or 'NRW') is the responsible body for water strategy in Wales.[9] In Scotland, Scottish Water is accountable to Scottish Ministers and the Scottish Parliament for water strategy.[10] Northern Ireland Water is the responsible body for Northern Ireland.[11] This section will predominantly focus on water management in England and Wales.

(iii) *Legal framework*

(a) Legislation

19.08 A patchwork of legislation regulates water and drainage management in England and Wales. There are five acts of principal importance:

- The Water Industry Act 1991 ('WIA 1991'), concerned with the privatisation and regulation of water and sewerage services.
- The Water Resources Act 1991 ('WRA 1991'), concerned with the protection of water resources.
- The Water Act 2014 ('WA 2014'), which implemented changes to the WIA 1991 as well as other water legislation.
- The Flood and Water Management Act 2010 ('FWMA 2010'), concerned with the management of flooding risks and coastal erosion.

19.09 The Environment Act 2021 ('EA 2021') provides that the Secretary of State must set at least one long-term (at least 15 years) target in each of the four priority areas, including water. Pursuant to that requirement, the Environmental Targets (Water) (England) Regulations 2023 (SI 2023/93) created four legally binding long-term targets in the priority area of water. In respect of water scarcity, this included a target to reduce the use of public water supply in England per capita by at least 20% by 31 March 2038, against a 2019–2020 baseline.[12]

(b) Water companies/undertakers

19.10 In 1989, the Water Act ('WA 1989') privatised the water industry by transferring the water supply and sewerage functions of publicly-owned regional water authorities to limited companies.[13] Pursuant to the WIA 1991, the Secretary of State has the power

---

9 Welsh Government, 'Water Strategy for Wales: Supporting the Sustainable Management of Our Natural Resources' (2015) <https://www.gov.wales/sites/default/files/publications/2019-06/water-strategy.pdf> accessed 23 April 2024.

10 Scottish Water, 'Strategic Plan: A Sustainable Future Together' (2021) <https://www.scottishwater.co.uk/Help-and-Resources/Document-Hub/Key-Publications/Strategic-Plan> accessed 23 April 2024.

11 Northern Island Water, 'Our Draft Strategy 2021 – 2046' (2021) <https://www.niwater.com/our-draft-strategy/files/assets/common/downloads/northern%20ireland%20water%20-%20our%20draft%20strategy%202021-2046.pdf> accessed 23 April 2024.

12 Department for Environment, Food and Rural Affairs, 'A Green Future: Our 25 Year Plan to Improve the Environment' (2018) <https://assets.publishing.service.gov.uk/media/5ab3a67840f0b65bb584297e/25-year-environment-plan.pdf> accessed 4 April 2024.

13 Water Act 1989 s 6 and The Water Authorities (Transfer of Functions) (Appointed Day) Order 1989. See also, John H Bates, *Water and Drainage Law* (Release 66, Sweet & Maxwell 2023) s 3A.01.

to appoint a company to be a water undertaker for an area within England and Wales.[14] There are currently 21 water companies.[15]

19.11 The WIA 1991 sets out the main powers and duties of the water and sewerage companies, replacing those set out in the WA 1989. A water undertaker has a statutory duty to maintain the water supply system,[16] to maintain the connection between the undertaker's water main and the service pipe by which that supply is provided to those premises[17] and to supply water to domestic premises.[18] Every water undertaker has a further duty to promote the efficient use of water.[19] The duty of water and sewerage undertakers to comply with the conditions of their appointments and the statutory requirements of the WIA 1991 may be enforced by the Secretary of State, under the provisions of sections 18 to 22.

19.12 In the absence of specific rights of action,[20] the provisions of the WIA 1991 create no cause of action for breach of statutory duty or other common law remedy for damages for a failure by a water undertaker to provide a service or benefit under the legislation.[21]

Regulation of water scarcity

(i) *Introduction*

19.13 The changing climate is expected to bring changes to the amount and pattern of rainfall expected across the UK, and the types of droughts confronted. Water is expected to become increasingly stretched. The challenge only becomes more formidable when the regional variations of water use are taken into account, caused by different types of industry and population levels, as well as water company leakage.[22]

(ii) *Water resource planning*

19.14 There is no statutory definition of water resources, but it is generally understood as being 'all sources of water that are capable of being exploited'.[23] For the purposes of the WRA 1991, water resources include any inland water (including any natural or artificial

---

14 WIA 1991 s 6.
15 Water Act 1989. A list of the current water companies may be found at Consumer Council of Water, 'Find Your Water Company' <https://www.ccw.org.uk/advice-and-support/households/water-companies/> accessed 23 April 2024.
16 WIA 1991 s 37.
17 ibid ss 45–46.
18 ibid s 52.
19 ibid s 93A as amended by WA 2014.
20 For example, a specific right of action is provided by WIA 1991 s 209. Subsection 1 provides that 'where an escape of water, however caused, from a pipe vested in a water undertaker causes loss or damage, the undertaker shall be liable, except as otherwise provided on this section, for the loss or damage'.
21 See *Dwr Cymru (Welsh Water) v Barratt Homes Ltd* [2013] EWCA Civ 233, where the Court of Appeal held that the scheme of the WIA 1991 did not permit the bringing of a claim for nuisance for wrongfully refusing connection to the public sewers under s 106.
22 Department for Environment, Food and Rural Affairs, 'Our Integrated Plan for Delivering Clean and Plentiful Water' (n 5) 15, 12–15.
23 Bates, *Water and Drainage Law* (n 13) s 4.00.

river or stream or watercourse), any lake pond or reservoir, and any channel, creek or bay or arm of the sea. Self-contained lakes, ponds or reservoirs are not considered a source of supply under the WRA 1991, as they do not discharge into any other inland water.[24]

(iii) *Water resource plans*

19.15 In 2020, the EA published a national framework for water resources. The plan observes that, 'if no action is taken between 2025 and 2050, around 3,435 million litres per day (Ml/d) extra capacity is likely to be needed in England by 2050 to meet future pressures on public water supply'.[25] It developed water resource planning by dividing England into five regional water resource planning groups. Those regional groups were instructed to prepare water resource plans for their region by September 2023.[26] The aims set out included the following:

- Building resilience to drought, so that emergency drought order restrictions, such as providing water only at certain times of the day, or through temporary taps in the streets, are expected to be implemented extremely rarely.

- Reducing water demand by increasing the efficiency of water using appliances, mandating labelling for water efficient appliances, and encouraging water metering to reduce water losses.

- Increasing water supply and moving water to where it is needed regionally. This will require the extensive development of supply side infrastructure, including options to increase storage, reuse water and transfer schemes.

19.16 Pursuant to the national framework for England and Wales, draft regional resource plans were developed by the five regional groups. The regional plans set out how the supply of water for people, business, industry, navigation and agriculture will be managed in the region. They observe the following challenges and regional disparities in water availability:

- Water Resources North – The North faces only modest pressures on public water supply in comparison with other regions and has significant surplus water in parts, likely offsetting the pressures it will face in the future.[27] The draft regional plan identifies particular pressures in the Kielder and Yorkshire grid zones, where water availability is expected to decrease due to climate change.[28]

---

24 WRA 1991 s 221(1).
25 Environment Agency, 'Meeting Our Future Water Needs: A National Framework for Water Resources' (n 4) 7.
26 Environment Agency, 'Appendix 2: Regional Planning Water Resources National Framework (Version 1)' (2020) <https://assets.publishing.service.gov.uk/media/5e6a2712d3bf7f269b07efbd/Appendix_2_Regional_planning.pdf> accessed 23 April 2024 s 4.3.
27 Environment Agency, 'Meeting Our Future Water Needs: A National Framework for Water Resources' (n 4).
28 Water Resources North, 'Draft Regional Plan for Consultation' (2022) 2 <https://www.waterresourcesnorth.org/our-region/wren-regional-draft-plan> accessed 23 April 2024.

- Water Resources West – The West sees the second greatest pressure on public water supply when viewed in total, although the pressures are smaller than those in the East, when expressed as a proportion of the water supplied. The draft plan observes that if demand reductions are not fully realised, deficits would be greater in all zones in the future and new deficits will appear in zones that were previously in surplus.[29]

- Water Resources East – The East faces significant pressure and has little surplus water available. The regional plan identifies its most urgent need as reducing the amount of water abstracted and leaving more water in the environment to help waterbodies and water dependent habitats in the future. Ambitious reductions in water use are outlined, as well as proposals to create additional capacity to meet higher needs in the future. Beyond the public water supply, consumptive water uses are most significant in the East, where agricultural use of spray irrigation dominates.[30]

- Water Resources South East – The South East faces the greatest pressure on public water supplies and the most significant challenges to water resources in the future. Most of the region is already classified as water stressed and its population is set to grow, with major growth corridors planned in some areas. Even if surplus water could be made available from other regions, the South East will still need to create significant new options to supply more water for both public and non-public water supply need. The draft plan proposes the creation of three new reservoirs, six water recycling schemes, six groundwater schemes, and an inter-regional water transfer scheme using the Grand Union Canal to transfer water from the Midlands to the South East.[31]

- West Country Water Resources – The West country sees relatively modest pressures when viewed as a whole, but are more significant when viewed as a proportion of the water supplied in the region. The region has historically good levels of sustainability in available water resources. However, the pressures of climate change are predicted to bring the current status quo to an end, unless changes are made to water use in the region.[32]

19.17 In addition to regional water resource management plans, water undertakers are required to develop their own plans under sections 37A to 37D of the WIA 1991. These plans should set out how the water undertaker will manage and develop water resources so as to be able, and to continue to be able, to meet its water supply duties under the

---

29 Water Resources West, 'Draft Regional Plan for Consultation' (2022) 24 <https://waterresourceswest.co.uk/publications> accessed 23 April 2024.

30 Water Resources East, 'Regional Water Resources Plan for Eastern England' (2023) <https://wre.org.uk/wp-content/uploads/2023/12/WRE-Regional-Water-Resources-Plan-for-Eastern-England.pdf> accessed 23 April 2024.

31 Water Resources South East, 'Revised Draft Regional Plan Water Resources South East' (2023) <https://www.wrse.org.uk/media/osjgqafk/wrse-revised-draft-regional-plan-august-2023-v1-1.pdf> accessed 23 April 2024.

32 West Country Water Resources, 'Draft Plan for Consultation and Comment' (2023) <https://www.wcwrg.org/siteassets/document-repository/reports/draft-west-country-water-resources-plan-31jan2023.pdf> accessed 23 April 2024.

WIA 1991.[33] These plans should reflect national and regional plans for water resource management and provide an estimate of the amount of water it will need.

(iv) *Water abstraction*

19.18 Water abstraction means the doing of anything as a result of which any water is removed from a source of supply, whether temporarily, or permanently, or whether it is transferred to another source of supply.[34] Abstraction provides essential water for public water supply, agriculture and industry. However, unsustainable levels of abstraction impact the ecology and resilience of the UK's rivers, wetlands and aquifers.[35]

(a) Legal framework

19.19 The abstraction of water in England and Wales is primarily regulated under Chapter II of Part II of the WRA 1991.[36] Licences to abstract water are granted by the EA/NRW to individuals or water undertakers, as set out by the eligibility restrictions under section 35. Generally, such persons must have, or be expected to have at the time the licence takes effect, a right of access to land contiguous to those waters at the place from which the abstraction will be made.[37]

19.20 Unlicensed abstraction is generally prohibited from any source of supply and a person will be guilty of an offence if they do so.[38] However, a licence is not required for abstractions of small quantities, provided such quantity does not exceed 20 cubic metres in any period of 24 hours, and the abstraction does not form part of a continuous operation or series of operations amounting to more than 20 cubic metres over that period.[39] Neither is an abstraction licence required in the course of land drainage operations,[40] nor during the course of an emergency to prevent damage, harm to health, or death.[41] The Secretary of State is empowered to make provision for further exemptions.[42]

19.21 There are three types of abstraction licence provided for by section 24A of the WRA 1991:

---

33 Environment Agency, 'Water Resources Planning Guideline' (2023) <https://www.gov.uk/government/publications/water-resources-planning-guideline/water-resources-planning-guideline> accessed 23 April 2024.

34 WRA 1991 s 221(1). Abstraction involves a positive act effected by an appliance, however to cause water to move to another source of supply is not a removal, and therefore not an abstraction from the waters moved: *British Waterways Board v Anglian Water Authority and another* [1991] (High Court, The Times).

35 Department for Environment, Food and Rural Affairs, 'Water Abstraction Plan: Environment (Policy Paper)' (2021) <https://www.gov.uk/government/publications/water-abstraction-plan-2017/water-abstraction-plan-environment> accessed 23 April 2024.

36 As amended by the WA 2003 and WA 2014, and regulated by the The Water Resources (Abstraction and Impounding) Regulations 2006.

37 Bates, *Water and Drainage Law* (n 13) s 4.74.

38 WRA 1991 s 24(1) and s 24(4).

39 ibid s 27(1). The Secretary of State may by order made by statutory instrument vary the small quantity threshold to another amount for a specified geographical area, class of inland waters and underground strata.

40 ibid s 29(1). The Spray Irrigation (Definition) Order 1992 s 3.

41 WRA 1991 s 29(2), (2A), (2B) and s 32(2).

42 ibid s 33A.

- *Full licence:* A licence to abstract water from one source of supply over a period of 28 days or more for any purpose. It must express the quantity of water that can be abstracted within a certain period, usually as a figure of gallons/cubic metres.

- *Transfer licence:* A licence to abstract water from one source of supply over a period of 28 days or more, for the purpose of either transferring water to another source of supply or to the same source but at another point, in the course of dewatering activities in connection with mining, quarrying, engineering, building or other operations.

- *Temporary Licence:* A licence to abstract water from one source of supply over a period of less than 28 days.[43]

19.22 An abstraction licence confers a 'right' to abstract water upon the licence holder, immunity from prosecution, and a defence to any civil action brought.[44] However, those who suffer loss and damage as a result of abstractions from inland waters or underground strata may have a claim for breach of statutory duty.[45]

19.23 An application for an abstraction licence must be made on the relevant form and be accompanied by such information, maps, and reports that the agency reasonably requires to determine it.[46] A copy of the notice must further be served on any relevant water undertaker for all applications and any relevant navigation, harbour, conservancy authority or internal drainage board for applications in respect of inland waters.[47] Where an application relates to abstraction in the area of a National Park or the Norfolk or Suffolk Broads, the agency must serve notice in writing of the application on the National Park authority for that National Park or the Broads Authority (as the case may be), and state that the authority may make written representations to the agency within 28 days from the date of service.

19.24 Groundwater abstraction or artificial groundwater recharge schemes, where the annual volume abstracted or recharged is equivalent to or exceeds 10 million cubic metres will be a Schedule 1 development under the Town and Country Planning (Environmental Impact Assessment) Regulations 2017/57, for which an environmental impact assessment ('EIA') must be carried out.[48] Deep drilling for water supplies or any groundwater abstraction or artificial groundwater recharge scheme that does not fall within Schedule 1, and where the area of the works exceeds 1 hectare will be a Schedule 2 assessment, and may require an EIA.[49]

---

43 ibid s 24A.
44 ibid s 48(2).
45 ibid s 48A.
46 ibid s 37(1); The Water Resources (Abstraction and Impounding) Regulations 2006 reg 6(1).
47 ibid s 37(2) and (3).
48 Town and Country Planning (Environmental Impact Assessment) Regulations 2017, SI 2017/571 sch 1, para 11.
49 Infrastructure Planning (Environmental Impact Assessment) Regulations 2017, SI 2017/572 sch 2, para 10(o).

(b) Abstraction Licensing Strategy

19.25 In 1999, the EA developed Catchment Abstraction Management Strategies ('CAMS') to make information on water resources availability and licensing more publicly available and to provide a more open, consistent and structured approach to water resources management. A catchment is a geographical area within which rainwater and groundwater collect and contribute to the flow of a specific river.[50] The EA considers CAMS to determine how much water is potentially available for further abstraction by taking into account likely rainfall, the amount of water already licensed for abstraction, how much is discharged and how much water the environment needs.[51] CAMS became 'Abstraction Licensing Strategies' ('ALS') in 2014. ALS set out how the EA/NRW are going to manage abstraction licensing in a particular area, and applicants for abstraction licences are advised to check their local water availability before applying.[52]

(c) Sustainable abstraction

19.26 Sustainable abstraction will be vital to ensure that river flows and groundwater levels support a healthy ecology, are resilient to drought and provide reliable water that supports economic growth.[53] The EA estimates that abstraction of 8% of surface water bodies and 28% of groundwater bodies is unsustainable.[54] A further 10% of surface water bodies are identified as potentially unsustainably abstracted, while 5% of surface water bodies and 15% of groundwater bodies have been identified as being at risk of deterioration.

19.27 Generally, the volume of water permitted to be abstracted over a period of time is larger than what will typically be used by the licensed abstractor over that period. The licences accommodate a larger volume, in order to permit abstractors to hold water in reserve and to meet short term peaks in demand. Volume licences are generally fixed and agreed upon based on an assessment of the environment at the time the licence was granted. However, changing environmental circumstances mean that ecological damage may still occur, even when abstraction licences are effected within their constraints. The EA attempts to mitigate the risk of future deterioration, by estimating future demand within licensed constraints and modelling the impact the additional abstraction would have on future flows and groundwater resources.[55] For rivers in England, the EA uses the 'Environmental Flow Indicator' to indicate where abstraction may start to have an undesirable impact on river habitats and species, unless there is better locally agreed information. For groundwater abstraction, the EA uses four quantitative tests that aim to protect surface water flows, groundwater levels, spring discharges and water quality.[56]

---

50 Department for Environment, Food and Rural Affairs, 'Water Abstraction Plan: Environment (Policy Paper)' (n 35).

51 The Water Services Regulation Authority (Ofwat) and Environment Agency, 'The Case for Change – Reforming Water Abstraction Management in England' (2011) <https://www.ofwat.gov.uk/wp-content/uploads/2015/11/pap_pos20111205abstraction.pdf> accessed 23 April 2024.

52 Environment Agency, 'Abstraction Licensing Strategies (CAMS Process)' (3 May 2023) <https://www.gov.uk/government/collections/water-abstraction-licensing-strategies-cams-process> accessed 23 April 2024.

53 Department for Environment, Food and Rural Affairs, 'Water Abstraction Plan: Catchment Focus' (2021) <https://www.gov.uk/government/publications/water-abstraction-plan-2017/water-abstraction-plan-catchment-focus> accessed 23 April 2024.

54 ibid.

55 ibid.

56 ibid.

19.28 In 2015, Ofwat and the EA published a case for change to the abstraction licensing regime to address unsustainable abstraction.[57] It was observed that many abstraction licences issued historically caused environmental harm and the system was not flexible enough to meet the needs of a changing environment. Abstraction licences can be difficult to change and may not reflect water availability over time and location. Where flows drop as a result of climate change or other factors, but abstraction continues, abstractions upstream can have a negative impact upon abstractions downstream, risking damage to the environment.[58] Even where licences are restricted by 'Hands Off Flow' conditions, those are usually fixed to a specific flow volume as opposed to a proportion of available flow, which does not reflect how flows change over time.

19.29 The EA runs a programme for restoring sustainable abstraction to address the problems caused by unsustainable water abstraction schemes. There are two processes available to the EA to change abstraction licences.

- *Voluntary.* Section 51 of the WRA 1991 permits the EA to agree to changes mutually with the licence holder. No time limit is added to the revised licence and no compensation is paid to the licence holder.
- *Compulsory.* Section 52 of the WRA 1991 permits the EA to make mandatory changes to a licence. The section 52 process requires the EA to develop a case to support each proposed licence change. Abstractors can object and may be eligible to claim compensation for any loss it will cause to their business.[59] In 2015, the EA and Ofwat observed that the overall process, from investigation to issue of a licence change, can take at least two years and cost between £50,000 and £100,000 per scheme in staff time and legal costs.[60]

19.30 Section 88 of the EA 2021 amended provisions of the WRA 1991 to provide that no compensation is payable for modifications to abstraction licences that are varied having regard to (i) a relevant environmental objective, or (ii) to otherwise protect the water environment from damage. Since 2008, the EA has made changes to over 270 abstraction licences to prevent over 30 billion litres of water per year from being removed from the environment where abstraction is unsustainable.[61]

(d) Transition to Environmental Permitting Regime

19.31 In September 2020, the government updated the Water Abstraction Plan to reflect its decision to delay moving water abstraction and impounding licensing into

---

57 The Water Services Regulation Authority (Ofwat) and Environment Agency, 'The Case for Change – Reforming Water Abstraction Management in England' (n 51).

58 ibid 18 s 4.1.

59 Under WRA 1991 s 54, the EA (or NRW) must pay the licence-holder compensation if they can show that they have either (i) incurred expenditure in carrying out work that has been rendered abortive by the revocation or variation or (ii) sustained other loss or damage that is directly attributable to the revocation or variation.

60 The Water Services Regulation Authority (Ofwat) and Environment Agency, 'The Case for Change – Reforming Water Abstraction Management in England' (n 51) 18–19. It is no longer the case that revocation of licences that are not time-limited can attract compensation.

61 Department for Environment, Food and Rural Affairs, 'Water Abstraction Plan: Environment (Policy Paper)' (n 35).

the Environmental Permitting Regime ('EPR') to 2023,[62] in light of the Covid-19 pandemic.[63] At the time of writing, no further update has been provided for the timeline to implementation. On the date of migration, existing water abstraction licences will automatically become environmental permits, with no change to existing licence conditions. However, all future applications will be determined under the EPR. The move to the EPR is part of the drive to modernise abstraction and to streamline the overall environmental regulatory framework.[64]

(v) *Water infrastructure*

19.32 In 2018, the National Infrastructure Commission ('NIC') estimated that around four billion litres (or 4,000 mega litres per day, Ml/day) of additional water a day will be needed in England by 2050.[65] In order to meet this demand, the NIC estimates that leakage in water infrastructure will need to be halved to supply an additional 1,400Ml/day, new supply and transfer infrastructures will have to be developed to supply at least 1,300Ml/day, and demand will need to be reduced through measures, including the installation of smart meters, to supply at least 1,400Ml/day.[66] The UK's long-term water resource needs will therefore require the development of infrastructure to increase supply and to address expected demand. The National Policy Statement for Water Resources Infrastructure identifies reservoirs, water transfer schemes and desalination plants as infrastructure necessary to address future pressures on the public water supply, including those from climate change.[67]

(a) Reservoirs

19.33 Reservoirs build resilience and capabilities for drought management due to their ability to conserve water for later use. They offer a variety of benefits. Primarily, reservoirs enable water to be captured during wet periods, or as a result of transfers, and reduce the need for increased abstraction when there would otherwise be a shortage. Additionally, they can provide compensatory flows to rivers to support downstream abstraction.[68]

19.34 Reservoirs typically require considerable areas of land for construction and as a result, they have associated local land use impacts. There are two types of reservoirs: those formed by constructing a dam across a stream to form a lake ('impounding reservoirs')

---

62 The Environmental Permitting (England and Wales) Regulations 2016, SI 2016/1154.
63 Department for Environment, Food and Rural Affairs, 'Water Abstraction Plan: Environment (Policy Paper)' (n 35) s 5.1.
64 Department for Environment, Food and Rural Affairs, 'Changes to the Regulatory Framework for Abstraction and Impounding Licensing in England Moving into the Environmental Permitting Regulations Regime (Consultation Document)' (September 2021) <https://consult.defra.gov.uk/water/abstraction-impounding-epr-consultation/supporting_documents/Consultation%20Document%20%20AI%20move%20into%20the%20EPR.pdf> accessed 23 April 2024.
65 National Infrastructure Commission, 'Preparing for a Drier Future: England's Water Infrastructure Needs' (2018) 3 <https://nic.org.uk/app/uploads/NIC-Preparing-for-a-Drier-Future-26-April-2018.pdf> accessed 23 April 2024.
66 National Infrastructure Commission, 'The Second National Infrastructure Assessment' (2023) 105 <https://nic.org.uk/app/uploads/Final-NIA-2-Full-Document.pdf> accessed 5 April 2024.
67 Department for Environment, Food and Rural Affairs, 'National Policy Statement for Water Resources Infrastructure' (2023) <https://www.gov.uk/government/publications/national-policy-statement-for-water-resources-infrastructure> accessed 5 April 2024.
68 ibid.

and those constructed either above or below ground and filled through a pipeline.[69] By effecting physical modifications to the local water environment, the construction of reservoirs, impounding reservoirs in particular, can cause adverse effects on health and/or protected species and habitats.

(b) Water transfer schemes

19.35 Water transfer schemes permit transfers of water from regions with a surplus to shortage areas. However, the required network of reservoirs, dams, aqueducts, canals and pipes are expensive to build. Transfers, especially over long distances, may also have significant energy costs associated with pumping. As a consequence, water transfers make up a small proportion of total supply, at around 4%. However, a report by the NIC suggests that strategic transfers could provide as much as 700 million litres extra capacity to the water supply system.[70] In particular, the National Policy Statement for Water Resources Infrastructure identified the possibility of strategic transfers from water resource zones with surpluses in the North and West of England, to zones in deficit in the East and South East.[71]

19.36 Water transfer schemes carry potential environmental impacts and risks. For example, they could potentially encourage the spreading of invasive non-native species between abstracted and receiving waters. Applications to develop water transfer schemes will generally require an EIA.[72]

(c) Water desalination

19.37 Desalination refers to the process of abstracting and treating saline or brackish water to drinking water standards and, in theory, can provide unlimited supplies of new water.[73] Supporting infrastructure, such as tanks or reservoirs for treatment, will often be required. At present, there is only one large scale desalination plant operating in England, which takes water from the Thames estuary.

(d) Water efficiency standards for housing

19.38 In April 2023, the government published a variety of proposed measures to improve water efficiency in homes across England.[74] They include:[75]

---

69 Bates, *Water and Drainage Law* (n 13) s 5.01.
70 Department for Environment, Food and Rural Affairs, 'National Policy Statement for Water Resources Infrastructure' (n 67) para 2.6.8–2.6.11.
71 ibid para 2.6.8.
72 Town and Country Planning (Environmental Impact Assessment) Regulations 2017 sch 1, para 12(b). Schedule 1 works for the transfer of water resources, other than piped drinking water, between river basins where the multi-annual average flow of the basin of abstraction exceeds 2,000 million cubic metres per year and where the amount of water transferred exceeds 5% of this flow. See also ibid, Sch. 2, para 10(o): Works for the transfer of water resources between river basins not included in Schedule 1; but where the area of the works exceeds 1 hectare, it may require an EIA.
73 Department for Environment, Food and Rural Affairs, 'National Policy Statement for Water Resources Infrastructure' (n 67) para 2.6.12.
74 Department for Environment, Food and Rural Affairs, 'Our Integrated Plan for Delivering Clean and Plentiful Water' (n 5) 15.
75 ibid. In particular, there is a planned review of the Building Regulations 2010, and the water efficiency, water recycling, and drainage standards (regulation 36 and Parts G2, H1, H2, H3 of Schedule 1).

- Developing minimum product standards for showers, taps and toilets, following the launch of mandatory water efficiency labelling;
- Encouraging water companies to rapidly increase smart meter installations for household and non-household customers;
- Strengthening consumer information on water usage, including leakage from everyday structures in the household, through billing and smart metering; and
- Developing clear guidance on 'net zero water' developments, reviewing water efficiency options in planning, building regulations and voluntary schemes for non-household buildings.

19.39 The proposed mandatory water efficiency labelling scheme is intended to be implemented in 2025, following the successful completion of a public consultation process in September 2022.[76]

Drought planning

19.40 While there is no single definition of drought, all droughts are characterised by some degree of rainfall shortage. The EA's drought response framework identifies three forms of drought:[77]

- *Environmental drought.* When a shortage of rainfall has a detrimental impact on the environment, often as a result of reduced river flows, exceptionally low groundwater levels and insufficient moisture in soils.
- *Agricultural drought.* When there is not enough rainfall and moisture in soils to support crop production or farming practices such as spray irrigation. These drought conditions often happen alongside environmental drought, but usually before public water supplies are affected.
- *Water supply drought.* When a shortage of rainfall causes water companies concern about supplies for their customers.

(i) *Drought plans*

19.41 Each water undertaker is under a duty to prepare and maintain a drought plan. The plan sets out how the water undertaker will continue, during a period of drought, to discharge its duties to supply adequate quantities of wholesome water, with as little

76 Department for Environment, Food and Rural Affairs, 'Consultation on Mandatory Water Efficiency Labelling' (2022) <https://consult.defra.gov.uk/water-efficiency-labelling/water-efficiency-labelling/supporting_documents/Water%20efficiency%20labelling%20consultation.pdf> accessed 23 April 2024.
77 Environment Agency, 'Drought Response: Our Framework for England' (2017) <https://assets.publishing.service.gov.uk/government/uploads/system/uploads/attachment_data/file/625006/LIT_10104.pdf> accessed 23 April 2024.

recourse as possible to drought orders or drought permits.[78] These drought plans should be prepared every five years.[79] In particular, they should set out which measures water undertakers expect they may need to take to restrain demand, obtain extra water and monitor the effects of drought measures.[80]

19.42 Drought plans should include 'drought triggers', such as rainfall levels, river flows, groundwater levels and reservoir stocks, that prompt particular actions to manage supplies and water demand. Demand side actions must prioritise actions that save water before taking more from the environment. They can include actions to reduce leakage, water efficiency campaigns, reducing mains pressure and restricting water use (for example, through temporary use bans). Supply side actions should prioritise actions that have the least effect on the environment. They can include carrying out engineering work to improve the supply, transferring water in bulk from other water companies, using drought permits and drought orders to abstract more water, using desalination, or using tankers to supply customers with water directly.[81]

(ii) *Temporary use bans*

19.43 Temporary use bans are generally the least onerous step that can be taken during a drought to relieve pressure on water resources. Pursuant to section 76 of the WIA 1991, a water undertaker may prohibit one or more specified uses of water supplied by means of its supply system, where it considers that it is experiencing, or may experience, a serious shortage of water for distribution. Uses that may be prohibited include various domestic uses of hosepipes, such as watering a garden, cleaning a private motor-vehicle and drawing water for recreational use.[82] An undertaker hoping to implement a temporary use ban must follow a specified procedure under section 76B. This includes requirements for publication online, circulating newspapers and providing the opportunity to make representations about the proposed prohibition.[83]

19.44 Once a temporary use ban is in force, the water undertaker may authorise a person to enter any premises to which the ban applies, to see if there has been any contravention of it.[84] Any person who contravenes a ban will be guilty of an offence.[85]

(iii) *Drought permits*

19.45 The Water Act 2003 ('WA 2003') introduced an abbreviated procedure by which the EA may issue a drought permit to a water undertaker without the involvement of

---

78 WIA 1991 s 39B.
79 Department for Environment, Food and Rural Affairs, 'Drought: How Water Companies Plan for Dry Weather and Drought (Policy Paper)' (2021) <https://www.gov.uk/government/publications/drought-managing-water-supply/drought-how-water-companies-plan-for-dry-weather-and-drought> accessed 23 April 2024.
80 ibid. See also The Drought Plan Regulations 2005.
81 Department for Environment, Food and Rural Affairs, 'Drought: How Water Companies Plan for Dry Weather and Drought (Policy Paper)' (n 79).
82 WIA 1991 s 76(2).
83 ibid s 76B(2).
84 ibid s 170.
85 ibid s 76(5).

the Secretary of State or Welsh Assembly.[86] The EA may enable a water undertaker to take water from a specified source or modify any restrictions which they are currently subject to, in respect of that source. A permit cannot, however, be obtained to protect wildlife via this procedure.[87]

19.46 Drought permits share similar procedure and compensation requirements as a drought order.[88]

(iv) *Drought orders*

19.47 Drought orders offer a more significant response to drought, and can only be made by the Secretary of State on application from the EA or a water undertaker.[89] There are two types of drought orders which may be made:

- *Ordinary Drought Order.* Where the Secretary of State is satisfied that there exists or there is a threatened serious deficiency of water supply, or a deficiency in flow or level of water posing a serious threat to any flora or fauna.[90] If the applicant is the EA, it may enable a person authorised by the EA to take water from a certain source or to discharge water to a specified place. It may prohibit an abstraction if it will seriously undermine the supplies available to the EA, water undertaker, or other abstractors.[91] If the applicant is a water undertaker, a similarly wide set of powers is laid out.[92] An ordinary drought order may last six months, but it is extendable to a maximum of twelve months.[93]

- *Emergency Drought Order.* Where the Secretary of State is satisfied that by reason of an exceptional shortage of rain, a serious deficiency of supplies of water in any area exists or is threatened, and that the deficiency is likely to impair the economic or social well-being of persons in that area. It may be in similar form to an ordinary drought order, but can additionally empower an undertaker to supply water via stand-pipes or water tanks in the area.[94]

19.48 Any person who takes or uses water, in contravention of a prohibition or limitation imposed under any drought order or drought permit, will be guilty of an offence.[95] They will likewise be guilty of an offence if they fail to allow an authorised person to inspect any apparatus or records in connection with that person.[96]

---

86 WA 2003 s 64(3)(b).
87 WRA 1991 s 79A.
88 ibid s 79A.
89 ibid ss 73 – 79.
90 ibid s 73(1).
91 ibid s 74(1).
92 ibid s 74(2).
93 ibid s 74(3).
94 ibid s 75(2).
95 ibid s 80.
96 ibid s 80.

19.49 Compensation is payable to occupiers under any drought order that requires the entry and occupation of their land, as well as all other persons injuriously affected by their entry.[97] Additionally, ordinary drought orders attract liability to pay compensation for loss and damage sustained, as a result of anything done or omitted in pursuance of an ordinary drought order.[98]

Flood protection

(i) *Introduction*

19.50 Flood protection is an important aspect of climate change mitigation and adaptation. Between 2018 and 2021, expenditure on flood and coastal erosion risk management in England alone increased from £777 million to £1.063 billion, reflecting the growing risk of flooding posed by climate change.[99]

19.51 In recent years, there have been a number of policy updates to address this increased risk, most notably the Flood and Coastal Erosion Risk Management Policy Statement (2020) and National Flood and Coastal Erosion Risk Management Strategy for England (2020). Important legislative changes are anticipated in 2024 with the implementation of Schedule 3 to the FWMA 2010, which will make sustainable drainage systems mandatory for nearly all developments in England.

19.52 The courts have also had to consider fundamental questions relating to private law liability for flood damage, as well as rights under the ECHR.[100]

(ii) *Policy framework*

(a) NPPF

19.53 National planning policy on managing flood risk is set out in chapter 14 of the National Planning Policy Framework ('NPPF') on 'Meeting the challenge of climate change, flooding and coastal change.' In its consultation response (published on 22 December 2023) concerning amendments to the latest version of the NPPF (published on 21 December 2023), the government advised that it intends:[101]

> to review national planning policy in due course to make sure it contributes to climate change adaptation as fully as possible. Responses will be used to inform any future consultation on the National Planning Policy Framework.

---

97 ibid s 79 and sch 9, para 1.
98 ibid sch 9, para 2.
99 Office for National Statistics, 'Investment in Flood Defences, UK: May 2023' <https://www.ons.gov.uk/economy/https://www.ons.gov.uk/economy/economicoutputandproductivity/output/articles/investmentinfloodde-fencesuk/may2023%202021%2C%20current%20prices.> accessed 23 April 2024.
100 *King v Environment Agency* (n 116).
101 Department for Levelling Up, Housing and Communities, 'Consultation Outcome: Government Response to the Levelling-up and Regeneration Bill: Reforms to National Planning Policy Consultation' (2023) <https://www.gov.uk/government/consultations/levelling-up-and-regeneration-bill-reforms-to-national-planning-policy/outcome/government-response-to-the-levelling-up-and-regeneration-bill-reforms-to-national-planning-policy-consultation> accessed 23 April 2024.

19.54 The cornerstone of national planning policy on flooding is the sequential test. This aims to steer new development to areas with the lowest risk of flooding, taking all sources of flood risk and climate change into account.

19.55 The EA designates land as falling within flood zone 1, 2 or 3, with flood zone 1 being land at the lowest risk of flooding.

19.56 A flood risk assessment ('FRA') is required for development in:

- Flood zones 2 or 3, including minor development and change of use;
- More than 1 hectare in flood zone 1;
- Less than 1 hectare in flood zone 1, including a change of use in development type to a more vulnerable class (for example from commercial to residential), where they could be affected by sources of flooding other than rivers and the sea (for example surface water drains, reservoirs); and
- An area within flood zone 1 which has critical drainage problems as notified by the EA.

19.57 All applications for development in flood zones 2 and 3 are required to apply the 'sequential' test. The sequential test must be undertaken where any part of the proposed development is located in an area at risk of flooding: see *Watermead Parish Council v Aylesbury Vale District Council*,[102] where planning permission was quashed due to failure to carry out a sequential approach. In that case, the majority of the development was to be located in flood zone 1 but the access roads and car park were to be located in flood zone 3.

19.58 Application of the sequential test requires consideration of reasonable alternatives, to demonstrate that there are no suitable locations appropriate for the proposed development on land at lower risk of flooding. Whether a location is 'appropriate' involves an exercise of planning judgment. However, in *Mead Realisations Ltd v Secretary of State for Levelling Up, Housing and Communities*,[103] the court rejected the claimant's argument that the sequential test required an assessment of the suitability of an alternative site for the specific development proposed in terms of its form, scale and timescales for delivery.

19.59 In *R (Substation Action Save East Suffolk Ltd) v Secretary of State for Energy Security and Net Zero & others*,[104] the Court of Appeal also confirmed that the requirement to consider alternative sites only applies in relation to the risk of fluvial flooding. There is no requirement to consider alternative sites in relation to the risk of surface water

---

102 *Watermead Parish Council v Aylesbury Vale District Council* [2018] PTSR 43.
103 *Mead Realisations Ltd v Secretary of State for Levelling Up, Housing and Communities* [2024] EWHC 279.
104 *R (Substation Action Save East Suffolk Ltd) v Secretary of State for Energy Security and Net Zero & others* [2024] EWCA Civ 12.

flooding. A sequential approach is still required at site level to minimise flooding risk from surface water, but how this is done is a matter for the decision-maker.

19.60 The NPPF requires the sequential test to be applied based upon the strategic flood risk assessment ('SFRA') produced by the relevant local authority, and not the EA's flood zone maps.[105]

19.61 The NPPF does not require a proposal to seek out and provide opportunities to reduce flood risk. The test is to ensure that flood risk is not increased elsewhere, although the benefit of reducing flood risk may be a positive factor in the planning balance, weighing in favour of the grant of planning permission.[106]

19.62 Paragraph 175 of the NPPF currently states that major developments should incorporate sustainable drainage systems, unless there is clear evidence that this would be inappropriate.

19.63 However, in January 2023, the government announced that it intends to legislate to make sustainable drainage systems mandatory in England from 2024 onwards, through the implementation of Schedule 3 to the FWMA 2010.[107] At the time of writing, Schedule 3 is awaiting implementation in England.

(b) PPG

19.64 The planning policy guidance ('PPG') contains further guidance on flooding, including on the use of climate change allowances in FRAs and SFRAs. These allowances are produced by the EA as predictions of anticipated change for peak river flow, peak rainfall intensity, sea level rise, offshore wind speed and extreme wave height. They were originally published in 2016, with updated versions (including changes to the approach to calculating peak river flow and peak rainfall intensity) published in July 2021 and May 2022.[108]

(iii) *Legal framework*

(a) Flood And Water Management Act 2010

19.65 The FWMA 2010 makes provision for the recommendations of Sir Michael Pitt in his independent review ('the Pitt Review'), following the severe flooding of 2007.

19.66 A 'flood' is defined to include any case where land not normally covered by water becomes covered by water, excluding flooding from a sewerage system 'unless wholly

---

105 *R (Martin) v Folkestone and Hythe District Council* [2020] EWHC 1614 (Admin).

106 *Menston Action Group v City of Bradford Metropolitan District Council* [2016] EWHC 127 (QB).

107 In Wales, SuDS (sustainable drainage systems) have been a mandatory requirement for all new developments of more than 1 dwelling house or where the construction area is 100 square meters or more, since 7th January 2019.

108 Environment Agency, 'Guidance: Flood Risk Assessments: Climate Change Allowances' (2022) <https://www.gov.uk/guidance/flood-risk-assessments-climate-change-allowances> accessed 23 April 2024.

or partly caused by an increase in the volume of rainwater (including snow and other precipitation) entering or otherwise affecting the system' or from a 'burst water main'.[109]

19.67 The FWMA 2010 defines the roles and responsibilities of Risk Management Authorities in England and Wales ('RMAs'), as the bodies who manage flood risk from different flood sources.

19.68 The EA, Lead Local Flood Authorities ('LLFAs'), District Councils (where there is no unitary authority), Internal Drainage Boards, Water and Sewerage Companies and Highway Authorities are defined as RMAs under the Act.[110]

19.69 Section 7 requires the EA to 'develop, maintain, apply and monitor a strategy for flood and coastal risk management in England'. The current strategy is the Flood and Coastal Erosion Risk Management Strategy, published in 2020. This was published alongside the Flood and Coastal Erosion Risk Management Policy Statement.

19.70 Lead local flood authorities are also required to develop local flood risk management strategies.[111] These must specify the objectives for managing local flood risk, the measures to achieve them, how and when these are expected to be implemented, their costs and benefits, and how they are to be paid for.[112]

19.71 The flood risk management strategy includes a commitment to local flood and coastal erosion risk planning 'so that every area of England will have a more strategic and comprehensive plan that supports long-term local action and investment' by 2026.[113]

19.72 In January 2023, the government announced its intention to implement Schedule 3 to the FWMA 2010 to make sustainable drainage systems mandatory for nearly all new developments in England from 2024 onwards. The details of the new legislative framework remain to be seen, including whether the automatic right for developers to connect to sewer networks will be removed in light of the recommendations in the Pitt review.

(b) Water Resources Act 1991

19.73 Part IV of the WRA 1991 confers functions in relation to works to manage flood risk relating to main rivers on the EA, which are functions of drainage boards in relation to other watercourses.

19.74 Under Part VII, the EA has extensive powers to take, enter and carry out works to land for the purpose of carrying out its flood defence functions. It must from time to

---

109 FWMA 2010 s 1(1) and s (3).
110 ibid s 6(13).
111 ibid s 9(1).
112 ibid s 9(4).
113 Department for Environment, Food and Rural Affairs, 'Local Flood Risk Management Planning Reform Advisory Group: Terms of Reference (Policy Paper)' (2021) <https://www.gov.uk/government/publications/local-flood-risk-management-planning-reform-advisory-group/local-flood-risk-management-planning-reform-advisory-group-terms-of-reference> accessed 23 April 2024.

time carry out surveys of the areas in relation to which it carries out those functions.[114] Ministerial authorisation may be given for the purchase of or the acquisition of rights over a person's land.[115] Under section 165, the EA has power to carry out flood defence works.[116] It also has a general power of entry under section 172, subject to obtaining a warrant from the Magistrates Court under Schedule 20.

19.75 Where the landowner does not consent to works on private land, the EA can rely on its powers of entry under section 172. It does not have to obtain a compulsory purchase order under section 154 nor a compulsory works order under section 168.[117]

(c) Land Drainage Act 1991

19.76 The Land Drainage Act 1991 ('LDA 1991') consolidates various enactments in relation to land drainage. It also establishes duties and powers in respect of the control of flow of watercourses and watercourse restoration/improvement works.

(iv) *Water Environment (Water Framework Directive) (England and Wales) Regulations 2017/407*

19.77 The Water Environment (Water Framework Directive) (England and Wales) Regulations 2017/407 ('WFD Regulations') transposed the European Union ('EU') Water Framework Directive[118] ('WFD') into national law. The WFD establishes a legal framework for the protection, improvement and sustainable use of surface waters, coastal waters and groundwater across Europe in order to promote sustainable water use, contribute to the mitigation of floods and droughts, prevent deterioration and enhance status of aquatic ecosystems, including groundwater, and reduce pollution.

(a) Flood Risk Regulations 2009

19.78 The Flood Risk Regulations 2009 ('FRR 2009') were revoked with effect from 31 December 2023, as they duplicate requirements to assess, plan for and manage flood risk set out in domestic English legislation through the FWMA 2010.[119]

19.79 However, updated flood risk management plans ('FRMPs') produced under Part 4 of the FRR 2009 were published by the EA in December 2022. These cover the period from 2021 to 2027 and remain in force. They cover areas of the river basin district where flood risk is significant. These areas are called flood risk areas.

19.80 The EA is responsible for producing FRMPs for flood risk areas that cover the sea, main rivers and reservoirs. LLFAs are responsible for producing FRMPs for flood risk areas that cover local sources of flooding in their area.

---

114 WRA 1991 s 105(2).
115 ibid s 154(1)–(2).
116 See the summary of these provisions at [22]–[27] of *King v Environment Agency* [2018] EWHC 65 (QB).
117 *Sharp v North Essex Magistrates' Court* [2017] EWCA Civ 1143.
118 Directive 2000/60/EC of the European Parliament and of the Council of 23 October 2000 establishing a framework for Community action in the field of water policy.
119 See Retained EU Law (Revocation and Reform) Act 2023 s 1(1) and sch 1.

(v) *Issues arising in practice*

(a) Flood Risk Assessment and Environmental Impact Assessment

19.81 The sequential test is an established and integral part of the planning system. Practitioners in this area can be expected to be familiar with the test, as now set out in the NPPF, and the legal principles governing its application.

19.82 As well as the requirement for FRA under the NPPF, likely environmental impacts in respect of water resources, including flooding, drainage and pollution, will also require assessment as part of any EIA required under the EIA Regulations.[120] This assessment may be required, even where no FRA is required under the NPPF.

19.83 FRA is also often accompanied by a drainage impact assessment, and there may be a requirement for such an assessment in local planning policy.

(b) Remedies (including damages claims)

19.84 Determining liability for damage caused by flooding is complex and this issue has been considered by the courts on a number of occasions.

19.85 In *King v Environment Agency*,[121] Dove J noted at [21] that:

> there is no legal right to be protected from flooding and its effect, and … at common law land owners are responsible for safeguarding their land and property when flooding occurs.

19.86 In *King*, the claimants argued that the EA had acted in breach of their property rights by adopting a policy that their land should be used to receive, hold or convey floodwater for the purpose of flood mitigation elsewhere, in particular in Gloucester. However, having reviewed the evidence, Dove J held that this did not amount to an interference with their rights under Article 1 Protocol 1 ('A1P1') of the ECHR and, in any event, there had been a fair balancing of the claimants' rights and the public interest.

19.87 The claim under Article 8 and A1P1 also failed in *Marcic v Thames Water Utilities Ltd.*[122] In that case, the claimant suffered flooding from an overloaded sewer and brought claims against the statutory sewerage undertaker, alleging failure to take steps to alleviate flooding under the WIA 1991. However, the legislation provided for an independent regulator of the defendant – with powers of enforcement – whose decisions were subject to judicial review. There was also a procedure for making complaints to the regulator, which the claimant did not pursue.

19.88 The House of Lords held that the claim under the Human Rights Act 1998 was inconsistent with the statutory scheme. A balance had to be struck between those

---

120 See, further, Chapter 7.
121 *King v Environment Agency* (n 116).
122 *Marcic v Thames Water Utilities Ltd* [2003] UKHL 66.

who were subject to sewer flooding and the financial interests of the defendant's other customers. Parliament had devised such a scheme.

(c) Compensation Claims

19.89 The WRA 1991 and LDA 1991 both make provision for compensation where 'injury' is sustained by reason of the exercise by the relevant authority of its flood defence or drainage powers: see Schedule 21, paragraph 5 of the WRA 1991 and sections 14 and 14A of the LDA 1991.[123]

Sea level rise and coastal management

(i) *Introduction*

19.90 Sea level change, with its implications for coastal management, is a serious consequence of climate change, as explained by the Divisional Court in *R (Spurrier) v Secretary of State for Transport*:[124]

> (i) concentration of GHGs in the earth's atmosphere is directly linked to average global temperatures, (ii) the concentration of GHGs has been rising steadily —and, with it, mean global temperatures—since the start of the Industrial Revolution and (iii) the most abundant GHG, accounting for at least two thirds of all GHGs, is CO_2 which is largely the product of burning fossil fuels. The increase in global temperature has resulted in (amongst other things) sea level change; a decline in glaciers, the Antarctic ice sheet and Arctic sea ice; alterations to various ecosystems; and in some areas a threat to food and water supplies. It is potentially catastrophic.

However, there is also growing interest in the positive role of the ocean and seas in climate mitigation, including its role as a natural carbon sink.

(ii) *Policy framework*

(a) NPPF

19.91 Paragraphs 176–179 of the NPPF set out national policies on coastal change. Paragraph 176 requires planning policies and decisions to take account of the UK Marine Policy Statement and marine plans; while paragraph 177 establishes the concept of Coastal Change Management Areas, defined as 'any area likely to be affected by physical changes to the coast', where additional constraints on development are imposed.

(b) UK Marine Policy Statement and Marine Plans

19.92 The UK Marine Policy Statement was adopted by the government in 2011 for the purposes of section 44 of the Marine and Coastal Access Act 2009. It sets the framework for a new system of marine planning through the formulation of marine

---

123 See *Robert Lindley Ltd v East Riding of Yorkshire Council* (2016) UKUT 6 (LC) for an example of a successful compensation claim under the LDA 1991.

124 *R (Spurrier) v Secretary of State for Transport* [2020] PTSR 240.

plans, and provides the high-level policy context within which national and sub-national marine plans will be developed and implemented. It also sets the direction for marine licensing and other relevant authorisation systems.

19.93 From 1 January 2021 onwards, the Marine Policy Statement must be read alongside DEFRA's statutory guidance, which explains how references to EU law should be interpreted following the UK's departure from the EU.

19.94 Marine plans are the responsibility of the Marine Management Organization ('MMO'). (See Chapter 4 for further discussion of other public bodies.) Like land use plans, they address the key issues for the area, setting a vision and objectives and establishing policies to inform decision-making for any activity or development which is in, or impacts on, a marine area.

19.95 There are 11 English marine plan areas covering the inshore and offshore waters of the English marine area. To date, six marine plans have been adopted covering the East, South, North East, North West, South East and South West regions. These plans cover a 20-year period with three-yearly reviews.

19.96 The Flood and Coastal Erosion Risk Management Policy Statement (2020) and National Flood and Coastal Erosion Risk Management Strategy for England (2020) also set out the government's strategic approach to managing the risks and consequences of sea level rises and coastal erosion.

(iii) *Legal framework*

(a) Coast Protection Act 1949

19.97 The Coast Protection Act 1949 ('CPA 1949') confers powers on coast protection authorities (defined under section 1 as the council of each maritime district), and the EA to carry out coast protection work where the authority thinks that work is desirable having regard to the national flood and coastal erosion risk management strategies under sections 7 and 8 of the FWMA 2010, and where the purpose of the work is to manage a coastal erosion risk. The CPA 1949 also contains further detailed provisions concerning the execution of those works.

(b) Water Resources Act 1991 and Land Drainage Act 1991

19.98 The WRA 1991 and LDA 1991 establish the main legislative framework for sea defence works for the prevention of flooding. 'Drainage' is defined for these purposes as 'defence against water, including sea water; irrigation and warping' and covers both coastal and inland flood defence.[125] The WRA 1991 also provides for drainage works for the purpose of defence against sea or tidal water.[126]

---

125 WRA 1991 s 113(1).
126 ibid s 165(2).

(c) Marine and Coastal Access Act 2009

19.99 The Marine and Coastal Access Act 2009 ('MCA 2009') established a new system for marine planning and licensing in the UK, including the establishment of the MMO, the requirement to produce a Marine Policy Statement and a new system of marine plans: see 19.92–19.96 above.[127]

19.100 Part 5 deals with Nature Conservation and the establishment of Marine Conservation Zones ('MCZs'). There are currently 91 MCZs in England (known collectively as the 'blue belt'). Under section 125, public authorities have a general duty to exercise their functions in the manner which the authority considers best furthers (or least hinders the achievement of) the conservation objectives stated for the MCZ. Section 129 confers powers on the MMO to make byelaws for the purpose of furthering the conservation objectives stated for an MCZ in England.[128]

(d) Water Environment (Water Framework Directive) (England and Wales) Regulations 2017

19.101 Estuarine and coastal waters are also covered by the WFD Regulations, where these fall within a river basin district for the purposes of regulation 4(1).[129]

19.102 Under the WFD Regulations, the EA (and NRW) are required to exercise their 'relevant functions' (including the preparation of river basin management plans and supplementary plans under regulation 32, and the implementation of measures to achieve the environmental objectives under regulation 13, discussed at paragraphs 19.128–19.129 below) to secure compliance with the WFD. Article 4 of the WFD requires member states to implement the necessary measures to prevent deterioration of the status of all bodies of surface water.

19.103 Under regulation 9, the EA (and NRW) may also designate any area of coastal or transitional water within a river basin district as a shellfish water protected area.

(iv) *Issues arising in practice*

19.104 In addition to the specific statutory duties and powers set out above, there may be a requirement to carry out an EIA, where the proposed development is a Schedule 1 or Schedule 2 development under the EIA Regulations, as well as a Habitats Regulations Assessment ('HRA'), where a plan or project has the potential to have an impact upon the designated features of a European site. The Habitats Regulations apply to European sites within England and Wales and their inshore waters, within 12 nautical miles of the coast.[130]

---

127 See *Powell v Marine Management Organisation* [2017] EWHC 1491 (Admin) [48]–[66] and *R (Tarian Hafren Severn Shield CYF) v MMO* [2022] EWHC 683 [46] onwards for a summary of the provisions of the MCA 2009.

128 See the summary at *R (Thomson) v Marine Management Organisation* [2019] EWHC 2368 (Admin), [6]–[12].

129 See, further, paras 19.127–19.131 below.

130 See *R (Sussex Wildlife Trust) v South Downs National Park Authority & Anor* (unreported), where the defendant consented to judgment on the grounds that the proposed reconstruction and extension of sea defences affecting the internationally important chalk reef at Cuckmere Haven should have been subject to EIA.

19.105 Indeed, major development projects affecting coastal areas may be caught by a number of overlapping regimes, including the EIA Regulations, the Habitats Regulations and the MCA 2009.

19.106 Whereas an EIA must be carried out at the earliest possible stage under the EIA Regulations, no such requirement arises under the Habitats Regulations. Accordingly, HRA may lawfully be completed at the reserved matters stage, even if it is not carried out prior to the grant of outline permission. By contrast, a failure to undertake an EIA at the outset cannot be remedied by assessment at a later stage in the approval process: see *R (Wingfield) v Canterbury City Council*[131] at [72]–[77].

Water as a constraint on development

(i) *Introduction*

19.107 The status of the UK's rivers, seas and other waterbodies has become a matter of widespread public interest and concern in recent years. However, water pollution also has serious implications for the delivery of development, particularly housing. Excess nutrients and phosphates in English waters caused by wastewater and agricultural run-off have resulted in eutrophication, disrupting healthy ecosystems and harming wildlife. Where this has the potential to impact upon habitats or species protected under the Habitats Regulations, this has led to an effective moratorium on new housing development, while an acceptable solution to ensure 'nutrient neutrality' in protected waterbodies is identified. Unsurprisingly, this has led to several high-profile legal challenges.

19.108 The statutory and policy framework discussed below also operates to constrain development, where this causes a deterioration of the status of a body of surface water or where it may give rise to an increased risk of flooding.

(ii) *Policy framework*

(a) NPPF

19.109 Paragraph 180(e) of the NPPF requires planning policies and decisions to contribute to and enhance the natural and local environment, by preventing new and existing development from contributing to, being put at unacceptable risk from, or being adversely affected by, unacceptable levels of water pollution.

19.110 Development should, wherever possible, help to improve local environmental conditions such as air and water quality, taking into account relevant information such as river basin management plans ('RBMPs').

(b) PPG

19.111 The PPG advises that local planning authorities must have regard to RBMPs in exercising their functions.

---

131 *R (Wingfield) v Canterbury City Council* [2020] JPL 154.

(c) River basin management plans and river basin planning guidance

19.112 The requirement to produce river basin management plans derives from the WFD Regulations: see, further, paragraphs 19.128–19.132 below. In England, the EA is responsible for producing RBMPs. These must be reviewed and updated every six years for approval by the Secretary of State for Environment, Food and Rural Affairs. There are 12 river basin districts in England, Scotland and Wales, with seven RBDs managed by the EA in England.

19.113 In December 2022, the EA published updated river basin management plans for each of the seven river basin districts in England. NRW and the Scottish Environment Protection Agency have also published river basin management plans for the river basin districts under their jurisdiction.

(iii) *Legal framework*

(a) Council Directive 92/43/EEC of 21st May 1992 on the Conservation of Natural Habitats and of Wild Flora and Fauna ('the Habitats Directive')

19.114 Article 6 of the Habitats Directive provides, insofar as relevant:

> 2. Member States shall take appropriate steps to avoid, in the special areas of conservation, the deterioration of natural habitats and the habitats of species as well as disturbance of the species for which the areas have been designated, in so far as such disturbance could be significant in relation to the objectives of this Directive.
>
> 3. Any plan or project not directly connected with or necessary to the management of the site but likely to have a significant effect thereon, either individually or in combination with other plans or projects, shall be subject to appropriate assessment of its implications for the site in view of the site's conservation objectives. In the light of the conclusions of the assessment of the implications for the site and subject to the provisions of paragraph 4, the competent national authorities shall agree to the plan or project only after having ascertained that it will not adversely affect the integrity of the site concerned and, if appropriate, after having obtained the opinion of the general public.

19.115 In *R (Harris) v Environment Agency*,[132] the court held that Article 6 of the Habitats Directive remains enforceable in the UK courts post-Brexit. Although Article 6(2) has not been recognised by the courts as having direct effect in domestic law, its obligations were of a kind recognised in cases decided prior to the UK leaving the EU. Consequently, the test in the European Union (Withdrawal) Act 2018, section 4(2)(b), is satisfied.[133]

19.116 In *Harris*, the claimant applied for judicial review of the EA's refusal to expand the scope of an investigation into the effect of abstraction of groundwater from wetland sites across the Norfolk Broads. The court held that the EA was in breach of Article 6(2). On the evidence, it was sufficient that a generalised risk to the Special Area of

---

132 *R (Harris) v Environment Agency* [2022] EWHC 2606 (Admin).
133 See, also, *CG Fry and Son Ltd v Secretary of State for Levelling Up Housing and Communities* [2024] JPL 1.15.

Conservation had been established for the duty to take proactive remedial steps under Article 6(2) to be engaged, applying the precautionary principle.

(b) Conservation of Habitats and Species Regulations 2017 ('the Habitats Regulations')

19.117 The Habitats Regulations transpose the Habitats Directive into domestic law.

19.118 Regulation 9 provides that:[134]

> (1) The appropriate authority, the nature conservation bodies and, in relation to the marine area, a competent authority must exercise their functions which are relevant to nature conservation, including marine conservation, so as to secure compliance with the requirements of the Directives.
>
> ...
>
> (3) Without prejudice to the preceding provisions, a competent authority, in exercising any of its functions, must have regard to the requirements of the Directives so far as they may be affected by the exercise of those functions.

19.119 Regulation 63(1) provides that:

> (1) A competent authority, before deciding to undertake, or give any consent, permission or other authorisation for, a plan or project which—
>
> (a) is likely to have a significant effect on a European site or a European offshore marine site (either alone or in combination with other plans or projects), and
> (b) is not directly connected with or necessary to the management of that site,
>
> must make an appropriate assessment of *the implications of the plan or project for that site in view of that site's conservation objectives.* (emphasis added)

19.120 The correct legal approach to HRA has been the subject of numerous European and domestic judgments. For a useful summary of the main authorities and principles, see the judgment of Sir Keith Lindblom in *R (Wyatt) v Fareham BC & Natural England*[135] at [9].

19.121 The requirement to demonstrate 'nutrient neutrality' arose following the judgment of the Court of Justice of the European Union ('CJEU') in *Cooperatie Mobilisation for the Environment UA, Vereniging Leefmilieu v College van Gedeputeerde Staten van Limburg* (the '*Dutch Nitrogen* case').[136] In that case, the CJEU held by reference to Article 6 of the Habitats Directive, that Dutch legislation which set generic threshold values for

---

134 The requirement under reg 9(3) to 'have regard to' the Habitats Directive does not impose a duty to secure compliance with it: see *Harris v Environment Agency* (n 132) above.

135 *R (Wyatt) v Fareham BC & Natural England* [2022] EWCA Civ 983.

136 *Cooperatie Mobilisation for the Environment UA, Vereniging Leefmilieu v College van Gedeputeerde Staten van Limburg* Case C-293/17.

nitrogen deposition failed to comply with the requirement for case-specific assessment. Moreover, any additional release of nutrients into protected sites which were already in 'unfavourable condition' would be unlawful.

19.122 In light of this decision, NE issued guidance to 32 local planning authorities that planning permission should not be granted where waters protected under the Habitats Regulations were already in unfavourable condition, unless the development could achieve 'nutrient neutrality'. This requires any nitrates entering a water system as a result of new development, including wastewater from new housing, to be offset by the removal of an equivalent number of nitrates, whether through mitigation or remedial measures, or by purchasing nitrogen 'credits' as part of a local authority wide scheme.

19.123 Between 2018 and 2020, NE also produced five versions of a technical advice note entitled 'Natural England's Advice on Achieving Nutrient Neutrality for New Development in the Solent Region'. This reflected the fact that local authorities in the Solent Region were particularly severely impacted by the nutrient neutrality issue.

19.124 The NE advice note(s), and the council's decision to grant permission in reliance upon this advice, were the subject of the unsuccessful judicial review challenge in *R (Wyatt) v Fareham BC & Natural England*.[137] The Court of Appeal upheld the High Court's judgment that the council had not erred in law in performing its duty under regulation 63 and had not acted unlawfully in relying on this advice to calculate the nutrient budget. It was open to the council:[138]

> to rely on the precautionary nature of several factors in the nitrogen budget to ground its own judgment that the use of an occupancy rate of 2.4 persons per dwelling was consistent with a sufficiently precautionary approach in this instance.

19.125 On 16 March 2022, NE issued updated nutrient neutrality guidance to a further 42 authorities, bringing the total number of affected authorities to 74.[139]

19.126 Since the judgment in *Wyatt*, NE has introduced a number of measures intended to provide a strategic approach to achieving nutrient neutrality. These include (i) the Nutrient Mitigation Scheme, introduced in July 2022, which enables developers to purchase nutrient credits as a form of mitigation[140] and (ii) the publication of a national methodology in November 2022 (the 'nutrient neutrality generic methodology') together with a nutrient budget calculator.[141]

---

137 *R (Wyatt) v Fareham BC & Natural England* (n 135).
138 ibid [62].
139 Natural England, 'NE785 Revised Edition Natural England Water Quality and Nutrient Neutrality Advice (16 March 2022)' (2022) <https://publications.naturalengland.org.uk/publication/4792131352002560> accessed 23 April 2024.
140 At the time of writing, the current scheme only applies to the Tees catchment area.
141 Natural England, 'NECR459 Edition 1 Nutrient Neutrality Generic Methodology' (2022) <https://publications. naturalengland.org.uk/publication/5143927928913920>.

19.127 In August 2023, the government also tabled an amendment to the Levelling Up and Regeneration Bill, to provide that consideration of nutrient flows from urban wastewater was no longer required as part of HRAs in nutrient neutrality catchments. However, this amendment was rejected by the House of Lords in September 2023 and it has not been added to the Bill, which received royal assent on 26 October 2023.

(c) Water Environment (Water Framework Directive) (England and Wales) Regulations 2017 and Water Framework Directive 2000/60/EC

19.128 The WFD Regulations transpose the WFD into UK law. They require the preparation and publication of river basin management plans; the setting of environmental objectives for groundwater and surface waters (including estuaries and coastal waters: see paragraph 19.102 above) and the devising and implementing of programmes of measures to meet those objectives.

19.129 Regulation 13 of the WFD Regulations establishes environmental objectives. Under regulation 12, river basin management plans must provide a programme of measures to address these objectives, including to prevent deterioration of the status of each body of surface water and to 'protect, enhance and restore each body of surface water (other than an artificial or heavily modified water body) with the aim of achieving good ecological status and (subject to paragraph (3)) good surface water chemical status, if not already achieved, by 22 December 2021. Regulation 16 permits the extension of the deadline for achieving good water status where this is not reasonably achievable. There is no power to extend the time to achieve the prevention of deterioration of status.[142]

19.130 The programme of measures required under regulation 12 is required to focus on whether, when and how the environmental objectives designated for the individual water body would be met. The programme and the objectives must be specific to the water body in question: a generic programme of measures at a national or river basin level will not satisfy the requirements of the WFD Regulations.[143]

19.131 In *Bund für Umwelt und Naturschutz Deutschland eV v Bundesrepublik Deutschland*,[144] it was held that Article 4(1)(a)(i)–(iii) of the WFD must be interpreted as meaning that Member States are required – unless a derogation is granted – to refuse authorisation for an individual project, where it may cause a deterioration of the status of a body of surface water or where it jeopardises the attainment of good surface water status or of good ecological potential and good surface water chemical status by the date laid down by the Directive.

19.132 However, there is no legal requirement under the WFD Regulations for a project to contribute positively towards the attainment of good surface water status

---

142 See *R (Pickering Fishery Association) v Secretary of State for the Environment, Food and Rural Affairs* [2023] EWHC 2918 (Admin) at [10]–[48] for an analysis of the statutory regime.
143 ibid [134].
144 Case C-461/13 *Bund für Umwelt und Naturschutz Deutschland eV v Bundesrepublik Deutschland* (2015) ECLI:EU:C:2015:43.

or good chemical status: see *Tarian Hafren Severn Shield CYF v Marine Management Organisation & another*[145] at [152] onwards.

(iv) *Issues arising in practice*

(a) Nutrient neutrality and planning applications

19.133 Although progress has been made towards providing a consistent methodology for calculating nutrient budgets, requirements to demonstrate nutrient neutrality will vary across different local planning authorities and different catchment areas.

19.134 An important question which arises in all cases concerns the stages of the consent process, when the requirement to demonstrate nutrient neutrality applies. This issue was considered by the High Court in *CG Fry and Son Ltd v Secretary of State for Levelling Up, Housing and Communities*,[146] where the court held that the requirement for appropriate assessment applies at all stages of the approval process, including the discharge of conditions. The court held that the council was entitled to decline to discharge the conditions attached to the grant of planning permission for 650 homes, in light of NE's advice at that time that the area was at risk of nutrient pollution. The court granted permission to appeal directly to the Supreme Court in light of the importance of this issue, but permission was refused.

(b) Water pollution: remedies

19.135 Where sewage discharges are unauthorised, persons directly impacted by these discharges may have a private law cause of action against the companies involved: see *Manchester Ship Canal Co Ltd v United Utilities Water Ltd.*[147]

19.136 The widespread public concern about water pollution and sewage discharges into UK waters has also resulted in several judicial review challenges, alleging a failure on the part of the relevant regulatory or government body to take sufficient measures or to regulate such discharges adequately. However, the courts will not readily hold that plans or measures implemented by the body with responsibility for such matters are so inadequate as to be unlawful: see, for example, *R (Wildfish Conservation); R (Marine Conservation Society & others) v Secretary of State for the Environment*,[148] which involved an unsuccessful challenge to the lawfulness of the Storm Overflows Discharge Reduction Plan ('the Plan') and *R (Wild Justice) v The Water Services Regulation Authority*,[149] where the claimant unsuccessfully argued that Ofwat had failed to discharge its obligations concerning the responsibilities of sewerage companies under the Urban Waste Water Treatment (England and Wales) Regulations 1994.

---

145 *R (Tarian Hafren Severn Shield CYF) v MMO* (n 127).
146 *CG Fry and Son Ltd v Secretary of State for Levelling Up Housing and Communities* [2023] EWHC 1622 (Admin).
147 *Manchester Ship Canal Co Ltd v United Utilities Water Ltd* [2024] UKSC 22 [2024] 3 WLR 356.
148 *R (Wildfish Conservation); R (Marine Conservation Society & others) v Secretary of State for the Environment* [2023] EWHC 2285 (Admin).
149 *R (Wild Justice) v The Water Services Regulation Authority* [2023] EWCA Civ 28.

PART III
PROPERTY

CHAPTER 20

IMPLICATIONS OF CLIMATE CHANGE FOR PROPERTY RIGHTS AND OBLIGATIONS

David Sawtell

Introduction

20.01 Property rights are capable of benefitting and binding parties who were uninvolved in their original creation.[1] They affect the relations between a person with respect to a thing, and provide a measure of autonomy and self-governance to the owner of the right.[2] We typically equate a degree of permanence and solidity to property rights, which persist as they are assigned or otherwise conveyed from person to person, sometimes over hundreds of years. The assumption that property rights in general and rights in respect of land in particular are enduring is undermined, however, when the thing that is the subject of the property right is damaged or destroyed. If land slides into the sea, collapses into a fissure in the ground, or is eroded or added to by riparian action, then difficult questions arise as to what happens to the rights in respect of that plot. These are not, however, new difficulties. Some of the rules that such events engage have their roots in Roman law. What climate change challenges, however, is the extent to which these rules will be rarely invoked. It may well be the case that these doctrines will come under increasing scrutiny in private law litigation.

20.02 What may also come under increased consideration is the extent to which the individual property owner is required to consider neighbouring plots when defending their own land from coastal erosion or flooding, and the extent to which they come under a positive duty to take active steps to prevent the property of adjacent landowners from being damaged or inundated.

20.03 The first part of this chapter considers coastal land, ground instability and extreme weather events. Climate change effects may well threaten the very existence of a landowner's property. The courts have been careful to limit the extent to which a landowner is obliged to take steps to protect the property of their neighbours. This, however, has a complex relationship with the old doctrine of defence against a common enemy, which actively allows a landowner to take steps to protect their land against flooding, even if those steps would worsen the flooding of neighbouring land.

---

1 Edward Burn and John Cartwright, *Cheshire and Burn's Modern Law of Real Property* (18th edn, Oxford University Press 2011) 3–6.
2 Hanoch Dagan, *A Liberal Theory of Property* (Cambridge University Press 2021) 26–31.

20.04 The second part of this chapter considers frustration and force majeure insofar as these rule sets affect property rights, and in particular, rights in respect of land. The common law has tended to require parties to keep to their bargains without providing relief on the grounds of frustration. This is especially the case where the subject matter of the dispute is a grant of an interest in land, such as a lease.

20.05 The third part of this chapter tackles the doctrines that relate to accretion to and destruction of land. The origins of these rules in the common law can be traced back to Roman law. They are still, however, current, and can be found in the Land Registration Act 2002 ('LRA 2002') and in cases across the common law world.

20.06 The fourth part of this chapter considers easements and freehold covenants as examples of incorporeal hereditaments. These rights are valuable, facilitating or restricting the full enjoyment of land. A number of the rule sets that are engaged by the possible effects of climate change are, however, potentially obscure. It remains to be seen whether climate change litigation will develop the law in these fields into new directions, or if older rules will remain essentially static.

Coastal land, flooding, ground instability and extreme weather events

(i) *Introduction*

20.07 The British Isles, surrounded by ocean in the north-east of the Atlantic, intersected by rivers, and studded with lakes and reservoirs, are vulnerably placed. As the Global Commission on Adaptation observed:[3]

> Climate risks manifest themselves in many ways—from the slow and inexorable rise in sea level to the erratic behavior of monsoons, and the strengthening of storms and heat waves.

20.08 Climate change, which would bring with it rising sea levels and increased precipitation, entails faster coastal erosion, increased risks of flooding, and the consequential destruction of property.[4] While the effect on the sea and on rivers might be the most obvious, the impact on smaller watercourses, groundwater, surface water and both natural and manmade slopes and hills would also be dramatic. It is estimated that over 5.2 million homes and properties in England are at risk from flooding and coastal erosion, but that only a third of people who live in areas at risk of flooding believe that their property is at risk.[5]

3 Global Commission on Adaptation, 'Adapt Now: A Global Call for Leadership on Climate Resilience' (2019) 9 <https://gca.org/reports/adapt-now-a-global-call-for-leadership-on-climate-resilience/> accessed 20 April 2024.
4 Paul D Bates and others, 'A Climate-Conditioned Catastrophe Risk Model for UK Flooding' (2023) 23 Natural Hazards and Earth System Sciences 891 <https://nhess.copernicus.org/articles/23/891/2023/> accessed 20 April 2024.
5 Environment Agency, 'National Flood and Coastal Erosion Risk Management Strategy for England' (2020) 15 <https://assets.publishing.service.gov.uk/media/5f6b6da6e90e076c182d508d/023_15482_Environment_agency_digitalAW_Strategy.pdf> accessed 20 April 2024. See Chapter 19 ('Water') for a discussion of flood protection.

20.09 Property law, as an aspect of private law more generally, is concerned with the jural relationships between individuals (whether they are natural or legal persons, or also happen to be public authorities) in respect of rights in property.[6] While the forces involved in climate change may well be very great and are global in scale, they also disrupt the rights, obligations and enjoyment of property holders. Different property law doctrinal regimes prescribe the limits placed on an owner in private law as to how they can use their own property without interfering with the use of others.[7] Property law acknowledges the interdependence between and potential impact on the lands of different owners. The early rule sets regulating the use of property as between landowners in respect of water discharge and flooding can be attributed to Ulpian.[8] The individual doctrines that English law has developed that respond to damage and destruction by water and ground instability have ancient roots. Climate change is likely to result in them becoming increasingly familiar.

(ii) *The destruction of Holbeck Hall Hotel and the measured duty of care*

20.10 The destructive power of the sea was considered directly by the Court of Appeal in *Holbeck Hall Hotel Ltd v Scarborough Borough Council*.[9] The Holbeck Hall Hotel stood on South Cliff, Scarborough, North Yorkshire. It commanded a panoramic view of the North Sea. The upper part of the cliff consisted of boulder clay deposited during an end of a period of glaciation. Below that was a layer of mudstones, which in turn was overlaid on a bed of harder quartz sandstone, which formed a nearly vertical base to the cliff. The cliff was subject to marine erosion, which made it inherently unstable.

20.11 The building which became the hotel was built in 1880 by Charles Alderson Smith, who at the time owned approximately nine acres of land extending to the sea. On 1 February 1887, he conveyed the northern part of the undercliff which formed the eastern slope of the property to the borough of Scarborough. There was no express covenant for support. On 2 August 1895, he conveyed the remaining, southern, part of the undercliff, this time including covenants for its maintenance.

20.12 From 1893 onwards, a series of slips and collapses took place along the coastline, including the stretch between the grounds of Holbeck Hotel and the sea. By 1912, sea defence works had been installed below the hotel, checking the retreat of the cliff. In 1982 a slip or slips occurred on Scarborough's land below Holbeck Hall. Geotechnical Engineering (Northern) Ltd ('GEN') tendered for an investigation into the works required to stabilise the cliffs; they identified the need for further investigations before remedial measures could be designed. In 1986, a further slip took place, doubling the

6 Kevin Gray and Susan Gray, *Elements of Land Law* (5th edn, Oxford University Press 2009); JE Penner, *The Idea of Property in Law* (Oxford University Press 1997) 25–31.
7 James Gordley, *Foundations of Private Law* (Oxford University Press 2007) ch 4.
8 Dig. 8.5.8.5 (Ulpian): '*it is not legal to discharge water or anything else from an upper on to a lower building, as the party has only the right to perform such acts on his own premises as will not discharge anything upon those of another*'. As for public law, we can identify the origins of the commissioners of sewers (with responsibility for the repairs of walls and watercourses as well as flood defences) to the 13th century: HG Richardson, 'The Early History of Commissions of Sewers' (1919) 34 The English Historical Review 385 <https://www.jstor.org/stable/551072> accessed 20 April 2024.
9 *Holbeck Hall Hotel Ltd v Scarborough Borough Council* [2000] QB 836.

size of the previous one. In 1989, remedial works were carried out, but they were incorrectly designed. In 1993, there were a series of major slips. First the lawn, and then the seaward wing of the main building itself, were destroyed. The remainder of the hotel became unsafe and had to be demolished.

20.13 The freehold owners, the first plaintiffs, leased the hotel to the second plaintiffs on a 21-year lease. Scarborough Borough Council were sued as the owners of the land between the hotel grounds and the sea. In turn, they claimed against GEN. The owners of the freehold and leasehold interests in the hotel claimed for damages arising out of the removal of support (relying on natural rights of support, implied reservation or prescription), breach of the Council's common law duty (as established in *Leakey v National Trust*[10]), and breach of covenant arising from the 1895 conveyance. The council claimed a contribution from GEN. At first instance, His Honour Judge Hicks QC rejected the claim for removal of support, holding that the occupier was not required to take active steps to maintain support; instead, some positive act amounting to removal of support was required. He also rejected the claim for breach of covenant. He allowed the claim, however, under the *Leakey*[11] duty.

20.14 The council's appeal regarding the *Leakey* duty went to the Court of Appeal. In *Leakey*, a number of houses had been built at the foot of a mound on land owned by the National Trust, who knew that there was a threat to the dwellings. In 1968, a large crack opened in the mound. Large quantities of earth fell on to the houses. The National Trust was held liable in nuisance; it was confirmed that the Privy Council decision of *Goldman v Hargrave*[12] also represented the law in England. In that case, a tall redgum tree on the defendant's land was struck by lightning and set on fire. Having taken limited steps to stop the spread of fire, the defendant did nothing further. The fire spread to his neighbour's land, damaging his property. It was held by the Privy Council that there was no difference in principle between a nuisance created by a trespasser and one created by the forces of nature, provided the defendant knew of the hazard. In particular, it was held that in order to give rise to a measured duty of care, the defendant must know or be presumed to know of the defect or condition giving rise to the hazard and must, as a reasonable man, foresee that the defect or condition will, if not remedied, cause damage to the plaintiff's land.

20.15 The Court of Appeal in *Holbeck Hall* stated that the extent of the foreseen damage was a relevant consideration when considering the scope of the duty, alongside the ease and expense of abatement and the ability of the defendant to achieve it. Stuart-Smith LJ stated that:[13]

> I do not think justice requires that a defendant should be held liable for damage which, albeit of the same type, was vastly more extensive than that which was foreseen or could have been foreseen without extensive further geological investigation; and this is particularly so where the defect existed just as much on the plaintiffs' land as on their own.

---

10 *Leakey v National Trust* [1980] 1 QB 485.
11 *Holbeck Hall Hotel Ltd v Scarborough Borough Council* [1997] 57 Con LR 113.
12 *Goldman v Hargrave* [1967] 1 AC 645.
13 *Holbeck Hall Hotel Ltd v Scarborough Borough Council* (n 9) [49].

20.16 It was held that the council's duty was confined to an obligation to take care to avoid damage to the plaintiffs' land which they ought to have foreseen without further geological investigation.[14] It was not necessarily incumbent on someone in the council's position to carry out extensive and expensive remedial work to prevent the damage which they ought to have foreseen; the scope of the duty may be limited to warning neighbours of such risk as they were aware of or ought to have foreseen, and sharing such information as they had acquired relating to it. The council's appeal was therefore allowed, as the damage was vastly more extensive than that which was foreseen.

20.17 The *Leakey* measured duty of care and the reasoning in *Holbeck Hall* has been extended to other natural phenomena. In *Vernon Knight Associates v Cornwall Council*,[15] the Court of Appeal considered flooding to a property in Cornwall that was being flooded by run off coming from a road where the highway authority had installed a series of drains, gullies and catchpits. The claimant's property was damaged when gratings in those drainage works became blocked. The first instance judge held that the highway authority had breached its duty of care by failing to perform checks during bad weather on the occasions when the damage occurred, and the Court of Appeal dismissed the appeal from his finding. It was considered that the measured duty of care required them to keep the drainage installation functioning properly. In *Green v Lord Somerleyton*,[16] a measured duty of care was imposed on the defendants in respect of naturally flowing water from marshes, but they were able to rely on a proviso in a drainage deed to exempt themselves from liability.

20.18 The decision in *Holbeck Hall* is a reminder that English law places only a limited duty on landowners to take active steps to take action against natural phenomena that arises from their land which affects neighbouring properties. The Court of Appeal placed particular emphasis on the fact that, save for the in-house expertise of the council, the owners of the freehold and leasehold were in as good a position as their neighbouring landowner to acquire knowledge about and take steps in respect of the encroaching sea.

(iii) *Limits on the responsibilities of landowners*

20.19 The courts are likely to have to reconcile the doctrinal rules which have grown up in respect of the passage of water with the expansion of the torts of negligence and nuisance in the 20th and 21st centuries. In *Home Brewery Co Ltd v William Davis & Co (Leicester) Ltd*,[17] water drained over and through the plaintiffs' land unchannelled, going into a disused clay pit on the defendants' land. The defendants filled in the clay pit, creating a partial barrier to the drainage, causing the plaintiffs' land to flood. It was held that the occupier of land had no cause of action against the occupier of higher adjacent land for permitting the passage of natural unchannelled water over or through the higher to the lower land.[18] At the same time, such an occupier was under no obligation

---

14 ibid [54].
15 *Vernon Knight Associates v Cornwall Council* [2013] EWCA Civ 950.
16 *Green v Lord Somerleyton* [2003] EWCA Civ 198, [2004] 1 P & CR 33.
17 *Home Brewery Co Ltd v William Davis & Co (Leicester) Ltd* [1987] QB 339.
18 This conclusion was approved by the Court of Appeal in *Palmer v Bowman* [2000] 1 WLR 842 [855] *per* Rattee J.

to receive such water and was entitled to take steps consistent with his reasonable user of the land to prevent it from entering, even if it caused damage to the higher land. It was only if the lower occupier's use of land was unreasonable and the damage to the higher land was foreseeable that an action in nuisance would lie. It was held that filling in the clay pit was a reasonable use, but that temporary flooding caused by ejecting water on to the higher land during the works did give rise to an action in nuisance. Piers Ashworth QC, sitting as a deputy High Court judge, doubted the authority of *Smith v Kenrick*,[19] which suggests that an occupier was not liable even if he had himself removed the barrier between his and his neighbour's land, thereby permitting the water to flow naturally from one land to the other, in the light of the development of the decision in *Leakey v National Trust*.[20]

20.20 In *Hudson v Tabor*,[21] it was held that a landowner whose land is adjacent to the coast is not required to maintain a barrier against the sea for the benefit of inland owners. There was a sea wall on the defendant's land, which reduced in height from time to time; he neglected to 'top' his wall, as a result of which the sea flowed over his wall and damaged the plaintiff's inland land. There was no evidence of an obligation to repair the wall for the benefit of the plaintiff arising by way of prescription: as the Court of Appeal noted, each frontage had a direct interest in keeping up his frontage wall to protect his own land. The argument that an obligation arose at common law was rejected, as it would 'lead to manifest hardships'.[22]

20.21 Beyond the measured duty of care seen in cases such as *Leakey v National Trust*, therefore, the common law imposes few responsibilities on landowners to maintain coastal or river flood defences. On the other hand, a landowner is not entitled to remove a natural barrier against the sea if this would cause injury to the land of a neighbouring landowner: 'although he is not bound to keep the sea out, yet he must not do an act which will let the sea in'.[23] Private law, therefore, imposes only very limited obligations on a landowner to take positive steps to defend neighbouring land from coastal action or flooding. Should climate change lead to increased risk of flooding, it is unlikely that English land law will impose additional burdens on landowners to take positive steps to erect new defences.

(iv) *Defence against a common enemy*

20.22 One question that occasionally emerges is the extent to which a private landowner can take steps to protect their land against flooding, if those steps would worsen the flooding of their neighbours' land. In *R v The Commissioners for the Levels of Pagham*,[24] commissioners of sewers erected groynes and other sea defences which caused the sea

19 *Smith v Kenrick* [1849] 7 CB 515.
20 *Home Brewery Co Ltd v William Davis and Co (Leicester) Ltd* (n 17) [346].
21 *Hudson v Tabor* [1877] 2 QBD 290.
22 ibid [293] *per* Lord Coleridge CJ.
23 *Attorney-General v Tomline* [1880] 14 ChD 58 [65] *per* Brett LJ. In that case, the action was brought by the Secretary of State for the War Department; it is unclear if the case would have been decided differently if the plaintiff was not the Crown. It is likely that the decision would be decided the same way today, but on the basis of the measured duty in *Leakey v National Trust*.
24 *R v The Commissioners of Sewers for the Levels of Pagham* [1828] 8 B & C 355.

to attack neighbouring land more fiercely, causing it to wash away. It was held that they were not liable to compensate the neighbouring landowner or to erect new works to protect them. Instead, landowners had a right to erect works that were necessary for their own protection, even though they might adversely affect others. Lord Tenterden CJ stated that, 'the sea is a common enemy to all proprietors on that part of the coast'.[25] He went on to state that:[26]

> [E]ach landowner for himself, or the commissioners acting for several landowners, may erect such defences for the land under their care as the necessity of the case requires, leaving it to others, in like manner, to protect themselves against the common enemy.

20.23 As Bramwell B set out in *Nield and Another v The London and North Western Railway Company*:[27]

> The law allows what I may term a kind of reasonable selfishness in such matters; it says, 'Let every one look out for himself and protect his own interest,' and he who puts up a barricade against a flood is entitled to say to his neighbour who complains of it, 'Why did not you do the same?'

20.24 The 'common enemy' rule was recognised in the 1741 case of *Farquharson v Farquharson*.[28] In a report taking the form of a note, it was recorded that it was found lawful for a party to build a fence on his own ground by the side of a river to prevent it overflowing on to his ground and hence damaging it, even though this would cause damage to his neighbour by diverting the overflow on to his land. It was not lawful, however, to carry out an operation in the *alveus*, or watercourse. Subsequently, the rule has been accepted in English cases.[29] These cases maintained the exception that the law prohibits interference with the *alveus*.

20.25 The Court of Appeal considered the doctrine of 'common enemy' in *Arscott v The Coal Authority*.[30] Laws LJ reviewed the earlier authorities, and noted that the doctrine has limitations. Firstly, the rule prevents interference with the *alveus*, or the established bed of the river or watercourse, or established flood channel. Secondly, while the rule permits the landowner to erect defences whose effect will be that water which would otherwise have flowed on to his land will be diverted onto his neighbour's, it does not permit the landowner to take measures so as to cause water which has already or will in any event come on to his land to flow from it on to that of his neighbour.[31] The rule, therefore, allows a landowner to protect his or her land from the incursions of the 'common enemy', but it does not allow the 'common enemy' to be exported from the

---

25 ibid [712].
26 ibid [713].
27 *Nield and another v The London and North Western Railway Company* [1874] L R 10 Ex 4 [7].
28 William Maxwell Morison, 'Deans of Court of Session' (1811) vol XXIX–XXX, 12779.
29 See, for example, *R v The Commissioners of Sewers for the Levels of Pagham* [1828] 8 B & C 355 (n 24); *R v Trafford* [1831] 1 B & Ad 874. and upon removal on error to the Court of Exchequer Chamber, sub nom *Trafford v R* [8].
30 *Arscott v The Coal Authority* [2004] EWCA (Civ) 892, [2005] Env LR 6.
31 See, for example, *Hurdman v NE Ry Co* [1878] 3 CPD 168; *Whalley v Lancs and Yorks Ry Co* [1884] 13 QBD 131.

landowner's land to another's land if the incursion has already happened or is about to happen.[32]

20.26 In the *Arscott* case,[33] the local council owned a large recreation area which was susceptible to flooding. The recreation area was built up with coal waste to raise the level to create a playing area. In 1998, the river Taff overflowed, causing damage to a number of residential buildings in the area; the recreation area, however, was not inundated. It was conceded by the council that the raised level was a cause of the damage, but they denied the claim in nuisance primarily on the basis of the 'common enemy' doctrine. They argued that a landowner was entitled to develop his land so as to prevent flood waters coming on to his land. It was held that this defence succeeded, both at first instance and on appeal.

20.27 Laws LJ set the common enemy rule within the context of the general law of nuisance. He noted that Lord Wright in *Sedleigh-Denfield v O'Callaghan*[34] had observed that, 'A balance has to be maintained between the right of the occupier to do what he likes with his own, and the right of his neighbour not to be interfered with.'[35] Laws LJ then went on to note that, in general, a landowner will not be liable in nuisance for the consequences of what would be recognised as a natural use of his land by him, unless the quality or extent of that use by him was unreasonable.[36] Secondly, it is necessary to establish reasonable foreseeability of damage as a condition of liability in nuisance.[37] The common enemy doctrine, including the distinction between the *alveus* and the flood plain, was one mechanism to achieve the correct balance between landowner and neighbour. Laws LJ held that, 'It represents a resolution of the balance between self interest and duty to neighbour which, in the broad context of land use of which it is a particular instance, makes up the body of law called nuisance.'[38] The limitations of no interference with an *alveus* and no discharge from one's own land were partial guarantors of reasonable user. Works done to protect land from the common enemy, within these limits, were a natural and reasonable use of the land.

20.28 On the facts of *Arscott v The Coal Authority*, the two limits to the doctrine were held to be met. Consequently, the defence was established. The submission that the rule did not apply where the claimant's properties were inland of the Taff (as opposed to abutting its banks) was rejected. It was also held that the doctrine was compatible with Article 8 of the European Convention on Human Rights, providing for the right to respect for private and family life and the home, and Article 1 of the First Protocol, providing for the right to the peaceful enjoyment of one's possessions.

32 *Arscott v The Coal Authority* (n 30) [39].
33 ibid.
34 *Sedleigh-Denfield v O'Callaghan* [1940] AC 880 [903].
35 ibid [903].
36 See also *Fearn and others v Board of Trustees of the Tate Gallery* [2023] UKSC 4, [2023] 2 WLR 339 [24] – [33], *per* Lord Leggatt.
37 *Arscott v The Coal Authority* (n 30) [30].
38 ibid [40].

20.29 It was considered in *Bourne Leisure (Hopton) Ltd v Great Yarmouth Port Authority*[39] that, for the common enemy rule to apply, the works must be erected for the purpose of protecting the land from water.

20.30 Different considerations may apply where the water floods from a watercourse. In the Scots case of *Menzies v The Earl of Breadalbane*,[40] the Court of Sessions held that a proprietor on the banks of a river was entitled to erect a bulwark on his own ground for the protection of his property against inundation. This was overturned on appeal; it was then held that a landowner was not entitled to carry out works to the banks of a river that would cause flooding to a neighbour in times of ordinary flood, diverting the stream of the river from its accustomed course.

20.31 Both the *Leakey* duty and the common enemy rule, therefore, have undergone review and modernisation in recent Court of Appeal decisions. The law has moved towards a more measured and gradated balance between neighbouring landowners.

Frustration and force majeure

(i) *The effect of climate change on obligations in respect of land*

20.32 Climate change is likely to bring with it increasingly unpredictable weather, rising sea levels, and other difficult to anticipate consequences. This can be broken down into different orders of events. Firstly, extreme weather events, changing sea levels and other phenomena is likely to lead to immediate physical destruction or damage.[41] At a second order, these direct physical events can cause immediate disruption to businesses, supply chains and markets.[42] At a third order, as discussed elsewhere in this book, there is likely to be regulatory change created by the government.[43] Fourthly, as an indirect result of these events and impacts, businesses and individuals may well make adaptations to their own business models and behaviour.[44]

20.33 Climate change, therefore, can make contracts in general, and agreements in respect of real property and leases in particular, substantially more onerous or even impossible. The common law response to sudden changes to the basis upon which parties have contracted is the doctrine of frustration. At the same time, parties may well

---

39 *Bourne Leisure (Hopton) Ltd v Great Yarmouth Port Authority* [2016] UKUT 44 (LC).

40 *Menzies v The Earl of Breadalbane* [1828] 3 Bligh (NS) 414, [1828] 4 ER 1387.

41 National Academies of Sciences, Engineering, and Medicine and others, *Attribution of Extreme Weather Events in the Context of Climate Change* (National Academies Press 2016) <https://www.nap.edu/catalog/21852> accessed 20 April 2024.

42 See, for example, Maximilian Auffhammer, 'Quantifying Economic Damages from Climate Change' (2018) 32 Journal of Economic Perspectives 33 <https://www.aeaweb.org/articles?id=10.1257/jep.32.4.33> accessed 20 April 2024; David J Frame and others, 'Climate Change Attribution and the Economic Costs of Extreme Weather Events: A Study on Damages from Extreme Rainfall and Drought' (2020) 162 Climatic Change 781 <https://doi.org/10.1007/s10584-020-02729-y> accessed 20 April 2024.

43 Navroz K Dubash and others, 'National and Sub-National Policies and Institutions', *Climate Change 2022 – Mitigation of Climate Change: Working Group III Contribution to the Sixth Assessment Report of the Intergovernmental Panel on Climate Change* (Cambridge University Press 2023) 1355 <https://www.cambridge.org/core/product/identifier/9781009157926%23c13/type/book_part> accessed 20 April 2024.

44 Kathryn Begg, Frans van der Woerd and David Levy (eds), *The Business of Climate Change: Corporate Responses to Kyoto* (Routledge 2017).

include force majeure provisions into their agreements, which expressly regulate their rights and obligations and potentially bringing such agreements to an end through contractual terms.

(ii) *The common law's approach*

20.34 The common law originally took a very restrictive approach to relieving parties from their obligations on the grounds of frustration and, in particular, appeared to reject the possibility of a lease being capable of being frustrated. The paradigm case was *Paradine v Jane*,[45] which was decided during the English Civil Wars of the 1640s. Jane held lands from Paradine as a tenant. Prince Rupert of the Rhine had come to England to assist King Charles I, his cousin, and was a prominent Royalist commander and cavalryman. He was associated with the sack of Leicester and was accused of other 'outrages', while the war overall was associated with property loss.[46] Jane alleged that Prince Rupert and his soldiers, described as an 'army of aliens', had driven away his cattle and expelled him from the lands, keeping him out of them for a time. He attempted to raise this as a defence to a claim for rent by Paradine. This defence was unsuccessful. The case did not, however, completely reject the possibility of frustration; it is, instead, an example of the old common law rule that the obligation of an express covenant is absolute.[47] There is a discussion in the case as to whether the tenant would have been liable if the 'lands had been surrounded by water'; again, despite acknowledging that in other cases this might raise a defence, it was no answer to a claim on the covenant.

20.35 The English common law was softened so as to allow for the possibility of frustration in contract in a series of cases in the 19th and early 20th century. The starting point for the modern law is Blackburn J's judgment in *Taylor v Caldwell.*[48] The defendants agreed to let out the Surrey Gardens and Music Hall to the plaintiffs for a series of concerts and fêtes; before they took place, the Gardens and Music Hall burned down. The plaintiffs sued the defendants for breach of contract. Blackburn J held that there was an implied condition in the contract that the subject of the agreement was to continue in existence, and that if it perished so that performance became impossible, the parties were excused from performance.[49] Blackburn J did not, however, import the post-classical civilian concept of changed circumstances.[50] This has continued to the present time, with the English common law adopting a narrower approach to post-agreement

45 *Paradine v Jane* [1647] 82 ER 519, Spty 47.
46 Imogen Peck, 'Civilian Memories of the British Civil Wars, 1642–1660' in Lloyd Bowen and Mark Stoyle (eds), *Remembering the English Civil Wars* (Routledge 2021).
47 Jeffrey Price, 'The Doctrine of Frustration and Leases' (1989) 10 The Journal of Legal History 90 <https://www.tandfonline.com/doi/abs/10.1080/01440368908530955> accessed 20 April 2024; Albert Kiralfy, 'Absolute Liability in Contract: A Historical and Comparative Note on the Rule in Paradine v. Jane (1648) Aleyn 26' (1980) 1 The Journal of Legal History 89 <https://doi.org/10.1080/01440368008530709> accessed 20 April 2024.
48 *Taylor v Caldwell* [1863] 3 B & S 826; 122 ER 309.
49 ibid 312–313. Blackburn J, in particular, cited the Digest, 45.1.23 ('If by reason of a legacy or as a result of a stipulation you owe me a certain man, you will not be liable to me after his death, except where it was your fault that you did not give him to me when he was still alive. This happens if you either failed to give him when requested or killed him.') and 45.1.33 ('If Stichus has been promised to be given on a certain date and dies before that date, the promisor is not liable.')
50 Reinhard Zimmermann, *The Law of Obligations: Roman Foundations of the Civilian Tradition* (Oxford University Press 1996) 579–580, where this is traced from a passage in Gratian's *Decretum.*

hardship.[51] By the time of the so-called 'Coronation Cases', Blackburn J's approach was extended to circumstances where an express condition or state of things that went to the root of the contract had ceased to exist.[52] In *Davis Contractors v Fareham UDC*,[53] Lord Radcliffe framed the test for frustration as whether the contracted performance would be rendered 'radically different' from that which had been undertaken by the contracting parties because the circumstances in which performance would be called for had changed without default of either party.

20.36 Lord Simon gave the definitive statement of the current English legal position in *National Carriers Ltd v Panalpina (Northern) Ltd*,[54] making it clear that it was not sufficient that performance would become more expensive or difficult:[55]

> Frustration of a contract takes place where there supervenes an event (without default of either party and for which the contract makes no sufficient provision) which so significantly changes the nature (not merely the expense or onerousness) of the outstanding contractual rights and/or obligations from what the parties could reasonably have contemplated at the time of its execution that it would be unjust to hold them to the literal sense of its stipulations in the new circumstances: in such case, the law declares both parties to be discharged from further performance.

20.37 In *Edwinton Commercial Corporation v Tsavliris Russ (Worldwide Salvage and Towage) Ltd, 'The Sea Angel'*,[56] the Court of Appeal adopted a multi-factorial approach to the question of whether or not an agreement has been frustrated.[57] It was held that among the factors which have to be considered are the terms of the contract itself, its matrix or context, the parties' knowledge, expectations, assumptions and contemplations, in particular as to risk, as at the time of contract, at any rate so far as these can be ascribed mutually and objectively, and then the nature of the supervening event, and the parties' reasonable and objectively ascertainable calculations as to the possibilities of future performance in the new circumstances.[58]

20.38 There are a number of limitations on the doctrine. Typically, it will not be engaged where the contract makes express provision for the event which has occurred; as set out in the above cases, the parties will have allocated the risks arising from the allegedly supervening event. Furthermore, if the parties have foreseen the event taking place, the

---

51 John P Dawson, 'Judicial Revision of Frustrated Contracts: Germany' (1983) 63 Boston University Law Review 1043–1058 <https://heinonline.org/HOL/Page?handle=hein.journals/bulr63&id=1047&div=&collection=> accessed 20 April 2024; Hannes Rösler, 'Hardship in German Codified Private Law: In Comparative Perspective to English, French and International Contract Law' (2008) 15 European Review of Private Law 483 <https://papers.ssrn.com/abstract=1154004> accessed 20 April 2024.
52 *Krell v Henry* [1903] 2 KB 740 [747]–[748], *per* Vaughan Williams LJ.
53 *Davis Contractors v Fareham UDC* [1956] AC 696 [729].
54 *National Carriers Ltd v Panalpina (Northern) Ltd* [1981] AC 675.
55 ibid [700].
56 *Edwinton Commercial Corporation v Tsavliris Russ (Worldwide Salvage and Towage) Ltd* [2007] EWCA Civ 547; [2007] 2 All ER (Comm) 634.
57 ibid.
58 ibid [111].

scope for the doctrine to operate is considerably circumscribed.[59] Finally, a party cannot rely on self-induced frustration, arising from their own conduct.[60]

(iii) *Frustration and agreements in respect of land*

20.39 Before the *National Carriers Ltd v Panalpina* case, it was considered that the doctrine of frustration did not apply to leases, and that the rule in *Paradine v Jane* operated so as to not relieve parties from their obligations. In an agreement for the sale of land, risk passes to the purchaser on exchange of contracts and not completion unless the parties make express contractual provision otherwise.[61] A lease is both an estate in land and an executory contract.

20.40 The House of Lords in *National Carriers Ltd v Panalpina* accepted that the doctrine of frustration could potentially apply to leases as a matter of principle. It was considered, however, that a case where the doctrine applied would be extremely rare. In that case, a warehouse was demised to the defendants for a term of 10 years. The only vehicular access to the warehouse was via a street which was closed for a likely period of up to 20 months, making the warehouse useless for the defendants. In an action for rent, the defendants argued that the lease had been frustrated. On the facts, this defence was rejected. Lord Hailsham cited the earlier decision of *Cricklewood Property and Investment Trust Ltd v Leighton's Investment Trust Ltd*,[62] where Viscount Simon LC had accepted the possibility that a lease could be frustrated if 'some vast convulsion of nature swallowed up the property altogether, or buried it in the depths of the sea'.[63] Lord Hailsham held that there was no point of principle that prevented a lease from being frustrated, but considered that this was a case 'hardly ever' as opposed to 'never'. As Lord Wilberforce noted, in most cases the tenant will have that which he or she bargained from namely, the leasehold estate, but that in some cases a lease may also be regarded as a subsidiary means to an end, not an aim or end of itself.[64]

20.41 The difficulty in establishing frustration in respect of a lease was illustrated by the European Medicines Agency's failure to show that the UK's withdrawal from the EU frustrated the lease of its headquarters in *Canary Wharf (BP4) T1 Ltd v European Medicines Agency*.[65] The parties entered into an agreement for a 25-year lease in August 2014, which was granted in 2014. On 29 March 2017, the UK gave notice under Article 50 of the Treaty on European Union to withdraw from the EU. The EMA argued that the UK's withdrawal from the EU would frustrate the lease. The first argument, that it would be illegal for the EMA to have its headquarters outside the EU, was rejected. As for the argument that the common purpose had been frustrated, Marcus Smith J adopted the *Sea Angel* multi-factorial approach. He held that, by taking on a 25-year lease without a break clause, the EMA had assumed the risk of change in that time. In

59 See, for example, *Dayah v Partners of Bushloe Street Surgery* [2020] EWHC 1375 (QB).
60 *J Lauritzen AS v Wijsmuller BV* [1990] 1 Lloyd's Rep 1.
61 The rule in *Paine v Miller* [1801] 6 Ves 349.
62 *Cricklewood Property and Investment Trust Ltd v Leighton's Investment Trust Ltd* [1945] AC 221.
63 ibid [229].
64 *National Carriers Ltd v Panalpina (Northern) Ltd* (n 54) [694]–[695].
65 *Canary Wharf (BP4) T1 Ltd v European Medicines Agency* [2019] EWHC 335 (Ch), [2019] L & TR 14.

any case, the risk of having to move out involuntarily was managed by the alienation provisions in the lease, as the EMA could assign the lease or find a new sub-tenant. The lease, therefore, was not frustrated.

20.42 This narrow approach to frustration and leasehold obligations was re-confirmed by the Court of Appeal in *Bank of New York Mellon (International) Ltd v Cine-UK Ltd; London Trocadero (2015) LLP v Picturehouse Cinemas Ltd*[66] in the context of the effect of Covid-19 on leasehold obligations. The lessees operated cinemas which had to close under mandatory government restrictions. They argued that the leases contained implied terms that rent would not be payable for periods when the properties could not be used for their intended use. While frustration was not argued, the Court of Appeal's analysis chimes with that in the *EMA* case. It was held that the leases allocated the risk that the premises cannot be used for their intended purpose to the tenant, so that the tenant is obliged to continue to pay rent where the express terms as to cesser of rent provisions did not apply; there was nothing unworkable or incoherent about that allocation of risk.[67]

20.43 Where the subject matter of the agreement extends beyond the grant of a leasehold estate, there is more scope for a party to argue that a supervening event has fundamentally changed the nature of the parties' contractual rights and obligations. In *Wong Lai Ying v Chinachem Investment Co Ltd*,[68] the vendor agreed to build a tower block and to sell some of the flats to the purchasers. The agreement provided for time to be of the essence. A landslip destroyed one of the blocks and delayed the sale of one of the flats for two and a half years, causing such devastation that the authorities regarded the area as unsafe and prevented the vendors from returning to site. The purchasers sought specific performance of the contract for sale. The Privy Council held that the landslip was a frustrating event, releasing the vendor from its obligation as it was a performance radically different from that which he originally undertook.

(iv) *Effect of a finding of frustration*

20.44 A finding of frustration is to bring the contract to an end automatically. The court does not have any discretion or power to adapt or modify the obligations of the parties.[69] A lease is an agreement for a leasehold estate to be vested in the lessee; if the subject matter of the grant is so vested, it has proved very difficult to argue that the fundamental nature of the parties' obligations has been affected by the supervening event, even in circumstances where the tenant themselves are not able to personally occupy the demised premises.[70]

66 *Bank of New York Mellon (International) Ltd v Cine-UK Ltd; London Trocadero (2015) LLP v Picturehouse Cinemas Ltd* [2022] EWCA Civ 1021.
67 *Bank of New York Mellon (International) Ltd v Cine-UK Ltd* [2022] EWCA Civ 1021 (n 66) [138].
68 *Wong Lai Ying v Chinachem Investment Co Ltd* [1979] 13 BLR 81.
69 *British Movietonews Ltd v London and District Cinemas Ltd* [1952] AC 166.
70 *London & Northern Estates Co v Schlesinger* [1916] 1 KB 20; *Amalgamated Investment & Property Co Ltd v John Walker & Sons Ltd* [1971] 1 WLR 164.

20.45 At common law, obligations which had accrued prior to the frustrating event were not adjusted; any liabilities which had already arisen at the time of the frustrating event (such as a payment obligation) were left intact. This was modified by the Law Reform (Frustration of Contracts) Act 1943. Section 1(2) states that all sums paid or payable to any party in pursuance of the contract before the discharge of the contract shall be recoverable (if paid) or shall cease to be payable (if not already paid). This is subject to a party who has incurred expenses before the discharge of the contract being allowed to retain or recover sums in respect of those expenses if the court considers it just by reference to all the circumstances of the case. By section 1(3), if a party has obtained a valuable benefit otherwise than by payment of money before the time of discharge, this is recoverable by the other party in a sum not exceeding the value of the benefit as the court considers just having regard to all the circumstances of the case and, in particular, (a) the amount of any expenses incurred before the time of discharge by the benefitted party in, or for the purpose of, the performance of the contract, including any sums paid or payable by him to any other party in pursuance of the contract and retained or recoverable by that party under the last foregoing subsection, and (b) the effect, in relation to the said benefit, of the circumstances giving rise to the frustration of the contract.

(v) *Frustration and climate change*

20.46 Climate change is likely to see an increase in low-probability, high-impact events, creating sudden shocks on legal relations and obligations. The English doctrine of frustration is geared to respond to the direct, first order, impact of such events. The destruction of land through flooding or coastal action is the model example of a force outside the control of the parties that they did not reasonably take into account when allocating risk between them. Whether the doctrine is engaged in such physical or direct examples depends, however, on the subject matter of the agreement as well as the other factors identified in the *Sea Angel.*

20.47 In the case of a lease, the destruction of the land comprising the subject matter of the grant (such as through a sudden coastal movement) may well amount to a frustrating event. On the other hand, it is arguable that a lessee takes on the risk of changes to the boundary of their demise where it abuts the coast, especially where there is only a partial destruction of the subject matter of the grant. As for destruction of buildings that form part of the grant through water, fire or other natural disasters, it is now common for leases to contain insurance and reinstatement clauses dealing with physical damage and destruction. It is more arguable that the parties to leases with such provisions have allocated the risk of such phenomena between themselves, reducing the prospect of a successful argument that the lease itself has been frustrated.

20.48 There is also a significant difference between a long lease measured in years and a short term let. As in the case of *National Carriers Ltd v Panalpina (Northern) Ltd* itself, the lessee under a long lease is likely to be regarded to have assumed the risks inherent in the land itself, to the point where a 999-year lease can be regarded as akin to a freehold grant. On the other hand, it is much more arguable that a supervening event that destroys the tenant's purpose in occupying the land under a very short lease is a frustrating event.

20.49 The analysis changes where the subject matter of a grant is not only the vesting of a leasehold estate, but also an agreement for works (as in a development agreement). As in the *Wong Lai Ying v Chinachem Investment Co Ltd* case, it may well be the case that the courts accept that the destruction of, or significant damage to, land comprising the subject matter of such an agreement represents a fundamental change of circumstances that amounts to a frustrating event.

20.50 The outlook for a successful plea of frustration is far more unlikely where the effect of climate change is merely to make one party's obligations more onerous or difficult to perform, as opposed to impossible or fundamentally changed. Changes in the regulatory environment, the market place or behavioural changes in response to climate change are far less likely to amount to a supervening event amounting to frustration. This was seen in the 2020 coronavirus pandemic, where it was considered very unlikely that changes in market behaviour or regulatory prohibitions on economic activity amounted to a frustrating event for the purpose of leases. This is illustrated in the *Bank of New York Mellon (International) Ltd v Cine-UK Ltd; London Trocadero (2015) LLP v Picturehouse Cinemas Ltd* case, where even though frustration was not cited in the Court of Appeal as a potential ground for relief, a similar analysis of the allocation of risk was performed. It is likely that a leaseholder will be considered to have assumed the risk of changes to the market place, especially pursuant to a long term agreement or lease.

20.51 It is also significant that the court's options on a finding that a lease or agreement has been frustrated are extremely limited: the relevant interest or contract is brought to an end from the date of the supervening event, while the Law Reform (Frustration of Contracts) Act 1943 makes some provision for the allocation of liabilities, expenses and benefits. The court has no power to make adjustments to the agreement in the light of the new circumstances as they are found. While this may not be significant in cases where a climate change-induced disaster has totally destroyed or neutered the subject matter of the grant (such as the examples of flooding or wholescale coastal destruction given in *Paradine v Jane* and *Cricklewood Property and Investment Trust Ltd v Leighton's Investment Trust Ltd*), this binary approach of frustration or no frustration may be unhelpful where there has been only a partial destruction of the subject matter of the grant.

(vi) *Force majeure*

20.52 There are considerable restrictions on the English doctrine of frustration. It is open to the parties to make express provision for the occurrence of low-probability, high-impact events, typically through what are generally referred to as 'force majeure' clauses. Such clauses set out the circumstances by which one or both of the parties is entitled to cancel the contract or is excused from performance of part or the whole of the contract, suspend performance, or extend the time for such performance. Such a clause defines the specified event or events (normally, but not necessarily, beyond the control of the parties) when the clause is engaged.

20.53 Force majeure clauses are varied, with different forms, effects and defined events.[71] Furthermore, despite the common use of the phrase, the words 'force majeure' do not amount to a term of art in English law.[72] Each clause should therefore be interpreted by reference to standard principles of contractual interpretation. The courts are, however, likely to require clear words before allowing a clause to give a party licence to terminate a contract or refrain from performing it.

20.54 The words 'force majeure' were considered in the influential judgment of McCardie J in *Lebeaupin v Richard Crispin & Co.*[73] He noted that if a party wishes to escape liability, then it must take care to use words of adequate clearness and width. He noted that the words 'force majeure' had been taken from French law, and referred to circumstances independent of the will of man, and which were not in his power to control, sufficient to justify the non-execution of a contract. The effect of a clause may, however, vary with each agreement.

20.55 The advantage of a force majeure clause compared to the English doctrine of frustration is that the parties may tailor the effect of a supervening event on their rights and obligations, rather than exposing themselves to the conceptual uncertainties and blunt consequences of frustration.[74]

20.56 Parties drafting leases, agreements for leases or development agreements, therefore, may well wish to consider the potential impact of climate change on their rights and obligations. In particular, they may well wish to consider the potential for low-probability, high-impact events, such as flooding, extreme weather or even the partial or total destruction of the land or buildings comprising part of the land.

20.57 The prospects of low-probability, high-impact events which cause significant disruption to interests in land (such as leases, development agreements or estate contracts) may well increase as a result of climate change. The doctrine of frustration in English law has only a very limited reach when it comes to unforeseen events that affect such interests. Instead, parties may well wish to consider including express terms that deal with the possible effects and consequences of climate change.

Accretion to and destruction of land

(i) *Introduction*

20.58 Climate change is likely to result in rising sea levels, extreme weather, and changes to precipitation levels.[75] The action of both tidal or coastal and non-tidal or riparian water bodies, including both the destruction and creation of areas of land, is

71 *Fairclough, Dodd & Jones Ltd v JH Vantol Ltd* [1957] 1 WLR 136 [143].
72 *Hackney BC v Doré* [1922] 1 KB 431 [437].
73 *Lebeaupin v Richard Crispin & Co* [1920] 2 KB 714.
74 William Swadling, 'The Judicial Construction of Force Majeure Clauses' in Ewan McKendrick (ed), *Force Majeure and Frustration of Contract* (2nd edn, Lloyd's of London Press 1995).
75 See paras 1.10–1.24 and 20.08.

likely to increase in both intensity and volume.[76] Coastal erosion, increased peak river flows and changes in the pattern of coastal and river deposits are not new phenomena: the destruction of one of England's most significant coastal ports, Dunwich in Suffolk, from 1286 onwards, is one striking example of the suddenness and power of coastal forces that continues to inspire historians and scientists alike.[77] While the common law has adopted and developed doctrinal rulesets in respect of the creation and destruction of land, it is likely that climate change will make disputes over their application more common. In particular, the common law has not developed a satisfactory explanation for the difference in approach between gradual and sudden changes in the extent of land.

20.59 English law recognises a difference between gradual accretion or diluvion to the land, such as where deposits by the sea, a river or a lake add to the extent of land that is only perceptible over a protracted period of time, and avulsion,[78] where the change is sudden. In the case of gradual accretion to the land which is not the result of the owner's deliberate action, the boundary of the land is taken to be extended to include those deposits. Sudden accretions, such as new islands in the sea or additions to the shore, however, are considered to belong to the Crown.[79]

(ii) *Origins and rationale*

20.60 The common law rules are derived from Roman law. *The Institutes of Gaius* stated that alluvial accretion by a river that is so gradual that it is not possible to judge at any one time what is being added becomes part of the owner's property. On the other hand, if the river cuts away a piece of land and carries it down to another owner's land, that piece remains in the ownership of the original landowner.[80] The same rule is found in Justinian's *Institutes*.[81] The 13th century treatise associated with Bracton, *De legibus et consuetudinibus Angliae* (On the Laws and Customs of England), adopted the wording set out in Justinian's *Institutes*.[82] As Palles CB in *Attorney General v M'Carthy*[83] noted, the principle was applied both to rivers and the action of coastal waters on the seashore.

---

76 See, for example, Keqi Zhang, Bruce Douglas and Stephen Leatherman, 'Global Warming and Coastal Erosion' (2004) 64 Climatic Change 41; Glenn Watts and others, 'Climate Change and Water in the UK – Past Changes and Future Prospects' (2015) 39 Progress in Physical Geography: Earth and Environment 6 <https://doi.org/10.1177/0309133314542957> accessed 20 April 2024.

77 Stefan Skrimshire, 'The View from Dunwich' (2021) 13(1) Environmental Humanities 264 <https://read.dukeupress.edu/environmental-humanities/article/13/1/264/173449/The-View-from-Dunwich> accessed 20 April 2024.

78 Avulsion takes place where land is suddenly torn off by an inundation or current from the property to which it previously belonged, or where a river changes its course, and instead of continuing to flow between two properties, cuts off part of one and joins it to the other (Daniel Greenberg, *Jowitt's Dictionary of English Law* (6th edn, Sweet & Maxwell 2023) <https://www.sweetandmaxwell.co.uk/Product/Academic-Law/Jowitts-Dictionary-of-English-Law/Hardback/43214566> accessed 20 April 2024). It is contrasted from accretion or diluvion by the suddenness with which it takes place.

79 See the discussion in Martin Dixon, Janet Bignell and Nicholas Hopkins, *Megarry & Wade The Law of Real Property* (10th edn, Sweet & Maxwell 2024) para 3-013. See also Alec Samuels, 'Winning Land from the Sea and Losing Land to the Sea' [2004] Journal of Planning and Environmental Law 692.

80 WM Gordon and OF Robinson (trs), *The Institutes of Gaius* (Duckworth 1988) II.70–71.

81 P Birks and G McLeod (trs), *The Institutes of Justinian* (Duckworth 1987) II.20–21.

82 Henry de Bracton, *De Legibus et Consuetudinibus Angliae: Libri Quinque in Varios Tractatus Distincti*, vol 6 (Travers Twiss ed, Cambridge University Press 2012) Book II, Chapter II, 68–71.

83 *Attorney General v M'Carthy* [1911] 2 IR 260.

20.61 What has proved to be elusive, however, is a reason or rationale for the difference in approach between gradual accretion and sudden avulsion. Blackstone, in his *Commentaries on the Law of England*, attempted to find a justification for the accretion rule in the maxim *de minimis non curat lex*, as well as the fact that this was consideration for the risk of loss as well; as for sudden changes, the land belonged to the Crown as the king was lord of the sea, and hence it was reasonable that it belonged to the king when it became dry.[84] This rationale has, however, been rejected in subsequent cases without a properly convincing replacement being advanced instead. Lord Chelmsford in *Attorney General v Chambers*[85] rejected this reason for the rule. Instead, he preferred Alderson B's explanation in *In re Hull and Selby Railway*:[86] 'That which cannot be perceived in its progress is taken to be as if it never had existed at all.' This analysis does not, however, withstand the fact that modern surveying and cartography can identify such progress. In the leading decision in this area, *Southern Centre of Theosophy Incorporated v State of South Australia*, Lord Wilberforce suggested that 'the rule is one required for the permanent protection of property and is in recognition of the fact that a riparian property owner may lose as well as gain from changes in the water boundary or level', while also accepting that a distinction should be made between imperceptible and large changes.[87]

20.62 This debate was given fresh impetus by Hanoch Dagan, who argued that the common law rules accord with a 'basic intuition about property: changes that are too big or too sudden undermine the owners' ability to plan', and therefore should not be 'imposed' on landowners as they are disruptive to individual autonomy.[88] As David Dana noted, however, this rationale does not explain those cases where a purchaser of property knows that the land is vulnerable to sudden changes in sea level: individual autonomy does not depend on the gradualness of the change, but on a full range of considerations.[89] In fact, many of the cases in respect of addition to land demonstrate that the landowner is very happy to take on the new area, and in fact would lose their access to important river or sea if they did not succeed.

(iii) *Application of the accretion rules*

20.63 The *Southern Centre of Theosophy Incorporated v State of South Australia*[90] case concerned Lake George in South Australia, a large inland lake. The Crown had granted a perpetual lease, with the eastern side bordered by the lake. The lake itself was not the subject of a grant. After the grant, the lake was connected to the sea. Between 1911 and 1975, approximately 20 acres was added to the eastern boundary of the land by gradual accretion coming from deposits from longshore drift, the retreat of water from the lake and sand blown from nearby dunes. The Privy Council reviewed the law of

---

84 William Blackstone, *Commentaries on the Laws of England* (4th edn, Clarendon Press 1770) vol. 2, 261–2.
85 *Attorney General v Chambers* [1854] 4 De GM & G 206.
86 *In re Hull and Selby Railway* [1839] 151 ER 139, (1839) 5 M. & W. 327.
87 *Southern Centre of Theosophy Incorporated v State of South Australia* [1982] AC 706 [721].
88 Dagan, *A Liberal Theory of Property* (n 2) ch 8.
89 David Dana, 'Individual Autonomy and Takings in a Liberal Theory of Property' (2022) 18(2) International Journal of Law in Context 229 <https://www.cambridge.org/core/journals/international-journal-of-law-in-context/article/abs/individual-autonomy-and-takings-in-a-liberal-theory-of-property/87339E6D20BC37B8B3FF24E7E4CD825B> accessed 20 April 2024.
90 *Southern Centre of Theosophy Incorporated v State of South Australia* (n 87).

accretion, giving the modern re-statement of the law. The Privy Council confirmed that the doctrine of accretion did apply to land on the edge of an inland lake, referring to authority from the USA.[91] It was also confirmed that the doctrine applied to land leased by the Crown.[92]

20.64 The Privy Council in *Southern Centre of Theosophy Incorporated v State of South Australia* identified that the doctrine gives recognition to the fact that where land is bounded by water, the forces of nature are likely to cause changes in the boundary between the land and the water.[93] Where these changes are gradual and imperceptible, the title to the land, as applicable to the land as it may be so, is changed. This is based on 'grounds of convenience and fairness'.[94] It is convenient to regard the boundary between land and water as being where it is from day to day or year to year. It is also fair: if land is taken by erosion or diluvion, it would be inconvenient to regard the boundary as extending into the water, so when an addition is made, it is only fair that title should extend to it. The doctrine does not apply where a substantial and recognisable change in the boundary has suddenly taken place.[95] The doctrine, therefore, 'arises from the nature of land ownership from, in fact, the long-term ownership of property inherently subject to gradual processes of change'.[96] The Privy Council extended the doctrine to include extensions caused by air (such as windborne sand) as well as water action.[97]

20.65 The requirement of imperceptibility has been part of the English common law from the time of Bracton, and has been interpreted in a number of cases. In *Rex v Lord Yarborough*,[98] it was stated that it must be understood as expressive only in respect of the manner of the accretion; it means imperceptible in progress, and not imperceptible after a long period of time. The issue of what is imperceptible has in the past been regarded as a jury question, and remains a question of fact.[99]

(iv) *Exclusion by agreement*

20.66 When land is conveyed, it is conveyed subject to and with the benefit of such subtractions and additions within the doctrine of accretion as may take place. Where land is granted with a water boundary, the title of the grantee extends to the land added to or detracted from by accretion or diluvion, whether or not the grant is accompanied by a map showing the boundary, or contains a parcels clause stating the area of the land,

---

91 *Banks v Ogden* [1864] 69 US 57 and *Lamprey v Metcalf* [1893] 53 NW Rep 1139 (Supreme Court of Minnesota). In so doing, the English case of *Trafford v Thrower* [1929] 45 TLR 502, which concerned the Norfolk Broads, was disapproved.
92 *Southern Centre of Theosophy Incorporated v State of South Australia* (n 87) [715]. See also *In re Hull and Selby Railway* (n 86) at 33–2 *per* Alderson B.
93 *Southern Centre of Theosophy Incorporated v State of South Australia* (n 87) [716].
94 ibid [716].
95 ibid [716].
96 ibid [716].
97 ibid [719]–[720].
98 *Rex v Lord Yarborough* [1824] 3 B & C 91 [107].
99 *Attorney General v M'Carthy* (n 83) [296].

and whether or not the original boundary can be identified.[100] It may be excluded by agreement, where the intention to exclude is plainly shown.[101]

20.67 The LRA 2002 maintains the common law approach. Section 61(1) of the LRA 2002 confirms that the fact that a registered estate in land is shown in the register as having a particular boundary does not affect the operation of accretion or diluvion; this is a distinct rule, separate from the general boundary rule in section 60. In the case of a registered estate (which would include longer leases), section 61(2) requires an agreement which modifies the operation of accretion and diluvion to be registered; this takes the form of a note in the property register, and must be made by or accompanied by the consent of the proprietor of the estate and any registered charge unless they are a party to the agreement.[102] The Law Commission expressly intended to preserve the common law rules set out in *Southern Centre of Theosophy Inc v State of South Australia*, confirming that the doctrines of accretion and diluvion will apply even if the exact line of the boundary has been determined under what is now section 60(3).[103]

(v) *Deliberate action*

20.68 The doctrine does not extend to additions caused by the deliberate action of the claimant. It does, however, extend to changes caused by human action other than deliberate action by the claimant. In *Brighton and Hove General Gas Co v Hove Bungalows Ltd*,[104] the accretion to land abutting the foreshore would not have taken place without the erection of groynes which had been installed to protect the shore from erosion. It was held that the doctrine of accretion still applied. Romer J made a declaration that the southern boundary of the plaintiff's land was the present high-water mark.

20.69 This case should be contrasted with the reasoning of the Privy Council in *Attorney-General of Southern Nigeria v John Holt and Company (Liverpool) Ltd*.[105] The respondents occupied land on the shore of the island of Lagos in Nigeria; all of the grants described the lands as bounded by the sea. The respondents carried out works to the foreshore to prevent incursion by the sea and erosion, which resulted in a strip of land being reclaimed. The respondents built stores and sheds on the reclaimed land. It was held that the reclaimed land had not been the result of natural accretion, and therefore vested in the Crown as the owner of the foreshore. The Privy Council noted that the distinction was that, 'Artificial reclamation and natural silting up are, however, extremely different in their legal results; the latter, if gradual and imperceptible in the sense already described, becomes an addition to the property of the adjoining land; the former has not this result, and the property of the original foreshore thus suddenly

---

100 *Southern Centre of Theosophy Incorporated v State of South Australia* [1982] (n 87) [716]–[720], affirming *Attorney General v M'Carthy* on this point; *Attorney-General of Southern Nigeria v John Holt & Co (Liverpool) Ltd* [1915] AC 599 [612].
101 *Southern Centre of Theosophy Incorporated v State of South Australia* (n 87) [716].
102 The Land Registration Rules 2003, SI 2003/1417, r 123.
103 Law Commission, *Land Registration for the Twenty-First Century: A Conveyancing Revolution* (Law Com No 271, 2001) <https://lawcom.gov.uk/project/land-registration-for-the-21st-century/> accessed 20 April 2024 paras 9.14–9.15.
104 *Brighton and Hove General Gas Co v Hove Bungalows Ltd* [1924] 1 Ch 372.
105 *Attorney-General of Southern Nigeria v John Holt & Co (Liverpool) Ltd* (n 100).

altered by reclamatory work upon it remains as before, i.e. in cases like the present, with the Crown.'[106] The difference between the two cases is one of fact and degree. The Privy Council noted that the reclamation did not consist of the erection of stakes, but the building of a solid wall with foundations sunk into the soil in the foreshore itself.[107] Ultimately, however, the riparian owners succeeded; the Privy Council held that there was presumed in the respondents' favour an irrevocable licence to erect buildings and store goods upon the reclaimed land, as the Crown had acquiesced in what the respondents had done.[108]

(vi) *Avulsion*

20.70 There are few examples of the sudden addition of land through natural processes. The common law rules, therefore, remain relatively untested. The most obvious examples include volcanic activity creating new land masses or sudden additions to existing ones. In Europe, one of the most picturesque and well-known examples is in Santorini, in Greece. At different times, the volcano in the island has destroyed and created new islands in the caldera. From 1707, a new volcano, Nea Kameni, grew before connecting with an earlier older volcanic island.[109]

20.71 Common law rules were applied to new land growing by way of lava extensions in Kehena, Puna, Hawaii, following volcanic activity in 1955. This led to a dispute as to the ownership of the new land between the owners of the bordering land, the Zimrings, and the State of Hawaii, which reached the Supreme Court of Hawaii in 1977.[110] This required an examination of the way in which the State claimed land, which would not arise in an English setting; ultimately, all land is held from the grant of the Crown. It was noted that in cases where there had been rapid, easily perceived and sometimes violent shifts of land, or avulsion, pre-existing legal boundaries are retained notwithstanding the fact that former riparian owners may have lost their access to the water. It was held that 'equity and sound public policy demand that such land inure to the benefit of all the people of Hawaii, in whose behalf the government acts as trustee', under public trust principles; the Zimrings would share in public access to the lava extension and to the ocean. This concept, which has its origins in Hawaiian history and traditional Hawaiian land use practices, does not have direct application in the English common law.[111] It does, however, illustrate how the avulsion doctrine (granting all sudden new

106 ibid [615].
107 ibid [616].
108 In the lower courts, the case of *Plimmer v Mayor of Wellington* [1884] 9 App Cas 699 was referred to, while the Privy Council held that the result was in accord with the principle set out in *Attorney-General v Tomline* (n 23). In *Tomline*, it was held that no subject is entitled to destroy a natural barrier against the sea, and that a neighbour is entitled to an injunction to retain it. Although the reasoning is unclear, it appears that the Privy Council held that the Crown could not raise an action against the respondents for erecting a sea defence which was, itself, the Crown's duty to install in any case.
109 Walter L Friedrich, *Santorini: Volcano, Natural History, Mythology* (Aarhus University Press 2009) 214–5 and 218–9; P Nomikou and others, 'The Emergence and Growth of a Submarine Volcano: The Kameni Islands, Santorini (Greece)' (2014) 1–2 GeoResJ 8 <https://www.sciencedirect.com/science/article/pii/S2214242814000047> accessed 20 April 2024.
110 *Kobayashi v Zimring* [1977] 566 P.2d 725 [729]–[733].
111 Ana Ching, 'Charting the Boundaries of Hawaii's Extensive Public Trust Doctrine Post-Waiāhole Ditch' [2020] Lewis & Clark College Paul L Boley Library <https://papers.ssrn.com/abstract=3642431> accessed 20 April 2024.

areas of land to the Crown) could be mitigated in its effect to avoid both 'windfall' gains to the coastal or riparian owner, as well as hardship caused by loss of rights of access. In this way, it can be compared to *Attorney-General of Southern Nigeria v John Holt and Company (Liverpool) Ltd*,[112] where the Privy Council had to consider how to ensure that non-accretion additions to land did not prejudice existing landowners. If avulsion cases become more common due to climate change, the need to balance these concerns will become more evident in the case law.

(vii) *Interaction with coastal defences*

20.72 The common law rules operate alongside the public law framework that is discussed elsewhere in this work. There is no absolute right to sea defence. The property owner's right to their property is contingent and limited, and subject to extinction or addition by natural processes. Furthermore, sea defences erected in one part of the coastline may lead to destruction or addition to another part of the coastline, without any right to compensation necessarily arising.[113] These rules, therefore, should be considered alongside the 'common enemy' rule discussed elsewhere in this section.

Easements and freehold covenants

(i) *Introduction*

20.73 Developed systems of real property have developed a concept of intangible property rights by which a parcel of land has non-possessory rights over neighbouring land. For example, one parcel of land may have a right of way over another, facilitating the use and enjoyment of the first plot without the landowner of the second having to surrender possession or control; one building may enjoy rights of light over another; while another building may enjoy a right of support from an adjacent structure. These are examples of easements, allowing for the efficient allocation of resources and enjoyment of a limited supply of land which would not be possible on a purely exclusionary basis to land law. English law also recognises, in prescribed circumstances, the proprietary nature of freehold covenants which are restrictive in nature; they provide for a mechanism of 'private law' or land management by regulating what a landowner can do with their land.[114]

20.74 Such incorporeal rights are, however, still vulnerable to the potential effects of climate change. The destruction of the land over which an easement (such as a right of way) runs, or the land with the benefit of a restrictive covenant (for example, if it falls into the sea), will most likely destroy the right itself.[115] While intangible, incorporeal rights are still strongly associated with the land: English land law refuses to acknowledge

---

112 *Attorney-General of Southern Nigeria v John Holt & Co (Liverpool) Ltd* (n 100).
113 Mark Stallworthy, 'Sustainability, Coastal Erosion and Climate Change: An Environmental Justice Analysis' (2006) 18(3) Journal of Environmental Law <https://www.jstor.org/stable/44248563> accessed 20 April 2024.
114 See Dixon, Bignell and Hopkins, *Megarry & Wade The Law of Real Property* (n 79) ch 31.
115 English private law does not acknowledge a concept of 'rolling easements', which allow the right of way to migrate inland as the coast is eroded, which are recognised in some circumstances in Texas and have been proposed as a solution to this issue: see, for example, Meg Caldwell and Craig Holt Segall, 'No Day at the Beach: Sea Level Rise, Ecosystem Loss, and Public Access Along the California Coast' (2007) 34 Ecology Law Quarterly 533 <https://www.jstor.org/stable/24114634> accessed 20 April 2024.

a proprietary nature capable of binding third parties to the original agreement in covenants in gross (that is, covenants belonging to a person without being appurtenant to land), which does not benefit the land itself.[116] Incorporeal hereditaments, therefore, may be disrupted or extinguished by events taking place on, or even destroying, the physical land with which they are associated.

(ii) *Destruction of the dominant or servient tenement*

20.75 Evershed MR in *Re Ellenborough Park*[117] identified four essential characteristics of an easement:

- There must be a dominant and a servient tenement.
- An easement must accommodate the dominant tenement, that is, be connected with its enjoyment and for its benefit.
- The dominant and servient owners must be different persons.
- The right claimed must be capable of forming the subject matter of a grant.

20.76 Where, therefore, the servient tenement or the dominant tenement has been destroyed, it is highly unlikely that the right will continue in gross.[118] It may be difficult to identify the servient tenement. For example, a right to discharge water or to receive water does not have a clear servient tenement, although the pipe or the adjoining property could be considered to be part of the servient land.[119]

20.77 Likewise, a freehold covenant that is enforceable against successors in title to the original parties requires both a benefitted land and a burdened land. The obligation created must be negative in nature. It is well established that a freehold covenant, to be enforceable beyond the parties to the agreement itself, must 'touch and concern' the land.[120] The destruction of either of the estates is likely to make the covenant purely personal, and hence unenforceable. They are, therefore, different to conservation covenants, which as well as running with the land, can create positive obligations.[121]

(iii) *Rights of support*

20.78 At common law, land in its natural state has a right of support from adjacent land; in other words, a plot of the land itself (without a building) is entitled to support

116 For a discussion of these rules and how they affect the enforceability of overage agreements, see David Sawtell, 'Overage Agreements and Temporal Aspects of Property Development in English Land Law' [2022] 4 Conveyancer and Property Lawyer 347 <https://uk.westlaw.com/Document/I5720C89072A511EDA278C0A6FF9F7A44/View/FullText.html> accessed 20 April 2024.
117 *Re Ellenborough Park* [1956] Ch 131.
118 *Rangeley v Midland Railway Co* [1868] 3 Ch App 306 [310].
119 *Paine & Co v St Neots Gas & Coke Co* [1939] 3 All ER 812 [823].
120 *Spencer's Case* [1583] 5 Co Rep 16a, 77 ER 72; *Federated Homes Ltd v Mill Lodge Properties Ltd* [1980] 1 WLR 594 [604].
121 See Chapter 21 ('Conservation Covenants').

from the land around it, so that it does not collapse. On the other hand, a right of support in respect of a building can only be acquired by way of a grant, in the usual ways in which an easement may be acquired (such as by prescription or by express or implied grant).[122] The right is most accurately described as a negative right not to have the support removed (as opposed to a positive right to maintain the support).[123] The servient owner is not, therefore, required to take active steps to maintain the building or other thing that gives support:[124]

> The owner of the servient tenement is under no obligation to repair that part of his building which provides support for his neighbour. He can let it fall into decay. If it does so, and support is removed, the owner of the dominant tenement has no cause for complaint.

20.79 Instead, the dominant tenement owner is entitled to effect repairs to the building or other thing giving support.

20.80 Importantly, therefore, there is no actionable interference with a right of support in cases where subsidence has taken place due to natural forces. This is illustrated in the case of *Rouse v Gravelworks Ltd*.[125] The defendant's gravel works became filled with water by rain and percolation, forming a pond. Wind action caused this body of water to erode material from a farmer's field, removing its lateral support and preventing its development. The Court of Appeal held that the farmer had no cause of action as the accumulation of water in the excavation and the subsequent erosion of support was caused by natural forces. It is, however, unclear if the farmer would now be able to rely upon the measured duty of care, considered below.

(iv) *Recreational easements*

20.81 English land law has refused to recognise indefinite and unregulated privileges of enjoyment over land, such as a right to wander at will over all and every part of another's field or park.[126] English law has, however, recognised more limited and certain rights. In *Re Ellenborough Park* itself, the Court of Appeal recognised the right to enjoy a collective park by the owners of adjacent dwellings to be capable of being an easement. This was considered more recently by the Supreme Court in *Regency Villas Title Ltd and others v Diamond Resorts (Europe) Ltd*.[127] A country house estate was converted into a country club with recreational facilities, a golf course, and other leisure facilities. A smaller house on the estate was sold for conversion into timeshare apartments with free rights of usage of the leisure complex's facilities. The transfer included the grant of

122 *Dalton v Henry Angus & Co* [1881] 6 App Cas 750 (HL).
123 *Byard v Co-operative Permanent Building Society Ltd* [1970] 21 P & CR 807 [821].
124 *Bond v Nottingham Corp* [1940] Ch 429 [438] *per* Sir Wilfred Greene MR.
125 *Rouse v Gravelworks Ltd* [1940] 1 KB 489.
126 This is often referred to as a 'ius spatiandi', although comparisons with the Roman law concept are problematic. English law recognises a number of rights which could be classified as profits à prendre which fall outside Paul's opinion that '*A servitude cannot be imposed permitting us to pick apples, or to walk about, or to eat our dinner, on the land of another*', in the *Digest* 8.1.8. See RN Gooderson, 'Easement—Jus Spatiandi' (1955) 13 The Cambridge Law Journal 24 <https://www.cambridge.org/core/journals/cambridge-law-journal/article/abs/easementjus-spatiandi/04E5B7AD220474E8D6EC521DD769503A> accessed 20 April 2024..
127 *Regency Villas Title Ltd and others v Diamond Resorts (Europe) Ltd* [2019] AC 553.

rights to use the facilities. The timeshare owners claimed the benefit of these rights as an easement. The Supreme Court held that the question of whether a right accommodated the dominant tenement was a matter of fact. Subject to the requirements for an easement being established, the grant over land of purely recreational or sporting rights, whether outdoor or indoor, which genuinely accommodated the servient land could be the subject matter of an easement.

20.82 Such recreational easements are likely to remain in use given the potential for shared communal green space. The difficulty for parties to such agreements is the cost of maintenance of such green spaces. Positive freehold covenants (such as obligations to pay money) generally fall foul of the *Austerberry* principle and are unenforceable against successors in title.[128] Easements, likewise, are essentially negative in character, imposing no obligation on the owner of the servient tenement to maintain them absent some other agreement. It is possible to include covenants on the part of the servient owner to repair, and a corresponding covenant by the dominant owner to pay a reasonable proportion of the costs of repair and maintenance carried out by the servient owner.

(v) *Rights of diversion*

20.83 If a right of way becomes impassable or inconvenient, such as if there is damage or destruction to the land over which it passes, the strict legal rights of the parties are relatively inflexible. The court, however, may refuse to grant equitable relief (such as an injunction or damages in lieu of an injunction) where interference with the right is wholly justified. The owner of the servient tenement over which a right of way runs has no right to alter its route, unless this is an express or implied term of the grant or the parties subsequently agree. The court may, however, refuse injunctive relief where the realignment is necessary to achieve an object of substantial public and local importance.[129] Likewise, a minor realignment as part of an improvement may result in the court refusing to order either injunctive relief or damages in lieu of an injunction.[130]

20.84 The owner of the dominant tenement, on the other hand, generally has no right to deviate from the route of the easement, such as a right of way, even if it becomes impassable.[131] The destruction of the land on which the right of way or other easement runs (such as by coastal erosion or river action), therefore, does not allow the owner of the dominant tenement to divert on to other parts of the servient tenement. Generally, the owner of the dominant tenement has a right to maintain (and, potentially, to improve) a right of way; it is conceivable that the right holder could repair the right of way and erect limited barriers or defences (depending on the terms of the grant and subject to accommodation of the servient tenement), but the possibilities for maintaining a right of way under attack from coast action are potentially very limited.

---

128 As set out above, for a freehold covenant to be enforceable against successors in title, it must be negative in its nature, and not create positive obligations, save for very limited exceptions: *Rhone v Stephens* [1994] 2 AC 310, [1994] UKHL 3, upholding *Austerberry v Corporation of Oldham* [1885] 29 Ch D 750.
129 *Greenwich NHS Trust v London & Quadrant Housing* [1998] 1 WLR 1749.
130 *Crane Road Properties LLP v Hundalani* [2006] EWHC 2066 (Ch).
131 *Bullard v Harrison* [1815] 4 M & S 387, 105 ER 877.

20.85 The party entitled to use a right of way has a right to deviate on to the adjoining land if a difficult to remove obstruction is actually placed across the right of way by the servient owner or occupier, or potentially another person.[132] The leading case remains *Selby v Nettlefold*.[133] Mr Selby had the right to pass along a private canal. Mr Nettlefold's predecessor in title built a bridge over the canal, obstructing the towpath with a solid wall. Mr Selby's servants had to divert around the foot of the bridge with their horses and to cross the road over the bridge, passing over Mr Nettlefold's land. He erected a fence to stop this diversion. In turn, Mr Selby sought and obtained an injunction preventing them from obstructing the towpath. On appeal, it was held that, due to the passage of time, Mr Selby could not obtain an order for the bridge to be removed, but it was accepted that he could go round to connect the two parts of his way on each side of the obstacle over the grantor's land without trespass. This, however, is a rule of equity, not of law: in *Dudley v Bishton*,[134] it was considered that it was subject to the owner of the servient tenement having notice of its existence, and it did not extinguish the original right of way. A right to divert, therefore, is potentially precarious, and not enforceable against an incoming purchaser without notice of the right. It is the original right that is the source of the right to divert. If, therefore, the right is wholly extinguished (such as by the complete destruction of the land over which the easement runs), it is unclear if the doctrine will apply, as there will be no legal right to which the right to divert applies.

---

132 *Stacey v Sherrin* [1913] 29 TLR 555, considered in *Secretary of State for Transport and High Speed Two (HS2) Ltd v Cucurean* [2020] EWHC 2614 (Ch) [117].
133 *Selby v Nettlefold* [1873–74] LR 9 Ch App 111.
134 *Dudley v Bishton* [2009] EWHC 607 (Ch) [27]–[28].

CHAPTER 21

NET ZERO AND ADAPTATION POLICIES RELEVANT TO RESIDENTIAL AND COMMERCIAL PROPERTY

Alexander Burrell

Introduction

21.01 This chapter summarises the legislation and policies relied upon by the government to achieve the transition to net zero in residential and commercial property, as well as those that are relevant to climate change adaptation.

21.02 Reducing emissions associated with residential and commercial property is widely acknowledged to be essential in achieving the UK's net zero commitments. As cited in the government's Heat and Buildings Strategy ('HBS'):[1]

> The UK is home to about 30 million buildings, which are responsible for around 30% of UK emissions. The majority of buildings still rely on burning high-carbon fossil fuels for heating, hot water and cooking, and have low thermal efficiency which means that much of the heat that is generated is wasted.
>
> To reach our Net Zero target, in the next 30 years, we need to decarbonise the way we heat and cool our homes and workplaces to near zero (between 0 and 2 MtCO2e). We also need to ensure that in the nearer-term we meet our fuel poverty targets and emission reduction targets …

21.03 However, as the Climate Change Committee ('CCC') states, policy progress is not on track, with 77% of the required emissions reduction by the Sixth Carbon Budget period judged to be either at significant risk or with insufficient plans. This is in part due to the costs of achieving net zero in residential and commercial property, and the recent twin crises of energy prices and cost of living, which have shifted the economics of building energy use and retrofits in various ways.[2]

1 Department for Energy Security and Net Zero, *Heat and Buildings Strategy* (CP 388, 2021) <https://assets.publishing.service.gov.uk/media/61a022788fa8f5037e8ccb4c/E02666137_CP_388_Heat_and_Buildings_Elay.pdf> accessed 27 March 2024.
2 Climate Change Committee, 'Progress in Reducing Emissions: 2023 Report to Parliament' (2023) 151–2 <https://www.theccc.org.uk/wp-content/uploads/2023/06/Progress-in-reducing-UK-emissions-2023-Report-to-Parliament.pdf> accessed 4 April 2024.

21.04 Further, whilst the majority of building emissions come from residential property,[3] policy is also needed in respect of non-residential buildings and as noted by the Climate Change Committee in its annual progress report 2023:[4]

> Non-residential buildings need attention. There is a large and increasingly concerning policy gap relating to non-residential buildings. We note some progress in public buildings, but a stable, long-term funding approach is urgently needed. There are no convincing plans to decarbonise commercial buildings. These properties get some benefits from schemes for residential decarbonisation (either directly or indirectly). However, this is not enough to drive improvements across the non-residential sector.

21.05 The government set out in the HBS on two categories of proposals and policies to transition to net zero:

- Those related to decarbonising heat, switching from high-carbon sources to low-carbon alternatives; and,
- Those concerned with improving the energy efficiency of buildings.[5]

Decarbonisation policies and legislation

21.06 In its HBS, the government splits its various current and future policies related to decarbonising heat into the following categories:[6]

- Phasing out fossil fuels;
- Heat pumps;
- Hydrogen;
- Heat networks;
- Bioenergy; and
- Using waste heat.

21.07 The proposals and legislation relating to heat networks is considered separately in paragraphs 21.24–21.29 below.

21.08 In respect of phasing out fossil fuels, the following proposals are relied upon within the HBS:[7]

---

3 ibid 148.
4 ibid.
5 See Chapter 22 for further details.
6 Department for Energy Security and Net Zero, *Heat and Buildings Strategy* (n 1).
7 ibid.

- Phasing out the installation of new and replacement natural gas boilers from 2035: This is envisaged to include a mix of low-carbon technologies used for heating: electrification of heat for buildings using hydronic (air-to-water or ground-to-water) heat pumps, heat networks and potentially switching the natural gas in the grid to low-carbon hydrogen.

- A consultation (expected to be published by 2025) on ending new connections to the gas grid in favour of alternative low-carbon heat sources from 2025: This prospective policy would prevent any expansion of reliance on natural gas and fossil fuels. It is not clear if/when a consultation response will now be published, given the confirmation by Rishi Sunak in September 2023, that there would be no prohibition on new connections until 2035.[8]

- A consultation on off gas-grid regulations for domestic buildings from 2026, possibly introducing regulations to end the installation of new fossil fuel heating systems in these homes from 2026; and a consultation on off gas-grid regulations for non-domestic buildings from 2024, bringing an end to the installation of new fossil fuel systems from 2024 at the earliest for the largest buildings, and bringing the remaining stock into scope from 2026. These consultations concluded in January 2022, however, the government response has not yet been published. Within the Carbon Budget Delivery Plan 2023 ('CBDP'), it is suggested these responses will be published in due course.[9]

21.09 In respect of heat pumps, the following proposals are relied upon within the HBS:[10]

- A Boiler Upgrade Scheme ('BUS'): Subsequent to the Heat and Buildings Strategy, on 22 May 2022, the Boiler Update Scheme (England and Wales) Regulations 2022[11] ('BUS Regulations') came into force, replacing the previous Domestic Renewable Heat Incentive Scheme (set out in the Domestic Renewable Heat Incentive Scheme Regulations 2014 which largely closed to new applicants on 31 March 2022). The purpose of the BUS is to assist customers overcome the high upfront capital costs of low-carbon heat technologies, in the transition away from fossil fuel systems.[12] The BUS is a renewable heat incentive scheme to facilitate and encourage the use of heat pumps and biomass boilers to provide space and water heating in domestic properties and small non-domestic properties. In respect of heat pumps, installers are able to apply for grants of £7,500 for both air source heat pumps and ground source heat pumps, and £5,000 for biomass boilers,[13] which

8 PM Rishi Sunak, 'PM Speech on Net Zero: 20 September 2023' (20 September 2023) <https://www.gov.uk/government/speeches/pm-speech-on-net-zero-20-september-2023> accessed 25 April 2024.
9 Department for Energy Security and Net Zero, 'Carbon Budget Delivery Plan' (2023) HC 1269 <https://assets.publishing.service.gov.uk/media/6424b2d760a35e000c0cb135/carbon-budget-delivery-plan.pdf> accessed 4 April 2024.
10 Department for Energy Security and Net Zero, *Heat and Buildings Strategy* (n 1).
11 The Boiler Upgrade Scheme (England and Wales) Regulations 2022, SI 2022/565.
12 Explanatory memorandum to The Boiler Upgrade Scheme (England and Wales) Regulations 2022.
13 'Boiler Upgrade Scheme (BUS) | Ofgem' <https://www.ofgem.gov.uk/environmental-and-social-schemes/boiler-upgrade-scheme-bus> accessed 2 April 2024.

meet the requirements set out in regulation 9 of the BUS Regulations, in respect of eligible properties.[14] There is £450 million of grant funding available over three years from 2022 to 2025.[15] The scheme is administered by Ofgem.[16]

- A consultation on a market-based mechanism for low-carbon heat: The intention of the mechanism is to increase the deployment of heat pumps from 35,000 to 600,000 installations (across domestic and non-domestic buildings) per year by 2028.[17] This consultation concluded with the government issuing its response, to the responses received, in May 2022.[18] A further 'clean heat market mechanism consultation' ran from 30 March 2023 to 8 June 2023.[19] Within the response, the government clarified what it is suggesting in respect of the market-based mechanism, namely to develop a rising standard (obligation) for the number of heat pump sales to end-consumers as a proportion of manufacturers' (of fossil fuel heating appliances) fossil fuel boiler sales; this would be achieved both through 'direct activities' and through trading in credits between parties.[20] This is envisaged to be similar to those in place for low-emissions vehicles.[21] Various other enabling actions the government intends to take were also highlighted, such as working with industry on training and skills for installers.[22]

- Support to low-income households through the Local Authority Delivery ('LAD') scheme: The primary purpose of the LAD scheme was concerned with the energy efficiency rating of homes, but it also applied to decarbonising heat supply. It was part of the Green Homes Grants scheme; and it ended in March 2022.

- The Social Housing Decarbonisation Fund: The primary purpose of this fund is the energy efficiency rating of homes, but it also applies to decarbonising heat supply by providing funding to assist the transition to low-carbon heating in social housing households. Social housing landlords are invited to apply for funding to be used to improve the energy performance of their social housing stock, with the aim to improve the energy performance of homes to EPC Band C.[23] Within the Carbon Budget Delivery Plan ('CBDP'), the government committed to begin the consultation process on a minimum energy efficiency standard for the social

14 See reg 5 or reg 14(1)(b) of the BUS Regulations.
15 'Boiler Upgrade Scheme (BUS) | Ofgem' (n 13).
16 See paras 4.46–4.50.
17 Department for Energy Security and Net Zero, *Heat and Buildings Strategy* (n 1).
18 Department for Business, Energy and Industrial Strategy, 'A Market-Based Mechanism for Low-Carbon Heat: Summary of Responses Received and Government Response' (2022) <https://assets.publishing.service.gov.uk/media/63bd6ba68fa8f55e2df4bd81/market-based-mechanism-for-low-carbon-heat-government-response.pdf>.
19 ibid.
20 ibid.
21 Department for Energy Security and Net Zero, 'Carbon Budget Delivery Plan' (n 9).
22 Department for Business, Energy and Industrial Strategy, 'A Market-Based Mechanism for Low-Carbon Heat: Summary of Responses Received and Government Response' (n 18).
23 Department for Energy Security and Net Zero, 'Social Housing Decarbonisation Fund: Wave 2.2 (Competition Guidance Notes).' (2023) <https://assets.publishing.service.gov.uk/media/658ed6f580a3bb000e9d05f8/shdf-wave-2-2-competition-guidance.pdf>.

rental sector, within six months of the Social Housing Regulation Bill receiving royal assent.[24]

- The Home Upgrade Grant: This grant is intended to provide energy efficiency upgrades and low-carbon heating via local authority funding, to eligible households[25] in England.[26]

- The Electrification of Heat Demonstration Project: The purpose of this project was to test the practical and technical feasibility of a large scale roll-out of heat pumps.[27] These were installed in October 2021, and the project now concerns the monitoring and optimisation phase where the Delivery Contractors will collect user feedback and detailed performance data on the installed heat pumps and look to ensure they are performing optimally.[28]

- Net Zero Innovation Portfolio ('NZIP'): £60 million has been invested in the 'Heat Pump Ready' programme to support the development of innovative solutions across the heat pump sector.[29]

- Reinforcing electricity networks: This is required, because the extent to which heat is electrified, and the way in which electrification of heat is deployed, will have implications for the timing and cost of requirements for new electricity generation capacity and transmission network reinforcements.[30]

21.10 In respect of hydrogen, the following proposals are relied upon within the HBS:[31]

- Hydrogen heating trials: Led by the gas networks, it will trial the conversion of existing gas network infrastructure in the local area, repurposing it for 100% hydrogen, conducting a first-of-a-kind 100% hydrogen village.[32] This was intended to start in 2023, with a village scale trial by 2025. However, it is now planned to start in Fife ('H100') in the second half of 2024.[33]

---

24 Department for Energy Security and Net Zero, 'Carbon Budget Delivery Plan' (n 9).
25 These are low income, off the gas grid, have an EPC between D and G and live in certain listed areas.
26 'Home Upgrade Grant: Successful Local Authorities' (GOV.UK) <https://www.gov.uk/government/publications/home-upgrade-grant-successful-local-authorities> accessed 2 April 2024.
27 HBS, [1.9].
28 'Electrification of Heat Demonstration Project' (*Energy Saving Trust*, 26 February 2024) <https://energysavingtrust.org.uk/electrification-of-heat-demonstration-project/> accessed 14 May 2024.
29 Department for Business, Energy and Industrial Strategy and Department for Energy Security and Net Zero, 'Information about the Heat Pump Ready Programme' (GOV.UK, 7 May 2023) <https://www.gov.uk/government/publications/heat-pump-ready-programme/information-about-the-heat-pump-ready-programme> accessed 14 May 2024.
30 Department for Energy Security and Net Zero, *Heat and Buildings Strategy* (n 1).
31 ibid.
32 ibid.
33 Leigh Collins, '"World First" 100% Green Hydrogen Heating Trial Struggling to Attract Households despite Offering "Bribes"' (*hydrogeninsight.com*, 9 December 2022) <https://www.hydrogeninsight.com/innovation/world-first-100-green-hydrogen-heating-trial-struggling-to-attract-households-despite-offering-bribes/2-1-1371068> accessed 14 May 2024.

- Hy4Heat programme: This programme explores the safety and feasibility of using 100% hydrogen for home heating, which includes the development of hydrogen heating appliance prototypes, with a consultation to follow on hydrogen-ready appliances.

- Consultation on hydrogen-ready boilers. This formed part of a wider consultation on improving boiler standards and efficiency. The government's response was published in March 2024. The government confirmed there was a range of views as to the mandating of hydrogen-ready boilers, it is working to assess the feasibility, costs and benefits of hydrogen (including the 'H100' trial), and its view is that there remains potential for hydrogen to play a role in slower time in some locations, but that heat pumps and heat networks will be the primary means of decarbonisation for the foreseeable future, and furthering the deployment of these technologies should remain the focus while questions remain on the role of hydrogen for domestic heating.[34]

- Net Zero Hydrogen Fund: The government is working with industry to attempt to deliver 1GW of low-carbon production capacity by 2025, and 5GW by 2030, by providing funds in respect of various competitions, finalising the design of a UK standard for low-carbon hydrogen and developing further detail on production strategy and twin track strategy.[35]

- Engaging with industry and regulators to develop assessments of blending 20% of hydrogen into the gas network: In December 2023, the government issued a strategic policy decision on blending, that it sees potential strategic and economic value in supporting the blending of up to 20% hydrogen into the GB gas distribution networks, and if outcomes from safety reviews support a decision to enable blending, the government would look to start the legislative process to deliver technical implementation activities and process required. The government doesn't anticipate blending at a commercial scale to commence until 2025–26 at the earliest.[36]

21.11 Developing the policy approach in relation to hydrogen further, the Energy Act 2023 received royal assent on 26 October 2023 and contains provisions in respect of the production and testing of hydrogen, of particular relevance to buildings is Chapter 2 of Part 4, concerning hydrogen grid conversion trials.[37] Hydrogen is considered further in paragraphs 16.49–16.65.

---

34 Department for Energy Security and Net Zero, 'Improving Boiler Standards and Efficiency: Summary of Responses Received and Government Response' (2024) <https://assets.publishing.service.gov.uk/media/660c52b9fb0f770011ec66da/improving-boiler-standards-and-efficiency-consultation-government-response.pdf> accessed 14 May 2024.

35 Department for Energy Security and Net Zero, 'Net Zero Hydrogen Fund Strands 1 and 2: Round 2 (Closed to Applications)' (GOV.UK, 27 February 2024) <https://www.gov.uk/government/publications/net-zero-hydrogen-fund-strand-1-and-strand-2> accessed 14 May 2024.

36 Department for Energy Security and Net Zero, 'Hydrogen Blending into GB Gas Distribution Networks: A Strategic Policy Decision' (2023) <https://assets.publishing.service.gov.uk/media/657a0a82254aaa0010050cde/hydrogen-blending-strategic-policy-decision.pdf> accessed 14 May 2024.

37 Energy Act 2023.

21.12 In respect of bioenergy (defined as all types of fuel of 'biogenic origin' (produced by living organisms), whether solid, liquid or gas),[38] three policies are relied upon within the HBS:[39]

- Grow UK biomethane gasification production capacity, a project to assess reasons for the failure of previous Advanced Gasification Technologies projects (thermal conversion technologies (gasification or pyrolysis) for conversion of biomass or waste into aviation fuel, diesel, hydrogen, methane and other hydrocarbons).[40]

- A Green Gas Support Scheme ('GGSS'): On 31 March 2021, the Green Gas Support Scheme Regulations 2021[41] came into force and the scheme runs to 31 March 2041. This scheme replaced the previous Renewable Heat Incentive Scheme which expired on 31 March 2021. The GGSS is a renewable heat incentive scheme to facilitate and encourage the production of biomethane by anaerobic digestion for injection into the gas grid; and is funded by levy payments from fossil fuel suppliers, under the Green Gas Levy. The scheme is also administered by Ofgem.[42] The government has further proposed to create a policy framework for commercial-scale gasification and to deliver increased production of biomethane and associated carbon savings subject to consultation.[43] Biomass is considered further at paragraphs 16.198–16.230.

- The BUS (see further details at paragraph 21.09 above) aims to encourage the installation and use of biomass boilers to provide space and water heating in domestic properties and small non-domestic properties.

21.13 In respect of waste heat, the government set out in the HBS one policy (though waste heat is of further relevance to heat networks):

- A call for evidence on Combined Heat and Power ('CHP'). This is a process which captures and utilises the heat that is a by-product of the electricity generation process.[44] In the government's consultation response, it was noted that due to the UK generation mix, and the increase of renewable and other low-carbon technology, from 2032, unabated natural gas CHP would displace an increasing proportion of low-carbon generation, effectively raising carbon emissions.[45]

---

38 Department for Energy Security and Net Zero, *Heat and Buildings Strategy* (n 1).
39 ibid.
40 AECOM and Fichtner Consulting Engineers, 'Advanced Gasification Technologies – Review and Benchmarking. Summary Report' (Department for Business, Energy and Industrial Strategy 2021) BEIS Research Paper Number 2021/038 <https://assets.publishing.service.gov.uk/media/615aa9cb8fa8f52985dd7475/agt-benchmarking-summary-report.pdf> accessed 14 May 2024.
41 The Green Gas Support Scheme Regulations 2021 SI 2021/1335.
42 See paras 4.46–4.50 in Chapter 4.
43 Department for Energy Security and Net Zero, 'Carbon Budget Delivery Plan' (n 9).
44 Department for Energy Security and Net Zero and Department for Business, Energy and Industrial Strategy, 'Combined Heat and Power' (GOV.UK, 6 October 2020) <https://www.gov.uk/guidance/combined-heat-and-power> accessed 14 May 2024.
45 Department for Business, Energy and Industrial Strategy, 'Combined Heat and Power: Pathway to Decarbonisation. Summary of Call for Evidence Responses' (2022) <https://assets.publishing.service.gov.uk/media/623ad327d3bf7f6ac1c770ed/chp-pathway-to-decarbonisation-summary-cfe-responses.pdf> accessed 14 May 2024.

Heat networks

21.14 Heat networks have been identified as one of the key existing solutions in achieving net zero within buildings and form a core part of the government's HBS. In particular heat networks will be a key technology in areas of high-density heat demand and where there are large low-carbon heat sources (likely urban centres).[46] In 2023, around 2–3% of heat in the UK is provided by heat networks. It is estimated that heat networks will need to be supplying almost 20% of heat by 2050 to enable the UK to reach net zero.[47]

21.15 A 'heat network' is defined in the Energy Act 2023 as:[48]

> A network that, by distributing a liquid or a gas, enables the transfer of thermal energy for the purpose of supplying heating, cooling or hot water to a building or persons in that building (and includes any appliance the main purpose of which is to heat or cool the liquid or gas).

21.16 The Energy Act 2023 describes two different forms of heat network:

- A district heat network, defined as 'a heat network by means of which heating, cooling or hot water is supplied to two or more buildings or persons in those buildings';[49]
- A communal heat network, defined as 'a heat network by means of which heating, cooling or hot water is supplied only to a single building divided into separate premises or persons in those premises'.[50]

21.17 Heat networks are central to government policy on decarbonising the delivery of heat to buildings, as stated in the Green Heat Network Fund Scheme Overview:[51]

> Heat networks will be vital to making net zero a reality in the UK. They are a proven, cost-effective way of providing reliable, efficient, low carbon heat at a fair price to consumers, while supporting local regeneration. In recognition of their importance to the future energy mix, the Committee on Climate Change have estimated that around 18 per-cent of UK heat will need to come from heat networks by 2050 if the UK is to meet its carbon targets cost effectively.[52]

46 Department for Energy Security and Net Zero, *Heat and Buildings Strategy* (n 1).
47 Department for Energy Security and Net Zero, 'Heat Network Zoning: Overview' (GOV.UK, 1 December 2024) <https://www.gov.uk/government/publications/heat-network-zoning-overview/heat-network-zoning-overview> accessed 14 May 2024.
48 Energy Act 2023 s 216(2).
49 ibid.
50 ibid.
51 Department for Energy Security and Net Zero, 'Green Heat Network Fund. Scheme Overview. Supporting the Commercialisation and Construction of Low-Carbon Heat Network Projects. Version 5.0' (2022) <https://assets.publishing.service.gov.uk/media/64a4a3167a4c230013bba17b/green-heat-network-fund-r6-overview.pdf> accessed 14 May 2024.
52 ibid 4.

21.18 In respect of heat networks, the government set out in the HBS eight policies:[53]

- The Green Heat Network Fund ('GHNF'): This fund is a capital grant programme that opened to applicants in March 2022, replacing the Heat Networks Investment Project (a government funded programme aiming to increase the number of heat networks and create conditions necessary for a sustainable heat network market to develop).[54] The GHNF provides targeted financial support to organisations in the public, private, and third sectors in England, supporting the development of low and zero carbon ('LZC') heat (and cooling) networks. This includes both the commercialisation and construction of new low and zero-carbon heat networks, along with the retrofitting and expansion of existing ones. Examples of support include:

  - accessing heat sources – such as capturing waste heat from an industrial process, energy from waste, wastewater, geothermal; low-carbon generation – energy centres, low-carbon generation and associated plant, control;

  - primary heat network distribution – distribution pipework – both above and below-ground for transmission and distribution of low-carbon heating and cooling.[55]

- The Heat Network (Metering and Billing) Regulations 2014 (as amended in 2015 and 2020) ('Heat Network 2014 Regulations'): It had been recognised that, whilst the Heat Network 2014 Regulations provided for some limited regulation, as discussed below, heat networks were largely unregulated, especially as compared with the supply of gas and electricity. The Heat Network 2014 Regulations set out the current regulations applicable to heat networks. They apply to 'heat suppliers', who are persons who supply and charge for the supply of heating, cooling or hot water to a final customer through 'communal heating' or a 'district heat network'[56] (as defined at regulation 2 of the Heat Network 2014 Regulations). The main obligation on heat suppliers is to submit a notification for each network they operate to the Office for Product Safety and Standards.[57] There are also obligations concerning *inter alia* the installation of meters, heat cost allocators, thermostatic radiator valves, and billing, which vary dependent on the class of building the heat is being supplied to.[58] Chapter 1 of Part 8 of the Energy Act 2023 now expressly provides for the issuing of regulations in respect of heat networks, and is intended to provide for regulations concerning authorisation and consumer protection. The regulator is Ofgem. The phase-in of authorisation and consumer protection

---

53 Department for Energy Security and Net Zero, *Heat and Buildings Strategy* (n 1).
54 <https://www.gov.uk/government/collections/heat-networks-investment-project-hnip-overview-and-how-to-apply> accessed 14 May 2024.
55 Department for Energy Security and Net Zero, 'Green Heat Network Fund. Scheme Overview. Supporting the Commercialisation and Construction of Low-Carbon Heat Network Projects. Version 5.0' (n 51) 4.
56 The Heat Network (Metering and Billing) Regulations 2014 s 2.
57 ibid 3.
58 ibid 4–9. In relation to the allocation of buildings, see Office for Product Safety & Standards, 'Guidance. Heat Network (Metering and Billing) Regulations 2014 (as Amended in 2015 and 2020).' (2020) <https://assets.publishing.service.gov.uk/media/5fce3739e90e07562aba0de7/heat-networks-guidance-on-metering-and-billing-regulations-2014.pdf>.

regulations is anticipated to start in 2025, with a new market framework for heat networks to be fully operational from 2026.[59]

- Heat network zoning: This enables the identification of areas where heat networks would provide the lowest cost low-carbon solution. Heat network zoning is now the subject of legislation. Pursuant to section 226 of the Energy Act 2023, the Secretary of State has the power to issue regulations making provision regarding heat network zones. Chapter 2 of Part 8 of the Energy Act 2023 provides that such 'zones regulations' may *inter alia* provide for regulations in respect of the identification, designation and review of prospective heat network zones, and regulations in respect of heat networks within those zones, the delivery of heat networks within zones, enforcement of zone regulations, and prospective penalties. The phase-in of heat network zoning regulations is anticipated to start in 2025,[60] with a new market framework for heat networks (addressed more below) to be fully operational from 2026.[61]

- A Heat Networks Market Framework: This framework (i.e. regulatory framework) will enable heat networks to be regulated, to ensure consumer protection, market growth and the decarbonisation of heating networks.[62]

- A Heat Network Skills Programme (which has led to the Heat Training Grant): This programme provides grant payments to support trainees, with the aim of improving the training and skills required to build the capacity of the supply chain to increase growth of heat networks.[63]

- A Heat Networks Investment Project (domestic and non-domestic). This is a grant and loan scheme for investments to fund the development and construction of heat networks for both domestic and non-domestic customers. As discussed above, this has now been replaced by the GHNF.

- Accessing low-carbon forms of heat, working with devolved authorities and industry to support commercially viable low-carbon sources to supply heat networks. This could include energy from waste plants, sewage systems and geothermal heat.

21.19 The government has acknowledged that heat networks will play a major role in carbonising heat; and has confirmed that it will publish a Heat Networks Strategy in 2024 including targets for low-carbon heat networks.[64]

---

59 'Coming Regulation' (*Heat Trust*) <https://www.heattrust.org/coming-regulation> accessed 4 April 2024.
60 Department for Energy Security and Net Zero, 'Heat Network Zoning' (n 47).
61 'Coming Regulation' (n 59).
62 Department for Energy Security and Net Zero, *Heat and Buildings Strategy* (n 1) para 119.
63 Department for Energy Security and Net Zero, 'Heat Training Grant: Heat Pumps. Guidance for Training Providers on How to Apply to Offer the Grant for Heat Pump Training' (2023) <https://assets.publishing.service.gov.uk/media/65dcd9a1f1cab30011fc474a/heat-training-grant-heat-pumps-training-provider-guidance.pdf> accessed 14 May 2024.
64 HM Government, *Responding to the Climate Change Committee's (CCC) 2023 Annual Progress Report to Parliament* (HC 2023, 1919) <https://assets.publishing.service.gov.uk/media/65393f4ae6c968000daa9b0e/ccc-annual-progress-report-2023-government-response.pdf> accessed 28 April 2024.

Policies and legislation related to improving the energy efficiency of buildings

21.20 In the HBS, the government categorises policies concerned with improving the energy efficiency of buildings as follows:[65]

- Energy-using products;
- New-builds;
- Retrofitting and insulation;
- Public sector buildings;
- Large and complete commercial and industrial buildings; and
- Small businesses and small commercial buildings.

21.21 The policies concerned with energy-using products are addressed in Chapter 32; and those dealing with new builds are set out in Chapter 36.

21.22 In respect of retrofitting and insulation, the government set out in the HBS the following policies:[66]

- Local Authority Delivery ('LAD') scheme. As discussed in paragraph 21.09 above, the scheme provided support to low-income households, which aimed to raise the energy efficiency of low income and low energy performance homes with a focus on energy performance certificate (EPC ratings of E, F or G).[67]
- The Home Upgrade Grant. Address above at paragraph 21.09, the grant is intended to provide energy efficiency upgrades and low-carbon heating via local authority funding, to eligible households (low income, off the gas grid, have an EPC between D and G and live in certain listed areas) in England.[68]
- The Energy Company Obligation ('ECO'). Under the ECO, obligated energy suppliers are required to install energy efficiency measures in eligible households (usually low-income, fuel poor and vulnerable households).[69] Measures include replacing or upgrading broken or inefficient heating systems and installing installation. Following various similar precursor schemes in respect of supplier

---

65 Department for Energy Security and Net Zero, *Heat and Buildings Strategy* (n 1).
66 ibid.
67 'Green Homes Grant Local Authority Delivery Scheme, Phase 2: Funding Allocated to Local Net Zero Hubs' (GOV.UK, 25 April 2022) <https://www.gov.uk/government/publications/green-homes-grant-local-authority-delivery-scheme-phase-2-funding-allocated-to-local-net-zero-hubs> accessed 4 April 2024.
68 'Home Upgrade Grant: Successful Local Authorities' (n 26).
69 'Energy Company Obligation (ECO)' (ofgem) <https://www.ofgem.gov.uk/environmental-and-social-schemes/energy-company-obligation-eco> accessed 14 May 2024.

commitments, the first version of the ECO was introduced by the Electricity and Gas (Energy Company Obligation) Order 2012.[70] Further orders updating the ECO scheme were made in 2014 (ECO2), 2018 (ECO3) and 2022 (ECO4). The current ECO4, pursuant to the Electricity and Gas (Energy Company Obligation Order) 2022, runs until 31 March 2026. Article 3 sets out the overall home-heating cost reduction target for the period. Article 4 sets out who must participate in the scheme. Part 3 sets out the process for apportionment of the target between participants. Part 4 requires that participants must achieve their obligations by 31 March 2026 and Part 5 contains provisions about what 'qualifying actions' participants can take to meet their target. Complementing the ECO is the Great British Insulation Scheme, administrated by Ofgem, designed to deliver improvements to the least energy-efficient homes. It is to mostly deliver single insulation measures, it is available to low-income and vulnerable households, and to those living in homes with EPC ratings of D–C, within Council Tax bands A–D in England and A–E in Scotland and Wales. The scheme places an obligation on medium and large energy companies to deliver measures that result in reduced energy usage and will run from April 2023 to March 2026.[71]

- A review of the Decent Homes Standard. This concerns a definition of what minimum standards constitutes a decent home, according to four criteria.[72] It is currently applicable to the social rented sector[73] and how this could best support decarbonisation and improved energy efficiency of social housing.

- The Social Housing Decarbonisation Fund ('SHDF'). As set out above at paragraph 21.09, this fund aims to upgrade a significant amount of the social housing stock that is currently below EPC rating of C up to that standard (i.e. EPC C), delivering warmer and more energy-efficient homes, and reducing carbon emissions and bills, as well as supporting green jobs. Wave 1 of the SHDF aimed to see energy performance improvements in up to 20,000 social homes.[74] Wave 2 allocated a further £800 million of funding.[75]

- Proposed expansion of minimum energy efficiency standards. Within the HBS, the government proposed that it would publish a response to a consultation on requiring all private-rented sector homes to meet minimum standards (EPC E by 2020 and EPC C by 2025 for new tenancies and 2028 for all tenancies) which closed on 8 January 2021. This response has never been published, and on 20

70 The Electricity and Gas (Energy Companies Obligation) Order 2012.
71 'Great British Insulation Scheme' (ofgem, 10 April 2024) <https://www.ofgem.gov.uk/environmental-and-social-schemes/great-british-insulation-scheme> accessed 14 May 2024.
72 Department for Communities and Local Government, 'A Decent Home: Definition and Guidance for Implementation. June 2006 – Update' (2006) <https://assets.publishing.service.gov.uk/media/5a7968b740f0b63d72fc5926/138355.pdf> accessed 4 April 2024.
73 ibid.
74 'Social Housing Decarbonisation Fund: Wave 2.1 (Closed to Applications)' (GOV.UK, 2 October 2023) <https://www.gov.uk/government/publications/social-housing-decarbonisation-fund-wave-2> accessed 4 April 2024.
75 ibid.

September 2023, Rishi Sunak confirmed the government was scrapping plans to impose such minimum standards.[76] EPC is discussed further in Chapter 22.

- Consulting with mortgage lenders to disclose information requiring EPC ratings of their lending portfolios, and proposed a voluntary target to reach an average of EPC band C across their portfolio by 2030. The government stated the response would be issued at the end of 2023,[77] but at date of publication, this had not yet been issued.

- Exploring opportunities to improve the energy performance of owner-occupier homes with plans for a consultation. Within the Carbon Budget Delivery Plan,[78] the government stated it was planning to consult by the end of 2023 on how to improve the efficiency of owner-occupied homes, however this has not yet taken place.

- Considering an ultimate backstop date to ensure all homes meet a net zero minimum energy performance standard before 2050.

21.23 In respect of public sector buildings, within the HBS there are three main policies:[79]

- A Public Sector Decarbonisation Scheme. This scheme aims to halve direct emissions from public sector buildings by 2032, against 2017 levels, and by 75% by 2037. Phase 1, which ran over the financial years 2020–2021 and 2021–2022, aimed to support up to 30,000 jobs in the low-carbon and energy efficiency sectors and reduce carbon emissions from the public sector and provided £1 billion in grants. Phase 2 provided £75 million of grant funding for the financial year 2021–2022 with a stronger focus on heat decarbonisation. Phase 3 is aiming to provide over £1.425 billion of grant funding over the financial years 2022 to 2023 and 2025 to 2026.[80] Phase 3 also has a stronger focus on heat decarbonisation.[81] The grants are for low-carbon heating measures, such as heat pumps, measures to reduce direct carbon emissions, like insulation; measures to reduce indirect carbon emissions (typically electricity savings); and measures that enable the installation of measures which save carbon (such infrastructure upgrades).[82]

- Greening Government Commitments. These are a set of sustainability targets, for government departments and their partner organisations to take to reduce their impacts on the environment. Though these targets have wider application than

---

76 PM Rishi Sunak (n 8).
77 Department for Energy Security and Net Zero, 'Carbon Budget Delivery Plan' (n 9).
78 ibid.
79 Department for Energy Security and Net Zero, *Heat and Buildings Strategy* (n 1).
80 'Public Sector Decarbonisation Scheme' (GOV.UK, 29 February 2024) <https://www.gov.uk/government/collections/public-sector-decarbonisation-scheme> accessed 4 April 2024.
81 Department for Energy Security and Net Zero, 'Public Sector Decarbonisation Scheme. Phase 3a Summary Report' (2023) <https://assets.publishing.service.gov.uk/media/65d89ceb87005a001a80f8e4/psds-phase-3a-summary-report.pdf> accessed 4 April 2024.
82 ibid.

only to property, reducing the carbon associated with each department's estate forms part of these targets.[83]

- A Public Sector Low Carbon Skills Fund. This fund supports public sectors that do not have the expertise to identify and develop projects for the Public Sector Decarbonisation Scheme. It provides grants for public sector organisations to engage the specialist and expert advice and skills required to develop heat decarbonisation plans.[84]

21.24 In respect of large and complex commercial and industrial buildings, within the HBS there are six principal projects:[85]

- Proposed performance-based energy rating. The government is developing and consulting on a mandatory framework for performance-based energy ratings for commercial and industrial buildings over 1,000m^2.

- Developing amendments to the Energy Efficiency (Private Rented Property) (England and Wales) Regulations 2015. The proposal within the HBS suggested requiring non-domestic private rented sector properties to increase to EPC band B by 2030, and a consultation was issued on this topic which closed in June 2021.[86] Within the Carbon Budget Delivery Plan, the government stated it would publish a response 'in due course', however to date no government response has been published.[87] Energy efficiency standards and EPC ratings are discussed in Chapter 22.

- PAS2038 Standards. The government has worked with the British Standards Institution to establish a framework specifying requirements for the installation of energy efficiency measures in non-domestic buildings. This resulted in the publication of PAS2038 in August 2021, a set of guidelines concerning the retrofitting of non-domestic buildings, with the aim of improving energy efficiency, reducing energy demand and ultimately reducing carbon emissions.

- The Energy Savings Opportunity Scheme ('ESOS'). This is a mandatory energy assessment scheme for large UK businesses, administered by the Environment Agency.[88] It came into force on 17 July 2014, pursuant to the Energy Savings

---

83 Department for Environment, Food and Rural Affairs, 'Policy Paper: Greening Government Commitments 2021 to 2025' (GOV.UK) <https://www.gov.uk/government/publications/greening-government-commitments-2021-to-2025/greening-government-commitments-2021-to-2025> accessed 4 April 2024. See Annex A for each department's respective target.
84 Department for Energy Security and Net Zero and Department for Business, Energy and Industrial Strategy, 'Public Sector Low Carbon Skills Fund' (GOV.UK, 3 October 2022) <https://www.gov.uk/government/collections/public-sector-low-carbon-skills-fund> accessed 14 May 2024.
85 Department for Energy Security and Net Zero, *Heat and Buildings Strategy* (n 1).
86 Department for Energy Security and Net Zero and Department for Business, Energy and Industrial Strategy, 'Non-Domestic Private Rented Sector Minimum Energy Efficiency Standards: EPC B Implementation' (GOV.UK, 17 March 2021) <https://www.gov.uk/government/consultations/non-domestic-private-rented-sector-minimum-energy-efficiency-standards-epc-b-implementation> accessed 14 May 2024.
87 Department for Energy Security and Net Zero, 'Carbon Budget Delivery Plan' (n 9).
88 The Energy Savings Opportunity Scheme Regulations 2014 s 5.

Opportunity Scheme Regulations 2014 ('ESOS Regulations 2014'),[89] implementing Directive 2012/27/EU. Organisations that qualify for ESOS must carry out ESOS assessments every four years,[90] including an audit of all energy used,[91] which would include energy used by their buildings. The scheme is designed to identify tailored and cost-effective measures to allow businesses to save energy and achieve carbon and cost savings.[92] A failure to comply with the ESOS Regulations 2014 may result in financial penalties.[93]

- Legislation requiring all large or listed UK businesses to report their annual carbon emissions and energy usage in Annual Reports. This is discussed in Chapter 30.

- Climate Change Agreements ('CCA'), and the Climate Change Levy. These are voluntary agreements made by high energy-using UK industry to reduce energy use and carbon emissions, and in return, operators receive a discount on the Climate Change Levy, a tax added to electricity and fuel bills (discussed in Chapter 34). The CCA scheme is administered by the Environment Agency.[94] The latest Climate Change Agreements Operations Manual (February 2022)[95] details eligible energy in the CCA scheme and how CCAs operate. The government opened a consultation, which closed on 14 February 2024, seeking views on proposals for a new 6-year Climate Change Agreements scheme to begin in 2025, which would add new target periods from 2025 to 2030, providing further reductions in the Climate Change Levy for eligible participants.[96]

21.25 In respect of small businesses and small commercial buildings, within the HBS there are four policies on energy efficiency:[97]

- The Boosting Access for SMEs to Energy Efficiency competition. This competition is aimed at developing innovative solutions that encourage the take up of energy efficiency and reduce barriers to SMEs. The competition closed in 2020.

- Developing amendments to the Energy Efficiency (Private Rented Property) (England and Wales) Regulations 2015. This is discussed above and in Chapter 22.

---

89 ibid 1.
90 ibid 4.
91 ibid 22(1).
92 'Guidance: Energy Savings Opportunity Scheme (ESOS)' (GOV.UK, 19 March 2024) <https://www.gov.uk/guidance/energy-savings-opportunity-scheme-esos> accessed 4 April 2024.
93 The Energy Savings Opportunity Scheme Regulations 2014 pt 8.
94 'Guidance: Climate Change Agreements' (GOV.UK, 2 March 2022) <https://www.gov.uk/guidance/climate-change-agreements--2> accessed 4 April 2024.
95 Environment Agency, 'Climate Change Agreements Operations Manual.' (2022) LIT7911 <https://assets.publishing.service.gov.uk/media/6216220cd3bf7f4f0399d084/Climate-Change-Agreements-Operations-Manual.pdf> accessed 4 April 2024.
96 Department for Energy Security and Net Zero, 'Climate Change Agreements: Consultation on a New Scheme' (2023) <https://assets.publishing.service.gov.uk/media/655b917fd03a8d001207fd07/climate-change-agreements-consultation-on-new-scheme.pdf> accessed 4 April 2024.
97 Department for Energy Security and Net Zero, *Heat and Buildings Strategy* (n 1).

- Non-domestic owner-occupier minimum standards consultation. The government's position on this, as clarified in its response to the CCC's June 2023 progress report,[98] is that it is still 'developing policy options to drive energy efficiency in owner-occupier properties with the aim of consulting in due course'.[99]

21.26 As set out above, reducing emissions associated with residential and commercial property is widely acknowledged to be essential in achieving the UK's net zero commitments,[100] and the CCC considers policy progress is not on track.[101] Within its response to the CCC's 2023 progress report, the government stated it would continue to develop and publish a suitable level of monitoring framework at scheme and portfolio level as appropriate by Autumn 2024.[102] The CCC also considers that clear direction on heat in buildings is needed.[103] The government has previously said that it will take a 'strategic decision' on the respective roles of hydrogen and electrification for heat in buildings by 2026.[104]

Climate change adaptation policies

21.27 As acknowledged by the government, within the UK, climate change will bring more regular drought, rising sea levels and changes in rainfall patterns.[105] At the date of publication, the latest programme setting out the government's proposals and policies in respect of adaptation is the Third National Adaptation Programme ('NAP3'),[106] published by the Department for Environment, Food and Rural Affairs on 18 July 2023. Within NAP3, the government sets out the adaptation challenges for the UK's building stock:

> The building stock in the UK will need to be improved to maintain safe and comfortable temperatures as summers become hotter due to climate change. The government is also working to address climate impacts on building fabric such as increased risks from moisture, wind, subsidence and wildfire.[107]

98 Climate Change Committee, 'Progress in Reducing Emissions: 2023 Report to Parliament' (n 2).
99 HM Government, 'Responding to the Climate Change Committee's (CCC) 2023 Annual Progress Report to Parliament Presented to Parliament Pursuant to Section 37 of the Climate Change Act (2008)' (HC 2023, 1919) <https://assets.publishing.service.gov.uk/media/65393f4ae6c968000daa9b0e/ccc-annual-progress-report-2023-government-response.pdf>.
100 Department for Energy Security and Net Zero, *Heat and Buildings Strategy* (n 1).
101 Climate Change Committee, 'Progress in Reducing Emissions: 2023 Report to Parliament' (n 2) 151–2.
102 HM Government, *Responding to the Climate Change Committee's (CCC) 2023 Annual Progress Report to Parliament* (n 64).
103 Climate Change Committee, 'Progress in Reducing Emissions: 2023 Report to Parliament' (n 2).
104 Department for Energy Security and Net Zero, 'Energy Efficiency Taskforce: Terms of Reference' (GOV.UK, 31 March 2023) <https://www.gov.uk/government/publications/energy-efficiency-taskforce-terms-of-reference/energy-efficiency-taskforce-terms-of-reference> accessed 14 May 2024.
105 Department for Environment, Food and Rural Affairs, 'The Third National Adaptation Programme (NAP3) and the Fourth Strategy for Climate Adaptation Reporting' (HC 2023,1649) <https://assets.publishing.service.gov.uk/government/uploads/system/uploads/attachment_data/file/1172931/The_Third_National_Adaptation_Programme.pdf>.
106 ibid 4.3.1.
107 ibid 77.

21.28 Besides NAP3, there is limited legislation concerning adaptation specific to residential and commercial property, beyond the government's wider flood management legislation, which is discussed in Chapter 19.

Third National Adaptation Programme: 'The built environment'

21.29 The relevant section of NAP3 for residential and commercial property is section 4.3, entitled 'The built environment'.

21.30 Within the action section (section 4.3.2), NAP3 refers to the introduction of Approved Document O of the Building Regulations, requiring, for new homes, housebuilders to mitigate the risk of overheating. Approved Document O is discussed in further detail in Chapter 36.

21.31 NAP3 further references taking action in respect of the government's own estate,[108] which includes research and the 2021–2025 Greening Government Commitments Framework for Government, addressed above at paragraph 21.23.[109] Section F of this framework references the headline commitment in respect of adaptation, which is for governmental departments to conduct climate change risk assessments across their estates and operations to better understand risk and target areas that need greater resilience, and for departments to develop a climate change adaptation action plan.[110]

21.32 Otherwise, NAP3 sets out that the government is still working to improve its understanding of the scale and variation of the impact of climate risks to the UK's building stock.[111] It will conduct research between 2023 and 2028 to further existing knowledge of the buildings, dwelling types, locations and groups most vulnerable from extreme heat.[112] It will carry out research to determine specific adaptation measures required to retrofit existing building stock; and it will manage research mapping out climate risks relevant to buildings at local scale, including extreme wind and wind-driven rain, and increase awareness of the public to potential risks posed by high temperatures and indoor air quality.[113]

21.33 Further actions are identified in respect of communities, and properties which constitute cultural heritage, including historic buildings, museums, heritage sites and archives.[114] NAP3 references better protecting communities through a £5.2 billion investment in flood and coastal erosion schemes in England by 2027, and providing

108 ibid 4.3.2.
109 'Greening Government Commitments 2021 to 2025' (GOV.UK) <https://www.gov.uk/government/publications/greening-government-commitments-2021-to-2025/greening-government-commitments-2021-to-2025> accessed 2 April 2024.
110 ibid.
111 Department for Environment, Food and Rural Affairs, 'The Third National Adaptation Programme (NAP3) and the Fourth Strategy for Climate Adaptation Reporting' (n 105) s 4.3.3.
112 ibid.
113 ibid.
114 ibid s 4.4.

support for local areas to utilise innovative ways to build resilience through the £200 million Flood and Coastal Innovation Fund.[115]

21.34 Through NAP3, the government also sets out actions it will take to increase resilience to future flood and coastal erosion, namely:[116]

- Updating the National Planning Policy Framework ('NPPF') to maximise its contribution to climate change, mitigation and adaptation;
- Build resilience to flooding and coastal change through the National Flood and Coastal Erosion Risk Management Strategy, Policy Statement and Roadmap by 2026;
- Reduce surface water flooding risk by standardising sustainable drainage systems in new developments through the implementation of Schedule 3 to the Flood and Water Management Act 2010;
- Refresh Shoreline Management Plans by the end of 2024;
- Help UK households that are at risk of flooding to access affordable insurance through the Flood Re scheme;
- NAP3 further states that DEFRA and the Environment Agency will improve the National Coastal Erosion Map, to provide an updated assessment of properties and infrastructure at risk from erosion, and improve the capability of forecasting floods in high-risk areas.[117]

21.35 There has been very limited litigation testing of the scope of the adaptation obligations on the government, though it is noted a judicial review claim has recently been brought concerning NAP3, in the case of *R (Friends of the Earth Ltd & others) v Secretary of State for Environment, Rood & Rural Affairs*[118] discussed further in Chapter 2.

21.36 The current policies and proposals concerning residential and commercial property in respect of adaptation are much more limited than the policies and proposals in respect of lowering emissions. However, as the effects of climate change on the built environment become more significant, adaptation policies and proposals are likely to become more developed.

---

115 ibid s 4.4.2.
116 ibid.
117 ibid s 4.4.3.
118 'R (Friends of the Earth Ltd, Mr Kevin Jordan and Mr Doug Paulley) v Secretary of State for Environment, Rood & Rural Affairs (Challenge to the Third National Adaptation Programme)' (Climate Change Litigation) <https://climatecasechart.com/non-us-case/rfriends-of-the-earth-ltd-mr-kevin-jordan-and-mr-doug-paulley-v-secretary-of-state-for-environment-rood-rural-affairs-challenge-to-the-third-national-adaptation-programme/> accessed 7 May 2024.

CHAPTER 22

GREEN LEASES AND SUSTAINABLE BUILDINGS

Niraj Modha

Introduction

22.01 This chapter considers green leases and policies to improve energy efficiency in the context of both rented and owner-occupied buildings.

Green leases

(i) *The concept*

22.02 There is no generally accepted definition of a green lease. There are perhaps three reasons for this.

22.03 First, the term is relatively novel. At the time of going to print, there are no reported cases in England and Wales in which the term 'green lease' has featured.[1] That detail by itself is not particularly illuminative, since it may only indicate that the concept has not generated notable litigation. However, the term appears to have been in existence since at least the time of the Climate Change Act 2008.[2] The absence of litigation suggests that the term has not been prevalent as a contentious issue in dispute resolution. That coincides with the author's professional experience.

22.04 Second, the term has not yet captured the close attention of the legislature or the executive. It does not appear in the Energy White Paper published by the Department for Energy Security and Net Zero and Department for Business, Energy and Industrial Strategy in December 2020.[3] There has been of course some consideration in Parliament of 'green' issues in property, such as the energy performance of leasehold property.[4] Yet, green leases hitherto have not been the subject of any real scrutiny. There are no reported instances of the use of the term in Hansard. There is no consideration of green leases

---

1 Also known as 'energy-aligned leases' for example in New York City.

2 See for example Susan Bright, 'The Green Lease: An Introduction' [2008] Conveyancer and Property Lawyer 485; Mark Hinnells, 'Greening the Commercial Leasehold Relationship' [2008] Conveyancer and Property Lawyer 487; Susan Bright, 'Drafting Green Leases' [2008] Conveyancer and Property Lawyer 498; Nick French, 'The Valuation of Sustainability and Green Leases' [2008] Conveyancer and Property Lawyer 518; Jeremy De Souza, 'Tax Editor's Notes (November/December)' [2008] Conveyancer and Property Lawyer 545.

3 Secretary of State for Business, Energy and Industrial Strategy, 'Energy White Paper: Powering Our Net Zero Future' (2020) CP 337 <https://assets.publishing.service.gov.uk/media/5fdc61e2d3bf7f3a3bdc8cbf/201216_BEIS_EWP_Command_Paper_Accessible.pdf> accessed 17 April 2024.

4 See Chapter 21, and see also paras 22.33–22.66 below.

in the Energy Act 2023, despite the wide scope of that significant legislation and the express reference therein to the energy performance of premises.[5]

22.05 Third, the term is not easily capable of definition. Arguably, it jars with the traditional view of leases. Leases comprise bundles of rights and obligations as between landowners and land users.[6] In this regard, a lease is much like any other contract, in that its terms are a matter for negotiation and agreement. Whilst there are common terms and standard forms, 'greening' provisions typically do not form part of these.[7] The principal purpose of a lease, at least in the context of commercial property, is the exploitation of the value of a parcel of land by someone other than the freeholder for a period of time in return for payment.[8] All other purposes or functions (whether described as 'green' or otherwise) customarily have been considered as secondary, even where land is to be occupied for public purposes or to provide a public benefit.

22.06 Consequently, it is perhaps currently impossible to define green leases with any particularity. It is equally unfeasible to identify a definitively 'green' lease. Commentators and professionals have nevertheless attempted to define the term.[9] It has been suggested that a 'green lease' means more than simply a typical full repairing and insuring ('FRI') lease with provisions that address environmental issues tacked on.[10] This reflects a view that green leases should be considered as fundamentally different to traditional leases, since they are underpinned by a different approach to negotiation and a specific focus on environmental issues and sustainability. They are said to require 'a far greater dialogue between a landlord and tenant to ensure that common objectives are set and achieved'.[11] This is understandable and unobjectionable as far as it goes. But the fact that the concept of a green lease is still in its relative infancy, and that the idea is underdeveloped, means that it may be considered unhelpful to limit its definition artificially.

(ii) *An attempt at definition*

22.07 The three reasons above for the absence of a clear definition of a green lease are connected. They represent a failing on the part of policymakers, stakeholders, investors and practitioners. Policymakers have appeared to ignore the opportunities for achieving efficiency gains – let alone making strides towards attaining net zero – through the concept of green leases. Stakeholders and investors have largely avoided implementing

---

5 Energy Act 2023 pt 10.
6 This was expressed in rather blunt terms for the first time by Lewis in the following terms: 'The dullest individual among the people knows and understands that his *property* in anything is a bundle of rights'. John Lewis, *A Treatise on the Law of Eminent Domain in the United States* (Callaghan & company 1888) 43.
7 See for example the business lease forms available at 'Business Leases Forms' (Law Society, 27 December 2023) <https://www.lawsociety.org.uk/topics/property/business-leases-forms> accessed 25 April 2024.
8 Green leases are associated exclusively with commercial property, but there is no obvious reason why the concept should be so limited and should not be applicable to residential property.
9 See Susan Bright and Hannah Dixie, 'Evidence of Green Leases in England and Wales' (2014) 6 International Journal of Law in the Built Environment 6; Kathryn B Janda and others, 'The Evolution of Green Leases: Towards Inter-Organizational Environmental Governance' (2016) 44 Building Research and Information: the International Journal of Research, Development and Demonstration 660.
10 Michael Barlow, 'Green Leases' [2008] 11 EIB 20.
11 ibid. This more expansive approach coincides with that of the authors of the series of articles in Issue 6 (2008) of Conveyancer and Property Lawyer (n 2).

greening provisions, preferring instead to focus on maximising returns on investment and short-term budgetary constraints, rather than any net zero goals. Practitioners are largely unfamiliar with, and as a result unlikely to advise their clients on the inclusion of, green clauses. As a result, green leases remain somewhat unknown, underappreciated and underutilised.[12]

22.08 In order to foster more engagement with the concept, it is suggested that it is in fact more helpful to think of leases with different 'shades of green'.[13] A lease of a building should be considered as a green lease if it contains clauses that are intended to improve the energy efficiency and sustainability of that building and reduce the environmental impact of its use. The more such clauses that a lease contains, the 'greener' it might be. A lease that imposes no duties or powers in this regard cannot be considered as a green lease at all. There should not be any additional requirement that the building be energy-efficient to any particular standard. It may not be, in light of its age, method or nature of construction, and purpose. What matters is that the landlord and tenant have, even if only tentatively, agreed a system for measuring, recording, and sharing data in order to formulate a plan for the more efficient and sustainable operation and management of that building. This is not to say that a green lease is purely aspirational. The provisions of a green lease should be workable, and indeed operated, so as to promote dialogue between a landlord and tenant on the efficient energy use of a building and improvements thereto.

22.09 From this perspective, green leases are not an especially radical concept. They do not fundamentally alter the bargain between a landlord and tenant or indeed disturb any canons of property law. Green leases do however represent a shift in emphasis from a traditionally adversarial relationship, or zero-sum approach, where a landlord's loss is a tenant's gain and vice versa, to a more cooperative relationship, where the parties to a lease may together reduce the carbon footprint of a building and potentially share in the resulting benefits.

(iii) *The energy use of land*

22.10 The virtues of green leases bear some explanation and analysis, particularly given the slow take-up of this concept.

22.11 It is no exaggeration to say that, notwithstanding the difficulty in defining a green lease, the concept has the potential to be an important – if not crucial – tool in achieving the UK's net zero target through improvement in the energy efficiency of commercial buildings in particular.[14]

---

12 Green leases do not appear to be mandatory in any major international legal jurisdiction.
13 This is the term used in Janet Bignell and Kim Lewison, *Lewison's Drafting Business Leases* (8th edn, Sweet & Maxwell, Thomson Reuters 2013). The Department of Climate Change and Energy Efficiency of Australia (as it then was) published a Green Lease Handbook on 1 September 2012 and this refers to 'hard' and 'soft' green leases in a similar vein. See Chris Wheeler, Alison Pratt and Beth Cox, 'The Green Lease Handbook: Council of Australian Governments (COAG) National Strategy of Energy Efficiency' (Department of Climate Change and Energy Efficiency 2012) <https://www.energy.gov.au/sites/default/files/green-lease-handbook-2012.pdf> accessed 24 April 2024.
14 See Chapter 1.

22.12 There is ample evidence of the potential importance of improving energy efficiency through green leases. In 2018, the capital value of commercial land in the United Kingdom was over £1 trillion.[15] As of 2017, it was estimated that about one-half of that commercial property was rented.[16] It is clear that leases are fundamental in unlocking the value of land and buildings, because it is trite that not all property owners are able or wish to occupy the land that they invest in or own. A shift in the dynamics of leasing arrangements towards a 'greener' approach could have significant positive consequences for how the majority of occupied buildings are used and operated.

22.13 Much of the commercial land referred to above is built. Buildings are responsible indirectly for 40% of the United Kingdom's carbon emissions and directly for 17% of yearly greenhouse gas emissions.[17] Of the energy consumed in the United Kingdom each year 40% is used to heat and provide power and water to buildings.[18] These statistics relate to commercial property. However, even in the residential context, approximately one-fifth of all dwellings in England were leased as of 2021–2022, albeit some 57% of those dwellings were owner-occupied.[19] These statistics without more demonstrate that there is significant potential for unlocking energy savings by improving efficiency and sustainability and reducing carbon consumption and energy use generally in the context of rented buildings, whether commercial or residential.

(iv) *Features of a green lease*

22.14 In order to appreciate the importance of green leases, it is worthwhile to consider their common features. A fundamental difference between a typical commercial lease and a green lease (defined broadly) is that a green lease is likely to impose a collaborative obligation on both the landlord and tenant, with the purposes of reducing energy use in some way or increasing sustainability. These twin aims essentially reflect the policy underpinnings of net zero and nature positive.

---

15 Values of retail, office, and industrial and other non-residential stock reduced in 2019 and 2020. See Fabrizio Varriale, 'UK Commercial Real Estate Impact Report' (RICS 2022) <https://www.rics.org/content/dam/rics-global/documents/market-surveys/UK_commercial_real_Estate_Impact_Report.pdf> accessed 25 April 2024.

16 'Property Data Report 2017. Facts and Figures about the UK Commercial Property Industry to Year-End 2016' (Property Industry Alliance 2017) <https://bpf.org.uk/media/3278/bpf-pia-property-report-2017-final.pdf> accessed 25 April 2024.

17 Simon Sturgis, 'The RICS Whole Life Carbon Assessment for the Built Environment: How, Why and What Next?' [2020] Construction Journal <https://ww3.rics.org/uk/en/journals/construction-journal/the-rics-whole-life-carbon-assessment-for-the-built-environment-how-why-and-what-next.html> accessed 25 April 2024. This percentage is coincidentally similar to the estimate by the World Economic Forum of the percentage of global carbon emissions which emanate yearly from buildings and infrastructure, totalling 15 gigatonnes. See World Economic Forum and Boston Consulting Group, 'Scaling Low-Carbon Design and Construction with Concrete: Enabling the Path to Net-Zero for Buildings and Infrastructure' (2023) <https://www3.weforum.org/docs/WEF_Scaling_Low_Carbon_Design_and_Construction_with_Concrete_2023.pdf> accessed 25 April 2024; Climate Change Committee, 'The Sixth Carbon Budget: Buildings' <https://www.theccc.org.uk/wp-content/uploads/2020/12/Sector-summary-Buildings.pdf> accessed 25 April 2024.

18 Department for Business, Energy and Industrial Strategy, 'Policy Paper: The Grand Challenge Missions' (GOV.UK, 1 March 2023) <https://www.gov.uk/government/publications/industrial-strategy-the-grand-challenges/missions> accessed 25 April 2024.

19 Department for Levelling Up, Housing and Communities, 'Official Statistics: Leasehold Dwellings, 2021 to 2022' (GOV.UK) <https://www.gov.uk/government/statistics/leasehold-dwellings-2021-to-2022/leasehold-dwellings-2021-to-2022> accessed 25 April 2024.

22.15 A green lease of a building may contain provisions relating to the following matters:

- The calculation, recording and reduction of energy consumption or the use of alternative and sustainable sources of energy and water supply.
- The identification and execution of methods to maintain and improve the environmental performance and sustainability of a building.
- Strategies and plans to reduce or re-utilise waste produced by a building and its occupiers.
- The use of energy-efficient materials and methods for construction, alteration, repair and improvement of a building.

22.16 A key conceptual difficulty mentioned above – and one reason for the comparative absence of sustained interest in green leases – is that leases are not frequently collaborative agreements. It is very unusual for any lease to require genuine collaboration, even where the lease is of premises in a mixed-use development or of part of a building where the owner occupies another part. It is far more common for a lease to provide one party (usually the landlord as the party with the stronger negotiating position) with a power or a veto, or to otherwise severely limit a tenant's freedom to execute alterations or improvements. Furthermore, commercial leases are rarely granted for very long terms in excess of 15 or 20 years. This contrasts with relational contracts in the fields of construction, franchising and distribution, or facilities management, where the contractual relationship between the parties may be more akin to a partnership and may be intended to last for many decades.

22.17 As a consequence, and notwithstanding the availability in most cases of renewal rights, commercial landlords and tenants are rarely focused on the long term in such a way as to foster a cooperative approach to improving energy efficiency or achieving sustainability goals. Both the landlord and tenant may be reluctant to incur the cost of efficiency improvements, given a perceived lack of security or returns, respectively, in a short- or medium-term lease. This means that green provisions relating to installations or alterations, for example, are often not considered at all, or the responsibility for them is at the discretion of a tenant who, without more, may face further costs in removing installations when reinstating premises at the end of the term of its lease. This conservative culture of landlord and tenant relations in the United Kingdom is firmly embedded.

22.18 In principle, however, there is no reason why a longer-term approach cannot be adopted between parties to a lease. Green leases can prove economically advantageous to both landlords and tenants, quite apart from contributing towards net zero. A green lease can help to achieve the following objectives:

- Reduction in energy costs and the realisation of greater costs savings in the medium- to long-term.

- Compliance with the landlord's and tenant's (internal) Corporate Sustainability and Reporting ('CSR') or Environmental, Social, and Governance ('ESG') policies.
- Improvement in the attractiveness and liveability of buildings for occupiers and visitors.
- Elevation of the inherent value of buildings so as to increase their desirability and market value.

22.19 Once these features and benefits of green leases are appreciated, it ought to become clear that green leases may be both commercially viable and beneficial to parties, over and above contributing towards achieving wider national policy objectives.

(v) *Practical considerations*

22.20 The 'lightest' green provisions in some ways are amongst the most important, because they represent the first step along the path to net zero. A landlord who lets a building on a typical FRI lease may have a good understanding of overall energy costs through its collection of contributions towards service charge. However, it may have very little visibility of a tenant's actual use of a building because, to all intents and purposes, it has no direct experience of how its tenant (to whom invariably it will have granted exclusive occupation) is using its building. In the example of office premises, unless a landlord can rely on widely-drafted access provisions, it might never re-enter those offices that it has demised during the subsistence of a lease. It would not know how efficiently a tenant controls heating and hot water services, how many and what types of appliances are used and for how long, or the steps a tenant might be taking to discourage carbon-intensive practices of its employees whilst in the workplace. The exchange of information is therefore key.

22.21 The interplay between green provisions and covenants for alterations, improvements and repair is also potentially important. Careful attention should be paid to whether a landlord and tenant wish to adopt an equitable approach towards the cost of efficiency improvements and a division of resultant savings. There is no obvious answer to the question of whether a landlord or a tenant should foot the bill for energy efficiency improvements or alterations. This is a matter for negotiation. In a typical FRI lease, a tenant may incur significant risk if it seeks to alter or improve in circumstances where a landlord is entitled to insist on reinstatement of the premises upon the termination of the lease. However, this should not be a prohibitive concern. Landlords and tenants typically agree rent-free periods of occupation at the start of a lease when premises are fitted out, for example. That could be an opportune moment to execute improvements to energy efficiency. Responsible tenants will likely recognise the sense in investing in the premises which they have leased, in order to promote a conducive working environment and achieve their own sustainability goals. Savvy landlords may likewise understand and appreciate that lasting energy efficiency improvements to their buildings could produce longer-term benefits through a higher yield.

22.22 Furthermore, not all commitments need to be binding. Parties may consider the extent to which they wish to make green clauses enforceable. Green clauses may be included within a lease itself or in a memorandum or side agreement. Whether or not contained in a lease, it is possible for green clauses to be expressed to be non-binding, such that breach would not result in the typical remedies of forfeiture, specific performance or injunctions, and damages. Whilst binding commitments are more likely to achieve longer-lasting and permanent improvements in the energy use of a building, there is no reason why non-binding commitments cannot be used at the outset. The most significant objection to optional commitments such as these is that they may not provide real impetus for change. However, some progress on this front is desirable and more important in moving the needle than insisting on binding provisions.

(vi) *Statutory considerations and guidance*

22.23 There is at present no direct obligation for a current or prospective landlord or tenant to consider the inclusion of greening provisions in an existing or new lease. This represents a fundamental failure and a missed opportunity. The majority of commercial property in the United Kingdom is leased. The only (indirect) obligations to improve the energy efficiency of existing buildings are contained in the MEES Regulations, (which are considered in more detail below). The lack of incentive or compulsion to include greening provisions in leases is a major reason for inertia.

22.24 At the same time, the introduction of an obligation to consider or adopt greening provisions may be difficult to implement. Landlords and tenants typically are free to agree whatever terms they wish in their lease, subject to compliance with relevant statutory provisions and regulations. Any imposition of greening obligations might be thought to jar against these principles of the freedom of contract.

22.25 Not only is there an absence of statutory obligations, but also the current (non-binding) guidance on green leases is limited. The Royal Institution of Chartered Surveyors ('RICS') Code for leasing business premises ('the 2020 Code')[20] refers to green leases and the consideration of green provisions in relation to management and operational performance. However, and despite the close attention paid by RICS to issues of energy efficiency and sustainability in its other publications, and a stated feature of the 2020 Code being the promotion of 'a less adversarial relationship between occupiers and owners and their advisors', these references are limited. They do very little to move the dial in terms of landlords' and tenants' commitments to considering greening provisions in new or existing leases.

20 RICS, 'Code for Leasing Business Premises. England and Wales. 1st Edition' (2020) para 10.2 <https://www.rics.org/content/dam/ricsglobal/documents/standards/February_2020_Code_For_Leasing_Business_Premises_England_And_Wales_1st_Edition.pdf> accessed 25 April 2024.

22.26 There are other sources of guidance. The Better Buildings Partnership has published a Green Lease Toolkit.[21] This contains best practice recommendations, model clauses for green leases, and memoranda of understanding. It may be noted that, until a very recent update, this toolkit had been last updated in 2013. Such toolkits contain well-drafted, practical precedents which parties may adopt and tailor to their requirements.[22] It is incumbent on those advising commercial parties that are seeking to enter into leases actively to consider the guidance in such toolkits. Similar materials are also published in other jurisdictions, for example by the Building and Construction Authority in Singapore and the California Sustainability Alliance. There is no reason why the principles which underpin this concept in other jurisdictions cannot be adapted to this jurisdiction.

(vii) *Future developments*

22.27 There is and ought to be scope for green leases to become central to the net zero agenda in the context of leased buildings. There are several ways in which the status quo (where uptake of greening provisions remains sluggish) might be addressed.

22.28 First, green leases might be considered more carefully in the context of renewals of business leases. There are limited if any relevant data on what percentage of commercial property that is presently leased is subject to the provisions on renewal comprised within Part II of the Landlord and Tenant Act 1954. It is thought that the majority of commercial property is leased on terms that provide for tenants' rights of renewal, with relatively fewer leases contracted out of the continuation provisions in Part II of the Landlord and Tenant Act 1954. Where commercial property is let on ten- or fifteen-year terms, the opportunities for revisiting covenants outside renewal processes therefore may be limited.

22.29 Even during the renewal process, the legislation and current position in case law simply is not designed to accommodate debates on green provisions.[23] In respect of proposed changes to existing terms when a lease to which Part II of the Landlord and Tenant 1954 Act applies is renewed, proposed changes are required to be fair and reasonable and justified on the grounds of 'essential fairness'.[24] However, the Landlord and Tenant Act 1954 is itself ripe for renewal. The Law Commission is currently reviewing the Act 'with a view to modernising commercial leasehold legislation'.[25] Net zero, together with 'levelling up', is an area on which there is likely to be further emphasis. It

21 'Green Lease Toolkit' (Better Buildings Partnership, 29 January 2024) <https://www.betterbuildingspartnership.co.uk/green-lease-toolkit-0> accessed 25 April 2024.
22 'Reduce Emissions Using the Power of Legal Documents and Processes' (The Chancery Lane Project) <https://chancerylaneproject.org/> accessed 25 April 2024.
23 See *Clipper Logistics plc v Scottish Equitable plc* (Sheffield County Court, 7 March 2022). In this case, the County Court determined that, in the course of modernising the terms of a lease upon renewal, the new lease should not contain various obligations relating to energy efficiency standards, since compliance with those were properly the landlord's obligations.
24 *O'May v City of London Real Property Company Limited* [1983] 2 AC 726; Kirk Reynolds and Wayne Clark, *Renewal of Business Tenancies* (5th edn, Sweet & Maxwell, Thomson Reuters 2017). Both were cited in *Clipper Logistics plc v Scottish Equitable plc* (n 23) para 19.
25 See 'Business Tenancies: The Right to Renew' (Law Commission) <https://lawcom.gov.uk/project/business-tenancies-the-right-to-renew/> accessed 25 April 2024.

remains to be seen to what extent green or levelling up policies bear on the reform of this Act. However, there is every reason for Parliament to ensure that, where a lease is renewed and updated, there is at least some careful consideration of how the terms of the new lease may contain 'greening' provisions.

22.30 Second, exemptions contained within the MEES Regulations (which are considered below), could be removed or gradually phased out, such that green leases are considered a more viable and mainstream option in order to enable landlords to comply with regulatory requirements. These exemptions currently permit landlords to avoid prohibitions on letting private rented property that fails to meet minimum energy efficiency standards in certain circumstances (and therefore avoid potential fines for non-compliance). A detailed consideration of these exemptions is outside the scope of this chapter, but the availability of exemptions reflects a general 'light touch' approach to regulation, whereas a more concerted effort is likely to be required in order to promote the use of green leases.

22.31 Third, there is a real opportunity to raise awareness of green leases and promote their legitimacy through more effective use by the government itself. This is an area where action can be taken without the government being seen to impinge on private law rights. Government departments and agencies such as the Ministry of Defence and Homes England are amongst the largest landowners in the UK. NHS England, which oversees the operation of the National Health Service in England, has produced a green leases framework which builds on the Green Leases toolkit published by the Better Buildings Partnership.[26] If public and local authorities and executive bodies adopted green leasing policies wholesale, then at the very least this would be likely to increase interest in, and engender debate surrounding, how leased property may be more efficiently used and occupied.

(viii) *Conclusion*

22.32 Green leases are not yet a mainstream concept. This is surprising and concerning. The mechanism of a green lease provides one of the most straightforward and effective methods to achieve reductions in energy use and promote efficiency in the operation of the built environment, much of which is leased. It is difficult to see how there can be real and timely progress towards net zero and nature positive in the context of leased buildings without a stronger focus on green leases.

Energy efficiency and the Minimum Energy Efficiency Standard Regulations (MEES Regulations)

(i) *Energy performance: certification*

22.33 The energy efficiency performance of buildings has been a target of national and EU policy over the past two decades. The key reforms which now support efforts

26 See 'Green Leases Framework' (NHS England) <https://www.england.nhs.uk/estates/green-leases-framework/#provisions> accessed 25 April 2024.

to improve the energy efficiency of buildings were initially introduced by the Energy Performance of Buildings (EPB) Directive in 2002 (following the adoption of the Kyoto Protocol).[27] The purpose of the EPB Directive 2002 was to create a framework for the assessment and promotion of energy efficiency in new and existing buildings in the EU.[28] The EPB Directive 2002 was recast in 2010 and 2018, and a further revised EPB Directive will likely soon be adopted.[29] The forthcoming revisions will further step up efforts to achieve net neutrality in the EU by 2050.

22.34 Following the EPB Directive 2002, The Energy Performance of Buildings (Certificates and Inspections) (England and Wales) Regulations 2007 ('the EPC Regulations'), which transposed the EPB Directive 2002, imposed various duties relating to the production, provision, and display of energy certificates for almost all buildings save for those excepted.[30] The EPC Regulations broadly applied to all non-dwellings and residential properties from 1 October 2008.

22.35 The main feature of the EPC Regulations was the creation of energy performance certificates ('EPCs') and display energy certificates ('DECs'). EPCs are certificates that are required to be issued in relation to commercial and residential property following the inspection and assessment of their energy efficiency. An EPC must include, amongst other information, an asset rating for the inspected property. The asset rating is a numerical value of between 1 to 100 (or greater for super-efficient buildings) with a corresponding band (from A – or A+ for non-dwellings – to G). The asset rating is somewhat theoretical, in that a higher number signifies that a property has a higher capacity for energy efficiency, but the rating itself does not take into consideration actual energy use. This means that a property with a comparatively lower asset rating (for example a rating of 68 (assigned the letter D) could outperform a higher-rated property (for example one that is rated 81, assigned the letter B), depending on how efficiently or wastefully that property is occupied. In addition to a rating, an EPC must contain narrative recommendations on how the energy efficiency of that property may be improved together with the anticipated effect of such improvements.

22.36 EPCs are required to be produced when properties are built, sold, or let. If a valid EPC has already been obtained within the past 10 years for that property, this EPC may be provided, such that there is no obligation to obtain a new EPC. EPCs are now a standard feature in almost all property transactions.

22.37 Duties in relation to DECs apply to larger buildings. They initially applied to premises with a floor area of more than 1,000 square metres that were occupied by public authorities, before duties relating to DECs were extended to public buildings with an area of 250 square metres or more and which are frequently visited by members of the public. DECs must be displayed prominently and show the actual energy

27 Council Directive 2002/91/EC of 16 December 2022 on the energy performance of buldings OJ L1/65.
28 ibid art 1.
29 Council Directive 2018/844/EU amending Directive 2010/31/EU on the energy performance of buildings and Directive 2012/27/EU on energy efficiency OJ L156/75. COM/2021/802, yet to be formally adopted.
30 The Energy Performance of Buildings (Certificates and Inspections) (England and Wales) Regulations 2007 s 4; The Energy Performance of Buildings (England and Wales) Regulations 2012.

consumption of a building over at least the preceding 12 months. There is no obligation yet for commercial (non-publicly occupied) premises to display DECs.

22.38 The introduction of EPCs (and to a lesser extent DECs) can be seen as largely facilitative. Whilst the EPC Regulations, both when promulgated in 2007 and later when consolidated in 2012, imposed sanctions for breach of the duties to obtain, provide, and where appropriate display certificates, they did not by themselves introduce new standards or oblige property owners to increase the energy efficiency of buildings. The recommendations which accompany EPCs and DECs remain non-binding only. However, through the adoption of the MEES Regulations, the government has begun to take steps to build on EPCs and require the improvement of the energy efficiency of rented property.

(ii) *The MEES Regulations*

22.39 The Energy Efficiency (Private Rented Property) (England and Wales) Regulations 2015 ('MEES Regulations')[31] were promulgated under the Energy Act 2011.[32]

22.40 The purpose of the MEES Regulations is to improve the energy efficiency of rented residential and commercial property by:

- introducing a minimum energy efficiency standard ('MEES');
- incentivising energy efficiency improvements (formerly, but no longer, through the Green Deal);[33] and
- applying sanctions for non-compliance.

22.41 The MEES Regulations represent the current most significant effort by the UK government to improve the energy efficiency of rented property.[34] However, matters of concern are the current absence of any direct, time-limited obligation to take further steps to improve energy efficiency, the lack of interest in and subsequent defunding of the Green Deal Finance Company – which operated the Green Deal Scheme and the Green Deal Home Improvement Fund – and a recent pronouncement by the UK government which suggests that further increases in minimum standards which were envisaged by the MEES Regulation are unlikely to be imposed in the near future.[35] They seriously jeopardise the policy objective of net zero, in light of the importance of improving the energy efficiency and sustainability of the United Kingdom's built environment. Whilst politically there is still conversation about a Green New Deal or New Green Deal, this is not in the context of property matters and energy efficiency, on which policy and action appears to have stalled.

---

31 The Energy Efficiency (Private Rented Property) (England and Wales) Regulations 2015.
32 Energy Act 2023 ch 2.
33 Previously known as the Green Deal Energy Efficiency Scheme.
34 See also paras 21.14–21.26 in Chapter 21 in respect of legislation and policy on heat networks and the Energy Savings Opportunity Scheme.
35 PM Rishi Sunak, 'PM Speech on Net Zero: 20 September 2023' (20 September 2023) <https://www.gov.uk/government/speeches/pm-speech-on-net-zero-20-september-2023> accessed 25 April 2024.

(iii) *Background*

22.42 Prior to the Energy Act 2011 ('EA 2011'), there was very little legislation in the United Kingdom on the issue of the energy efficiency of existing buildings.[36] The only significant measures in the period prior to EA 2011 were focused on energy efficiency in the context of the publication and production of energy performance certificates.[37]

22.43 The Climate Change Act 2008 ('CCA 2008') provided the impetus for further legislative action. Following CCA 2008, the EA 2011 implemented recommendations from the Annual Energy Statement and the Carbon Plan. The principal purposes of the EA 2011 were to:

- improve energy efficiency;
- enhance energy security; and
- make provision for energy infrastructure.

(iv) *The structure of the MEES Regulations*

22.44 The relevant sections of the EA 2011 concerning rented property are contained in Chapter 2 of Part 1. These apply to England and Wales. Chapter 3 of Part I applies equivalent provisions to the private rented sector in Scotland.

22.45 Chapter 2 of Part 1 defines 'domestic private rented property' (hereafter domestic PR property) and 'non-domestic private rented property' (hereafter commercial PR property) (section 42). Sections 43 and 49 respectively impose an obligation on the Secretary of State to make regulations to secure that a landlord of residential PR property and commercial PR property 'may not let the property' until the landlord has complied with various obligations as set out in those sections. The intended effect of these provisions is to prevent a landlord from letting out (or continuing to let out) property where its energy efficiency (as demonstrated by a relevant EPC) falls below a prescribed minimum level.

22.46 The MEES Regulations were made under the EA 2011. The substantive elements of the MEES Regulations deal with:

- tenants' energy efficiency improvements (Part 2); and
- MEES, sanctions, and enforcement (Part 3).

36 Planning and Energy Act 2008 s 1(c) introduced the concept of 'energy efficiency standards' (defined in s 1(2)) in relation to building development.
37 See Council Directive 2002/91/EC of 16 December 2022 on the energy performance of buldings OJ L1/65; The Energy Performance of Buildings (Certificates and Inspections) (England and Wales) Regulations 2007.

22.47 Parts 1 and 2 of the MEES Regulations came into force on 1 April 2016.[38] Part 3 came into force on 1 April 2017 in relation to commercial PR property and on 1 October 2017 in relation to domestic PR property.[39]

(a) Part 2 of the MEES Regulations

22.48 Part 2 of the MEES Regulations provides a right for tenants of domestic PR property to seek consent from their landlord to execute particular energy efficiency improvement works to their rented properties. Property is outside the definition of domestic PR property if it is, or forms part of, a building which is excluded by provisions in the Energy Performance of Buildings Regulations.[40] These exclusions relate to temporary buildings with a time of use of two years or less and buildings which were demonstrably suitable for demolition and redevelopment.

22.49 Under Part 2 of the MEES Regulations, a tenant of domestic PR property is entitled to serve a notice requesting the landlord's consent to the making of one or more relevant energy efficiency improvements to the domestic PR property let to it. The MEES Regulations prescribes the information required by any written notice.[41] In particular, a tenant is obliged to provide copies of any reports setting out recommended improvements and evidence of funding. A tenant is not entitled to make a request in certain circumstances. These include where it or the landlord has served a notice to terminate the tenancy or it has notified the landlord that it would vacate the property let at the expiry of the term, or possession proceedings are on foot.[42]

22.50 Energy efficiency improvement is defined broadly as:[43]

- a measure for improving efficiency in the use of energy in the property; or
- where indicated, a measure installed for the purposes of enabling the supply of gas through a service pipe to the property in any case where the property—
  - is not fuelled by mains gas; and
  - is situated within 23 metres from a relevant main of a gas transporter.

22.51 The MEES Regulations entitle a tenant to apply to the First-tier Tribunal (Property Chamber) if, following its written request, the landlord does not engage properly or at all as required by regulation 12.

(b) Part 3 of the MEES Regulations

22.52 Part 3 of the MEES Regulations prohibited a landlord from letting out property that fell below an 'E' rating unless it first made energy efficiency improvements or

38 reg 1(2).
39 reg 1(2)–(3).
40 regs 5, 8.
41 reg 8(2).
42 reg 9.
43 The Energy Efficiency (Private Rented Property) (England and Wales) Regulations 2015, reg 2(1).

availed itself of an exemption. The MEES Regulations were amended by The Energy Efficiency (Private Rented Property) (England and Wales) (Amendment) Regulations 2019, with effect from 1 April 2019 (the MEES Regulations as amended).[44]

22.53 The three key dates for implementation of the MEES Regulations were:

- By 1 April 2018, the MEES Regulations applied only upon the grant of a new tenancy to a tenant of residential PR property or commercial PR property. Tenancies that had already been granted before that date were not affected.

- From 1 April 2020, the MEES Regulations applied to all residential PR property, whether or not the property was already let or occupied.

- From 1 April 2023, the MEES Regulations applied to all commercial PR property, whether or not the property was already let or occupied.

22.54 It remains to be seen whether the professed long-term target of increasing MEES to EPC rating 'B' by 2030 will be implemented. The MEES Regulations remain in their relative infancy and only target leasehold property. There is considerable scope for not only the extension of the MEES Regulations but also their reframing, to impose stronger commitments on landlords and owner-occupiers to increase the efficiency of existing stock.

(v) *Green Deal*

22.55 The Green Deal was a policy initiative of the UK coalition government from 2010. The intention behind the policy was to bring about increases in the energy efficiency of buildings by subsidising the initial cost of certain energy efficiency improvements. It was envisaged that the cost of those improvements would be financed at the outset by private, unsecured funding supported by the United Kingdom government. Those costs would then be recouped over time through charges applied to occupiers of improved properties through their electricity bills. Chapter 1 of Part 1 of the EA 2011 implemented the Green Deal. Those provisions were brought into force in 2012–2013.[45]

22.56 The Green Deal was underpinned by the Golden Rule. This provided that the increased charges applied to the electricity bills of improved properties would be no greater than the sums saved by the improvements.

22.57 There were 46 different types of energy efficiency improvements which were specified under the Green Deal.[46] These included the following broad areas:

---

44 The Energy Efficiency (Private Rented Property) (England and Wales) (Amendment) Regulations 2019.
45 The Energy Act 2011 (Commencement No 1 and Saving) Order 2012; The Energy Act 2011 (Commencement No 2) Order 2013.
46 The Green Deal (Qualifying Energy Improvements) Order 2012 Article 3 and para 1(a)–(ss) of the Schedule, as amended by The Green Deal (Qualifying Energy Improvements) (Amendment) Order 2014.

- Insulation;
- Heating and hot water systems;
- Heat pumps, biomass and condensing boilers, and solar panels;
- Double glazing and draught-proofing.

22.58 The Green Deal Regulations provided for assessment by qualified energy assessors, who were tasked with providing recommendations for energy efficiency improvements. In order to take advantage, the occupier or homeowner was thereafter required to enter into a Green Deal plan. In order to foster greater interest in the Green Deal, the government provided for a cashback scheme and a Green Deal Home Improvement Fund.

22.59 The Green Deal Finance Company was a consortium which made funding available for Green Deal energy efficiency improvements. The government ceased funding the GDFC by way of loans in 2015. Only around 10,000 households took up financing under the Green Deal, and only about £100 million was loaned. The Green Deal did not extend to commercial property, despite this having been the original intention of the policy.

22.60 The Green Deal has been effectively abolished. Whilst it is still possible for a building owner to seek finance for energy efficiency improvements, the incentives to do so are much reduced in circumstances where there is no subsidisation of initial costs. The Green Deal has not been replaced with any alternative scheme.

(vi) *Future developments*

22.61 It remains uncertain whether and when the government will further increase MEES or begin to tighten the exemptions presently available to landlords. The current situation is marked by stasis, since the upward trend in MEES remains stalled without further developments in sight.

22.62 In 2021, the government proposed a timeline for the continued increase in MEES in order to satisfy the net zero target. The timeline envisaged that, by 1 April 2027, all non-domestic rented properties would be required to have a minimum EPC rating of C or be registered as exempt, and by 1 April 2030 all non-domestic rented properties would be required to be B-rated or registered as exempt.

22.63 Subsequently, on 20 September 2023, the Prime Minister of the United Kingdom confirmed that the 'plans [to increase MEES by 1 April 2025] will be scrapped'.[47]

47 PM Rishi Sunak (n 35).

22.64 There are no current plans to change MEES. The Green Deal has not been reformed or replaced. The future pathway towards higher MEES remains uncertain.

22.65 Progress towards increasing the energy efficiency of housing stock generally remains slow. The MEES Regulations affect *rented* property but not owner-occupied or vacant buildings. According to the Office for National Statistics, of all homes with an EPC, around 8 million homes in England (58% of the total) and 460,000 homes in Wales (62% of the total) were rated *below* band C.[48] Band D is the median energy efficiency rating of dwellings in England and Wales.[49] Around 40% of properties in England and Wales (more than 11 million) did not have an EPC as of 2021, so there are no comparable data on the energy efficiency of these dwellings.[50] Until there are more onerous or intrusive obligations to obtain an EPC or undertake energy efficiency measures, particularly in relation to freehold property that is not subject to the MEES regime, the efficiency of these properties will remain an unknown quantity.

22.66 The position in the United Kingdom contrasts with the ongoing efforts being made in the European Union. The recently revised EPB Directive and Energy Efficiency Directive 2023/1791 seek to '[put] Europe on track to achieve a fully decarbonised building stock by 2050'.[51] The EPB Directive as revised will mandate all new buildings to be emission-free from 2028. Residential buildings will be required to have a minimum efficiency rating of E by 2030 and D by 2033. There is a real danger that the lack of progress currently being made in the UK will lead to heavier burdens on landowners and tenants as the UK seeks to catch up as it must over the next decade.

Retrofitting leasehold properties and repurposing[52]

22.67 Retrofitting and repurposing are strategies which can successfully rejuvenate existing buildings through renewal and adaptation, in order to reduce energy consumption and achieve decarbonisation.[53]

22.68 In practical terms, these strategies involve the re-use and recycling of materials, and the re-utilisation of existing buildings, in a manner that is more advantageous and efficient than demolition and rebuilding. Retrofitting is a wide umbrella term. It is apt to include insulation, and the replacement of inefficient installations with new low-carbon or renewable technologies and energy systems. Repurposing refers to the

48 'Who Is Most Likely to Live in Homes That Are Harder to Keep Warm?' (Office for National Statistics, 14 December 2023) <https://www.ons.gov.uk/peoplepopulationandcommunity/housing/articles/whoismostlikelytoliveinhomesthatarehardertokeepwarm/2023-12-14> accessed 25 April 2024.
49 'Energy Efficiency of Housing in England and Wales; 2023' (Office for National Statistics, 11 January 2024) <https://www.ons.gov.uk/peoplepopulationandcommunity/housing/articles/energyefficiencyofhousinginenglandandwales/2023> accessed 25 April 2024.
50 'Who Is Most Likely to Live in Homes That Are Harder to Keep Warm?' (n 49).
51 European Commission, 'Questions and Answers on the Revised Energy Performance of Buildings Directive (EPBD)' <https://ec.europa.eu/commission/presscorner/api/files/document/print/en/qanda_24_1966/QANDA_24_1966_EN.pdf> accessed 15 May 2024.
52 See Chapter 38 on the legal framework for retrofitting.
53 See Robert Brazier, 'What a Retrofit-First Approach Offers the UK' [2024] RICS Property Journal <https://ww3.rics.org/uk/en/journals/property-journal/retrofit-first-approach.html> accessed 25 April 2024.

adaptation of buildings to suit different purposes in order to maximise efficient use and avoid unnecessarily mothballing or the uneconomic effects of long-term vacancy.

22.69 Retrofitting and repurposing are important concepts in the net zero discourse. The UK Green Building Council estimates that 80% of the buildings that will be standing in the United Kingdom in the year 2050 have already been built.[54] New buildings that are built to exceptionally high energy standards and optimised for efficient occupation may be eye-catching and important in demonstrating the possibilities of new technologies. But the manner in which existing stock is improved and re-tooled is likely to achieve greater gains in the short- and medium-term.

22.70 Other trends also point towards the need for retrofitting and repurposing. The rate of housebuilding in the United Kingdom is low. It is both limited by the scarcity of land that is available for development and also subject to the vicissitudes of the economy and policy aims of the government of the day. The energy requirements to demolish and rebuild a building are necessarily greater than the effort required to unlock efficiency savings in existing buildings. Coupled with this, there is uncertainty as to the future of the 'zero carbon' policy, which was introduced by the UK government in 2006.[55] The aim of that policy was to require that all new homes built from 2016, and all new commercial buildings from 2019, would be net zero in their operation. That policy was subsequently abandoned and has never been replaced in terms. In residential property, as of March 2023, in England and Wales, 'the median estimated CO_2 emissions for existing dwellings were more than double the estimated emissions of new dwellings'.[56] Retrofitting existing stock is therefore a method of improving energy efficiency more swiftly, and at lower expense when compared with waiting for buildings to reach the end of their lifecycles before being demolished and rebuilt – which themselves are potentially highly carbon-intensive activities.

22.71 However, retrofitting in particular is problematic in relation to leasehold property. There are several reasons for this. First, a tenant with an FRI lease is typically required to maintain and repair, not repurpose or improve, the buildings or land which they lease. At the outset, therefore, the first stumbling block will be that, however well-intentioned a tenant may be, there is no right to carry out improvements which alter the fabric of or installations within the building.

22.72 Second, leases hitherto granted are extremely unlikely to acknowledge the concepts of retrofitting and repurposing. A lease will commonly require a tenant to use the property leased for permitted purposes or for whatever lawful purposes they may be appropriate, but it would be highly unusual for a standard (non-development) lease

54 'Non-Domestic Retrofit: Retail and Logistics Project Task Group' (UKGBC) <https://ukgbc.org/get-involved/non-domestic-retrofit-retail-and-logistics-project-task-group/> accessed 25 April 2024; Government Property Function, 'Net Zero Estate Playbook. A Guide to Decarbonising Government Property. Version 1.0' (2021) 5 <https://assets.publishing.service.gov.uk/media/619cfd62e90e070441bcf731/Net_Zero_Estate_Playbook__1_.pdf> accessed 25 April 2024.
55 Matt Weaver, 'Brown Pledges to Build 'Zero Carbon' Homes' *The Guardian* (6 December 2006) <https://www.theguardian.com/environment/2006/dec/06/politics.greenpolitics> accessed 25 April 2024.
56 'Energy Efficiency of Housing in England and Wales; 2023' (n 49) fig 8.

to make provision for the regeneration of premises. The lease will therefore be silent on where the cost burden of retrofitting and repurposing falls. The default outcome in such a case where improvements are permitted is that it is for the tenant to pay for them, without any obligation on a landlord or other tenants of the same building to contribute towards the cost through payments towards service charge or otherwise.

22.73 Third, and connected with these issues, there may be a reduced incentive for a tenant to execute energy efficiency works on account of cost. On a pure cost–benefit analysis, there may be limited reasons for a tenant to effect improvements at its own cost when it may not take advantage of any returns during the currency of (or until the termination of) its lease.

22.74 Some of these issues may be resolved by the adoption of greening provisions in new and existing leases by variation (see paragraph 22.29 above). It may also be that further innovation is required in how landlords and tenants consider and deal with their obligations. The Green Deal, discussed above (see paragraphs 22.55–22.60 above), included a mechanism by which costs savings would be passed on to residential occupiers through credits against their electricity bills. The creation of a similar fund in relation to leasehold property, through which a tenant may be compensated for the initial outlay on retrofitting works in the event of a disposal or termination of the lease could help to promote retrofitting.

22.75 Retrofitting and repurposing of course are not the sole strategies for optimising energy efficiency. Much can also be done by inspecting and repairing existing systems to identify leaks, faults, and other defects which result in inefficiency, and increasing awareness generally of the benefits of reducing energy consumption. A renewed focus on increasing MEES combined with a 'retrofit-first' approach would be much more likely to achieve carbon reductions and net zero goals.

Conclusion

22.76 In recent years, there has been little progress in establishing a successful, progressive approach towards sustainability in the use of privately rented and existing buildings. This lag is largely due to uneven and incompletely executed or stunted policies, as well as a lack of awareness and debate.

22.77 Considerable potential improvements and energy efficiency gains may be unlocked in the way that existing buildings are used, occupied, and altered or improved. However, without more concerted efforts to promote green leases and tighten energy efficiency requirements, the sustainability potential for existing buildings is likely to remain largely untapped.

CHAPTER 23

CONSERVATION COVENANTS

Rebecca Cattermole

Introduction

23.01 Conservation covenants were introduced by Part 7 of the Environment Act 2021 ('EA 2021').[1] They are agreements between a landowner and a responsible body containing positive and/or restrictive obligations on land for a conservation purpose and intended to be for the public good. It only applies to land in England.[2] The environment is not a reserved matter and thus a devolved power of the National Assembly for Wales.[3]

23.02 Whereas conservation obligations can be entered into as personal agreements between parties to a contract, such contracts fail to bind future owners owing to the law of freehold covenants. Further, freehold restrictive covenants cannot bind the burdened land unless there is neighbouring land which benefits from it. There has been limited circumnavigation of the general rule: for example, by the National Trust Act 1937 and the Forestry Act; use of section 106 agreements in the planning context;[4] and legally complex solutions, such as transferring freehold land to a conservation organisation with a leaseback to the landowner.[5]

23.03 In several other jurisdictions the law has created an exception for covenants which are intended to help conservation such as Scotland, the USA, Canada, Australia and New Zealand.[6] Many of these places also have the traditional rules about covenants which exist in England and Wales (unsurprising given they derived from English common law).

Historical context

23.04 The Law Commission was asked to investigate whether there was a case for introducing conservation covenants into the law of England and Wales and, if so, what

1 Environment Act 2021, Pt 7, s 117–139, Sch 18. These provisions came into force on 30 September 2022 (Environment Act 2021 (Commencement No.2 and Saving Provision) Regulations 2022, SI 2022/48.
2 See s 117(2)(a). Environment Act 2021, Sch 19 makes provision about the application of Pt 7 to Crown land.
3 Government of Wales Act 2006 as amended by the Wales Act 2017.
4 The National Trust Act 1937 and the Forestry Act 1967 can only restrict the landowner's activities. Whereas these statutory provisions avoid the need to have neighbouring land benefitting from the restriction in order for the covenant to be binding on successors, it cannot create positive obligations.
5 e.g. transferring freehold land to a conservation organisation with a leaseback to the landowner; a third party taking the benefit of covenants contained in the original contract under the Contracts (Rights of Third Parties) Act 1999; or a chain of covenants.
6 See Christopher Rodgers and David Grinlinton, 'Covenanting for Nature: A Comparative Study of the Utility and Potential of Conservation Covenants' (2020) 83 The Modern Law Review 373.

elements might be needed in a new statutory scheme. The Consultation Paper was published on 28 March 2013.[7]

23.05 The final report was published on 24 June 2014 and recommended introducing a new statutory scheme of conservation covenants in England and Wales. The Law Commission Report included a draft Conservation Covenants Bill.

23.06 On 23 June 2016, the United Kingdom voted to leave the European Union; and in a speech the following year, the Secretary of State, Rt Hon Michael Gove MP, stated that 'in this unfrozen moment new possibilities occur'.[8] DEFRA published its 25-Year Environment Plan in January 2018, 'A Green Future: Our 25 year Plan to Improve the Environment report'.[9] It pledged: 'Working with landowners, conservation groups and other stakeholders we will review and take forward the Law Commission's proposals for a statutory scheme of conservation covenants in England.'[10]

Conservation covenant agreement

23.07 A conservation covenant 'is so much of a conservation covenant agreement as is given statutory effect'.[11] Accordingly, it is necessary to consider in the first instance the meaning of conservation covenant agreement.

23.08 A conservation covenant agreement is an agreement between a landowner[12] and a responsible body[13] which satisfies the following conditions:[14]

- The agreement contains provision which:
  - is of a qualifying kind;
  - has a conservation purpose;
  - is intended to be for the public good;
- It appears from the agreement that the parties intend to create a conservation covenant;[15]
- The agreement is executed as a deed by the parties.

---

7 Law Commission, *Conservation Covenants: A Consultation Paper* (CP 211, 2013).
8 Gove, 'The Unfrozen Moment – Delivering A Green Brexit' (Speech at WWF Living Planet Centre Woking, 21 July 2017) at <https://www.gov.uk/government/speeches/the-unfrozen-moment-delivering-a-green-brexit> accessed 1 April 2024.
9 United Kingdom Government, 'A Green Future: Our 25 Year Plan to Improve the Environment' (2018).
10 ibid.
11 EA 2021 s 118(1).
12 See paras 23.20–23.22 below for meaning of landowner.
13 See paras 23.12–23.14 below for meaning of responsible body.
14 EA 2021 117(1).
15 Note that it is not that the parties intend to create a conservation covenant but that it *appears* that is the intention. Quaere whether this is to avoid difficulties with agreements which may not expressly state that this is a conservation covenant.

(i) *Provision 'of a qualifying kind'*

23.09 The provision of a qualifying kind is one which:[16]

- requires the landowner to do or not to do something on specified land in respect of which the landowner holds a specified qualifying estate; or
- allows the responsible body to do something on such land; or
- requires the responsible body to do something on such land.

(ii) *Conservation purpose*

23.10 There are three categories of conservation purpose:[17]

- First, to conserve the land itself, that is, the natural environment[18] of land or natural resources of land;[19]
- Secondly, to conserve the value of the land, namely as a place of archaeological, architectural, artistic, cultural or historic interest;[20] or
- Thirdly, to conserve the setting of the land (natural environment or natural resources or which is a place of archaeological, artistic, cultural or historic interest).[21]

Conservation covenant

23.11 The provisions in the conservation agreement which take effect as a conservation covenant are those of the qualifying kind which have a conservation purpose and are intended to be for the public good and those which are ancillary to them.[22] Where the agreement includes public access,[23] it will be treated as ancillary.

Responsible body

23.12 A responsible body may be either the Secretary of State or a body designated by the Secretary of State.[24]

---

16 EA 2021 s 117(2).
17 EA 2021 s 117(3).
18 That is, its plants, animals and other living organisms and their habitats, and the land's geographical features (EA 2021 s 117(4)).
19 EA 2021 s 117(3)(a).
20 ibid s 117(3)(b).
21 ibid s 117(3)(c).
22 ibid s 118(2).
23 The public access provision must relate to another provision in the agreement which falls within s 118(2)(a) (i.e. meets the conditions in s 117(1)(a)).
24 EA 2021 s 119(1).

(i) *Designation of responsible body*

23.13 A body may apply to be designated, but the Secretary of State must be satisfied that it is suitable to be a responsible body.[25] Where the body is not a local authority,[26] in addition to suitability, the Secretary of State must also be satisfied that, in the case of a public body or charity,[27] that some of its main purposes or functions relate to conservation, and in other cases, at least some of its body's main activities relate to conservation.

23.14 The Secretary of State may determine the criteria to be applied in deciding whether a body is suitable to be, or to remain, a responsible body and must publish a document setting out the criteria and a list of designated bodies.[28] The government guidance published sets out the criteria for becoming and remaining a responsible body under eligibility, financial security, operational capacity and capability, and ongoing suitability.[29]

(ii) *Annual return*

23.15 The responsible body is under a duty to complete an annual return to the Secretary of State stating whether there were any conservation covenants under which an obligation was owed to it, and to provide certain details.[30]

(iii) *Revocation*

23.16 A designation as a responsible body may be revoked by the Secretary of State.[31] This is achieved by serving notice of revocation on the responsible body if:[32]

- The body has applied to the Secretary of State for its revocation;
- The Secretary of State is satisfied that it is not suitable to remain a responsible body; or
- The Secretary of State is satisfied that in the case of a public body or charity, it does not meet the condition that some of its main purposes or functions do not relate to conservation, and in other cases, at least some of its body's main activities relate to conservation.[33]

---

25 ibid s 119(2–3).
26 i.e. a county or district council, a London Borough Council, the Common Council of the City of London; the Council of the Isles of Scilly: EA 2021 s 119(9).
27 A charity registered under the Charities Act 2011 or an exempt charity within the meaning of the Charities Act 2011: EA 2021 s 119(9).
28 EA 2021 s 119(8). The criteria may be found at https://www.gov.uk/government/publications/conservation-covenants-apply-to-become-a-responsible-body.
29 DEFRA, 'Getting and Using a Conservation Covenant Agreement' (GOV.UK, 6 February 2024) <https://www.gov.uk/guidance/getting-and-using-a-conservation-covenant-agreement> accessed 1 April 2024.
30 EA 2021 s 136. The Secretary of State may make provision about annual returns under EA s 136(4).
31 ibid s 119(6).
32 ibid.
33 i.e. the conditions in EA 2021 s 119(5).

(iv) *Replacement*

23.17 A responsible body has a power to appoint its replacement unless the covenant otherwise provides,[34] exercisable by agreement executed as a deed.[35] The appointment has the effect of transferring the benefit of every obligation of the landowner and the burden of every obligation of the responsible body under the conservation covenant[36] but it does not transfer any right or liability in respect of an existing breach.[37] The new responsible body must notify the appointment to every landowner who is bound by an obligation under the covenant.[38]

(v) *Body ceasing to be a designated body*

23.18 If a body under a conservation covenant is no longer a designated body, it ceases to be the responsible body under the conservation covenant and the benefit and burden transfer to the Secretary of State as custodian.[39] Importantly, no right or liability in respect of an existing breach is transferred,[40] nor does the Secretary of State have any liability for performance of any obligation of the responsible body during any period in which it is custodian.[41]

(vi) *Acquisition and disposal of land by responsible body*

23.19 If the responsible body acquires an estate in land to which an obligation under a covenant relates (whether that is of the landowner or the responsible body), it does not extinguish the obligation and binds as successor of the landowner and as responsible body.[42]

Landowner and qualifying estate

23.20 'Landowner' is not defined. By a somewhat convoluted route of the provisions in the EA 2021, however, a landowner may be a freehold owner or certain qualifying tenants:

- Section 117(1)(a) states that a conservation covenant agreement is an agreement where, *inter alia,* it contains 'provision which – (i) is of a qualifying kind'

34 EA 2021 s 131(1).
35 EA 2021 s 131(2). Note that it only has effect when the appointor responsible body supplies the information to enable amendment of the local land charges register: EA 2021 s 131(3–4).
36 ibid 2021 s131(5).
37 ibid 2021 s131(6).
38 ibid 2021 s131(7).
39 EA 2021 s 132(1–2). The Secretary of State is custodian until an appointment of the replacement responsible body, or election, by the Secretary of State: EA 2021 s 131(5) and (6). The Secretary of State may enforce any obligation or exercise any power of the responsible body under the conservation covenant during the period of custodianship: EA 2021 s131(7).
40 ibid s 132(4).
41 ibid s 132(8).
42 ibid s 133.

- 'Provision of a qualifying kind' means a provision, *inter alia*, '(a) requiring the landowner (i) to do, or not to do, something on land in England specified in the provision in relation to which the landowner holds a qualifying estate specified in the agreement for the purposes of the provision' (s 117(2))

- Section 117(4) defines qualifying estate as:

  (a) an estate in fee simple absolute in possession, or
  (b) a term of years absolute granted for a term of more than seven years from the date of the grant and in the case of which some part of the period for which the term of years was granted remains unexpired; ...

23.21 Therefore, the landowner may either be the freehold owner or a tenant of a tenancy of a fixed term of more than seven years from the date of grant *and* some period of that term remains unexpired. It will not apply to periodic tenancies.[43]

23.22 The following tenants, for example, will not hold a qualifying estate to be a landowner:

- a tenant under a farm business tenancy of a fixed term of less than seven years;

- a tenant under a farm business tenancy which has expired and has continued as a periodic tenancy under section 5(1) of the Agricultural Tenancies Act 1995;[44]

- a tenant under a periodic tenancy governed by the Agricultural Holdings Act 1986.

Duration of obligation under conservation covenant

23.23 A conservation covenant itself may specify the duration of the obligations contained therein.[45] Any obligation, however, has effect for the default period unless the covenant provides for a shorter period.[46] Therefore, where the covenant provides for a longer period than the default period, the default period will apply.

23.24 The default period depends on the nature of the qualifying estate.

23.25 If the qualifying estate in relation to the obligation is freehold, the default period is a period of indefinite duration.[47] This will be useful where the conservation covenant needs to be sufficiently long enough for the purposes of a particular scheme.

---

43 See, however, the successor provisions at paras 23.28ff below which, in general terms, have the effect of binding periodic tenancies granted after the person who qualified as landowner entered into the conservation covenant.
44 'A farm business tenancy for a term of more than two years shall, instead of terminating on the term date, continue as from that date as a tenancy from year to year but otherwise on the terms of the original tenancy so far as applicable…' Agricultural Tenancies Act 1995 s 5(1). The 'term date' means the date fixed for the expiry of the term (s 5(2) ATA 1995).
45 Environment Act 2021 s 121(1).
46 ibid.
47 ibid s 121(2).

Nonetheless, a conservation covenant of an indefinite length might be less palatable to a freehold landowner. It also calls into question the impact of a conservation covenant of indefinite length on the value of the land.

23.26 Where the qualifying estate is a tenancy, the default period is a period corresponding in length to the remaining period left before expiry of the fixed term.[48] It will not be possible for the conservation covenant to impose a period which exceeds the remaining part of the fixed term of the tenancy. But it seems that where a conservation covenant does impose a longer length, the covenant itself will still be effective for the default period (that is, it does not void the covenant).[49]

23.27 A landlord and tenant may increase the length of the term of a tenancy by agreement which will take effect as a surrender and re-grant of the tenancy by operation of law.[50] Section 134 of the Environment Act 2021 provides that where a tenancy which is the qualifying estate is deemed to be surrendered and regranted by operation of law, in the application of sections 122 (benefit and burden of landowner), 123 (benefit of an obligation of a responsible body) and 127 (discharge of obligation) to the period after the deemed surrender, references to the qualifying estate are to be read as including a reference to the term of years deemed to be granted. Section 121 of the Environment Act 2021, dealing with the default duration of the covenant, is not specified.[51] It seems that the effect of this is that whilst the default period cannot be extended by a deemed surrender and regrant where the original covenanting party is concerned, in the case of a successor, a surrender and regrant of the tenancy would extend the duration of the covenant.

Benefit and burden of obligation of landowner

23.28 Generally, freehold covenants will not bind successors because positive covenants do not run with the land; and restrictive covenants require the benefitting party to have an interest in neighbouring land that will benefit from the covenant.[52]

23.29 Section 122 of the Environment Act 2021 provides a further statutory exception to address the difficulties of the general law regarding freehold covenants and secures that the benefit and burden of the obligation of landowner binds successive owners.[53]

---

48 ibid s 121(2)(b).
49 ibid s 121.
50 *Well Barn Farming v Backhouse* [2005] 3 EGLR 109.
51 In the application of ss 122, 123 and 127 to the period after the deemed surrender, references to the qualifying estate are to be read as including a reference to the term of years deemed to be granted. But there is no equivalent provision under s 121.
52 There are certain statutory exceptions. For example, National Trust Act 1937 s 8 although this is limited to restrictive covenants; and Town and County Planning Act 1990 s 106 which enables both positive and negative obligations to bind successors in title without the need for neighbouring land to be benefitted.
53 Leases can include positive and restrictive covenants but the concept of transferring the freehold to a charity and the lease being granted to the former freehold owner is obviously unattractive to most landowners.

(i) *Circumstances where an obligation will be binding on a successor*

23.30 An obligation of the landowner under a conservation covenant is owed to the responsible body[54] and binds the landowner under the covenant and any person who becomes a successor of the landowner under the covenant.[55]

23.31 The binding of the covenant on the successor requires more explanation. The successor means:

> a person who holds, in respect of any of the land to which the obligation relates- (a) the qualifying estate; or (b) an estate in land derived (whether immediately or otherwise) from the qualifying estate[56] after the creation of the covenant.[57]

23.32 A conservation covenant will bind any successors of the original covenantor, that is, anyone who acquires the original covenantor's estate in any of the land to which the obligation under the conservation covenant relates.[58] The reference to 'any' has the effect of applying where only part of the land is sold.

23.33 The holder of an estate in land derived from the qualifying estate after the creation of the covenant will also be a successor.[59] This will also apply to part of the land to which the obligation relates.[60] Thus, for example, where a periodic tenancy of the whole or part of the land is granted after the covenant was entered into, that tenant is 'a successor' and will be bound by the covenant.

(ii) *Circumstances where an obligation will not bind a successor*

23.34 There are exceptions to the rule that a successor who holds an estate in land derived from the qualifying estate will be bound by an obligation contained in the covenant.[61] They are as follows:

23.35 A successor tenant will not be bound by a positive obligation.[62] Accordingly, where a freeholder creates a conservation covenant which is registered as a local land charge and then grants a periodic tenancy, the lessee will be bound by negative obligations in the conservation covenant but not by positive ones. The same result follows where a tenancy of a fixed term of more than seven years is granted after the creation of a conservation covenant, or where a conservation covenant is created by a tenant under a tenancy of a term of seven years or more who then sub-lets the land. It is important to note that the positive obligations, and any related ancillary obligations will, however, continue to be binding on the landlord.[63]

---

54 EA 2021 s 122(1).
55 ibid s 122(2).
56 The qualifying estate is the freehold or the qualifying tenancy as described above at paras 23.20–23.22.
57 EA 2021 s 122(2).
58 ibid s 122(3)(a).
59 ibid s 122(3)(b).
60 ibid s 122(2).
61 ibid s 122(5).
62 ibid s 122(5)(a).
63 DEFRA guidance (n 29).

23.36 A successor will not be bound where the conservation covenant was not registered in the local land charges register[64] at the time the successor acquired the estate in land.[65] Nor will it bind a successor where his immediate predecessor[66] was not bound by the obligation.[67]

(iii) *Cessation of landowner's obligation*

23.37 An obligation of the landowner under a conservation covenant ceases to bind the landowner or a person who becomes a successor of that landowner in the following circumstances:[68]

- where land ceases to be land to which the obligation relates;
- in the case of a landowner under the covenant land in relation to which the landowner ceases to be the holder of the qualifying estate; or
- in the case of a successor, land in relation to which the successor ceases to be the holder of the qualifying estate or of the estate derived from the qualifying estate.

(iv) *Effect of determination of lease*

23.38 The provisions are not entirely clear as to what happens when the original party was the tenant, the tenancy is not assigned but is determined, and therefore reverts to the freehold owner.

23.39 The duration of the obligation is governed by the conservation covenant itself or in default, in the case of a tenancy, 'for a period corresponding in length to the remainder of the period for which the term of years was granted'. Therefore, if the landowner is the tenant under a fixed term, and there are three years remaining on the tenancy, the covenant will continue for that three year period.

23.40 *Prima facie,* that would suggest that the obligations under the conservation covenant do not terminate on early determination of the tenancy. But it may not be so clear cut.

23.41 On early termination of the tenancy, the question is whether the person immediately entitled to the reversion is then bound by the conservation covenant. A simple

---

64 Or to the appropriate local land charges register where Local Land Charges Act 1975 s 3 does not yet have effect.

65 EA 2021 s 122(5)(b). EA 2021 s 122(7) provides that the reference in s 122(5)(b) to the time when the successor acquired the estate in land concerned is, if the successor acquired that interest under a disposition which took effect at law only when registered in the register of title kept under the Land Registration Act 2002, to be read as a reference to the time when the disposition was made.

66 This means the immediate predecessor in title. However, if the successor is the first holder of an estate in land derived from another estate in land (i.e. there is no immediate predecessor in title), then the successor's immediate predecessor is the holder of the other estate when the derived estate was created: s 122(9). Thus, for example, if the periodic tenant's landlord was not bound by the bound by the obligation in respect of that tenanted land.

67 EA 2021 s 122(5)(c).

68 ibid s 122(4).

scenario is where the tenancy is forfeited, and possession of the land reverts to the landlord who is the freehold owner.

23.42 Section 122(3)(a) would suggest the landlord is a successor: a successor means a person who holds, in respect of any of the land to which the obligation relates, the qualifying estate.[69] The qualifying estate means the freehold.[70]

23.43 Section 117(4), however, also goes on to provide that:

> a reference to qualifying estate, in relation to an obligation under a conservation covenant, is to *the estate in land* by virtue of which the condition in subsection (1)(a)(i) *was met* in relation –
>
> (a) if the obligation is not an ancillary obligation, the provision giving rise to the obligation, or
> (b) if the obligation is an ancillary obligation, the provision giving rise to the obligation to which it was ancillary;
>
> (and for this purpose 'ancillary obligation' means an obligation under provision falling within section 118(2)(b)); … [emphasis added]

23.44 Section 117(1)(a)(i) provides:

> For the purposes of this Part, a 'conservation covenant agreement' is an agreement between a landowner and a responsible body where—
>
> (a) the agreement contains provision which—
> (i) is of a qualifying kind …

23.45 At risk of repetition, 'of a qualifying kind' means provision, *inter alia*, requiring the landowner to do, or not to do, something on land in England specified in the provision in relation to which the landowner holds a qualifying estate specified in the agreement.

23.46 Whereas the landlord would hold a qualifying estate if he were the person entering into a conservation covenant agreement, or would be a successor on transfer of the freehold where the freeholder was the landowner under the agreement, the condition was not met by him holding the freehold but by the tenant holding the fixed term tenancy. Thus, on early termination of the tenancy, it seems there is no successor.

---

69 ibid s 122(3)(a).
70 ibid s 117(4)(a).

Benefit of obligation of responsible body

23.47 An obligation of the responsible body under a conservation covenant is owed to the landowner under the covenant and to any person who becomes a successor[71] of the landowner.[72] An obligation of the responsible body ceases in the same circumstances as in the case of an obligation of the landowner.[73]

Pre-existing rights

23.48 It is important to note that conservation covenant agreements do not override pre-existing rights and obligations, such as statutory rights; private property rights (e.g. under tenancy agreements); planning restrictions; statutory designations. Accordingly, some of the difficulties already identified relating to restrictive terms in the tenancy agreement will remain relevant. Landlord and tenant collaboration is likely to be required.

23.49 Pre-existing rights binding the land are still enforceable (e.g. right to use common land, statutory undertakers to inspect and maintain infrastructure, such as water companies, easements or a restrictive covenant, public rights of way).

Registration

23.50 A conservation covenant is a local land charge.[74] It is an exception to the rule[75] that a covenant or agreement made between a landlord and tenant cannot amount a local land charge.[76] Responsible bodies must register conservation covenants as a local land charge and only from that point forward will they bind successors in title (in contrast to obligations under the Town and County Planning Act s 106).

Breach and enforcement

23.51 A negative obligation is breached where the person bound does something which it prohibits or permits or suffers[77] another person to do such a thing.[78] The positive covenant will be breached if the obligation is not performed.[79]

---

71 Successor means a person who holds the qualifying estate or an estate in land derived (whether immediately or otherwise) from the qualifying estate after the creation of the covenant: EA 2021 s 123(2). Note that it does not apply if the obligation ancillary to an obligation under the covenant which does not bind the successor.
72 EA 2021 s 123(1).
73 ibid s123(3); and see above at para 23.37 above.
74 ibid s 120.
75 Under the Local Land Charges Act 1975 s 2(a) and (b).
76 EA 2021 s 120(3).
77 The meaning of 'permit' was considered by the House of Lords in *Tophams Ltd v Earl of Sefton* [1967] 1 AC 50 in the context of a breach of a restrictive covenant. 'Suffer' may have a slightly different meaning: see *Berton v Alliance Economic Investment Co* [1922] 1 KB 742 [759], per Atkin LJ; and *Barton v Keeble* [1928] Ch 517 and *Barton v Reed* [1932] 1 Ch 362 [375]. Where a covenantor does all that can reasonably be done to prevent the acts prohibited by the covenant, he will not 'permit or 'suffer' that act.
78 EA 2021 s 124(1)(a).
79 ibid s 124(2).

23.52 It is a defence to show:[80]

- that the breach occurred as a result of a matter beyond the defendant's control;
- that the breach occurred as a result of doing, or not doing, something in an emergency in circumstances where it was necessary for that to be done, or not to be done, in order to prevent loss of life or injury to any person; or
- that at the time of breach the obligation relates or was within an area designated for public purpose and compliance would have involved a breach of any statutory control.[81]

23.53 The remedies available for breach of an obligation[82] under a conservation covenant are specific performance,[83] an injunction,[84] damages[85] and order for payment of an amount due under the obligation.[86]

Discharge, modification and declarations

23.54 The responsible body and the person who holds the qualifying estate or the successor of the landowner may by agreement discharge from the obligation any of the land to which it relates.[87] The agreement should be executed as a deed.[88] Similar provisions apply for the discharge of the obligation by the responsible body.[89]

23.55 A person bound by, or entitled to a benefit of, an obligation under a conservation covenant may, by agreement with the responsible body, modify the obligation by deed.[90] However, the parties cannot make a change which, had it been included in the original agreement, would have prevented it from being a conservation agreement.[91] Such modification will bind successors.[92]

---

80 This does not apply if the designation for public purpose was already in force at the time the conservation covenant was created: EA 2021 s 124(3). If the sole failure is to obtain authorisation, the defendant must also show that all reasonable steps had been taken to do so: EA 2021 s 126(2).
81 This does not apply if the designation for public purpose was already in force at the time the conservation covenant was created: EA 2021 s 124(3). If the sole failure is to obtain authorisation, the defendant must also show that all reasonable steps had been taken to do so: EA 2021 s 126(2).
82 For the purposes of the Limitation Act 1980, conservation contract to be treated as a simple contract: EA 2021 s 125(5).
83 In considering the appropriate remedy, the court must take into account any public interest in the performance of the obligation concerned: EA 2021 s 125(2).
84 ibid.
85 Contract principles apply to damages save that the court may award exemplary damages in such circumstances as it thinks fit: EA 2021 s 125(3) and (4).
86 EA 2021 s 125(1).
87 ibid s 127(1)–(3).
88 ibid s 127(5).
89 ibid s 128.
90 ibid s 129(1) and (3).
91 ibid s 129(2).
92 ibid s 129(4). A successor of a person bound by the modification means a person who holds in respect of the land to which the modification relates: (a) the estate held by the person bound by the modification when it was agreed; or (b) an estate in land derived (whether immediately or otherwise) from that estate after the modification is agreed: EA 2021 s 129(5).

23.56 The Upper Tribunal has the power to discharge or modify an obligation.[93] Where proceedings are taken by action[94] or otherwise[95] to enforce an obligation, the defendant may apply to the High Court or county court for an order giving leave to apply to the Upper Tribunal and staying the proceedings.

23.57 The court[96] and the Upper Tribunal have the power on an application of any person interested to make a declaration:

- whether anything purporting to be a conservation covenant is a conservation covenant;
- whether any land is land to which an obligation under a conservation covenant relates;
- whether any person is bound by, or entitled to the benefit of, any obligation under a conservation covenant and, if so, in respect of what land;
- on the true construction of any instrument, the nature of the obligation under a conservation covenant.[97]

Conclusion

23.58 The advantage of conservation covenants is that they are a statutory means of creating obligations to carry out works (or allow them to be carried out) which run with the land in a way that would be otherwise cumbersome to achieve. This is useful in securing biodiversity net gain on planning applications, as opposed to planning conditions or section 106 agreements.

23.59 To what extent they will be taken up remains to be seen. Unlike private covenants and easements, conservation covenants are less for private and more for public benefit. There are likely to be issues where land is let.

---

93 ibid 2021 s 130(1) and Sch 18. This is different to the Upper Tribunal's power to discharge or modify a restrictive covenant under the Law of Property Act 1925, s 84(1). Environment Act 2021 s 130(3) expressly excludes an application being made under that provision in relation to an obligation under a conservation covenant.
94 This refers to proceedings started in a civil court.
95 It is not clear to what 'otherwise' refers. The phrase is used in the Law of Property Act 1925 s 146, in relation to forfeiture; a landlord may proceed by action or otherwise to enforce a right of re-entry or forfeiture. Subject to certain statutory restrictions, a landlord may enforce a right of re-entry by physical re-entry rather than issuing proceedings. In *Iveagh v Harris* [1929] 2 Ch 142, however, it was held that forfeiture proceedings were not proceedings 'by action or otherwise' *to enforce a restrictive covenant* but action or otherwise for the recovery of possession. Arguably, the same would apply here. Thus, a leaseholder who applies for relief in response to a claim or action by a landlord for forfeiture will not be able to seek a stay in order to apply for modification or discharge of the conservation covenant.
96 The court means the High Court or the county court: EA 2021 s 135(3).
97 EA 2021 s 135(1). Note that an application cannot be made under the Law of Property Act 1925 s 84(2) as for other restrictive covenants.

CHAPTER 24

AGRICULTURAL HOLDINGS

Rebecca Cattermole

Introduction

24.01 The departure from the European Union on 31 January 2020 gave the United Kingdom control over its agricultural policies for the first time in over 40 years. Indeed, the Agricultural Act 2020[1] was the first major piece of legislation in a post-Brexit world, closely followed by the Environment Act 2021.[2] Environmental preservation and improvement was at the forefront of the Conservative government's policy in the move away from the Common Agricultural Policy and subsidies on the basis of land ownership and farming. A suite of environmental land management schemes[3] were, and may still be, introduced and are discussed elsewhere in this book.[4]

24.02 This chapter concerns matters of relevance to entering such schemes in the context of agricultural tenancies.[5] As to whether the parties are entitled to enter any agreement relating to the scheme and/or need consent, will depend on the terms of the agreement (whether that is written or oral).[6] The consequences for a tenant may be significant: it may lead the tenant to be in breach in the absence of any variation or remove security of tenure because statutory conditions are no longer satisfied.

24.03 The law governing agricultural holdings is complex and readers are advised to consult the standard textbooks on the subject.[7] Nonetheless an understanding as to the terms of such tenancies and how they operate is required given how they may restrict participation in environmental schemes and the extent to which conservation

---

1 See consultations: Health and Harmony: The future or Food, Farming and the Environment in a green Brexit, February 2018, DEFRA for England; Brexit and Our Land: Securing the future of Welsh Farming, Welsh Government, July 2018; and Sustainable Farming and our lands: Simplifying Agricultural Support, Welsh Government, July 2020; and Tenancy Reform Industry Group.
2 Following the Agricultural Transition Plan released in 2018.
3 e.g. Sustainable Farming Incentive, Local Nature Recovery, Landscape Recovery.
4 See Chapters 11 and 12. A green future: Our 25 Year Plan to improve the Environment, January 2018, DEFRA and Environmental Improvement Plan 2023. Environmental land management schemes, productivity schemes, tree planting schemes, and offer to new entrants into the tenanted sector. See also Country Land and Business Association and Tenant Farmers Association guidance published in March 2022. Note this is likely to change in light of the Labour government's budget delivered on 30 October 2024.
5 These have been well aired. In 2017 the Tenancy Reform Industry Group (TRIG) made recommendations to government on reforming landlord and tenant legislation. The House of Lords Science and Technology report on Natural Capital in 2019; 2021 National Food Strategy. Note also that concern about food production was evident long before Brexit with the introduction of area payments in 1993.
6 Agreements would have been drafted in a very different era where production was the focus.
7 e.g. *Scammell, Densham & and Williams on Law of Agricultural Holdings*, (11th edn, Lexis Nexis 2023) and *Muir, Watt and Moss: Agricultural Holdings* (16th edn, Sweet & Maxwell 2024).

covenants may be entered in relation to tenanted land and by whom. Conversely, such an understanding demonstrates how tenanted land may be able to play an active role in the pursuit of net zero and nature positive goals.

24.04 This chapter will therefore consider the following:[8]

- Recent policy developments with references to agricultural holdings
- A brief outline of the different tenancy regimes governing agricultural holdings
- Length of tenancy
- Good husbandry
- Other restrictive terms and conditions of tenancy
- Reservations
- Loss of security of tenure
- Forcing a tenant to give up land under the Agricultural Holdings Act 1986
- Consent and variation
- Environment improvements: fixtures and fittings
- Rent Review.

Recent policy developments

24.05 In February 2022, the Tenancy Working Group chaired by Baroness Rock was asked by the Secretary of State to consider how the new government financial schemes should be accessible to tenant farmers. The 'Rock Review: Working together for a thriving agricultural tenanted sector' was published in October 2022.[9] The Rock Review found that the government had a 'long way to go to make its schemes open to tenants' and that current legislation and tax incentives[10] did not align to government policy of farmers delivering long-term environmental benefits.[11]

24.06 Tenant farmers are facing multiple pressures, *inter alia*, demands from non-agricultural land use such as solar, development, tree planting and biodiversity, net zero

---

8 For tax, see Chapter 34.
9 Tenancy Working Group, 'The Rock Review: Working Together for a Thriving Agricultural Tenanted Sector' (2022) <https://assets.publishing.service.gov.uk/media/6347da6ae90e0731ac4a55c0/The_Rock_Review_-_Working_together_for_a_thriving_agricultural_tenanted_sector.pdf>.
10 For tax, see Chapter 34.
11 Rock Review (n 9) 10. Note there will be changes given the Labour government budget delivered on 30 October 2024.

ambitions, water quality and climate change, all of which take land out of production, as well as a change to a Labour government.[12]

24.07 DEFRA's response to the Rock Review was published in May 2023 and stated:[13]

> We strongly agree that tenant farmers should be able to:
>
> - access 'farm offers';
> - make their essential contribution to restoring the natural environment;
> - produce food for the nation.

24.08 Importantly, DEFRA promised that a new 'Farm Tenancy Forum' would be established which will have the primary role of supporting the implementation of the government response to the Rock Review.[14] The Forum was established in May 2023 and will explore all issues relating to the tenant farming sector in England and act as a conduit between DEFRA and tenant farmers. The objective is to find practical ways in which landlord and tenant may vary tenancy agreements and allow tenants to diversify and enter into farming schemes. An important development has been the publication of The Agricultural Landlord and Tenant Code of Practice in April 2024[15] which is founded on three principles of clarity, communication and collaboration. Whereas it is a voluntary code and does not override contractual and statutory rights, it provides guidance on the standards of behaviour expected by landlords and tenants and their professional advisers. There is specific provision regarding environmental schemes.

Security of tenure under the agricultural tenancy regimes

(i) *Tenancies governed by the Agricultural Holdings Act 1986*

24.09 The Agricultural Holdings Act 1986 was a consolidating Act and applies to a tenancy of an agricultural holding[16] entered into before 1 September 1995 which satisfies certain conditions. All tenancies entered into on or after that date will be farm business tenancies governed by the Agricultural Tenancies Act 1995 subject to the saving

12 The Rock Review emphasises that 'Defra needs to define food security as a public good alongside other environmental objectives such as clean air, clean water, lower carbon emissions, and improving biodiversity': ibid.
13 DEFRA, 'Government Response to the Rock Review' (2023) < https://www.gov.uk/government/publications/rock-review-on-agricultural-tenancies-government-response/government-response-to-the-rock-review-full-report> accessed 9 October 2024.
14 The Farm Tenancy Forum is made up of members of industry organisations which represent tenant farmers, landlords and professional advisors working in the sector. The terms of reference outline how the Forum will work. See <https://www.gov.uk/government/publications/farm-tenancy-forum-terms-of-reference/farm-tenancy-forum-terms-of-reference> accessed 9 October 2024.
15 The Agricultural Landlord and Tenant Code of Practice has been endorsed by other industry bodies including the Tenant Farmers Association, Country Land and Business Association, National Farmers Union, Central Association of Agricultural Valuers and the Agricultural Law Association. This will build on other guidance: e.g. Country Land and Business Association and Tenant Farmers Association guidance published in March 2022; and TRIG Code of Good Practice.
16 'Agricultural holding' means the aggregate of the land (whether agricultural land or not) comprised in a contract of tenancy which is a contract for an agricultural tenancy, not being a contract under which the land is let to the tenant during his continuance in any office, appointment or employment held under the landlord, Agricultural Holdings Act 1986 s1(1).

provisions in the Agricultural Tenancies Act 1995 section 4.[17] The Agricultural Holdings Act 1986 Act will therefore continue to provide significant statutory protection for a considerable period in the future.[18]

24.10 The importance of the agricultural aspects is seen in the statutory definition of an agricultural holding governed by the Agricultural Holdings Act 1986. A contract of tenancy relating to any land is a contract for an agricultural tenancy if, having regard to the terms of the tenancy, the actual or contemplated use of the land at the time of the conclusion of the contract and subsequently, and any other relevant circumstances, the whole of the land comprised in the contract, subject to such exceptions only as do not substantially affect the character of the tenancy, is let for use as agricultural land.[19]

24.11 The common law rights to determine a yearly tenancy including forfeiture, surrender and notice to quit are preserved.

24.12 Parliament, however, intervened for the benefit of agricultural tenants in respect of the landlord's common law right to terminate a yearly tenancy in two ways:

- Agricultural Holdings Act 1986 section 25 provides that a notice to quit which would at common law be effective will be invalid if it purports to terminate the tenancy before the expiry of 12 months from the then current year of the tenancy (subject to certain exceptions).

- Agricultural Holdings Act 1986 section 26 provides that the tenant shall have the power to give a counter-notice within one month of the notice to quit requiring referral to the First-tier Tribunal (Property Chamber) (Agricultural Land and Drainage)[20] for consent under Agricultural Holdings Act 1986 section 27. This does not apply if the notice to quit relies upon one of the Cases set out in Part I of Schedule 3.

24.13 Where a landlord gives a notice to quit complying with Agricultural Holdings Act 1986 section 25 and specifying one of the Cases, the tenant is given no power other than to seek arbitration, and then only in order to query whether or not the special Case on which the landlord expressly relies actually applies on the facts.

---

17 e.g. a tenancy granted by way of succession to an agricultural holding or to a qualifying close relative of a deceased or retiring tenant.
18 See 'Agricultural tenancy consultation and call for evidence on mortgage restrictions and repossession protections for agricultural land in England' issued by Department for Environment and Rural Affairs in April 2019 and, in particular, [3.1]–[3.5].
19 Agricultural Holdings Act 1986 s 1(2); 'agricultural land' means (a) land used for agriculture which is so used for the purposes of a trade or business, and (b) any other land which, by virtue of a designation under the Agriculture Act 1947 s 109(1) is agricultural land within the meaning of that Act: Agricultural Holdings Act 1986 s 1(4).
20 As defined by the Agricultural Holdings Act 1986 s 96(1).

24.14 The Agricultural Holdings Act 1986 imposes a complex regime governing landlord and tenant relations including, *inter alia*, the imposition of certain terms and conditions.[21]

(ii) *Farm business tenancies*

24.15 The Agricultural Tenancies Act 1995 marked a liberalisation of the tenancy regime governing agricultural holdings thus enabling diversification from agriculture. The parties are free to agree detailed terms of the contract without statutory interference. Importantly, the conditions to be satisfied to be a farm business tenancy have diversification in mind.

24.16 A tenancy will be a farm business tenancy if it meets the business conditions together with either the agricultural condition or the notice conditions.[22]

24.17 The business conditions are:[23]

- that all or part of the land comprised in the tenancy is farmed for the purposes of a trade or business; and

- that, since the beginning of the tenancy, all or part of the land so comprised has been so farmed.

24.18 The agriculture condition is that the character of the tenancy is primarily or wholly agricultural.[24]

24.19 The notice conditions are that the landlord and the tenant each gave the other a written notice containing, *inter alia,* a statement to the effect that the tenancy or proposed tenancy is to be, and remain, a farm business tenancy.[25] Further, that at the beginning of the tenancy, having regard to the terms of the tenancy and any other relevant circumstances, the character of the tenancy must be primarily or wholly agricultural.[26]

24.20 The combination of the business and notice conditions enables diversification within the farm business tenancy regime.

---

21 The terms of the tenancy agreement are governed by express terms, terms implied at common law and terms implied by statute including the model clauses incorporated by Agricultural Holdings Act 1986 s7, and other relevant terms by Agricultural Holdings Act 1986 s 8.
22 Agricultural Tenancies Act 1995 s 1(1).
23 Agricultural Tenancies Act 1995 s 1(2) having regard to having regard to the terms of the tenancy, the use of the land comprised in the tenancy, the nature of any commercial activities carried on that land, and any other relevant circumstances.
24 Agricultural Tenancies Act 1995 s 1(3).
25 ibid s 1(4)(a).
26 ibid s 1(4)(b).

- The business condition does not require that the part farmed[27] should be substantial or that the business itself is agricultural.

- If the notice conditions are satisfied, the tenancy only needs to be primarily or wholly agricultural at the commencement but not thereafter.

- So long as there is minimal commercial farming to comply with the business condition, the tenancy will remain a farm business tenancy.[28]

24.21 However, if the notice conditions do not apply,[29] the agricultural condition will need to be satisfied. This poses a problem if the tenant wishes to diversify its operations and activities on the holding, and the landlord is uncooperative or not agreeable to a variation of the tenancy, or the grant of a new tenancy. This is likely to arise where a tenancy has been granted on a short-term basis and contains covenants restricting any non-agricultural use.

24.22 The security of tenure under a farm business tenancy is as follows:

- A fixed term of two years or less than two years will terminate on expiry without the need for a notice to quit.[30]

- A fixed term of more than two years shall continue as a tenancy from year-to-year unless at least 12 months' notice before the term date has been given.[31]

- A fixed term of two years or more given pursuant to a break clause must give at least 12 months' notice.[32]

- The periodic tenancy (at commencement or after the two-year period) depends on the periods of the tenancy: a tenancy from year-to-year requires at least 12 months' notice;[33] shorter periods will determine in accordance with common law rules.[34]

- The landlord has a right to entry or forfeiture if such provision is included in the agreement.[35]

---

27 It does not say it should be used for agriculture. Agricultural Tenancies Act 1995 s 38(2) states that references to farming the land include the carrying out in relation land of an agricultural activity. Thus farming may go beyond agricultural activity.
28 And indeed avoids the risk of a tenancy being inadvertently conferred protection under the Landlord and Tenant Act 1954.
29 Either because they were not served or were defective.
30 Agricultural Tenancies Act 1995 s 5.
31 ibid s 5(1).
32 ibid s 7(1). Whereas there is no provision for repossession for non-agricultural use or short notice, the landlord is able to give notice to quit part of the holding.
33 ibid s 6(1).
34 i.e. a quarter's notice to terminate a quarter, a month's notice to terminate a monthly periodic tenancy.
35 The common law rules and Law of Property Act 1925 s 146 will apply.

Length of tenancy

24.23 The length of the tenancy will be relevant to the level of commitment required in partaking or implementing schemes. There will be an inevitable difficulty with long term schemes which amount to a one-off up-front payment, 30-year biodiversity net gain agreements or 80-year nutrient neutrality agreements, and Woodland Carbon Code and Peatland Code, which require long term land use change to generate carbon units for sale. The fear, articulated by the Rock Review, was that landowners may look to take back in hand tenanted land in order to access scheme payments.[36]

24.24 Tenancies governed by the Agricultural Holdings Act 1986 have a high degree of security of tenure and some tenants will enjoy succession rights,[37] the effect being that these are long term tenancies (albeit such tenancies, however, are more restrictive of use).[38]

24.25 The length of a farm business tenancy will vary from short to long term and possesses the degree of flexibility which is more likely to be suitable for environmental schemes.[39] The average length, however, for those farm business tenancies granted on or after 1 September 1995 and governed by the Agricultural Tenancies Act 1995 is between 4 and 5 years.[40] Lettings tend to be longer for larger and better equipped holdings, and shorter lettings where land may be required for development or testing out a new tenant.[41] It remains to be seen whether the new schemes will lead to landlords being willing to grant longer term tenancies if they choose not to take the land back in hand.[42] A longer term tenancy with a break clause at 5 or 10 years during the fixed term may be attractive where a longer term commitment is required because it minimises the risk of the 12 months' notice to quit early on during its term.

24.26 There will be three main matters of concern for a tenant requiring long term commitment:

- Whether any sums paid over will be required to be repaid and to whom under the scheme if the tenancy comes to an end.[43] If the landowner or the incoming tenant takes on the balance of the agreement this may not arise. But if that is not the case then the tenant could be required to repay the money paid to him.

---

36 DEFRA queries whether this was as prolific as suggested by the Rock Review (see DEFRA (n 13)).
37 Agricultural Holdings Act 1986 s 26, 27 and Part IV.
38 See below at paras 24.30, 24.35, 24.40–24.41.
39 See paras 24.15–24.22 above in relation to security of tenure.
40 Central Association of Agricultural Valuers, CAAV Agricultural Land Occupation Surveys 2020 (2021).
41 See Rock Review (n 9) and response from government (n 13).
42 There may be good reason for shorter term tenancies, e.g. landlord intending to farm in hand, crop rotation, new entrants avoiding long term risk, flexibility for the landowner. One means of encouraging longer term tenancies is to restrict agricultural property relief from inheritance tax to tenancies for a term of 8 years or more: see Chapter 34. However, this may change under the new Labour government.
43 A tenant may be subject to an unforeseen notice to quit or termination that does not arising from tenant default and it may be that some protection will be afforded by force majeure provision.

- Whether a successor occupier (the landlord on reversion of the tenancy or a new tenant) take on the balance of any agreement. In the case of a long term scheme (for example, one of 30 years), this becomes more critical.

- Tenant's fixture or improvement for which see below.

24.27 Some attempt has been made to overcome the difficulties posed by length of term. Where a tenant does not have security of tenure for the duration of a countryside stewardship agreement,[44] the landlord can also sign and agree to take responsibility for delivering the agreement if the tenancy expires before agreement of completion.[45]

24.28 Where tenants are eligible to apply for the England Woodland Creation Offer, both landlord and tenant need to agree to the proposal and agreement transfers to the landlord or new tenant on expiry of the original tenancy. This will merge into the Countryside Stewardship scheme in 2025 and the same approach may be taken to cover all environment land management activities.[46]

24.29 In relation to the future, the parties will wish to consider whether, if a scheme has already been implemented or will be adopted, the tenancy is of an appropriate length to provide sufficient security of tenure to accommodate the type of scheme and the commitment required. A potential tenant will also need to be alert to any conservation covenants which may be binding on any tenancy.[47]

Good husbandry

24.30 It is common to find a covenant in a tenancy governed by the Agricultural Holdings Act 1986 requiring the tenant to observe the rules of good husbandry set out in the Agriculture Act 1947 section 11.[48] An occupier of agricultural land is considered to be farming it in accordance with the rules of good husbandry if, having regard to the character and situation of the unit, the standard of management by the owner and other relevant circumstances, the occupier is maintaining a reasonable standard of efficient production, as respects the kind of produce and the quality and quantity of the produce, while keeping the farming unit in a condition to enable such a standard to be

---

44 Under the Countryside Stewardship scheme. This provides financial incentives for farmers, foresters and land managers to look after and improve the environment. See Chapter 12.
45 DEFRA response to the Rock Review (n 13) 21/57.
46 ibid 22/57. The creation of woodland on high quality agricultural land will have a detrimental impact on food production. One of the concerns raised by the Rock Review was the purchase of land by large business to convert agricultural land into non-agricultural use.
47 See Chapter 23 ('Conservation Covenants').
48 The Agriculture Act 1947 was introduced after the Second World War with the aim of increasing and intensifying food production.

maintained in the future.[49] It is the minimum standard. Therefore, taking the land out of production to take advantage of various environmental schemes may well be in breach of the rules of good husbandry.[50]

24.31 Where Agriculture Act 1947 section 11 is included in an agreement, it will in consequence be a term of the tenancy thus enabling a landlord to rely on Case D[51] should he need to enforce.

24.32 Breaches of the rules of good husbandry may also enable a landlord to make a successful application to the Tribunal for a certificate of bad husbandry and thereafter serve notice to quit under Case C:[52]

> Not more than six months before the giving of the notice to quit, the Tribunal granted a certificate under paragraph 9 of Part II of this Schedule that the tenant of the holding was not fulfilling his responsibilities to farm in accordance with the rules of good husbandry, and that fact is stated in the notice.

24.33 Unusually for the Agricultural Holdings Act 1986 (which, as with previous legislation, was focused on productivity, in determining whether to grant a certificate of bad husbandry), the Tribunal shall disregard any practice adopted by the tenant in pursuance of any provision of the tenancy contract, or of any other agreement with the landlord, which indicates (in whatever terms) that its object is the furtherance of one or more of the following purposes, namely:

- the conservation of flora or fauna or of geological or physiographical features of special interest;
- the protection of buildings or other objects of archaeological, architectural or historic interest; or

---

49 Agriculture Act 1947 s 11(1). In determining whether the manner in which a unit is being farmed in accordance with rues of good husbandry regard shall be had to the extent to which: (a) permanent pasture is being properly mown or grazed and maintained in a good state of cultivation and fertility and in good condition; (b) the manner in which arable land is being cropped is such as to maintain that land clean and in a good state of cultivation and fertility and in good condition; (c) the unit is properly stocked where the system of farming practised requires the keeping of livestock, and an efficient standard of management of livestock is maintained where livestock are kept and of breeding where the breeding of livestock is carried out; (d) the necessary steps are being taken to secure and maintain crops and livestock free from disease and from infestation by insects and other pests; (e) the necessary steps are being taken for the protection and preservation of crops harvested or lifted, or in course of being harvested or lifted; (f) the necessary work of maintenance and repair is being carried out.

50 Although see the matters that may be disregarded for the purposes of obtaining a certificate of bad husbandry under the Agricultural Holdings Act 1986, Part III, Case C. The Rock Review called for the definition of good husbandry to be redefined to avoid conflict with environmental schemes; (n 9) 86–89.

51 Agricultural Holdings Act 1986. Case D reads: 'At the date of the giving of the notice to quit the tenant had failed to comply with a notice in writing served on him by the landlord, being either—(a) a notice requiring him within two months from the service of the notice to pay any rent due in respect of the agricultural holding to which the notice to quit relates, or (b) a notice requiring him within a reasonable period specified in the notice to remedy any breach by the tenant that was capable of being remedied of any term or condition of his tenancy which was not inconsistent with his responsibilities to farm in accordance with the rules of good husbandry, and it is stated in the notice to quit that it is given by reason of the said matter'.

52 ibid Sch 3, Part I, Case C.

- the conservation or enhancement of the natural beauty or amenity of the countryside or the promotion of its enjoyment by the public.[53]

24.34 Further, in determining whether to grant a certificate under this paragraph, the Tribunal shall disregard any practice adopted by the tenant in compliance with any obligation accepted by or imposed on the tenant under the Water Resources Act 1991 section 94 or 95.

Other restrictive terms and conditions

24.35 There may be other covenants contained in the agreement restricting use of the land comprised in the holding which would preclude parties entering into environmental land management schemes.[54] For example, a prohibition by the tenant on tree planting as land use would be not agricultural unless its use was ancillary to the farming of other land for other agricultural purposes.[55] Note the England Woodland Creation Offer reduced the scale of some tree planting (hedges, verges, screening and shelter belts) thus retaining focus on food production.[56] The Agricultural Landlord and Tenant Code of Practice discourages the blanket ban on participation in environmental schemes in new agreements.

Reservations

24.36 Most tenancy agreements will contain rights over the demised land which are reserved to the landlord. Thus, for example, the landlord may reserve the right to enter private schemes and retain ownership of the natural capital thus preventing the tenant entering environmental schemes.[57]

24.37 Existing trees, and trees which are planted during the term of the tenancy, are commonly reserved to the landlord and Agricultural Holdings Act 1986 section 31 allows part resumption for tree planting by the landlord.

24.38 Furthermore, the landlord may reserve use of resources on the demised land (such as peat for biodiversity net gain or carbon credits). The terms of the tenancy may exclude tenants from carrying out or receiving income from change of use to deliver environmental benefits such as increasing biodiversity.[58]

---

53 ibid Sch 3, para 9(2). The Rock Review called for good husbandry to be redefined; (n 9) 35–36.
54 DEFRA, 'Agricultural Tenancy Consultation and Call for Evidence on Mortgage Restrictions and Repossession Protections for Agricultural Land in England' <https://consult.defra.gov.uk/ahdb-sponsorship-and-agricultural-tenancies/agricultural-tenancy-consultation/> accessed 9 April 2024. This consultation led to the Agriculture Act 2020 and variations under the Agricultural Holdings Act 1986.
55 Agricultural Holdings Act 1986 s 31 allows a landlord to recover part of land demised for the purposes of tree planting.
56 See DEFRA farm woodland standard through SFI pilot: <https://defrafarming.blog.gov.uk/farm-woodland-standard/> accessed 9 October 2024.
57 Unsurprising given that the natural capital is the trees, soil and water resources. The Rock Review recommended that the trade and income from that land via management of the land should belong to the tenants (n 9) 76–79.
58 Dustin Benton and others, 'Natural Capital: The Battle for Control' (Green Alliance 2022) <https://green-alliance.org.uk/wp-content/uploads/2022/01/Natural_capital_the_battle_for_control.pdf> accessed 9 October 2024.

24.39 In addition, environmental schemes may be inconsistent with the landlord's reserved rights and interfere to the extent that they would lead to tenant breaches of the tenancy. For example, entering an environmental scheme may interfere with the landlord's shooting rights.

Loss of security of tenure

24.40 A tenant risks losing his security under the Agricultural Holdings Act 1986 if the tenancy no longer satisfies the conditions under section 1 (for example, where the land is still used for the purposes of a business but the character of the business itself ceases to be substantially agricultural and the income is derived from non-agricultural activity).

24.41 Thus, for example, agroforestry[59] does not fall within the meaning of agriculture. DEFRA is currently investigating how best to define agroforestry as an agricultural activity.[60]

Forcing a tenant to give up land under the Agricultural Holdings Act 1986

24.42 This depends on the nature of the scheme and the terms of the tenancy.

24.43 If the scheme is in breach of the tenancy (without consent or variation sought) that may enable the landlord to serve notice under Case D,[61] seek a certificate of bad husbandry, or even contend that the protection afforded by the Agricultural Holdings Act 1986 is lost.

24.44 A landlord may seek possession under Case B[62] on the ground that possession is required for a use, other than for agriculture, where planning permission is required.

24.45 Furthermore, a landlord may serve a notice to quit and seek consent for its operation from the Tribunal on the basis that he proposes to terminate the tenancy for the purpose of a use other than for agriculture, and which does not fall within Case B. There are circumstances where a landlord may resume possession of part of the holding.[63]

Consent and variation of tenancy terms

24.46 The restrictions or prohibitions contained in a tenancy agreement may be qualified permitting change of user or entering of schemes with the consent of the landlord. There may be situations where the tenancy itself will need to be varied.

---

59 Agroforestry sits between agricultural and trees. See Chapter 12.
60 DEFRA response to the Rock Review (n 13) 30/57.
61 Agricultural Holdings Act 1986 Sch 3, Pt 1.
62 ibid.
63 e.g. Agricultural Holdings Act 1986 s 31 allows part resumption for tree planting.

(i) *Collaborative approach*

24.47 DEFRA strongly encourages a collaborative approach to enable parties to take advantage of the various environmental schemes. For example, DEFRA suggests applications being made jointly by the landlord and tenant in order to overcome any requirement for consent and restrictive covenants contained in the tenancy agreement, the ideal outcome for both parties being to share 'work and rewards'.[64] DEFRA is considering joint applications for more productivity and innovation grants.[65]

24.48 There has been some attempt to address the difficulties in obtaining consent. Sustainable Farming Incentive schemes previously required landlord consent before the tenant could apply. That is no longer the case nor is there any requirement to pay a penalty in the event the tenant unexpectedly loses control of management of land. It does not, however, of itself overcome the question of seeking consent vis-à-vis the landlord and gives rise to the issue of whether, if the landlord does successfully recover possession, it could be said to be unexpected.

24.49 In response to the concerns raised in the Rock Review that landlord agents were an impediment to obtaining consent from a landlord, DEFRA's suggestion is that aggrieved tenants raise the issue directly with the landlord, and refer the landlord and agent to the guidance published by Tenant Reform Industry Group, Tenant Farmers Association and Countryside Land and Business Association, and engage in mediation.[66]

24.50 Importantly, the Agricultural Landlord and Tenant Code of Practice for England says that consent for new schemes should not be withheld unreasonably. Landlords and tenants should be able to discuss environmental opportunities openly and constructively. Reasonable grounds for withholding consent relate to matters of taxation, rental income, capital value, mortgage terms, and long term estate plans.

(ii) *Consent or variation under Agricultural Holdings Act s 19A*

24.51 The difficulties surrounding tenant participation in environmental schemes had been anticipated by the government. A new section of the Agricultural Holdings Act has gone some way to address this. By Agricultural Holdings Act 1986, section 19A the Secretary of State is given power to make regulations providing for the tenant of an agricultural holding to refer a request for consent or variation to arbitration.[67] Parts 1, 2 and 4 of the Agricultural Holdings (Requests for Landlord's Consent or Variation of Terms and the Suitability Test) (England) Regulations 2021[68] came into force on 21 June 2021; Part 3 came into force on 1 September 2024.

---

64 DEFRA response to the Rock Review (n 13) 33/57. Perhaps an inelegant echo of that ancient farmer poet, Hesiod, in *Works and Days*.
65 ibid. DEFRA, however, also recognised the unwelcome result in forcing landlords to enter schemes jointly with their tenants, namely, dissuading landlords from letting land at all where there is already a short supply.
66 An arbitrator may also be appointed under the Agricultural Holdings Act 1986 from the Central Association of Agricultural Valuers, Royal Institution of Chartered Surveyors and the Agricultural Law Association.
67 As defined in Agricultural Holdings Act 1986 s 19A(3) where no agreement has been reached with the landlord.
68 SI 2021/619.

24.52 This marks an important statutory intervention because it enables a tenant to enter and take advantage of various schemes from which they would otherwise be barred. For that reason, it merits some consideration.

24.53 A tenant's request[69] is one which satisfies these conditions:

- it is a request for–
  - the landlord's consent to a matter which under the terms of the tenancy requires such consent; or
  - a variation of the terms of the tenancy,

  and

- it is made for the purposes of–
  - enabling the tenant to request or apply for relevant financial assistance; or
  - complying with a statutory duty, or a statutory duty of a description applicable to the tenant in respect of the use of the holding.[70]

24.54 The relevant financial assistance[71] is that under:[72]

- Agriculture Act 2020 section 1 (powers of Secretary of State to give financial assistance);
- Agriculture Act 2020 section 21 (powers of Secretary of State to give financial assistance in exceptional market conditions); or
- a scheme of the sort mentioned in Agriculture Act 2020 section 2(4) (third party schemes).

24.55 Where there has been no agreement following the request, the landlord and tenant may agree in writing to refer the matter to third party determination.[73]

---

69 The right to refer to arbitration under Agricultural Holdings Act 1986 s 19A is not permitted where a valid notice to quit under Sch 3, Pt 1 or Sch 5 has been served which can no longer be contested by the tenant.

70 Agricultural Holdings Act 1986 s 19A(3) and Agricultural Holdings (Requests for landlord's Consent or Variation of Terms and the Suitability Test) (England) Regulations 2021, reg 3(1).

71 Agriculture Act 2020 s 2(4). 'Financial assistance may be given to the maker or operator of a third-party scheme in connection with expenditure involved in establishing or operating the scheme (including the provision of financial support'.

72 Agricultural Holdings (Requests for Landlord's Consent or Variation of Terms and the Suitability Test) (England) Regulations 2021, reg 2.

73 Agriculture Act 2020 s 19A. and Agricultural Holdings (Requests for landlord's Consent or Variation of Terms and the Suitability Test) (England) Regulations 2021 reg 3(1). The tenant can refer the request to arbitration.

24.56 In summary, the procedure is as follows:

- The tenant raises a request in writing for consent or variation;
- The tenant serves notice on the landlord;[74]
- The landlord then has two months to serve a counter-notice;[75]
- Where the landlord does not serve a counter-notice, or the landlord consents but on conditions which are not acceptable to the tenant, or refuses the request, the tenant may refer the request to arbitration within four months of the service of the tenant's notice;[76]
- The matter is then referred to arbitration (or third party determination if the parties agree).

24.57 The arbitrator[77] may order the landlord to comply with the request or make such other award as he considers reasonable and just as between the landlord and the tenant having regard to all relevant matters including:

- the tenant's quiet enjoyment of the holding;
- the landlord's reversionary interest in the holding;
- other property of the landlord and the tenant;
- evidence as to the settled objectives of the landlord and tenant;
- the desirability of making the least change to the tenancy that is reasonably necessary to give effect to such variation or approval that the arbitrator or third party may direct.[78]

24.58 The arbitrator may also include such awards as they consider reasonable and just as between the landlord and the tenant in respect of:

- the payment of costs;
- conditions relating to the making of a successful application for financial assistance.[79]

---

74 Complying with Agricultural Holdings (Requests for landlord's Consent or Variation of Terms and the Suitability Test) (England) Regulations 2021 regs 3(5) and (6).
75 ibid reg 3(8).
76 ibid reg 3(9).
77 Or third party determination where applicable.
78 An arbitrator may also be appointed under the Agricultural Holdings Act 1986 from the Central Association of Agricultural Valuers, Royal Institution of Chartered Surveyors and the Agricultural Law Association.
79 Agricultural Holdings (Requests for landlord's Consent or Variation of Terms and the Suitability Test) (England) Regulations 2021 reg 4(2).

24.59 The arbitrator does not have jurisdiction to make an award which includes variation as to rent or compensation.[80]

(iii) *Consent or variation under farm business tenancies*

24.60 No equivalent provisions were introduced under the Agricultural Tenancies Act 1995. The Rock Review recommended legislation to extend protection against an unreasonable refusal of scheme entry and access to arbitration for farm business tenancies.[81] This is unlikely to happen in the short term; DEFRA has adopted a wait and see approach on how schemes progress and encourages collaboration.[82] Thus, at present, it will depend on the particular terms and conditions contained in individual agreements.

Environment improvement: tenant's fixture or improvement

24.61 If a landlord consent or variation of the tenancy will be required before entering into a scheme, the question over the tenant's fixture or improvement should be addressed when drawing up the agreement or as part of the arbitral award (or third party determination).

24.62 Where physical works are required, the question is whether they be treated at the end of the tenancy as the tenant's improvements or tenant's fixture. Consideration will need to be given as to whether the scheme itself addresses this or whether it is left to the individual landlord and tenant agreement. It will, of course, be very specific to the particular works required.

24.63 The relevance of fixtures is this: Agricultural Holdings Act 1986 section 10 applies to fixtures of whatever description affixed to an agricultural holding by the tenant whether for the purpose of agriculture or not. It varies the common law rule that anything fixed to the freehold becomes part of the freehold, and thus the property of the landlord. In other words section 10 allows the tenant to remove fixtures (so long as certain conditions are met). But a fixture cannot be removed if it has been agreed that it is a tenant's improvement.[83] One example is in the case of agroforestry where trees could be approved as a tenant's fixture and thus removed if feasible or lawful at the end of the tenancy.

24.64 Under the Agricultural Tenancies Act 1995, if it is a fixture and also an improvement then it is the tenant's choice to remove it or claim compensation for the improvement.[84] The tenant's right to remove is as follows:

---

80 ibid regs 4(3) and 4(4).
81 See Rock Review (n 9) 12–14; 35–36, 38, 42 and for this, and other recommendations, see 53–55.
82 The Rock Review recommendations included redefining agriculture and good husbandry and dispute resolution process where there had been unreasonable refusal to consent. DEFRA declined to do so (see Response to Rock Review (n 13) 49–57). Obviously, unreasonable refusal to consent there is actionable. The Rock Review was really leading calls to impose variation/consent equivalent to Agricultural Holdings Act 1986 s 19A.
83 Agricultural Holdings Act 1986 s 10(2)(b).
84 cf Agricultural Holdings Act 1986 which does not apply to buildings or where the landlord decides to elect to take a fixture.

- A tenant can remove any fixture he put or previously added and any building erected by him or a previous tenant;
- It is not confined to agricultural fixtures and the Agricultural Tenancies Act 1995 anticipates non-agricultural activities;
- A tenant is always entitled to remove a fixture regardless of the terms of the tenancy;[85]
- But if it is a fixture or a building erected pursuant to some contractual or statutory obligation, a tenant is not entitled to remove it.[86]

Rent review

24.65 The potential effect on the market value of the land by environmental schemes and the generating of non-farming income[87] may be relevant factors for the purposes of rent review under both the Agricultural Holdings Act 1986 and the Agricultural Tenancies Act 1995.[88]

85 Agricultural Tenancies Act 1995 s 8.
86 e.g. in relation to pollution control measures where it would be an improvement for the landlord to remove it, but the tenant is entitled to compensation.
87 e.g. BNG, nutrient neutrality schemes.
88 *JW Childers Trustees v Anker* (1995) 7 P&CR 458 and Court of Session in *Morrison-low v Paterson* SLC/233/08 (2010).

CHAPTER 25

PROPERTY-BASED AND OTHER TORTS

Ashley Pratt

Introduction

25.01 The Court of Appeal of New Zealand in the case of *Smith v Fonterra*[1] posed the question: 'What should be the response of tort law to climate change?'[2]

25.02 Discussions concerning property-based torts and climate change will inevitably have to consider and balance the historical foundations of the law against a rapidly changing environment. The fact is that courts, both nationally and internationally, are already having to deal with the complex interplay between the existing legal framework, the traditionally incremental common law response to change, and an increasing pressure to react timeously to the climate change crisis.[3]

25.03 Statutory intervention is going to be very important since the complexity of the problem is 'quintessentially a matter that calls for a sophisticated regulatory response at a national level supported by international co-ordination'.[4]

25.04 The courts have traditionally trodden carefully in developing tort law, rightly wary of stepping into the political arena.[5] In the environmental law context, the Supreme Court reiterated in *Vedanta Resources plc and another v Lungowe and others*,[6] a case concerning toxic emissions from a mine in Zambia, that the courts will rigorously analyse any claims that concern 'novel and controversial extension of the boundaries of the tort of negligence, beyond any established category, calling for a cautious incremental approach by analogy with established categories'.[7]

1 *Smith v Fonterra* [2021] NZCA 552 [1], which has been overturned by the Supreme Court in [2024] NZSC 5.
2 *Smith v Fonterra* (n 1) [1].
3 There have been 2,341 international climate change claims reported in the Sabin Centres climate change database as of 31 May 2023 and rising; see Joana Setzer and Catherine Higham, 'Global Trends in Climate Change Litigation: 2023 Snapshot' (Grantham Research Institute on Climate Change and the Environment 2021).
4 *Smith v Fonterra* (n 1) [16].
5 See e.g. *Hunter v Canary Wharf* [1997] AC 655 [696], Lloyd LJ, '…But it is one thing to modernise the law by ridding it of unnecessary technicalities; it is another thing to bring about a fundamental change in the nature and scope of a cause of action'.
6 *Vedanta Resources plc and another v Lungowe and others* [2019] UKSC 20.
7 *Vedanta Resources plc v Lungowe* (n 6) [46].

25.05 Given the scientific consensus on the long-lasting effects of climate change,[8] will the courts have to adopt a policy-driven approach to the development of property-based torts? Should novel torts be created? How will the law adapt to the effects of climate change when considering property rights balanced against the collective benefits of environmental protectionism? Is there a distinction to be drawn by the courts between environmental mitigation and adaptation cases and cases concerning negligence?

25.06 Who should pay the costs of the effects of climate change? Lord Bingham suggested rhetorically:[9]

> But if a member of the public whom a public service exists suffers a significant injury or loss through the culpable fault or reprehensible failure of that service to act as it should, is it not consistent with ethical and, perhaps, democratic principle that the many, responsible for funding the service, should bear the cost of compensating the victim.

These are complex ethical policy issues that will continue to vex both the legislature and the courts.

25.07 At present the courts of England and Wales are yet to decide a case concerning property-based torts and net zero. In the field of environmental law there are, however, some helpful decisions upon which assistance can be drawn. There are also a number of recent international net zero cases that are considered in this section.

25.08 It is anticipated that the courts' usual approach to the incremental change of tort law may come under increasing challenge depending on the rate of climate change, public pressure, and the extent of any statutory intervention.

25.09 This section will deal with the difficult questions raised above in the context of property-based and other torts in the areas of:

- public nuisance;
- statutory nuisance;
- private nuisance;
- *Rylands v Fletcher*;[10]
- statutory undertakers;

8 *Smith v Fonterra* [2024] NZSC 5 [14] in reliance on IPCC, 'Climate Change 2023: Synthesis Report' (2023) <https://www.ipcc.ch/report/ar6/syr/downloads/report/IPCC_AR6_SYR_FullVolume.pdf> accessed 12 April 2024.
9 Bingham, *Lives of the Law: Selected Essays and Speeches: 2000–2010* (Oxford University Press 2011), Chapter 17 'A Duty of Care. The Uses of Tort' 269 at 282.
10 *Rylands v Fletcher* (1868) LR 3 HL 330.

- trespass;
- negligence;
- novel torts; and
- causation.

Public nuisance

25.10 Public nuisance is usually concerned with particular types of damage relating to the inconvenience and injury suffered over and above that endured by the general public.[11] The historical basis for civil liability in public nuisance actions is derived from the criminal law:[12]

> The relevance of these miscellaneous criminal misdemeanours to the law of tort was that no private action could be brought to recover damages for a nuisance which was common to the whole locality. If it were otherwise, a wrongdoer might be subject to hundreds of actions for the same offence. The proper course was for an indictment to be preferred against an offender.

25.11 The criminal law relating to public nuisance has very recently been enshrined in the Police, Crime, Sentencing and Courts Act 2022 which retains civil liability. The Act provides:[13]

> (3) Intentionally or recklessly causing public nuisance
> 78.-(1) A person commits an offence if- …
>
> (a) the person-
> (i) does an act, or
> (ii) omits to do an act that they are required to do by any enactment or rule of law,
> (b) the person's act or omission
> (i) creates a risk of, or causes, serious harm, to the public or a section of the public, or
> (ii) obstructs the public or a section of the public in the exercise or enjoyment of a right that may be exercised or enjoyed by the public at large, and
> (c) the person intends there that their act or omission will have a consequence mentioned in paragraph (b) or is reckless as to whether it will have such consequence.

---

11 See Anthony Dugdale, *Clerk & Lindsell on Torts* (24th edn, Sweet & Maxwell 2023) paras 19–03.
12 Baker, *Introduction to English Legal History* (5th edn, Oxford University Press 2019) 463 (1465) Y.B. Pas. 5 Edw. IV, fo 2, pl. 4, per Heydon.
13 In force since 28 June 2022.

(2) In subsection (1) (b) (i) 'serious harm' means-

(a) death, personal injury, or disease,
(b) loss of, or damage to, property, or
(c) serious distress, serious annoyance, serious inconvenience, or serious loss of amenity…

(8) This section does not affect- …

(b) the civil liability of any person for the tort of public nuisance.

25.12 Whilst there is now in place a statutory offence for public nuisance, where the common law offence continues to apply:[14]

a person is guilty of a public nuisance (also known as a common nuisance) who:-
Does an act not warranted by law; and
Omits to discharge a legal duty,
If the effect of the act or omission is to endanger life, health, property, or comfort of the public, or to obstruct the public in the exercise or enjoyment of rights common to all Her Majesty's subjects.

25.13 In the context of civil liability, the tort of public nuisance is actionable by private individuals so long as they are found to have suffered from 'particular damage over and above the general inconvenience and injury suffered by the public in general'.[15]

25.14 How should the courts expand public nuisance as a tort, if at all, to respond to claims caused by domestic and international emitters of greenhouse gases? Should the courts provide injunctive relief against future emissions if national targets are not met or impose requirements to provide for adaptations to mitigate future damage? Is this simply a role for the legislature? Any development in the law applicable generally to members of the public would clearly be a departure from the current law of public nuisance.

25.15 In the New Zealand case of *Smith v Fonterra*[16] a claim was brought in public nuisance, negligence and a novel tort, described in the Supreme Court's judgment[17] as a 'proposed climate system damage tort', against seven New Zealand companies that were described as being 'in an industry that either emits [GHGs] or supplies products which release GHGs when burned'.[18] The claim alleged that the defendants had contributed to:[19]

14 *Archbold: Criminal Pleading, Evidence and Practice* (2024 edn, Sweet & Maxwell) paras 31–40. The normal course will be to prosecute for the statutory offence see, *R v Rimmington; R v Goldstein* [2006] 1 AC 459.
15 *Clerk & Lindsell on Torts* (24th edn, Sweet & Maxwell 2023) (n 11) paras 19–03.
16 *Smith v Fonterra* (NZSC) (n 8).
17 ibid [71].
18 ibid [3].
19 *Smith v Fonterra* (n 1) [4].

dangerous anthropogenic interference with the climate system and to the adverse effects of climate change. These are particularised as increased temperatures, loss of biodiversity and biomass, loss of land, risks to food and water security, increasing extreme weather events, ocean acidification, geopolitical instability, population displacement, adverse health consequences, economic losses and an unacceptable risk of social and economic loss and mass loss of human life. It is also alleged that poor and minority communities will be disproportionately burdened by the adverse effects of climate change.

25.16 The action relied on the concept of 'net zero' and sought injunctive relief. The claim for injunctive relief required the defendants to 'produce (or contribute to …) zero net emissions by 2030, by linear reductions in net emissions each year until that time (to be supervised by the Court), or to otherwise cease their emission creating activities immediately'.[20]

25.17 The allegations brought by the claimant were ground-breaking. The claim submitted that the court should extend the law of public nuisance to include all citizens of New Zealand – a wholesale departure from the existing test for public nuisance. It was submitted to the court that the case was a 'watershed moment' in the law and that the court should be 'courageous' as were the judges in *Donoghue v Stevenson*.[21]

25.18 In short, the Court of Appeal refused to accede to such claims, it said:[22]

> [T]he issue of climate change cannot be effectively addressed through tort law. Rather, this pressing issue calls for a sophisticated regulatory response at a national level, supported by international co-ordination … As is well known, relevant international agreements include the United Nations Framework Convention on Climate Change, the Kyoto Protocol and the Paris Agreement.

25.19 The Supreme Court overturned the Court of Appeal and allowed the appeal in respect of the public nuisance claim. The claim was thus reinstated and sent for trial.[23]

25.20 The Supreme Court stated in its reasoning that:[24]

> It is here beyond question that the respondents are either very substantial emitters of GHGs or are (or have been) very substantial suppliers of fossil fuels that release GHGs when burned by others. Further, as we are here dealing with a strike out application, where pleaded facts are assumed to be capable of proof, we have been required to assume for present purposes that the consequences of the activities is harm to the land and other pleaded interests held by Mr Smith …

---

20 ibid [20].
21 *Donoghue v Stevenson* [1932] AC 562 (HL).
22 *Smith v Fonterra* (n 1) [28]–[29].
23 *Smith v Fonterra* (NZSC) (n 8) [172]–[173].
24 ibid [155]–[156].

> The common law has not previously grappled with a crisis as all-embracing as climate change. But in the 19th and 20th centuries it [the common law] had to deal with…the industrial revolution… The law's response was a mixture of the flawed (e.g. the common employment rule restricting claims by employees for injury) and the inspired (e.g. the duty of care based on neighbourhood, expounded by Lord Atkin in *Donoghue v Stevenson*). Importantly, where the common law's response proved flawed, it was revised by the legislature either enlarging or limiting its reach …

25.21 The Supreme Court concluded:[25]

> real caution is necessary before pre-emptively disposing of a claim where seriously arguable non-trivial harm is in issue. The courts in New Zealand have barely touched (let alone grappled with) the law of public nuisance in the last century … The principles governing public nuisance ought not to stand still in the face of massive environmental challenges attributable to human economic activity …

25.22 The principal difference in the reasoning between the Court of Appeal and the Supreme Court appears to have been the reluctance to strike out the claimant's claim without:[26] (i) the courts providing an answer at trial to whether, and if so to what extent, the law of public nuisance should develop in response to climate change cases and (ii) considering the effect of any climate change attribution evidence. It is cautiously suggested that the prospects of success will be dependent on the quality of the attribution evidence, as it is likely that the court will develop the law of public nuisance if provided with positive evidence that emitters had at least contributed to climate change related damage. Developments in relation to causation are dealt with below. It is difficult to say how the UK courts might react to a similar set of facts. At present the tests for strike out in the UK[27] and New Zealand[28] are very similar and as such the UK Courts may take a similar approach and let the arguments and evidence unravel at trial.

Statutory nuisance

25.23 Statutory nuisance must be distinguished from the tort of private nuisance: the former is concerned with harm to people whilst the latter protects private property rights.[29] The key difference is that statutory nuisance can give rise to criminal liability, whereas private law nuisance is concerned with civil liability.

25.24 Section 79 of Environmental Protection Act 1990 ('EPA 1990') sets out the statutory nuisances; and insofar as relevant states that:

---

25 ibid [172]–[173].

26 See para 25.69 below.

27 CPR 3.4(2)(a) (applicable to England and Wales) states: 'The Court may strike out a statement of case if it appears to the court – That the statement of case brings no reasonable grounds for bringing or defending the claim'.

28 Rule 15.1(1)(a) of the New Zealand High Court Rules 2016 states that the test for strike out is a pleading or part of a pleading that 'discloses no reasonably arguable cause of action'.

29 Robert McCracken, Gregory Jones and James Pereira, *Statutory Nuisance* (4th edn, Bloomsbury Publishing 2019) para 1.10.

(1) … the following matters constitute 'statutory nuisances' for the purposes of this Part …

(a) any premises in such a state as to be prejudicial to health or a nuisance;
(b) smoke emitted from premises so as to be prejudicial to health or a nuisance;
(c) fumes or gases emitted from premises so as to be prejudicial to health or a nuisance;
(d) any dust, steam, smell or other effluvia arising on industrial, trade or business premises and being prejudicial to health or a nuisance;
(e) any accumulation or deposit which is prejudicial to health or a nuisance; …
(g) noise emitted from premises so as to be prejudicial to health or a nuisance;
(ga) noise that is prejudicial to health or a nuisance and is emitted from or caused by a vehicle, machinery or equipment in a street or in Scotland, road;
(h) any other matter declared by any enactment to be a statutory nuisance; …

25.25 The EPA 1990 defines 'fumes' as 'any airborne solid matter smaller than dust'; 'gas' as 'vapour and moisture precipitated from vapour'; and 'smoke' to include 'soot, ash, grit and gritty particles emitted in smoke'.[30]

25.26 In respect of each statutory nuisance, there are two limbs; either there is a statutory nuisance because the existence of something is 'prejudicial to health' or because it is a 'nuisance'.[31] 'Prejudicial to health' is defined by the EPA 1990 as 'injurious, or likely to cause injury, to health'.[32] What is 'prejudicial to health' is a matter of judgment based on expert opinion and guidance.[33] 'Nuisance' bears the common law meaning with two important differences: (i) statutory nuisance is only concerned with harm to property when it causes harm to people's comfort or amenity; and (ii) a complainant in relation to statutory nuisance does not need to have any property rights.[34]

25.27 Ultimately, statutory nuisance could address GHG emissions at source, provided the other conditions in the EPA 1990 are met, because it may well be that the GHG emissions are present in the fumes, gas or smoke, but this would not address the wider issue of GHG emissions. Further, given that s 79(1)(c) only applies to private dwellings, a statutory nuisance claim in relation to fumes or gases could not be pursued against commercial emitters.[35]

30 EPA 1990 s 79(7).
31 ibid s 79(1).
32 ibid s 79(7).
33 McCracken, Jones and Pereira, *Statutory Nuisance* (n 29) para 1.04.
34 *National Coal Board v Neath BC* [1976] 2 All ER 478 (DC); *Clerk & Lindsell on Torts* (n 11) para 19-04; McCracken, Jones and Pereira, *Statutory Nuisance* (n 29) para 1.10.
35 EPA 1990 s 79(4) where a 'private dwelling' is defined as 'any building, or part of a building, used or intended to be used, as a dwelling', see EPA 1990 s 79(7).

Private nuisance

25.28 A private nuisance is usually an act that arises out of lawful acts performed on a person's own land but the consequences of those acts encroach, cause physical damage, or unduly interfere with neighbouring enjoyment of land.[36]

25.29 During the reign of Henry II (1154–1189), there is said to have been lost legislation that included '... acts done to the nuisance of a free tenement'.[37] From about that time there was a right known as the 'assize of nuisance' that could be 'lay to abate a nuisance'.[38] A little later there is a reported case in 1342[39] concerning a claim for damages arising out of a failure to repair a sea wall. It was found that this failure to repair amounted to a nonfeasance and the claimant succeeded in his claim for damages, as well as obtaining an order for repair.[40] By the Tudor period there was some pushback against 'the spread of the new remedy'.[41] In 1582 an action for passive continuance[42] failing to put an end to a nuisance (that was already existing on land when it came into his possession) was allowed, confined to 'man-made nuisance'.[43]

25.30 Turning to the current law, the often-quoted test for private nuisance[44] is taken from Professor Francis Newark's classic article, 'the Boundaries of Nuisance',[45] which states, 'The term "nuisance" is properly applied only to such actionable user of land as interferes with the enjoyment by the plaintiff of rights in land.' The article continues:[46]

> [T]he interest of the plaintiff which is invaded is not the interest of bodily security but the interest of liberty to the exercise of rights over land in the amplest manner. A sulphurous chimney in a residential area is not a nuisance because it makes householders cough and splutter but because it prevents them from taking their ease in their gardens.

25.31 The leading case on the law of private nuisance is *Fearn & others v Board of Trustees of the Tate Gallery*,[47] which confirmed Professor Newark's statement and added:[48]

> As generally in the law of property, the legal concept of land includes here not only the earth itself but also buildings and other things which are physically attached to it and rights, for example easements, which attach in law to the land.

---

36 *Clerk & Lindsell on Torts* (n 11) paras 19–05.
37 Baker, *Introduction to English Legal History* (n 12) 452.
38 ibid 452.
39 ibid 453. *Bernadeston v Heighlynge* (1342) B & M 644, 102 SS117, 105 SS291–2.
40 Baker, *Introduction to English Legal History* (n 12) 453.
41 ibid 454. *Orwell v Mortoft* (1505) B & M 448, 451, Kingsmill J.
42 Baker, *Introduction to English Legal History* (n 12) 455. *Beswick v Cunden* (No.2) (1596) Cro Eliz 520.
43 Baker, *Introduction to English Legal History* (n 12) 455.
44 See also *Hunter v Canary Wharf* (1997) AC 655 at 688; *Coventry v Lawrence* [2014] UKSC 13, Lord Neuberger [2]; *Fearn & others v Board of Trustees of the Tate Gallery* [2023] UKSC 4, Lord Leggatt.
45 Newark, 'The Boundaries of Nuisance' (1949) 65 LQR 480.
46 ibid 488–489.
47 *Fearn & others v Board of Trustees of the Tate Gallery* [2023] UKSC 4.
48 ibid [9].

25.32 The recent UK Supreme Court case of *Jalla & others v Shell International Trading and Shipping Co Ltd & another*[49] summarised the tort of private nuisance as follows:[50]

> In general terms, the tort of private nuisance is committed where the defendant's activity, or a state of affairs for which the defendant is responsible, unduly interferes with (or, as it has commonly been expressed, causes a substantial and unreasonable interference with) the use and enjoyment of the claimant's land ... Nearly always the undue interference with the use and enjoyment of the claimant's land will be caused by an activity or state of affairs on the defendant's land so that the tort is often described as one dealing with respective rights of neighbouring landowners or occupiers ... But the creator of the nuisance can be sued whether or not that person still has (or perhaps ever had) any interest in the land from which the nuisance emanates.

25.33 The case of *Jalla* concerned claims arising out of a major oil spill off the coast of Nigeria. The question to be decided was whether the oil spill amounted to a continuing private nuisance and thus a continuing action for the purposes of limitation. The court decided that a single oil spill did not constitute an 'ongoing state of affairs'[51] and to accept the contrary would be to undermine the law on limitations and allow a 'continual restarting of the limitation period until the oil was removed or cleaned up'.[52]

25.34 There were two further points raised in *Jalla*, which are apposite:[53]

> Moreover, it is being assumed for the purposes of this appeal that the tort of private nuisance may be committed where the nuisance emanates from the sea. It is also being assumed that the tort of private nuisance may be committed to a one-off single event such as the oil spill in this case.

25.35 Whilst the two points were considered by the court, *de bene esse*, it refused to address them as *Shell* had failed to properly apply to cross-appeal the decision and had succeeded on limitation. Given the importance of environmental and climate change cases it may be that in circumstances where the court has the opportunity to decide points such as those in *Jalla* it should grasp the nettle. In the context of climate change litigation deciding what was a one-off event was may have assisted future jurisprudence in relation to continual emitters of GHGs.

25.36 The Court of Appeal took the opportunity to consider the strike-out principles in relation to Brazilian law (the law similar to private nuisance) in response to the Fundao Dam disaster that occurred on 5 November 2015 when the dam in south-eastern Brazil collapsed.[54] The collapse and consequential flood killed 19 people, destroyed villages, and resulted in a widespread impact on individuals, companies, and communities up to 400 miles away. The Brazilian prosecutor estimated that the damage might amount to

---

49 *Jalla & others v Shell International Trading and Shipping Co Ltd & another* [2023] UKSC 16 [2].
50 ibid [2].
51 ibid [26].
52 ibid [39] the court referred to Law Commission Paper No 151, Limitation of Actions (1998) paras 1.22–1.38.
53 *Jalla & others v Shell International Trading and Shipping Co Ltd & another* (n 49) [2].
54 *Municipio De Mariana & others v (1) BHP Group (UK) Ltd (2) BHP Group Ltd* [2022] EWCA Civ 951.

£25 billion. As a result of the disaster an action was launched in England by 202,600 claimants seeking compensation for losses (there are now 732,000 claimants).[55] Brazilian law applied, which allowed the claimants to pursue damages for losses associated with claims arising out of environmental damage.[56] Indirect polluters in Brazil are subject to strict liability rules. There are some features akin to the domestic law of private nuisance.

25.37 At first instance,[57] Turner J struck out the claims as an abuse of process. The judge's reasons were (i) there were likely to be irreconcilable judgments between those in the English and the Brazilian courts and (ii) that cross-contamination of judgments would lead to 'irredeemably unmanageable' cases in England. Had the judge not struck out the claims he would have stayed them due to the risk of irreconcilable judgments.

25.38 The Court of Appeal decided:[58] (i) a properly advanced claim even if it is 'unmanageable' does not make it an abuse, (ii) the judge's conclusion that the proceedings were 'irredeemably unmanageable' could not be sustained, (iii) the judge was wrong to rely on *forum non conveniens* factors when considering abuse of process, (iv) the judge's view that there was nothing to be gained in the English courts was premised on an unjustified view that the claims were unmanageable and (v) the judge incorrectly treated the claimants as a single indivisible group whose applications must succeed or fail altogether. The Court of Appeal considered the strike out application for abuse afresh stating:[59]

> In summary, the risk of unmanageability, or as the judge put it 'utter chaos', due to the existence of proceedings in Brazil is not clear and obvious, whether by reference to the claimants as a whole, or, as in fact required considering their position on an individual basis. As the claimants rightly recognise, it may be that 'down the line' some individual claims may need to be reviewed by releases signed by particular claimants… The potential for such issues arising in due course cannot be said to make them abusive on the grounds that the claims are unmanageable.

25.39 What is apparent from the Court of Appeal's decision is that the courts are ready to hear substantial environmental law claims involving many hundreds of thousands of claimants. This is likely to be important in the climate change context because the effects of climate change do not recognise international boundaries and may be brought by many claimants in group actions.[60]

25.40 It is therefore likely that UK GHG emitters will be pursued both in the domestic and international courts if climate change continues at its current rate. Transboundary

---

55 *Vale SA vs BHP Group* [2023] EWCA Civ 1388.
56 ibid [11].
57 *Municipio De Mariana v (1) BHP Group (UK) Ltd (2) BHP Group Ltd* [2020] EWHC 2930 (TCC).
58 *Municipio De Mariana v (1) BHP Group (UK) Ltd (2) BHP Group Ltd* (n 54).
59 ibid [194].
60 Post Brexit, Rome II on the law applicable to non-contractual obligations Recitals 24 and 25 are applicable and provide for claims arising out of environmental damage. Article 25 provides that there should be a high level of environmental protections and the polluter pays principle. For further analysis see causation section below para 25.69. Also see *Dicey, Morris & Collins on the Conflict of Laws* (16th edn, Sweet & Maxwell 2023) paras 35–076 for full commentary on this complex area.

environmental harm is already being considered by international bodies such as the International Law Commission.[61]

25.41 The Court of Appeal in New Zealand was of the view that the common law should not provide wholesale solutions to such complex regulatory issues which have international ramifications.[62] Whilst statutory intervention will be required it is far from certain when and to what extent legislation will assist. The courts should decide questions such as those posed in *Jalla* when they arise to assist the gradual development of this important area. Taking an incremental approach will assist the development of the common law and may assist in creating a richer array of policy options to assist Parliament when these important issues are considered. The extent to which the court will intervene in developing the law remains to be seen. What is clear is that the court is willing and able to manage large scale international environmental litigation.

Rylands v Fletcher

25.42 The rule in *Rylands v Fletcher*[63] can be stated as follows:

- a defendant that brings onto its land anything likely to do mischief if it escapes is on the face of it responsible if it does escape and affects the use of the claimant's land;
- the rule does not apply to anything that is naturally on the defendant's land;
- the defendant will be responsible for the foreseeable consequences of the escape (see *Cambridge Water Co Ltd v Eastern Counties Leather plc*);[64] and
- the rule is engaged only where the defendant's use of the land is shown to be extraordinary and unusual – 'the ordinary user test'.[65]

25.43 The rule in *Rylands v Fletcher* was restated by Bingham LJ in the case of *Transco v Stockport MBC*:[66]

> The rule in Rylands v Fletcher is a sub-species of nuisance, which is itself a tort based on the interference by one occupier of land with the right in or enjoyment of land by another occupier of land as such …
>
> It has from the beginning been a necessary condition of liability under the rule in Rylands v Fletcher that the thing which the defendant has brought on his land should be 'something which…will naturally do mischief if it escapes out of his land' … 'anything likely

61 For support of this view, see Foster, 'Novel Climate Tort? The New Zealand Court of Appeal Decision in Smith v Fonterra Co-Operative Group Limited and Others' (2022) 24 Environmental Law Review 224.
62 *Smith v Fonterra* (n 1) [16].
63 *Rylands v Fletcher* (1866) LR1 Ex 265.
64 *Cambridge Water Co Ltd v Eastern Counties Leather plc* [1994] 2 AC 264 [306].
65 *Transco v Stockport MBC* [2004] 2 AC 1.
66 ibid [8]–[11].

> to do mischief if it escapes', 'something … harmless to others so long as it is confined to his own property, but which he knows to be mischievous if it gets on his neighbour's' … Bearing in mind the historical origin of the rule, and also that its effect is to impose liability in the absence of negligence for an isolated occurrence, I do not think the mischief or danger test should be at all easily satisfied. It must be shown that the defendant has done something which he recognised … as giving rise to an exceptionally high risk of danger or mischief if there should be an escape, however unlikely an escape may have been thought to be.
>
> … I think it clear that ordinary user is a preferable test to natural user, making it clear that the rule in Rylands v Fletcher is engaged only where the defendant's use is shown to be extraordinary and unusual. This is not a test to be inflexibly applied: a use may be extraordinary and unusual at one time or in one place but not so at another time or in another place…Again, as it seems to me, the question is whether the defendant has done something which he recognises, or ought to recognise, as being quite out of the ordinary in the place and at the time he does it.

25.44 The rule in *Rylands v Fletcher* is concerned with isolated escapes. For this rule to be applicable in the context of climate change emissions, in cases such as *Smith v Fonterra*,[67] there would have to be some modifications to include extensions for continual escapes from GHG emitters and to the ordinary user test. As it stands it is unlikely that the rule will be of much use in the context of climate change litigation. It may be better to simply start with a new or novel tort. In the case of *Smith v Fonterra*,[68] the claimant chose to develop a novel tort called 'climate system damage tort'.[69]

Statutory undertakers

25.45 Statutory undertakers are bodies who perform obligations under statutory powers, for example, utility companies.[70]

25.46 The Water Industry Act 1991 s 209 (1) states: 'Where an escape of water, however caused, from a pipe vested in a water undertaker causes loss or damage, the undertaker shall be liable, except as otherwise provided in this section, for the loss or damage.' The exception to s 209 (1) is where the claimant is at fault. In the instance of an act of God the undertaker would be liable.

25.47 In the construction of sewers by statutory undertakers the converse rule applies. It is only when negligence is proven that the claimant can succeed in his claim.[71] Generally speaking statutory undertakers are subject to the proof of negligence rule unless

67 *Smith v Fonterra* (n 1).
68 ibid.
69 *Smith v Fonterra* (NZSC) (n 8) [71] and dealt with below at para 25.67.
70 'Statutory Undertaker Definition | Legal Glossary | LexisNexis' <https://www.lexisnexis.co.uk/legal/glossary/statutory-undertaker> accessed 3 May 2024.
71 *Clerk & Lindsell on Torts* (24th edn, Sweet & Maxwell 2023) (n 11) paras 19–130. Negligence is applicable to the construction of sewers, *Collins v Middle Level Commission* (1869) LR 4 C & P 279, and for failure to properly manage the sewer following their construction *Dixon v Metropolitan Board of Works* (1881) 7 QBD 418. For a more recent example see *Oldcorn v Southern Water Services Ltd* [2017] EWHC 62 (TCC).

statute dictates otherwise. Other examples of statutory intervention in the nuisance arena include the Clean Air Act 1993 and the Environmental Protection Act 1990 Pt III.

25.48 As stated in the statutory nuisance section[72] there would have to be some modification to current statute to make it relevant to climate litigation cases in the context of property-based and other torts.

Trespass

25.49 The tort of trespass differs from the tort of private nuisance and the tort of negligence in that it is actionable without proof of damage.[73] In the property-based torts context, trespass may become a feature of litigation where, for example, energy infrastructure projects infringe on private land. This could arise during the development of adjoining land, such as in the construction of wind and solar farms where damage may occur. There could also be arguments relating to carbon capture and subsoil trespass. Attempts may be made to claim damages for diminution in value of land.[74] Trespass could also extend to the depositing of waste on private land[75] and where flooding has arisen, and adaptations have not been installed either adequately or at all.

Negligence

25.50 The law of negligence is not limited to particular kinds of interests and as such is wide ranging in its scope.[76] It includes cases such as the protection of reputation, personal injuries, public rights and for present purposes property interests. The law of negligence has a long history.

25.51 The 1466 *Case of Thorns*,[77] well-known to legal historians, concerned a claim for damages arising out of the defendant entering his neighbours land to remove thorns following his clipping a hedge. The judge, Choke J, said, 'If he wants to make a good plea out of this, he should show what he did to prevent the thorns from falling, so that we can judge whether he did enough to excuse himself'.[78] By 1856, the tort of negligence was said to be: '... the omission to do something which a reasonable man ... would do, or something which a prudent and reasonable man would not do'.[79] The famous case of *Donoghue v Stevenson*[80] developed the test of negligence to include 'persons who are so closely and directly affected by my act that I ought reasonably to have them in

72 See para 25.23.
73 *Clerk & Lindsell on Torts* (n 11) paras 18-08 and 19-02 '... Trespass is a direct entry on the land of another, and is actionable per se, without proof of special damage'.
74 See *Crazy Bear Group v Patel* [2020] EWHC 3023 (Ch) and *Clerk & Lindsell on Torts* (n 11) paras 18–68.
75 There is statutory provision for civil liability for damages arising out of depositing waste; see Environmental Protection Act 1990 s 73(6).
76 *Clerk & Lindsell on Torts* (n 11) paras 7-01.
77 *Hulle v Orynge* (1466) B & M 369.
78 ibid 430.
79 ibid 442.
80 *Donoghue v Stevenson* [1932] AC 562.

my contemplation as being so affected when I am directing my mind to the acts or omissions which are called in question'.

25.52 The modern principles of negligence were distilled in the recent case of *Manchester Building Society v Grant Thornton*:[81]

(1) Is the harm (loss, injury, and damage) which is the subject matter of the claim actionable in negligence? (the actionability question)

(2) What are the risks of harm to the claimant against which the law imposes on the defendant a duty to take care? (the scope of duty question)

(3) Did the defendant breach his or her duty by his or her act or omission? (the breach question)

(4) Is the loss for which the claimant seeks damages the consequence of the defendant's act or omission? (the factual causation question)

(5) Is there a sufficient nexus between a particular element of the harm for which the claimant seeks damages and the subject matter of the defendant's duty of care analysed at stage 2 above? (the duty nexus question)

(6) Is a particular element of harm for which the claimant seeks damages irrecoverable because it is too remote, or because there is a different effective cause (including novus actus interveniens) in relation to it or because the claimant has mitigated his or her loss or has failed to avoid loss which he or she could reasonably have been expected to avoid? (the legal responsibility question)[82]

25.53 *Smith v Fonterra*[83] dealt with the tort of negligence as a separate cause of action. The New Zealand Court of Appeal accepted, at least at a general level, that the claim in negligence met the foreseeability test:[84]

> If knowledge and foreseeability are pitched at that more general level, then we agree that reasonable foreseeability of harm is arguably a trial issue and not of itself a ground for striking out.

81 *Manchester Building Society v Grant Thornton* [2021] UKSC 20 (n 1). *Clerk & Lindsell on Torts* (n 11) provides at para 7-04 a five stage as opposed to six stage test for negligence. See also, in the context of negligence and breach of duty, the court also has to take into account Compensation Act 2006, s 1ff whether the defendant should have taken particular steps to meet a standard of care, have regard to whether taking such steps would (a) prevent a desirable activity from being undertaken at all, to a particular extent or in a particular way, or (b) discourage persons from undertaking functions in connection with a desirable activity. The Act does not apply to claims in nuisance.
82 *Manchester Building Society v Grant Thornton* (n 81) [6].
83 *Smith v Fonterra* (n 1).
84 ibid [100].

25.54 The case however failed in the Court of Appeal in negligence on the basis that:[85]

> Proximity however is a different concept to foreseeability. It concerns the closeness of the connection between the parties in terms of their physical, temporal, relational and causal proximity. The notion of proximity requires the isolation of facts … that the defendant's act or omission closely and directly affected the plaintiff and that the parties are in this sense neighbours.

25.55 The Supreme Court of New Zealand disagreed with the Court of Appeal's analysis, its view was that negligence was at the very least a triable issue:[86]

> These authorities articulate what are long-established principles: a measured approach to strike out is appropriate where a claim- whether in negligence, nuisance or otherwise- is novel, but at least founded on seriously arguable non-trivial harm. That is so even if attribution to individual respondents remains difficult. In such a case the common law should lean towards receipt of the claim, and full evaluation and argument at trial, over pre-emptive elimination.

25.56 The Court of Appeal noted that were it to accede to such arguments in relation to extending the proximity of claimants there would be 'a limitless class of potential plaintiffs as well as a limitless class of potential defendants'.[87] The Supreme Court did not see this as justifying strike out,[88] but interestingly did not dive into the arguments raised by the Court of Appeal.

25.57 In the case of *Minister for the Environment v Sharma*[89] the Federal Court of Australia found that the Minister for the Environment did not have a duty to exercise her powers to refuse the expansion of a coal mine when considering the effects of climate change on children in accordance with the Environment Protection and Biodiversity Conservation Act 1999 ('EPBC 1999'). Sections 130 and 133 of the EPBC 1999 required the Minister for the Environment to take reasonable care to avoid 'causing injury or death to persons who were under 18 years of age and ordinarily resident in Australia'.[90]

25.58 The Federal Court considered *inter alia* whether the Minister for Environment could be said to be negligent in failing to exercise her powers. The Federal Court stated:[91]

> all these considerations: lack of control over the harm (as opposed to the tiny contribution of the risk), the conduct of countless others around the world, the lack of any special vulnerability, and lack of reliance, are only really features or reflections of the essential problem for the respondents: the relationship that founds the duty is one between the government and the governed and lacks the relevant nearness and proximity necessary for the imposition of a duty of care.

---

85 ibid [101].
86 *Smith v Fonterra* (NZSC) (n 8) [83].
87 ibid [116].
88 ibid [83].
89 *Minister for the Environment v Sharma* [2022] FCAFC 35.
90 ibid [10].
91 ibid [344].

25.59 Thus, the Federal Court has left questions regarding climate change and its effects on the public, in this case children, to the legislature as was suggested by the Court of Appeal in *Smith v Fonterra*.[92]

Novel torts

25.60 Where property-based torts are unable to develop incrementally, is there scope for the development of novel torts?

25.61 Bringing an action using a novel tort is nothing new. For example, a claim was brought in 1569 for nuisance by nonfeasance. '[I]f one who has a horrible sickness be in my house, and will not depart, an action will lie against him; and yet he taketh not any air from me, but infecteth that which I have.'[93] One could reasonably argue that greenhouse gases do 'infecteth the air'. Is there then scope for a novel property-based tort that encompasses property damage. It has been said that 'there is scope for the creation of a novel common law climate tort. This tort must be forward-looking and preventative in orientation and may differ fundamentally from existing torts.'[94]

25.62 The view above differs from the New Zealand Court of Appeal in *Smith v Fonterra*.[95] The proposed new tortious duty, as presented in *Smith,* was pleaded as follows:[96]

> The defendants owe a duty, cognisable at law, to cease contributing to damage to the climate system, dangerous anthropogenic interference with the climate system, and the adverse effects of climate change through their emission of Greenhouse Gasses into the atmosphere (or their production or exportation of coal in the case of BT Mining; and their production and supply of Fuel Products ...

25.63 The Supreme Court in *Smith v Fonterra*, quoting the above pleading,[97] described the novel tort as a 'proposed climate system damage tort.'[98]

25.64 The first instance decision in *Smith v Fonterra*[99] found:

> It may, for example, be that the special damage rule in public nuisance could be modified: it may be that climate change science will lead to an increased ability to model the possible effects of emissions. These are issues which can only be properly explored at trial. I am not prepared to strike out the third cause of action [novel tort] and foreclose on the possibility of the law of tort recognising a new duty which might assist Mr Smith.

---

92 *Smith v Fonterra* (n 1) [16].
93 Baker, *Introduction to English Legal History* (n 12) 458; *Hales' Case* (1569) BM 652, 653, per Mounson.
94 Foster, 'Novel Climate Tort? The New Zealand Court of Appeal Decision in Smith v Fonterra Co-Operative Group Limited and Others' (2022) 24 Environmental Law Review 224.
95 *Smith v Fonterra* (n 1).
96 ibid [118].
97 *Smith v Fonterra* (NZSC) (n 8) [71].
98 ibid [71].
99 *Smith v Fonterra Co-operative Group Ltd* [2020] NZHC 419, [2020] 2 NZLR 394 [High Court Judgment].

25.65 The Court of Appeal refused to extend the law of tort and allowed the defendants' cross-appeal. In its reversal of the judge's ruling at first instance it stated:[100]

> The bare assertion of the existence of a new tort without any attempt to delineate its scope cannot of itself be sufficient to withstand strike out on the basis of speculation that science may evolve by the time that matters gets to trial. Yet that is the effect of the decision.

25.66 The Supreme Court reversed the Court of Appeal's decision to strike out the proposed climate system damage tort; it stated:[101]

> Where the primary cause of action is not struck out, the authorities generally discourage striking out any remaining causes of action as a point of principle, unless it can be said they both meet the criteria for striking out and are likely to add materially to costs, hearing time and deployment of other court resources.
>
> In this case, there are good reasons to follow that approach. As the pleading itself demonstrates, the same facts are alleged, and are alleged to be relevant, in all three causes of action. Striking out the remaining claims in negligence and the proposed climate system damage tort would be unlikely to produce a material saving…And, although each cause of action has its own doctrinal underpinning, the deeper questions of necessary relationship, proximity, causation, disproportionality and indeterminacy raise issues common to all.

25.67 The Supreme Court allowed the claimants to obtain attribution evidence reports to establish their claims under the proposed climate system damage tort.[102] Attribution evidence will be important in establishing the proposed climate system damage tort because the claimant will inevitably have to establish that the defendants bear at least some responsibility for the damage claimed. This is discussed further in the causation section.[103] The Supreme Court's decision accords with the views of Stuart-Smith and others[104] that attribution evidence is available to meet a proposed system damage tort claim:[105]

> In our view these findings are not a product of technical limitations preventing the production of required evidence. Scientific evidence on the influence of individual actors' GHG emission is available for existing and projected impacts.

25.68 Whether or not it is the courts or Parliament who will develop novel property-based and other tort law in respect of climate change is difficult to tell.[106] Whilst the courts will often readily leave Parliament to develop new laws or radically alter existing

---

100 *Smith v Fonterra* (n 1) [124].
101 *Smith v Fonterra* (NZSC) (n 8) [174]–[175].
102 ibid [174]–[175].
103 See para 25.69 below.
104 Rupert F Stuart-Smith and others, 'Filling the Evidentiary Gap in Climate Litigation' (2021) 11 Nature Climate Change 651.
105 ibid line 150.
106 A search of the Law Commission's website did not disclose any results that reveal it is considering torts and climate change.

law, it is not always a straightforward process. Take for example the case of *McLoughlin v O'Brien*[107] where the House of Lords refused to expand the law concerning recovery arising out of psychiatric injury. Whilst the Law Commission recommended a change in the law, the government proposed that it should be left to the courts to develop the law in this area.[108] The consultation stated, '[T]he arguments in this complex and sensitive area are finely balanced. On balance the Government continues to take the view that it is preferable for the courts to have the flexibility to continue to develop the law rather than impose a statutory solution.'[109]

Causation

25.69 Claimants in climate change tort actions will inevitably deploy arguments surrounding contribution.[110] There will have to be scientific evidence, which is arguably available, to support such claims:[111]

> Courts evaluate scientific evidence by applying tests that set evidentiary thresholds for establishing causation. Across jurisdictions, causal analysis focuses on the relationship between defendants' conduct and plaintiffs' losses, but the tests and standards of proof applied vary … In some cases, claimants have had to show that the defendant's actions constituted material contributions to harm; others applied causality tests more flexibly. However, plaintiffs have been unable to overcome even the more flexible causation tests applied in several jurisdictions which ask if damages are 'fairly traceable' to defendant's actions. This is typically due to courts' finding that the evidence provided does not substantiate the connection between individual emitters' actions and plaintiffs' losses. In our view, in most cases concerning impacts for which the causal link to climate change does not exist, existing scientific methodologies could fill the evidentiary gap.

25.70 Proving causation in climate change litigation has proven to be difficult in numerous jurisdictions.[112] It is apparent that for cases to succeed they need to rely on up-to-date scientific attribution evidence. The problem thus far for claimants has been establishing breach of duty. *Smith v Fonterra*[113] should prove to be illuminating as attribution evidence has been allowed and will be considered at the trial.

---

107 *McLoughlin v O'Brien* [1983] 1 AC 410.

108 Ministry of Justice, 'Response to Consultation: The Law on Damages' (2009) CP(R) 9/07 <https://data.parliament.uk/DepositedPapers/Files/DEP2009-1863/DEP2009-1863.pdf> accessed 13 September 2024. See *Clerk & Lindsell on Torts* (n 11) paras 1–24.

109 Ministry of Justice, 'Response to Consultation: The Law on Damages' (n 108) 51.

110 Smith v Fonterra (n 1) [106]–[107].

111 It has been hypothesised that '… greater appreciation and exploitation of existing methodologies in attribution science could address obstacles to causation and improve the prospects of litigation as a route to compensation for losses'. Stuart-Smith and others, 'Filling the Evidentiary Gap in Climate Litigation' (n 104). Cases concerning material contribution and climate change have been tested abroad see for example *City of Oakland v BP plc,* No. C 17-06011 WHA (N.D. Cal. Jul. 27, 2018).

112 Stuart-Smith and others, 'Filling the Evidentiary Gap in Climate Litigation' (n 104). In the study of 73 cases on climate change only 8 succeeded the main problems being associated with causation.

113 *Smith v Fonterra* (NZSC) (n 8).

25.71 The claimants in *Smith v Fonterra*[114] inevitably relied upon case law supporting scientific attribution in relation to the material contribution test. The claimant cited[115] in support *Fairchild v Glenhaven Funeral Services*[116] and *Barker v Corus UK Ltd.*[117] The *Fairchild* exception is reserved for those cases where there is scientific uncertainty about which one or more of multiple defendants are responsible for causing harm where an increase in material risk should be treated as if it had materially increased the damage.[118] The exception to the usual rule is that a claimant must prove that but for the defendant's breach of duty it would not have suffered loss.[119]

25.72 The *Fairchild* exception arose out of claims surrounding exposure to asbestos at work which later caused mesothelioma. The science in support of the claim was reasonably clear in that it was known that the disease probably arose from exposure to asbestos. What was not however possible to say was which employer was likely to have been responsible for the exposure, and thus caused the disease. In establishing the *Fairchild* exception to causation, harm is proven against one or all of the defendants if:[120]

> C cannot (because of the current limits of human science) prove, on the balance of probabilities, that his mesothelioma was the result of his inhaling asbestos dust during his employment by A or during his employment by B or during his employment by A and B taken together.

25.73 There appears to be no common law principle that extends the *Fairchild* exception to cases outside of actionable harm.[121] However, that does not mean that causation should take a mechanical approach to new situations that arise. The common law should provide common sense answers to different torts. After all there is no 'uniform causal requirement for liability in tort'.[122]

25.74 In *Smith v Fonterra*[123] the New Zealand Court of Appeal accepted that there were some limited similarities to *Fairchild* in that there were multiple tortfeasors and a single causative agent: GHGs. However, the Court of Appeal refused to draw a further analogy. They said that in *Fairchild* the tortfeasors were either known or readily identifiable. In *Smith v Fonterra* however any one or more of unknown emitters could have been responsible. The extension of the *Fairchild* principle to 'limitless' defendants that may or may not be identifiable, let alone amenable to jurisdiction, appeared to the court to be insuperable.

---

114 ibid.
115 ibid [107].
116 *Fairchild v Glenhaven Funeral Services* [2003] 1 AC 32.
117 *Barker v Corus UK Ltd* [2006] 2 AC 572.
118 See *Clerk & Lindsell on Torts* (n 11) paras 2-56 and 2-57 which also addresses *McGhee v National Coal Board* [1973] 1 WLR 1.
119 See *Clerk & Lindsell on Torts* (n 11) paras 2-56 and 2-57.
120 *Fairchild v Glenhaven Funeral Services* (n 116) [2].
121 *Saunderson v Hull* [2008] EWCA Civ 1211.
122 See Lord Hoffmann's decisions in *Kuwait Airways Corpn v Iraqi Airways Co (Nos 4 and 5)* [2002] AC 883 [128] and *Environment Agency (formerly National Rivers Authority) v Empress Car (Abertillery) Ltd* [1999] 2 AC 22.
123 *Smith v Fonterra* (n 1) [110]–[113].

25.75 The Supreme Court disagreed:[124]

> How the law of torts should respond to cumulative causation in a public nuisance case involving newer technologies and newer harms (GHGs, rather than sewage and other water pollution) is a matter that should not be answered pre-emptively, without evidence and policy analysis exceeding that available on a strike out application. Accordingly, suppliers of fuels producing GHGs … should not in our view be eliminated as parties until these difficult but fact- and policy driven questions have been resolved by a full trial and (potential) appeal.

25.76 Whilst it is highly unlikely that any one of the multiple defendants can be said to have probably caused the damage claimed, can it be said that each of them had materially contributed to the risk of harm? Only the results of the attribution evidence will be able to tell whether the defendants did in fact materially increase the risk of harm to the claimant and if so to what extent.[125]

25.77 An alternative approach to causation posited in *Smith v Fonterra*[126] was the 'market share liability' approach arising out of *Sindell v Abbott Laboratories*, a product liability case decided in California.[127] In *Sindell*, the claimant alleged she developed cancer as a result of taking medication during pregnancy. She could not prove which of the major manufacturers of the drug had manufactured the medication. The court arrived at the practical solution that each manufacturer would be responsible by reference to its market share. Such an approach would be a dramatic departure from both the but for test and the *Fairchild* exception, but would it be a practical solution to the causation conundrum in such claims? Might such an approach be justified on the basis of a redistributive approach to tort law using the polluter pays principle, which appears to have been adopted to environmental protections by the UK government.[128] The Court of Appeal in *Smith v Fonterra*, cognisant of the liberal market share approach, was concerned that the defendants did not constitute a market share as 'the prerequisites to liability include that a substantial share of the manufacturers who produced the product must be named as defendants in the action'.[129] The Supreme Court, as set out above, did not develop the approach to causation; they simply left it to the trial judge to react to the results of the attribution evidence.[130]

---

124 *Smith v Fonterra* (NZSC) (n 8) [166].
125 There is a German decision currently on appeal *Luciano Lliuya v RWE AG* case no: 2 O 285/15 [2015] which concerns a Peruvian farmer that is pursuing Germany's largest electricity producer for declaratory relief and damages arising out of melting mountain glaciers near his home. The case is going to consider attribution evidence and as such may prove to be useful.
126 *Smith v Fonterra* (n 1) [109].
127 *Sindell v Abbott Laboratories* 26 Cal 3d 588 (Cal 1980).
128 DEFRA, 'Environmental Principles Policy Statement' (2023) <https://www.gov.uk/government/publications/environmental-principles-policy-statement/environmental-principles-policy-statement> accessed 26 April 2024. Also see para 25.39 above re: Rome II.
129 *Smith v Fonterra* (n 1) [111].
130 See para 25.69 above.

Conclusion

25.78 Statutory intervention would be the sensible approach to addressing some of the complex liability issues surrounding both breach of duty and causation as they require a 'sophisticated regulatory response'.[131] At present there is no governmental proposal that will affect the law of property-based or other torts and climate change. As such, unless there is a change, the courts will inevitably have to deal with these complex issues. The common law's usual incremental approach to the development of torts may come under increasing pressure.

25.79 Given that *Smith v Fonterra*[132] is heading for trial the decision is likely to be at least *prima facie* persuasive to the English Courts. However, the unknown factors are how the New Zealand Court will develop the law of public nuisance, negligence, and the proposed climate system damage tort. The uncertainty is heightened by the fact that the courts are still to deal with causation attribution evidence in respect of the said heads of loss.

25.80 There are further uncertainties in how the law of trespass will develop, how the role of the statutory undertaker might evolve and how statutory nuisance might become a feature of future litigation.

25.81 If climate change continues at its current pace what is certain is that property-based and other torts will need to develop rapidly to take account of the growing body of international legal obligations and case law.[133]

131 *Smith v Fonterra* (n 1) [16].
132 *Smith v Fonterra* (NZSC) (n 8).
133 See para 25.02 above.

CHAPTER 26

PROPERTY LEGAL ADVICE, INSURANCE AND CLIMATE RISK

Ashley Pratt

Introduction

26.01 On 19 April 2023 the Law Society of England and Wales ('Law Society') produced pioneering guidance thought to be the first in the world of its kind addressing 'the impact of climate change on solicitors' ('the Guidance').[1] The Guidance follows the Law Society's earlier ambitious 'Climate Change Resolution' policy.[2]

26.02 This section considers the evolving duties of solicitors in the wake of climate change specifically in respect of property transactions and insurance.

26.03 The Guidance provides that 'climate-related risks will affect most clients and nearly all areas of legal practice'.[3] The importance of the Guidance on all solicitors cannot therefore be overstated.

26.04 Annex 2 of the Guidance provides a non-exhaustive list of areas of law that it envisages will be affected by climate change. It includes corporate governance, corporate reporting and due diligence, disputes,[4] real estate and asset-based transactions, commercial contracts and agreements, human rights and social governance.[5]

26.05 Given the far-reaching impact of the Guidance, how should the profession respond to these challenges?[6] How might these challenges evolve as climate change predictably worsens and progressively affects an increasing number of vulnerable properties in the UK?[7]

---

1 The Law Society of England and Wales, 'Guidance on the Impact of Climate Change on Solicitors' (2023) <https://www.lawsociety.org.uk/topics/climate-change/impact-of-climate-change-on-solicitors> accessed 22 May 2024.
2 The Law Society of England and Wales, 'Climate Change Resolution' (2021) <https://prdsitecore93.azureedge.net/-/media/files/topics/climate-change/the-law-society--climate-change-resolution.pdf?rev=d6a92119541d43239f73a76cbc4e4f14&hash=DDA1BD6CB66FFD3F499EA9A654F67D6D> accessed 22 May 2024.
3 The Law Society of England and Wales, 'Guidance on the Impact of Climate Change on Solicitors' (n 1) pt B[2].
4 See for example Chapter 41.
5 The Law Society of England and Wales, 'Guidance on the Impact of Climate Change on Solicitors' (n 1). (The duties of other professionals is considered in Chapter 41.)
6 See para 26.30 below.
7 See para 26.40 below.

26.06 Climate change is forecast to affect the provision and cost of insurance.[8] The impact of this is considered in respect of solicitors' professional indemnity insurance, and lending.[9]

26.07 Finally, the risk of failing to discharge solicitors' duties is considered.[10]

26.08 The Guidance categorises the legal risks owed by solicitors to their clients in relation to climate change in six sections:[11]

(i) duty of care;

(ii) duty to warn;

(iii) duty to disclose;

(iv) duty to uphold service and competency levels;

(v) actions to take when there are gaps in your competence; and

(vi) the SRA Principles.

This section expands upon these six categories.

26.09 Before turning to the issues raised in the Guidance, we set out the broader financial risks that may affect businesses and individuals collectively as a result of climate change. The Prudential Regulation Authority issued the world's first set of supervisory expectations in 2019 in relation to the management of climate-related risk.[12] The Bank of England in its latest guidance reported that:[13]

> The PRA expects firms to develop and embed effective risk management processes to manage their climate risks. Further progress by firms to address capability gaps is important in the short term to provide a better foundation for the identification, measurement, and management of climate risks.

---

8 The Law Society of England and Wales, 'Guidance on the Impact of Climate Change on Solicitors' (n 1) at 4.5.
9 See para 26.54 below.
10 See para 26.62 below.
11 The Law Society of England and Wales, 'Guidance on the Impact of Climate Change on Solicitors' (n 1).
12 Prudential Regulation Authority, 'Enhancing Banks' and Insurers' Approaches to Managing the Financial Risks from Climate Change' (2019) <https://www.bankofengland.co.uk/prudential-regulation/publication/2019/enhancing-banks-and-insurers-approaches-to-managing-the-financial-risks-from-climate-change-ss> accessed 22 May 2024.
13 Prudential Regulation Authority, 'Climate-Related Financial Risk Management and the Role of Capital Requirements: Climate Change Adaptation Report 2021' (2021) <https://www.bankofengland.co.uk/-/media/boe/files/prudential-regulation/publication/2021/october/climate-change-adaptation-report-2021.pdf> accessed 22 May 2024.

26.10 In its earlier guidance the Bank of England categorised climate risk into two broad groups, (i) physical risks and (ii) transition risks.[14] By physical risks it meant 'extreme weather events (floods and heatwaves etc.) and longer-term changes to our climate (sea level rise etc.)', and by transition risks, 'changes that governments, industries and consumers make in pursuit of a greener world'.[15]

26.11 These two risks taken together are important as, individually and collectively, they have real world consequences. In taking into account the physical and transition risks in conveyancing, the following issues arise:

- what advice should be provided to clients prior to purchasing a property?[16]
- what are the potential lending implications of such advice?[17] and
- how might climate risk affect insurance?[18]

26.12 In other areas of law solicitors will have to consider corporate governance issues including: the effects of 'greenwashing',[19] commercial contract drafting,[20] compliance issues, and climate risk disclosure issues.[21] What is clear is that climate risks will affect the advice that practitioners provide to their clients in many different areas of law for the foreseeable future, despite the fact that the precise effects of climate change may still be unknown.

Law Society guidance

(i) *Duty of care*

26.13 Duties owed by solicitors to their clients arise either contractually, usually in the form of a written retainer, or tortiously under statute and common law.

---

14 See also the view of Stephen Tromans KC: Stephen Tromans, 'In the Matter of Conveyancers' Duty of Care to Advise Clients about Climate Risk and How to Discharge Such Duty' (2022) <https://content.groundsure.com/stephen-tromanskc-legal-opinion> accessed 22 May 2024.
15 Bank of England, 'Climate Change' (2024) <https://www.bankofengland.co.uk/climate-change> accessed 22 May 2024.
16 See for example para 26.27 below.
17 See para 26.54 onwards below.
18 ibid.
19 Competition and Markets Authority, 'Guidance – Green Claims Code: Making Environmental Claims' (2021) <https://www.gov.uk/government/publications/green-claims-code-making-environmental-claims> accessed 22 May 2024. See Chapter 30, para 30.52, on greenwashing.
20 See Chapter 40, paras 40.59ff, on measurement.
21 For example, see The Companies (Directors' Report) and Limited Liability Partnerships (Energy and Carbon Report) Regulations 2018, SI 2018/1155, and see Chapter 30.

26.14 A solicitor's contractual duty[22] to his client includes:[23]

i) ... to carry out the tasks which the client has instructed and the solicitor has agreed to undertake.

ii) It is implicit in the solicitor's retainer that he/she will proffer advice which is reasonably incidental to the work that he/she is carrying out.

iii) In determining what advice is reasonably incidental, it is necessary to have regard to all the circumstances of the case, including the character and experience of the client.

iv) In relation to iii), it is not possible to give definitive guidance but one can give fairly bland illustrations. An experienced businessman will not wish to pay for being told that which he/she already knows. An impoverished client will not wish to pay for advice which he/she cannot afford. An inexperienced client will expect to be warned of risks which are (or should be) apparent to the solicitor but not to the client.

v) The solicitor and client may, by agreement, limit the duties which would otherwise form part of the solicitor's retainer. As a matter of good practice the solicitor should confirm such agreement in writing. If the solicitor does not do so, the court may not accept that any such restriction was agreed.

26.15 When providing legal advice, a solicitor owes a duty to exercise reasonable care and skill in accordance with section 13 of the Supply of Goods and Services Act 1982.[24] Prior to the Act this was in any event the common law position.

26.16 The duty of care and skill has been observed to comprise:[25]

the following:

(1) To be skilful and careful;

(2) To advise his client on all matters relevant to his retainer, so far as may be reasonably necessary;

(3) To protect the interest of his client;

(4) To carry out his instruction by all proper means;

22 Roger Stewart, Hugh Evans, and Kieran Lee Marshall (eds), *Jackson & Powell on Professional Liability* (9th edn, Sweet & Maxwell 2023) [11-007].
23 *Minkin v Landsberg* [2015] EWCA Civ 1152, [2016] 1 WLR 1489 [38].
24 In relation to consumer contracts, Consumer Rights Act 2015 s 49 applies the same test.
25 See Stewart, Evans, and Marshall (eds), *Jackson & Powell on Professional Liability* (n 22) [11-088]; *Millican v Tiffin Holdings Ltd* [1964] 49 DLR (2d) 216 as approved by the Supreme Court of Canada [1967] SCR 183, [1967] 60 DLR (2d) 469.

(5) To consult with his client on all questions of doubt which do not fall within the express or implied discretion left to him;

(6) To keep his client informed to such an extent as may be reasonably necessary, according to the same criteria.

26.17 The duty a solicitor owes his client was considered in the case of *Midland Bank v Hett, Stubbs and Kemp*.[26] Oliver J held that:[27]

> Now no doubt the duties owed by a solicitor to his client are high, in the sense that he holds himself out as practising a highly skilled and exacting profession ... It may be that a particularly meticulous and conscientious practitioner would, in his client's interests, take it upon himself to pursue a line of inquiry beyond the strict limits comprehended by his instructions. But that is not the test. The test is what the reasonably competent practitioner would do having regard to the standards normally adopted in his profession ... the duty is directly confined to the confines of the retainer.

26.18 The Guidance on solicitors' duty of care in the context of climate risks states:[28]

> Climate change will impact different areas of the law ... solicitors may have to look beyond the narrow scope of an instruction by a client to consider whether and to what extent climate legal risks are relevant.

26.19 The standard of care applied to a solicitor is that of a reasonably competent practitioner.[29] In the context of conveyancing, the standard of care is accordingly judged against that of a reasonably competent conveyancer, and in commercial property transactions, a reasonably competent conveyancer and a commercial lawyer.[30] In the absence of specific authority on the point it is anticipated that different professional bodies, such as Licensed Conveyancers, will have to accord with same, or at least similar, duties.

26.20 Whilst the Guidance does not amount to law,[31] the Law Society guides are persuasive. *Jackson & Powell* states:[32]

> The Law Society has issued a number of publications to assist solicitors in practice, the most important of which is probably the Law Society's conveyancing Handbook, which is reissued annually. These various guides are likely to carry great weight with the courts (a) as evidence of the general practice of the profession and (b), in certain situations, such as an indication of what specific steps a reasonably careful and competent solicitor would take. Although these various sources are generally intended to reflect the existing

---

26 *Midland Bank v Hett, Stubbs and Kemp* [1979] Ch 384. See Stewart, Evans, and Marshall (eds), *Jackson & Powell on Professional Liability* (n 22) [11-087].
27 *Midland Bank Trust Company Ltd v Hett, Stubbs & Kemp* (n 26) [402]–[403].
28 The Law Society of England and Wales, 'Guidance on the Impact of Climate Change on Solicitors' (n 1) [3.1].
29 Stewart, Evans, and Marshall (eds), *Jackson & Powell on Professional Liability* (n 22) [11-100].
30 ibid. See also *Hurlingham Estates Ltd v Wilde Partners* [1997] 1 Lloyd's Rep 525.
31 *Johnson v Bingley* [1997] PNLR 392. See also Stewart, Evans, and Marshall (eds), *Jackson & Powell on Professional Liability* (n 22) [11-099].
32 ibid [11-098].

practices of the profession, they have also led to a greater uniformity of practice. Thus it has become increasingly difficult for a solicitor to justify conduct which falls short of that described in the guides.

26.21 It is likely that the courts will place substantial weight on the Guidance as evidence that a duty has arisen.[33] However, was there a duty prior to the Guidance?

26.22 Stephen Tromans KC's view is that a duty to advise on climate risks:[34]

> probably arose first as a result of the transition risks becoming clear in 2021 as a result of the attitudes of financial regulators, leading banks and building societies; and secondly with a search tool in 2022 which could pinpoint risk on specific properties.

26.23 There is support in Australia for the view that there exists a duty of care to warn in relation to transition risks:[35]

> Lawyers in NSW owe a duty to their clients to warn them of the risks associated with a property transaction including any physical risks to the property which they are purchasing … One of these emerging risks is climate change.

26.24 The Australian view on when the duty first arose reflects our understanding of the UK's position:[36]

> Precisely when any duty of care on the part of real estate lawyers to advise and warn their clients of climate risks arose is factually dependent and will vary case to case.
> However, we are of the view that many real estate lawyers are likely to be currently obliged to advise on climate risks, and were potentially obliged to do so as early as 2021.

26.25 The standard of duty of care will naturally increase as experience in the understanding of climate risks develops.[37]

26.26 There is a growing consensus that a duty of care applies to solicitors advising clients as to the risks of climate change. Although the domestic courts have yet to determine whether such a duty arises, it would be very surprising if the courts were to come to an alternative conclusion. The precise moment when the duty of care to advise in relation to climate-related risks arose is unclear. Whilst it is likely that a duty initially arose in 2021–2022 each case will turn on its own facts.

---

33 ibid.
34 Stephen Tromans, 'In the Matter of Conveyancers' Duty of Care to Advise Clients about Climate Risk and How to Discharge Such Duty' (n 14) 23.
35 Elizabeth Wild, 'Legal Opinion: Do Real Estate Lawyers in NSW Owe Their Clients a Duty of Care to Advise and Warn in Relation to Climate Risk?' (2023) <https://www.infotrack.com.au/wp-content/uploads/Legal-Opinion_Groundsure_Norton-Rose-Fulbright-1.pdf> accessed 22 May 2024.
36 ibid 2.
37 Stewart, Evans, and Marshall (eds), *Jackson & Powell on Professional Liability* (n 22) [11-091]. A solicitor should be judged by the standards of time when the transaction took place. See *Bell v Strathairn* [1954] 104 LJ 618.

(ii) *Duty to warn*

26.27 The Guidance suggests that the scope of duty in respect of advising on climate risks may extend to information obtained whilst fulfilling the retainer and to matters outside its original scope.

26.28 In considering how such an extended duty will affect a lawyer's duty to warn, the underlying test to be applied was set out in *Credit Lyonnais SA v Russell Jones Walker*[38] in the often quoted passage of Laddie J:[39]

> A solicitor is not a general insurer against his client's legal problems. His duties are defined by the agreed retainer … obligations may arise outside of the retainer or where there is no retainer at all … if in the course of doing that for which he is retained, he becomes aware of a risk or a potential risk to the client, it is his duty to inform the client.

26.29 The Guidance states:[40]

> Presently, climate change may have an impact on a solicitors' duty to warn clients of the legal risks in certain contexts. The steps involved in fulfilling your duty to warn will be fact and context dependent but should be addressed by a solicitor at all stages of their advice.

26.30 In order to practically manage these risks in the real estate context, conveyancers regularly request third party searches for their clients such as environmental searches and local searches, which usually form part of the advice contained in the report on title. Such searches may reveal flood risks, local developments, land contamination risks, etc.

26.31 Search tools are available in the UK which provide climate risk property reports.[41] It is likely that a climate search tool will become a standard feature in domestic conveyancing although it is not necessarily available internationally.[42]

26.32 Solicitors are not required to warn clients of every risk. Whether risks are advisable or not can depend on the experience of the client. As Lord Donaldson stated in *Carradine Properties Ltd v DJ Freeman & Co*:[43]

> An inexperienced client will need and be entitled to expect the solicitor to take a much broader view of the scope of his retainer and of his duties than will be the case with an experienced client.

---

38 *Credit Lyonnais SA v Russell Jones & Walker* [2002] EWHC 1310.
39 See Stewart, Evans, and Marshall (eds), *Jackson & Powell on Professional Liability* (n 22) [11-168].
40 The Law Society of England and Wales, 'Guidance on the Impact of Climate Change on Solicitors' (n 1) [3.2].
41 Stephen Tromans, 'In the Matter of Conveyancers' Duty of Care to Advise Clients about Climate Risk and How to Discharge Such Duty' (n 14) 23.
42 Elizabeth Wild, 'Legal Opinion: Do Real Estate Lawyers in NSW Owe Their Clients a Duty of Care to Advise and Warn in Relation to Climate Risk?' (n 35): a search tool was not available in NSW Australia as of 4 April 2023.
43 *Carradine Properties Ltd v DJ Freeman & Co* [1999] Lloyd's Rep PN 483 [487].

26.33 Clients are generally unlikely to have experience of the risks posed by climate change. Thus for the foreseeable future all clients should be advised on climate risks which may include advising on risks such as flooding, coastal erosion and land contamination.

26.34 Such advice may simply amount to a general warning as to the risks of climate change where a search is unavailable. The advice should be set out in the report on title.

26.35 Where a climate risk report is available it is important that the solicitor not only passes on the report to the client, but also explains any risks identified. If the solicitor is not qualified to advise on a particular aspect of the report, then third party expertise should be recommended.

26.36 Although a solicitor may have discharged their duty by advising a client on climate risks, a client may decline to accept such advice. If the client fails to accept the advice the solicitor should make a written note of the advice given, as is common practice.

26.37 A situation may also arise where a solicitor and/or his client wishes to limit the terms of the retainer. The Guidance provides:[44]

> A solicitor and client may, by agreement, limit the terms of the retainer which may limit the solicitor's duties. In certain circumstances, it may be possible to exclude climate issues specifically from your retainer, for instance where you are not competent to advise or where the client is directed to more expert technical advice …
>
> However, where climate legal risks are relevant, it is becoming less realistic in practice to exclude consideration of such matters from the instruction completely, given that they impact so many areas of activity.

26.38 It is highly unlikely at present that a client will have the experience to fully understand and thus contract out of climate risks. A solicitor should be very careful before agreeing to such terms. A client will need to be advised in writing if the retainer is going to be restricted.

(iii) *Duty to disclose*

26.39 The Guidance states:[45]

> When acting on a matter, solicitors have a duty to disclose to their client all information material to the matter of which they have actual knowledge.
>
> In the context of climate change, this means that a solicitor who becomes aware in the course of acting on a retainer that there are climate legal risks that might impact the client's interests in-scope of the retainer should disclose such risks to their client in a

44 The Law Society of England and Wales, 'Guidance on the Impact of Climate Change on Solicitors' (n 1) [4.4].
45 ibid [3.3].

clear and understandable way. Regard should also be given to the relevant regulatory obligations (see Rule 6.4 of the SRA Code of Conduct for Solicitors).

26.40 A duty to disclose is enmeshed with a duty to warn. If matters arise outside of the retainer, it will be for the solicitor to decide whether to warn the client of such risks when taking into account both his extended contractual duty and tortious obligations.

26.41 As climate risks are evolving, the duties owed to the client may change during the course of the retainer. As such solicitors should be careful before completing any transaction to check to see whether the duty has changed.

(iv) *Duty to uphold service and competence levels*

26.42 The Guidance states:[46]

> You must ensure that you provide a proper standard of service to your clients. In doing so, you should have regard to the SRA's regulatory requirements, including those relating to the continuing competencies[47] that it expects solicitors to demonstrate.

26.43 The SRA's advice is less prescriptive than it used to be,[48] the Guidance continues:[49]

> The SRA Code of Conduct for Solicitors, RELs and RFLs (SCCS) and the Code of Conduct for Firms (SCCF) (the SRA Codes) each require that 'you ensure that the service you provide to clients is competent and delivered in a timely manner' and that the service takes account of client's attributes, needs and circumstances.

26.44 Solicitors are required to understand the regulatory framework in respect of their competencies. As part of their continuing duty to uphold service and competence levels, they should take account of key documents such as the Law Society's Conveyancing Handbook, as well as the Guidance.

(v) *Actions to take where there are gaps in competence*

26.45 The Guidance has put solicitors on notice that they have a duty of care to advise their clients on climate risks.

26.46 The Guidance states:[50]

> Not all solicitors have expertise or training in matters relating to climate legal risks. However, as solicitors undertake training as part of their professional development, widespread awareness and acknowledgment will grow over time.

---

46 The Law Society of England and Wales, 'Guidance on the Impact of Climate Change on Solicitors' (n 1) [3.4].
47 Solicitors Regulation Authority, 'Statement of Solicitor Competence' (2022) <https://www.sra.org.uk/solicitors/resources/continuing-competence/cpd/competence-statement/> accessed 22 May 2024.
48 Stewart, Evans, and Marshall (eds), *Jackson & Powell on Professional Liability* (n 22) [11-89].
49 The Law Society of England and Wales, 'Guidance on the Impact of Climate Change on Solicitors' (n 1).
50 ibid [3.5].

> This may intensify the expectation that a reasonably competent solicitor should be aware of the impact and the relevance of climate change to their practice area and be able to advise clients accordingly.
>
> Therefore, the general standards that solicitors are required to meet to discharge their duty of care to clients in this area may shift accordingly.

26.47 Whilst the Law Society provides that not all solicitors will have undertaken training on climate risks, solicitors advising on property transactions should complete such training or at the very least be aware of the Guidance and its underlying principles.

26.48 Conveyancing solicitors should continue to use third party experts to assist where they do not have the necessary expertise. Solicitors' advice on climate change risks may evolve during the transaction. It would therefore be sensible for the retainer to reserve the right to seek further third-party expertise in relation to climate risks.[51]

(vi) *The SRA Principles*

26.49 The SRA Principles require solicitors to act:[52]

> [i] in a way that upholds the constitutional principle of the rule of law, and the proper administration of justice,
>
> [ii] in a way that upholds public trust and confidence in the solicitors' profession and in legal services provided by authorised persons,
>
> [iii] with independence,
>
> [iv] with honesty,
>
> [v] with integrity,
>
> [vi] in a way that encourages equality, diversity and inclusion, and
>
> [vii] in the best interest of each client.

26.50 The Guidance reiterates that the way in which solicitors 'interact with climate-related issues is likely to change as the narrative on climate change develops'.[53] In relation to climate risks solicitors will have to identify the needs of each client taking account of the SRA principles. It is difficult at this stage to see how the interaction between the SRA principles and climate risks will change the shape of the duties owed by solicitors to their clients until there is further legal development.

---

51 See *Credit Lyonnais SA v Russell Jones & Walker* (n 38).
52 The Law Society of England and Wales, 'Guidance on the Impact of Climate Change on Solicitors' (n 1) [3.6].
53 ibid.

26.51 The Guidance then sets out two ways that solicitors will have to consider their duties under the SRA principles and climate risks:[54]

> **I. Duty to maintain public trust and confidence**
>
> …This duty is one that you may wish to consider when assessing client instructions that may give rise to climate legal risks or impacts. Over time, this duty may fall under closer scrutiny as climate change becomes more pronounced …
>
> **II. Duty to act with integrity**
>
> There may be some client matters where solicitors decide that they cannot act (or continue to act) for a certain client as this is incompatible with a duty of integrity…Note, however, that a solicitor is not generally responsible for their client's actions providing that they have advised correctly and competently and explained the implications of any breaches unless they have contributed or colluded in any breach.

26.52 In property transactions it is suggested that for solicitors to comply with their duty to maintain public trust and confidence, and act with integrity they should, as a minimum, warn clients of the effects of climate risks. Such a warning may simply include advising on the relevant searches, and next steps if anything is revealed. If a solicitor is acting for a lender the same duty will apply.

Insurance and lending

26.53 Climate-related risks are likely to affect professional indemnity insurance. The Guidance provides:[55]

> Insurers are also giving greater attention to climate issues and the risks they pose to their business. Solicitors should be mindful of current and prospective requirements of professional indemnity insurers so that solicitors can obtain affordable cover for the areas of practice upon which they wish to advise … To obtain PII cover, in the future solicitors may need to advise on climate legal risks and identify when they are not competent to advise.

26.54 The Guidance confirms that there is a duty of care to advise clients in relation to climate risks. Therefore, it is important that solicitors properly plan and prepare to identify the risks to their practice. Professional indemnity insurers may, as part of their due diligence processes, request confirmation as to whether such risks have been properly identified and assessed.

26.55 The process of climate risk identification and assessment is likely to become one of the transition costs faced by solicitors in providing legal advice. Even if such risks are properly identified and assessed, the additional risks placed on law firms may increase

---

54 ibid.
55 ibid [4.5].

the costs of insurance premiums. Inevitably the increased costs of legal services will be passed on to the consumer.

26.56 The Bank of England in its Climate Biennial Exploratory Scenario ('CBES')[56] were of the view that the costs of future climate litigation may make obtaining insurance prohibitively expensive:

> Liability insurance contracts typically provide cover for periods of 12 months, allowing insurers to annually reassess, amend, and re-price products to reflect any changes in risk. Annual re-pricing mitigates some but not all the risk of increasing climate litigation – new contracts could be at risk from a rapid shift in the legislative environment and expected professional standards.
>
> Under such circumstances, future insurance cover could become prohibitively expensive for businesses, or in extremis not available at all, particularly if insurers feel they can no longer accurately calibrate the risks. Potential difficulties in securing insurance coverage for directors, officers and professional advisors would have a substantial impact on businesses. And though it could incentivise firms to focus on developing and implementing credible climate transition plans, it may also make firms more risk averse, and reduce innovation.

26.57 Work already undertaken on the risks of climate change has revealed startling results.[57] In the short term it is thought that 2 million domestic properties are at risk from surface water flooding, rising to 2.5 million by 2050, and to 3 million by 2070. This will inevitably affect lending. The CBES report predicts that if there is a failure to properly manage climate risk there could be as much as £225 billion in credit losses.[58]

26.58 Mortgage terms in the UK can last up to 40 years,[59] as such a mortgage provided today could be affected by the predicted effects of climate change. How the lending market will react to this remains to be seen.

26.59 Issues that may arise include whether a mortgage company will provide lending following an unfavourable climate search result, whether the property is insurable, whether there are transitional costs such as the construction of flood defences that are able to mitigate the risk, and whether further expertise is required. Similar issues will arise in respect of climate-related subsidence and coastal erosion.

26.60 Climate risk is an issue that faces solicitors and clients and it is crucial that solicitors put in place proper systems to identify and assess such risks.

---

56 Bank of England, 'Results of the 2021 Climate Biennial Exploratory Scenario (CBES)' (2022) <https://www.bankofengland.co.uk/stress-testing/2022/results-of-the-2021-climate-biennial-exploratory-scenario> accessed 22 May 2024.

57 Stephen Tromans, 'In the Matter of Conveyancers' Duty of Care to Advise Clients about Climate Risk and How to Discharge Such Duty' (n 14) [6].

58 Bank of England, 'Results of the 2021 Climate Biennial Exploratory Scenario (CBES)' (n 56).

59 Vicky Shaw, 'HSBC Offers Its Longest-Ever Mortgage Term to Help First-Time Buyers' *The Independent* (30 August 2023) <https://www.independent.co.uk/money/hsbc-40year-mortgage-firsttime-buyers-b2401805.html> accessed 22 May 2024.

Failure to discharge duty

26.61 Failing to properly manage climate risks is likely to affect not only individual law firms, but the legal profession as a whole. As has already been discussed, the CBES reports that failure to properly manage climate risk could lead to credit losses of up to £225 billion.[60]

26.62 Professional negligence claims arising out of climate risks will, without proper identification, assessment and advice, lead to higher indemnity premiums. These increases may continue to have a disproportionate effect on smaller law firms, especially in respect of conveyancing work.[61]

26.63 Conveyancing is already viewed by insurers as a high-risk legal activity.[62]

26.64 Professional negligence claims, and breaches of the SRA Code, also bring about a risk of reputational damage. To avoid this, solicitors should identify and assess such risks to their clients both prior to and during any transaction.

26.65 If a professional negligence action is brought arising out of a failure to advise on climate risks, it is likely to include a claim for misevaluation. *Jackson & Powell* states:[63]

> Where the purchaser's solicitor errs in his advice he gives or in the investigations which he makes on the client's behalf, the property purchased may prove to be less valuable than was assumed at the time of purchase. The normal measure of damages in such circumstances, as in the case on surveyor's negligence, is the amount by which the sum paid by the client exceeds the true value of the property at the date of purchase.

26.66 Thus, in a claim for professional negligence, subject to issues concerning remoteness and foreseeability, a surveyor or valuer will provide evidence to quantify such losses.

Conclusion

26.67 Climate risks are going to affect nearly every area of legal practice. Solicitors owe a duty of care to their clients to advise on climate risks, such duty probably arose at a point in time in 2021–2022. When and whether a duty previously arose will be dependent on the facts of the case. Regardless, the Guidance issued has made clear that a duty of care exists.

26.68 Given the evolving duty of care, solicitors' obligations are becoming increasingly complex. Considering the rapid pace of change, solicitors should be particularly conscious of developments in relation to their duty of care to advise on climate risks. Some

---

60 Bank of England, 'Results of the 2021 Climate Biennial Exploratory Scenario (CBES)' (n 56).
61 David Green, 'Property and PII: How Does It or How Could It Affect Your Firm?' (3 August 2023) <https://www.lawgazette.co.uk/practice/property-and-pii-how-does-it-or-how-could-it-affect-your-firm/5116870.article> accessed 22 May 2024.
62 ibid.
63 Stewart, Evans, and Marshall (eds), *Jackson & Powell on Professional Liability* (n 22) [11-291].

conveyancing transactions take many months, so it follows that it is readily conceivable that the duty to advise in such cases will evolve between the commencement of the retainer and its termination.

26.69 Conveyancers should make use of climate risk search tools; the risk of failing to do so may lead to increased professional indemnity premiums, professional negligence claims, and reputational damage. Increased premiums pose an existential threat to small law firms. Law firms should identify and assess the climate risks to each area of law on which it provides advice. A failure to do so is likely to breach the SRA guiding principles.

PART IV

ENVIRONMENTAL PROTEST

CHAPTER 27

ENVIRONMENTAL PROTEST

Rachel Sullivan

History of protest rights in domestic law

27.01 Freedom of speech has long been perceived as a key feature of English common law. However, the approach of the common law to recognising any right to protest was 'hesitant and negative, permitting that which was not prohibited'. See Lord Bingham in *R (Laporte) v Chief Constable of Gloucestershire Constabulary*:[1]

> The approach of the English common law to freedom of expression and assembly was hesitant and negative, permitting that which was not prohibited. Thus although Dicey in *An Introduction to the Study of the Law of the Constitution*, 10th ed (1959), in Part II on the 'Rule of Law', included chapters VI and VII entitled 'The Right to Freedom of Discussion' and 'The Right of Public Meeting', he wrote of the first, at pp 239–240, that 'at no time has there in England been any proclamation of the right to liberty of thought or to freedom of speech' and of the second, at p 271, that 'it can hardly be said that our constitution knows of such a thing as any specific right of public meeting'. Lord Hewart CJ reflected the then current orthodoxy when he observed in *Duncan v Jones* [1936] 1 KB 218, 222, that 'English law does not recognise any special right of public meeting for political or other purposes'. The Human Rights Act 1998, giving domestic effect to articles 10 and 11 of the European Convention, represented what Sedley LJ in Redmond-Bate v Director of Public Prosecutions 163 JP 789, 795, aptly called a 'constitutional shift'.

27.02 Protest in domestic law is therefore subject on the one hand to the protections afforded by the European Convention on Human Rights ('ECHR'), and on the other, the restrictions imposed through the statutory framework of policing powers and requirements for those organising protests. We consider these in turn, before turning to consider the development of the civil law and injunctions restraining protest.

Human rights and the development of protest law

27.03 The United Kingdom ratified the ECHR in 1951. The Human Rights Act 1998 incorporated the Convention into domestic law, enabling courts to adjudicate on allegations of breaches of those rights set out in Schedule 1 of the Act.[2]

---

1 *R (Laporte) v Chief Constable of Gloucestershire Constabulary* [2006] UKHL 55 [34].
2 See Human Rights Act 1998 Schedule 1. In particular, Articles 2–12, 14, 16–18, Articles 1–3 of the First Protocol, Article 1 of the Thirteenth Protocol, and Articles 1–2 of the Sixth Protocol.

27.04 Of particular relevance in relation to environmental protest are Articles 10 and 11 of the Convention, which protect the right to freedom of expression and freedom of association respectively. Article 5 (right to liberty) has also been held to be engaged in some cases.

(i) *Applicable rights*

27.05 Article 10 protects the right to freedom of expression. It provides:

> (1) Everyone has the right to freedom of expression. This right shall include freedom to hold opinions and to receive and impart information and ideas without interference by public authority and regardless of frontiers. This right shall not prevent States from requiring the licensing of broadcasting, television or cinema enterprises.
>
> (2) The exercise of these freedoms, since it carries with it duties and responsibilities, may be subject to such formalities, conditions, restrictions or penalties as are prescribed by law and are necessary in a democratic society in the interests of national security, territorial integrity or public safety, for the prevention of disorder or crime, for the protection of health or morals, for the protection of the reputation or rights of others, for preventing the disclosure of information received in confidence or for maintaining the authority and impartiality of the judiciary.

27.06 Article 11 protects the right to freedom of assembly, providing that:

> (1) Everyone has the right to freedom of peaceful assembly and to freedom of association with others, including the right to form and to join trade unions for the protection of his interests.
>
> (2) No restrictions shall be placed on the exercise of these rights other than such as are prescribed by law and are necessary in a democratic society in the interests of national security or public safety, for the prevention of disorder or crime, for the protection of health or morals or for the protection of the rights and freedoms of others. This article shall not prevent the imposition of lawful restrictions on the exercise of these rights by members of the armed forces, of the police or of the administration of the State.

27.07 The European Court has described Article 11 as forming the *lex specialis* governing protest cases, while Article 10 is the *lex generalis*;[3] however, whichever article a case is considered under, the outcome is likely to be the same.[4]

27.08 Article 5, which protects the right to liberty, has also been held to be engaged by restrictions on the freedom of movement of protestors where controls go beyond mere restrictions and amount to a deprivation of liberty. Thus in *Austin v UK*, 'kettling' of protestors did not amount to a deprivation of liberty on the facts of the case, although

3 *Kudrevičius v Lithuania* (2016) 62 EHRR 34 [85].
4 *Ziegler v Director of Public Prosecutions* [2021] UKSC 23 [61].

the European Court of Human Rights recognised that in principle there could be a breach of Article 5 in a crowd control case.[5]

(ii) *Scope of protected rights*

27.09 The right to freedom of assembly includes the right to choose the time, place and manner of protest,[6] in recognition that the purpose of an assembly is often linked to a certain location or time.[7] This has been held to extend to protests taking the form of impeding activities the organisers disapprove of, although the court has distinguished between such activities (as well as 'reprehensible acts committed in the preparation of a publication or broadcast'), which are capable of falling within the ambit of Article 10, and actions which infringe domestic criminal law 'in a manner unrelated to the exercise of freedom of expression'.[8]

27.10 In *Steel v United Kingdom*, the applicant had been arrested for breach of the peace after protesting against grouse shooting by walking in front of a member of a shooting party as he lifted his gun. The European Court of Human Rights held that while 'these protests took the form of physically impeding the activities of which the applicants disapproved … the Court considers nonetheless that they constituted expressions of opinion within the meaning of Article 10' (although in the event holding that her arrest and detention for 44 hours, as well as her subsequent conviction, were a proportionate means of meeting the legitimate aim of preventing disorder).[9] Similarly, in *Hashman and Harrup v United Kingdom*, the European Court of Human Rights held that a protest which took the form of interrupting a hunt constituted an expression of opinion within the meaning Article 10.[10]

27.11 In *Kudrevičius v Lithuania*, the European Court of Human Rights considered whether obstruction of roads by protestors (in that case, farmers protesting against the Lithuanian government) fell within Article 11. The Court recognised that disruption of traffic was 'not an uncommon occurrence in the context of the exercise of freedom of assembly in modern societies', but held that such conduct was not at the core of that freedom as protected by Article 11, which might have implications when considering the 'necessity' of any interference.[11] The consequence in that case was that the arrest and conviction of the applicants was held to be proportionate.

27.12 Likewise, the Court has recognised that 'any large-scale gathering in a public place inevitably creates inconvenience for the population'[12] and has held accordingly that public authorities are required to show 'a certain degree of tolerance towards peaceful gatherings' if Article 11 is not to be deprived of its substance.[13] When considering the

5 *Austin v United Kingdom* [2012] ECHR 459.
6 *Sáska v Hungary* App no 58050/08 (ECtHR, 27 February 2013) [21].
7 *Lashmankin v Russia* App no 57818/09 (ECtHR, 29 May 2017) [405].
8 *Kotlyar v Russia* App no 38825/16 (ECtHR, 12 October 2022) [41–2].
9 *Steel and others v United Kingdom* App no 24838/94 (ECtHR, 23 September 1998) [92].
10 *Hashman and Harrup v United Kingdom* App no 25594/94 (ECtHR, 25 November 1999).
11 *Kudrevičius v Lithuania* (n 3) para 97.
12 *Primov & Ors v Russia* App no 17391/06 (ECtHR, 13 October 2014) [145].
13 ibid [118], [145].

appropriate degree of tolerance, the court will consider the particular circumstances of the case and in particular the extent of interruption to ordinary life.

27.13 The Court has emphasised that the notion of peaceful assembly protected by Article 11 does not cover demonstrations 'where the organisers and participants have violent intentions', incite violence, 'or otherwise reject the foundations of a democratic society'.[14] However, it has also suggested that this must be systematic, or at least more than sporadic outbursts of violence from protestors, holding that:[15]

> an individual does not cease to enjoy the protections the right to peaceful assembly as a result of sporadic violence or other punishable acts committed by others in the course of the demonstration if the individual in question remains peaceful in his or her intentions or behaviour.

27.14 A protest does not cease to be a peaceful protest even though it may annoy or cause offence to the persons opposed to the ideas or claims that the protest is seeking to promote.[16]

27.15 The European Court has also held that the rights to protest under Article 10 and 11 may impose positive obligations on states: in a case involving the detention and fining of the applicant for refusing to put away a flag he was displaying at a demonstration as a form of counter-protest, the Court considered that the State had a positive obligation to protect the rights of both parties and to find the least restrictive means that would have enabled both demonstrations to take place.[17]

(iii) *Qualified rights*

27.16 Articles 10 and 11 are qualified rights: interference with freedom of expression or assembly may therefore be justified, providing that the interference is prescribed by law and necessary in democratic society in pursuit of a legitimate aim. Both Articles prescribe the relevant legitimate aims.

27.17 Interference with the rights can take the form of both measures taken before and during a gathering, as well as punitive measures taken afterwards such as conviction for participation in demonstrations.[18]

27.18 While the European Court of Human Rights has afforded contracting states a wide margin of appreciation in relation to measures for the prevention of crime and disorder, it has also held that a narrow margin of appreciation may be called for where such measures interfere with freedom of assembly and expression other than in cases

14 *Kudrevičius v Lithuania* (n 3) [92].
15 *Primov & Ors v Russia* (n 12) [155].
16 *Alexseyev v Russia* App nos 4916/07, 25924/08 and 14599/09 (ECtHR, 11 April 2011) [73].
17 *Fáber v Hungary* App no 40721/08 (ECtHR, 24 October 2012) [43].
18 *Kudrevičius v Lithuania* (n 3) [100].

of incitement to violence or rejection of democratic principles.[19] Such measures 'do a disservice to democracy and often even endanger it'.

27.19 The court has also held that a particularly narrow margin of appreciation applies in relation to measures restricting freedom of expression where that contributes to an important public debate (*Mamère v France*, where the impugned measures were analysed by reference to the legitimate aim of the protection of the environment and public health).[20]

(iv) *Key domestic cases*

27.20 The leading authority on the scope of protected protest rights in domestic law is the Supreme Court's decision in *Director of Public Prosecutions v Ziegler*[21] (which concerned appellants who had been acquitted of obstructing the highway during a protest against the arms trade at the ExCel centre in London, and then convicted following an appeal by way of case stated by the respondent). After considering the authorities above, the Supreme Court noted

> (a) that deliberate obstructive conduct which has a more than de minimis impact on others, still requires careful evaluation in determining proportionality; and, (b) that there is a separate evaluation of proportionality in respect of each restriction.[22]

27.21 In *Steel*, that necessitated separate analysis of the proportionality of removing her from the scene, her detention before being brought before a magistrate and the penalties imposed.[23] Determination of the proportionality of an interference with ECHR rights is a fact-specific enquiry which requires the evaluation of the circumstances in the individual case.[24]

27.22 In *Ziegler*, the appellants' convictions for obstructing the highway were quashed: the effect of Article 10/11 was that they had a lawful excuse for obstructing the highway, which was a defence under the relevant statute. The district judge had therefore been entitled to reach the view that the prosecution had not proved that the appellant's conduct was such as to lose the protection of Articles 10–11, and thus amount to an unreasonable obstruction of the highway.[25]

27.23 However, subsequent cases have clarified the scope of *Ziegler* and the extent to which a freestanding assessment of proportionality is required. Thus, in *DPP v Cuciurean*,[26] Mr Cuciurean was convicted of aggravated trespass, for which no defence

19 *Kuznetsov v Russia* App no 3079/18 (ECtHR, 27 October 2022) [45].
20 *Mamère v France* App no 12697/03 (ECtHR, 07 November 2007) [20]. See also *Hertel v Switzerland* 1998-VI 2330.
21 *Ziegler v Director of Public Prosecutions* (n 4).
22 ibid [64].
23 *Steel and others v United Kingdom* (n 9) [102]–[107].
24 *Ziegler v Director of Public Prosecutions* (n 4) [59].
25 ibid [80]–[87].
26 *Director of Public Prosecutions v Elliott Cuciurean* [2022] EWHC 736 (Admin).

of lawful excuse is available,[27] having dug a tunnel which he then occupied to protest against the construction of the HS2 railway line. His appeal on the grounds that conviction was a disproportionate interference with his Article 10/11 rights was dismissed. The High Court distinguished *Ziegler*, and held that the interference with Article 11 was minimal as trespass is not 'at the core of' protest.[28] Conviction of the offence was, further, intrinsically justified as an interference with Articles 10 and 11 without the need for a freestanding assessment of proportionality.[29]

27.24 At the time of writing, the Court of Appeal's judgment in the 'Colston Four' case (concerning four individuals charged with causing criminal damage to a statue of a merchant who profited from the slave trade during a peaceful protest as part of the Black Lives Matter movement)[30] is the most authoritative statement of the limits of the principle in *Ziegler*. The protestors had been acquitted by a jury following their trial. The Attorney General referred the case to the Court for decisions on the following questions of law:

- Did criminal damage fall within that category of offences where conviction for the offence was, intrinsically and without the need for a separate consideration of proportionality in individual cases, a justified and proportionate interference with any rights engaged under Articles 9, 10 and 11?
- If not, what principles should Crown Court judges apply when determining whether the qualified rights found in those Articles were engaged by the potential conviction of defendants purporting to be carrying out acts of protest?
- If those rights were engaged, under what circumstances should any question of proportionality be withdrawn from a jury?

27.25 The Court of Appeal held that *Ziegler* does not establish any broad principle that conviction for any offence arising out of a peaceful protest amounts to an interference with Article 9, 10 or 11 ECHR. For some offences, proof of the offence itself was sufficient and there was no need for a separate fact-sensitive proportionality assessment: the jurisprudence of the European Court of Human Rights did not establish that a general criminal measure could not, itself, strike the balance of proportionality. However, in other cases, a fact-sensitive assessment will generally be required unless that would be inconsistent with the statutory language governing the offence.

27.26 The Court held that criminal damage was not in the category of offences where proof of the ingredients of the offence was itself sufficient to justify conviction of the offence as a proportionate interference with the rights engaged under Articles 9, 10 and 11. However, the need of an assessment of proportionality would be limited, as the conduct in question would generally occur only where protests had been violent

27 Criminal Justice and Public Order Act 1994 s 68.
28 *Director of Public Prosecutions v Elliott Cuciurean* (n 26) [36]–[45], [76].
29 ibid [79], [81].
30 *Attorney General's Reference No 1 of 2022* [2022] EWCA Crim 1259.

and not peaceful (and so outside the protection of Article 11) or because the issue of proportionality would be clear.[31] Issues of proportionality should not therefore be left to a jury.[32]

27.27 In *Attorney General v Crosland*,[33] the Supreme Court gave short shrift to the argument that the respondent's contempt of court through publicising an embargoed judgment was justified as he was motivated by his concerns about global warming. Although accepting that he was so motivated, the Court considered that this did not justify his conduct: 'there is no principle which justifies treating the conscientious motives of a protestor with impunity'.[34] However, it was accepted that greater clemency is normally required to be shown in cases of civil disobedience than in other cases.[35]

27.28 In *Attorney General's Reference (No 1 of 2023)*,[36] the Court of Appeal similarly held that the right to protest did not amount to a defence to charges of criminal damage under the Criminal Damage Act. While the reason for the damage (the protestors' belief in the urgent need for action to confront climate change) was a relevant circumstance within the meaning of section 5(2) of the Act, the merits or otherwise of protest was not. The section was not intended 'to afford a defence to protestors based on the merits, urgency or importance of their cause'.[37]

Key legislation

27.29 The right to peaceful protest now exists within a framework of legislation which provides for policing powers to restrict protest. The below is an overview of the main legislative provisions but it is not intended to be comprehensive.

(i) *Public Order Act 1986*

27.30 The Public Order Act 1986 requires written notice to be given to the police of at least six clear daysbefore any public procession in support of or opposing a cause, publicising a cause or campaign, or marking or commemorating an event, unless it is not reasonably practicable to give advance notice.[38] It is an offence for the organisers not to give such notice (or having given it, for the date, time or route of the protest to differ from that set out in the notice)[39] subject to a defence of not knowing of – or not suspecting and not having cause to suspect – such a failure.[40]

---

31 ibid [114]–[116].
32 ibid [120].
33 *Attorney General v Crosland* [2021] UKSC 15.
34 ibid [47].
35 ibid. The court cited *Cuadrilla Bowland Ltd v Persons Unknown* [2020] EWCA Civ 9; *Cuciurean v Secretary of State for Transport* [2021] EWCA Civ 357.
36 *Attorney General's Reference No 1 of 2023* [2024] EWCA Crim 243.
37 ibid [47]–[50].
38 Public Order Act 1986 s 11.
39 ibid s 11(7).
40 ibid s 11(8).

27.31 It also provides police (in the form of the most senior police officer present, or where that does not apply the Chief of Police) with powers to impose conditions on public processions if he reasonably believes that:[41]

(a) it may result in serious public disorder, serious damage to property or serious disruption to the life of the community,

(aa) in the case of a procession in England and Wales, the noise generated by persons taking part in the procession may result in serious disruption to the activities of an organisation which are carried on in the vicinity of the procession,

(ab) in the case of a procession in England and Wales—
(i) the noise generated by persons taking part in the procession may have a relevant impact on persons in the vicinity of the procession, and
(ii) that impact may be significant, or

(b) the purpose of the persons organising it is the intimidation of others with a view to compelling them not to do an act they have a right to do, or to do an act they have a right not to do.

27.32 The conditions at section 12(aa) and (ab) were inserted by the Police, Crime, Sentencing and Courts Act 2022 in the face of concern as to the potential for a 'chilling' effect on lawful protest and the exercise of protestors' Article 10 and 11 ECHR rights.

27.33 Such directions may be given by the chief officer of police in relation to a procession which is intended to be held but has not yet begun to assemble (in which case they must be in writing),[42] or by the senior police officer present at the scene in relation to a procession which is being held or where people are assembling with a view to taking part in a procession.

27.34 It is an offence not to comply with such conditions, whether as an organiser or a participant (knowingly in Scotland; in England and Wales, if one knows or ought to know that the condition has been imposed).[43] On conviction, organisers may be liable to imprisonment for up to 51 weeks (or 3 months in Scotland) or to a fine,[44] while protestors may be liable to a fine.[45] It is a defence to show that the failure to comply arose from circumstances outside the individual's control.

27.35 Similar provisions apply in relation to protests which take the form of public assemblies rather than processions.[46] However, any conditions imposed under these powers must be clear enough that compliance is possible, otherwise the conditions will

41 ibid s 12(1).
42 Public Order Act 1986 s 12(3).
43 ibid s 12(4–5A).
44 ibid s 12(8).
45 ibid s 12(9).
46 ibid s 14. There is also a power to impose conditions on one-person protests on the grounds relating to noise only: ibid s 14ZA.

be unlawful, as demonstrated by the acquittal of Greta Thunberg in February 2024 from a charge of breaching conditions imposed under section 14 of the Act.[47]

27.36 The Act also provides that the chief officer of police may apply to the relevant council to make an order prohibiting a public procession in a district or part of a district if he reasonably believes that because of the conditions existing in that district, the powers under section 12 would be insufficient to prevent a procession from resulting in serious public disorder if held.[48] It is an offence to organise or participate in a procession which the individual knows is prohibited by such an order.[49] There is a similar power in relation to assemblies where the chief officer of police reasonably believes that the assembly is to be held on land to which the public has no, or only a limited, right of access, is likely to be held without (or in excess of any) permission, and may result in serious disruption to the life of the community or significant to land, a building or monument which is of historical, archaeological, architectural or scientific importance.[50]

(ii) *Public Order Act 2023*

27.37 The Public Order Act 2023 has established a number of new criminal offences in relation to protest, including offences of: causing serious disruption by locking-on;[51] being equipped to lock-on;[52] causing serious disruption by tunnelling,[53] by being present in a tunnel,[54] or by going equipped for tunnelling;[55] obstructing major transport works,[56] and interfering with key national infrastructure.[57]

27.38 It also provides, when in force, for serious disruption prevention orders ('SDPOs') to be made on conviction.[58] For a summary of the details of this long section see the Explanatory Notes.[59]

Injunctions to restrain protest

(i) *Introduction*

27.39 In addition to restrictions on the right to protest imposed through criminal law, increasing use is also being made of civil injunctions to restrain protest.

---

47 See the dicta of Ouseley J in *James v Director of Public Prosecutions* [2015] EWHC 3296 (Admin) [39]. See also Bean LJ in *Director of Public Prosecutions v Eastburn* [2023] EWHC 1063 (Admin) [17].
48 Public Order Act 1986 s 13.
49 ibid s 13(7–8).
50 ibid s 14A.
51 Public Order Act 2023 s 1 (as at the date of writing, only ss 1–8, 10–17, 30–31 and 34–35 are in force).
52 ibid s 2.
53 ibid s 3.
54 ibid s 4.
55 ibid s 5.
56 ibid s 6.
57 ibid ss 7–8.
58 ibid s 20.
59 'Explanatory Notes to the Public Order Bill (HL Bill 61)' paras 108–17 <https://bills.parliament.uk/publications/48142/documents/2370> accessed 24 April 2024.

27.40 Section 37 of the Senior Courts Act 1981 provides:

> 37 Powers of High Court with respect to injunctions …
>
> (1) The High Court may by order (whether interlocutory or final) grant an injunction … in all cases in which it appears to the court to be just and convenient to do so.
> (2) Any such order may be made either unconditionally or on such terms and conditions as the court thinks just.[60]

27.41 An injunction may be granted on the basis of an anticipated (actionable) wrong (sometimes referred to as *quia timet* injunctions): the claimant must prove that there is a real and imminent threat of the defendant committing or causing the torts feared, rather than having to prove that such torts have already been committed.[61]

27.42 An injunction is a discretionary remedy. The court will only grant an injunction where the balance of convenience (or justice) favours doing so.[62]

27.43 When considering whether to grant summary judgment for a final anticipatory injunction, the standard test for summary judgment applies, of whether the defendant has no real prospect of successfully defending the claim and there is no other compelling reason for the claim to go to trial.[63]

(ii) *Injunctions against persons unknown*

27.44 The following guidelines apply where an injunction is sought against persons unknown:[64]

- The 'persons unknown' must be people who have not been identified (since known and identified persons must be joined as individual defendants) but are capable of being identified and served with proceedings: in principle, this includes both anonymous defendants who are identifiable but whose names are unknown when proceedings commence, and newcomers;

- The 'persons unknown' must be defined in the application by reference to their alleged unlawful conduct;

- Interim injunctive relief may only be granted if there is a sufficiently real and imminent risk of a tort being committed;

---

60 Senior Courts Act 1981 s 37.
61 *Boyd & Anor v Ineos Upstream Ltd & Others* [2019] EWCA Civ 515 [34].
62 *American Cyanamid v Ethicon* [1975] AC 396.
63 Civil Procedure Rules s 24.2; *National Highways Ltd v Persons Unknown* [2023] EWCA Civ 182 [40].
64 *Canada Goose UK Retail Ltd v Persons Unknown* [2020] 1 WLR 2802.

- The defendants must be named in the order if known, or if described as 'persons unknown' must be capable of being identified and served with the order; if service is to be effected by alternative means, the method must be set out in the order;

- The acts prohibited must correspond to the threatened tort; they may include otherwise lawful conduct if, and only to the extent that, there is no other proportionate means of protecting the claimant's rights;

- The terms of the injunction must be sufficiently clear and precise as to enable persons potentially affected to know what they must not do. They should not be described in terms of a cause of action (such as trespass or nuisance). Unless it is strictly necessary to refer to the defendant's intention to correspondence to the threatened tort, they should not be formulated by reference to intention if the prohibited can be described in ordinary language without having to do so;

- Any interim injunction should have clear geographical and temporal limits.

(iii) *Newcomer injunctions*

27.45 The Supreme Court has held that there is 'no immovable obstacle' in the way of granting injunctions against newcomers: that is to say, persons unknown at the time of the application who may come to the threatened tort.[65] However, as the Supreme Court observed, 'this by no means leads straight to the conclusion that they ought to be granted, either generally or on the facts of any particular case'.[66] Although the Court expressly acknowledged that it was dealing with the specific circumstances of applications for injunctions brought by local authorities against Travellers, and that nothing said in that contexts should be taken as prescriptive in relation to newcomer injunctions in other contexts;[67] much of the Court's guidance is of general applicability. Newcomer injunctions are only likely to be justified where:

- There is a compelling (and sufficiently evidenced) need for an injunction for the protection of civil rights or a statutory objective (such as enforcement of planning control or prevention of anti-social behaviour) which cannot be adequately met by any other measures available. The need for an applicant to satisfy the court by detailed evidence that there is a compelling justification for the order sought is 'an overarching principle which must guide the court at all stages of its consideration';[68]

- There is procedural protection for the rights (including Convention rights) of affected newcomers which is sufficient to overcome the strong prima facie objection of subjecting them to a without notice injunction other than as an emergency measure. This includes an obligation to take all reasonable steps to draw the application and any order to the attention of all those likely to be affected, in advance of

---

65 *Wolverhampton City Council & others v London Gypsies and Travellers & others* [2023] UKSC 47 [167].
66 ibid.
67 ibid [235].
68 ibid [188].

the application being made,[69] and the most generous provision for liberty to apply to have the order varied or set aside;

- There has been compliance with the most stringent form of disclosure duty by the applicant, 'so as both to research for and then present to the court everything that might have been said by the targeted newcomers against the grant of injunctive relief'.[70] This is a continuing obligation, and if there is any doubt, the evidence before the court should err on the side of caution: the court and not the applicant should be the judge of relevance;[71]

- The injunction is both geographically and temporally limited to ensure (as far as practicable) that they neither 'outflank nor outlast' the circumstances relied on to justify them. Injunctions of this kind should be subject to periodic review, and should (absent any application for renewal) come to an end after no more than a year;[72]

- It is, on the facts, just and convenient that such an injunction is granted.

27.46 It is still necessary to define the actual or intended respondents as precisely as possible: insofar as it is actually possible to identify persons affected, this should be done, and the fact that an injunction is also sought against newcomers is not of itself a justification for failing to do so.[73]

27.47 Although (at the time of writing) a recent development, and made in the very different context of local authorities and Travellers, the case has been applied already in the context of environmental protest. Indeed, the Supreme Court recognised that cases including 'those directed at protestors who engage in direct action by, for example, blocking motorways, occupying motorway gantries or occupying HS2's land with the intention of disrupting construction' may all, depending on the circumstances, justify the grant of an injunction against persons unknown including newcomers.[74] The Court emphasised that such cases called for a full and careful assessment of the justification for the order sought, the rights which are or may be interfered with by the grant of the order, and the proportionality of that interference.[75]

27.48 In *Valero Energy v Persons Unknown*,[76] the claimants applied for an injunction to prevent protestors connected with Just Stop Oil/Extinction Rebellion/Insulate Britain/Youth Climate Swarm from blocking access to an oil refinery and various oil terminals. Granting an injunction (although not in the terms sought), the Court gave

69 ibid [226].
70 ibid [167].
71 ibid [220].
72 ibid [222].
73 ibid [221].
74 ibid [235].
75 ibid [236].
76 *Valero Energy Ltd & others v Persons Unknown & others* [2024] EWHC 134 (KB).

the following guidance as to the substantive and procedural requirements for obtaining an injunction:[77]

(A) Substantive Requirements

Cause of action

(1) There must be a civil cause of action identified in the claim form and particulars of claim. The usual quia timet (since he fears) action relates to the fear of torts such as trespass, damage to property, private or public nuisance, tortious interference with trade contracts, conspiracy with consequential damage and on-site criminal activity.

Full and frank disclosure by the Claimant

(2) There must be full and frank disclosure by the Claimant (applicant) seeking the injunction against the PUs.

Sufficient evidence to prove the claim

(3) There must be sufficient and detailed evidence before the Court on the summary judgment application to justify the Court finding that the immediate fear is proven on the balance of probabilities and that no trial is needed to determine that issue. The way this is done is by two steps. Firstly stage (1), the claimant has to prove that the claim has a realistic prospect of success, then the burden shifts to the defendant. At stage (2) to prove that any defence has no realistic prospect of success. In PU cases where there is no defendant present, the matter is considered ex-parte by the Court. If there is no evidence served and no foreseeable realistic defence, the claimant is left with an open field for the evidence submitted by him and his realistic prospect found at stage (1) of the hearing may be upgraded to a balance of probabilities decision by the Judge. The Court does not carry out a mini trial but does carry out an analysis of the evidence to determine if it the claimant's evidence is credible and acceptable. The case law on this process is set out in more detail under the section headed 'The Law' above.

No realistic defence

(4) The defendant must be found unable to raise a defence to the claim which has a realistic prospect of success, taking into account not only the evidence put before the Court (if any), but also, evidence that a putative PU defendant might reasonably be foreseen as able to put before the Court (for instance in relation to the PUs civil rights to freedom of speech, freedom to associate, freedom to protest and freedom to pass and repass on the highway). Whilst in *National Highways* the absence of any defence from the PUs was relevant to this determination, the Supreme Court›s ruling in *Wolverhampton* enjoins this Court not to put much weight on the lack of any served defence or defence evidence in a PU case. The nature of the proceedings are 'ex-parte' in PU cases and so the

77 ibid [58].

Court must be alive to any potential defences and the Claimants must set them out and make submissions upon them. In my judgment this is not a 'Micawber' point, it is a just approach point.

Balance of convenience – compelling justification

(5) In interim injunction hearings, pursuant to *American Cyanamid v Ethicon [1975] AC 396*, for the Court to grant an interim injunction against a defendant the balance of convenience and/or justice must weigh in favour of granting the injunction. However, in PU cases, pursuant to *Wolverhampton*, this balance is angled against the applicant to a greater extent than is required usually, so that there must be a 'compelling justification' for the injunction against PUs to protect the claimant's civil rights. In my judgment this also applies when there are PUs and named defendants.

(6) The Court must take into account the balancing exercise required by the Supreme Court in *DPP v Ziegler [2021] UKSC 23*, if the PUs› rights under the European Convention on Human Rights (for instance under Articles 10(2) and 11(2)) are engaged and restricted by the proposed injunction. The injunction must be necessary and proportionate to the need to protect the Claimants› right.

Damages not an adequate remedy

(7) For the Court to grant a final injunction against PUs the claimant must show that damages would not be an adequate remedy.

(B) Procedural Requirements

Identifying PUs

(8) The PUs must be clearly and plainly identified by reference to: (a) the tortious conduct to be prohibited (and that conduct must mirror the torts claimed in the Claim Form), and (b) clearly defined geographical boundaries, if that is possible.

The terms of injunction

(9) The prohibitions must be set out in clear words and should not be framed in legal technical terms (like 'tortious' for instance). Further, if and in so far as it seeks to prohibit any conduct which is lawful viewed on its own, this must also be made absolutely clear and the claimant must satisfy the Court that there is no other more proportionate way of protecting its rights or those of others.

The prohibitions must match the claim

(10) The prohibitions in the final injunctions must mirror the torts claimed (or feared) in the Claim Form.

Geographic boundaries

(11) The prohibitions in the final injunctions must be defined by clear geographic boundaries, if that is possible.

Temporal limits – duration

(12) The duration of the final injunction should be only such as is proven to be reasonably necessary to protect the claimant's legal rights in the light of the evidence of past tortious activity and the future feared (quia timet) tortious activity.

Service

(13) Understanding that PUs by their nature are not identified, the proceedings, the evidence, the summary judgment application and the draft order must be served by alternative means which have been considered and sanctioned by the Court. The applicant must, under the Human Rights Act 1998 S.12(2), show that it has taken all practicable steps to notify the respondents.

The right to set aside or vary

(14) The PUs must be given the right to apply to set aside or vary the injunction on shortish notice.

Review

(15) Even a final injunction involving PUs is not totally final. Provision must be made for reviewing the injunction in the future. The regularity of the reviews depends on the circumstances. Thus such injunctions are 'Quasi-final' not wholly final.

(iv) *Contempt of court*

27.49 Breach of an order may amount to contempt of court, where the following factors are proved to the criminal standard:

- Having received notice of the order (which must be an unambiguous order) the alleged contemnor did an act prohibited by the order or failed to do an act required by the order;
- He intended to do the act (or fail to do the act);
- He had knowledge of all the facts which would make the carrying out of the prohibited act or the omission to act a breach of the order.[78]

---

78 *FW Farnsworth Ltd v Lacy* [2013] EWHC 3487 (Ch) [20].

27.50 The act constituting the breach must be deliberate rather than merely inadvertent, but an intention to commit a breach is not necessary. Intention (or lack thereof) to flout an order is relevant to penalty.[79]

27.51 Stringent procedural requirements apply to the making of applications for committal for contempt of court, and for service of any application on the alleged contemnor.[80]

27.52 Although it must be proved that the alleged contemnor had notice of the order (ordinarily through the requirements of service being satisfied), the court has the power to dispense with personal service retrospectively.[81] In particular, the Court of Appeal has held that the requirement for personal service could not be interpreted so as to provide the respondent to an *ex parte* application for injunction, who had been notified by telephone or email of the terms of the injunction, with 'the perfect opportunity to do the very act restrained before he can be served'.[82] Although the general position is that an application for committal for breach of an injunction can only be brought where there has been personal service of the injunction which is sought to be enforced, this has never been an absolute requirement if it could be shown that the respondent had actual knowledge of the terms of the order.[83] As noted above, the power to dispense with personal service can be exercised retrospectively.[84]

27.53 Turning to penalties for breach, the object of the penalty is both to punish conduct in defiance of the court's order as well as serving a coercive function by holding out the threat of future punishment as a means of securing the protection which the order is designed to achieve. A committal order is appropriate where there is serious contumacious flouting of orders of the court.[85]

27.54 Following the entry into force of the Public Order Act 2023, a Serious Disruption Prevention Order may be made following a finding of contempt of court for a protest-related breach of an injunction.[86]

79 ibid.
80 Civil Procedure Rules pt 81.
81 *Business Mortgage Finance 4 U v Hussain* [2022] EWCA Civ 1264 [56]–[84].
82 ibid [67].
83 ibid [78]–[79].
84 ibid [80].
85 *Crystalmews Ltd v Metterick* [2006] EWHC 3087 (Ch).
86 Public Order Act 2023 s 20.

PART V

PUBLIC INTERNATIONAL LAW

CHAPTER 28

PUBLIC INTERNATIONAL LAW

Grace Cheng, Vivek Kapoor and Christopher Staker

Introduction

28.01 The main focus of this book is the domestic law and policy of the United Kingdom ('UK') relating to net zero and nature positive issues. However, domestic law and policy has a strong international dimension. Certain domestic legislation and policy is designed specifically to discharge the UK's obligations under public international law dealing with climate change, such as the obligations arising under the Paris Agreement of 22 April 2016.[1] Furthermore, arguments are being advanced to the effect that other international treaties and principles of customary international law dealing with more general matters, such as the law of the sea, international human rights, and international criminal law, may be of specific significance to climate change issues.

28.02 The first part of this chapter describes recent activity before international courts, tribunals and organisations involving the application of public international law to issues of climate change. It is of interest to note that much of this activity has focused not on multilateral treaties dealing specifically with climate change issues such as the Paris Agreement, but rather on principles of customary international law, on bilateral or regional conventions, or on multilateral treaties such as the Statute of the International Criminal Court and regional human rights treaties.

28.03 The second part of this chapter then deals with recent cases before international investment treaty arbitration tribunals. Investment protection treaties are designed to protect the legitimate expectations and ensure fair treatment of nationals of one State that make a protected investment in the territory of another State. Measures taken by a host State with a view to furthering environmental protection may negatively impact the economic interests of the investor. Where this occurs, issues may arise as to whether the measures taken by the host State are compatible with the investment protection treaty, and whether the host State is obliged to compensate the investor for the negative effects of such measures.

28.04 The third and final part of this chapter then moves on to consider circumstances in which public international law issues may be relevant in proceedings before domestic courts. Although domestic courts do not administer public international law directly as such, it may nonetheless be relevant in domestic proceedings, for instance, when courts

1 See discussion on Paris Agreement at paras 2.35–2.53 in Chapter 2.

have to interpret domestic legislation that has been enacted to give effect to the UK's obligations under international law, or judicially review executive action that is claimed to be inconsistent with such obligations. It will be seen that many recent cases have placed reliance on the European Convention on Human Rights ('ECHR'), a regional international treaty that has to a significant extent been incorporated into domestic law by the Human Rights Act 1998 ('HRA').

Proceedings before international courts and organisations[2]

(i) *The general context*

28.05 The number of claims and requests for advisory opinions involving climate rights brought before international courts and other international quasi-judicial and adjudicatory bodies has steadily risen over the years. This is not surprising in the wake of recent developments, including the historic resolution unanimously reached[3] by the United Nations General Assembly ('UNGA') in recognising the right to a clean, healthy and sustainable environment as a human right. This is likely to reinforce rights-based claims before adjudicatory bodies in years to come.

(ii) *International Court of Justice*

28.06 The International Court of Justice ('ICJ'), also known as the 'world court', is the principal judicial organ of the United Nations ('UN'). It was established by the United Nations Charter ('UN Charter') in June 1945 in The Hague (Netherlands) and has a twofold role: (i) to settle, in accordance with international law, legal disputes submitted to it by States, through judgments which as per Article 94 of the UN Charter, have a binding force (as between the parties and in respect of that particular case) and are without appeal for the parties concerned; and (ii) to give advisory opinions on legal questions referred to it by duly authorised UN organs and specialised agencies.[4] It is the only international court that adjudicates general disputes between countries, with its rulings and opinions serving as primary sources of international law.

28.07 On 18 November 2010, Costa Rica instituted proceedings against Nicaragua in the ICJ, alleging an 'incursion into, occupation of and use by Nicaragua's army of Costa Rican territory' as well as alleged breaches of Nicaragua's obligations towards Costa Rica under a number of international treaties and conventions.[5] Compensation was sought for the loss of environmental goods and services due to Nicaragua's excavation of channels on Costa Rica's territory and removal of nearly 300 trees and clearing of 6.19 hectares of vegetation which was said to have resulted in the impaired ability of the area to provide 'gas regulation and air quality services, such as carbon sequestration'.[6]

---

2 This part of this chapter has been authored by Grace Cheng. She is grateful to Dhara Pandya and Rupal Shah for the research assistance provided in preparing this part of the chapter.
3 UNGA Resolution A/RES/76/300 (28 July 2022).
4 Statute of the International Court of Justice. See also 'How the Court Works | INTERNATIONAL COURT OF JUSTICE' <https://www.icj-cij.org/how-the-court-works> accessed 3 April 2024.
5 *Certain Activities Carried Out by Nicaragua in the Border Area (Costa Rica v Nicaragua)*, Compensation, Judgment, ICJ Reports 2018, p 15 paras 19–20 [1].
6 ibid 64.

28.08 The ICJ handed down a ruling on 16 December 2015, establishing Nicaragua's activities as unlawful and having violated Costa Rica's territorial sovereignty and navigational rights. It was found that Costa Rica should be compensated for these unlawful activities.[7] Subsequently, the ICJ determined on 2 February 2018 that Nicaragua must compensate Costa Rica *inter alia* for the loss of environmental services in the sum of US$120,000 for the impairment or loss of the environmental goods and services of the impacted area in the period prior to recovery.[8]

28.09 This was the first case in which the ICJ adjudicated a claim for compensation for environmental damage and provides guidance as to how the Court may approach damages claims in cases of environmental harm. It is notable that the Court recognised ecosystem services as part of the compensable damage to the environment, stating that 'damage to the environment, and the consequent impairment or loss of the ability of the environment to provide goods and services, is compensable under international law. Such compensation may include indemnification for the impairment or loss of environmental goods and services in the period prior to recovery and payment for the restoration of the damaged environment'.[9]

28.10 The ICJ has further ruled that a State must ascertain whether there is a risk of significant transboundary harm prior to undertaking an activity having the potential to affect adversely the environment of another State. The State in question must conduct an environmental impact assessment if it considers that there is a risk of significant transboundary harm.[10] In addition, the ICJ has also made limited pronouncements on environmental issues, including on the issue of whaling in the Antarctic.[11]

28.11 Article 96 of the Charter gives the UNGA and the Security Council the power to request an advisory opinion from the ICJ on any legal question. Although ICJ advisory opinions lack binding effect, they are said to carry great legal weight and moral authority[12] since they are often an instrument of preventive diplomacy and contribute to the development of international law, thereby helping to strengthen peaceful relations between States.

28.12 On 29 March 2023, the UNGA adopted a resolution by consensus[13] requesting an advisory opinion from the ICJ in accordance with Article 96 of the Charter on the obligations of States with respect to climate change; in particular, whether States have specific obligations under international law to prevent and redress the adverse effects of climate change in order to protect the climate system as well as present and future generations.

---

7 *Certain Activities Carried Out by Nicaragua in the Border Area (Costa Rica v Nicaragua) and Construction of a Road in Costa Rica along the San Juan River (Nicaragua v Costa Rica)*, Judgment, ICJ Reports 2015, p 740 [229].
8 *Certain Activities Carried Out by Nicaragua in the Border Area (Costa Rica v Nicaragua)* (n 5) para 157.
9 ibid p 28 [42].
10 *Pulp Mills on the River Uruguay (Argentina v Uruguay)*, Judgment, ICJ Reports 2010, pp 59–60 [119]. See Chapter 7 for a more detailed discussion of environmental impact assessments.
11 *Whaling in the Antarctic (Australia v Japan: New Zealand intervening)*, Judgment, ICJ Reports 2014, p 226.
12 'Advisory Jurisdiction | INTERNATIONAL COURT OF JUSTICE' <https://www.icj-cij.org/advisory-jurisdiction> accessed 3 April 2024.
13 UNGA Res A/RES/77/276 (29 March 2023).

28.13 The initiative was spearheaded by the Government of Vanuatu and follows similar attempts by Palau[14] and the Marshall Islands previously to request an advisory opinion which were ultimately unsuccessful due to strong political opposition.[15] Although it will not be legally binding, any opinion from the ICJ on climate change is likely to be transformative for climate justice by creating a basis for climate accountability in international law.[16] The matter remains pending.

(iii) *International Criminal Court*

28.14 The International Criminal Court ('ICC') was established in 2002 and is a permanent institution in The Hague that has the power to exercise jurisdiction over persons for the most serious crimes of concern to the international community as a whole, namely genocide, war crimes, crimes against humanity, and the crime of aggression.[17]

28.15 There are 124[18] State Parties to the Rome Statute of the ICC ('Statute') which is the treaty that established the ICC. Attempts have been made to bring cases of 'climate crime' before the ICC, by incorporating the term 'ecocide' in the Rome Statute. For the purposes of the Statute, Article 7 'crime against humanity' is defined to mean, *inter alia*, '[o]ther inhumane acts of a similar character [to murder, deportation, persecution etc.] intentionally causing great suffering, or serious injury to body or to mental or physical health' when committed as part of a widespread or systematic attack directed against any civilian population, with knowledge of the attack.

28.16 On 12 October 2021, AllRise[19] submitted a request[20] to the Office of the Prosecutor of the ICC requesting an investigation into Brazilian President, Jair Messias Bolsonaro for his role in crimes against humanity resulting from ongoing deforestation and related activities in the Amazon rainforest. This follows previous communications sent to the ICC alleging serious crimes against humanity taking place in the Brazilian Amazon.[21] The request was made pursuant to Article 15 of the Statute which allows the

---

14 'Palau Seeks UN World Court Opinion on Damage Caused by Greenhouse Gases | UN News' (22 September 2011) <https://news.un.org/en/story/2011/09/388202> accessed 3 April 2024.
15 Maria Antonia Tigre and Jorge Alejandro Carrillo Bañuelos, 'The ICJ's Advisory Opinion on Climate Change: What Happens Now?' (*Climate Law Blog*, 29 March 2023) <https://blogs.law.columbia.edu/climatechange/2023/03/29/the-icjs-advisory-opinion-on-climate-change-what-happens-now/> accessed 4 March 2024.
16 Fred Lewsey, 'Seeking Climate Justice at the "World Court"' (University of Cambridge, 29 March 2023) <https://www.cam.ac.uk/stories/climate-ICJ> accessed 3 April 2024.
17 Rome Statute of the International Criminal Court 1998 Article 5.
18 On 14 November 2023, Armenia formally ratified the Rome Statute. Its ratification entered into force on 1 February 2024. See 'The States Parties to the Rome Statute | International Criminal Court' <https://asp.icc-cpi.int/states-parties> accessed 3 April 2024.
19 AllRise is a non-profit organisation and registered law clinic for climate and environmental justice located in KwaZulu Natal, South Africa. See 'AllRise' (*AllRise*) <https://www.allrise.at> accessed 4 April 2024.
20 AllRise, 'Communication under Article 15 of the Rome Statute of the International Criminal Court Regarding the Commission of Crimes Against Humanity against Environmental Dependents and Defenders in the Brazilian Legal Amazon from January 2019 to Present, Perpetrated by Brazilian President Jair Messias Bolsonaro and Certain Former and Current Principal Actors of His Administration' <https://climatecasechart.com/wp-content/uploads/non-us-case-documents/2021/20211012_14633_na.pdf> accessed 4 April 2024.
21 Human Rights Advocacy Collective (CADHu) and ARNS Commission, 'Informative Note to the Prosecutor International Criminal Court Pursuant to Article 15 of the Rome Statute Requesting a Preliminary Examination into Incitement to Genocide and Widespread Systematic Attacks Against Indigenous Peoples by President Jair Messias Bolsonaro in Brazil' <https://apublica.org/wp-content/uploads/2019/11/e-muito-triste-levar-um-brasileiro-para-o-tribunal-penal-internacional-diz-co-autora-da-peticao.pdf?ref=the-wave.net> accessed 4 April 2024.

Prosecutor to make a request to the Pre-Trial Chamber to authorise an investigation into crimes within the jurisdiction of the Court on the basis of information from third parties.

28.17 It was alleged that President Bolsonaro promoted and facilitated a 'widespread attack' on the Amazon Biome in furtherance of a State policy amounting to crimes against humanity contrary to Article 7[22] and contrary to Article 25(3)c) of the Rome Statute which provides for the facilitation of the commission of a crime. It was alleged that:[23]

> in addition to contributing to the general destruction or degradation of the rainforest, large infrastructure projects disrupt rivers; agriculture expansion impoverishes and contaminates soils and rivers with pesticides; gold-mining activities generate dangerous mercury pollution; and land-grabbing and invasions of territories cause the spread of infectious zoonotic diseases and COVID-19.

28.18 It was submitted that since the Brazilian authorities are unable to carry out proceedings against the President, the complaint should be admissible before the ICC under Article 17 (Issue of Admissibility) of the Statute. If an investigation materialises, this would be the first time that an investigation relating to crimes against humanity is based on alleged environmental and climate harm.

28.19 On 8 December 2022, another request was made to the Office of the Prosecutor. Students for Climate Solutions New Zealand and the UK Youth Climate Coalition submitted a request to open investigations into, and request reparations from, BP Senior Executives, pursuant to Article 15 of the Statute and Article 8 of the Paris Agreement, respectively.[24] It was alleged that BP Senior Executives have committed a crime against humanity by knowingly causing and perpetuating climate change by pursuing activities in the oil and gas industry; more specifically, maximising profits from fossil fuels which are said to be responsible for 91% of global industrial greenhouse gas emissions.[25]

28.20 Both cases are pending before the ICC. In 2016, Chief Prosecutor of the ICC at the time, Fatou Besouda said that her office would 'give particular consideration' to crimes committed by or resulting in 'the destruction of the environment, the illegal exploitation of natural resources or the illegal dispossession of land'.[26] However, the only current reference to the environment in the Statute is in relation to war crimes which criminalises an act of:[27]

---

22 Specifically, Article 7(1)(a) (murder); Article 7(1)(h) (persecution against any identifiable group); Article 7(1)(k) (other inhumane acts).
23 AllRise (n 20) para 37.
24 New Zealand Students for Climate Solutions and UK Youth Climate Coalition, 'Request to Open Investigations & Request for Reparations Regarding the Crimes against Humanity of Climate Change Submitted under Article 15 of the Rome Statute of the International Criminal Court' <https://climatecasechart.com/wp-content/uploads/non-us-case-documents/2022/20221208_19343_points-of-claim.pdf> accessed 4 April 2024.
25 ibid 5.
26 Office of the Prosecutor (ICC), 'Policy Paper on Case Selection and Prioritisation' para 41 <https://www.icc-cpi.int/sites/default/files/itemsDocuments/20160915_OTP-Policy_Case-Selection_Eng.pdf> accessed 4 April 2024.
27 Rome Statute of the International Criminal Court 1998 Article 8.2.b.iv.

> [i]ntentionally launching an attack in the knowledge that such attack will cause … widespread, long-term and severe damage to the natural environment which would be clearly excessive in relation to the concrete and direct overall military advantage anticipated.

28.21 There have been various calls for the inclusion of a crime of 'ecocide' in the Statute, and calls to include climate charge harm within the definition of ecocide.[28] In 2021, a definition of ecocide was drawn up which was intended to be adopted by the ICC to prosecute the most egregious offences against the environment.[29] The UN Special Rapporteur on the promotion and protection of human rights in the context of climate change has recommended that the ICC include an indictable offence of ecocide.[30] This has also received support from the UN High Commissioner for Human Rights.[31]

28.22 With ecocide being officially a crime in 10 countries and being actively discussed in another 27 countries,[32] it remains to be seen whether the ICC will follow suit. In the meantime, whether ecological damage and destruction will be considered a 'crime against humanity' by the ICC will also be keenly followed with interest, with potential far reaching effects and implications.

(iv) *International Tribunal for the Law of the Sea*

28.23 The International Tribunal for the Law of the Sea ('ITLOS') is an independent judicial body that was established by the 1982 United Nations Convention on the Law of the Sea ('UNCLOS') to adjudicate disputes arising out of the interpretation and application of UNCLOS. Disputes relating to UNCLOS may concern the conservation and management of the living resources of the sea, and protection and preservation of the marine environment.

28.24 The connection between climate change and the oceans is well-established. It is recognised that the oceans are an integral part of the global climate system in which most of the heat accumulating in the Earth's energy system is stored.[33] In the Report of the Conference of the Parties ('COP') regarding the 25th Session, a commendation was made regarding:

---

28 UNGA, 'Promotion and Protection of Human Rights in the Context of Climate Change: Note by the Secretary-General. A/77/226' para 90.
29 The proposed definition of 'ecocide' by the Independent Expert Panel convened by the Stop Ecocide Foundation is 'unlawful or wanton acts committed with knowledge that there is a substantial likelihood of severe and either widespread or long-term damage to the environment being caused by those acts'. See 'Legal Definition of Ecocide Drafted by Independent Expert Panel' (*Stop Ecocide International*) <https://www.stopecocide.earth/legal-definition> accessed 4 April 2024.
30 UNGA (n 28) para 90.f.
31 'Türk: Human Rights Are Antidote to Prevailing Politics of Distraction, Deception, Indifference and Repression' (OHCHR) <https://www.ohchr.org/en/statements/2023/09/turk-human-rights-are-antidote-prevailing-politics-distraction-deception> accessed 4 April 2024.
32 Mark Hillsdon, 'Society Watch: Drive to Make Ecocide an International Crime Gains Momentum' *Reuters* (20 February 2023) <https://www.reuters.com/business/sustainable-business/society-watch-drive-make-ecocide-an-international-crime-gains-momentum-2023-02-20/> accessed 4 April 2024.
33 Our Children's Trust and Oxfam International, 'Case No. 31. Responsibilities and Obligations of States with Respect to Climate Change and International Law. Request for Advisory Opinion Submitted to the Tribunal by the Commission of Small Island States. Amicus Curiae Submission' <https://climatecasechart.com/wp-content/uploads/non-us-case-documents/2023/20230616_Case-No.-312022_opinion-31.pdf> accessed 4 April 2024.

> the efforts of the President of the Conference of the Parties at its twenty-fifth session to highlight the importance of the ocean, including as an integral part of the Earth's climate system, and of ensuring the integrity of ocean and coastal ecosystems in the context of climate change.[34]

28.25 Despite the clear interplay between the oceans and climate change (as shown in the scientific literature and recent reports from the International Panel on Climate Change)[35] there is no mention in UNCLOS of greenhouse gas emissions, global warming, climate change, sea level rise, or ocean acidification. This is not surprising since the convention was adopted in 1982, prior to the rise in concerns of climate change.

28.26 On 12 December 2022, the Commission of Small Island States on Climate Change and International Law[36] submitted a request for an advisory opinion from ITLOS on the specific obligations of State Parties to UNCLOS to: (i) prevent, reduce and control pollution of the marine environment in relation to the deleterious effects that result or are likely to result from climate change; and (ii) protect and preserve the marine environment in relation to climate change impacts.[37] Written statements were submitted by States Parties to UNCLOS, as well as intergovernmental and other organisations. A public hearing was held on 11 September 2023 and a unanimous advisory opinion was delivered on 21 May 2024.[38]

28.27 This was the first time that an international judicial body had been asked to clarify States' obligations to protect the world's oceans from fossil fuel-driven climate change which threatens human rights, biodiversity, and the very existence of many island nations.[39] The advisory opinion rendered is particularly momentous given that ITLOS was the first of the three international judicial bodies to deliver its opinion. It is to be seen whether this may have implications for the opinions to be rendered by the ICJ as well as by the Inter-American Court of Human Rights.

---

34 'Report of the Conference of the Parties on Its Twenty-Fifth Session, Held in Madrid from 2 to 15 December 2019. FCCC/CP/2019/13' (UNFCCC 2020) 4 <https://unfccc.int/documents/210472> accessed 20 May 2024.
35 Armando Rocha, 'The Advisory Jurisdiction of the ITLOS in the Request Submitted by the Commission of Small Island States' (*Climate Law Blog*, 4 December 2023) <https://blogs.law.columbia.edu/climatechange/2023/04/12/the-advisory-jurisdiction-of-the-itlos-in-the-request-submitted-by-the-commission-of-small-island-states/> accessed 8 April 2024.
36 The Commission of Small Island States on Climate Change and International Law was established on 31 October 2021 as an international organisation with Antigua and Barbuda and Tuvalu as the original signatories. It was duly registered with the Secretariat of the United Nations in accordance with Article 102 of the Charter of the United Nations. Pursuant to Article 3(1) of the Agreement, Membership in the Commission is open to all Members of the Alliance of Small Island States. Instruments of accession have been deposited by the Republic of Palau, Bahamas, Niue, St. Kitts and Nevis, St. Lucia, St. Vincent and the Grenadines, Tuvalu and the Republic of Vanuatu.
37 Commission of Small Island States on Climate Change and International Law, 'Request for Advisory Opinion' <https://www.itlos.org/fileadmin/itlos/documents/cases/31/Request_for_Advisory_Opinion_COSIS_12.12.22.pdf> accessed 8 April 2024.
38 *Request for an Advisory Opinion Submitted by the Commission of Small Island States on Climate Change and International Law (Advisory Opinion) Case No 31 (21 May 2024)* (ITLOS).
39 'Climate Opinion Awaited as Historic Hearings Conclude at ITLOS' (Center for International Environmental Law, 25 September 2023) <https://www.ciel.org/news/climate-opinion-awaited-as-historic-hearings-conclude-at-itlos/> accessed 8 April 2024.

(v) *Regional cases*

28.28 The Inter-American Court of Human Rights ('IACtHR') is one of the world's three regional human rights tribunals, together with the European Court of Human Rights ('ECtHR')[40] and the African Court of Human and Peoples' Rights ('ACHPR'). The IACtHR is an autonomous judicial body whose objective is to interpret and apply the American Convention on Human Rights, an international treaty that entered into force on 18 July 1978. The ACHPR is a continental court established by African countries to ensure the protection of human and people's rights in Africa which complements and reinforces the functions of the African Commission on Human and Peoples' Rights.

28.29 On 9 January 2023, Chile and Colombia submitted a joint request to the IACtHR for an advisory opinion to clarify the scope of State obligations for responding to the climate emergency under the framework of international human rights law.[41]

28.30 The request covered the following topics: (i) the scope of States' duty of prevention against extreme and slow onset climate effects in light of the Paris Agreement and the scientific consensus not to increase beyond 1.5°C of global temperature; (ii) States' obligation to preserve the right to life against the climate emergency in light of science and human rights; (iii) the obligations of States to protect the rights of children and future generations from climate change; (iv) the nature of State obligations to provide judicial actions for adequate protection and reparation of rights affected by climate emergency; (v) the obligations of States to protect environmental defenders, especially indigenous people and women; and (vi) cooperation between States to confront climate change in the region.[42]

28.31 The IACtHR has previously issued an advisory opinion in response to a request from Colombia in which the court concluded that the right to a healthy environment is a human right under the American Convention on Human Rights.[43] The opinion noted that the adverse effects of environmental degradation and climate change both affect human rights. Coupled with any advisory opinion that may be rendered in due course by the Court, this is likely to pave the way towards claims being brought before the Court in relation to climate change related harms.

28.32 An initiative is also underway to request an advisory opinion from the ACHPR on the human rights obligations of African States with respect to climate change.[44] This

---

40 Addressed below at paras 28.104–28.134.

41 'Chile and Colombia Join Forces to Ask Regional Human Rights Court for Guidelines to Respond to Climate Emergency | CEJIL' <https://cejil.org/en/blog/chile-and-colombia-join-forces-to-ask-regional-human-rights-court-for-guidelines-to-respond-to-climate-emergency/> accessed 8 April 2024.

42 Republic of Colombia and Republic of Chile, 'Request for an Advisory Opinion on Climate Emergency and Human Rights to the Inter-American Court of Human Rights from the Republic o Colombia and the Republic of Chile' <https://climatecasechart.com/wp-content/uploads/non-us-case-documents/2023/20230109_18528_petition-2.pdf> accessed 20 May 2024.

43 *Advisory Opinion Oc-23/17 of November 15, 2017 Requested by the Republic of Colombia* (Inter-American Court of Human Rights).

44 'Increased Scrutiny of Climate Crisis Emerging before International Courts' (*ESCR-Net*) <https://www.escr-net.org/news/2023/increased-scrutiny-climate-crisis-emerging-international-courts> accessed 8 April 2024.

will be a historic milestone if rendered, given that no advisory proceedings in relation to climate change have been requested as of now, despite the African human rights system offering a relatively easier avenue to make such a request.[45]

28.33 The Court of Justice of the European Union ('CJEU') is tasked with implementing and interpreting the Charter ('EU Charter') of Fundamental Rights of the European Union ('EU'). In contrast to the European Convention of Human Rights ('ECHR'), the EU Charter contains a self-standing provision on the environment in Article 37 (environmental protection) which states that:[46]

> [a] high level of environmental protection and the improvement of the quality of the environment must be integrated into the policies of the Union and ensured in accordance with the principle of sustainable development.

28.34 However, the EU Charter including Article 37 has, to-date, been seldomly invoked in climate litigation, with parties preferring to rely on the ECHR due to its more developed case law in environmental matters at the ECtHR, even though the ECHR does not enshrine any right to a healthy environment as such. The ECtHR has been called upon to develop its case law in environmental matters since it is considered that the exercise of rights under the ECHR may be undermined by the existence of harm to the environment and exposure to environmental risks.[47]

28.35 The CJEU has recently had two climate cases brought before it, but both were dismissed due to a lack of standing.[48] Although all non-governmental organisations can challenge violations of environmental law at the CJEU,[49] the Court applies a strict test of standing whereby applicants must show an individual concern particular to them or their group.[50] In the case of *Armando Ferrão Carvalho and Others v the European Parliament and the Council*,[51] the Court held that since everyone is impacted by climate change one way or another, the applicants could not demonstrate that they were individually impacted by the EU's climate policy. This makes it difficult for individuals and environmental groups to challenge EU law measures of general application before the court, even when human rights are affected.

28.36 In addition to the human rights tribunals referred to above, there are also other bodies that are involved with climate litigation. In the case of *Daniel Billy and Others v Australia (Torres Strait Islanders Petition)*,[52] a group of eight indigenous Torres Strait

45 Yusra Suedi and Marie Fall, 'Climate Change Litigation before the African Human Rights System: Prospects and Pitfalls: Practice Note: GNHRE Climate Litigation in Global South Project' [2024] 16(1) Journal of Human Rights Practice 146.
46 Charter of Fundamental Rights of the European Union Article 37.
47 See section D.IV below.
48 Case T-141/19 *Peter Sabo et al v European Parliament and Council of the European Union* (2020) ECLI:EU:T:2020:179; Case T-330/18 *Armando Ferrão Carvalho & Others v the European Parliament and the Council* (2021) ECLI:EU:C:2021:324.
49 Case C-873/19 *Deutsche Umwelthilfe v Germany* (2022) ECLI:EU:C:2022:857.
50 Treaty establishing the European Community (Nice consolidated version) Article 230.4; Case 25/62 *Plaumann & Co v Commission of the European Economic Community* [1963] ECR 95.
51 *Armando Ferrão Carvalho and Others v the European Parliament and the Council* (n 48).
52 *Daniel Billy et al v Australia*, CCPR/C/135/D/3624/2019 (UN Human Rights Committee).

Islanders with Australian nationality and six of their children submitted a petition against the Australian Government to the United Nations Human Rights Committee. It was alleged that the Islanders' rights had been violated since Australia had failed to adapt to climate change by *inter alia* failing to upgrade seawalls on the islands and to reduce greenhouse gas emissions.

28.37 On 23 September 2022, the UN Human Rights Committee found that Australia's failure to take timely and adequate measures to protect the Islanders against the adverse impacts of climate change violated their rights to enjoy their culture and be free from arbitrary interferences with their private life, family and home. It was held that although Australia had already taken some measures, the effects of climate change may expose individuals to a violation of their right to life without robust national and international efforts in place and therefore, additional timely and appropriate measures were required to avert a risk to the Islanders' lives. Australia was ordered to compensate the Islanders for the harm suffered, engage in meaningful consultation with their communities to assess their needs, and take measures to continue to secure the communities' safe existence on their respective islands.[53]

(vi) *Need for a new International Environmental Court?*

28.38 The international legal system is decentralised with jurisdiction stemming from consent of the relevant actors. A striking feature of environmental cases that have been decided over the past decade is the assortment of bodies that have been involved in the process. A survey of significant international environmental law cases has included decisions of permanent courts and tribunals, as well as *ad hoc* mechanisms; global institutions and regional bodies; courts of general jurisdiction and specialist tribunals.

28.39 For this reason, there have been calls for the establishment of an international court for the environment, dedicated to dealing with environmental disputes.[54] The bilateral approach of existing courts which were set up to resolve disputes between two parties does not fit the complex realities of environmental issues involving collective action problems for a large number of actors. Moreover, various of the international courts deal only with disputes between States, thereby precluding individual persons or non-State actors from bringing a claim.

28.40 However, the difficulties with singling out areas that are exclusively environmental, and whether States would be prepared to do so, poses another thorny question. In 1993, the ICJ created a Chamber for Environmental Matters. However, no State requested that a case be dealt with by the Chamber before it was eventually disbanded in 2006.[55]

---

53 ibid.
54 'ICE Coalition' (ICE Coalition) <http://www.icecoalition.org> accessed 8 April 2024.
55 'Chambers and Committees | INTERNATIONAL COURT OF JUSTICE' <https://icj-cij.org/chambers-and-committees> accessed 8 April 2024.

(vii) *Conclusion*

28.41 Climate litigation and the involvement of international courts and quasi-judicial bodies is becoming an integral part of securing climate action and justice. With advisory opinions currently being sought from three international bodies, it is clear that actors are increasingly turning to international courts and bodies to combat the climate crisis. With governments taking further steps to reduce emissions and adapt to the impacts of climate change, and with recent initiatives including talks on a worldwide pact to prevent plastic pollution,[56] and vows to protect dwindling biodiversity,[57] it is expected that there will be increased use of international courts in future to tackle climate issues.

Proceedings before international arbitration tribunals[58]

(i) *The general context*

28.42 In July 2023, the European Commission proposed that the EU, its Member States, and Euratom withdraw, in a coordinated manner, from the Energy Charter Treaty ('ECT'). The stated reason was that the ECT was no longer compatible with the EU's enhanced climate ambition under the European Green Deal and the Paris Agreement.[59] From late-2022 until the announcement in July 2023, several EU States had already withdrawn from the ECT. On 22 February 2024, the UK government confirmed that the UK would withdraw from the ECT, stating that the decision to do so 'will support the UK's transition to net zero and strengthen its energy security'. The Minister of State for Energy Security and Net Zero stated that the ECT 'is outdated and in urgent need of reform but talks have stalled and sensible renewal looks increasingly unlikely', and that '[r]emaining a member would not support our transition to cleaner, cheaper energy, and could even penalise us for our world-leading efforts to deliver net zero'.[60]

28.43 The stated purpose of the ECT is to establish a legal framework 'in order to promote long-term cooperation in the energy field, based on complementarities and mutual benefits, in accordance with the objectives and principles of the [European Energy] Charter'.[61] The ECT is an example of an international (multilateral) investment treaty that includes investor–state dispute settlement mechanism ('ISDS'). ISDS was designed to protect foreign investors from excessive interventions by host states. ISDS provides foreign investors access to international arbitration, where they can pursue damages against a host state for policies and regulations that harm their protected investments. However, there is growing concern that ISDS may limit States' right to regulate, even

56 'Historic Day in the Campaign to Beat Plastic Pollution: Nations Commit to Develop a Legally Binding Agreement' (UN Environment, 2 March 2022) <http://www.unep.org/news-and-stories/press-release/historic-day-campaign-beat-plastic-pollution-nations-commit-develop> accessed 8 April 2024.
57 UNEP, 'Kunming-Montreal Global Biodiversity Framework' (19 December 2022) <http://www.unep.org/resources/kunming-montreal-global-biodiversity-framework> accessed 8 April 2024.
58 This part of this chapter has been authored by Vivek Kapoor.
59 'European Commission Proposes a Coordinated EU Withdrawal from the Energy Charter Treaty' <https://energy.ec.europa.eu/news/european-commission-proposes-coordinated-eu-withdrawal-energy-charter-treaty-2023-07-07_en> accessed 8 April 2024.
60 'UK Departs Energy Charter Treaty' (GOV.UK) <https://www.gov.uk/government/news/uk-departs-energy-charter-treaty> accessed 8 April 2024.
61 Energy Charter Treaty Article 2.

when pursuing legitimate public policy objectives, particularly in the context of climate policies and regulations.

28.44 There are over 2,500 similar treaties in force globally that potentially allow international energy investors to sue States for climate policies and regulations.[62]

(ii) *The Investment Protection Regime and the Promise of International Arbitration*

28.45 Beyond their considerably diverse formulations, investment treaties advance a distinctive conception of property protection and sanctity of contract, which sets them apart from other legal regimes. They establish protections for protected investments, beyond the arrangements available under the domestic legal regime.[63]

(a) The Investment Protection Regime

28.46 The principle of *pacta sunt servanda* applied under international law provides for the binding nature of treaties.[64] Under international investment law, the principle uniquely amalgamates private and public-law dimensions. It requires States to honour their contractual obligations made to another sovereign State for the protection of investors of the latter, and the breach of which allow the investors of the latter State to make a claim against the former State.

28.47 Investment treaties – whether bilateral, multilateral or those forming part of trade treaties – essentially protect investment by guaranteeing standards of protections for investors such as compensation for expropriation, national treatment of foreign investors or most favoured nation treatment.[65]

28.48 To be clear, investment treaties protect investment, rather than property. The two notions overlap but do not coincide.[66] Investment can take many forms, including arrangements outside property relations. It is a dynamic concept connected to running a business enterprise and usually involves capital contributions, a duration, risk taking and the aim of generating returns.[67] Arbitral tribunals applying international investment law have typically favoured such dynamic notions of property. For instance, in *Methanex Corporation v United States of America*,[68] the tribunal observed that the restrictive notion of property as a material thing is obsolete and has ceded its place to a contemporary conception which includes managerial control over components of a process that is wealth producing. In the view of the tribunal, items such as good will and market share

62 Bilateral Investment Treaties (BITs): total – 2828, in force – 2219; Treaties with Investment Provisions (TIPs): total – 451, in force – 371. See 'International Investment Agreements Navigator | UNCTAD Investment Policy Hub' <https://investmentpolicy.unctad.org/international-investment-agreements> accessed 8 April 2024.
63 Lorenzo Cotula, 'International Investment Law and Climate Change: Reframing the ISDS Reform Agenda' (2023) 24 The Journal of World Investment & Trade 766.
64 Vienna Convention on the Law of Treaties Article 26.
65 Brian Preston, 'Investor-State Dispute Resolution and the Environment: A Case for Appropriate Dispute Resolution' (A New Era for IDR: Breaking the Stronghold of International Arbitration, Singapore, 4 August 2024).
66 Zachary Douglas, 'Property, Investment, and the Scope of Investment Protection Obligations' in Zachary Douglas, Joost Pauwelyn and Jorge E Viñuales (eds), *The Foundations of International Investment Law: Bringing Theory into Practice* (Oxford University Press 2014) 374.
67 See *Nova Scotia Power Incorporated v Bolivarian Republic of Venezuela*, ICSID Case No ARB(AF)/11/1 [84].
68 *Methanex Corporation v United States of America, Final Award of the Tribunal on Jurisdiction and Merits.*

may constitute an element of the value of an enterprise and hence, may figure in valuation. But it is difficult to see how they might stand alone.

28.49 The historical development of capitalist economies and the rise of enterprise as source and storage of wealth have made property also a dynamic notion.[69] While a static concept of property emphasises holding assets, a more dynamic notion centres on expectations and revenue generating potential, as reflected in the proposition. As Jeremy Bentham in *Theory of Legislation*[70] noted: property is nothing more than the basis of a certain expectation.

28.50 The concept of expectation has gained substance and strength under international investment law. Successive arbitral tribunals have interpreted fair and equitable treatment as protecting the 'legitimate expectations' that the investors had when they made the investment – the frustration of which could be redressed by way of damages.

28.51 The tribunal in *Técnicas Medioambientales Tecmed, SA v Mexico*[71] was one of the first to refer, within its discussion of the fair and equitable treatment standard, to protection of legitimate expectations. The tribunal tied fair and equitable treatment to the good faith principle established by international law and thus concluded that fair and equitable treatment required 'the Contracting Parties to provide to international investments treatment that does not affect the basic expectations that were taken into account by the foreign investor to make the investment'.[72] This has been referred to by several subsequent tribunals with approval.[73]

28.52 The protection of property against expropriation too has been strengthened under international law. It is no longer limited to direct expropriation. It includes indirect expropriations and measures equivalent or tantamount to expropriation. As the UNCTAD[74] study on 'Taking of Property' has described: it is not the physical invasion of property that characterises nationalisations or expropriations that has assumed importance, but the erosion of rights associated with ownership by State interferences. So, methods have been developed to address this issue.[75]

---

69 For a discussion, see Stefano Rodotà, *Il Terribile Diritto: Studi Sulla Proprietà Privata e i Beni Comuni* (2nd edn, Il Mulino 1990) 149–71.
70 Jeremy Bentham, *Theory of Legislation* (Trübner & Company 1871).
71 *Técnicas Medioambientales Tecmed, SA v The United Mexican States,* ICSID Case No ARB (AF)/00/2 Award.
72 ibid 154.
73 See, among others, *LG&E Energy Corp, LG&E Capital Corp, and LG&E International, Inc v Argentine Republic,* ICSID Case No ARB/02/1 Decision on liability [127]; *MTD Equity Sdn Bhd and MTD Chile SA v Republic of Chile,* ICSID Case No ARB/01/7 Award [114]; *Occidental Exploration and Production Company v The Republic of Ecuador,* LCIA Case No UN3467 Final Award [185]; *CMS Gas Transmission Company v The Republic of Argentina,* ICSID Case No ARB/01/8 Award [279]; *Sempra Energy International v The Argentine Republic,* ICSID Case No ARB/02/16 Award [298].
74 The United Nations Conference on Trade and Development is an intergovernmental organisation within the United Nations Secretariat that promotes the interests of developing countries in world trade.
75 UNCTAD, 'Taking of Property. UNCTAD/ITE/IIT/15' <https://unctad.org/system/files/official-document/psiteiitd15.en.pdf> accessed 8 April 2024.

28.53 The decisive element is the substantial loss of control or economic value of a foreign investment without a physical taking.[76] That may be as a result of regulatory measures. A protected investment, to the extent affected by regulatory measures, may be deemed to have been expropriated. For instance, in *Metalclad v Mexico*[77] the investment had been assured by the federal government that his project for a landfill facility had complied with all relevant environmental and planning regulations. Subsequently the local municipal authorities denied a construction permit. In addition, the regional government declared the land in question a national area for the protection of rare cactus. The tribunal upheld the investor's claim under the North American Free Trade Agreement ('NAFTA')'s provision on expropriation. It held that expropriation includes:

> not only open, deliberate and acknowledged takings of property, such as outright seizure or formal or obligatory transfer of title in favour of the host State, but also covert or incidental interference with the use of property which has the effect of depriving the owner, in whole or in significant part, of the use or reasonably-to-be expected economic benefit of property even if not necessarily to the obvious benefit of the host State.[78]

28.54 Further, protection from expropriation relates not only to tangible property or physical assets but also to a broad range of rights that are economically significant to the investor. As UNCTAD described:[79]

> in the past, the concern was only with the physical property of a foreign investor. In modern times, the concern is not so much with the physical property but with the antecedent rights that are necessary for the enjoyment of these property rights as well as with incorporeal property.

(b) The Promise of International Arbitration

28.55 In relation to protected investments, investors can enforce their rights through international arbitration, often without the need to exhaust local remedies. Unlike human rights treaties, which typically require claimants to first pursue domestic litigation, investment treaties usually enable foreign investors to access international arbitration directly.

28.56 It falls on to the arbitral tribunals constituted under these investment treaties to award damages for violations of the investment protections. Even though, most investment treaties do not specify how to calculate damages if the State violates the treaty. The general guiding principle of international law is the principle stated in the *Chorzów Factory*[80] case that compensation 'should wipe out all the consequences of the

---

76 James Crawford and Ian Brownlie, *Brownlie's Principles of Public International Law* (9th edn, Oxford University Press 2019).

77 *Metalclad Corporation v The United Mexican States*, ICSID Case No ARB(AF)/97/1 Award.

78 *CME Czech Republic BV v The Czech Republic*, UNCITRAL Partial Award [606].

79 UNCTAD Series on issues in international investment agreements, Taking of Property 36 (2000). UNCTAD (n 75) 36.

80 *Factory at Chorzów (Merits) PCIJ Series A No 17* (PCIJ).

illegal act and re-establish the situation which would, in all probability, have existed if that act had not been committed' by the State.[81]

28.57 The current state of arbitral practice in relation to the calculation of compensation/damages is based on three fundamental pillars.[82] The first is the principle of full compensation (in cases of lawful expropriation) or reparation (in cases of treaty breach).[83] That means that the investor must recover the entirety of the value lost as a result of the State's expropriation/breach, with neither any overcompensation nor any under compensation. The second is the standard of 'fair market value' (i.e. an estimate of the price that the investment would be sold for in an open market, hereinafter, 'FMV').[84] The principle of full compensation/reparation is given a more precise meaning – to compensate/repair fully means to award the harmed investor an amount of money equal to the decrease in FMV of its investment. The third is a marked preference, in terms of how to determine FMV, for an income-based approach, i.e. to estimating FMV as equal to the present value of the investment's anticipated future benefits, and in particular for the discounted cash flow ('DCF') valuation method, which involves first projecting future cash flows and then subjecting them to a discount rate to account for the time value of money (a dollar today is worth more than a dollar tomorrow) and risk of the cash flows not actually materialising.[85]

28.58 Because of these substantive, procedural and remedial specificities, investment treaties have enabled foreign investors to obtain compensation in circumstances where damages might not have been available under national law, or in amounts that exceed the damages they would have received through national courts.[86]

(iii) *Net Zero, Energy Security and Investment Protection*

28.59 The competing goals of States to achieve net zero and energy security do not always align with the protections qualifying investments enjoy under investment treaties. Nevertheless, it would be naïve to expect that the goals of net zero and energy security can be achieved without the investment protection regime.

28.60 The International Renewable Energy Agency estimates that the transformation of the energy system alone will require investments of $5.7 trillion per year until 2030 to keep the rise in global temperatures to well below 2°C and towards 1.5°C during this century.[87] While most of the additional capital is expected to come from the private

---

81 ibid 125.
82 Toni Marzal, 'Quantum (In)Justice: Rethinking the Calculation of Compensation and Damages in ISDS' (2021) 22 The Journal of World Investment & Trade 249.
83 ibid.
84 ibid.
85 ibid.
86 For instance, the amounts awarded by the European Court of Human Rights and by an investor–State arbitral tribunal in connection with the *Yukos* disputes were widely differing (around US$1.8 billion and US$50 billion, respectively), partly reflecting different findings on the merits. See E De Brabandere, 'Yukos Universal Limited (Isle of Man) v The Russian Federation: Complementarity or Conflict? Contrasting the Yukos Case before the European Court of Human Rights and Investment Tribunals' (2015) 30 ICSID Review 345.
87 'World Energy Transitions Outlook 2022' (*IRENA*) <https://www.irena.org/Digital-Report/World-Energy-Transitions-Outlook-2022> accessed 8 April 2024.

sector, public financing will also have to double in order to catalyse private finance and create an enabling environment for speedy transition with optimal socio-economic outcomes.[88]

28.61 The jury may be out on whether protections against discrimination and uncompensated expropriation and guarantees of fair and equitable treatment rank as factors for investment generally, but investment protections and ISDS are vital to the energy industry's investments. UNCTAD suggests that fossil fuel investors have initiated over 15% of all known treaty-based ISDS cases.[89]

28.62 The Paris Agreement requires States to prepare, maintain and account for NDCs to reduce greenhouse gas ('GHG') emissions, and to increase their climate ambition over time.[90] Meeting these contributions may require phasing out emission-intensive activities such as coal-fired energy generation. It will also include changes to the investment framework for renewables as the roll-out of solar and wind power occurs. Similar policies have already given rise to investor–State claims.

28.63 In February 2021, German utility RWE filed a claim against the Netherlands under the ECT, seeking up to €1 billion in compensation for the Dutch government's decision to phase out coal power by 2030. RWE says its Eemshaven coal-fired plant, which was completed in 2015 at a cost of €3 billion, was built at the request of the Dutch government.[91] In April 2021, Uniper, another German utility, filed a similar claim under the ECT against the Dutch state.[92] In March 2024, a split ICSID tribunal reportedly ordered Romania to pay a group of European solar investors more than €46 million in an ECT claim over the state's cuts to its renewable energy incentive scheme.[93] Also in March 2024, ICSID registered a case by a UK investor, Kiabod Tutonian Mashad, a claim against Belarus under the UK-Belarus bilateral investment treaty, alleging that the state expropriated a solar power project after withdrawing renewables incentives.[94]

28.64 Italy has seen a number of claims arising out of a series of governmental decrees to cut tariff incentives for some solar power projects.[95] *Rockhopper*[96] filed claims against

88 ibid.
89 'Energy Transition Calls for Faster Investment Treaty Reforms | UNCTAD' (30 August 2023) <https://unctad.org/news/energy-transition-calls-faster-investment-treaty-reforms> accessed 8 April 2024.
90 Paris Agreement (adopted 12 December 2015, entered into force November 4, 2016) Article 4(2), 13.
91 *RWE AG and RWE Eemshaven Holding II BV v Kingdom of the Netherlands*, ICSID Case No ARB/21/4.
92 *Uniper SE, Uniper Benelux Holding BV and Uniper Benelux NV v Kingdom of the Netherlands*, ICSID Case No ARB/21/22.
93 Toby Fisher, 'ICSID Panel Orders Romania to Pay European Solar Investors' (*Global Arbitration Review*, 20 March 2024) <https://globalarbitrationreview.com/article/icsid-panel-orders-romania-pay-european-solar-investors> accessed 8 April 2024.
94 Tom Jones, 'UK Solar Investor Files ICSID Claim against Belarus' (*Global Arbitration Review*, 20 March 2024) <https://globalarbitrationreview.com/article/uk-solar-investor-files-icsid-claim-against-belarus> accessed 8 April 2024.
95 *Blusun SA, Jean-Pierre Lecorcier and Michael Stein v Italian Republic*, ICSID Case No ARB/14/3; *Silver Ridge Power BV v Italian Republic*, ICSID Case No ARB/15/37; *Belenergia SA v Italian Republic*, ICSID Case No ARB/15/40; *CEF Energia BV v Italian Republic*, SCC Case No 158/2015; *Greentech Energy Systems A/S, et al v Italian Republic*, SCC Case No V 2015/095; *Eskosol S.pA in liquidazione v Italian Republic*, ICSID Case No ARB/15/50.
96 *Rockhopper Italia S.pA, Rockhopper Mediterranean Ltd, and Rockhopper Exploration plc v Italian Republic*, ICSID Case No ARB/17/14.

Italy's decision not to award the claimants a production concession following the government's re-introduction of a general ban on oil and gas exploration and production activity within the 12-mile limit of the coastline. Similarly, Spain has seen claims arising out of a series of energy reforms undertaken by the government affecting the renewables sector, including a 7% tax on power generators' revenues and a reduction in subsidies for renewable energy producers.[97] Germany saw claims from *Strabag and other* arising out of the government's legislative changes to its renewable energy regime, including for offshore wind energy production, which allegedly caused the claimants to abandon their offshore wind projects.[98] In 2022, Slovenia saw a claim arising out of its decision to conduct an environmental impact assessment of Ascent's proposed fracking project, which allegedly destroyed the value of Ascent's investments in Slovenia's energy sector.[99]

28.65 The claims have not been limited to Europe. In September 2023, a pair of Guatemalan renewable energy investors are pursuing a DR-CAFTA claim against Honduras, as a group of US claimants drop their bid to revive a case against Nicaragua under the same free trade agreement.[100]

28.66 The Paris Agreement also calls on States to conserve and enhance, as appropriate, sinks and reservoirs of GHG, including forests.[101] Doing so might require restricting or terminating investments in sensitive ecosystems.[102] Hence, measures to implement the Paris Agreement can adversely affect protected foreign investments.[103] Investment treaties do not differentiate between high and low-carbon investments that qualify for protection. That means that investors, whose investments are harmed by climate policies and regulations, are likely to turn to investment treaties. And States cannot ignore the normative standards established under investment law in formulating climate policies and regulations.

28.67 In 2010, the Czech Republic introduced retroactive changes to its Feed-in-Tariff support scheme for solar power production that was first put in place in 2005. This led to a reduction in fixed tariffs and revenues for generators. A number of foreign investors in Czech solar power projects challenged the decision before international tribunals.

---

97 *Isolux Netherlands, BV v Kingdom of Spain*, SCC Case V2013/153; *9REN Holding S.a.r.l v Kingdom of Spain*, ICSID Case No ARB/15/15; *AES Solar and others (PV Investors) v The Kingdom of Spain*, PCA Case No 2012–14.

98 Lisa Bohmer and Luke Eric Peterson, 'As Vattenfall nuclear case sees new round of submissions, Germany faces another energy charter treaty arbitration following modification of renewables incentives regime' (https://www.iareporter.com/articles/as-vattenfall-nuclear-case-sees-new-round-of-pleadings-germany-faces-another-energy-charter-treaty-arbitration-following-modification-of-renewables-incentives-regime/) accessed 8 April 2024.

99 *Ascent Resources plc and Ascent Slovenia Ltd v Republic of Slovenia*, ICSID Case No ARB/22/21.

100 Toby Fisher, 'Guatemalan Renewables Investors Bring Claim against Honduras' (22 September 2023) <https://globalarbitrationreview.com/article/guatemalan-renewables-investors-bring-claim-against-honduras> accessed 8 April 2024.

101 Paris Agreement (adopted 12 December 2015, entered into force November 4, 2016) Article 5.

102 ibid 61.

103 ibid 61. Also see, Kate Miles, 'International Investment Law and Climate Change: Issues in the Transition to a Low Carbon World' (2 July 2008) <https://papers.ssrn.com/abstract=1154588> accessed 8 April 2024; Jorge E Viñuales, 'Foreign Investment and the Environment in International Law: An Ambiguous Relationship' (2010) 80 British Yearbook of International Law 244; Ximena Fuentes Torrijo, 'Chapter I.26: Climate Change and International Investment Treaties' in Michael Faure (ed), *Elgar Encyclopedia of Environmental Law.* (Edward Elgar Publishing 2016) <https://www.elgaronline.com/view/book/9781785369520/b-9781783477616-I_26.xml> accessed 8 April 2024.

The outcomes of the arbitrations were broadly favourable for the Czech state as most of the tribunals took the view that the retroactive changes introduced were reasonable and proportionate. However, in the *Natland* case,[104] involving foreign investors in a solar PV project in the Czech Republic, a tribunal found in an interim award that the retroactive changes breached the fair and equitable treatment standard under the ECT.

28.68 In 2012, Swedish investor Vattenfall commenced an arbitration claim against Germany before the International Centre for Settlement of Investment Disputes ('ICSID') relating to the nuclear phase-out plans. After years of wrangling, the German government recently entered into a settlement agreement with Vattenfall and will pay €1.4 billion to the Swedish investor.[105] Although investor–state arbitration is the preserve of the foreign investor, German companies affected by the phase-out decision will also receive compensation from the government: RWE, for example, was awarded €880 million.

28.69 Taking the example of nuclear power, investors in nuclear power are also exposed to regulatory risks in states with no phase-out plans. Nuclear power is fundamentally dependent on government-backed subsidies, such as Contracts for Difference ('CfDs'). The UK's Hinkley Point C, for example, has secured a CfD agreement worth £92.50/MWh over a 35-year period, meaning the government will guarantee that price even if wholesale market prices are lower.[106]

28.70 But a lot can change in a 35-year period as governments come and go and energy markets evolve. It is worth noting that the UK has since moved away from the CfD model to support nuclear power. The government says CfDs put too much construction risk on developers and that this has led to investors walking away from big projects. This was exemplified by Japanese firm Hitachi's decision to cancel the 2.9GW Wylfa plant in Wales. In October 2021, the government put forward a new funding model for nuclear power known as Regulated Asset Base (RAB). Under the RAB model, investment costs for nuclear projects are passed on to end-users' bills during the construction period.[107]

28.71 Even though these climate goals do not target 'brown' investments directly, it is evident that they will have an impact on their profitability and lifespan over time.[108] The renewables expansion means that coal and gas plants will not run as many hours

---

104 *GIHG Limited, Natland Group Limited, Natland Investment Group NV, and Radiance Energy Holding SARL v Czech Republic*, PCA Case No 2013-35.
105 Lisa Bohmer, 'Long-Running Vattenfall v. Germany Arbitration Is Discontinued, Following Settlement between the Parties' (*Investment Arbitration Reporter*, 11 November 2021) <https://www.iareporter.com/articles/long-running-vattenfall-v-germany-arbitration-is-discontinued-following-settlement-between-the-parties/> accessed 8 April 2024.
106 Contracts for the Hinkley Point C, which from 2025 is expected to provide 3.2GW of clean, reliable, electricity generation capacity. See, 'Investor–State Arbitration in the Energy Sector Likely as Green Transition Accelerates' (*Cleary Gottlieb*) <https://content.clearygottlieb.com/dispute-resolution/investor-state-arbitration-in-the-energy-sector-likely-as-green-transition-accelerates/> accessed 8 April 2024.
107 Department for Business, Energy and Industrial Strategy, 'Guidance on Development Costs and the Nuclear Regulated Asset Base Model' (2022) <https://assets.publishing.service.gov.uk/media/6384ae9ce90e0778a2122668/development-costs-nuclear-rab-model-guidance.pdf> accessed 8 April 2024.
108 'Investor–State Arbitration in the Energy Sector Likely as Green Transition Accelerates' (n 106).

as anticipated when the investments were made.[109] These plants may also be exposed to lower wholesale prices driven down by periods of 'cheap' electricity from wind and solar plants which do not incur fuel costs.[110] This increases the risk of assets being 'stranded' as the investment environment changes, particularly for coal plants, but also for gas plants in the longer term. As the economics of energy generation change, investors may seek to recoup diminishing returns by bringing claims.[111]

28.72 With an increasing number of states introducing cap-and-trade, green certificates or other types of carbon markets, there is also likely to be a rise in the number of arbitration cases.

28.73 Prices for carbon allowances have surged in recent years, eating into the profitability of coal-fired power generation in particular.[112] Gas-fired power generators, particularly older and less efficient plants, may also see profit margins reduced if carbon prices continue to rise in the future.[113]

28.74 In 2020, Koch Industries initiated claims under NAFTA[114]/USMCA[115] arising out of Ontario's cap-and-trade system which was launched in 2016 but cancelled in 2018. The claims relate to the lack of compensation received following the revocation of the system in 2018 after they allegedly purchased allowances for over $30 million.[116]

28.75 In 2020, 44 renewables investors initiated ECT arbitration against Romania concerning the country's green certificate scheme.[117] Green certificates are issued in exchange for electricity produced by renewable installations and are tradable. Changes in the quotas of certificates allocated to producers are said to have triggered the legal action.

28.76 The energy crisis in Europe has also refocused minds on the dependency on fossil fuels – and the urgent need to scale renewable energy generation, transmission, and storage. Again, the private sector and private finance will play an important role in scaling renewable energy infrastructure. Much of this investment will be cross-border, with capital and technology flows.

28.77 A fundamental peril is that until energy transition is somewhat achieved, there will be continued and significant investment in fossil fuels in the interim. That is likely to bring a wave of investor–State claims, when these high-carbon investments are retired.

---

109 ibid.
110 ibid.
111 ibid.
112 ibid.
113 ibid.
114 North American Free Trade Agreement.
115 The United States–Mexico–Canada Agreement.
116 *Koch Industries, Inc and Koch Supply & Trading, LP v Canada*, ICSID Case No ARB/20/52.
117 Lisa Bohmer, '44 Renewables Investors Initiate ECT Arbitration against Romania' (*Investment Arbitration Reporter*, 18 September 2020) <https://www.iareporter.com/articles/44-renewables-investors-initiate-ect-arbitration-against-romania/> accessed 20 May 2024.

Proceedings before national courts[118]

(i) *The general context*

28.78 The UK has a 'dualist' legal system, in which the rules and principles of public international law are not part of the domestic legal order except to the extent that they have been incorporated into it either by the common law or by legislation.[119] Thus, international treaties, except to the extent that they have been so incorporated, are not a source of rights or obligations in UK domestic law.[120]

28.79 Issues of public international law nonetheless arise in various ways before UK domestic courts. For instance, where rules of international law have been incorporated into domestic law, the courts may need to determine the content of the international law rules in order to apply the domestic common law or legislation into which it has been incorporated. Even where legislation does not expressly purport to incorporate international law rules, the legislation may nonetheless be interpreted in the light of a presumption that it is intended to be consistent with both customary international law and the UK's treaty obligations.[121] In some areas, the relationship between international law and domestic law may be more controversial,[122] or more fluid, in particular in the realm of administrative law and judicial review.

28.80 Litigation before domestic courts involving climate change issues has risen appreciably in many jurisdictions in recent years. The Sabin Center for Climate Change Law at Columbia University in New York maintains databases of such cases before both international and domestic courts.[123] According to the 'Global Climate Litigation Report: 2023 Status Review' published by the United Nations Environment Programme (UNEP),[124] as at 31 December 2022, the Sabin Center's databases included 2,180 climate change cases in 65 jurisdictions (both international and domestic, some pending

118 This part of this chapter has been authored by Christopher Staker.

119 'The UK takes a fundamentally dualist view of international law. In other words, it sees domestic and international law as operating on different planes. International law has of course inspired the common law. The UK's international commitments are also the basis of much domestic legislation. But the reception of international law into domestic law depends upon its acceptance in one of two ways: either by Parliament through legislation or by the judges through the common law'. Lord Mance, 'International Law in the UK Supreme Court' para 1 <https://www.supremecourt.uk/docs/speech-170213.pdf> accessed 8 April 2024.

120 For recent reaffirmations, see *Ukraine v Law Debenture Trust Corp plc* [2023] UKSC 11 [157]; *R (SC, CB and 8 children) v Secretary of State for Work and Pensions and others* [2021] UKSC 26 [78]–[79]; *R (Miller) v Secretary of State for Exiting the European Union* [2017] UKSC 5 [55]–[58]. In relation to Scotland, see *Donaldson v Scottish Legal Aid Board* [2014] CSIH 31 [33]–[37]. In relation to Northern Ireland, see for instance *In re Allister and others* [2023] UKSC 5 [28]–[32]; *SPUC Pro-life Ltd v Secretary of State for Northern Ireland* [2023] NICA 35 [59].

121 *Halsbury's Laws: International Law and Foreign Relations*, vol 61 (5th edn, LexisNexis 2018) para 22 <https://www.lexisnexis.co.uk/legal/commentary/halsburys-laws-of-england/international-law-foreign-relations> accessed 8 April 2024.

122 For instance, in relation to the question of whether the UK's treaty obligations may also be taken into account in determining or developing the common law, see ibid para 23.

123 These databases are found at 'Climate Change Litigation Databases' (Sabin Center for Climate Change Law) <https://climatecasechart.com> accessed 8 April 2024. One database deals with litigation in the United States. Another deals with litigation before other domestic jurisdictions and before international jurisdictions.

124 UNEP, 'Global Climate Litigation Report: 2023 Status Review' (2023) <https://wedocs.unep.org/bitstream/handle/20.500.11822/43008/global_climate_litigation_report_2023.pdf> accessed 8 April 2024.

and some concluded).[125] When compared with a corresponding figure of 1,550 cases in 39 jurisdictions as at 1 July 2020,[126] this shows the commencement of significant numbers of new proceedings over a period of 18 months.

28.81 According to the Director of UNEP's Law Division, 'people are increasingly turning to the courts to combat the climate crisis', and 'the legal grounds for these cases are also widening'.[127] Although many of these cases do not involve public international law issues, the number of cases before domestic courts that do may potentially increase if this trend continues.

28.82 The 'Global Climate Litigation Report' notes in particular that there are 'ongoing and increasing numbers of cases relying on human rights enshrined in international law and national constitutions'.[128] This is of significance, given that one international human rights treaty, the European Convention on Human Rights ('ECHR') has to a considerable extent been incorporated into the UK's domestic law through the Human Rights Act 1998 ('HRA').

28.83 This section of this chapter gives examples of how issues of public international law relating to net zero and nature positivity may potentially arise before UK domestic courts.

(ii) *Common law*

28.84 There is a presumption that a rule of customary international law will 'shape the common law' unless there is 'some positive reason based on constitutional principle, statute law or common law that it should not', and that it is 'the policy of the common law that it should be in alignment with the common customary law applicable between nations'.[129]

28.85 Customary international law rules on climate change might therefore theoretically influence certain principles of common law, such as the duty of care in negligence.

---

125 It is reported that 1,522 of these were in the United States and 658 were in all other jurisdictions combined, including 127 in Australia, 79 in the UK, 62 in the European Union, 34 in Canada and 26 in New Zealand. ibid 13, 17.

126 See the corresponding earlier report from 2020: UNEP, 'Global Climate Litigation Report: 2020 Status Review' (2020) 4, 13 <https://wedocs.unep.org/bitstream/handle/20.500.11822/34818/GCLR.pdf> accessed 8 April 2024. According to this report, 1,200 of these cases were filed in the United States of America and 350 in other jurisdictions combined, including 97 in Australia, 58 in the UK, and 55 in the European Union.

127 UNEP, 'Global Climate Litigation Report: 2023 Status Review' (n 124) IX–X. See also Joana Setzer and Catherine Higham, 'Global Trends in Climate Change Litigation: 2021 Snapshot' (2021) <https://www.lse.ac.uk/granthaminstitute/wp-content/uploads/2021/07/Global-trends-in-climate-change-litigation_2021-snapshot.pdf> accessed 8 April 2024; Climate Financial Risk Forum, 'Climate Financial Risk Forum Guide 2022 Scenario Analysis Working Group: Climate Litigation Risk Chapter' (2022) <https://www.fca.org.uk/publication/corporate/cfrf-guide-2022-scenario-analysis-working-group-climate-litigation-risk-chapter.pdf> accessed 8 April 2022.

128 UNEP, 'Global Climate Litigation Report: 2023 Status Review' (n 124) 74. The report also indicates that 12 of the cases identified are before the European Court of Human Rights, five are before the Inter-American Court of Human Rights, and two are before the United Nations Human Rights Committee. ibid 17.

129 *R (Freedom and Justice Party) v Secretary of State for Foreign and Commonwealth Affairs* [2018] EWCA Civ 1719 [117]. See also *Halsbury's Laws: International Law and Foreign Relations* (n 121) para 16.

Such potential influence may however be constrained by the consideration that domestic courts 'will not give effect at common law to a rule of customary international law which does not directly implicate the rights or interests of natural or municipal legal persons but which regulates purely interstate relations'.[130] A further constraint in this respect may be uncertainty as to what obligations with respect to climate change are in fact part of customary international law, and as to whether customary international law obligations are any more onerous or precise than treaty obligations.[131]

28.86 This issue has so far not been a focus of exploration in the UK. In other jurisdictions where arguments have been advanced as to the influence of climate change issues on private law duties of care, customary international law principles have not specifically been relied on.

28.87 In *Smith v Fonterra Co-Operative Group Ltd*, the Court of Appeal of New Zealand upheld the striking out of a claim that the release of greenhouse gases by the respondent, due to its effect on the climate, gave rise to common law causes of action for public nuisance and negligence. The Court also struck out a claim that there exists under the common law of New Zealand a new tort of breach of 'duty, cognisable at law, to cease contributing to damage to the climate system'. The Court considered that:

> Private litigation against a small subset of emitters, requiring them to comply with requirements that are more stringent than those imposed by statute, will not be effective to address climate change at a national level, let alone globally.[132]

28.88 The New Zealand Court of Appeal also stated that litigation of this sort would be 'costly and inefficient', and 'arbitrary in its application and impact', and 'not consistent with the policy goals … of ensuring that this country's response to climate change is effective, efficient and just'.[133] Any reliance on international law principles to develop common law duties of care might be met by similar arguments.

28.89 This decision to strike out the claim was overturned by the New Zealand Supreme Court. However, the Supreme Court did not determine whether or not such a tort existed. It merely found that the claim was not so unarguable as to satisfy the test for a strike-out, such that the question fell to be argued at trial.

28.90 In *Minister for Environment v Sharma*, the Full Court of the Federal Court of Australia held that the Minister for the Environment did not owe a duty of care at common law when exercising a statutory power to approve an extension of a coal mine.

---

130 *Halsbury's Laws: International Law and Foreign Relations* (n 121) para 16 and the cases there cited.
131 See generally Benoit Mayer, 'Climate Change Mitigation as an Obligation under Customary International Law' (2023) 48(1) Yale Journal of International Law 105–151 <https://ssrn.com/abstract=4086746> accessed 4 November 2024; Moise Jean, 'Customary International Law and the Challenge of Climate Change: How to Deal with the Stagnation of the Paris Agreement' (October 14, 2021) New York University Journal of International Law and Politics (JILP), Vol. 54, 2021 <https://ssrn.com/abstract=3942517> accessed 4 November 2024; Pierre-Marie Dupuy, Ginevra Le Moli, and Jorge E Viñuales, 'Customary International Law and the Environment' (December 2018) <https://papers.ssrn.com/sol3/papers.cfm?abstract_id=3785239> accessed 4 November 2024.
132 *Smith v Fonterra Co-operative Group Ltd* [2021] NZCA 552 [33].
133 ibid.

In a detailed judgment, all three of the judges gave different reasons for this conclusion but were unanimous that no duty of care in tort should be imposed.[134]

28.91 However, not all jurisdictions have decided in the same way. In a decision which has generated some interest in the common law world (unusually for a case from a civil law jurisdiction), the District Court of The Hague in the Netherlands in *Vereniging Milieudefensie v Royal Dutch Shell plc* held that a corporation had a duty of care under Article 6:162 of the Dutch Civil Code (a general provision on tortious acts) to reduce its CO_2 emissions by at least 45% at the end of 2030 relative to 2019 levels.[135] The court referred in that case amongst other things to the International Covenant on Civil and Political Rights and the European Convention on Human Rights, in addition to the Paris Agreement. A comparative law analysis may be of interest and relevance in any future case in which principles of customary international law are relied on.

(iii) *Administrative law*

28.92 There are subtleties surrounding the extent to which the UK's international obligations may be relevant in the sphere of administrative law, particularly in the case of unincorporated treaties such as the Paris Agreement.[136]

28.93 The courts have rejected the argument that statutory provisions conferring administrative powers must be interpreted as impliedly empowering only such action as is in conformity with the UK's international obligations. Thus, as a matter of general principle, executive action will not without more be unlawful merely because the decision-maker failed to take the UK's obligations under an unincorporated treaty into account, or acted in a way that was inconsistent with those obligations.[137]

28.94 The general proposition that the government, by ratifying an international treaty, creates a legitimate expectation for administrative law purposes that the government will henceforth act in a way that is consistent with the obligations under that treaty, has been described as 'at least, controversial'.[138]

28.95 However, while a decision-maker may generally not be required to take into account the UK's obligations under an unincorporated international treaty, it is generally lawful for the decision-maker to do so.[139]

134 *Minister for the Environment v Sharma* [2022] FCAFC 35.
135 *Vereniging Milieudefensie v Royal Dutch Shell plc and others* [2021] C/09/571932/HA ZA 19-379 (The Hague District Court), unofficial English translation prepared by the court available at <https://uitspraken.rechtspraak.nl/details?id=ECLI:NL:RBDHA:2021:5339> accessed 16 October 2024. On 12 November 2024 the Hague Court of Appeal handed down its judgment in the appeal, 200.302.332/01.
136 For the proposition that the Paris Agreement is an unincorporated treaty for domestic law purposes, see for instance *R (Packham) v Secretary of State for Transport and The Prime Minister* [2020] EWCA Civ 1004 [102].
137 *R v Secretary of State for the Home Department, Ex p Brind* [1991] 1 AC 696; *Heathrow Airport Ltd v HM Treasury and HMRC* [2021] EWCA Civ 783 [148].
138 *R (SG) v Secretary of State for Work and Pensions* [2015] UKSC 16 [246] (Lord Kerr). International human rights treaties may be in a different position: ibid [247]–[262] (Lord Kerr).
139 *R (Friends of the Earth Ltd and others) v Heathrow Airport Ltd* [2020] UKSC 52 [116]–[122]; *R (Packham) v Secretary of State for Transport and The Prime Minister* [2020] EWCA Civ 1004 (n 136) [102]–[103].

28.96 Furthermore, some legislation may positively require a decision-maker to take into account obligations under otherwise unincorporated treaties, and in certain circumstances, the UK's obligations under an unincorporated treaty may be 'so obviously material to the decision ... that it [would be] irrational not to take it into account'.[140]

28.97 In *R (Plan B Earth) v Secretary of State for Transport*, a provision in the Planning Act 2008 stated that policy statements adopted by the Secretary of State under that Act were required to 'include an explanation of how the policy set out in the statement takes account of government policy relating to the mitigation of, and adaptation to, climate change'. The Court of Appeal found that the Paris Agreement was part of 'government policy' for purposes of this provision.[141] Thus, although the legislation did not require the Secretary of State to act in accordance with government policy, it required the government to take government policy (including the Paris Agreement) into account.[142] It was found that the Secretary of State had not considered the Paris Agreement due to legal advice that he was legally obliged not to take it into account at all, and that this was a misdirection of law that vitiated the decision.[143] The court considered that 'the only reasonable view open to him was that the Paris Agreement was so obviously material that it had to be taken into account'.[144]

28.98 However, the Supreme Court allowed an appeal against the Court of Appeal's judgment in *R (Friends of the Earth Limited) v Heathrow Airport Ltd.* The Supreme Court found that the Paris Agreement itself was not government policy for purposes of the legislative provision in question, and nor was a 'policy commitment' to the Paris Agreement.[145] The Supreme Court further found that the Secretary of State had taken the Paris Agreement into account to the extent that the obligations under it were already covered by the measures under the Climate Change Act 2008,[146] that he had asked himself the question of whether he should take into account the Paris Agreement beyond that extent, and that he had concluded in the exercise of his discretion that it would not be appropriate to do so.[147] This conclusion was found to have been a rational one.[148]

28.99 Subsequently, in *R (Friends of the Earth Ltd) v Secretary of State for International Trade*, the Court of Appeal found that a decision-maker was entitled, but not required, to take the Paris Agreement into account when approving an investment by UK Export Finance in a liquified natural gas project in Mozambique. The Court added that if the

---

140 *R (Plan B Earth) v Secretary of State for Transport* [2020] EWCA Civ 214 [234]; *R (Friends of the Earth Ltd and others) v Heathrow Airport Ltd* (n 139) [118]; *R (Packham) v Secretary of State for Transport and The Prime Minister* [2020] EWCA Civ 1004 (n 136) [102]; *R (Global Feedback Ltd) v HM Treasury* [2024] EWHC 1810 (Admin) [29]–[34], [43]–[46], [58].
141 *R (Plan B Earth) v Secretary of State for Transport* (n 140) [222], [228].
142 ibid [223], [226], [231], [238].
143 ibid [227], [233], [236].
144 ibid [237].
145 *R (Friends of the Earth Ltd and others) v Heathrow Airport Ltd* (n 139) [112].
146 ibid [125].
147 ibid [129].
148 ibid [132], [149]–[150]. See also *R (Transport Action Network) v Secretary of State for Transport* [2021] EWHC 2095 (Admin) [112]–[117]; *R (Packham) v Secretary of State for Transport and The Prime Minister* [2020] EWCA Civ 1004 (n 136) [92]–[103].

decision-maker did take it into account, it was not for the Court to allocate weight as between competing factors.[149]

28.100 In that case, the decision-maker had reached the conclusion that the funding of the project was aligned with the UK's international obligations under the Paris Agreement. The Court of Appeal held that the question whether it was an error of law for the decision-maker to have so concluded was a justiciable issue in judicial review proceedings. However, the Court found that this question had to be judged by considering whether the decision-maker adopted a tenable view of that question at the time that the decision was taken (even if, with the benefit of hindsight, a different conclusion might be reached). That is to say, if it was tenable for the decision-maker to reach the view that funding the project was aligned with the UK's obligations under the Paris Agreement, the Court could not and should not hold that the decision-maker had made an error of law.[150]

28.101 This conclusion followed from the fact that the Paris Agreement 'is pre-eminently an unincorporated international treaty that does not give rise to domestic legal obligations'.[151] The court considered that 'the court cannot and should not second guess the executive's decision-making in the international law arena where there is no domestic legal precedent or guidance', regardless of whether or not the executive had formed a definitive view of the matter.[152] The court considered that the view taken by the decision-maker in that case had been a tenable view.[153]

28.102 Notwithstanding the above, in other contexts it has been held that if the government has a policy that administrative guidance should comply with obligations under an unincorporated treaty, then it may be open to the courts to decide whether the guidance does or does not do so, and to hold the guidance to be unlawful if it does not do so.[154]

---

149 *R (Friends of the Earth Ltd) v Secretary of State for International Trade/UK Export Finance* [2023] EWCA Civ 14 [40].
150 ibid; *R (Corner House Research and others) v Director of The Serious Fraud Office* [2008] UKHL 60 [44].
151 *R (Friends of the Earth Ltd) v Secretary of State for International Trade/UK Export Finance* (n 149) [40].
152 ibid.
153 The Supreme Court refused an application for permission to appeal against this decision on 9 June 2023, on the ground that the application did not raise an arguable point of law. See also *R (Elliott-Smith) v Secretary of State for Business, Energy and Industrial Strategy* [2021] EWHC 1633 (Admin) [55], in which the Court said: 'The Paris Agreement is an obvious instrument to be reflected in the architecture of national measures to address climate change and abate greenhouse gas emissions. The real substance of the claimant's contentions relates to their interpretation of the Paris Agreement and what they contend is the element of urgency contained in particular within article 4.1 for the short to medium term. In my view it is not for this court to resolve definitively any questions of construction in relation to an unincorporated international treaty for the reasons set out in the earlier authorities. The Paris Agreement is an international instrument to which 197 states are parties. It contains a mechanism for enforcing the implementation of the Agreement within article 14 of its text, along with other mechanisms for dispute resolution. There are, therefore, strong policy reasons as well as practical considerations which clearly militate against the court embarking on an exercise of construing the terms of the Paris Agreement. At most, in accordance with the approach set out in the authorities set out above, the court should assess whether or not the defendants' view of the Paris Agreement was one which was tenable in examining the question posed by the claimant'.
154 By way of example from a different context, see *R (EOG) v Secretary of State for the Home Department* [2022] EWCA Civ 307, which concerned the Council of Europe Convention on Action against Trafficking in Human Beings 2005.

28.103 In *Greenpeace v Secretary of State for Energy Security and Net Zero*, the Court dismissed an application for judicial review of the government's decision to grant further drilling licences in the North Sea.[155] The claimant in this case did not rely on the Paris Agreement as such, but proponents and opponents of the grant of further licences disagreed as to whether the grant of further licences would be compatible with achieving the UK's net zero target following an amendment to the Climate Change Act 2008 in response to the Paris Agreement. The Court said that 'plainly this is a matter of judgment and not law'.[156]

(iv) *European Convention on Human Rights*

28.104 The European Convention on Human Rights ('ECHR') is one international treaty that has to a large extent been incorporated into UK domestic law by legislation, by means of the Human Rights Act 1998 ('HRA'). However, the incorporation is not complete. In particular, the HRA provides that primary legislation which cannot be read and given effect in a way that is compatible with ECHR rights will nonetheless continue to operate, and that acts of public authorities contrary to the ECHR that are positively required by such legislation will not be unlawful.[157]

28.105 Nevertheless, the HRA establishes that both primary and subordinate legislation will, so far as it is possible to do so, be read and given effect in a way that is compatible with ECHR rights, and that it is unlawful for a public authority (including a court or tribunal) to act in a way that is incompatible with ECHR rights when not compelled by primary legislation to do so.[158] This particular international treaty is therefore of considerable significance in cases before UK domestic courts.

28.106 The case law of the European Court of Human Rights ('ECtHR') is similarly of significance, given that UK courts when determining questions arising in connection with ECHR rights must take account of the case law of the ECtHR,[159] and given that a claimant who fails to succeed in an ECHR claim before the domestic courts can go on to bring a case against the UK before the ECtHR. Case law of the domestic courts of other ECHR Contracting States may also be of persuasive authority as to the correct interpretation and application of the ECHR.

28.107 The potential significance of the ECHR has been recognised by applicants in climate change litigation. Various climate change cases have been brought before the ECtHR against various ECHR Contracting States.[160] The applicants in these various cases have contended that their governments' failings in their responses to climate change and climate protection amount to violations of the positive obligation under

---

155 *R (Greenpeace Ltd) v Secretary of State for Energy Security and Net Zero* [2023] EWHC 2608 (Admin).
156 ibid [13].
157 Human Rights Act 1998 ss 3, 6(1)–(2).
158 ibid. As to the corresponding position in Ireland, see European Convention on Human Rights Act 2003 (Ireland).
159 Human Rights Act 1998 s 2(1).
160 See European Court of Human Rights, 'Factsheet – Climate Change' <https://www.echr.coe.int/documents/d/echr/FS_Climate_change_ENG> accessed 8 April 2024.

ECHR Article 2 to protect life effectively, and to violations of ECHR Articles 2 (right to life), 3 (prohibition of inhuman or degrading treatment or punishment), 8 (right to respect for private and family life), and/or 14 (prohibition of discrimination). The lack of effective means in domestic law to ensure compliance is also said in some cases to violate ECHR Articles 6 (right to a fair trial) and 13 (right to an effective remedy). In some of these cases, it is argued that ECHR rights must be read in the light of undertakings under the Paris Agreement.[161]

28.108 In three of these cases,[162] Chambers of the Court relinquished jurisdiction in favour of the Grand Chamber,[163] and six other cases pending before the ECtHR were adjourned in order to await the outcome in the three cases to be decided by the Grand Chamber.[164] The Grand Chamber gave judgments in these three cases on 9 April 2024.

28.109 One of these cases, *Verein KlimaSeniorinnen Schweiz and Others v Switzerland*,[165] is particularly significant for two reasons.

28.110 First, the Grand Chamber made important findings in relation to who has standing (*locus standi*) to bring climate change cases before the ECtHR. Under Articles 34 and 35 ECHR, an applicant before the ECtHR can only invoke a violation of the ECHR if they are a victim of that violation.[166] There were five applicants in this case, namely a Swiss non-profit association, and four individuals who were members of the association and who claimed that their health and daily routines were affected by heatwaves.[167] The Grand Chamber found that the four individual applicants did not fulfil the victim-status criteria under Article 35 ECHR, and therefore lacked standing, but that the non-profit association could bring a claim.

28.111 In relation to the four individuals, the Grand Chamber reiterated that the ECHR does not provide for the institution of an *actio popularis*, that is to say, it 'does not permit individuals or groups of individuals to complain about a provision of national

---

161 But compare *R (Plan B Earth) v Prime Minister & others* [2021] EWHC 3469 (Admin) [48]–[54], which considered that compliance with the Paris Agreement could not be used as a test for compliance with Arts 2 and 8 ECHR in proceedings before domestic courts, as this would amount to enforcing the Paris Agreement, an unincorporated treaty. See further, in a different context, *R (HZ) v Secretary of State for the Home Department* [2023] EWHC 660 (Admin) [99].

162 *Verein KlimaSeniorinnen Schweiz v Switzerland* [GC], no 53600/20, 9 April 2024 (ECtHR); *Carême v France* (dec.) [GC], no 7189/21, 9 April 2024 (ECtHR); *Duarte Agostinho v Portugal and 32 Others* (dec.) [GC], no 39371/20, 9 April 2024 (ECtHR).

163 Article 30 of the ECHR provides: 'Where a case pending before a Chamber raises a serious question affecting the interpretation of the Convention or the Protocols thereto, or where the resolution of a question before the Chamber might have a result inconsistent with a judgment previously delivered by the Court, the Chamber may, at any time before it has rendered its judgment, relinquish jurisdiction in favour of the Grand Chamber'.

164 *Uricchio v Italy and 31 Others* (application no 14615/21) (ECtHR); *De Conto v Italy and 32 Others* (application no 14620/21) (ECtHR); *Müllner v Austria* (application no 18859/21) (ECtHR); *Greenpeace Nordic and Others v Norway* (application no 34068/21) (ECtHR); *The Norwegian Grandparents' Climate Campaign and Others v Norway* (application no 19026/21) (ECtHR); *Soubeste and 4 other applications v Austria and 11 other States* (application nos 31925/22, 31932/22, 31938/22, 31943/22, and 31947/22) (ECtHR); *Engels v Germany* (application no 46906/22) (ECtHR).

165 *Verein KlimaSeniorinnen Schweiz and Others v Switzerland* (n 162).

166 See European Court of Human Rights, 'Practical Guide on Admissibility Criteria' <https://www.echr.coe.int/documents/d/echr/admissibility_guide_eng> accessed 20 May 2024.

167 *Verein KlimaSeniorinnen Schweiz and Others v Switzerland* (n 162) [10]–[21].

law simply because they consider, without having been directly affected by it, that it may contravene the Convention'.[168] The Grand Chamber found that while heatwaves may have affected these applicants' quality of life, it was not apparent that they were exposed 'with a degree of intensity giving rise to a pressing need to ensure their individual protection', or that they 'suffered from any critical medical condition whose possible aggravation linked to heatwaves could not be alleviated'.[169]

28.112 However, in relation to the non-profit association, the Grand Chamber found that the principles of standing are as follows:

> In order to be recognised as having *locus standi* to lodge an application under Article 34 of the Convention on account of the alleged failure of a Contracting State to take adequate measures to protect individuals against the adverse effects of climate change on human lives and health, the association in question must be: (a) lawfully established in the jurisdiction concerned or have standing to act there; (b) able to demonstrate that it pursues a dedicated purpose in accordance with its statutory objectives in the defence of the human rights of its members or other affected individuals within the jurisdiction concerned, whether limited to or including collective action for the protection of those rights against the threats arising from climate change; and (c) able to demonstrate that it can be regarded as genuinely qualified and representative to act on behalf of members or other affected individuals within the jurisdiction who are subject to specific threats or adverse effects of climate change on their lives, health or well-being as protected under the Convention.[170]

28.113 The Court added that such an association is not required to show that those on whose behalf the case has been brought would themselves have met the victim-status requirements for individuals.[171]

28.114 Secondly, the Grand Chamber made important findings in relation to the merits. The non-profit association complained of violations of ECHR Articles 2, 6, 8 and 13.[172] The Grand Chamber found that in this case, there had been violations by Switzerland of Article 8 and Article 6 of the ECHR.

28.115 As to Article 8 ECHR, the Grand Chamber found amongst other matters as follows. In cases involving environmental issues, Contracting States have a positive obligation under Article 8 to put in place and to apply effectively in practice a relevant legislative and administrative framework designed to provide effective protection of human health and life.[173] While Contracting States have a wide margin of appreciation in devising and/or implementing the relevant measures, they must have an adequate decision-making process that allows the authorities to strike a fair balance between the various conflicting interests at stake. Furthermore, the public must have access to the

---

168 ibid [460].
169 ibid [533].
170 ibid [502].
171 ibid.
172 ibid [291].
173 ibid [538].

conclusions of the relevant studies, allowing them to assess the risk to which they are exposed, and individuals concerned must have an opportunity to protect their interests in the environmental decision-making process.[174] The Grand Chamber found, more specifically, that 'effective respect for the rights protected by Article 8 of the Convention requires that each Contracting State undertake measures for the substantial and progressive reduction of their respective greenhouse gas ('GHG') emission levels, with a view to reaching net neutrality within, in principle, the next three decades', and that they must 'act in good time, in an appropriate and consistent manner'.[175] The Grand Chamber also found that these measures must 'be supplemented by adaptation measures aimed at alleviating the most severe or imminent consequences of climate change, taking into account any relevant particular needs for protection'.[176]

28.116 The Grand Chamber found in this case that there had been a violation of Article 8 ECHR by Switzerland because it had exceeded its margin of appreciation and failed to comply with its positive obligations due to certain critical lacunae in putting in place the relevant domestic regulatory framework.[177] These lacunae included a failure to quantify national GHG emissions limitations, and a failure to meet its past GHG emission reduction targets.[178] Although the applicant relied on Article 2 ECHR as well as on Article 8, the Grand Chamber considered it appropriate to consider the complaint from the angle of Article 8 alone.[179]

28.117 As to Article 6 ECHR, the Grand Chamber found amongst other matters as follows. 'Article 6 does not guarantee a right of access to a court with power to invalidate or override laws enacted by Parliament', and 'Article 6 cannot be relied upon to institute an action before a court for the purpose of compelling Parliament to enact legislation'.[180] However, Article 6 may be applicable 'where domestic law does provide for individual access to proceedings before a Constitutional Court or another similar superior court which does have the power to examine an appeal lodged directly against a law'.[181] The Grand Chamber found that the proceedings taken by the association at domestic level fell outside Article 6 to the extent that they 'concerned issues pertaining to the democratic legislative process', but that they fell within Article 6 to the extent that they pertained 'specifically to alleged failures in the enforcement of the existing domestic law affecting the protection of the rights defended by the applicant association'.[182] The Grand Chamber found that '[t]he domestic courts did not engage seriously or at all with the action brought by the applicant association',[183] and this was found to be a violation of Article 6 ECHR. The Grand Chamber considered that Article 13 ECHR was absorbed by the more stringent requirements of Article 6.

174 ibid [538]–[554].
175 ibid [548].
176 ibid [552].
177 ibid [555]–[574].
178 ibid [573].
179 ibid [537]. The Grand Chamber noted, however, at [538] first sub-paragraph, that the principles under Article 2 are to a very large extent similar to those under Article 8.
180 ibid [609].
181 ibid.
182 ibid [633].
183 ibid [636].

28.118 Of the other two cases in which judgments were given by the Grand Chamber on the same day, in *Carême v France*[184] the Grand Chamber decided that the applicant, an individual who was the former mayor of a town in France but who no longer lived in that municipality, did not have victim status for purposes of a complaint concerning alleged risks linked to climate change threatening that municipality. In *Duarte Agostinho and Others v Portugal and 32 Others*,[185] the Grand Chamber decided that the applicants were not under the jurisdiction of any Contracting State other than Portugal, the country of their nationality and residence, and that their complaints against other Contracting States were therefore inadmissible. Furthermore, their complaint against Portugal was found to be inadmissible due to non-exhaustion of local remedies.

28.119 The findings of the Grand Chamber in *Verein KlimaSeniorinnen Schweiz* concerning victim status will be of considerable significance at domestic level in the UK, since section 7 of the HRA provides that a person can only bring proceedings under the HRA if he or she would be a victim for the purposes of Article 34 ECHR. The Grand Chamber's findings on the merits in that case are of potentially landmark importance both at domestic level in ECHR Contracting States as well as in future cases before the ECtHR. However, given the affirmation by the Grand Chamber of the wide margin of appreciation of Contracting States, future cases must be expected to be fact specific, and the precise significance of the case will need to be evaluated in the light of future developments.

28.120 The cases before the ECtHR were preceded by litigation before the domestic courts of the respondent States concerned. Details can also be found in the Sabin Center Database[186] of other environmental litigation cases raising ECHR issues that are currently pending before or have recently been decided by domestic courts in other ECHR Contracting States.

28.121 Given the recency of developments in the case law, and given that six further cases before the ECtHR still remain to be decided, it would be premature to express firm conclusions. It is merely noted that the limited case law at domestic level in the UK so far indicates that there are limitations on the reliance that can be placed on the ECHR as a basis for claims in climate litigation cases. However, it needs to be taken into account this domestic case law all predates the decision of the ECtHR in *Verein KlimaSeniorinnen Schweiz*.

28.122 In *Plan B Earth v Secretary of State for Business, Energy and Industrial Strategy*, the High Court refused permission to apply for judicial review in a case where the claimants argued that the refusal by the Secretary of State to revise the 2050 carbon target under the Climate Change Act 2008 was (amongst other things) a breach of their rights under ECHR Articles 2 and 8, and Article 1 of Protocol 1 (deprivation of property), individually and in conjunction with ECHR Article 14. The court considered that

---

184 *Carême v France* (n 162).
185 *Duarte Agostinho and Others v Portugal and 32 Others* (n 162).
186 See 'Climate Change Litigation Databases' (n 123).

this is an area where the executive has a wide discretion to assess the advantages and disadvantages of any particular course of action, not only domestically but as part of an evolving international discussion.[187]

28.123 In *R (Plan B Earth) v Prime Minister*, the High Court refused permission to apply for judicial review in a case where the claimants were seeking a declaration that their rights under ECHR Articles 2, 8 and 14 were being breached by the defendants' failure to take effective measures to meet their commitments arising under the Paris Agreement. The court considered that 'there is an administrative framework to combat the threats posed by climate change, in the form of the [Climate Change Act 2008] and all the policies and measures adopted under it', and that this framework is 'constantly evolving' and 'consists of high level economic and social measures involving complex and difficult judgments'. The court concluded that it was 'not well equipped to form its own views on the matters in question', and 'does not have and cannot acquire expertise in this complex area and will always be dependent on competing extracts from a global debate'. The court considered that 'the judgment of the executive or legislature in such areas will generally be respected unless it is manifestly without reasonable foundation', and that the legislation should be allowed to operate, noting that it 'contains provision for debate, and that debate occurs in a political context with democratic, rather than litigious, consequences'. The court also expressed concern that the claimants were seeking to enforce domestically an unincorporated treaty, namely the Paris Agreement.[188]

28.124 Plan B Earth subsequently brought proceedings before the ECtHR against this decision, which declared the application inadmissible in an unpublished decision.[189]

28.125 In *R (Friends of the Earth Ltd) v Secretary of State for Business, Energy and Industrial Strategy*, the court affirmed that section 3(1) HRA is applicable only if the ordinary interpretation of a legislative provision is incompatible with a Convention right, in which case the effect of that provision is to modify the ordinary interpretation to that which is necessary to achieve compatibility. The court rejected the suggestion that section 3(1) HRA requires the court to adopt an interpretation that would be more, rather than less, conducive to the protection of ECHR rights.[190]

28.126 In *R (Humane Being) v Secretary Of State For Environment, Food and Rural Affairs*, the High Court refused permission to apply for judicial review in a case where the claimants contended that the Secretary of State's failure to take reasonable steps to put an end to intensive farming practices was amongst other things contrary to ECHR Articles 2, 3 and 8. The court found that the claimants had no realistic prospect of

---

187 *Plan B Earth v Secretary of State for Business, Energy and Industrial Strategy* [2018] EWHC 1892 (Admin) [48]–[49].

188 *R (Plan B Earth) v Prime Minister & others* (n 161) [48]–[54]. The court referred to *R (SC, CB and 8 children) v Secretary of State for Work and Pensions and others* (n 120), which affirmed that the HRA gives effect only to the ECHR, and not to other unincorporated treaties. For the more general proposition that non-compliance with an unincorporated treaty is irrelevant when considering ECHR rights, see *Assange v USA* [2024] EWHC 700 (Admin) [96].

189 *Plan B Earth and Others v the United Kingdom* (application no 35057/22) (ECtHR).

190 *R (Friends of the Earth Ltd) v Secretary of State for Business, Energy and Industrial Strategy* [2022] EWHC 1841 (Admin) [264]–[266].

establishing that the defendant was in breach of any positive obligation under ECHR Articles 2, 3 or 8, or had acted irrationally.[191] The claimant subsequently brought proceedings before the ECtHR, which declared the application inadmissible in an unpublished decision.[192]

28.127 In *R (Richards) v Environment Agency*, the Court of Appeal found that the court could not grant a declaration requiring a public authority to undertake specified activities in order to comply with its obligations under Article 2 ECHR. The Court of Appeal said that the declaration made by the court below was 'in substance a mandatory order indicating that the appellant must achieve certain outcomes within a prescribed timetable'.[193] The Court of Appeal considered that in circumstances where there has been no finding of actual or proposed unlawfulness, and where an advisory declaration was neither sought nor would be appropriate, such a declaration was neither justified nor required to remedy any unlawful act or failure to act.

28.128 Some climate change claims based on the ECHR brought before the domestic courts of other ECHR Contracting States have also been unsuccessful.[194] However, in *State of the Netherlands (Ministry of Economic Affairs and Climate Policy) v Stichting Urgenda*, the Supreme Court of the Netherlands held that 'Articles 2 and 8 ECHR relating to the risk of climate change should be interpreted in such a way that these provisions oblige the contracting states to do "their part" to counter that danger',[195] and upheld the judgment of the courts below ordering the State to reduce emissions by the end of 2020 by at least 25% compared to 1990.[196] Claims in Belgium and Germany have also been partially successful.[197]

---

191 *R (Humane Being) v Secretary of State for Environment Food and Rural Affairs* [2022] EWHC 300 (Admin).
192 *Humane Being and Others v United Kingdom* (application no 36959/22) (ECtHR).
193 *R (Richards) v Environment Agency* [2022] EWCA Civ 26. See also *R (Wildfish Conservation) v Secretary of State for Environment, Food and Rural Affairs* [2023] EWHC 2285 (Admin) (unsuccessful challenge based on ECHR Article 8 and Article 1 of Protocol 1); *R (Friends of the Earth Ltd and others) v Heathrow Airport Ltd* (n 139) (unsuccessful challenge based on Arts 2 and 8 ECHR); *Re McAleenon's Application for Leave to Apply for Judicial Review* [2022] NIQB 39 (unsuccessful challenge based on Article 8 ECHR).
194 For instance, in Austria, Verfassungsgerichtshof (Constitutional Court), 30 September 2020, G 144/2020 <https://www.vfgh.gv.at/downloads/VfGH_Beschluss_G_144_2020_vom_30._September_2020.pdf> (claim rejected on grounds of standing); *Friends of the Irish Environment CLG v Government of Ireland* [2019] IEHC 747 [142]–[146] (claim under the European Convention on Human Rights Act 2003 (Ireland) refused substantively); *Friends of the Irish Environment v Ireland* [2020] IESC 49 (Supreme Court of Ireland) [7.23]–[7.25] (claim rejected on grounds of standing).
195 *State of the Netherlands (Ministry of Economic Affairs and Climate Policy) v Stichting Urgenda*, Hoge Raad (Supreme Court of the Netherlands), 20 December 2019, ECLI:NL:HR:2019:2007, unofficial English translation prepared by the court available at <https://uitspraken.rechtspraak.nl/details?id=ECLI:NL:HR:2019:2007> accessed 16 October 2024.
196 This case has been cited in argument in cases before domestic courts in the UK and Ireland: *R (Friends of the Earth Ltd) v Secretary of State for Business, Energy and Industrial Strategy* (n 190) [268]–[270]; *Coyne v An Bord Pleanala* [2023] IEHC 412 [295]–[299]; *R (Plan B Earth) v Prime Minister & others* (n 161) [55].
197 Belgium: Michel de Muelenaere, 'La Belgique une nouvelle fois condamnée pour son inaction climatique', *Le Soir*, 30 November 2023 <https://www.lesoir.be/552575/article/2023-11-30/la-belgique-une-nouvelle-fois-condam-nee-pour-son-inaction-climatique>. Germany: Bundesverfassungsgericht (Federal Constitutional Court), Order of the First Senate of 24 March 2021 – 1 BvR 2656/18, English translation available at <https://www.bundesverfassungsgericht.de/SharedDocs/Entscheidungen/EN/2021/03/rs20210324_1bvr265618en.html>.

28.129 Apart from claims that failure to tackle climate change is itself a breach of ECHR rights, the ECHR and the HRA may be of relevance in other ways in the area of climate change more generally.

28.130 Environmental protestors convicted of criminal offences in respect of conduct causing disruption during protests have relied on the ECHR as a basis for challenging their convictions or sentences, or for challenging the prosecutorial decision not to charge them with less serious offences.[198] Such challenges have however tended to be unsuccessful.[199] Nor have ECHR considerations generally prevented the courts from granting injunctions against both known and unknown persons, restraining them from committing acts of trespass or nuisance in connection with such protests,[200] or prevented the courts from dealing with breaches of such injunctions as contempt of court.[201]

28.131 Article 1 of Protocol 1 to the ECHR, which provides that '[n]o one shall be deprived of his possessions except in the public interest and subject to the conditions provided for by law and by the general principles of international law', has also been relied on as a shield rather than a sword, to argue that legislation imposing environmental measures, or imposing penalties for violations of such measures, constitute a violation of this right. Such arguments have also generally been unsuccessful.[202]

28.132 However, in *AXB Air Inc v Environment Agency*, the First-tier Tribunal held that a literal interpretation of legislation providing for an excessive emissions penalty would contravene Article 1 of Protocol 1 ECHR, and that, for the legislation to be interpreted compatibly with the ECHR, 'the decision maker (and the Tribunal on appeal) must assess whether, in the individual circumstances, the imposition of the penalty would establish a fair balance between the public interest pursued and the protection of the

---

198 Reliance has been placed in particular on ECHR Arts 10 (freedom of expression), 11 (freedom of assembly and association) and 14.

199 See for instance *R v Trowland (Morgan)* [2023] EWCA Crim 919 [49], [70]–[91]; *DPP v Eastburn* [2023] EWHC 1063 (Admin) [24]–[26]; *R v Brown* [2022] EWCA Crim 6 [9]–[39]; but compare *R v Roberts* [2018] EWCA Crim 2739. In relation to the proposition that the right to protest does not give a right to cause damage to property, see *Attorney-General's Reference (No 1 of 2023)* [2024] EWCA Crim 243.

200 *North Warwickshire BC v Baldwin* [2023] EWHC 1719 (KB); *Transport for London v Persons Unknown* [2023] EWHC 1201 (KB); *Shell UK Ltd v Persons Unknown* [2023] EWHC 1229 (KB); *National Highways Ltd v Persons Unknown* [2023] EWHC 1073 (KB); *Transport for London v Persons Unknown* [2023] EWHC 1038 (KB); *National Highways Ltd v Persons Unknown* [2023] EWCA Civ 182; *Transport for London v Lee* [2022] EWHC 3102 (KB); *Three Counties Agricultural Society v Persons Unknown* [2022] EWHC 2708 (KB); *Thurrock Council v Adams* [2022] EWHC 1324 (QB); *Shell UK Oil Products Ltd v Persons Unknown* [2022] EWHC 1215 (QB); *Balfour Beatty Group Ltd v Persons Unknown* [2022] EWHC 874 (QB); *National Highways Ltd v Persons Unknown* [2021] EWHC 3081 (QB). But compare *National Highways Ltd v Persons Unknown* [2022] EWHC 1105 (QB); *Valero Energy Ltd v Persons Unknown* [2022] EWHC 911 (QB); *Boyd & Anor v Ineos Upstream Ltd & others* [2019] EWCA Civ 515.

201 *National Highways Ltd v Lancaster* [2021] EWHC 3080 (KB) [21]; *National Highways Ltd v Heyatawin* [2021] EWHC 3078 (QB) [44]; *North Warwickshire BC v Litten* [2022] EWHC 2777 (KB) [15]; see also *National Highways Ltd v Russenberger* [2024] EWHC 566 (KB).

202 See for instance *John Paton and Sons Ltd v Glasgow City Council* [2023] CSOH 74; *Heaney v Secretary of State for Business, Energy and Industrial Strategy* [2022] UKFTT 416 (GRC) [101]–[103]. A first-instance court in the Netherlands has held that legislation phasing out coal-fired power stations by 2030 did not violate the rights of energy companies under Article 1 of Protocol 1 to the ECHR: *RWE Generation NL BV v De Staat der Nederlanden (Het Ministerie van Economische Zaken en Klimaat)*, Rechtsbank Den Haag (The Hague District Court), 30 November 2022, ECLI:NL:RBDHA:2022:12635.

operator's right to property.'[203] The tribunal said that this was a fact-sensitive question, and that the imposition of the penalty in that particular case was not disproportionate within the meaning of Article 1 of Protocol 1 ECHR.

28.133 Beneficiaries of governmental environmental policies may also have difficulty relying on Article 1 of Protocol 1 ECHR to challenge changes in policy to their detriment, such as reductions in subsidies.[204]

28.134 Application for consent for development of a wind farm may be subject to the right under Article 6 ECHR right to a determination within a reasonable time.[205] However, a future hope of obtaining a planning permission is not a 'possession' within the meaning of ECHR Protocol 1 Article 1.[206]

203 *AXB Air Inc v Environment Agency* [2023] UKFTT 847 (GRC) [50].
204 *See Solaria Energy UK Ltd v Department for Business Energy and Industrial Strategy* [2019] EWHC 2188 (TCC). But see *Solaria Energy UK Ltd v Department for Business, Energy and Industrial Strategy* [2020] EWCA Civ 1625 (certain but not all contracts may be 'possessions' within the meaning of ECHR Protocol 1 Article 1).
205 *North Lowther Energy Initiative Ltd v Scottish Ministers* [2021] CSOH 104.
206 *Re ABO Wind NI Ltd's Application for Judicial Review* [2021] NIQB 96 [115]–[116].

PART VI

COMMERCIAL AND FINANCIAL SERVICES

CHAPTER 29

THE ROLE OF FINANCE IN ACHIEVING NET ZERO NATURE POSITIVE

Juan Lopez, Joe-han Ho and Philippe Kuhn

The role of finance in achieving net zero and nature positive ambitions

29.01 Finance has a crucial role to play in achieving net zero and nature positive targets.

29.02 To give a flavour of this, according to recent estimates:

- Achieving net zero requires US$125 trillion of finance globally to support the scale up of low-carbon solutions and the transition of high-emitting sectors.[1]
- The adaptation finance gap is between US$194 billion to US$366 billion per year.[2] This refers to the difference between the estimated costs of meeting a given adaptation target and the amount of finance available for adaptation.[3]

29.03 This chapter will consider:

- Global and UK efforts to finance the transition to net zero.
- The scope for making investment decisions by reference to net zero and nature positive goals.

29.04 The Paris Agreement specifically addressed climate finance in Article 9. By Article 9(1), the Paris Agreement required developed country Parties[4] to provide financial resources to assist developing country Parties in relation to both mitigation and adaptation. This built upon the financial commitments made in the United Nations Framework Convention on Climate Change ('UNFCCC').[5] The Paris Agreement coined the phrase 'climate finance', and refers to mobilising such finance from 'a wide

1 Pietro Rocco and Nina Foster, 'Financing Net Zero: How to Incentivise Credible Climate Action through Sustainability-Linked and Transition Finance' (Carbon Trust, 2 June 2023) <https://www.carbontrust.com/news-and-insights/insights/financing-net-zero-how-to-incentivise-credible-climate-action-through-sustainability-linked-and-transition-finance> accessed 15 May 2024.
2 UNEP, 'Adaptation Gap Report 2023. Underfinanced. Underprepared. Inadequate Investment and Planning on Climate Adaptation Leaves World Exposed' (2023) <https://wedocs.unep.org/bitstream/handle/20.500.11822/43796/adaptation_gap_report_2023.pdf?sequence=1&isAllowed=y>.
3 ibid.
4 This is the capitalisation used in the Paris Agreement itself.
5 See Articles 4(3), (5), (7), and 11 of the UNFCCC.

variety of sources, instruments and channels.'[6] The UNFCCC also requires that COPs[7] should seek to mobilise finance in accordance with the UNFCCC.[8] Accordingly, the Green Climate Fund was established at COP 16 in Cancún 2010, and received a boost at COP 28 in Dubai with pledges of $3.5 billion.[9]

Definitions: Climate finance and related concepts

29.05 The term 'climate finance' is not a term of art. It is, however, widely used to describe funding processes for investments related to climate change mitigation and adaptation.

29.06 The UNFCCC does not formally define 'climate finance'. Its Standing Committee on Finance explained in a 2014 report that data collectors and aggregators use different operational definitions but suggested that the various definitions converge as follows:[10]

> Climate finance aims at reducing emissions, and enhancing sinks of greenhouse gases and aims at reducing vulnerability of, and maintaining and increasing the resilience of, human and ecological systems to negative climate change impacts.

29.07 The UNFCCC website describes 'climate finance' as 'local, national or transnational financing—drawn from public, private and alternative sources of financing—that seeks to support mitigation and adaptation actions that will address climate change'.[11] This is broadly consistent with previous descriptions, and again emphasises the breadth of the concept.

29.08 'Climate finance' is related to the concepts of 'green finance', 'sustainable finance', and 'transition finance'. Like 'climate finance', while there remains fluidity in their respective parameters, these other concepts have increasingly settled definitions:

- 'Green finance' may be understood as financial flows (such as banking, micro-credit, insurance and investment) from the public, private and not-for-profit sectors to sustainable development priorities.[12] It therefore includes climate finance, but it is not limited to it as it may include a wider range of other environmental objectives such as industrial pollution control, water sanitation, or biodiversity protection.[13]

---

6 Paris Agreement, Article 9(3).
7 Defined at para 2.18.
8 UNFCCC, Article 7(2)(h). This forms part of the COP's role in ensuring the effective implementation of the UNFCCC.
9 See para 2.21.
10 UNFCCC, '2014 Biennial Assessment and Overview of Climate Finance Flows Report' (2014) <https://unfccc.int/files/cooperation_and_support/financial_mechanism/standing_committee/application/pdf/2014_biennial_assessment_and_overview_of_climate_finance_flows_report_web.pdf> accessed 19 September 2024.
11 UNFCCC, 'Introduction to Climate Finance | UNFCCC' <https://unfccc.int/topics/introduction-to-climate-finance> accessed 15 May 2024.
12 UNEP, 'Green Financing' (UNEP – UN Environment Programme, 23 January 2018) <http://www.unep.org/regions/asia-and-pacific/regional-initiatives/supporting-resource-efficiency/green-financing> accessed 15 May 2024.
13 UNFCCC, '2014 Biennial Assessment and Overview of Climate Finance Flows Report' (n 10).

- 'Sustainable finance' may be understood as financial flows which are directed taking into account environmental, social and governance considerations, leading to more long-term investments in sustainable economic activities and projects.[14] Environmental considerations may include climate change mitigation and adaptation.[15] Social considerations may include inclusiveness, inequality issues, and human rights issues.[16] Governance considerations may include management structures, employee relations, and executive remuneration.[17]

- 'Transition finance' may be understood as financial flows which are directed to support higher emitting companies and activities to decarbonise over time.[18] These instruments are generally used by companies seeking to reduce greenhouse gas emissions and should be part of a credible decarbonisation pathway that is consistent with global climate and nature goals.[19]

Climate finance and the transition to net zero

29.09 Article 14 of the Paris Agreement requires a 'global stocktake'. The parties agreed to 'periodically take stock of the implementation of this Agreement to assess the collective progress towards achieving the purpose of this Agreement and its long-term goals'.

29.10 The first 'global stocktake' took place in 2023. It reflected rocky progress in the transition to net zero. In relation to finance, some of its observations were as follows:[20]

- The adaptation finance gap, estimated to be up to US$366 billion per year, must be urgently addressed. Doubling adaptation finance by 2025 is a step in the right direction. However, the scale of overall adaptation finance must be dramatically increased, including through improved access to grants and highly concessional adaptation finance for all developing countries.

- A step-change is needed to mobilise climate finance to meet the scale required to deliver the Paris Agreement. This necessitates the enhanced scale and quality of concessional finance,[21] as well as a broader shift in public and private financial flows, consistent with a pathway towards low greenhouse gas emissions and climate-resilient development.

---

14 EU, 'Overview of Sustainable Finance' <https://finance.ec.europa.eu/sustainable-finance/overview-sustainable-finance_en> accessed 15 May 2024.

15 ibid.

16 ibid.

17 ibid.

18 Department for Energy Security and Net Zero and HM Treasury, 'Transition Finance Market Review: Terms of Reference' (2023) <https://www.gov.uk/government/publications/transition-finance-market-review/transition-finance-market-review-terms-of-reference> accessed 15 May 2024.

19 ibid.

20 UNFCCC, 'First Global Stocktake High-Level Committee Summary of High-Level Events' (2023) <https://unfccc.int/sites/default/files/resource/GST_HLE%20branded%20V2.pdf> accessed 15 May 2024.

21 'Concessional finance' refers to below market rate finance provided by major financial institutions.

- While there has been progress in mobilising climate finance, it is crucial to urgently meet all relevant pledges, including the delivery of the pledged US$100 billion, and to set an ambitious new collective quantified goal on climate finance. Such a goal would take account of finance from all sources – public, private, domestic and international – including guarantees and blended finance, green bonds and innovative instruments. Public finance is key and can also incentivise private finance flows towards economy-wide decarbonisation.

29.11 The rocky progress in the transition to net zero is also reflected in other analysis at the corporate level. An analysis of the Financial Times Stock Exchange 100 Index is instructive. In November 2021, the British Government's Transition Plan Taskforce ('TPT') released a Draft Disclosure Framework setting out guidance for companies to create credible and reliable decarbonisation plans. However, analysis conducted by EY in January 2023 has shown that 95% of FTSE 100 companies have not published detailed plans regarding how they intend to achieve their net zero transition goals and are missing key TPT framework requirements.[22] Even for the remaining 5%, significant gaps remain in their transition plans, primarily in their implementation strategies relating to financial planning or metrics.[23]

Making investment decisions by reference to net zero and nature positive goals

29.12 A key challenge in the transition to net zero is the clash between more traditional metrics and more modern metrics for assessing the suitability of investments. Where traditional investment models rely heavily on factors such as revenue growth, price-to-earnings ratios, and price-to-book ratios, net zero and nature positive-focused investors place significant weight on other factors such as absolute and normalised emissions, carbon intensity, and other less tangible factors such as the analysis of due diligence conducted in assessing the credibility and overall sustainability of such investments.[24] Further, as considered below, there have historically been legal impediments to trustees and asset managers taking into account ethical or moral considerations in making investment decisions.

29.13 In addition, a general lack of climate change business expertise across all levels of management and staff may be hampering efforts to undertake greener investments. There have been warnings by captains of industry about a lack of climate-based talent, from engineers who can implement decarbonisation of heat and power generation to C-suite executives who possess technical knowledge and expertise to accurately assess and price risk in green investments.[25]

---

22 Rob Joyce, 'Only 5% of FTSE 100 Have Published Net Zero Plans That Would Be Deemed 'Credible' under Government's Transition Plan Guidance' (2023) <https://www.ey.com/en_uk/news/2023/04/only-five-percentage-of-ftse-100-have-published-net-zero-plans> accessed 15 May 2024.
23 ibid.
24 Alastair Fraser and Tanya Fiedler, 'Net-Zero Targets for Investment Portfolios: An Analysis of Financed Emissions Metrics' (2023) 126 Energy Economics 106917.
25 Rob Joyce, 'UK Sustainability Leaders Warn Lack of Climate Talent at All Levels Could Stall Net Zero Progress' (2023) <https://www.ey.com/en_uk/news/2023/06/uk-sustainability-leaders-warn-lack-of-climate-talent> accessed 15 May 2024.

29.14 However, there have been positive cultural changes led by the Financial Conduct Authority ('FCA'). As explained in more detail in Chapter 30, particularly from paragraph 30.37, the FCA recently issued rules and guidance to improve trust and transparency to the market for sustainable investment products by its Policy Statement PS23/16 entitled 'Sustainability Disclosure Requirements (SDR) and investment labels'. These aim to inform and protect consumers and improve trust in the market for sustainable investments, and the measures include an anti-greenwashing rule for all authorised firms, four investment labels, and new rules and guidance for firms marketing investment funds on the basis of their sustainability characteristics.

The Financial Services and Markets Act 2023

29.15 In June 2023, after more than two and a half years of review and consultation, the Financial Services and Markets Act 2023 ('FSMA 2023') became law. This was the second piece of financial services legislation passed following the UK's exit from the EU single market (the first piece being the largely technical Financial Services Act 2021), and it substantially rewired the UK's financial regulatory architecture for a post-Brexit world.

29.16 This legislation makes important strides forward in the context of net zero and nature positive.[26]

29.17 Its section 27 introduces, for the first time, a regulatory principle requiring the FCA and the Prudential Regulation Authority ('PRA') to have regard to the need to contribute towards achieving compliance with section 1 of the Climate Change Act 2008 (the target of reaching net zero by 2050), replacing the existing principle relating to sustainable economic growth. This therefore statutorily embeds at the core of financial regulation the importance of complying with the 2050 net zero target.

29.18 Its section 21 also empowers the Treasury to prepare a Sustainability Disclosure Requirement policy statement, to which the FCA and the PRA must have regard when making rules or issuing guidance in connection with disclosure concerning matters relating to sustainability. At the time of publication, the Treasury has yet to prepare such a policy statement.

29.19 Its section 79 also requires the Treasury to carry out a review and report to Parliament on the extent to which regulation of the UK financial system is adequate for the purpose of eliminating the financing of the use of prohibited forest risk commodities. At the time of publication, this has yet to be completed.

---

26 James Fotherby, 'The Financial Services and Markets Act Must Deliver for Climate and Nature' (*Aldersgate Group*, 2023) <https://www.aldersgategroup.org.uk/blog/the-financial-services-and-markets-act-must-deliver-for-climate-and-nature/> accessed 15 May 2024.

Financing the transition to net zero

(i) *Financing the transition: an introduction*

29.20 In December 2020, the Advisory Group on Finance for the Climate Change Committee,[27] published 'The Road to Net-Zero Finance',[28] which assessed the UK financial system's ability to deliver its net zero target. Its recommendations included the following:[29]

> A 2. Make net-zero projects and plans investable, by increasing the predictability of cash flows and reducing risks through sector pathways, carbon pricing, and de-risking.

29.21 This section addresses the financing of projects that contribute to the transition to net zero carbon emissions. In particular, it addresses: project finance; offtake agreements, and legal issues to consider in respect of them; the government's Contracts for Difference scheme; the Green Finance Strategy; and sustainable finance and bonds.

(ii) *Project finance*

29.22 The development of net zero projects, such as renewable energy technology and infrastructure, typically goes hand in hand with a need for substantial, upfront capital financing at often high levels of risk.[30]

29.23 The financing method that has traditionally been, and will continue to be, used for long-term, capital-intensive infrastructure and industrial developments (key to the transition to net zero) is project finance. The structure of project finance usually includes non-recourse financing, limited recourse (limited to the assets or revenue of the project), or mezzanine financing:

- Non-recourse financing[31] means that the lender will only have recourse to, or security over, the assets being financed, generally held by a special purpose vehicle ('SPV'): the lender would not have recourse to the developer (or sponsor)'s other assets.
- Limited recourse financing[32] will allow the lender, in addition to recourse to the assets being financed, limited rights to pursue the borrower personally, for example for damages for breach of contract.

---

27 The Advisory Group on Finance is a body created by the CCC in order so that it may best evaluate how finance – not strictly limited to renewables projects' financing – may promote the meeting of the Carbon Budget 2033–2037 and UK's net zero target.
28 Climate Change Committee, 'The Road to Net-Zero Finance' (2020) <https://www.theccc.org.uk/publication/the-road-to-net-zero-finance-sixth-carbon-budget-advisory-group/> accessed 19 September 2024.
29 ibid.
30 Risks include political risk, economic risk, regulatory risk, and risk of construction or technical failure, in addition to the many financial risks associated with costs and margins of return.
31 <https://www.tradefinanceglobal.com/trade-finance/recourse-non-recourse/> accessed 19 September 2024.
32 Naman Bansal, 'Limited Recourse Financing in Project Finance' (2021) 4(5) International Journal of Law Management & Humanities 2189 <https://ijlmh.com/paper/limited-recourse-financing-in-project-finance/> accessed 19 September 2024.

- Mezzanine financing[33] is a method of financing by which the investor accumulates rolled interest rather than regular interest payments and is able to convert debt into an equity, upon any payment default.

29.24 The financing (through debt and equity) is usually repaid by the cash flow generated by the project itself.

(iii) *Parties and capital structures*

29.25 Parties under typical project finance structures for a renewable energy generation project will be the project sponsor or developer company (typically the creator of the project which commands renewables technology expertise, and the delivery body), the landowner, the lender (typically, a bank, debt fund or other financial institution) and the investor.

29.26 An individual SPV will usually be created for each project, with investors buying into the SPV, not the sponsor (developer) company. An SPV will have a separate legal identity, usually as a separate corporate body, from the project sponsor company, with distinct assets and liabilities. The SPV will manage and limit the sponsor's financial risk.

29.27 With so many contractual parties there will frequently be a complex contractual matrix. A conventional relationship between project financing parties will be as follows: the sponsor will find an investor for the renewables project; the investor will then buy the project infrastructure, for installation by the sponsor. The investor will then lease the operating facility to the sponsor or landowner, at a reduced rate that takes some account of the tax incentives benefitting the investor. The energy product generated by the facility is then sold, to offtakers, the buyers of the energy produced.

(iv) *Offtaking*

29.28 One way in which risk is mitigated in the financing of large infrastructure and energy projects is through the securing of offtake agreements. These are agreements made in advance to buy or sell the energy (or goods) produced by a project. These agreements give proof and guarantee of demand, certainty of future income, and, therefore, comfort to potential investors, making the investment a viable proposition.

29.29 The general law of contract will apply to offtake agreements, however, in this section we consider two issues that may concern parties to an offtake agreement, given the level of risk involved and the generally long-term nature of the projects which are subject to the agreements:

- Force majeure clauses; and

- Take or pay provisions.

---

33 <https://www.fundingoptions.com/knowledge/mezzanine-finance/> accessed 19 September 2024.

(a) Force majeure clauses

29.30 Most offtake agreements will include a force majeure clause, a clause that allows a party to cancel a contract or suspend the performance of obligations where it is prevented from performing due to the occurrence of a certain (factual or legal) event. Force majeure clauses may include as defined force majeure events: acts of God, floods, droughts, earthquakes or other natural disasters. The term, force majeure, is not a term of art,[34] so whether an event is a force majeure event will depend on the construction of the force majeure clause. It is, therefore, vital that a force majeure event is properly defined in the contract.[35]

29.31 The world increasingly experiences extreme, climate-change-related weather events. These weather events may – and already do – cause physical (and immediate) disruption to the industry in terms of delays, and damage to work on site. In addition to the physical disruption climate change may bring, net zero-related policy and legislative changes (in terms of measures to adapt and mitigate) could also increase as governments step in to regulate or legislate with little notice, which could also disrupt a project.

29.32 There are various forms of words commonly used in force majeure clauses that may be relevant to climate events, including, for example, the expression 'act of God'. An act of God was described by Cockburn CJ in *Nugent v Smith* as:[36]

> such a direct and violent and sudden and irresistible act of Nature as the defendant could not, by any amount of ability, foresee would happen, or, if he could foresee that it would happen, he could not by any amount of care and skill resist, so as to prevent its effect.

29.33 Extreme weather events could be seen to be acts of God according to *the Nugent v Smith* definition, however, it is worth noting the definition given by Lord Hobhouse in *Transco plc v Stockport Metropolitan Borough Council*:[37]

> It was a metaphorical phrase (like 'fate') with a religious origin used to describe those events which involved no human agency and which it was not realistically possible for a human to guard against: an accident which the defendant can show is due to natural causes, directly and exclusively, without any human intervention and could not have been prevented by any amount for foresight, pains and care, reasonably to be expected of him.

29.34 It might be arguable that climate-change-related extreme weather events are events against which it was reasonably possible for a human to guard, and there may be scope for a party to argue that such an event was not, in fact, an act of God.

(b) Take or pay provisions

29.35 A take or pay provision is a commonly used clause in an offtake agreement, under which the offtaker is obliged to pay for a certain amount of energy, whether or

---

34 *Tandrin Aviation Holdings Ltd v Aero Toy Store LLC and another* [2010] EWHC 40 (Comm) [43].

35 For a full review of the operation of force majeure clauses and the doctrine of frustration, see for example Chapter 27 of *Chitty on Contracts*, (35th edn, Sweet & Maxwell 2023).

36 *Nugent v Smith* (1876) 1 CPD 423, 426.

37 *Transco plc v Stockport Metropolitan Borough Council* [2003] UKHL 61 per Lord Hobhouse at [59].

not it is taken. Parties to an offtake agreement should bear in mind that there is a risk that such clauses are unenforceable by virtue of the law against penalties.[38] There is little judicial guidance on this point, but we note that in *M&J Polymers Ltd v Imerys Minerals Ltd*,[39] Burton J reviewed the authorities in relation to the law of penalties and held that, although in his view, 'take or pay clause' was capable of being a penalty clause, (and that that the concept of penalty could apply equally to a debt claim as to a claim for damages), the specific take or pay clause did not offend the rule against penalties, the judge being satisfied that it was:[40]

> commercially justifiable, did not amount to oppression, was negotiated and freely entered into between parties of comparable bargaining power, and did not have the predominant purpose of deterring a breach of contract nor amount to a provision 'in terrorem'.

29.36 Whilst not in relation to 'take or pay' clauses, the Supreme Court provided clear guidance in relation to contractual penalty clauses in *Cavendish Square Holding BV v El Makdessi* and *ParkingEye Ltd v Beavis*.[41] The test for a penalty clause was set out by Lords Neuberger and Sumption as follows:[42]

> The true test is whether the impugned provision is a secondary obligation which imposes a detriment on the contract-breaker out of all proportion to any legitimate interest of the innocent party in the enforcement of the primary obligation …

29.37 Thus, the risk of a take or pay clause violating the rule against penalties could be mitigated by ensuring that: a) it serves a legitimate business interest; and b) the provision does not impose on a contract breaker a detriment out of proportion[43] to the legitimate interest.

(v) *The Contracts for Difference Scheme*

29.38 In 2013 the government introduced a set of reforms, the Electricity Market Reform ('EMR') to incentivise investment in secure, low-carbon electricity.[44]

29.39 In order to pursue its aims under the EMR, in 2014, the government launched the Contracts for Difference Scheme, which aims to support low-carbon electricity

---

38 *M&J Polymers Ltd v Imerys Minerals Ltd* [2008] EWHC 344 (Comm); [2008] Bus LR D68. Here, Burton J was satisfied that in relation to the take or play clause, the rule against penalties applied [44].
39 ibid.
40 ibid [45]–[48].
41 *Cavendish Square Holding BV v El Makdessi and ParkingEye Ltd v Beavis* [2015] UKSC 67, [2015] 3 WLR 1373.
42 ibid [32]. The test was articulated by Lord Mance at [152]: 'What is necessary in each case is to consider, first, whether any (and if so what) legitimate business interest is served and protected by the clause, and, second, whether, assuming such an interest to exist, the provision made for the interest is nevertheless in the circumstances extravagant, exorbitant or unconscionable'; and by Lord Hodge at [293]: 'I therefore conclude that the correct test for a penalty is whether the sum or remedy stipulated as a consequence of a breach of contract is exorbitant or unconscionable when regard is had to the innocent party's interest in the performance of the contract.'
43 Or extravagant, exorbitant or unconscionable.
44 Department for Energy and Climate Change, 'Review of Electricity Market Arrangements (REMA): Second Consultation' (GOV.UK, 12 March 2024) <https://www.gov.uk/government/consultations/review-of-electricity-market-arrangements-rema-second-consultation> accessed 10 May 2024.

generation, by addressing the lack of investment in it. The scheme supports many large infrastructure projects that are funded or seek funding through project finance. A developer who meets certain eligibility requirements[45] can apply by sealed bid for a Contract for Difference ('CfD').

29.40 CfDs are intended to incentivise investment in renewable (or low-carbon) energy by providing protection from volatile energy prices, with the lowest cost to the consumer. A CfD is a contract between a low-carbon electricity generator developer and the Low Carbon Contracts Company ('LCCC'),[46] a company classified as a central government organisation whose sole shareholder is the Secretary of State for Energy Security.[47] The LCCC issues and manages the contracts.

29.41 The CfD scheme guarantees that low-carbon generators benefit from fixed ('strike price')[48] power output unit pricing for electricity produced over a 15-year period.[49] Under the scheme, payment is made to the generator either by way of a subsidy up to the strike price[50] or is required to be paid back into the scheme by the generator, if the reference price[51] is above the strike price.[52]

29.42 Pursuant to section 11 of the Energy Act 2013, the Secretary of State may issue standard terms and conditions of CfDs,[53] and may from time to time revise[54] these in accordance with provision made in regulations.[55] In issuing or revising terms under section 11 of the Energy Act 2013, the Secretary of State must have regard to the matters in section 5(2).[56]

---

45 Applicable eligibility requirements can be found at, for Allocation Round 6, <https://www.gov.uk/government/publications/contracts-for-difference-cfd-allocation-round-6-allocation-framework> accessed 13 October 2024.
46 See <https://www.lowcarboncontracts.uk/> accessed 13 October 2024.
47 Department for Energy Security and Net Zero and Low Carbon Contracts Company, 'Low Carbon Contracts Company Framework Document' (2023) <https://www.lowcarboncontracts.uk/resources/guidance-and-publications/lccc-framework-document-2023/> accessed 13 October 2024.
48 Defined by the Contracts for Difference (Standard Terms) Regulations 2014 as 'in relation to a CFD, means a price specified in or determined under the CFD which is compared to the reference price determined under that CFD so as to enable the determination of the amount (if any) which is payable by the CFD counterparty or a generator under the CFD in respect of the generation of electricity by that generator.'
49 Nicole Watson and Paul Bolton, 'Contracts for Difference Scheme' (House of Commons Library 2023) <https://commonslibrary.parliament.uk/research-briefings/cbp-9871/> accessed 13 October 2024.
50 See reg 3(a) of the Contracts for Difference (Standard Terms) Regulations 2014, SI 2014/2012, as amended by reg 2 of the Contracts for Difference (Standard Terms) (Amendment) Regulations 2017, SI 2017/112.
51 A 'reference price' is defined by the Contracts for Difference (Standard Terms) Regulations 2014 as, 'in relation to a CFD, means a price determined under the CFD which is intended to represent a market price of electricity in respect of a period specified in that CFD'.
52 See reg 3(b) of the Contracts for Difference (Standard Terms) Regulations 2014, SI 2014/2012, as amended by reg 2 of the Contracts for Difference (Standard Terms) (Amendment) Regulations 2017, SI 2017/112.
53 Energy Act 2013 s 11(1).
54 ibid s 11(2).
55 ibid s 11(3).
56 ibid s 11(4).

29.43 The matters set out in section 5(2) of the Energy Act 2013 are as follows:[57]

5(2) The matters are –

(a) the duties of the Secretary of State under sections 1 and 4(1)(b) of the Climate Change Act 2008 (carbon targets and budgets);
(b) the duty of the Secretary of State under section 1(1) of this Act (decarbonisation target range);
(c) ensuring the security of supply to consumers of electricity;
(d) the likely cost to consumers of electricity;
(e) the target set out in Article 3(1) of, and Annex 1 to, the renewables directive (use of energy from renewable sources).

29.44 The 2023 auction round for CfD delivered 'a record number' of solar, onshore wind, tidal, and geothermal projects.[58] In previous auction rounds, offshore wind had been the 'dominant technology'.[59] The CfD scheme is, at the date of publication, the subject of governmental review and consultation, including as regards whether it should incorporate wholesale pricing or calculate generator revenues by reference to predictive (rather than actual) generator output determined by location.[60]

(vi) *The Green Finance Strategy*

29.45 In July 2019, the government published the Green Finance Strategy, a plan to use the UK's financial services sector to support its climate and environmental aims. The strategy for achieving this included the following: ensuring climate and environmental factors are integrated into long-term public financial policy and private financial decision-making, promoting robust green financial market frameworks, and encouraging the development of new green financial products and services.

29.46 The Green Finance Strategy was updated in March 2023.[61] This policy document set out the UK's plans to:

- Develop a 'UK Green Taxonomy,' a UK-specific set of definitions of economic activities that should be classed as 'environmentally sustainable'. Companies would ultimately be required to report against these definitions. Controversially, the government proposed that the generation of nuclear energy be classified as 'environmentally sustainable'.

- Require large companies to publish their net zero transition plans.

---

57 By s 5(3) of the Energy Act 2013, In subsection (2)(e) 'the renewables directive' means Directive 2009/28/EC of the European Parliament and of the Council of 23 April 2009 on the promotion of the use of energy from renewable sources.
58 Watson and Bolton, 'Contracts for Difference Scheme' (n 49).
59 ibid 4.
60 ibid 17.
61 'Mobilising Green Investment' (2023) <https://assets.publishing.service.gov.uk/media/643583fb877741001368d815/mobilising-green-investment-2023-green-finance-strategy.pdf> accessed 19 September 2024.

- Review the regulatory framework for UK pension funds (in which over £2.5 trillion are invested) in order to promote green investment decisions and clarify the content of trustees' fiduciary duties in making such decisions.

- Review the regulatory framework for the UK insurance industry in order to facilitate its investment in green assets that were previously considered too illiquid, such as renewable energy infrastructure.

29.47 Additionally, the publication by the government of net zero 'investment roadmaps'[62] is intended to aid in the identification of investment needs. Roadmaps have already been produced for the hydrogen and carbon capture usage and storage markets. The government also aims for the UK to become the first net zero-aligned financial centre.[63] 'Power project' financing is also to be actively brought forward, as is the promotion of a comprehensive range of finance, in the form of debt, hybrid products, as well as equity and guarantees, supportive of the delivery of private sector infrastructure projects.[64]

29.48 In 2021, the European Commission separately renewed its sustainable finance strategy, which included further regulation requiring companies to report against the EU (Green) Taxonomy and a standard for European Green Bonds.[65]

(vii) *Sustainable finance and bonds*

29.49 Bonds play an important role in sustainable finance.[66] Three forms of bond are particularly significant:

- Sustainability bonds, which are bonds used to finance or re-finance environmental and social projects.

- Green bonds, which are bonds where the proceeds will be used to finance or re-finance projects or activities with clear, positive environmental impacts. The first green bonds were issued by the World Bank and European Investment Bank in 2007. The International Capital Market Association issued guidelines for issuing

62 HM Government, 'CCUS Net Zero Investment Roadmap' (2023) <https://assets.publishing.service.gov.uk/government/uploads/system/uploads/attachment_data/file/1167167/ccus-investment-roadmap.pdf> accessed 19 September 2024.
63 HM Treasury, 'Chancellor: UK Will Be the World's First Net Zero Financial Centre' (GOV.UK, 2021) <https://www.gov.uk/government/news/chancellor-uk-will-be-the-worlds-first-net-zero-financial-centre> accessed 15 May 2024.
64 ESFC Investment Group, 'Project Finance in Energy Sector' (ESFC Investment Group) <https://esfccompany.com/en/articles/project-finance/project-finance-in-energy-sector/> accessed 15 May 2024.
65 European Parliament, 'Renewed Sustainable Finance Strategy | Legislative Train Schedule' (European Parliament) <https://www.europarl.europa.eu/legislative-train/theme-a-european-green-deal/file-renewed-sustainable-finance-strategy> accessed 15 May 2024.
66 Defined at para 29.08 above.

Green Bonds in 2021 – the Green Bond Principles[67] – which were adopted by the government when setting up the framework for UK green gilts and savings bonds.[68]

- Sustainability linked bonds, in which the interest rate payable is linked to the achievement (or failure to achieve) defined environmental standards or goals.

29.50 Critics of the green (and wider sustainability) bond scheme have pointed to the following failings and challenges:

- The lack of a standard definition for what constitutes a 'green' project has seen environmentally controversial projects financed by the issuance of green bonds – one example is the expansion of the runways at Hong Kong International Airport.[69] While standards such as the EU and UK Green Taxonomies remain unsettled and at odds, there is much scope for greenwashing in bond issuance.[70]

- Without sensible and clearly defined key performance indicators, it is often difficult to measure the environmental impact of the investment or the underlying project.

- The difficulty in enforcing obligations relating to the use of bond proceeds where the issuer is a sovereign or quasi-sovereign entity.

The scope for making investment decisions by reference to net zero nature positive goals: trustees' powers of investment under English law

29.51 Trustees and asset managers of pension funds, charities, and other large institutional investors are likely to be key players in providing the necessary capital for the investments required to achieve net zero nature positive goals globally. The UK has the largest pension market in Europe, worth over £2.5 trillion.[71]

29.52 However, trustees and asset managers operating in common law jurisdictions face a potential fetter when making investment decisions. There is a long-standing legal principle which may be broadly stated as requiring such officers to focus on financial prudence and the maximisation of returns for assets under their management. Accordingly, there has been concern that taking into account non-financial considerations – such as by preferring investments that are consistent with the achievement of net zero nature positive goals – may be a breach of duty.

---

67 ICMA, 'Green Bond Principles' (2021) <https://www.icmagroup.org/assets/documents/Sustainable-finance/2022-updates/Green-Bond-Principles-June-2022-060623.pdf> accessed 19 September 2024.
68 HM Treasury and UK Debt Management Office, 'UK Government Green Financing Framework' (2021) <https://assets.publishing.service.gov.uk/media/60f008d78fa8f50c7f08ae6e/20210630_UK_Government_Green_Financing_Framework.pdf> accessed 19 September 2024.
69 Reclaim Finance, 'High-Flying Greenwashing around a New Green Bond for Hong Kong Airport' (Reclaim Finance, 2022) <https://reclaimfinance.org/site/en/2022/01/04/high-flying-greenwashing-around-a-new-green-bond/> accessed 15 May 2024.
70 Bertrand Rocher and Marc Briand, 'How Green Are Green Bonds?' (9 March 2023) <https://www.im.natixis.com/uk/esg/how-green-are-green-bonds> accessed 15 May 2024.
71 HM Treasury, 'Mansion House 2023' (GOV.UK, 11 July 2023) <https://www.gov.uk/government/collections/mansion-house-2023> accessed 15 May 2024.

29.53 In England, the law of trusts has historically been very cautious, and indeed prohibited trustees from taking into account ethical or moral considerations in making investment decisions. For a long time, the law required trustees to make investment decisions guided solely by financial prudence, having regard to risk and diversification, and in accordance with the objects of the relevant trust.[72]

29.54 Notably, the leading English authorities on ethical investments have arisen in the charities context. Accordingly, some of the detailed factual considerations and application of legal principles are limited to charitable trusts. However, these authorities are of wider relevance and application given the English courts have made clear that the general law of trusts applies to charities as to other trusts (albeit with certain qualifications and differences, including as a result of different legislative regimes).

29.55 Before turning to the case law in the charities context, it is helpful to start with the current law on investment decisions by trustees of non-charitable pension funds, in particular occupational pension schemes. This is derived from a variety of sources, including legislation, the general law of trusts and fiduciary duties as well as guidance from the Law Commission for England and Wales (the 'Law Commission') and the Department for Work and Pensions ('DWP'). What follows below is a brief overview of what is necessarily a specialist area of pensions law.

Investment decisions by pension trustees – Law Commission 2014 report

29.56 The modern starting point is the Law Commission's 2014 report 'Fiduciary Duties of Investment Intermediaries'.[73] This report clearly distinguished between the consideration of financial and non-financial factors in relation to investment decisions by what it terms 'investment intermediaries', which includes but is not limited to pension trustees. Amongst other things, the Law Commission considered the extent to which such persons may, or must, consider: (1) factors relevant to long-term investment performance which might not have an immediate financial impact, including questions of sustainability or environmental and social impact; (2) interests beyond the maximisation of financial return; and (3) generally prevailing ethical standards, and/or the ethical views of their beneficiaries, even where this may not be in the immediate financial interest of those beneficiaries.[74]

29.57 The Law Commission concluded that pension trustees should start with consideration of the purpose for which the power of investment has been given to them under the applicable trust or other instrument, followed by consideration of applicable legislation. Relevant legislation may include the Pensions Act 1995, the Pensions Act 2004 and the Occupational Pension Scheme (Investment) Regulations 2005 (considered below). Within the confines of that legislative framework, pension trustees enjoy a

---

72 See generally *Cowan v Scargill* [1985] Ch 270 and *Harries v Church Commissioners for England* [1992] 1 WLR 1241.
73 Law Commission, *Fiduciary Duties of Investment Intermediaries* (Law Com No 350, 2014).
74 ibid para 6.1.

degree of discretion or flexibility, provided always a sound procedure has been followed before pursuing a particular investment policy or decision.[75]

29.58 Specifically in relation to the question of how far pension trustees may (or must) consider factors relevant to long-term investment performance; interests beyond the maximisation of financial returns; and ethical views, even where this may not be in the immediate financial interest of those beneficiaries, the Law Commission concluded:

- It is not helpful to suggest that trustees should only maximise financial returns.[76]
- 'Trustees may take account of any factor which is financially material to the performance of an investment, including environmental, social and governance factors.'[77]
- 'Whilst it is clear that trustees may take into account environmental, social and governance factors in making investment decisions where they are financially material, we think the law goes further: trustees should take into account financially material factors.'[78]
- However, it is not helpful to approach the exercise on the basis that 'ESG or ethical factors must always be taken into account.' These labels are not clearly defined. Nor do they neatly track onto the financial and non-financial factors terminology. Instead, according to the Law Commission, '[i]n every case, the test must be: what are the risks associated with this investment?'[79]
- The approach to taking into account non-financial factors in making investment decisions is more limited than in relation to financial factors.[80]

29.59 Specifically as to non-financial factors, the Law Commission proposed a two-stage test:[81]

> In general, non-financial factors may only be taken into account if two tests are met:
>
> (1) trustees should have good reason to think that scheme members would share the concern; and
> (2) the decision should not involve a risk of significant financial detriment to the fund.

29.60 It is in particular in relation to investment decisions influenced by non-financial factors, including what are commonly referred to as ESG considerations, that the leading English cases, namely *Cowan v Scargill*, *Harries v Church Commissioners for*

75 ibid para 6.5–6.11.
76 ibid para 6.21–6.22.
77 ibid para 6.27.
78 ibid para 6.30.
79 ibid para 6.31.
80 ibid para 6.33.
81 ibid para 6.34.

England (*'Harries'*) and *Butler-Sloss & others v Charity Commission for England and Wales* (*'Butler-Sloss'*),[82] contain helpful guidance which is of wider application than their immediate factual context. These cases are discussed below, but as the Law Commission explains its two-stage test is substantially derived from the leading decision in *Harries*.

29.61 The two-stage test is explained by the Law Commission in its report.[83] As to stage one, in particular, it states that '[t]he courts have made clear that trustees may not impose their own ethical views on their beneficiaries', citing Harries.[84] As to stage two, it concluded that, having regard to Harries, in its view 'it is clear that non-financial factors can be used if they do not cause significant financial detriment, but there has been considerable debate about how this test should be applied'.[85]

29.62 Helpfully, the Law Commission published a 6-page summary guidance document entitled 'Pension trustees' duties when setting an investment strategy: Guidance from the Law Commission' together with its full report.[86]

29.63 The Law Commission's observations must now also be read in light of the more recent guidance of the High Court in *Butler-Sloss* (considered below). Moreover, as explained below, there have been relevant changes to the legislation which applies in this area following the Law Commission's 2014 report.

Investment decisions by pension trustees – amendments to legislation and departmental guidance

29.64 Moving on to survey more recent developments, with effect from 1 October 2019, regulation 2 of the Occupational Pension Schemes (Investment) Regulations[87] (the '2005 Regulations') was amended by regulation 4 of the Pension Protection Fund (Pensionable Service) and Occupational Pension Schemes (Investment and Disclosure) (Amendment and Modification) Regulations 2018.[88] The main effect of that change in the law, for present purposes, was to introduce into legislation the distinction between consideration of financial and non-financial factors. Specifically, the new regulation 2(3)(vi) requires a 'statement of investment principles' ('SIP') within the meaning of the 2005 Regulations to cover 'financially material considerations over the appropriate time horizon of the investments, including how those considerations are taken into account in the selection, retention and realisation of investments' and regulation 2(3)(vii) requires such statements to cover 'the extent (if at all) to which non-financial matters are taken into account in the selection, retention and realisation of investments'.

---

82 *Cowan v Scargill* (n 72); *Harries v Church Commissioners for England* (n 72); *Butler-Sloss & others v Charity Commission for England and Wales* [2022] EWHC 974 (Ch); [2022] Ch 371.
83 Law Commission, *Fiduciary Duties of Investment Intermediaries* (n 73) para 6.57–6.78.
84 ibid para 6.57.
85 ibid para 6.69.
86 Available at https://lawcom.gov.uk/project/fiduciary-duties-of-investment-intermediaries/, accessed 27 September 2024.
87 SI 2005/3378.
88 SI 2018/988.

29.65 Regulation 2(4) of the 2005 Regulations (as amended) defines 'financially material considerations' as including (but not limited to) 'environmental, social and governance considerations (including but not limited to climate change), which the trustees of the trust scheme consider financially material' (regulation 2(4)). The term 'non-financial matters' is defined as 'the views of the members and beneficiaries including (but not limited to) their ethical views and their views in relation to social and environmental impact and present and future quality of life of the members and beneficiaries of the trust scheme'.

29.66 Further guidance on the approach to these provisions and the 2005 Regulations more generally was provided by the DWP in 2022.[89] Materially:

- The DWP stressed in relation to the general duty to invest scheme assets in scheme members' and beneficiaries' best interests (commonly known as the best interests duty) found in regulation 4(2) of the 2005 Regulations that '[t]he line between financial and non-financial factors is not always clear. DWP encourages trustees, if it is practical to do so, to keep under review non-financial factors that may not immediately present as financially material but have the potential to become so, particularly for schemes with a long-term horizon.'[90]

- The DWP addressed the relationship between the selection of so-called stewardship priorities or themes and the legislative requirements as to the recording and taking into account of non-financial factors.[91]

- More specific guidance in relation to regulations 2(3)(vi)–(vii) is also provided, reiterating that requirements in relation to 'financially material considerations' (including ESG considerations such as climate change) are more stringent and extensive than in relation to 'non-financial factors'.[92] Even so, the DWP guidance makes clear that '[w]hile trustees are not required to take account of non-financial matters, trustees or managers of relevant multi-employer schemes are required to make arrangements to encourage members of the scheme, or their representatives, to make their views on matters relating to the scheme known to the trustees or managers. This could include views about its investments and its stewardship.'[93]

89 Department for Work and Pensions, 'Reporting on Stewardship and Other Topics through the Statement of Investment Principles and the Implementation Statement: Statutory and Non-Statutory Guidance' (2022) <https://www.gov.uk/government/consultations/climate-and-investment-reporting-setting-expectations-and-empowering-savers/outcome/reporting-on-stewardship-and-other-topics-through-the-statement-of-investment-principles-and-the-implementation-statement-statutory-and-non-statutory> accessed 27 September 2024.
90 ibid para 30.
91 ibid paras 50–52.
92 ibid paras 112–118.
93 ibid para 117.

29.67 The breadth of application of the DWP's guidance cannot be overstated. As it states:[94]

> Trustees of occupational pension schemes with 100 or more members, that are required to prepare a Statement of Investment Principles (SIP), are required to publicly state their policy on the exercise of the rights attaching to the investments, and on undertaking engagement activities in respect of the investments via the SIP, which they are required to publish so that the SIP is available free of charge to the public. Trustees of such schemes are also required to report on how and the extent to which they have followed this policy during the scheme year and to describe the voting behaviour by, or on behalf of trustees, including the most significant votes cast, during the scheme year and state any use of the services of a proxy voter during that year via an annual published Implementation Statement (IS). *Pension schemes subject to these requirements account for more than 99% of savers.* (Emphasis added.)

29.68 Following the 2022 DWP guidance, the government issued its 2023 Green Finance Strategy paper in March 2023.[95] Amongst other things, this noted the two-stage test proposed by the Law Commission in its 2014 report and the 2022 DWP guidance. A review of this regime was announced. At the time of publication, the outcome of that review is unclear.

English case law on investment decisions

29.69 As noted above, the leading English cases on ESG considerations in investment decisions are from the charities context. The leading cases are *Cowan v Scargill*, *Harries* (also commonly known as the *Bishop of Oxford* case) and *Butler-Sloss.*[96]

29.70 The *Butler-Sloss* case provides a helpful modern statement of the law. It provides welcome clarity as to the approach to ethical investments for charity trustees and is also of interest to other trustees (subject to certain qualifications and relevant differences, including as a result of legislation). As noted above, the guidance provided by the Law Commission in its 2014 report predates the *Butler-Sloss* decision.

29.71 The High Court in *Butler-Sloss* confirmed that its previous decision in *Harries* did not render unlawful the pursuit of ethical investments *provided that* the general law of trusts was complied with. The Court also firmly rejected an absolutist approach to the issue of whether investments conflicted with the objects or purposes of a charitable trust. The decision in *Butler-Sloss* has been supplemented by helpful guidance from the

---

94 ibid para 2.
95 'Mobilising Green Investment' (n 61).
96 *Cowan v Scargill* (n 72); *Harries v Church Commissioners for England* (n 72); *Butler-Sloss & others v Charity Commission for England and Wales* (n 82).

Charity Commission for England and Wales on the general principles[97] and their legal underpinning.[98]

29.72 The claimants in *Butler-Sloss* were the trustees of two charities, the principal purposes of which included environmental protection. These trusts had assets of approximately £42 million and £22 million respectively. The trustees proposed adopting a new investment policy that excluded potential investments that were not aligned with the goals set down in the Paris Climate Agreement for limiting the increase in global temperatures despite the risk of consequent financial detriment to the charity. In particular, Michael Green J observed at [27] that the proposed investment policy would necessarily exclude over half of publicly traded companies and many commercially available investment funds, because of a requirement to be in the top two quartiles of ESG ratings. The claimants sought a declaration as to the proper approach for charity trustees to follow when considering whether to adopt an ethical investment policy, and a declaration that they were permitted to adopt the proposed investment policy and would be acting lawfully in doing so.

29.73 At the outset of his legal analysis, Michael Green J reiterated at [48] that the standard investment criteria that must be considered and followed by trustees in exercising their power of investment are set out in section 4 of the Trustee Act 2000. This forms part of the general law of trusts in England and Wales and requires trustees, *inter alia*, to have regard to the standard investment criteria, which are suitability and diversification. Michael Green J then conducted a helpful survey of *Cowan v Scargill* and *Harries*.

29.74 *Cowan v Scargill* raised the question whether the trustees of the mineworkers pension scheme, half of whom were appointed by the National Union of Mineworkers ('NUM'), including the representative claimant, Mr Arthur Scargill, were acting in breach of their duties in blocking an investment plan which included an increase in overseas investment and investments in energy companies that were in direct competition with coal. It was accepted that such investments would be contrary to the NUM's policy and principles. Sir Robert Megarry V-C concluded in that case that given that the trust was for the provision of financial benefits to individuals, and not for a charitable purpose, the power of investment had to be exercised to yield the best financial return for the beneficiaries. However, he qualified this by adding that there may be non-financial benefits that the beneficiaries of the trusts may wish to obtain even if they might as a result receive lesser financial benefits. For this, however, Sir Robert Megarry V-C considered the consent of the beneficiaries would effectively be required. Michael Green J in *Butler-Sloss* pointed out at [52] that 'In the case of charities, there are no beneficiaries who can give such consent.' This absence of beneficiaries to provide consent

97 Charity Commission, 'Investing Charity Money: A Guide for Trustees' (2023) <https://www.gov.uk/government/publications/charities-and-investment-matters-a-guide-for-trustees-cc14/charities-and-investment-matters-a-guide-for-trustees> accessed 27 September 2024.
98 Charity Commission, 'Charities and Investment Matters: Legal Underpinning' (2023) <https://www.gov.uk/government/publications/charities-and-investment-matters-a-guide-for-trustees-cc14/charities-and-investment-matters-legal-underpinning> accessed 27 September 2024.

for a particular investment policy gave rise to the applications for court declarations in *Harries* and *Butler-Sloss*.

29.75 *Harries* was a factually involved case and contained extensive discussion of the applicable legal principles by Sir Donald Nicholls V-C. For brevity, the focus here is on how the decision in *Harries* has now been interpreted in *Butler-Sloss*. *Harries* concerned reservations in relation to investments by the Church Commissioners. The Church Commissioners already had in place an ethical investment policy that excluded investments in armaments, gambling, tobacco and newspapers. They also had an express policy in relation to investments in South African companies but the claimants considered that it did not go far enough and sought stricter investment criteria. Wide declarations were sought.[99] These were refused by the High Court on the grounds of ambiguity and lack of necessity.

29.76 In *Harries*, Sir Donald Nicholls V-C observed that 'In most cases the best interests of the charity require that the trustees' choice of investments should be made solely on the basis of well-established investment criteria, having taken expert advice where appropriate and having due regard to such *matters as the need to diversify, the need to balance income against capital growth, and the need to balance risk against return.*'[100] To that extent, *Harries* reaffirmed the orthodox investment approach also endorsed in *Cowan v Scargill* previously.

29.77 However, *Harries* has become a prominent case because it also addressed, in obiter dicta, questions as to how charitable trustees should deal with (1) direct conflict with the charity's purposes, (2) indirect conflict with the charity's purposes and (3) moral considerations. These questions are explored at length in *Butler-Sloss* at [58]–[76]. Briefly:

- As to direct conflicts, there was debate in *Butler-Sloss* as to whether the view in *Harries* was that there was an absolute prohibition on investments that directly conflict with the charity's purposes. Michael Green J considered that *Harries* did not go as far as that and, even if it did, that that dictum should not be followed: see at [60]–[61], [69]–[75]. His primary conclusion at [75] was that 'I do not believe that the passage of the Vice-Chancellor's judgment [in *Harries*] should be read as imposing, as a matter of law, an absolute prohibition against directly conflicting investments. It will all depend on the particular facts of the case but the trustees have a discretion in relation to the exercise of their powers of investment and that includes in relation to potential situations of direct conflict.'

- As to indirect conflicts, the view in *Harries* was that this calls for a balancing exercise. Michael Green J in *Butler-Sloss* agreed with this approach and held further that there is no difference in approach between direct and indirect conflict cases: see at [62], [71]–[72].

---

99 Specifically: '(1) that the commissioners ... are obliged to have regard to the object of promoting the Christian faith through the established Church of England; and (2) that in the exercise of those functions ... may not act in a manner which would be incompatible with that object.'
100 *Harries v Church Commissioners for England* (n 72) [1246E–F].

- As to moral considerations, the view in *Harries* was that there is limited scope for taking into account such considerations. Specifically, Sir Donald Nicholls V-C explained at page 1247H: 'Trustees may, if they wish, accommodate the views of those who consider that on moral grounds a particular investment would be in conflict with the objects of the charity, so long as the trustees are satisfied that course would not involve a risk of significant financial detriment.' Michael Green J in *Butler-Sloss* agreed that morality has a limited place in relation to investment decisions, if any: see at [63]–[65].

29.78 As noted above, this part of the decision in *Harries* has proved influential beyond the charitable trusts context and appears to have provided the legal underpinning for the Law Commission's two-stage test in its 2014 report, as discussed above. This illustrates the wider relevance of the *Harries* line of authority, including *Butler-Sloss*.

29.79 Michael Green J's analysis in *Butler-Sloss* concludes with an authoritative summary of the principles at [78] which repays careful reading. It is an important modern statement of English law on investment decisions and the approach to non-financial considerations for charitable trustees, and is of interest beyond that specific context.

29.80 On the facts, Michael Green J concluded that it was appropriate to grant a declaration to the effect that the proposed investment policy was lawful. Notably, in his discussion at [85]–[88], the judge had considerable sympathy with the claimant trustees and recognised the uncertainties surrounding the impact on financial returns of the exclusion of investments on ESG grounds. He was satisfied that they had struck an acceptable balance.

29.81 To comment briefly on the Charity Commission's current guidance,[101] this *inter alia* stresses the general application of the comments in *Butler-Sloss* to charitable trustees and the genesis of these principles in the general law of trusts. In addition, the guidance includes helpful examples of different approaches to investment decisions with net zero nature positive or ESG considerations in mind.[102] As to investments that conflict with a charity's purposes, the guidance states 'Where you identify that an investment (current or planned) could conflict with your charity's purposes or harm its reputation, this is a relevant factor for your decision-making. The law says that it is up to you to decide whether to make or not make the investment, acting in compliance with your trustee duties, and balancing the following: [a] all the factors that are relevant to your charity's circumstances and investment decisions [b] the extent of any potential conflict and how likely and serious it is [c] any potential financial effect of a decision to exclude the investment and how likely and serious this is'.[103] The guidance also reiterated the importance of trustees taking advice and, where appropriate, using the services of investment managers.

---

101 Charity Commission, 'Investing Charity Money: A Guide for Trustees' (n 97).
102 ibid 'Example approaches – financial investments'.
103 ibid 'Investments that conflict with your charity's purpose'.

29.82 Overall, in terms of advancing net zero nature positive goals, English law now seems more open to ESG considerations, including the pursuit of net zero nature positive goals, forming a material part in investment decisions, although trustees remain under the general obligations imposed by trusts law, both statutory and common law.

International parallels

29.83 Across the Atlantic, there is also growing interest in the legal issues arising from net zero nature positive compatible investment decisions. Most recently, there has been a high-profile challenge to the divestment from companies involved in fossil fuel extraction by New York City public pension funds, which is playing out in the New York courts at the time of writing.

29.84 Specifically, in *Wong v New York City Employees' Retirement System* ('*Wong v NYCERS*'),[104] four New York City employees and a non-profit organisation filed a civil complaint against three New York City public employee retirement systems (including the New York City Employees' Retirement System, NYCERS) in the Supreme Court of the State of New York, New York County, in May 2023. It is alleged by the plaintiffs that the defendants breached fiduciary duties owed to them and other pension plan participants and beneficiaries by divesting approximately US$4 billion from companies involved in fossil fuel extraction. The complaint alleges that this divestment was 'a misguided and ineffectual gesture to address climate change' and that '[t]his unlawful decision to elevate unrelated policy goals over the financial health of the Plans is flatly inconsistent with the Defendants' fiduciary responsibilities, and jeopardizes the retirement security of Plan participants and beneficiaries'.[105] The factual allegations include a striking allegation that 'Defendants have willingly cooperated in a plan initiated by former Mayor Bill de Blasio, former Comptroller Scott Stringer, and other City politicians to dragoon Plan assets into an ineffectual, inappropriate campaign to address climate change.'[106] The plaintiffs assert breach of fiduciary duty claims under New York common law and New York insurance regulations. They seek monetary damages, an order requiring the defendants to make the pension plans whole for losses caused by the divestment actions, declaratory relief, injunctive relief, appointment of a monitor to assure compliance, and appointment of an independent fiduciary to make a report on what fossil fuel-related investments should be added to the plans' portfolios.[107]

29.85 The case is at the pre-trial stage and, notably, a jury trial has been demanded. A motion to dismiss was filed by the defendants on 7 August 2023 and the New York court has been briefed on that motion. *Wong v NYCERS* will be watched with great interest by pension trustees and asset managers across the United States and globally.

104 *Wong v New York City Employees' Retirement System* (Case No. 652297/2023).
105 Complaint dated 11 May 2023, *Wong v NYCERS*, para 1, available at: https://climatecasechart.com/wp-content/uploads/case-documents/2023/20230511_docket-6522972023_complaint.pdf, accessed 27 September 2024.
106 ibid [21].
107 ibid [23]–[24].

Challenges to regulated companies and their regulators

29.86 Challenges to regulated companies and their regulators are a further emerging variant of climate finance litigation. The recent *FCA/Ithaca* litigation is a case in point.

29.87 Ithaca Energy plc ('Ithaca') is a British oil and gas company operating in the North Sea. In 2022, it sought to list on the London Stock Exchange. As part of the listing process Ithaca submitted a prospectus for the approval of the FCA. After the FCA had approved and published Ithaca's registration document for listing purposes in mid-October 2022, ClientEarth corresponded with the FCA in relation to alleged deficiencies in Ithaca's prospectus, specifically in relation to the treatment of climate-related financial risks. Despite these contentions, the FCA proceeded to approve Ithaca's final prospectus in November 2022.

29.88 ClientEarth applied for permission for judicial review. Permission was refused on the papers by Sir Ross Cranston, sitting as a High Court judge, on 18 April 2023. ClientEarth renewed its application for judicial review at an oral hearing in the High Court (Administrative Court) pursuant to CPR 54.12. That hearing was held before Lang J and judgment was given on 13 December 2023: *R (ClientEarth) v The Financial Conduct Authority*[108] ('*ClientEarth v FCA*'). Ithaca was represented as an interested party.

29.89 Under Ground 1, ClientEarth argued that the prospectus did not disclose, adequately or at all, Ithaca's assessment of its climate-related financial risks, by reference either to the probability of their occurrence, or the expected magnitude of their negative impact on Ithaca. Instead, it was argued, the prospectus only refers to climate change, the Paris Agreement and the net zero commitment in broad generic terms. ClientEarth submitted this is contrary to Article 16 of Regulation (EU) 2017/1129 (the 'Prospectus Regulation') and the European Securities and Markets Authority 'Guidelines on Risk Factors under the Prospectus Regulation' ('ESMA Guidelines'). More specifically, as to the legal framework, ClientEarth argued that the FCA had erred in two ways. First, in assuming that the obligation to assess materiality under Article 16 is discharged by the process of identifying and presenting risk factors and that there is no obligation for the issuer to describe that assessment on the face of the prospectus. Secondly, that the FCA was wrong in its view that it is for it (i.e. the FCA) to be 'satisfied' under section 87A of the Financial Services and Markets Act 2000 ('FSMA 2000') that the prospectus complies with Article 16 and that its decision can only be challenged on public law grounds.[109]

29.90 Relatedly, under Ground 2, ClientEarth submitted that the prospectus failed adequately to disclose or describe the specificity of the climate-related risks associated with Ithaca's securities in breach of Article 16 and the ESMA Guidelines. The particular criticism levelled against Ithaca's prospectus was that references to the possibility of climate activism negatively impacting the process of obtaining approval for further development and to material adverse effect on the hydrocarbon industry were not

108 *R (ClientEarth) v The Financial Conduct Authority* [2023] EWHC 3301 (Admin).
109 ibid [16]–[17].

sufficiently specific to Ithaca. ClientEarth argued that what is required is a focus on risks to Ithaca's particular situation, rather than the situation of the industry in general.[110]

29.91 Lang J concluded as to Grounds 1–2 that they are both unarguable and have no realistic prospect of success. In particular, Lang J considered that 'Parliament has conferred upon the FCA responsibility for approving a prospectus. Section 87A FSMA 2000 provides that the FCA may not approve a prospectus unless it is satisfied that the prospectus contains the information required by Article 6(1) or 14(2) of the Prospectus Regulation and all of the other requirements imposed by or in accordance with the Prospectus Regulation and the relevant provisions of the FSMA… It follows that the FCA's decision to approve Ithaca's prospectus can only be challenged on public law grounds, i.e. that it has misdirected itself on the meaning of the law it has to apply, or failed to take relevant considerations into account, or made an irrational decision.'[111]

29.92 Moreover, Lang J agreed with the FCA that 'the requirements of Article 16(1) are not hard-edged and whether they have been met requires an evaluative judgment which may admit of more than one view.' As a matter of established public law principles, this meant that 'the court may not substitute its own view if the FCA's assessment is rational'. Lang J not only considered the FCA's analysis of Article 16 of the Prospectus Regulation and of the ESMA Guidelines was rational, but went further in concluding that in particular as to Article 16 it was 'plainly correct'. In particular, Lang J concluded that 'Article 16 requires the disclosure of those risk factors that are material but it does not impose a separate requirement for the issuer to disclose its assessment of risk and materiality' and that '[t]here is no separate requirement in Article 16(1) [nor in the ESMA Guidelines] for the issuer to disclose its assessment of risk and specificity.'[112]

29.93 As to Ground 3, ClientEarth argued that the FCA acted irrationally in concluding that the prospectus complied with Article 6 of the Prospectus Regulation. ClientEarth referred in particular to a technical note by the FCA, TN801.2, which states: 'In order to provide adequate information to the market for this purpose, information on climate change and other ESG-related matters may need to be provided where relevant to the issuer. For instance, in the context of the UK government's target to achieve net-zero carbon emissions by 2050 and to achieve the goals of the Paris Agreement more generally, many companies are likely to need to consider significant changes to their business. Such changes may be material to an investor's assessment of the prospect of the company and the risks and opportunities shaping it.' According to ClientEarth, Ithaca was in a comparable position to the companies referred to in this technical note and had failed, in its prospectus, to deal adequately with the potential impacts of the Paris Agreement.[113]

29.94 Lang J gave short shrift to this ground for judicial review. She concluded that it was unarguable and had no realistic prospect of success. In particular because (1) 'the

110 ibid [16]–[17].
111 ibid [20]–[21].
112 ibid [22]–[26].
113 ibid [27].

Paris Agreement was identified as a material risk for the business in the prospectus' and ClientEarth and Ithaca had 'presented competing arguments as to its compatibility with the Paris Agreement and the difference of view was referenced in the prospectus' and (2) ClientEarth did not come close to demonstrating that the FCA had acted irrationally in concluding that the prospectus complied with Article 6, this being a 'high hurdle'.[114]

29.95 While this attempted judicial review failed, it represents a creative use of financial services regulations and established public law principles to target a significant player in the UK oil and gas industry. Importantly, the High Court's judgment should not be regarded as shutting the door on any challenge in the capital markets context. Ultimately, ClientEarth was seeking to second-guess the FCA's assessment, as an experienced and expert regulator, of Ithaca's prospectus. That was a tall order, and is likely to be in most cases. However, the mere prospect of scrutiny by way of judicial review, which might be supplemented by other types of claims against the share issuer directly (such as under section 90A FSMA 2000 for misrepresentation) or against the directors (under section 172 of the Companies Act 2006 in respect of the duty to promote the success of the company),[115] could materially affect the actions of companies in relation to their net zero nature positive policies post-*ClientEarth v FCA*.

29.96 Moreover, the nexus between net zero nature positive goals and financial services regulation is now even clearer in light of FSMA 2023. As discussed in Chapter 4,[116] the FCA must now *inter alia* have regard to the regulatory principles in section 3B FSMA 2000. Those regulatory principles were amended by FSMA 2023 to include at section 3B(1)(c) '[T]he need to contribute towards achieving compliance by the Secretary of State with section 1 of the Climate Change Act 2008 (UK net zero emissions target) and section 5 of the Environment Act 2021 (environmental targets) where each regulator considers the exercise of its functions to be relevant to the making of such a contribution.' While the Hansard debates discussed at paragraph 4.63–4.64 make clear that this regulatory principle is not intended to take priority over the FCA's core (and traditional) functions of protecting the integrity of the financial markets, the safety and soundness of firms within the financial system and consumers, it is no doubt a reflection of the growing importance of environmental targets in the UK that FSMA 2023 has expressly introduced such a requirement on the regulator.

29.97 While it remains for the FCA to decide how best to meet these environmental targets, it is to be expected that greater consideration will be given by the FCA and regulated persons to the environmental targets contained in the Climate Change Act 2008, Environment Act 2021 and other applicable legislation. The amendment to the UK's flagship financial services legislation at this time also underscores the growing importance of climate policy in all areas of commerce, including the financial services industry, which is, of course, a mainstay of the UK's economy.

114 ibid [28]–[29].
115 See, e.g., the paper delivered by Lord Sales, 'Directors' Duties and Climate Change: Keeping Pace with Environmental Challenges' (2019) <https://www.supremecourt.uk/docs/speech-190827.pdf> accessed 27 September 2024.
116 Specifically, at paras 4.58–4.66.

CHAPTER 30

ESG, DISCLOSURE AND REPORTING

David Hopkins

The role of ESG, disclosure, and reporting in achieving net zero and nature positive targets, and policy development

30.01 ESG stands for Environmental, Social and Governance. Companies are increasingly expected to report against these three criteria: the environmental impact of operations and products; the social impact of labour practices, supply chain management and products; and corporate governance practices including board room diversity, executive compensation, and shareholder rights.

30.02 Underpinning the increasing importance of ESG is the hypothesis that regulatory and corporate focus on these matters promotes better markets and better companies. Better markets because the sustainable development of the global economy should promote stable and predictable markets. Better companies because companies that properly manage ESG risks may, as a result, derive a competitive advantage.

30.03 By focusing on transparency and reporting, regulators have tried to create ESG frameworks that are fundamentally market-led: if companies whose environmental, social and corporate governance is superior to others provide better returns in the long run, investors will prefer those companies; thus investors are incentivised to endeavour to identify those companies; and those who entrust their money to others to invest will prefer investors who choose those companies, since they provide better returns. In turn, companies should be required to make ESG disclosures to improve investors' decision-making and are incentivised to improve their environmental, social and corporate governance, as doing so makes them more attractive to investors.

30.04 With increased policy focus on achieving net zero and nature positive, investors are increasingly demanding that companies produce ESG plans, and make environmental disclosures, which demonstrate they are on a path to net-zero carbon emissions. This makes ESG, disclosure, and reporting key tools in achieving the goal of net zero and nature positive across the economy and society at large.

Environmental, social and governance

30.05 The UN Global Compact describes itself as 'the world's largest corporate sustainability initiative'[1] and espouses ten principles derived from the Universal Declaration of

1 'What Is the UN Global Compact | UN Global Compact' <https://unglobalcompact.org/what-is-gc> accessed 19 April 2024.

Human Rights and other documents, under the headings of Human Rights, Labour, Environment and Anti-Corruption.[2] It was launched in July 2000 by then UN Secretary-General Kofi Annan.[3] Membership of the compact is voluntary and 'open to any company that is serious about its commitment to work towards implementation of the UN Global Compact principles', save for companies who meet the exclusionary criteria.[4]

30.06 In January 2004, Secretary-General Annan wrote to the CEOs of 55 financial institutions inviting them to join an initiative under the UN Global Compact's auspices to: 'develop guidelines and recommendations on how to better integrate environmental, social and governance issues in asset management, securities brokerage services and associated research functions.'[5] Between March 2004 and May 2004, 18 financial institutions participated in a working group.[6] The results of their work were published in July 2004 in a report titled 'Who Cares Wins: Connecting Financial Markets to a Changing World' ('*Who Cares Wins*').[7] *Who Cares Wins* has been described as having 'laid the foundations of environmental, social and governance investing ... based on the principle that better investment leads to more sustainable societies'.[8] The report states:[9]

> Ultimately, successful investment depends on a vibrant economy, which depends on a healthy civil society, which is ultimately dependent on a sustainable planet. In the long-term, therefore, investment markets have a clear self-interest in contributing to better management of environmental and social impacts in a way that contributes to the sustainable development of global society. A better inclusion of environmental, social and corporate governance (ESG) factors in investment decisions will ultimately contribute to more stable and predictable markets, which is in the interest of all market actors.

30.07 *Who Cares Wins* makes 25 recommendations, including:[10]

> a. We are convinced that it is in the interest of investors, asset managers and securities brokerage houses alike to improve the integration of ESG factors in financial analysis. This will contribute to better investment markets as well as to the sustainable development of the planet.

2 'The Ten Principles | UN Global Compact' <https://unglobalcompact.org/what-is-gc/mission/principles> accessed 19 April 2024.
3 The Global Compact, 'Who Cares Wins' (2004) viii <https://www.unepfi.org/fileadmin/events/2004/stocks/who_cares_wins_global_compact_2004.pdf> accessed 19 April 2024.
4 Excluded companies are those who: are subject to a UN sanction; are listed on the UN Ineligible Vendors List for ethical reasons; derive revenue from the production, sale and/or transfer of antipersonnel landmines or cluster bombs; or derive revenue from the production and/or manufacture of tobacco. See <https://unglobalcompact.org/about/faq> accessed 19 April 2024.
5 The Global Compact, 'Who Cares Wins' (n 3) page vii.
6 ibid page x.
7 ibid page x.
8 Gillian Lofts, 'Who Cares Wins in the Brave World of ESG' *Financial Times* (2018) <https://www.ft.com/content/64ce9225-0c55-3256-967c-5fae6622c637> accessed 19 April 2024.
9 The Global Compact, 'Who Cares Wins' (n 3) 3.
10 ibid 5, 10, 22.

b. We invite all financial market actors, including investors, asset managers, analysts, financial advisers and consultants to improve their understanding and consideration of these trends and related potential impacts. This will not be possible without adequate disclosure on these matters by companies.

…

e. We call on financial analysts to take an active role in testing and refining the investment rationale for ESG integration in research and investment decisions. We invite analysts not only to focus on ESG risks and risk management, but also to consider ESG issues as a potential source of competitive advantage.

…

g. We encourage pension fund trustees and their selection consultants to consider integrating ESG issues into the formulation of investment mandates and the selection of investment managers, taking into account their fiduciary obligations to participants and beneficiaries. We believe that governments and multilateral agencies should proactively consider the investment of their pension funds according to the principles of sustainable development, taking into account their fiduciary obligations to participants and beneficiaries.

Climate-Related Financial Disclosures

30.08 In 2015, G20 finance ministers and central bank governors asked the Financial Stability Board ('FSB') to review how the financial sector could take account of climate-related issues. The FSB identified a need for better information to support investment, lending, and insurance underwriting decisions. It established the Task Force on Climate-Related Financial Disclosures ('TCFD'), chaired by Michael Bloomberg, to help identify the information needed by investors, lenders, and insurers to appropriately assess and price climate-related risks and opportunities.[11]

30.09 The TCFD published its final report, 'Recommendations of the Task Force on Climate-Related Financial Disclosures' in June 2017 ('TCFD Final Report'). The report includes, in particular, four recommendations and eleven recommended disclosures[12] (the 'TCFD Recommendations and Recommended Disclosures'). The TCFD Final Report states the recommendations are structured around four thematic areas that represent core elements of how organisations operate – governance, strategy, risk management, and metrics and targets – and are supported by the eleven key recommended climate-related financial disclosures. The TCFD's intention is that these disclosures will help investors and others understand how reporting organisations think about and assess climate-related risks and opportunities.

11 'About | Task Force on Climate-Related Financial Disclosures (TCFD)' (Task Force on Climate-Related Financial Disclosures) <https://www.fsb-tcfd.org/about/> accessed 19 April 2024.
12 At Section C, Figure 4 and quoted in the text herein.

30.10 The TCFD Recommendations and Recommended Disclosures are:

Governance	Strategy	Risk management	Metrics and targets
Disclose the organization's governance around climate-related risks and opportunities.	Disclose the actual and potential impacts of climate-related risks and opportunities on the organization's businesses, strategy, and financial planning where such information is material.	Disclose how the organization identifies, assesses, and manages climate-related risks.	Disclose the metrics and targets used to assess and manage relevant climate-related risks and opportunities where such information is material.
Recommended disclosures	**Recommended disclosures**	**Recommended disclosures**	**Recommended disclosures**
(a) Describe the board's oversight of climate-related risks and opportunities.	(a) Describe the (climate-related risks and opportunities the organization has identified over the short, medium, and long term.	(a) Describe the organization's processes for identifying and assessing climate-related risks.	(a) Disclose the metrics used by the organization to assess climate-related risks and opportunities in line with its strategy and risk management process.
(b) Describe management's role in assessing and managing climate-related risks and opportunities.	(b) Describe the impact of climate-related risks and opportunities on the organization's businesses, strategy, and financial planning.	(b) Describe the organization's processes for managing climate-related risks.	(b) Disclose Scope 1, Scope 2, and, if appropriate, Scope 3 greenhouse gas (GHG) emissions, and the related risks.
	(c) Describe the resilience of the organization's strategy, taking into consideration different climate-related scenarios, including a 2°C or lower scenario.	(c) Describe how processes for identifying, assessing, and managing climate-related risks are integrated into the organization's overall risk management.	(c) Describe the targets used by the organization to manage climate-related risks and opportunities and performance against targets.

30.11 The TCFD Final Report contains guidance on how organisations can develop climate-related financial disclosures consistent with the TCFD Recommendations and Recommended Disclosures. In addition, TCFD issued supplemental guidance for the financial sector and supplemental guidance for non-financial industries. Reference should also be made to the TCFD's 2021 Annex 'Implementing the Recommendations of the Task Force on Climate-Related Financial Disclosures', which updated and superseded the guidance issued in 2017. All of TCFD's publications are available at: <https://www.fsb-tcfd.org/publications/>.

30.12 In October 2023, the FSB announced that the TCFD had fulfilled its remit and was disbanded. The FSB asked the International Financial Reporting Standards Foundation ('IFRS') to take over the monitoring of the progress of companies' climate-related disclosures. Prior to this, on 3 November 2021, the IFRS's trustees had announced the formation of the International Sustainability Standards Board ('ISSB') at COP 26 in Glasgow.

30.13 The IFRS stated[13] that the ISSB was 'developing—in the public interest—standards that will result in a high-quality, comprehensive global baseline of sustainability disclosures focused on the needs of investors and the financial markets' and that the ISSB's four key objectives are:

1. to develop standards for a global baseline of sustainability disclosures;
2. to meet the information needs of investors;
3. to enable companies to provide comprehensive sustainability information to global capital markets; and
4. to facilitate interoperability with disclosures that are jurisdiction-specific and/or aimed at broader stakeholder groups.

30.14 The ISSB published its first two IFRS Sustainability Disclosure Standards on 26 June 2023:

- IFRS S1 General Requirements for Disclosure of Sustainability-Related Financial Information, effective for annual reporting periods beginning on or after 1 January 2024 with earlier application permitted as long as IFRS S2 is also applied;[14] and
- IFRS S2 Climate-related Disclosures, effective for annual reporting periods beginning on or after 1 January 2024 with earlier application permitted as long as IFRS S1 is also applied.[15]

30.15 IFRS S1 and S2 both require an entity to disclose information that could reasonably be expected to affect the entity's cash flows, its access to finance or cost of capital over the short, medium or long term. IFRS S1 requires disclosure of such information about sustainability-related risks and opportunities, while IFRS S2 requires disclosure of such information about climate-related risks and opportunities.

30.16 IFRS has stated:[16]

> Companies applying IFRS S1 General Requirements for Disclosure of Sustainability-Related Financial Information and IFRS S2 Climate-Related Disclosures will meet the TCFD recommendations as the recommendations are fully incorporated into the ISSB's Standards.

---

13 'IFRS – International Sustainability Standards Board' <https://www.ifrs.org/groups/international-sustainability-standards-board/#about> accessed 19 April 2024.
14 'IFRS – IFRS S1 General Requirements for Disclosure of Sustainability-Related Financial Information' <https://www.ifrs.org/issued-standards/ifrs-sustainability-standards-navigator/ifrs-s1-general-requirements/> accessed 19 April 2024.
15 'IFRS – IFRS S2 Climate-Related Disclosures' <https://www.ifrs.org/issued-standards/ifrs-sustainability-standards-navigator/ifrs-s2-climate-related-disclosures/> accessed 19 April 2024.
16 'IFRS – ISSB and TCFD' <https://www.ifrs.org/sustainability/tcfd/> accessed 19 April 2024.

> Companies can continue to use the TCFD recommendations should they choose to do so, and some companies may still be required to use the TCFD recommendations. Using the recommendations is a good entry point for companies as they move to use the ISSB's Standards.

30.17 The 'Core Content' of each of IFRS S1 and S2 is structured around the same four themes as in the TCFD Recommendations and Recommended Disclosures, namely: governance, strategy, risk management, and metrics and targets. However, IFRS S1 and S2 do not use wording which is identical to the TCFD Recommendations and Recommended Disclosures. For example, the requirements in IFRS S2 for disclosure of information about climate resilience[17] do not expressly refer to consideration of 'a 2°C or lower scenario'. IFRS has published a comparison between the TCFD Recommendations and Recommended Disclosures and IFRS S2.[18]

National law and policy

(i) *Environmental, social and governance*

30.18 In the UK, ESG policy has been implemented (in terms of requiring persons actively to take steps with respect to ESG) mostly in pensions legislation. One reason for this is likely that, although they are not themselves policy developers, legislators or regulators, pension funds have a powerful impact on companies' behaviour due to the vast sums they invest. The requirements for entities other than pensions funds are better characterised as requirements to make disclosures and reports (the rationale for such disclosures being to aid investors' decision-making). These requirements are dealt with in the following subsection.

30.19 In England, Wales and Scotland, the Occupational Pension Schemes (Investment) Regulations[19] enacted the year after *Who Cares Wins*, included requirements for pension schemes in relation to social and environmental considerations. Regulation 2(3)(b)(vi), as originally enacted, provided that the statement of investment principles prepared for a trust scheme under Pensions Act 1995 section 35, must cover, among other matters, the extent (if at all) to which social, environmental or ethical considerations are taken into account in the selection, retention and realisation of investments.

30.20 However, this initial implementation of ESG requirements for pension schemes was not without flaws. In its 2014 report on Fiduciary Duties of Investment Intermediaries,[20] the Law Commission found from responses to its consultation that 'the reference to ethical factors alongside social and environmental factors is a major source of confusion for trustees because it leads to the conflation of ESG with ethics'.[21]

---

17 IFRS S2 para 22 and Annex B to IFRS S2 paras B1–B18.
18 IFRS, 'Comparison: IFRS S2 Climate-Related Disclosures with the TCFD Recommendations' (2023) <https://www.ifrs.org/content/dam/ifrs/supporting-implementation/ifrs-s2/ifrs-s2-comparison-tcfd-july2023.pdf> accessed 19 April 2024.
19 SI 2005/3378.
20 Law Commission, *Fiduciary Duties of Investment Intermediaries* (Law Com No 350, 2014).
21 ibid para 7.80.

30.21 The Commission recommended that the government should review 'the reference to "social, environmental or ethical considerations" in regulation 2(3)(b)(vii) [sic], to ensure that it accurately reflects the distinction between financial factors and non-financial factors'.[22] The government implemented this recommendation in the Pension Protection Fund (Pensionable Service) and Occupational Pension Schemes (Investment and Disclosure) (Amendment and Modification) Regulations 2018,[23] which amends Occupational Regulation 2 of the Pension Schemes (Investment) Regulations. Regulation 2, as amended, provides:

> (1) The trustees of a trust scheme must secure that the statement of investment principles prepared for the scheme under section 35 of the [Pensions Act 1995] is reviewed—
>
> (a) at least every three years; and
> (b) without delay after any significant change in investment policy.
>
> …
>
> (3) A statement of investment principles must be in writing and must cover at least the following matters—
>
> …
> (b) [the trustees'] policies in relation to—
> …
>
> (vi) financially material considerations over the appropriate time horizon of the investments, including how those considerations are taken into account in the selection, retention and realisation of investments; and
> (vii) the extent (if at all) to which non-financial matters are taken into account in the selection, retention and realisation of investments;
>
> …
>
> (4) For the purposes of this regulation—
>
> …
> 'financially material considerations' includes (but is not limited to) environmental, social and governance considerations (including but not limited to climate change), which the trustees of the trust scheme consider financially material;
> 'non-financial matters' means the views of the members and beneficiaries including (but not limited to) their ethical views and their views in relation to social and environmental impact and present and future quality of life of the members and beneficiaries of the trust scheme;

22 ibid para 7.94(2).
23 SI 2018/988, reg 4.

30.22 Thus, a pension scheme's statement of investment principles must cover:

- ESG considerations, including how those considerations are taken into account in the selection, retention and realisation of investments, but only if the trustees consider those ESG considerations financially material; and
- the extent (if at all) to which the views of members and beneficiaries in relation to social and environmental impact are taken into account in the selection, retention and realisation of investments.

(ii) *Disclosure and reporting*

30.23 Companies Act 2006 section 414A(1) provides that the directors of a company must prepare a strategic report for each financial year of the company. However, that requirement does not apply if the company is entitled to the small companies exemption: Companies Act 2006 section 414A(2).[24] Companies Act 2006 section 414C(1) provides that the purpose of the strategic report is to inform members of the company[25] and help them assess how the directors have performed their duty under Companies Act 2006 section 172 (the duty to promote the success of the company).

30.24 Companies Act 2006 section 414C(7)(b) provides that, in the case of a quoted company, the strategic report must, to the extent necessary for an understanding of the development, performance or position of the company's business, include information about:

(i) environmental matters (including the impact of the company's business on the environment),

(ii) the company's employees, and

(iii) social, community and human rights issues,
including information about any policies of the company in relation to those matters and the effectiveness of those policies.

30.25 Quoted companies are thus required to make ESG disclosures, albeit only to the extent necessary for an understanding of the development, performance or position of their business. The proviso to Companies Act 2006 section 414C(7) provides that if the report does not contain information of each kind mentioned in paragraphs (b)(i), (ii) and (iii), it must state which of those kinds of information it does not contain.

30.26 The Companies (Strategic Report) (Climate-Related Financial Disclosure) Regulations 2022[26] were introduced to compel some of those companies which are required

---

24 In turn, s 414B provides: 'A company is entitled to the small companies exemption in relation to the strategic report for a financial year if— (a) it is entitled to prepare accounts for the year in accordance with the small companies regime, or (b) it would be so entitled but for being or having been a member of an ineligible group.'
25 In the case of a company with share capital, that is, its shareholders.
26 SI 2022/31.

to provide a strategic report to provide climate-related financial disclosures therein. The Regulations apply in respect of any financial year of a company which commences on or after 6 April 2022: Regulation 1(2). Regulation 5 provides, among other things:

- The Secretary of State must from time to time carry out a review of the regulatory provision contained in the Regulations and publish a report setting out the conclusions of the review.

- The first such report must be published before 6 April 2027 and subsequent reports must be published at intervals not exceeding five years.

30.27 The substance of the Regulations is the amendments made to Companies Act 2006 sections 414C, 414CA and 414CB by Regulations 2–4. Those amendments include:

- Section 414CA(A1), as amended, provides: 'A strategic report of a company to which this subsection applies must include a non-financial and sustainability information statement'; and

- Section 414CB(A1), as amended, provides: 'The non-financial and sustainability information statement must contain the climate-related financial disclosures of the company'.

30.28 Companies Act 2006 section 414CB(2A) defines 'climate-related financial disclosures'. The definition is broadly consistent with the TCFD Recommendations and Recommended Disclosures (see above).

30.29 The types of companies required to provide climate-related financial disclosures by virtue of Companies Act 2006 sections 414CA(A1) and 414CB(A1) are summarised in the explanatory notes to the Regulations as follows:

> The requirement applies to a traded company, a banking company, an authorised insurance company and a company carrying on insurance business which in each case satisfy various conditions, including that of having more than 500 employees. The companies are listed in section 414CA(1) of the Companies Act 2006 and the requirement for more than 500 employees is set out in section 414CA(4) as applied by section 414CA(1B). In addition, these Regulations require two further types of company, with more than 500 employees, to make climate-related financial disclosures. These are a company which has securities admitted to trading on the Alternative Investment Market and a high turnover company which is a company which does not fall within another category but which has a turnover of more than £500 million (see regulation 3).

30.30 See also, below, the climate-related financial disclosures required by the Listing Rules of the Financial Conduct Authority ('FCA'). The requirements in Companies Act 2006 do not apply to all companies covered by the FCA's Listing Rules: for example, a company whose shares are listed, but which has fewer than 500 employees. Similarly, the requirements in the FCA's Listing Rules do not apply to all companies covered by the Companies Act 2006: for example, a company with more than 500 employees which is a traded company because its shares are admitted to trading on an EU regulated market (see Companies Act 2006 section 360C).

(iii) *Transition plans*

30.31 At COP 26, the UK government announced its intention for the UK to become the world's first net zero-aligned financial centre and that it would launch a Transition Plan Taskforce ('TPT') with a mission to produce a gold standard Disclosure Framework for transition plans. In March 2023, the government published its 2023 Green Finance Strategy, 'Mobilising Green Investment'.[27] It stated that the 'Government commits to consulting on the introduction of requirements for the UK's largest companies to disclose their transition plans if they have them' and that the consultation would take place following the finalisation of the TPT's Disclosure Framework.[28]

30.32 The TPT issued its Disclosure Framework[29] and supporting guidance on 9 October 2023. In the introduction to the Disclosure Framework, the TPT states:

> The world urgently needs to make an orderly transition to a low-greenhouse gas (GHG) and climate-resilient economy. One that captures opportunities, while safeguarding the natural environment. And one that is as fair and inclusive as possible to everyone, creating decent work opportunities and leaving no-one behind.
>
> To meet this challenge a fundamental transformation in business and finance is required.
>
> **The role of transition planning and transition plans**
>
> Transition planning and the disclosure of transition plans are core to this transformation. A robust approach to transition planning provides a blueprint for strategic delivery. Disclosure of transition plans can equip investors with the information they need to finance the transition at the speed and scale required.

30.33 The 'guiding principles' of the Disclosure Framework are 'Ambition, Action and Accountability'.[30] The TPT recommends that:

> in setting its Strategic Ambition and designing its transition plan, an entity take a 'strategic and rounded' approach. ... That is, the entity should consider the actions that it can take now to capture opportunities, minimise future risks and protect and enhance its long-term value. Applying a strategic mindset, the entity can also design its transition plan in a way that will protect and enhance long-term value for the stakeholders, society, economy and natural environment on which it depends.

---

27 'Mobilising Green Investment' (2023) <https://assets.publishing.service.gov.uk/media/643583fb877741001368d815/mobilising-green-investment-2023-green-finance-strategy.pdf> accessed 1 March 2024.
28 ibid 10.a.
29 Transition Plan Taskforce, 'Disclosure Framework' (2023) <https://transitiontaskforce.net/wp-content/uploads/2023/10/TPT_Disclosure-framework-2023.pdf>.
30 ibid s 2.2.

30.34 'Strategic Ambition' is defined as:[31]

> An entity's overarching aims for its transition plan. This will comprise the entity's objectives and priorities for responding and contributing to the transition towards a low-GHG emissions, climate-resilient economy, and set out whether and how it is pursuing these objectives and priorities in a manner that captures opportunities, avoids adverse impacts for stakeholders and society, and safeguards the natural environment.

30.35 The Disclosure Framework identifies five key elements of a good practice transition plan:[32]

- Foundations: 'An entity shall disclose the Strategic Ambition of its plan';
- Implementation strategy: 'An entity shall disclose the actions it is taking within its business operations, products and services, and policies and conditions to achieve its Strategic Ambition';
- Engagement strategy: 'An entity shall disclose how it is engaging with its value chain, industry peers, government, public sector, communities, and civil society in order to achieve its Strategic Ambition';
- Metrics and targets: 'An entity shall disclose the metrics and targes that it is using to drive and monitor progress towards its Strategic Ambition'; and
- Governance: 'An entity shall disclose how it is embedding its transition plan within its governance structures and organisational arrangements in order to achieve the Strategic Ambition of its transition plan'.

30.36 The TPT's Disclosure Framework breaks these elements down into 19 sub-elements, each of which is supported by a series of Disclosure Recommendations. The TPT states that its Disclosure Recommendations 'are designed to be consistent with, and build on, the wider climate-related disclosure requirements in the ISSB Standards [that is, IFRS S1 and S2]'.[33]

FCA rules and guidance

(i) *Environmental, social and governance*

30.37 In November 2023, the FCA issued its Policy Statement PS23/16, 'Sustainability Disclosure Requirements (SDR) and investment labels'.[34] The policy statement,

31 ibid Glossary, p 44.
32 ibid s 4.
33 ibid Appendix 1.
34 Financial Conduct Authority, 'Sustainability Disclosure Requirements (SDR) and Investment Labels' (2023) PS23/16 <https://www.fca.org.uk/publication/policy/ps23-16.pdf> accessed 1 March 2024.

following Consultation Paper CP22/20,[35] announced the FCA's rules and guidance aimed 'to improve trust and transparency to the market for sustainable investment products'.[36] The FCA stated:[37]

> 1.5 We have been concerned that some firms may be making misleading or exaggerated sustainability-related claims about their investment products.
>
> 1.6 So we are introducing a package of measures which aim to inform and protect consumers and improve trust in the market for sustainable investments. The regime should help underpin the UK's position as a world-leading competitive centre for asset management and sustainable finance.
>
> 1.7 The measures include an anti-greenwashing rule for all authorised firms, 4 investment labels, and new rules and guidance for firms marketing investment funds on the basis of their sustainability characteristics.

30.38 Those rules and guidance are contained in various parts of the FCA Handbook, including the Environmental, Social and Governance sourcebook ('FCA ESG'). FCA ESG rules apply only to a firm within the meaning of the FCA Handbook, that is, in this context, an authorised person.[38] An authorised person is a person who: has a Financial Services and Markets Act 2000 ('FSMA') Part 4A permission to carry on one or more regulated activities; is an investment company with variable capital; or is the Society of Lloyd's.[39] It does not apply, for example, to a company which is not an authorised person but whose shares are listed on the London Stock Exchange (although the disclosure and reporting requirements in the FCA Listing Rules do: see below).

30.39 Not all parts of FCA ESG apply to all authorised persons:

- The specific application of the rules and guidance in FCA ESG 2, FCA ESG 4 and FCA ESG 5 is set out in FCA ESG 1A and FCA ESG 3.
- The table at FCA ESG 1.2.4G(2) provides a general overview as to how the rules in FCA ESG 2, FCA ESG 4 and FCA ESG 5 apply to firms.
- The climate-related disclosure requirements in FCA ESG 2 apply only to firms of the types listed in Column 1 of the table under FCA ESG 1A.1.1R(2), that is, asset managers (such as managers of UK UCITS) and asset owners (such as insurers and pensions schemes). FCA ESG 1A.1.2R provides that a firm is exempt from the disclosure requirements under FCA ESG 2 if and for as long as

35 Financial Conduct Authority, 'Sustainability Disclosure Requirements (SDR) and Investment Labels' (2022) CP22/20 <https://www.fca.org.uk/publication/consultation/cp22-20.pdf> accessed 1 March 2024.
36 Financial Conduct Authority, 'Sustainability Disclosure Requirements (SDR) and Investment Labels' (n 34) para 1.1.
37 ibid para 1.5–1.7.
38 Financial Conduct Authority, 'Glossary of Definitions' (2023). FCA Handbook, Glossary, Release 32, December 2023 ('FCA Glossary').
39 FCA Glossary (n 38).

the assets under administration or management in relation to its TCFD in-scope business[40] amount to less than £5 billion calculated as a 3-year rolling average on an annual assessment.

30.40 However, FCA ESG 4.1.1R(1) and 4.3.1R apply to all firms: see FCA ESG 3.1.2R(1).

30.41 FCA ESG 4.1.1R(1), the sustainability labelling rule, provides:

(1) Subject to ESG 4.1.1R(2), a firm must not make use of the following sustainability labels:
'Sustainability focus';
'Sustainability improvers';
'Sustainability impact'; or
'Sustainability mixed goals'.

(2) A manager may, from 31 July 2024, make use of a sustainability label in ESG 4.1.1R(1) where the manager is undertaking sustainability in-scope business[[41]] in relation to a sustainability product[[42]]:

(a) that is not a feeder fund if it satisfies the requirements set out in ESG 4.2; or
(b) that is a feeder fund if it satisfies the requirements in ESG 4.1.2R.

30.42 See Chapter 29 for further detail on sustainable finance and the role of finance in achieving Net Zero Nature Positive more generally.

30.43 FCA ESG 4.3.1R (in force from 31 May 2024), the anti-greenwashing rule, provides:

(1) This rule applies to a firm (whether it is undertaking sustainability in-scope business or not) which:

(a) communicates with a client in the United Kingdom in relation to a product or service; or
(b) communicates a financial promotion to, or approves a financial promotion for communication to, a person in the United Kingdom.

---

40 That is, the following activities, as set out in more detail in FCA ESG 1A.1.1R(2): (1) portfolio management; (2) managing a UK UCITS; (3) managing an AIF; (4) providing insurance-based investment products; (5) operating a personal pension scheme (excluding a SIPP) or stakeholder pension scheme; and (6) operating a SIPP, but only in relation to SIPPs which contain an insurance-based investment product, a unit, an interest in a closed-ended investment fund or a pre-set investment portfolio provided by the firm: FCA Glossary (n 38).
41 FCA Glossary (n 38): 'the following activities, as set out in more detail in ESG 3.1.2R: (1) managing a UK UCITS; and (2) managing an AIF which is a UK AIF.'
42 FCA Glossary (n 38): 'any of the following: (1) an authorised fund, including, where the authorised fund is an umbrella scheme, each sub-fund of the umbrella; or (2) an unauthorised AIF that is a managed by a full-scope UK AIFM or a small authorised UK AIFM, unless it is: (a) a non-UK AIF; (b) a closed-ended AIF that makes no additional investments after 22 July 2013 …; (c) a [qualifying social entrepreneurship fund (as defined in the SEF Regulation)]; or (d) [a qualifying venture capital fund (as defined in the RVECA Regulation)].'

(2) A firm must ensure that any reference to the sustainability characteristics of a product or service is:
consistent with the sustainability characteristics of the product or service; and
fair, clear and not misleading.

30.44 On 23 April 2024, following consultation, the FCA published FG24/3, 'Finalised non-handbook guidance on the Anti-Greenwashing Rule'.[43] Paragraph 2.17 of FG24/3 states:

> In practice, the effect of the anti-greenwashing rule and the other rules mentioned above mean the following:
> Sustainability references should be:
>
> - Correct and capable of being substantiated
> - Clear and presented in a way that can be understood
> - Complete – they should not omit or hide important information and should consider the full life cycle of the product or service
> - Comparisons to other products or services are fair and meaningful

30.45 The reader is referred to the full guidance set out in FG24/3 which includes, among other things, examples to help firms understand what the core principles of the guidance mean in practice.

(ii) *Disclosure and reporting*

30.46 The group accounts of a parent company whose securities are, on its balance sheet date, admitted to trading on a UK regulated market must be prepared in accordance with UK-adopted international accounting standards (that is, IFRS standards as adopted by the UK): Companies Act 2006 section 403(1).[44] For now, however, in respect of climate-related financial reporting, the FCA Listing Rules ('LR') continue to require companies whose shares are listed[45] to use the TCFD Recommendations and Recommended Disclosures in their annual financial reports rather than IFRS S1 and S2 (see further above).

30.47 In August 2023, the FCA stated:[46]

> We expect to consult in the first half of 2024 on proposals to implement disclosure rules referencing UK-endorsed IFRS S1 and IFRS S2 for listed companies. We'll take into

---

43 <https://www.fca.org.uk/publication/finalised-guidance/fg24-3.pdf> accessed 24 April 2024.
44 See also the International Accounting Standards and European Public Limited-Liability Company (Amendment etc.) (EU Exit) Regulations 2019, SI 2019/685.
45 For the purposes of LR, a listed company is a company that has any class of its securities listed, that is, a company that has any class of its securities admitted to the official list maintained by the FCA in accordance with s 74(1) of the Financial Services and Markets Act 2000 ('FSMA') for the purposes of Part VI of FSMA: FCA Glossary (n 38). However, the climate-related financial disclosure rules in LR apply only to companies whose shares, or certificates representing those shares, are listed.
46 'Primary Market Bulletin 45' (FCA, 3 August 2023) <https://www.fca.org.uk/publications/newsletters/primary-market-bulletin-45> accessed 19 April 2024.

account inputs to the Government's endorsement process and our own cost-benefit analysis. Assuming the Government's endorsement process is completed in the timeframe envisaged, our aim is to finalise our policy position by the end of 2024, with a view to bring new requirements into force for accounting periods beginning on or after 1 January 2025. The first reporting would begin from 2026.

30.48 LR 9.8.6R(8)(a) and (c) provide that a listed company incorporated in the United Kingdom with a premium listing[47] must state, in its annual financial report, whether the company has included in its annual financial report climate-related financial disclosures consistent with the TCFD Recommendations and Recommended Disclosures (see above) and where in the report those climate-related financial disclosures can be found.

30.49 Where the company has:

- made such disclosures other than in the annual financial report, it must include in the annual financial report a statement setting out: (A) which recommendations and/or recommended disclosures are not included in the report; (B) a description of the other document in which those disclosure can be found; and (C) the reasons for not including the disclosures in the annual financial report: LR 9.8.6R(8)(b)(i); and

- not made such disclosures either in the annual financial report or elsewhere, it must include in the annual financial report a statement setting out: (A) which recommendations and/or recommended disclosures are not included in the report or elsewhere; (B) the reasons for not including the disclosures; and (C) any steps it is taking or plans to take in order to be able to make those disclosures in the future, and the timeframe within which it expects to be able to make those disclosures: LR 9.8.6R(8)(b)(ii).

30.50 LR 14.3.27R makes the same provisions for listed companies (other than investment entities and shell companies) which have a standard listing of their shares.[48]

30.51 See also, at paragraphs 30.23–30.30 above, the climate-related financial disclosures required by the Companies Act 2006. Practitioners are advised to note well the not entirely overlapping domains of the two regimes.

Issues in practice: Greenwashing, green hushing and green bleaching

30.52 'Greenwashing' is likely to be the term most familiar to the reader. Examples of greenwashing are set out in paragraph 32.51 below. See also the FCA's anti-greenwashing rule and associated guidance at paragraphs 30.43–30.45 above.

---

47 As explained in the guidance in LR 1.5.1G, premium listing only exists for: equity shares of commercial companies, closed-ended investment funds, and sovereign controlled commercial companies; and certificates representing shares of sovereign controlled commercial companies. An issuer has a choice under LR as to whether it has a standard listing or a premium listing. The type of listing it applies for will therefore determine the requirements it must comply with.

48 Which may include preference shares, as well as equity shares: FCA Glossary (n 38).

30.53 Some companies' responses to the past two decades' increased focus on ESG and to their disclosure and reporting obligations are more subtly problematic than greenwashing:

- 'Green hushing' has been described as 'companies ... choosing not to publicise details of their climate targets in an attempt to avoid scrutiny and allegations of greenwashing'[49] or 'the act of corporate management teams under-reporting or hiding their sustainability credentials in order to evade investor scrutiny'.[50]

- Meanwhile, 'green bleaching' has been used to describe a situation in which 'a provider of investment services or products that is [sic] in practice 'green' chooses not to claim that it is ... to avoid extra regulatory requirements and a potential regulatory or legal risk'.[51]

30.54 These tactics are, plainly, contrary to the goals envisaged by ESG and the related disclosure and reporting requirements outlined above. In December 2023, the International Organization of Securities Commissions, a global association of financial regulators, issued its final report on Supervisory Practices to Address Greenwashing.[52] The report notes:[53]

> There is no global definition of greenwashing. ... However, many authorities have provided guidance on the identification of greenwashing and the risks associated with it. In addition to greenwashing, other malpractices such as greenhushing and green-bleaching are becoming prominent. While there are no specific frameworks to regulate these concepts, some regulators noted ways in addressing these malpractices.
>
> ...
>
> While steps have been taken by both regulators and market participants, greenwashing remains a fundamental concern that poses risks to both investor protection and market integrity. Ensuring that the proliferation of sustainability-related products does not increase the risk of greenwashing is also a matter of culture. Greenwashing will remain a high risk to the reputation of global sustainable finance markets until the quality and reliability of information available to investors improve.

49 Madeleine Speed, '"Green Hushing" on the Rise as Companies Keep Climate Plans from Scrutiny' *Financial Times* (2022) <https://www.ft.com/content/5fd513c3-e23f-4daa-817e-aa32cf6d18d4> accessed 2 January 2024.
50 Planet Tracker, 'The Greenwashing Hydra' (2023) <https://planet-tracker.org/wp-content/uploads/2023/01/Greenwashing-Hydra-3.pdf> accessed 2 January 2024.
51 ESMA, 'Advice to ESMA: SMSG Advice to ESMA on the ESAs' Call for Evidence on Greenwashing' (2023) ESMA22-106–4384 <https://www.esma.europa.eu/sites/default/files/2023-01/esma22-106-4384_smsg_advice_on_greenwashing.pdf> accessed 2 January 2024 at para 10 fn 6.
52 IOSCO, 'Supervisory Practices to Address Greenwashing' (2023) <https://www.iosco.org/library/pubdocs/pdf/IOSCOPD750.pdf> accessed 2 January 2024.
53 ibid 4–5.

CHAPTER 31

CONTRACTUAL DRAFTING

Rebecca Drake and Celia Reynolds

Introduction

31.01 Contractual drafting has a dual role in achieving net zero nature positive goals: first, drafting can be used to promote the performance of contracts in a manner that accords with net zero nature positive; and second, parties may draft in a manner that manages climate change risks in relation to the performance of contractual duties.

31.02 In this chapter, we look first at how the standard forms for the oil and gas, shipping, and healthcare industries allocate environmental risks and responsibilities. For each of these three industries, we consider how contractual terms allocate risk for the effect of climate change on the performance of contractual duties, and the national or international regulation of contractual terms in relation to net zero nature positive.

31.03 We next consider how The Chancery Lane Project ('TCLP') has created draft climate clauses for use in both standard form and bespoke contracts. It has worked to find solutions to concerns about the costs of meeting net zero nature positive obligations, which often form barriers to compliance.

Standard form contracts

(i) *Oil and gas industry*

31.04 Companies in the oil and gas sector are among those with the highest environmental risk profile. Given the hazardous nature of oil spills and the impact of fossil fuel emissions on the environment, environmental provisions have long been a standard feature of oil and gas contracts.

31.05 This section will focus on two types of agreements reached within the oil and gas industry: sale and purchase agreements and joint operating agreements.

(a) Sale and Purchase Agreements

31.06 A Sale and Purchase Agreement ('SPA') may occur either through an asset SPA, where the 'Purchaser' or 'Buyer' purchases the target oil and gas interests directly; or by a share SPA, where the Buyer purchases shares in a company that owns the oil and gas interests.[1] The standard market position is that Sellers can generally expect to have no residual environmental liability after the completion of the agreement. However, the Seller will remain responsible for all liabilities that arose under the interest documents during its period of ownership. The dividing point of allocation is sometimes the completion of the sale and purchase, but it is more common for there to be an alternative agreed 'Economic Date'. The Economic Date is the date from which the Buyer will bear the economic burden and take on the economic benefit of the assets – in other words, the agreement will have economic effect. It is usually the same date as the last day of the Seller's financial year.[2]

31.07 It follows that environmental risk will typically be allocated to the Buyer.[3] In the UK, the standard SPA is the Oil & Gas UK ('OGUK') Model SPA. The OGUK model 'clean break' clause provides a sweeping environmental indemnity in favour of the Seller, with no environmental warranties to protect the Buyer from unforeseen liabilities:[4]

> 5.3(b) Without prejudice to the generality of the foregoing, the Purchaser agrees to indemnify, keep indemnified and hold harmless the Seller against any Decommissioning Liabilities and any Environmental Liabilities of whatsoever nature and howsoever arising before or after the Post Economic Date.[5]
>
> 'Environmental Liabilities' means all costs, charges, expenses, liabilities and obligations (other than Decommissioning Liabilities) incurred in respect of the Asset in relation to cleaning up, removing debris or any Asset Property from and for reinstating any area of land, foreshore, or seabed, wherever situated, whether such costs, charges, expenses, liabilities, and obligations are incurred pursuant to any statutory, common law or other obligation and regardless of negligence on the part of the Seller.

31.08 The purpose of a 'clean break' is to facilitate the transfer of assets between industry buyers and sellers with ease, on the understanding that neither will be accumulating residual liability in relation to past ownership. However, the OGUK 'clean break' clause enables the Buyer to be held liable for taking over a state of affairs that is non-compliant with national and/or international law or gives rise to environmental liability, even where such liability has been caused by the Seller's actions before the Economic Date. The Buyer would, regardless, be held responsible for bringing the target asset back into compliance and bearing the costs associated with that responsibility.[6] Effectively, it allocates *all* environmental risk to the Buyer, even if the Seller has acted negligently or is required to remediate or reinstate on the basis of third-party contractual obligations or a court order on foot of a successful third-party claim.[7]

---

1 Hussain Kubba, Holly Stebbing and Kimberly Wood, 'Liabilities and Indemnities: Allocation and Limitations on Liability, and the Use of Indemnities', in John LaMaster and Caroline-Lucy Moran (eds), *Oil and Gas Sale and Purchase Agreements* (2nd edn, Global Law and Business 2000).
2 ibid 197.
3 ibid 220.
4 Julie Vaughan, 'Environmental Provisions in Oil and Gas Transactions', in John LaMaster and Caroline-Lucy Moran (eds), *Oil and Gas Sale and Purchase Agreements* (2nd edn, Global Law and Business 2000) 228.
5 See definition of Economic Date in [1.06]. The Post Economic Date may be defined by the parties.
6 Vaughan, 'Environmental Provisions in Oil and Gas Transactions' (n 4) 217.
7 ibid 229.

31.09 Of course, environmental warranties may be negotiated to guard the Buyer against such unexpected liabilities. Vaughan provides a sample of 'typical drafting' for an environmental warranty as follows:[8]

> The [Company] complies and has at all times [in the 2 years prior to the date of this Agreement] complied with Environmental Law.
>
> The [Company] has not received any complaint (whether or not in writing) or a notice alleging a breach of, or a liability under, Environmental Law.
>
> The [Company] is not engaged in any prosecution, litigation, investigation, arbitration, action or other proceedings or settlement under any Environmental Law, or concerning any Environmental Permit or any Hazardous Substance, and so far as the seller is aware, there are no facts or circumstances which are likely to give rise to any such prosecution, litigation, investigation, arbitration, action, proceedings or settlement by or against the [Company].
>
> The [Company] has obtained and complies, and at all times [in the 2 years] prior to the date of this Agreement has obtained and complied, with each Environmental Permit required to carry on its business.
>
> No action has been taken to vary, revoke, or suspend an Environmental Permit obtained by the [Company] and so far as the Seller is aware, no circumstances exist which may give rise to this kind of action.
>
> There is no application currently pending made by the [Company] to vary, transfer, or surrender any Environmental Permit.

31.10 This warranty should cover the failure of the Seller to disclose past and ongoing non-compliance with regulations, difficulties adapting to forthcoming changes in the law,[9] an outstanding proposal by a regulator to revoke or suspend a permit, and the existence of any ongoing regulatory investigations or third-party claims arising from the environmental impacts caused by the business.[10] The warranty offers a contractual assurance of a target's circumstances on a particular date, and the burden will be on the Buyer to prove breach of contract and loss.[11] However, warranty protection is usually limited to a short period (18 months to two years), and would not protect against problems that come to light long after the ability to claim on the warranties.[12]

31.11 Moving forward, indemnities and warranties within SPAs will play an increasingly important role in managing climate change risks in the transfer or purchase of oil and gas assets and changing government policy on net zero. It may be that as risks

---

8 ibid 217–218.
9 Environmental Law will often be a defined term in the particulars.
10 Vaughan, 'Environmental Provisions in Oil and Gas Transactions' (n 4) 218.
11 Caroline-Lucy Moran, 'Oil and Gas Warranties', in John LaMaster and Caroline-Lucy Moran (eds), *Oil and Gas Sale and Purchase Agreements* (2nd edn, Global Law and Business 2000).
12 Vaughan, 'Environmental Provisions in Oil and Gas Transactions' (n 4) 218.

become more uncertain, the industry standard will cease to be that Buyers assume all environmental risk. It is already the case, as Vaughan observes, that where non-industry participants (such as private equity funds) enter the market, they are generally less willing to provide all-encompassing 'clean-break' indemnities, and require the Seller to provide an indemnity for pre and post-completion liabilities.[13]

(b) Joint Operating Agreements

31.12 A Joint Operating Agreement ('JOA') is a binding arrangement by which businesses come together as one to explore and exploit an area for oil and gas, typically under a licence obtained from the government, with the purpose of minimising risks and sharing costs. In contrast to an SPA, which is a more 'discrete' contract, JOAs are relational and lay down rules of conduct which are to apply during the course of their relationship.[14] A JOA will usually provide for the creation of an operating committee to make key decisions relating to the conduct of the joint venture ('JV').[15] However, most of the duties under a JOA rest with the operator – the party responsible for the administration of the day-to-day activities of the JV.[16] The state's participation is usually limited to certain approvals required by the host government, as the resources tend to belong to the host government, unless state participation is required in a particular jurisdiction (e.g. Norway, Nigeria, Saudi Arabia and Iran).[17]

31.13 During the operation phase, Pereira and others identify the major environmental risks as being:[18]

- A well blow-out at a drilling or production site, or the rupture of a pipeline and subsequent release of large amounts of oil into the environment – i.e. and oil spill; and

- Loss of well or hydrocarbon control, including the release of toxic gases such as hydrogen sulphide, marine oil spills, and ignition of explosive gases, land and marine pollution, including contamination of groundwater sources and productive marine environments.

31.14 As with SPAs, standardised forms of agreement have been adopted to minimise the time spent on contractual negotiations. In the USA, the standard form frequently used is the Association of Petroleum Landsmen ('AAPL') Model Form Operating Agreement Form. In the UK Continental Shelf ('UKCS'), the most influential standard form contract is the OGUK Model JOA. For international petroleum projects, the Association of International Energy Negotiators ('AIEN', formerly Association of

---

13 ibid.
14 Mohammad Alramahi, *Oil and Gas Law in the UK* (2nd edn, Bloomsbury Publishing 2021) 101–102, section 3.40.
15 ibid section 3.71–75.
16 Eduardo Pereira, *Joint Operating Agreements* (1st edn, Globe Law and Business 2018) 11.
17 ibid 38–39.
18 Eduardo Pereira, Anna Ovcharova and Reg Fowler, *Joint Operating Agreements: A Comparison Between the IOC and NOC Perspectives* (2nd edn, Globe Law and Business 2022) 166.

International Petroleum Negotiators, or 'AIPN') has developed a model form international JOA.

31.15 Model clauses generally require operators to avoid harmful methods of working by, for example, operating in accordance with 'good oilfield practice' and taking all steps practicable to prevent the escape of petroleum.[19] For example, the AIPN JOA requires operators to conduct joint operations in a 'diligent, safe, and efficient manner in accordance with good and prudent petroleum industry practices and field conservation principles generally followed by the international petroleum industry under similar circumstances'.[20] This has no particular meaning under the JOA, but approximates what might be understood as the standard of a 'reasonable and prudent operator'.[21] From an environmental perspective, this requires joint operations to be undertaken in accordance with the environmental requirements of local legislation.[22]

31.16 Usually, the operator's liability will be restricted in some respect. The JOA will typically provide that the operator will not be responsible for any loss or liability suffered by a party (or third-party) and claimed against the operator, that results from the operator having exercised (or having failed to exercise) its rights under the JOA, or from having performed (or from having failed to perform) the obligations that it has under the JOA. Under the OGUK agreement, the exclusion of liability and the indemnity in favour of the operator for such loss or liability suffered by a party (or third party) generally apply, irrespective of the operator's negligence or breach of duty.[23]

31.17 The key exception to the above is where the loss or liability suffered is attributable to 'wilful misconduct' on the part of the operator.[24] The OGUK agreement defines 'wilful misconduct' as:

> an intentional or reckless disregard by Senior Managerial Personnel of [those methods and practices customarily used in good and prudent oil and gas field practice in the United Kingdom Continental Shelf with that degree of diligence and prudence reasonably and ordinarily exercised by experienced operators engaged in the UK Continental Shelf in a similar activity under similar circumstances and conditions] or any of the terms of the [agreement] in utter disregard of avoidable and harmful consequences.

31.18 In any case, the JOA will usually contain a prohibition on the operator's liability for consequential losses.[25] In other words, the JOAs exclude consequential loss even when gross negligence or wilful misconduct is clearly established, in order to give more

19 Mohammad Alramahi, *Oil and Gas Law in the UK* (n 14) 238, s 4.17.
20 Association of International Energy Negotiators, 'The 2023 Model International Joint Operating Agreement' (2023) s 4.2.B.2. See also Eduardo Pereira, Peter Roberts and Reg Fowler, *The AIPN Joint Operating Agreement: A Practical Guide* (1st edn, Globe Law and Business 2019) 33–42.
21 Pereira, Roberts and Fowler, *The AIPN Joint Operating Agreement: A Practical Guide* (n 20) 39–40, point 5.
22 Pereira, Ovcharova and Fowler, *Joint Operating Agreements: A Comparison Between the IOC and NOC Perspectives* (n 18) 166.
23 Peter Roberts and Reg Fowler, *Joint Operating Agreements: A Practical Guide* (4th edn, Globe Law and Business 2020) 307–308, s 17.1.
24 Pereira, Roberts and Fowler, *The AIPN Joint Operating Agreement: A Practical Guide* (n 20) 308. See also Mohammad Alramahi, *Oil and Gas Law in the UK* (n 14) 101–102, s 3.67.
25 Roberts and Fowler, *Joint Operating Agreements: A Practical Guide* (n 23) 311.

protection to the operator.[26] Under the OGUK agreement, consequential losses are defined as 'indirect or consequential loss, including in relation to delay or loss of petroleum production, loss of use, profit, revenue, bargain or opportunity or any reservoir damage.'[27] Often, consequential loss will include environmental loss, although this may be a matter of dispute between parties.[28]

31.19 It is usually a requirement under the JOA that the operator will establish a suitable Health, Safety, and Environment ('HSE') plan for the operation of the JOA.[29] Generally, the stricter the HSE obligations in the JOA, the greater the liability the operator should bear in relation to the standards in the hydrocarbons operations, subject to the restrictions on liability set out above.[30]

31.20 The 2012 AIEN/AIPN Model Clause provides some of the most robust HSE provisions in comparison to other model JOAs:[31]

> HSE Plan
> Operator shall in the conduct of Joint Operations:
> Prepare and establish an HSE Plan designed to achieve safe and reliable conduct of operations and activities, to avoid significant and unintended impact on the safety and health of people, on property and on the environment, and to comply with Laws relating to HSE;
> Carry out the HSE Plan in conformance with Laws relating to HSE and in a manner [consistent] with standards and procedures [generally] followed in the international petroleum industry under similar circumstances.
> Plan and conduct Joint Operations consistent with the HSE Plan; and the Operating Committee shall at least annually review and approve:
>
> ALTERNATIVE PROVISION, CHOOSE ONE
>
> ALTERNATIVE #1
> The details of the HSE Plan, the implementation of the HSE Plan, and the effectiveness of the HSE Plan
> ALTERNATIVE #2
> An HSE report and letter of assurance from Operator in a form acceptable to the Operating Committee providing adequate evidence that the [HSE] Plan fulfils the requirements of Article 6.6.A and is in place, that Operator is [properly] carrying out the HSE Plan, that any major HSE issues have been brought to the attention of the

26 Pereira, Ovcharova and Fowler, *Joint Operating Agreements: A Comparison Between the IOC and NOC Perspectives* (n 18) 25.
27 Oil & Gas UK, 'Joint Operating Agreement Pack' section 1.1 <https://oeuk.org.uk/product/joint-operating-agreement-pack/> accessed 1 May 2024.
28 See *BHP Petroleum Ltd v British Steel plc* [1999] 2 Lloyd's Rep 583 for a debate of consequential loss.
29 Roberts and Fowler, *Joint Operating Agreements: A Practical Guide* (n 23) 370, s 20.5. See also, AAPL JOA s 5.10; OGUK JOA s 6.12.1.
30 Pereira, Ovcharova and Fowler, *Joint Operating Agreements: A Comparison Between the IOC and NOC Perspectives* (n 18) 170.
31 ibid 168.

Operating Committee and are being properly managed, and that the HSE Plan as carried out is effective.

ALTERNATIVE PROVISION, [CHOOSE] 1

ALTERNATIVE # 1
Establish and carry out a program of regular HSE assessments. The purpose of such assessments is to periodically review HSE systems and procedures, including actual practice and performance, to verify that the HSE Plan is in place and fulfils the requirements of Article 6.6.A, that the HSE Plan is being properly caried out and that the HSE Plan as carried out is effective. Operator shall, at a minimum, conduct such an assessment before entering into significant new Joint Operations and before undertaking any major changes to existing Joint Operations. Upon reasonable notice given to the Operator, Non-Operators shall have the right to participate in such HSE assessments.
ALTERNATIVE #2
Establish an annual audit program in which independent auditors review and verify that the HSE Plan is in place and fulfils the requirements of Article 6.6.A, that the HSE Plan is being properly carried out, and that the HSE Plan as carried out is effective.
Operator shall require its contractors, consultants and agents undertaking activities for the Joint Account to manage HSE risks in a manner consistent with the requirements of the HSE Plan. In the conduct of Joint Operations, Operator shall Operator shall establish and enforce rules consistent with those generally followed in the international petroleum industry under similar circumstances.

31.21 Under this JOA, the operator is required to supply HSE key performance data and monthly reports to the operations committee, promoting compliance with objectives. In addition, the detailed provisions and options presented support the conduct of audits to ensure HSE objectives are met, and mandate that the operator require contractors to comply with the HSE's rules and regulations.[32] Bhargava and others criticise model JOAs for failing to contain express, detailed provisions governing operations with respect to greenhouse gases ('GHGs') and compliance with local government laws:[33]

> Quite often, those drafting these agreements are concerned first and foremost about minimizing their company's environmental liability rather than negotiating clauses that establish strong pro-environment standards. While understandable, this orientation has the unintended effect of limiting a non-operating partner's ability to hold the operator to strong environmental standards which could stop environmental problems before such clauses are needed.

---

32 ibid 168–170.
33 Shishir Bhargava and others, 'Fixing Flawed Environmental Clauses in Joint Venture Legal Agreements: How Operators and Non-Operators Can Live Up to Their Environmental Stewardship Promises' [2020] OGEL Energy Law Journal 5. Cited in Pereira, Ovcharova and Fowler, *Joint Operating Agreements: A Comparison Between the IOC and NOC Perspectives* (n 18).

31.22 Pereira and others challenge this criticism, contending that it would be inappropriate for a JOA to add an additional level of environmental rule-making, on top of the national and international standards that will apply as a matter of law and will have an obligatory effect by default. To the extent that the JOA would impose rules that duplicate or conflict with those standards, that understanding must be right. Yet, it should not be otherwise 'inappropriate' for industry bodies to devise more rigorous standards where they choose and agree to do so. In any case, Pereira and others acknowledge that the JOA should play an important role in promoting and ensuring compliance by, for example, requiring operators to present its procedures for meeting environmental requirements to the Operating Committee for approval.

(ii) *Shipping*

31.23 Large ships are significant individual contributors to GHG emissions.[34] The International Maritime Organization estimates that shipping is responsible for approximately 3% of global anthropogenic GHG emissions.[35] While most international maritime trade is invisible to consumers, 80% of world trade is transported by sea and contributes to the carbon footprint of most consumer products.[36]

31.24 As Zografakis and others posit, re-shaping the standardised contractual framework will play a central role in achieving global emission targets, because 'no maritime decarbonization target can be achieved without an appropriate and realistic re-consideration of the contractual architecture of international maritime trade, rather than simply the regulation of ships by the IMO [International Maritime Organization]'.[37] There is no widely adopted international convention for the purchase and sale of goods carried by sea – therefore, the trade of commodities is almost exclusively the domain of contracts.[38] Maritime trade is facilitated by trade associations, such as the Baltic and International Maritime Council ('BIMCO'), who produce contractual templates that structurally regulate trade relationships.

(a) Charter parties

31.25 When a shipowner contracts to place at the disposal of another the employment of a ship on a given voyage or voyages for a given period of time, the contract is almost always contained in a document called a charter party.[39] Under a time charter party, the owner retains possession and navigational control of the vessel, provides the master and crew, remains responsible for the vessel's fitness to trade, and continues to pay the vessel's normal running costs. In return for payment, the charterer obtains the right to

34 Greenhouse gas emissions include carbon dioxide, methane, and nitrous oxide.
35 International Marine Organization, 'Fourth IMO Greenhouse Gas Study' (2020) <https://wwwcdn.imo.org/localresources/en/OurWork/Environment/Documents/Fourth%20IMO%20GHG%20Study%202020%20-%20Full%20report%20and%20annexes.pdf> accessed 1 May 2024.
36 Haris Zografakis and others, 'Decarbonize Shipping or Decarbonize International Maritime Trade: The Present Contractual Framework and the Need for a New Contractual Architecture', in Mikael Lind, Wolfgang Lehmacher, Robert Ward (eds), *Maritime Decarbonization: Practical Tools, Case Studies and Decarbonization Enablers* (1st edn, Springer 2023) 204.
37 ibid 219.
38 ibid 203.
39 David Foxton and others, *Scrutton on Charterparties and Bills of Lading* (24th edn, Sweet & Maxwell 2019) s 1-006.

direct the vessel's use for the period of time fixed in the charter.[40] The shipowner may be entitled, either by implication of law or by express agreement, to be indemnified by the time charterer against loss falling upon him in consequence of the charterer's acts or the consequence of compliance with the charterer's requests. However, it does not extend to navigation or incidents of navigation, which remain the responsibility of the shipowner.[41]

31.26 In contrast, in a voyage charter party, a charterer hires a vessel for a voyage or multiple voyages in return for the payment of freight by the charterer calculated according to the quantity of cargo carried. The shipowner retains possession and navigational control, and there is no transfer to the charterer of the right to exploit the vessel's earning capacity.[42]

31.27 Time charter parties contain 'speed and fuel consumption' warranties which determine the speed at which voyages will be performed. The New York Produce Exchange ('NYPE') 2015 Charter Party is the most widely used standard time charter party in the dry cargo sector. Clause 12 provides as follows:[43]

> (a) Upon delivery and throughout the duration of this Charter Party the Vessel shall be capable of speed and daily consumption rates as stated in Appendix A in good weather on all sea passages with wind up to and including Force four (4) as per the Beaufort Scale and sea state up to and including Sea State (3) as per the Douglas Sea Scale (unless otherwise specified in Appendix A). Any period during which the Vessel's speed is deliberately reduced to comply with the Charterers' orders/requirements (unless slow steaming or eco speed warranties have been given in Appendix A) or for reasons of safety or while navigating within narrow or restricted waters or when assisting a vessel in distress or when saving or attempting to save life or property at sea, shall be excluded from performance calculations.
>
> (b) The Charterers shall have the option of using their preferred weather routing service. The Master shall comply with the reporting procedure of the Charterers' weather routing service and shall follow routing recommendations from that service provided that the safety of the Vessel and/or cargo is not compromised.
>
> (c) The actual route taken by the Vessel shall be used as the basis of any calculation of the Vessel's performance.
>
> (d) If the speed of the Vessel is reduced and/or fuel oil consumption increased, the Charterers may submit to the Owners a documented claim limited to the estimated time list and/or the additional fuel consumed supported by a performance analysis from the

40 ibid s 1-007.
41 ibid s 17-042 to 17-044.
42 ibid ss 1-006 and 1-008.
43 The Baltic and International Maritime Council (BIMCO), 'NYPE 2015' <https://www.bimco.org/contracts-and-clauses/bimco-contracts/nype-2015#> accessed 1 May 2024. Please note that BIMCO is the copyright holder for NYPE 2015.

weather routing service established in accordance with his Clause. The cost of any time lost shall be off-set against the cost of any fuel saved and vice versa.

(e) In the event that the Owners contest such claim then the Owners shall provide copies of the Vessel's deck logs for the period concerned and the matter shall be referred to an independent expert or alternative weather service selected by mutual agreement, whose report shall take Vessel's log data and the Charterers' weather service data into consideration and whose determination shall be final and binding on the parties. The cost of such expert report shall be shared equally.

31.28 The first subclause provides a continuing warranty by the owners that the ship is capable of performing at the speed and with the fuel consumption set out in Appendix A throughout the charter period. Claims by the charterers are expressly limited to compensation for time lost as a result of the underperformance or the cost of any additional fuel consumed. Credit is given for under-consumption offset against the time lost and vice versa.[44]

31.29 'Slow steaming' is the practice of operating ships at significantly less than their maximum speed in order to reduce fuel consumption and GHG emissions. The NYPE 2015 Time Charter Party makes provision for an optional slow steaming clause:[45]

38. (a) The Charterers may at their discretion provide, in writing to the Master, instructions to reduce speed or Revolutions Per Minute (main engine RPM) and/or instructions to adjust the Vessel's speed to meet a specified time of arrival at a particular destination.

(i) *Slow Steaming – Where the Charterers give instructions to the Master to adjust the speed or RPM, the Master shall, subject always to the Master's obligations in respect of the safety of the Vessel, crew and cargo and the protection of the marine environment, comply with such written instructions, provided that the engine(s) continue(s) to operate above the cut-out pint of the Vessel's engine(s) auxiliary blower(s) and that such instructions will not result in the Vessel's engine(s) and/or equipment operating outside the manufacturer's designers' recommendations as published from time to time.

(ii) *Ultra-Slow Steaming – Where the Charterers give instructions to the Master to adjust the speed or RPM regardless of whether this results in the engine(s) operating above or below the cut-out point of the Vessel's engine(s) auxiliary blower(s), the Master shall, subject always to the Master's obligations in respect of the safety of the Vessel, crew and cargo and the protection of the marine environment, comply with such written instructions, provided that such instructions will not result in the Vesel's engine(s) and/or equipment operating outside the manufacturers'/designers' recommendations issued subsequent to the date of this Charter Party require additional physical modifications to the engine or

44 The Baltic and International Maritime Council (BIMCO), 'Explanatory Notes NYPE 2015' 14 <https://www.bimco.org/contracts-and-clauses/bimco-contracts/nype-2015#> accessed 1 May 2024.
45 The Baltic and International Maritime Council (BIMCO), 'NYPE 2015' (n 43). Please note that BIMCO is the copyright holder for NYPE 2015.

related equipment or require the purchase of additional spares or equipment, the Master shall not be obliged to comply with these instructions.

*(*Sub-clauses (a)(i) and (a)(ii) are alternatives)*

(b) At all speeds the Owners shall exercise due diligence to ensure that the Vessel is operated in a manner which minimises fuel consumption, always taking into account and subject to the following:

(i) the Owners' warranties under this Charter Party relating to the Vessel's speed and consumption
(ii) the Charterers' instructions as to the Vessel's speed and/or RPM and/or specified time of arrival at a particular destination;
(iii) the safety of the Vessel, crew and cargo and the protection of the marine environment; and
(iv) the Owners' obligations under any bills of lading, waybills or other documents evidencing contracts of carriage issued by them or on their behalf.

(c) For the purposes of Sub-clause (b), the Owners shall exercise due diligence to minimise fuel consumption:

(i) when planning voyages, adjusting the Vessel's trim and operating main engine(s) and auxiliary engine(s);
(ii) by making optimal use of the Vessel's navigation equipment and any additional aids provided by the Charterers, such as weather routing, voyage optimization and performance monitoring systems; and
(iii) by directing the Master to report any data that the Charterers may reasonably request to further improve the energy efficiency of the Vessel.

(d) The Owners and the Charterers shall share any findings and best practices that they may have identified on potential improvements to the Vessel's energy efficiency.

(e) For the avoidance of doubt, where the Vessel proceeds at a reduced speed or with reduced RPM pursuant to Sub-clause (a), then provided that the Master has exercised due diligence to comply with such instructions, this shall constitute compliance with, and there shall be no breach of, any obligation requiring the Vessel to proceed with utmost and/or due (or any other such similar/equivalent expression).

(f) The Charterers shall procure that this Clause be incorporated into all sub-charters and contracts of carriage issued pursuant to this Charter Party. The Charterers shall indemnify the Owners against all consequences and liabilities that may arise from bills of lading, waybills or other documents evidencing contracts of carriage being issued as presented to the extent that the terms of such bills of lading, waybills or other documents evidencing contracts of carriage impose or result in breach of the Owner's obligation to proceed with due or are to be held to be a deviation or the imposition of more onerous liabilities upon the Owners than those assumed by the Owners pursuant to this Clause.

31.30 Ordinarily, time charter parties do not include a right for the charterer to order the ship to proceed at a reduced speed or to adjust its speed to arrive at a specified time. The slow steaming clause provides charterers with such a right and protects the shipowner against the risk of claims from third parties.[46] This is achieved through the Charterer's indemnification of the Owners against any consequences and liabilities, in relation to issuing bills of lading where the terms of the bill result in the imposition of liabilities greater than those assumed by the owners under the clause. Additionally, the Charterers are obliged to incorporate the Slow Steaming clause in any bills of lading issued under the time charter party, where possible.[47]

31.31 Further difficulties are created by the fact that many contracts for the commercial employment of dry bulk vessels and tankers are on a spot-contract basis. While this encourages competitive pricing, it is not conducive to the long-term investments needed for the required energy transition.[48] Zografakis and others identify short-term sale contracts as the root of many carbon emission inefficiencies observed in chartering.[49] For example, whereas engine designers have advised that slow steaming above the cut-out point of the auxiliary blowers can be achieved by most ships, 'ultra slow steaming' below the cut-out point will require engine modification and additional equipment in most cases.[50] The owner of a time-chartered vessel has no direct financial interest in energy efficiency measures and has little interest in paying for such modifications as a consequence of the short-termism of most trade contracts.[51] Zografakis and others call this one of the common 'split incentive' problems in shipping contracts.[52]

31.32 In addition, contracts may include clauses which provide for the monitoring of GHG emissions, particularly where emission trading schemes ('ETS') are in place. The EU operates the world's largest ETS and utilises a 'polluter-pays' principle by ensuring the passing of costs onto time charterers. BIMCO provides an example of the following fuel efficiency clause to be used in a time charter party:[53]

> Notwithstanding any other provision in this Charter Party, the Owners and the Charterers (the 'Parties' and each individually a 'Party') agree as follows:
>
> 'Emission Allowances' means an allowance, credit, quota, permit or equivalent, representing a right of a vessel to emit a specified quantity of greenhouse gas emissions recognised by the Emission Scheme.

46 The Baltic and International Maritime Council (BIMCO), 'Explanatory Notes NYPE 2015' (n 44) 22.
47 ibid 24.
48 Zografakis and others, 'Decarbonize Shipping or Decarbonize International Maritime Trade: The Present Contractual Framework and the Need for a New Contractual Architecture' (n 36) 204.
49 ibid.
50 The Baltic and International Maritime Council (BIMCO), 'Explanatory Notes NYPE 2015' (n 44) 23.
51 Zografakis and others, 'Decarbonize Shipping or Decarbonize International Maritime Trade: The Present Contractual Framework and the Need for a New Contractual Architecture' (n 36) 208.
52 ibid.
53 The Baltic and International Maritime Council (BIMCO), 'ETS – Emission Trading Scheme Allowances Clause for Time Charter Parties 2022' <https://www.bimco.org/contracts-and-clauses/bimco-clauses/current/etsa_clause> accessed 1 May 2024. Please note that BIMCO is the copyright holder for the ETS Allowances Clause.

'Emission Scheme' means a greenhouse gas emissions trading scheme which for the purposes of this Clause shall include the European Union Emissions Trading System and any other similar systems imposed by applicable lawful authorities that regulate the issuance, allocation, trading or surrendering of Emission Allowances.

(a) The Owners and the Charterers shall co-operate and exchange all relevant data and information in a timely manner to facilitate compliance with any applicable Emission Scheme and enable the Parties to calculate the amount of Emission Allowances in respect of the Vessel that must be surrendered to the authorities of the applicable Emission Scheme for the period of the Charter Party.

(b) The Owners shall monitor and report the relevant greenhouse gas emissions of the Vessel for verification by an independent verifier in accordance with the applicable Emission Scheme.

(c)

- (i) Throughout the Charter Party period the Charterers shall provide and pay for the Emission Allowances corresponding to the Vessel's emissions under the scope of the applicable Emission Scheme: 1. Within the first seven (7) days of each month, the Owners shall notify the Charterers in writing of the quantity of Emission Allowances for the previous month; and 2. No later than fourteen (14) days prior to the expected date of redelivery the Owners shall notify the Charterers in writing of the estimated quantity of Emission Allowances for the final month or part thereof.
- (ii) The Owners' notifications in subclause (c)(i) shall include the relevant calculations and the data used to establish the quantities.
- (iii) Within seven (7) days of notification under subclause (c)(i), the quantity of Emission Allowances notified by the Owners above shall be transferred by the Charterers and received into the Owners' nominated Emission Scheme account. If the estimated quantity of Emission Allowances for the final month or part thereof is higher or lower than the actual quantity calculated by the Owners as at the time and date of redelivery, any difference in Emission Allowances shall be transferred by the Charterers or returned by the Owners, as the case may be, and received into the nominated account of the receiving Party within seven (7) days of written notification from that Party.
- (iv) During any period of off-hire, the Charterers shall have the right to offset against any Emission Allowances due or require the Owners to return a quantity of Emission Allowances equivalent to the emissions that the Charterers would otherwise have been responsible for, had the Vessel remained on hire.

(d) If the Charterers fail to transfer any of the Emission Allowances in accordance with subclause (c), the Owners shall, by giving the Charterers' five (5) days' notice, have the right to suspend the performance of any or all of their obligations under this Charter Party until such time as the Emission Allowances are received in full by the Owners. Throughout any period of suspended performance under this subclause, the Vessel shall remain on hire and the Owners shall have no responsibility whatsoever for any consequences arising out of the valid exercise of this right. The Owners' right to suspend performance under this Clause shall be without prejudice to any other rights or claims they may have against the Charterers under this Charter Party.

31.33 ETS require cooperation between charterers and owners for the timely sharing of data and information on emissions. Pursuant to the above clause, owners are obliged to follow mandatory reporting obligations. Clause (c) provides for the 'polluter-pays' principle.

31.34 A voyage charterer does not have the same powers to dictate how a ship is operated as a time charterer has. However, if a shipowner were to choose, without prior agreement of the charterer, to slow-steam, they may be held liable for wrongful deviation as they are obliged to prosecute voyages with utmost dispatch. Additionally, shipowners are required to pay for a vessel's delay in port (also known as 'demurrage'). In effect, this incentivises the practice of 'sail fast, then wait', which Zografakis and others identify as 'the largest systemic carbon inefficiency in maritime trade'.

(b) Bills of Lading

31.35 A bill of lading is a document issued by a carrier, which states that specific goods have been shipped onto a particular vessel. It is a document of title to the goods described and contains or evidences the terms of the contract of carriage.[54]

31.36 The paramount obligation of the carrier under a bill of lading is to exercise due diligence to provide a seaworthy vessel, but this does not include any concept of carbon emissions efficiency, or 'greenworthiness'

31.37 Furthermore, given that a shipowner usually undertakes to proceed with the utmost dispatch to the discharge port (and, absent contrary agreement in the charter party, common law implies a warranty of reasonable dispatch), speed reduction is often treated as a breach of contract.[55] Consequently, bills of lading themselves do not appear to provide great scope for the introduction of decarbonisation measures.

(iii) *Healthcare – the NHS*

31.38 Whilst there are specific legal frameworks that apply to public sector procurement in general,[56] some government departments have their own particular procurement rules. We consider in this section that of the NHS.

---

54 Foxton and others, *Scrutton on Charterparties and Bills of Lading* (n 39) s 5-001.

55 Zografakis and others, 'Decarbonize Shipping or Decarbonize International Maritime Trade: The Present Contractual Framework and the Need for a New Contractual Architecture' (n 36) 209.

56 See for example Procurement Policy Note 01/24 published alongside The Carbon Reduction Schedule which provides standard terms and conditions to support contract specific decarbonisation objectives to be set and delivered, and which provides a framework to monitor and assess the Supplier's decarbonisation performance. Found at Cabinet Office, 'Procurement Policy Note: Carbon Reduction Contract Schedule' (2024) Action Note 01/24 <https://assets.publishing.service.gov.uk/media/65f80672af6a0daea190d501/2023-12-01_Carbon_clauses_PPN_01_24.pdf> accessed 1 May 2024.

31.39 Since 1 April 2022, all NHS organisations have been required to comply with Procurement Policy Note PPN 06/20[57] when commissioning and buying goods and services, i.e. when awarding contracts and running and participating in procurements.

31.40 PPN 06/20 contains guidance published by NHS England to formally adopt central government policy requiring contracting authorities to take account of social value when awarding contracts. 'Social value' comprises both net zero carbon targets, as well as wider social value priorities, although we only consider the former in this chapter.

31.41 NHS England also published a social value model alongside PPN 06/20, which contains net zero emissions requirements; the reduction of NHS carbon emissions is a particular focus when aiming to meet targets, as more than 60% of NHS carbon emissions occur in the supply chain.[58]

31.42 The requirements in the new guidance build on the government's 'Taking Account of Carbon Reduction Plan' (PPN 06/21) and are outlined in the NHS Net Zero Supplier Roadmap,[59] which builds on the requirements set out in PPN 06/20.

31.43 NHS England's guidance in PPN 06/20 sets out detail on how to support the delivery of net zero across the NHS through the social value theme of 'Fighting climate change'. The guidance suggests that to this end, all NHS procurement should include activities that 'deliver additional environmental benefits in the performance of the contract including working towards net zero greenhouse gas emissions' or 'influence staff, suppliers, customers and communities through the delivery of the contract to support environmental protection and improvement'.

31.44 This could include measures such as:

- Reducing single use plastics;
- Increasing efforts to recycle products;
- Requiring the use of electric vehicles;
- Using materials that are locally sourced and manufactured; and
- The use of meetings virtually rather than in person.

---

57 Cabinet Office, 'Procurement Policy Note – Taking Account of Social Value in the Award of Central Government Contracts' (2020) PPN 06/20 <https://assets.publishing.service.gov.uk/media/5f6ccf89d3bf7f7237cf4015/PPN-06_20-Taking-Account-of-Social-Value-in-the-Award-of-Central-Government-Contracts.pdf> accessed 1 May 2024.
58 East of England NHS Collaborative Procurement Hub, 'Empowering Procurements That Deliver Social, Economic and Environmental Benefit to Local Communities and the Wider NHS' <https://www.eoecph.nhs.uk/buyers/sustainability-and-social-value/> accessed 1 May 2024.
59 NHS, 'NHS Net Zero Supplier Roadmap' (2023) <https://www.england.nhs.uk/greenernhs/wp-content/uploads/sites/51/2024/04/NHS-Net-Zero-Supplier-Roadmap-2024.pdf> accessed 1 May 2024.

31.45 It is intended that PPN 06/20 requirements are incorporated into the NHS Standard Contracts.

31.46 For example, the Schedules to the NHS Modern Services Contract v 2.1, one of the NHS standard contracts, provide *inter alia* the following decarbonisation clauses:

- Clause 1.3.7:

  The Balanced Scorecard Report shall be presented in the form of an online accessible dashboard and, as a minimum, shall contain a high level summary of the Supplier's performance over the relevant Service Period, including details of the following
  ...
  sustainability indicators, for example net zero carbon, waste minimisation or performance to support a circular economy.

- Clause 3.3.1:

  In performing its obligations under the Contract the Supplier shall, where applicable to the Contract, to the reasonable satisfaction of the Authority:
  demonstrate low carbon resource efficiency, including minimising the use of resources and responding promptly to the Authority's reasonable questions.

- Clause 3.3.5:

  3.3 In performing its obligations under the Contract the Supplier shall, where applicable to the Contract, to the reasonable satisfaction of the Authority:
  ...
  in circumstances that a permit, licence or exemption to carry or send waste generated under this Contract is revoked, the Supplier shall cease to carry or send waste or allow waste to be carried by any Subcontractor until authorisation is obtained from the Environment Agency; minimise the release of greenhouse gases (including carbon dioxide emissions), air pollutants, volatile organic compounds and other substances damaging to health and the environment.

- Clause 3.3.6:

  In performing its obligations under the Contract the Supplier shall, where applicable to the Contract, to the reasonable satisfaction of the Authority:
  ...
  reduce and minimise carbon emissions by taking into account factors including, but not limited to, the locations from which materials are sourced, the transport of materials, the locations from which the work force are recruited and emissions from offices and on-site equipment.

- Clause 3.4:

> In performing its obligations under the Contract, the Supplier shall to the reasonable satisfaction of the Authority (where the anticipated Charges in any Contract Year are above £5 million per annum (excluding VAT)), where related to and proportionate to the contract in accordance with PPN 06/21), publish and maintain a credible Carbon Reduction Plan in accordance with PPN 06/21.

(iv) *The Chancery Lane Project*

31.47 TCLP was founded in 2019 and describes itself as 'the largest global network of lawyers and business leaders using the power of climate contracting to deliver fast and fair decarbonisation'.[60]

31.48 It holds a library of over one hundred free access 'climate clauses' for use in agreements and contracts. There are clauses available for a number of different jurisdictions; at the time of publishing, those comprised England and Wales (129), New Zealand (10), the USA (10), Germany (8) and Ireland (3).

31.49 At the time of publishing, TCLP works with 375 different participating organisations over 113 different countries, ranging from small businesses to large multinational corporations, such as Nestlé, Bank of America and IKEA.[61]

31.50 TCLP's climate clauses aim to meet objectives such as setting decarbonisation targets, measuring and reporting on emissions, cooperating to reduce environmental impact, and allocating costs for environmental improvements. The clauses that aim to do this are written in collaboration with law firms and businesses, then peer reviewed. They are regularly updated.

(a) Model climate aligned clauses

31.51 Each of TCLP's model clauses aims to address a specific climate change issue that can be mitigated or addressed by adopting contractual obligations to change the behaviour of the parties. While most of the model clauses are intended to be

---

60 Consolidated press pack downloaded at The Chancery Lane Project, 'About' <https://chancerylaneproject.org/> accessed 1 May 2024.
61 ibid.

incorporated into transactional contracts, some model clauses take other forms, such as questionnaires,[62] licences,[63] scorecards,[64] charters[65] and board minutes.[66]

31.52 Most of the model clauses contain alternative drafting options dependent on the end user's characteristics and desires, along with explanatory notes as to when each option is relevant. Some are adapted for different jurisdictions. Most of the model clauses also have a link to a separate document which contains essential notes and guidance, which in turn explains the purpose of the clause, the practice areas to which it applies, the climate issue at stake, the drafting solution, the impact of the clause on net zero, the stakeholders who are affected, and the potential barriers and challenges to using or implementing the relevant clause.

31.53 Each model clause is prefaced by the relevant glossary terms applicable to that particular model clause, which are all taken from the longer list of standard TCLP glossary terms which are found on the TCLP website.

31.54 Each model clause has two different alternative titles. The first reflects the purpose of the clause, whilst the second is a child (or children's) name or names. TCLP's use of children's names is intended to reflect the fact that the next generation will be the most affected by the climate crisis, and accordingly is intended to promote long-term thinking.

31.55 An example of one of TCLP's more far-reaching model climate-aligned clauses is Sebastian's Clause. Based on feedback to TCLP, both internal and external, and data gathered from its website, Sebastian's clause is one of the most popular clauses amongst users. The others are Austen, David, Eddie, Griff, Jess and Rory, Lola and Harry, Marni, Matilda, Owen, Raphael and Zoe and Bea. Sebastian's Clause enables a party to ensure that counterparties have robust Paris Agreement aligned targets, implementation strategies, governance, and policies. It provides:[67]

> Additional Definitions
> [Drafting note: Capitalised terms relate to either a defined term in this clause or a defined term in the main agreement that this clause is designed to be inserted into.]
> Carbon Footprint means the total annual GHG Emissions relating to the [Obligor]'s business.

---

62 The Chancery Lane Project, 'Drew's DDQ: Climate Change Due Diligence Questionnaire' (19 September 2023) <https://chancerylaneproject.org/clauses/climate-change-due-diligence-questionnaire/> accessed 1 May 2024.

63 The Chancery Lane Project, 'Vincent and George's Licence: Climate Solutions IPR Licence' (1 September 2023) <https://chancerylaneproject.org/clauses/climate-solutions-ipr-licence/> accessed 1 May 2024.

64 The Chancery Lane Project, 'Maria's Scorecard: Supply Chain Emissions Scorecard' (27 September 2021) <https://chancerylaneproject.org/clauses/supply-chain-emissions-scorecard/> accessed 1 May 2024.

65 The Chancery Lane Project, 'Chloe's Clause: Environmental Business Charter' (4 November 2022) <https://chancerylaneproject.org/clauses/environmental-business-charter/> accessed 1 May 2024.

66 The Chancery Lane Project, 'Darcy's Board Minutes: Board Minutes: Consideration of Climate Change Factors' (1 November 2022) <https://chancerylaneproject.org/clauses/board-minutes-consideration-of-climate-change-factors/> accessed 1 May 2024.

67 The Chancery Lane Project, 'Sebastian's Clause: Entire Business Net Zero Objectives' (22 April 2022) <https://chancerylaneproject.org/clauses/entire-business-net-zero-objectives/> accessed 1 May 2024.

Carbon Footprint Data means the full figures and details of the measurement and calculations carried out by the [Obligor] in the assessment of its Carbon Footprint at any point in time.

GHG Emissions means the [Obligor]'s emissions of GHGs classified as scope 1, 2 and 3 emissions by The Greenhouse Gas Protocol: A Corporate Accounting and Reporting Standard, Revised Edition 2015 as updated periodically. [Drafting note: Scope 1, 2 and 3 emissions are defined on page 27 of the GHG Protocol.]

Greenhouse Gases (GHGs) means the gases that trap thermal radiation in the earth's atmosphere. They are specified by the United Nations Framework Convention on Climate Change (UNFCCC) in Annex A to the Kyoto Protocol and may be updated periodically.

Net Negative means the GHGs removed from the atmosphere [by the Obligor] are greater than [its] GHG Emissions.

[Drafting note: See also TCLP Glossary: Net Negative. On a global scale, removals of GHGs should be consistent with the mitigation pathways that would limit global warming to 1.5°C, with little to no overshoot. See IPCC Special Report on Global Warming of 1.5°C (2018), Summary for Policymakers, Part C Emission Pathways and System Transitions Consistent with 1.5°C Global Warming and Working Group III Contribution to the IPCC Sixth Assessment Report (AR6), Climate Change 2022: Mitigation of climate change (4 April 2022).]

Net Zero Target means a target to reduce and remove GHG Emissions, including by offsetting Residual Emissions, to achieve a balance between the [Obligor's] sources and sinks of GHGs. This must be achieved by [2050/Insert earlier date] and align with Paris Agreement Goals.

Net Zero Transition Plan means a plan to deliver the Net Zero Target and then remain Net Negative, that:

(a) includes an Offsetting Strategy;

(b) sets interim GHG Emission reduction targets that align with Paris Agreement Goals;

(c) links executive remuneration to achieving the interim targets;

(d) is updated to address developments in science and technology;

(e) is reviewed and approved annually by the Board; and

(f) promotes a just transition to a low carbon economy.

* [Drafting note: If the Net Zero Target will be validated by the Science Based Targets Initiative, consider replacing 'interim GHG Emission reduction targets' with the defined term '[Short/Near] Term Science Based Targets'. See TCLP's Glossary: Science Based Target for suggested drafting.]

Offsetting Strategy means a plan specifying:

(a) the verified credits from a recognised offset provider that may be used by the [Obligor] to offset its Residual Emissions;

(b) how [the Obligor] will [transition:

(i) from using credits from offsetting projects that avoid or reduce emissions of GHG to projects that remove emissions of GHG; and

(ii) to GHG removals that involve long-term storage methods with a low risk of reversal;*

(c) how the [Obligor] will reduce its use of credits by reducing its Residual Emissions [by [•]%] by 2050; and

(d) the impact of the relevant offsetting projects on a just transition and wider social and environmental goals.

* [Drafting note: The Oxford Principles for Net Zero Aligned Carbon Offsetting 2020 state that 'an immediate transition to 100% carbon removals is not necessary, nor is it currently feasible, but organisations must commit to gradually increase the percentage of carbon removal offsets they procure with a view to exclusively sourcing carbon removals by mid-century. Most offsets available today are emission reductions, which are necessary but not sufficient to maintain net zero in the long run. Carbon removals scrub carbon directly from the atmosphere. This counteracts ongoing emissions after net zero is achieved and creates the possibility of net removal for actors choosing to remove more carbon than they emit.']

Paris Agreement Goals means the goals in Articles 2.1 and 4.1 of the UNFCCC's Paris Agreement, in particular limiting global temperature increase to 1.5 degrees Celsius above pre-industrial levels.

Residual Emissions means [the Obligor's] GHG Emissions that are emitted after all reasonable efforts have been made [by the Obligor] to reduce them. [Drafting note: See TCLP Glossary: Residual Emissions.]

Additional Clauses

1. Sustainability Objectives

[Drafting note: This is a menu of suggestions and these objectives should be tailored to the parties' requirements and made 'darker' or 'lighter' green accordingly.]

The [Obligor] shall: [Drafting note: Consider changing to 'the Parties shall' and making all obligations mutual]

1.1 within [time period] of entering into this agreement publicly set an organisational Net Zero Target [validated by the Science Based Targets initiative][and sign up to Race to Zero];

1.2 develop and immediately begin implementation of the Net Zero Transition Plan;

1.3 [no later than six months after the date of this agreement, sign up to the Carbon Trust Standard for Supply Chain (as published from time to time) [which the [Obligor] will demonstrate by providing the [Counterparty] with a copy of the relevant declaration signed by a Director of the [Obligor];]

[OR]

1.3 [regularly measure and report on the [Obligor]'s Carbon Footprint in accordance with the The Greenhouse Gas Protocol: A Corporate Accounting and Reporting Standard, Revised Edition 2015;]

1.4 [reduce its Carbon Footprint, as originally assessed, by [15]% within [three (3)] calendar months of the signing of this agreement, as reasonably demonstrated by Carbon Footprint Data;]

1.5 establish a sustainability committee as a committee of its board of directors to oversee the development, implementation and review of the Net Zero Transition Plan. The sustainability committee shall be chaired either by a [non-executive] director with experience of improving sustainability and mitigating carbon footprints, or by an appropriately qualified climate, sustainability or environmental consultant with the skills and experience to diligently, competently and professionally advise on improving sustainability and mitigating [the Obligor]'s Carbon Footprint;

1.6 report [annually] [and publicly] on:*

1.6.1 the climate risks and opportunities to the [Obligor] and its business in accordance with the recommendations of the Task Force on Climate-Related Financial Disclosures (TCFD);

1.6.2 how the effects on key stakeholders (including but not limited to employees, clients, end customers and supply chain partners) of the measures taken by the [Obligor] to mitigate its GHG Emissions can align with a just transition to net zero; and
1.6.3 all climate policy engagement, climate leadership, lobbying activities, trade association memberships and public policy positions that directly or indirectly relate to the UNFCCC's Paris Agreement;
* [[Drafting note: Consider adding CDP or Sustainability Accounting Standards Board (SASB) disclosure]]
1.7 provide an environmental and sustainability training programme on a regular basis (at least annually) for employees, personnel and contractors during their usual working hours (and online as required). As a minimum, the training will cover:
1.7.1 details of [the Obligor]'s public and contractual commitments, targets and governance in relation to climate change and sustainability;
1.7.2 the latest climate science presented by the Intergovernmental Panel on Climate Change (the United Nations body for assessing the science related to climate change);
1.7.3 climate change policy and relevant legal context (including core terms of the Paris Agreement and any national implementation measures);
1.7.4 the economic and social (e.g. health) benefits to [the Obligor] in reducing the workplace's environmental impact; and
1.7.5 sustainable lifestyle changes and issues relating to the workplace;
1.8 include in the Net Zero Transition Plan contractual clauses (for example, climate clauses published by The Chancery Lane Project) to embed the Net Zero Target in the [Obligor]'s activities and relationships. The Obligor shall also include climate contract clauses in most of its standard form precedent contracts[; and
1.9 establish its pension scheme with an ESG/green investment fund].

31.56 The various different options for the clause can be seen within the clause itself as set out above. When read together with the explanatory notes for the clause, this demonstrates how bespoke the TCLP's clauses are intended to be; they are not intended to be simple cut and paste clauses that are the same in every agreement in which they are used.

31.57 Because net zero is a specific target with precise measurable deliverables, Sebastian's Clause is in the minority of the TCLP's model clauses when it comes to meeting net zero objectives definitively. Rather, a majority of the TCLP clauses state that, whilst they bring climate considerations to drafting, they are not yet net zero aligned. Instead, they go some way to meeting net zero objectives and principles, but cannot guarantee that the precise criteria for net zero are met. TCLP therefore suggests that in order to align those clauses with net zero, the user should use the TCLP toolkit and join one of TCLP's events, with links to both.

31.58 The net zero toolkit contains a number of different elements: a net zero explainer; a net zero dashboard; a net zero drafting checklist; definitions and sample wording; a discussion document on offsets, insets and carbon credits; and a discussion document on commerciality and climate ambition in drafting. The use of the dashboard and checklist, in particular, permits checks to be made in relation to different benchmarks, being 'minimal ambition', 'moderate ambition' and 'higher ambition'. Minimal ambition permits warming by over 2 degrees, moderate ambition by only 2 degrees, and higher ambition by only 1.5 degrees.

31.59 One such clause, which requires further use of the TCLP toolkit, relates to Electronic Notices (Arthur and Charlie's Clause). This aims to minimise travel and the use of paper when notices are provided. It is clear from its scope that use of this clause alone will not necessarily reach net zero goals, but it can be understood how it goes towards reaching them. The toolkit allows additional considerations to be made, and would in this instance probably require a wider range of clauses in the contract itself to be used in order to meet net zero targets, as notices alone are a small part of the operation of a contractual framework. It provides:[68]

> 1. Electronic notices preferred
> 1.1 Any party providing a notice under this [document] will do so electronically, provided that, if that party is unable to effect or confirm delivery of the notice electronically, or delivery of the notice electronically is not permitted by law, it will [to the extent practicable][use reasonable endeavours (to the extent practicable)]*:
>
> (a) use [FSC-certified**][recycled] paper and non-solvent-based ink when printing a notice; and
> (b) if the notice is being delivered by hand, courier or post, use a delivery method that minimises the associated [greenhouse gas emissions]*** [(for example, by using a courier service that utilises electric vehicles or is certified as carbon neutral)].
>
> * [Drafting note: The second option can be used where the parties want to include an additional qualifier (where 'to the extent practicable' alone might impose a standard they do not consider they can meet). If using the second option, add 'to' before 'use' in 1.1(a).]
> ** [Drafting note: FSC refers to the Forest Stewardship Council, an international non-governmental organisation dedicated to promoting responsible management of the world's forests.]
> *** [Drafting note: If this clause is being used in a document that contains other TCLP clauses, this could be replaced with the defined term 'Greenhouse Gas Emissions'.]

31.60 Again, the bespoke nature of the clause with its various different options, together with explanatory notes, can be seen.

31.61 TCLP launched a set of eight guides on 20 February 2024 following user feedback, distilling from its clause collection the core, best practice principles for writing contracts in a climate-aligned way. The guides are designed to open up climate-aligned contracting to many more lawyers, use cases and business needs than the clauses (necessarily bespoke) were ever able to.

68 The Chancery Lane Project, 'Arthur and Charlie's Clause: Electronic Notices' (23 May 2023) <https://chancerylaneproject.org/clauses/electronic-notices/> accessed 1 May 2024.

CHAPTER 32

CONSUMER PROTECTION

Hannah McCarthy and Alexander Burrell

The role of the consumer in achieving net zero and nature positive targets

32.01 Improving the energy efficiency and sustainability of consumer products and services is an essential part of the transition to net zero and nature positive. European and North American regulators have primarily relied on two tools in pursuit of this goal: first, requiring the provision of accurate information about the environmental impact of consumer goods and services, so as to permit the consumer to make informed choices; second, regulating the characteristics of the goods and services themselves.[1]

32.02 Actual or perceived consumer pressure on manufacturers and suppliers to produce 'green' goods and services has led to a proliferation of false claims as to the environmental credentials of goods and services. This, in turn, has necessitated the further development of consumer protection regulation to combat such 'greenwashing.'

Consumer information

(i) *Introduction*

32.03 Consumer information has an important role to play in relation to net zero and nature positive goals: well-informed consumers can choose to exercise their buying power in a manner that is consistent with the transition to net zero and nature positive, which can, in turn, shape supplier and producer decision-making.

32.04 The government expressly recognised the importance of providing clear information to consumers in its 2021 Net Zero Strategy: Build Back Greener:[2]

> Consumer preference can shape producers' decisions, but sometimes consumers and businesses lack clear information to make informed choices. As announced by the chancellor in his Mansion House speech in July 2021, we will work with the Financial Conduct Authority to introduce a sustainable investment label – a quality stamp – so that consumers and retail investors can clearly compare the impacts and sustainability of their investments for the first time.

---

1 Regulators have also demonstrated a willingness to impose restrictions in relation to products that cause indirect damage to the environment. For a more detailed commentary on the regulation of products associated with deforestation, please see paras 8.116–8.157 in Chapter 8.

2 Department for Energy Security and Net Zero, 'Net Zero Strategy: Build Back Greener' (2021) 278 <https://www.gov.uk/government/publications/net-zero-strategy> accessed 28 September 2023.

> We plan to help empower people to make informed choices about the goods and products they buy and services they use by exploring how we better label these with their emission intensity and environmental impact. We are also exploring the use of product labelling to show the durability, repairability and recyclability of products, as well as their environmental footprint with a view to stimulating demand for better quality items. We continue to explore the evidence base for environmental labelling within food production and disposal, including the most accurate methodologies to monitor and verify the carbon emissions, and environmental impact, of food items.

(ii) *Current product labelling requirements*

32.05 Within its 2021 Net Zero Strategy, the government references future plans as to product labelling and the impact this is hoped to have on consumers.[3] However, there has been longstanding legislation, primarily deriving from EU law, which requires the provision of information to consumers in respect of certain energy consuming products.

32.06 The purpose of such information, and its relevance to reducing energy consumption, and thus to net zero, is cited within the relevant EU legislation. For example, as stated at recital (1) and (2) of Regulation (EU) 2017/1369:[4]

> (1) The Union is committed to building an Energy Union with a forward looking climate policy. Energy efficiency is a crucial element of the Union's 2030 Climate and Energy Policy Framework and is key to moderating energy demand.
>
> (2) Energy labelling enables customers to make informed choices based on the energy consumption of energy-related products. Information on efficient and sustainable energy-related products makes a significant contribution to energy savings and to reducing energy bills, while at the same time promoting innovation and investments into the production of more energy efficient products. Improving the efficiency of energy-related products through informed customer choice and harmonising related requirements at Union level benefits also manufacturers, industry and the Union economy overall.

32.07 One of the first pieces of UK legislation on mandatory labelling concerned with energy efficiency (and thereby net zero) was the Energy Information (Refrigerators and Freezers) Regulations 1994,[5] implementing EU legislation, Council Directive 92/75/EEC(3) and Commission Directive 94/2/EC. Applicable to refrigerators, frozen food storage cabinets and food freezers, these regulations introduced requirements on suppliers and dealers in respect of labels and information notices, denoting categories of appliance and energy efficiency class. Schedule 1 of these regulations was the first to introduce the now ubiquitous label denoting categories from A to G, together with the products energy consumption in kWh per year.

---

3 ibid 52, 61, 131 and 278.
4 Regulation (EU) 2017/1369 of the European Parliament and of the Council of 4 July 2017.
5 SI 1994/3076.

32.08 The current primary UK legislation on labelling is the Energy Information Regulations 2011. These regulations initially implemented the requirements of Directive 2010/30/EU, and later implemented and referred to Regulation (EU) 2017/1369. These regulations have been variously updated over the years by way of amendment regulations, including dealing with the UK's exit from the European Union.

32.09 The latest version of the Energy Information Regulations 2011[6] applies to energy-related products. An 'energy-related product' is defined as any good that has an impact on energy consumption during use which is placed on the market and/or put into service (including parts intended to be incorporated).[7]

32.10 The latest amended Energy Information Regulations 2011 refer to and rely upon various Articles of Regulation (EU) 2017/1369, referred to as 'the EU Energy Labelling Regulation', which continue to apply to dealers and suppliers of such products.

32.11 Article 3 of the EU Energy Labelling Regulation sets out various obligations on suppliers, requiring that products are placed on the market with accurate printed labels and product information sheets. 'Label' is defined as a graphic diagram, including a closed scale, using only letters from A to G, representing a class corresponding to energy savings, in seven colours from dark green to red.[8]

32.12 Article 5 of the EU Energy Labelling Regulation provides for various obligations on dealers, to display these labels and product information sheets.

32.13 Article 11 of the EU Energy Labelling Regulation provides for powers for the Secretary of State to introduce and rescale 'labels', in particular to make product-specific measures to introduce labels for a product group if certain criteria are met, to ensure a homogenous A to G scale.

32.14 Regulation 11 of the updated Energy Information Regulations 2011 provides that it is an offence for a dealer or supplier to fail to comply with the obligations placed on dealers and suppliers under the EU Energy Labelling Regulation, and Regulation 4 of the Energy Information Regulations 2011 provides that the local weights and measures authority may enforce the applicable Articles of the EU Energy Labelling Regulation. Regulation 11 clarifies that the penalty for both summary conviction and conviction on indictment is a fine.

32.15 Schedule 1 of the updated Energy Information Regulations 2011 sets out in Column 1 the various products to which the labelling requirements apply.

32.16 Schedule 4 of the updated Energy Information Regulations 2011 sets out powers of the market surveillance authority to impose sanctions, including:

---

6 SI 2011/1524.
7 Article 2(1) of Regulation (EU) 2017/1369.
8 Article 2(19) of Regulation (EU) 2017/1369.

- On persons which it is satisfied beyond reasonable doubt have committed an offence:
  - Issuing a 'compliance notice', imposing on that person a requirement to take steps to secure that the offence does not continue/recur.[9]
  - Imposing a variable monetary penalty in such amount as it may determine (there is no limit).[10]
- Issuing a 'stop notice' on persons carrying on an activity which the market surveillance authority reasonably believes involves or is likely to involve the commission of an offence, prohibiting the person from carrying out that activity until they take steps specified in the notice.[11]
- Imposing a non-compliance penalty for any failure to comply with a compliance notice, stop notice, third party undertaking or enforcement undertaking.[12]

(iii) *Future product labelling requirements*

32.17 As discussed above, as part of its Net Zero Strategy, the government highlighted how it planned to further explore the use of product labelling to show the durability, repairability and recyclability of products, as well as their environmental footprint.[13]

32.18 On 19 July 2021, Kwasi Kwarteng as then Secretary of State for Business, Energy and Industrial Strategy, sent a letter to the Competition and Markets Authority ('CMA'), asking the CMA's advice on how the UK can better use the tools available under competition and consumer law to achieve net zero and sustainability goals, including climate adaptation. Three questions were asked of the CMA:[14]

i. If, and how, do current competition and consumer legal frameworks constrain or frustrate initiatives that might support the UK's Net Zero and sustainability goals?

ii. Are there changes to the UK's competition and consumer law that would help to achieve the UK's Net Zero and sustainability goals?

iii. Are there other opportunities within the UK's competition and consumer policy toolbox that would support the UK's Net Zero and sustainability goals, which the government should be considering.

---

9 Energy Information Regulations 2011, Schedule 4, Paragraph 3.
10 ibid Schedule 4, Paragraph 4.
11 ibid Schedule 4, Part 2.
12 ibid Schedule 4, Part 4.
13 Department for Energy Security and Net Zero, 'Net Zero Strategy: Build Back Greener' (n 2) 278.
14 Kwasi Kwarteng, 'Letter from Kwasi Kwarteng, BEIS Secretary of State, to Andrea Coscelli on Sustainability' (2021) <https://assets.publishing.service.gov.uk/government/uploads/system/uploads/attachment_data/file/1004016/sos-letter-to-andrea-coscelli-on-sustainability.pdf>.

32.19 In respect of product labelling, the CMA responded with the following recommendations, in correspondence published on 14 March 2022:[15]

- Legislating to create standardised definitions of commonly used environmental terms, to which businesses must adhere in marketing and labelling their products.
- Confirming in legislation a requirement for mandatory disclosure of certain information (such as environmental impact, recyclability, repairability and durability).
- Legislating to require businesses to provide better environmental information to their business customers.

32.20 In particular, the CMA made the following recommendations:[16]

> Create statutory definitions of commonly used environmental terms, such as biodegradable, compostable and carbon neutral. We believe this could be achieved either by amendments to the CPRs and the Consumer Contracts (Information, Cancellation and Additional Charges) Regulations 2013 (CCRs), or through another appropriate legislative vehicle. This would enable consumers to more easily compare products and stop unscrupulous businesses deliberately misusing these terms.
>
> Confirm an express positive obligation to disclose environmental information. We believe this could be achieved by amending the definitions of material information [footnote 26] in the CPRs and CCRs to confirm explicitly that environmental information must be provided to consumers. This would put beyond doubt the requirement to disclose such information in all circumstances. This would be particularly helpful for consumers to identify less environmentally-friendly products which might not otherwise disclose their impact.

32.21 The government has not yet implemented these recommendations, but it is likely there will be future legislation addressing some or all of these points.

(iv) *Fuel Mix Disclosure and Renewable Energy Guarantees of Origin*

32.22 Consumers must also be provided with information in respect of energy supply. The Electricity (Fuel Mix Disclosure) Regulations 2005[17] introduced a requirement on all electricity suppliers in Great Britain to disclose to their customers the mix of fuels used to generate the electricity supplied annually, provided that electricity is supplied for a full disclosure period (1 April – 31 March).[18]

---

15 CMA, 'Environmental Sustainability and the UK Competition and Consumer Regimes: CMA Advice to the Government' (2022) <https://www.gov.uk/government/publications/environmental-sustainability-and-the-uk-competition-and-consumer-regimes-cma-advice-to-the-government/environmental-sustainability-and-the-uk-competition-and-consumer-regimes-cma-advice-to-the-government#fnref:4> accessed 19 September 2024.
16 ibid.
17 SI 2005/391.
18 See https://www.ofgem.gov.uk/environmental-and-social-schemes/renewable-energy-guarantees-origin-rego/electricity-suppliers-and-generators/fuel-mix-disclosure-fmd.

32.23 Pursuant to the Electricity (Fuel Mix Disclosure) Regulations 2005, the standard conditions in electricity supply licences were amended, requiring electricity suppliers to specify, in or with bills, and in promotional materials made available to final customers, certain information regarding the contribution of each energy source to the fuel mix of the supplier over the preceding year.[19]

32.24 The information which is required to be provided is: the contribution of each energy source, even if expressed as zero, to the total amount of electricity purchased for supply by the supplier, and the environmental impact, per kWh of electricity supplied resulting from the total amount of electricity purchased for supply by the supplier, in terms of emissions of carbon dioxide and production of radioactive waste.[20] This information is required to be provided annually.

32.25 The provision of this information is a requirement of energy suppliers' licences[21] and, as such, any failure to provide this information may constitute a breach of licence.

32.26 The Renewable Energy Guarantees of Origin scheme, as administered by Ofgem, provides for the issuance of certificates referred to as REGOs (Renewable Energy Guarantees of Origin), for each megawatt hour (MWh) of eligible renewable output. REGOs are issued to generators of renewable electricity and are used to fulfil Fuel Mix Disclosure obligations.[22] The EU derived legislation providing for REGOs comprises the Electricity (Guarantees of Origin of Electricity Produced from Renewable Energy Sources) Regulations 2003,[23] and the Guarantees of Origin of Electricity Produced from High Efficiency Cogeneration Regulations 2007.[24]

Sustainable design

(i) *Introduction*

32.27 The design characteristics of consumer products – such as their energy and resource efficiency – is another area of focus for governments managing the transition to net zero and nature positive.

32.28 The government's 2021 Net Zero Strategy states:

> We are taking action to ensure that products are more sustainable, both in relation to their energy efficiency during use and use of materials over their lifetime (resource efficiency) through developing proposals for new regulatory product standards and better consumer information. We are exploring updating and expanding 'Ecodesign' product regulation

---

19 Explanatory Notes to Electricity (Fuel Mix Disclosure) Regulations 2005; Condition 21 of Standard conditions of electricity supply licence.
20 Electricity (Fuel Mix Disclosure) Regulations 2005, reg 4.
21 Condition 21 of Standard conditions of electricity supply licence.
22 See <https://www.ofgem.gov.uk/environmental-and-social-schemes/renewable-energy-guarantees-origin-rego> accessed 19 September 2024.
23 SI 2003/2562.
24 SI 2007/292.

which sets minimum requirements to phase out the least energy and resource efficient products from the market.[25]

32.29 Existing legislation sets out minimum requirements for certain specific products, primarily derived from EU legislation.

32.30 Further, consumer rights focused legislation, and in particular the Consumer Rights Act 2015, has an indirect effect on ensuring the sustainability of products. Possible future legislation would include strengthening this legislation.

(ii) *Ecodesign legislation*

32.31 Ecodesign means 'the integration of environmental aspects into product design with the aim of improving the environmental performance of the product throughout its whole life cycle'.[26]

32.32 Some of the first ecodesign-related legislation in the UK was the Boiler (Efficiency) Regulations 1993,[27] implementing Directive 90/396/EEC, which set efficiency requirements for boilers. Then followed various further EU derived legislation, including the Energy Efficiency (Refrigerators and Freezers) Regulations 1997[28] and the Energy Efficiency (Ballasts for Fluorescent Lighting) Regulations 2001.[29] The Ecodesign for Energy-Related Products Regulations 2007[30] revoked all these previous regulations, implementing Directive 2005/32/EC, and these regulations were themselves revoked by the current Ecodesign for Energy-Using Products Regulations 2010,[31] which implemented Directive 2009/125/EC.

32.33 The Ecodesign for Energy-Related Products Regulations 2010 are still in place, but have been amended by various amendment provisions, including provisions dealing with the UK's exit from the EU. This is a lengthy piece of legislation, but the key provisions can be summarised as follows.

32.34 These Regulations apply to 'energy-related products' which are defined as 'any good that has an impact on energy consumption during use which is placed on the market or put into service' and certain related parts (reg 2(1)).

32.35 Manufacturers must not place on the market or put into service energy-related products unless they comply with the applicable implementing measures and bear either the CE marking or UK marking (reg 3). Compliance requires that the manufacturer assesses whether the energy-related product complies with the applicable implementing

---

25 Department for Energy Security and Net Zero, 'Net Zero Strategy: Build Back Greener' (n 2) 278.
26 Directive 2009/125/EC, Article 2(23).
27 SI 1993/3083.
28 SI 1997/1941.
29 SI 2001/3316.
30 SI 2007/2037.
31 SI 2010/2617.

measure, and if so, makes a declaration of conformity, and affixes the CE or UK marking (as applicable) (reg 4).[32]

32.36 The Secretary of State is required to make implementing measures in respect of products which meet certain criteria (reg 22). These criteria include that the product has a significant environmental impact, and presents a significant potential for improvement in terms of its environmental impact without entailing excessive cost. There are various provisions detailing what the Secretary of State must take into consideration in making implementing measures. The implementing measures themselves must, among other things, lay down ecodesign requirements in accordance with Annex 1 and 2 of Directive 2009/125/EC. Schedule 1 sets out the various energy-related products, and the related implementing measures which they must conform to.

32.37 There are various mechanisms for dealing with non-compliance with these regulations. The Secretary of State (as the marketing surveillance authority) has the power to impose civil sanctions. These include issuing compliance notices (requiring steps to be taken to secure that offence does not continue, or requiring products to be withdrawn), stop notices (prohibiting persons from carrying on an activity specified in a notice, or prohibiting/restricting products from coming onto the market), and requiring payment of a variable monetary penalty or non-compliance penalty (Schedule 5).

32.38 Further, various criminal offences for breaching certain regulations are specified within Part 6 of the Ecodesign for Energy-Related Products Regulations 2010. Upon conviction, the court may also make a 'remediation order', requiring the convicted person to remedy any matter of which he/she was convicted.

32.39 The latest ecodesign regulations are the Ecodesign for Energy-Related Products and Energy Information Regulations 2021[33] and the Ecodesign for Energy-Related Products and Energy Information (Lighting Products) Regulations 2021.[34] Both provisions were made pursuant to powers contained within the Ecodesign for Energy-Related Products Regulations 2010.

32.40 The Ecodesign for Energy-Related Products and Energy Information Regulations 2021 set out various ecodesign requirements for a range of energy-related products, including welding equipment, household washing machines and washer-dryers, refrigerating appliances, electric motors and variable speed drives, and electronic displays. Meanwhile the Ecodesign for Energy-Related Products and Energy Information (Lighting Products) Regulations 2021 set out various ecodesign requirements for light sources and separate control gears.

---

32 Following the UK's exit from the EU, pursuant to the Ecodesign for Energy-Related Products and Energy Information (Amendment) (EU Exit) Regulations 2019, regs 3 and 4 provide that goods placed onto the market or put into service in England, Wales and Scotland bear the UK marking, and goods placed onto the market or put into service in Northern Ireland bear the CE marking.
33 SI 2021/745.
34 SI 2021/1095.

32.41 One of the prescribed ecodesign requirements for these products under the Ecodesign for Energy-Related Products and Energy Information Regulations 2021 concerns resource efficiency and is often described as the 'right to repair'. In particular, these regulations provide that in respect of certain products to which they apply, the manufacturer (or authorised representative or importer) must make available to professional repairers certain spare parts and repair and maintenance information, and must ensure that spare parts are delivered within 15 working days of receiving an order.[35]

32.42 Further UK legislation related to ecodesign are the Waste Electrical and Electronic Equipment Regulations 2013,[36] which provide for the prevention, and recovery, of waste electrical and electronic equipment. These Regulations transpose the main provisions of Directive 2012/19/EU on waste electrical and electronic equipment ('WEEE'). This Directive provides that producers of electrical and electronic equipment will be financially responsible for managing the waste that arises from products they place on the Union market. This policy is intended to promote greater efficiencies in the management of waste from this type of equipment. These Regulations provide for all WEEE that arises in the United Kingdom to be collected at designated collection facilities and transported to an 'approved authorised treatment facility' or approved exporter for treatment, recovery, recycling or reuse.[37]

(iii) *Consumer Rights Act 2015*

32.43 The Consumer Rights Act 2015 provides that a contract between a consumer and a trader for the sale of goods will be treated as including a term that the quality of the goods is satisfactory (section 9). The quality of goods includes their state and condition, their fitness for purpose, their appearance and finish, their freedom from minor defects, safety and durability. Further, if the consumer makes known to the trader a particular purpose for the goods, and the consumer reasonably relies on the skill or judgment of the trader, then the contract will be treated as containing a term that the goods are reasonably fit for that purpose (section 10).

32.44 If the goods are not of satisfactory quality, or not fit for purpose, the consumer has various rights, including the short term right to reject (section 20 and 22), the right to repair or replacement (section 23), and the right to a price reduction or final right to reject (section 20 and 24).

32.45 Importantly, goods which do not conform (including not being of satisfactory quality or fit for purpose) within the period of six months from the day the goods were delivered, must be taken not to have conformed to it on that day (section 20(14)).

32.46 The relevance of this to net zero is that this legislation incentivises product manufacturers to make their products more durable (and therefore sustainable), as there

35 e.g. para 3(11) of Schedule 1 of the Ecodesign for Energy-Related Products and Energy Information Regulations 2021.
36 SI 2013/3113.
37 Explanatory Memorandum to the Waste Electrical and Electronic Equipment Regulations 2013, 2013.

is an automatic presumption that non-conformities found within the first six months if there is a non-conformity are regarded as present on the day of sale.

(iv) *Future Legislation*

32.47 In response to Kwasi Kwarteng's letter to the CMA of 19 July 2021, referred to in paragraph 32.18 above, in respect of product design and durability, the CMA stated in correspondence published on 14 March 2022:[38]

> Some CFI respondents suggested an extension of the statutory guarantees in the Consumer Rights Act 2015, as a means of incentivising businesses to design longer-lasting products. Other jurisdictions have taken a different approach, banning premature obsolescence altogether.
>
> While the CMA does not yet have sufficient evidence to recommend specific changes to consumer law at present, the Secretary of State may wish to undertake further work to explore potential benefits of changes to the law to:
>
> - expressly prohibit planned premature obsolescence. This could be achieved by adding planned or premature obsolescence to Schedule 1 to the CPRs or through freestanding legislation
> - broadening of the 'right to repair' under the Ecodesign for Energy-Related Products and Energy Information Regulations 2021 to include other categories of product.'

32.48 A consultation launched by DEFRA and the devolved governments, which sought views on reforms to the Waste Electrical and Electronic Regulations 2013, closed on 7 March 2024. Suggested reforms included producer responsibility for WEEE, to support a drive to a more circular economy (being an economy where waste becomes a resource that is reintroduced into the production cycle).[39]

32.49 It appears highly likely that further ecodesign legislation will be developed in the near future.

Greenwashing

32.50 As the regulatory tools for tackling climate change develop and gain traction, so too does a range of marketing practices known as 'greenwashing', by which companies lead consumers to believe that products or company practices are doing more to protect the environment than is actually the case. Greenwashing creates a false sense of consumer confidence by way of exaggerated or even false solutions, at the expense of credible action to address climate change.

---

38 CMA, 'Environmental Sustainability and the UK Competition and Consumer Regimes: CMA Advice to the Government' (n 15).

39 DEFRA, 'Consultation on Reforming the Producer Responsibility System for Waste Electrical and Electronic Equipment' (2023) <https://consult.defra.gov.uk/product-regulation-and-producer-responsibility/consultation-on-reforming-the-producer-responsibil/supporting_documents/WEEE%20Reforms%20Consultation%20Document%20Final%202023%20.pdf> accessed 18 September 2024.

32.51 Greenwashing can take many forms, for example:

- Overstatement of an organisation's actions or initiatives in respect of climate change, also known as 'climate-washing';[40]
- Deliberately vague environmental claims, such as 'kinder' or 'healthier' to 'our planet';[41]
- Vague or unsubstantiated claims of 'net zero' plans or strategies;
- False or exaggerated claims of 'carbon neutral' or 'low emission' business practices, events or products;[42]
- The use of non-regulated terms to describe products and services, such as 'green' or 'eco friendly' without proper basis;[43]
- Emphasising a single sustainable or positive element of an environmental policy or product in isolation from any wider factors;[44]
- Selective use of data to mislead the public as to environmental claims;[45]
- Strategic investment or sponsorship to distract from polluting business practice;[46]
- Use of environmental offset schemes such as plastic credits or reforestation without addressing more polluting business practices.

32.52 Not only does greenwashing take many forms, but it has increased exponentially with the global encouragement of responsible commercial practice – environmental, social and corporate governance ('ESG') – since COP 21 and the Paris Agreement. The

---

40 For example, making selective or misleading claims about an organisation's carbon emissions, including carbon offset initiatives or net zero pledges, now increasingly referred to as 'carbonwashing': See <https://sfi.stanford.edu/sites/sfi/files/media/file/carbonwashing-_a_new_type_of_carbon_data-related_esg_greenwashing_working_paper_0_0_0_0.pdf> accessed 16 September 2024.
41 Persil TV advertisement, banned by ASA in August 2022 for unclear use of the word 'kinder'; Alpro cautioned by ASA for claiming that its oat milk was 'your recipe to a healthier planet'.
42 FIFA was successfully reported to ASA in 2022 for its claims that the 2022 Qatar FIFA World Cup was completely carbon neutral: see <https://climatecasechart.com/non-us-case/new-weather-institute-v-fifa/> accessed 16 September 2024; Ryanair was banned from advertising 'lowest emissions' with little substantiation; Etihad Airways banned from making claims of 'sustainable aviation' in 2023.
43 Perfectly Green Limited, an artificial grass company, was banned by ASA from claiming that its product was recyclable, and that it could be called 'Eco-grass'. See <https://www.asa.org.uk/rulings/perfectly-green-ltd-a22-1156075-perfectly-green-ltd.html> accessed 16 September 2024.
44 HSBC claiming that it was aiming to produce up to £1 trillion in net zero financing, whilst omitting significant information about its investment in the fossil fuel industry.
45 Oatly Limited claimed that its product generated 75% less CO_2 than milk; however, ASA found that some of the data supporting this claim had been carefully selected and presented in a misleading fashion. See <https://www.asa.org.uk/rulings/oatly-uk-ltd-g21-1096286-oatly-uk-ltd.html> accessed 16 September 2024.
46 Coca Cola Limited's sponsorship of COP 27 in 2022, in spite of the fact that the company has been exposed as the world's worst plastic polluter for five years prior to COP 27. See <https://www.breakfreefromplastic.org/2022/11/15/the-coca-cola-company-named-worst-plastic-polluter-for-five-years-in-a-row-brand-audit-2022-report/> accessed 16 September 2024.

problem is particularly acute in the European and North American markets.[47] Greenwashing occurs across a range of consumer products and services, and in the example of Coca Cola's sponsorship of COP 27, might be said to have infiltrated even the United Nations' highest committee to address climate change. That said, consumer awareness of this practice has developed considerably, as can be seen by the number of references to the Advertising Standards Agency ('ASA') (discussed further below). There has been a corresponding increase in regulatory measures to tackle greenwashing, which means that it has become more difficult for companies to make claims designed to mislead consumers, or to reassure them of environmental credentials on a false basis. These are discussed below.

(i) *National law*

32.53 In the UK, greenwashing practices relating to consumers currently fall within the Consumer Protection from Unfair Training Regulations 2008 ('CPRs').[48] These do not address greenwashing practices directly, but instead regulate all aspects of business to consumer transactions with to a view to protecting consumers from misleading claims or other unfair commercial practices. The CPRs most likely to be engaged by greenwashing practices are:

- Regulation 3 of the CPRs prohibits 'unfair commercial practices', described as contravening the requirements of professional diligence, likely to materially distort the economic behaviour of the average consumer, misleading for the purposes of Regulations 5 and 6, or contained within the list of unfair practices at Schedule 1;

- Regulation 5 bans three types of misleading action: any practice containing false information, any comparison with another product likely to confuse, and a failure to comply with a code of conduct;

- Regulation 6 prohibits misleading omissions, which includes the provision of material information in an unclear or ambiguous manner, in addition to omitting or concealing material information itself;

- Schedule 1 sets out a list of commercial practices which are in all circumstances unfair and prohibited. The relevant practices for greenwashing include falsely claiming to be a signatory to a code of conduct (paragraph 1), displaying a quality mark or equivalent without the necessary authorisation (paragraph 2), falsely claiming that a trader or its product has been approved by another body (paragraph 4), and presenting the consumer's legal rights as a distinctive feature of the trader's offer (paragraph 10).

32.54 The CPRs are enforced by the Competition and Markets Authority ('CMA'), and, in Great Britain, weights and measures authorities (as defined at regulation 2(1)).

47 <https://www.reprisk.com/news-research/reports/on-the-rise-navigating-the-wave-of-greenwashing-and-social-washing> accessed 16 September 2024.

48 SI 2008/1277. The Business Protection from Misleading Marketing Regulations 2008, SI 2008/1276 (known as the BPRs) provide similar protection for business-to-business advertising and comparative advertising.

32.55 The Digital Markets, Competition and Consumers Bill was introduced in 2023, and is anticipated to make sweeping changes to consumer protection laws. It is intended to replace the CPRs by consolidating the prohibition of unfair commercial practices. It is also anticipated to extend the powers of the regulatory bodies, discussed in more detail below. Although the Bill does not explicitly refer to the term 'greenwashing', it is envisaged that these powers will enable the CMA and other bodies to tackle greenwashing as a form of misleading commercial practice.

(ii) *National guidance*

32.56 Most greenwashing claims arise in the context of public communications, notably advertising as well as organisational ESG credentials or carbon claims. The codes that govern advertising in Britain are the UK Code of Non-Broadcast Advertising, Sale Promotion and Direct Marketing ('the CAP Code'), which applies to non-broadcast advertising such as print, internet, cinema or social media, and the UK Code of Broadcast Advertising ('the BCAP Code'), which applies to radio and television. The formal guidance on the application of the CAP and BCAP Codes ('Advertising Guidance') advises advertisers as follows:[49]

- Avoid using unqualified 'carbon neutral', 'net zero' or similar claims. Information explaining the basis for these claims helps consumers' understanding, and such information should therefore not be omitted.

- Marketers should ensure that they include accurate information about whether (and the degree to which) they are actively reducing carbon emissions or are basing claims on offsetting, to ensure that consumers do not wrongly assume that products or their manufacture generate no or few emissions.

- Claims based on future goals relating to reaching net zero or achieving carbon neutrality should be based on a verifiable strategy to deliver them.

- Where claims are based on offsetting, they should comply with the usual standards of evidence for objective claims set out in this guidance, and Advertising Guidance 14 marketers should provide information about the offsetting scheme they are using.

- Where it is necessary to include qualifying information about a claim, that information should be sufficiently close to the main aspects of the claim for consumers to be able to see it easily and take account of it before they make any decision. The less prominent any qualifying information is, and the further away it is from any main claim being made, the more likely the claim will mislead consumers.

49 ASA, 'The Environment: Misleading Claims and Social Responsibility in Advertising: Advertising Guidance (Non-Broadcast and Broadcast)' (2023) <https://www.asa.org.uk/static/d819e399-3cf9-44ea-942b82d5ecd6dff3/4d3c736f-1e59-471f-bf77e10614544b3b/CAP-guidance-on-misleading-environmental-claims-and-social-responsibility.pdf> accessed 16 September 2024.

32.57 Both CAP and BCAP Codes are enforced by the ASA, to which complaints can be made for review and determination. The ASA has been at the forefront of efforts to tackle greenwashing, as its recent rulings have demonstrated:

- UK adverts for Air France, Lufthansa and Etihad were banned in December 2023 for misleading consumers about the airlines' environmental impact;[50]
- A Shell UK Limited TV and print campaign alleging that 'the UK is READY for Cleaner Energy' was banned in June 2023 for having mislead the public about the proportion of Shell's business that comprised lower-carbon energy products;
- A TV advert for Anglian Water in June 2023 was banned for having misleadingly omitted material information about its release of sewage into the environment;[51]
- HSBC UK Bank plc was banned in October 2021 from using posters that promoted its green initiatives because these omitted significant information about the company's contribution to carbon dioxide and greenhouse gas emissions.[52]

32.58 There is no direct financial consequence to any such review by ASA, however, and it is of note that both Lufthansa and Etihad were found to have misled consumers on more than one occasion in 2023.[53]

32.59 In 2021, this regulatory regime was boosted by CMA's issue of the Green Claims Code ('GCC'), to apply to all advertising and any product or service supplied to UK consumers, whether the business itself is based in the UK or not. The object of the GCC is to eradicate greenwashing by providing a code of conduct for businesses to assist compliance with the CPRs and BPRs. It comprises six key 'principles' for businesses when making an environmental or 'green' claim:[54]

- It must be truthful and accurate, and businesses must live up to all claims made;
- It must be clear and unambiguous, i.e. a customer should be able to understand the claims being made;

---

50 ASA, 'ASA Ruling on Etihad Airways' (2023) <https://www.asa.org.uk/rulings/etihad-airways-a23-1206008-etihad-airways.html> accessed 21 April 2024; ASA, 'ASA Ruling on Deutsche Lufthansa AG t/a Lufthansa' (2023) <https://www.asa.org.uk/rulings/deutsche-lufthansa-ag-a23-1206007-deutsche-lufthansa-ag.html> accessed 21 April 2024; ASA, 'ASA Ruling on Air France-KLM' (2023) <https://www.asa.org.uk/rulings/air-france-klm-a23-1206006-air-france-klm.html> accessed 21 April 2024.

51 ASA, 'ASA Ruling on Anglian Water Services Ltd t/a Anglian Water' (2023) <https://www.asa.org.uk/rulings/anglian-water-services-ltd-g22-1171967-anglian-water-services-ltd.html> accessed 21 April 2024.

52 ASA, 'ASA Ruling on HSBC UK Bank Plc' (2023) <https://www.asa.org.uk/rulings/hsbc-uk-bank-plc-g21-1127656-hsbc-uk-bank-plc.html> accessed 21 April 2024.

53 A poster for Lufthansa was banned by ASA for making misleading environmental claims in March 2023, and Etihad had already had a Facebook campaign banned by ASA in April 2023.

54 CMA, 'Making Environmental Claims on Goods and Services' (2021) <https://www.gov.uk/government/publications/green-claims-code-making-environmental-claims/environmental-claims-on-goods-and-services#principles>.

- It must not omit or hide important information, such that the consumer has the full picture to be able to make an informed choice;
- Comparisons must be fair and meaningful, between products that meet the same needs or be intended for the same purpose;
- It must be substantiated, that is, backed up with robust and credible evidence;
- The claim should include consideration of the full life cycle of the product or service, i.e. its overall impact from creation to disposal.

32.60 The GCC (unlike the CPRs and BPRs) is not itself legally binding, but its introduction in September 2021 marked an increased vigilance on the part of the CMA in respect of environmental claims made to consumers. In 2022, the CMA went on to conduct detailed reviews of environmental claims made by the fast fashion sector, as well as household products.[55] In the same year, it also commenced investigations into the advertising and provision of 'green' heating solutions, followed by a more detailed investigation of Worcester Bosch, the leading UK heating boiler brand, amid concerns that it was misleading consumers with inaccurate or confusing green claims.[56]

32.61 These efforts will soon be supported by the Digital Markets, Competition and Consumers Bill, which is anticipated to arm the CMA with far greater powers, in particular in respect of enforcement of consumer laws. At the date of going to press, the Bill had had its third reading, however, the proposed provisions include enabling the CMA to:

- Enforce consumer laws directly without recourse to the courts;
- Investigate any suspected infringements of consumer laws;
- Issue infringement notices and award compensation to consumers;
- Impose fines of up to 10% of a company's annual global turnover, and further financial sanctions if a company fails to comply with an information request from the CMA.

32.62 The Bill will therefore incorporate the GCC guidance and the critical role of the CMA within the new statutory regime, and afford the CMA the powers it currently lacks to identify and effectively penalise greenwashing practices.

---

55 CMA, 'ASOS, Boohoo and Asda Investigated over Fashion "Green" Claims' (2022) <https://www.gov.uk/government/news/asos-boohoo-and-asda-investigated-over-fashion-green-claims> and CMA, 'Unilever's "Green" Claims Come under CMA Microscope' (2023) <https://www.gov.uk/government/news/unilevers-green-claims-come-under-cma-microscope>.

56 CMA, 'Investigation into Boiler Company over "Green" Claims' (2023) <https://www.gov.uk/government/news/investigation-into-boiler-company-over-green-claims>.

(iii) *EU legal framework*

32.63 Within the EU legislative framework, greenwashing falls under the Unfair Commercial Practices Directive (2005/29/EC). The interpretation of the Directive was updated in December 2021, and now includes the following interpretative principles relevant to misleading or false environmental claims:[57]

- Green claims must be truthful, not contain false information and be presented in a clear and specific, accurate and unambiguous manner, so that consumers are not mislead (based on Article 6 of the Directive);

- Green claims can be misleading if they consist of vague and general statements of environmental benefits, and to avoid being deemed so should be supplemented by prominent specifications or explanatory statements on the product's environmental impact (based on Article 7 of the Directive);

- Traders must have evidence to support their claims (based on Article 12 of the Directive).

32.64 The guidance also identifies which of the unfair practices contained in Annex I of the Directive are particularly relevant to environmental claims, including claiming to be a signatory to a code of conduct without having done so or displaying a trust mark or equivalent without having obtained the necessary authorisation.

32.65 The need to address greenwashing was identified as a priority by the European Commission in the New Circular Economy Action Plan (11 March 2020) and the New Consumer Agenda (13 November 2020). In March 2023, the Commission proposed the Green Claims Directive, specifically to address greenwashing. The proposed Directive also incorporates the objectives of the 2019 European Green Deal 2019, which aimed at empowering consumers to make better informed choices and thereby take an active role in the 'green transition'.[58] The main goals of the Directive are:

- To harmonise the minimum requirements for traders to provide evidence when making environmental claims;

- A standardised EU labelling system;

- New enforcement procedures and penalties for non-compliance.

---

57 Commission Notice on the interpretation and application of the Unfair Commercial Practices Directive, at Section 4 https://eur-lex.europa.eu/legal-content/EN/TXT/?uri=CELEX%3A52021XC1229%2805%29 accessed 16 September 2024.

58 European Commission, 'Proposal for a Directive of the European Parliament and of the Council on Substantiation and Communication of Explicit Environmental Claims (Green Claims Directive)' (2023) COM(2023) 166 final <https://eur-lex.europa.eu/legal-content/EN/TXT/PDF/?uri=CELEX:52023PC0166> accessed 16 September 2024.

32.66 At the date of going to press, the draft Directive was awaiting the Council's first reading position.

(iv) *International guidance*

32.67 The development of international reporting standards will also alleviate the problem of greenwashing by standardising environmental metrics and required disclosures. In June 2023, the International Sustainability Standards Board ('ISSB') published two new international standards for corporate sustainability disclosures: IFRS S1, which addresses environmental impact, including emissions, and IFRS S2, which addresses specific items such as climate mitigation and adaptation.[59] These are due to come into effect in January 2024, and the government has already confirmed that it will publish its own sustainability disclosure standards based on IFRS S1 and S2.[60] In August 2023, the International Auditing and Assurance Standards Board ('IAASB'), opened a consultation on a global sustainability assurance standard, for the purpose of enabling confidence in sustainability reporting.[61] We address this in more detail in Chapter 30.

59 IFRS, 'IFRS – New and Updated Resources to Help Companies Apply IFRS S1 and IFRS S2 from 2024' (2023) <https://www.ifrs.org/news-and-events/news/2023/12/new-and-updated-resources-to-help-companies-apply-ifrs-s1-ifrs-s2/> accessed 21 April 2024.
60 Department for Business, Energy and Industrial Strategy, 'UK Sustainability Disclosure Standards' (2023) <https://www.gov.uk/guidance/uk-sustainability-disclosure-standards> accessed 16 September 2024.
61 IAASB, 'IAASB Launches Public Consultation on Landmark Proposed Global Sustainability Assurance Standard | IAASB' (2023) <https://www.iaasb.org/news-events/2023-08/iaasb-launches-public-consultation-landmark-proposed-global-sustainability-assurance-standard> accessed 21 April 2024.

CHAPTER 33

ENFORCEMENT AND RELAXATION OF CORPORATE RESPONSIBILITIES

James Shaerf and Anna Lintner

33.01 Corporate net zero nature positive obligations are of little value if they are not enforced. A notable theme in this developing area of law has been 'enforcement' by the market. As noted in Chapter 4, regulators have prioritised transparency and the provision of detailed and accurate information about the environmental credentials of products and services, in the hope that an informed market will incentivise production that is aligned with net zero and nature positive goals.

33.02 The increased availability of information as to the environmental practices of corporate entities has also led to creative attempts to deploy established private law rights, against such entities, in aid of net zero and nature positive goals. As discussed below, law of tort and company law relating to the rights of shareholders have been deployed with mixed results.

33.03 Another notable trend has been the relaxation of the regulatory regime relating to anti-competitive practices in order to permit companies to pursue environmental goals that might otherwise be unattainable. This development is discussed below.

Shareholder claims

33.04 This section is concerned with what rights might be available to a shareholder to vindicate interests associated with climate change policy generally.

33.05 The reality is that the claims that have been pursued to date have invariably been pursued by minority shareholders, meaning they must pursue their action through the derivative claims mechanism – that is, they must sue on behalf of the company, and the claim will only be permitted to proceed if it is one that the directors would have pursued acting in accordance with their fiduciary obligations.

33.06 This section considers:

- The UK statutory framework under the Companies Act 2006 ('CA 2006').
- Two recent decisions of the English courts dealing with duties under CA 2006 and derivative claims.

- Claims by shareholders in respect of listing particulars and prospectuses under the Financial Services and Markets Act 2000 ('FSMA').

- Other potential avenues for shareholder redress.

(i) *The UK statutory framework*

33.07 Section 170 of CA 2006 provides that the general duties enumerated in sections 171 to 177 are owed by a director of the company to the company.

33.08 Section 171 requires directors to act in accordance with the company's constitution and only to exercise their powers for the purposes for which those powers are conferred.

33.09 The statute goes on to state expressly that section 171 may be breached even though the director has acted in accordance with all his other duties, and in particular the duties to act in good faith and with care. In determining whether there has been a breach of section 171, the court must:

- First, construe the power and determine the limits within which it must be exercised, and second consider the purpose actuating the exercise of the power and determine whether it falls within the proper limits.

- Assess whether the exercise of the power is an abuse of power, even if the power is exercised within the scope of the rule.[1]

33.10 Section 172 of CA 2006 imposes a duty to promote the success of the company in the following terms:

> (1) A director of a company must act in the way he considers, in good faith, would be most likely to promote the success of the company for the benefit of its members as a whole, and in doing so have regard (amongst other matters) to–
>
> (a) the likely consequences of any decision in the long term,
> (b) the interests of the company's employees,
> (c) the need to foster the company's business relationships with suppliers, customers and others,
> (d) the impact of the company's operations on the community and the environment,
> (e) the desirability of the company maintaining a reputation for high standards of business conduct, and
> (f) the need to act fairly as between members of the company.
>
> (2) Where or to the extent that the purposes of the company consist of or include purposes other than the benefit of its members, subsection (1) has effect as if the reference to promoting the success of the company for the benefit of its members were to achieving those purposes.

1 *Eclairs Group Ltd v JKX Oil & Gas plc* [2015] UKSC 71 [15].

(3) The duty imposed by this section has effect subject to any enactment or rule of law requiring directors, in certain circumstances, to consider or act in the interests of creditors of the company.

33.11 Like section 171(1)(b), the duty imposed on directors is to act bona fide in the interests of the company and is assessed subjectively:[2]

> The question is not whether, viewed objectively by the court, the particular act or omission which is challenged was in fact in the interests of the company; still less is the question whether the court, had it been in the position of the director at the relevant time, might have acted differently. Rather, the question is whether the director honestly believed that his act or omission was in the interests of the company. The issue is as to the director's state of mind.

33.12 Among the duties that are further enumerated, we find:

- Section 173(1), which provides for the duty to exercise independent judgment.
- Section 174 which provides for the duty to exercise reasonable care, skill and diligence.
- Section 175, which provides for the duty to avoid conflicts of interest.

33.13 The framework for derivative claims is found in Part 11 of the Act. Relevantly:

- A derivative claim may only be brought in respect of a cause of action involving a legal wrong by a director of the company.[3]
- Where a shareholder of the company commences a derivative claim, it must apply to the Court for permission (in Northern Ireland, leave) to continue it. If the Court considers that the application for permission and the supporting evidence filed by the applicant in support of it do not disclose a prima facie case for giving permission, the court must dismiss the application.[4]
- Permission must be refused if a person acting in accordance with section 172 would not seek to continue the claim,[5] or if the act or omission in issue has been authorised or ratified by the company.[6]
- The court must take into account a number of factors, including whether the member seeking permission is acting in good faith in seeking to continue the

2 *Re Regentcrest plc v Cohen* [2001] 2 BCLC 80 [120] per Jonathan Parker J.
3 Companies Act 2006 s 260(3).
4 ibid s 261(2).
5 ibid s 263(2)(a).
6 ibid s 263(2)(b) and (c).

claim, and the importance that a person acting in accordance with section 172 would attach to continuing the claim.[7]

(ii) *The English courts' approach to climate-related derivative claims*

33.14 Shareholder derivative claims in respect of the directors' or company's failure to pursue climate change-friendly corporate policies are a relatively new phenomenon. There is an increasing realisation that change in the private sector might be encouraged through the use of existing levers of company law. After all, in principle if a court were to be persuaded that climate change-friendly policies are an undoubted public good, it might take the position that a board of directors failing to consider, if not pursue, such policies (if the context of the company's field of activity reasonably requires them to be considered or pursued) is acting in a way that is harmful to the planet. The company's success may be said to be tied to that of the planet. In that case, not pursuing the policies is not promoting the company's success.

33.15 The problem with this line of argument is that innately it espouses a particular political point of view. Were the courts to sanction a derivative claim in these circumstances they would effectively be requiring the directors to take the company's climate change policies in a given direction, which would inevitably involve trespassing on the directors' exercise of their independent commercial judgment. That is all the more so in circumstances where there is no consensus as to how the company can best implement climate policy. The door is opened to an applicant saying that the company has not adopted the applicant's favoured approach, where there are many approaches available. How is the court to decide which approach is best without taking a position on the relative importance of climate policy in the range of considerations which directors must apply in their best commercial judgment?

33.16 *McGaughey v Universities Superannuation Scheme* concerned a company limited by guarantee whose sole object was to act as trustee of a superannuation scheme.[8] The claimants, who were academics, were members of the superannuation scheme and pursued claims against the past and present directors of the company, alleging various breaches of fiduciary and statutory duties. The action was pursued as a common law derivative claim, thus requiring the court's permission to proceed. The claimants alleged that in breach of sections 171 and 172 of the Companies Act, the directors continued to invest in fossil fuels without a plan for divestment, contrary to the company's long-term financial interests and scheme's public statements to the effect that it intended to be carbon neutral by 2050.

33.17 Leech J rejected this part of the claim, finding that the claimants had only made their allegation of a financial loss in the abstract and had failed to point to any immediate financial loss suffered by the company. The Court also found that the claimants' interest in climate change and their disagreement with the directors' approach to investment did not give them standing to bring a derivative claim.

7 ibid s 263(2)(a) and (b).
8 *McGaughey v Universities Superannuation Scheme* [2022] EWHC 1233 (Ch).

33.18 The Court further held that the company was under a duty to exercise its powers of investment in a manner calculated to ensure the security, quality, liquidity, and profitability of the portfolio as a whole, and diversifying the assets in such as a way to avoid excessive reliance on any particular asset, issuer, or group of undertakings.[9] The Court found that the company's approach was 'well within the discretion of the Company in exercising the powers of its investment' and was not prepared to allow an allegation to the contrary to go to trial.

33.19 The Court of Appeal dismissed an appeal, stating that, in effect, the claimants' fossil fuels claim was 'an attempt to challenge the management and investment decisions of [the company] as trustee without any ground upon which to do so', and that there was nothing to suggest the company had exercised its powers in an improper fashion.[10] The Court of Appeal also suggested that the claim should not have been brought derivatively in the name of the company, and that there was no reason – apart from the claimants' desire to avoid difficulties in relation to costs and representation – for proceeding in the Court's derivative jurisdiction. The claimants could, after all, have proceeded directly against the company for breach of trust.

33.20 The limits of the derivative claim procedure in climate change cases were further put to the test by a single (and very much minority) shareholder of Shell plc, in *ClientEarth v Shell plc*.[11] ClientEarth ('CE') (which held 27 shares) sought permission to issue a derivative claim against Shell's directors under section 260 (1) of CA 2006. CE alleged that the directors had breached their section 172 and section 174 duties because they had failed to establish appropriate emissions targets, strategies to manage climate change risk, establish a reasonable basis for achieving the net zero target and align with the 1.5 degree Paris Agreement goal. Additionally a breach was said to arise out of a failure to comply with the judgment of The Hague District Court in *Vereniging Milieudefensie v Royal Dutch Shell plc* (in which the Court had ordered Shell to reduce its CO_2 emissions, and which is discussed further below at paragraphs 33.67–33.74).[12]

33.21 The legal question before the Court was whether CE established a prima facie case for giving permission to bring a derivative claim against the company, a process designed to weed out unmeritorious or clearly undeserving cases.[13] Under rule 19.15 of the Civil Procedure Rules, the procedure for a derivative claim is that the court shall determine on the papers in the first instance whether a prima facie case has been established. If the court is not satisfied that such a case has been established, the application must be dismissed, but the petitioning shareholder has the right to an oral hearing

9 In this case this was in accordance with the Occupational Pensions (Investment) Regulations 2005, SI 2005/3378, consistent with the common law's approach articulated by Sir Robert Megarry V-C in *Cowan v Scargill* [1985] Ch 270 [286H]–[288G].
10 *McGaughey v Universities Superannuation Scheme Ltd* [2023] EWCA Civ 873 [174].
11 *ClientEarth v Shell plc* [2023] EWHC 1137 (Ch); [2023] EWHC 1897 (Ch). There were two judgments as CE's application was initially dismissed on the papers, leading to a second judgment in which Trower J further explained his reasoning following an oral hearing. References are to the later judgment.
12 *Vereniging Milieudefensie v Royal Dutch Shell plc and others* [2021] C/09/571932/HA ZA 19-379 (The Hague District Court). On 12 November 2024 the Hague Court of Appeal handed down its judgment in the appeal, 200.302.332/01.
13 See *ClientEarth v Shell plc* [2023] EWHC 1897 (Ch) (n 11) [8].

within 7 days. Trower J dismissed CE's application for permission, both on the papers and following an oral hearing as requested by CE.

33.22 CE contended that the statutory duties in sections 172 and 174 encompassed a number of 'incidental' duties to comply with strategies to mitigate the risk of climate change. These duties are set out at paragraph 22 of the judgment and effectively would have required Shell to act to mitigate climate risk and accord appropriate weight to it, make judgments regarding climate risk based upon a reasonable consensus of scientific opinion. In particular, it was alleged that Shell had 'a duty to implement reasonable measures to mitigate the risks to the long-term financial profitability and resilience of Shell in the transition to a global energy system and economy aligned with the global temperature objective of 1.5°c under the Paris Agreement'. CE accordingly sought a mandatory injunction requiring the directors to (a) adopt and implement a strategy to manage climate risk in compliance with their statutory duties and (b) to comply immediately with the Dutch Order.

33.23 The Court confirmed that, given the emphasis on subjectivity in the assessment of a breach of the section 172 duty, the question was whether the directors of Shell has acted in good faith, not simply whether they had acted irrationally: an honest but unreasonable and mistaken belief that a particular course of action is in the company's best interests is not sufficient to amount to a breach of section 172.[14]

33.24 The Court rejected the claimants' formulation of the duties incumbent upon Shell as being inconsistent with the established principle that it is for directors of the company to determine (acting in good faith) how best to promote the success of a company for the benefit of its members as a whole. This is essentially a commercial decision which the court is ill-equipped to take, except in a clear case.[15] Trower J said at [37] that:[16]

> The way in which ClientEarth puts its case seeks to impose absolute duties on the Directors which cut across their general duty to have regard to the many competing considerations as to how best to promote the success of Shell for the benefit of its members as a whole. The impact of Shell's operations on the community and the environment is a matter which the Directors are required to weigh in the balance in that context (s.172(1)(d)), but their responses to the business risks for Shell associated with climate change, whether they be the adoption of a strategy or its implementation, are part of the decision making process by which the Directors manage Shell's business.

33.25 Trower J also found that even if, as a matter of Dutch law, the directors owe duties to Shell to take reasonable steps to ensure the order made by the Court in Milieudefensie was to be obeyed, that would be irrelevant to the assessment of their claims made in the instant proceedings, which were governed by English law. The judge said that English law knew of no specific duty (separate from the general duties owed

---

14 ibid [29]–[30].
15 ibid [28], citing *Lesini v Westrip Holdings Ltd* [2010] BCC 420 [85] per Lewison J.
16 *ClientEarth v Shell plc* [2023] EWHC 1897 (Ch) (n 11) [37].

by directors) which required them to take reasonable steps to ensure that the order of a foreign court is obeyed.[17]

33.26 After indicating his view on the scope of Shell's obligations, Trower J considered the alleged breaches of duty. CE put forward voluminous evidence (in the form of a witness statement and exhibits made by a senior lawyer employed by CE) to establish its allegations that the directors failed to set an appropriate emissions target, and that they did not have a management strategy in place which was a reasonable basis for achieving the net zero target. The evidence implicated Shell's responsibility for direct emissions from the production of oil and gas (scope 1), indirect emissions from the generation of energy used to carry out operations (oil refining) (scope 2) and indirect emissions arising from the use of Shells' products by its customers (scope 3). While CE's evidence before Trower J canvassed all of Shell's directors' public statements as to how to mitigate its emissions risk, CE's claim criticised the inadequacy of Shells' targets for reducing its scope 1 and 2 emissions, and for failing to set any target at all for the reduction of scope 3 emissions.

33.27 After carefully summarising the evidence, Trower J rejected CE's claims, saying that:

- The court could place very little weight on the opinions expressed by CE's lawyer (the genuineness of which the judge described as being 'plainly insufficient').[18] Neither CE's lawyer nor CE were able to give expert evidence on which the court could rely.

- The evidence did not establish that there was a universally accepted methodology by which Shell might be able to achieve the targeted reduction of emissions. Hence it was difficult to treat what CE was saying as a:[19]

  > proper evidential basis for alleging that no reasonable board of Directors could properly conclude that the pathway to achievement is the one they have adopted. While it is plain that there are fundamental disagreements between ClientEarth and the Directors as to the right way to achieve the NZ 2050 targets that Shell has set itself, the law respects the autonomy of the decision making of the Directors on commercial issues and their judgments as to how best to achieve results which are in the best interests of their members as a whole.

- The directors did have policies and targets in place to achieve net zero by 2050 (as CE conceded) but CE's complaint was that those were manifestly unreasonable and inadequate. This fact was inconsistent with the suggestion that the directors had not in fact considered what was in the best interests of Shell and its members as a whole when addressing the most appropriate manner to deal with climate risk.[20]

---

17 ibid [36].
18 ibid [46].
19 ibid [47].
20 ibid [65].

33.28 Trower J said that CE's case had missed the fundamental point that directors' general duties required them to take into account a whole range of considerations in the management of Shell's business, and there was no recognition of the directors' obligations to balance the significance of climate change against other competing commercial considerations. CE could not provide any explanation of how the directors had gone so wrong in balancing those competing considerations.

33.29 Trower J then turned to consider the discretionary factors enumerated in section 263(3) of the Companies Act, and agreed with Shell's submission that CE's claim was an attempt to publicise and advance its own policy agenda, amounting to an abuse of the derivative claim procedure and supporting the conclusion that CE's application was not brought in good faith. Trower J first confirmed that if CE had such an ulterior motive, it would by definition be using the derivative action for a purpose other than that which the legislation intended, and '[i]f, on the evidence adduced by the applicant, that remains an open and unanswered question irrespective of what Shell might say at the substantive hearing, the court cannot be satisfied that ClientEarth is acting in good faith'.[21]

33.30 Trower J then said that the very fact that CE was proposing to seek relief on behalf of Shell in a claim of considerable size, complexity, and importance – whilst at the same time holding only 27 shares – gave rise to an inference that its real interest was not how best to promote the success of Shell for the benefit of its members as a whole. CE 'adopted a single-minded focus on the imposition of its views and those of its supporters as to the right strategy for dealing with climate change risk', and this led to the inference of an ulterior motive.[22] Trower J confirmed that having reached the conclusion that CE's application was brought for a collateral motive, a person acting in accordance with the duty in section 172 would 'attach little if any importance to continuing the claim', because CE had not established a prima facie case that Shell had a good cause of action arising out the directors' alleged breaches of their duties.

33.31 Stepping back, it is clear from the results in *McGaughrey* and *ClientEarth* that:

- There is apparent hostility to progressing claims related to alleged failures to adopt climate-friendly policies by way of derivative action.

- The court will stick firmly to the injunction in section 260 of CA 2006 that a claim cannot be continued unless a director acting in accordance with her obligations under section 172 would have continued it. There is a wide margin of appreciation given to directors in making their assessment of what constitutes an action to promote the success of the company.

---

21 ibid [64].
22 ibid [93].

- In other words, as Lord Wilberforce put it in *Howard Smith Ltd v Ampol Ltd*:[23]

> [t]here is no appeal on merits from management decisions to courts of law: nor will courts of law assume to act as a kind of supervisory board over decisions within the powers of management honestly arrived at.

- Where the directors of the company have weighed up the implications of climate change policy and documented that exercise, it will be very difficult to proceed by way of derivative claim.

33.32 The view expressed in the above bullet points has not been met with universal approbation. In February 2024, Lord Carnwath published a paper[24] in which he found Trower J's judgment 'unpersuasive', and criticised the Court for having dismissed CE's witness evidence. Lord Carnwath also thought it was beside the point that there was no 'universally accepted methodology' for strategies reducing emissions – the point, said Lord Carnwath, is that Shell had not adopted *any* such methodology.

33.33 No doubt the point will be litigated in again. Accordingly, as a recent legal opinion prepared by leading environmental law practitioners states:[25]

> a prudent director wishing to gain protection from allegations of breach of duty under s. 174 would be well advised to identify and consider the nature-related risks the company faces. Keeping informed of the risks facing the company is a central facet of the s. 172 duty.

(iii) *Claims in respect of listing particulars and prospectuses*

33.34 Section 90 of FSMA creates liability for listing particulars and prospectuses (and supplementary listing particulars and prospectuses) to compensate a person who has (1) acquired or contracted to acquire securities to which those materials apply; and (2) suffered a loss as a result of either an untrue or misleading statement in the materials or the omission from them of any matter required to be included.[26] The statute requires that such materials must contain all information that investors and their advisers reasonably require and would reasonably expect for the purposes of making an informed assessment of the business.[27]

33.35 Section 90A of FSMA separately provides for the liability of issuers of securities to pay compensation to persons who have suffered loss as a result of (a) a misleading

23 *Howard Smith Ltd v Ampol Ltd* [1974] AC 821 [832].
24 Lord Robert Carnwath, 'ClientEarth v Shell: What Future for Derivative Claims?' (Grantham Research Institute on Climate Change and the Environment 2024) <https://www.lse.ac.uk/granthaminstitute/wp-content/uploads/2024/02/ClientEarth-v-Shell-what-future-for-derivative-claims.pdf> accessed 27 May 2024.
25 Sharif A Shivji KC and others, 'Opinion: Nature-Related Risks and Directors' Duties under the Law of England and Wales' (2024) [128] <https://commonwealthclimatelaw.org/wp-content/uploads/2024/03/Nature-related-risks-and-directors-duties-under-the-law-of-England-and-Wales.pdf> accessed 27 May 2024.
26 By certain provisions of FSMA: see ss 80–82 in the case of listing particulars and supplementary listing particulars and ss 87A–B, and G in the case of prospectuses and supplementary prospectuses.
27 FSMA 2000 ss 80(1) and 87A(2).

statement or dishonest omission in certain published information relating to the securities; or (b) a dishonest delay in publishing such information.

33.36 The basis of the issuer's liability for a misstatement in published information is fraud on the part of at least one person discharging managerial responsibilities ('PDMR'). As to this:

- As with common law deceit, it must be shown that a PDMR knew the statement to be untrue or misleading, or is reckless as to whether it is untrue or misleading.
- It is not sufficient that a person knows the facts which render a statement untrue: he will only be liable if those facts were present to his mind at the moment when the statement is made, such that he appreciates that the statement is untrue.[28]
- Recklessness is not caring about the truth of the statement so as to lack an honest belief in its truth – in other words, honest belief in the truth of a statement defeats a claim in recklessness, no matter how unreasonable the belief '(though of course the more unreasonable the belief asserted the less likely the finder of fact is to accept that it was genuinely held)'.[29]

33.37 Greenwashing is, in essence, misrepresentation as to green credentials or characteristics. The guilty party will have sought to create an impression to the market that the company is more environmentally friendly than it is (if it is at all).

33.38 The strict evidential burden on claimants under sections 90 and 90A to demonstrate dishonesty means that cases under these provisions (and still less successful claims) are very rare. With that said, companies promoting their net zero or climate change credentials must take care to ensure that they have reasonable grounds to believe in the truth of what is being published in company materials released to the market. They would also be advised to document their decision-making in relation to any positive statement as to climate change credentials contained in such materials.

33.39 This point is borne out on recent proposed changes to both FSMA and the FCA's listing rule requirements:

- The Companies (Strategic Report) (Climate-Related Financial Disclosure) Regulations 2022 will require certain companies to include information relating to sustainability in their strategic reports.[30]

---

28 See *ACL Netherlands BV v Lynch* [2022] EWHC 1178 (Ch) [369], referring to and discussing *Derry v Peek* [1889] 14 App Cas 337.

29 And it is not a requirement that the defendant must have appreciated that his conduct was dishonest by the standards of ordinary decent people; dishonesty is assessed by reference to the individuals' subjective statement of mind with the reasonableness of that belief being a matter for evidence going to whether the belief was in fact held: *Ivey v Genting Casinos (UK) Ltd* [2018] AC 391 (UKSC) [74] and see *ACL Netherlands BV v Lynch* (n 28) [369].

30 Companies (Strategic Report) (Climate-Related Financial Disclosure) Regulations 2022, SI 2022/31.

- This accompanies an FCA listing rule requirement to make disclosures consistent with reporting requirements set out by the FCA's climate-related financial disclosures task force.

33.40 At the time of writing there is ongoing litigation in the Southern District of New York alleging that the Oatly Group, an oat milk producer, made false statements and failed to disclose adverse facts that deceived the public into investing and artificially inflated Oatly's stock price. The litigation is ongoing but was dealt a blow by the court in June 2023, when US District Judge Hellerstein stated that the claimants had failed to plead a legally sufficient and plausible set of allegations, inviting the claimants to replead and avoid 'superfluous verbiage, unnecessary allegations, puzzle pleading, inactionable statements of opinion, and mere puffery'.[31]

Tort claims

33.41 Damage to property and to the person that is sustained as a consequence of environmental damage can be catastrophic for affected individuals. Potential claimants face a number of obstacles to obtaining redress from perpetrators, particularly where such damage occurs in the poorest parts of the world, including: (a) the economics of pursuing a claim without adequate resources; (b) navigating domestic legal systems which lack experience of litigating such claims; and (c) the corporate structures of multinational corporations, which often silo the operational (polluting) aspects of the business in local subsidiary companies which lack resources to meet any substantial award of damages. In order to circumvent these obstacles, in recent years there has been an increase in the use of group litigation to seek compensation for environmental damage caused by multinational energy and mining companies; in particular, by pursuing claims against the parent companies of environmental polluters before the courts of the country in which the parent company is incorporated.

(i) *Environmental damage caused by overseas subsidiaries: English[32] case law*

33.42 The use of group claim forms[33] and the availability of formal collective action procedures,[34] along with the growth of the third-party funding market, make the English courts an attractive forum in which to litigate group claims arising from environmental damage where the parent company is English-registered.

33.43 Claimants wishing to litigate such actions before the English courts must seek the permission of the English court to serve the foreign-registered subsidiary out of the jurisdiction.[35] On an application for service out of the jurisdiction, a claimant must

31 *In re Oatly Group AB Securities Litigation*, Order Granting Motion to Dismiss, SDNY 21 Civ. 6360, 1 June 2023.
32 References in this chapter to 'English' case law and the 'English' courts are to the courts of England and Wales and case law emanating from them.
33 In relation to which see the decision of the Divisional Court in *Abbott & others v Ministry of Defence* [2023] EWHC 1475 (KB), pursuant to which some 3,500 claimants were permitted to use a single claim form to bring a claim in which there were significant common issues, albeit varying facts in individual cases.
34 The representative claimant procedure under CPR 19.8 and group litigation orders pursuant to CPR 19.22.
35 Pursuant to CPR Rule 6.36.

establish that the claim falls within one of the service 'gateways' provided for in the Civil Procedure Rules.[36] These include where (a) there is between the claimant and the English-registered parent company (the 'anchor defendant') a real issue which it is reasonable for the English court to try; and (b) the subsidiary is a necessary and proper party to that claim.[37] Further, the court will not give permission to serve out unless satisfied that England and Wales is the proper place in which to bring the claim.[38]

33.44 Given the need to establish a serious issue to be tried as between the claimant and the parent company as the anchor defendant, an important development in the recent jurisprudence has been the clarification of the law in relation to the duty of care owed by a parent company to those harmed by the actions of its subsidiaries. This is illustrated by two decisions of the Supreme Court in relation to jurisdictional challenges that were handed down within months of each other: *Vedanta Resources plc v Lungowe* ('*Vedanta*')[39] and *Okpabi v Royal Dutch Shell plc* ('*Okpabi*'),[40] the decision in each of which is summarised below.

(a) *Vedanta Resources v Lungowe*

33.45 The claimants in *Vedanta* were 1,826 Zambian citizens, living in Zambia, who were 'by any standards, very poor members of rural farming communities served by watercourses'.[41] They alleged that their health and farming activities had been damaged by repeated discharges of toxic matter from the Nchanga Copper Mine into watercourses 'which provide their only source of water for drinking (by themselves and their livestock) and irrigation for their crops', from 2005 onwards. They brought claims in negligence against a UK-domiciled company ('Vedanta'), the anchor defendant, and its Zambian subsidiary, alleging personal injury, damage to property and loss of income, amenity and enjoyment of land due to pollution and environmental damage caused by discharges from a Zambian copper mine which was owned and operated by the second defendant subsidiary ('KCM').

33.46 The negligence and breach of statutory duty causes of action pleaded against Vedanta were said to arise by reason of the 'very high level of control and direction that the first defendant exercised at all material times over the mining operations of the second defendant and its compliance with applicable health, safety and environmental standards'.[42] The essence of the claimants' case against Vedanta was that 'it exercised a sufficiently high level of supervision and control of the activities at the mine, with sufficient knowledge of the propensity of those activities to cause toxic escapes into surrounding watercourses, as to incur a duty of care to the claimants'.[43] Vedanta had

---

36 Set out in Practice Direction 6B para 3.1.
37 Practice Direction 6B para 3.1(3) provides that a claimant may serve a claim form out of the jurisdiction with the permission of the court under CPR rule 6.36 where: (3) A claim is made against a person ('the defendant') on which the claim form has been or will be served and (a) there is between the claimant and the defendant a real issue which it is reasonable for the court to try; and (b) the claimant wishes to serve the claim form on another person who is a necessary and proper party to that claim.
38 CPR Rule 6.37(3).
39 *Vedanta Resources plc and another v Lungowe and others* [2019] UKSC 20.
40 *Okpabi and others v Royal Dutch Shell plc and another* [2021] UKSC 3.
41 *Vedanta Resources plc v Lungowe* (n 39) [1].
42 ibid [3].
43 ibid [55].

published material in which it asserted its responsibility for the establishment of appropriate group-wide environmental control and sustainability standards, for their implementation throughout the group by training, and for their monitoring and enforcement. These included a report entitled 'Embedding Sustainability' which stressed that the oversight of all Vedanta's subsidiaries rested with the board of Vedanta itself, made particular reference to problems with discharges into water and to the particular problems arising at the mine.

33.47 Vedanta contended that the claimants' pleaded case disclosed no real triable issue against Vedanta, because it could not be shown to have done anything in relation to the operation of the mine sufficient either to give rise to a common law duty of care in favour of the claimants, or a statutory liability as a participant in breaches of Zambian environmental protection, mining and public health legislation. On Vedanta's case it was a mere indirect owner of KCM and no more than that.[44] That being so, Vedanta contended that 'a conclusion that Vedanta had incurred a duty of care to the claimants would involve a novel and controversial extension of the boundaries of the tort of negligence, beyond any established category'.[45]

33.48 The Supreme Court (Lord Briggs JSC giving the unanimous judgment) comprehensively rejected this argument. It held unequivocally that the liability of parent companies in relation to the activities of their subsidiaries was to be determined on ordinary, general principles of the law of tort regarding the imposition of a duty of care and did not form a distinct category of liability in common law negligence. The Supreme Court rejected the Court of Appeal's identification of specific categories of parent company liability, because:[46]

> There is no limit to the models of management and control which may be put in place within a multinational group of companies. At one end, the parent may be no more than a passive investor in separate businesses carried out by its various direct and indirect subsidiaries. At the other extreme, the parent may carry out a thoroughgoing vertical reorganisation of the group's businesses so that they are, in management terms, carried on as if they were a single commercial undertaking, with boundaries of legal personality and ownership within the group becoming irrelevant, until the onset of insolvency, as happened within the Lehman Brothers group.

33.49 The Supreme Court further rejected the submission made on behalf of Vedanta that there is 'a general principle that a parent could never incur a duty of care in respect of the activities of a particular subsidiary merely by laying down group-wide policies and guidelines, and expecting the management of each subsidiary to comply with them', with Lord Briggs stating:[47]

---

44 ibid [17].
45 ibid [46].
46 ibid [51].
47 ibid [53].

> I am not persuaded that there is any such reliable limiting principle. Group guidelines about minimising the environmental impact of inherently dangerous activities, such as mining, may be shown to contain systematic errors which, when implemented as of course by a particular subsidiary, then cause harm to third parties.

33.50 Expanding on the circumstances in which a parent company's actions may give rise to a duty of care to third parties, the Supreme Court found that:[48]

> Even where group-wide policies do not of themselves give rise to such a duty of care to third parties, they may do so if the parent does not merely proclaim them, but takes active steps, by training, supervision and enforcement, to see that they are implemented by relevant subsidiaries. Similarly, it seems to me that the parent may incur the relevant responsibility to third parties if, in published materials, it holds itself out as exercising that degree of supervision and control of its subsidiaries, even if it does not in fact do so. In such circumstances its very omission may constitute the abdication of a responsibility which it has publicly undertaken.

33.51 On the facts, it was arguable that Vedanta had exercised a sufficient level of control over the activities of its subsidiary, KCM, so as to make Vedanta liable in negligence to the claimants and that there was accordingly a real issue to be tried between the claimants and Vedanta:[49]

> I regard the published materials in which Vedanta may fairly be said to have asserted its own assumption of responsibility for the maintenance of proper standards of environmental control over the activities of its subsidiaries, and in particular the operations at the mine, and not merely to have laid down but also implemented those standards by training, monitoring and enforcement, as sufficient on their own to show that it is well arguable that a sufficient level of intervention by Vedanta in the conduct of operations at the mine may be demonstrable at trial, after full disclosure of the relevant internal documents of Vedanta and KCM, and of communications passing between them.

33.52 The Supreme Court affirmed the first instance judge's decision that, notwithstanding that Zambia was the proper place for the claims to be brought, the claim would be allowed to proceed in the English court because there was a real risk that the claimants would not be able to obtain substantial justice in Zambia since: (i) the claimants were at the poorer end of the poverty scale in one of the poorest countries in the world, had no sufficient resources of their own with which to fund the litigation, would not obtain legal aid for the claim and it could not be funded by way of a conditional fee agreement because such agreements are unlawful in Zambia; and (ii) the Zambian legal profession lacked the resources and experience with which to conduct such litigation successfully.[50] Accordingly, the Supreme Court held that the English litigation should be allowed to proceed.

---

48 ibid [53].
49 ibid [61].
50 ibid [90]–[91].

33.53 In reaching this conclusion, the Supreme Court highlighted the difficulties outlined at the outset of this section that are faced by claimants seeking to litigate in the poorest parts of the world, by referring to a similar case that had proceeded before the Zambian court. In that case, liability was established but on appeal just 12 out of 2,000 claimants had their damages award upheld because the remaining claimants had failed to file medical evidence to establish that they had suffered loss. The Supreme Court in *Vedanta* observed that there was evidence that the reason why so few of the claimants had medical evidence deployed on their behalf was that this would have required funding from the claimants which they could not afford.[51] The Supreme Court also referred to a further case, *Shamilimo v Nitrogen Chemicals of Zambia Ltd*, in which there was evidence that the claim had failed on causation because the claimants could not fund the necessary expert evidence to prove it.[52]

33.54 A further practical difficulty that is often faced by claimants seeking to litigate against parent companies on the basis of their involvement in the subsidiary's business is that the evidence required to establish that control and/or involvement by a parent company is likely to be internal to the group companies and not publicly available to the claimants. This informational asymmetry was acknowledged by Lord Briggs in *Vedanta*, who said:[53]

> I make no apology for having suggested during argument that it is blindingly obvious that the proof of that particular pudding [being the level of intervention by Vedanta in the conduct of operations at the mine] would depend heavily upon the contents of documents internal to each of the defendant companies, and upon correspondence and other documents passing between them, currently unavailable to the claimants, but in due course disclosable.

(b) *Okpabi v Royal Dutch Shell*

33.55 The decision in *Vedanta* was said by the Supreme Court to be 'very relevant' to that court's decision in *Okpabi v Royal Dutch Shell*, also known as the Bille and Ogale Group Litigation. This was another application to set aside service of the claim form out of the jurisdiction on a subsidiary company alleged to have caused environmental damage. The similarities with *Vedanta* were such that the Supreme Court in *Okpabi* observed that 'It might reasonably have been expected that the guidance provided by that decision would resolve this appeal without the need for a hearing'.[54]

33.56 The appeal involved two sets of claimants who lived in the Niger Delta region of Nigeria: In the Ogale proceedings the claimants were a Nigerian farming and fishing community of approximately 40,000 individuals in River State, Nigeria. That claim was brought by the leadership of the Ogale community, namely the King, HRH Emee Godwin Bebe Okpabi and the Council of Chiefs, suing both for themselves and in a representative capacity on behalf of the people of the Ogale Kingdom. In the Bille

---

51 ibid [99].
52 ibid [100]; *Shamilimo v Nitrogen Chemicals of Zambia Ltd* (2007/HP/0725) (unreported) 20 January 2016, High Court of Zambia.
53 *Vedanta Resources plc v Lungowe* (n 39) [44].
54 *Okpabi v Royal Dutch Shell plc* (n 40) [2].

proceedings the claimants were 2,335 individuals who live in the Bille Kingdom, a remote riverine community in River State, Nigeria. The second defendant Nigerian company operated oil pipelines and ancillary infrastructure in the Niger Delta region. The claimants claimed that persistent oil leaks from the pipelines and associated infrastructure caused widespread environmental damage, including serious water and ground contamination, which was not adequately cleaned up or remediated. The claimants said that, as a result of the spills, the natural water sources in the claimants' communities could not safely be used for drinking, fishing, agricultural, washing or recreational purposes.

33.57 The claimants commenced proceedings in England for damages in negligence against the Nigerian-registered company that operated the oil pipelines and ancillary infrastructure (The Shell Petroleum Development Company of Nigeria Ltd ('SPDC')) and its UK-domiciled parent company (Royal Dutch Shell plc ('RDS')). The claimants contended that the subsidiary's efforts to prevent oil leaks or remediate their impact were inadequate and in breach of a duty of care owed to them by both the subsidiary and the parent company. The duty alleged against the parent was on the basis that it exercised a high degree of control, direction and oversight in respect of the subsidiary's pollution and environmental compliance and the operation of its oil infrastructure and/or that it assumed responsibility for the subsidiary's operations including by the promulgation and imposition of mandatory health, safety and environmental policies, standards and manuals.

33.58 As part of their case against RDS, the claimants alleged that it was clear that RDS had for many years had detailed knowledge about widespread pollution in the Niger Delta caused by spillages and leakages of oil from infrastructure operated by SPDC. RDS was said to have knowledge of the frequency, location and size of oil spills, of the causes of oil spills and of SPDC's systemic failure to prevent spills, including its failure to protect its oil infrastructure against the risk of damage caused by the criminal acts of third parties.

33.59 Although much of the Supreme Court's judgment is directed at the proper approach to the resolution of a jurisdictional challenge, the Court made some important findings in relation to the relationship between parents and subsidiaries. In particular, the Supreme Court:

- Confirmed that to the extent that the Court of Appeal had indicated that the promulgation by a parent company of group-wide policies or standards can never in itself give rise to a duty of care, that is inconsistent with *Vedanta* and there is no general principle that the promulgation by a parent company of group-wide policies can never in itself give rise to a duty of care.[55]

- Held that control is just a starting point when determining parent company liability:[56]

---

55 ibid [143].
56 ibid [147].

> The issue is the extent to which the parent did take over or share with the subsidiary the management of the relevant activity (here the pipeline operation). That may or may not be demonstrated by the parent controlling the subsidiary. In a sense, all parents control their subsidiaries. That control gives the parent the opportunity to get involved in management. But control of a company and de facto management of part of its activities are two different things. A subsidiary may maintain de jure control of its activities, but nonetheless delegate de facto management of part of them to emissaries of its parent.

- Confirmed that, as the decision in *Vedanta* makes clear, there is no special doctrine in the law of tort of legal responsibility on the part of a parent company in relation to the activities of its subsidiary, vis-a-vis persons affected by those activities.[57]

- Rejected the Court of Appeal's analysis of the case by reference to the threefold test set out in *Caparo Industries plc v Dickman*.[58] As acknowledged in *Vedanta*, the liability of parent companies in relation to the activities of its subsidiaries is not, of itself, a distinct category of liability in common law negligence.[59]

33.60 On the facts of the case, the Supreme Court found that there were real issues to be tried and that the action could proceed, subject to RDS successfully challenging the English courts' jurisdiction on other grounds it had raised. In relation to the claimant's contention that RDS owed them a duty of care by reason of it having assumed responsibility for the subsidiary's operations, the Supreme Court referred to a document entitled the RDS Control Framework, which showed that the responsibilities of the CEO and the RDS ExCo included 'the safe condition and environmentally responsible operation of Shell's facilities and assets'.[60] Further, the Supreme Court found that 'it is of significance that the Shell group is organised along Business and Functional lines rather than simply according to corporate status. This vertical structure involves significant delegation.'[61] Although formal binding decisions were taken at corporate level, they were taken on the basis of advice and consent from the vertical Business and Functional lines and corporate approval generally followed organisational authority.[62] The claimants contended that this vertical organisational structure meant that RDS was comparable to the example given by Lord Briggs at paragraph 51 of *Vedanta,* of group businesses which 'are, in management terms, carried on as if they were a single commercial undertaking, with boundaries of legal personality and ownership within the group becoming irrelevant'.[63]

33.61 On the issue of disclosure of relevant documents (also referred to by Lord Briggs in *Vedanta*, see above) the Supreme Court held that the proper approach on a jurisdictional challenge is to ask 'are there reasonable grounds for believing that disclosure may

---

57 ibid [149].
58 *Caparo Industries plc v Dickman* [1990] 2 AC 605.
59 *Okpabi v Royal Dutch Shell plc* (n 40) [151].
60 ibid [157].
61 ibid [156].
62 ibid [157].
63 ibid [150].

materially add to or alter the evidence relevant to whether the claim has a real prospect of success?'[64] As noted in relation to *Vedanta*, this is of particular importance in the context of claims against the parent company of a polluting subsidiary because '[t]he importance of internal corporate documents is well recognised in the context of cases concerning the negligence liability of a parent company for the acts of its subsidiary'.[65]

33.62 Further claims before the English courts against multinational corporate polluters in respect of damage sustained abroad have followed on from the decisions in the Supreme Court in *Vedanta* and *Okpabi*.

33.63 In *Municipio de Mariana v BHP Group (UK) Ltd (formerly BHP Group plc)*,[66] a large number of claimants brought claims in the High Court against an English company and an Australian company in respect of losses flowing from the collapse of a dam in Brazil. The claims, which were brought under Brazilian law, were founded on strict liability, fault-based liability and shareholder liability. The judge at first instance struck out the claims as an abuse of process for 'irredeemable unmanageability' and held that, had he not done so, he would have stayed them on jurisdictional grounds. The Court of Appeal allowed an appeal by the claimants and at the time of writing the claim is proceeding through the English courts.

33.64 *Bravo v Amerisur Resources Ltd* is a further recent example of a multinational corporation being held to account before the English courts in respect of damage sustained overseas.[67] The claimants lived in remote rural communities in the Putumayo region of Colombia. They brought an action against the defendants pursuant to the Colombia Civil Code seeking damages in respect of environmental contamination caused by a spill of crude oil which resulted from deliberate acts by the terrorist organisation, FARC.

33.65 On a trial of preliminary issues, the defendants contended that there was no parent company liability under Colombian law for the acts or omissions of a subsidiary. Steyn J found that under Colombian law, the question of a parent company's liability could only be determined on the facts; it was not precluded by operation of Colombian law. In cross-examination, the defendants' Colombian law expert was taken to paragraph 51 of the Supreme Court's decision in *Vedanta* and gave evidence that there is nothing in Colombian law that would prohibit the same spectrum of possibilities in terms of the degree of control exercised by a parent company.[68]

(ii) *The Hague District Court: a duty to prevent CO_2 emissions?*

33.66 The use of class actions in climate change litigation is of course not unique to the UK jurisdiction. Class actions are also permissible under the Dutch Civil Code,

---

64 ibid [128].
65 ibid [129].
66 *Municipio de Mariana v BHP Group (UK) Ltd (formerly BHP Group plc)* [2022] EWCA Civ 951, [2022] 1 WLR 4691.
67 *Bravo v Amerisur Resources Ltd* [2023] EWHC 122 (KB).
68 *Okpabi v Royal Dutch Shell plc* (n 40) [150].

pursuant to which a foundation or association with full legal capacity may institute proceedings for the protection of similar interests of other persons.[69]

33.67 A recent decision of The Hague District Court – *Milieudefensie and Others v Royal Dutch Shell* – is of interest because, unlike the claims discussed in the previous section that were brought before the English courts, the claim was not founded on damage to property or personal injury caused by environmental damage.[70] Instead, the claim related to the alleged failure of Royal Dutch Shell ('RDS') to meet its obligation to reduce the CO_2 emissions of the Shell group.

33.68 The case was brought by Milieudefensie (a Dutch environmental organisation), Greenpeace Netherlands ('Greenpeace') and others, on behalf of 17,379 claimants, against RDS (a UK-registered company with its head office in The Hague). Greenpeace claimed that RDS had breached its obligation, derived from an unwritten standard of care under the Dutch Civil Code,[71] to contribute to the prevention of dangerous climate change through the corporate policy it determined for the Shell group. In interpreting the unwritten standard of care, the claimants relied upon the right to life and the right to respect for private and family life, as well as soft law endorsed by RDS such as the UN Guiding Principles on Business and Human Rights, the UN Global Compact and the OECD Guidelines for Multinational Enterprises. The claimants contended that RDS had an obligation to ensure that its CO_2 emissions will have been reduced by 45% before the end of 2030, relative to 2019 levels, through the corporate policy of the Shell group. They argued that RDS was violating, or was at risk of violating, this obligation 'with a hazardous and disastrous corporate policy for the Shell group, which in no way is consistent with the global climate target to prevent a dangerous climate change for the protection of mankind, the human environment and nature'.[72]

33.69 In a landmark ruling, the Hague District Court found in substantive part for the claimant Milieudefensie and determined that:

> RDS is obliged to reduce the CO_2 emissions of the Shell group's activities by net 45% at end 2030 relative to 2019 through the Shell group's corporate policy. This reduction obligation relates to the Shell group's entire energy portfolio and to the aggregate volume of all emissions (Scope 1 through to 3). It is up to RDS to design the reduction obligation, taking account of its current obligations and other relevant circumstances. The reduction obligation is an obligation of result for the activities of the Shell group, with respect to which RDS may be expected to ensure that the CO_2 emissions of the Shell group are reduced to this level. This is a significant best-efforts obligation with respect to the business relations of the Shell group, including the end-users, in which context RDS may be expected to take the necessary steps to remove or prevent the serious risks ensuing from the CO_2 emissions generated by the business relations, and to use its influence to

69 Book 3 s 305a Dutch Civil Code.
70 *Milieudefensie v Royal Dutch Shell plc* (n 12).
71 Book 6 s 162 Dutch Civil Code provides that acting in conflict with what is generally accepted according to unwritten law is unlawful.
72 *Milieudefensie v Royal Dutch Shell plc* (n 12) para 3.2.

> limit any lasting consequences as much as possible. This obligation is also designated hereinafter as 'RDS' reduction obligation'.

33.70 The Court acknowledged the 'twin challenge' of curbing dangerous climate change by reducing CO_2 emissions while meeting the global energy demand of the rapidly growing world population, but held that 'the importance of access to reliable and affordable energy, as pointed out by RDS, and the Shell group's role in it, have no bearing on RDS' reduction obligation. That interest must always be served within the context of climate targets.'[73]

33.71 In reaching its conclusion, the Court observed that:

- The fact that companies within the Shell group were responsible for the implementation and execution of policy did not alter the fact that RDS determines the general policy of the Shell group, which consists of about 1,100 companies and operates in 160 countries all over the world;[74]
- The total CO_2 emissions of the Shell group exceeds the CO_2 emissions of many states, including the Netherlands;[75] and
- Taking those factors, amongst others, into account '[t]he court is of the opinion that much may be expected of RDS' in relation to the means through which RDS meets its responsibility to respect human rights including with respect to climate change.[76]

33.72 Importantly, the obligation that the Court found RDS to be under was not limited to RDS's own actions and those of its group companies. Having distinguished between the CO_2 emissions of: (1) the Shell group (RDS and the other Shell companies); and (2) the business relations of the Shell group, including the end-users of its products, the Court found that:[77]

> Due to the policy-setting influence RDS has over the companies in the Shell group, it bears the same responsibility for these business relations as for its own activities. The far-reaching control and influence of RDS over the Shell group means that RDS' reduction obligation must be an obligation of result for emissions connected to own activities of the Shell group.
>
> ...
>
> As regards the business relations of the Shell group, including the end-users, RDS may be expected to take the necessary steps to remove or prevent the serious risks ensuing from the CO_2 emissions generated by them, and to use its influence to limit any lasting

73 ibid para 4.4.40 approved English translation.
74 ibid para 4.4.4.
75 ibid para 4.4.5.
76 ibid paras 4.4.16 and 4.4.37.
77 ibid paras 4.4.23–4.4.24.

> consequences as much as possible. … This is a significant best-efforts obligation, which is not removed or reduced by the individual responsibility of the business relations, including the end-users, for their own CO_2 emissions.

33.73 In relation to the end-users of its products, RDS had sought to contend that it had contractual obligations, as well as obligations ensuing from long-term concessions, which limited its freedom as regards the energy package offered by the Shell group. This argument was rejected by the Court, which held that:[78]

> This limitation does not alter the fact that ultimately RDS determines the energy package of the Shell group – and consequently, the range of energy products. With due observance of its current obligations, RDS is free to decide not to make new investments in explorations and fossil fuels, and to change the energy package offered by the Shell group.

33.74 The Court considered that imposing the obligation to meet CO_2 reductions across the Shell group, rather than on individual companies, afforded RDS greater freedom in how it achieved the reduction:[79]

> RDS has total freedom to comply with its reduction obligation as it sees fit, and to shape the corporate policy of the Shell group at its own discretion. The court notes here that a 'global' reduction obligation, which affects the policy of the entire Shell group, gives RDS much more freedom of action than a reduction obligation limited to a particular territory or a business unit or units.

On 12 November 2024 the Hague Court of Appeal handed down its judgment in relation to Shell's appeal, allowing the appeal and quashing the previous judgment. The Court concluded that while Shell may have obligations to reduce its scope 3 emissions, it could not be bound by a 45% reduction standard because this percentage does not apply to every country and every business sector individually.

Competition law

33.75 The Competition and Markets Authority ('CMA') is the body tasked with enforcing breaches of competition law in the UK. The CMA's powers of enforcement are presently contained in the Competition Act 1998, as amended by the Enterprise Act 2002, but at the time of writing are due to be overhauled by the Digital Markets, Competition and Consumers Act 2024 as and when it is brought into force. The new powers of the CMA in relation to 'greenwashing' (i.e. the making of misleading environmental claims about goods and services) are addressed in Chapter 32.

33.76 A comprehensive review of the CMA's enforcement powers is beyond the scope of this work. However, competition law is relevant to the enforcement of corporate duties in relation to climate change because compelling companies to act competitively

---

78 ibid para 4.4.25.
79 ibid para 4.4.54 approved English translation.

risks undermining or even precluding the cooperation that is required in order to bring about sector-wide transition to net zero.

33.77 On 12 October 2023, the CMA published guidance on the application of the Chapter I prohibition in the Competition Act 1998 (the 'CA 1998') to environmental sustainability agreements ('ESAs') between businesses operating at the same level of the supply chain: the 'Green Agreements Guidance'.[80] The Chapter 1 prohibition in the CA 1998 prohibits agreements between businesses that are restrictive of competition. However, the CMA acknowledges that 'there are circumstances where collaboration between competitors may be needed to promote environmental sustainability'.[81] Examples given by the CMA include:

- Where a business that acts first to promote environmental sustainability could sustain a competitive disadvantage compared with its rivals. This kind of 'first mover disadvantage' might disincentivise businesses from switching to more sustainable but costlier options without some form of collaboration.

- Where businesses individually lack the resources and capabilities to achieve more environmentally sustainable outcomes but could achieve them (or could achieve them more quickly) collectively.

33.78 ESAs are described by the CMA as 'agreements between competitors which are aimed at preventing, reducing or mitigating the adverse impact that economic activities have on the environment or assist with the transition towards environmental sustainability'. The CMA notes that '[a]t a general level, economic activity may, directly or indirectly, cause negative environmental externalities, including through causing pollution, reducing biodiversity, or contributing to climate change from greenhouse gas emissions'.[82] Examples given by the CMA include:

- An agreement between fashion manufacturers to stop using certain fabrics that contribute to microplastic pollution in bodies of water; and

- An agreement between waste management companies to commit to recycle a waste product rather than incinerating it.

33.79 Climate change agreements are identified by the CMA as a subset of ESAs, which will typically reduce the negative externalities[83] arising from greenhouse gases, such as carbon dioxide and methane, that are emitted from the production, distribution

---

80 Competition and Markets Authority, 'Green Agreements Guidance: Guidance on the Application of the Chapter I Prohibition in the Competition Act 1998 to Environmental Sustainability Agreements' (2023) CMA 185 <https://assets.publishing.service.gov.uk/media/6526b81b244f8e000d8e742c/Green_agreements_guidance_.pdf> accessed 27 May 2024.
81 ibid para 1.8.
82 ibid para 2.1.
83 Being the costs borne by parties external to the commercial transaction in dealing with the by-products of the transaction – such as pollution.

or consumption of goods and services.[84] Examples given by the CMA of climate change agreements include:

- An agreement between delivery companies to switch to using electric vehicles; and

- An agreement to pool funds, technology or expertise to support the development of more effective technology to capture and store carbon dioxide.

33.80 The CMA has sought in its Green Agreements Guidance to provide reassurance to business by confirming that it does not expect to take enforcement action in respect of ESAs, including climate change agreements, provided that they correspond with the principles set out in the guidance.[85]

33.81 Certain types of ESA are unlikely to infringe competition law. The categories of ESA identified by the CMA as falling into this category include:

- ESAs which do not affect or engage with the way that businesses compete.[86] An example of this is an agreement to pool funds, to use for training activities for people working in the industry, to encourage the use of more sustainable practices.

- ESAs to do something jointly which none of the parties could do individually (e.g. because they do not have the technical capabilities, or because of the level of risk involved or the level of the investment required).[87] An example of this that is given by the CMA is where several housing corporations, which individually lack technical expertise to undertake the project, participate in a pilot project to develop zero-energy housing using a novel, more efficient technology.

- Where competitors collaborate to develop environmental sustainability standards aimed at making products or processes more sustainable, provided that: the process for developing the standard is transparent; it is possible for any business in affected markets to participate (though no business is obliged to); any business can implement the standard on reasonable and non-discriminatory terms and can go beyond the standard if desired; and it is unlikely to result in an appreciable reduction in the availability of suitable products for consumers to purchase.[88] An example of this might be a logo used by publishers to certify that a book is published using a certain percentage of recycled paper and environmentally friendly printing processes.

- Where competitors agree to phase out particular non-environmentally sustainable processes, or cease procuring or supplying certain non-environmentally sustainable products, where it does not involve either an appreciable increase in price

84 Competition and Markets Authority, 'Green Agreements Guidance: Guidance on the Application of the Chapter I Prohibition in the Competition Act 1998 to Environmental Sustainability Agreements' (n 80) para 2.4.
85 ibid para 1.13.
86 ibid para 3.6.
87 ibid para 3.7.
88 ibid para 3.15.

or reduction in product quality or choice for consumers and provided that this does not have the object of eliminating or harming the parties' competitors or market sharing.[89]

- The setting of non-binding targets or ambitions for the whole industry with regard to environmental sustainability objectives, such as the reduction of CO_2 emissions, provided that the participating businesses remain free to determine their own contribution and the way in which the targets are realised.[90]

- Agreements between shareholders to vote for promoting corporate policies that pursue environmental sustainability.[91]

33.82 Other types of ESAs could infringe the Chapter I prohibition. If these ESAs have the object or effect of restricting competition, they will be prohibited unless they benefit from exemption on the grounds stipulated in the Green Agreements Guidance. Those ESAs which involve price fixing, market or consumer allocation, limitations of output or limitations of quality or innovation typically have as their object the restriction of competition (and are therefore only permissible if they engage the exemptions). An example of this type of ESA is an agreement between competitors on the price at which they will sell products meeting an agreed environmental sustainability standard.[92]

33.83 In order to benefit from the exemptions set out in the Green Agreements Guidance, parties must be able to demonstrate that their agreement meets each of the following four conditions:[93]

- The agreement must contribute to certain benefits, namely, improving production or distribution or contribute to promoting technical or economic progress. Such benefits could include eliminating or reducing the harmful effects arising from the production or consumption of particular goods or services, e.g. reducing greenhouse gas emissions; shortening the time it takes to bring environmentally sustainable products to the market; and improving production or distribution processes, e.g. the introduction of new cleaner technologies.[94] The benefits of an agreement need to be substantiated and cannot be assumed; they must be objective, concrete and verifiable;[95]

- The agreement and any restrictions of competition within the agreement must be indispensable to the achievement of those benefits. This requires the parties to the agreement to show that it is no more restrictive of competition than is reasonably necessary to achieve the benefits.[96] In practice, this means that an agreement is

89 ibid para 3.19.
90 ibid para 3.21.
91 ibid paras 3.24–3.27.
92 ibid para 4.6.
93 ibid Section 5.
94 ibid para 5.4.
95 ibid para 5.5.
96 ibid para 5.8.

likely to be considered indispensable, or reasonably necessary, if either (i) in the absence of the agreement the parties would not otherwise be able to achieve the level of benefits which the agreement seeks to achieve (e.g. for economic reasons or given a lack of expertise or scale); or (ii) the agreement enables the parties to achieve the benefits more efficiently, e.g. at reduced cost or more quickly.[97] One of the examples given by the CMA is where a less polluting material has been developed, but manufacturers individually lack incentives to use it as it would increase costs and would give rise to a 'first mover disadvantage' of requiring manufacturers to make additional investments to promote their more sustainable (and expensive) products. A collective agreement between manufacturers in that industry to use the new material might be necessary to overcome the first mover disadvantage and ensure that environmental benefits can materialise;[98]

- UK consumers must receive a fair share of the benefits that result from the agreement and those benefits must outweigh the harm that UK consumers will suffer as a result of the agreement.[99] Benefits can include future as well as current benefits, and those benefits that accrue to indirect users (i.e. not just the direct customers of the parties to the agreement, but also those who purchase from those customers).[100] Benefits can be direct (e.g. an agreement to use more sustainable packaging, which makes it easier for consumers to recycle the packaging or reduces price), or indirect (e.g. an agreement not to import or produce furniture made from unsustainable wood sources, which benefits consumers indirectly by not contributing to deforestation);[101] and

- The agreement must not eliminate competition in respect of a substantial part of the products concerned, i.e. there must be meaningful remaining competition on the market(s) affected by the agreement.[102]

33.84 The criteria for exemptions applicable to climate change agreements (as opposed to ESAs more generally) are the same as the conditions listed above, save that when considering the third condition – that consumers must receive a fair share of the benefits – the CMA considers that a more permissive approach is appropriate when assessing who are the relevant consumers. In the context of ESAs, the consumer benefit requirement is assessed with reference to whether the harm to consumers of the ESA's products is offset by benefits to substantially the same set of consumers. In the context of climate change agreements, 'there is a concern that having regard only to the climate change benefits accruing to the consumers in the relevant market would have a perverse and harmful effect'.[103] As such, in the case of climate change agreements, the 'fair share to consumers' condition can be satisfied taking into account the totality of the climate

97 ibid para 5.9.
98 ibid para 5.11.
99 ibid para 5.16.
100 ibid para 5.17.
101 ibid paras 5.18–5.19.
102 ibid para 5.29.
103 ibid para 6.3.

change benefits to all UK consumers arising from the agreement.[104] The CMA considers this justified:

> because of the exceptional nature of the harms posed by climate change (and therefore the exceptional nature of the benefits to consumers from combating or mitigating climate change or its impact); climate change represents a special category of threat that sets it apart and requires a different approach to the pass-on criteria. This reflects the sheer magnitude of the risk that climate change represents (including the need for urgent action), the degree of public concern about it, and the binding national and international commitments that successive UK governments have entered into.

33.85 However, greenwashers take note: in order to benefit from this approach the parties to the agreement would need to demonstrate that the climate change benefits are in line with, or exceed, existing legally binding requirements or well-established national or international targets including the overarching climate change goals set out in the Paris Agreement.[105]

33.86 Provided ESAs, including climate change agreements, 'correspond clearly to the principles set out in [the Green Agreements Guidance]', the CMA has made clear that it does not expect to take enforcement action in respect of such agreements.[106]

---

104 ibid para 6.4.
105 ibid para 6.6.
106 ibid para 7.1.

PART VII

FISCAL MEASURES

CHAPTER 34

GOVERNMENT FUNDING: FISCAL MEASURES AND SUBSIDIES

Kelly Stricklin-Coutinho, Alexander Burrell and Rachel Sullivan

Introduction

34.01 Taxes and subsidies are two ways in which governments may use their financial functions to influence behaviour. In respect of taxes, there are at least two reasons for introducing a tax.[1] First, taxes may help a government to achieve its economic and social objectives, encourage growth or change the behaviour of those subject to tax.[2] Second, taxes may raise revenue for a government. The tension between taxes which have the predominant purpose to raise revenue and those with the main objective of effecting behaviour change, differs according to the policy the government seeks to implement. Some taxes (such as Value Added Tax) predominantly have the function of raising revenue, but the social and behavioural impacts are also relevant. Other taxes (such as landfill tax) have a main focus on changing behaviour (by charging a considerably higher rate of tax for damaging deposits of waste than the rate applicable for less damaging waste, which is intended to have a dissuasive effect). Measures such as landfill tax also raise significant funding alongside their predominant purpose. The Office for Budget Responsibility ('OBR') has indicated their view that as emissions fall as the UK transitions to net zero, receipts generated from these emissions-linked taxes will be affected.[3]

34.02 Taxes can have a powerful and immediate impact on behavioural change, because (depending on the design of the system) they can become relevant very quickly and if so designed, can have a commercial cost which is unlikely to be ignored. Taxes therefore can become a commercial issue to taxpayers, whilst being a tool to implement a policy objective for government.

34.03 Subsidies (or state aid in the context of the EU) can also be used by a government for similar purposes as a tax: to further its economic and social objectives, to encourage growth and in some cases at least, to influence the behaviour of those to whom it grants

---

1 See, for example, Reuven S Avi-Yonah, 'The Three Goals of Taxation' (2006) 60 Tax Law Review <https://repository.law.umich.edu/cgi/viewcontent.cgi?article=1039&context=articles> accessed 28 April 2024.

2 See, for example, para 1.1 of the government's call for evidence in relation to Landfill Tax, which sets out that Landfill Tax was introduced to encourage the diversion of waste away from landfill and towards more environmentally friendly waste management options: HM Treasury, 'Landfill Tax: Call for Evidence Ensuring the Tax Continues to Support Environmental Objectives' (2021) <https://assets.publishing.service.gov.uk/media/61a5ff9c8fa8f5038358c0c3/LfT_review_CfE.pdf> accessed 28 April 2024.

3 Office for Budget Responsibility, 'Working Paper No.18 Emissions and Our Tax Forecasts' (2023) <https://obr.uk/docs/dlm_uploads/Emissions-working-paper.pdf> accessed 28 April 2024.

the subsidy.[4] Subsidies do the opposite of raising revenue for a government – they are a mechanism under which a government can distribute its resources directly, rather than to gather resources. However, taxes and subsidies may both be seen as tools with which a government can influence behaviour and financial positions.

34.04 Taxes and subsidies can be remarkably similar and have some crossover, such as where a tax system gives an advantage to a taxpayer, by letting them off or relieving a tax liability. Tax reliefs in this way can be subsidies (or state aid) and from a policy perspective, can perform the same function: like more traditional subsidies, they are a way for governments to 'dish out sweets'.

34.05 There are some emissions which are not (yet) taxed in the UK. By mapping industry sectors against the tax base for emissions generating activities, the OBR identified a number of areas where there are emissions, but they are not taxed. These include agriculture, which accounted for 10.7% of territorial emissions in 2019 (relating to livestock, direct and indirect soil emissions, and combustion) and land use, land use change and forestry (in which there are some large source emissions, but they are largely offset by some large sinks of carbon, such as forests). The OBR identifies that overall, 76% of UK territorial emissions map onto tax bases to some extent.

34.06 Further, while there are specific taxes targeted at pursuing particular policy objectives, it should not be forgotten that aspects of other taxes which apply more generally may have some policy specific provisions. Those include reliefs which only apply to certain items or in certain circumstances, or an additional regime under the legislation designed to encourage (or discourage) certain behaviours. For example, the UK's tax system has long encouraged research and development in the UK, such as through reliefs available for research and development activity, and the Patent Box regime, which allows companies to elect to pay a corporation tax rate of 10% to profits attributable to qualifying patents and other qualifying intellectual property rights.[5]

34.07 A final important aspect to note in the landscape of tax and subsidies is the EU and international picture. At the highest level (since it is not within the scope of this chapter to set out the relationship between the UK, the EU and international law), in respect of tax, the UK has full jurisdiction to set its tax system as it wishes to do so. Before Brexit, the UK had the same jurisdiction, albeit that the tax system was subject to international law (as it is now) and to EU law. Notably, there is a long history of the application of EU law to UK tax law, in particular the fundamental freedoms and state aid law.[6] Since Brexit, that position has changed to the extent that provisions of EU law such as the fundamental freedoms, state aid and the principles of EU law which had previously been highly relevant to the UK's tax system, are no longer applicable. As to state aid, the UK now has its own subsidy regime, which is derived from the

---

4 See, for example, Kelyn Bacon, *European Union Law of State Aid* (3rd edn, Oxford University Press 2017) at para 1.12 as to policy objectives, economic welfare and 1.13 as to market failures.
5 See HM Revenue & Customs, 'HMRC Internal Manual: Corporate Intangibles Research and Development Manual' (2024) <https://www.gov.uk/hmrc-internal-manuals/corporate-intangibles-research-and-development-manual/cird200110> accessed 28 April 2024.
6 See Chapter 28.

EU–UK Trade and Co-operation Agreement ('TCA'). The UK also has other international law obligations in respect of state aid and subsidies (as set out in more detail at paragraph 34.53 below).

34.08 In the UK, there are a number of fiscal measures and subsidy measures which have either direct, or indirect, environmental objectives and consequences. This chapter considers current taxes on emissions, current structured subsidies on emissions, and taxes with an impact on nature positive goals.

Current taxes on emissions

(i) *Introduction*

34.09 There are various fiscal measures applicable to different aspects of the economy that have the effect of either direct or indirect taxation on emissions. Some of these are classified as 'environmental taxes', as they have explicit environmental objectives (such as the UK Emissions Trading Scheme, or the Climate Change Levy). Others are indirect taxes on products which cause emissions (such as fuel duties). These fiscal measures are summarised below.

(ii) *UK Emissions Trading Scheme*

34.10 The UK Emissions Trading Scheme ('UK ETS') is the closest thing the UK has to an explicit emissions tax.[7] It is a cap-and-trade scheme, where a cap is set on the total amount of greenhouses gases ('GHGs') that can be emitted by sectors covered by the scheme, thus limiting the total amount of carbon which can be emitted, which is to decrease over time.[8] The UK ETS is covered in more detail in Chapter 14.

(iii) *Climate Change Levy, Climate Change Agreements, Carbon Price Support and Carbon Price Floor*

34.11 The Climate Change Levy ('CCL') is a tax on energy (electricity, gas, liquefied petroleum gas and solid fuels) supplied to businesses, set pursuant to the Finance Act 2000, which commenced in April 2001.[9] It excludes businesses that use small amounts of energy, domestic energy users, and charities.

34.12 At the time of its introduction, it was the second biggest component in the 'UK Climate Change Programme' by estimated size of carbon savings,[10] its aim being

7 Institute of Fiscal Studies, 'Chapter 8: Tax Policies to Help Achieve Net Zero Carbon Emissions', IFS Green Budget 2021 (2021) 18 <https://ifs.org.uk/sites/default/files/output_url_files/8-Tax-policies-to-help-achieve-net-zero-carbon-emissions-.pdf> accessed 28 April 2024.

8 Department for Business, Energy and Industrial Strategy and Department for Energy Security and Net Zero, 'Guidance: Participating in the UK ETS' (GOV.UK) <https://www.gov.uk/government/publications/participating-in-the-uk-ets/participating-in-the-uk-ets> accessed 17 April 2024.

9 Finance Act 2000 Sch 6.

10 House of Commons Environmental Audit Committee, *Reducing Carbon Emissions from UK Business: The Role of the Climate Change Levy and Agreements* (HC 2008, 354) 3 <https://publications.parliament.uk/pa/cm200708/cmselect/cmenvaud/354/354.pdf> accessed 28 April 2024.

to encourage organisations to use energy more efficiently, and thereby reduce GHG emissions.

34.13 The CCL is paid at either main rates, or reduced rates arising from Climate Change Agreements, or Carbon Price Support ('CPS') rates.

34.14 The system of Climate Change Agreements was introduced because of the need for special consideration of energy-intensive industries exposed to international competition. By those agreements, energy-intensive firms are allowed an 80% reduction in the levy, provided they agree to increase energy efficiency and reduce emissions.[11]

34.15 CPS rates are paid in respect of the quantity of energy supplied by businesses that own electricity generating stations, or are operators of combined heat and power stations.[12]

34.16 CPS rates were introduced as part of the Carbon Price Floor ('CPF'), a government policy implemented to support the EU ETS. The CPF was introduced on 1 April 2013 to underpin the price of carbon at a level that drives low carbon investment, which some considered the EU ETS had not achieved.[13]

34.17 The CPF consists of two components, which are paid for by energy generators in different ways: the EU ETS allowance price, and the CPS rates, which top up the EU ETS allowance price to the CPF target. Since the implementation of the CPF, there have been significant falls in coal electricity generation, which some commentators suggest can partly be attributed to the CPF.[14]

(iv) *Carbon Border Adjustment Mechanism*

34.18 On 18 December 2023, the government committed to introducing a Carbon Border Adjustment Mechanism ('CBAM') by 2027.[15]

34.19 A CBAM places a carbon tax on certain emissions intensive industrial goods which are imported into the country. The sectors currently identified by the government include the aluminium, cement, ceramics, fertiliser, glass, hydrogen, iron and steel sectors.[16]

---

11 ibid 5; Finance Act 2000 paras 44–52 of sch 6.
12 Finance Act 2000 paras 24A, 24B and 42A of sch 6.
13 David Hirst, *Carbon Price Floor (CPF) and the Price Support Mechanism* (Briefing Paper No 05927, 2018) 3 <https://researchbriefings.files.parliament.uk/documents/SN05927/SN05927.pdf> accessed 28 April 2024.
14 ibid.
15 Department for Energy Security and Net Zero, 'Consultation Outcome Factsheet: UK Carbon Border Adjustment Mechanism' (2023) <https://www.gov.uk/government/consultations/addressing-carbon-leakage-risk-to-support-decarbonisation/outcome/factsheet-uk-carbon-border-adjustment-mechanism#:~:text=After%20careful%20review%20and%20giving,a%20UK%20CBAM%20by%202027> accessed 28 April 2024.
16 ibid.

34.20 The primary purpose of a CBAM, including both the anticipated UK CBAM,[17] and the EU's CBAM is to resolve the issue of carbon leakage.[18]

34.21 Carbon leakage refers to the situation that may occur if, for reasons of costs related to climate policies, businesses in certain industry sectors or subsectors transfer production to other countries, or imports from those countries replace equivalent products that are less intensive in terms of GHG emissions. Such situations could lead to an increase in total global emissions.[19]

34.22 The 'climate policies', in respect of the UK and the EU, primarily refer to the ETS. As set out in paragraph 34.10 above and in Chapter 14, the UK ETS (and EU ETS) provides for a cap-and-trade scheme for certain sectors. Under this scheme, certain carbon intensive sectors at particular risk of carbon leakage receive free allowances of carbon credits, to safeguard their competitiveness.[20] The intention of a CBAM is to enable the phase out of free allowances, whilst enabling these industries to remain competitive, by taxing the carbon of imported products at an equivalent rate to domestic products.[21]

34.23 Whilst the primary objective of a CBAM is to prevent carbon leakage, the introduction of a CBAM is also intended to encourage the use of more GHG emissions-efficient technologies by third countries. This is because applicable industries will now be taxed for importing into territories covered by the CBAM, unless they were already subject to an equivalent carbon tax in their origin country, thus incentivising third countries to introduce such taxes, so they receive the tax income rather than the territory imposing the CBAM.[22]

34.24 At the time of writing, there is no current UK draft legislation in respect of the UK CBAM. However, it is likely that it will closely reflect the EU CBAM.

34.25 Listed below are some of the key features of the EU CBAM:

- The EU CBAM should ensure that imported products are subject to a regulatory system that applies carbon costs equivalent to the ones borne under the EU ETS, resulting in an equivalent carbon pricing for imports and domestic products;[23]

- The EU CBAM was approved on 10 May 2023, and its transitional period commenced on 1 October 2023 and runs until 31 December 2025, during which it is

---

17 ibid.
18 Regulation (EU) 2023/956 of the European Parliament and of the Council of 10 May 2023 establishing a carbon border adjustment mechanism recital 12.
19 ibid recital 9.
20 Department for Energy Security and Net Zero, 'Consultation Outcome Factsheet: UK Carbon Border Adjustment Mechanism' (2023) (n 15).
21 Regulation (EU) 2023/956 of the European Parliament and of the Council of 10 May 2023 establishing a carbon border adjustment mechanism recital 12.
22 ibid recital 14.
23 ibid recital 15.

limited to a reporting obligation as set out within Articles 33–35 of the regulation, e.g. the CBAM report detailed in Article 35;[24]

- From 1 January 2026,[25] only authorised declarants will be permitted to import covered products.[26] The declarants will need to report on the direct and indirect embedded emissions in the imported covered products on an annual basis, and will need to surrender a corresponding amount of 'CBAM certificates' covering the assessed and declared embedded emissions of the imported products.[27] A 'CBAM certificate' means a certificate in electronic format corresponding to one metric tonne of CO_2e of embedded emissions in goods;[28]

- The products which are covered under the EU CBAM are listed in Annex I to Regulation (EU) 2023/956.[29] The initial industrial sectors covered include iron and steel, refineries, cement, aluminium, organic basic chemicals, hydrogen and fertilisers.[30] However, the ultimate objective of the CBAM is a broad product coverage;[31] and

- The price of CBAM certificates should reasonably reflect the EU ETS market price of allowances released onto the market via auctions, through averages calculated on a weekly basis.[32]

(v) *Fuel duties*

34.26 The Treasury and HM Revenue & Customs define environmental taxes narrowly, as taxes with explicit environmental objectives.[33] This does not include fuel duty, as the government does not consider this to have environmental objectives as its primary or sole purpose.[34] As such, it is not managed as an environmental tax.[35] However, it is accepted that fuel duty has an impact on the government's environmental objectives, as it may contribute to the UK's commitment to reduce CO_2 emissions and improve air quality.[36]

34.27 A much wider definition of environmental taxes comes from the Office for National Statistics ('ONS').[37] Its definition covers taxes based 'on a physical unit that

---

24 ibid Article 32.
25 ibid Article 36(2).
26 ibid Article 4.
27 ibid Article 6.
28 ibid Article 3(24).
29 ibid Article 2.
30 ibid recital 32.
31 ibid recital 30.
32 ibid recital 23.
33 HM Treasury, 'Press Release: Definition of Environmental Tax Published' (2012) <https://www.gov.uk/government/news/definition-of-environmental-tax-published> accessed 28 April 2024.
34 House of Commons Committee of Public Accounts, *Environmental Tax Measures* (HC 2021, 937) 4 <https://committees.parliament.uk/publications/5649/documents/55743/default/> accessed 28 April 2024.
35 National Audit Office, *Environmental Tax Measures* (HC 2021, 1203) 11 <https://www.nao.org.uk/wp-content/uploads/2021/02/Environmental-Tax-Measures.pdf> accessed 28 April 2024.
36 ibid 6.
37 Institute for Government, 'Net Zero and the Tax System' (2021) 7 <https://www.instituteforgovernment.org.uk/sites/default/files/publications/net-zero-tax.pdf> accessed 28 April 2024.

has a proven negative impact on the environment'.[38] On top of the taxes identified by the Treasury, it includes fuel duty and air passenger duty ('APD'). While neither was introduced with a primary or sole environmental objective, both increase the cost of travel and hence affect transport emissions.[39]

34.28 Fuel duty is levied per unit of fuel purchased; and it is included in the price paid for the fuel. The rate depends on the type of fuel.

34.29 Fuel duty was first introduced by Section 85 of the Finance Act 1908 at three pence per gallon.[40] The current legislation concerning fuel duty is the Hydrocarbon Oil Duties Act 1979 ('HODA 1979'). Section 6 of the HODA 1979 sets out the various charging provisions for the different fuels. The current rate for petrol, diesel, biodiesel and bioethanol, is 52.95 pence per litre.[41]

34.30 The HODA 1979 sets out various other provisions relevant to rebate and certain reliefs, and certain excepted machines, such as an 'agricultural vehicle' at a time when it is used for purposes relating to agriculture, horticulture, pisciculture or forestry.[42]

34.31 VAT is then applied on fuel after fuel duty is applied.[43] In respect of fuel used for road transportation, VAT is 20%; however, if the fuel is to be used as domestic fuel, it has a reduced rate of 5%.[44]

34.32 Fuel duty represents a substantial revenue stream for the government. In 2023–24, the OBR estimates that fuel duties will raise £24.3 billion, which would represent 2.3% of all receipts.[45] As a result, there are concerns about the impact of net zero policy on government revenue. In 2021, the Treasury identified risks to £37 billion of revenue from taxes that are wholly dependent on the consumption of fossil fuels or the emission of GHGs. A large part of this risk concerns the likely impact to revenues from fuel duty, which will decline as a result of government policy to end the sale of new petrol and diesel vehicles.[46]

34.33 The House of Commons Public Accounts Committee set out in its report on environmental tax measures, published on 28 April 2021, that the Treasury would need to act soon to identify and consult on options for motoring taxes, and should set out a timetable for how it will consult on options for replacing declining revenues from fuel duty.[47]

---

38 ibid.
39 ibid.
40 HC Deb 29 October 1909, vol 12.
41 'Tax on Shopping and Services' <https://www.gov.uk/tax-on-shopping/fuel-duty> accessed 28 April 2024.
42 Hydrocarbon Oil Duties Act 1979 para 2(1)(a) of sch 1A.
43 Office for Budget Responsibility, 'Fuel Duties' (2024) <https://obr.uk/forecasts-in-depth/tax-by-tax-spend-by-spend/fuel-duties/> accessed 28 April 2024.
44 Value Added Tax Act 1994 group 1 of sch 7A.
45 Office for Budget Responsibility, 'Fuel Duties' (n 43).
46 House of Commons Committee of Public Accounts, *Environmental Tax Measures* (n 34) 7.
47 ibid 7.

(vi) *Air passenger duty*

34.34 Air passenger duty ('APD') is charged on all passenger flights from UK airports. The rate of duty varies according to passenger destination and the class of passenger travel.[48] It is the principal tax on the aviation sector, because tickets are VAT-free and aviation fuel incurs no duty.[49]

34.35 As with fuel duty, APD is not considered (or administered) as an environmental tax, as it does not have environmental objectives as its primary or sole purpose (albeit the consultation on APD in 2021 set out three objectives, one of which was environmental).[50] As such, it is not managed as an environmental tax.[51] However, as with fuel duty, it is accepted that APD has an impact on the UK's environmental objectives, as it may contribute to the commitment to reduce CO_2 emissions and improve air quality.[52]

34.36 APD was first introduced in the November 1993 Budget, coming into effect on 1 November 1994,[53] through Chapter IV of the Finance Act 1994 ('FA 1994'), which is still in place.

34.37 Section 28 of the FA 1994 provides that APD is to be charged on the carriage on a chargeable aircraft of any chargeable passenger. Section 29 defines chargeable aircraft. Section 30 sets out the applicable rates, which for standard class travel currently stand at £6.50 if the passenger's journey ends at a place in the UK, £13 if the passenger's journey ends at a place in a territory specified in Part 1 of Schedule 5A (largely European destinations), £87 if the passenger's journey ends in a territory specified in Part 1A of Schedule 5A, and £91 if the passenger's journey ends at any other place.

34.38 There is criticism of APD, and more broadly the taxation of aviation, in connection with the net zero strategy, particularly in the context of direct demand management ('DDM') measures.[54] There are currently two claims before the High Court challenging the government's 'Jet Zero strategy', focusing on DDM measures (see paragraphs 18.24–18.28).

34.39 There have been suggestions for APD to be amended or replaced with a frequent flyer levy which would progressively tax passengers increasing per flight or mile which they fly, or other demand management measures.[55] The Climate Change Committee

48 Anthony Seely, *Air Passenger Duty: Introduction* (Briefing Paper No 413, 2019) 3 <https://researchbriefings.files.parliament.uk/documents/SN00413/SN00413.pdf> accessed 28 April 2024.
49 HM Treasury, 'Consultation on Aviation Tax Reform: Summary of Responses to the Consultation' (2021) <https://assets.publishing.service.gov.uk/media/61782a01d3bf7f55fc098efa/APD_Summary_of_Responses_IN_TEMPLATE__002_.pdf> accessed 28 April 2024 para 1.2.
50 House of Commons Committee of Public Accounts, *Environmental Tax Measures* (n 34) 4.
51 National Audit Office, *Environmental Tax Measures* (n 35) 11.
52 ibid 6.
53 Anthony Seely, *Air Passenger Duty: Introduction* (n 48) 3.
54 Green Alliance, 'Written Response Submitted by Green Alliance' (2021) ZAS0022 <https://committees.parliament.uk/writtenevidence/38595/pdf/> accessed 28 April 2024.
55 House of Commons Environmental Audit Committee, *Net Zero and the UK Aviation Sector* (HC 2023, 404) 44 <https://committees.parliament.uk/publications/42703/documents/212154/default/> accessed 28 April 2024.

advises that DDM is the most effective way of reducing aviation CO_2 and non-CO_2 emissions.[56]

34.40 However, the government does not support the DDM measures, and these do not form part of its Jet Zero Strategy.[57]

(vii) *Vehicle excise duty*

34.41 In contrast to fuel duty, vehicle excise duty ('VED') is now considered to be an environmental tax.[58]

34.42 A duty of excise for carriages (a precursor tax to VED) was first introduced for motor vehicles in the UK from 1 January 1889, pursuant to the Customs and Inland Revenue Act 1888.[59]

34.43 One of the early objectives of VED was to finance the building and maintenance of the road system.[60] It was only in 2001, following recommendations in the 1990s by the Royal Commission on Environmental Pollution to graduate the VED to encourage environmentally friendly behaviour, that VED was graduated according to carbon emissions (pursuant to Budget 2000). The Budget in 2000 introduced a new system of VED for all cars registered after 1 March 2001, based on four bands according to their average CO_2 emissions per kilometre.[61] Since then, further changes have been made, such as the introduction of new bands and different charges, but throughout VED has been graduated according to carbon emissions.

34.44 The current legislation concerning vehicle tax is the Vehicle Excise and Registration Act 1994. Section 1 of this Act provides that a duty of excise is charged in respect of every mechanically propelled vehicle that is registered under the Act, or is not registered but is used or kept on a public road in the UK. The relevant chargeable rates as applicable to different vehicles are detailed within Schedule 1 of this Act. Part II of the Act sets out provisions for the registration of vehicles, and Part III of the Act sets out offences for using or keeping an unlicensed vehicle and for failure to pay licence fees.

---

56 Climate Change Committee, 'Progress in Reducing Emissions: 2023 Report to Parliament' (2023) <https://www.theccc.org.uk/wp-content/uploads/2023/06/Progress-in-reducing-UK-emissions-2023-Report-to-Parliament.pdf> accessed 4 April 2024.

57 Department for Transport, 'Jet Zero Consultation: Summary of Responses and Government Response' (2022) <https://assets.publishing.service.gov.uk/government/uploads/system/uploads/attachment_data/file/1096928/jet-zero-consultation-summary-of-responses-and-government-response.pdf> accessed 28 April 2024; HM Government, *Responding to the Climate Change Committee's (CCC) 2023 Annual Progress Report to Parliament* (HC 2023, 1919) <https://assets.publishing.service.gov.uk/media/65393f4ae6c968000daa9b0e/ccc-annual-progress-report-2023-government-response.pdf> accessed 28 April 2024.

58 House of Commons Environmental Audit Committee, *Vehicle Excise Duty as an Environmental Tax* (HC 2008, 907) <https://publications.parliament.uk/pa/cm200708/cmselect/cmenvaud/907/907.pdf> accessed 28 April 2024; House of Commons Committee of Public Accounts, *Environmental Tax Measures* (n 34).

59 Francesco Masala, *Vehicle Excise Duty* (Research Briefing No CBP-1482, 2023) 35 <https://researchbriefings.files.parliament.uk/documents/SN01482/SN01482.pdf> accessed 28 April 2024.

60 House of Commons Environmental Audit Committee, *Vehicle Excise Duty as an Environmental Tax* (n 58) 9.

61 ibid.

34.45 Whilst this tax has an effect on reducing emissions, some commentators state that it is not closely targeted at emissions, as whilst it may discourage ownership of emissions heavy vehicles, it does not discourage car owners to drive less.[62]

34.46 As with fuel duty, there is concern about future revenue from VED, as low emissions vehicle ownership increases. This has led to a new proposed measure, announced in the Autumn Statement 2022, to introduce VED for all zero emission vehicles from April 2025.[63]

34.47 In addition to national legislation, there are also various local schemes which take into account environmental criteria to tax the use of vehicles on public roads. Most notably, these are the Central London Congestion Charging Scheme[64] and the London Low Emission Zone ('LEZ') and Ultra Low Emission Zone ('ULEZ').[65]

(viii) *Renewable Transport Fuel Obligation*

34.48 The Renewable Transport Fuel Obligation ('RTFO') was one of the government's main policies for reducing GHG emissions from road transport in the UK, intending to reduce CO_2 emissions by encouraging the supply of renewable fuels. It is considered, by the Department of Transport, to be meeting this objective.[66]

34.49 Pursuant to the Renewable Transport Fuel Obligations Order 2007 ('RTFO Order 2007'), implementing Chapter 5 of Part 2 of the Energy Act 2004 ('EA 2004'), the obligation imposes on transport fuel suppliers (including refiners, importers and others) who supply more than 450,000 litres of relevant hydrocarbon oil in the UK,[67] an obligation to produce evidence that a certain amount of renewable transport fuel has been supplied in the UK.[68] The percentage of required renewable transport fuel, and formula for calculation, is set out at Article 4(6C) of the RTFO Order 2007. It is set at 13.563% for 2024, increasing to 17.676% by 2032.

34.50 In addition, this order provides for a similar obligation in respect of 'development fuel', a specific sub-set of advanced fuels as defined in Article 3, set at 1.379% for 2024 and increasing to 3.390% by 2032.

34.51 Renewable transport fuel is defined in Section 132(1) of the EA 2004 as: '(a) biofuel; (b) blended biofuel; (c) any solid, liquid or gaseous fuel (other than fossil fuel

---

62 Institute of Fiscal Studies, 'Chapter 8: Tax Policies to Help Achieve Net Zero Carbon Emissions', IFS Green Budget 2021 (n 7) 21–22.
63 HM Revenue & Customs, 'Policy Paper: Introduction of Vehicle Excise Duty for Zero Emission Cars, Vans and Motorcycles from 2025' (2022) <https://www.gov.uk/government/publications/introduction-of-vehicle-excise-duty-for-zero-emission-cars-vans-and-motorcycles-from-2025/introduction-of-vehicle-excise-duty-for-zero-emission-cars-vans-and-motorcycles-from-2025> accessed 28 April 2024.
64 Established under The Greater London (Central Zone) Congestion Charging Order 2004.
65 Established under The Greater London Low Emission Zone Charging Order 2006.
66 Department for Transport, *Renewable Transport Fuel Obligation Annual Report 2021* (CP 856, 2023) 4 <https://assets.publishing.service.gov.uk/media/648881a4b32b9e000ca966af/rtfo-annual-report-2021-web-version.pdf> accessed 28 April 2024.
67 Part 2 of The Renewable Transport Fuel Obligations Order 2007.
68 Energy Act 2004 s 124.

or nuclear fuel) which is produced—(i) wholly by energy from a renewable source; or (ii) wholly by a process powered wholly by such energy; or (d) any solid, liquid or gaseous fuel which is of a description of fuel designated by an RTF order as renewable transport fuel'.

34.52 Relevant transport fuel suppliers who can evidence the use of renewable transport fuel must apply for RTF certificates, certifying the use of such fuel, which can then be credited to the supplier.[69] A supplier who does not wholly discharge the RTFO for an obligation period must pay a 'buy out sum'. The calculation for the 'buy out sum' is set out within Article 21 of the RTFO Order 2007, which comes to £0.50 per litre for each litre of shortfall of renewable transport fuel, and £0.80 per litre for each litre of shortfall of development fuel.

Current structured subsidies on emissions

(i) *Meaning of subsidies*

34.53 It is not within the scope of this book to offer a thorough overview of subsidy control laws, and readers should refer to specialist texts on the subject.[70] However, in broad terms, there are three applicable regimes on subsidies: domestic, EU and international. Although there are differences between the regimes, all define a subsidy as (i) a measure which amounts to aid, financial assistance or a financial contribution, (ii) granted through state resources, (iii) which is selective/threatens to distort competition and (iv) which affects trade.

(ii) *Legal regimes governing subsidies*

34.54 In the domestic regime, the Subsidy Control Act 2022 ('SCA 2022') defines a subsidy as:

> [F]inancial assistance which (a) is given, directly or indirectly, from public resources by a public authority, (b) confers an economic advantage on one or more enterprises, (c) is specific, that is, is such that it benefits one or more enterprises over one or more other enterprises with respect to the production of goods or the provision of services, and (d) has, or is capable of having, an effect on: (i) competition or investment within the United Kingdom; (ii) trade between the United Kingdom and a country or territory outside the United Kingdom, or (iii) investment as between the United Kingdom and a country or territory outside the United Kingdom).[71]

34.55 This includes through a direct transfer of funds (such as grants or loans), contingent transfers of funds (such as guarantees), the foregoing of revenue that is otherwise due, and the provision or purchase of goods and services.[72]

69 Part 4 and 5 of The Renewable Transport Fuel Obligations Order 2007.
70 See for instance Kelyn Bacon, *European Union Law of State Aid* (n 4).
71 SCA 2022 s 2(1).
72 ibid s 2(2).

34.56 Part 2 of the SCA 2022 sets out the requirements for subsidy control. These include application of the subsidy control principles set out in Schedule 1,[73] and the energy and environment principles set out in Schedule 2,[74] as well as general prohibitions and other requirements.

34.57 The energy and environment principles require that subsidies for renewable energy 'shall be determined by means of a transparent, non-discriminatory and effective competition process'; see principle C(1)(c).[75]

34.58 Regulations made under the SCA 2022 set out the details for how subsidies of interest or in sensitive areas are to be handled.[76] Statutory guidance has also been published:[77]

- EU law – Articles 107–109 on the Treaty of the Functioning of the European Union ('TFEU') prohibit state aid.[78] In the UK context, following the UK's withdrawal from the EU, Article 10(1) and Annex 5 of the Northern Ireland Protocol apply EU state aid rules to measures which affect trade between Northern Ireland and the Union.[79]

- International law – the TCA and the WTO Agreement on Subsidies and Countervailing Measures all make provision in respect of subsidy controls in international law. The TCA concluded between the EU and the UK following the latter's withdrawal from the EU contains preferential arrangements in various areas of trade, including energy.[80] While Article 302 of the TCA preserves the right of each party 'adopt, maintain and enforce measures necessary to pursue legitimate public policy objectives, such as securing the supply of energy goods and raw materials, protecting society, the environment, including fighting against climate change', this is subject to the other provisions of the Agreement, including the principle of non-discrimination.[81] The WTO Agreement on Subsidies and Countervailing Measures differentiates between prohibited subsidies (subsidies prohibited in their own right, namely subsidies contingent on export performance and subsidies

---

73 ibid s 12.
74 ibid s 13.
75 ibid s 13, sch 2.
76 The Subsidy Control (Subsidies and Schemes of Interest or Particular Interest) Regulations 2022.
77 Department for Business & Trade, 'Statutory Guidance for the United Kingdom Subsidy Control Regime: Subsidy Control Act 2022' (2023) <https://assets.publishing.service.gov.uk/media/658025b295bf65000d719140/uk_subsidy_control_regime_statutory_guidance.pdf> accessed 28 April 2024.
78 See on this the analysis in Kelyn Bacon, *European Union Law of State Aid* (n 4) para 2.02: a measure will amount to state aid within the meaning of Article 107(1) if it amounts to (a) an economic advantage; (b) granted directly or indirectly through State resources and imputable to the State; (c) it favours certain undertakings or the production of certain goods ('selectivity'); and (d) is liable to distort competition and affect trade between Member States.
79 See The Protocol on Ireland/Northern Ireland, and see also *R (British Sugar) v Secretary of State for International Trade* [2022] EWHC 393 (Admin) as to the circumstances in which the NIP is engaged.
80 Trade and Cooperation Agreement between the European Union and the European Atomic Energy Community, of the one part, and the United Kingdom of Great Britain and Northern Ireland, of the other part [2021] OJ L 149/10.
81 TCA 2021 Article 302; see in respect of non-discrimination recital 19, and Articles 303–307 in respect of energy markets.

contingent on the use of domestic goods over imported) and actionable subsidies (which can be challenged if they cause adverse effects to the interests of another member).[82]

34.59 There are a number of fiscal measures currently in use which are capable of amounting to subsidies, including contracts for difference, feed-in tariffs and renewables obligations, which we will now examine in turn. The latter two schemes are closed to new entrants but remain relevant for existing participants.

(iii) *Contracts for Difference*

34.60 A Contract for Difference ('CfD') sets a 'strike price' for the cost of energy.[83] A generator selling electricity into the market may achieve a variable price which exceeds the strike price: however, if the strike price is higher than the market price, the generator receives a top-up payment from the government-owned Low Carbon Contracts Company, to the level of the strike price. The CJEU has held that CfDs are capable of amounting to state aid, as the strike price mechanism ensures payment if price drops below the strike price.[84]

34.61 Section 6 of the Energy Act 2013 ('EA 2013'), as amended by Section 18 of the Energy Prices Act 2022, provides:

> (1) The Secretary of State may for the purpose of encouraging low carbon electricity generation make regulations about contracts for difference between a CFD counterparty and an eligible generator.
>
> (1A) The reference in subsection (1) to encouraging low carbon electricity generation includes encouraging the continuation of, or an increase in, low carbon electricity generation by existing generation stations.
>
> (2) A contract for difference is a contract—
>
> (a) certain payments under which are to be funded by electricity suppliers (see further section 9), and
> (b) which a CFD counterparty is required to enter into by virtue of section 10 or 14;
>
> and such a contract is referred to in this Chapter as a 'CFD'.

34.62 The purposes for which CfD regulations may be made therefore includes encouraging the continuation of, or an increase in, low carbon electricity generation by existing generating stations, as well as new generating stations. A number of types of generating

82 For a more detailed summary, see World Trade Organization, 'Agreement on Subsidies and Countervailing Measures ('SCM Agreement')' <https://www.wto.org/english/tratop_e/scm_e/subs_e.htm> accessed 28 April 2024.
83 Department for Energy Security and Net Zero, 'Contracts for Difference' (16 November 2023) <https://www.gov.uk/government/collections/contracts-for-difference> accessed 28 April 2024.
84 Case C-594/18 *Austria v Commission* [2020] ECLI:EU:C:2020:742.

stations are eligible for CfDs.[85] CfDs are allocated by way of a framework established by government through regulations, including the Contracts for Difference (Allocation) Regulations 2014,[86] and the Contracts for Difference (Standard Terms) Regulations 2014.[87] Bespoke CfDs can also be entered into (and indeed for nuclear are required, as contracts relating to nuclear are not eligible under the Allocation Regulations).[88]

34.63 Following the closure of the Renewables Obligation Scheme (addressed more below), CfDs are the primary method of support for large-scale renewable energy generation.

(iv) *Green Gas Support Scheme and Levy*

34.64 The Green Gas Support Scheme provides financial incentives to facilitate and encourage the production of methane, through anaerobic digestion plants which produce methane. The scheme is open to applicants for four years from 30 November 2021: producers who produce biomethane which they will commence to inject before 30 November 2025 may apply for a tariff guarantee.[89] If approved, Ofgem will confirm the guaranteed tariff, specifying the date by which injection must commence, the equipment to be used, the information the applicant must supply and any other conditions it considers necessary.[90]

34.65 The Scheme is supported through a levy on suppliers of gas from fossil fuels, unless they are an exempt supplier (meaning at least 95% of the gas they supplied in a tariff year was certified biomethane).[91]

(v) *Feed-in Tariff Scheme*

34.66 The Feed-in Tariffs (FITs) Scheme was designed to incentive small-scale renewable energy generation.[92] In effect, the scheme introduced guaranteed payments to small-scale producers for a fixed period. Generators would apply for accreditation: solar photovoltaic, wind, hydro, anaerobic digestion and micro combined heat and power installations with total installed capacity of less than 5MW were eligible.[93] The process for accreditation depended on the type of installation in terms of the technology employed and the size.[94] There were exceptions, including installations which had previously received support or which had received support under the Renewables Obligation scheme.[95]

85 The Contracts for Difference (Definition of Eligible Generator) Regulations 2014 sch 1.
86 SI 2014/2011.
87 SI 2014/2012.
88 The Contracts for Difference (Definition of Eligible Generator) Regulations 2014 reg 14.
89 The Green Gas Support Scheme Regulations 2021, SI 2021/1335 reg 4.
90 ibid reg 4(6).
91 ibid reg 38.
92 The Feed-in Tariffs Order 2012, SI 2012/2782 ('FITs Order 2012').
93 FITs Order 2012 Article 3.
94 ibid Articles 4–5.
95 ibid Article 7.

34.67 FITs were generally payable to the owner of the installation, who could however nominate a recipient. Two forms of tariffs were payable: a generation tariff (a fixed payment per kilowatt hour generated, based on the type of technology and size of the installation) and an export tariff (a minimum payment for each kilowatt hour exported). Ofgem was required to publish the payment table for each year.[96] Generators could opt out of the export tariff in favour of selling their electricity on the market.

34.68 The FITs scheme closed in 2019.[97]

(vi) *Renewables obligation*

34.69 The Renewables Obligation was introduced to incentivise renewable generation. The Renewables Obligation Order 2015[98] provided that electricity suppliers in England were required to source a proportion of energy from renewable sources.[99] Generators would apply for accreditation and once accredited, they would be issued with Renewables Obligation Certificates ('ROCs'). ROCs were issued per megawatt hour (mW/h) based on features of the generating station. Failure to provide accurate information could result in withdrawal of accreditation.[100]

34.70 Generators would then sell ROCs to suppliers, who were obliged to hold a given number to meet their Renewables Obligation. ROCs were tradeable and could therefore be supplied directly or indirectly.

34.71 All suppliers licensed under the Electricity Act 1989 were required to submit the relevant number of ROCs to Ofgem for each mW/h of electricity supplied.[101]

34.72 The level of the Renewables Obligation was calculated by the Secretary of State in accordance with the Order (until the final scheme closure date, see below).[102] If a supplier had a shortfall in the number of ROCs they were required to pay into a shortfall fund.[103] Money in the fund would then be paid back out (once the running costs of the Renewables Obligation had been met) to suppliers who had met their RO.[104]

---

96 ibid Article 16.
97 Ofgem, 'Feed-in Tariffs (FIT)' <https://www.ofgem.gov.uk/environmental-and-social-schemes/feed-tariffs-fit> accessed 28 April 2024.
98 SI 2015/1947.
99 The equivalent Scottish and Northern Irish equivalents being the The Renewables Obligation (Scotland) Order 2009 and The Renewables Obligation Order (Northern Ireland) 2009.
100 *R (Gravis Solar) v Gas and Electricity Markets Authority* [2021] EWHC 490 (Admin).
101 The Renewables Obligation Order 2015, SI 2015/1947 Article 7.
102 ibid Articles 8–14.
103 ibid Article 67.
104 ibid Articles 69–71. See further the guidance published by Ofgem at Ofgem, 'Guidance for Generators That Receive or Would like to Receive Support under the Renewables Obligation (RO) Scheme' (2019) <https://www.ofgem.gov.uk/sites/default/files/docs/2019/04/ro_generator_guidance_apr19.pdf#page7> accessed 28 April 2024.

34.73 The Renewables Obligation closed to new capacity in 2017,[105] with a view to suppliers transitioning to CfDs. Generators that were already accredited will continue to receive support until the final scheme closure date of 2037.[106]

(vii) *Non-domestic renewable heat incentive*

34.74 The non-domestic renewable heat incentive is a further scheme through which the government sought to incentivise production of renewable energy, under which accredited installations receive payments in proportion to the amount of heat generated from renewable sources.[107] The non-domestic renewable heat incentive closed to new applicants in 2021, and extensions for applications closed in 2023.[108]

Other schemes administered by Ofgem

34.75 Ofgem also administers environmental schemes aimed at supporting consumers, such as the Boiler Upgrade Scheme (which provides grants to cover part of the cost of replacing fossil fuel heating systems with a heat pump or biomass boiler)[109] and the domestic renewable heat incentive (which closed to new applicants in 2022).[110]

Environmental taxes

34.76 In addition to the taxes identified above, there are a number of environmental taxes designed to reduce environmental impacts of landfill, plastics, mining, etc. The key relevant taxes in the UK are the landfill tax, the Aggregates Levy and the Plastic Packaging tax.

(i) *Landfill Tax*

34.77 The purpose of landfill tax is to encourage efforts to minimise the amount of waste produced, and to encourage the use of non-landfill waste management options, which might include recycling, composting and recovery.[111] Broadly, landfill tax in England and landfill disposals tax in Wales are payable in relation to taxable disposals of waste in licensed landfill sites (i.e. those with a permit), and at unlicensed waste sites (i.e. those where the disposal is of a type which requires a permit, but the deposit is made elsewhere than at a licensed landfill site).[112]

105 Renewables Obligation Closure Order 2014, SI 2014/2388.
106 The Renewables Obligation Order 2015, SI 2015/1947 Article 44.
107 Ofgem, 'Non-Domestic Renewable Heat Incentive (RHI)' <https://www.ofgem.gov.uk/environmental-and-social-schemes/non-domestic-renewable-heat-incentive-rhi> accessed 28 April 2024; see also The Renewable Heat Incentive Scheme Regulations 2018 SI 2018/611.
108 Ofgem, 'Non-Domestic Renewable Heat Incentive (RHI)' (n 107).
109 HM Government, 'Apply for the Boiler Upgrade Scheme' <https://www.gov.uk/apply-boiler-upgrade-scheme> accessed 28 April 2024.
110 Ofgem, 'Non-Domestic Renewable Heat Incentive (RHI)' (n 107).
111 See HM Revenue & Customs, 'Excise Notice LFT1: A General Guide to Landfill Tax' (2024) <https://www.gov.uk/government/publications/excise-notice-lft1-a-general-guide-to-landfill-tax/excise-notice-lft1-a-general-guide-to-landfill-tax> accessed 28 April 2024.
112 HM Revenue & Customs, 'Guidance: Check If You Need to Pay Landfill Tax' (2024) <https://www.gov.uk/guidance/landfill-tax-rates-exemptions-and-taxable-activities> accessed 28 April 2024.

34.78 Certain activities at landfill sites are also to be treated as disposals. They include:

- The use of material to cover the disposal area during a short-term cessation in landfill disposal activity;

- The use of material to create or maintain a temporary haul road or temporary hardstanding;

- The use of material to create or maintain a cell bund or create or maintain a temporary screening bund (except where the material is naturally occurring material extracted from the site);

- The temporary storage of ashes; and

- The use of material placed against the drainage layer or liner of the disposal area to prevent damage to that layer or liner.[113]

34.79 Landfill tax was introduced in the Finance Act 1996 ('FA 1996'), and the regime was amended by the Finance Act 2018 ('FA 2018'). To supplement the statute, there are regulations including the Landfill Tax Regulations 1996,[114] the Landfill Tax (Miscellaneous Provisions) Regulations 2019[115] and the Landfill Tax (Prescribed Landfill Site Activities) Order. A variety of Guidance[116] has also been produced, including a landfill tax manual (although the manual has been withdrawn for an update and, at the time of writing, that update has not been published).

34.80 A taxable disposal takes place in one of two ways. Either material is disposed of and the disposal is made at a landfill site (defined as requiring a permit), or the disposal requires a permit or licence but the disposal is made elsewhere. This means that there is a close relationship between the environmental permitting regime[117] and the landfill tax regime.

34.81 Landfill tax is charged at one of two rates, depending on the type of waste deposited. A lower rate of tax (£3.30 per tonne from 1 April 2024)[118] applies to inert waste, which is listed in the Schedule to the Landfill Tax (Qualifying Material) Order 2011.[119] Examples of inert waste include unused minerals, furnace slags, ash, low activity inorganic compounds and naturally occurring rocks and soils. From 1 April 2025, the lower rate will be £4.05 per tonne.[120]

---

113 The Landfill Tax (Prescribed Landfill Site Activities) Order 2009, SI 2009/1929 para 3.
114 SI 1996/1527.
115 SI 2018/396.
116 HM Revenue & Customs, 'Landfill Tax: Detailed Information' (30 January 2024) <https://www.gov.uk/government/collections/landfill-tax-detailed-information> accessed 28 April 2024.
117 See Chapter 13.
118 FA 1996 s 42, as amended.
119 SI 2011/1017.
120 HM Treasury, *Spring Budget 2024* (HC 2024,560) <https://assets.publishing.service.gov.uk/media/65e8581eea2f36001a3c8970/E03057752_HMT_Spring_Budget_Mar_24_TEXT_20pt_LP_PRINT__2_.pdf> accessed 28 April 2024.

34.82 The other rate, described as the standard rate, applies to all other taxable wastes, and in practical terms includes active wastes or those which might be regarded as more toxic. The rate is £103.70 from 1 April 2024. Both rates are now to be uprated in line with the Retail Price Index ('RPI') (whereas in the past increases to rates were made by legislation). From 1 April 2025, the standard rate will be £126.15 per tonne.

34.83 Disposals which have been made at places other than at a landfill site became taxable only after the amendments to the FA 2018, i.e. on or after 1 April 2018.[121] Those amendments include transitional deeming provisions for disposals made before 1 April 2018, to the effect that they may be treated as having been made on 1 April 2018 and may therefore be subject to tax.[122] There is a limit, however, to the deeming provision, such that a person cannot be guilty of an offence or liable to a civil penalty solely as a result of the retrospective effect of the provision deeming disposals to have been made on or after 1 April 2018.[123]

34.84 There are a number of exemptions from the landfill tax regime, which include material removed (or dredged) from water,[124] mining and quarrying,[125] filling quarries[126] and pet cemeteries.[127]

34.85 There has been a raft of case law testing the question of whether certain materials used in a landfill site are subject to landfill tax. These include *Waste Recycling Group v HMRC*,[128] in which it was held that material that had been used, rather than discarded at a landfill site, was not taxable. Following that case, HMRC published Revenue & Customs Brief 58/08 in which claims for repayment of tax were invited, and which referred to examples of non-taxable use.[129] Claims were made for the material used to line the bottom and sides of landfill sites (known as base and side fluff).

34.86 Following those claims was the case of *R (Veolia ES Landfill Ltd) v HMRC*,[130] in which two taxpayers sought judicial review of HMRC's reversal of the decision to repay the overpaid tax. The applications were refused on the basis that when the tax was paid, it was paid on the basis that the material was taxable, and the claimants therefore did not have a legitimate expectation.

34.87 *R (Biffa Waste Services Ltd) v HMRC*[131] concerned the layer between the upper part of the soft waste at the site and the sealing cap of the landfill site (known as top fluff). In that case, HMRC initially determined that the layer would not be subject to

---

121 FA 2018 paras 29, 31 and 32 of sch 12.
122 ibid para 31(1) of sch 12.
123 ibid para 31(2) of sch 12.
124 FA 1996 s 43.
125 ibid s 44.
126 ibid s 44A.
127 ibid s 45.
128 *Waste Recycling Group v HMRC* [2008] EWCA Civ 849.
129 HM Revenue & Customs, 'Revenue & Customs Brief 50/08' (2008) <https://webarchive.nationalarchives.gov.uk/ukgwa/20090211133613/http:/www.hmrc.gov.uk/briefs/excise-duty/brief5008.htm> accessed 29 April 2024.
130 *R (Veolia ES Landfill Ltd) v HMRC* [2016] EWHC 1880 (Admin).
131 *R (Biffa Waste Services Ltd) v HMRC* [2016] EWHC 1444 (Admin).

landfill tax, but then revoked its decision. The Court considered that HMRC's determination was a general statement and the relevant factor was whether the material was 'used' in the layer, which was determinative of liability.

34.88 There was also a later case *HMRC v Devon Waste Management*,[132] in which certain fluff and EVP (black bag waste that had been shredded and could be used in the same way as fluff) was argued to be not subject to landfill tax, because it was not a disposal of waste and was being used. The First Tier Tribunal ('FTT') had held that it was chargeable waste, the Upper Tribunal ('UT') held that the materials were used and therefore not discarded. HMRC appealed, and their appeal was allowed by the Court of Appeal. Other recent cases have also concerned whether something is waste or recycled[133] and the intention of the landfill company when disposing of the waste.[134]

34.89 Recent proposals for the reform of landfill tax include a landfill tax grant scheme to fund the costs of landfill tax to public bodies in England, since costs of disposal are acting as a barrier to the remediation and redevelopment of contaminated land.[135]

(ii) *Aggregates Levy*

34.90 The Aggregates Levy is a tax on bulk properties of sand, gravel and rock that has either been dug from the ground, dredged from the sea in UK waters or imported. The Aggregates Levy was introduced to ensure that the environmental impacts of aggregates extraction not already addressed by regulation are more fully reflected in the prices.[136] It is charged at £2.03 per tonne of sand, gravel or rock. Smaller amounts are charged less (i.e. £1.015 on half a tonne). From 1 April 2024, increases will be linked to RPI.

34.91 The legislation was introduced in the Finance Act 2001 ('FA 2001'), and is supplemented by various regulations including Aggregates Levy (Registration and Miscellaneous Provisions) Regulations 2001, Aggregates Levy (General) Regulations 2002 and Aggregates Levy (Registration and Miscellaneous Provisions) (Amendment) Regulations 2016.

34.92 Exemptions apply to certain aggregates and certain aggregate producing processes. They include soil, vegetable and other organic matter, drill cuttings from oil exploration in UK waters and from land drilling in the UK, and material arising from utility works.[137] Also exempt are aggregates arising from laying foundations, pipes or cables for any building, navigation dredging, highway construction and the construction or improvement of railways, tramways and motorways.[138] Spoil, waste or by products

---

132 *HMRC v Devon Waste Management* [2021] EWCA Civ 584.
133 See *Parkwood Landfill Ltd v Customs and Excise Commissioners* [2002] EWCA Civ 1707.
134 See *Patersons of Greenoakhill Ltd v Revenue & Customs* [2014] UKFTT 334 (TC).
135 HM Treasury, *Spring Budget 2023* (HC 2023, 1183) para 4.03 <https://assets.publishing.service.gov.uk/media/6419c87d8fa8f547c267efca/Web_accessible_Budget_2023.pdf>.
136 HM Treasury, 'Review of the Aggregates Levy: Summary of Responses to the Discussion Paper and Government next Steps' (2020) para 2.1 <https://assets.publishing.service.gov.uk/media/5f15db5f3a6f405c00b44567/2020.07.20_Review_of_the_Aggregates_Levy_summary_of_responses_to_the_discussion_paper_and_government_next_steps.pdf> accessed 28 April 2024.
137 FA 2001 s 17(4).
138 ibid s 17(3).

of industrial combustion processes and smelting or refining metal are also exempt.[139] Exempt processes include cutting rock to produce stone with a flat surface, extraction or separation of a substance, the production of lime or cement from limestone and processes using shale.[140]

34.93 Key relevant cases include *PJ Thory Ltd v HMRC*[141] which concerned whether sand and gravel arising from the construction of a marina, which included dredging, were exempt. The FTT held that the activities were not exempt and the UT agreed, deciding that a generous interpretation of the legislation would detract from the general purpose of the legislation, and that the ordinary meaning of 'dredging' should be applied.

34.94 In addition, the British Aggregates Association brought an important challenge in 2001, complaining to the European Commission that the exclusion of certain materials from the scope of the levy was constituted prohibited state aid. The ECJ considered the case and decided[142] that the European Commission had been wrong to decide that the exemptions did not constitute prohibited state aid. Following that case the UK government disapplied the exemptions, and following further consideration by the European Commission, it reinstated many of the exemptions in Section 48 of Finance (No.2) Act 2015.

(iii) *Plastic Packaging Tax*

34.95 Plastic Packaging Tax ('PPT') was introduced in the Finance Act 2021 ('FA 2021'). The aim of the tax is to provide a 'clear economic incentive for businesses to use recycled plastic in the manufacture of plastic packaging, which will create greater demand for this material'.[143] It is intended that this will in turn stimulate increased levels of recycling and collection of plastic waste, thereby diverting it from landfill or incineration.[144] PPT was introduced following a call for evidence in 2017 into using the tax system or charges to tackle single-use plastic waste. The tax is payable when chargeable plastic packaging is produced or imported into the UK. The tax is charged per tonne for packaging with less than 30% recycled plastic. The rate is £210.82 per tonne from 1 April 2023[145] and £217.85 per tonne from 1 April 2024.[146] Where the volume is less than a tonne, the tax is charged proportionately. There is an exemption for components used in the delivery of goods to the UK that are transport packing, tertiary packaging or rail, road, ship and air containers.[147] There is also no charge of PPT for

---

139 ibid s 17(3).
140 See ibid s 18(2), and as regards the cutting of rock produce stone with one or more flat surfaces, *Jones Brothers Ruthin (Civil Engineering) Company Ltd v HMRC* [2011] UKFTT 206 (TC).
141 *PJ Thory Ltd v HMRC* [2016] UKFTT 568 (TC).
142 Case T-210/02 *British Aggregates Association v Commission of the European Communities* [2006] ECR II-02789.
143 HM Revenue & Customs, 'Policy Paper: Increase to Plastic Packaging Tax rates from 1 April 2024' <https://www.gov.uk/government/publications/changes-to-plastic-packaging-tax-rates-from-1-april-2024/increase-to-plastic-packaging-tax-rates-from-1-april-2024> accessed 22 October 2024.
144 HM Revenue & Customs, 'Policy Paper: Introduction of Plastic Packaging Tax from April 2022' (2021) <https://www.gov.uk/government/publications/introduction-of-plastic-packaging-tax-from-april-2022/introduction-of-plastic-packaging-tax-2021> accessed 28 April 2024.
145 Finance (No. 2) Act 2023 s 329.
146 Finance Act 2024 s 31.
147 FA 2021 s 52(1).

plastic packaging components which are stores within the meaning of the Customs and Excise Management Act 1979, or for packaging a medicinal product.[148]

34.96 Plastic is defined as material consisting of a polymer, other than cellulose-based polymer that has not been chemically modified or had additives (e.g. calcium) or other substances added. Recycled plastic is defined as plastic that has been reprocessed from recovered material by means of a chemical or manufacturing process, other than organic recycling, so that it can be used for its original purpose or other purposes.[149]

34.97 Primary liability for the tax is imposed on the taxable person, which is the person who produces in the course of business or imports on behalf of a person acting in the course of a business the plastic packaging.[150] Secondary liability for the tax is imposed on businesses in the supply chain who know that the primary payer has not paid the PPT.[151] Liability for the tax can also be deferred or cancelled for exports.[152]

Other adjustments to the tax system

34.98 While the tax measures above are ones which are bespoke regimes to deal with specific tax issues, it is also notable that generally applicable tax measures may be adjusted with specific policy objectives in mind, which may include environmental objectives. One example of this is Inheritance Tax, about which the government has recently consulted on matters, including whether it would be appropriate to extend the existing scope of agricultural property relief to land managed under an environmental agreement with, or on behalf of the UK government, devolved administrations, public bodies, local authorities or approved bodies.[153] Other measures include an 80% investment allowance in the Energy Profits Levy, for qualifying expenditure which relates to decarbonising upstream oil and gas production.[154] Reliefs are also given in the VAT system for use of energy efficient materials.[155]

---

148 ibid s 52.
149 ibid s 49.
150 ibid s 43.
151 ibid part 1 of sch 9.
152 ibid s 51(1).
153 HM Treasury, 'Consultation Outcome: Taxation of Environmental Land Management and Ecosystem Service Markets' (2024) <https://www.gov.uk/government/consultations/taxation-of-environmental-land-management-and-ecosystem-service-markets> accessed 28 April 2024.
154 HM Revenue & Customs, 'Policy Paper: Energy Profits Levy: Decarbonisation Allowance' (2023) <https://www.gov.uk/government/publications/the-decarbonisation-allowance-in-the-energy-profits-levy/energy-profits-levy-decarbonisation-allowance> accessed 28 April 2024.
155 HM Revenue & Customs, 'Guidance: Energy-Saving Materials and Heating Equipment (VAT Notice 708/6)' (2024) <https://www.gov.uk/guidance/vat-on-energy-saving-materials-and-heating-equipment-notice-7086> accessed 28 April 2024.

PART VIII

CONSTRUCTION

CHAPTER 35

CONSTRUCTION: OVERVIEW

Camilla ter Haar

35.01 The year 2023 was the hottest year since records began,[1] a year in which greenhouse gas ('GHG') levels continued to rise, and which saw widespread extreme weather and climate events globally, including 'major floods, tropical cyclones, extreme heat and drought, and associated wildfires'.[2] The impacts of these weather events affect buildings and infrastructure, causing damage to their construction, as well as posing a risk to the life, safety and health of the human beings inhabiting and working in these buildings.

35.02 The built environment sector contributes to 21% of global GHG emissions,[3] and 25% of the United Kingdom's GHG emissions.[4]

35.03 The construction industry therefore has a critical role to play in both:

- The design and build of buildings which are adaptable and resilient to the impacts of climate change; and
- The development and use of methods and materials,[5] in order to reduce carbon emissions and to meet the target of achieving net zero carbon emissions by 2050.[6]

35.04 This is a challenge and a necessity. It is also an opportunity as tenants, funders, developers and owners increasingly demand more sustainable buildings, which can command higher rental and purchase prices. There is also a corresponding risk, as

---

1 World Meteorological Organization, 'Press Release – 2023 Shatters Climate Records, with Major Impacts' (2023) <https://wmo.int/news/media-centre/2023-shatters-climate-records-major-impacts> accessed 10 March 2024.
2 ibid.
3 Intergovernmental Panel on Climate Change, 'Climate Change 2022: Mitigation of Climate Change. Contribution of Working Group III to the Sixth Assessment Report of the Intergovernmental Panel on Climate Change' (2022) <https://www.ipcc.ch/report/ar6/wg3/> accessed 22 March 2024.
4 Daisy Everingham, 'The Whole Life Carbon Roadmap: Answering Your Data FAQs Received to Date' [2022] UK Green Building Council <https://ukgbc.org/news/the-whole-life-carbon-roadmap-answering-your-data-faqs-received-to-date/> accessed 22 March 2024.
5 More than 4 billion tonnes of cement are produced annually, which contributes to approximately 8% of global carbon emissions. See Felix Preston and Johanna Lehne, 'Making Concrete Change, Innovation in Low-Carbon Cement and Concrete' [2018] Chatham House Report 1.
6 The Climate Change Act 2008 (as amended) sets out the Net Zero Target which is that:
'1 The target for 2050
(1) It is the duty of the Secretary of State to ensure that the net UK carbon account for the year 2050 is at least 100% lower than the 1990 baseline.
(2) "The 1990 baseline" means the aggregate amount of—
(a) net UK emissions of carbon dioxide for that year, and
(b) net UK emissions of each of the other targeted greenhouse gases for the year that is the base year for that gas.'

reflected in the chapters in this section, if the industry fails to adapt to the demands posed by climate change.

Net zero and construction

35.05 The definition of net zero is addressed in Chapter 1 of this book. However, it is instructive to consider the way in which the term is understood in relation to the built environment. The UK Green Building Council ('UKGBC') 'Net Zero Carbon Buildings: A Framework Definition', sets out two approaches for net zero:

- Net zero carbon in relation to construction:[7]

> When the amount of carbon emissions associated with a building's product and construction stages up to practical completion is zero or negative, through the use of offsets or the net export of on-site renewable energy.

- Net zero carbon in relation to operational energy:[8]

> When the amount of carbon emissions associated with the building's operational energy on an annual basis is zero or negative. A net zero carbon building is highly energy efficient and powered from on-site and/or off-site renewable energy sources, with any remaining carbon balance offset.

35.06 The UKGBC has indicated that its Framework Definition of Net Zero is likely to be superseded by the UK Net Zero Carbon Buildings Standard, when it is published in 2024. At the date of publication, the UK Net Zero Carbon Buildings Standard gave the following explanation of a Net Zero Carbon Building:[9]

> A building whose operational and embodied carbon performance is within limits which allow the UK built environment to stay within its own allocation of remaining carbon budget, in order to limit warming to 1.5°C.
>
> We are currently seeking input via consultation on whether the Standard should require offsets to be purchased to balance the asset-level emissions.

Statistics and data

(i) *Statistics*

35.07 At paragraph 35.02 above, we cite a statistic for the percentage of GHG emissions contributed by the built environment sector. However, competing statistics exist.

7 UK Green Building Council, 'Net Zero Carbon Buildings: A Framework Definition' (2019), 1.1, <https://ukgbc.org/wp-content/uploads/2019/04/Net-Zero-Carbon-Buildings-A-framework-definition.pdf> accessed 22 March 2024.
8 ibid 1.2.
9 'UK Net Zero Carbon Buildings Standard Frequently Asked Questions' <https://www.nzcbuildings.co.uk/questions> accessed 22 March 2024.

35.08 A commonly cited statistic is that the built environment sector contributes to 40% of the UK's carbon emissions. This is the statistic cited by the UK government in its September 2022 Guidance Note, *Promoting Net Zero Carbon and Sustainability in Construction.*[10] As set out in the footnote, this includes the operation of surface transport.

35.09 The UKGBC figure, that 25% of UK emissions are directly attributable to the built environment, is comprised of: embodied carbon, regulated operational carbon, unregulated operational carbon and F-Gas.[11] This figure has been 'translated' from the Climate Change Committee's Sixth Carbon Budget report.

35.10 Even taken at its lowest percentage share of UK GHG emissions, the built environment is responsible for the largest share of GHG emissions after surface transport.[12] There is enormous potential for buildings to contribute to significant GHG emissions reduction and an important role for the industry to play in achieving net zero carbon emissions by 2050.

(ii) *Operational Carbon and Embodied Carbon*

35.11 The built environment's carbon emissions comprise both operational carbon and embodied carbon. Operational carbon is the carbon emitted during the time in which a building is in use. In other words, the emissions resulting from a building's operation, including the heating, cooling and lighting of a building. Embodied carbon is the carbon emitted during the construction, maintenance, refurbishment and demolition of a building (i.e. emissions connected to construction processes over the whole lifetime of a building).[13]

International commitments

35.12 The year 2023 saw the twenty-eighth conference of the parties ('COP 28') of the United Nations Framework Convention on Climate Change ('UNFCCC'), one of the key outcomes of which was an agreement to transition away from fossil fuels.[14]

35.13 COP 28 concluded the first 'global stocktake' which was intended to evaluate progress against the goals of the Paris Agreement, and to inform nationally determined

---

10 UK Government Commercial Function, 'Promoting Net Zero Carbon and Sustainability in Construction: Guidance Note' (2022) <https://assets.publishing.service.gov.uk/government/uploads/system/uploads/attachment_data/file/1102389/20220901-Carbon-Net-Zero-Guidance-Note.pdf> accessed 28 November 2023; para 2.2.2 which explains that 'This includes emissions linked to heating buildings, the energy they consume to support operations and the operation of transport infrastructure. Construction activity accounts for around 50m tonnes of CO_2 emissions, over half of which is linked to construction product and materials production, particularly materials such as steel and cement, which account for around 15% of global carbon emissions.'

11 Everingham, 'The Whole Life Carbon Roadmap: Answering Your Data FAQs Received to Date' (n 4).

12 UK Green Building Council, 'Climate Change Mitigation' <https://ukgbc.org/our-work/climate-change-mitigation/> accessed 22 March 2024.

13 UK Green Building Council, 'Operational & Embodied Carbon: Explainer Guide' <https://ukgbc.org/wp-content/uploads/2023/02/operational-and-embodied-carbon-1.pdf> accessed 22 March 2024.

14 Nuala Burnett, *What Was Agreed at COP28* (Briefing Paper No CBP 9909, 2024) <https://researchbriefings.files.parliament.uk/documents/CBP-9909/CBP-9909.pdf> accessed 22 March 2024.

contributions ('NDCs'), the next round of climate action plans under the Paris Agreement.

35.14 The September 2023 Global Stocktake Synthesis Report made a key finding[15] that achieving net zero CO_2 and GHG emissions requires systems transformations across all sectors and contexts, and that:[16]

> Measures to implement systems transformations in industry, transport, buildings and other sectors must rapidly reduce process and energy emissions. Ambitious implementation of measures to address GHG emissions from industry, transport, buildings and other sectors can reduce emissions in those sectors and across their supply chains while reducing costs and delivering co-benefits.

35.15 Paragraph 123 of the Global Stocktake Synthesis Report also noted that:[17]

> Buildings currently account for roughly 6% of global GHG emissions. Both existing and yet-to-be-built buildings can be net zero emissions by mid-century if they use low-carbon construction materials, reduce energy demand and implement mitigation options in design, construction, use and retrofits.

35.16 Following the conclusion of the Global Stocktake, the Buildings Breakthrough[18] was launched at COP 28 by the UN Environment Programme with the support of the UK government. The aim of the Buildings Breakthrough is to make near-zero emissions and climate resilient buildings the 'new normal' by 2030.[19]

35.17 At the time of writing, the world is not on track to achieve the Paris Agreement goals, as the Global Status Report for Buildings and Construction 2023 reported that the overall energy demand and emissions of the building sector have risen by 1% since 2021.[20]

35.18 In March 2024, ministerial delegations from countries, including the United Kingdom, endorsed the Ministerial Declaration ('Declaration de Chaillot')[21] at the

---

15 United Nations Framework Convention on Climate Change, 'Technical Dialogue of the First Global Stocktake, Synthesis Report by the Co-Facilitators on the Technical Dialogue' Key Finding 6 (2023) <https://unfccc.int/sites/default/files/resource/sb2023_. 09_adv.pdf> accessed 22 March 2024.
16 ibid para 20.
17 ibid para 123.
18 Preston and Lehne, 'Making Concrete Change, Innovation in Low-Carbon Cement and Concrete' (n 5) 1.
19 The Global Alliance for Buildings and Construction gives the following explanations of phrases used: 'Near-zero emission buildings' are defined as 'high energy-efficient buildings with a low carbon footprint taking into account a whole life cycle assessment approach (meaning using a low GHG energy source, and built with low GHG building materials and equipment'; 'Resilient Buildings' are defined as 'buildings that integrate specifications related to the future climate in their design, construction, and operation maintenance'; 'New normal' is defined as meaning that 'the above concepts are generalized in engineered buildings (formal and semi-formal).' See UN Environment Programme and the Global Alliance for Buildings and Construction, 'Fostering Collaboration: Buildings Breakthrough' <https://globalabc.org/our-work/fostering-collaboration> accessed 10 March 2024.
20 UN Environment Programme and the Global Alliance for Buildings and Construction, 'Global Status Report for Buildings and Construction' (2024) <https://www.unep.org/resources/report/global-status-report-buildings-and-construction> accessed 14 March 2024.
21 The Ministerial Declaration of the Buildings and Climate Global Forum, 'Declaration de Chaillot' (2024) <https://www.ecologie.gouv.fr/sites/default/files/declaration-de-chaillot-forum-batiments-climat.pdf> accessed 14 March 2024.

inaugural Buildings and Climate Global Forum, dedicated to the decarbonisation and climate resilience of buildings. The Ministerial Declaration set out its objectives at point 5, which acknowledged 'the importance of accelerating the transition towards a buildings sector consistent with the long-term goals of the Paris Agreement in 2015 … and keeping the 1.5 C goal within reach' and set out objectives including:[22]

> 5.2 Construction/Retrofitting: Plan, design, build, operate and manage all-round sustainable, culturally, functionally, socially and economically climate adapted, resource efficient, zero-emission, healthy, safe, flexible and resilient buildings through a whole life cycle approach.

35.19 Point 5.2.1–5.2.8 sets out the ways in which this is to be done. Point 6 of the Declaration then sets out the commitment to take into account point 5's operational objectives and to implement national policies and measures necessary to attain them, including:[23]

> 6.1 Implementing long-term regulatory roadmaps and frameworks, mandatory building and energy codes for buildings, or supporting the adoption of these at the subnational level; requiring integrated comprehensive design;
>
> …
>
> 6.3 Advancing and promoting the adoption of standards, labels and certifications in the buildings and construction sector or supporting the adoption of these at subnational level.

35.20 Developments such as these reflect both the growing awareness in the construction industry of its role in achieving net zero as well as the growing attention which the industry will receive in this area.

Net zero and related material considerations in construction

35.21 The below is an overview of this section of the book.

35.22 'A new and evolving legislative and regulatory context'. In order to meet international targets and pledges, the government has, and will continue to, introduce new regulations and legislation. In Chapter 36 we set out the current statutory framework for the energy efficiency of buildings, as well as the various consultations, government strategies and proposed industry guidance, being put forward to address the changes needed to achieve net zero in the industry by 2050.

35.23 'Construction: methods and materials'. In order to meet the target of net zero carbon emissions by 2050, pressure will be felt by the construction industry to reduce carbon emissions of both the materials used and the construction methods employed. At Chapter 37 we will consider how changes may be made to the construction phase

22 ibid 7.
23 ibid 8.

(e.g. procurement, supply chain, project delivery, modern methods of construction, and circularity) in order to achieve net zero targets.

35.24 'Increased retrofitting'. According to the UKGBC, embodied carbon contributes to 20% of the built environment's carbon emissions. Thus, reuse (and retrofitting) of buildings, rather than the demolition of buildings, is likely to become increasingly common.[24] Retrofitting will be increasingly common in light of the need for buildings to be adapted to new climate and weather conditions, as well as to increase energy efficiency. We look at key considerations in relation to retrofitting at Chapter 38.

35.25 'Insurance'. Insurance is a critical financial support mechanism to address the risks of events arising in building projects. At Chapter 39 we will address the current insurance landscape in relation to the route to net zero.

35.26 'Measurement'. Underlying the net zero carbon aspirations and obligations of the construction industry is the question of measurement: that is, how to frame measures of carbon reduction so as to ensure an objective, consistent and agreed approach towards compliance with those obligations. We look at measurement and assessment of carbon emissions at Chapter 40.

35.27 'Professional duties and standards of construction professionals to advise'. Construction professionals will increasingly be expected to work towards ensuring their clients acquire climate resilient buildings and infrastructure, as well as to work within the new standards expected in creating and refurbishing buildings that are compliant with net zero related targets. At Chapter 41 we consider various types of claims a construction professional might face.

24 UK Green Building Council, 'Advancing Net Zero: Embodied Carbon' <https://ukgbc.org/our-work/topics/advancing-net-zero/embodied-carbon/> accessed 22 March 2024.

CHAPTER 36

STATUTORY FRAMEWORK, STANDARDS AND INDUSTRY GUIDANCE

Melissa Shipley

Introduction

36.01 The current statutory framework for the energy efficiency of buildings is set out in the Building Regulations 2010 (as amended) ('the Building Regulations'). The Building Regulations are supplemented by Approved Documents, which are intended to give practical guidance on the Building Regulations, together with standards and industry guidance.

36.02 It has been recognised that the construction industry has a key role to play in achieving net zero by 2050, and various consultations, government strategies and proposed industry guidance have suggested further changes to the legislative and regulatory framework. Some of these have been summarised in the 'Future standards' section below. Given the scale of changes needed to achieve net zero, and that these changes have not yet been implemented, this area of law is in flux. The contents of this chapter are correct at the time of writing (29 October 2024).

Building Regulations and Approved Documents

36.03 The Building Regulations impose requirements in relation to 'building work'. This is defined in regulation 3, and includes, amongst other things, the erection or extension of a building and the material alteration of a building.

36.04 Part 6 of the Building Regulations concerns energy efficiency requirements. It requires, for example:

- Pursuant to regulation 21, that the energy efficiency requirements apply to: the erection of a building falling within regulation 21(2); the extension of any such building, other than an extension falling within regulation 21(4); and the carrying out of any work to or in connection with any such building or extension.
- The 'energy efficiency requirements' are defined in regulation 2(1) as the requirements of regulations 23, 25A, 25B, 26, 26A, 26C, 28, 40 and 43 and Part L of Schedule 1.[1]

---

1 This definition was amended by reg 3(a) of the Building Regulations etc (Amendment) (England) Regulations 2021/1391, subject to the transitional provisions set out in reg 17.

- These requirements are many and various, and a detailed consideration of them falls outside the scope of this book. To give an example, regulation 25B states: 'Where a building is erected, it must be a nearly zero-energy building'. Regulation 35 defines a 'nearly zero-energy building' as:

> a building that has a very high energy performance, as determined in accordance with a methodology approved under regulation 24,[2] where the nearly zero or very low amount of energy required should be covered to a very significant extent by energy from renewable sources, including energy from renewable sources produced on-site or nearby.

36.05 On 15 June 2022, the Building Regulations etc (Amendment) (England) Regulations 2021 came into force. They amended the Building Regulations 2010,[3] including by:

- Introducing a target primary energy rate for new buildings in regulation 26C of the Building Regulations:

> Where a building is erected it must not exceed the target primary energy rate for the building which has been approved pursuant to regulation 25(c), applying the methodology of calculation and expression of the energy performance of buildings approved pursuant to regulation 24.

- The target primary energy rate is the maximum primary energy use for the dwelling in a year, expressed as kWhPE/(m^2 year) and determined using the Standard Assessment Procedure.[4]

- Where a system for on-site electricity generation is installed, regulation 40A(2) of the Building Regulations provides that:

> The person carrying out the work must, not later than five days after the work has been completed, provide to the owner sufficient information about the system for on-site electricity generation in respect of its operation and maintenance requirements so that the system may be operated and maintained in such a manner as to produce the maximum electricity that is reasonable in the circumstances and delivers this electricity to the optimal place for use.

---

2 The latest notice of approval of the methodology for reg 24 can be found online at Department for Levelling Up, Housing and Communities, 'Notice of Approval of the Methodologies of Calculation of the Energy Performance of New Buildings to Demonstrate Compliance with the Building Regulations 2010 in England' (2022) <https://www.gov.uk/government/publications/methodologies-for-calculating-the-energy-performance-of-new-buildings-in-england-notice-of-approval/notice-of-approval-of-the-methodologies-of-calculation-of-the-energy-performance-of-new-buildings-to-demonstrate-compliance-with-the-building-regulati> accessed 28 November 2023.

3 See Section 2 of the Building Regulations etc (Amendment) (England) Regulations 2021/1391. The Standard Assessment Procedure is defined on the same page as 'The current approved procedure for assessing the performance of dwellings in line with this document (Approved Document L, Volume 1). The Standard Assessment Procedure is detailed in The Government's Standard Assessment Procedure for Energy Rating of Dwellings version 10'.

4 Approved Document L Volume 1 to the Building Regulations 2010, page 76.

- Part O1 of Schedule 1 of the Building Regulations provides that:

  (1) Reasonable provision must be made in respect of a dwelling, institution or any other building containing one or more rooms for residential purposes, other than a room in a hotel ('residences') to—(a) limit unwanted solar gains in summer; (b) provide an adequate means to remove heat from the indoor environment…

- Regulation 40B(2) of the Building Regulations consequently provides that:

  The person carrying out the work must, not later than five days after the work has been completed, give sufficient information to the owner about the provision made in accordance with Part O so that the systems in place further to Part O can be operated in such a manner as to protect against overheating.

36.06 Approved Documents[5] are designed to give practical guidance with respect to the requirements of the Building Regulations.[6] In relation to energy efficiency, the most relevant Approved Documents are:

- Approved Document L: Volume 1 (dwellings)[7] and Volume 2 (buildings other than dwellings).[8] Approved Document L concerns the conservation of fuel and power, and supports Part L of Schedule 1 of the Building Regulations.

- Approved Document F: Volume 1 (dwellings)[9] and Volume 2 (buildings other than dwellings).[10] Approved Document F concerns ventilation, and supports Part F of Schedule 1 of the Building Regulations.

- Approved Document O, which covers the overheating mitigation requirements in Part O of Schedule 1 to the Building Regulations. Approved Document O applies to new residential buildings only.[11]

Standards and industry guidance

(i) *BS EN 15978*

36.07 BS EN 15978[12] sets out a framework for assessing the environmental impacts of buildings, including the principles of carbon measurement. However, BS EN 15978 has been subject to various differing interpretations. Also, as noted by the House of

5 The Approved Documents can be accessed online at Department for Levelling Up, Housing and Communities, 'Approved Documents' <https://www.gov.uk/government/collections/approved-documents> accessed 3 April 2024.
6 The Building Act 1984 s 6.
7 Approved Document L Volume 1 to the Building Regulations 2010.
8 Approved Document L Volume 2 to the Building Regulations 2010.
9 Approved Document F Volume 1 to the Buildings Regulations 2010.
10 Approved Document F Volume 2 to the Buildings Regulations 2010.
11 Approved Document O to the Building Regulations 2010.
12 The British Standards Institution, 'BS EN 15978:2011, Sustainability of Construction Works. Assessment of Environmental Performance of Buildings. Calculation Method' (2011).

Commons Environmental Audit Committee, 'the embodied carbon cost of the construction is not required by current policy to be assessed or controlled, other than on a voluntary basis'.[13] The Committee noted that the UK is therefore falling behind other European countries in monitoring and controlling embodied carbon in construction.

(ii) *RICS Whole life carbon assessment for the built environment*

36.08 In order to provide greater consistency to the measuring and reporting of carbon throughout the life cycle of a built asset,[14] the first edition of the Royal Institute of Chartered Surveyors' ('RICS's') *Whole life carbon assessment for the built environment* was published in November 2017. The second edition was published in September 2023 and has been effective since 1 July 2024.[15]

36.09 The standard applies to all types of built assets.[16] There are two main types of carbon impacts in the built environment: operational carbon impacts (which are those that arise from the running of the asset); and embodied carbon impacts (which are those that arise from sourcing the materials for and constructing the asset).[17] In addition, there are user carbon impacts, such as the impact of commuting to an office.[18] A whole life carbon assessment ('WLCA') assesses operational, embodied and user carbon. The assessment runs from a building's construction, throughout its operation and use, to its demolition. We look at this in further detail in Chapter 40 ('Measurement').

36.10 The standard sets out a RICS-approved methodology for carrying out a WLCA.[19] However, whilst the standard is intended for RICS members, it aims to be adopted more widely across the industry to '…enhance the quality, comparability and accuracy of data'.[20] We note in particular that the London Plan 2021 requires schemes which will be referred to the Mayor of London to include a whole life cycle carbon emission assessment, as set out in paragraph 5.25 of Chapter 5 ('Land Use Planning').[21] Part Z, an industry-proposed amendment to the Building Regulations that would ensure that embodied carbon is assessed and limited, aligns with the RICS standard.[22]

---

13 Environmental Audit Committee, *Building to Net Zero: Costing Carbon in Construction, First Report of Session 2022–23*, page 3 (HC 2022–23, 103) <https://committees.parliament.uk/publications/22427/documents/165446/default/> accessed 28 November 2023.

14 'Whole Life Carbon Assessment for the Built Environment', page 9 <https://www.rics.org/profession-standards/rics-standards-and-guidance/sector-standards/construction-standards/whole-life-carbon-assessment> accessed 28 November 2023.

15 'Whole Life Carbon Assessment for the Built Environment' (second edition) <https://www.rics.org/profession-standards/rics-standards-and-guidance/sector-standards/construction-standards/whole-life-carbon-assessment> accessed 29 October 2024.

16 ibid 12.

17 ibid 9.

18 ibid.

19 ibid 11.

20 ibid.

21 Mayor of London, 'The London Plan 2021' (2021) 395–396, 399 <https://www.london.gov.uk/sites/default/files/the_london_plan_2021.pdf> accessed 4 April 2024.

22 'Proposed Building Regulations Amendment Part Z' <https://part-z.uk/proposal> accessed 24 January 2024.

(iii) *PAS 2080:2023*

36.11 PAS 2080:2023 ('PAS 2080') is a standard which came into effect on 31 March 2023[23] and specifies requirements for the management of whole life carbon in buildings and infrastructure: 'By following the PAS 2080 approach, value chain members across the built environment can work collaboratively towards the common goal of net zero carbon transition'.[24] The scope of PAS 2080 includes managing carbon to reduce whole life emissions in the built environment and provide consistency in the process of carbon management.[25]

Government guidance

36.12 Various guidance notes and policies in relation to public sector contracts and estates were issued during the previous Conservative governments. For example:

- Procurement Policy Note 06/21[26] requires suppliers who are bidding on central government contracts (over £5 million p/a) to commit to achieving net zero by 2050.[27]

- The Net Zero Estate Playbook provides guidance to support government departments and public sector bodies in transitioning their estate towards net zero.[28]

- 'The Construction Playbook, Government Guidance on sourcing and contracting public works projects and programmes', provides that all contracting authorities should have strategies and plans in place for achieving net zero by 2050 across their entire estate.[29] We consider this in more detail at paragraphs 37.07–37.10 of Chapter 37 ('Construction Phase').

---

23 The British Standards Institution, 'PAS 2080: 2023, Carbon Management in Buildings and Infrastructure' 5.
24 ibid 7.
25 ibid 11.
26 Cabinet Office, 'Procurement Policy Note – Taking Account of Carbon Reduction Plans in the Procurement of Major Government Contracts' (2021) PPN 06/21 <https://assets.publishing.service.gov.uk/media/62066d5ae90e077f7dec749e/PPN-0621-Taking-account-of-Carbon-Reduction-Plans-Jan22__1_.pdf> accessed 28 November 2023.
27 UK Government Commercial Function, 'Promoting Net Zero Carbon and Sustainability in Construction: Guidance Note' (2022) <https://assets.publishing.service.gov.uk/government/uploads/system/uploads/attachment_data/file/1102389/20220901-Carbon-Net-Zero-Guidance-Note.pdf> accessed 28 November 2023.
28 UK Government Property Function, 'Net Zero Estate Playbook, A Guide to Decarbonising Government Property' (2021) <https://assets.publishing.service.gov.uk/media/619cfd62e90e070441bcf731/Net_Zero_Estate_Playbook__1_.pdf> accessed 28 November 2023.
29 Cabinet Office, 'The Construction Playbook, Government Guidance on Sourcing and Contracting Public Works Projects and Programmes' (2022) Version 1.1, page 6 <https://assets.publishing.service.gov.uk/government/uploads/system/uploads/attachment_data/file/1102386/14.116_CO_Construction_Playbook_Web.pdf> accessed 28 November 2023.

Future standards

36.13 One frequently cited statistic is that 'around 40% of UK carbon emissions are linked to the built environment'.[30] Unsurprisingly, therefore, the construction industry is the focus of future standards and policies designed to achieve net zero.

(i) *Conservative government policies*

(a) Future Homes Standard and Future Buildings Standard

36.14 Starting in 2019, the government conducted a two-stage consultation: the Future Homes Standard and the Future Buildings Standard. The first stage, the Future Homes Standard, proposed changes to Part L and Part F of the Building Regulations to increase the energy efficiency of new homes.[31] The second stage, the Future Buildings Standard, set out changes to Part L and Part F of the Building Regulations for non-domestic buildings and dwellings, and overheating in new residential buildings.[32]

36.15 As a result of these consultations, amendments were made to the Building Regulations, as described at paragraph 36.05 above. In addition, five new versions of Approved Documents were released (Approved Document L Volumes 1 and 2, Approved Document F Volumes 1 and 2 and Approved Document O).

36.16 However, these changes were interim measures only; they were designed to be stepping stones to the implementation of the Future Homes Standard and Future Buildings Standard by 2025:

- The intention was that an average semi-detached home built to meet the Future Homes Standard would produce 75–80% less carbon dioxide emissions than one built to the 2013 Part L requirements.[33]

- The Future Buildings Standard was designed to transition non-domestic buildings to use low-carbon heat sources for heating and hot water,[34] and to deliver highly efficient non-domestic buildings.[35]

---

30 UK Government Commercial Function, 'Promoting Net Zero Carbon and Sustainability in Construction: Guidance Note', page 8.

31 Ministry of Housing, Communities and Local Government, 'The Future Homes Standard 2019 Consultation on Changes to Part L (Conservation of Fuel and Power) and Part F (Ventilation) of the Building Regulations for New Dwellings' (2019) <https://assets.publishing.service.gov.uk/media/5df78ecee5274a0910cb6d4d/Future_Homes_Standard_2019_Consultation.pdf> accessed 28 November 2023.

32 Ministry of Housing, Communities and Local Government, 'The Future Buildings Standard Consultation on Changes to Part L (Conservation of Fuel and Power) and Part F (Ventilation) of the Building Regulations for Non-Domestic Buildings and Dwellings; and Overheating in New Residential Buildings' (2021) <https://assets.publishing.service.gov.uk/media/60113d70e90e07143e58f16e/Future_Buildings_Standard_consultation_document.pdf> accessed 28 November 2023.

33 Ministry of Housing, Communities and Local Government, 'The Future Homes Standard 2019 Consultation' para 2.15.

34 Ministry of Housing, Communities and Local Government, 'The Future Buildings Standard Consultation' para 1.4.4.

35 ibid para 2.2.1.

(b) The Ten Point Plan for a Green Industrial Revolution

36.17 In November 2020, the government published *The Ten Point Plan for a Green Industrial Revolution* (the 'Ten Point Plan').[36] The plan was to 'build back better'[37] from Covid-19 with a 'green recovery'.[38]

36.18 The first three points all concerned energy:

- Point 1 was to advance offshore wind. The government announced an intention to quadruple offshore wind capacity by 2030.[39]
- Point 2 was to drive the growth of low carbon hydrogen, which could provide a clean source of fuel. The aim was to develop 5GW of low carbon hydrogen production capacity by 2030.[40]
- Point 3 was to deliver new and advanced nuclear power. The government stated that it was pursuing large-scale new nuclear projects, subject to value-for-money, together with research and development in the next generation of nuclear technology.[41]

36.19 Point 7 was greener buildings. The government announced that it would implement the Future Homes Standard in the shortest possible timeline and consult on increased standards for non-domestic buildings.[42] The government also aimed to install 600,000 heat pumps per year by 2028.[43] It was estimated that the green home finance initiatives could help improve the energy efficiency of around 2.8 million homes.[44]

(c) Energy White Paper Powering our Net Zero Future

36.20 In December 2020, the government issued the *Energy White Paper Powering our Net Zero Future* ('the Energy White Paper').[45] This built on the Ten Point Plan, setting out the government's 'long-term strategic vision for our energy system, consistent with net zero emissions by 2050'.[46] It underlined the government's commitment to transforming energy, including through the expansion of offshore wind and growing the installation of electric heat pumps.

36 Department for Energy Security and Net Zero, 'The Ten Point Plan for a Green Industrial Revolution' (2020) <https://assets.publishing.service.gov.uk/media/5fb5513de90e0720978b1a6f/10_POINT_PLAN_BOOKLET.pdf> accessed 28 September 2023.
37 ibid 3.
38 ibid.
39 ibid 8.
40 ibid 10.
41 ibid 12.
42 ibid 20.
43 ibid.
44 ibid 21.
45 Department for Energy Security and Net Zero, *Energy White Paper: Powering Our Net Zero Future* (White Paper, CP 337, 2020) <https://www.gov.uk/government/publications/energy-white-paper-powering-our-net-zero-future> accessed 28 September 2023.
46 ibid 15.

(d) Net Zero Strategy: Build Back Greener

36.21 The Ten Point Plan and the Energy White Paper were followed in October 2021 by the 'Net Zero Strategy: Build Back Greener' ('the Net Zero Strategy').[47] This was presented to Parliament pursuant to section 14 of the Climate Change Act 2008, which provides:

> (1) As soon as is reasonably practicable after making an order setting the carbon budget for a budgetary period, the Secretary of State must lay before Parliament a report setting out proposals and policies for meeting the carbon budgets for the current and future budgetary periods up to and including that period.

36.22 Energy was at the forefront of the Net Zero Strategy: the '... net zero economy will be underpinned by cheap clean electricity, made in Britain'.[48] The aim was that, by 2035, the UK would be powered entirely by clean electricity, subject to security of supply.[49] Increasing offshore wind capacity and new nuclear power stations were key to meeting this target.

36.23 In relation to heat and buildings, the Net Zero Strategy noted that heating for homes and workspaces made up almost a third of all UK carbon emissions.[50] The aim was therefore to improve the energy efficiency of buildings. In addition, there was an ambition that, by 2035, no new gas boilers would be sold.

(e) The Heat and Buildings Strategy

36.24 The government published the *Heat and Buildings Strategy* in October 2021.[51] This set out the immediate and long-term strategies to reduce emissions from buildings to near zero by 2050.[52] Decarbonising buildings was central to achieving net zero by 2050.[53] Of all UK carbon emissions 23% come from heating buildings,[54] and therefore the focus of the strategy was to reduce emissions from heating.[55] The measures included:

- Phasing out the installation of gas boilers by 2035.[56]
- Reducing the costs of installing a heat pump by 25–30% by 2025 and ensuring that heat pumps are no more expensive to buy and run than gas boilers by 2030.[57]

---

47 Department for Energy Security and Net Zero, 'Net Zero Strategy: Build Back Greener' (2021) <https://www.gov.uk/government/publications/net-zero-strategy> accessed 28 September 2023.
48 ibid 19.
49 ibid.
50 ibid 22.
51 Department for Energy Security and Net Zero, *Heat and Buildings Strategy* (CP 388, 2021) <https://assets.publishing.service.gov.uk/media/61a022788fa8f5037e8ccb4c/E02666137_CP_388_Heat_and_Buildings_Elay.pdf> accessed 27 March 2024.
52 ibid 27.
53 ibid 28.
54 ibid.
55 ibid 31.
56 ibid 20.
57 ibid.

- Developing hydrogen for heating buildings by thoroughly assessing the feasibility, safety, consumer experience and other costs and benefits, by the middle of the decade.[58]

(ii) *Labour government policies*

36.25 Keir Starmer became Prime Minister on 5 July 2024, leading a Labour government. Green energy was a central part of the Labour Party Manifesto 2024. For example, one of Labour's first steps for change was to set up Great British Energy, which it described as 'a publicly-owned clean power company, to cut bills for good and boost energy security, paid for by a windfall tax on oil and gas giants'.[59] Labour committed to making Britain a 'clean energy superpower'; clean energy by 2030 was Labour's second mission.[60] Labour's aims included:[61]

- Working with 'the private sector to double onshore wind, triple solar power, and quadruple offshore wind by 2030'.[62]

- Investing in carbon capture and storage.[63]

- Building new nuclear power stations, including Hinkley Point C and Sizewell C.[64]

- Investing £6.6 billion over the next parliament to upgrade the energy efficiency of five million homes under the Warm Homes Plan.[65]

- Requiring UK-regulated financial institutions and FTSE 100 companies to 'implement credible transition plans that align with the 1.5°C goal of the Paris Agreement'.[66]

36.26 In the King's Speech on 17 July 2024, the government's commitment to green energy was reconfirmed. It was noted that the government was 'committed to a clean energy transition which will lower energy bills for consumers over time'.[67] A Bill (the Great British Energy Bill) would be introduced to establish Great British Energy, as discussed at paragraph 35.25 above.

36.27 The Great British Energy Bill was introduced into the House of Commons on 25 July 2024 and at the time of writing is at the Report stage.[68] The Bill allows

---

58 ibid 23.
59 'Change: Labour Party Manifesto 2024', page 10 <https://labour.org.uk/wp-content/uploads/2024/06/Change-Labour-Party-Manifesto-2024-large-print.pdf> accessed 28 October 2024.
60 ibid 13.
61 ibid 51–57.
62 ibid 51.
63 ibid.
64 ibid 52.
65 ibid 56.
66 ibid 57.
67 The text of the King's Speech can be found at <https://www.gov.uk/government/speeches/the-kings-speech-2024> accessed 28 October 2024.
68 <https://bills.parliament.uk/bills/3738> accessed 28 October 2024.

for the designation of a company called Great British Energy. Under section 3(2) of the Bill, the objects of the company will be restricted to facilitating, encouraging and participating in:

- The production, distribution, storage and supply of clean energy, meaning energy produced from sources other than fossil fuels.[69]
- The reduction of greenhouse gas emissions from energy produced from fossil fuels.
- Improvements in energy efficiency.
- Measures for ensuring the security of the supply of energy.

36.28 Under section 4 of the Bill, the Secretary of State is empowered to provide financial assistance to Great British Energy. The government's intention is to provide Great British Energy with £8.3 billion in the current parliament.[70]

(iii) *The UK Net Zero Carbon Buildings Standard*

36.29 The pilot version of the UK Net Zero Carbon Buildings Standard was launched in September 2024. The standard has been in development since May 2022, through a collaboration of leading industry bodies. The aim was to develop a standard to define requirements for buildings in the UK to be net zero carbon.[71] The pilot version contains details of how to meet the standard, 'including what limits and targets it needs to meet, the technical evidence needed to demonstrate this and how it should be reported'.[72]

69 See section 3(3).
70 <https://commonslibrary.parliament.uk/research-briefings/cbp-10088/> accessed 28 October 2024.
71 <https://www.nzcbuildings.co.uk/_files/ugd/6ea7ba_33db26ba808b4212801457963d2ed225.pdf> accessed 29 October 2024.
72 <https://www.nzcbuildings.co.uk/pilotversion> accessed 29 October 2024.

CHAPTER 37

CONSTRUCTION PHASE

Hannah Fry

Introduction

37.01 In 2019, the Climate Change Act 2008 was amended to introduce a target of at least a 100% reduction in the net UK carbon account.[1] This created a statutory net zero target of a 100% reduction of greenhouse gas ('GHG') emissions compared to 1990 levels by 2020.[2] Around 40% of UK carbon emissions are linked to the built environment and construction activity accounts for around 50 million tonnes of CO_2 emissions, over half of which is linked to construction product and materials production.[3]

37.02 Historically, the construction industry has operated with construction projects being delivered for the lowest price, in the quickest timeframe and governed by contractual provisions which have little regard for net zero carbon targets.

37.03 In order for the construction sector to achieve its net zero carbon targets, it is 'not an option, [but] an imperative',[4] that there are significant procurement changes to construction operations. The question is: how will such targets be achieved, and what changes are needed to the construction phase in order to achieve such targets?

37.04 This part of the chapter will consider:

- The legislative framework and industry guidance;
- Procurement;
- The supply chain;
- Project delivery;
- Modern methods of construction;

1 The Climate Change Act 2008 (2050 Target Amendment) Order 2019, SI 2019/1056.
2 UK Government Commercial Function, 'Promoting Net Zero Carbon and Sustainability in Construction: Guidance Note' (2022) <https://assets.publishing.service.gov.uk/government/uploads/system/uploads/attachment_data/file/1102389/20220901-Carbon-Net-Zero-Guidance-Note.pdf> accessed 28 November 2023 para 2.2.2.
3 ibid para 2.2.2.
4 King's College London Centre of Construction Law & Dispute Resolution and others, 'Procuring Net Zero Construction' (2022) 2 <https://www.scl.org.uk/sites/default/files/2022-03/Procuring%20Net%20Zero%20Construction%20Report%20for%20SCL%2018%20March%202022.pdf> accessed 26 April 2024.

- Whole life cost and digital information management; and
- Circularity in construction and construction products.

The legislative framework and industry guidance

(i) *Specific considerations in government contracts*

37.05 The government has made it clear that all contracting authorities must make immediate progress towards achieving net zero.[5] Procurement Policy Note PPN 05/21 states that 'all contracting authorities should consider the following national priority outcomes alongside any additional local priorities in their procurement activities: … tackling climate change and reducing waste'.[6]

37.06 Further, from October 2021, Procurement Policy Note PPN 06/21 requires all companies bidding for UK government contracts worth more than £5 million per annum to submit a Carbon Reduction Plan ('CRP') which includes but is not limited to:

- Confirming the bidding supplier's commitment to achieving net zero by 2050 for their UK operations;
- Providing the supplier's current emissions for the sources included in Scope 1 (direct emissions linked to operations) and Scope 2 (indirect emissions linked to energy, heating and cooling used) of the Green House Gas Protocol, and a defined subset of Scope 3 emissions (indirect emissions within the firm value chain);
- Providing emissions reporting in CO_2e (Carbon Dioxide Equivalent) for the six GHGs covered by the Kyoto Protocol;[7]
- Setting out the environmental management measures in effect, including certification schemes or specific carbon reduction measures it has adopted, that it will be able to apply when performing the contract and that support achieving net zero by 2050; and
- Publication of the CRP on the supplier's website.[8]

---

5 Cabinet Office, 'Procurement Policy Note – National Procurement Policy Statement' (2021) PPN 05/21 1, para 2 <https://assets.publishing.service.gov.uk/media/60b0c01d8fa8f5488e618b93/PPN_05_21-_National_Procurement_Policy_Statement.pdf> accessed 26 April 2024. 'Contracting Authorities' are defined in section 39(2) and (4) of the Small Business Enterprise and Employment Act 2015 and whose functions are wholly or mainly reserved. This includes central government departments, executive agencies, non-departmental public bodies, local authorities, NHS bodies and the wider public sector.

6 Cabinet Office, 'Procurement Policy Note – National Procurement Policy Statement' (n 5) 1, para 6.

7 Carbon dioxide (CO_2), Methane (CH_4), Nitrous Oxide (N_2O), Hydrofluorocarbons (HFCs), Perfluorocarbons (PFCs) and Sulphur Hexafluoride (SG_6).

8 Cabinet Office, 'Procurement Policy Note – Taking Account of Carbon Reduction Plans in the Procurement of Major Government Contracts' (2021) PPN 06/21, 2, para 8 <https://assets.publishing.service.gov.uk/media/62066d5ae90e077f7dec749e/PPN-0621-Taking-account-of-Carbon-Reduction-Plans-Jan22__1_.pdf> accessed 28 November 2023.

(ii) *The Construction Playbook*

37.07 Collaboration between the government and the construction industry led to the development of the December 2020 'Construction Playbook, Government Guidance on Sourcing and Contracting Public Works Projects and Programmes' ('Construction Playbook'), which identifies key procurement and contracting changes to achieve net zero.[9] The Construction Playbook states that all contracting authorities should set out strategies and plans for achieving net zero GHG emissions by or ahead of 2050 for their entire estate and infrastructure portfolio.[10]

37.08 The Construction Playbook applies to all public works projects and programmes. It is mandated for central government departments and arm's-length bodies on a 'comply or explain' basis and the wider public sector is encouraged to take account of the Construction Playbook.[11] For central government, compliance to the Construction Playbook is being driven through departments' governance processes, central Cabinet Office controls (projects over £10 million per transaction) and the Treasury Approval process.[12]

37.09 The Construction Playbook is aimed at Commercial, Finance, Project Delivery, Policy sectors and any professionals across the public sector contracting authorities who are responsible for the planning and delivery of public work projects and programmes.[13] Ministers, Permanent Secretaries, Accounting Officers, Commercial Directors and project sponsors will also find the Construction Playbook useful when acting as decision-makers or approvers, or when conducting checks within the capacity of scrutiny and assurance.[14] Its principles and policies have been co-developed with input from public officials and industry stakeholders. They can be considered good practice for all professionals involved in public work projects and programmes across the public sector.[15]

37.10 The Construction Playbook establishes 14 new policies which are mandated for central government departments and arm's length bodies on a 'comply or explain' basis and will be enforced through spending controls.[16] This includes commercial pipelines; market health and capability assessments; portfolios and longer term contracting; harmonise, digitise and rationalise demand; further embed digital technologies; early supply chain involvement; outcome-based approach; benchmarking and Should Cost Models ('SCM'); delivery model assessments; effective contracting; risk allocation; payment mechanism and pricing approach; assessing the economic and financial

---

9 Cabinet Office, 'The Construction Playbook, Government Guidance on Sourcing and Contracting Public Works Projects and Programmes' (2022) Version 1.1 12 <https://assets.publishing.service.gov.uk/government/uploads/system/uploads/attachment_data/file/1102386/14.116_CO_Construction_Playbook_Web.pdf> accessed 28 November 2023.
10 ibid 6.
11 ibid 34.
12 ibid.
13 ibid 78.
14 ibid.
15 ibid.
16 ibid 12–15.

standing of suppliers; and resolution planning. Such principles insofar as they relate to the construction phase and net zero will be considered in this part of the chapter.

(iii) *Non-government initiatives*

37.11 There are also a significant number of non-government initiatives within the construction industry, focused on changes in the construction phase to achieve net zero. For example:

- The UK Green Building Council's A Framework Definition provides organisations with guidance on how to deliver a net zero carbon building.[17] Further, the UK Green Building Council's Net Zero Whole Life Carbon Roadmap includes Stakeholder Action Plans, which set out specific recommended actions for 14 key industry stakeholders;[18]

- CO2nstructZero, developed by the UK Construction Leadership Council, is the construction sector's response to the government's ten point plan for a Green Industrial Revolution, which is based on nine strategic objectives.[19] The UK Construction Leadership Council works with industry and government to identify and deliver actions supporting UK construction in building greater efficiency, skills and growth.[20] While CO2nstructZero's role is not to develop new solutions, roadmaps or pathways, the UK Construction Leadership Council has a critical role in bringing people together from the construction sector to consolidate collective action and plans for the sector by sharing innovative solutions and setting transparent goals and clear actions; and[21]

- The Carbon Reduction Code for the Built Environment, published by the UK Construction Leadership Council, aims to facilitate action and collaboration by relevant parties towards reducing carbon emissions related to design, construction, maintenance, operation and decommissioning of built assets.[22] It provides a framework for organisations to make a public commitment to and report progress towards achieving net zero. The Code contains core commitments for all organisations; core commitments for client organisations; core commitments for supply chain organisations and three levels of commitment: pledger, signatory, and champion.

---

17 UK Green Building Council, 'Net Zero Carbon Buildings: A Framework Definition' (2019) <https://ukgbc.org/wp-content/uploads/2019/04/Net-Zero-Carbon-Buildings-A-framework-definition.pdf> accessed 22 March 2024.
18 UK Green Building Council, 'Net Zero Whole Life Carbon Roadmap: A Pathway to Net Zero for the UK Built Environment' (2021) <https://ukgbc.org/wp-content/uploads/2021/11/UKGBC-Whole-Life-Carbon-Roadmap-A-Pathway-to-Net-Zero.pdf> accessed 18 April 2024.
19 UK Construction Leadership Council, 'CO2nstructZero' <https://www.constructionleadership council.co.uk/workstream/co2nstructzero/> accessed 26 April 2024.
20 UK Construction Leadership Council, 'Construction Leadership Council: Leading Transformation Across The Construction Industry' <https://www.constructionleadership council.co.uk/> accessed 26 April 2024.
21 UK Construction Leadership Council, 'CO2nstructZero' (n 19).
22 UK Construction Leadership Council, 'Carbon Reduction Code for the Built Environment' (2023) Issue 30 <https://www-smartinfrastructure.eng.cam.ac.uk/carbon-reduction-code> accessed 27 April 2024.

Procurement

(i) *Procurement strategy*

37.12 The Construction Playbook sets out that the procurement strategy should clearly state the client's commitments to tackling climate change and the ways in which the client expects these to be matched by commitments from the construction industry.[23]

37.13 The Construction Playbook requires that 'projects and programmes should adopt an outcome-based approach focused on whole life value, performance, sustainability and cost'.[24] Such an approach is said to help suppliers understand Contracting Authorities' ambitions without being prescriptive about how to deliver outcomes.[25] Further, Contracting Authorities should adopt 'value-based procurement', which is consideration of the outcomes they are trying to achieve, identification of the wider value drivers beyond speed, cost and quality, and how these outcomes align to government's wider priorities, including net zero GHG emissions.[26]

37.14 The Construction Innovation Hub Value Toolkit has been developed to support Contracting Authorities in defining what constitutes value in relation to a project or programme.[27] Whilst it does not specify what the outcomes should be, it aims to provide a suite of five complementary streams, which can be deployed over the lifecycle of a project and enable Contracting Authorities to consider the definition of value and approach to delivery of a project in a structured way.[28] The Value Definition Framework provides a model to define outcomes based on four capitals: natural capital; human capital; social capital and produced capital.[29]

37.15 'Procuring Net Zero Construction', a 2022 research paper by King's College Centre of Construction Law & Dispute Resolution led by Professor David Mosey, provides that a net zero construction procurement strategy should state:[30]

- How net zero proposals from consultants, contractors and supply chain members will form part of the quality criteria, that move the evaluation focus away from lowest price and towards a deeper understanding of the bidders' capabilities;

23 King's College London Centre of Construction Law & Dispute Resolution and others, 'Procuring Net Zero Construction' (n 4) 16.
24 Cabinet Office, 'The Construction Playbook, Government Guidance on Sourcing and Contracting Public Works Projects and Programmes' (n 9) 30.
25 ibid.
26 ibid 62.
27 Construction Innovation Hub, 'Value Toolkit' <https://constructioninnovationhub.org.uk/our-projects-and-impact/value-toolkit> accessed 27 April 2024.
28 UK Government Commercial Function, 'Promoting Net Zero Carbon and Sustainability in Construction: Guidance Note' (n 2) 17–18, para 3.5.
29 ibid.
30 King's College London Centre of Construction Law & Dispute Resolution and others, 'Procuring Net Zero Construction' (n 4) 17; Professor David Mosey, 'Constructing the Gold Standard: An Independent Review of Public Sector Construction Frameworks' (2021) 42 <https://assets.publishing.service.gov.uk/media/61b9cb41e90e07043e8ff5cc/Constructing_The_Gold_Standard_Final.pdf> accessed 27 April 2024.

- The purpose of seeking competitive supplier net zero proposals, including the processes by which these proposals are reviewed, developed, and adopted once a team member is appointed;
- How confidentiality and intellectual property rights in net zero proposals will be respected;
- By what process the clients, consultants, contractors, and supply chain members will seek agreement to share approved net zero proposals with other clients, consultants, contractors, and supply chain members; and
- How the success of consultant, contractor, and supply chain proposals in delivering improved net zero outcomes will affect the award of future work and other incentives.

37.16 The objective of the net zero construction procurement strategy and the approach to delivering it should be reflected in projects and programmes commissioned by the Contracting Authority. These strategies should form the start of a clear line of sight that informs the development of outcome specifications, decisions on the delivery model, contractual terms and contract management arrangements, the setting of Key Performance Indicators ('KPIs') and the monitoring and reporting of progress.[31]

(ii) *Procurement process*

37.17 In terms of the procurement process, according to 'Procuring Net Zero Construction', the system for the selection of construction team members should use balanced evaluation criteria that take into account net zero carbon proposals submitted by prospective consultants, contractors and supply chain members, and should make clear the procedures by which the approved net zero carbon proposals from successful bidders will be developed, agreed and implemented.[32]

37.18 An effective valued-based, net zero procurement process should:[33]

- Use specifications that focus on the net zero carbon client outcomes;
- State how intellectual property rights may arise from supplier proposals and how these intellectual property rights will be managed through the life of the contract;

---

31 UK Government Commercial Function, 'Promoting Net Zero Carbon and Sustainability in Construction: Guidance Note' (n 2) 9, para 2.2.5.
32 King's College London Centre of Construction Law & Dispute Resolution and others, 'Procuring Net Zero Construction' (n 4) 18.
33 Professor David Mosey, 'Constructing the Gold Standard: An Independent Review of Public Sector Construction Frameworks' (n 30) 42; King's College London Centre of Construction Law & Dispute Resolution and others, 'Procuring Net Zero Construction' (n 4).

- Evaluate supplier solutions accompanied by whole life carbon assessments and proposals for minimising GHG emissions across the lifecycle of the assets procured; and

- Make clear the criteria for net zero carbon performance measurement, how they will be applied and how they will affect the award of future work and other supplier incentives.

37.19 The Construction Playbook emphasises that the evaluation criteria should focus on 'the whole life cost, not the lowest purchase price'.[34] Further:[35]

> While cost is an important evaluation criterion, there will be many occasions where quality will be weighted higher than cost, recognising the importance of delivering quality public works projects and programmes, or meeting legal obligations such as net zero by 2050. The quality evaluation criteria need to be sufficiently well developed and detailed to allow for the differentiation in scores between competing bids, to avoid too close or identical scores from bidders.

37.20 The Construction Playbook states that 'contracting authorities should evaluate bids for public works projects and programmes by determining the most economically advantageous tender ('MEAT') based on their published award criteria'.[36]

37.21 Regulation 67(2) of the Public Contracts Regulations 2015 provides that Contracting Authorities should base the award of public contracts on the MEAT approach. This should be identified on the basis of the price or cost using a cost-effectiveness approach, such as lifecycle costing, and may include the best price–quality ratio, which should be assessed on the basis of criteria, such as qualitative, environmental and/or social aspects, linked to the subject-matter of the public contract in question.[37]

37.22 The government's Green Paper on 'Transforming Public Procurement' proposed requiring the evaluation of bids to be based on the Most Advantageous Tender ('MAT'), instead of MEAT, which 'should provide greater reassurance to contracting authorities that they can take a broader view of what can be included in the evaluation of tenders in assessing value for money including social value as part of the quality assessment'.[38] This approach was already provided for in the Public Contracts Regulations 2015. Under MEAT, the proposed change was focused on reinforcing and adding clarity rather than changing scope.[39]

---

34 Cabinet Office, 'The Construction Playbook, Government Guidance on Sourcing and Contracting Public Works Projects and Programmes' (n 9) 62.
35 ibid 64.
36 ibid 63.
37 The Public Contracts Regulations 2015 reg 67(2).
38 Cabinet Office, *Transforming Public Procurement: Government Response to Consultation* (CP 556, 2021) 38, para 101 <https://assets.publishing.service.gov.uk/media/61addef38fa8f5037ac 74399/Transforming_Public_Procurement_Government_response_to_consultation.v3_.pdf> accessed 27 April 2024.
39 ibid.

37.23 Following the Green Paper, the MAT approach was implemented by Section 19(1) of the Procurement Act 2023, which provides that Contracting Authorities may award a public contract to the supplier that submits the most advantageous tender in a competitive tendering procedure.[40]

37.24 The difficulty that may arise in practice is shifting the industry's perspective from traditionally important criterion such as lowest purchase price, to factors such as net zero considerations. However, such a shift is likely to be ameliorated by the legal and industry obligations described above, consideration in the procurement strategy of how the success in delivering improved net zero outcomes will affect the award of future work and other incentives, as well as the inclusion of performance incentives within contracts.

37.25 In addition, it is important to have a procurement process that allows sufficient time for the careful examination, investigation, and agreement of net zero proposals submitted by the select suppliers.[41] This is why early conditional appointments of contractors and supply chain members are an essential part of the procurement process, in order for clients and their consultants to gain the best insights as to what net zero solutions are on offer.[42]

The supply chain

(i) *Early supply chain involvement and supply chain collaboration*

37.26 Contractors and supply chain members should be appointed early during the pre-construction phase of a project, on the basis of clear contractual systems through which they work with the client and consultants in developing and agreeing viable and affordable net zero carbon proposals as preconditions to the commencement of the construction phase of the project.[43]

37.27 Firms within the sector possess different levels of capabilities to manage delivery of objectives including carbon and environmental outcomes, and Contracting Authorities need to actively engage with the supply chain to achieve intended outcomes.[44]

37.28 The Construction Playbook requires that public works projects and programmes contract for early supply chain involvement ('ESI') to achieve the planned outcomes, value for money and whole life value.[45] Further, ESI extends the principle of early contractor involvement by formally engaging the Tier 1 contractor alongside Tier 2 and 3 sub-contractors and suppliers in the pre-construction phase to input into the design

---

40 Procurement Act 2023 s 19(1).
41 King's College London Centre of Construction Law & Dispute Resolution and others, 'Procuring Net Zero Construction' (n 4) 21.
42 ibid.
43 ibid 21.
44 UK Government Commercial Function, 'Promoting Net Zero Carbon and Sustainability in Construction: Guidance Note' (n 2) 25, para 4.1.3.
45 Cabinet Office, 'The Construction Playbook, Government Guidance on Sourcing and Contracting Public Works Projects and Programmes' (n 9) 28.

(including the use of standards for products and interfaces), costing, risk, management and structuring of a project or programme.[46] Further, the Construction Playbook warns against a separate pre-construction phase as:[47]

> The procurement process, evaluation approach and contract should generally be structured to cover both the ESI and the construction phase. Whilst it is possible to follow ESI with a further competitive procurement process, this can undermine the benefits of using ESI.

37.29 The UK government recommends the following procurement models using ESI systems:[48]

- 'Two Stage Open Book', comprising the pre-construction phase conditional appointment of team members as a means to develop early collaboration and to encourage proposals for cost savings and improved value, within a stated budget, prior to confirming construction phase appointments;
- 'Cost Led Procurement', comprising the use of a framework mini-competition as a means to encourage speculative proposals for savings and improved value, within a stated cost ceiling, prior to making team appointments; and
- 'Integrated Project Insurance', comprising appointment at outset of an alliance team to develop a delivery solution within a target budget and a collective commitment to achieve the required outcomes, supported by a client-funded, non-recourse insurance policy covering latent defects and cost overruns.[49]

37.30 'Supply Chain Collaboration' is a recommended type of ESI, which can be used in conjunction with the above procurement methods whereby the Tier 1 contractors propose their preferred supply chains; the client then works with the appointed Tier 1 contractor to re-engineer that supply chain to ensure best value, quality and net zero carbon targets.[50] This process allows earlier involvement and better understanding by Tier 2 supply chain members, and the potential sharing of supply chain members among more than one Tier 1 contractor on more favourable common terms.[51]

---

46 ibid.
47 ibid.
48 Cabinet Office, 'New Models of Construction Procurement: Introduction to the Guidance for Cost Led Procurement, Integrated Project Insurance and Two Stage Open Book' (2014) 7–9 <https://assets.publishing.service.gov.uk/media/5a7d97fce5274a6b89a50fc4/New_Models_of_Construction_Procurement_-_Introduction_to_the_Guidance_-_2_July_2014.pdf> accessed 27 April 2024.
49 King's College London Centre of Construction Law & Dispute Resolution and others, 'Procuring Net Zero Construction' (n 4) 24.
50 Cabinet Office, 'New Models of Construction Procurement: Introduction to the Guidance for Cost Led Procurement, Integrated Project Insurance and Two Stage Open Book' (n 48) 10.
51 ibid.

(ii) *Supply chain decarbonisation*

37.31 A 2021 report by the World Economic Forum states that construction supply chains account for more than 10% of global CO_2 emissions.[52] The importance of collaboration, for example by the use of ESI, is central to supply chain decarbonisation:[53]

> Beyond defining procurement standards, supply-chain emission reductions often require more intensive supplier collaboration – to educate suppliers about decarbonization levers, provide technical advice, enable longer-term asset upgrades and cultivate continuous improvement.

37.32 In major construction projects, supply chains will contribute significantly to GHG emissions. As set out above, the UK government has implemented PPN 06/21 which will encourage supply chain decarbonisation, as failure to comply is likely to lead to exclusion at the supplier selection stage.[54]

Project delivery

37.33 In terms of project performance, Contracting Authorities should:[55]

- Regularly review the suite of project and programme documentation, and ensure that these are aligned around key objectives, including those relating to sustainability and achieving net zero;
- Ensure that the sustainability and carbon objectives incorporated into the output specification are included in the SCM;
- Select a delivery model that will support collaboration between clients and the supply chain in relation to sustainability objectives, informed by early supply chain engagement and best practice sharing with other client organisations and academia;
- Identify KPIs that enable reporting against strategic outcomes and can be used to monitor progress in each phase of the project or programme delivery process and that these are practical for the supply chain to gather and report;
- Embed sustainability and carbon objectives and associated KPIs in contractual documentation. Review and update this documentation regularly to take account of developing best practice and learning from other projects; and

52 World Economic Forum, 'Net-Zero Challenge: The Supply Chain Opportunity' (2021) 12 <https://www3.weforum.org/docs/WEF_Net_Zero_Challenge_The_Supply_Chain_Opportunity_2021.pdf> accessed 27 April 2024.
53 ibid 30.
54 UK Government Commercial Function, 'Promoting Net Zero Carbon and Sustainability in Construction: Guidance Note' (n 2) 9, para 2.3.2.
55 ibid para 4.1.3.

- Ensure sustainability and carbon objectives are embedded in project and programme management structures, and these have the resources required to deliver these objectives.

(i) *Delivery model assessment*

37.34 Consideration of a delivery model should be undertaken by a delivery model assessment ('DMA') which is an analytical, evidence-based approach to reach a recommendation on how a Contracting Authority should structure the delivery of a project or programme.[56] This should take place early enough to inform the first business case stage, the Strategic Outline Business Case, in parallel with the development of the value model and outcome specification.[57]

37.35 To ensure the delivery model can deliver sustainability and carbon objectives, Contracting Authorities should:[58]

- Consider organisational strategies and objectives in relation to sustainability, including net zero carbon, and the objectives that they are seeking to deliver through the project and programme;

- Assess the market capability to deliver these objectives, and what level of engagement will be required with the supply chain to enable this;

- Determine the KPIs and reporting methodologies to use to track and measure outcomes over the life of a project, and what capability will be required, including to meet mandatory requirements e.g. PPN 06/21;

- Review the key risks and potential for developments in the market that could jeopardise the achievement of these objectives;

- Identify the whole life costs and value linked to the delivery of these objectives, and incorporate these into the SCM; and

- Consider which delivery model, approach to contract management, project management and supplier relationship management best align with the intended outcomes.

37.36 In practice, there will be many, often competing, objectives to consider during the project delivery stage. It is important to expressly consider sustainability and carbon objectives from the outset and to explore how their interrelationship with other seemingly competing objectives, such as cost, can instead be mutually beneficial.

---

56 Cabinet Office, 'The Construction Playbook, Government Guidance on Sourcing and Contracting Public Works Projects and Programmes' (n 9) 38.
57 ibid.
58 UK Government Commercial Function, 'Promoting Net Zero Carbon and Sustainability in Construction: Guidance Note' (n 2) 26–27, para 4.2.2.

(ii) *Should Cost Model*

37.37 The Construction Playbook requires that all projects and programmes should produce a SCM, which provides a forecast of what a project or programme 'should' cost over its whole life, including both the build phase and the expected design life.[59] The level of investment in producing a SCM will vary with the complexity and significance of the procurement; for major works projects, a SCM will be more detailed and, while the level of detail will evolve, they should be produced during the planning and preparation stage to support the DMA.[60]

37.38 In practice, the difficulty may be that there will be increased costs linked to the delivery of reduced carbon emissions. However, these may be more than offset by improved performance of the asset and reduced operational costs, like improved heat and energy efficiency, or from reduced costs for the disposal of waste, due to the incorporation of more sustainable materials.[61] This is why consideration of the circularity of construction products at the outset of a project is key.

Modern methods of construction

37.39 Modern methods of construction ('MMC') is a wide term, covering a range of offsite and onsite techniques which provide alternatives to traditional methods and have the potential to deliver significant improvements in productivity, efficiency, safety, and quality.[62]

37.40 A joint government and industry working group, the MHCLG Joint Industry Working Gorup on MCC, published the MMC Definition Framework, which allocates the spectrum of construction techniques into seven MMC categories:[63]

- Category 1 – Pre-Manufacturing – 3D primary structural systems;
- Category 2 – Pre-Manufacturing – 2D primary structural systems;
- Category 3 – Pre-Manufacturing – Non-systemised structural components;
- Category 4 – Pre-Manufacturing – Additive manufacturing;
- Category 5 – Pre-Manufacturing – Non-structural assemblies and sub-assemblies;

59 Cabinet Office, 'The Construction Playbook, Government Guidance on Sourcing and Contracting Public Works Projects and Programmes' (n 9) 42.
60 ibid.
61 UK Government Commercial Function, 'Promoting Net Zero Carbon and Sustainability in Construction: Guidance Note' (n 2) 27, para 4.3.2.
62 Cabinet Office, 'The Construction Playbook, Government Guidance on Sourcing and Contracting Public Works Projects and Programmes' (n 9) 2.
63 Ministry of Housing, Communities and Local Government, 'Modern Methods of Construction: Introducing the MMC Definition Framework' (2019) 4 <https://www.cast-consultancy.com/wp-content/uploads/2019/03/MMC-I-Pad-base_GOVUK-FINAL_SECURE.pdf> accessed 27 April 2024.

- Category 6 – Traditional building product led site labour reduction/productivity improvements; and
- Category 7 – Site process led labour reduction/productivity improvements.

37.41 For example, these technologies support:[64]

- Improved designs that require fewer materials, and which are produced to support higher levels of reuse and recycling;
- Designs that deliver improved energy and heat performance, and which allow the use of new and more sustainable products and materials;
- The precision manufacturing of buildings to achieve these specifications, and reduce material waste and emissions linked to the construction processes;
- The opportunity for firms based at a distance from where a project is being delivered to benefit from participating;
- Increased incentives for investment in technologies, capital equipment and workforce skills;
- Improved management of construction operations, logistics and the supply chain, as well as built assets; and
- Accurate monitoring, quantification and reporting of carbon emissions, and the comparison of projects and programmes, identifying best practice and supporting performance improvement.

37.42 The Construction Playbook requires that Contracting Authorities develop a comprehensive strategy at an organisational level, which should run through their portfolios and down to individual projects and programmes.[65] Contracting Authorities should consider whether, how and to what extent the use of MMC can drive wider value and achieve the project or programme outcomes.

37.43 The Modern Methods of Construction Guidance Note states that appropriate uptake of MMC will help to drive greener, faster, better construction portfolios in the public sector space through:[66]

---

64 UK Government Commercial Function, 'Promoting Net Zero Carbon and Sustainability in Construction: Guidance Note' (n 2) 10, para 2.4.1.
65 Cabinet Office, 'The Construction Playbook, Government Guidance on Sourcing and Contracting Public Works Projects and Programmes' (n 9) 20.
66 Cabinet Office, 'Modern Methods of Construction Guidance Note' (2022) 5, para 2.4 <https://assets.publishing.service.gov.uk/media/631222468fa8f5423fb0c7c0/20220901-MMC-Guidance-Note.pdf> accessed 27 April 2024.

- Shared requirements and standards will encourage investment into readily available interoperable components to drive faster delivery;
- Greater use of offsite construction can deliver efficiencies, higher quality and safer solutions with lower GHG emissions quicker than traditional construction methods; and
- Further embedding digital technologies, including the UK Building Information Management ('BIM') Framework and digital twins, will improve the performance, sustainability and value for money of projects and programmes, allowing for building information to be passed effectively and efficiently on from the design team to the facility operator via the contractor.

37.44 The difficulty that may arise in practice is the investment that is needed to develop MMC and skills. One way of achieving this is adopting longer term contracting. However, the Construction Playbook itself acknowledges that the industry needs to actively consider how it can collectively maximise the use of MMC.[67]

Whole life cost and digital information management

37.45 The Construction Playbook focuses in particular on whole life cost/procurement which takes into account the total cost over the life of an asset, including capital, maintenance, management, operation and exit.[68]

37.46 The construction industry remains focused primarily on the procurement of the capital expenditure phase that covers project design and construction, rather than on procurement of the repair, maintenance and operation phase and its potential for long-term efficiencies.[69] Digital management of whole lifecycle asset information is a possible solution to this approach.

37.47 The Construction Playbook requires Contracting Authorities and suppliers to apply the BIM Framework.[70] This includes standards, guidance, and other resources that will deliver BIM interoperability and government soft landings. These include standardised approaches to defining information requirements, generating and classifying data, information security and data exchange. The standards include ISO 19650 which is the international standard for managing information over the whole life cycle of a built asset using building information modelling.[71]

---

67 Cabinet Office, 'The Construction Playbook, Government Guidance on Sourcing and Contracting Public Works Projects and Programmes' (n 9) 20.
68 ibid 62.
69 King's College London Centre of Construction Law & Dispute Resolution and others, 'Procuring Net Zero Construction' (n 4) 43.
70 UK BIM Framework, 'UK BIM Framework Standards' <https://www.ukbimframework.org/standards/> accessed 27 April 2024.
71 The British Standards Institution, 'ISO 19650 – Managing Information With Building Information Modelling (BIM)' 196 <https://www.bsigroup.com/en-GB/capabilities/buildings-and-construction/iso-19650-building-information-modelling-bim/> accessed 27 April 2024.

Circularity in construction and construction products

37.48 The construction sector generates around 60% of waste in the UK.[72] Reducing waste and increasing levels of reuse and recycling is essential to achieving net zero. A 2021 report by the World Economic Forum listed as two of the eight major abatement levers to decarbonisation:[73]

- Circularity/recycling: increasing the share of recycled materials; and
- Material and process efficiency: lowering the amount of waste and/or improving efficiency in the production process to reduce power and/or heat consumption. This can be done by using the newest available process and heat technologies (such as motors, drives, pumps or ovens), more efficient process steering, by using waste heat from other processes, or reducing material waste in production.

37.49 Further, the report details that within the global construction supply chain, approximately 5% of emissions can be abated by introducing circularity in cement, aluminium or plastics from demolition waste or via increasing the share of scrap in existing electric arc furnaces; while some 20% of emissions can be tackled through material and process efficiency levers, such as cement clinker substitution, and more efficient transport vehicles.[74]

37.50 Contracting Authorities should consider how they can promote increased levels of reuse and recycling through their projects and programmes.[75] This could be achieved through including requirements for these within tenders or specifications, the adoption of standards, or by encouraging the supply chain to demonstrate best practice through participation in private or other non-government sector initiatives, which includes:[76]

- BES 6001: a standard that enables construction product manufacturers to prove that their products have been produced with responsibly-sourced materials.[77] It provides a framework for governance, supply chain management and environmental and social management, and can be used by a manufacturer of any construction product that uses a foundation product such as cement, steel, timber, plastics or ceramics. Certification of meeting the standard is provided by independent third party bodies;

---

72 UK Government Commercial Function, 'Promoting Net Zero Carbon and Sustainability in Construction: Guidance Note' (n 2) 23, para 3.8.2.1.
73 World Economic Forum, 'Net-Zero Challenge: The Supply Chain Opportunity' (n 52) 14.
74 ibid 38.
75 UK Government Commercial Function, 'Promoting Net Zero Carbon and Sustainability in Construction: Guidance Note' (n 2) 23, para 3.8.2.2.
76 ibid.
77 Building Research Establishment, 'BES 6001 Framework Standard for Responsible Sourcing' <https://bregroup.com/services/standards/sourcing/BES-6001-responsible-sourcing>.

- BS 8001: a voluntary guidance standard for the circular economy.[78] It aims to provide a practical framework and advice for organisations of any size or sector to implement the principles of the circular economy, through evaluating how their business models, processes, products and services are managed to maximise the economic, social and environmental benefits; and

- Cradle to Cradle: a global standard for certifying product safety and environmental impact.[79] It assesses these against five criteria: safety of materials used in production; reusability and recyclability; air quality and carbon reduction; water and soil quality; and social impact. Assessments are undertaken by independent assessment bodies to ensure they meet the required criteria every two years.

37.51 Complex and multi-faceted problems often require complex and multi-faceted answers; the changes required in the construction phase to achieve net zero are both complex and multi-faceted. However, through collaboration and innovation in the procurement process, the supply chain and project delivery; adopting modern methods of construction and digital information management; as well as awareness of whole life value and circularity; the construction industry is making progressive steps in the construction phase towards achieving net zero. The continued progression of such change is reliant on educating industry users and further capital investment. Legal and industry obligations, as well as net zero performance incentives built into contracts, continue to mandate and encourage the changes required in the construction phase to achieve net zero.

78 The British Standards Institution, 'BS 8001:2017 Framework for Implementing the Principles of the Circular Economy in Organizations' <https://knowledge.bsigroup.com/products/framework-for-implementing-the-principles-of-the-circular-economy-in-organizations-guide?version=standard> accessed 27 April 2024.
79 Cradle to Cradle Products Innovation Institute, 'Cradle to Cradle Certified' <https://c2ccertified.org/the-standard> accessed 27 April 2024.

CHAPTER 38

RETROFITTING

Ruth Keating

Introduction

38.01 Retrofitting is the process of upgrading an existing building to improve its energy efficiency and reduce its carbon emissions. As decarbonising the UK's building stock is a major priority for meeting climate goals, retrofitting existing properties will become more important for the government and, in turn, developers. Given that 80% of the buildings with us today will still be in use in 2050,[1] retrofitting will have an increasingly important role in the construction industry.

38.02 Embodied carbon (carbon emitted during the construction of a building) means that even the greenest of new buildings can be detrimental to global climate goals. As such, rather than demolition, reuse and retrofitting will become increasingly common.

38.03 Retrofitting is a broad process that encompasses many different types of changes to existing buildings. In the context of climate goals and net zero targets, these changes seek to reduce the energy consumption of buildings, such that operational carbon emissions are ultimately reduced. This usually means improvements like the installation of renewable or low-carbon energy technologies, or measures to improve energy efficiency, such as insulation or smart lighting.

38.04 In June 2021, the Committee on Climate Change ('CCC') published its third UK Climate Change Risk Assessment ('CCRA3') Report.[2] The report highlighted several priority risk areas that required immediate attention, in order to mitigate the threat posed by climate change. Among other things, the CCC recommended updating building regulations to cater for a warmer climate, given that overheating poses a genuine risk to life. Therefore, it is plain that in the future, further updated regulations will develop in this area, which the industry will have to adapt to.

---

1 UK Green Building Council, 'Climate Change Mitigation' <https://ukgbc.org/our-work/climate-change-mitigation/> accessed 22 March 2024.

2 Climate Change Committee, 'Independent Assessment of UK Climate Risk: Advice to Government For the UK's Third Climate Change Risk Assessment (CCRA3)' (2021) <https://www.theccc.org.uk/wp-content/uploads/2021/07/Independent-Assessment-of-UK-Climate-Risk-Advice-to-Govt-for-CCRA3-CCC.pdf> accessed 1 April 2024. Note that Part 4 of the Climate Change Act 2008 requires the CCC to assess UK climate risk, both under current conditions and over the long term, on behalf of the government.

38.05 Further, decisions like the well-known *Marks and Spencer* decision (in relation to Marks and Spencer's proposal to demolish and rebuild their Marble Arch flagship),[3] demonstrate that there is likely to be an increasing emphasis on retrofitting existing buildings, rather than demolishing them.[4] In turn, this means that employers and contractors will need to adapt to a different manner of construction, than what they may be used to. In the *Marks and Spencer* decision, the High Court expressed the view that the Secretary of State for Levelling Up, Housing and Communities had erred in refusing planning permission for the construction of a new mixed office and retail store at the western end of London's Oxford Street, contrary to the planning inspector's recommendation. For the purposes of this chapter, the conclusions the court reached at paragraph 152 of the National Planning Policy Framework ('NPPF') are particularly relevant. Paragraph 152 of the NPPF states:

> The planning system should support the transition to a low carbon future in a changing climate, taking full account of flood risk and coastal change. It should help to: shape places in ways that contribute to radical reductions in greenhouse gas emissions, minimise vulnerability and improve resilience; encourage the reuse of existing resources, including the conversion of existing buildings; and support renewable and low carbon energy and associated infrastructure.[5]

38.06 In the High Court decision, Lieven J held that:

> There is in paragraph 152 some encouragement for the reuse of buildings, but nothing that comes close to a presumption. Mr Shadarevian's argument that paragraph 152 is seeking to achieve a radical reduction in carbon, and thus a presumption of retailing [sic] buildings can be inferred, ignores the rest of the paragraph which refers to a number of other very general policy aspirations. There is nothing in the paragraph that supports the application of a policy presumption for one part of the paragraph alone.[6]

38.07 Therefore, there is no presumption in favour of reuse of buildings by virtue of paragraph 152 of the NPPF. Rather, there is encouragement. Nonetheless, this is but one factor that is relevant to the decision of whether to reuse or retrofit a building, rather than demolish it.

The legal framework for retrofitting in England and Wales

(i) *Statutory and regulatory duties*

38.08 In light of the government's target of reducing greenhouse gas emissions to net zero by 2050, the government will increasingly consider ways to achieve this net zero

---

3 *Marks and Spencer plc v Secretary of State for Levelling Up, Housing and Communities* [2004] EWHC 452 (Admin).
4 In this decision, the Secretary of State agreed with the inspector that, at [24], 'there should generally be a strong presumption in favour of repurposing and reusing buildings as reflected in paragraph 152'.
5 Department for Levelling Up, Housing and Communities, 'National Planning Policy Framework' (2023) para 152 <https://assets.publishing.service.gov.uk/media/65a11af7e8f5ec000f1f8c46/NPPF_December_2023.pdf> accessed 2 April 2024.
6 *Marks and Spencer plc v Secretary of State for Levelling Up, Housing and Communities* (n 3) [55].

target. Retrofitting existing buildings is one of the most cost-effective ways to achieve this target.

38.09 Many existing laws and regulations will also be relevant to retrofitting in England and Wales.

38.10 The Building Regulations 2010 ('the 2010 Regulations') apply in England and Wales and provide a minimum standard relating to the construction and alteration of premises. The 2010 Regulations apply to 'building work', which is defined in regulation 3 of the 2010 Regulations. The definition of building work includes:

- The erection or extension of a building;[7]
- The installation or extension of a service or fitting that is controlled under the building regulations;[8]
- The material alteration of a building or controlled service or fitting;[9]
- Work required where there is a material change of use of the whole building;[10]
- Insertion of insulating material into the cavity wall of a building;[11]
- Work involving the underpinning of a building;[12]
- Work required by regulation 22 (requirements relating to a change of energy status);[13]
- Work required by regulation 23 (requirements relating to thermal elements);[14]
- Work required by regulation 28 (consequential improvements to energy performance).[15]

38.11 One can readily appreciate the variety of different ways in which a retrofit project could bring the 2010 Regulations into scope. The practical requirements for carrying out building work are set out in Parts A to S of Schedule 1 to the 2010 Regulations, which are in turn supplemented by detailed technical guidance contained in Approved

---

7 The Building Regulations 2010 reg 3(1)(a).
8 ibid reg 3(1)(b).
9 ibid reg 3(1)(c).
10 ibid reg 3(1)(d).
11 ibid reg 3(1)(e).
12 ibid reg 3(1)(f).
13 ibid reg 3(1)(g).
14 ibid reg 3(1)(h).
15 ibid reg 3(1)(i).

Documents.[16] Approved Documents give practical guidance on common building situations and how to meet the requirements of the 2010 Regulations.

38.12 Applying the 2010 Regulations is fairly straightforward when it comes to building new homes. However, the added complexity with retrofitting projects is that with retrofitting, employers and contractors will need to be mindful that certain obligations may vary in practice. For example, contractors will need to consider the extent of the works undertaken: what may initially appear to be a limited piece of work, might in practice require much larger works to be carried out to comply with the 2010 Regulations. For example, regulation 23 generally provides that where a thermal element is renovated or replaced, work shall be carried out to ensure the whole thermal element complies with Part L of the 2010 Regulations. Therefore, depending on the circumstances, contractors will need to consider the extent to which more minimal works may ultimately require more significant works to be undertaken, such that the work is compliant with the 2010 Regulations.

38.13 Further, the latest revisions of Approved Documents often introduce increased efficiency standards (this is demonstrated, for example, by Part L).[17] Therefore, employers and contractors must also consider whether retrofit projects have been adequately designed to meet the expected standards – bearing in mind that those standards will undoubtedly develop and change over time.

38.14 Equally, other statutory duties may be relevant. For example, section 1(1) of the Defective Premises Act 1972 provides that the Act's provisions apply to a person taking on work for or in connection with the provision of a 'dwelling', whether the dwelling is provided 'by the erection or by the conversion or enlargement of a building'.[18] The provisions are therefore apt to cover a retrofitting project, depending on the circumstances of the project. Those duties include the following:

- Pursuant to section 1, to 'build dwellings properly'.
- Pursuant to section 1(1)(b), the duty-holder must carry out his work in a 'workmanlike' or, 'as the case may be, professional' manner. The duty-holder must also 'use proper materials' and the dwelling must be 'fit for habitation' when completed.[19]

---

16 The Approved Documents can be found online at Department for Levelling Up, Housing and Communities, 'Approved Documents' <https://www.gov.uk/government/collections/approved-documents> accessed 3 April 2024.

17 For example, Part L came into force on 15 June 2022 – it addresses the conservation of fuel and power and applies to all building projects in England. This includes that non-domestic buildings must achieve an average of 27% reduction in CO_2 and dwellings must achieve a 31% reduction, relative to 2013 standards. Volume 1 concerns dwellings and Volume 2 concerns buildings other than dwellings.

18 Toulmin HHJ provided guidance in *Catlin Estates Ltd and another v Carter Jonas (a firm)* [2005] EWHC 2315 (TCC) [296] on the meaning of 'dwelling', stating that 'a dwelling house is a building used or capable of being used as a dwelling house, not being a building which is used predominantly for commercial and industrial purposes'. See also other authorities such as Edwards-Stuart J in *Rendlesham Estates plc and others v Barr Ltd* [2014] EWHC 3968 (TCC), in which he concluded that an entire block could not be considered a dwelling.

19 As per *Bayoumi v Protim Services Ltd* [1996] EWCA Civ 885, the Claimant must prove: 'on a balance of probability, that the defendant's failure to do his work in a workmanlike manner has caused the property to be unfit for human habitation'.

- When considering whether a dwelling is 'unfit for human habitation', it appears that a high threshold applies: in *Andrews v Schooling*, Balcombe LJ considered that this would be the case when the dwelling is without 'some essential attribute'.[20] Nonetheless, given the authorities have confirmed that the defect or defects may be latent at the time of completion, there is potential for a defect to arise due to a failure to account for climate change adaptation or mitigation.

38.15 Finally, in the context of retrofitting and statutory duties, we mentioned that from 15 June 2022, the Revised 2022 Part L Target Thermal U-Values[21] apply. The effect is that the maximum permitted U-values have decreased. For example, in existing building extensions, the U-values for walls are to be tightened from $0.28W/m^2$ K to $0.18W/m^2$ K, and roofs tightened from $0.18W/m^2$ K to $0.15W/m^2$ K. Again, this demonstrates how there is likely to be an increased focus on energy consumption and use in the coming years, and therefore on the energy performance of buildings.

(ii) *Contractual duties and challenges*

38.16 Like the statutory and regulatory duties considered above, many contractual duties that parties are already familiar with will apply with the same force to a retrofitting project. The difficulty is that contracting parties will have to consider the extent to which the fact the project is a retrofit project, as compared with a demolish and build. Consequently, this will change their understanding of their contractual rights and duties.

38.17 The complex issues that arise in existing case law, as summarised directly below, may arise in the context of retrofitting projects. We consider some of those potential challenges below:

38.18 New industry standards and guidance. The relevance of industry standards and guidance to professionals has been covered in Chapter 36. The standards and guidance referred to in that chapter reflect that competence is not a static achievement and must be revisited and updated. Therefore, contractors and parties will need to ensure that they understand new guidance and standards referred to in contracts.[22] This is particularly so given this is an area where one could expect a growing body of relevant standards and guidance. We discuss guidance and standards in more detail in Chapter 36.

---

20 See Balcombe LJ in *Andrews v Schooling* [1991] 1 WLR 783: 'If when the work is completed, the dwelling is without some essential attribute e.g. a roof or a damp course – it may well then be unfit for human habitation though the problems resulting from the lack of that attribute have not become patent. A house without a roof is unfit for habitation even though it does not rain until some months after the house has been completed.'
21 U-value (or thermal transmittance) is the rate of transfer of heat through a structure.
22 This is an area where there will be increasingly new standards and guidance. For example, on 31 January 2022, the British Standards Institution published PAS 2035/2030:2019+A1:2022 'Retrofitting dwellings for improved energy efficiency. Specification and guidance'. In terms of PAS 2035/2030: (i) PAS 2035 on retrofitting dwellings, covers retrofitting dwellings including how to assess dwellings for retrofit, identify improvement options, design and specify Energy Efficiency Measures ('EEM') and monitor retrofit projects. (ii) Meanwhile, PAS 2030, which was redeveloped in conjunction with PAS 2035, covers the installation, commissioning, and handover of retrofit projects. Organisations that trade using the Trustmark government-endorsed Quality scheme are required to comply with PAS 2035.

38.19 Fitness for purpose. A retrofit project works towards a desired outcome – for example, the improved energy efficiency of a building. Therefore, contracts for retrofitting are likely to include several fitness for purpose outcomes, to ensure the works achieve a desired level of efficiency or carbon output. Where these obligations relate to design, they may be classed as fitness for purpose clauses. As fitness for purpose clauses, these will impose duties which go beyond a duty to exercise reasonable skill and care in carrying out the works, in that the contractor will be under a contractual obligation to achieve a specified result in terms of performance. Construction professionals should be alive to any fitness for purpose clauses in the contracts, particularly in light of *MT Hojgaard v E.ON Climate and Renewables UK Robin Rigg East Ltd.*[23] The background of this appeal arose from the failure of the foundation structure of two offshore wind farms, designed and installed by the respondent, MTH, shortly after completion of the construction and installation. The contract, which contained a provision that the foundations be fit for purpose, incorporated E.ON's Technical Requirements which referred to the international design standard for the design of offshore wind turbines, J101. The Technical Requirements also stated that the design of the foundations should ensure a lifetime of 20 years in every aspect without planned replacement.

38.20 The central question considered by the Supreme Court was whether, in the light of the provision in the Technical Requirements, which referred to ensuring a life for the foundations, and the works, of 20 years, MTH had been in breach of contract, despite the fact that it used due care and professional skill, adhered to good industry practice, and had complied with J101.

38.21 The Supreme Court, in allowing the appeal, held that the Technical Requirements of the project, which ensured a lifetime of 20 years, either provided a warranty that the foundations would actually have a lifetime of 20 years, or an undertaking to provide a design that could objectively be expected to have a lifetime of 20 years. The Court emphasised, however, that the reconciliation of inconsistent terms must be decided by reference to ordinary principles of contractual interpretation and therefore by reference to the provisions of the particular contract and its commercial context.

38.22 Lord Neuberger held that where the two provisions imposed different or inconsistent standards or requirements, rather than concluding that they are inconsistent, the correct analysis in this case was that 'the more rigorous or demanding of the two standards or requirements must prevail, as the less rigorous can properly be treated as a minimum requirement'.

38.23 Therefore construction professionals should be aware of any net zero requirements in the contract which are more rigorous than the relevant international standards and should understand the requirements imposed by any fitness for purpose obligation, which references climate commitments or performance, contained in the contract. It is particularly important to consider the requirements given that fitness for purpose obligations may not be covered by professional indemnity insurance.

---

23 *MT Hojgaard v E.ON Climate and Renewables UK Robin Rigg East Ltd* [2017] UKSC 59.

38.24 Design liability matrix. Retrofitting can entail the management of different components of a building, and thus the need to understand how they interrelate to impact overall performance. For example, a beneficial change to one component may cause deterioration in another. This will often require bespoke and complicated design solutions. An employer may seek to amend a design and build contract to impose a 'single point of responsibility', whilst a contractor may be unwilling to take on this risk if multiple third party designers have contributed to achieving the solution. This will raise issues that frequently arise in the context of design responsibility, including the need to thoroughly investigate the employer's design for which the contractor is assuming responsibility.

38.25 Existing standards, legislation and case law will continue to develop. The following points should be kept in mind:

- Retrofitting is encouraged under paragraph 152 of the NPPF.

- There are growing regulatory and commercial reasons to consider retrofitting buildings.

- The RICS Red Book Global Standards require the valuer to consider 'any sustainability and ESG factors that could affect the valuation'.[24] The UK Green Building Council has noted that explicit reflection of sustainability in market or investment values is still limited.[25] Nonetheless, this is an area where there is likely to be increased attention in the future.

- Any claims as to the energy efficiency or performance of a building need to be capable of being evidenced. This is just as relevant to a retrofit project, as any other type of project.

24 Royal Institution of Chartered Surveyors, 'Red Book Global Standards RICS Valuation VPS 2' (2021) para 2.3 <https://www.rics.org/profession-standards/rics-standards-and-guidance/sector-standards/valuation-standards/red-book/red-book-global> accessed 3 April 2024.
25 See discussion at section 3.7 of UK Green Building Council, 'Building the Case for Net Zero: Retrofitting Office Buildings' (2024) <https://ukgbc.org/wp-content/uploads/2024/01/Retrofitting-Office-Buildings-Building-the-Case-for-Net-Zero.pdf> accessed 3 April 2024.

CHAPTER 39

INSURANCE AND CONSTRUCTION

Hannah McCarthy

Insuring construction projects

39.01 Insurance is a critical element of construction, as it provides a mechanism of financial support to address the risks of the occurrence of inopportune events, whether arising in the course of the construction works or in other circumstances. The risks inherent to building projects are such that insurance will normally be a requirement for the project itself.[1] The two main categories of insurance for a construction project are insurance for property damage and loss, and insurance in respect of liabilities to third parties. The first of these, often taken out in an 'All Risks' policy described below, will cover the construction works themselves and any other damage to property. For the second category, contractors may avail themselves of professional indemnity insurance, personal injury insurance for workers, and insurance cover for risks to third parties incurred in the course of the project. Beyond these categories of insurance, construction contracts may also include a requirement for additional forms of insurance, such as a guarantee in respect of the contractor's or employer's obligations, or a bond, in which the bondsman may be required to make payment on demand to the beneficiary without any need to demonstrate fault.

39.02 Insurance for property loss and damage is usually a contractual requirement, stipulated as insurance of the works during construction. It will include insurance of the completed construction project, and of any temporary works to achieve the completed project, as well as plant and any existing property on the relevant site. These policies will include a list of identified risks against which damage to the works will be covered, such as fire, earthquakes, floods or other natural disasters. The standard form contracts now propose an 'All Risk' policy, whereby the relevant property is simply insured against any loss, destruction or damage, with exclusions identified rather than particular risks. Although such a policy may insure both contractors and employers, it is more common for contractors to obtain 'Contractor's All Risk' ('CAR') insurance policies.

39.03 Liability insurance, which covers any liabilities to third parties, comprises four main categories in a construction context. The first of these is public liability insurance, whereby either the contractor or the employer is insured against any loss, damage, or personal injury suffered by a third party arising in the course of the construction

1 See for example, NEC4, 'Engineering and Construction Contract' clauses 83–85; The Joint Contracts Tribunal Limited, 'Design and Build Contract 2016' Contract Particulars (items 6.4.1, 6.5.1, 6.7, 6.10, 6.15), Section 6 and Schedule 3.

works. Employers' liability insurance is the second category, which covers any personal injury sustained by an employee in the course of the works. An employer for these purposes is one who has control of that employee's action at the relevant time, which means that contractors and sub-contractors must ensure that these policies include circumstances in which an employee is not acting on the instructions of the original employer.[2] Professional indemnity insurance is the third category, and attaches to the liability of construction professionals, including architects, engineers and designers. It is often a requirement of a professional's contract with an employer, and will cover claims brought against the consultant in contract and in tort. A fourth, although less frequently employed, category is product liability insurance, which protects against loss, damage or injury to third parties arising from products installed within the constructed building. All of these varieties of liability insurance are generally included within a CAR policy.

39.04 A construction contract may include additional insurance beyond the two categories discussed above. Latent defects insurance can be obtained to protect the owner of a building – for example, the defects insurance or 'guarantee' is now offered only by the National House Building Council ('NHBC') in respect of newly constructed residential property. Latent defects insurance may also be obtained after reconstruction of an existing building, if contractual warranties or indemnities are not provided by the contractor. Furthermore, construction contracts may attract additional insurance for other risks, such as strict liability insurance or, rarely, liquidated damages insurance, which would not normally be covered under a CAR policy. Other more general insurance policies obtained may include property insurance, business interruption insurance or motor insurance.

39.05 Environmental risks arising from a construction project do not normally fall within the public liability policies discussed above. Environmental insurance developed in the United States in the 1970s as a discrete category of insurance to address liabilities arising from accidental pollution in the course of construction or other works. Specialist contractors may obtain contractors' pollution liability ('CPL') policies to address the risk of loss or damage occurring as a result of contamination carried out on third party sites.[3] Less common are Contractors Operations and Professional Services ('COPS') policies, which combine CPL cover with professional indemnity insurance for liabilities arising from a contractor's design.

Construction insurance market

39.06 Insurance is thus a fundamental feature of construction projects, and the construction insurance market in the UK alone is estimated to reach £6.5 billion by 2026.[4] This is notwithstanding a recent challenging period for the industry itself. The market faced a huge increase in claims arising from the impact of the Covid-19 crisis in 2020, as well as new supply chain disruptions as a result of Brexit, and geopolitical instability

2 *Mersey Docks and Harbour Board v Coggins* [1947] AC 1.
3 CPL policies are offered in the UK by insurers such as AXA, Chubb and others.
4 Allied Market Research, 'Contractor Insurance Market Global Opportunity Analysis and Industry Forecast, 2023–2032' (2024).

in Ukraine and elsewhere. Insurers faced a significant increase in large claims made under pre-2020 CAR policies, issued in a very different global market. Similarly, the professional indemnity insurance market in the UK has been affected since the 2017 Grenfell Tower disaster, by claims relating to the increased costs of cladding remediation and fixing fire safety defects. The Building Safety Act 2022 ('BSA') has also brought in significant changes to the Defective Premises Act 1972 ('DPA'), particularly in respect of limitation periods.[5] This has increased both costs and the likely number of future claims. New policies now routinely restrict or exclude coverage for cladding and other fire based issues.

39.07 Unsurprisingly, even beyond the wider factors of Covid-19, Brexit and the BSA, the construction insurance market is in a state of caution, if not vigilance. Insurers are increasingly concerned about some modern methods of construction ('MMC'), such as modular and prefabrication construction, which had been heralded as an environmentally friendly and quick solution to the UK's housing shortage.[6] Insurers have less appetite for these, as they are concerned about manufacturing failures that would require large-scale remediation, and fearful about the specification or quality of the material.

39.08 The challenge of meeting net zero for construction insurance companies takes place against this background of several years of difficult, if not catastrophic, global developments, and at a time when industry profitability has been particularly badly hit by increased claims across the market. But even before these events, insurers were already being asked to consider their role in the undeniable truth about the construction industry: in 2019, the global construction industry was responsible for 40% of the world's energy consumption, at least 40% of its greenhouse gas emission, and 16% of the world's water supply consumption.[7] The need for insurance providers to enable the transition of the construction industry towards a circular economy, create more specialised underwriting to support new construction technology (3D printing, for example) as well as to encourage the reuse of existing materials, and even seize an opportunity for its own investments was increasingly clear.

Global insurance market and climate change

39.09 However, even before the events of 2020, the insurance market contained sufficient scepticism about the role of insurers within any such transition. In one 2019 study, respondents queried the role of insurers at all, pointing out that the industry model was to insure legal business operations and entities, rather than operate as a moral compass.[8] The same study revealed that the insurance market held the impression

5 The BSA has widened the categories of causes of action under the DPA to include claims for defective remedial works and maintenance (section 2A DPA), and extended limitation periods to 30 years retrospectively and 15 years prospectively as of 28 June 2022.
6 David Thame, 'After 3 Major Failures, Does UK Modular Housebuilding have a Future?' [2023] *Bisnow UK* <https://www.bisnow.com/london/news/construction-development/modules-119586> accessed 8 April 2024.
7 Gholamreza Heravi and Mohammad Mehdi Abdolvand, 'Assessment of Water Consumption during Production of Material and Construction Phases of Residential Building Projects' [2019] 51 Sustainable Cities and Society 101785.
8 David Worsfold, 'Climate Change: The Role of Insurers in Reducing Carbon Emissions' [2020] *Kennedys Law and Insurance Post* <https://kennedyslaw.com/en/thought-leadership/article/climate-change-the-role-of-insurers

that only 15% of its corporate clients considered an insurer's position on climate change, when placing insurance. Currently, pressure is certainly increasing, driven by factors such as an increase in extreme weather events, as well as global initiatives like the annual Conference of Parties to the United Nations Framework Convention on Climate Change ('COP').[9] However, despite this pressure, the industry's shift from discussion to action has been neither linear nor swift. At COP 26 in April 2021, the Net Zero Insurance Alliance ('NZIA') was convened by Glasgow Financial Alliance for Net Zero ('GFANZ'). Twenty-two international insurers became founder members and committed to working to decarbonise their insurance underwriting portfolios, and to align their pathways to net zero emissions.[10] By May 2023, however, ten of the founder members, including Lloyd's of London, Swiss Re, Axa, Allianz and QBE, had all left NZIA. They cited a variety of concerns with NZIA's approach, although some believe that this was actually a response to anti-ESG pressure from Republican lawmakers in the United States.[11]

39.10 At COP 27, held in 2022, the Sharm El-Sheikh Adaptation Agenda increased the pressure on insurers to take action. The Agenda recommended that the focus for global action be concentrated on adaptation and resilience in the face of climate change, and recognised the particular need for increased private sector investment in climate finance, especially in respect of vulnerable communities.[12] At COP 28 in 2023, the UN Climate Change High-Level Champions, along with Marsh McLennan, issued 'Building a Climate Resilient Future: five priorities for the Global Insurance Industry' ('the Marsh McLennan Report'), with reference to the Agenda's focus on adaptation and resilience. The Marsh McLennan Report presented five recommendations on how the global insurance industry could address the obstacles preventing it from fulfilling a wider role in adaptation and resilience:[13]

- *Prioritise resilience as a strategic imperative*, in order to steer products, distribution and investment towards areas of the portfolio that are most at risk;

- *Collaborate with the public sector and civil society to expand coverage*: public–private partnerships could offer more effective insurance penetration, and will likely become increasingly important as the frequency and severity of weather-related disasters continues to rise;

-in-reducing-carbon-emissions/> accessed 8 April 2024.
9 See paras 2.08–2.27 in Chapter 2.
10 UN Environment Programme Finance Initiative, 'Statement from the UN Environment Programme on the Net-Zero Insurance Alliance' <https://www.unepfi.org/wordpress/wp-content/uploads/2023/07/UNEP-Statement-on-the-NZIA-5-July.pdf> accessed 8 April 2024.
11 Saumya Jain, 'Lloyd's Becomes the 10th Major Player to Mark Its Exit from NZIA' [2023] *Reinsurance News* <https://www.reinsurancene.ws/lloyds-becomes-the-10th-major-player-to-mark-its-exit-from-nzia/> accessed 8 April 2024.
12 COP 27, 'Sharm-El-Sheikh Adaptation Agenda' (2022) para 1.1 <https://climatechampions.unfccc.int/wp-content/uploads/2022/11/SeS-Adaptation-Agenda_Complete-Report-COP27_FINAL-1.pdf> accessed 8 April 2024.
13 United Nations Climate Change High-Level Champions, 'Building a Climate Resilient Future: Five Priorities for the Global Insurance Industry' (2023) section 1 <https://www.marshmclennan.com/content/dam/mmc-web/insights/publications/2023/december/Marsh_McLennan_Building_A_Climate_Resilient_Future.pdf> accessed 8 April 2024.

- *Improve accuracy and availability of climate-related data and analytics*: insurers should improve data quality and availability, not only to improve their own risk pricing models, but with a view to sharing data with public bodies to facilitate adaptation and resilience activities;

- *Create an industry standard around the concept 'build back better'*, so that adaptation and resilience, and therefore structural improvements, can be at the forefront of reconstruction efforts; and

- *Advocate for public policies and regulations that support resilience*: i.e. engaging with government and community stakeholders to influence planning, building code regulations, and land-use decisions.

39.11 Notwithstanding this clarion call, the Report then acknowledged:[14]

> Supporting adaptation and resilience has clear commercial value for the insurance industry and fulfills an important social good. Insurers already have many to the tools at hand to expand their role beyond transitional risk transfer, but many have not undertaken the mindset shift that allows this potential to be realized. Successfully fulfilling this agenda will improve societal resilience and drive long-term success for insurers in the face of climate change.

39.12 Climate change and the need to achieve net zero are fast becoming a commercial reality, rather than an inconvenient truth, for insurers around the world. In view of the magnitude and impact of the construction industry, its insurers are particularly well placed to engage in the terms envisaged by the Marsh McLennan Report. The question, however, is whether the 'mindset shift' identified in the Report will occur in time or at all, in order to realise these goals of adaptation and resilience and to achieve long term success for insurers themselves.

Net zero: What can construction insurers do?

39.13 The global insurance industry has had a roadmap for action since 2012. The United Nations Environment Programme ('UNEP')[15] Finance Initiative's 'Principles for Sustainable Insurance' were issued in 2012, to offer a global framework for the insurance industry to address environmental risks and opportunities. Principle 1 requires insurers to 'embed in our decision-making environmental, social and governance issues relevant to insurance business'.[16] This has been termed 'impact underwriting', and refers to using insurance to promote economic, social and environmental sustainability. It has been suggested that this includes providing insurance coverage for sustainable activities,

---

14 ibid section 1.
15 See footnote 24 in Chapter 2.
16 UN Environment Programme Finance Initiative, 'PSI: Principles for Sustainable Insurance' (2012) 4 <https://www.unepfi.org/psi/wp-content/uploads/2012/06/PSI-document.pdf> accessed 10 April 2024.

developing insurance products to shift non-sustainable behaviour, and reducing underwriting activities that harm sustainability.[17]

39.14 At present, the route to net zero for the construction industry remains unchartered in the UK: there are no specific targets to reduce carbon emissions of building materials or construction, although the industry is increasingly implementing standards such as the assessment of the impacts of the built environments (BS EN 15978:2011), discussed further at paragraph 40.44, and adopting non-obligatory industry targets and policies in respect of climate resilience.[18] In 2023, the UK Green Building Council issued the 'Systems Enablers for a Circular Economy', which is a self-described 'toolkit' to address the barriers to a circular economy.[19] It identified a single general initiative, that the industry needed to shift from a linear to a circular economy. This strategic focus would ensure that planetary resources would not be exceeded, and that the true cost of non-regenerative materials would tip the balance in favour of secondary material and shift the industry towards a zero carbon trajectory.[20] However, the report acknowledged that this approach is completely contrary to the traditional model of insurance, which favours a linear economy, to which the insurance industry remains regrettably committed. The challenge of the 'mindset shift' identified above must not be oversimplified, but a single transformative approach to be adopted by insurers would be the engagement, support and enabling of the industry's transition from a linear to a circular economy. To enable this strategic objective, there are three key action points:

- Adjust and expand risk assessment management and underwriting to encourage a circular economy (and other environmentally sound client behaviour);
- Innovate on product offerings; and
- Engage with climate change as market leaders and use influence to effect this change.

39.15 Insurers are uniquely placed to encourage clients towards more environmentally sound behaviour, including a circular economy, by adjusting assessment management and underwriting principles. For example, at present, there is little financial incentive for insurers to encourage newly developed or even recycled low carbon alternatives to traditional materials, such as concrete, cement and plasterboard. This is because insurers are focused on short or medium-term premium costs, rather than the whole life costs of these materials. Yet, the dramatic rise in extreme weather events within the last half century is directly connected to high carbon levels: insurers need to recognise that a longer-term outlook on low-carbon alternatives would benefit their own business model.

---

17 Franziska Arnold-Dwyer, 'A Legal Framework for Net Zero Aligned Insurance Products' [2023] 29(2) Connecticut Insurance Law Journal 6.

18 In October 2023, the UK Green Building Council announced its Climate Resilience Roadmap, which had the purpose of setting metrics to help measure climate resilience, establishing industry and industry wide targets, and policies to achieve these. In addition, the pilot version of the UK Net Zero Carbon Buildings Standard was released in September 2024, although this is again a voluntary scheme.

19 UK Green Building Council, 'System Enablers for a Circular Economy' (2023) <https://ukgbc.org/wp-content/uploads/2023/01/Circular-Economy-System-Enablers-Report.pdf> accessed 8 April 2024.

20 ibid 4.

Although the benefits of this approach have been recognised by some,[21] in practical terms, it requires a complete shift in risk assessment, underwriting and indeed insurance policies themselves. This could be done with the engagement of the insured contractor, which should be encouraged and expected to demonstrate its own commitment to the risks posed by climate change, by reference to materials, its construction approach, and its own business model.

39.16 The second means by which insurers can encourage this shift towards a circular economy and net zero is to innovate on the approach to insurance products offered. They could incentivise climate related risk prevention, for example, by offering lower premiums to contractors who can demonstrate their climate related adaptation and resilience measures. Such an initiative would echo measures already taken by insurers in other areas of construction, for example, where cover is predicated on fire precautions being taken. A contractor who has sourced low carbon or recycled materials within the UK could benefit from a lower premium than one who sources an equivalent material without questioning its environmental credentials. Insurance products could actively incentivise existing circular economy practices such as leasing or sharing of equipment. Products could also foster a more collaborative and long-term approach to construction generally, such as integrated project insurance ('IPI'). IPI is a method of procurement and delivery introduced by the UK government in 2014, which insures the client along with all other parties to the project. By reconfiguring the traditional model of liability and risk allocation, the product fosters a holistic team approach, which has benefits far beyond incentivising positive climate change behaviour. That said, insurance companies have obligations to their shareholders, and the very real financial risk of approaches like impact underwriting could be properly incentivised by way of publicly funded initiatives and grants. Further, government engagement will be required from a regulatory position, for example, on how insurance products could be designed to encourage impact underwriting.[22]

39.17 Finally, insurers can effect considerable influence on the construction industry's approach to achieving net zero and a circular economy simply by leading by example, through impact investment. Like impact underwriting, impact investment is a financial approach that pursues ethical or social goals, including sustainability.[23] Insurers are at the top of the global financial model, being a cash-rich industry with huge and widespread investment influence.[24] Beyond vocal commitments to net zero, insurers could harness their considerable financial resources to ensure that their own operations and investments shift to a carbon neutral and truly environmentally beneficial model. As elsewhere, however, the industry response has been inclined to follow rather than to lead. The Association of British Insurers ('ABI') estimates its members could support up to 33% of the £2.7 trillion of investment needed to achieve the UK government's

---

21 Allianz, 'Supporting Customers with Eco-Construction: An Insurance View' (22 February 2022) <https://www.allianz.co.uk/news-and-insight/insight-and-expertise/supporting-customers-with-eco-construction-an-insurance-view.html> accessed 10 April 2024.

22 Arnold-Dwyer, 'A Legal Framework for Net Zero Aligned Insurance Products' (n 15) 27–29.

23 ibid 6–7.

24 Association of British Insurers, 'Insurers as Investors' <https://www.abi.org.uk/data-and-resources/tools-and-resources/regulation/insurers-as-investors/> accessed 10 April 2024.

target of achieving a 78% reduction in carbon emissions by 2035 (as part of its initiative to achieve Net Zero by 2050). Yet, its focus appears to be turned towards what the government can do to support the insurance industry, rather than the other way around.[25] As outlined above, publicly funded support should be available to support the industry's shift in approach – but effective collaboration will require initiative from both the insurance industry itself and public bodies.[26]

Looking forward

39.18 The route to net zero in respect of construction insurance is hampered by the same factors that impede other industries: a lack of a unified approach within the industry itself, poor private–public agreement and dialogue regarding meaningful action, and little financial incentive to shift from a linear economy. A collaborative approach between the public and private sectors is critical to addressing this impasse. That said, the shifting legal and regulatory landscape within the UK and abroad offers some hope that the promises made by the industry to date will indeed be realised in the years to come.

25 Association of British Insurers, 'Pillar Two: Unleashing Investment Capacity' <https://www.abi.org.uk/about-the-abi/sustainability/climate-change-roadmap/pillar-two-unleashing-investment-capacity/> accessed 10 April 2024. See also Department for Business, Energy and Industrial Strategy, 'UK Enshrines New Target in Law to Slash Emissions by 78% by 2035' <https://www.gov.uk/government/news/uk-enshrines-new-target-in-law-to-slash-emissions-by-78-by-2035> accessed 10 April 2024.

26 Arnold-Dwyer, 'A Legal Framework for Net Zero Aligned Insurance Products' (n 15) 38–43.

CHAPTER 40

MEASUREMENT

Patrick Hennessey

Introduction

40.01 The UK built environment is responsible for approximately 25% of the UK's total greenhouse gas ('GHG') emissions.[1] The built environment sector is therefore of critical importance to the UK's Net Zero Strategy, but it is recognised within the construction industry that without a change in the way in which infrastructure projects are delivered, increased carbon emissions associated with construction and operation are likely to contribute to the UK failing to meet its net zero target. As aptly summarised by the Net Zero Infrastructure Industry Coalition, 'whilst net-zero compatible national infrastructure cannot guarantee a net-zero economy, inaction or fragmented action on national infrastructure will all but guarantee that aspirations for a net zero economy will not be achieved'.[2]

40.02 Underlying all the net zero carbon aspirations and obligations of the construction industry is the question of measurement: that is, how to frame measures of carbon reduction, so as to ensure an objective, consistent and agreed approach to compliance with those obligations. A sufficiently clear and common framework for the actual measurement of carbon reduction is a pre-requisite to the objective assessment of carbon reduction measures and the assessment of whether contractual and statutory obligations with respect to carbon reduction are being met.

40.03 At the 26th United Nations Climate Change Conference UK 2021 ('COP 26'), the UK Green Building Council ('UKGBC') launched the 'Net Zero Whole Life Carbon Roadmap' project, with the aim of outlining a common vision and establishing industry wide actions for achieving net zero in the construction, operation and demolition of buildings and infrastructure in the UK. In the 'Net Zero Whole Life Carbon Roadmap: A pathway to Net Zero for the UK Built Environment', the UKGBC identified five key net zero carbon priorities for the government and industry to support and implement, one of which was a unified approach to measurement:

---

1 Environmental Audit Committee, *Building to Net Zero: Costing Carbon in Construction, First Report of Session 2022–23*, 3 (HC 2022–23, 103) <https://publications.parliament.uk/pa/cm5803/cmselect/cmenvaud/103/report.html> accessed 22 October 2024.

2 Net Zero Infrastructure Industry Coalition, 'Is Our Carbon Wallet Empty?: The Embodied Carbon of the National Infrastructure Pipeline' (2021) <https://www.skanska.co.uk/498048/siteassets/about-skanska/media/features/embedded-carbon-infrastructure/nziic-embedded-carbon-in-infrastructure.pdf> accessed 22 October 2024.

> Whole life carbon measurements and agreed limits. To start with mandatory measurement, followed by the phased introduction of embodied carbon limits for new buildings to reduce demand, alongside changes to planning and VAT to incentivise the reuse of existing buildings.[3]

40.04 As explained further below, despite widespread acknowledgment of the importance of establishing a consistent approach to measurement and progress in that direction, there is presently no settled consensus as to measurement, and no single agreed methodology for making net zero claims. It is widely hoped that this situation will be significantly remedied by the UK Net Zero Carbon Buildings Standard, the pilot version of which was launched in September 2024.

40.05 This chapter describes the construction industry's current approach to carbon measurement, seeks to identify relevant contractual terms and standards, and examines certain issues likely to arise in connection with carbon measurement.

40.06 By way of introduction, it is necessary to define certain terms. In particular, the priority with regard to measurement in the 'Net Zero Whole Life Carbon Roadmap' refers to 'whole life carbon' ('WLC'), which is the combined total of two distinct elements: 'operational carbon' and 'embodied carbon'. Operational carbon emissions are the emissions associated with the use of energy within a building. Embodied carbon emissions are the emissions associated with materials, construction, maintenance, repair, demolition and disposal of a building.

40.07 Operational carbon is responsible for a significantly greater proportion of global carbon emissions than embodied carbon, but not to the extent that justifies the disparity with which the two have, until relatively recently, been considered. In 2021, the UN Environment Programme estimated that embodied carbon was responsible for approximately 12% of global carbon emissions: on its own a hugely significant figure. By the same estimate, operational carbon was responsible for approximately 28% of global carbon emissions.

40.08 Until very recently, government policy in respect of carbon emissions has focused entirely on 'operational carbon emissions', seeking to reduce these emissions by increasing the energy efficiency of the built environment. In contrast, 'embodied carbon emissions' have been ignored and are not required by current policy to be assessed or controlled, other than on a voluntary basis. This uneven approach is inadequate and incapable of supporting the UK's Net Zero Strategy.

40.09 A disproportionate focus on operational carbon emissions not only ignores the substantial contribution and effect of embodied carbon emissions, but may also be counterproductive. Hitherto insufficient consideration has been given to balancing the anticipated operational carbon benefit to be derived from, for example, installing

---

3 UK Green Building Council, 'Net Zero Whole Life Carbon Roadmap: A Pathway to Net Zero for the UK Built Environment' (2021) 10 <https://ukgbc.org/wp-content/uploads/2021/11/UKGBC-Whole-Life-Carbon-Roadmap-A-Pathway-to-Net-Zero.pdf> accessed 18 April 2024.

additional thermal efficiency measures or using a specific material, against the potential embodied carbon burden of that same measure or material. In certain instances, over the life of a building, the embodied carbon emissions associated with a specific material or element may actually cancel out or even outweigh any reduction in operational carbon emissions, thereby undermining the ultimate carbon reduction goal.

40.10 Self-evidently, any coherent approach to reducing carbon emissions must include and consider together both embodied carbon and operational carbon and be aimed at reducing WLC emissions. However, in the absence of any national policy requiring them to be measured or controlled, there is no agreed methodology for the assessment of embodied emissions, which it is suggested remains 'unfamiliar territory' to developers.[4]

40.11 This concern is borne out by the Royal Institute of Chartered Surveyors ('RICS') Sustainability Report 2023, which reports that of nearly 4,600 real estate and construction professionals from across more than 30 countries, 43% of respondents took no measurement of carbon across projects at all, while only 16% measured carbon and used this to guide their selection of materials and components. The significance of a coordinated approach to measurement is perhaps best demonstrated by the 25% of respondents, who stated that they would like to measure carbon if there was a standardised approach to doing so.[5] A key conclusion of the RICS Sustainability Report 2023 is that 'the measurement of carbon emissions across the whole life cycle must become common practice'.[6]

Whole life carbon approach

40.12 Notwithstanding the current lack of national policy with regard to embedded carbon emissions, the government recognises that in order to achieve net zero, the construction industry must adopt a whole life approach. By definition, this includes (and therefore requires consistent measurement of) embodied carbon omissions.

40.13 In July 2021, the UK government proposed that the Building Regulations 2010 be amended by the addition of a new Part Z, providing specific guidance on WLC and requiring *inter alia* the assessment and reporting of WLC emissions, and reasonable provision to be made to reduce WLC. It subsequently identified the need to improve reporting and develop shared approaches to embodied emissions in its 'Net Zero Strategy: Build Back Greener' in October 2021. The Net Zero Strategy was published at the same time that 'Procurement Policy Note 06/21: Taking account of Carbon Reduction Plans in the procurement of major government contracts' came into effect – which required all companies bidding for UK government contracts worth more than £5 million per annum to commit to achieving net zero by 2050.

4 Environmental Audit Committee, *Building to Net Zero: Costing Carbon in Construction, First Report of Session 2022–23* (n 1) 10.
5 Royal Institution of Chartered Surveyors, 'RICS Sustainability Report' (2023) 15 <https://www.rics.org/news-insights/rics-sustainability-report-2023> accessed 22 October 2024.
6 ibid 18.

40.14 Further, since September 2022, all central government departments, their executive agencies and non-departmental public bodies have been required to take a whole life approach to reducing carbon emissions and specifically to require a Whole-Life Carbon Assessment ('WLCA') pertaining to the procurement of new built assets or the large-scale refurbishment of existing buildings and infrastructure.[7]

40.15 In turn, the construction industry has also recognised the importance of establishing a baseline for and targeting reduction in embodied carbon emissions[8] and adopting a whole life approach.[9] The UKGBC's Net Zero Whole Life Carbon Roadmap includes a 'Stakeholders Action Plan' which identified the establishment of WLC as a 'first order' consideration in initial site development appraisals and decision making. It also proposed the establishment of a net zero carbon client brief on all development projects, which establishes WLC as a 'primary decision-making metric to be evaluated at each RIBA Stage'.[10]

Carbon measurement

40.16 As neatly summarised in the RICS Sustainability Report 2023: 'what we can measure, we can then manage – understanding the scale and scope of emissions is a key first step.'[11] This section looks at the differences in approaches to the measurement of operational carbon, embodied carbon and WLC emissions.

(i) *Operational carbon*

40.17 As described above, to date the construction industry (and government and other industries and stakeholders) has focused mainly on the reduction of operational carbon through energy reduction targets. The Building Act 1984 gave the Secretary of State power to make Building Regulations for the purposes *inter alia* of furthering the conservation of fuel and power, which was a functional requirement of Approved Document Part L. In 1995, the Building Regulations were amended to introduce the Standard Assessment Procedure for Energy Rating of Dwellings ('SAP'). All new build dwellings were required to be subject to a SAP calculation and to have a resultant SAP Rating.

40.18 A SAP Rating is based on the energy costs associated with space heating, water heating, ventilation and lighting, less costs savings from on-site energy generation technologies. It is adjusted for floor area to give an objective expression on a scale from 1 to 100. The higher the SAP Rating, the lower the running costs.

---

7 UK Government Commercial Function, 'Promoting Net Zero Carbon and Sustainability in Construction: Guidance Note' (2022) para 3.2.3 <https://assets.publishing.service.gov.uk/media/631222898fa8f54234c6a508/20220901-Carbon-Net-Zero-Guidance-Note.pdf> accessed 22 October 2024.
8 Construction Leadership Council, 'Construct Zero Performance Framework' (2023) <https://www.constructionleadershipcouncil.co.uk/workstream/co2nstructzero/the-performance-framework/> accessed 22 October 2024.
9 UK Green Building Council, 'Net Zero Whole Life Carbon Roadmap: A Pathway to Net Zero for the UK Built Environment' (n 3).
10 ibid.
11 Royal Institution of Chartered Surveyors, 'RICS Sustainability Report' (n 5) 2.

40.19 In 2002, Approved Document Part L was divided into parts L1 and L2, applying to domestic and non-domestic buildings respectively. In Part L1, the SAP Ratings energy rating method was replaced by a new 'Carbon Index Method'; while Part L2 included a carbon performance calculation methodology for non-domestic buildings. In order to comply with Part L1, the Carbon Index for a dwelling could not be less than 8.0. In order to comply with Part L2, using the Carbon Emissions Calculation Method, the calculated annual carbon emissions of a proposed building could be no greater than those from a notional building of the same size and shape designed to comply with the Elemental Method.

40.20 In 2006, the Building Regulations were amended *inter alia* to implement the requirement of Directive 2002/91/EC on the energy performance of buildings, that EU member states adopt a whole-building calculation method for assessing the carbon emissions of new buildings. The 2006 amendments marked a significant change in approach, by introducing specific carbon emissions targets. New regulation 17B provided that the Secretary of State 'shall approve minimum energy performance requirements for new buildings, in the form of target CO_2 emission rates'. By new regulation 17C, new buildings were not permitted to exceed the relevant approved target carbon emissions rate.

40.21 Part L2 as amended replaced the Elemental, Whole Building and Carbon Emissions Calculation Methods with a single, unified approach to compliance with energy efficiency requirements, by reference to five criteria. The first of which was: 'the calculated CO_2 emission rate for the building as constructed (the building emission rate, ('BER')) must not be greater than the target rate (the target emission rate, ('TER')).'[12] The TER and BER are expressed as the mass of CO_2 emitted per year per square metre of the total useful floor area of the building, calculated using either the Simplified Building Energy Model ('SBEM') or another approved software tool.

40.22 The SBEM applies the National Calculation Methodology, as defined by the Health and Safety Executive, by calculating the annual energy use for proposed buildings and comparing it with the energy use of a comparable notional building making use of standard data sets.

40.23 In respect of residential dwellings, Part L1 was also amended to introduce the requirement for an Energy Performance Certificate ('EPC') – a publicly visible rating of the energy efficiency of a building (from A being the most efficient, to G being the least efficient) based on the SAP calculation.

40.24 In 2013, the Building Regulations were amended *inter alia* to deliver a 6% reduction in carbon emission rates for residential dwellings and a 9% reduction in carbon emission rates for non-domestic buildings, with updated references to the National Calculation Methodology modelling guide.

---

12 Approved Document L2A to The Building Regulations 2010 section 1, para 1.4.

40.25 In 2021, the government announced further amendments to the Building Regulations, specifically intended to form part of the Net Zero Strategy. The amendments introduced what were, in effect, interim measures expressly anticipating a further set of amendments in 2025 to implement the planned Future Homes Standard.

40.26 In respect of residential dwellings, Part L1 introduced new carbon emissions targets requiring that all new homes produce 31% less carbon emissions and introduced a new SAP calculation *inter alia* setting greater insulation requirements. For existing homes, a new minimum standard for fabric efficiency was introduced. In respect of non-domestic buildings, Part L2 introduced a new carbon emissions target requiring all new buildings to produce 27% less carbon emissions.

40.27 The development of Part L has provided an effective framework for the calculation of operational carbon measured as $kgCO_2e/yr$ in respect of the development of new buildings, but as described above, this alone is insufficient to implement the whole life approach and consideration must also be given to embodied carbon.

(ii) *Embodied carbon*

40.28 As described above, embodied carbon is the amount of CO_2 emitted during a product's entire life cycle including raw material extraction, transport, manufacture, assembly, installation, maintenance, disassembly or demolition and decomposition.

40.29 It has been relatively straightforward for manufacturers to provide data on embodied carbon emissions up to the point a material leaves the factory – so-called, cradle to gate embodied carbon. In contrast, later embodied emissions in the life cycle – cradle to site (of the building) and/or cradle to grave (end of life of a building) have been overlooked. For example, the University of Bath's Inventory of Carbon and Energy ('ICE') lists embodied carbon to the end of the manufacturing process for various materials. Nonetheless, the ICE database is a useful source of embodied carbon data and is widely used within the construction industry.[13]

40.30 The development of the life-cycle approach in the 1970s resulted in the development of Life Cycle Assessment methodologies incorporating embodied carbon and subsequently, the development of International Standards to provide consistency in evaluation. Construction products tend to use a wide range of raw materials and different processes to produce different products used in many different ways. In general terms, consideration to embodied carbon must be given during *inter alia*; (i) extraction of virgin resources; (ii) manufacturing; (iii) packaging; (iv) transport; (v) waste impacts; (vi) site impacts; (vii) maintenance and refurbishment; and (viii) demolition and disposal.

40.31 Since the early 2000s, it was recognised by the European Commission that different national schemes for assessing the environmental impact of buildings risks confusion. Thus, the EU Member States agreed to ask the European Committee for

---

13 Circular Ecology, 'Embodied Carbon – The ICE Database' <https://circularecology.com/embodied-carbon-footprint-database.html> accessed 22 October 2024.

Standardization ('CEN') to develop a horizontal approach to the measurement of embodied and operational environment impacts of construction products and whole buildings across the entire life cycle. Since 2005, the European Standards Technical Committee ('CEN/TC 350') has been developing these standards. In Britain, the work of CEN/TC 350 is mirrored by the British Standards Institution ('BSI') Committee B/558.

40.32 From this came the requirement to produce Environmental Product Declarations ('EPDs') to provide a standardised way to collect data (including embodied carbon data), assess impact, communicate the information and review the environmental performance of construction products. EPDs can produce credible information as to environmental performance in a variety of situations *inter alia*: (i) by reference to individual units (e.g. per m^3 of cement); (ii) by reference to performance based on function of a product installed (e.g. per unit of thermal resistance for insulation per linear metre of beam); and (iii) performance at a building level over the full life cycle.

40.33 Databases are key to any approach measuring embodied carbon. The working groups under CEN/TC 350 compile databases for the purpose of undertaking Life Cycle Assessments ('LCAs') and EPDs. In the UK, the BRE Green Guide provides cradle to grave embodied greenhouse gas emissions (CO_2E) data per m^2 for each element of a project. Similar cradle to gate embodied carbon data can be found in pricing books, such as the Hutchins UK Blackbook.[14]

40.34 EPDs have a wide application: (i) to inform product designers; (ii) to promote the credible and transparent marketing of products; (iii) to provide important information in the supply chain; (iv) to inform procurement; (v) to be incorporated into and set performance specifications; (vi) to inform purchasers and end users; and (vii) as a regulatory lever. Brighton & Hove City Council is the first UK council requiring an embodied carbon assessment of developments as part of its planning permission process.

40.35 However, the various approaches to measuring embodied carbon mean that is very difficult to make comparisons between buildings with any certainty. For example:

- Is the scope for the EPD cradle to gate or cradle to grave? Is Transport included? Is Site Waste included?
- Is the assumed Building Life 50, 60 or 100 years (or longer)?
- What reporting indicators are being used? Is it CEN/TC 350, BRE Ecopoints, Embodied Carbon, or Embodied Greenhouse Gases?
- Which elements of the building are included?
- Which data sources are used? Is it ICE, EPD, LCA?

14 *Hutchins UK Building Blackbook 2010: The Capital Costs and Embodied CO2 Guide, Volume 2 – Major Works* (Franklin & Andrews 2010).

40.36 Without a single, standardised approach to measuring embodied carbon, it has proven difficult to provide any sort of 'benchmark' data.

40.37 In the UK, the primary methods and standards for measuring a product's embodied carbon are:

- LCA is a technique to assess the environment impacts associated with a product or service over its full life cycle and was one of the original methods to provide embodied carbon data. ISO Standards ISO 14040:2006 and ISO 14044:2006 were developed to define LCA studies which, subject to peer review, can be used to make public comparison between different products;
- EPDs are standardised documents, freely available in Europe and elsewhere, covering a wide range of construction products. In the UK, this includes the BRE's Certified Environmental Profiles (the Green Book);[15]
- A carbon footprint for a construction product is analogous to its embodied carbon. In the UK, the Carbon Trust, the BSI and DEFRA developed PAS 2050:2008 as a standard method for calculating the carbon footprint of products and services.

40.38 BS EN 15804 provides the core set of Product Category Rules ('PCRs') for the Europe-wide generation of EPDs for construction products. It defines the methods for data collection, calculation of environmental impact and presentation of information. BS EN 15804 also defines the various building life cycle stages that can be included with LCAs and EPDs:

- Modules A1–A3 relate to the product stage;
- Modules A4–A5 relate to the construction process stage;
- Modules B1–B7 relate to the use stage;
- Modules C1–C4 relate to the end of life stage; and
- Module D relates to supplementary information beyond the life cycle of construction works.

40.39 In the latest version of EN 15804, reporting of Module C and D impacts in EPDs is mandatory. Clause 5.2 states that 'all construction products and materials shall declare modules A1–A3, modules C1–C4 and module D'.

40.40 In the absence of UK regulation of embodied carbon and a standard approach to assessment or benchmarks, recent industry guides and initiatives have proposed embodied carbon targets:

---

15 'Green Book Live' <https://www.greenbooklive.com/> accessed 22 April 2024.

- The London Energy Transformation Initiative ('LETI') Climate Emergency Design Guide[16] proposes following baseline and 2020 and 2030 best practice targets for embodied carbon (Modules A1–A5).

- The RIBA 2030 Climate Challenge, version 2 (2021) proposes baseline, 2025 and 2030 targets by reference to the RICS WLC (modules A1–A5, B1–B5, C1–C4 etc.) and requires WLC Analysis.

40.41 Organisations are adopting these methods and approaches to measure and set targets for the reduction of embodied carbon emissions (see for example, Westminster City Council's January 2024 Embodied Carbon Evidence Base study which followed *inter alia* the UKGBC, LETI and RIBA guidance). However, further progress and direction are required in order to support the WLC approach as described below.

(iii) *Whole life carbon*

40.42 As described above, it is fast becoming accepted that achieving net zero will require a whole life approach and assessment of the carbon emissions associated with the design, construction, operation and ultimate disposal of buildings and civil engineering structures. Support for WLCA comes from a number of recently published embodied carbon guides:

- The RICS Professional Standard: Whole life carbon assessment for the built environment, version 2 November 2023 (effective from 1 July 2024) ('the RICS WLCA'),[17] which states at 4.1:

  > A complete WLCA undertaken in compliance with this standard must account for carbon removals and emissions arising over the entire life cycle of a built asset (modules A–C). It must also separately account for the loads and benefits beyond the system boundary considered in module D.

- The Institution of Structural Engineers ('IStructE') guide on how to calculate embodied carbon, dated 31 March 2022,[18] which states:

  > [B]est practice is to consider whole life embodied carbon (Stages A–C, with D reported separately) so that we not only minimise embodied carbon emissions today but also consider the future emissions impacts of using the asset, durability, longevity, end of life scenarios, reusability, and recyclability. Structural engineers should take ownership for all of the emissions that they cause. This will ensure that future

---

16 London Energy Transformation Initiative, 'Climate Emergency Design Guide' (2020) <https://www.leti.uk/_files/ugd/252d09_3b0f2acf2bb24c019f5ed9173fc5d9f4.pdf> accessed 22 April 2024.

17 'Whole Life Carbon Assessment for the Built Environment' <https://www.rics.org/profession-standards/rics-standards-and-guidance/sector-standards/construction-standards/whole-life-carbon-assessment> accessed 28 November 2023.

18 The Institution of Structural Engineers, 'How to Calculate Embodied Carbon (Third Edition)' (2024) 3rd edn <https://www.istructe.org/journal/volumes/volume-102-(2024)/issue-9/whats-new-institution-carbon-calculation-tools/> accessed 22 October 2024.

emissions and resource consumption are also kept to a minimum. Industry guidance on calculating emissions for Modules B1–B5, C1–C4 and D1–D2 has improved since this guide was first published[8]. If Stages A–C are calculated, it is important to report upfront carbon (A0–A5) results alongside A–C results so that the short-term and long-term emissions impacts can be considered alongside each other.

- The latest version of the ICE database (v3.0),[19] which states:

  The modular approach of the EU wide standards EN 15978 and EN 15804 is particularly encouraged, due to the transparency it brings to method for recycling. These standards require that the lifecycle results are broken down by lifecycle stage. Module A being cradle to gate. Module B is in-use. Module C is end of life. Module D is benefits and burdens beyond the lifecycle.

- The Whole Life-Cycle Carbon Assessments draft guidance published by the Mayor of London,[20] which states:

  In developing a WLC assessment for compliance with Policy SI 2, applicants should follow BS EN 15978 using the RICS PS as the methodology for assessment.

  A WLC assessment should cover the entirety of modules A, B, C and D to comply with Policy SI 2. Applicants should note that they will be expected to report against all of these life-cycle modules in their WLC assessment, not just the minimum requirements identified in the RICS PS.

  In order to transform London to a resource-efficient, zero-carbon economy, it is essential that these issues are given careful consideration at the design stage. The Circular Economy Statement for the development will set out the carbon reduction activities undertaken for Module D. The potential carbon costs or benefits associated with these activities should be calculated and included in the appropriate section of the WLC assessment.

  The objective is to facilitate future reuse, recovery and recycling at the highest possible level. The applicant is required to develop realistic and feasible scenarios, supported by evidence, to support any carbon benefits included in the reporting of Module D. Due to the speculative nature of these scenarios this module is reported separately. Module D is essentially (in combination with module C3) the 'circular economy' module. Its importance is that it provides a carbon emissions quantification of the potential circular benefits of a scheme.

- The Whole Life-Cycle Carbon Assessments draft guidance published by the Mayor of London also proposed the following WLC benchmarks and aspirational targets:

---

19 Circular Ecology, 'Embodied Carbon – The ICE Database' (n 13).
20 Mayor of London, 'London Plan Guidance Whole Life-Cycle Carbon Assessments' (2022) <https://www.london.gov.uk/sites/default/files/lpg_-_wlca_guidance.pdf> accessed 22 April 2024.

Benchmark
- Carbon at Completion (A1–A5) 900 to 1000 kg $CO2e/m^2$ GIA
- Carbon over Life Cycle 400 to 500 kg $CO2e/m^2$ GIA

Aspirational Benchmark
- Carbon at Completion (A1–A5) 550 to 600 kg $CO2e/m^2$ GIA
- Carbon over Life Cycle 250 to 300 kg $CO2e/m^2$ GIA

Calculation methods and standards

40.43 Certain calculation methods and standards in respect of operational carbon and embodied carbon are identified above. In respect of WLC, any assessment must account for a building's:

- operational carbon emissions (both regulated and unregulated);
- embodied carbon emissions; and
- any future potential carbon emissions 'benefits' post end of life, including benefits from reuse and recycling of building structure and materials.

40.44 In the UK, the methods of calculation and standards for the assessment of the environmental impacts of the built environment are provided in BS EN 15978:2011.[21]

40.45 The practical implementation of BS EN 15978:2011 in the context of WLCA is the RICS WLCA. The RICS WLCA is a particularly significant document in the current landscape and stands as the most effective and increasingly widely adopted standard currently in existence, in large part due to the following features:

- Methodological consistency;
- Comprehensiveness and modularity – expanding on the life cycle modules introduced in BS EN 15978:2011 to better cover and differentiate between sources of carbon;
- Process integration – provides guidance on integrating WLCAs into all aspects and stages of a project as a core decision making and feedback tool;
- Alignment with cost planning – including established frameworks such as ICMS 3 and RICS NRM;
- Consistency with carbon management – it works with the GHG Protocol and any carbon management framework;

21 The British Standards Institution, 'BS EN 15978:2011, Sustainability of Construction Works. Assessment of Environmental Performance of Buildings. Calculation Method' (2011).

- Digital integration; and
- Holistic approach – it provides a combined method to assess embodied and operational carbon together.

40.46 While it strictly only applies to members of RICS undertaking a WLCA, as stated above, the standard is increasingly being adopted more widely and, importantly, by statutory and regulatory authorities. For example, the Mayor of London expressly identifies the RICS WLCA as 'underpinning' BS EN 15978:2011, and requires it to be followed and applied in order that a WLCA complies with Policy SI 2 Policy SI 2 regarding planning applications in Greater London.

40.47 In December 2023, the Breakthrough Agenda[22] was launched at COP 26. It provided a collaborative framework to accelerate international action on climate change and close the 'collaboration gap', which was identified in the Breakthrough Agenda Report 2022 as undermining progress towards meeting the Paris Agreement's global decarbonisation targets.

40.48 The Breakthrough Agenda aims to make near-zero emissions and resilient buildings a new normal in all regions by 2030. One of the key recommendations to achieve this goal is that the built environment sector harmonise key definitions and assessment methodologies and align certification schemes.

40.49 In support of this goal, in March 2024, RICS published its Implementation Guide: Global harmonisation of whole life carbon assessments ('RICS Harmonisation Guide').[23] The RICS Harmonisation Guide provides a clear framework for achieving that recommendation, by creating a global harmonized WLCA framework and standard (essentially the RICS WLCA standard). RICS also made available various resources to make the adoption and implementation of the WLCA standard as straightforward as possible including, as discussed further below, the RICS National playbook for implementing whole life carbon assessments (the 'RICS WLCA Playbook').[24]

Acting on WLC measurements

40.50 The Mayor of London's Whole Life-Cycle Carbon Assessments draft guidance provides perhaps the most useful illustration of how WLC measurements can be most effectively acted upon – that is, by providing the framework for the assessment of performance and ultimately compliance with both contractual and legal obligations.

40.51 As described above, the development of Part L of the Building Regulations and the incorporation of successively more effective and accurate methods and calculations *inter alia* for measuring operational carbon emissions, has allowed the government

22 'Breakthrough Agenda' <https://breakthroughagenda.org/> accessed 22 April 2024.
23 Royal Institution of Chartered Surveyors, 'Global Harmonisation of Whole Life Carbon Assessments' (2024).
24 Royal Institution of Chartered Surveyors, 'National Playbook for Implementing Whole Life Carbon Assessments' (2024).

to legislate for specific targets and thresholds for the reduction of operational carbon emissions. The adoption of a standard approach to the measurement of WLC emissions will allow for the setting of specific targets and thresholds, as contractual requirements and legal requirements.

40.52 It is unfortunate, therefore, that the government's planned further revisions to the Building Regulations still fail to have any regard to embodied carbon emissions and therefore make no provision for WLC measurement. As this book goes to press, it remains the government's intention to publish new regulations and associated guidance in 2024 implementing the 2025 Future Homes and Buildings Standards, which will come into force in 2025.

40.53 The 2025 Future Homes and Buildings Standards are intended to deliver significant carbon savings and establish new homes and non-domestic buildings that are 'zero-carbon ready'. It is difficult to see how this can be achieved if no provision is made for the measurement of embodied and WLC emissions. The UK government appears to acknowledge this fundamental shortcoming in the 'Future Homes and Buildings Standards: 2023 consultation' document. The perfunctory statement that embodied carbon 'is beyond the scope of this consultation and the existing Building Regulations' is immediately followed by the assertion that '[w]e recognise, however, that embodied carbon is a significant contributor to the WLC of a building and that it is therefore crucial that we take steps to address it. The government intends to consult on our approach to measuring and reducing embodied carbon in new buildings in due course.'

40.54 There is a dissonance between the government's express recognition of the significance of embodied carbon on the one hand, and its statement of vague intent to consult on its approach to measuring and reducing it 'in due course', on the other hand. This chapter does not comment on the specific measures expected to be implemented by the new standards, but by failing to provide for the measurement of embodied and WLC emissions – which has been a universally recognised key recommendation and/or priority to reduce carbon emissions for a number of years – the 2025 Future Homes and Buildings Standards are effectively out-of-date before they have even been published.

40.55 A more comprehensive and effective approach to WLC measurement is expected of the UK Net Zero Carbon Building Standard, the pilot version of which was launched in September 2024. The UK Net Zero Carbon Building Standard is the product of an unprecedented cross-industry initiative jointly founded by members of RIBA, CIBSE, IStructE, BBP, LETI, RICS and UKGBC and it is supported by representatives from almost every sector of the built environment industry. It is envisaged that this Standard will influence the specification criteria for buildings through mandating certain performance limits, targets and requirements to allow buildings to be classified as net zero carbon. These limits, targets and requirements will influence systems, material choices and specification.

40.56 While the planned UK Net Zero Carbon Building Standard will be voluntary, it is noteworthy that it expressly states that 'it could however, be used to support policymakers in setting robust requirements that deliver buildings aligned with a 1.5°C decarbonisation pathway for the UK. The Governance Board and Technical Steering Group are open to engagement with local and national planning authorities to enable this.' Until both standards are published, further speculation is futile, but it is not hard to imagine the 2025 Future Homes and Building Standards being rapidly superseded, while the UK Net Zero Carbon Building Standard and RICS WLCA provide a framework for future contractual and legal obligations with regards to WLC measurements.

40.57 Pending the publication of either standard and in the absence of substantive guidance or direction from the government to facilitate significant progress in WLC measurement, there are interim actions and steps which can be taken to generate and support the WLC framework necessary to achieve net zero. In the RICS WLCA Playbook,[25] RICS identified the following 7 recommended actions on the part of national governments and stakeholders to implement WLCA:

- Define national WLCA methodology;
- Develop local capacity and knowledge;
- Set decarbonisation pathways for buildings;
- Establish national data repository and reporting platforms;
- Make WLCA mandatory for all buildings;
- Update regulations, building codes and public procurement;
- Track progress and update targets.

40.58 The description of the UK as a 'world-leader' on climate change can be compared with the effective extent to which it has progressed, let alone completed, these recommended actions.

Contractual terms and mechanisms

40.59 This chapter started with noting that despite the widespread acknowledgement of the importance of a unified approach to measurement as a pre-requisite to the objective assessment of carbon reduction measures, there is presently no such common framework. The various plans, proposals, projects and protocols described above could be said to be moving towards this goal, but arguably too slowly and haphazardly.

40.60 Until such time as a clear and common framework for effective measurement of carbon reduction is firmly entrenched, universally accepted and understood, it is difficult to establish standard contractual terms and model mechanisms relating to measurement. Furthermore, until such time as required by law and industry practice

---

25 ibid.

and custom, no matter how well intentioned, contracting parties are unlikely to agree to potentially onerous provisions and or obligations.

40.61 It is unsurprising therefore that at present, standard form construction contracts do not contain specific measurement clauses, even where they do include sustainability provisions such as:

- The FIDIC Red, Yellow and Silver Books contain provisions requiring the contractor to take steps to protect the environment. This includes clause 4.18, which ensures that emissions do not exceed those stated in the specification or prescribed by law;

- The JCT Design and Build Contract 2024 has introduced a provision within the Contractor's Obligations at 2.1.5 as follows:

  > The Contractor is encouraged to suggest economically viable amendments to the Works which, if instructed as a Change, may result in an improvement in environmental performance and sustainability in the carrying out of the Works or of the completed Works and a reduction in environmental impact, provided that no instruction shall extend the Contractor's obligations in relation to design under this Contract.

40.62 However, steps are already being taken to promote more detailed and stringent contractual provisions to achieve net zero, for example:

- In November 2021, FIDIC published a 'Climate Change Charter' aiming *inter alia* to reduce the carbon footprint of the industry. FIDIC has pledged to provide best practice templates and clauses and guidance, including with respect to how embodied and operational carbon can be reduced;[26]

- In April 2022, NEC published a consultation on a new optional 'sustainability' clause X29 which as finalised in June 2022, provides *inter alia*: (i) for the inclusion of 'Climate Change Requirements' in the scope; and (ii) for the production of a 'Climate Change Execution Plan'.

40.63 The Chancery Lane Project ('TCLP') is referred to numerous times throughout this book as befits the importance of the work it does. Its library of model 'climate clauses' contains *inter alia* the following model clauses relevant to measurement:

- 'Willow's Clause' – which sets a carbon budget for construction projects along with the financial budget, to reduce GHG emissions (similarly 'Tristan's Clause');

---

26 Presumably along the lines of the TCLP model clause 'Olivia's Clause', which sets targets for contractors and subcontractors to reduce greenhouse gas emissions. Scope 3 emissions often account for the biggest chunk of an organisation's total inventory, to be included in the FIDIC EPC contracts.

- 'Daniel's Clause' – which sets assessment criteria for sustainable practices in construction works task orders to drive improvement in environmental and sustainability performance during the contract term;
- 'Dharna & Keshan's Clause' – which requires parties to measure their emissions and report on them, in line with the climate reporting framework in Aotearoa New Zealand's Financial Reporting Act 2013;
- 'Millie's Clause' – which incentivises insured parties to meet emissions reduction targets by actively transitioning their business operations to net zero, for example, by engaging green suppliers and consuming renewable energy; and
- 'Ming's Clause' – which provides a Target Product Carbon Footprint budget (which reduces over time) for each product manufactured and supplied pursuant to the contract.

40.64 These are just a small illustration of the various detailed model clauses produced by TCLP which, in conjunction with its guides and toolkit, provide an impressive basis for the development and incorporation of meaningful contractual terms and mechanisms.

CHAPTER 41

CONSTRUCTION PROFESSIONALS AND THE DUTY TO ADVISE ON NET ZERO AND CLIMATE CHANGE

Marion Smith KC, Ruth Keating and Camilla ter Haar

Overview

41.01 In 2020, Sir James Bevan, the chief executive of the Environment Agency, said that '[t]ackling climate change must become a default position for everyone.'[1]

41.02 Construction professionals are no exception. They will increasingly be expected to work towards ensuring the delivery of climate resilient buildings and infrastructure which are able to withstand extreme weather events, as well as constructing or renovating in a manner which reduces operational and embodied carbon emissions. This will require construction professionals to keep up to date with relevant regulations, legislation, technology and building materials. Existing and well-developed duties are likely to be applied to address situations where there may have been a failure to mitigate the effects of a changing climate on a project, or where there has been a failure to adapt to the effects of a changing climate.

41.03 The various types of claims a construction professional might face include:

- Claims in relation to the methodologies of building, or how buildings are built. Claims may include those in relation to the development and use of new, cutting-edge technologies and untested methods, as well as relating to material selection, with the goal of reducing operational and embodied carbon emissions; and

- Claims in relation to the finished building, or what is built. Claims may include those in relation to the failure to take into account climate change and climate-change-related events and in relation to the failure to design and/or build a more climate-resilient building.

1 Said in the context of the Environment Agency launching its five year plan. See Environment Agency, 'Press Release: Business as Usual Won't Tackle the Challenges We Face, Warns Environment Agency' (2020) <https://www.gov.uk/government/news/business-as-usual-won-t-tackle-the-challenges-we-face-warns-environment-agency> accessed 3 May 2024.

41.04 The general law of contract and tort applies to net zero and climate change disputes in the same way as it does to any other form of dispute.[2] In this section, we focus on seven key questions of particular concern to professional construction designers, such as architects, engineers and those who undertake design obligations in relation to these disputes:

- To what extent will the standard of reasonable skill and care be assessed by reference to professional Codes of Practice?
- How should a professional designer approach the use of an untested design or technique, to minimise the risk of a finding of sub-standard performance of his or her retainer?
- What is the extent of a professional designer's duty to warn the client of the risk in relation to untried materials or techniques?
- When, if ever, is the fact that other professionals may have acted just as negligently, sufficient to avoid liability?
- To what extent, if at all, will an audit trail and records of the design process be important?
- When will strict liability be imposed on the professional designer?
- What express obligations in relation to net zero and climate change are imposed on a contractor who undertakes design and build responsibilities under major standard form contracts?

2 For guidance on this topic, reference can be made to standard textbooks such as *Chitty on Contract*, *Clerk & Lindsell on Torts* and *Jackson & Powell on Professional Liability*. In this context, see particularly Richard Wilmot-Smith and Paul Darling, *Wilmot-Smith on Construction Contracts* (4th edn, Oxford University Press 2021) chapter 5.

Duties owed by construction professionals: Standards of care with reference to professional guidance and codes of conduct

41.05 Professional codes of practice may be good,[3] but not conclusive,[4] evidence of what is reasonable care and skill when considering a professional's obligations. Whilst the term 'construction professional' potentially encompasses a wide range of disciplines, for the purposes of this section, we focus on those who have a pivotal role in the design process: architects and engineers.

41.06 The codes of conduct issued by professional bodies relevant to architects and engineers reveal clear obligations in relation to climate change and net zero. We note, in particular, the obligations:

- To keep up to date; and
- To consider the work's impact on the environment.

(i) *Architects*

41.07 The architecture profession is regulated by the Architects Registration Board ('ARB').[5] Section 13(1) of the Architects Act 1997 requires the ARB to issue a code laying down standards of professional conduct and practice, expected of those registered as architects under the Architects Act 1997.[6] The ARB is to keep the code under review and vary its provisions whenever it considers it appropriate to do so.[7] The current form of the Architects Code is dated January 2017.

41.08 The Royal Institution of British Architects ('RIBA') is a professional voluntary membership organisation for architects. The RIBA Code of Professional Conduct sets out the standards of conduct and practice that RIBA requires of its members. The

---

3 See Anthony Dugdale, *Clerk & Lindsell on Torts* (24th edn, Sweet & Maxwell 2023) para 7-200. For example, in relation to financial advisers, see *Seymour v Caroline Ockwell & Co* [2005] EWHC 1137 (QB) per His Honour Judge Havelock-Allan QC at [77]: 'I accept that whilst the ambit of the duty of care owed by a financial adviser at common law is not necessarily co-extensive with the duties owed by that adviser under the applicable regulatory regime, the regulations afford strong evidence as to what is expected of a competent adviser in most situations (see *Lloyd Cheyham & Co. Ltd v Eversheds* (1985) 2 PN 154).' This was cited by the Court of Appeal in *Green and Rowley v The Royal Bank of Scotland plc* [2013] EWCA Civ 1197 [18].

4 *Snow v Royal United Hospitals Bath NHS Foundation Trust* [2023] EWHC 42 (KB), in which HHJ Richard Roberts sitting as a Judge of the High Court cited Birss J in *Price v Cwm Taf University Health Board* [2019] PIQR P14 and held at [69] that whilst failure to follow NICE guidance was 'not prima facie evidence of negligence, there would need to be an explanation for not following NICE's guidance'. See also *Mrs Marion O'Brien (Administratrix of the Estate of Mr John Berry (Deceased)) v Guy's & St Thomas' NHS Trust* [2022] EWHC 2735 (KB) in which HHJ Tindal, sitting as a Judge of the High Court, reviewed the authorities in relation to the law on *Bolam* and held at [88(5)] that 'What ultimately matters is whether the conduct fell within a Bolam-compliant practice in the usual way. … Just as guidelines are no substitute for clinical judgment and expert evidence, they are no substitute (nor a shortcut) for the *Bolam/Bolitho* approach. However, as clinical guidelines are relevant, practitioners and experts should consider whether any national clinical guidelines were applicable – and if any 'in-house' guidelines should be disclosed.'

5 Under the Architects Act 1997, the ARB, as the profession's regulator, maintains a UK register of all qualified architects.

6 Architects Act 1997, SI 1997/22 s 13(1).

7 ibid s 13(2).

current version is dated April 2021. It is used to judge the conduct of members in relation to disciplinary complaints.

(a) The duty to keep up to date

41.09 Standard 2, paragraph 2.4 of the Architects Code states that an architect is:[8]

> Expected to keep your knowledge and skills relevant to your professional work up to date and be aware of the content of any guidelines issued by ARB from time to time.

41.10 Guidance issued on 11 May 2022, in relation to Standard 2 of the Architects Code, addresses the competence expected of an architect. Notably, the guidance states:[9]

> Competence is not a static achievement but an evolving standard, so the knowledge and skills relevant to your professional work must be kept up date – particularly in response to advancements in technology and methods within the built environment, or changes in regulatory guidelines.

41.11 In March 2021, the ARB published detailed 'Competence Guidelines: Sustainability' to expand on the high-level wording of the Architects Code, to provide sufficient guidance to architects on how to approach the challenges of 'the climate emergency',[10] and 'to ensure [registered architects] are fully competent in all areas of sustainability that apply to buildings and all areas of architecture'.[11]

41.12 The RIBA Code of Professional Conduct[12] similarly includes at paragraph 1.11, a duty to continue to 'develop and update' 'skills, knowledge and expertise to maintain and improve their competence … for the benefit of the … natural environment.' Members must also, pursuant to paragraph 1.15, be familiar (and up-to-date) with relevant codes of practice and guidelines issued or endorsed by RIBA, especially those concerned with sustainability and protection of the environment.

(b) The duty to consider the work's impact on the environment

41.13 Standard 5 paragraph 5.1 of the Architects Code sets out that:[13]

> Where appropriate, you should advise your client how best to conserve and enhance the quality of the environment and its natural resources.

---

8 ARB, 'Architects Code: Standards of Conduct and Practice' (2017) <https://arb.org.uk/wp-content/uploads/2016/05/Architects-Code-2017.pdf> accessed 4 May 2024.
9 ARB, 'Advisory Note, Standard 2: Competence' 1 <https://arb.org.uk/architect-information/architects-code-standards-of-conduct-and-practice/advisory-notes/competence/?download_pdf=9864> accessed 4 May 2024.
10 ARB, 'ARB Competence Guidelines: Sustainability' (2021) 1 <https://arb.org.uk/wp-content/uploads/ARB-Competence-Guidelines_-Sustainability.pdf> accessed 4 May 2024.
11 ARB, 'Advisory Note, Standard 5: Considering the Wider Impact' 5 <https://arb.org.uk/architect-information/architects-code-standards-of-conduct-and-practice/advisory-notes/wider-impact/> accessed 4 May 2024.
12 Royal Institute of British Architects, 'RIBA Code of Professional Conduct' (2021) <https://www.architecture.com/knowledge-and-resources/resources-landing-page/code-of-professional-conduct> accessed 4 May 2024.
13 ARB, 'Architects Code: Standards of Conduct and Practice' (2017) <https://arb.org.uk/wp-content/uploads/2016/05/Architects-Code-2017.pdf> accessed 4 May 2024.

41.14 The ARB's Sustainability Guidelines appear to add the words 'in pursuit of sustainability' to Standard 5.[14] The Competence Guidelines: Sustainability cover ethics and professionalism, sustainable design principles, environmental and building physics, and construction technology. It is particularly noteworthy that by Guideline SB1, an architect should 'be able to design low and zero carbon buildings'; and, by Guideline SD1, an architect should '[u]nderstand the embodied carbon and resource implications of different methods of construction and performance of building materials'.

41.15 Principle 2 of RIBA's Code of Professional Conduct states that:[15]

> Members should continuously strive to improve their professional knowledge and skill. … Members should strive to protect and enhance heritage and the natural environment.

41.16 At paragraph 3.2(c) of Principle 2 of RIBA's Code of Professional Conduct, the following is stated: 'Members should endeavour to deliver projects that … minimise negative impacts on the environment during their anticipated life cycle.'

41.17 Other provisions dealing with the environment include those at paragraph 13 of Principle 2, and the provision that members should use reasonable endeavours to 'specify and use sustainable materials on their projects', and to 'minimise whole-life carbon and energy use.'[16]

(ii) *Engineers*

41.18 There are various professional bodies relating to engineers including: the Institution of Civil Engineers (ICE) (governed by Royal Charter and regulated by the Engineering Council); the Institution of Structural Engineers (I.Struct.E); the Institution of Mechanical Engineers (I.Mech.E) and the Institution of Engineering and Technology. All of these bodies include provisions relating to the environment and sustainability in their respective codes of conduct.

(a) The duty to keep up to date

41.19 The ICE Rules of Professional Conduct (October 2022 version) includes at Rule 5 that 'all members shall develop their professional knowledge, skills and competence on a continuing basis.' It provides the following guidance at page 8:

> All members have a duty to improve and update technical knowledge, and to keep abreast of relevant developments, including new or changed statutory provisions.

41.20 Likewise, the Institution of Structural Engineers' Code of Conduct (January 2022) requires, at Article 4, that members maintain and broaden their competence where appropriate; the Institution of Mechanical Engineers' Code of Conduct Regulations (revised 2021) includes at CR1 that members are to maintain their professional

14 ARB, 'ARB Competence Guidelines: Sustainability' (n 10).
15 Royal Institute of British Architects (n 12).
16 Royal Institute of British Architects, 'RIBA Code of Professional Conduct' (n 12) paras 13.7–13.8.

knowledge; and the Rules of Conduct of the Institution of Engineering and Technology (October 2019) state at Rule 5 that members shall keep their knowledge and skills up-to-date through planned professional development and seek to broaden and deepen that knowledge throughout their working life.

(b) The duty to consider the work's impact on the environment

41.21 The ICE Rules of Professional Conduct (October 2022 version) includes at Rule 4: 'All members shall show due regard for the environment and for the sustainable management of natural resources.'[17]

41.22 The Institution of Structural Engineers' Code of Conduct (January 2022) includes explicit obligations in relation to sustainability and climate change. Article 2 states that its members must: 'Have regard to the public interest as well as the interests of all those affected by their professional activities'. Members shall:[18]

> carry out their professional duties cognisant of the short term and long term impacts of their actions, taking measures to protect those affected by their advice and the laws that are relevant to their work. The Institution of Structural Engineers supports a policy of sustainability and renewable resources.

41.23 The related Guidance Note 7 ('Sustainability and Climate Change') states that:[19]

> Members should be aware of the impact their professional duties have on the environment and take proactive measures to operate in a sustainable manner. In doing so, members should consider the effects of their design and the impact of that design on the environment, by considering the whole life cycle of the building through design, construction, use, re-use and demolition such that it reduces unnecessary consumption of resources, and minimises waste.

41.24 In addition, the Code of Conduct requires its members to comply with the Statement of Ethical Principles published by the Engineering Council and the Royal Academy of Engineering. The 2017 edition includes the following Statement of Ethical Principles:[20]

> 2. Respect for life, law, the environment and public good. Engineering professionals have a duty to obey all applicable laws and regulations and give due weight to facts, published standards and guidance and the wider public interest. They should: … protect, and where possible improve, the quality of built and natural environments; maximise the public good

17 Institute of Civil Engineers, 'Code of Professional Conduct' (2022) <https://www.ice.org.uk/download-centre/code-of-conduct> accessed 4 May 2024.

18 The Institution of Structural Engineers, 'Code of Conduct' (2022) Article 2 <https://www.istructe.org/about-us/istructe-code-of-conduct/> accessed 4 May 2024.

19 The Institution of Structural Engineers, 'Guidance Note 7: Sustainability and Climate Change in Code of Conduct' (2022) <https://www.istructe.org/getattachment/About-us/istructe-code-of-conduct/IStructE-Code-of-Conduct-(2022).pdf?lang=en-GB> accessed 4 May 2024.

20 Engineering Council and Royal Academy of Engineering, 'Statement of Ethical Principles for the Engineering Profession' (2017) Article 2 <https://www.engc.org.uk/media/2337/statement-of-ethical-principles-2014.pdf> accessed 4 May 2024.

> and minimise both actual and potential adverse effects for their own and succeeding generations; take due account of the limited availability of natural resources …

41.25 The Institution of Mechanical Engineers includes in its Code of Conduct Regulations (revised 2021) at CR3:[21]

> All members shall engage responsibly with the environment: They shall recognise the importance of socio-economic and environmental factors; They shall comply with obligations for environmental protection; They shall take account of the needs of a diverse environment, while never knowingly or deliberately wasting or carelessly using natural resources; They shall balance the needs of the present with the needs of future generations.

41.26 The Rules of Conduct of the Institution of Engineering and Technology (October 2019) states at Rule 2 that 'members shall observe the provisions of the current Statement of Ethical Principles published by the Engineering Council and the Royal Academy of Engineering'. Further, Rule 15 states that 'members shall take all reasonable steps to avoid waste of natural resources, damage to the environment, and damage or destruction of man-made products'.

How should a professional designer approach the use of an untested design or technique to minimise the risk of a finding of sub-standard performance of his or her retainer?

41.27 Special considerations apply when a design or technique is untested. The fact that the design is untried may require the consultant to act with particular caution or to take particular care to test and assess its merits.

41.28 However, the position is in practice more nuanced than this. For example, *IBA v EMI and BICC*[22] concerned the design of a television mast by the sub-contractors BICC. In their defence, BICC had argued that they had no experience in the design of cylindrical masts,[23] and that the design and building of such masts was work which was 'both at and beyond the frontier of professional knowledge at that time'.[24]

41.29 The House of Lords nevertheless held that they were in breach of their duty to exercise reasonable skill and care in the design of the mast. The relation of the required standard to the novel design was considered by Lord Edmund-Davies:[25]

> Justice requires that we seek to put ourselves in the position of BICC when first confronted by their daunting task, lacking all empirical knowledge and adequate expert advice in dealing with the many problems awaiting solution. But those very handicaps

21 Institution of Mechanical Engineers, 'Code of Conduct Regulations (Revised 2021)' (2021) Article 3 <https://www.imeche.org/docs/default-source/1-oscar/About-us/governance/code_of_conduct_02_03_02.pdf?sfvrsn=2> accessed 4 May 2024.
22 *IBA v EMI and BICC* [1980] 14 BLR 1.
23 ibid [3].
24 ibid [5].
25 ibid 196.

created a clear duty to identify and to think through such problems, including those of static and dynamic stresses, so that dimensions of the 'venture into the unknown' could be adequately assessed and the ultimate decision as to its practicability arrived at.

41.30 *IBA v EMI and BICC* has been cited with approval in other authorities. For example, in *Baylis Farms Ltd v RB Dymott Builders Ltd*,[26] it was stated that if the client is warned in suitably clear terms of the risk of failure of the works, and despite that clear warning the client instructs the contractor to proceed, in such circumstances there would be a consensual shifting of the risk of failure of the works from contractor to employer.

41.31 One can imagine a similar situation arising in respect of a project which requires adaption or mitigation against the effects of climate change. Simply because a particular issue has not been encountered before is not sufficient to absolve a professional in exercising their duties. The 'unknown' must be 'adequately assessed', even in circumstances where a project or technology used may be novel. This is also supported by the codes above, which for example, impose the duty to improve and update technical knowledge and stipulate that competence is not a 'static achievement but an evolving standard'.[27]

What is the extent of a professional designer's duty to warn the client of the risk in relation to untried materials or techniques?

41.32 As set out in the section above, there may be potential claims against those involved in using and developing new techniques and materials aimed to reduce our carbon footprint. This may be particularly relevant where there are new technologies, where construction professionals have limited or no experience of designing or using those technologies, and where very little data, in relation to those technologies, is available.

41.33 In *University of Manchester v Hugh Wilson & Lewis Womersley (A Firm)*,[28] Judge Newey QC said:[29]

> For architects to use untried, or relatively untried, materials or techniques cannot in itself be wrong, as otherwise the construction industry can never make any progress. I think, however, that architects who are venturing into the untried or little tried would be wise to warn their clients specifically of what they are doing and to obtain their express approval.

41.34 The duty to warn will therefore be, depending on the circumstances, important. In the case of *Baylis Farms Ltd v RB Dymott Builders Ltd* referred to above, a warning given by a builder to its client about the adequacy of proposed drainage works had been insufficiently clear to displace the implied warranty of fitness for purpose. The builder was therefore liable in damages for the defective drainage installed. In that case, the warning included the following evidence given at trial by one of the witnesses: 'It might

---

26 *Baylis Farms Ltd v RB Dymott Builders Ltd* [2010] EWHC 3886 (QB) [21].
27 ARB, 'Advisory Note, Standard 2: Competence' 1 (n 9).
28 *University of Manchester v Hugh Wilson & Lewis Womersley (A Firm)* [1984] CILL 126.
29 For a critique of this case's dictum on the duty to warn generally see Richard Wilmot-Smith and Paul Darling, *Wilmot-Smith on Construction Contracts* (n 2) para 1.160.

not be ideal, but in my opinion from experience it should still work.'[30] The evidence did not show that a 'clear warning' had been given, while on the contrary the professional opinion given was that it 'should work'. Clarity is therefore important.

41.35 The construction industry has adapted constantly to new methods and challenges. Climate change and net zero considerations are no different in this respect. However, where a professional is in uncharted territory, it is prudent to warn the client and explain the risks clearly. This is particularly apt in the context of net zero and climate change, where new or novel approaches may be adopted.

When, if ever, is the fact that other professionals may have acted just as negligently sufficient to avoid liability?

41.36 When considering the standard expected of a designer when dealing with the effects of climate change and mitigation techniques, reference may be made to the practice of other professionals and to the defence that since it was commonplace, it cannot have been negligent.

41.37 The starting point is the relevant standard expected of a professional person. It is that of competent practitioners, prevailing at the time when the particular professional services are performed. In *Bolam v Friern Hospital Management Committee*[31] McNair J said:[32]

> I myself would prefer to put it this way, that he is not guilty of negligence if he has acted in accordance with a practice accepted as proper by a responsible body of medical men skilled in that particular art … Putting it the other way round, a man is not negligent, if he is acting in accordance with such a practice, merely because there is a body of opinion who would take a contrary view.

41.38 This was explained in relation to an architect by Stephen Browne LJ in *Nye Saunders & Partners v Alan E Bristow* as follows:[33]

> the courts approach the matter upon the basis of considering whether there was evidence that at the time a responsible body of architects would have taken the view that the way in which the subject of enquiry had carried out his duties was an appropriate way of carrying out the duty and would not hold him guilty of negligence merely because there was a body of competent professional opinion which held he was at fault.

41.39 However, it is not enough to establish that the professional acted in accordance with a 'responsible body of opinion'. There has to be a logical basis for any such body of opinion. In *Bolitho v City & Hackney Health Authority*, Lord Browne-Wilkinson held that:[34]

---

30 *Baylis Farms Ltd v R B Dymott Builders Ltd* (n 26) at [28].
31 *Bolam v Friern Hospital Management Committee* [1957] 1 WLR 582.
32 ibid 587.
33 *Nye Saunders & Partners v Alan E Bristow* [1987] 37 BLR 92 [103].
34 *Bolitho v City & Hackney Health Authority* [1998] AC 232 [241]–[242].

> The Court is not bound to hold that a defendant doctor escapes liability for negligent treatment or diagnosis just because he leads evidence from a number of medical experts who are genuinely of opinion that the defendant's treatment or diagnosis accorded with sound medical practice … the court has to be satisfied that the exponents of the body of opinion relied upon can demonstrate that such opinion has a logical basis. In particular in cases involving, as they so often do, the weighing of risks against benefits, the judge before accepting a body of opinion as being responsible, reasonable or respectable, will need to be satisfied that, in forming their views, the experts have directed their minds to the question of comparative risks and benefits and have reached a defensible conclusion on the matter.

41.40 This imports a two-stage test that must be fulfilled before a body of opinion will be considered to have a 'logical' basis. In *Khoo James v Gunapathy*, it was said that the 'threshold test' was, first, that the body must have 'directed his mind … to the comparative risks and benefits relating to the matter'.[35] At this stage, 'it is … the process and not the result of the expert's reasoning that is material in the eyes of the court'. Secondly, as a result of that process, a 'defensible conclusion' must have been reached. This requires that the 'opinion must be internally consistent on its face. It must make cogent sense as a whole, such that no part of the opinion contradicts with another'. In addition, it cannot 'fly in the face of proven extrinsic facts relevant to the matter. It should not ignore or controvert known medical facts or advances in medical knowledge.'

41.41 Thus, a court is not simply focused on what conclusion a body of opinion reached. It will also examine the way in which that body of opinion reached its conclusion. If it cannot be demonstrated that this was reached as the result of a process by which the risks had been actively considered, it cannot be logical.

41.42 This approach was adopted by Edwards-Stuart J in *Knightsbridge Development Ltd v WSP UK Ltd*.[36] A defendant to a professional negligence claim may be exonerated if there is: 'evidence of a responsible body of opinion that has identified and considered the relevant risks or events and which can demonstrate a logical and rational basis for the course of conduct or advice that is under scrutiny'. That is what is needed.

41.43 This defence, described as 'everyone else was doing it', clearly does not operate as a 'get out of jail free card'. In *Martlet Homes Ltd v Mulalley & Co Ltd*,[37] a contractor was liable to the owner of four tower blocks for the cost of replacing combustible external cladding which it had installed between 2005 and 2008 pursuant to a design and build contract. The judge accepted the claimant's argument that the mere fact other professionals were acting or advising in the same way at the time is not sufficient. At paragraph [271], the judge held:

> I accept the claimant's argument in closing submissions that the argument that 'everyone else was doing it' does not, on a proper application of the 'Bolam' principle, operate as a get out of jail free card. Following the analysis of Edwards-Stuart J in 199 Knightsbridge

35 *Khoo James v Gunapathy* [2002] 2 SLR 414 [64]–[65].
36 *Knightsbridge Development Ltd v WSP UK Ltd* [2014] EWHC 43 (TCC).
37 *Martlet Homes Ltd v Mulalley & Co Ltd* [2022] EWHC 1813 (TCC).

Development Ltd v WSP UK Ltd [2014] EWHC 43 (TCC), at paragraphs 101 to 120, for the Bolam principle to operate to exonerate a defendant, there must be 'evidence of a responsible body of opinion that has identified and considered the relevant risks or events and which can demonstrate a logical and rational basis for the course of conduct or advice that is under scrutiny' (paragraph 120). 'A defendant is not exonerated simply by proving that others … [were] … just as negligent' (paragraph 106). Both of these observations would apply in this case.

41.44 This approach is particularly relevant for professionals discharging their duties in relation to net zero and climate change. A professional will not be exonerated from their duties simply by proving that others were just as negligent at the relevant time. The defence that 'everyone else was doing it' did not – in *Martlet Homes Ltd v Mulalley & Co Ltd* – satisfy the *Bolam* principle. Readers will not fail to forget the Grenfell Tower fire and the tragedy which shook the industry, and brought to stark attention to the gravely inadequate levels of performance. The disaster highlighted clear obligations to keep up to date and to understand the impact of the materials being used on a building.

Records of and an audit trail in relation to the design process

41.45 Professional codes of conduct highlight the importance of keeping records.

41.46 The RIBA Code of Professional Conduct sets out at 13.2 (under Principle 2) that 'Members should practise evidence-informed design and should keep records of the evidence used in reaching design decisions'.[38]

41.47 The ICE Rules of Professional Conduct (October 2022 version) includes at rule 4: 'All members shall show due regard for the environment and for the sustainable management of natural resources.'[39] The following guidance is given at page 8:

> In all the work that members do, they must be able to demonstrate, by an appropriate audit trail, that they have taken all reasonable steps to take account of all the relevant factors in relation to the impact upon the environment and the sustainable management of natural resources. It is increasingly the case that engineers are called to account for their decisions, especially where projects are controversial or are opposed by particular interest groups.

41.48 As we have identified above, in *IBA v EMI and BICC*, Lord Edmund-Davies stated that when confronted by a 'daunting task' with handicaps including a lack of empirical knowledge and adequate expert advice, those handicaps:[40] 'created a clear duty to identify and to think through such problems, including those of static and dynamic stresses, so that dimensions of the venture into the unknown could be adequately assessed and the ultimate decision as to its practicability arrived at.' It follows, in our

---

38 Royal Institute of British Architects, 'RIBA Code of Professional Conduct' (n 12).
39 Institute of Civil Engineers, 'Code of Professional Conduct' (n 17).
40 *IBA v EMI and BICC* (n 22) 196.

view, that where there is a duty to identify and to think through problems, it would be prudent to keep a record of that analytical process.

When will strict liability be imposed on the professional designer?

41.49 In the context of professional duties, it is important to emphasise that professionals will need to be mindful of not only clauses that directly deal with climate change and net zero considerations, but also those that are indirectly relevant such as design life requirements.

41.50 The impact of climate change on the life expectancy of buildings needs to be carefully considered. A project being built now may have to deal with a climate significantly different from that in which it was procured and designed. The significance of this to the UK construction industry is evidenced by the fact that, for example, millions of people in the UK live on flood plains and in coastal areas and are thus at risk of flooding.

41.51 Recent cases have concentrated on whether a design life obligation imposes strict liability. Whilst the decision in each case depends on the particular contract terms considered by the court, these cases highlight the need to take care as to the nature of the obligation undertaken. *MT Højgaard v E.ON*[41] concerned the foundation structures of two offshore wind farms at Robin Rigg in the Solway Firth. They were designed, manufactured, and installed by the respondent, MT Højgaard. They failed shortly after completion of the project. The agreement referred to a 'design life' of 20 years. The agreement also included detailed technical requirements, including that the design of the foundations be in accordance with an international standard DNV-OS-J101 (J101). MT Højgaard performed the works in accordance with J101 but, due to an error in the international standard, the design did not have a service life of 20 years. The dispute concerned who was responsible for the remedial costs.

41.52 The Supreme Court considered whether clause 3.2.2.2(ii) of the Technical Requirements of the contract document, which required that 'the design of the foundations shall ensure a lifetime of 20 years without replacement', operated when read with clause 8.1(x) of the contract as a strict warranty and had been breached. The Supreme Court ultimately allowed the employer's appeal, holding that the clause should be construed as a strict liability obligation which had been breached on the basis of the facts as found. As with all of these decisions, the facts are context specific. In *MT Højgaard v E.ON*, Lord Neuberger was of the view at [30] that the clause on its proper construction was a contractual term that the foundations had been designed to last for 20 years without replacement, as opposed to being a warranty that they would last 20 years without replacement. He observed at [31] that, given the forces of nature, a lifetime of any specified period could never, in practice, be guaranteed. In that case, it appears from [31] that it was possible to give the design life obligation specific meaning in terms of annual probability of failure by reference to a contractually incorporated

41 *MT Højgaard v E.ON* [2017] UKSC 59.

design standard. However, as he said in [32], he did not consider it necessary to decide the question on the basis that whichever the answer, the same result would follow in that case. The decision is also relevant because, as appears from the judgment of Lord Neuberger at paragraphs [45] and [50], if there are two clauses imposing design obligations with different or inconsistent standards or requirements, treating the clause imposing the less demanding obligation as a minimum requirement makes more sense than treating it as qualifying the clause imposing a more demanding obligation, since to do so would give that clause a meaning which in effect renders it redundant.

41.53 The strict nature of these design life requirements – depending on the specific contractual context – was reiterated in *Blackpool BC v Volkerfitzpatrick Ltd.*[42] Here, the local authority brought a claim against a contractor for breach of contract in respect of the design and construction of a tram depot on the seafront in Blackpool. The tram depot was sited directly on the coastline, adjacent to the promenade at its southern end point. Directly to the south and west of the tram depot, on the other side of the promenade, lay the Irish Sea. It was not disputed that the tram depot was regularly subjected to wind-driven sea spray and salty sands. The claimant complained that significant parts of the tram depot as designed and constructed did not meet their intended design life of 50 years; nor were they suitable for the exposed coastal marine environment where the tram depot was located and suffered from regular exposure to the elements. It was held that there was 'no basis for treating … the design life obligations … as being only "reasonable care" obligations'.[43] The court was satisfied that they had the 'same essentially strict character' as the Supreme Court held that the clauses in issue did in *MT Hojgaard v E.ON.*[44] The judge emphasised that it was important to understand what is meant by 'design life' and that there was no contractual definition of the phrase.[45] However, the judge reviewed the relevant standards which were available at the time to understand the meaning of 'design life'. In that case, those were BS ISO 15686-1:2000 entitled 'buildings and constructed assets – service life planning' and BS EN 1990:2002 entitled 'basis of structural design'. HHJ Davies said at [157] that although it could not realistically be thought that a structure should be intended to be maintenance-free for the whole of its design life, it could reasonably be assumed that it ought not to need major repairs over that period. Therefore, the distinction lay between anticipated maintenance and major repair – which would be a question of fact and degree in any given case.[46]

41.54 Professionals should consider all design life requirements provided for in the contract: in terms of what they mean and what they require. At the very least, designers should consider the design life requirements that are provided for in the contract, and consider whether the positioning of the building or project might mean it is at an increased risk in light of storms or changing weather patterns.

---

42 *Blackpool Borough Council v Volkerfitzpatrick Ltd and others* [2020] EWHC 1523 (TCC).
43 ibid [152].
44 ibid.
45 ibid [153].
46 See also *Martlet Homes Ltd v Mulalley & Co Ltd* (n 37); *LDC (Portfolio One) Ltd v (1) George Downing Construction Ltd and (2) European Sheeting Ltd* [2022] EWHC 3356 (TCC) [46]. Distinguished in *Lendlease Construction (Europe) Ltd v AECOM Ltd* [2023] EWHC 2620 (TCC) [134]–[136].

41.55 We note that the JCT 2024 Design and Build contract includes an amended clause 2.17 in relation to the Contractor's liability in respect of design. This provides that the Contractor shall have no greater duty, obligation or liability than to exercise reasonable skill and care as provided in clause 2.17.1.1, caveated to the extent permitted by the Statutory Requirements. There is an express exclusion of any fitness for purpose obligation in relation to design. We set out clause 2.17.1 in full below:

> 2.17.1.1 Insofar as its design of the Works is comprised in the Contractor's Proposals and in what it is to complete in accordance with the Employer's Requirements and these conditions (including any further design that it is required to carry out as a result of a Change), the Contractor warrants, subject to clause 2.17.1.2, that it shall use the reasonable skill and care in such design to be expected of a qualified and experienced architect (or other appropriate professional designer) undertaking the design of the works similar in scope and character to such design of the Works.
>
> 2.17.1.2 To the extent permitted by the Statutory Requirements, the Contractor shall have no greater duty, obligation or liability than to exercise reasonable skill and care as provided in clause 2.17.1.1 in respect of such design and under no circumstances shall the Contractor be subject to any duty, obligation or liability which requires that any design shall be fit for its purpose.

41.56 The JCT Design and Build Contract Guide 2024 explains that the intended level of design liability, that of reasonable skill and care, is that of 'any qualified and experienced architect or other professional designer undertaking the design of the works of a similar type'.[47]

What express obligations in relation to net zero and climate change are imposed on a contractor who undertakes design and build responsibilities under major standard form contracts?

41.57 As we have set out in Chapter 31, contractual drafting will play a central role in managing climate change risks between the parties whilst also presenting an opportunity to promote contract performance in line with the objective of achieving net zero goals.

41.58 In the main standard form contracts, the contractor will often take on design responsibilities, so it is important to consider the climate-related clauses proposed in some of the main standard construction contracts.

(i) *Standard Forms of Contract*

41.59 Parties to construction contracts will often use standard forms of contracts, which increasingly include provisions in relation to net zero. We set out, by way of example, some of the climate-related clauses in some of the main standard form contracts, should

---

47 The Joint Contracts Tribunal Limited, 'Design and Build Contract Guide' (2024) para 45 <https://www.jctltd.co.uk/product/design-and-build-contract-guide-2024> accessed 4 May 2024.

parties wish to incorporate clauses which seek to mitigate the carbon emissions of the construction project.

(a) FIDIC

41.60 Looking first at the International Federation of Consulting Engineers ('FIDIC') standard contracts, sub-clause 4.18 of the 2017 Red, Yellow and Silver Books provides that:

> The Contractor shall take all necessary measures to:
>
> (a) protect the environment (both on and off the Site);
> (b) comply with the environmental impact statement for the Works (if any); and
> (c) limit damage and nuisance to people and property resulting from pollution; noise and other results of the Contractor's operations and/or activities.
>
> The Contractor shall ensure that emissions, surface discharges, effluent and any other pollutants from the Contractor's activities shall exceed neither the values indicated in the Specification, nor those prescribed by applicable Laws.

41.61 Parties should note the ambiguity in this sub-clause: namely, 'environment' is not defined, 'necessary measures' are not spelled out, and 'environment impact statement' is not a defined term.

41.62 FIDIC published its Climate Change Charter on 11 November 2021.[48] This sets out actions for FIDIC to take 'a leadership position on climate action and carbon emission reduction' including addressing the relevant challenges through its 'contractual guidance'.[49] In its Climate Change Charter, FIDIC committed to 'providing best practice templates and clauses that can be incorporated at the scheme, project, and programme level'.[50] It is likely, therefore, that more specific, net zero-related provisions will be developed by FIDIC.

(b) JCT

41.63 JCT has placed a greater emphasis on sustainable development in the new JCT Design and Build Contract 2024. This includes, under clause 2.1.5 within the main text, the previously optional Supplemental Provision 8.1 relating to sustainable development and environmental impact, designed to promote positive environmental performance. The JCT Design and Build Contract Guide, 2024 explains[51] that this change reflects a key industry focus area and forms part of JCT's response to the Construction Playbook (which we cover in more detail in Chapter 37 Construction Phase).

---

48 FIDIC, 'FIDIC Climate Change Charter' (2021) <https://issuu.com/fidic/docs/climate_charter_with_fore word> accessed 4 May 2024.
49 ibid 2.
50 ibid 12.
51 The Joint Contracts Tribunal Limited, 'Design and Build Contract Guide' (n 47) para 4 of the Introduction.

41.64 Clause 2.1.5 of JCT's Design and Build Contract 2024 states as follows:

> The contractor is encouraged to suggest economically viable amendments to the Works which, if instructed as a Change, may result in an improvement in environmental performance and sustainability in the carrying out of the Works or of the completed Works and a reduction in environmental impact, provided that no instruction shall extend the Contractor's obligations in relation to design under this Contract.

41.65 By this clause, the contractor is 'encouraged', but not required, to suggest economically viable amendments to the works which may result in an improvement in environmental performance in the carrying out of the works or the completed works. This clause contains neither carrot nor stick to encourage compliance.

41.66 Clause 2.2.2 of JCT's Design and Build Contract 2024 incorporates previously optional Supplemental Provision 8.2 and states as follows:

> The Contractor shall provide to the Employer all information that the Employer reasonably requests regarding the environmental impact of the supply and use of materials and goods which the contractor selects.

41.67 We also note that the obligation under Clause 2.2.2 to provide the Employer with all information that he reasonably requests regarding the environmental impact of the supply and use of the materials and goods selected only arises when the Employer requests it, so the implementation of this in practice will depend on the Employer's appetite.

(c) NEC

41.68 In July 2022, the New Engineering Contract ('NEC') published Option X29 Climate Change for all NEC4 main, and main subcontract, forms: the first detailed clause relating to climate change in a standard form construction contract. Option X29 is designed to help parties 'in their drive towards achieving net zero greenhouse gas emissions and other related climate change and biodiversity targets'.[52] It is intended to reduce the impact of the creation, operation, maintenance and demolition of assets on climate change. Since, according to the NEC, this is mainly a technical issue, it is usually addressed in the Scope. The NEC sought to address the limitation of this approach which had relied on users linking the required content in the Scope to contractual processes in the contract. Option X29 was developed to signpost climate related issues in the body of the contract, namely the Climate Change Requirements.[53]

41.69 Option X29 Climate Change includes by way of example, the following optional clauses for the Design Build and Operate Contract:

---

52 NEC, 'X29 Climate Change' <https://www.neccontract.com/resources/x29-climate-change-working-group> accessed 4 May 2024.

53 The X29 Guidance states that, 'Climate Change Requirements could include things such as levels of recycling, use of renewable power or electric vehicles, reducing waste generation, designing out waste, designs that reduce carbon emission etc. but are likely to focus more on the operation of the completed asset under a design build and operate contract.'

- A requirement for the Contractor to collaborate with other Climate Change Partners[54] identified in the Climate Change Requirements;[55]

- The provision for submission of a Climate Change Plan, which shows how the Contractor plans to meet the Climate Change Requirements;[56]

- A clause allowing for the use, disclosure and publication of information relating to climate change as stated in and for the purposes of the Climate Change Requirements;[57] and

- The provision for the Contractor to propose changes in the Scope in order to reduce the impact of creation, operation, maintenance or demolition of the property on climate change.[58]

41.70 As set out above, the Climate Change Requirements are to be stated in the Scope and are, therefore, requirements with which the Contractor must comply (or provide); a failure to do so will be a breach of the Contractor's obligations and a defect the Contractor will have to address. The Climate Change Requirements are to be stipulated by the Client (or employer) and could be in relation to any aspect of the work, including:[59]

> levels of recycling, use of renewable power of electric vehicles, reducing waste generation, designing out waste, designs that reduce carbon emissions etc. but are likely to focus more on the operation of the completed asset under a design build and operate contract.

(ii) *Key Performance Indicators*

41.71 A range of contractual techniques exist which encourage building with a net zero target in mind. These include provisions regarding key performance indicators ('KPIs') relating to net zero and nature positive.

41.72 For example, the JCT Suite of Contracts includes Supplemental Provision 7 which states:[60]

> 7.1 The Employer shall monitor and assess the Contractor's performance by reference to any performance indicators stated or identified in the Contract Documents.

---

54 NEC, 'Option X29 Climate Change' X29.1(3) states that 'The Climate Change Partners are the people or organisations who contribute to the achievement of the Climate Change Requirements and are identified in the Climate Change Requirements.'
55 ibid X29.2.
56 ibid X29.4.
57 ibid X29.5.
58 ibid X29.6.
59 NEC, 'Option X29 Climate Change Guidance Notes' (2022) <https://www.neccontract.com/news/final-version-of-x29-released> accessed 4 May 2024.
60 The Joint Contracts Tribunal Limited, 'Design and Build Contract (DB 2024)' supplemental provision 7 in part 2 of sch 2 <https://www.jctltd.co.uk/product/design-and-build-contract-db-2024-tracked-change-document> accessed 4 May 2024.

41.73 The NEC includes optional Clause X20 in NEC4, which states as follows:[61]

> A Key Performance Indicator is an aspect of performance by the Contractor for which a target is stated in the Incentive Schedule.

41.74 The Chancery Lane Project[62] ('TCLP') has drafted a bespoke clause which employers and contractors may incorporate into their contracts entitled 'Sustainability Key Performance Indicators in Construction Works Task Orders' ('Daniel's Clause'). This identifies KPIs for contractual performance against the employer's environmental and sustainability targets, in order to incentivise the contractor to embed climate change considerations within design and construction.

41.75 Performance against any requirements must be capable of being assessed and measured. The UK Green Building Council ('UKGBC')[63] and the Royal Institution of Chartered Surveyors ('RICS') have produced guidance in relation to the measurement of climate-related performance. One example is Version 2 of RICS's whole life carbon assessment (WLCA) standard for the built environment. This is effective from 1 July 2024. It has been produced to enable assessors to estimate 'the amount of carbon emitted throughout the life cycle of a constructed asset, from the early stages of development through to the end of life'.[64]

41.76 Parties must be careful to ensure that the key performance indicators are clearly defined. *Sutton Housing Partnership Ltd v Rydon Maintenance Ltd*[65] demonstrates this need for clear contractual drafting, albeit that the Court of Appeal in this case did construe the clauses in order to uphold them, and found that 'example' 'minimal acceptable performance' figures for the KPIs in a contract were binding (rather than merely illustrative) on the parties.

---

61 NEC4, X20.1.

62 The Chancery Lane Project (TCLP) is a 'network of lawyers and business leaders using the power of climate contracting to deliver fast and fair decarbonisation.' TCLP has drafted over one hundred climate clauses and over 70 glossary terms along with a suite of tools in order to assist partes in decarbonising contracts including in relation to procurement, Modern Methods of Construction, energy efficiency and environmental obligations. See https://chancerylaneproject.org/.

63 UK Green Building Council, 'Embodied Carbon: Developing a Client Brief' (2017) <https://ukgbc.org/wp-content/uploads/2017/09/UK-GBC-EC-Developing-Client-Brief.pdf> accessed 4 May 2024.

64 'Whole Life Carbon Assessment for the Built Environment' <https://www.rics.org/profession-standards/rics-standards-and-guidance/sector-standards/construction-standards/whole-life-carbon-assessment> accessed 28 November 2023.

65 *Sutton Housing Partnership Ltd v Rydon Maintenance Ltd* [2017] EWCA Civ 359. At [49] Jackson LJ restated Lord Neuberger's guidance on the interpretation of contractual provisions at [15]–[20] of *Arnold v Britton* [2015] UKSC 36.

INDEX